THE CAMBRIDGE HANDBOOK OF PRIVATE LAW AND ARTIFICIAL INTELLIGENCE

Artificial Intelligence (AI) appears to disrupt key private law doctrines and threatens to undermine some of the principal rights protected by private law. The social changes prompted by AI may also generate significant new challenges for private law. It is thus likely that AI will lead to new developments in private law. This Cambridge Handbook is the first dedicated treatment of the interface between AI and private law and the challenges that AI poses for private law. This Handbook brings together a global team of private law experts and computer scientists to deal with this problem and to examine the interface between private law and AI, which includes issues such as whether existing private law can address the challenges of AI and whether and how private law needs to be reformed to reduce the risks of AI while retaining its benefits.

Ernest Lim is Professor of Law at the National University of Singapore. A prize-winning researcher, he has published on the legal implications of AI and comparative corporate law and governance. He is the sole author of three acclaimed monographs with Cambridge University Press: *Social Enterprises in Asia: A New Legal Form* (2023), *Sustainability and Corporate Mechanisms in Asia* (2020), and *A Case for Shareholders' Fiduciary Duties in Common Law Asia* (2019). He obtained his doctorate from Oxford. He used to practise law at Davis Polk & Wardwell LLP.

Phillip Morgan is Reader in Law at the University of York. A leading expert in tort law, his work on AI and tort has been funded by the European Research Council, and UK Research and Innovation (amongst others). He has held visiting positions at Oxford, Cambridge, the University of Hong Kong, Trinity College Dublin, and Georgetown. Phillip is a graduate of Cambridge (MA), Oxford (BCL), and UCL (PhD), and a Barrister of the Middle Temple. He also holds appointments as a part-time ('fee-paid') Judge in the Employment Tribunals, and in the First-tier Tribunal.

"This Handbook is timely and significant, with no other work considering with such insight the interface between AI and private law. The Handbook asks the challenging questions for private lawyers and seeks to provide answers, both as to how private law will need to adapt to meet the challenges and fulfil the potential of AI but also what role private law will need to play to control and regulate AI. The editors have brought together private lawyers and computer scientists from around the globe to reflect on these important issues. I have no doubt that this Handbook will be both ground-breaking and influential."

– Graham Virgo KC (Hon), Professor of English Private Law, University of Cambridge

"AI is now an everyday topic of conversation. All lawyers and policy-makers need to think about the issues raised. This multi-authored book will be invaluable in assisting them to do so. It is the first book dedicated to the role of AI in relation to private law. It makes a fascinating read whether dipped into or taken as a whole. Within its pages, the reader will find the familiar areas of private law, such as contract, tort, property law and commercial law, excitingly exposed to the full glare of the AI revolution."

– Lord Burrows FBA, Justice of the United Kingdom Supreme Court

"If artificial intelligence stands to remake society—as its greatest proponents and critics both claim—then among the things that must change are law and legal institutions. This book—featuring an international and interdisciplinary cadre of some of the wisest contemporary voices on AI law—will be indispensable to the faculty, students, and policymakers engaged in this effort."

– Ryan Calo, Lane Powell and D. Wayne Gittinger Professor, The University of Washington School of Law

"This Handbook brings together an impressive team of contributors to offer a panoramic view of the interface between private law and AI. At this already disrupted interface, we now see AI-enabled processes and products generating a broad sweep of new questions for private law as well as AI tools that are insinuating themselves into governance practices. If we want to understand more about why, where, and how the tectonic plates of private law governance are being put under stress during this time of extraordinary development of AI, this Handbook is one to read."

– Roger Brownsword, Professor of Law, King's College, London

"Our social and economic environment is increasingly saturated with AI. Covering a wide range of timely topics, this rich Handbook carefully examines some of the most important challenges that AI poses for private law. Benefitting from the perspective of multiple jurisdictions, it explores some of the most significant risks and opportunities as well as the possible reforms required in order to properly recalibrate private law. This exciting Handbook is thus an essential resource for private law scholars, lawmakers, and practitioners in the AI era."

– Hanoch Dagan, Professor of Law, UC Berkeley School of Law

"It's vital to track and, to the extent possible today, understand the complex and evolving intersection of AI and private law. This Handbook is a valuable resource for those both newly interested and long-standing experts, exploring legal issues alongside technological challenges that call for policy response."

– Jonathan Zittrain, Professor of Law, Computer Science and Public Policy, Harvard University; co-founder, Berkman Klein Center for Internet & Society

"Social change drives legal change. Statutes respond to new social problems and court decisions resolve disagreements between litigants whose interactions are conditioned by evolving social context. The causal flow also goes the other way: legislation and judgments aim to alter social relations and sometimes have this effect (though not always in the way that lawmakers intend). Technological developments provide well-known examples of these phenomena and developments in artificial intelligence are set to do the same, in more or less-predictable ways. Until now, the focus of academic discussion of the interplay between AI and the law has been on regulation, but as the wide-ranging contributions to this important new volume make clear, the interplay between AI and private law is another rich field for scholarly examination."

– Charles Mitchell KC (Hon), FBA, Professor of Laws, University College London

The Cambridge Handbook of Private Law and Artificial Intelligence

Edited by

ERNEST LIM
National University of Singapore

PHILLIP MORGAN
University of York

CAMBRIDGE
UNIVERSITY PRESS

CAMBRIDGE UNIVERSITY PRESS

Shaftesbury Road, Cambridge CB2 8EA, United Kingdom

One Liberty Plaza, 20th Floor, New York, NY 10006, USA

477 Williamstown Road, Port Melbourne, VIC 3207, Australia

314–321, 3rd Floor, Plot 3, Splendor Forum, Jasola District Centre, New Delhi – 110025, India

103 Penang Road, #05–06/07, Visioncrest Commercial, Singapore 238467

Cambridge University Press is part of Cambridge University Press & Assessment, a department of the University of Cambridge.

We share the University's mission to contribute to society through the pursuit of education, learning and research at the highest international levels of excellence.

www.cambridge.org
Information on this title: www.cambridge.org/9781108845595

DOI: 10.1017/9781108980197

First published 2024

A catalogue record for this publication is available from the British Library

Library of Congress Cataloging-in-Publication Data
NAMES: Lim, Ernest, 1977– editor. | Morgan, Phillip, 1984– editor.
TITLE: The Cambridge handbook of private law and artificial intelligence / edited by Ernest Lim, National University of Singapore; Phillip Morgan, University of York.
DESCRIPTION: Cambridge, United Kingdom ; New York, NY :
Cambridge University Press, 2024. | Includes bibliographical references and index.
IDENTIFIERS: LCCN 2023044961 | ISBN 9781108845595 (hardback) | ISBN 9781108980197 (ebook)
SUBJECTS: LCSH: Artificial intelligence – Law and legislation. | Civil law. |
Artificial intelligence – Law and legislation – European Union countries. |
Civil law – European Union countries.
CLASSIFICATION: LCC K564.C6 C3593 2024 | DDC 343.09/99–dc23/eng/20231005
LC record available at https://lccn.loc.gov/2023044961

ISBN 978-1-108-84559-5 Hardback

For Edwin and Edmund

Ernest Lim

For Molly and James

Phillip Morgan

Contents

Figures

Table

Contributors

Jeremias Adams-Prassl is Professor of Law, University of Oxford, and a Fellow of Magdalen College, Oxford

Deirdre Ahern is Professor in Law, Trinity College Dublin

Nadia Banteka is Gary & Sallyn Pajcic Professor of Law, Florida State University College of Law

Anthony J. Casey is Donald M Ephraim Professor of Law and Economics, and Director of the Center on Law and Finance, University of Chicago Law School

Eric C. Chaffee is Professor of Law, Peter M. Gerhart Distinguished Research Scholar, and Associate Director, Centre for Business Law, Case Western Reserve University School of Law

Thomas Cheng is Professor of Law, Faculty of Law, University of Hong Kong

Iris H.-Y. Chiu is Professor of Corporate Law and Financial Regulation, Faculty of Laws, University College London

Dev S. Gangjee is Professor of Intellectual Property Law, University of Oxford, and a Fellow of St Hilda's College, Oxford

James Goudkamp is Professor of the Law of Obligations, University of Oxford, and a Fellow of Keble College, Oxford

Özlem Gürses is Professor of Commercial Law, Dickson Poon School of Law, King's College London

Ibrahim Habli is Professor of Safety-Critical Systems, Department of Computer Science, University of York

Gérard Hertig is Emeritus Professor of Law, ETH Zurich, and Principal Investigator, Future Resilient System Programme

Ying Hu is Assistant Professor of Law, Faculty of Law, National University of Singapore

Yan Jia is Research Associate, Department of Computer Science, University of York

Ernest Lim is Professor of Law, Faculty of Law, National University of Singapore

Kelvin F. K. Low is Professor of Law, Faculty of Law, National University of Singapore

Adrian Mak is Arbitration Associate, Singapore and Hong Kong

Yvette Maker is Senior Lecturer, University of Tasmania, and Honorary Senior Fellow, Melbourne Law School, University of Melbourne

John A. McDermid is Professor, Department of Computer Science, and Director of Lloyd's Register Foundation Assuring Autonomy International Programme, University of York

Anke Moerland is Associate Professor of Intellectual Property Law, European and International Law Department, Maastricht University

Phillip Morgan is Reader in Law, York Law School, University of York

Anthony Niblett is Professor of Law and the Canada Research Chair in Law, Economics, and Innovation, University of Toronto Faculty of Law

Ugo Pagallo is Professor of Jurisprudence, Department of Law, University of Turin

Jeannie Marie Paterson is Professor of Law, and Director of the Centre for Artificial Intelligence and Digital Ethics, University of Melbourne

Serena Quattrocolo is Professor of Italian and European Criminal Procedure, Department of Law, University of Turin

Anselmo Reyes is International Judge, Singapore International Commercial Court, and Arbitrator

Ernestina Sacchetto is Post-Doctoral Researcher, University of Turin, Italy

Daniel Seng is Associate Professor of Law and Director of the Centre for Technology, Robotics, Artificial Intelligence & the Law, Faculty of Law, National University of Singapore

Sandy Steel is Professor of Law and Philosophy of Law, University of Oxford, and Lee Shau Kee's Sir Man Kam Lo Fellow in Law, Wadham College, Oxford

Harry Surden is Professor of Law, University of Colorado Law School, and Associate Director of the Stanford Center for Legal Informatics (CodeX)

T. T. Arvind is Professor of Law and Head of Department, York Law School, University of York

Tan Cheng Han is Professor of Law, Faculty of Law, National University of Singapore

Sean Thomas is Reader in Law, York Law School, University of York

Vibe Ulfbeck is Professor of Private Law and Director of the Centre for Private Governance, Faculty of Law, University of Copenhagen

Wan Wai Yee is Adjunct Professor, City University of Hong Kong School of Law

Wu Ying-Chieh is Associate Professor of Law, Seoul National University School of Law

John Zerilli is Chancellor's Fellow (Assistant Professor) in AI, Data, and the Rule of Law, Edinburgh Law School, University of Edinburgh

Acknowledgements

It is a pleasure to work with a group of outstanding contributors from multiple jurisdictions. We are grateful to Joe Ng, the commissioning editor of Cambridge University Press (CUP), for his patience, professionalism and helpfulness, to the ten CUP anonymous reviewers for their constructive feedback on this Handbook, and to the anonymous referees of each of the twenty-nine chapters for their thoughtful comments.

We would like to extend our appreciation to the commentators and participants at the online conference for this project, especially Vincent C Müller, Zoe Porter, Jenny Steele, Isra Black, Tan Zhong Xing, Francis Reynolds, Orian Dheu, Peter Harrison, Jeremiah Lau, Benjamin Wong, Rory Gregson, Kenneth Khoo, Michael Bridge, Yeo Hwee Ying, Christian Hofmann, Kirsty Hughes, Andrew Tettenborn, and Ryan Whalen, who provided invaluable comments on the draft chapters. We would also like to thank Jochem Koers for his excellent editorial assistance with formatting.

York Law School and the Faculty of Law, National University of Singapore, provided helpful and collegial environments in which to complete this project. Work on this project was also carried out by one of us during visiting fellowships at the University of Hong Kong, the Trinity Long Room Hub, Trinity College Dublin, and by both of us at Magdalen College, Oxford; these periods were formative in the conceptual development of this project, and we are most grateful for the time spent in these intellectually invigorating environments, and for the energy this provided at formative stages of this project. We acknowledge the financial support provided by these institutions for these visits. We are also grateful to our families for the help and support they have provided throughout the duration of this project.

Finally, we acknowledge the support we received from the National University of Singapore EW Barker Centre for Law and Business and the Centre for Technology, Robotics, Artificial Intelligence & the Law, and funding from the European Research Council, under the European Union's Horizon 2020 research and innovation programme (grant agreement No 824990). We have endeavoured to state the law as of 1 December 2023.

Abbreviations

AAIP	Assuring Autonomy International Programme, University of York
ACPR	*Autorité de Contrôle Prudentiel et de Résolution*
AEV	Automated and Electric Vehicles Act 2018
AGI	artificial general intelligence
AI	artificial intelligence
AIA	Artificial Intelligence Act
AMF	*Autorité des Marchés Financiers*
ARMD	adverse reaction to metal wear debris
AUC-ROC	area under the curve receiver operating characteristic
AustLII	Australasian Legal Information Institute
AV	autonomous vehicle
BaFin	*Bundesanstalt für Finanzdienstleistungsaufsicht*
BMI	body mass index
BNs	Bayesian networks
BoE	Bank of England
BTC	Bitcoin
B2B	business-to-business
CAHAI	Committee on Artificial Intelligence
CCPA	California Consumer Privacy Act
CDA	Communications Decency Act
CD-ROM	compact disc read-only memory
CEO	chief executive officer
CEPEJ	European Commission for the Efficiency of Justice
CERN	*Conseil Européen pour la Recherche Nucléaire* (European Council for Nuclear Research)
CFR	European Union Charter of Fundamental Rights
CIDRA	Consumer Insurance (Disclosure and Representations) Act 2012
CIO	chief information officer
CJEU	European Union Court of Justice
CNN	convolutional neural network

COMPAS	Correctional Offender Management Profiling for Alternative Sanctions
Covid-19	coronavirus disease
CPA	Consumer Protection Act 1987
CPRs	common-pool resources
CSA	Canadian Securities Administrators
CSRD	Corporate Sustainability Reporting Directive
CSV	comma-separated values
CTO	chief technology officer
CV	curriculum vitae
CWU	Communication Workers Union
DABUS	Device for the Autonomous Boot-strapping of Unified Sentience
DARPA	United States Defense Advanced Research Projects Agency
DLT	distributed ledger technologies
DMCA	Digital Millennium Copyright Act
DNN	deep neural network
DPIA	Data Protection Impact Assessment
DPR	Data producer's right
DSA	Digital Services Act
DVD	digital video disc
DVR	digital video recorder
EBA	European Banking Authority
EC	European Commission
ECB	European Central Bank
EIOPA	European Insurance and Occupational Pensions Authority
EPC	Convention on the Grant of European Patents
EPO	European Patent Office
ESG	environment, sustainability and governance
ETH	Ethereum
EU	European Union
FBI	Federal Bureau of Investigation
FCA	Financial Conduct Authority
FDA	Food and Drug Administration
FINMA	Swiss Financial Market Supervisory Authority
FinTech	financial technology
FRAND	fair, reasonable and non-discriminatory
FPR	false positive rate
FREMP	fundamental rights, citizens' rights and free movement of persons
FSB	Financial Stability Board
FTC	Federal Trade Commission
GANs	generative adversarial networks
GAO	United States Government Accountability Office

GDPR	European Union General Data Protection Regulation
GPS	global positioning system
G20	Group of Twenty
HLEG	European Union High Level Experts Group on Artificial Intelligence
HR	human resources
IA	Insurance Act 2015
ICTs	information and communication technologies
ID	identification
InsurTech	insurance and technology
IoT	Internet of Things
IP	intellectual property
IT	information technology
JRC	Joint Research Centre
LIBE	Committee on Civil Liberties, Justice and Home Affairs
LU	leading underwriter
MAS	Monetary Authority of Singapore
MIT	Massachusetts Institute of Technology
ML	machine learning
MPI	Max Planck Institute for Innovation and Competition
NASAA	North American Securities Administrators Association
NDVR	network digital video recording
NIST	National Institute of Standards and Technology
NNs	neural networks
NLP	natural language processing
OECD	Organisation for Economic Co-operation and Development
OEM	original equipment manufacturer
PAI	Predictive Analytics Artificial Intelligence
PCP	provision, criterion, or practice
PETA	People for the Ethical Treatment of Animals
PGMS	probabilistic graphical models
PLD	European Union Product Liability Directive 1985
P2P	peer to peer
P&I	protection and indemnity
R&D	research and development
RDR	retail distribution review
RF	random forest
RL	reinforcement learning
ROC	receiver operating characteristic
RS-DVR	remote storage digital video recorder
RTA	Road Traffic Act 1988
SaMD	software as a medical device

SDV	self-driving vehicle
SEC	United States Securities and Exchange Commission
SGA	Sale of Good Act
TCRP	Trusted Copyright Removal Program
TFEU	Treaty on the Functioning of the European Union
TPR	true positive rate
UBI	usage-based insurance
UETA	Uniform Electronic Transactions Act
UK	United Kingdom
UKIPO	United Kingdom Intellectual Property Office
UNCITRAL	United Nations Commission on International Trade Law
US	United States
VAEs	variational autoencoders
VITAL	Validating Investment Tool for Advancing Life Sciences
VLOPs	very large online platform
VLOSEs	very large online search engines
WINnERS	weather index-based risk services
WIPO	World Intellectual Property Organisation
XAI	explainable artificial intelligence

Introduction

Private Law and Artificial Intelligence

Ernest Lim and Phillip Morgan

I INTRODUCTION

Much attention has been given in both academic work and the media to the social, economic, and political impacts of AI.[1] Unsurprisingly, several research handbooks have been published, exploring the benefits and risks of AI and addressing how AI impacts on democracy, privacy, free speech, and other fundamental freedoms in relation to legal and ethical rules, in a variety of domains (including but not limited to healthcare, armed conflict, finance, policing, and politics). AI also produces significant new legal challenges.[2] However, so far, there has been no dedicated treatment of the interface between AI and private law, and the challenges that AI will pose for private law.

It is not uncommon for the pace of technological development to initially outpace developments in the law.[3] Frequently the law needs to shift to reflect the pace of change.[4] However, a careful balance needs to be struck. Where legal change is too slow, it can create significant risks, whereas where it is too fast, and perhaps ill-thought through, it can stifle technological advances.[5] The introduction of AI has

1 Defining AI has proven problematic both for computer scientists and lawyers. There is no standard accepted definition (W Barfield, 'Towards a Law of Artificial Intelligence' in W Barfield and U Pagallo (eds), *Research Handbook on the Law of Artificial Intelligence* (Edward Elgar 2018) 21–22). For a detailed survey and taxonomy of existing definitions see Sofia Samoili and others, *AI WATCH. Defining Artificial Intelligence* (Publications Office of the European Union 2020) 11. For a detailed discussion of AI, how it works, and definitions see Chapter 1. Given proposed European Union regulation the EU has been at the forefront of legally defining AI. For an overview of attempts to legally define AI at an EU level see Chapters 22 and 29.

2 Ryan Calo, 'Robotics and the Lessons of Cyberlaw' (2015) 103 *Calif LR* 513.

3 See Lyria Bennett Moses, 'Recurring Dilemmas: The Law's Race to Keep Up with Technological Change' (2007) 2007 *U Ill JL Tech & Pol'y* 239.

4 Deirdre Ahern, 'Corporate Law, Corporate Governance and AI: Are We Ready for Robots in the Boardroom?' in Ernest Lim and Phillip Morgan (eds), *The Cambridge Handbook of Private Law and Artificial Intelligence* (Cambridge University Press 2024). Note also Lyria Bennett Moses, 'Agents of Change' (2011) 20 *Griffith Law Review* 763.

5 Gregory N Mandel, 'Legal Evolution in Response to Technological Change' in Roger Brownsword, Eloise Scotford and Karen Yeung (eds), *The Oxford Handbook of Law, Regulation and Technology* (Oxford University Press 2017) 226.

been widely described as the fourth industrial revolution.[6] Each previous industrial revolution led to major challenges to private law, and significant legal developments.[7] Previously, technological changes and their accompanying social changes radically reshaped a number of areas of private law.[8] New types of disputes arose, and existing legal categories in some cases proved problematic.[9] No private lawyer can ignore the legal developments which were driven by advances such as the steam engine, motor car, mass production, the printing press, modern communications, photography, computing, and the internet.[10] AI appears to generate unique challenges for private law. Features including autonomy, complexity, opacity, data-drivenness, vulnerability, unpredictability, machine learning, openness, and the distance between the systems and those responsible for them are commonly cited as problems generated by AI technologies for the existing legal settlement,[11] and which will disrupt key private law doctrines. In doing so, AI also threatens to undermine some of the key rights protected by private law. It is further likely that social changes prompted by AI will also generate significant new challenges for private law. Consequently, as the chapters of this Handbook demonstrate, it is likely that AI will lead to new developments in private law.

Previous experience shows that such legal developments will also impact private law doctrines more broadly and not simply when these doctrines interface with the new technologies.[12] However, it is not just the challenges that AI causes to private law doctrines that should be of interest to private lawyers. Private law also has a regulatory role. This role may be pronounced in some fields such as consumer law, competition law, or corporate law, but, at its core, law, including private law, regulates relationships. How AI is regulated is of pressing concern to policymakers who have proposed a range of ex-ante regulatory measures. This issue has additionally attracted the attentions of human rights, anti-discrimination, and criminal law scholarship, amongst others, but it is also important to consider the private law regulation of AI.

6 For example, Klaus Schwab, *The Fourth Industrial Revolution* (WEF 2016).

7 Donald Gifford, 'Technological Triggers to Tort Revolutions: Steam Locomotives, Autonomous Vehicles, and Accident Compensation' (2018) 11 *J Tort L* 71; Ken Oliphant, 'Tort Law, Risk, and Technological Innovation in England' (2014) 59 McGill LJ 819.

8 Reinhard Zimmermann, *The Law of Obligations, Roman Foundations of the Civilian Tradition* (Clarendon Press 1996) 1130; Gert Brüggemeier, 'The Civilian Law of Delict: A Comparative and Historical Analysis' (2020) 7 *European Journal of Comparative Law and Governance* 339, 340; Gifford (n 7) 126.

9 Mandel (n 5).

10 Oliphant (n 7) 837; John Bell and David Ibbetson, *European Legal Development, The Case of Tort* (Cambridge University Press 2012) 38.

11 See HLEG, 'Liability for Artificial Intelligence and Other Emerging Technologies' (Report from the European Commission's Group of Experts on Liability and New Technologies, 2019) <www.op.europa.eu/en/publication-detail/-/publication/1c5e30be-1197-11ea-8c1f-01aa75ed71a1/language-en>.

12 Phillip Morgan, 'Tort Liability and Autonomous System Accidents – Challenges and Future Developments' in Phillip Morgan (ed), *Tort Liability and Autonomous System Accidents, Common and Civil Law Perspectives* (Edward Elgar 2023).

This Handbook brings together a global team of private law experts and computer scientists to deal with this problem and examine the interface between private law and AI, which includes issues such as whether existing private law can address the challenges of AI and whether and how private law needs to be reformed to reduce the risks of AI while retaining its benefits.

Private law can be generally and broadly understood as the rights that persons have against one another that are conferrable or enforceable judicially or extra-judicially. This can be further broken down into questions of who has the rights, what the rights are, and how these rights can be enforced.[13] However, rather than dividing the Handbook into these subcategories, it is more reader-friendly and neater to simply categorise the chapters into the traditional areas of private law (i.e., the law of obligations such as contract, torts, trusts, and unjust enrichment), property law (including intellectual property and information technology law), and the more regulatory aspects of private law (such as corporate law, insurance law, competition law, and consumer law). It should be noted that the regulatory aspects of private law are also covered in the leading compendium of private law work in the common law world.[14] At least nineteen distinct areas of private law, spanning major jurisdictions such as the UK, US, and EU are covered in this Handbook.[15]

II INITIAL CHAPTERS

Chapters 1 and 2 deal with general issues which straddle all areas of private law. Systems employing AI technologies are already in use, and it is likely that there will be an increase in the use of such technologies. Chapter 1 is written by three leading computer scientists. It aims to introduce basic concepts of AI to lawyers in order to assist lawyers in understanding how, if at all, the private law framework needs to be adjusted to enable AI systems to be treated appropriately by lawyers. This understanding of the technology is essential since it is important to base our analysis on the current state of the art, not scenarios unreflective of current or future technologies. The chapter deals with key concepts, and the capabilities and limitations of AI and identifies technological challenges which might require legal responses.

In Chapter 2, which deals with 'computable law', Harry Surden makes the case for law to be 'computable', in order to make retrieval and analysis easier. Computable

13 Andrew Burrows (ed), *English Private Law (Oxford Principles of English Law)* (3rd edn, Oxford University Press 2013) ix. The public law and private law divide has a long history, see WW Buckland, *Manual of Roman Private Law* (Cambridge University Press 1925) 30. However, the distinction is often blurred within the common law, note Steve Hedley 'Is Private Law Meaningless?' (2011) 64 *CLP* 89.

14 For example, Burrows (n 13) includes family law, company law, property (including intellectual property), banking, insurance, insolvency, carriage of goods, civil procedure, and private international law.

15 These include contract, torts, consumer law, product liability law, privacy law, agency law, trusts, unjust enrichment, property law, intellectual property law, corporate law, financial regulation, competition law, commercial law, insurance law, commercial dispute resolution, securities law, employment law, and data protection and governance.

law takes aspects of law, which are implicit in legal texts and aims to model them as data, rules, or forms which are amenable to computer processes. He argues that we should supplement statutory language, proposing that laws should be labelled with computable structural data to permit advanced computational processing and legal analysis. For instance, this structural data could be used to indicate important features such as sunset provisions. His thesis is that the law itself should be changed to make it easier for computers to best administer it. Surden advances that these labels should be capable of unambiguous processing by a computer and simultaneously convey sensible information to the human reader.

Surden considers that even with current advances in natural language processing (NLP), the current error margins are still significant enough to warrant the use of computable legal data in certain contexts. However, he considers that recent advances in NLP AI technologies may generate a bridge between written law and computable law, through the ability to produce reliable first-draft translations of written law into comparable computer instructions and data. Through leveraging this technology, structured data may be more easily added to many existing natural language documents.

Whilst other chapters primarily focus on analysing law from the angle of how it can accommodate AI, the need to subject AI to regulation and law, and required legal reforms, Chapter 2 instead considers how law itself may be best served by AI and how law should change to adapt to this. However, Surden recognises limits on this notion of labelling and modelling, considering it not always beneficial or appropriate in every context. This model requires legislators to change their approach to drafting and enacting law. However, contract law may be one of the first potential applications, since parties can through their own private law-making render their own contracts computable.

III PART I: LAW OF OBLIGATIONS

Part I deals with the law of obligations, broadly defined. Chapter 3 deals with AI-infused contracting. In Chapter 3, TT Arvind advances that AI has the potential to overcome problems concerning the existing approaches to contract drafting, management, and implementation, whilst also having the potential to exacerbate these problems. To deal with this risk and to create AI which is trustworthy in relation to contracting Arvind argues that such systems require channelling in a new direction, which he terms 'transactional responsibility'. His chapter addresses how AI practices and contract law may be developed so that AI-infused contracting serves responsible and responsive ends rather than being extractive and oppressive.

Arvind notes that the nature of algorithmic systems may make it easy for these systems to lapse into contract law minimalism, unless the systems are expressly designed not to do so. Consequently, he argues that the legal regulation must be structured around the entirety of the socio-technical system which underpins AI.

He discusses questions that must be addressed by contract law for it to be able to regulate AI-infused contracting and related social concerns. To deal with these concerns, he proposes a relationally informed principle of transactional responsibility which he argues should be infused into the way in which AI contracting systems are designed, deployed, and regulated. He argues that systems of governance should consider all categories of transactors likely to be subject to a particular system. Further, he proposes that contract law itself will need to change, specifying disclosure and transparency requirements so as to require the provision of accessible explanations as to how the relevant AI-infused contracting system functions, makes decisions, exercises discretions, and is assured.

Chapter 4, which again concerns contract law, deals with self-driving contracts and AI. Anthony Casey and Anthony Niblett examine the role of AI in automated private contracts. They expand on their previous work on micro-directives, that is, legal technologies 'that use AI-augmented algorithms to translate the purpose of a law into a specific legal directive'.[16] Casey and Niblett have previously argued that these can be used to produce self-driving contract, that is, a contract which instead of relying on a human referee to fill gaps, update, or reform the provisions of the contract, use data-driven predictive algorithms to do so instead.[17] These micro-directives draw on real-world data and factor in the purpose of the contract.

Within Chapter 4, Casey and Niblett respond to scholarly criticisms of their previous work. They distinguish between self-driving contracts and mere smart contracts. Chapter 4 explores existing contracts and technologies and makes the case that not only are self-driving contracts possible, they are in fact already with us. They also examine existing AI augmentation and prediction technologies that are, or can be used, to create self-driving contracts. Numerous examples of current and potential self-driving provisions and technologies are considered in Chapter 4. These include dynamic pricing clauses using a pricing algorithm instead of a human arbitrator, refitting litigation prediction systems for the purpose of automating terms regarding contractual non-performance and also to fill contractual gaps, and using technology currently used to flag unlawful or problematic terms of a contract. They also consider the use of existing technologies which automate contractual negotiation and discuss the potential to use such technologies to update a contract during its lifespan.

Casey and Niblett also discuss the risks of such automation which include the replication of existing biases and party weaknesses and the problems of data manipulation and security. They also consider the question of who drafts the self-driving contract algorithms and potential solutions to ensure that these algorithms do not intentionally or systematically favour one party. By examining existing technologies and considering how they are or could be used to create self-driving contracts, Casey

[16] Anthony J Casey and Anthony Niblett, 'Self-Driving Contracts and AI: Present and Near Future' in Lim and Morgan (n 4).

[17] Anthony J Casey and Anthony Niblett, 'Self-Driving Laws' (2016) 66 *University of Toronto Law Journal* 429; Anthony J Casey and Anthony Niblett, 'Self-Driving Contracts' (2017) 43 *J Corp L* 1.

and Niblett demonstrate that the notion of self-driving contracts is not simply science fiction but also a genuine possibility for the present.

In Chapter 5, Jeannie Marie Paterson and Yvette Maker examine the interface between consumer protection law and AI. Consumers are at the forefront of market uses of AI, from targeted advertising, to differential pricing, and automated decision-making for services. There are also myriad consumer uses of AI products to assist them in their everyday lives. However, they have the potential to endanger consumer autonomy and welfare, ranging from erosions of consumer privacy, the perpetuation of undesirable bias and unlawful discrimination, susceptibility to hacking and security issues, to proving unreliable or unsafe. Such systems collect large volumes of data on consumers. The insights provided by such data may also be used to nudge consumers into making decisions that might not be welfare-enhancing, and which are not the autonomous decisions of the consumer.

Paterson and Maker note that consumer protection law justifies greater responses where the interactions involve significant risks and relevant consumer vulnerability. They argue that both such elements are present in the current and predicted AI uses concerning consumers. They advance that consumer protection law is likely to be able to be sufficiently flexible to adapt to AI, although there is a need to recalibrate consumer protection law for AI. They also suggest the possibility of fiduciary duties for some systems, such as digital assistants, or, given the potential intimate relationships between smart devices and consumers, that there may be scope to expand the doctrine of undue influence.

Chapters 6–10 focus on tort law. In Chapter 6, Phillip Morgan considers the difficulties in applying existing tort law to AI systems. He argues that AI will disrupt the existing tort settlement. Morgan introduces the notion of tech-impartiality within torts, that is, tort law should not encourage or discourage the adoption of new technologies where they generate the same level of risk, and victim rights should not be eroded by the use of new technologies in place of existing systems of work.

Chapter 6 advances that existing tort law is poorly suited to address some AI challenges. In particular, Morgan highlights the liability gap which will emerge as systems replace employees, as AI does not have legal personality and cannot commit a tort. The chapter identifies the key problems with various alternative claims in tort, from negligence, and non-delegable duties, to product liability, when applied in an AI context, and the UK's Automated and Electric Vehicles Act 2018. Chapter 6 argues that these alternative claims do not adequately address the liability gap, and the present law thus violates tech-impartiality.

Chapter 6 examines a wide range of alternative liability proposals including those based on liability for children, slaves, and animals, to no-fault funds and also proposed European-level reforms. Morgan argues for a form of AI statutory vicarious liability to apply in commercial settings to address the liability gap and as the tech-impartial solution. The chapter also explores what standards of care should apply in this statutory claim context.

Given the tort liability gap, which Chapter 6 discusses in detail, the UK Parliament has already pre-emptively legislated for a compensation solution for autonomous vehicle accidents. As the UK Parliament is one of the first movers on this issue, and since other jurisdictions may be tempted to transplant this approach, it is worth thorough consideration. In Chapter 7, James Goudkamp subjects the Automated and Electric Vehicles Act 2018 to a detailed analysis. The Act is a response to the fact that the ordinary approach to motor vehicle accidents cannot apply in an AV context. This is since there is no human driver. The Act plugs this gap in insurance coverage by providing AV accident victims with a direct claim against the vehicle's insurer. The Act contains a number of technical provisions and ambiguities.

Goudkamp situates the Act within the major shifts that tort law has undergone in response to motor vehicles, considering that we are again on the cusp of another motor-vehicle-inspired revolution in tort law. He also identifies a previously unarticulated statutory preference for victims of AV accidents. This preference does not appear to have been identified by the Act's architects, nor was its appropriateness considered, since it is a matter of luck whether a victim's claim is under the AEV Act or whether the victim needs to establish a claim in negligence against a human driver. Examining the Act's legislative history, Chapter 7 argues that there was inadequate consideration of alternative approaches.

In Chapter 8, Sandy Steel examines private law's causal rules in an AI context. This is an issue of particular importance in claims for compensation where a right holder must prove a causal connection between the relevant conduct and the harm. Chapter 8 identifies two core problems: (1) a problem of proof due to opacity and (2) autonomy. Steel notes that if AI is capable of being considered an intervening agent, this would mean that using AI would have liability-avoiding effects. He also considers the issue of foreseeability.

Steel identifies three kinds of causal uncertainty which also pertain to an AI context: uncertainty due to lack of expertise; uncertainty due to causation evidence being destroyed, tampered with, or not gathered; and finally uncertainty which is present even with sufficient expertise, and in the absence of evidence destruction, tampering, or non-collection. The first he considers does not pose a problem for the private law rules of causation. The second is not unique to AI, nor are we uniquely vulnerable to this problem in an AI context. Indeed, AI may in some contexts provide us with an enhanced ability to record and access relevant facts. However, Steel considers that there may be particular problems with informational and decisional AI, particularly where machine learning takes into account an extraordinarily large number of features, which are given subtle and complex weightings, and are not recoverable after a decision has been made. Chapter 8 discusses principles which have been developed for situations where a party bears some responsibility for a lack of causal evidence and also the EU Expert Group's proposals in relation to logging and recording data duties.

Chapter 8 argues that the third form of uncertainty is inevitable in any legal system and that most systems retain the orthodox burden of proof in this context, resulting in a claimant losing the factual causation issue. However, some systems depart from this where the impossibility of proving causation is recurrent and predictable. Steel considers whether AI involves this form of uncertainty and if it justifies a departure from the ordinary principles. Chapter 8 also makes the case that the issue of the foreseeability of harm in an AI context is less problematic than sometimes suggested in the literature.

Increasing use of AI systems will mean that there will be a consequent shift from liability for human errors to liability for malfunctioning products, which will bring product liability to the fore. In Chapter 9, Vibe Ulfbeck focuses on product liability law and AI. She argues that AI will greatly challenge product liability, since it is based on assumptions as to physical objects distributed through organised linear value chains which do not necessarily apply in the AI context. Ulfbeck also argues that AI systems further challenge both liability compartmentalisation based on separate risk spheres and the notion of defectiveness.

Ulfbeck examines the current European product liability regime and proposed amendments. The regime is based on a linear value chain, and it channels liability to the producer as the best risk avoider. However, she notes that with AI, systems may be distributed differently, with more complex value chains which are more in the nature of a network. Further, AI blurs the line between product and service. Chapter 9 considers a range of other aspects of the current regime which are challenged by AI; for instance, later defect defences which are based on the fact that producers no longer have control of a product. She advances that the realities of new value chains call for a number of adjustments to central product liability concepts, which will widen the scope of product liability rules. Further, she considers that AI may in fact have the potential to ultimately dissolve the very notion of product liability itself.

Certain current uses of AI demonstrate the inadequacy of the current private law settlement to deal with new harms. In Chapter 10, John Zerilli focuses on the problem of deep fakes and the appropriation of personality. Deep fakes are a special kind of counterfeit image which are difficult to distinguish from an authentic image. They may be used to represent a person doing any act and are generated through using advanced machine learning techniques. Such techniques have become widely available through easy-to-use apps. Chapter 10 considers privacy law and demonstrates that currently, such an appropriation of personality is only actionable if the circumstances disclose one of a number of largely unrelated causes of action. Actions such as passing off, defamation, injurious falsehood, nuisance, intentional infliction of psychiatric injury, and trespass were never intended to cover such cases. Although he notes that given the manner in which deep fakes are created and the motivations behind their most objectionable uses, such actions may be more effective against deep fakes than with traditional photographs and video recordings. Nevertheless, Zerilli demonstrates the inadequacy of existing causes of action to protect claimants from the appropriation of their personality. He thus argues for a new independent tort or statutory action for the appropriation of personality which is grounded in the protection of a person's dignitary interests.

AI systems will supplant and automate processes which formerly required human intervention. Such systems may also act in an extra-legal manner or take unanticipated actions. This raises questions as to how to characterise AI interactions. Underlying many of the problems identified in Part I concerning the interface between AI systems and tort and contract law, lays the issue of agency. In Chapter 11, Daniel Seng and Tan Cheng Han deal with this issue.

There have been a number of scholarly proposals that AI systems should in some contexts be treated as legal agents and also to recognise such systems as legal persons. Engaging with these proposals Seng and Tan reject the arguments for AI agency. They argue that the AI agency problem is overstated and that many of the issues concerning AI contracting and liability can be solved by treating artificial agents as instrumentalities of persons or legal entities. In particular, they reject characterising AI systems as agents for liability purposes (cf Morgan in Chapter 6). Seng and Tan advance that this approach best accords with their functionality and places the correct duties and responsibilities on their human developers and operators.

In Chapter 12, which addresses trust law, Anselmo Reyes makes the case that AI will greatly assist in the administration of express and charitable trusts and also be of significant benefit to trust law in acting as an adjudicator – by forcing a clarification and simplification of the law of constructive trusts.

Reyes considers that AI should be able to act as an acceptable trustee of an express trust. He also makes the case that resulting trusts do not insurmountably challenge AI, either as trustees or adjudicators. He rejects the proposition that discretionary trusts are unsuited to AI administration and further rejects the notion that the discretionary nature of remedies makes this area of law unsuited to AI adjudication. Reyes acknowledges that constructive trusts may pose some difficulties for AI. Whilst he suggests that determining when a constructive trust has arisen can be ascertained by reference to a database of case patterns, he accepts that there are difficulties in assessing the respondent's mental state. However, Reyes notes this is also a problem for human adjudicators and criticises the current system of elaborate states of minds used within the law of constructive trusts which cannot be easily implemented by either human adjudicators or AI. His solution is to suggest legal reform to simplify the tests used.

In Chapter 12, Reyes strongly advocates for AI trustees. He argues that the difficulties they will create are not incapable of practical solutions. For instance, whilst lack of personality may be an obstacle, he considers practical workarounds, including a proposed form of in rem claim against trust property which would operate by analogy to the Admiralty jurisdiction in rem.

Chapter 13 concerns unjust enrichment. Data is key to AI. It is a valuable commodity which is collected and sold. This theme will also emerge in Part II of this Handbook. In Chapter 13, Ying Hu addresses whether data subjects should be allowed to seek gain-based remedies against defendants who collect or use their data to train, develop, or improve their systems or who have sold their data for such purposes. Hu argues that one advantage of a gain-based remedy in this context is that it may be relatively easy to ascertain the gain, but demonstrating loss will be considerably harder. Further, a defendant may seek to defeat a class action (for losses) by requiring individualised evidence of loss from each putative class member, whereas the benefits received by a defendant from unauthorised data collection or use can often be established without requiring each claimant to provide individualised evidence.

Hu advances that unjust enrichment is a plausible cause of action for individuals whose data has been collected and used without their consent, and that disgorgement of profits may be possible in some situations where the defendant has unlawfully collected or used personal data. However, Hu acknowledges that contractual pre-emption may limit the utility of claims in unjust enrichment, where the defendant collects personal data pursuant to a valid and binding contractual provision. The chapter considers a range of scenarios, and how such claims would operate.

IV PART II: PROPERTY

Part II deals with property law. Data, agency, and personhood again emerge as key themes in this part. In Chapter 14, Kelvin Low, Wan Wai Yee, and Wu Ying-Chieh probe the divide between property and personhood, examining AI through both lenses. They consider the arguments for legal personhood for (some) AI systems and the challenges that this would create. They note that the conferral of personhood is a choice made by legal systems but argue that just because it can be done, does not mean that it should. They advance that the analogies which are made between AI systems and corporations are superficial and flawed. For instance, the demand for asset partitioning does not apply to AI systems in the same way that it does to corporations, and it may in fact lead to moral hazards. Chapter 14 considers that conferring personhood on AI systems would also need to be accompanied with governance structures equivalent to those that accompany corporate legal personhood. The authors also explore the issues that would arise if legal personality was granted to some AI systems. In particular, they consider the mechanisms used in corporate law to prevent exploitation of the corporate form, and how they might apply (if at all), to an AI context. The authors also consider the interface between data and property, arguing that it is time that the metaphorical ghost of data as property be exorcised.

In Chapter 15, Dev Gangjee examines data from an intellectual property perspective. Data is one of the most valuable resources in the twenty-first century, seemingly straddling the divide between goods and services. Property rights are a tried and tested legal response to regulating valuable assets. Chapter 15 considers whether non-personal, machine-generated (or generative AI) data is protected by

IP law, concluding that within an EU context, mainstream IP options are not available, although certain types of machine-generated data may be protected as trade secrets or within *sui generis* database protection. Gangjee also considers whether a new IP right is needed for data and argues that it is not. His chapter is framed as an obituary for the EU data producer's right, which he advances is a cautionary tale for jurisdictions considering a similar model. He argues that a new property right would both strengthen the position of de facto data holders and drive up costs. However, with data, he considers that there are valuable lessons to be learned from constructed commons models.

Intellectual property is again the subject of Chapter 16. In this chapter, Anke Moerland considers if and when IP law comes into play when AI technologies are used to generate technical inventions or to make creative works. Moerland considers the fit of the current human-centric justifications for IP law in the context of AI creations, noting that the protection of AI-assisted, and AI-generated (or generative AI) works causes problems for the existing law. She suggests that it is doubtful whether the purposes of patent law would be served by granting patents for AI-generated inventions. Further, she notes that AI systems are unable to make the creative choices to bring their outputs into the realm of copyright protection. Chapter 16 advances that AI fundamentally challenges the anthropocentric copyright regime. However, with AI-assisted outputs, there may still be sufficient creative choices of the programmer or user to bring the output into the domain of IP protection. Moerland further addresses whether new rights should be constructed for AI-generated outputs.

Moerland's chapter also considers the broader impact of AI on IP law, arguing that AI technologies will require us to rethink fundamental concepts. In particular, she considers that widespread use of AI technologies may mean that the standard of obviousness applied within patent law will change. When considering the obviousness of an invention to the skilled person, will the skilled person be deemed to be the skilled person using an AI tool? If so, the standard of obviousness will change, with the result that it will be harder to obtain patents on non-obvious inventions.

Chapter 17 by Daniel Seng examines the issue of whether an Internet intermediary – a company that does not create or control the content of information – is liable for providing access to such information, in light of new technologies in data aggregation and machine learning. He analyses two of the most important US pieces of legislation in this regard – the Communications Decency Act (CDA) of 1996 and the Digital Millennium Copyright Act (DMCA) of 1998. He notes that the basic principle is that an intermediary is not liable for providing automated services to disseminate content which it was not involved in creating. Even if an intermediary uses automation to greatly expand its 'editorial' role to arguably create or develop new and illicit content from user-supplied information, he notes that the courts have interpreted the CDA in such a way as to exempt the intermediaries from liability. However, where intermediaries use automation to provide online services to users, such that the infringing activities committed by the users could not be ascribed to the service provider's 'volitional conduct', he notes that service providers have not always succeeded in shifting responsibilities to the users under the DMCA. He argues that law reform is needed to recognise the impact of automation and machine learning systems on the services provided by the intermediary, while requiring intermediaries to minimise illicit or harmful content.

V PART III: CORPORATE AND COMMERCIAL LAW

The third part of the Handbook deals with the corporate and commercial law implications of AI. This part begins with Chapter 18 by Deirdre Ahern where she explores how AI has, and could, impact the content, application, and processes of corporate law and corporate governance, and the interactions of corporate law actors including directors, shareholders, and regulators. Specifically, this wide-ranging chapter covers the effects and usage of algorithms on legislative design (such as tagged machine-readable legislation and the use of codes to draft bespoke model articles), post-incorporation corporate administration and compliance (such as allotment of shares and maintenance of the register of members), corporate reporting (such as the use of digital tagging of reported information), and regulatory enforcement (such as recording failure to file accounts and the penalty that should be meted out). Further, Ahern considers the relationship between AI and the directors' duty to act in the company's best interests and the duty of care. On the former, she takes the view that directors will be insulated against liability for good-faith decisions regarding whether and, if so, how the company should use AI. On the latter, to discharge the duty of care, directors need to become AI proficient, obtain expert advice and put in place governance structures.

In Chapter 19, Gérard Hertig provides a broad overview of how AI has been used and regulated by financial institutions. He points out that the private sector has been increasingly relying on AI for managerial decision-making because AI improves the process by which governance structures are chosen, predicts bank distress, and improves risk management. For example, in the banking sector, he notes that AI has been deployed for credit scoring, fraud detection, claims management, and automated execution. However, Hertig notes the risks that come from using AI, including perpetuating biases, the possibility of infringing competition laws, overreliance on AI, and an inadequate understanding of AI models. He then briefly describes the proposed or existing regulatory measures to address these risks that have been adopted by international organisations (such as the OECD, the Council of Europe, the European Commission, the Financial Stability Board, the European Central Bank, and the European Banking Authority) and regulatory authorities (in the European Union and Asia).

In Chapter 20, Iris Chiu argues that the development of robo-advice – 'automated forms of investment interfaces' – in the EU and UK has been influenced by the existing investment advice regulation in three key ways. First, the law has affected the development of robo-advice in that the robo-advisory process is programmed in such a way that the robo-adviser will elicit the relevant information from the customer and then rationally match the customer's profile with the categorised financial products, which is aligned with the regulatory duty to advise on suitable investments. Second, the regulation on mitigating the adverse impact of conflicts of interest on the quality of investment advice has also shaped robo-advice. Because the law requires advisers to be the end-product provider to their customers and to be independent of any particular product distributors, the law makes it more difficult for the robo-advice industry to offer independent advice and personalised financial planning. Finally, she offers several detailed suggestions on how the regulations can be reformed so that the robo-advice industry can offer personalised planning across a range of products.

Chapter 21 is concerned with the impact of AI on competition law. Thomas Cheng addresses the legal treatment of autonomous algorithmic collusion in light of its technical feasibility and various theoretical considerations. This is an important issue because autonomous algorithmic collusion raises difficult questions concerning the attribution of conduct by algorithms to firms and reopens the long-standing debate about the legality of tacit collusion. He distinguishes and examines two main types of autonomous algorithmic collusion, namely, direct communication between algorithms, which amounts to express collusion and is hence illegal and intelligent and independent adaptation to competitors' conduct by algorithms with no direct communication between them, which is tacit collusion and is regarded as generally legal. He also critically assesses the three main dimensions by which algorithmic collusion has been analysed: the existence of direct communication among the colluding firms or algorithms, the degree of algorithmic autonomy, and the extent of collusive human intent. He is inclined towards the view that there should be ex ante regulation to reduce algorithmic collusion.

The relationship between AI and sales law is explored by Sean Thomas in Chapter 22. He explains the differences between AI software and normal software as this has implications for how a transaction of AI software will be treated under sales law. Next, he explores what it means to own an AI system – whether it is a chattel, merely a software, or something more than a software. If AI is merely a software, he takes the view that it will be protected by copyright, but he notes that there will be problems with licensing. But if AI is encapsulated in a physical medium, he notes that the transaction may be treated as one of sale of goods or a *sui generis* position may be taken. He then provides a detailed analysis of the Court of Justice of the European Union's decision in *Computer Associates v The Software Incubator*.[18] He takes the position that, from a policy and doctrinal perspective, an AI transaction can be regarded as a sale of goods. Because he considers the sale of goods regime to

[18] Case C-410/19 *Software Incubator Ltd v Computer Associates (UK) Ltd* EU:C:2021:742, [2022] 2 CMLR 3.

be insufficient, Thomas then explores what sort of transaction regimes there should be for AI systems. He analyses the elements that have to be taken into account in developing this regime including ownership and fair use (assuming AI is regarded as merely a software) and the right to repair (whether AI is treated as goods or software).

Chapter 23 concerns AI and commercial dispute resolution. Anselmo Reyes and Adrian Mak address the concerns about using AI to resolve commercial disputes. They distinguish two areas where AI will be used – where AI is used to assist in dispute adjudication and where AI is used to adjudicate disputes entirely. On the former, the authors identify and address various concerns including biases (such as automation bias, anchoring bias, contrarian bias, and herd bias) and ethical worries (such as human adjudicators ceasing to be decision-makers, excessive standardisation of decisions, and the fact that judges may be pressured to conform to the AI's predictions). Next, the authors suggest how adjudicators should use AI to assist them in their decisions by distinguishing three stages in which AI may be used: training and implementation; actual use; and monitoring. They conclude that because AI will not be able to provide the legal justifications underlying its predictions, the human adjudicator will have to explain why the AI-generated prediction is legally justified. On the issue of using AI to replace human adjudicators entirely, the authors are doubtful that AI can and should do so. One reason is that AI cannot perform the balancing or probability reasoning process that adjudicators perform in assessing factual disputes. Another is that AI is not able to provide a reasoned justification for an outcome that it arrives at where there are no precedents or where there are two equally viable precedents or interpretations.

In Chapter 24, Özlem Gürses analyses the impact of AI on insurance law. She argues that InsurTech has had a major disrupting effect on the industry in five areas: algorithmic underwriting; data profiling and risk pooling; presentation of the risk to the insurer; inducement; and actuarial fairness. On algorithmic underwriting, she notes that there is now a fully digital and algorithmically driven Lloyd's of London syndicate offering instant capacity, accessible anywhere, at any time. On data profiling and risk pooling, she notes that there may be unfairness caused to individuals because it is impossible for an individual to know the accuracy with which the AI has profiled him or her or the accuracy or suitability of the risk pool to which AI has allocated the individual. On presentation of the risk to the insurer, AI will reduce this burden imposed on the assured because AI will predict or assume the assured's answers to the questions that are posed in the proposal form. On inducement, she argues that AI will not make it easier for the insured to establish that had the assured complied with the duty of disclosure, the insurer would not have entered into the contract at all, because it is difficult to prove causality in the algorithms. On actuarial fairness, she examines the concern that algorithmic prediction will lead to the demise of risk-pooling, on which the principle of risk-spreading is based. Finally, Gürses explores whether AI promotes or undermines trust in insurance.

In Chapter 25, Eric Chaffee considers robo-advisers. However, this chapter is different from that by Iris Chiu. Chiu explains how the law influences the development of robo-advice in the UK and EU. But Chaffee critically evaluates seven different models for regulating this industry, focusing on the United States: agency law, design intervention, merit-based regulation, disclosure-based regulation, fiduciary duties, investor education, and regulation by litigation. He argues that although design intervention and merit-based intervention are not suitable because they hinder innovation, disclosure-based regulation, fiduciary duties, and investor education can strike the appropriate balance between promoting innovation and protecting investors. He takes the view that the best model for regulating the robo-adviser industry is a combination of mandatory disclosure; fiduciary duties for those developing, marketing, and operating robo-advisers; investor education; regulation by litigation; and regulation by survey. The last mechanism involves regular standardised surveying of the investors who are using them and the release of that data to the general public.

Chapter 26 by Jeremias Adams-Prassl examines the effect of AI on employment law, specifically the individual and collective dimensions of employment relations, as well as regulatory domains, including data protection and anti-discrimination law. He notes that digital workplace surveillance via algorithmic management from the inception till the termination of employment can pose moral, physical, and legal problems. He argues that algorithmic management poses two novel challenges: the amount and kind of data collected, and the ways in which that information is then processed and controlled. Adams-Prassl explains the implications of these challenges for the implied term of trust and confidence as well as collective agreements negotiated between trade unions and workers. He notes that on the one hand, algorithmic management enables employers to exercise considerable control over the workers and, on the other hand, enables them to diffuse responsibility. Chapter 26 also examines the effect of algorithmic management on employment status. Given that only those employed under a contract of service are entitled to certain legal benefits and protections, Gig economy platforms' attempts to classify workers as independent contractors have been rejected by courts as a result of the courts' analysis of the platform's algorithmic management techniques that control the workers' performance. Further, he observes that there are difficulties in holding that algorithmic management amounts to indirect discrimination. Moreover, he points out that data protection law like the GDPR is unlikely to provide effective protection against the collection and use of employee data in algorithmic management.

VI PART IV: COMPARATIVE PERSPECTIVES

Chapter 27 is concerned with the EU data protection law and the US information privacy law. Ugo Pagallo explains that there is a convergence on the protection of the traditional right to privacy and today's right to data protection, as evidenced by judicial rulings. However, he argues that there are still distinct differences among the jurisdictions based on how personal data is conceived (as a personality or proprietary right) and on the aims of the regulation. These have implications for how the use of AI will impact on the laws of these two jurisdictions. For example, under the EU approach, the focus is on access to, and protection and control over, information in digital environments. But under the US approach, the focus is on protecting reasonable expectations of privacy and thus on ensuring transparency, due process and accountability for algorithmic operators. Nevertheless, he takes the view that there are some regulatory convergences between US and EU laws by examining the realignment of traditional rights through data-driven technologies, the convergence between data protection safeguards and consumer law, and the dynamics of legal transplantation and reception in data protection and consumer law.

Chapter 28 analyses the issue of giving legal personhood to AI. This is a theme that is raised in a number of the previous chapters. Nadia Banteka argues that the debate over whether AI should be given legal personhood should not be framed in binary terms. Instead, she argues that this issue should be analysed in terms of a sliding-scale spectrum. On one axis, there is the quantity and quality of the bundle of rights and obligations that legal personhood entails. The other axis is the level of the relevant characteristics that courts may include in conferring legal personhood. She argues that the more the AI system acts in an autonomous, intentional, or conscious manner, such that it can function with negligible or no human intervention, the narrower the rights and duties that should be conferred on the AI system. The reason is that the more autonomous an AI system is, the more difficult it would be to attribute the acts or knowledge of the AI system to the AI developer. By contrast, where the AI system operates with human supervision, a more extensive bundle of rights and duties can be conferred on it because, in the worst-case scenario, the persons who exercise supervision over the AI system can be held accountable.

The final chapter, chapter 29, examines the EU approach to AI. Since the EU has sought to be a thought leader in AI law, EU developments are worth paying close attention to. Serena Quattrocolo and Ernestina Sacchetto give an overview of the different legislation, proposals, and statements that have been issued by the EU. They first examine the evolution of the EU definitions of AI which moved from a narrow one to a broad one because the EU policy is to govern the phenomenon of AI in the broadest way that includes a wide range of situations. But the authors note that vague and broad definitions of AI will lead to uncertain applications of the law. Next, they analyse the key contents of the main EU AI documents including the European Parliament Resolution with recommendations to the Commission on Civil Law Rules on Robotics, the Ethics Guidelines for Trustworthy AI, the proposed AI Act, and the proposal for an AI Liability Directive. They conclude by elaborating on the distinction between accessibility and transparency, which are the two cornerstones of the EU regulatory framework, and they suggest that the concept of Explainable Artificial Intelligence would play an important role.

AI offers the potential to revolutionise many fields. This Handbook seeks to be a dedicated treatment of the interface between AI and private law and the challenges that AI will pose for private law. Although it is not possible for this Handbook to answer all such questions concerning private law and AI, new questions will indeed arise as the technology develops further and as the direction of societal change becomes more apparent; this Handbook aims to prompt debate amongst private law scholars and AI law scholars. We also hope that the issues and themes raised in this Handbook prove useful to future scholars, policymakers, legislators, and practitioners grappling with the ramifications of AI. AI has the potential both to unlock great benefits for society and engender great harm. Private lawyers will need to have the right tools and need to ask the right questions, to play their part.

1

AI for Lawyers

A Gentle Introduction

John A. McDermid, Yan Jia and Ibrahim Habli

I INTRODUCTION

This chapter introduces the basic concepts of artificial intelligence (AI) to assist lawyers in understanding in what way, if any, the private law framework needs to be updated to enable systems employing AI to be treated in an 'appropriate' manner. What 'appropriate' means is a matter for legal experts and ethicists, insofar as the law reflects ethical principles, so the chapter seeks to identify the technological challenges which *might* require a legal response, not to prejudge what such a response might be.

AI is a complex topic, and it is also moving very fast, with new methods and applications being developed all the time[1]. Consequently, this chapter focuses on principles that are likely to be stable over time, and this should help lawyers to appreciate the capabilities and limitations of AI. Further, it illustrates the insights with 'concrete' examples from current applications of AI. In particular, it discusses the state of the art in application of AI and machine learning (ML) and identifies a range of challenges relating to use of the technology where it can have an impact on human health and wellbeing.

The rest of the chapter is structured as follows. Section II introduces the key concepts of AI including ML and identifies some of the main types and uses of ML. Section III sets out a view of the current 'state of the art' in AI applications, the strengths and weaknesses of the technology and the challenges that this brings. This is supported by concrete examples. Section IV presents conclusions including arguing that a multidisciplinary approach is needed to evolve the legal framework relating to AI and ML.

[1] Z Somogyi, *The Application of Artificial Intelligence: Step-by-Step Guide from Beginner to Expert* (Springer 2021).

II ARTIFICIAL INTELLIGENCE: KEY CONCEPTS

The concept of AI is generally said to originate with Alan Turing[2] who proposed an 'imitation game' where a human held a conversation through a textual interface either with another human or a computer (machine).[3] If a human cannot distinguish the machine from another human, then the machine is said to have 'passed the test' – we now refer to this as the 'Turing Test',[4] although Turing didn't use that term himself. Technology has advanced to an enormous degree in the seventy years since Turing's original paper but the concept of a machine imitating a human remains valid and indicative of the aims of AI.[5]

A *Artificial Intelligence and Machine Learning*

First, we give a more direct definition of what is meant by AI and then introduce the concept of ML:

- AI involves developing computer systems to perform tasks normally regarded as requiring human intelligence, for example, deciding prison sentences,[6] or medical diagnosis.[7]

At the moment, there is no consensus on a standard definition of AI.[8] The European Commission's Communication on AI proposed the following definition of AI:

> Artificial intelligence (AI) refers to systems that display intelligent behaviour by analysing their environment and taking actions – with some degree of autonomy – to achieve specific goals. AI-based systems can be purely software-based, acting in the virtual world (e.g., voice assistants, image analysis software, search engines, speech and face recognition systems) or AI can be embedded in hardware devices (e.g., advanced robots, autonomous cars, drones or Internet of Things applications).[9]

Some other definitions of AI tend to describe the technology in terms of its most widely used techniques, for example, ML, logic, and statistical approaches.[10]

[2] SB Cooper and J van Leeuwen (eds), *Alan Turing: His Work and Impact* (Elsevier 2013).

[3] A Turing, 'Computing Machinery and Intelligence' (1950) 59(236) *Mind* 433.

[4] J Moor (ed), *The Turing Test: The Elusive Standard of Artificial Intelligence*, vol 30 (Springer 2003).

[5] A Darwiche, 'Human-Level Intelligence or Animal-Like Abilities?' (2018) 61(1) Communications of the ACM 56.

[6] J Ryberg and JV Roberts (eds), *Sentencing and Artificial Intelligence* (Oxford University Press 2022).

[7] EJ Topol, 'High-Performance Medicine: The Convergence of Human and Artificial Intelligence' (2019) 25(1) *Nature Medicine* 44.

[8] R Calo, 'Artificial Intelligence Policy: A Primer and Roadmap' (2017) 51 *UCDL Rev* 399.

[9] <https://ec.europa.eu/futurium/en/system/files/ged/ai_hleg_definition_of_ai_18_december_1.pdf>.

[10] T Madiega, 'Briefing, EU Legislation in Progress, Artificial Intelligence Act, PE 698.792' (*European Parliamentary Research Service*, January 2022) <www.europarl.europa.eu/RegData/etudes/BRIE/2021/698792/EPRS_BRI(2021)698792_EN.pdf>.

Early AI systems, often called expert systems,[11] were generally based on well-defined rules, and these rules were normally defined by humans reflecting knowledge of the domain in which the system was to be used, for example, clinical decision-support tools that utilise a knowledge repository and a predefined ruleset for the prescribing of medications for common conditions.[12] ML is a form of AI, developing computer systems that *learn* to perform a task from training data, guided by performance measures, for example, accuracy.[13] ML is intended to generalise beyond the training data so the resultant systems can work effectively in situations on which they were not trained, for example, learning to identify the presence or absence of diabetic retinopathy from thousands of historic retinal scans labelled with outcomes.[14] We will use the term AI to include ML, but not *vice versa*.

It is common to distinguish 'narrow AI' from 'general AI', often referred to as artificial general intelligence (AGI).[15] The key difference is that 'narrow AI' is focused on a specific task, for example, recognising road signs, whereas AGI is not – indeed we would expect AGI to have the breadth of capabilities of humans including the ability to hold conversations, drive a car, interpret legal judgments, and so on. Modern AI systems can be classed as 'narrow' and some view AGI as unattainable[16] (see also the discussion of the 'state of the art' later).

ML is used in most modern AI systems as a cost-effective way of solving problems that would be prohibitively expensive or impossible to develop using conventional programming – and the key to this is the ability of ML to generalise beyond training data.[17] For example, an ML-based system used for medical diagnosis should work for any patient in the system's intended scope of application. This is similar to the way that humans apply their knowledge – doctors can treat patients they have not seen before, we can drive on new roads, including those that weren't built when we learnt to drive. This can be seen as generalising Turing's imitation game to a wider range of capabilities than textual communication.

11 J Liebowitz (ed), *The Handbook of Applied Expert Systems* (CRC Press 2019).

12 J Fox, N Johns and A Rahmanzadeh, 'Disseminating Medical Knowledge: The Proforma Approach' (1998) 14(1–2) *Artificial Intelligence in Medicine* 157.

13 Most definitions of ML centre on learning from experiences that are captured via a training dataset. For example, Mitchell defines ML as 'the scientific study of computer algorithms that improve automatically through experience'. T Mitchell, *Machine Learning* (McGraw Hill 1997).

14 Y Liu, PHC Chen, J Krause and L Peng, 'How to Read Articles that Use Machine Learning: Users' Guides to the Medical Literature' (2019) 322(18) *Jama* 1806.

15 G Marcus and E Davis, *Rebooting AI: Building Artificial Intelligence We Can Trust* (Vintage 2019).

16 Despite the impressive performance of many ML-based systems that have exceeded human ability, say for object recognition in images, no 'new theory of the mind' has emerged that could be seen as paving the way for AGI. A Darwiche, 'Human-Level Intelligence or Animal-Like Abilities?' (2018) 61(10) *Communications of the ACM* 56.

17 I Goodfellow, Y Bengio and A Courville, *Deep Learning* (MIT Press 2016).

B *Types of Machine Learning*

There are many different ML methods, but they can generally be divided into three classes.[18] We provide some contextual information then give descriptions of these three classes before giving some examples of different ML methods.[19]

Data plays a key role in ML and learning algorithms are used to discover knowledge or patterns from data without explicit (human) programming.[20] The result of learning is referred to as the ML model. The dataset used for training may be labelled, saying what each datum means, for example, a cat or a dog in an image, or it may be unlabelled.[21] The data is normally complex, and we will refer to the elements of each datum as features. The dataset is often split into a training set and a test set, with the test set used to assess the performance, for example, accuracy, of the learnt ML model.[22]

1 Supervised Learning

Supervised learning uses a labelled dataset and this *a priori* knowledge is used to guide the learning process. Supervised learning tries to find the relationships between the feature set and the label set. The knowledge extracted from supervised learning is often utilised for classification or for regression problems. Where the labels are categorical, the learning problem is referred to as *classification*.[23] On the other hand, if the labels correspond to numerical values, the learning problem is defined as *regression* problem.[24]

Figure 1.1 gives a simple illustration of the use of ML for object identification and classification. The ML models have classified dynamic objects in the image and placed bounding boxes around them; in general, such algorithms will distinguish different classes of vehicle, for example, vehicles from people, as this helps in predicting their movement. Here, regression may be used for predicting the future position or trajectory of a vehicle based on its past positions.[25]

18 S Shalev-Shwartz and S Ben-David, *Understanding Machine Learning: From Theory to Algorithms* (Cambridge University Press 2014).

19 The descriptions and illustrations in the rest of this section are mainly drawn from: Y Jia, 'Embracing Machine Learning in Safety Assurance in Healthcare' (PhD thesis, University of York 2021).

20 JC Mitchell and K Apt, *Concepts in Programming Languages* (Cambridge University Press 2003).

21 R Raina and others, 'Self-Taught Learning: Transfer Learning from Unlabeled Data' (*Proceedings of the 24th International Conference on Machine learning*, June 2007) 759–766.

22 R Ashmore, R Calinescu and C Paterson, 'Assuring the Machine Learning Lifecycle: Desiderata, Methods, and Challenges' (2021) 54(5) *ACM Computing Surveys (CSUR)* 1.

23 G Haixiang and others, 'Learning from Class-Imbalanced Data: Review of Methods and Applications' (2017) 73 *Expert Systems with Applications* 220.

24 A Géron, *Hands-On Machine Learning with Scikit-Learn, Keras, and TensorFlow: Concepts, Tools, and Techniques to Build Intelligent Systems* (O'Reilly Media 2019).

25 A Benterki, M Boukhnifer, V Judalet and M Choubeila, 'Prediction of Surrounding Vehicles Lane Change Intention Using Machine Learning' (*10th IEEE International Conference on Intelligent Data Acquisition and Advanced Computing Systems: Technology and Applications (IDAACS)*, September 2019) 839–843.

FIGURE 1.1 Object classification (courtesy of AAIP)
Note: Assuring Autonomy International Programme at the University of York, funded by the Lloyd's Register Foundation.

2 Unsupervised Learning

Unsupervised learning uses unlabelled data and can draw inferences from the dataset to identify hidden patterns.[26] Unsupervised learning is often used for clustering (grouping together related data) and finding associations among features. An active area of work is so-called 'self-supervised learning' (the self here is a computer, not a person) which learns good generic features from an enormous unlabelled dataset.[27] These features can then be used to solve a specific task with a smaller labelled dataset, that is, feeding into supervised learning.

The 'recommender' systems for online shopping systems produce outputs such as: 'people who bought this item also bought…'.[28] Practical recommender systems use a mixture of ML methods, and this may include unsupervised learning.[29] Thus, it is likely that most readers of this chapter will have used a system that employs unsupervised learning, without being aware of it.

[26] M Alloghani and others, 'A Systematic Review on Supervised and Unsupervised Machine Learning Algorithms for Data Science' in M. Berry, A. Mohamed, B. Yap (eds), *Supervised and Unsupervised Learning for Data Science* (Springer 2020) 3.

[27] D Hendrycks, M Mazeika, S Kadavath and D Song, 'Using Self-Supervised Learning Can Improve Model Robustness and Uncertainty' (2019) *Advances in Neural Information Processing Systems* 32.

[28] I Portugal, P Alencar and D Cowan, 'The Use of Machine Learning Algorithms in Recommender Systems: A Systematic Review' (2018) 97 *Expert Systems with Applications* 205; M Beladev, L Rokach and B Shapira, 'Recommender Systems for Product Bundling' (2016) 111 *Knowledge-Based Systems* 193.

[29] See: Luciano Strika, 'K-Means Clustering: Unsupervised Learning for Recommender Systems' (*Towards Data Science*, 3 April 2019) <www.towardsdatascience.com/k-means-clustering-unsupervised-learning-for-recommender-systems-397d3790f90f> 18 August 2022.

3 Reinforcement Learning

Reinforcement learning (RL) is a learning method that interacts with its environment by producing actions and discovering errors or receiving rewards.[30] Trial-and-error search and delayed reward are the most relevant characteristics of RL. In this class of learning, there are three primary components: the agent (the learner or decision-maker), the environment (everything the agent interacts with) and actions (what the agent can do).

The environment gives the agent a state (e.g., moving or stationary), the agent takes an action, then the environment gives back a reward as well as the next state. By analogy, this is like a children's game where one child is blindfolded (the agent), this child can move forwards, backwards, left and right (the actions) in a room (the environment) to find an object and is given hints (rewards), for example, warm, hot, cold, freezing, depending on how close they are to the object, by other children.

This loop continues until the environment gives back a terminal state and a final reward (perhaps some chocolate in the children's game), which ends the episode. The objective is for the agent to automatically determine the ideal behaviour in this environment to maximise its performance. Normally RL development is carried out in a simulated environment or on historical data before the agent is used in real-world applications, for example, optimising the treatment of sepsis.[31]

RL can be used in planning and prediction problems, for example, identifying safe paths for a robot to move around a factory, and recommending medication for a patient.[32] In constrained environments with concrete rules, for example, board games, RL has demonstrated outstanding performance. This is best illustrated by DeepMind's AlphaGo computer program that utilised RL, amongst other ML models, and defeated the world champion in the game of Go, which is much more complex than chess.[33]

C *Developing ML Models*

Following the identification and analysis of a problem in a specific context, ML models can be developed through three primary phases: data management, model learning and model testing.[34] Data management involves collecting or creating, for example, by simulation, data on which to train the models. The data needs to be representative of the situation of interest, for example, roads for autonomous vehicles (AVs),[35] patient treatments and outcomes in healthcare, and perhaps successful and unsuccessful cases

30 RS Sutton and AG Barto, *Reinforcement Learning: An Introduction* (MIT Press 2018).

31 M Komorowski and others, 'The Artificial Intelligence Clinician Learns Optimal Treatment Strategies for Sepsis in Intensive Care' (2018) 24(11) *Nature Medicine* 1716.

32 I Kavakiotis and others, 'Machine Learning and Data Mining Methods in Diabetes Research' (2017) 15 *Computational and Structural Biotechnology Journal* 104.

33 DeepMind, 'AlphaGo' <www.deepmind.com/research/highlighted-research/alphago>.

34 Ashmore, Calinescu and Paterson (n 22).

35 We use the AVs term to embrace all driver assistance system, for example, adaptive cruise control, that reduce the need for the driver to engage in the dynamic driving task whether or not they are 'fully autonomous'.

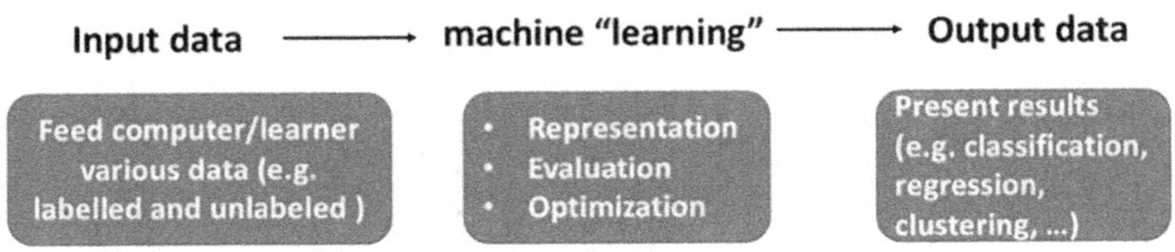

FIGURE 1.2 A simple illustration of machine learning process
Jia, 'Embracing Machine Learning in Safety Assurance in Healthcare' (n 19).

for a legal assistant. As well as splitting a dataset into a training dataset and a test data set, a validation dataset can also be used for model parameter tuning during model learning. For model learning itself, it is necessary to consider how to represent the knowledge derived from the training data, that is, what type of ML method to use, how to evaluate the ML model performance and then how to optimise the learning process. This is illustrated in Figure 1.2.

In model testing, the performance of the ML models is assessed using various metrics on the test dataset. It is easiest to explain this concept by considering classification of objects for an AV. The ML model output is therefore the assessed class for the observed object. For simplicity, assume we are only interested in identifying dynamic objects, that is, those that can move, and distinguishing them from static objects. In this case, we can have:

- True positive – correct classification, for example, a person is identified as a dynamic object.
- True negative – correct classification, for example, a lamppost is not identified as dynamic.
- False positive – incorrect classification, for example, a statue[36] is classified as dynamic.
- False negative – incorrect classification, for example, a person is not classified as dynamic.

It is common to convert these cases into rates and measures,[37] for example, a true positive rate (TPR), which is the proportion of positives correctly identified, that is, true positives, out of all the positives. Similarly, other measures are defined, for example, accuracy, which is the proportion of correct outputs (true positives plus true negatives) out of all the ML model outputs.

Some ML methods, for example neural networks (NNs), produce a score or probability qualifying the output,[38] for example, dynamic object with 0.6 probability. If the threshold in this case was 0.5, then the output would be interpreted as saying that the object was

36 Although, of course, statues might move when being installed or if being toppled in a revolution or other form of protest – but this simply serves to show the difficulty of the problems being addressed by ML.
37 T Fawcett, 'An Introduction to ROC Analysis' (2006) 27(8) *Pattern Recognition Letters* 861.
38 MA Nielsen, *Neural Networks and Deep Learning*, vol 25 (Determination Press 2015).

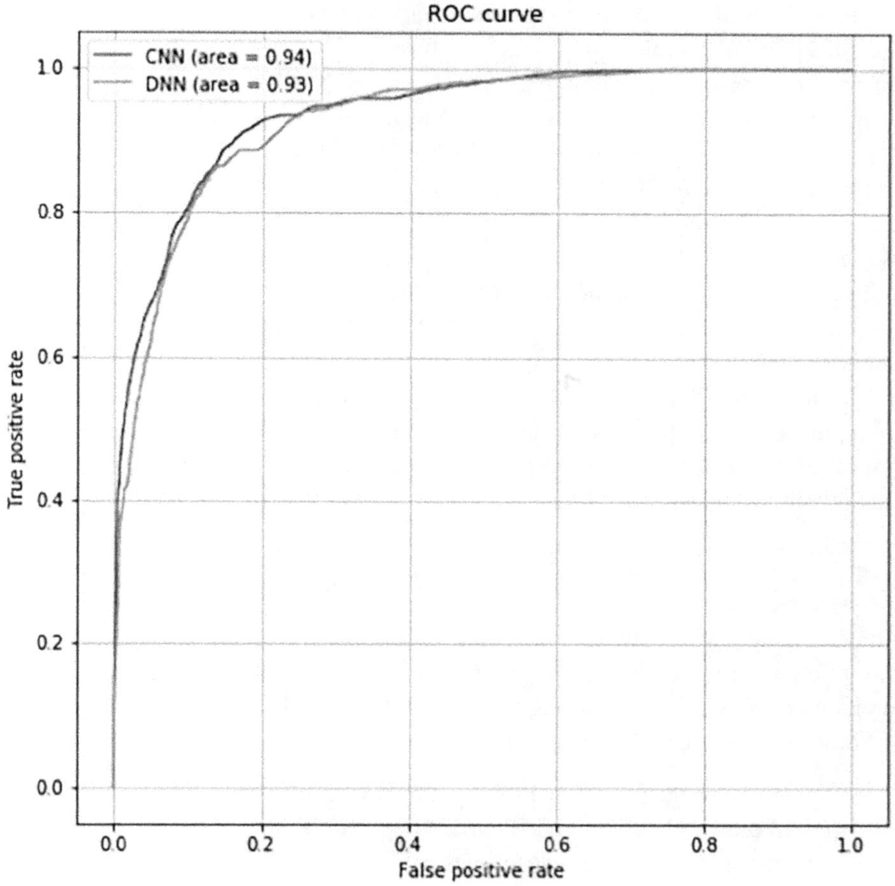

FIGURE 1.3 Illustration of ROC
JA McDermid, Y Jia, Z Porter and I Habli, 'Artificial Intelligence Explainability: The Technical and Ethical Dimensions' (2021) 379(2207) *Phil. Trans. R. Soc. A.*

dynamic. However, if the threshold was set at 1, then the use of the NN would never give a positive output (saying the object was dynamic), thus the TPR would be 0, and so would the false positive rate (FPR). Similarly, a threshold of 0 would mean that everything was treated as positive, so both TPR and FPR would be 1. Intermediate thresholds, for example 0.5, would give a different value for TPR and FPR. TPR and FPR are combined into a measure known as the receiver operating characteristic (ROC)[39] which plots TPR vs. FPR as the threshold varies with different values, see Figure 1.3 for an example. It is also common to use the area under the curve ROC (AUC-ROC) to report the model performance, and the closer the AUC is to 1, the better the performance is.[40]

39 The origin of the concept was in the development of radars in the 1940s, hence the slightly unintuitive name.

40 T Fawcett, 'An Introduction to ROC Analysis' (2006) 27(8) *Pattern Recognition Letters* 861.

The AUC-ROC can be used to compare different ML models to choose the best one for a particular application. Figure 1.3 illustrates the use of a ROC curve for this purpose, comparing a convolutional neural network (CNN) with a fully connected deep neural network (DNN).[41] A random ML model (prediction) would produce a diagonal line on the ROC and the AUC-ROC would be 0.5. A perfect ML model would give an AUC-ROC of 1, and the 'curve' would follow the axes in the diagram. The example in Figure 1.3 shows that the two ML models have similar performance as measured by the AUC-ROC.

The intent of the evaluation criteria for ML models is to illuminate how well the model performs, contrasting desired behaviour with erroneous or undesirable behaviour.

In practice, development of ML models is highly iterative[42] and model developers frequently build and test new models, evaluating them to see if the performance has improved. Once ML models are put into operation they may still be updated, for example if new data is available.

D *Examples of ML Methods*

There are many ML methods as we mentioned earlier. The aim here is to illustrate the variety and their capabilities to inform the discussion on the use of ML methods later, and on strengths, limitations, the state of the art and challenges in Section III.

Some of the more widely used ML methods are:

- NNs – a network of artificial (computer models of) neurons, inspired by the human brain.[43] NNs are good at analysing complex data, for example images, and can be used supervised, for example, with labelled images, or unsupervised.[44] There are many variants, for example, CNN and fully connected DNN as illustrated in Figure 1.3.
- Random forest (RF) – a collection of decision trees which is normally more robust (less susceptible to error in a single input) than a single decision tree.[45] Usually, RF is developed using supervised learning, and they are well-suited to decision problems, for example, for clinical diagnosis.[46]

41 NNs have an input layer (of neurons), and an output layer with hidden layers in between. Here, the fully connected DNN means all of the hidden layers are fully connected. CNN means that at least one of the hidden layers uses convolution instead of being fully connected.

42 R Hawkins and others, 'Guidance on the Assurance of Machine Leaning in Autonomous Systems (AMLAS)' (2021) <arXiv:2102.01564>.

43 MA Nielsen, *Neural Networks and Deep Learning*, vol 25 (Determination Press 2015).

44 M Alloghani and others, "A Systematic Review on Supervised and Unsupervised Machine Learning Algorithms for Data Science' in M. Berry, A. Mohamed, B. Yap (eds), *Supervised and Unsupervised Learning for Data Science* (Springer 2020) 3.

45 M Belgiu and L Drăguţ, 'Random Forest in Remote Sensing: A Review of Applications and Future Directions' (2016) 114 *ISPRS Journal of Photogrammetry and Remote Sensing* 24.

46 KR Gray and others, 'Random Forest-Based Similarity Measures for Multi-Modal Classification of Alzheimer's Disease' (2013) 65 *NeuroImage* 167.

- Probabilistic graphical models (PGMs) – a graph of variables (features) of interest in the problem domain and probabilistic relationships between them. There are several types of PGM including Bayesian networks (BNs) and Markov networks.[47] They can be used both supervised and unsupervised.

Generally, the learnt models, most notably DNNs, are very complex and 'opaque' to humans, that is, not open to scrutiny. PGMs are more amenable to human inspection, and it is possible to integrate human domain knowledge into PGMs. The primary difference between DNNs and PGMs lies in the structure of the machine learnt model in that PGMs tend to reflect human reasoning more explicitly, including causation.[48] This aids the process of interrogating the model for understanding the basis of its output. This level of transparency is harder to achieve with DNNs and therefore the majority of the techniques that are used to explain the output of DNN models rely on indirect means,[49] for example, examples and counterfactual explanations.[50]

E *Uses of ML Models*

There are many uses of ML models. Some are embedded in engineered systems, for example, AVs, whereas others are IT systems, that is, operating on a computer, phone, or similar device.

AVs are an example of embedded ML. AVs often use ML for camera image analysis and understanding, for example classifying 'objects' into dynamic vs static, and identifying subclasses of dynamic objects – cars, bicycles, pedestrians, and so on. Typically, the systems employ a form of NN, for example, CNNs.[51] Many employ conventional computational methods of path planning (local navigation) but some use RL to determine safe and optimal paths.[52]

ML is increasingly being proposed for use in healthcare for both diagnosis and treatment;[53] most of such applications are IT systems. Some of the systems also involve image analysis, for example, identifying tumours in images, with performance exceeding that of clinicians in some cases.[54] There are online systems, for

47 J Pearl, *Probabilistic Reasoning in Intelligent Systems: Networks of Plausible Inference* (Morgan Kaufmann 1988); D Lowd and A Rooshenas, 'Learning Markov Networks with Arithmetic Circuits' (2013) 31 *Artificial Intelligence and Statistics* 406.

48 J Pearl and D Mackenzie, *The Book of Why: The New Science of Cause and Effect* (Basic Books 2018).

49 J McDermid, Y Jia, Z Porter and I Habli, 'Artificial Intelligence Explainability: The Technical and Ethical Dimensions' (2021) 379(2207) *PhilTrans*.

50 S Wachter, B Mittelstadt and C Russell, 'Counterfactual Explanations without Opening the Black Box: Automated Decisions and the GDPR' (2017) 31 *Harv JL & Tech* 841.

51 S Ren, K He, R Girshick and J Sun, 'Faster R-CNN: Towards Real-Time Object Detection with Region Proposal Networks' (2015) 28 *Advances in Neural Information Processing Systems* 91.

52 AE Sallab, M Abdou, E Perot and S Yogamani, 'Deep Reinforcement Learning Framework for Autonomous Driving' (2017) 19 *Electronic Imaging* 70.

53 E Topol, *Deep Medicine: How Artificial Intelligence Can Make Healthcare Human Again* (Hachette 2019).

54 EJ Hwang and others, 'Development and Validation of a Deep Learning Based Automatic Detection Algorithm for Active Pulmonary Tuberculosis on Chest Radiographs' (2019) 69(5) *Clinical Infectious Diseases* 739–747.

example, from Babylon Health,[55] which employs an ML-based symptom checker. Applications which recommend treatments are also being explored, for example, delivery of vasopressors as part of sepsis treatment.[56]

Legal uses of AI are also IT systems. The applications include predicting the outcome of tax appeals[57] and helping with the production of legal letters which correctly phrase non-expert text in support of claims, and other legal actions.[58] Some of the benefit of such tools arises from currently available computational power to trawl large volumes of documents, and there are now commercially available tools that use ML (including supervised and unsupervised learning) to find appropriate legal documentation to support a case.[59]

III STATE OF THE ART AND CHALLENGES

AI, particularly ML, has enormous potential. As noted above, this arises out of its ability to generalise from the data used for training to new situations; this is perhaps the strongest justification for the use of the term 'intelligence'. However, some would argue that the potential hasn't been fully realised.[60] The aim in this section is to try to characterise the state of the art in the use of ML, noting that it differs across application domains, and to identify some of the challenges in achieving more widespread use of the technology. The focus here is on technical and ethical issues, rather than on legal challenges.

A *State of the Art*

ML is already pervasive in a range of online applications (IT systems). As indicated above, online platforms, which many use daily, such as Google search and online shopping, make massive use of ML.[61] Arguably, Google's search engine is one of the most impressive applications of ML providing extensive results to arbitrary textual queries in a very short space of time. This is all the more impressive as the learning is necessarily unsupervised. As well as good algorithms, this is made possible by access to massive computational power in data centres (sometimes referred to as 'cloud computing').[62]

55 www.emed.com/uk 18 August 2022.

56 Y Jia and others, 'Safety-Driven Design of Machine Learning for Sepsis Treatment' (2021) 117 *Journal of Biomedical Informatics* 103762.

57 <www2.deloitte.com/nl/nl/pages/tax/articles/tax-i-outcome-predictions-dutch-tax-cases.html>.

58 <www.donotpay.com>.

59 <www.luminance.com>.

60 Demis Hassabis, 'Royal Society Lecture on the History, Capabilities and Frontiers of AI' <www.royalsociety.org/science-events-and-lectures/2018/04/you-and-ai-history/>.

61 See: <www.blog.hubspot.com/marketing/rankbrain-guide>.

62 R Buyya, J Broberg and AM Goscinski (eds), *Cloud Computing: Principles and Paradigms* (Wiley & Sons 2010).

Such capabilities are becoming 'commoditised' and companies, for example, Amazon Web Services,[63] now provide access to data centres as a commercial offering. Further, the software to build ML applications is now widely available. For example, TensorFlow,[64] originally developed by Google is readily available; it can be used to build applications with a wide range of ML models including NNs, although it still requires extensive programming skills; there is also support for developing popular classes of system such as recommenders.

Further, there is a growing availability of skills to develop such systems with most computer science departments in universities teaching ML at undergraduate and postgraduate level. Thus, the ingredients are there for widespread development of AI and ML applications.

Most application domains where ML is being applied can be viewed as emergent or nascent. Whilst there are examples of systems, for example, in healthcare and legal practice, their adoption is not widespread. We will illuminate some of the reasons for this when we consider challenges.

There has been work on ML in embedded systems for some time, for example, in robotics, but the 'autonomous vehicle challenge' set up by the US Defense Advanced Research Projects Agency ('DARPA') about fifteen years ago can perhaps be seen as prompting a step-change in research in this area.[65] Although there is work using ML systems across transportation and in other sectors, for example, factory automation,[66] mining[67] and robotic surgery,[68] perhaps the greatest investment and development has been seen in AVs. Waymo (a spin off from Google) is now offering a 'ride hailing' service known as Waymo One;[69] whilst this service is only available in limited areas, for example, in Phoenix Arizona,[70] the service does operate without a human driver and the vehicles have now operated for about 20 million miles on the roads.[71] Waymo has also now forged partnerships with several automotive Original Equipment Manufacturers ('OEMs'), for example, Jaguar Land Rover.[72] However, whilst extremely impressive, the systems are not 'perfect',

63 <www.aws.amazon.com/>.

64 <www.tensorflow.org>.

65 M Buehler, K Iagnemma and S Singh (eds), *The DARPA Urban Challenge: Autonomous Vehicles in City Traffic*, vol 56 (Springer 2009).

66 DH Kim and others, 'Smart Machining Process Using Machine Learning: A Review and Perspective on Machining Industry' (2018) 5(4) *International Journal of Precision Engineering and Manufacturing-Green Technology* 555.

67 Z Hyder, K Siau and F Nah, 'Artificial Intelligence, Machine Learning, and Autonomous Technologies in Mining Industry' (2019) 30(2) *Journal of Database Management (JDM)* 67.

68 M Bhandari, T Zeffiro and M Reddiboina, 'Artificial Intelligence and Robotic Surgery: Current Perspective and Future Directions' (2020) 30(1) *Current Opinion in Urology* 48.

69 <www.waymo.com/waymo-one/>.

70 At the time of writing, services were being extended to San Francisco to 'trusted testers', see for example: <www.arstechnica.com/gadgets/2021/08/waymo-expands-to-san-francisco-with-public-self-driving-test/>.

71 <www.reuters.com/article/us-autonomous-waymo-idUSKBN1Z61RX>.

72 <www.theverge.com/2018/3/27/17165992/waymo-jaguar-i-pace-self-driving-ny-auto-show-2018>.

and there have been several examples of vehicles getting confused or 'stuck', for example, by traffic cones.[73]

Note that these systems are computationally expensive (particularly for image analysis)[74] and are only practicable because of the availability of super-computer levels of performance at affordable prices.[75] Further, computational power is doubling roughly every eighteen months[76] which should facilitate the broader adoption of ML.

B *Challenges*

There are many challenges in developing ML-based systems, so that they can be used with confidence that their behaviour will be sound, safe, legal, and so on, where their use can give rise to harm. The aim here is to identify some of the key technical challenges and to outline some of the possible approaches to addressing these challenges.

First, and most fundamentally, there is a transfer of decision-making or responsibility for recommending a course of action from a human to a computer and its ML components. From a legal perspective, this raises issues about agency and liability which are discussed elsewhere in this volume.

Second, humans have a semantic model, for example, know what a bicycle is and its likely behaviour; computers, even those incorporating ML, do not have these models.[77] Similarly, humans have contextual models, for example, know what a roundabout is and the effects on driver behaviour, and the ML does not.[78] These semantic and contextual models allow humans to generalise beyond their experience to reliably deal with new situations. However, for systems using ML the lack of such models can contribute to 'gaps' between what is required and what is achieved, which may be significant in engineering, ethical and legal terms.[79] The solution to this is to encode enough additional information in the systems to cope with the limitations in the ML components to enable effective operation – note that this is potentially feasible as we are considering 'narrow AI' not AGI[80] – but, as the example of the Waymo getting stuck encountering traffic cones shows, doing this remains a major challenge.

[73] <www.vice.com/en/article/y3dv55/waymo-self-driving-car-gets-stuck-by-cones-drives-away-from-assistance>.

[74] F Dufaux, 'Grand Challenges in Image Processing' (2021) 1 *Frontiers in Signal Processing* 3.

[75] <www.qblocks.medium.com/how-much-did-it-cost-to-build-the-fastest-supercomputer-in-the-world-8e9e30a56f60>.

[76] This claim is often made in reference to Gordon Moore's prediction that the number of components in an integrated circuit would double every two year (referred to as 'Moore's law'), <www.britannica.com/technology/Moores-law>.

[77] A Darwiche, 'Human-Level Intelligence or Animal-Like Abilities?' (2018) 61(10) *Communications of the ACM* 56.

[78] C Paterson and others, 'DeepCert: Verification of Contextually Relevant Robustness for Neural Network Image Classifiers' (*International Conference on Computer Safety, Reliability, and Security*, September 2021) 3–17.

[79] S Burton and others, 'Mind the Gaps: Assuring the Safety of Autonomous Systems from an Engineering, Ethical, and Legal Perspective' (2020) 279 *Artif Intell* 103201.

[80] G Marcus and E Davis, *Rebooting AI: Building Artificial Intelligence We Can Trust* (Vintage 2019).

Third, the way the ML systems work, generalising from training data, identifies correlations not causation.[81] A recent study[82] used ML to assess the relationship between body shape and income, and identified correlations which differ across genders, for example that obesity in females correlates with lower income. It would be a mistake, however, to infer that body shape *causes* low income – it may be that those on low income cannot afford a good diet and that might lead to obesity. Further, there may be other causally relevant factors that have not been considered in the ML model. This does not mean that the ML model is wrong; just that care needs to be taken when acting on the outputs of the ML model.

Fourth, the learnt ML models are 'opaque', that is not amenable to human scrutiny.[83] This means that it is hard to understand why the ML models produce their outputs. This can, in turn, give rise to doubts – why was that recommendation made, and was it biased? This has legal implications, for example, in terms of complying with the General Data Protection Regulations,[84] as well as ethical ones in terms of fairness. A partial solution is via so-called explainable AI methods, where simpler approaches are used to make the workings of the ML model human interpretable.[85] One of the most commonly used explainable AI methods is feature importance which illustrates the relative weight of each input feature for the ML model as a whole (global importance) or for a particular output (local importance).[86] This is illustrated in Figure 1.4, for a system concerned with weaning intensive care patients from mechanical ventilation. Here, the longer bars show greater influence of that input feature on the ML model output, with those bars close to zero length being of least importance.

This figure is for the two ML models shown in Figure 1.3. The two ML models have similar performance as shown in Figure 1.3, but the feature importance is quite different. Clinicians can judge the relevance and validity of these weightings to see which, if either, of the ML models is preferable. It is also notable that gender, ethnicity, and age are close to zero (low importance) for the CNN but age and gender in the fully connected DNN are relatively important, so this model might be thought to show bias. Care needs to be taken here. Age and gender might be clinically relevant, so a judgement about whether a system is biased or not needs to be

81 JG Richens, CM Lee and S Johri, 'Improving the Accuracy of Medical Diagnosis with Causal Machine Learning' (2020) 11(1) *Nature Communications* 1.

82 S Song and S Baek, 'Body Shape Matters: Evidence from Machine Learning on Body Shape-Income Relationship' (2021) 16(7) *PLoS One* e0254785 <https://doi.org/10.1371/journal.pone.0254785>.

83 C Molnar, 'Interpretable Machine Learning' (Lulu.com, 2021).

84 C Kuner and others, 'Machine Learning with Personal Data: Is Data Protection Law Smart Enough to Meet the Challenge?' (2017) 7(1) *International Data Privacy Law* 1, 1–2.

85 D Doran, S Schulz and TR Besold, 'What Does Explainable AI Really Mean? A New Conceptualization of Perspectives' (2017) <arXiv preprint arXiv:1710.00794>.

86 LH Gilpin and others, 'Explaining Explanations: An Overview of Interpretability of Machine Learning' (*IEEE 5th International Conference on Data Science and Advanced Analytics (DSAA)*, October 2018) 80–89.

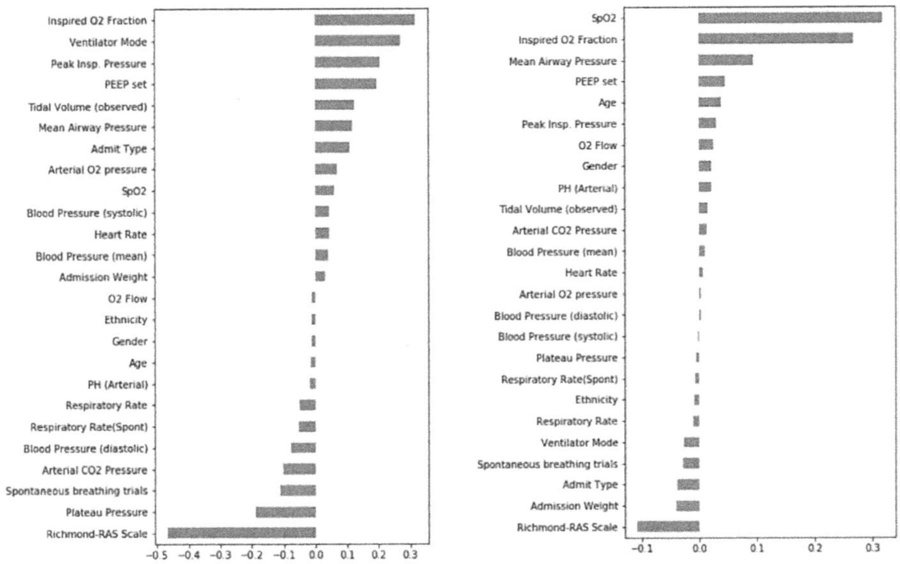

(a) CNN (b) DNN

FIGURE 1.4 Global feature importance for CNN and fully connected DNN McDermid, Jia, Porter and Habli, 'Artificial Intelligence Explainability: The Technical and Ethical Dimensions' (n 49).

considered carefully; in this case, ethical considerations need to be treated alongside clinical ones.

Fifth, there is an issue of trust and human control over the system employing ML. As noted above, some ML systems produce outputs with a probability; in all cases, there is uncertainty in the accuracy of the results.[87] Users should be (made) aware of this intrinsic uncertainty. However, even if they are aware, there can be automation bias where users tend to trust the system's outputs without questioning them.[88] Further, the user might have no practical way of cross-checking the output of the ML system – they might not have access to the 'raw' data and there may simply be insufficient time to assess the data and to intervene. Such issues might, in part, be addressed using techniques such as explainable AI methods but there remain legal and ethical issues, for example, the ethical conditions for carrying responsibility might not be met for those who carry legal responsibility for the effects of using the system[89].

[87] MA Nielsen, *Neural Networks and Deep Learning*, vol 25 (Determination Press 2015).

[88] R Parasuraman and V Riley, 'Humans and Automation: Use, Misuse, Disuse, Abuse' (1997) 39(2) *Human Factors* 230.

[89] Burton and others (n 79).

FIGURE 1.5 Partial timeline in Uber Tempe accident

Sixth, many embedded systems operate in situations where they can pose a threat to human health or safety, for example, in unmanned aircraft for reconnaissance.[90] However, this is perhaps most apparent with AVs although it can arise in other cases, for example, robotic surgery. Figure 1.5 presents a partial timeline for the accident

[90] JA McDermid, Y Jia and I Habli, 'Towards a Framework for Safety Assurance of Autonomous Systems' (CEUR Workshop Proceedings, August 2019) 1–7.

caused by an Uber ATG vehicle in March 2018 in Tempe Arizona that led to the death of Elaine Herzberg.[91] This example enables us to illustrate the importance of some of the concepts introduced earlier.

Figure 1.5 shows the positions of Elaine Herzberg and her bicycle (labelled as pedestrian) and the Uber ATG vehicle (shown in green) at four times prior to the impact. The Highway Accident Report published by the National Transportation Safety Board stated that the Automated Driving System 'never accurately classified her as a pedestrian or predicted her path'.[92] Critically, the predicted motion depended on the classification so when she was on one of the left turn lanes and classified as a car, she was predicted to leave the main road. Her movement history was discarded each time the vehicle reclassified her so at no time was her trajectory predicted as crossing the road. An impending collision was predicted 1.2S before the actual accident took place but the system did not act automatically (due to a concern over false positives leading to unnecessary emergency braking) with the expectation that the safety driver would respond. The safety driver (Rafaela Vasquez) didn't initiate timely braking – reportedly she was not paying attention, perhaps due to lack of training or due to automation bias (the vehicle had already successfully navigated the 'circuit' on which she was driving once). However, it may have been the case that she had insufficient time to react – see the previous discussion about legal and ethical responsibility. Uber was found to have no (legal) (criminal) case to answer for the accident, but the safety driver is facing a trial for negligent homicide.[93] There is no currently accepted solution to assuring the safety of autonomous systems.[94] There is relevant work on the assurance of the ML components of autonomous systems[95] but this remains an active area of research.

Finally, ML models can be set up to continue learning in operation – sometimes referred to as online learning.[96] This is, of course, analogous to the way humans learn. Most current ML-based systems learn off-line with the ML models being updated periodically by the developers (perhaps via over-the-air updates in the case of AVs).[97] As systems move towards online learning this introduces new challenges including how to assure continued safety, and it raises further questions about human control and agency.

91 National Transportation Safety Board, 'Collision between Vehicle Controlled by Developmental Automated Driving System and Pedestrian' (2019) *NTSB Tech Rep* <www.ntsb.gov/investigations/AccidentReports/Reports/HAR1903.pdf>.

92 Ibid.

93 <www.bbc.co.uk/news/technology-54175359>.

94 McDermid, Jia and Habli 'Towards a Framework for Safety Assurance of Autonomous Systems' (n 90).

95 R Hawkins and others, 'Guidance on the Assurance of Machine Leaning in Autonomous Systems (AMLAS)' (2021) <arXiv:2102.01564>.

96 GI Parisi, 'Continual Lifelong Learning with Neural Networks: A Review' (2019) 113 *Neural Networks* 54.

97 J Bauwens, 'Over-the-Air Software Updates in the Internet of Things: An Overview of Key Principles' (2020) 58(2) *IEEE Communications Magazine* 35.

IV CONCLUSIONS

AI, especially ML, is already a key component of many systems affecting society – not least online search and other online services. The capability of current ML systems and the trends in the power of computer systems means that these uses are likely to expand over time from current applications which are predominantly IT systems to include embedded systems, for example, in AVs, implantable medical devices and manufacturing. Further, the range of application domains is likely to expand. These capabilities bring with them challenges in technical, ethical and legal terms.

Technically, the biggest challenge is to develop and assure systems employing ML models so that they can be used with confidence that they are safe and have other desirable properties, including being free from bias. This links to the broader issues of trust and the ability for humans to exercise informed control or consent when this is appropriate. There are many legal questions, including those around the notion of agency and liability. This is a complex and intellectually challenging area, but also one requiring urgent attention since systems employing ML models are already being used and there is potential for considerable growth in applications.

This chapter has tried to give an accessible (gentle) introduction to the concepts of AI and ML for lawyers. Some technical details have been presented, for example, explaining the concept of feature importance for ML models, to give an idea of the depth and subtlety of the issues raised by the use of AI and ML models. It is hoped that this makes clear the need to take a multi-disciplinary approach to studying and evolving the legal framework relating to AI and ML and gives an adequate basis to help lawyers engage in constructive discussions with technical specialists.

2

Computable Law and AI

Harry Surden

I WHAT IS COMPUTABLE LAW?

'Computable Law' is a research area focused on the creation and use of computer models of laws. What does it mean to model a law computationally? There are a few broad approaches. In one method, researchers begin with traditional, written legal sources of law – such as statutes, contracts, administrative regulations, and court opinions – and identify legal rules that they wish to model.[1] They then aim to 'translate' aspects of these legal obligations into comparable sets of organised data, programming instructions, and other forms of expression that computers can easily process. In that approach, one begins with a familiar legal text written in a 'natural language'[2] such as English, and then aims to represent qualities of the legal obligations described – such as their *structure, meaning, or application* – in terms of data, programming rules and other highly organised forms of expression that are easier for computers to handle.

The other approach allows us to express legal obligations as *data from the outset*. There, one begins with laws expressed as computer data in their initial form – a departure from the written-language through which laws have traditionally been conveyed. An example of this approach can be found in the so-called data-oriented,

[1] For an example of some interesting work in this area, see A Malerba, A Rotolo and G Governatori, 'A Logic for the Interpretation of Private International Law' in S Rahman, M Armgardt and HCN Kvernenes (eds), *New Developments in Legal Reasoning and Logic: From Ancient Law to Modern Legal Systems* (Springer 2022) 149–169; Carla L Reyes, 'Creating Cryptolaw for the Uniform Commercial Code' (2021) 78 *Wash & Lee L Rev* 90; H Diedrich, *Lexon Bible: Hitchhiker's Guide to Digital Contracts* (2020); MJ Sergot and others, 'The British Nationality Act as a Logic Program' (1986) 29 *Communications of the ACM* 370; S Lawsky, 'Form as Formalization' (2020) 16 *Ohio St LJ* 114; H Bhuiyan and others, 'A Methodology for Encoding Regulatory Rules' (CEUR Workshop Proceedings, 2020) 14.

[2] As will be described, 'natural language' is the term that computer scientists use to refer to the ordinary spoken and written languages that people use to communicate with one another, such as French, English, or Spanish. The term 'natural language' is used to contrast against the highly structured, 'formal languages' of computer instructions and data that are used, among other things, to program computers.

'computable contracts'.[3] These are legal agreements created electronically, whose core terms are expressed largely as data rather than as written paragraphs, and which are frequently used in finance, electronic commerce, cryptocurrency,[4] and other areas. Through this 'data-oriented' method we are still ultimately able to display legal obligations in forms that people can understand, such as in language or visually on a computer screen. However, what is interesting is that the human-understandable versions are typically *derived* upwards from the underlying data. In other words, one can present to users what appear to be ordinary written legal documents on a screen or on paper, but the contents of those documents are actually generated by processing lower-level computer data. In those cases, it is sometimes best to think of the law's native data-oriented representation as the authoritative version (or source of 'ground-truth') for information about the legal obligations.

Why model laws in computer-processable form? Doing so can enable new and useful analytical capabilities that are not generally possible today. An example involving contract law will help illustrate this. Traditionally in the United States, the terms of a contract – such as an insurance agreement – are expressed in writing, in an English-language document.[5] However, if such an insurance contract were developed

[3] Computable contracts (and computable law generally) should not be confused with the so-called 'smart contracts'. Computable contracts is a broader research area devoted to modelling any legal agreement in computational form, whereas 'smart contracts' refers to a much narrower subset of these ideas. I described the idea of 'computable contracts' here, in Harry Surden, 'Computable Contracts' (2012) 46 *UC Davis L Rev* 629 and work is ongoing here <www.law.stanford.edu/projects/stanford-computable-contracts-initiative/> to develop a general, robust and theoretically supported data-oriented, legal contracting framework for expressing contractual relations. By contrast, the term 'smart contracts' is a somewhat misleading name that refers to distributed *computer programs* (that are not necessarily, or even usually, legal contracts) that are running on a blockchain in a virtual machine. Examples include programs written in the Solidity language running on the Ethereum blockchain. The term 'smart contract' is confusing for a few reasons. For one, it suggests that most smart contracts are also legal contracts. This is not the case. Legal contracts are, approximately speaking, formal promises to exchange something of value, under certain conditions, with remedies available under some legal system. By contrast, 'smart contracts' are simply arbitrary computer programs and need not resemble legal contracts at all. It is true that some subset of these distributed 'smart contract' computer programs resemble legal contracts in that their programmatic function is to exchange some virtual or tangible good of value and might, in fact, be valid legal contracts in that jurisdiction. But the vast majority of 'smart contracts' that could be created are simply generic computer programs that have no resemblance to legal contracts. Computable law can be thought of a superset of smart-contracts, one whose theoretical structures allow for representing a much broader range of aspects of laws and contractual obligations computationally while also being consciously grounded in legal theory and practice.

[4] The other major area is cryptocurrency and the blockchain, in addition to finance and e-commerce. Although the concepts of this chapter do apply to the blockchain space and programmatic efforts to represent certain legal obligations, this chapter will largely not address the cryptocurrency/blockchain space specifically because it is rapidly changing and still maturing. This chapter aims to take a more general approach to computable law that are applicable to multiple technologies, rather than specific implementations.

[5] Although often contracts are 'memorialised' and expressed in a single written document, sometimes contracts span multiple documents or exist across time with new versions that amend or supplement previous versions. For our purposes, we will think of a contract as a single document, although that is not necessarily always the case.

according to the principles of computable law, it would contain additional information that would facilitate computer processing. Along with the familiar written document, the computable version of the contract would also include well-defined data and rules that describe core aspects of the contract in a machine-processable format. Such additional data could enable capabilities – such as automated compliance checking, risk assessment, or enable predictive analytics – activities that are challenging to perform within the constraints of today's natural language contract environment.

Because laws and legal documents are complex, there are many distinct aspects of legal obligations that we may wish to represent as data. To account for this, computable law categorises computable legal data into different types depending upon the different characteristics of laws that we are aiming to capture. Some of the main categories include *structural, semantic, control-flow, and legal application data*, each of which will be illustrated briefly below.

'Structural data' is the term for information that clearly identifies and distinguishes the key components of legal obligations. For instance, contracts often have individual provisions with specific purposes, such as a 'Force Majeure'[6] (or 'Act of God') clause that excuses obligations in the case of a major disruptive event, or a 'Choice of Law'[7] provision that specifies the jurisdiction whose law governs the contract. In the insurance contract discussed earlier, structural data might be used to uniquely label the role of the various provisions, uniquely distinguishing a 'Force Majeure' provision from a 'Choice of Law' provision. The addition of such structural data to a written language contract allows a computer to reliably identify the intended function of each provision and also dependably extract core information about the contract terms.

Structural data can also be used to describe how portions of a legal document are organised, presented, or otherwise related to one another. For instance, contracts often have dependencies – portions whose meanings are intrinsically linked to other sections of the contract or to external sources. For example, a contract provision might rely upon a condition or described elsewhere in the document. Traditionally, such connections within a contract might not be explicitly stated, leaving it up to the astute reader to infer these links through careful cross-referencing. This implicitness can lead to misunderstandings or oversight. By contrast, structural data can be used to make explicit any dependencies, constraints, or relationships that exist in a legal document. For example, if the parties were to change the governing law from one state (New York) to another (Delaware) in

6 A 'Force Majeure' provision is a common contractual clause that relieves parties of various responsibilities in the case of extraordinary circumstances, such as war and natural disaster, that make performance impractical or impossible.

7 A 'Choice of Law' or 'Governing Law' provision is a common contractual clause which clarifies which state jurisdiction's laws should be applied in case of disputes over interpretation or application of the contract.

the Choice of Law provision, other parts of the contract may need to be altered to ensure consistency. Structural data can thus be used to explicitly flag and systematically capture such interdependencies.

Additional structural data might be used to demarcate important information within provisions, such as contract expiration dates, price terms, the identities of contracting parties, and other related agreements, in a form that computer can reliably read and identify. Consider the type of structural data that might be added to the traditional legal language for a contract's 'Choice of Law' provision (e.g., 'This agreement shall be governed by the law of the State of Delaware…'):

Example of Structural Data (simplified):

```
{ Contract_Role   : 'Choice_Of_Law',
  Jurisdiction    : 'Delaware_State',
  Dependencies    : ['Termination_Clause', 'Dispute_Resolution_Clause']
}
```

This example, although simplified[8] for explanatory purposes, illustrates the general idea of a structural data – a consistent data format for conveying legal information that computers can reliably process. In this example, we imagine that the parties have agreed that the keyword 'Contract_Role': will indicate to a computer that the subsequent data will describe the function of that specific contract provision (e.g., 'Choice of Law'). For the moment, the details of the data format illustrated is not important. Rather, the crucial point is that it allows information about legal obligations to be conveyed according to a precise set of rules that a computer can follow, and it has human-readable labels that sensibly describe the legal information that is being expressed.

Although the addition of such basic structural data to a legal document might seem rudimentary from a technological standpoint, this simple step is one of the foundations that enables more advanced legal analytics. Structural data, such as that shown earlier, allows computers to consistently identify and extract important legal information, such as the fact that Delaware state law governs any disputes under the example contract. Once extracted, that data, in turn, can then be used for more sophisticated legal analysis by other computing systems that can analyse, visualise, simulate, or otherwise make use of such legal information. Without such structural data, seemingly basic tasks such as determining the parties, the governing law, the prices, or other core contract information are surprisingly difficult for computers to do accurately today in the typical environment in which legal instruments are composed of ordinary written sentences. Such 'natural language' legal documents are comparatively easy for people to read but challenging for contemporary computers to process with the reliability and conceptual sophistication of a literate person.

[8] To improve clarity and readability, I have included only partial and simplified examples of structural and semantic data that would, in more realistic cases, be somewhat more complex.

In addition to structural data, a computable law document, such as an insurance contract might also contain *semantic data*.[9] 'Semantic data' is conceptually distinct from structural data and refers to information about the *meaning* of legal language. At its core, semantic data essentially involves providing a computer with data or programming instructions that reasonably reflect what was intended by legal language, but that, unlike ordinary language, once expressed as data it can also be reliably processed by a computer. The reason that semantic data is needed is that computers do not, on their own, necessarily understand language in the cognitively sophisticated way that people do. Although natural language processing abilities are improving, computers must generally be provided with instructions or patterns that associate words with computer-processable actions that sensibly reflect the meaning of those words in order to ensure consistency and reliability. For instance, imagine (based upon a real example) that the insurance agreement had a provision restricting coverage to the so-called 'Qualified Hospitals' that stated, 'A "Qualified Hospital" under this agreement is one licensed under state law and which has a minimum of 1000 beds.' On its own, a typical computer would not be able to interpret the meaning of that provision sensibly. However, it is sometimes possible to 'decompose' (or 'conceptually break apart') such a seemingly abstract legal criterion into an analogous set of computable programming rules that the parties agree suitably reflects its meaning, such as:

Qualified_Hospital = IsCurrentlyLicensed & (Minimum_Bed_Count >= 1000)[10]

The rule earlier instructs a computer that the meaning of the condition 'Qualified_Hospital' (whether a hospital is qualified for insurance coverage according to the contracting parties' agreed upon terms) can be decomposed into two distinct subcomponents that can be automatically assessed: 'IsCurrentlyLicensed' (which represents whether or not a particular hospital is actively licensed under state law) and 'Minimum_Bed_Count > 1000' (which requires a source of data about any particular hospital's actual count of patient beds).[11]

Consider another example: a different abstract contract criterion, such as 'Force Majeure', might be partially broken down into an enumerated list of the most

[9] The term 'semantics' in computer science has more limited connation than its use in linguistics. In linguistics, semantics generally refers to the entire complex relationship by which words acquire their literal or non-literal meanings in society, whereas in computer science, the term semantics generally means relating programming keywords (e.g., 'print') to a series of computer instructions or data that usually correspond to a sensible understanding of that keyword (e.g., linked to instructions causing the symbols to 'print' or appear on a screen or on paper). See, for example, CA Gunter, *Semantics of Programming Languages: Structures and Techniques* (2nd edn, MIT Press 1993).

[10] This computer rule is expressed in the so-called 'pseudo-code'. 'Pseudo-code' is an informal way of expressing computer programming rules in an approximate, casual and readable way, but that is not tied to the details of any specific programming language such as Python, Java, or C.

[11] We need to provide additional semantic instructions and data for a computer (described later) defining IsCurrentlyLicensed and Minimum_Bed_Count, so that for any particular hospital, it can determine whether it is actively licensed and what that hospital's count of hospital beds is.

common disruptive events that potentially excuse a party from performing the contracts obligations (e.g., Force_Majeure = [war, pandemic, natural disaster]). This is a slightly different approach from the rules-based method just described because it involves decomposing indefinite legal criterion such as 'Force Majeure' into a concrete list of common examples, rather than computer instructions. However, this enumeration approach can be useful for computer processability in the event of legal 'easy cases' where the parties are not disputing that conditions are satisfied (e.g., a pandemic occurs and both parties agree obligations should be excused), to assess the impact of this change on contractual obligations.[12] Although attorneys tend to focus on 'hard-cases' where parties are disputing legal criteria, there is also significant and under-recognised value in computationally processing commonly occurring 'easy cases' (where parties agree that conditions have been met), because routine but important contractual data can then be automatically passed on to other operational systems for further relevant actions. At the same time, the semantic data technique can also preserve the flexibility to handle unexpected 'hard-cases' that are not explicitly listed by alerting the parties that something unexpected or disputed has arisen.

In sum, adding *semantic data* can facilitate automated analysis of legal language under the right circumstances. Of course, not all legal language can be meaningfully (or desirably) represented in terms of enumerated data or rules that computers can automatically process, as in the examples above.[13] But it is interesting to observe is that it *sometimes* is possible to provide counterparts to legal language that are computable.[14]

In addition to structural and semantic data, *computable law* principles allow us to model other important aspects of laws. Consider two more facets: control flow and application data. *Control-flow* refers to information about the logical structure of legal rules and the individual subcomponents that comprise them.[15] Many legal rules implicitly have a general 'IF-THEN' structure within their language, as in 'If these criteria are met, then these legal consequences will follow.' (i.e., Criteria-Consequences Form). For instance, the US Constitution states (paraphrasing slightly for clarity), 'No person except a natural born citizen … shall be eligible to the Office

[12] In the common case where contract criteria are triggered without dispute, it is still often helpful to pass on data about changed contract conditions to other computing systems.

[13] It is common to have 'hybrid' models of legal obligations where some are amenable to being represented in terms of both semantic rules and ordinary language, and where other portions are expressed only as language.

[14] Of course, given the diversity of language used in contracts (e.g., 'reasonable efforts'), it is not always useful or feasible to translate language into data or rules, but it is possible and helpful more often than attorneys typically expect.

[15] For examples of programming tools capable of representing control flow, see Andrew Mowbray, Graham Greenleaf and Philip Chung, 'Law as Code: Introducing AustLII's DataLex AI' (UNSW Law Research Paper No 21-81, 2021) (describing the 'yscript' rules-as-code language); Harold Boley and others, 'A Datalog+ RuleML 1.01 Architecture for Rule-Based Data Access in Ecosystem Research' in Antonis Bikakis, Paul Fodor and Dumitru Roman (eds), *Rules on the Web: From Theory to Applications* (Springer 2014) 112–126.

of President … [nor anyone] … who shall not have attained to the age of thirty-five years…'[16] A statement like this can be reformulated into *criteria-consequence* form. *Control-flow* data makes the implicit logical structure within such an English-language law more explicit in terms of 'IF X and Y Then Z' (or similar) style programming rules that model the conditions, constraints and consequences, such as:

Control Flow Data:
IF (NaturalBornCitizen) AND (Age >= 35) THEN potentiallyEligiblePresident

Of course, this example is not meant to suggest that this Constitutional provision (or any other) would benefit from computational law or should be automated in any way. Nor does it reflect the fact that legal rules, such as constitutional provisions, are often subject to interpretation by courts that can diverge from their plain textual meaning. Rather this example is simply meant to illustrate that a wide range of legal rules and obligations, emanating from public sources as diverse as federal and state constitutions, statutes,[17] administrative regulations, court opinions, to private law sources such as contracts and wills, contain basic structural characteristics that are, at a basic level, compatible with computable law principles of control-flow modelling. As a practical matter, modelling control flow becomes most useful when one is aiming to assess compliance with large numbers of legal rules or obligations, an example of which is assessing an individual or corporation navigating a complex legal environment with hundreds of statutory, administrative, or contractual obligations.

Finally, *legal application data* refers to data about how legal rules are intended to be applied (or are actually applied) to factual scenarios that arise. Such legal application data might include instructions about conditions in the world that are relevant to whether legal obligations have been triggered, or explicit processes for assessing the consequences of legal rules once triggered. For instance, in the insurance agreement described earlier with *'IsCurrentlyLicensed'*, *legal application data* might be used to specify a precise computational procedure to query an official, government hospital licensing database to determine whether a specific hospital is actively licensed, according to some criteria, in order to meet the contract's conditions.[18] Together, computable law principles allow us to use *structural data, semantic data, control-flow data, and legal application data,* to represent aspects of laws, or legal documents in terms of consistently structured computer data.

16 See US Const Art II, Section I, Paragraph 5. ('No person except a natural born citizen, or a citizen of the United States, at the time of the adoption of this Constitution, shall be eligible to the office of President; neither shall any person be eligible to that office who shall not have attained to the age of thirty-five years, and been fourteen years a resident within the United States.')

17 This point is important because readers might get the misimpression from the examples given that computable law principles are relevant only to contract law. However, computable law methods have also been applied to US income tax law and several other areas of public law.

18 This is a concept similar to that sometimes referred to in the cryptocurrency area as an 'oracle', although I consider the oracle concept too narrow compared to the more general idea of assessing data indicative of a legal condition or criterion.

Taking a step back from the details, we can see how the examples above illustrate some of the central themes of computable law. One core idea involves taking aspects of laws that are today expressed using ordinary language such as English, and *where appropriate*,[19] modelling them as comparable, structured data-oriented forms that are amenable to computer processing. In that spirit, we can think of the contract discussed above as having been expressed, in parallel, in two different forms: one a traditional text document describing the contractual obligations in a way that people can read, and the other as data and rules that represent aspects of these same obligations, but in a manner more easily handled by computers. This is not so conceptually different from what happens today when individuals read legal contracts and necessarily must informally 'translate' them into a series of real-world actions that they believe to be consistent with the contract's specifications. For instance, when a firm's contract stipulates that a good be delivered by a specific date, an employee reading the contract must deconstruct this requirement and convert it into a set of actionable steps to ensure the delivery occurs as agreed. Thus, the sequence of actions taken to fulfil nearly any contract effectively becomes an informal translation of its stipulations and conditions – from the language of the contract to the language of actions, with the larger point being that, even today, most contracts inherently require some form of subjective 'translation', to some degree, from the original natural language version.

Another core computable law idea is concerned with *taking aspects of law that are today largely implicit and making them more explicit*. For instance, within official legal texts many substantively meaningful components are conveyed only implicitly through headings, formatting, organisation, or unstated background context. Where appropriate, computable law aims to foreground as data certain aspects of laws that are substantively meaningful but are today only implicitly (and often ambiguously) conveyed through visual or other contextual cues in legal texts. More broadly, although the prior examples primarily focused upon contract law, observe that many of these same computational principles can apply to statutory, administrative, judicial, and other sources of law, to varying degrees, depending upon the context.

Before discussing the benefits of computable law, it is important to clarify some potential misunderstandings. One common misperception is that computable law stands for a variety of naïve positions such as 'all laws should be computerised', 'automated-based laws are inherently better than current legal approaches' or 'law would be improved if we removed human discretion in favour of automation' or

[19] As I will frequently state throughout this chapter, I am *not arguing that computational law is always possible or appropriate* in every legal context. I am also *not arguing that converting a traditional natural-language area of law to computational law is necessarily better*. Also, it is important to acknowledge that even where possible in law, it is not always beneficial or appropriate to make computable aspects of every area of law, and as with any legal approach or tool, there are always trade-offs. Rather, my argument is simply that in the law it is *sometimes* possible and potentially beneficial to use computable law, and we must take care to appropriately identify those contexts and their trade-offs.

similar, viewpoints. This is decidedly not what I am suggesting, nor, in my experience, does it represent the position of researchers in this area. Those who research in computable law take seriously the insights from the Legal Realist, Critical Legal Studies, Legal Process, Science and Technology Studies literatures, and other relevant scholarly traditions that aim to bring a more nuanced view of law, legal processes, legal actors, technology, and legal institutions. Rather, computable law researchers aim to make a much more modest point: under the right circumstances, modelling laws in terms of structured forms that computers can process can enable new legal analytical and computational abilities that are today difficult to do using traditional methods. This potentially useful approach has tended to be underappreciated within the field of law.

At the same time, researchers do recognise and emphasise the limitations of computable law methods. For instance, certain areas of law are plainly more suitable for computable law than others. There are those legal contexts where meanings are heavily disputed, where background policies rather than legal texts dominate, where values are politically contested, where interpretations are disputed, where process is core, or where there are other fundamental concerns with translating law to data. In these areas, computable law methods may be less appropriate than others. Additionally, some areas of law contain structural features that make it easier to create computer models (e.g., Federal Income Tax Code) than others (e.g., US First Amendment doctrine), when considering issues such as legal uncertainty, judicial discretion, indeterminacy, abstract bodies of case law, interpretative methodologies, and institutional and political economy. Again, computable models of law may be less feasible in those areas. Finally, the 'translation' of law to code is not value-free and involves judgment and subjectivity. On the other hand, just because computable law methods may be less appropriate or feasible in some areas than others, does not mean that there are no legal contexts where the concerns just discussed are less present and where computable law methods may be suitable and useful. Like any methodology, computable law should be thought as a tool that requires judgment to be used well, with some applications more suitable than others.

The interesting point is that, in contexts where it both is feasible and appropriate, computable law methods can enable new legal analytical capabilities that are not readily available today. Adding data about the *meaning*, *structure*, *control-flow*, or *application* of legal obligations to their text allows us to harness the analytical abilities of computers to acquire new insights, visualisations, and other novel computational functionalities within law that are not presently available. Consider a few examples.

For one, computable law allows us to 'query' large collections of legal rules to ask and answer questions about obligations in ways that are difficult to reliably do currently. Consider a common situation: a corporation that has hundreds of thousands of active contracts that are housed in a document-management system. Overwhelmingly, such contracts are 'ordinary, natural language' documents, which refers to familiar legal documents written on a computer (often by a lawyer) and stored as a PDF or Word document. Notably, such written contracts typically do not have additional structural or semantic data representing the legal obligations described within (unlike those created using computable law methods). In such a text-based context, it is difficult for that corporation to reliably ask and answer even basic questions about its own contractual obligations across such a large expanse of language-only agreements.

For instance, imagine that there is an unexpected but disruptive event, such as a world-wide pandemic. A corporation might want to quickly determine, which (if any) of their thousands of active contracts would likely excuse them from meeting their contractual obligations under a 'Force Majeure' or similar provision. They might also want to analyse the effects of any changes to contractual obligations on their business operations, by passing this relevant contract data to their logistics, finance, or other affected internal computing systems for simulation, prediction, or analysis.

Readers might be surprised to learn that under the current paradigm – in which contracts and other sources of legal obligations are written only as ordinary text (without additional computer data) – seemingly straightforward analyses like this are quite hard to conduct *reliably* using the most sophisticated automation available today. This is true despite recent technological improvements within Artificial Intelligence (AI). Since 2022, there have been enormous advances in AI systems that can analyse and 'understand' written text documents. This is exemplified by large language model (LLM) AI systems, such as GPT-4 from OpenAI (which, as of the writing of the chapter is the most advanced AI technology of this type), which have reached unprecedented capabilities, approaching and in many contexts matching or exceeding human-like understanding of written documents. Nonetheless, for certain legal tasks, reliably analysing natural language documents still poses considerable challenges for even the most advanced AI large language model systems.

I emphasise the word 'reliably' because although recent NLP techniques have become quite sophisticated, they still produce approximate predictions when analysing ordinary text documents. As such, such systems may miss relevant documents or language that are actually relevant but that use uncommon language – such as – 'Emergency Performance Relief' – rather than 'Force Majeure' (false negatives); or erroneously find documents whose underlying meaning is completely different in terms of legal substance but that bear a superficial linguistic or statistical resemblance (false positives). Thus, for certain legal tasks, such as compliance, which require high degrees of precision, the error rates of these NLP approximation techniques that analyse ordinary text may be unsuitable. By contrast, had the contracts had structural data added on top of the ordinary written language, the relevant legal language and terms could have been reliably retrieved and processed. Thus, the types of structured legal data, described by the principles of computable law, are still very much relevant even as AI approaches to natural text continue improve.

More powerfully, depending upon the data available, computable legal obligations have the capability of being seamlessly inputted as data to other relevant business systems. For instance, if the 'Force Majeure' provisions explicitly listed a 'pandemic' as an excusable event, the firm might consider this an 'easy-case' from a legal perspective and perform automated business simulations under an analytical condition that they are excused from relevant contractual obligations. Or, in a different scenario, an insurance company might be able to automatically assess its total exposure to pandemic liability based upon the terms of its issued policies, something that is nearly impossible to do accurately today with only ordinary language insurance contracts. By contrast, ordinary written documents (without additional computable data) cannot robustly be used as inputs to interface with a typical firm's existing computer systems, such as accounting, finance, compliance, the way that data-oriented versions of those legal obligations can.

Nevertheless, the gap between what advanced AI can achieve with ordinary languages and the precision required for certain legal tasks is narrowing. The future may see these AI technologies that can read ordinary text without data match the level of precision and interoperability of structured computer data. Yet, as it stands, the error margins, although reduced, are still significant enough to warrant use of computable legal data.[20]

In sum, the field of *computable law* researches the theory and methods for modelling legal rules and obligations in forms that computers can reliably process. There are many different aspects of legal obligations that might be modelled in terms of data. *Structural data* is focused upon making legal information easy for a computer to identify, organise, and process, *semantic information* is focused upon modelling the meaning of legal rules in automatable form where possible, *control-flow* data is focused upon representing the logic of legal rules, and *legal application data* is focused upon how legal rules are activated or applied when relevant events occur in the world.

II HOW IS COMPUTABLE LAW DIFFERENT FROM TRADITIONAL LEGAL APPROACHES

To understand computable law, it is helpful to understand the difference between 'natural languages' and artificial 'formal languages'. 'Natural language' is the computer science term for the everyday spoken and written languages that people use to communicate with each other, such as English, French, or Spanish.[21] The text of emails, letters, SMS messages, social media posts, books, academic articles, conversation, and all the other common ways in which people speak or write to one another are considered natural language communications.

[20] See, for example, T Rostain, 'Techno-Optimism & Access to the Legal System [2019] *Daedalus*, 93–97; T Carter, 'Professor Tanina Rostain Has Her Students Developing Access-to-Justice Apps' (2015) *ABA Journal* <www.abajournal.com/legalrebels/article/tanina_rostain_profile>.

[21] See, for example, EM. Bender (ed), *Linguistic Fundamentals for Natural Language Processing: 100 Essentials from Morphology and Syntax* (Morgan and Claypool Publishers 2013); S Bird, E Klein and E Loper (eds), *Natural Language Processing with Python* (NLTK 2009).

Computer scientists use the description 'natural' to contrast such familiar human language communication against artificially developed 'formal languages'. The term 'formal language' refers to explicitly designed symbolic languages such as C, JavaScript, or Python that are used, among other things, to program computers.[22] Such formal languages are highly structured according to precise patterns and rules but also extremely constrained in what they can express. In addition to computer programming languages, data files, HTML documents, Comma Separated Files (CSV), JavaScript JSON objects, and other sorts of highly organised data documents are considered 'structured, formal language' communications. Roughly speaking, natural language communications are intended for other people, whereas formal language communications are intended to be processed by computers (or in similar contexts that require extreme precision and reliability).[23]

Today, we would classify most official sources of legal rules and obligations as *natural language* communications. This is because official legal texts – such as statutes, contracts, administrative regulations, legal opinions, and wills – are primarily intended to be read by other people. Thus, lawmakers creating public statutes, or private actors creating contracts or other private law obligations, have historically expressed the *substance* of legal rules using written sentences in the ordinary languages of their jurisdiction (albeit with specialised legal words familiar to lawyers).

It makes sense that society has traditionally communicated laws using ordinary language. Natural languages are extremely flexible and expressive enough to convey a nearly infinite variety of concepts. Moreover, as the name suggests, it is the way that most people communicate 'naturally' and by default and understand their primary language almost effortlessly. So, to be clear, a core principle of computable law is than we *supplement* natural language law with formal, structured data where it is helpful, *not* that we *replace* natural language as the primary mode of communicating law to the public.

One reason for doing so is to harness the power of computing to manage legal obligations. Computers excel at organising, processing, analysing, and visualising information in complex environments. For instance, in many complex contexts, it would be helpful to use computers to manage and assess compliance with legal obligations. In other domains, computers are similarly used for powerful organisational, analytical, simulation, or predictive tasks. Moreover, computable law has the promise to enable socially beneficial activities, such as making legal queries more accessible to underrepresented communities.[24] Attorneys are often enlisted to

22 Contemporary computers tend to work best when given highly structured 'formal languages', such as Python or Java, which although are less expressive and flexible than natural languages, have a format that can be unambiguously processed.

23 This is not strictly accurate as mathematics uses formal symbolic languages that are intended to be read by other people and not just computer processing. But for our purposes, this approximation suffices.

24 See, for example, SAEF Legal Aid, at <www.saeflegalaid.org/> (providing free, structured computable answers to family law questions to those unable to afford a lawyer) supported by the Duke Law School Tech Lab, and Illinois Legal Aid Online (providing free automated answers to common legal

focus on complex legal questions that involve questions of uncertainty. But there also are many basic legal topics with clear answers that remain an impediment to those without access to legal expertise (e.g., 'Do I qualify for a particular government service?'). With computable law, many simple but important legal queries can potentially be analysed through common computing devices (such as smartphones) for those without access to attorneys. By contrast, when sources of legal obligations are expressed in natural language *only* as they typically are today (without having important aspects also modelled in terms of formal, computer-processable data), such advanced, and potentially socially beneficial legal analytics tasks are infeasible and unreliable.

The reason that it is important to supplement written law with structured data in order to enable advanced computational analytics has to do with current limitations in the way computers are able to process written texts such as statutes or contracts. Although the landscape of NLP has recently progressed rapidly with the advent of GPT-4 and similar large language model technologies, in many cases, the flexibility and ambiguity inherent in natural languages can still pose challenges for these systems. While modern NLP AI systems can today grasp context, infer meaning, and process complex language structures more effectively than ever, variations in language, nuances in content and subtle concepts often elude even the most advanced AI systems. Therefore, the integration of structured data remains a crucial complement to NLP capabilities, ensuring that computational analytics can achieve the precision and reliability demanded in legal contexts.

This is made clear when we consider the power of natural languages like English or Spanish. One benefit of natural languages is that they are flexible enough to allow us to express the same, or similar concepts in a myriad of different ways. Those who craft legal documents can take advantage of this linguistic flexibility to convey nuances, handle complex scenarios, or simply avoid repetition. However, this same linguistic flexibility can be problematic for computer processing, which often relies upon clear patterns. For example, contracts often have headings that simply identify the role of a particular clause for the reader. Recall that a 'Force Majeure' clause is a common contract provision that legally excuses parties from contractual obligations that they would otherwise be expected to perform in the event of a major disruption outside of their control that makes compliance infeasible, such as a war or a pandemic. Consider the multiple ways in which natural language permits one to convey just the *heading* for a contract's 'Force Majeure' clause. Such a header could be expressed as an 'Act of God', 'Emergency Relief of Obligations', 'Excuse of Performance', 'Impossibility', 'Unexpected Disruption', 'Infeasibility of Performance', 'Undue Hardship', or numerous other linguistic formulations that can be used to convey the same or similar legal concept.

issues) at <www.illinoislegalaid.org/>, supported by the Center for Access to Justice & Technology at the Chicago Kent College of Law.

If there is that much potential linguistic variability in just a contract's descriptive heading, one can imagine that there are innumerable more distinct ways to compose the actual legal language describing the substance of that provision. For instance, an attorney could write, 'If either party is unable to perform their obligations due to Force Majeure…' or 'Neither party shall be liable for failure to perform for major events beyond their control including war, pandemic…' or 'A party shall not be in breach of the contract if it is prevented from carrying out its obligations due to an Act of God…' and so on. This same linguistic variability applies to any contract provision, statutory or administrative obligation. Given the flexibility of natural language, lawmakers can express legal rules and obligations in a nearly infinite variety of formulations that are more or less equivalent to one another.

Due to powerful cognitive processes, people are adept at reading and understanding even completely new natural language text that they have never encountered before and comprehending similarities between different wordings that express the same, or similar, ideas. Additionally, individuals have incredible facility to understand visual or contextual clues about meaning or function. Thus, a lawyer encountering any of the various 'Force Majeure' heading variations would have little problem understanding the contractual function of the clause regardless of the wording variations used. Additionally, people are very good at identifying and understanding text based upon implicit and subtle contextual cues. For example, if language expressing the essential concept of a 'Force Majeure' provision was buried deep within a contract document, without any identifying header, a competent and careful lawyer would be able to recognise the significance of such language even without specific identification. People are also excellent at resolving ambiguous language based upon context, and also extracting key information (e.g., dates, prices, parties) embedded in sentences. All of these natural language tasks that are nearly effortless for attorneys – understanding similar concepts despite linguistic variations, identifying key information within sentences, resolving ambiguous language through context, understanding substance from visual cues, understanding the real world meaning of sentences – are challenging for all but the most advanced contemporary systems to reliably do today.

The area of computer science and artificial intelligence (AI) devoted to automatically analysing ordinary text documents such contracts written in English (as opposed to analysing formal, structured computer data or programming instructions) is known as 'Natural Language Processing' (NLP). Modern NLP systems, such as GPT-4, display remarkable abilities to 'understand' human text, and now manage tasks that only recently extremely were nearly impossible for prior NLP systems, such as discerning context, reducing ambiguity, handling abstractions, and understanding complex document structures to a certain extent.

Yet, despite these improvements, the requirement for precision in certain legal contexts highlights the limitations of even the most sophisticated NLP techniques within law. While GPT-4 and similar technologies have narrowed the gap in understanding and generating complex language patterns compared to its predecessors, it is not without its limitations, especially when it comes to legal analysis and computational legal tasks. Most NLP systems, even those as advanced as GPT-4, still fundamentally rely on pattern recognition to interpret text. For example, if a corporation sought to identify 'Force Majeure' clauses across a vast array of contracts, GPT-4 would analyse the corpus, recognising patterns and inferring context to a highly accurate degree. Using NLP, this process would largely amount to scanning the text of these contracts to extract patterns likely to be indicative of 'Force Majeure' language.

By contrast, certain critical legal tasks, such as compliance analysis, risk assessment, and binding legal interpretation, require a level of exactitude and legal reasoning that goes beyond statistical pattern matching. NLP systems can produce errors – false positives and false negatives – that, while decreasing in frequency, remain significant when the task demands absolute certainty. Beyond problems with consistently recognising linguistic variations of the same legal concepts, NLP approaches also are unable to reliably do other language tasks that people are able to do almost effortlessly when reading legal documents: identifying and extracting key information – such as the identity of parties, delivery dates, and price terms – buried within other text, resolving ambiguous language through context, understanding legally substantive information from visual cues, understanding the structure of legal documents, understanding dependencies and references and most importantly understanding what legal language actually means in terms of its effects on the world. Thus, when it comes to identifying legal obligations for the purpose of legal analysis, legal prediction, compliance, visualisation, simulation, and other important activities involving the underlying meaning and substance of law, such partial approximations provided by NLP systems alone may be inadequate.

That said, modern NLP approaches have proven suitable for many other tasks within law which require less precision. For example, in litigation discovery, such automated NLP scanning approaches have been successfully used to help attorneys sort through huge collections of litigation documents. In this context, high precision in extracting exact legal information is not the goal. Rather, these automated systems excel at winnowing down huge collections of written emails and other natural language documents into much smaller, more tractable collections that can then be manually inspected by attorneys for legal relevance or privilege. In this context, NLP approaches that have reasonably high, but imperfect, accuracy rates of 90% are still quite useful. Such automated detection can dramatically reduce the amount of potentially relevant documents that need to be manually reviewed by lawyers, who can then quickly identify and disregard irrelevant selections. Similarly, GPT-4 has proven quite capable at summarising complex legal documents and legislation, producing first drafts of legal documents, and answering broad questions about laws and legal obligations written in natural language – capabilities which were largely out of reach in previous years. Thus, when approximation is sufficient, or when further manual review is expected, NLP approaches can work well in law.

To be clear, the point of this discussion is not to denigrate natural language processing techniques – they have become extremely impressive and have proven useful for many activities both within law and elsewhere. Rather, the point is to emphasise for the reader that despite the attention such artificial intelligence techniques have received in the media, for the task of advanced analysis of legal obligations, given the current state of the technology, NLP alone may not be appropriate technological tool.[25] Rather, as shall be discussed, complimenting natural language with structured data according to the methods of computable law is likely to improve the performance of both NLP and computational systems within law.

A *Computable Law as a Link for Natural Language Law*

The alternative approach in computer science to bridge the gap between natural human communication and artificial computer processing has been through formal computer languages that are precisely defined but limited. The principle of computable law follows this well-trodden path. Computable law essentially uses constrained computer languages and data formats to supplement the flexible natural languages that have historically been used in law. Thus, we can think of computable law not so much as a solution to the limitations of natural language processing of laws just described, as much as it is a partial compromise. It uses communicative bridges to transmit relevant legal information to computers in forms that they can reliably process but at the expense of some of the flexibility and expressiveness that ordinary written and spoken natural language communication permits.

The use of structured data and formal languages has a long history in computer science in providing a link between the word-based communications that people naturally use and the limitations in the way computers can reliably process language. This is the reason that today, most sophisticated computer software is created using formal, structured programming languages such as C, Java, or Python rather than using sentences in ordinary, natural languages such as English or French. In many contexts, computers require constrained, unambiguous instructions to perform well. Because these formal programming languages are standardised, structured, and limited, programmers can use the precisely defined keywords and formatting rules of these artificially created programming language to unambiguously instruct computers. This would be difficult to reliably do if the programmers were instead using the types of natural language sentences that people can understand with ease but computers often have difficulty processing. Such precision is not without a trade-off: one must give up the nearly infinite flexibility, expressiveness, and adaptability of natural

[25] Despite some advances in NLP technology – such as transformer-based models – limitations like this for precision-based language tasks are likely to persist into the near future.

language, for a much more limited subset of terms or actions that must be explicitly and precisely pre-defined in ways that computers can reliably process. However, in many cases, one can express enough information in this constrained form to provide a meaningful link between human intention and computer processing.

As described in the introduction, computable law provides a series of conceptual methods for modelling legal obligations as formatted data and computer rules, aiming to represent many of the distinct facets that such legal obligations have as they are situated within the legal system. This includes things such as the specific parties or organisations that they affect, the legal, private, and government institutions who create or evaluate them, and activities or conditions in the wider world which affect or are affected by their application. Some of the major categories described earlier of computable law data categories that can be used to characterise legal obligations and their situational context include: *structural data* (i.e., data used to identify legal obligations, key information, dependencies and relationships in unique, machine-processable form), *semantic legal data* (i.e., data that aims to specify what legal components mean in terms of comparable computer rules or data, which is not always possible but it sometimes is), *control-flow data* (i.e., data that models the If-Then or conditional structure of many legal rules, where legal rules have a condition that must be satisfied and then some legal consequence fallows from it), and *legal application data* (i.e., data that specifies information about events, states, or changes in the outside world that can sometimes be used to automatically assess legal conditions and consequences). We can think of these different categories of computable law data as ranging from more basic to more advanced and sophisticated in terms of computational theory and functionality, the most basic of which is structural data.

A central suggestion of this chapter is to emphasise that one does not necessarily need to focus on the latest and most advanced technologies to facilitate new and useful analytical abilities in law. Rather, major improvements in computable law functionality can be enabled by technologically simple, but mature computing approaches such as structural data. By contrast, computable law methods that involve semantic, control-flow, and application data are newer and more sophisticated technologically but provide more high-level functionality that is not likely to be as immediately useful, nor bring as much noticeable improvement to current legal analysis as would the foundational step of simply adding structural data to legal obligations that today do not have it.

At its core, structural data amounts to little more than labelling important information in legal documents in consistent and understandable ways to allow computers to reliably identify and extract different legal elements. Notably, structural data involves adding labels to law without further instructing the computer about what those labels actually 'mean'. Meaning is the role *of semantic* data, which requires supplementing the computer with additional instructions about the substantive or procedural meaning of those structural data labels, when helpful. Thus, as a technological approach, structural data is comparatively simpler than semantic data. Its main purpose is simply to tag legal data consistently in ways that both allows computers to find and capture that information while also using sensibly chosen label words that convey basic legal meaning to human readers as well. As discussed, without structured data, even the most advanced NLP systems have a difficult time performing basic identification and extraction tasks at a high enough level of precision.

The difference can between basic structural data and more sophisticated techniques can be illustrated by imagining that we supplement a contract's Force Majeure clause with a structural data label such as {Contract_Role: 'Force_Majeure'}. In that case, we are simply labelling the contract's legal language in a consistent way that it can be reliably identified and later extracted by a computer. By contrast, if we were to further add *semantic data* to that label, that would require additional information, actually linking that 'Force Majeure' data label to other automatable processing rules that reasonably reflect some aspect of the meaning of Force Majeure, such as an enumerated list of common activities that the parties agree will be common, legal easy-cases under Force-Majeure, such as ('Force_Majeure = [war, pandemic, rebellion]'), or a set of computer instructions that the parties agree represent that condition. Even more sophisticated legal analytical abilities could be enabled by adding control-flow or legal application data.

Although much of the research focus has been on these more advanced techniques, the benefits of adding basic structural data to legal obligations should not be underestimated. Even without employing the more sophisticated *semantic*, *control-flow*, and *legal application* approaches, simply supplementing legal obligations with structural data can actually bring large improvements in terms of analysis compared to the state of legal computation today. For one, the basics of structural data methodologies – adding consistent, identifying data keywords and labels to convey computer-processable information about legal text – are comparatively easy to do and are part of a mature and common set of techniques widely used in computing at large. Additionally, while it is true that semantic, and other more advanced computational law techniques bring along new and high-level automation capabilities, they also require more resources to implement and are more recent from a research standpoint and therefore less conceptually familiar.

Moreover, for the vast majority of legal analytics use cases, the improvements in querying, analysis, sorting, and retrieval of legal obligations enabled by adding structural data alone will bring significant marginal improvements compared to the state of the art today using ordinary natural language documents alone. This is important to emphasise because much of the focus from the media and computer science scholarly community has been on the more advanced legal automation and computational capabilities potentially enabled by semantic, control-flow, and application data, as in the focus on the so-called 'smart contracts'[26] and other legal automation

[26] 'Smart contracts' can be thought of as somewhat limited versions of the computable law data methods described more broadly here.

technologies, all the while paying comparatively little attention to the much simpler and technologically mundane but likely more impactful addition of basic, structured legal data.

Consider another example – this time from statutory law – of the ways in which adding just basic *structural* data to natural language legal expression can enable useful computer processing that is otherwise difficult to do today (based, in part, upon an actual research project).[27] It is not uncommon for statutory law to have 'sunset provisions' – which is statutory language that causes that law to automatically expire on a certain date unless it is explicitly renewed. One might think that it would be a somewhat trivial task to ask and answer a seemingly basic legal question such as, 'Which current federal US statutes have sunset provisions that are expiring this year?' For example, an organisation that is aiming to comply with its legal obligations might want to determine, which, if any, currently applicable statutes will potentially no longer apply the following year due to expiration under a sunset clause. It turns out, given contemporary technology and the fact that statutes are written primarily in natural language (and largely without computable data), such a superficially basic question becomes difficult to reliably answer.[28]

A seemingly straightforward query like this would involve at least several basic tasks. The first would be to identify all of the active federal statutes that have explicit sunset provisions, or that have language with more or less legal equivalent sunset-like, language with some time-based expiration or reauthorisation process. The second would be to determine which of those provisions are likely relevant to the organisation or individual in question. The third would be to extract, from the language of the relevant statutes, the key sunset dates and time periods, so that one could determine when the law was no longer in effect and when it needed reauthorisation. The fourth would be to find a way of determining if, in fact, a law expired or was reauthorised by a certain date, and a way of storing that information for later access. And the fifth would be to conduct legal analysis about changes to obligations based upon the additional information that a particular statutory provision might no longer be in effect after a certain point in the future.

In principle, these queries could be answered manually, by having one or more people with the appropriate expertise read the entire text of all of the statutes in the

[27] See S Adler and S Langehennig, 'Tracking Statutory Reauthorizations: Creating a New Metric for Legislative Productivity' (APSA White Papers on Congressional Capacity, 2016).

[28] This example is based upon an actual research project conducted to see how reliably one could identify 'sunset provisions' in the US Code. Due to the huge variance in natural language used by lawmakers to describe sunset provision, ranging from 'sunset' to 'pilot program' to 'reauthorization' and many others, it turned out to be nearly impossible to do so reliably by using general rules, or detected patterns. See S Adler and S Langehennig, 'Tracking Statutory Reauthorizations: Creating a New Metric for Legislative Productivity' (APSA White Papers on Congressional Capacity, 2016).

US Code. However, the total number of federal statutory provisions is extremely large. The US Code – where federal statutes are codified and housed – is a collection of (largely)[29] natural language documents that comprise fifty-four separate titles. These titles collectively house hundreds of thousands of distinct legal rules and obligations. Moreover, there are innumerable other queries, that would each require their own distinct close reading of the text to answer. Generally speaking, in contexts such as this involving large amounts of information, the analytical organisational, automation, visualisation, and processing power of computers can prove useful.

For reasons mentioned earlier, NLP approaches to scanning the US code for patterns, although improving, may be inadequate to answer this query with the level of precision needed. NLP techniques involving basic manual keyword pattern matching designed with expert assistance – perhaps searching for text matching 'sunset*' or 'expirat.*' or 'reauthor.*', or machine-learning approaches based upon analysing pre-identified examples of 'sunset provision' language to produce statistical patterns in likely signalling that some provision is possibly a sunset provision – may be inadequate to answer this query with precision. These NLP approaches produce too many false-positive and false-negative errors and furthermore may be unable to reliably extract key information – such as the date the provision expires – for further automated processing.

But by far the much more reliable approach is to supplement the statutory language with consistent, structural data. This is the approach suggested by computable law. Such structural data could be used to indicate important substantive or procedural features of a statute (or collection of statutory rules), such as whether a statutory section has a sunset mechanism or conceptually equivalent expiration or reauthorisation condition. Additional structural information might be used to indicate the date upon which the law expires, or the scope of the sunset provision (which specific statutory portions it effects), and other useful information regarding laws.

Let's imagine a different scenario in which all of the statutes in the US Code that had sunset provisions has been previously supplemented with structural data. Perhaps, each relevant section of the US Code with a sunset provision, had been marked with a sensible data such as:

Sample Structural Data Indicating that a Section of the US Code Has a Sunset Provision

[29] The qualifier 'largely' acknowledges that some aspects of the US code are partially in computable form, just not enough for legal analysis purposes. The U.S. House of Representatives, Office of Law Revision Council, has for several years released versions of the US Code that have been marked up with some meta-data about the structure of the code. See, Office of Law Revision Council at <www.uscode.house.gov/download/download.shtml>. This is actually a terrific start and is an example of 'structural data' described in this chapter. However, to do more advanced computational processing and legal analysis, much more computable data needs to be added, such as labelling statutes that have sunset provisions with appropriate data labels indicating this – either officially under the imprimatur of the US Government, or unofficially by those in the public.

```
{ Section_Duration: 'Sunset_Provision',
  Sunset_Expiration_Date: '01/01/2025',
  Scope_of_Sunset: '[35 USC Sections 124]'
  ...
}
```

Once again, this data example has been oversimplified for explanation; moreover, the particular formatting and labels used above are not the focus. For computable law purposes, the important point is that someone has chosen a consistent and unique way of asserting and capturing as data some aspect of legal interest (such that a specific statutory section will expire at some date under a sunset provision), and that the data labels chosen not only can be unambiguously processed by a computer but also convey sensible information to a human reader as well.

This is the simple but powerful principle behind how formal programming languages and data provide a (limited) link between human and computer communications. In essence, when it comes to formal computing languages and data, people agree to use some consistent, unique, and precisely defined set of keywords and labels such as 'Force_Majeure' or 'Sunset_Provision' that convey information to human readers but also can be processed by computers. These keywords are then linked to some set of computer activities (or human analysis) that make sense in light of whatever information is being conveyed by the chosen keywords. In some cases, the keywords chosen might come through a formal 'data standard' administered by an official organisation, such as the way in which the standard words and format of HTML – the mark-up language used to produce web pages – is created and maintained by the World Wide Web Consortium. But just as often people create ad-hoc and informal but sensible data labels (e.g., 'First Name') for their own use and those around them that convey enough information even in the absence of an official, formal standard and can still be reliably processed by a computer. Whether the standards are formal or informal, with such consistent data in place in law, anyone can use same formatting and labelling rules to accurately extract information using a computer.

It is the use of consistent structural data, rather than open-ended natural language, to convey substantive or procedural legal information, which allows computers to answer queries and reliably gather the relevant statutes in the sunset provision example above. As opposed to the NLP techniques which make probabilistic estimates based upon patterns in natural language text and have false-positive and false-negative errors, and have difficult extracting core information reliably, the structured text approach is much more accurate, assuming the data has been properly labelled. Once a consistent and unique data label such as 'Sunset_Provision' has been chosen and uniformly applied, it is a simple matter of scanning all of the data for sections that exactly match this label, something contemporary computers can do quickly and with no errors. Moreover, such scanning need not be done multiple times – the results can be captured in another database for quick reference, and updated to reflect changes in the actual law. It goes without saying that the procedure just described does not apply only to 'sunset provisions', but to any innumerable other substantive or procedural features of laws that people might want to be able to later accurately query and identify using computer systems. Further, we could imagine not just the US code, but nearly any other source of law, including administrative law and state statutory or administrative law, with supplemental data signalling various substantively important aspects that others might be interested in knowing and using computers to process.

One could also imagine adding *semantic data* to instruct a computer what a sunset provision actually means. Again, this would involve providing some sort of computational link between a human-understandable label such as 'Sunset_Provision' and a set of actionable computer rules that reasonably reflect the meaning of the label. The meaning of such a statutory sunset provision could be approximately represented in terms of semantic computer rules such as:

```
Sunset_Provision =
  If Current_Date <= Sunset_Expiration_Date Then
    Statute_In_Effect = TRUE
  Else
    Statute_In_Effect = FALSE
```

Again, adding such semantic data on top of structural labelling data may not always be possible or necessary. But where it is possible, it can enable advanced computation, as a computer could, based upon the rule above, perform slightly more sophisticated automated legal analytics by excluding laws that have expired.

B *Other Potential Benefits of Computable Law*

Computable law can, under the right circumstances, facilitate the automated analysis of legal liability and compliance. To understand this, consider first an analogy. Attorneys, in significant part, help clients understand their obligations under the law: what is or is not permitted within client goals, whether clients have met their existing legal duties, what they still are obligated to do and the official process for doing it, and whether clients risk liability (or other legal consequences) for future or past activity, and so on. Given a client's particular circumstances, lawyers are trained to determine the legal rules[30] that are likely relevant (i.e., statute, case law, regulation, contract provisions, etc.), apply those legal rules to their client's situation and make recommendations going forward. For instance, a tax attorney might take a

[30] Please note that I use the term 'legal rule' as simply a generic word for any written law or legal obligation, such as an individual statutory or contract provision that requires some entity to do something or that sets out requirements. Notably, I am *not* using the word 'rule' as in the legal theory 'rules and standards' sense of the word.

holistic look at a client's financial and earning situation within their web of personal and business relations, determine the potentially relevant federal and state tax rules and regulations, and advise about future tax strategies or current liability.

Under the right circumstances, fully or partially automated 'first cut' or *prima-facie* legal analysis is possible. Such first-cut automated analysis may not be legally comprehensive in all instances, as in the case where there is significant legal uncertainty or abstraction, and more sophisticated manual lawyerly analysis may need to be brought to bear to provide additional insight. Attorneys are typically involved when there is significant uncertainty or disagreement, and where something has gone wrong in unexpected ways. But in many other real-world scenarios, where there is little to no uncertainty, and everything goes as expected, automated assessment of legal obligations can produce useful, if legally tentative, results. This ability can be facilitated by the modelling of legal obligations in terms of structural, semantic, control-flow, application, and other categories of data under the computable law research area.

Outside of law, such computable models are more familiar. In these areas, it is common to model aspects of the real world in computer systems in order to learn something new. For example, meteorologists create computer models of weather systems, representing enough of the key features of the weather and its interactions, in computer-friendly form (i.e., computer data and programming), so that they can derive hopefully accurate information about the world (e.g., will it rain tomorrow?). Similarly, in medicine, doctors use computer models of disease and symptoms to aid in diagnosis.

More generally, a computer model involves creating a simplified representation of some aspect of the real world. The goal is to capture enough of the essential aspects of the thing that we are modelling (e.g., temperature or pressure in weather, test results, or symptoms medicine), and how this model approximately interrelates with the world, so that the computer can give predictions or analysis that are useful and accurate within a context where its limitations are understood.

As illustrated, we are similarly able to make at least partial computer models of legal rules, obligations, and other aspects of liability or obligation. However, there are some important differences between the field of law on the one hand and the areas like medicine, science, or engineering on the other hand that make *legal* computational models sometimes more difficult to create and sometimes less useful. One obvious distinction is that meteorology, science, medicine, and others analyse (more or less) objective phenomena that exist in the real world. By contrast, law is a completely human-created area of endeavour. For this reason, law is sometimes more subjective and indeterminate. This is because, unlike a relatively objective measurement of weather temperature, laws often deliberately embody subjective principles or judgments and political, social, and normative values. Moreover, laws are ultimately interpreted through subjective and value-laden lenses by humans and applied to arrange societal affairs and resolve conflicts among societal actors.

Nonetheless, it would be a mistake to conclude that, because of these complications, computer models of law are neither possible nor useful. To the contrary, there are many areas of the law that currently are and can be modelled and analysed computationally, and the reasons why it may be easier or harder to do so. For example, as shall be discussed, the commonly used tax preparation software Turbotax remains a good illustration of computable law. Through various engineering processes, the creators of tax preparation software have faithfully represented, in computer-processable form, the structure and logic of many of the tax legal rules. Applying these computer-representation of legal rules to data about individual taxpayers (e.g., income and deductions), the computer model is able to produce reliable and partially automated results concerning tax liability.

Another aspect to consider: are we computationally modelling *existing laws* or creating *new*, computable laws? Much of the consideration around computable law might contemplate how we might model on a computer, some existing legal rule, such as a particular tax rule from the Internal Revenue Service, or the negligence doctrine from the law of tort. If we want to computationally model such an English-language law in the United States, there is a necessary translation step.

As shall be discussed, in the past, this mostly involved a person reading the English-language version of a law, understanding its meaning, and then translating that law into a set of comparable computer programming rules and data that faithfully reflect the English meaning. More recently, modern NLP systems like GPT-4 have developed the capability to automatically translate natural language laws into a draft of comparable computer instructions or data, thereby reducing some of the manual labour. At this point, it is still very much necessary to have a person verify this translation for fidelity and accuracy. More broadly, much of computable law is concerned with modelling existing laws created by federal or state legislators, or common law judges, and wondering which laws can be more easily and usefully represented than others on an automated platform. I will certainly discuss that process here. However, most existing laws were created largely without computability in mind (for good reason). A typical law has been created to designed to be read, interpreted, and applied by people, and not computers.

By contrast, it is important to point out that it is possible to create *new* laws with the intention of making them computer-processable at the outset. In other words, rather than creating English-language laws (in the United States) intended to be understood by people and then translating those English-language laws into a comparable computer-processable counterpart, it is possible to create laws that are expressed as rules and data, and that are intended to be processed by computers, from the outset. A good example of this, which will be discussed within, involves the so-called 'computable contracts' discussed earlier. As it is sometimes said, the creation of contracts is sometimes referred to as 'private law-making'. This is because when two people or companies create a contract with one another, they are voluntarily creating a set of legal rules that they each are bound by (e.g., the provisions of the contract). In a sense, those who enter into a contract are like mini-legislators, creating a tiny set of laws (e.g., contractual obligations) that apply only to them. Once we understand that contracting parties can create the substance of law (e.g., what exactly they are legally obligating themselves to do), we can also see that these mini-lawmakers can also choose the *form* of their contractual obligations (i.e., shall we write the contract in English to be read by people or express it as data to be read by computers).

Thus, in the realm of contracting, particularly in the area of finance and Internet purchasing, we are seeing mini-law-making contracting parties choosing to express their laws, from the outset, as computer-rules and data, with the intention to be primarily processable by computers. This is simply to illustrate a large point that anyone who creates law, whether a federal legislator or judge, or a 'mini-lawmaker' who is a contracting party that is creating rules that bind only themselves, can, in principle, choose to express that law intentionally in a form primarily designed to be processable by computers ('data native law'), rather than expressing it only in English (or other natural languages) and requiring an intermediate translation step. This is not to say that every law should or would necessarily benefit from being expressed computationally by those who create the laws. Rather, the point is that creating laws to be computable at the outset (rather than creating a translation of an English language law after the fact) is in principle possible, and should be considered a related, but distinct aspect of computable law, rather than simply 'translating' natural language laws from legislatures to computer code.

III ISSUES WITH TRANSLATING LAW INTO DATA

Of course, the Computable Law approach, while improving some aspects, also brings its own new set of issues: if adding data to the law can bring analytical benefits, who (or what) is adding all this data to the law? Each of the techniques described earlier, in one way or another, involves some sort of translation: someone is examining a law or legal obligation and is expressing some feature or aspect of that legal obligation – a role of a contract provision, or the fact that a federal statute has a sunset provision – as data. In other words, ultimately some person, or some computer system, is going to have to examine a particular legal obligation and make a translation from the law's logical structure and meaning, taking into account nuances of language, law, and context, into a comparable computer-processable data enabled form.

From one perspective, this is not so different from what lawyers do today. Computational law involves creating computer models – simplified version – of legal obligations. In general, humans create simplified mental or conceptual models in order to make otherwise complex phenomenon more manageable. Broadly speaking, such models are useful when they are simple enough to allow us to comprehend and manage the phenomenon, but nonetheless contain still enough of the underlying core features that model can still be reliably used to analyse, understand, predict, or otherwise simulate the actual phenomenon.

By this account, attorneys today already engage in a sort of informal modelling when they engage in legal analysis and other related tasks. For instance, when an attorney considers a standard legal statement such as, 'The *prima-facie* cause of action of negligence has four elements: Duty, Breach, Causation, and Injury' – this is an example of informal modelling using natural language. In other words, there is some complex legal phenomenon – the tort of negligence, law, doctrine, and practice that has been spelled out in countless natural language documents, such as court decisions or legislation – and that statement is a partial simplification of tort law used to make it tractable for attorneys – a conceptual model. A statement such as that does not imply that it fully describes negligence law, or that there is nothing more to negligence law than that described in that sentence. Rather, it is a recognition that for the purposes of analysis, it is helpful to boil down some of the more essential aspects of negligence law to a simpler model for analytical, conceptual, or predictive purposes.

Similarly, when it comes to 'translations', attorneys inevitably have used their judgment to interpret textual sources of law, and they always rely upon treatises and other secondary sources that purport to translate the law into authoritative form. In the end, the very act of providing legal advice to clients requires attorneys to form simpler, conceptual models of the law – articulating which features of the law that attorneys think matter and distinguishing it from those that matter less – and to make interpretations and translations from official sources of law. Thus, in some ways, the acts of translating aspects of law into computer instructions and data are not so different from the informal processes that attorneys use to conceptually model and simplify the law today to make it practically tractable.

Moreover, organisations and individuals must ultimately comply with the law as best as they are able to give their assessment of what laws are likely apply to them and their interpretation of those laws, either directly or with the expert help of an attorney. In order to comply with the laws, it is quite common today for companies in particular to engage in *ad-hoc*, informal, computational modelling of the law. These are often modelled as internal company business rules or policies. In many cases, these policies are implemented by administrators or managers within the company who try to come up with actionable rules that they believe result in actions by the company that are in compliance with the law. Often these informal rules or structured rules are entered into entirely separate business operations computing systems, sometimes as informally as being only captured in a solitary Excel spreadsheet and sometimes more formally as being captured in an internal company logistics or operations database.

The important point is that these translations from abstract law to formal, structured, actionable, computable instructions that are deemed to be compliant with a corporation's legal obligations are already occurring today – in company compliance, logistics, operations, and other departments – just in a more ad-hoc, informal, and less considered manner than the more comprehensive modes described by computable law. One of the points of computable law research is to ground such ad-hoc and informal approaches in a more rigorous, comprehensive, deliberately considered, and legally theoretically grounded methodology.

So, in many respects, the principles of computable law are not so foreign from practices that are already accepted as part of legal practice. For example, when an attorney reads a contract and recognises language as describing a 'Choice of Law' provision, that conceptual step of mental identification is not so different from simply explicitly formally capturing that feature in structural data, as would be done in computable law. Computable law just makes explicit and captured in computer-processable data, many of the existing simplifications and interpretations that attorneys and others aiming to understand legal obligations law, informally or implicitly do.

A different issue is concerned with the following: who is doing the modelling of aspects of law as data? When it comes to public law – such as federal or state statutory or administrative law, one might think that such modelling with have to come from lawmakers themselves. Indeed, in some cases, having data with the imprimatur of the legal officials who created the laws can be useful. One example of this is a version of the US Code in the form of data that is released and maintained by the Office of Law Revision Counsel of the United States House of Representatives. This version of the US Code has some (very limited) structural data[31] and actually exemplifies basic computable law principles. It is quite a good start on the path described in this chapter, but to fully take advantage of computable law, this version could be supplemented with much more additional useful structural and semantic data. However, the larger point is that because such structural data is added by an official arm of a federal law-making body, presumably these data-based demarcations would acquire some more authority.

However, an important point is that computable law data need not be added only by government officials, nor need it always have the official imprimatur of lawmakers. This is a common misconception. To reiterate the point – computational law is about modelling different aspects of the law, and individuals, attorneys, and businesses are constantly having to create simplified mental or written models of what they think their legal obligations are. Thus, while it might be helpful to have computable data that has the official imprimatur of lawmakers – such as if the US House of Representatives Office of Law Revision Counsel were to add supplemental data to every provision in the US Code with a sunset provision, one need not wait for that. Rather, attorneys and others with sufficient expertise are capable of recognising legal elements – such as the language of a sunset provision – and confidently identifying them even without explicit disambiguation from a government official. Indeed, this is what attorneys do as a matter of course but implicitly in legal memos or briefs in which they make statements by reading the language of statutes, such as, 'Section XYZ has a sunset provision and will expire on 01/01/2025 unless

[31] See n 31.

reauthorized', even if that section has not been explicitly demarcated as such by lawmakers.

In other words, it is true that some legal assessments involve uncertainty, whereas others are fairly clear. In those cases, it is perfectly legitimate for attorneys, or other members of the public with sufficient understanding, to capture that implicit expert knowledge explicitly in data outside of the official realms of government. Indeed, we see similar aspects of interpretation captured in more limited data, in private services such as Westlaw and Lexis, and in the internal private knowledge bases of laws and regulations that are maintained by law firms. Similarly, corporations such as Turbotax represent aspects of the personal income tax laws in a formal, computable form.

In some ways, we can think of these organisations as engaged in early variants of computational law. The computational law research aims to make this process more coherent and theoretically unified, leveraging some of the emerging concepts from computer science and legal informatics. These include more recent concepts, such as semantic and application data, which have tended not to be included in existing legal knowledge systems as they have only more recently been developed.

It is important to emphasise that not every use of computers in law is an example of *computable law*. *Computable law* refers to a distinct use of computers in law and only applies to instances where we have represented the *meaning* and *structure* of law computationally. Thus, for example, although attorneys use computers to carry out legal research using a platform like Westlaw and retrieve the content of laws, this is *decidedly not* an example of computational law, even though it superficially involves legal rules, computers, and some organisational structure. The reason is that a research platform such as Westlaw presents law in a form friendly to human attorneys – plain text – but that is not meaningful to a computer. While an attorney can read a legal rule on Westlaw and understand its meaning, in general, computers only 'understand' exactly what we tell them, and will not be able, on their own, to extract sufficient meaning from ordinary human text that has not been otherwise deliberately prepared by people. By contrast, computable law refers to legal rules whose content and meaning have been represented in computer-friendly form. This representation can occur either explicitly (as in a programming rule that mimics the logic of a tax provision) or implicitly (as in a machine-learning model that has learned a pattern in which a legal rule tends to be applied), but in any case, must exist in a form that a computer can do something useful with (e.g., structured data or computer rules).

From a public benefit point of view, one of the problems is that this expert knowledge is private and not accessible to the public. One of the benefits of computable law is that once you capture certain legal knowledge and represent it as data, you do not have to continually redo it each time, and you can leverage the existing knowledge. There already exist terrific public service legal resources, such as the Legal Information Institute at Cornell University in the United States and the Australasian

Legal Information Institute (AUSTLII) at UTS and UNSW Universities in Australia, that provide the public access to high-quality, searchable databases of natural language law. We could imagine further supplementing these non-profit, natural language law legal resources with structural or semantic data in ways that would allow the general public to harness this data and engage in more sophisticated analysis and queries using the power of computational law. In that way, we could harness the wisdom of the crowds to intelligently supplement open, public law sources with useful and reliable computational legal data, without necessarily having to wait for official government sources, such as the Office of Law Revision Counsel, to add this.

Another concern might be, how does one go about adding such data, as a practical matter? Would lawyers have to manually input data? Lawyers are not typically computer scientists, and the whole concept of computable law might seem to conceive of lawyers as coding in data. This too is largely a misconception. Outside of law, much of daily interaction today is mediated electronically, performed on a computer, and often through controlled interfaces in which users convey information by selecting options or inputting information. Similarly, much of the research in the field of computable law involves studying and creating computer interfaces in which structural or semantic legal data is added in the background as attorneys or others put together or work with legal obligations, largely beneath the awareness of the attorneys using them.

By way of analogy, consider two relatively common activities on the web: electronically trading stock or purchasing a product from an online store. In each of these cases, the user selects from multiple different options – such as selecting the financial security and the amount to purchase or selecting items to purchase, using a controlled interface. However, in the background, these different selections about user choices are information conveyed to the computer system that can be stored or acted upon automatically. In these processes, important structural data is captured in the background, almost invisible to the user, who is simply interacting with the computer interface. Thus, adding identifying and useful structural data to legal obligations needs not be labour-intensive, and can often be captured implicitly as lawyers, and others, interact through electronic interfaces, such as web pages.

Moreover, as discussed, recent and rapid advances in natural language AI processing technology, such as exemplified by GPT-4, offer a new bridge between written law and computable law. Such systems are now able to read written legal obligations and produce reliable first-draft translations of into comparable computer instructions and data. To emphasise, at this stage, such automated translations from written legal texts to data, should be considered first-drafts, and require manual double-checking to ensure quality and fidelity. But the interesting to thing to note is that only recently have such reasonably reliable, automated translation even technologically possible. Prior to 2022, such automation of computable law was not technologically feasible. Such advances open up the possibility of adding structured data more broadly to many existing natural language documents, such as corpuses of contracts, or legislation, by leveraging NLP state-of-the-art NLP automation.

A separate concern has to do with fundamental legal theoretical issues in translating law to fixed data. Many legal concepts and rules are politically contested, and nearly all legal rules contain some embedded political or social values. In some cases, the very act of translation to data is an implicit choice to elect one interpretation over another, or to elevate a certain political value over another. These are all valid points and have been previously raised by the various legal theoretical literatures that critique simple, formalist views of the law. To be clear, computable law respects these insights, and its methods should not be conflated with older, naïve views such as 'Legal Formalism', which fictitiously characterised the US legal process as the mechanistic, objective application of 'objective' legal rules to 'objective' facts producing deterministic and syllogistically mandated legal outcomes. This is not at all the view of those who research computable law. Rather, computable law involves *modelling* legal obligations in a structured manner, in which approximate representations of legal obligations in terms of formal data can be useful when concerns of indeterminacy, abstraction, political values, or uncertainty are less present. Similarly, researchers take seriously the related concerns from the computer science community who study the role of fairness, accountability, and transparency, as well as the problems of embedding bias or values in computational systems.

IV WHAT ASPECT OF THE LAW DO WE NEED TO MODEL IN A COMPUTER SYSTEM?

As mentioned, the computable law process involves creating some computer-based representation of the meaning and structure of legal rules. It also requires some way to analyse relevant data about the world under those rules, to produce useful, computer-based assessments as to liability, compliance, or other legal matters.

But this description leaves open many questions. What aspects of the law are we modelling, exactly? Is it the formal sources of written law, such as federal and state statutes, administrative regulations, court decisions, constitutions, contracts, wills, and other official documents? These are the official, written sources of law, promulgated by legal officials (lawmakers, judges, regulators), or created through an officially sanctioned process (i.e., formalities for creating a valid will). Must a computer model contain complete computational representations of *all* of these formal sources of law? What about the complex chains of common law written court decisions known as 'case law' that create implicit legal or rules or which layer official interpretations or procedures on top of statutory or administrative law? Do we have to come up with an entire computationally representative system for that as well?

For that matter, must we also take into account the so-called 'informal' aspects of law? These are aspects of law and society that are distinct from written statutes or regulations that affect the interpretation and administration of the law, sometimes more than the formal, written law itself. Such informal sources of law include 'law on the ground' – which refers to what people actually do with respect to laws and legal obligations, which may be distinct from what the law actually says. For instance, police may have an informal habit of not ticketing drivers whose driving speed is only five miles per hour over the speed limit, even though these drivers are technically violating the formal speed limit statute. Similarly, businesses are known to routinely include provisions in contracts that they voluntarily choose not to enforce for business relations purposes, although they could as a matter of formal contract law. Other informal sources of law include customary practices among businesses. Must a computer model necessarily include representation of all these informal sources that affect law as well? Finally, all of law is built in a context of larger society, and in an incredibly complex web of shared societal understandings and practices, political and social values, institutions, and individual citizens and businesses. Must all of society be modelled as well?

The short answer is 'no'. One of the principles of computable law is that one does not have to create a model of the entire legal universe in order to create helpful legal computational models. As in any area of endeavour, a computer model is necessarily a simplification of the underlying phenomenon that we are trying to represent. Thus, a meteorological model strips away the vast complexities of weather systems into helpful measurements, geographic mapping, and interactions, and medical diagnostic systems can produce useful outcomes despite the ferocious complexity of the human body and diseases. The creators of these computer models aim to select the relevant features that they hope preserve the essential elements of the underlying phenomena, while making the computer model simple and tractable enough. As in any of these areas, one of the most important criteria for judging a computer model is whether it produces helpful and accurate computer-based results.

We can adopt a similar point of view in law. We need not necessarily create a computer representation of every provision of every statute, regulation, contract, or judicial opinion, in order to create a useful computer model. Rather, we can certainly pick and select certain essential features among the various sources that capture essentials of the legal rules that we are aiming to represent. Our computer model of legal rules and obligations, as elsewhere, will necessarily be a *simplified* representation of the underlying phenomenon that we are trying to represent. One major criterion for judging the computer model will be whether it produces useful, accurate automated results about legal liability or compliance.

V CONCLUSION

This chapter provided an overview of the theory, limits, and methods of computable law. Computable law involves representing the *structure*, *meaning*, or *application* of laws in a form that a computer can readily process. In general, this involves identifying legal rules and obligations found in statutes, contracts, and other sources of law, and representing the *structure*, *meaning*, or *application* of these rules in forms that computers can readily process. In other context, legal obligations can start out in computer-processable data from the outset, and readable and understandable natural language views of legal information can still be produced from that data.

A central idea of computable law is to take aspects of law that are today largely implicit in legal texts, and *where appropriate*,[32] make them more explicit by modelling them as data, rules, or other highly structured forms that are amenable to computers. Importantly, this must be done in a way that reasonably reflects the underlying organisation and shared meaning. This is not always possible or beneficial in every legal context. However, where it is appropriate, it opens some interesting new possibilities.

Once rendered as data, computable legal obligations or documents can be used as inputs to other computer systems for the purpose of analysis or simulation or compliance analysis. One important point to realise is that from the computable law perspective, the structure, meaning, and application of a legal rule are distinct things that can be modelled separately. This is important because in some cases, it may be easier to create a computer model of, say, the structural aspects of a document (e.g., identifying a contract's provisions uniquely), without being able to translate a particular contract provision into a meaningful semantic counterpart (e.g., inability to translate a 'reasonable efforts' provision into an actionable computer rule). That is not a problem because computational law doesn't demand that every aspect of a legal document such as a contract be modelled computationally – rather only those that make sense. And in some legal contexts, it will be possible to model multiple aspects of legal obligations such as the structure, meaning, and application, such as a contract payment provision that can be faithfully represented as a series of computer rules that transfer and confirm that payment has occurred.[33]

This chapter also emphasised a core point: the simple act of labelling existing laws and legal documents with structural meta-data can bring multiple computational benefits that have been somewhat under-appreciated. One reason may be the following: adding meta-data to natural language text to make it easier to identify and extract is a technological approach that has been around for a long time, and as such, it may not be particularly interesting to researchers exploring the frontiers of legal informatics and AI and law. Rather, it seems that researchers in legal informatics have largely focused on newer theoretical areas, such as adding semantic legal meaning to contract data. But this has meant that a simple, conventional, and well-understood technology – structural meta-data – has largely gone overlooked and under-utilised in legal research and practice, because it may be seen as not particularly cutting-edge. One point is to emphasise that this basic step alone – labelling contracts and other legal documents with structural meta-data that uniquely identify the parts of elements of the document in a form that computer can reliably extract – even without

[32] See n 21.

[33] Although modelling meaning in addition to structure opens up additional possibilities, modelling structure alone can still bring significant benefits.

adding the more theoretically advanced *semantic data, control-flow data, and application data* – concepts that have primarily gotten the attention of researchers and corporations – is likely to unlock tremendous capabilities going forward in terms of computational law.

In conclusion, although certain ideas underlying computable law have been around for some time, the modern research programme is still very much under development and rapidly changing. Moreover, with the rapid improvements in natural language processing AI systems such as GPT, the interplay between natural language law, automated computer analysis, and structured data, will continue to evolve. The goal of this chapter has been to both synthesise some of the foundational concepts of computational law as well as introduce some new ideas, organisation, and terminology in the area.

PART I

Law of Obligations

3

Contract Law and AI

AI-Infused Contracting and the Problem of Relationality – Is Trustworthy AI Possible?

T. T. Arvind

I INTRODUCTION: THE RISE OF AI-INFUSED CONTRACTING

The focus of this chapter is on a relatively new, but rapidly growing, phenomenon which I term 'AI-infused contracting'.[1] AI has increasingly come to be used both in contracts themselves and in the broader transactional processes within which contracts are embedded. Its use can be classified into four archetypes: making transactional decisions, creating self-enforcing contractual mechanisms, managing the contractual lifecycle, and producing contractual terms. I refer to these processes, used individually or in combination, as 'AI-infused contracting.'

AI-infused contracting has the potential to significantly improve the quality and effectiveness of commercial and non-commercial transactions. Nevertheless, this chapter argues that its rise is not problem-free. Making AI systems resilient and trustworthy involves non-trivial challenges, which go to the heart of the nature of the law and practice of contracting. Most branches of private law – including tort, equity, and property law – are concerned directly with interests and interpersonal relations. Although interests and relations do also matter to contract law, its primary focus of contract law is the medium through which these interests and relations are created – that is, the parties' contract.

The work underlying this paper was partially funded by UK Research and Innovation Project EP/V026747/1, 'Resilient Autonomous Socio-cyber agents (REASON)', which is part of UKRI's Trustworthy Autonomous Systems programme. I am grateful to UKRI for its support. I am also grateful to Tan Zhong Xing, Jeannie Marie Paterson, and participants at the workshop for their comments on an earlier version of this paper, and to Daithí Mac Síthigh for drawing my attention to the relevance of Marshall McLuhan's work to the present day.

[1] I use the term 'AI' in this chapter to cover not just artificial intelligence in the strict sense, but also the broader category of algorithmic and autonomous systems, including deterministic systems as well as those based on machine learning and stochastic processes. Most of my argument is in fact concerned with algorithmic systems that function at least partially autonomously and that use a mix of deterministic and stochastic processes, but are not 'intelligent' in a technical sense. I use 'AI' rather than the more accurate 'AS' purely to reflect popular usage.

While bodies of sectoral regulation such as consumer and even construction law may focus on the substance of a transactional relationship,[2] the general law of contract does not. As far as contract law is concerned, the medium is very much the message.[3]

The tendency of contract law to focus on the medium rather than the substance of transactions has important implications for AI. The transactional heart of contracts lies in the potential they offer for joint maximisation.[4] However, as a growing body of research not just in law but also in management has shown, the actual practice of contracting deploys and depends on techniques of drafting and management that not only fail to further joint maximisation but, frequently, achieve its precise opposite by facilitating opportunistic and extractive behaviour in ways that have transactional and systemic effects.[5]

The argument of this chapter is that this makes AI something of a double-edged sword in the domain of contracts. AI in the real world is not simply a technical system but a socio-technical system. Its real-world use depends not just on the technology underpinning it but also on the manner in which and ends towards which that technology is deployed, and on the predispositions, asymmetries, and biases that characterise the specific social contexts in which those ends are pursued. As a result, although AI has the potential to overcome the problems caused by existing approaches to the drafting, management, and implementation of contracts, it also has the potential to exacerbate these problems. Addressing this risk and creating AI that is trustworthy in relation to contracting will require channelling its use in a new direction, which this chapter describes as 'transactional responsibility'.

Achieving transactional responsibility requires rethinking not just contract law but also general programming practices and approaches in the field of contract-related AI. The purpose of this chapter is to begin that process of rethinking by analysing the nature of AI's dual potential in relation to contracting, the roots of that duality in the structure of AI, and the challenge it presents for law as well as for the computational design of AI. Part II discusses the use of AI in the domain of

[2] See for example, the discussion of construction law in C Ellis, 'Regulating Commercial Contracts: What Can We Learn from Part II of the Housing Grants, Construction and Regeneration Act 1996?' in TT Arvind and J Steele (eds), *Contract Law and the Legislature: Autonomy, Expectations, and the Making of Legal Doctrine* (Hart Publishing 2020).

[3] The idea of a medium being the message comes from the work of Marshall McLuhan. See M McLuhan, *Understanding Media: The Extensions of Man* (MIT Press 1994) 7–21. McLuhan is discussed in more detail in Section IV. For an in-depth discussion of its relevance to law, see D Mac Síthigh, *Medium Law* (Routledge 2018).

[4] For a recent overview of the theoretical literature on joint maximisation, see RE Scott, 'A Joint Maximization Theory of Contract and Regulation' in H Dagan and BC Zipursky (eds), *Research Handbook on Private Law Theory* (Edward Elgar 2020).

[5] In law, the starting point is the classic work of Ian Macneil and Stewart Macaulay. See D Campbell (ed), *The Relational Theory of Contract: Selected Works of Ian Macneil* (Sweet and Maxwell 2001); D Campbell (ed), *Stewart Macaulay: Selected Works* (Springer 2020). For a review of the management literature, see DJ Schepker and others, 'The Many Futures of Contracts: Moving beyond Structure and Safeguarding to Coordination and Adaptation' (2014) 40(1) *Journal of Management* 193; F Lumineau, 'How Contracts Influence Trust and Distrust' (2017) 43(5) *Journal of Management* 1553.

contracting and the manner in which its processes differ from those used by human transactors. I argue that for the use of AI to be sustainable, it must meet two baseline conditions: the condition of resilience and the condition of trustworthiness. The nature of the socio-technical process underpinning the use of AI, however, means that AI is not naturally given to meeting these conditions, and achieving them will therefore require a high degree of attentiveness to the techniques used to design AI as well as the social context in which AI is used.

Part III discusses how current contracting practice affects joint maximisation in a range of social contexts. I argue that contracts can have a range of effects on a transaction, not all of which are beneficial, and that the deleterious effects are a particularly strong risk in asymmetric transactions. Part IV builds on this by demonstrating how and why these issues with contracting practice lead to AI having a dual potential to either ameliorate or exacerbate the problems of contracting.

Part V presents an outline of the key components of what I term the principle of transactional responsibility, which I argue can resolve these challenges in a manner that contributes to the resilience and trustworthiness of AI. I conclude by discussing how programming practices in relation to AI as well as the law of contract can be developed to create conditions in which AI-infused contracts serve ends that are responsive and responsible, rather than extractive and oppressive.

II CONTRACTS AND AI: MAPPING THE TERRAIN

As things stand, there are four uses to which AI is put that are relevant to the law and practice of contracting. The first, and probably the most straightforward, is in smart contracts. Smart contracts are, in essence, computerised transaction protocols that, when initiated, are capable of automatically executing some or all of the terms of a contract.[6] In a modern context, smart contracts typically take the form of a script in a programming language that is stored on a blockchain and triggered when a transaction is addressed to it. The content of the script is the functional equivalent of the terms of a traditional contract and determine precisely what transpires when the transaction is executed. The classic application of a smart contract is the trading of cryptocurrency, but they are also capable of being used in any commercial transaction capable of being executed electronically. They have been used in areas ranging from trade finance to creating an automated system for buying and selling excess energy generated by domestic solar panels.[7] The systems used in this application are typically deterministic and function in accordance with hard-coded

[6] This was the definition used by Nick Szabo in the paper that is generally taken to have developed the idea of a smart contract. See N Szabo, 'Smart Contracts' (1994) <www.fon.hum.uva.nl/rob/Courses/InformationInSpeech/CDROM/Literature/LOTwinterschool2006/szabo.best.vwh.net/smart.contracts.html>.

[7] K Christidis and M Devetsikiotis, 'Blockchains and Smart Contracts for the Internet of Things' (2016) 4 *IEEE Access* 2292, 2298.

parameters rather than on the basis of parameters or considerations autonomously derived through machine learning.

A second use of AI, which is probably the most studied, is in making transactional decisions, for example, decisions on whether to transact and, if so, at what price. Here, unlike in the first example, the AI is operating at least in part on the basis of non-deterministic logic and usually on the basis of patterns autonomously detected through the analysis of large volumes of data. Examples range from high-frequency trading, in which market actors use algorithms based on complex and typically proprietary computational models to identify and execute large volumes of security trades automatically and rapidly, to dynamic pricing in which algorithms automatically adjust the price of goods or services to take into account market factors such as demand. Somewhat more controversially, it also includes discriminatory pricing, in which enterprises use complex data-derived profiles of customers to make individualised pricing decisions with the result that identical products and services are offered at different prices to different customers based on the inferred characteristics of that customer.[8] This applies not just to pre-contractual decision-making but also to instances of in-contractual decision-making, such as the exercise by a credit provider of a contractual discretionary power to reduce a customer's credit limit.[9]

A third use, less explored in legal scholarship, is in the area of what has come to be called contract lifecycle management. The complexity of the obligations involved in large-scale transactions creates a need for managerial capacity, which many organisations lack.[10] The idea of a 'contract lifecycle' was devised by management theorists as a way of conceptualising the manner in which an organisation's focus shifts to different aspects of the transaction over its lifecycle and, thus, for better structuring and directing managerial resources within organisations. There is now a significant amount of software that assists organisations with contract lifecycle management, and ongoing work to use machine learning and natural language processing to infuse these tools with a greater degree of artificial intelligence and autonomy. A particularly promising line of work in relation to commercial contracts lies in combining contract lifecycle management with blockchains, in the form of both distributed ledgers and smart contracts. Examples of the former already exist in sectors such as international trade and transport, which involve large numbers of relatively standard and well-understood contracts, documents, risk mitigation measures, and contractual processes, and therefore lend themselves readily to automation.[11] Similarly, attempts

[8] For a critical analysis of this trend in the context of anti-discrimination law, see TB Gillis and JL Spiess, 'Big Data and Discrimination' (2019) 86 *University of Chicago Law Review* 459.

[9] See for example, M Hurley and J Adebayo, 'Credit Scoring in the Era of Big Data' (2016) 18 *Yale Journal of Law and Technology* 148, 157–183.

[10] See for example, TL Brown and M Potoski, 'Contract-Management Capacity in Municipal and County Governments' (2003) 63(2) *Public Administration Review* 153, analysing the limits on the capacity of local government bodies to manage outsourcing contracts.

[11] In one frequently used scheme, these are described as involving, successively, transactional architecture, negotiation, operation, and regeneration. See S Cullen, *The Contract Scorecard: Successful*

have been made to specify and develop smart contract trees that are capable of handling the entire transactional lifecycle in the context of transactions taking place between members of a decentralised manufacturing network.[12]

A fourth and final potential use of AI lies in the field of the actual drafting of contracts. Contract drafting software already exists, but the most common ones are only slightly more sophisticated than the document assembly engines that emerged in the 1990s. As such, they continue to be based on a deterministic processes, and use questionnaires to trigger logic trees which lead to particular clauses being selected from a bank of pre-drafted clauses.[13] Although no non-deterministic systems exist in the wild as yet, it is generally accepted that 'predictive contracting' approaches based on machine learning, which draw on prior decisions in relation to the effects of particular types of clause and on the cumulative sum of past experience in relation to the types of risks that have been known to eventuate in the context of transactions of that type, have the power to transform the practice of contracting and the recent successes of predictive systems for generating programming code, such as GPT-3,[14] suggest that the creation of predictive systems for generating contracts is feasible, as is the possibility of combining them with smart contracts and contract lifecycle management.

Nevertheless, there are two obvious and crucial baseline conditions that must be met if these developments are to underpin a sustainable and socially acceptable approach to contracting. These are, firstly, the systems and processes that underpin any autonomous system used in contracting must be resilient and, secondly, they must be trustworthy. Resilience requires systems to be capable of dealing effectively with the very wide range of requirements, interests, and contexts in which contracting is used; of avoiding, withstanding, or responding sensibly to unexpected and uncertain circumstances; and of identifying potential points of failure and responding appropriately to them. Trustworthiness is more complex. Trustworthiness involves an evaluative judgment not just in relation to the technical dimensions of the functioning of an autonomous system, but more fundamentally in relation to the social aspects of its operation: the outcomes it has a propensity to produce, the interests it has a propensity to prioritise, and the impact these propensities have on different categories of social actors. In other words, as a baseline condition, trustworthiness requires not just that the AI be reliably able to produce outcomes under a range of conditions but also that those outcomes conform to a particular normative standard or set of standards.

Outsourcing by Design (Routledge 2016) 96–97; F Munari, 'Blockchain and Smart Contracts in Shipping and Transport' in B Soyer and A Tettenborn (eds), *New Technologies, Artificial Intelligence and Shipping Law in the 21st Century* (Informa Law 2020) 9–11.

12 J Leng and others, 'Makerchain: A Blockchain with Chemical Signature for Self-Organizing Process in Social Manufacturing' (2019) 234 *Journal of Cleaner Production* 767, 773–774.

13 For an overview, see KD Betts and KR Jaep, 'The Dawn of Fully Automated Contract Drafting: Machine Learning Breathes New Life into a Decades-Old Promise' (2017) 15 *Duke Law and Technology Review* 216, 218–224.

14 S Williams, 'Predictive Contracting' [2019] *Columbia Business Law Review* 621; TB Brown and others, 'Language Models are Few-Shot Learners' (22 July 2020) <https://arxiv.org/abs/2005.14165>.

Historically, the assessment of trustworthiness tended to be focused on technical properties, such as reliability, safety, security, availability, usability, and data safeguarding.[15] More recently, however, computer scientists have begun to argue for a more broadly based and socially grounded conceptualisation of trustworthiness, which incorporates not just technical standards but also social standards, including fairness, accountability, ethical use, accountability, and interpretability of outcomes.[16] There is sound logic behind this broader conception. An AI that reliably produces a one-sided outcome – ensuring, in Llewellyn's evocative phrase, that 'what Big Fist wants, he gets'[17] – may well meet the baseline condition of resilience, but it is extremely unlikely to meet the condition of trustworthiness. Nor should it.

Creating autonomous systems that are resilient and trustworthy in this broader sense involves three sets of challenges. The first relates to the technical side of AI. Although it is common to use human metaphors in relation to AI processes, these metaphors are neither accurate nor appropriate. The AI systems that we currently have and those that are likely to be capable of being deployed in contracting in the near future are not intelligent in any sense comparable to human intelligence. They do not think, and they exercise neither judgement nor discernment. What algorithmic systems do have is a high level of competence, far exceeding that of humans, at certain types of tasks that require an ability to layer ideas or representations, to map the conceptual territory covered by those ideas and representations, and to formulate, identify, and execute actions on the basis of those maps.[18] To put it in the language of analytical philosophy, algorithmic systems have significant strengths in the field of practical reasons but are inherently incapable of framing new grounds for epistemic reasons beyond those set out in hard-coded instructions and identified through pattern recognition. In consequence, a system will only meet the baseline condition of trustworthiness if it has either been hard-coded with directives that have a propensity to produce the types of outcomes associated with trustworthiness, or been trained on materials that give it an ability to identify and build into its workings patterns that reliably produce such outcomes. The nature of the heuristic processes on which the functioning of algorithmic systems is predicated makes it very easy for these systems to lapse into contract law minimalism, behaving like the proverbial 'steely-eyed utility maximisers', unless the system has been explicitly designed not to do so. This makes it crucial to appreciate, and structure legal regulation around, the entirety of the socio-technical system underpinning AI.

The second challenge relates to the legal consequences of the character of the processes that underpin the functioning of AIs. Contract law plays a strong regulatory

[15] JM Wing, 'Trustworthy AI' (2020) 64(10) *Communications of the ACM* 64, 65.

[16] Ibid. 66.

[17] K Llewellyn, 'The Normative, the Legal, and the Law-Jobs: The Problem of Juristic Method' (1940) 49(8) *Yale Law Journal* 1355, 1376.

[18] A Kremer, 'Computers Do Not Think, They Are Oriented in Thought' (2021) 36 *AI and Society* 401.

role in relation to contract:[19] law does not just facilitate the practice of contracting and give effect to contracting, but also creates structures and scaffolding whose express purpose is to channel contracting in particular directions and to impose limits on the types of social relations and interests that contract can be used to order and govern.[20] The tools law uses, however, assume human decision-making processes. The law sets limits on opportunism, for example, by implying terms that require the parties to conduct themselves in a particular co-operative manner, by limiting the way in which and ends for which a contractual discretion may be validly exercised, by structuring the remedies available for breach in a manner that incentivises particular types of conduct, and so on.[21] The tests and concepts on which these tools rely, however, are framed in a language that, whilst capable of easily being applied to humans, poses considerable difficulties in relation to AI.

The effect is to raise serious, and non-trivial, questions that contract law must answer if it is to exercise regulatory capacity over AI-infused contracting, but to which there are at present no obvious answers. Would, for example, a person with no ability to read programming code be able to avail of the non est factum defence in relation to a contract implemented in the form of a computer programme?[22] If parties misunderstand the way in which an algorithm is designed to function – for example, in dynamically devising new terms to deal with emerging circumstances – does that trigger a remedy of mistake? Should a party who is in a superior position to understand the manner in which an algorithm functions be under a duty to disclose or correct a misunderstanding that the other party has (unlike the current position at common law)? These questions do not represent a mere doctrinal querulousness. It is doctrines such as these and remedies such as rectification that enable the courts to exercise regulatory power over contracts, and if those doctrines are no longer operational, a different system of assurance will have to be found for AI to meet the baseline condition of trustworthiness and for the overall system of contracting to meet the baseline condition of resilience when the AI fails to function as expected.

Underpinning both of these is a third challenge, which goes to the heart of the impact of AI on contracting. As the introduction argued, the functioning of AI is underpinned not just by its technical design but also by the social context within which it operates. As the literature has long noted, this gives AI a marked propensity to inherit biases and limitations from that social context. AI itself is morally neutral as a matter of definition if it has not been programmed to apply a particular

[19] H Collins, *Regulating Contracts* (Oxford University Press 1999).

[20] S Hedley, 'Two Laws of Contract, or One?' in TT Arvind and J Steele (eds), *Contract Law and the Legislature: Autonomy, Expectations, and the Making of Legal Doctrine* (Hart Publishing 2020).

[21] D Campbell, 'The Relational Constitution of Remedy: Co-operation as the Implicit Second Principle of Remedies for Breach of Contract' (2005) 11 Texas Wesleyan Law Review 455.

[22] The defence in its current form is generally taken to require legal incapacity. See for example, *Saunders v Anglia Building Society* [1971] AC 1004 (HL) and *Ford v Perpetual Trustees Victoria Ltd* [2009] NSWCA 186 (2009), 257 ALR 658.

moral framework, but that does not mean that it will operate in a morally neutral manner. To the extent an AI replicates functions that, in humans, constitute 'judgment', those judgments are wholly derivative of the human-constructed systems that enable an AI to exercise those functions.[23] An AI that emerges from a social context that displays particular biases and predispositions, and that has not been designed to avoid those biases and predispositions, is therefore likely to have a propensity to replicate them.

The fact that the applications towards which the development of AI-infused contracting has been directed continue to follow the pattern of focusing on the medium of the contract rather than the substance of the transaction instantiates the extent to which the functionality of AI is shaped by the worldviews implicit in the human-constructed systems that underpin their design. But the social context also exerts a deeper shaping influence, which can be illustrated with reference to the analogy between contracts and narratives which is frequently deployed in the literature on contracting.[24] If a contract contains a transactional narrative, then an AI's strengths – its particular 'competence', in the terminology used above – lies in its ability to identify where we are in the narrative, what possible endings exist, and what path needs to be followed to get to a particular ending (or, at least, to increase the chances of arriving at that ending). An AI does not, however, have an independent ability to form a view on what constitutes an optimal ending, or an optimal way of dealing with an unexpected contingency, in the context of a specific transaction. Its 'views' are wholly shaped by the material it was given, which in turn are shaped by biases and predispositions that arise from the social context in which it is designed.[25] To achieve the baseline conditions of trustworthiness and resilience, it is essential that the processes by which AIs are designed, and the manner in which they are legally regulated, are oriented towards addressing these biases and predispositions. It is, accordingly, to examining the types of biases that the present contracting environment creates that we now turn.

III THE MANY PRESENTS OF CONTRACT: SOCIAL AND COMMERCIAL CONTEXTS

Since the formulation in the 1960s of what has come to be termed 'relational contract theory', it has been clear that there is a real, and growing, disjunction between the transactional and legal aspects of contract. In the last twenty years, a considerable body of empirical and theoretical work on contracts and contracting has given us new and important insights into the nature of this disjunction and the impact it

[23] J Malpas, 'The Necessity of Judgment' (2020) 35 *AI and Society* 1073, 1074.

[24] See for example, LM Ingram and LS Jensen, 'The Utility of Narrative Voices in the Federal Procurement Contract' (2018) 4(1–2) *Journal of Strategic Contracting and Negotiation* 58.

[25] D Varona, Y Lizama-Mue and JL Suárez, 'Machine Learning's Limitations in Avoiding Automation of Bias' (2020) 36 *AI and Society* 197.

has on transactions. This disjunction and its impact are a fundamental part of the social context against whose backdrop AI is used in the field of contracting, and three aspects of it are of particular importance in considering the impact of AI on contracting and identifying the challenges that creating trustworthy and resilient AI is likely to pose for the law as well as for the practice of AI design.

Firstly, in contrast to the older literature on relational contract,[26] recent empirical studies have shown that interorganisational relations tend to involve both relational and contractual governance, with the two playing complementary roles rather than being substitutes for each other.[27] Empirical work has also shown that combining relational and contractual governance has a positive effect on transactions, improving outcomes for both parties and reducing opportunistic behaviour.[28] This work, in turn, has led to a more nuanced view of the diverse range of functions that contracts serve in transactions. Apart from the safeguarding function familiar to lawyers, contracts also serve as devices to structure transactional adaptation in the face of changing circumstances,[29] to structure communication and coordination during the lifetime of a transaction (e.g., by creating steering groups)[30] as well as to support internal management and medium-term planning in the context of a transaction.[31]

The manner in which contracts are drafted, however, is not oriented towards enabling them to discharge these functions in a systematic or reliable way. Macneil criticised traditional approaches to drafting contracts for their reliance on foreseeing and planning for all future contingencies, a goal he argued was unachievable.[32] Recent research suggests that little has changed since his day. Legal scholars working within a broadly relational and empirical tradition have argued that contracts require a more 'proactive' element if they are to serve as an effective transactional management tool, but notwithstanding this they tend instead to be drafted reactively in a manner that prioritises safeguarding the parties' interests in a litigated dispute,[33] and focuses on risk allocation rather than on the strategic dimensions of

[26] S Macaulay, 'Non-contractual Relations in Business: A Preliminary Review' (1963) 28(1) *American Sociology Review* 55.

[27] L Poppo and T Zenger, 'Do Formal Contracts and Relational Governance Function as Substitutes or Complements' (2002) 23(8) *Strategic Management Journal* 707.

[28] Z Cao and F Lumineau, 'Revisiting the Interplay between Contractual and Relational Governance: A Qualitative and Meta-Analytic Investigation' (2015) 33–34 *Journal of Operations Management* 15, 30.

[29] R Klein Woolthuis, B Hillebrand and B Nooteboom, 'Trust, Contract and Relationship Development' (2005) 26(6) *Organization Studies* 813.

[30] Y Chen and others, 'Understanding the Multiple Functions of Construction Contracts: The Anatomy of FIDIC Model Contracts' (2018) 36(8) *Construction Management and Economics* 472.

[31] A Hurmerinta-Haanpää and S Viding, 'The Functions of Contracts in Interorganizational Relationships: A Contract Experts' Perspective' (2014) 40(1) *Journal of Management* 193, 107–109.

[32] IR Macneil, 'Restatement (Second) of Contracts and Presentation' (1974) 60 *Virginia Law Review* 589.

[33] G Berger-Walliser, 'The Past and Future of Proactive Law: An Overview of the Development of the Proactive Law Movement' in G Berger-Walliser and K Østergaard (eds), *Proactive Law in a Business Environment* (DJØF Publishing 2012) 23.

contracting.[34] The effects of this on contract performance have not been happy. Research has shown, for example, that control-oriented provisions tend to be favoured by lawyers, even though contracts which rely on control-oriented provisions tend to exacerbate conflict in environments that are subject to rapid change.[35]

Much of this literature has focused on contracts where the parties are in a position of relative equality and are thus free to bargain in pursuit of their interests. Yet this is only rarely true in the real world. The practice of contracting is marked by asymmetry and inequality of bargaining power far more frequently than it is by symmetry, and it is in this area – where the failure to structure contracts to further joint maximisation combines with terms that are heavily tilted towards one side in terms of their safeguarding function – that the transactional impact of contracting practices becomes particularly problematic. In recent work, Jenny Steele and I have devised a framework which, drawing on Mary Douglas's grid-group cultural theory, identifies four distinct approaches or perceptions of markets within legal regulation.[36] Figure 3.1 presents an adaptation of that framework which charts four different ways in which the drafting of contracts can affect a transaction.

At the bottom end, transactions are largely symmetric. Positions are not fixed, and parties may be a seller one day and a buyer the next. At the top end, transactions are asymmetric, and positions are fixed: a consumer of payday lending services, for example, is unlikely to become a provider of such services, and the head contractor on a construction project and an electrical subcontractor are unlikely to ever find themselves in the opposite position. Similarly, at the left extreme contracts are treated as being autonomous of the commercial transaction: there is a sharp distinction between the 'paper deal' and the 'real deal'. At the right extreme, there is a close and embedded relationship between the contract and the transaction: the paper deal at least partially furthers the commercial purposes of the real deal.

As the dashed lines indicate – the two axes represent a continuum rather than hard-edged discrete categories. The more a transaction moves away from the extreme end of an axis, the more it displays a mixture of characteristics. At the bottom end, the effect of contracts on transactions is relatively benign. In transactions that are genuinely autonomous and symmetric – such as a commercial sale of commodified industrial goods – a contract which follows a pattern of transactional safeguarding will support the transaction relatively well: its provisions efficiently communicate to the parties how they need to reorient conduct and channel their expectations

[34] LA DiMatteo, GJ Siedel and H Haapio, 'Strategic Contracting: Examining the Business-Legal Interface' in G Berger-Walliser and K Østergaard (eds), *Proactive Law in a Business Environment* (DJØF Publishing 2012).

[35] O Schilke and F Lumineau, 'The Double-Edged Effect of Contracts on Alliance Performance' (2018) 44(7) *Journal of Management* 2827.

[36] TT Arvind and J Steele, 'Remapping Contract Law: Four Perceptions of Markets' in TT Arvind and J Steele (eds), *Contract Law and the Legislature: Autonomy, Expectations, and the Making of Legal Doctrine* (Hart Publishing 2020) 439–445.

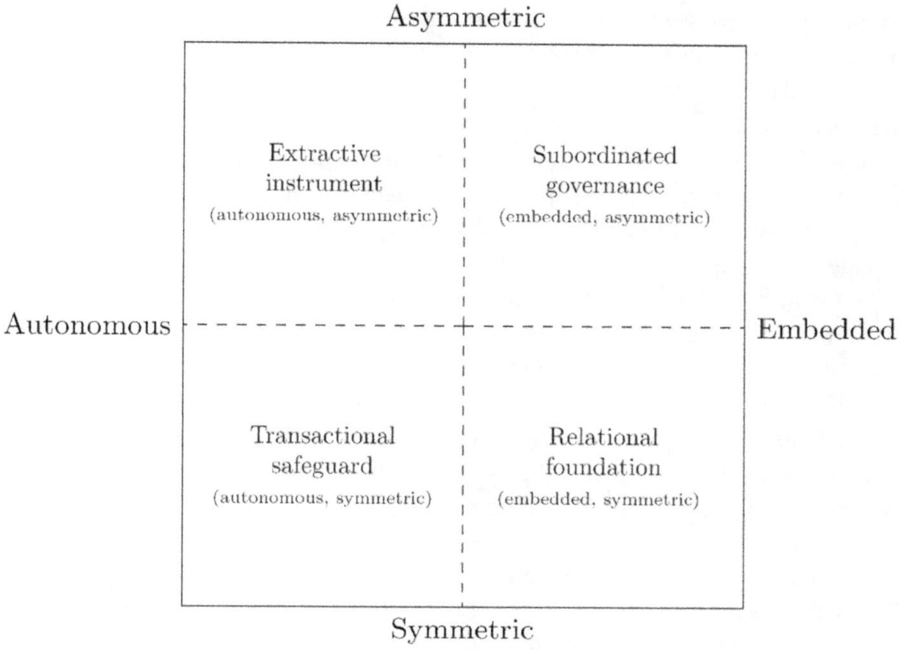

FIGURE 3.1 Four different ways in which the drafting of contracts can affect a transaction

to avoid transactional conflict.[37] Similarly, a contract which relates to a symmetric transaction and is sufficiently well-specified to embed the key requirements of the transaction – for example, a well-drafted relationally oriented joint venture agreement – will operate efficiently in its role of providing a relational foundation for the transaction, which serves to define, plan, and organise the parties efforts around a positive and constructive shared goal.[38]

As we move higher along the vertical dimension into more asymmetric transactions, however, this begins to change. A contract embedded in asymmetry will create a hierarchical system of governance, in which one party – and its interests and goals – is subordinated to the other. The context and specificities of the transaction infuse the contract's terms, but the ultimate say – the right to determine how transactional governance operates, how unforeseen surpluses and losses are allocated, and how the transaction is adapted to deal with emergent circumstances – is vested

[37] There is a strong parallel between this transactional function of contracts and the law-job which Llewellyn termed 'channelling' (Llewellyn (n 21) 1376–1380). I have previously discussed the parallels between grid-group cultural theory and Llewellyn's law-job theory in TT Arvind, S Halliday and L Stirton, 'Judicial Review and Administrative Justice' in J Tomlinson and others (eds), *The Oxford Handbook of Administrative Justice* (Oxford University Press 2021), on which the account in this chapter is largely based.

[38] In this, it closely resembles the law-job Llewellyn termed 'net drive'. See Llewellyn (n 21) 1387–1391.

in the superior party who has considerable discretion in relation to how much and in what circumstances regard will be had to the interests of other parties.[39]

The situation is not much better at the left extreme. Here, contracts serve as extractive instruments, with the contract terms becoming one-sided tools whose purpose is primarily to enable one of the parties to extract as much value as feasible from their counterparty. The paper deal displaces the real deal, because the stronger party's interests are better served through disembedding the transaction from broader social expectations. The party in a weaker position has little ability to influence the terms of the contract, giving contracts a systemic propensity to operate in a manner that is contrary to the other party's interests, while the party in a superior position has little interest or incentive to have regard to the other party's interests save to the extent necessary to prevent the transaction from disintegrating in a manner that harms the superior party's commercial interests.[40]

These propensities are real and they are deeply entrenched in the fabric of modern contracting. And whilst AI has the potential to ameliorate these propensities, it also has the ability to exacerbate them. As the discussion in Section II has shown, when viewed as a socio-technical system, the processes that create AIs have a strong tendency to replicate biases inherited from existing social practices, and to the extent the purposes for which they are deployed remain subject to the same asymmetries as existing contracting practices, those biases will also be reflected in their use. Section IV considers this issue in more detail, with reference to the four types of use to which AI is actually put. As I show, the solution lies in a new standard of transactional responsibility, which must be placed at the heart of the processes by which AI systems in the field of contracting are conceptualised, designed, built, and regulated.

IV THE PROMISE AND PERILS OF AI-INFUSED CONTRACTING

In principle, AI-infused contracting should be readily able to overcome the biases outlined in Section III. The biases and challenges in question are to a very significant extent a product of the drafting and negotiating practices of lawyers and, in particular, their reliance on 'legalese' in drafting and on a heavily legalised and legalistic approach to negotiation.[41] Both of these make sense if viewed as an example of a 'fast and frugal' heuristic in action.[42] 'Fast and frugal' heuristics

39 Cf the law-job which Llewellyn terms 'the say': ibid. 1383–1387.

40 Cf Llewellyn's discussion of the law-job he terms 'the trouble-case': ibid. 1375–1376.

41 P Hietanen-Kunwald and H Haapio, 'Effective Dispute Prevention and Resolution through Proactive Contract Design' (2021) 5 *Journal of Strategic Contracting and Negotiation* 3 <https://doi.org/10.1177/20555636211016878>.

42 See G Gigerenzer and PM Todd, 'Fast and Frugal Heuristics: The Adaptive Toolbox' in G Gigerenzer, PM Todd and the ABC Research Group (eds), *Simple Heuristics that Make Us Smart* (Oxford University Press 1999). For a discussion of its application to law, see C Engel and G Gigerenzer, 'Law and Heuristics: An Interdisciplinary Venture' in C Engel and G Gigerenzer (eds), *Heuristics and the Law* (MIT Press 2006).

use familiar, tested forms that are known to reduce the chance of bad outcomes even though those forms may not necessarily promote good outcomes or a positive transactional culture.[43] Although this makes sense as a technique to deal with the cognitive limitations of human actors, AI is not subject to these limitations. The superior competence (discussed in Section II above) which AI-infused contracting exhibits in relation to layering and mapping a conceptual field and connecting those maps to patterns of outcomes provides a very different heuristic that has a clear and obvious potential to avoid the limitations of the default heuristic that underpins standard legal drafting practices. In their work on 'self-driving contracts', Casey and Niblett have argued that technology creates the potential for a wholly new type of contract oriented around dynamically generated 'micro-directives' that translate a general objective into a specific set of actions that are likely to achieve the objective, and can be programmed to do so on the fly thus eliminating both the need for gap-filling and the disputes that arise when gaps are not properly filled.[44] Similar arguments have been made in relation to predictive AI which, it has been suggested, can eliminate a lot of the legal uncertainty around the question of what precisely a given term or set of terms requires parties to do under a particular set of circumstances.[45]

Realising these possibilities in practice, however, faces two issues. Firstly, from a technical standpoint, although AI-infused contracting does indeed offer the potential to significantly improve contracting through the dynamic generation of 'micro-directives' and a more rigorously evidence-based approach to the formulation of contract terms – whether in the form of code-based micro-directives or more conventional terms – the practical utility of these terms will be diminished unless those terms, and the contract lifecycle management processes the AI follows, takes due account of the role played by relational governance in contractual transactions. Although there was at one stage a significant strand of the literature which took the view that reliance on relational techniques such as trust and flexibility was a response to transaction costs, the empirical work discussed in Section III has unambiguously demonstrated that relational governance plays a distinctive role that is wholly independent of techniques to respond to transaction costs.[46] Eliminating the problem of contract gaps will not, therefore, eliminate the need for relational governance; and given the distinctiveness of relational governance and its importance to the quality of transactional outcomes, it is unlikely that AI-infused contracting will meet the baseline condition of resilience unless it is able to develop, deploy,

43 CA Hill, 'Why Contracts are Written in "Legalese"' (2001) 77(1) *Chicago-Kent Law Review* 59.

44 A Casey and A Niblett, 'Self-Driving Contracts' (2017) 43 *Journal of Corporation Law* 1.

45 Williams (n 17).

46 For a recent overview, see B Petersen and K Østergaard, 'Reconciling Contracts and Relational Governance through Strategic Contracting' (2002) 33(3) *Journal of Business and Industrial Marketing* 265, 265–267.

and embed techniques of relational governance in circumstances where they are appropriate.[47]

Obtaining the data needed to create an AI capable of dealing with relational governance is far from straightforward. Not all relational governance techniques are codified in a contract, and even where they are the type of relationality they are intended to facilitate may not be apparent from the wording of the clause. There is, in consequence, a non-trivial risk of a conflict between the relational world of contract and the logical world of AI, in which an AI's focus on 'micro-directives' risks shrinking the room available for relational governance.[48] Equally, although predictive contracting can build on a good understanding of the legal consequences of specific types of provisions based on a machine analysis of the text of judicial dicta, the data on their relational and transactional consequences is far less choate, making these consequences considerably harder to estimate through traditional machine learning techniques.

Secondly, and from a social standpoint, AI-infused contracting runs a non-trivial risk of exacerbating the problems discussed in Section III. The costs of AI, the non-transparency of the (typically proprietary) algorithms that underpin it, and the legal and practical hurdles associated with acquiring access to the large quantities of data required to design functional AI, cumulatively give it an inherent propensity to accentuate pre-existing knowledge- and power-asymmetries. The further we move beyond the ideal-typical example of a business-to-business transaction between equally resourced parties, the likelier it becomes that the systems used in AI-infused contracting will be trained on material which disproportionately represents the preferences of a subset of transactors – for example, larger enterprises – without that material being counterbalanced by material representing broader preferences. If transactors in the 'subordinated governance' quadrant outlined in Figure 3.1 lack the ability to exercise a proportionate say in the making of contractual determinations, it is difficult to see how they will be able to exercise any form of say in relation to the particular type of algorithmic system that should be used to govern a contract or the propensities and predilections that system should be designed to have. This is even truer of transactors who would normally be required to accept a contract in the 'extractive instrument' quadrant as a condition of transacting. Indeed, in both cases, the proprietary character which the technology underlying the algorithmic system is likely to have will, if anything, further erode the capacity of transactors in an asymmetric transaction to influence or even have full knowledge of the nature

[47] The qualification is important, as empirical work has shown that there are circumstances in which an excessive reliance on relationality negatively affects transactional outcomes. See JH Dyer, H Singh and WS Hesterley, 'The Relational View Revisited: A Dynamic Perspective on Value Creation and Value Capture' (2018) 39 *Strategic Management Journal* 3140.

[48] Cf D'Acquisto's discussion of the (closely-related) conflict between the ethical principles that underpin human action and the logical principles that underpin the operation of AI, in G D'Acquisto, 'On Conflicts between Ethical and Logical Principles in Artificial Intelligence' (2020) 35 *AI and Society* 895.

TABLE 3.1 *The tetrad of effects of AI on contracting*

Type of effect	Manifestation in AI-infused contracting
Enhances	The ability to create proactive contracts customised to the specific circumstances of a transaction
Obsolesces	Boilerplate, standard form, reactive contracts drafted according to routinised professional heuristics
Retrieves	The return of a role for inaccessible, technical processes in taking action that produce legal effects
Reverses into	A return from contract to status

of the predispositions that the algorithm in question exhibits. And yet, it is hard to see AI-infused contracting can meet the baseline condition of trustworthiness unless transactors who would be placed in these quadrants by existing contracting practices do in fact have such an ability.

McLuhan's tetrad of effects of technologies provides a useful way of conceptualising and pulling together the full range of social consequences that a system of AI-infused contracting subject to these limitations is likely to have. McLuhan's work, like this chapter, was concerned with aspects of technology that seek to extend the capabilities of the physical human body or mind, and it was motivated by the insight that the effects of technology were mediated, firstly, by the fact that technologies were always characterised by at least some element of social distrust in relation to the manner in which they were actually used and, secondly, by the learning processes through which the know-how underpinning the technology is communicated and transmitted.[49]

Based on this, McLuhan suggests that technologies are never neutral or passive. Rather, they tend to have a 'tetrad' of four effects. Firstly, they enhance, intensify, accelerate or make possible some type of human action or some aspect of the human situation. Secondly, they also displace or render obsolete other types of action or aspects of situations. Thirdly, they retrieve or bring back older forms of action that may have previously lapsed into obsolescence. Fourthly and finally, they have a reverse potential of inverting their original characteristics when pushed to their limits. These effects are complementary: they operate simultaneously and when taken together and read cumulatively, they provide a means to examine how a given technology acts and affects human action.[50]

Table 3.1 summarises the manner in which these effects play out in AI-infused contracting. The first two effects – enhancement and obsolescence – are both positive. AI-infused contracting enhances the ability of parties to, through AI, create

[49] M McLuhan and E McLuhan, *The Laws of Media: The New Science* (University of Toronto Press 1988) 93–97.

[50] Ibid. 98–99.

contracts and transactional management systems that are neither dependent on nor influenced by the fast-and-frugal heuristic that currently underpins virtually all of the contract lifecycle that is informed or influenced by the legal aspects of the transaction. For much the same reason, it also renders obsolete the apparatus of boilerplate contracts, as well as the reliance on complex, legalistic, and reactive documents that characterises current contract practice. Both these practices serve as a heuristic to reduce transaction costs by using clauses which have the advantage of being tried-and-tested, even if they only imperfectly fit the facts of a case. AI-infused contracting does not, however, require this heuristic.

The other two effects, in contrast, require a more detailed explanation. AI-infused contracting operates through stochastic processes that differ fundamentally from the processes that underpin ordinary human reasoning. In consequence, the reasoning underpinning the decisions made in AI-influenced contracting inherently and necessarily recedes from the level of accessibility that characterises ordinary human decision-making. The consequence is a return, as far as the processes necessary to give legal effect to actions are concerned, to something not dissimilar to Sir Edward Coke's description of the law as 'an artificial perfection of reason'.[51] To Coke, this 'artificial reason' was critical to understanding the evaluative judgments embedded in legal rules, and the implications of those embedded evaluative judgments for the manner in which the legal system would treat individual cases. However, it was not accessible to the ordinary subject of the law. It could only be properly acquired through 'long study, observation, and experience' rather than through the application of the natural reason that all persons possess.[52] This way of thinking about the law was characteristic of the late mediaeval and early modern common law, and there are a number of pieces of popular literature from the period depicting the struggles of ordinary people to navigate the system, written from perspectives sympathising with the system,[53] as well as from perspectives sympathising with ordinary people.[54] The parallel with the position of a party, particularly parties in an inferior position in asymmetric transactions, is obvious, and it suggests a strong need to pay close attention to the potentially deleterious social consequences of AI-infused contracting.

This is also true of the fourth effect, described in Table 3.1 as a return from contract to status. Henry Maine, famously, described the movement of progressive societies as having been 'from Status to Contract',[55] and his statement points to

[51] Co Litt 97b.

[52] Ibid.

[53] See for example, 'The Complaints of the People of Stoughton', MS. Bodl. 57, f. 191v.

[54] See for example, 'A Satyre on the Consistory Courts', BL MS Harley 2253, f. 70v <www.bl.uk/manuscripts/FullDisplay.aspx?ref=HarleyMS2253>. For a translation, see <www.d.lib.rochester.edu/camelot/text/fein-harley2253-volume-2-article-40>.

[55] HS Maine, *Ancient Law: Its Connection with the Early History of Society, and Its Relation to Modern Ideas* (John Murray 1861) 170.

the important role self-determination through contract played in the emergence of modern social thought. A fundamental premise of this school of thought is the idea that markets operate as an information-communication framework, which enables individual market participants to improve their position by learning from market signals. As I have argued elsewhere, this function is threatened at a fundamental level by the growing use of data-driven autonomous algorithms which, in an asymmetric social environment, operate to limit both the amount of information communicated by market mechanisms to non-dominant participants and the ability of non-dominant participants to influence the opportunities open to them.[56] To the extent AI-infused contracting relies on data-driven algorithmic systems, it is likely to have precisely the same propensity to producing social effects of this type as other data-driven algorithms.

V THE PRINCIPLE OF TRANSACTIONAL RESPONSIBILITY

How, then, can these issues be resolved, and how can AI-infused contracting be brought closer to satisfying the baseline conditions of resilience and trustworthiness? The answer, as I argue in this section, lies in developing a relationally informed principle of transactional responsibility, and embedding that principle into the processes and systems by which AI-infused contracting systems are designed, implemented, deployed, and regulated.

Until recently, the focus of contract law on the medium of contracts rather than the substance of transactions exercised a high degree of influence over the manner in which the normative ends of contracting have been conceptualised. The ends of the law were largely seen in terms of giving effect to the message contained in the medium of the contract, by providing a forum in which the requirements of that message could be authoritatively determined and in which breaches of contract could be remedied.[57] The normative core of contract law was, accordingly, conceptualised in terms that were closely related to the medium of contracts rather than the substance of transactional relations: as being about the promises made by the parties to each other,[58] or about the duties assumed by the parties to each other,[59] or about the fact and consequences of the parties' mutual consent,[60] and so on. That the law sometimes intervened to alter or compel a deviation from the contractual framework was not denied, but it was compartmentalised: as a consumer-welfarist

[56] TT Arvind, 'Personalisation, Markets, and Contract: The Limits of Legal Incrementalism' in U Kohl and J Eisler (eds), *Data-Driven Personalisation in Markets, Politics and Law* (Cambridge University Press 2021) 114–116.

[57] This is the position taken by the corrective justice account of contracts. See esp. E Weinrib, *The Idea of Private Law* (Harvard University Press 1995).

[58] C Fried, *Contract as Promise: A Theory of Contractual Obligation* (Harvard University Press 1981).

[59] B Coote, *Contract as Assumption: Essays on a Theme* (Hart Publishing 2010).

[60] RE Barnett, 'Some Problems with Contract as Promise' (1992) 77 *Cornell Law Review* 1022.

exception to contract law's default market-individualist orientation, or as a policy-based, distributive exception to the corrective and vindicatory goals that were considered to be the normative core of contract.[61]

Recent work has begun to challenge this picture and demonstrate that contract law can only provide a sustainable basis for contracting if it builds on a relational understanding of the tasks and ends of contract law and of the types of outcomes that an effective law would promote. This insight, of course, lay at the heart of the work of the original relational contract theorists, but more recently, their insight has been taken up by scholars working within a much broader set of approaches. Wielsch, for example, has put forward a relational legal analysis which argues that all legal rights have social dimensions, and the social institutions and systems on which these dimensions depend have a normativity of their own, which the law must provide the room to consider comprehensively.[62] Similarly, Tan has recently put forward a helpful distinction between 'macro' and 'micro' justice and has argued that although contract theorists have traditionally assumed that contract is focused solely on a corrective conception of micro justice, contract law embeds a distinctive, relationally oriented and relationally constrained conception of micro justice which underpins a range of positions taken by contract law in areas ranging from employment law to pre-nuptial contracts.[63] By bringing these insights into dialogue with recent work on the distributive implications of AI and the challenges of making AI more socially responsive, we can begin to construct a framework to define and bring into operation a principle of transactional responsibility which, if it underpins AI-infused contracting systems, can help make those systems resilient and trustworthy by avoiding the biases and predilections discussed in Sections II and IV. In the remainder of this section, I describe the five core elements on which such a framework will be built.

Firstly, in place of the focus on the medium of contract which the current approach to AI-infused contracting has inherited from the conceptual frameworks on which contract practice is currently based, a transactionally responsible approach will have its heart the understanding that Macneil termed the 'solidary belief.' The solidary belief reflects a common belief in continued future interdependence, which is sufficiently deep and extensive to ensure that no participant in a contractual system has the power to unilaterally appropriate an undue share of the surplus generated by a transaction. Macneil argued that the solidary belief was of fundamental importance to contractual systems of private ordering. Contracts frequently incorporate terms that give one party the ability to cause disproportionate harm to another party, and if there is a widespread belief that those terms will be used by systemically stronger parties to further their interests at the expense of systemically weaker parties, the

[61] See, for example, RA Epstein, 'In Defense of the Contract at Will' (1984) 51(4) *University of Chicago Law Review* 984.

[62] D Wielsch, 'Relational Justice' (2013) 76 *Law and Contemporary Problems* 191.

[63] ZX Tan, 'Where the Action Is: Macro and Micro Justice in Contract Law' (2020) 83(4) *Modern Law Review* 725.

ultimate effect will be to threaten the viability of the contractual system.[64] That AI-infused contracting carries the potential to threaten the solidary belief should be obvious from the discussion in Sections III and IV, and task of making it trustworthy therefore requires that it is the preservation of the solidary belief, rather than inherited ideas such as gap-filling or outcome-prediction, that must be its central function.

Secondly, in terms of the principles that inform the design of algorithmic systems in the field of contracting, it is vital that the systems be designed to be not just contractually and legally aware but also socially, contextually, sectorally, and transactionally aware. Much of the work on designing systems for AI-infused contracting has focused on developing their ability to analyse contractual texts to extract lifecycle-relevant information and on developing predictive capabilities in relation to the impact of legal rules on the contract's provisions. Yet as the discussion above has demonstrated, a resilient AI system must also be able to work constructively with relational dimensions of contracts, including relational dimensions or aspects of relational governance that commonly inform transactional practice but are not codified in the actual terms of contracts. This does not require an AI to exercise judgment or discernment. Within the frameworks of non-monotonic logic that are used in programming autonomous system, it rather requires the system to be programmed to have an awareness of when relational considerations have priority over other considerations. This does not mean that creating systems with this awareness is straightforward: as Section IV has discussed, there are challenges in actually ascertaining what these relational practices are, and when they are triggered and thus acquire priority, these challenges are not insurmountable. There are established methods for ascertaining relevant social norms that are regularly deployed in relation to other autonomous systems, such as care robots,[65] which can with some adaptation be applied to the design of systems for AI-infused contracting, as can the experience of designing systems for broader public input into policy formation processes.[66]

Thirdly, in terms of the process that underpins the design of systems for AI-infused contracting, it is vital to institute systems of governance that ensure that the system is designed to have due regard to, and give due weight to, the interests of all categories of transactors who are likely to be subject to a particular algorithmic system. This is of particular importance in systemically asymmetric transactions, where neither transactional power nor transactional positions are equally distributed. As the discussion above has shown, whatever claims may be made in relation to the moral neutrality of an algorithm, the actual pattern of outcomes produced by AI-infused

[64] IR MacNeil, *The New Social Contract: An Inquiry into Modern Contractual Relations* (Yale University Press 1980) 102–104.

[65] See, for example, N McBride, 'Developing Socially Inspired Robotics through the Application of Human Analogy: Capabilities and Social Practice' (2020) 35 *AI and Society* 857.

[66] BS Noveck, 'Crowdlaw: Collective Intelligence and Lawmaking' (2018) 40 *Analyse & Kritik* 359.

contracting will reflect the biases and predispositions of the social circles involved in its design, which could stretch as far as tolerating the propensity of an algorithmic system to cause disproportionate harm to certain categories of transactors. One possible way of creating such systems lies in the system of the 'negotiated economy'. The negotiated economy as a concept was advanced to explain features of governance that are common in Nordic countries. In place of the emphasis on individual choice and economic rationality that characterises traditional approaches to contracting, the negotiated economy emphasises structuring governance processes in a manner that enables all key interest groups to be represented, and to achieve mutually acceptable outcomes through a process of negotiation and persuasion.[67] By elevating the negotiations to the level of interest groups, rather than individual transactors, the institutions of the negotiated economy deal effectively with the problems of asymmetry discussed in Section III. At the same time, the direct involvement of the user groups themselves also deals effectively with the problems of limited regulatory capacity – a problem that is particularly acute in relation to algorithmic systems – and regulatory capture. It is easy to see how this system can be adapted to meet the needs of AI-infused contracting, and a robust design system will address a significant proportion of the obstacles to its trustworthiness.

Fourthly, transactionally responsible systems of AI-infused contracting will require robust systems of assurance. Assurance as a concept has a technical meaning in the field of system safety. Assurance requires the production of: 'a structured argument, supported by evidence, intended to justify that a system is acceptably assured relative to a concern (such as safety or security) in the intended operating environment.'[68]

As the quotation suggests, assurance cases are typically associated with physical properties of a system, such as safety. The methodology and the techniques used, however, are not limited to these concerns. Any property capable of observation or inference from observation is capable of being assured for, and it is therefore possible to extend existing techniques and systems of assurance to assure a system for AI-infused contracting for its social, relational, and transactional awareness, as well as its distributive propensities. Achieving this will require a high level of transparency about the risks which the system has been designed to mitigate, the safeguards that have been put in place to mitigate those risks, the evidence for the effectiveness of those safeguards at actually mitigating the risks, and the manner in which the accuracy of the claims underpinning the assurance case can be tested. Assurance cases make a significant contribution to a system's actual ability to avert the risks that are the subject of the concern (and, thus, to its performance and resilience) as well

[67] K Nielsen, 'The Mixed Economy, the Neoliberal Challenge, and the Negotiated Economy' (1992) 21 *Journal of Socio-Economics* 325.

[68] A Piovesan and E Griffor, 'Reasoning about Safety and Security: The Logic of Assurance' in E Griffor (ed), *Handbook of System Safety and Security* (Syngress 2017).

as to confidence in the system's design (and, thus, to its trustworthiness). They are, therefore, an essential component of systems of transactional responsibility.

Fifthly and finally, actually achieving transactional responsibility will require reworking the role of law, so that it provides a scaffold for the design of transactionally responsible systems of AI-infused contracting, as well as a backstop to deal with the consequences of situations in which AI systems fail for one reason or another. The first of these will entail the creation of a statutory framework to ensure that systems for AI-infused contracting are in fact designed in conformity with the principle of transactional responsibility. The second will require a fundamentally revised and updated approach to the manner in which the law regulates contracts. The law of contract will need to specify requirements in relation to disclosure and transparency requiring the provision of accessible explanations of how a system of AI-infused contracting functions, the basis on which it identifies the specific micro-directive it formulates to deal with a situation and the basis on which the allocative decisions implicit in that micro-directive are made, the data and processes that underpin decisions on the exercise of contractual discretion, the systems of assurance used to measure and evaluate an algorithm's propensities, and so on. Some of these are already provided for under the GDPR, albeit in a limited way, and the growing literature on contract visualisation suggests other ways in which it might be done.[69] An agreed visualisation of an AI-infused contract's expected functioning will be particularly important in determining cases where the question of whether an AI has in fact functioned as expected is at issue, and in assisting the court to remedy situations where it has not so functioned – including where appropriate, rectification, annulment, and restitution. As case law in some jurisdictions has begun to demonstrate, these questions do in fact arise in AI-infused contracting, and it is not obvious that the law as it currently stands provides a satisfactory solution.[70] It goes without saying that the process of reorienting the law will not be straightforward, and is likely to require a statutory scaffold at least in part. However, the purpose of this chapter is not to provide an easy solution as much as to highlight the importance of incorporating it into our research programmes on AI and private law.

VI CONCLUSIONS: TOWARDS (ARTIFICIALLY) INTELLIGENT CONTRACT DESIGN

The practice of contracting in its current form is far from problem-free, and the rise of AI-infused contracting on its face offers a powerful tool with which to begin addressing some of these problems. Nevertheless, as this chapter has sought to show,

[69] See, for example, L Shi and DA Plewe, 'Contract Visualisation: Sketches for Generic Interfaces' in FF-H Nah and C-H Tan (eds), *HCI in Business, Government and Organizations: Part II* (Springer 2017).

[70] See, for example, the decision of the Singapore Court of Appeal in *Quoine Pte Ltd v B2C2* [2020] SGCA(I) 02.

there are real and non-trivial risks that systems of AI-infused contracting will replicate, or even exacerbate, these problems. As this chapter has shown, while these risks can be mitigated, doing so will require a significant shift in the manner in which AI-infused contracting is currently approached in legal scholarship.

This chapter has suggested two baseline conditions which AI-infused contracting must satisfy for its use to be socially acceptable: a condition of resilience and a condition of trustworthiness. I have argued that meeting these conditions requires leaving behind the long shadow cast on AI by traditional contracting practices and anchoring AI in a new principle, which I have called the principle of transactional responsibility. As I have shown, closer attentiveness to the five elements I have identified as central to transactional responsibility can go a long way to making AI less prone to reproducing the negative social effect of existing asymmetries and to perpetuating the problems in the current approach to contracting that make contract law a frequent source of, rather than remedy for, transactional friction. In making these points, my purpose has not been to criticise the rise of AI-infused contracting or the elements of the scholarship that have been supportive of – and, indeed, enthusiastic about – its rise. My purpose has, rather, been to place the focus on another set of issues to which somewhat less attention has been paid but which are nevertheless of considerable importance to the success of AI-infused contracting.

4

Self-Driving Contracts and AI

Present and Near Future

Anthony J. Casey and Anthony Niblett

I INTRODUCTION

Over the last decade or so, there has been a tidal wave of research examining the potential effects of artificial intelligence (AI)[1] on the law.[2] As some early predictions from that literature begin to play out, small changes in the legal landscape are taking shape. This provides an opportune moment to take stock. In this chapter, we do that with regard to AI's effects on automated private contracts. We assess where some relevant technology stands today, where things are headed in the near future, and what this means for contract law.

As this latest AI trend in legal scholarship was taking early form in 2015, we introduced the idea of the micro-directive – a legal technology that uses AI-augmented algorithms to translate the purpose of a law into a specific legal directive.[3] That

Casey acknowledges financial support from the Richard M Weil Faculty Research Fund and the Paul H Leffmann Fund. Niblett acknowledges financial support for this project from SSHRC and the Canada Research Chair program. In the interests of full disclosure, Niblett is the co-founder of Blue J, a start-up bringing machine learning to tax law and employment law. We wish to thank Rachel Chang, Robin Chang, and Ryan Fane for excellent research assistance. We also wish to thank all the participants at the AI and Private Law workshop held online, 19–23 July 2021, for their helpful questions and comments. In particular, we wish to thank TT Arvind, Ernest Lim, and Phillip Morgan.

1 Much of the literature has discussed the growth and importance of predictive technologies such as supervised machine learning. In this article, we use the term 'artificial intelligence' or 'AI' broadly – and somewhat imprecisely – to encompass these various predictive technologies that facilitate automated decision-making based on data analytics.

2 See generally Catalina Goanta, Gijs van Dijck and Gerasimos Spanakis, 'Back to the Future: Waves of Legal Scholarship on Artificial Intelligence' in Sofia Ranchordás and Yaniv Roznai (eds), *Time, Law, and Change: An Interdisciplinary Study* (Hart Publishing 2020) 327 (showing the increased attention artificial intelligence has received in legal scholarship in recent years); see also Benjamin Alarie, 'The Path of the Law: Towards Legal Singularity' (2016) 66 *UTLJ* 443; Gillian K Hadfield, *Rules for a Flat World* (Oxford University Press 2016); Rory Van Loo, 'Rise of the Digital Regulator' (2017) 66 *Duke LJ* 1267; Aziz Z Huq, 'A Right to a Human Decision' (2020) 106 *Virginia LR* 611.

3 Anthony J Casey and Anthony Niblett, 'The Death of Rules and Standards' (2015) <www.chicagounbound.uchicago.edu/cgi/-viewcontent.cgi?article=2444&context=law_and_economics>. For the final published version see Anthony J Casey and Anthony Niblett, 'The Death of Rules and Standards' (2017) 92 *Indiana LJ* 1401. All citations to this paper below are to the published version.

directive is communicated to the relevant party at the moment it becomes useful. Importantly, the directive is context specific, and so the content of the law effectively changes to fit each situation to which it is applied.[4]

In 2016, we took this idea in a new direction, exploring the possibility of using micro-directives in private contracts.[5] In that context, private parties use micro-directives to fill gaps or update contract provisions that would otherwise be incomplete or inflexible.[6] We posited that data-driven predictive algorithms, specified up front, could give the parties context-specific directives on how to comply with a contract's purpose. Thus, rather than relying on human referees to fill gaps and reform provisions after disputes arise, these contracts would rely on micro-directives – which gather data about the current state of the world and factor in the purpose of the contract – to update the parties' obligations at the time of performance.

We referred to these automated private agreements as 'self-driving contracts.'[7] Just as passengers in a self-driving car input a destination and let the car do the rest, parties to a self-driving contract simply specify their ex ante objective (e.g., maximise joint surplus) and let the contract's algorithms flesh out the details of their relationship. And just as the car collects data and updates its route to account for changing traffic patterns and road conditions, the contract's algorithms utilise data and update the parties' rights and obligations to account for the changing context of their relationship.[8]

The ideas of the micro-directive and the self-driving contract have been the subject of much scrutiny and critique.[9] Some scholars were sceptical that micro-directives

4 Ibid. 1410.

5 Anthony J Casey and Anthony Niblett, 'Self-Driving Laws' (2016) 66 *University of Toronto Law Journal* 429, 440–441. We expanded on this analysis in Anthony Casey and Anthony Niblett, 'Self-Driving Contracts' (2017) 43 *J Corp L* 1.

6 Casey and Niblett, 'Self-Driving Contracts' (n 5) 13–15.

7 Others have referred to these and similar contracts as 'algorithmic contracts.' See Lauren Henry Scholz, 'Algorithmic Contracts' (2018) 20 *Stan Tech LR* 128. In an earlier article, Harry Surden referred to a related concept of a 'Data-Oriented Contract.' See Harry Surden, 'Computable Contracts' (2012) 46 *UC Davis LR* 629.

8 Importantly, self-driving contracts are distinct from 'smart contracts.' The former involves contracts that use micro directives to automate the creation of substantive terms, while the later involves certain technologies, like blockchain, to provide a self-execution mechanism. See generally, Nick Szabo, 'The Idea of Smart Contracts' (1997) <www.szabo.best.vwh.net/smart_contracts_idea.html>. Much has been written on smart contracts in recent years. See, for example, Dirk A Zetzsche, Ross P Buckley and Douglas W Arner, 'The Distributed Liability of Distributed Ledgers: Legal Risks of Blockchain' (2018) *UIll LR* 1361. While we view smart contracts as distinct from self-driving contracts, some view the self-driving contracts as an advanced type of smart contract. See, for example, Michele M van Eck, 'The Disruptive Force of Smart Contracts' in Wesley Doorsamy, Babu Sena Paul and Tshilidzi Marwala (eds), *The Disruptive Fourth Industrial Revolution* (Springer, 2020) 21; Joshua S Gans, 'The Fine Print in Smart Contracts' (2019) NBER Working Paper No w25443.

9 For discussions and criticisms of our earlier work, see Jamie Susskind, *Future Politics* (Oxford University Press 2018); Frank Pasquale, 'A Rule of Persons, Not Machines: The Limits of Legal Automation' (2019) 87 *Geo Wash LR* 1; Mark A Lemley and Bryan Casey, 'Remedies for Robots' (2019) 86 *UChi LR* 1311; Dan L Burk, 'Algorithmic Fair Use' (2019) 86 *UChi LR* 283; Christoph

and self-driving contracts were even possible.[10] And, at a high level of abstraction, the idea of a fully self-driving contract does bring to mind science fiction examples of conscious automatons controlling human behaviour.

Yet when one considers things at a more specific level, it becomes clear that micro-directives have actually existed in early form for decades. The standard traffic light can be viewed as a micro-directive.[11] Similarly, self-driving contracts cannot accurately be classified as science fiction when, for example, insurance companies have been using them for years.[12]

But what of our claims that advanced self-driving contracts will proliferate? The most compelling evidence exists in the advances that have already taken or are about to take hold. And so, while our previous work on this topic has taken the form of longer-term thought experiments, this chapter explores existing data-driven AI technologies that can facilitate the automation of specific contract provisions today. The purpose of this exploration is to uncover the present and near future of self-driving contracts.

The remainder of this chapter proceeds as follows. In Section II, we explore specific examples of existing technologies that are being or can be used to construct real-life self-driving contract provisions. We illustrate what the technology can do and describe how it will be deployed in the near future. In Section III, we discuss broader implications and lessons emerging from these examples.

II EXISTING SELF-DRIVING CONTRACT TECHNOLOGY

As we discuss in this section, several recent developments in AI contracting represent meaningful early steps in the evolution of self-driving contracts. These advances

Busch, 'Implementing Personalized Law: Personalized Disclosures in Consumer Law and Data Privacy Law' (2019) 86 *UChi LR* 309; Carla L Reyes and Mireille Hildebrandt, 'Law as Computation in the Era of Artificial Legal Intelligence: Speaking Law to the Power of Statistics' (2018) 68 *UTLJ* 12; David Freeman Engstrom, Daniel E Ho, Catherine M Sharkey, and Mariano-Florentino Cuellar, 'Government by Algorithm: Artificial Intelligence in Federal Administrative Agencies' (2020) NYU School of Law, Public Law Research Paper No 20–54; Katherine J Strandburg, 'Rulemaking and Inscrutable Automated Decision Tools' (2019) 119 *Colum LR* 1851.

10 Many criticisms take issue with the idea of a fully self-updating contract. These critiques question the extent to which AI is able to tailor contractual positions for all or nearly all possible contingencies. See, for example, Spencer Williams, 'Predictive Contracting' (2019) 2019 *Colum Bus LR* 621, 674; Eric Tjong Tjin Tai, 'Force Majeure and Excuses in Smart Contracts' (2018) 26 *Eur Rev Priv L* 787; Benito Arruñada, 'Prospects of Blockchain in Contract and Property' (2020) 8 *Eur Prop LJ* 231, 234; Ralph Schuhmann, 'Quo Vadis Contract Management? Conceptual Challenges Arising from Contract Automation' (2020) 16 *Eur Rev Contract L* 489, 500.

11 See Casey and Niblett, 'Death of Rules and Standards' (n 3) 1416–1417.

12 See, for example, Yiyang Bian and others, 'Good Drivers Pay Less: A Study of Usage-Based Vehicle Insurance Models' (2018) 107 *Transportation Research Part A: Policy and Practice* 20; Angelo Borselli, 'Insurance by Algorithm' (2018) 2018 *Eur Ins LR* 40; Angelo Borselli, 'Smart Contracts in Insurance: A Law and Futurology Perspective' in Pierpaolo Marano (ed), *InsurTech: A Legal and Regulatory View* (Springer 2020) 101, 108 (on dental insurance companies adjusting rates based on a smart toothbrush that tracks an individual's oral hygiene).

provide proofs of concept, as well as a set of prototypes for examining the opportunities and challenges that self-driving contracts present for private law.

While the theoretical ideal of a complete self-driving contract would govern every aspect of a private relationship, the technology developments we discuss here support and advance the automation of specific and often narrow contract provisions.[13] Such provisions are, after all, the building blocks of the complete self-driving contract. Indeed, the automation of a single provision governing even a narrow aspect of a private transaction does itself represent the emergence of a self-driving contract. It is therefore useful to start our analysis with technologies that facilitate these discrete provisions.

We provide four current examples of how existing AI-augmentation and prediction technology can automate the operation of different types of contract provisions.

A *Dynamic Pricing: Automating Price of Performance*

1 Technology

Perhaps the term most obviously susceptible to automation in a contract is the price term. Of course, there is nothing particularly new about AI-augmented pricing algorithms. Dynamic pricing algorithms are used in many contexts to better reflect rapid changes in demand and supply. Uber's pricing mechanism presents a familiar example of dynamic pricing.[14] The price of an Uber journey adjusts automatically and frequently depending on how many users demand rides and how many drivers are available. Such algorithmic pricing technologies are pervasive in spot markets. Other prominent examples include Amazon's pricing strategies[15] and pricing in the airline industry.[16]

2 Application to Self-Driving Contracts

Just as pricing algorithms are used to specify spot market prices, AI-augmented algorithms can dynamically and automatically adjust the prices in longer-term contracting relationships. Instead of 'agreeing to agree' to a future price based on changed circumstances – as they often do – the parties can agree to abide by the algorithmically derived price, even though it is unknown at the time of contracting.

Such dynamic pricing clauses are already in use. As we noted in 2017:

[13] In discussing the development of technology in the law, David Freeman Engstrom and Jonah B Gelbach point out that the adoption of legal technology will be incremental and arrive sooner in areas with abundant data and regulated conduct that takes repetitive, stereotypical forms. See David Freeman Engstrom and Jonah B Gelbach, 'Legal Tech, Civil Procedure, and the Future of Adversarialism' (2020) 169 *UPa LR* 1001.

[14] See Uber, 'How Uber's Dynamic Pricing Model Works' <www.uber.com/en-GB/blog/uber-dynamic-pricing/>.

[15] See, for example, Robert M Weiss and Ajay K Mehrotra, 'Online Dynamic Pricing: Efficiency, Equity and the Future of E-Commerce' (2001) 6 *Va JL&Tech* 11.

[16] See, for example, R Preston McAfee and Vera te Velde, 'Dynamic Pricing in the Airline Industry' in T Hendershott (eds), *Handbook of Economics and Information Systems*, vol 1 (Elsevier Science 2007).

> The most familiar example can be found in the auto-insurance industry, where parties agree to price terms that adjust automatically based on computer-driven analytics. Similar pricing terms can be found in dental insurance, in short-term rental agreements, and in transportation services.[17]

With these clauses, parties have an ongoing relationship and the price of the contract changes with respect to the changing environment and actions of the parties. If you drive safely, you will pay lower premiums for your auto-insurance. If you brush your teeth more, you will pay lower premiums for your dental insurance. The algorithm is learning more about the riskiness of the customer. The prices adjust accordingly.

3 How It Changes the Contract

Any price term in a long-term relationship implicitly allocates risks among the parties. For example, if parties to a long-term production contract agree to a fixed price, the producer bears the risk that production costs might increase. In a labour or supply shortage, the producer may realise a smaller profit (or even a loss) on the contract. In some cases, the change in production costs may be such that the producer chooses to cease performance and pay damages on the contract.[18]

Price adjustments can therefore be important in drafting a long-term contract. Conventional contract provisions give the parties some risk allocation options. Changing a fixed-price term to a cost-plus formula, shifts the production-cost risk from the supplier to the buyer. More complex formulas set prices based on data compiled and made available by third parties.[19] For example, many financial contracts set interest rates and other prices by reference to indices reflecting market conditions.[20] Likewise, supply contracts often use industry pricing reports to create formulas.[21]

Alternatively, if the parties think that pricing formulas will be too rigid or subject to abuse, they might leave the price decision to be decided at a later date. They will thus agree to renegotiate the price as the market changes (essentially agreeing to agree), or perhaps they will let an arbitrator set the price when the market changes.[22]

[17] Casey and Niblett, 'Self-Driving Contracts' (n 5) 3.

[18] The buyer, on the other hand, might bear the risk that the good being produced will become less valuable or obsolete while she still has to pay full price for it.

[19] See Gabriel V Rauterberg and Andrew Verstein, 'Index Theory: The Law, Promise and Failure of Financial Indices' (2013) 30 *Yale J Reg* 101.

[20] Until recently LIBOR, discussed later when we talk about data manipulation. See infra, text accompanying notes 56–60.

[21] See, for example, Frederic R Curtiss, Phillip Lettrich, and Kathleen A Fairman, 'What Is the Price Benchmark to Replace Average Wholesale Price (AWP)?' (2010) 16 *Journal of Managed Care & Specialty Pharmacy* 492.

[22] Andrew Verstein refers to these arrangements as 'ex tempore contracting,' where parties will intentionally leave gaps in the terms of their contract and delegate determination to third parties who update the contract on an ongoing basis. Examples of such contracts include dispute boards in construction contracts that inspect projects and update contractual responsibilities on an ongoing basis. See Andrew Verstein, 'Ex Tempore Contracting' (2014) 55 *Wm&M LR* 1869.

Each method has pros and cons. Fixed-prices don't adjust to changing conditions. But they are less susceptible to ex post abuse and manipulation. Formulas provide some flexibility, but they can be manipulated. Renegotiation allows total flexibility, but renegotiation is costly and the parties can abuse the flexibility.[23] Arbitration provides flexibility, but it can also be unpredictable and subject to the human arbitrator's idiosyncratic decisions and biases.

AI-augmented pricing technology provides new options. The cost-plus pricing term is an algorithm, but a very simple one. Index pricing is more complex and introduces third-party data. But with AI-augmented pricing technologies, the algorithms are more sophisticated, processing complex data and updating more frequently.

These existing AI-pricing technologies can mitigate problems associated with incomplete contracts. Suppose a long-term contract includes an AI-augmented algorithm that determines the price. The pricing algorithm is developed with a specific objective in mind (maximise the joint surplus of the parties). Such a predictive algorithm would likely factor in the historical market prices of similar deals. It would also consider the parties' willingness to continue the relationship as the price changes.

In this setting, the parties agree to insert this algorithm into the agreement *at the time of contracting*. The actual price schedule is not known at that time, but the parties agree that this AI algorithm will fill that gap in the future.

The pricing algorithm is doing the work that is currently done by the human arbitrators, without the accompanying costs and uncertainty. The *ex-ante* commitment to the algorithm replaces the ex-post arbitration mechanism for resolving disputes. It reduces the likelihood of disputes about whether changed circumstances require or justify a new price.

In this way, self-driving contracts have the potential to improve matters on all fronts. A well-designed algorithm with quality data can provide flexible pricing that accounts for all sorts of changed circumstances and allocates risk according to the parties' joint preferences. It may even help the parties identify relevant price factors that they previously ignored.

Moreover, because the parties commit to the algorithm ahead of time, a self-driving contract limits opportunistic abuse and eliminates renegotiation costs. The parties are in essence committing to an automated arbitration that provides flexibility but prevents the parties from opportunistically trying to rewrite the contract.

Finally, well-designed algorithms can in some (but not all)[24] cases reduce the biases and idiosyncratic variance associated with human arbitration.[25]

[23] Patrick W Schmitz, 'The Hold-Up Problem and Incomplete Contracts: A Survey of Recent Topics in Contract Theory' (2001) 53 *Bulletin of Econ Res* 1.

[24] We discuss the potential for algorithm bias and variance below when we discuss the lessons and challenges for the near future of self-driving contracts.

[25] Other scholars have explored the use of algorithms to reduce bias in other areas of the law. See, for example, Jon Kleinberg, Jens Ludwig, Sendhil Mullainathan, and Cass R Sunstein, 'Discrimination in the Age of Algorithms' (2018) 10 *J Leg Analysis* 113; Alex Chohlas-Wood and others, 'Blind Justice: Algorithmically Masking Race in Charging Decisions' (2020) Technical Report.

4 Potential Use Example

Consider the following possible application of pricing technology.[26] A building owner and a bank negotiate a long-term rental agreement for commercial real estate. The bank wishes to locate its corporate headquarters in the building. Together, the two parties agree that they wish to maximize their joint surplus. With this objective in mind, the parties initially agree that the lease shall last five years. The parties also agree on a monthly rental price for the five years of the lease.

The parties also include a renewal term. The renewal term is a signal that the parties wish to enter into a longer-term agreement, but are unsure about how the market for commercial leasing will look in five years. Each party acknowledges that the other party is specifically investing in the relationship.

But there is enormous uncertainty. While the parties could undertake the expense of trying to work out the most likely best price for each month of the lease for ten or fifteen years, including such a price would be costly and create enormous risk for both parties. And so the parties include an agreement to negotiate a new rental price at the time of renewal.

That agreement could require them to 'renegotiate the price in good faith.' But what if they can't reach an agreement? They might also include arbitration as a mechanism for resolving such disputes should they arise. This mechanism reduces some hold-up behaviour and renegotiation costs. But, parties may be uncomfortable with uncertainty about the identity and bias of the arbitrator.

The missing content of the renewal price term thus introduces costly uncertainty, leaving the parties vulnerable to opportunistic hold up by the other side during renegotiation or arbitration. These problems reduce the parties' incentives to invest in the relationship in the first place.

But with dynamic pricing technology, the parties can do away with the fixed price portion of the lease and simply rely upon the pricing algorithm to provide month-by-month updated pricing. This is true not only for the renewal period but also for the initial five years. Indeed, the parties might implement the updates the moment the contract begins, and they might set the updates to run on a weekly or daily schedule to get an even more well-calibrated pricing schedule. If the algorithm is calibrated properly, it would reduce the need for renegotiation in the event of booms or slumps or changes in the parties' circumstances.

B *Litigation Analytics: Automating Terms of Non-performance*

1 Technology

AI-augmented technology that is currently being used for litigation prediction can be refitted for the purpose of automating terms regarding non-performance.

[26] The underlying facts here are loosely based on *Empress Towers Ltd v Bank of Nova Scotia* (1990) 73 DLR (4th) 400 (BCCA). But these arrangements are common and often litigated.

In the last decade, there has been a dramatic acceleration in the development of algorithms that predict how courts and arbitrators will decide cases. Previous judicial decisions can be collected to build a dataset that machine learning algorithms use to provide a prediction of how a judge or arbitrator will resolve questions if the parties seek ex post dispute resolution. These predictions include the likelihood that a judge will rule in one party's favour and probabilities associated with different damage awards.

These algorithms factor in the relevant features of the case; they compare these factors to all similarly litigated cases in the dataset.[27] Such predictive algorithms are already in use by lawyers and accountants to determine the merits of their positions in patent law, employment law, and tax law, as well as by litigation finance firms.

2 Application to Self-Driving Contracts

One might think that these algorithms are exclusively relevant in litigation. The thinking here is that once the parties are involved in a dispute, they can use the algorithm to better determine the strength of their position.[28] While this no doubt represents one use case of the algorithms, the parties can just as easily use them to fill gaps in their contracts.

Because the definition and price of non-performance are common subjects of litigation, parties can incorporate into their self-driving contracts existing technologies originally designed for predicting litigation outcomes and damages. The contract – rather than an arbitrator or judge – could turn those predictions into micro-directives available at the relevant moment that update the definition and price of non-performance. These micro-directives could dictate what price parties will pay if they fail to perform a certain obligation, or they might define exactly what constitutes non-performance in specific contexts.

3 How It Changes the Contract

Conventional contracts do sometimes set a price for non-performance. For example, a contract may include a liquidated damages provision, specifying damages that are payable in the event that one side fails to perform its obligations. But these prices are difficult to set and do not update to take the parties' actual situation into account. As a result, most contracts are silent on the matter, leaving it to the courts to set the price in ex post litigation.

[27] See generally, Benjamin Alarie, Anthony Niblett and Albert H Yoon, 'Using Machine Learning to Predict Outcomes in Tax Law' (2016) 58 *Can Bus LJ* 231; Benjamin Shmueli and Moshe Phux, 'Small Data, Not (Only) Big Data: Personalized Law and Using Information from Previous Proceedings' (2019) 35 *Ohio State J Disp Resol'n* 331.

[28] We have elsewhere discussed how the use of tools that predict litigation outcomes based on data from prior cases will affect litigation outcomes and settlement. See Anthony J Casey and Anthony Niblett, 'Will Robot Judges Change Litigation and Settlement Outcomes? A First Look at the Algorithmic Replication of Prior Cases' (2020) *MIT Comp L Rep* 2.0.

As parties incorporate this technology, setting a self-driving price for non-performance, they will have clarity about how they should or should not perform. At the time of deciding whether to perform, they will have full information about the cost of not performing.

Similarly, where the contract incorporates prediction algorithms to define non-performance, the parties will know at the time they choose to perform whether a certain action is allowed.

Combining the two points, they will know both what path of action constitutes non-performance and the price they will pay for going down that path.[29] In some sense, this eliminates the possibility of 'breach' since 'damages' simply become the prices attached to one option. While labelling something as an option or a breach is semantic, the important feature here is that the party makes the decision with full information, and there is little reason to litigate because the contract terms themselves match the predicted outcome of litigation.[30]

4 Potential Use Example

An illustrative example of a potential use for this technology comes from Canadian employment law. When an employment contract is silent on the question of notice, the common law implies a default term of reasonable notice. If a worker is dismissed without cause, they are entitled to a reasonable notice period, or as is more common to payment in lieu of that notice.[31] For the employer, this is the price of terminating the contract.

Reasonable notice is a vague term. What is reasonable depends on the circumstances. The frequently cited statement of law stipulates that '[t]here can be no catalogue laid out for determining what is reasonable.'[32] The calculation is complex, factoring in not only the years of service, but also the age of the terminated worker, the characteristics of the job, and the availability of similar employment.

Employers and dismissed employees frequently disagree about what constitutes *reasonable* notice. While larger employers no doubt have their own formulas for assessing what the notice period should be for dismissed employees, these formulas typically understate what an employee is entitled to under the common law. Thus, after failing to negotiate, parties seek the assistance of a referee to determine the employer's price of non-performance. Indeed, this specific legal issue is one of the most litigated legal matters in Canada, with thousands of published cases on this narrow question in the past half century.[33]

29 See, for example, Borselli, 'Smart Contracts in Insurance' (n 12) 115.
30 Casey and Niblett, 'Self-Driving Contracts' (n 5) 22–23.
31 *Bardal v Globe & Mail Ltd* (1960) 24 DLR (2nd) 140 (ON SC).
32 *Bardal* (n 31) 145.
33 See Anthony Niblett, 'Algorithms as Legal Decisions: Gender Gaps and Canadian Employment Law in the 21st Century' (2020) 71 *UNBLR* 112.

Parties may want to specify up front what is reasonable for all points in time over the employment relationship. But that can be difficult to do considering how much can change during the term of the agreement. But now parties can instead insert a provision agreeing to use the machine learning algorithm to calculate a specific employee's reasonable notice period at the specific moment when that employee is dismissed.

The employment contract could use predictive technology to replicate what a judge or arbitrator would do in any given situation. The provision would be a highly contextual and tailored provision that pertains only to the employee at that point in time. As time and circumstances change, so will the self-driving contractual provision. But it would not be subject to some of the problems of ex-post adjudication that contracting parties are commonly concerned about.[34]

Note that data predicting Canadian litigation can even be useful in self-driving contracts involving parties who are not subject to Canadian law. Imagine parties in another jurisdiction that has no rules. The parties want to contract for reasonable notice, but they have trouble defining it, and there is no precedent in their jurisdiction. They might choose to use the Canadian system as their model and create a self-driving provision that uses the Canadian data to produce micro-directives.

The applications just described would entrench the content of the Canadian judicial precedent on reasonable notice into any contract that uses it. But some parties may want a different measure of reasonable notice. For them, there are alternative sources of contract substance available. The parties may use other technologies to seek an algorithm that better describes what *they* think is 'reasonable.' For example, the algorithm could be built around data that measures how long it takes dismissed employees to find a new job. Using data on employment statistics, such an algorithm may be able to predict how long it will take a particular worker in a particular industry in a particular economy to find a similar job. This algorithm would implement a reasonable-notice rule, but it would be one that achieves a different objective to one that mimics precedent.

C *Legal Review Technology: Automating Legal Compliance*

1 Technology

Today's AI-augmented algorithms can help determine whether a contractual clause is enforceable or not. Compliance logic is relatively straightforward where the law is based on bright-line rules. For example, in a promissory note, if the interest rate

34 These problems include judicial bias and uncertainty. See Thomas J Miles and Cass R Sunstein, 'The New Legal Realism' (2008) 75 *UChi LR* 831; Jeffrey J Rachlinski and Sheri Lynn Johnson, 'Does Unconscious Racial Bias Affect Trial Judges?' (2009) 84 NDLR 1195; Anthony Niblett, 'Tracking Inconsistent Judicial Behavior' (2013) 34 *Int'l RL&Econ* 9; Allison P Harris and Maya Sen, 'Bias and Judging' (2019) 22 *Ann'l Rev of Pol Sci* 241.

coded by the 'contract drafter' exceeds the legislative maximum, then the software will 'raise an error' to the coder.[35]

But even more advanced technology that can detect the meaning of a particular clause is in development. Even with more general terms, studies have shown that machine learning technology can automatically identify contract clauses that are potentially not enforceable.[36] And recent scholarship has sought to use computational language models to interpret contractual clauses and provide advice. Noam Kolt, for example, has empirically tested Open AI's GPT-3 model to answer questions about whether consumers are permitted to take certain actions under standard forms.[37] Kolt finds that the technology is able to predict the 'correct' answer in 77% of his sample questions. Along a similar line, Yonathan Arbel and Samuel Becher have explored the potential of 'smart readers' that can 'read, analyze, and assess contracts, disclosures, and privacy policies.'[38]

The ability to detect and translate meaning implies a broader ability to identify and change problematic terms. This ability will facilitate the emergences of important self-driving provisions.

2 The Application to Self-Driving Contracts

Technology that flags illegal, unenforceable, or otherwise problematic provisions can also be adapted to automatically remove or rewrite provisions that become problematic as the law changes after the contract is agreed to.

Thus, as clauses that were enforceable when the contract was formed become unenforceable before the time of performance, the contract will update to account for the change. This change might come in the form of legislation or a court decision rendering particular provisions unenforceable. Once the technology can identify provisions that have become unenforceable, it is a small step to automatically update and adjust the contract to account for the changes in the legal environment.

3 How It Changes the Contract

To return to our self-driving car analogy: if the police temporarily block a road, the self-driving car needs to update its information and find a different route to reach

[35] See Joe Dewey, 'What if We Developed Legal Contracts like We Developed Software Applications?' (*Medium*, 3 April 2016) <www.medium.com/@jndewey/what-if-we-developed-legal-contracts-like-we-developed-software-applications-6f8305256c5c#.6z774clv2>. See also Irene Ng, 'The Art of Contract Drafting in the Age of Artificial Intelligence: A Comparative Study Based on US, UK and Austrian Law' (2017) TTLF Working Papers No. 26, Stanford Transatlantic Technology Law Forum <www.law.stanford.edu/wp-content/uploads/2017/02/Irene-Ng-TTLF-Working-PAper-26-Art-of-Contract-Drafting.pdf>.

[36] Machine learning has been used to tag clauses of contracts that are 'potentially' unfair under European consumer law. See, for example, Marco Lippi and others, 'CLAUDETTE: An Automated Detector of Potentially Unfair Clauses in Online Terms of Service' (2019) 27 *AI&L* 117. More generally, see, Hans-W Micklitz, Przemyslaw Palka, and Yannis Panagis, 'The Empire Strikes Back: Digital Control of Unfair Terms on Online Services' (2017) 40 *J Cons Pol'y* 367.

[37] Noam Kolt, 'Predicting Consumer Contracts' (2022) 37 *Berkeley Journal of Law & Technology* 71.

[38] Yonathan A Arbel and Samuel Becher, 'Contracts in the Age of Smart Readers' (2022) 90 *Geo Wash LR* 83.

the desired destination. Similarly, should a contractual clause be 'blocked' by lawmakers, an AI-automated referee can find a new way to achieve the parties' objectives within the new legal constraints.[39]

Conventional contracts require renegotiation, invalidation, or judicial gap-filling when certain provisions become unenforceable. Questions arise about whether the invalidated term can be separated from the other contractual obligations and, if so, how the change might alter the price or other obligations in the contract.

By agreeing in advance to allow the self-driving contract to reform the provision, the parties avoid the costs of renegotiation or litigation. Because the new term may affect other terms in the contract and alter the parties' allocation of risk and division of surplus, they may want to combine this technology with the pricing technology above to adjust the price to account for the changes in the law and in the content of the reformed provision. In some instances, they may also include provisions that invalidate the entire contract if the price effect is too great.

4 Potential Use Example

This technology could be used in the context of a non-compete clause in an employment contract. Such a clause may prohibit an employee from working for a firm that competes with the employer for a period of time after the current employment relationship has ended.

These clauses are treated differently in different jurisdictions. For example, such clauses are generally not enforceable in California.[40] There, the legislature has expressly prohibited the inclusion of such provisions. But in other jurisdictions, the law is vague. In Canada, for example, courts will only enforce such a clause if the employer has legitimate interests to protect and the restrictions imposed are reasonable and unambiguous.[41] Whether it is reasonable will turn on factors such as the activity that is being restricted, the geographic scope of the restriction, and the duration of the restriction.

It would be somewhat trivial to develop software that produces a red flag for any employment contract in California that includes such a clause, or one that automatically drops any such non-compete provisions from the contract.

But employers in Canada who wish to adopt a non-compete clause need to write specific and clear provisions that are tailored to the employee's role in the organisation and the employer's legitimate interests. They need to be reasonable in all the circumstances.

39 In discussing the development of personalised default rules in the law, Francesco Paolo Patti envisions these rules as a benchmark that can be used to assess whether a term is unfair. Patti notes that if the term is declared unfair, a self-driving contract can act as a personalised gap-filler to supplement the now incomplete contract through a personalised default rule. See Francesco Paolo Patti, 'Personalization of the Law and Unfair Terms in Consumer Contracts' (2019) Bocconi Legal Studies Research Paper No. 3466214 15.

40 California Business and Professions Code § 16600 (2020).

41 *Shafron v. KRG Insurance Brokers (Western) Inc* (2009) 1 SCR 157 (SCC).

The lawyers might spend time crafting a provision that they know the courts will enforce. But what if the law changes? If Canada suddenly prohibited all non-compete clauses in employment contracts, the algorithm could simply drop the provision from the contract, and the employee could be notified that they are entitled to move positions without fear of a restrictive injunction or other remedies.[42]

But the change might be more nuanced. A court may hold that a similar – but not identical – restrictive provision is not enforceable. This move by the courts may give some partial indication about whether judges will enforce similar provisions. The self-driving contract might automatically amend the content of the contract to account for the new information. Depending on the parties' comfort with uncertainty, it might drop the provision or amend it and other related clauses to account for changes in probabilities about what a court will enforce.

Combined with litigation prediction, these review technologies can update a self-driving contract to account for even small changes reflecting incremental steps in the evolution of judicial precedent. If, in a recent case, a court held that a 12-month provision was unreasonably long, the predictive algorithm may suggest reducing a 10-month provision to 8 months, depending on the algorithm's new predictions with regard to the probability estimates and the parties' tolerance for uncertainty, which would have been incorporated in the algorithm at the time the contract was agreed to.

D *Negotiation Technology: Automating Substantive Obligations*

1 Technology

Perhaps the most advanced potential comes from existing technology that automates contract negotiation.[43] AI technologies have recently been deployed to automate contract negotiation. Data describing the terms of a contract and associated outcomes could greatly inform which specific terms are included in the contract. Automated technologies can be used to mark-up contracts and suggest new terms.[44] They promise to find solutions and compromise solutions that the lawyers did not see.[45]

Sean Williams gives the example of using data to help determine which clause to include in a procurement contract:

> [A] predictive contracting system with data on the terms and outcomes of thousands of prior procurement contracts could inform a contract drafter that version A of a delivery term is ten percent more likely to result in late performance by a particular type of counterparty than version B.[46]

[42] Given that this change affects the division of surplus between the parties, a more complex self-driving contract may also adjust prices accordingly.

[43] See Schuhmann, 'Quo Vadis Contract Management?' (n 10) 501–502.

[44] See Roy Strom, 'Automated Contract Negotiation Race Heats Up with Seal Entry' (*Bloomberg Law*, 2 October 2019) <www.news.bloomberglaw.com/us-law-week/automated-contract-negotiation-race-heats-up-with-seal-entry>.

[45] *See* Jonathan Gratch, 'The Promise and Peril of Automated Negotiators' (2021) 37 *Negotiation Journal* 13.

[46] Williams (n 10) 629.

2 Application to Self-Driving Contracts

The step from automated negotiation to self-driving contract provisions is small. Automated negotiation technology is valuable because it can identify terms that are acceptable to both parties. But instead of using the technology to write the contract at the time of agreement, the parties could instead agree to use the technology at the time of performance with updated data. At that point, the automated negotiation technology produces a micro-directive telling the parties how to fulfil their agreement. The technology is the same; the only difference is the timing and the data.

3 How It Changes the Contract

Whereas parties have always been able to agree to renegotiate certain terms in the future, they can now agree to let the technology do the future negotiating for them. This provides the flexibility of renegotiation but the commitment of ex ante formulas and fixed terms.

This is the same idea we explored with regard to pricing above, but the automated negotiation technology goes further. It can, for example, create tailored instructions that indicate what *actions* constitute performance.

This can be especially useful for complex contract terms where the substantive obligations required for optimal performance turn on facts that are not known at the time of agreement and it is difficult to define the proper course of action up front. In those cases, conventional contracts often include provisions framed as vague standards using terms like 'reasonable' or 'material.' Automated negotiation technology can replace these vague standards with precise micro-directives delivered at the time of performance.

4 Potential Use Example

Take, for example, a marketing agreement where one party agrees to market and sell software created by another. It is difficult to spell out in the contract exactly what the salesperson should do in any given sales situation. Instead, the obligations of the marketer may be defined by vague guidelines such as 'best efforts' or 'reasonable commercial efforts.' But the software company may have a very different view of what *reasonable* commercial efforts mean compared to the company selling the product. The software company may be disappointed by low sales and attribute this to poor effort on the part of the sales team. This vagueness creates a gap in the contract.

Automated negotiation technology could fill this gap, and when used ex post to define the parameters of the parties' obligations, it could do so in the form of micro-directives embedded in a self-driving contract.

III IMPLICATIONS, LESSONS, AND CHALLENGES

The examples in Section II reveal a number of lessons and challenges for self-driving contracts. We turn to those now. We explore *who* provides the algorithms and whether regulations may be necessary to ensure that automated private ordering achieves its promise. We look at what data is required for these AI-augmented algorithms to work, considering the data required for the underlying architecture of the self-driving provision and the data required to assess the context of parties' positions. The use of such data raises issues of privacy and security and how the data will be collected, processed, used, and maintained. Further, we explore the degree to which the algorithms in the contract can actually align with the parties' objectives.

A *Who 'Drafts' the Algorithms?*

One challenge to the emergence of self-driving contracts is trust.[47] Sophisticated parties may not trust each other to design algorithms that will be true to their joint purpose. If one side creates that algorithm, the other side may suspect that they will corrupt the programme to favour the creator in application.

Similarly, if one party is more sophisticated than the other, there may be public policy concerns that the sophisticated party may take advantage of the unsophisticated.[48] This concern is similar to those voiced with regard to lengthy form contracts that large businesses use when contracting with consumers.[49]

One solution is government regulation of the algorithms that requires them to include certain features. Such regulation may be difficult to enforce, and in some instances, it may stifle innovation. A more attractive solution is to look to third parties to provide the algorithm, and – when necessary – the government could create regulations with regard to the independence of the provider rather than the substance of the algorithm.

We suspect that third-party developers will generate most of the content of self-driving contracts.[50] The providers of AI-augmented algorithms for self-driving

47 For greater discussion on this point, *see* TT Arvind, 'AI and Contract Law' in Ernest Lim and Phillip Morgan (eds), *The Cambridge Handbook of Private Law and Artificial Intelligence* (Cambridge University Press 2024).

48 Gerhard Wagner and Horst Eidenmueller raise similar concerns, arguing that the risks of an extremely unequal distribution of the gains of digital dispute resolution will be to the detriment of less vigilant parties. This could impact on the rule of law. They argue in favour of regulatory tools to control the power of large, sophisticated commercial actors. See, Gerhard Wagner and Horst Eidenmueller, *Digital Dispute Resolution* <https://papers.ssrn.com/sol3/papers.cfm?abstract_id=3871612>.

49 See, for example, Margaret Jane Radin, *Boilerplate: The Fine Print, Vanishing Rights, and the Rule of Law* (Princeton University Press 2013).

50 See Andrew Verstein, 'Privatizing Personalized Law' (2019) 86 *UChi LR* 551; see also Greg Buchak, 'Micro-Regulation in the Platform Economy' <www.law.uchicago.edu/files/2019-01/buchak1_0.pdf>; Mateusz Grochowsk, 'Default Rules beyond a State: Special-Purpose Lawmakers in the Platform Economy' in Stefan Grundmann and Mateusz Grochowski (eds), *European Contract Law and the Creation of Norms* (Intersentia 2021). We also discuss the role of these platform providers in our previous work. See Casey and Niblett, 'Self-Driving Contracts' (n 5) 22.

contracts are likely to evolve from various existing markets. New start-up software developers, harnessing the power of big data and machine learning techniques, will arise. Insurance companies, with access to enormous swathes of data on risk, may elect to use their data to create contractual plug-ins that allocate risks between commercial parties.[51] Commercial arbitrators may use data from their prior decisions to create ex ante arbitration tools. Finally, consumer protection agencies and advocates may develop competing algorithms to offset potential biases.

This raises new questions about the neutrality of the algorithms used in self-driving contract provisions. When both contracting parties are sophisticated, the market will likely do a good job of ensuring neutrality. As we noted in our 2017 piece:

> In a well-functioning market, … private firms will compete over how well calibrated their ultimate terms are to the parties' objectives…[52]

Still, not all markets are well functioning. And when transactions involve unequal parties, third-party providers may favour sophisticated repeat players.[53]

In those cases, the regulation of the market for providers will be necessary. These concerns are similar to those related to arbitration today. Human arbitrators can be unpredictable or biased and that imposes costs on parties. AI-augmented algorithms can also be unpredictable or have biases that favour one party entrenched in their programming or data.[54]

And so, in the same way that the neutrality of arbitrators can be regulated by legislation or court supervision, the neutrality and competence of the providers of algorithms for self-driving contracts can be regulated. Courts might void contracts that are based on algorithms that are intentionally or systematically biased in favour of one party.[55] Likewise, in the same way that arbitration clauses can be struck down as unconscionable if the arbitrator is not neutral, AI in a self-driving contract could be invalidated if it were not neutral.[56]

[51] See Borselli, 'Smart Contracts in Insurance' (n 12) 119.

[52] See Casey and Niblett, 'Self-Driving Contracts,' (n 5) 27. As we also note, at 27, the market for self-driving contracts is similar to, and takes inspiration from, recent work by Gillian Hadfield, who argues that law is moving toward a private provision of substantive contract law. Hadfield suggests that private firms could fill gaps and compete for the right to arbitrate. Hadfield, *Rules for a Flat World* (n 2) 249–251.

[53] A similar problem exists with rating agencies, see, for example, Robert J Rhee, 'Incentivizing Credit Rating Agencies under the Issuer Pay Model through a Mandatory Compensation Competition' (2014) 33 *Banking & Financial Services Policy Report* 11.

[54] Examples of algorithmic bias include studies suggesting that algorithmic risk assessment tools used in the criminal justice system are biased against black defendants. See Julia Angwin and others, 'Machine Bias' (*ProPublica*, 23 May 2016) <www.propublica.org/article/machine-bias-risk-assessments-in-criminal-sentencing>; see also Megan Garcia, 'Racist in the Machine: The Disturbing Implications of Algorithmic Bias' (2016) 33 *World Policy Journal* 111; David Danks and Alex John London, 'Algorithmic Bias in Autonomous Systems' (Paper delivered at the Proceedings of the 26th International Joint Conference on Artificial Intelligence, 2017).

[55] See Marco Rizzi and Natalie Skead, 'Algorithmic Contracts and the Equitable Doctrine of Undue Influence: Adapting Old Rules to a New Legal Landscape' (2020) 14 *J of Equity* 301.

[56] When the parties are equally sophisticated, they might agree to use a provider that was not neutral. The court would only invalidate that if the contract promised neutrality. With consumer contracts, the law might require neutrality in all instances.

B *Data Sources*

Additional regulation of how these companies create and use their data may be required. The integrity of the data is important, as are privacy and security issues. There are two broad categories of relevant data: data about the world and data about the parties to the contract.

1 Training Data: Data That Describe the World

Data about the world is necessary for self-driving contracts to work. Most of the technologies discussed use data about the past to predict future outcomes. Thus, large datasets about the past are necessary.

These datasets may include prior legal decisions when the algorithm is using predictions about what a human referee would do in a future case. In those instances, the AI referee is trying to replicate the decisions of the human referee. That is the objective of the algorithm here. These outcome data are used to find likely ex-post decisions and transform those into a contract term.

Alternatively, the datasets may use broad information about events in the world. The parties may not want to replicate a prior judicial outcome. Instead, they may want to achieve a certain real-world outcome.[57] In those cases, the parties use data that measure the objectives that they care about, and the algorithms predict what actions will lead to the realization of those objectives. Such algorithms can improve upon the default rules offered by human referees or address matters where litigation data are sparse.

The integrity and quality of these data sets will determine the quality of the automated contract provisions.[58] Bad data inputs will produce bad outputs. Data can be bad for various reasons, some intentional and some unintentional. Parties may use the best observable proxy for something they wish to measure – for example, using the S&P500 as a metric for the strength of the economy – but such a proxy may not represent the specific movements in the economy that the parties intended. Further, proxies based on indices are subject to the whims and discretion of those constructing the indices.[59] Again, the variation in the indices may not align with the expectations of contracting parties.

Of greater concern, contracting parties can intentionally manipulate algorithms if they can control or influence the data sources. There are a few high-profile examples of data manipulation with simpler non-AI contract formulas. For example, the LIBOR scandal involved financial institutions colluding to submit false data to manipulate the LIBOR index, which was used in their contract formulas.[60] Similarly, in the medical industry, pharmaceutical companies were accused of

[57] See, for example, Williams, 'Predictive Contracting' (n 10).

[58] See Van Eck, 'Disruptive Force of Smart Contracts' (n 8) 28.

[59] See, for example, Adriana Z Robertson, 'The (Mis)uses of the S&P 500' (2023) 2 *University of Chicago Business Law Review* 137.

[60] See Andrew Verstein, 'Benchmark Manipulation' (2015) 56 *BCLR* 215.

colluding with third-party data providers to manipulate the industry price benchmarks that were used in determining how much insurance companies and the government paid for medications.[61]

These examples suggest that data regulation will be one of the most important government roles in the evolution of self-driving contracts.

2 Use Data: How Contract Provisions Update

Once the data for the underlying algorithms is created, the tailoring of terms will require data about the parties themselves. For example, suppose the parties insert a self-driving notice-period provision into an employment contract. In order to provide a context-specific directive, the algorithm needs to be fed a variety of information about the parties' circumstances.

Some of that information may be personal. For example, one question that would affect the length of a notice period – irrespective of whether the algorithm was based on the current state of the law or on the likely length of time to secure new employment – is whether the employee is suffering from illness or disability. This may raise privacy concerns for individuals. Similarly, with insurance contracts, where the premiums adjust based on data on driving or brushing teeth, privacy advocates have clashed with insurance companies, arguing that the costs of privacy invasions outweigh the benefits.[62]

Firms, too, may not be comfortable sharing proprietary information with third-party algorithm providers. In the example of a bank renewing a lease for a large commercial space in a building, the bank may object to revealing sensitive information about their future plans.

There are, of course, incredibly important questions about the security of these data once they are provided to third parties. As with algorithm design, there will likely be a need for some form of regulation of the data. Without sufficient regulation, the reluctance of parties to share private or proprietary information with third-party providers could pose a real barrier to the adoption of self-driving contracts.[63] Empirical evidence, however, suggests that parties are often willing to waive privacy in exchange for some economic benefit.[64]

C *Difficulty in Specifying Parties' Objectives*

In our earlier piece on self-driving contracts, we assumed – to make the point – that parties to the contract had a shared objective that they could easily specify. For

61 See Curtiss and others (n 22).

62 See, for example, Robson Fletcher, 'New Alberta Law Would Make It Easier for Insurance Companies to Track Driving Habits through Your Phone' (*Canada Broadcasting Corporation*, 26 November 2020) <www.cbc.ca/news/canada/calgary/alberta-bill-41-usage-based-insurance-driver-tracking-1.5810597>.

63 See Kathryn D Betts and Kyle R Jaep, 'The Dawn of Fully Automated Contract Drafting: Machine Learning Breathes New Life into a Decades-Old Promise' (2017) 15 *Duke L&TechR* 216, 229–231.

64 See, for example, Sebastian Derikx, Mark de Reuver, and Maarten Krosen, 'Can Privacy Concerns for Insurance of Connected Cars Be Compensated?' (2016) 26 *Electronic Markets* 72.

the most part, we presupposed that that objective was to maximise joint surplus. But specifying these ultimate objectives may be difficult. Parties may have conflicting interests and differing preferences.[65] Indeed, parties may even agree to contractual ambiguity to facilitate agreement when they cannot agree on an ultimate objective.[66]

The parties may also find it difficult to define these objectives in ways that can be cleanly translated for the algorithm. That is, even where both parties share an objective, it may be difficult to specify that objective in a way that is easily measurable by data. The popular literature on AI is replete with examples of reinforcement learning algorithms gone awry because the objective and reward functions were not adequately aligned with what the human designer wished the AI to do.[67]

There is thus a real risk that an algorithm in a self-driving contract provision will implement an objective that doesn't fully align with what the parties actually intended. In this way, AI referees are not so different from human judges!

To the extent that AI algorithms will be able to learn what objective contracting parties wish to achieve, such problems may be capable of being overcome. While this is a real challenge, there are promising signs that it can be met. For example, recent scholarship has shown that AI agents are able to, through machine-learning technology, adopt socially beneficial norms in multi-agent settings.[68] It is plausible that such AI agents will be able to identify the purpose of a relationship and set out obligations by observing past relationships.

IV CONCLUSION

We concluded our 2017 piece by predicting that self-driving contracts will 'be greeted with a healthy mixture of scepticism, trepidation, and fear.'[69] This was certainly our most accurate prediction.

But much of the scepticism is poorly focused. All-knowing, all-seeing general AI machines will perhaps remain in the realm of Hollywood movies and science fiction literature. But AI technologies are advancing. The success stories of AI are primarily narrow applications developed for specific tasks such as parking a car, playing chess, or predicting real estate prices. Machines are outperforming humans in more of these narrow tasks every day. As narrow AI subsumes more tasks previously

65 See Anthony J Casey and Anthony Niblett, 'A Framework for the New Personalization of Law' (2019) 86 *UChi LR* 333.

66 Albert Choi and George Triantis, 'Strategic Vagueness in Contract Design: The Case of Corporate Acquisitions' (2010) 119 *Yale LJ* 848.

67 See Brian Christian, *The Alignment Problem: Machine Learning and Human Values* (WW Norton 2020); Stuart Russell, *Human Compatible: Artificial Intelligence and the Problem of Control* (Viking 2020).

68 Eugene Vinitsky and others, 'A Learning Agent the Acquires Social Norms from Public Sanctions in Decentralized Multi-Agent Settings' (16 June 2021) <https://arXiv.org/abs/2106.09012v1>.

69 Casey and Niblett, 'Self-Driving Contracts' (n 5) 31.

performed by humans, the technology is becoming more generally applicable and dramatically changing our everyday lives.

The story is the same for the emergence of self-driving contracts. AI provisions that outperform human-drafted content are replacing conventional contracts, one provision at a time. The clumsy fixed-price term and the simple cost-plus formula will fall by the wayside in favour of more tailored and dynamic automated pricing algorithms. The objectives underpinning a vague standard describing performance may be better captured by an algorithm's better-calibrated and more appropriate micro-directives, providing fewer opportunities for parties to engage in ex-post exploitation.

The predictive technology and data underlying these advances will continue to improve – and, piece-by-piece, more and more contractual clauses will become dynamic, self-correcting, and self-driving.

5

Consumer Protection Law and AI

Jeannie Marie Paterson and Yvette Maker

I INTRODUCTION

As this handbook demonstrates, there is ongoing debate about the ability of private law to adapt to technological change. These debates remain relevant even in the face of legal and regulatory initiatives directed directly at data-driven technologies and artificial intelligence (AI). Potentially private law has a role in complementing these more specific initiatives, for example, by providing compensation for harms caused by AI, an incentive for businesses to take reasonable care in their design and deployment or by focusing the minds of parties in the supply chain on the most efficient allocation of risk. However, to fulfil this role, private law, which typically develops in a cautious manner by reference to precedent and analogy, must prove itself capable of responding to the burgeoning use of AI in social, business, and government applications.[1]

These questions also apply to the rights and obligations imposed by legislation, albeit in a somewhat different form, including statutory consumer protection regimes, which are the focus of this chapter. In many ways, consumers are at the forefront of the market uses of AI.[2] The uses of data and algorithms associated with AI increasingly inform targeted advertising,[3] differential

[1] See Chapter 1.

[2] There are different views about what kinds of software are included in the description 'artificial intelligence'. Stuart Russell and Peter Norvig, *Artificial Intelligence: A Modern Approach* (4th edn, Pearson 2021) focus on the extent to which computer programs act as rational agents, which means being able to perform actions autonomously, perceive their environment and pursue goals to achieve the best possible outcomes (para 1.1.4) – ideally with those outcomes beneficial to humans (para 1.5). This approach avoids the philosophical question of whether machines merely replicate intelligence or can actually think: see John R Searle, 'Is the Brain's Mind a Computer Program?' (1990) 262 *Scientific American* 26. In a consumer protection context, we consider that the performance of actions is precisely the right focus. For consumers, what is or is not strictly AI is less important than how the product performs and the claims made about it. Accordingly, our use of the term in this chapter refers to the kinds of performance claims made about the product in question.

[3] See further Ryan Calo, 'Digital Market Manipulation' (2014) 82 *Geo Wash L Rev* 995; Jeannie Marie Paterson and others, 'The Hidden Harms of Targeted Advertising by Algorithm and Interventions

pricing,[4] and the automated decision-making that increasingly determines access to a variety of commercial services,[5] including insurance[6] and credit.[7] Additionally, consumers are now able to purchase products that use AI to assist them in their day-to-day lives.[8] Indeed, these products provide a good exemplar of the risks to consumers and challenges to consumer protection law arising from AI technologies.

Prominent examples of AI consumer products include digital assistants, such as Siri or Alexa, that respond to voice commands to provide information; 'internet of things' or 'smart' devices that embed computing capacity, sensors, and internet connectivity in everyday devices; and chatbots, such as ChatGPT, Bard, and Bing, for text-based conversations, written explanations, and code. AI consumer products create opportunities to free consumers from mundane tasks and to assist consumers in making more informed decisions about all sorts of matters, from shopping to investing and gaining new skills.[9] AI consumer products also give rise to a number of risks of harm to consumer autonomy and well-being. Such risks include the potential to erode privacy and perpetuate undesirable bias and unlawful discrimination inherent in most data-driven technologies.[10] AI consumer products also carry risks that arise from their status as products: they may not work very well, they may be unreliable or unsafe, or they may fail to live up to representations about their utility.[11] Although AI consumer products have been promoted for their potential to

from the Consumer Protection Toolkit' (2021) 9 *International Journal on Consumer Law and* Practice 1–24; Gerhard Wagner and Horst Eidenmüller, 'Down by Algorithms? Siphoning Rents, Exploiting Biases, and Shaping Preferences: Regulating the Dark Side of Personalized Transactions' (2019) 86 *U Chi L Rev* 581.

4 Frederik Zuiderveen Borgesius and Joost Poort, 'Online Price Discrimination and EU Data Privacy Law' (2017) 40 *J Consum Policy* 347, 351; Maurice E Stucke and Ariel Ezrachi, 'How Digital Assistants Can Harm Our Economy, Privacy, and Democracy' (2017) 32 *Berkeley Tech LJ* 1239, 1264; Jeannie Paterson, Gabby Bush and Tim Miller, 'Transparency to Contest Differential Pricing' (2021) 93 *Computers & Law* 49.

5 See Danielle Keats Citron and Frank Pasquale, 'The Scored Society: Due Process for Automated Predictions' (2014) 89 *Wash L Rev* 1.

6 See for example, Michele Loi and Markus Christen, 'Choosing How to Discriminate: Navigating Ethical Trade-Offs in Fair Algorithmic Design for the Insurance Sector' (2021) 34 *Philos Technol* 967.

7 See for example, Nikita Aggarwal, 'The Norms of Algorithmic Credit Scoring' (2021) 80 *CLJ* 42; Frank A Pasquale, 'Humans Judged by Machines: The Rise of Artificial Intelligence in Finance, Insurance, and Real Estate' in Joachim von Braun and others (eds), *Robotics, AI, and Humanity: Science, Ethics, and Policy* (Springer 2021).

8 Cf Russell and Norvig (n 2) vii.

9 John Danaher, 'Towards an Ethics of AI Assistants: An Initial Framework' (2018) 31 *Philos Technol* 629, 636. See also The Treasury, Commonwealth of Australia, 'Inquiry into Future Directions for the Consumer Data Right' (Final Report, 2020) 20 <https://treasury.gov.au/sites/default/files/2021-02/cdrinquiry-final.pdf>.

10 Mireille Hildebrandt and Bert-Jaap Koops, 'The Challenges of Ambient Law and Legal Protection in the Profiling Era' (2010) 73 *MLR* 428; Stucke and Ezrachi (n 4).

11 See also See Jeannie Marie Paterson, Tim Miller and Henrietta Lyons, 'Demystifying Consumer Facing Fintech' in Zofia Bednarz and Monika Zalnieriute (eds), *Money, Power and AI: From Automated Banks to Automated States* (Cambridge University Press, 2023).

facilitate or improve social, market, and other forms of participation for some people, such as people with disabilities, there has been little scrutiny of the degree to which such products are actually accessible or promote greater social equity.

While new laws and regulatory initiatives have been proposed in response to concerns about variously defined high-risk uses of AI,[12] there has been much less attention given to how to regulate AI consumer products. Our view is that the challenges for consumer protection law in responding to the risks of harm arising from AI consumer products are primarily technical and evidential, rather than demonstrating a fundamental mismatch between the impacts of the technologies and the precepts of consumer protection law.[13] We think that, by and large, the open-textured standards relied upon by most statutory consumer protection regimes should be sufficiently flexible to adapt to AI and emerging digital technologies. However, there will need to be some recalibration of the way in which those principles are understood and applied in order to respond to the kinds of harms presented by AI consumer products[14] and the ways in which responsibility for those harms are established.[15]

It is also important to recognise the limits of this body of law. As we shall see, consumer protection law tends to focus on the processes of contracting for and the performance of consumer products. It has less to say about issues of bias, equity, and the relationships humans should have with AI. Thus, some concerns about the harms to humans arising from the widespread use of AI consumer products need to be addressed in different legal domains, in particular through human rights and anti-discrimination law. In some contexts, responses to the relationship between AI and consumers will need to be informed by policy and values rather than law. In all of these inquiries, the principles developed through the domain of responsible, trustworthy or ethical AI may prove useful. These principles provide a lens for identifying the risks inherent in AI consumer products, insights into possible technical approaches for establishing a contravention of consumer protection law in the use of AI in consumer products, and a way of beginning to think about the broader ethical challenges posed by these technologies.

In this chapter, Section II sets the scene for this discussion. We consider the core imperatives of consumer protection law in reducing the risk of harm to consumers

12 For example, European Commission, 'Proposal for a Regulation of the European Parliament and of the Council Laying Down Harmonised Rules on Artificial Intelligence (Artificial Intelligence Act)' COM(2021) 206 final, 21 April 2021. See also UK Government, 'Establishing a Pro-innovation Approach to Regulating AI' (July 2022); President Biden, *Executive Order on Safe Secure and Trustworthy AI* (30 October, 2023).

13 See more generally Lyria Bennett Moses, 'How to Think about Law, Regulation and Technology: Problems with Technology as a Regulatory Target' (2013) 5 *Law Innovation & Tech* 1; Eliza Mik, 'The Resilience of Contract Law in Light of Technological Change' in Michael Furmston (ed), *The Future of the Law of Contract* (Routledge 2020).

14 See Kayleen Manwaring, 'Emerging Information Technologies: Challenges for Consumers' (2017) 17 *OUCLJ* 265.

15 Ibid. 287–288.

in the use of everyday products. We raise the possible role of frameworks of AI ethics in informing legal responses to the risks associated with AI consumer products. We then outline the nature of AI consumer products, focusing on the services provided by digital assistants and chatbots (generative AI or otherwise). We then turn to the responses that may be provided by consumer protection law to three identified categories of possible harm arising from AI consumer products. Section III considers harms associated with the use of personal data. Section IV considers the harms to consumers arising from the status of AI consumer products as consumer goods and services. Section V returns to ethics, noting that the deepest ethical concerns about AI in the home arise from questions about human character and human relationships. Responses to these ethical questions may be beyond the scope of the law, though even here they may point to the need for specific legislative responses.

II SETTING THE SCENE

A *Consumer Protection Law*

Statutory consumer protection law has its origins in private law but provides additional protections for consumers in market-based transactions for goods and services.[16] Statutory consumer protection regimes usually contain provisions that scrutinise the full life of a transaction. Thus, statutory prohibitions on unfair commercial practices[17] misleading practices,[18] and aggressive commercial practices[19] scrutinise the contracting process to invalidate contracts tainted by conduct that undermines any notion of free and informed consent.[20] Provisions that invalidate unfair terms address concerns about substantive fairness of the terms of consumer contracts.[21] Implied terms of satisfactory quality,[22] liability for product defects,[23] and rendering void terms that purport to exclude responsibility for product failings provide baseline standards to ensure products are reasonably safe and meet reasonable consumer expectations.[24]

Statutory consumer protections that intervene in market-based transactions are usually premised on an assessment of the risks to consumers and the degree to

[16] The consumer protected by consumer protection statutes is commonly defined by reference to the purpose of the transaction: see, for example, Consumer Rights Act 2015 (UK) (CRA 2015) s 3.

[17] Consumer Protection from Unfair Trading Regulations 2008 (UK) (CPUTR 2008), SI 2008/1277, Reg 3. See also Jeannie Paterson and Elise Bant, 'Should Australia Introduce a Prohibition on Unfair Trading? Responding to Exploitative Business Systems in Person and Online' (2020) 55 *J Consum Policy* 1.

[18] See CPUTR 2008 Reg 5.

[19] See ibid. Reg 7.

[20] Ibid.

[21] CRA 2015 pt 2.

[22] Ibid. s 9.

[23] See Chapters 6 and 9.

[24] CRA 2015 ss 63 and 65.

which consumers may themselves be expected to respond to those risks, recognising the information asymmetries and inequalities of bargaining power that make it difficult for consumers themselves to protect their own best interests.[25] Stronger statutory responses are usually thought to be justified for interactions involving significant risk and relevant vulnerability on the part of consumers, which magnifies their exposure to those risks.[26] Both of these elements are present in the current and predicted uses of AI. AI consumer products carry a number of potential risks for consumers' autonomy and well-being. Yet consumers are at a significant disadvantage in assessing the relative merits of or the veracity of claims made about such products. AI consumer products are a relatively recent arrival on the market and, moreover, are rapidly changing, which means consumers may have little experience with them. Moreover, the innermost workings of AI products are often opaque and complex, and unreadable and incomprehensible terms typically govern their use.[27] Consumers may, additionally, misunderstand, or be misled, by the 'intelligence' of such products, which, although able to follow commands, answer questions, and engage in conversation, fundamentally do not understand the meaning of language or the sentiments behind it.[28]

Consumer protection statutes typically contain a combination of precise rules and open-textured standards.[29] The standards perform a 'safety net' function, catching conduct that is not covered by the specific rules yet is nevertheless judged unacceptable by reference to the values embedded in the legislation.[30] This feature should ensure that consumer protection law is capable of responding to the risks to consumers raised by new consumer products, such as those using AI. Accordingly, we suggest that a key challenge lies not in the 'fit' of the law to AI but in establishing a contravention of that law. It will often be challenging for consumers or, more particularly, regulators to investigate the operations of AI products to prove a breach of the statutory standards, largely because of the combined impact of novelty and complexity of the products, referred to above.[31] Here, we suggest that the field of AI ethics may provide some assistance.

[25] Jeannie Paterson, 'The Australian Unfair Contract Terms Law: The Rise of Substantive Unfairness as a Ground for Review of Standard Form Consumer Contracts' (2009) 33 *Melb U L Rev* 934.

[26] See, for example, Federal Trade Commission Act 1914 (US) s 45.

[27] See, for example, Guido Noto La Diega and Ian Walden, 'Contracting for the "Internet of Things": Looking into the Nest' (2016) 7(2) *EJLT* 3.

[28] See further Michael L Littman and others, 'Gathering Strength, Gathering Storms: The One Hundred Year Study on Artificial Intelligence (AI100) 2021 Study Panel Report' (Stanford University, September 2021) <www.ai100.stanford.edu/2021-report>, 13.

[29] Jeannie Paterson and Elise Bant, 'Misrepresentation, Misleading Conduct and Statute through the Lens of Form and Substance' in Andrew Robertson and James Goudkamp (eds), *Form and Substance in the Law of Obligations* (Hart Publishing 2019).

[30] Jeannie Paterson and Gerard Brody, '"Safety Net" Consumer Protection: Using Prohibitions on Unfair and Unconscionable Conduct to Respond to Predatory Business Models' (2015) 38 *Journal of Consumer Policy* 3.

[31] See Manwaring (n 14) 285.

B *Frameworks for Responsible or Ethical AI*

Principles of responsible, trustworthy, or ethical AI have been put forward as a way of responding to the risks of increasing human reliance on data-driven technologies. There are many formulations of these principles, and they may be expressed in different ways.[32] Nonetheless, there are some common themes.[33] Principles of responsible or ethical AI typically emphasise the need for applications of the technology to respect values of privacy and fairness, or an absence of bias, along with equity and accessibility. AI should be safe, robust, and reliable. The principles typically require AI to be transparent, explainable, or explicable and to provide mechanisms for ensuring accountability and contesting adverse outcomes. AI ethical principles usually emphasise an overriding goal of non-maleficence or, ideally, beneficence, meaning AI should enrich rather than harm human lives.

Some scholars and activists have been concerned that principles of responsible or ethical AI may be co-opted by firms deploying AI to entrench their market power and cloak the need for stronger controls over high-risk developments of AI.[34] They have also criticised codes of AI ethics as being too general to provide effective guidance or sanction.[35] We do not suggest that principles of AI ethics should be treated as the only or even the main mechanism for responding to the risks of AI consumer products. However, we do think that principles of AI ethics have a useful role to play in this inquiry. AI-specific laws will not cover the field in addressing all possible concerns about AI applications. Additionally, principles of responsible AI strongly influence current ways of thinking about the design and oversight of AI, as well as the standards relevant to AI operations. Treated merely as one form of regulatory intervention, we suggest that principles of responsible or ethical AI ethics are useful as a way of identifying the risks of harm that may arise from AI in particular contexts,

[32] See for example, Dave Dawson and others, 'AI Ethics Framework' (*Australian Government Department of Industry, Innovation and Science*, 2019) <www.industry.gov.au/data-and-publications/australias-artificial-intelligence-ethics-framework>; Independent High-Level Expert Group on Artificial Intelligence, 'Ethics Guidelines for Trustworthy AI' (European Commission 2019) <https://ec.europa.eu/digital-single-market/en/news/ethics-guidelines-trustworthy-ai.Intelligence>. See also United Kingdom Government, *The Bletchley Declaration by Countries Attending the AI Safety Summit* (1-2 Nov 2023).

[33] See Brent Daniel Mittelstadt and others, 'The Ethics of Algorithms: Mapping the Debate' (2016) 3(2) *Big Data & Society* 1; Anna Jobin, Marcello Ienca and Effy Vayena, 'The Global Landscape of AI Ethics Guidelines' (2019) 1 *Nat Mach Intell* 389.

[34] Luke Stark, Daniel Greene and Anna Lauren Hoffmann, 'Critical Perspectives on Governance Mechanisms for AI/ML Systems' in Jonathan Roberge and Michael Castelle (eds), *The Cultural Life of Machine Learning: An Incursion into Critical AI Studies* (Palgrave Macmillan 2020) 257; Australian Human Rights Commission, 'Article Intelligence and Human Rights' (Discussion Paper, 2019) 54. See also Carly Kind, 'The Term "Ethical AI" is Finally Starting to Mean Something' (*VentureBeat*, 23 August 2020) <https://venturebeat.com/2020/08/23/the-term-ethical-ai-is-finally-starting-to-mean-something/>.

[35] Kind (n 34). See also Brent Mittelstadt, 'Principles Alone Cannot Guarantee Ethical AI' (2019) 1 *Nat Mach Intell* 501.

possible technical responses to concerns about these risks and contexts where hard boundaries should be placed on the use of particular techniques.[36] In this way, principles of responsible or ethical AI can complement a legal analysis by highlighting the kinds of concerns about AI consumer products to which consumer law should respond and providing insights into the kinds of evidence and strategic lines of argument that may assist in enforcing the law more effectively.

C *AI in Consumer Products*

The AI available to consumers to buy for use is typically embedded in everyday devices enhanced with networked capacity or in readily available apps and websites. The usual stated purpose of these products is to assist consumers by performing simple tasks and, more substantively, by reducing the cognitive load involved in running their daily lives.[37] Thus, AI consumer products might include internet of things or smart devices such as fridges that monitor what foods need replacing, vacuum cleaners that navigate their own cleaning map, sensors that control lighting and heating, and doorbells that monitor visitors and passers-by.[38] More interactive offerings are digital assistants, such as Alexa (Amazon), Google Assistant (Google), Siri (Apple), and Bixby (Samsung).[39] The prime purpose of these kinds of digital assistants is to assist consumers in performing a range of tasks in response to voice commands, such as providing recommendations and reminders, playing music, or controlling other networked devices in the home. More sophisticated options are constantly emerging. At the time of writing, the tech hype cycle was focused on new generation chatbots like ChatGPT (Open AI), Bing (Microsoft), or Bard (Google) which use text-based prompts to provide information or code.[40]

Although often promoted as using AI, many of these products rely on relatively simple processes. Robot vacuum cleaners use sensors to navigate the home. Smart fridges similarly use sensors and an internet connection to detect low stock and reorder items. Digital assistants, or smart speakers, provide far more interactive services but are relatively simple in their front-end or direct-to-consumer interactions. Such devices typically record human conversations to relay them to the internet for processing and performance of the desired function. In this back-end role, digital

[36] See for example, Cynthia Rudin, 'Stop Explaining Black Box Machine Learning Models for High Stakes Decisions and Use Interpretable Models Instead' (2019) 1 *Nat Mach Intell* 206. See also Virginia Dignum, *Responsible Artificial Intelligence: How to Develop and Use AI in a Responsible Way* (Springer Nature 2019).

[37] See generally Roger Brownsword, 'From Erewhon to AlphaGo: For the Sake of Human Dignity, Should We Destroy the Machines?' (2017) 9(1) *Law, Innovation and Technology* 117, 128–131.

[38] See Noto La Diega and Walden (n 27). Also US Congressional Research Service, 'The Internet of Things (IoT): An Overview' (2020) <https://fas.org/sgp/crs/misc/IF11239.pdf>.

[39] Judith Shulevitz, 'Alexa, How Will You Change Us?' (2018) 322 *The Atlantic Magazine* 96, 96 <www.theatlantic.com/magazine/archive/2018/11/alexa-how-will-you-change-us/570844/>.

[40] Ian Bogost, 'ChatGPT is Dummer than You Think' (8 December 2022) *The Atlantic*.

assistants generally work on natural language generation and processing to interact with human users through voice commands and responses.[41] Conversational chatbots rely on similar text-based processes. While they use increasingly large language models, they rely on statistical or pattern recognition methods for producing responses, rather than human-like understanding.[42] These interactions are used to retrieve information or to link with other networked devices to control their functions. Unlike popular media representations and dystopian visions of robots in the home, AI consumer products are typically physically unassuming and unobtrusive, embedded in familiar or discrete objects.[43] Their functionality arises from using their position in the home to gather data about consumers' behaviour, which is processed by algorithmic methods to predict future preferences.

AI consumer products potentially offer tremendous benefits to many consumers. They are a labour-saving device that creates opportunities for consumers to spend less time on mundane tasks, benefit from increased access to relevant information, and make more informed and rational decisions.[44] AI consumer products may provide significant assistance to people whose participation in social, civic, and market interactions is affected by distance, lack of physical mobility, disability, language, or limited literacy.[45] Products using generative AI open the possibility of producing fluid, persuasive writing for those who do not have the skills themselves to do so, at least in the language required for written communication. Voice-activated bots or digital assistants may provide a new way for people to access essential public information, including crisis management strategies, news, and goods and services. They can facilitate social, civic and political interactions by bringing information and the opportunity for engagement to people's homes without the obtrusive act of opening a device.[46] The voice-to-text capacity of these devices broadens the possibility of communication for people who cannot otherwise write or write in the language required for the institutions they need to communicate with.

Yet while AI consumer products offer convenience, they also carry a number of risks of harm to consumers. As with any use of personal data, these harms include undermining privacy, hacking, data breaches, and biased processes and decisions. The risks of harm also include those arising from the status of AI products as goods

[41] See for example, Alistair Charlton, 'Voice Shopping with Amazon Alexa and Google Assistant: Everything You Need to Know (*Gearbrain*, 11 March 2020) <www.gearbrain.com/voice-shopping-with-alexa-explained-2534870941.html>.

[42] See in particular concerns raised in Emily M. Bender, Timnit Gebru, Angelina McMillan-Major, and Shmargaret Shmitchell. 'On the Dangers of Stochastic Parrots: Can Language Models Be Too Big?' in *Conference on Fairness, Accountability, and Transparency* (FAccT '21), 3–10 March 2021, Virtual Event, Canada. ACM, New York, NY, USA, 14 pages. <https://doi.org/10.1145/3442188.3445922>.

[43] See Shulevitz (n 39).

[44] Michal S Gal and Niva Elkin-Koren, 'Algorithmic Consumers' (2017) 30 *Harv J L & Tech* 309, 319–320.

[45] See, for example, Lyndsie M Koon, Kenneth Blocker and W Rogers, 'Voice-Activated Digital Assistants: Perceptions from Novice Users with Long-Term Mobility Disability' (2019) 3 *Innov Aging* 759.

[46] See Shulevitz (n 39) 96–97.

or services, such as problems of safety, reliability, and consistency with consumer expectations of performance. Further risks include the increasingly ubiquitous embedding of AI in human lives, which may impact on human autonomy and human relationships. In the following sections, we examine these harms in turn and consider possible responses, drawing primarily on consumer protection law as well as the insights provided by principles of AI ethics, particularly as a way of promoting explicability and accountability.

III RISKS ARISING FROM THE USE OF PERSONAL DATA IN AI CONSUMER PRODUCTS

A *Privacy*

AI consumer products give rise to the risks of harm to consumer autonomy and well-being inherent in many data-driven automated processes.[47] AI consumer products have been criticised as collecting large volumes of data that may be used for purposes well beyond providing the immediate service offered by the product.[48] This is a particular concern of devices such as smart speakers or doorbells. Not only may the product collect information about the consumer who purchased it, the product may also upload information about everyone who lives in or even visits the home in which the device is installed. Bystander surveillance raises concerns where AI products 'listen' to guests or visitors without their knowledge or opportunities to refuse consent.[49] The increased surveillance of individuals enabled by AI products and smart devices may undermine privacy and have a chilling effect on individual expression. This concern is particularly pertinent for AI products designed to be used in the home, which often rely on collecting intimate data about individuals to perform their function.[50] It is not clear that consumers understand these risks, especially given the length and complexity of online privacy policies associated with the use of digital technologies.[51] Firms have been accused of using choice architecture, or 'dark patterns', to push consumers towards privacy-reducing options by making these more salient while downplaying the value of other options.[52]

Concerns about unbounded data collection lie primarily in the domain of privacy and data protection law. These regimes commonly rely on consent as a key jurisdiction

47 Hildebrandt and Koops (n 10); Stucke and Ezrachi (n 4).

48 Noto La Diega and Walden (n 27) 9–12; Stucke and Ezrachi (n 4) 1284.

49 See also Meredith Whittaker and others, 'Disability, Bias, and AI' (Report 2019) 23–24 <https://ainowinstitute.org/disabilitybiasai-2019.pdf>.

50 Stucke and Ezrachi (n 4) 1279.

51 See above text at n 27.

52 See for example, Norwegian Consumer Council, 'Deceived by Design: How Tech Companies Use Dark Patterns to Discourage Us from Exercising Our Rights to Privacy' (Report, 2018). See also Katharine Kemp, 'Concealed Data Practices and Competition Law: Why Privacy Matters' (2020) 16 *Europ Competition J* 628; Lauren E Willis, 'Deception by Design' (2020) 34 *Harv J L & Tech* 115.

for data processing.[53] The UK's Data Protection Act 1998, following the GDPR, imposes robust requirements for what amounts to valid consent for these purposes, requiring it to be a 'freely given, specific, informed and unambiguous'.[54] Notably, however, these requirements do not ensure that consumers have read or understood the terms, and indeed, issues around the behavioural biases of consumers in decision-making and the likelihood of information overload in the face of frequent requests for consent to data processing undermine the impact of these protections.[55] This has led to recognition of a role for substantive protections for consumers in contracting, such as through unfair terms regimes, which render void substantively one-sided or overreaching terms.[56] Prohibitions on misleading[57] or aggressive[58] practices may be used to sanction firms that use 'choice architecture' to lay out terms and conditions in a manner likely to 'nudge' consumers into agreeing to provisions that work against their interests.[59]

A related concern around the collection and use of personal data is over the potential to manipulate consumer decision-making. One primary purpose of data collection is to enable the creation of digital profiles which are aggregated and used to make predictions about behaviour and preferences. These insights may be used to nudge consumers into purchasing and other decisions that may not be welfare-enhancing and which do not, in any real sense, represent autonomous decision-making. The most commonly discussed manifestation of this concern is targeted behavioural advertising through social media.[60] The AI consumer product may be conceived to operate as an in-home channel for targeted advertising, thus amplifying the effect of such strategies. In some scenarios, the conduct may infringe prohibitions on unfair commercial practices. Proposals have also been made for more comprehensive interventions, such as through bans and warnings,[61]

53 Damian Clifford, Inge Graef and Peggy Valcke, 'Pre-formulated Declarations of Data Subject Consent—Citizen-Consumer Empowerment and the Alignment of Data, Consumer and Competition Law Protections' (2019) 20 *German L J* 679.

54 Council Regulation (EU) 2016/678 of 27 April 2016 on the protection of natural persons with regard to the processing of data and on free movement of such data, and repealing Directive 95/46/EC (General Data Protection Regulation) [2016] OJ L119/1 (GDPR), art 4(11).

55 See Damian Clifford and Jeannie Paterson, 'Consumer Privacy and Consent: Reform in the Light of Contract and Consumer Protection Law' (2020) 94 *ALJ* 741.

56 CRA 2015, pt 2.

57 See CPUTR 2018, Reg 5.

58 Ibid. Reg 7.

59 See, for example, Jeannie Marie Paterson, Elise Bant and Henry Cooney, 'Australian Competition and Consumer Commission v Google: Deterring Misleading Conduct in Digital Privacy Policies' (2021) 26 *Communications L – J of Computer, Media and Telecommunications Law* 136. See also Cobun Keegan and Calli Schroeder, 'Unpacking Unfairness: The FTC's Evolving Measures of Privacy Harms' (2019) 15 *J L Econ & Pol'y* 19; Dennis D Hirsch, 'From Individual Control to Social Protection: New Paradigms for Privacy Law in the Age of Predictive Analytics' (2020) 79 *Md L Rev* 439.

60 See Calo (n 3); Wagner and Eidenmüller (n 3).

61 Emma Wollacott, 'European Regulator Calls for Ad Targeting Ban' (*Forbes*, 11 February 2021) <www.forbes.com/sites/emmawoollacott/2021/02/11/european-regulator-calls-for-ad-targeting-ban/?sh=6504969a2523>. See also Gilad Edelman, 'Why Don't We Just Ban Targeted Advertising' (*Wired*, 22 March 2020) <www.wired.com/story/why-dont-we-just-ban-targeted-advertising>.

on the ground that this is a socially unacceptable intrusion on market choice and decision-making.[62]

B *Bias and Discrimination*

A second key concern arising from the data-driven processes that inform the uses of AI is the risk of endemic bias, which perpetuates and amplifies discrimination.[63] Bias in the outputs informed by AI arises in a number of ways. It may arise from the prejudices of the people creating or applying the system.[64] Biased outcomes may also arise from the data used to train the system, which may lead to the systems being 'indirectly, unintentionally and unknowingly discriminatory'[65] and moreover these kinds of discriminatory outputs may arise through the use of proxies for protected attributes even where the data is formally blind to those attributes.

Problems of bias have most commonly been considered in conjunction with public and private sector decision-making that determines access to services, entitlements, and employment.[66] AI consumer products also carry a risk of bias. As we have seen, AI consumer products commonly provide information, text, or recommendations in response to user requests. These responses may be affected by historical patterns of discrimination that influence the algorithmic prediction of what is being asked or what information should be provided in response to a request. Biased recommendations from AI consumer products may provide results that perpetuate undesirable stereotypes or discriminatory attitudes. They may have the effect of excluding people from accessing products and services on the basis of protected characteristics such as gender or race.[67]

Consumer protection laws might be used to address bias in AI consumer products, responding, for example, to misleading claims or unfair outcomes.[68] However,

62 See Paterson and others, 'Hidden Harms' (n 3).

63 See Committee for Economic Development of Australia, *How Unequal? Insights on Inequality* (Report, April 2018) 124–128; Select Committee on Artificial Intelligence, AI in the UK: Ready, Willing and Able? (HL 2017–19) 41. See also Virginia Eubanks, *Automating Inequality: How High-Tech Tools Profile, Police and Punish the Poor* (St Martin's Publishing Group 2018).

64 Lilian Edwards and Michael Veale, 'Slave to the Algorithm? Why a "Right to an Explanation" is Probably Not the Remedy You Are Looking For' (2017) 16 *Duke L & Tech Rev* 18, 28.

65 Ibid.

66 Cathy O'Neil, *Weapons of Math Destruction* (Penguin Books 2016).

67 The Editorial Board, 'Facebook Faces Redlining Reckoning' *The New York Times* (New York City, 30 March 2019) <www.nytimes.com/2019/03/29/opinion/facebook-discrimination-civil-rights.html>; Jon M Garon, 'Dysregulating the Media: Digital Redlining, Privacy Erosion, and the Unintentional Deregulation of American Media' (2020) 73 *Me L Rev* 45, 75. See also Sandra Wachter, 'Affinity Profiling and Discrimination by Association in Online Behavioural Advertising' (2020) 35 *Berkeley Tech LJ* 367, 370–372.

68 See warnings to companies to ensure against bias in algorithms as contrary to fairness in trading from the Federal Trade Commission: Federal Trade Commission, 'Aiming for Truth, Fairness, and Equity in Your Company's Use of AI' (April 2021) <www.ftc.gov/news-events/blogs/business-blog/2021/04/aiming-truth-fairness-equity-your-companys-use-ai>.

the more direct approach is through human rights, along with anti-discrimination law.[69] The difficulty in this approach is likely to be primarily evidential. It may be difficult to establish bias in automated recommendations or decisions.[70] For example, an individual consumer may find it difficult to determine whether a recommendation that differs from that given to a friend or colleague is discriminatory or personalised to his or her unique circumstances. At least part of the solution may lie in mechanisms for explanations and a systematic framework for governance or accountability.

Explanations in this context do not involve the detail of the algorithms providing the service, which is, in any event, unlikely to be available due to concerns about commercial confidentiality and too complex to be useful in many instances. Scholars working in the field of algorithmic fairness have suggested that unlawful discrimination may be identified through counterfactual explanations,[71] which work by identifying the factors that would need to change to produce a different outcome. There are, unfortunately, limits to this approach, mainly when dealing with proxies for protected attributes.[72] Another, albeit complementary, response is to require firms producing AI products to implement rigorous assurance or accountability frameworks, including systems for scrutinising training and testing data, design decisions, and performance outputs to identify patterns of exclusion or discrimination.[73] There have also been suggestions for regular reporting obligations or algorithmic impact statements from those deploying AI as a civil rights protection.[74] There are currently no rules in consumer protection law that would require this kind of systematic oversight of AI consumer products. Here, mandated assurance frameworks, accompanied by product certification may be valuable as a coregulatory approach for reducing the risk of unfair bias and prompting more robust product performance.[75]

69 See Australian Human Rights Commission, *Human Rights and Technology Final Report* (2021) 105.

70 Matt J Kusner and Joshua R Loftus, 'The Long Road to Fairer Algorithms' (2020) 578 *Nature* 34. See also Pak-Hang Wong, 'Democratizing Algorithmic Fairness' (2020) 33 *Philos Technol* 225.

71 Matt Kusner and others, 'Counterfactual Fairness' (*31st Conference on Neural Information Processing Systems*, arXiv 2017) 16 <https://arxiv.org/pdf/1703.06856.pdf> <www.perma.cc/4SVN-7J9D>; Sandra Wachter, Brent Mittelstadt and Chris Russell, 'Counterfactual Explanations without Opening the Black Box: Automated Decisions and the GDPR' (2018) 31 *Harv J L & Tech* 841, 853.

72 Sandra Wachter, Brent Mittelstadt and Chris Russell, 'Why Fairness Cannot Be Automated: Bridging the Gap between EU Non-discrimination Law and AI' (2020) 41 *Comput L Sec Rev* 105567 <www.sciencedirect.com/science/article/pii/S0267364921000406>.

73 Kusner and Loftus (n 70). See also Wong (n 70) 233–234; Dawson and others (n 32) 8.

74 Dillon Reisman and others, 'Algorithmic Impact Assessments: A Practical Framework for Public Agency Accountability' (Report 2018) <www.ainowinstitute.org/aiareport2018.pdf>.

75 See Australian Human Rights Commission, *Human Rights and Technology Final Report* (n 69) 95–97. Also Proposal for a Regulation of the European Parliament and of the Council (EU) COM(2021) 206 arts 17 and 19, and requirements in ch 2.

IV AI CONSUMER PRODUCTS AS GOODS AND SERVICES

A *Meeting Consumers' Performance Expectations*

In addition to the risks inherent in data-driven technology, AI consumer products give rise to risks that arise from their status as products, namely that they may prove unsafe, unreliable, or defective. The relevant legal responses to such problems vary according to whether the issue in question relates to the status of the product as a good or a service.

1 Goods

The devices that house AI products, such as the fridge, doorbell, speaker or device in which the AI element sits, are goods, sometimes accompanied by software, which in the UK is similarly regulated as a 'digital product'.[76] As such, they are subject to the standards of satisfactory quality and fitness for purpose applying to the supply of consumer goods.[77] This means that they should operate for a reasonable time without failure and should be relatively safe; for example, they should not be unstable or have parts likely to splinter or short-circuit. An additional concern is cybersecurity. So-called 'smart home' devices have been found to be particularly vulnerable to cyberattacks which challenge the integrity of the service being provided and the security of the home in which it is located.[78] Hacking is often made possible through the low processing power of the devices, which results in lower levels of encryption and limited capacity for software updates, along with user inexperience.[79]

Concerns over cybersecurity have led to the development of codes of conduct for web-connected AI products,[80] along with calls for legislation.[81] This susceptibility to hacking and security generally would also appear to be core consumer protection issues (as well as ones pertaining to security and domestic and family violence). One of the elements to consider in determining whether goods are of satisfactory quality is the degree to which the device is safe.[82] The statutory expectations of quality and safety in networked devices should include a reasonable level of cyber resilience, at

[76] CRA 2015, ch 3.

[77] CRA 2015, ss 9 and 10. Also ss 34–35 (for digital content).

[78] Manwaring (n 14) 270–272.

[79] Swaroop Poudel, 'Internet of Things: Underlying Technologies, Interoperability, and Threats to Privacy and Security' (2016) 31 *Berkeley Tech LJ* 997, 1015; Kayleen Manwaring and Roger Clarke, 'Is Your Television Spying on You? The Internet of Things Needs More than Self-Regulation' (2020) 93 *Computers & Law* 31, 33.

[80] UK Department for Digital, Culture, Media & Sport, 'Code of Practice for Consumer IoT Security' (2018) <www.gov.uk/government/publications/code-of-practice-for-consumer-iot-security>.

[81] See 'Government Response to the Call for Views on Consumer Connected Product Cyber Security Legislation' (*Department for Digital, Culture, Media & Sport*, April 2021) <www.gov.uk/government/publications/regulating-consumer-smart-product-cyber-security-government-response>.

[82] CRA 2015, s 9(3)(d).

least to the degree demanded by the various codes. This is an example of the ability of standards-based regulation to respond to new technical demands.

2 Services and Reasonable Care

In many instances, the core function of AI consumer products is providing a service. The prime examples are digital assistants and chatbots for which the device, such as a speaker, phone, or software, is less significant than the service provided.[83] Typically, consumers will be expecting AI consumer products to provide them with useful, or even beneficial, information, text, recommendations, or advice. Consumers might legitimately look for a remedy where this is not forthcoming. Legitimate consumer complaints might arise where, for example, an AI consistently misunderstands commands, fails to activate reminders, or makes recommendations that the consumer does not like. Still worse are scenarios where the AI gives advice that is positively contrary or dangerous, for example, suggesting children play a drinking game or insert a metal object into a power point.[84]

Providers of services are subject to a duty of reasonable care and skill implied under general law[85] and statute.[86] The standard of reasonable care for the purpose of consumer law is usually determined by reference to industry practice and the circumstances in which the product is marketed and sold.[87] It is not straightforward to decide how this standard would be applied to the service offered by an AI consumer product, which is essentially a set of algorithms. The AI product is not itself performing the service of a human or performing like a human, so that cannot be a relevant standard for assessment.[88]

Perhaps the relevant reference point is the skill of the firm that has designed and deployed the product, along with the technical capacities of the product and the promotion that was used to sell it. Not all outputs from a generative AI chatbot will be accurate; such products infamously can make very wrong predications about the kind of answer being sought or even create seeming accurate new factual information. Nonetheless, a firm that offers an AI consumer product that is technically incapable of performing the service offered, unreliable in doing so, or produces discriminatory recommendations may be unlikely to have used reasonable care and skill in making the product available on the market. Blame for these outcomes placed on the training data set or the algorithms used is hardly relevant to the liability of the supplier under consumer protection law regimes.

83 See above n 39.

84 'Alexa Tells 10-Year-Old Girl to Touch a Live Plug with a Penny' *BBC News* (28 December 2021); 'How a Chatbot Encouraged a Man Who Wanted to Kill the Queen' *BBC News* (6 October 2023).

85 *Greaves & Co (Contractors) Ltd v Baynham Meikle & Partners* [1975] 1 WLR 1095 (CA), 1100; *Voli v Inglewood Shire Council* (1963) 110 CLR 74 (HCA), 85.

86 CRA 2015, s 49.

87 See, for example, *Rogers v Whitaker* (1992) 175 CLR 479 (HCA), 483–484.

88 Cf Ryan Abbott, *The Reasonable Robot* (Cambridge University Press 2020) advocating technological neutrality. See also discussion in Chapter 6 (Phillip Morgan).

While the legal standard for such claims may be relatively easily stated, in practice it may be more difficult to prove. Much of the promised attraction of AI consumer products lies in the capacity for personalisation. Consumers are often told that such products learn through personal interactions to become better at predicting their behaviour and preferences.[89] If the service provided by an AI consumer product is highly personalised then, aside from patently dangerous or random responses, it may be difficult to establish that the product has failed to meet the standard of reasonable care and skill in any particular instance.[90] It may be possible for an AI product to provide what appear to be personalised outputs but which are a very poor fit for a consumer's circumstances. Conversely, suppose a consumer does not like an AI's recommendation. It may be difficult to tell if the AI simply got it wrong on one occasion, missed better options within a ballpark range of valid predications, or used selection criteria that were not related to the preferences of the consumer.[91] Only the last option would amount to a breach of the supplier's obligation of reasonable care and skill.

A useful starting point for this inquiry may be in principles of explainable and accountable AI, discussed earlier.[92] Starting with explanations, it is important to note that the concept is not quite the same as disclosure requirements in consumer law. Disclosure operates to inform consumers of the risks inherent in particular products and is offered as a means of allowing consumers to take responsibility for their purchasing choices. Overreliance on disclosure as a central tool for consumer protection has been criticised.[93] This is on the ground that it ignores the inevitable bounded rationality of consumers and the inequality of bargaining power that limits their ability to bargain for better-quality consumer products and fairer contract terms.[94] Explanations in AI may be a way for consumers or, importantly, regulators to verify claims about the quality or capacity of services informed by complex computer systems. Rather than a technical description of the relevant code, explanations in this sense should be tailored towards the information needs of the recipient.[95] This kind of explanation, perhaps using counterfactuals,[96] should reveal whether the key determinants of the automated recommendation were peculiar to the consumer's inquiry, in some way off-the-shelf, or even self-serving.[97] Additionally, as

89 Stucke and Ezrachi (n 4) 1255.

90 Ibid. 1269.

91 Cf ibid. 1296.

92 See above text at n 71.

93 See generally Omri Ben-Shahar and Carl E Schneider, *More Than You Wanted to Know: The Failure of Mandated Disclosure* (Princeton UP 2014).

94 See generally Robert A Hillman and Jeffrey J Rachlinski, 'Standard-Form Contracting in the Electronic Age' (2002) 77 *NYU L Rev* 429; Russell Korobkin, 'Bounded Rationality, Standard Form Contracts, and Unconscionability' (2003) 70 *U Chi L Rev* 1203.

95 Wachter, Mittelstadt and Russell (n 71) 843. See also Tim Miller, 'Explanation in Artificial Intelligence: Insights from the Social Sciences' (2019) 267 *Artif Intell* 1.

96 Ibid.

97 See also Jeannie Marie Paterson, 'Making Robo Advisers Careful' (2023) 15 *Law and Financial Markets Review* 278.

already noted, a commitment to AI accountability may require firms to implement assurance systems, such as auditing outputs, as a way of monitoring the performance provided by AI consumer products. In addition to providing scrutiny of possible discrimination, statistical audits may reveal trends of self-serving recommendations or patterns of results that undermine claims to fitness for purpose in the service provided to consumers.

There is no specific obligation to provide processes for explainable or accountable AI in consumer products,[98] at least currently.[99] It is possible that these practical and technical measures might be applied to give content to the duty of reasonable care and skill.[100] We suggest that this is a reasonable demand from those responsible for providing AI-informed products. This is on the basis that measures are necessary to ensure the quality of AI consumer products and that they meet the expectations created by consumers about their performance. Even with explanations and a systematic approach to accountability, it may be unrealistic to expect consumers to scrutinise the performance and impact of AI products. However, these governance mechanisms may allow better regulatory oversight, and in this way, allow the quality of performance of AI products to be contested and enforced.

3 Services That Mislead Consumers

In some instances, the supplier of an AI product may mislead consumers, and contravene consumer protection law.[101] A supplier may, for example, mislead by promoting sentience or superhuman insight in a bot informed by statistical predictions or suggesting the product's 'intelligence' lies in the use of sophisticated data analytics and machine learning when it does nothing of the kind.[102] A different kind of misrepresentation may arise where the AI product itself provides consumers with false, inaccurate, or misleading information. In some instances, this may merely be inconvenient or disappointing, such as when a bot produces a supposedly award-winning cake recipe that is not very tasty. An AI cannot be blamed for information about inherently variable outcomes, such as a weather or share market prediction, unless it is wildly wrong or out of any reasonable margin of error. However, inaccuracy may have more significant consequences when consumers are directed to

98 The GDPR 'right' to an explanation applies only to decisions based 'solely' on automated processing that produce legal or similar effects – on automated decisions that significantly affect consumer rights: see GDPR art 22.

99 Some such processes are envisaged by the EU's Draft AI Act (n 72) but only for high-risk products. See also Bryan Casey, Ashkon Farhangi and Roland Vogl, 'Rethinking Explainable Machines: The GDPR's "Right to Explanation" Debate and the Rise of Algorithmic Audits in Enterprise' (2019) 34 *Berkeley Tech LJ* 143, 176.

100 See also Paterson (n 98).

101 CPUTR 2018, Reg 5.

102 See Jeannie Marie Paterson, 'Misleading AI: Regulatory Strategies for Algorithmic Transparency in Technologies Augmenting Consumer Decision-Making (2023) 34(Symposium) *Loyola Consumer Law Review* 558.

expensive or unsuitable decisions, for example, high-risk purchases dressed up as a bargain or recommendations for dangerous or harmful behaviours said to be safe.

If an AI consumer product makes a misleading statement or omission, then liability for that conduct will lie with the firm that supplies the AI product. In the case of products that produce information through sophisticated machine learning or neural networks, the firm in question may have had no direct or immediate control over the information produced or any specific intention to mislead.[103] However, statutory prohibitions on misleading actions do not require fault in the form of intentional wrongdoing, negligence or even foresight that the misleading conduct may occur.[104]

B *Equity and Accessibility*

AI consumer products are sometimes promoted for their potential to provide information and assistance to people with disabilities. Certainly, smart devices, digital assistants, and chatbots offer the potential to assist with everyday tasks for some people.[105] They might, for example, control lighting and temperature around the home, access information about available services, manage medication, make phone calls, send text messages, or assist with completing forms and applications. There is, however, little sustained research on the functionality or fitness for purpose of such devices in these roles and, equally, whether they are genuinely accessible and equitable.

There are again real risks here of the products failing to meet the assertions about their enabling potential. It is unclear, for example, whether voice assistants are responsive to the full range of voices of people with disabilities, and they may not work at all for some people with speech impairments or people who are deaf or hard of hearing.[106] Is access to information sufficient if people with disabilities receiving the information are precluded by entrenched social hierarchies from acting on or making use of that information to their benefit?[107] Even the issue of who sets up the device (and hence who decides the privacy settings and consents to the terms of use) and the scope of interaction available to the person impact the extent to which it has benefits for the user.[108] Concerns about privacy and surveillance that arise for

[103] Stucke and Ezrachi (n 4) 1271.

[104] See for example, CPUTR 2008, Regs 3 and 7.

[105] Koon, Blocker and Rogers (n 45).

[106] Shaun K Kane and others, '"At Times Avuncular and Cantankerous, with the Reflexes of a Mongoose": Understanding Self-Expression through Augmentative and Alternative Communication Devices' (Association for Computing Machinery Conference on Computer Supported Cooperative Work and Social Computing, Portland, Oregon, USA, 25 February–1 March 2017) 1166 <https://doi.org/10.1145/2998181.2998284>.

[107] Anna Lauren Hoffmann, 'Where Fairness Fails: Data, Algorithms, and the Limits of Antidiscrimination Discourse' (2019) 22 *Information, Communication & Society* 900, 907–908.

[108] Noting also the potential for surveillance technology to be used to facilitate abuse: eSafety Commissioner, Australian Government, '"For My Safety": Experiences of Technology-Facilitated Abuse among Women with Intellectual Disability or Cognitive Disability' (Report 2021) <www.esafety.gov.au/sites/default/files/2021-09/TFA%20WWICD_accessible.pdf>.

all users of AI consumer products may be exacerbated for people with disabilities where, for example, a person feels that they must choose between maintaining their privacy and accessing life-enhancing assistance, or where data on their activities and actions may be used to assess and limit future access to disability-specific funding and other resources.[109]

Additionally, reliance on inaccurate and incomplete data may produce inequitable outcomes that reinforce the existing exclusion of people with disabilities.[110] People whose attributes are not well represented in a data set or have unique circumstances, are unlikely to be well served by predictions drawn from that data. Where there is no data on a group, there may be no outcomes that are suitable for them – they miss out or must make do with suboptimal results.[111] There is no easy solution to these concerns. One response is to ensure that principles of universal design are respected by including the experiences of a wide range of users in the development of the product and recognising and acknowledging its limits.[112] Importantly, from both human rights and consumer protection perspectives, it is important not to exaggerate the capacity of AI consumer products to change the lives of people with disabilities and other 'marginalised' consumer groups, without strong evidence that this is possible and desired by those communities. Requirements for greater transparency around design features and auditing of performance outcomes would go some way towards allowing claims of accessibility and equity in AI products to be robustly assessed.

V CONCERNS ABOUT EMBEDDING AI PRODUCTS IN HUMAN LIVES

Even if we assume that AI consumer products are capable of operating in a manner that is free of unacceptable bias and broadly accessible, they may still carry the risk of harms to consumer autonomy and welfare that arise from their aspiration to personalised recommendations and their deployment in the private sphere of the home.

[109] Whittaker and others (n 46) 24–25; Jillian Weise, 'Common Cyborg' (*Granta*, 24 September 2018) <https://granta.com/common-cyborg/>, using the example of her prosthetic leg, which collects and transmits data, and the possibility that she will not be approved for a new leg in the future if she does not follow medical advice about how often and far she should be walking every day.

[110] Select Committee on Artificial Intelligence (n 63) 119; Phuong Nguyen and Lauren Solomon, 'Consumer Data and the Digital Economy: Emerging Issues in Data Collection, Use and Sharing' (Consumer Policy Research Centre 2018) 34 <https://apo.org.au/sites/default/files/resource-files/2018-07/apo-nid241516.pdf>.

[111] See also Edwards and Veale (n 64).

[112] See further Eduardo Velloso and others, 'Challenges of Emerging Technologies for Human-Centred Design: Bridging the Gap between Inquiry and Invention' (*Proceedings of the 30th Australian Conference on Computer-Human Interaction, Association for Computing Machinery* 2018) <https://doi.org/10.1145/3292147.3293451>.

A *Autonomy, Welfare, and Influence*

As already noted, one of the purposes of AI products is to unburden consumers from some of the mundane administrative tasks that come with running a home. Thus, consumers are encouraged to rely on digital assistants to provide them with reminders, information, and assistance in their day to day lives, and to use generative AI tools for a variety of study, work and creative tasks.[113] Some of these uses may be relatively mundane, such as the latest TikTok trend or a new cake recipe. Other kinds of assistance have more impact, such as providing information about fitness, health, high-value purchases or investments, not to mention information about politics and news.[114] Reliance on these kinds of AI produced recommendations may assists consumers in finding their way through a myriad of potentially conflicting sources of information. But it also risks misdirecting consumers away from the purchasing options that would suit them best, as well as broader political misinformation.[115]

Consumers' reliance on AI recommendations or information may also restrict the scope of the very choices available to them, as processes informed by data analytics not only produce but also hide information.[116] This misdirecting and narrowing of consumer choice may arise as a result of a failing in the design or development of the product. It may also be more deliberate.[117] An AI may learn, or be programmed, to prioritise product recommendations from firms that have a commercial affiliation with its corporate manufacturer.[118] This conduct may produce no material harm. Nonetheless, consumers may reasonably expect that their AI products will act in their best interests in providing information, recommendations or advice. Should a fiduciary duty be in place, this behaviour may manifest as a conflict of interest.[119] In other circumstances, it may be misleading for an AI product to depart from consumers' expectations of personalised loyalty.

A further concern may be with AI consumer products, learning not merely to promote outcomes beneficial to the manufacturer but also to manipulate consumers' decision-making to achieve these outcomes.[120] John Danaher suggests that we

[113] See further Eliza Mik, 'The Erosion of Autonomy in Online Consumer Transactions' (2016) 8 *Law Innov Tech* 1.

[114] Stucke and Ezrachi (n 4) 1271.

[115] Karen Yeung, '"Hypernudge": Big Data as a Mode of Regulation by Design' (2019) 20 *Inf Commun Soc* 118, 121.

[116] See Wagner and Eidenmüeller (n 3) 599–603; ibid. 129. See also Paterson and others, 'Hidden Harms' (n 3).

[117] See above text at n 52.

[118] Stucke and Ezrachi (n 4) 1253.

[119] Simone Degeling and Jessica Hudson, 'Financial Robots as Instruments of Fiduciary Loyalty' (2018) 40 *Sydney L Rev* 63; Jeannie Paterson and Elise Bant, 'Mortgage Broking, Regulatory Failure and Statutory Design' (2020) 31 *J Banking and Finance: Law and Practice* 7, 12–13, 26.

[120] Cf Willis (n 52).

should not exaggerate this concern, noting that individuals may choose not to rely on such devices.[121] However, the evolving relationship may be closer than between a consumer and a mere electronic device. Indeed, the risk arises precisely from the potential intimacy of the relationship.[122] The AI in consumer products is commonly marketed as clever, effective, and omnipresent, even fulfilling the role of wife or servant.[123] The voiced presence of digital assistants may exaggerate this feeling of closeness felt by consumers in their interactions with the device.[124] Even disembodied and voiceless chatbots are often given appealing robot faces and communicate in a quirky, positive tone. We might, therefore, ask whether this nurtured sense of friendliness or intimacy should carry a responsibility with regard to the well-being and autonomy of the consumer.

The private law doctrine that responds to these kinds of concerns is undue influence.[125] The equitable doctrine is not (yet) applicable to a relationship with a smart device in which the intimacy arises from data-driven predictions. The Consumer Protection from Unfair Trading Regulations 2008 (UK) and similar legislation contain prohibitions on unfair commercial practices[126] and aggressive practices.[127] The prohibition on aggressive practices is explicitly concerned with practices that involve the exercise of 'undue influence'.[128] This is not entirely the same concept as that deployed in equity.

Undue influence under the Regulations is defined to mean 'exploiting a position of power in relation to the consumer so as to apply pressure … in a way which significantly limits the consumer's ability to make an informed decision'.[129] Whether the concept extends so far as to encompass subtle relational influence remains to be seen.[130] Nonetheless, the statutory doctrine might be used to respond to such concerns; ultimately, they raise exercise of information asymmetries that undermine the capacity of consumers to make informed decisions. Again, in practice, there may be issues with obtaining evidence of such influence, given that the line between personalised functionality and influence may be blurred. Interestingly, the record of interactions made by AI consumer products in communicating with consumers

121 Danaher (n 9) 645. See also John Danaher, 'The Ethics of Algorithmic Outsourcing in Everyday Life' in Karen Yeung and Martin Lodge (eds), *Algorithmic Regulation* (Oxford University Press 2019) 98.

122 Stucke and Ezrachi (n 4) 1271.

123 Yolande Strengers and Jenny Kennedy, *The Smart Wife: Why Siri, Alexa, and Other Smart Home Devices Need a Feminist Reboot* (MIT Press 2020). See also Thao Phan, 'Amazon Echo and the Aesthetics of Whiteness' (2019) 5 *Catalyst Feminism Theory Technoscience* <https://catalystjournal.org/index.php/catalyst/article/view/29586/24800>.

124 Shulevitz (n 39).

125 Paterson and Bant (n 21) 14.

126 CPUTR 2008, s 4.

127 Ibid. Reg 7.

128 Ibid. Reg 7(1)(a).

129 Ibid. Reg 7(3)(b).

130 Chris Willett, 'Fairness and Consumer Decision Making under the Unfair Commercial Practices Directive' (2010) 33 *J Consum Policy* 247, 260.

may be useful in establishing the point at which the virtual assistant has overstepped its boundaries.

B *Beneficence, Human Character, and Human Relationships*

Most frameworks of AI ethics include principles relating to beneficence.[131] The aspiration to a positive obligation to do well goes beyond most consumer protection statutes, which typically focus on avoiding harm. The ethical principle of beneficence may mean refusing to deploy or rely on AI in some circumstances. Thus, there may be tasks that should not be delegated, and especially not to an AI consumer product.[132] One such limit may be in contexts that involve sustaining meaningful or authentic human relationships. While these are not questions that can be addressed by law, they are not trivial concerns.

Danaher argues that our inner life may flourish if routine and mundane tasks can be delegated to a machine.[133] However, different kinds of considerations may apply in contemplating relying on AI products to perform tasks that traditionally are done to show our care for another human, such as buying a present or sending a get-well card. Reliance on an AI to complete or coordinate these tasks potentially carries a risk of stripping our lives of the small intimacies that create meaning for humans.[134] However, Danaher notes that not all tasks carry inherent moral worth because they are done by ourselves rather than being delegated, pondering that as long as it is a human who has the thought to benefit another, that should be the key consideration both ethically and emotionally.[135] In other words, if the human thinks about others by initiating an action that benefits them through an AI, does it really matter that a machine, not the human, completes the task?

Like Danaher, we suggest that the answer to this question lies in being discerning in our use of AI.[136] Some kinds of personal tasks carry value primarily because a human does them. In these scenarios, outsourcing the task to a machine may well be considered to be inherently 'uncaring' and as undermining the relational merit of the action. For example, programming an AI to say 'goodnight' to a child will have different moral worth and relational weight than the parent saying goodnight themselves.[137] Similarly, we should consider whether reliance on AI companions

[131] See also Frank A Pasquale, 'Toward a Fourth Law of Robotics: Preserving Attribution, Responsibility, and Explainability in an Algorithmic Society' (2017) 78(5) *Ohio State Law Journal* 1243.

[132] One such check may be sustaining an arm's length relationship with the device. See further Joanna J Bryson, 'Robots Should Be Slaves' in Yorick Wilks (ed), *Close Engagements with Artificial Companions: Key Social, Psychological, Ethical and Design Issues* (John Benjamins Publishing 2010).

[133] Danaher (n 9) 636.

[134] Ibid. 630.

[135] Ibid. 650.

[136] Ibid. 638.

[137] Berenice Fisher and Joan Tronto, 'Toward a Feminist Theory of Caring' in Emily K Abel and Margaret K Nelson (eds), *Circles of Care: Work and Identity in Women's Lives* (SUNY Press 1990).

may create or worsen the isolation of older people before we deploy them in pursuit of more efficient models of care or support.[138]

One important consideration in weighing up the significance of a task must be the perspective of the 'recipient' or supposed beneficiary of that task. For instance, an elderly parent might find it more meaningful and valuable to have a child or other family member they care about, and have chosen, doing a personal task for them rather than it being delegated, even if the person performing the task finds it repetitive or dull, and even if an AI product might perform the task more effectively or efficiently. There may be something important in humans retaining control over the actions or interactions to which they are subject, even when they may be less than objectively optimal. Equally, however, another elderly parent might prefer to disclose personal information to an AI rather than their child when completing medical or legal paperwork. We may need to consider equipping both parties to these relational activities with information and options about the potential benefits and risks of delegating tasks to AI products.

VI CONCLUSION

We have argued that statutory consumer protection law, typically designed as open-textured standards promoting fair market conduct and safe and reliable products, is capable of responding to the challenges to consumer autonomy and well-being raised by AI consumer products. In this role, consumer law will complement other regimes, such as data protection and human rights law, in addressing the increasingly widespread use of AI technologies in market and civic dealings. In our opinion, one key challenge in this context is to equip those enforcing the law with the tools to be able to identify and respond to significant consumer harms stemming from the use of AI consumer products. The other is to address the profound, and even existential, questions about the relationship we as humans want to have with the disembodied machines increasingly embedded in our homes and private lives.

See also Aimee van Wynsberghe, 'Designing Robots for Care: Care Centered Value-Sensitive Design' (2013) 19 *Sci Eng Ethics* 407.

138 Amanda Sharkey and Noel Sharkey, 'Granny and the Robots: Ethical Issues in Robot Care for the Elderly' (2012) 14 *Ethics Inf Technol* 27.

6

Tort Law and AI

Vicarious Liability

Phillip Morgan

I INTRODUCTION: THE REPLACEMENT OF EMPLOYEES

The introduction of AI technologies has been widely described as the fourth industrial revolution.[1] Each previous industrial revolution led to significant challenges to the law of tort, and it is difficult to underestimate the changes to tort law that resulted. For instance, industrialisation, and the development of the railways radically changed personal injury torts and nuisance and led many jurisdictions to adopt worker's compensation schemes.[2] With the previous digital revolution new cyber torts emerged, and torts such as defamation were found wanting, necessitating legal reform.[3]

AI produces new challenges for tort.[4] This chapter focuses on the replacement of employees, and the disruption this will cause to the existing tort settlement. Particular problems arise with fully autonomous systems, rather than with human in the loop, or human on the loop systems.

The replacement of employees with technology, alongside the creation of new technology-focused jobs is not a new phenomenon. However, the replacement of employees with autonomous AI technologies poses significant new challenges, which the current law of tort is poorly suited to address.

Whilst such technologies may offer both significant productivity and safety benefits over the use of human actors, their use may result in unpredictable, unforeseen negative

I acknowledge funding from the European Research Council under the European Union's Horizon 2020 research and innovation programme (grant agreement No 824990). I also acknowledge visiting research fellowships at Magdalen College, Oxford, the University of Hong Kong, and the Trinity Long Room Hub, Trinity College Dublin. I am grateful to Prof Jenny Steele, and the participants at workshops at the University of Hong Kong, the Trinity Long Room Hub, and a joint National University of Singapore/ University of York workshop for feedback and discussion. All errors remain my own.

1 For example, Klaus Schwab, *The Fourth Industrial Revolution* (WEF 2016).

2 Donald Gifford, 'Technological Triggers to Tort Revolutions: Steam Locomotives, Autonomous Vehicles, and Accident Compensation' (2018) 11 *J Tort L* 71; Ken Oliphant, 'Tort Law, Risk, and Technological Innovation in England' (2014) 59 *McGill LJ* 819.

3 See Trevor Hartley, 'Libel Tourism and Conflict of Laws' (2010) 59 *ICLQ* 25; in the UK this was in the shape of the Defamation Act 2013.

4 And for law generally, see: Ryan Calo, 'Robotics and the Lessons of Cyberlaw' (2015) 103 *Calif LR* 513.

outcomes, resulting in harm to individuals or society, even in situations where a human actor would not have caused such harm,[5] or they may be misused.[6] This is of increasing relevance to the law of tort since such systems are now able to take on non-standardised tasks, are operating outside closed laboratory or factory settings, are interacting with third parties, and are deployed in complex, random, and uncertain environments. They are also increasingly used in high-risk contexts, and in safety critical roles.[7]

The diversity in uses of AI will also put significant pressure on the law of tort.[8] The potential range of rights that may be violated and harms committed by AI systems is extremely broad, ranging from publishing defamatory materials, providing inaccurate advice or information, making discriminatory decisions, invading privacy, to causing accidents (and so on). Using such systems autonomously, particularly when accompanied by machine learning may result in negative outcomes which are not traceable to the fault of any party, resulting in a liability gap. This chapter makes the case for a statutory system of vicarious liability to bridge this gap.

II TECHNOLOGY IMPARTIALITY

Tech-impartiality[9] has two aspects: deterrence and victim rights.

The risk of tort liability, whether direct or vicarious, factors into the decision making of actors, including as to how they carry out work, the level of care they exercise, and the precautions they implement.[10] Properly deployed tort law deters harmful conduct and encourages the use of safer methods.[11] Deterrence is present even in the presence of insurance since insurers reduce moral hazards through a range of sophisticated devices and also provide a governance function.[12]

5 Harry Surden and Mary-Anne Williams, 'Technological Opacity, Predictability, and Self-Driving Cars' (2016) 38 *Cardozo LR* 121, 123–126.

6 Corrine Cath, 'Governing Artificial Intelligence: Ethical, Legal and Technical Opportunities and Challenges' (2018) *Phil Trans R Soc A* 376.

7 Ibid.

8 Neil Richards and William Smart, 'How Should the Law Think about Robots?' in Ryan Calo, A Michael Froomkin and Ian Kerr (eds), *Robot Law* (Edward Elgar Publishing 2016) 12.

9 Note Simon Burton and others, 'Mind the Gaps: Assuring the Safety of Autonomous Systems from an Engineering, Ethical, and Legal Perspective' (2020) 279 *Artificial Intelligence* 103201; note also legal neutrality: Ryan Abbott, *The Reasonable Robot* (Cambridge University Press 2020) 3; cf Brad Greenberg, 'Rethinking Technology Neutrality' (2016) 100 *Minn LR* 1495 (laws untethered to particular technologies).

10 Richard Posner and Francesco Parisi (eds), *Economic Foundations of Private Law* (Edward Elgar Publishing 2002) 5; Richard Posner, *Tort Law: Cases and Economic Analysis* (Little Brown and Company 1982) 1–9; Steven Shavell, *Economic Analysis of Accident Law* (Harv UP 1987) 5; Don Dewees, David Duff and Michael Trebilcock, *Exploring the Domain of Accident Law* (Oxford University Press 1996); Gary Schwartz, 'Reality in the Economic Analysis of Tort Law: Does Tort Law Really Deter?' (1994–1995) 42 *UCLA LR* 377; Peter Cane and James Goudkamp, *Atiyah's Accidents, Compensation and the Law* (9th edn, Cambridge University Press 2018) 405–433.

11 Posner and Parisi (n 10) 5; Posner (n 10) 1–9; Shavell (n 10) 5.

12 See Malcolm Clarke, *Policies and Perceptions of Insurance* (Clarendon Press 1997) 216–226; Rob Merkin and Jenny Steele, *Insurance and the Law of Obligations* (Oxford University Press 2013) 322; R Ian McEwin, 'No-Fault and Road Accidents: Some Australasian Evidence' (1989) 9 *IRLE* 13, 18; Tom

Within tort law, there is a calculus between safety and technological innovation.[13] The first aspect of tech-impartiality is that tort law should neither encourage nor discourage the use of new technologies, where the risk of legally recognised harms that such technologies pose to third parties are the same when compared to older technologies and methods of work. Tort should only play a role in encouraging or discouraging the use of new technologies where the systems are more or less safe than the alternatives. This aspect prevents a perversion of tort's deterrence role. Measuring this in fine grain can be difficult, and where data is lacking this needs to be assessed with a broad brush, examining if particular causes of action are absent for, or materially differ between technologies, or if additional hurdles within claims exist between technologies.[14]

Victims also have legally recognised rights which are protected by and vindicated through the law of tort,[15] including rights of bodily security and freedom, reputational rights, and rights in property.[16] Such rights may be rendered nugatory from a tort law perspective by the elimination of causes of action or remedies. The second aspect of tech-impartiality insists that an actor cannot strip a victim of their rights through the use of new technology in place of existing systems of work. If the same harm is inflicted on a person, a similar remedy, or remedies of equal value, should be provided in tort whether or not that harm is inflicted by a person, or a new technology. For instance, a pedestrian injured by a collision with a vehicle driven in a manner which falls below the standard of that of the reasonable driver has their right to bodily integrity violated whether or not the vehicle is autonomous or driven by a human driver. Likewise, to take a hypothetical future example, a victim's right of bodily freedom is equally violated if they are wrongfully detained by a human security guard, or an AI security system.[17] Tech-impartiality's requirement for remedial equivalence is particularly important in a common law context since the historical approach of the common law of tort, unlike civil law systems, has been *ubi remedium ibi ius* (where there is a remedy, there is a right).[18]

Baker and Peter Siegelman, 'The Law & Economics of Liability Insurance' in Jennifer Arlen (ed), *Research Handbook on the Economics of Torts* (Edward Elgar Publishing 2013) ch 7; Richard Ericson, Aaron Doyle and Dean Barry, *Insurance as Governance* (University of Toronto Press 2003); Tom Baker and Rick Swedloff, 'Regulation by Liability Insurance: From Auto to Lawyers' Professional Liability' (2013) 60 *UCLA LR* 1412; Gary Schwartz, 'The Ethics and Economics of Tort Liability Insurance' (1990) 75 *Cornell LR* 312, 356.

13 F Patrick Hubbard, 'Allocating the risk of physical injury from "sophisticated robots": efficiency, fairness, and innovation' in Calo, Froomkin and Kerr (n 8) 26.

14 This point relates to safety. However, it is recognised that there are a limited number of torts to which this statement does not apply, for instance, with defamation, which represents a balance of the rights of the claimant to reputation, and the defendant to free speech – the balance of these competing rights may differ in the context of AI speech when compared to human speech.

15 Robert Stevens, *Torts and Rights* (Oxford University Press 2007) 2–3.

16 *Allen v Flood* [1898] AC 1, 29 (Cave J).

17 Currently robot security guards are merely surveillance systems, and do not restrain individuals.

18 Harold Potter, *Introduction to the History of English Law* (Sweet & Maxwell 1924) 4; John Salmond and WTS Stallybrass, *Law of Torts* (8th edn, Sweet & Maxwell 1934) 1; Patrick O'Callaghan, 'Reversing Ubi Remedium Ibi Jus in the Common Law: The Right of Privacy' (2007) 15 *European Review of Private Law* 659.

III VICARIOUS LIABILITY

Vicarious liability is a core feature of tort litigation. In a US context, the doctrine is also referred to as respondeat superior. Given that many significant actors in society are legal persons, and since division of labour is core to the modern economic system, without such a doctrine or an analogous doctrine, the tort system would look very different, and would be unlikely to fully discharge its present functions. It is key in holding companies and other enterprises to account in tort.

Vicarious liability multiplies the number of possible defendants, increasing the probability of finding a solvent or insured defendant.[19] The doctrine makes one party, A, strictly liable for the torts of another, B. There are two stages to establishing vicarious liability. Firstly, there must be a relationship between A and B which is sufficient to trigger the doctrine; secondly, the tort committed by B must be sufficiently connected with that relationship to render A vicariously liable for the tort.[20] Its typical use is in making employers liable for their employees' torts.

Vicarious liability is not the only way for the victim to bring a claim against an employer. The employer may also owe the victim a direct duty of care, for instance in the case of a duty to take reasonable care to select a competent employee,[21] or the employer may also owe the victim a non-delegable duty.[22] However, a vicarious liability claim is usually less evidentially complex, and often more likely to succeed than such a direct duty claim. This is since there is no need to prove employer fault, and it bites even where the employer has followed all proper standards and processes. Vicarious liability is thus a powerful accountability mechanism, particularly where evidence is lacking or difficult to obtain; where there are disputes over the proper industry standards; and where the harm does not meet the foreseeability requirements from the employer's perspective required by the tort of negligence.[23] Of course, the victim retains the ability to sue the tortfeasing employee, although they may often be a man of straw.

Vicarious liability has proven flexible in accommodating long-term social changes, and changes in the nature of work. Particularly important in this context was the development that the 'employee' tortfeasor did not need to have a contract with the employer,[24] nor did they need to be an employee, being akin to an employee was sufficient.[25] However, vicarious liability faces its greatest challenge

19 Cane and Goudkamp (n 10) 217.

20 Phillip Morgan, 'Vicarious Liability on the Move' (2013) 129 *LQR* 139, approved: *Allen v The Chief Constable of the Hampshire Constabulary* [2013] EWCA Civ 967 [17]; approach also adopted in *Various Claimants v Catholic Child Welfare Society* [2012] UKSC 56, [2013] 2 AC 1 ('*CCWS*') [21], and *Trustees of the Barry Congregation of Jehovah's Witnesses v BXB* [2023] UKSC 15 ('*BXB*') [4], [58] (Lord Burrows).

21 For example, *Attorney General of the British Virgin Islands v Hartwell* [2004] UKPC 12, [2004] 1 WLR 1273; *Mattis v Pollock* [2003] EWCA Civ 887, [2003] 1 WLR 2158.

22 For example, *Rogers v Night Riders* [1983] RTR 324 (CA).

23 *Bazley v Curry* [1999] 2 SCR 534 (SCC) ('*Bazley*') [32] (McLachlin J).

24 Phillip Morgan, 'Recasting Vicarious Liability' (2012) 71 *CLJ* 615, 623–625.

25 *JGE v English Province of Our Lady of Charity* [2012] EWCA Civ 938, [2013] QB 722 ('*JGE*'); *CCWS* (n 21); *BXB* (n 21) [36] (Lord Burrows).

yet, which risks rendering it obsolete in many commercial contexts – the replacement of employees with autonomous AI systems.

A *Obsolescence?*

Much ink has been spilled on how vicarious liability can be justified, as Williams notes, '[v]icarious liability is the creation of many judges who have different ideas of its justification or social policy, or no idea at all.'[26] Presently, the courts adopt a pluralist approach invoking enterprise liability, insurance, loss-spreading, deterrence, deep pockets, acting on behalf of the employer, and control justifications for the doctrine.[27] This approach, although criticised,[28] is a compromise reflecting the organic development of tort within an environment where no single theory has predominated,[29] although enterprise liability and loss-spreading tend to feature more strongly within vicarious liability and control has been downplayed.[30] Whilst none of these theories can alone explain the current doctrine, this is not problematic, provided an adequate method is available to balance their competing demands.

The akin to employment category of vicarious liability offers the possibility of the doctrine applying to the torts of non-natural persons.[31] Further, the vicarious liability justifications used by courts, broadly point towards vicarious liability for AI systems when used in the place of employees. Applying these justifications, enterprises which use such technologies should internalise the risks that they generate and spread this loss or their related insurance costs to their customers, shareholders, or others with financial interests in their activities. It would also encourage them to introduce risk management systems in their use of AI systems, for instance regularly monitoring their behaviour, promoting safety, and ensuring that the systems are regularly updated. Whilst the control justification has been downplayed, in some cases, employer control over AI systems may be lacking, or control may be exercised by more than one entity or instead by the manufacturer/producer/developer. It is also possible that the employer's relationship with the system may be more in the nature of a relationship with a true independent contractor,[32] with the system not being integrated into or controlled by the employer. However, vicarious liability is able to cope

26 Glanville Williams, 'Vicarious Liability and the Master's Indemnity' (1957) 20 *MLR* 220, 231.

27 *CCWS* (n 21) [34]–[37] (Lord Phillips); *BXB* (n 21) [58] (Lord Burrows).

28 Stevens, *Torts and Rights* (n 16) 259.

29 *JGE* (n 26) [10] (MacDuff J); TT Arvind, 'Scholars of Tort Law' (2021) PN 114, 116–7; note also Williams, 'Master's Indemnity' (n 27) 231.

30 For example, *Cox v Ministry of Justice* [2016] UKSC 10, [2016] AC 660 [29] (Lord Reid); *Various Claimants v Barclays Bank plc* [2020] UKSC 13, [2020] AC 973 [13]–[14] (Baroness Hale).

31 Phillip Morgan, 'Vicarious Liability for Group Companies: The Final Frontier of Vicarious Liability?' (2015) 31 *PN* 276.

32 There being no vicarious liability for true independent contractors: *D & F Estates Ltd v Church Commissioners for England* [1989] AC 177 (HL), 208 (Lord Bridge); *Salsbury v Woodland* [1970] 1 QB 324 (CA), 336 (Widgery LJ).

with these eventualities via dual vicarious liability or by considering if the system is in fact akin to an employee of the manufacturer/producer/developer instead. The latter may be the case where the employer leases the system and where the system is integrated into the lessor's enterprise and controlled by the latter. However, there is currently a fundamental objection to establishing vicarious liability for AI systems.

1 Property Not Person

To facilitate modern commerce and investment we grant legal personality to companies. Legal personality for AI systems has been debated amongst scholars.[33] At one stage, the European Parliament suggested a form of electronic personhood.[34] This has, however, been rejected[35] by most legal systems. Denying AI systems legal personality appears to be influenced by the fact that making them legal persons would potentially shift risk and responsibility away from those currently responsible, protecting them from liability,[36] and shift liability to an impecunious entity. It would inadvertently replicate judgment-proofing structures which are used by enterprises, particularly in hazardous industries, to evade the payment of damages for the harms that their activities cause to others.[37] To insulate technology companies from liability and place liability on an impecunious system seems odd, and is counter both to correcting harm caused by such systems, making those that benefit from them pay for the harm that they cause, and deterring future harms.[38] Additionally, there are many forms of AI system, and legal personality, if it ever proves required for a particular form of AI, is unlikely to be required for most systems – it would be strange to say the least to grant legal personality to an iPhone. However, this is an over-simplistic approach to legal personality as it fails to consider that there may be different forms of personhood that the law can accommodate.

The rejection of legal personality means that the AI systems themselves are not persons, they are property – either a form of personal property (where they are embodied), real property when embodied in a building, or intellectual property, or

[33] Simon Chesterman, 'Artificial Intelligence and the Limits of Legal Personality' (2020) 69 *ICLQ* 819; Robert van den Hoven van Genderen, 'Legal Personhood in the Age of Artificially Intelligence Robots' in Woodrow Barfield and Ugo Pagallo (eds), *Research Handbook on the Law of Artificial Intelligence* (Edward Elgar Publishing 2018).

[34] European Parliament Resolution with Recommendations to the Commission on Civil Law Rules on Robotics (2015/2103(INL)) (16 February 2017) [59(f)].

[35] Janosch Delcker, 'Europe Divided over Robot "Personhood"' (*Politico*, 11 April 2018) <www.politico.eu/article/europe-divided-over-robot-ai-artificial-intelligence-personhood/>; cf Ugo Pagallo, 'Apples, Oranges, Robots: Four Misunderstandings in Today's Debate on the Legal Status of AI Systems' (2018) 376 *Phil Trans R Soc A* 20180168.

[36] Chesterman (n 34); Caroline Cauffman, 'Robo-Liability: The European Union in Search of the Best Way to Deal with Liability for Damage Caused by Artificial Intelligence' (2018) 25 *MJECL* 527, 531–532; Jacob Turner, *Robot Rules* (Palgrave 2019) 191.

[37] See generally Stephen Gilles, 'The Judgment-Proof Society' (2006) 63 *Washington & Lee LR* 603; Lynn LoPucki, 'The Death of Liability' (1996) 106 *Yale LJ* 1; Steven Shavell, 'The Judgment Proof Problem' (1986) 6 *IRLE* 45; Lynn LoPucki, 'Virtual Judgment Proofing: A Rejoinder' (1998) 107 *Yale LJ* 1413; Lynn LoPucki, 'The Essential Structure of Judgment Proofing' (1999) 51 *Stanford LR* 147.

[38] Chesterman (n 34).

a combination thereof. Only persons, legal or natural, can commit torts.[39] We do not hold property to account at law. Property cannot commit a tort. It also cannot hold assets sufficient to meet judgment. Given the abolition of deodands,[40] apart from rare cases, it is not subject to legal seizure if it causes harm. Instead we hold those associated with it to account.[41]

B *Rejection of Master's Tort Theory*

That an AI system itself cannot commit a tort has significant consequences for vicarious liability. There are two theoretical models of how such liability works, which are known as the master's tort model and the servant's tort model. The first is an agency model which attributes conduct, such that the master themselves commits the tort. The second, which has become the orthodox model, attributes liability, and is a strict liability model.[42]

The distinction between the two models was of some importance in the era of widespread tort immunities. Where the employee has a substantive immunity, a master's tort model meant that the master remains liable since their liability is not parasitic on their employee's liability. Although, where the employee's immunity is merely procedural, and not substantive, it does not make any difference which of the two models is adopted.[43] With the elimination of most such immunities, there were few circumstances where the adoption of either theory over the other would make a practical difference.[44] This may explain why the distinction is often ignored by both courts and commentators. Where the theory adopted would make a difference, courts are guided by 'pragmatic considerations',[45] rather than theory.

Typical objections to the master's tort theory model include the fact that it is an artificial legal fiction, which has the potential to blur the distinction between primary and secondary liability and does not fit within either; that with vicarious liability, both the master and the servant are jointly liable, whereas a master's tort theory makes only the master liable; that the theory is inconsistent with how such cases are pleaded,[46] since an employer is not held liable for their own tort, but rather they are held vicariously liable for their employee's tort; and that it also conflicts with the rules otherwise used to attribute actions to companies.[47] It also fails to account for how the tort is established; for instance, where it is alleged that the employer is

39 See Gerhard Wagner, 'Robot, Inc.: Personhood for Autonomous Systems?' (2019) 88 *Fordham LR* 591.
40 Deodands Act 1846.
41 Note Van Genderen (n 34) 245–246.
42 Patrick Atiyah, *Vicarious Liability in the Law of Torts* (Butterworths 1967) 6.
43 Ibid. 7–8.
44 Stevens, *Torts and Rights* (n 16) 262.
45 Atiyah (n 43) 7.
46 Paula Giliker, *Vicarious Liability in Tort: A Comparative Perspective* (Cambridge University Press 2010) 13–15; Atiyah (n 43) 8–10; cf Stevens, *Torts and Rights* (n 16) 260.
47 Nicholas McBride and Roderick Bagshaw, *Tort Law* (6th edn, Pearson 2018) 856.

vicariously liable for their employee's negligence, we examine the employee's duty of care and whether or not the employee is in breach of it. Questions concerning standards of care and remoteness are also assessed from the employee's position.[48]

Perhaps more problematically for the master's tort theory is that it brings into question the scope of vicarious liability. Vicarious liability now includes an employee's intentional torts, for instance, sexual abuse torts in a residential care setting. This expansion was heavily influenced by loss-spreading theories of vicarious liability,[49] which are intimately connected with insurance. If the employer had committed the intentional tort, rather than merely being liable for the tort of the employee, it would not be insurable since one cannot insure oneself for one's own intentional tort.[50] The master's tort theory renders insurance-based loss-spreading arguments in such contexts otiose.

Notwithstanding academic attempts to revive the master's tort doctrine,[51] perhaps motivated by the fact that a servant's tort model is a problematic obstacle to attempts to explain tort in solely corrective justice terms,[52] the master's tort theory has been rejected by the highest courts in Canada, Australia, and the United Kingdom.[53]

Although the servant's tort theory may accommodate an employee's procedural immunities, which do not prevent vicarious liability claims against their employer, where the servant themselves does not owe a duty to the victim, this is fatal to the vicarious liability claim. This is highly significant for AI systems. AI systems are property not persons. They thus enjoy both a substantive and a procedural immunity.[54] They cannot owe duties and therefore cannot commit torts. They also cannot be subject to a tort claim. Under the existing common law, whereby vicarious liability is parasitic on a servant's tort, there is therefore no vicarious liability for AI systems. An obscure technical doctrine within the law of vicarious liability, which does not consider the justifications and purposes of vicarious liability, appears to rule out common law vicarious liability for AI systems.

C *A Liability Gap*

Systems will stand in the shoes of employee tortfeasors, and systems cannot commit torts. With human in/on the loop systems, it will still be possible to bring

[48] Atiyah (n 43) 7–8.

[49] *Bazley* (n 24); *Lister v Hesley Hall Ltd* [2001] UKHL 22, [2002] 1 AC 215.

[50] Note Merkin and Steele (n 12) 322; also Anthony Gray, *Vicarious Liability: Critique and Reform* (Hart Publishing 2018) 179–180.

[51] Stevens, *Torts and Rights* (n 16). Note also Glanville Williams, 'Vicarious Liability: Tort of the Master or of the Servant?' (1956) 72 *LQR* 522.

[52] Note Ernest Weinrib, *The Idea of Private Law* (Oxford University Press 2012) 186.

[53] Gray (n 51) 264; *Dubai Aluminium Company Ltd v Salaam* [2002] UKHL 48, [2003] 2 AC 366 [155] (Lord Millett); *Majrowski v Guy's and St Thomas's NHS Trust* [2006] UKHL 34, [2007] 1 AC 224 [7], [14–] [15] (Lord Nicholls), [68] (Baroness Hale); *Staveley Iron and Chemical Co v Jones* [1956] AC 627 (HL); *Imperial Chemical Industries Ltd v Shatwell* [1965] AC 656 (HL).

[54] Although there are rare exceptions, for example, admiralty claims in rem. Applying analogous procedures to AI systems would be odd in the context of unembodied systems, and even where embodied in many cases, they will not be embodied in large, high-value products such as ships.

actions against the operator or supervisor for negligence in their operation or supervision of the system and also against their employer via vicarious liability for the operator's/supervisor's tort. However, this route is not available for fully autonomous systems. The failure of vicarious liability to account for autonomous AI systems prima facie appears to violate tech-impartiality, unless this substitution of technology for employees does not create a liability gap and sufficient victim protection is found in alternative claims of equal value. If not, there is a risk that employing enterprises will no longer be held to account, tort deterrence will be perverted, and victims will be stripped of their rights. We must now examine the alternative actions.

Whilst some AI manufacturers, particularly those in the autonomous vehicle ('AV') domain, such as Volvo, have publicly declared that they will accept liability if their system causes an accident,[55] most deployed AI technologies are not accompanied by such assurances. Further, accidents are only one of a wide range of potential harms that may be caused by AI systems. Notwithstanding the absence of vicarious liability, unlike employees, with AI systems there will be potential alternative claims against a broad range of actors including manufacturers, designers, developers, testers, maintainers, and not just the employer of the system. However, as set out below, due to a number of serious problems with these claims in an AI context, particularly if the system is evolving and deploys machine learning, this will not offset the loss of the vicarious liability action.

IV NEGLIGENCE

Negligence is a fault-based tort. Its flexibility means that it has the potential to be deployed in an AI context.[56] It requires a duty of care between the defendant and the claimant, that duty must be breached, that breach must cause the claimant injury (which must be of a legally recognisable type of damage), the duty must relate to the kind of damage suffered,[57] and that damage cannot be too remote. Such claims may potentially be brought against manufacturers, programmers, designers, employers/users, and so on, provided they owe a duty of care to the claimant.

Analogously to their position with employees, it is likely that employers of AI technologies will owe a duty of care to select an appropriate system for the task, to appropriately monitor it, and to maintain it.[58] That said, it should be noted that AI

[55] 'Who Is Responsible for a Driverless Car Accident?' (*BBC*, 8 October 2015) <www.bbc.co.uk/news/technology-34475031>.

[56] Note Jonathan Morgan, 'Torts and Technology' in Roger Brownsword, Eloise Scotford and Karen Yeung (eds), *The Oxford Handbook of Law, Regulation and Technology* (Oxford University Press 2017) 522.

[57] *Caparo Industries Plc v Dickman* [1990] 2 AC 605 (HL); *South Australia Asset Management Corp v York Montague Ltd* [1997] AC 191 (HL).

[58] Expert Group on Liability and New Technologies, *New Technologies Formation, Liability for Artificial Intelligence and Other Emerging Digital Technologies* (European Union 2019) 44.

technologies are becoming so ubiquitous that some who employ such technologies will not understand them or be able to predict their behaviour,[59] or they may not be aware that the system uses such technology. Manufacturers also owe duties of care to the world at large for negligence in the production of their goods and duties to warn of non-obvious risks, and analogous duties have also been placed on designers, repairers, maintainers, and distributors of products.[60] It is likely that programmers, developers, and those responsible for training data will hold similar duties. Particularly in the context of machine leaning and interconnected Internet of Things systems, producers may also owe a duty of care to monitor the product after they have put it into circulation.[61]

In assessing whether there is a breach of duty, courts will consider whether the defendant met the required standard of care, which is that of the reasonable person in the position of the defendant, which in this context is that of the ordinary competent practitioner in the relevant calling.[62] Thus, the standard is that of a reasonable AI designer, programmer, and so on. This will require examining relevant industry practices and opinions,[63] and it is likely that courts will be guided by soft law, such as ISO and IEEE standards and Government Guidelines, to determine what the appropriate standards of care are. Industry practices may therefore gain binding legal effect through their incorporation into the tort of negligence.[64] Thus, there may be a breach of duty where harm has resulted from the manufacturer using the wrong type of sensors in an embodied AI system, where the user deployed the system in an inappropriate context, or where a designer, without good reason, did not follow widely used international design practices, guidelines, and codes.

It is important to realise that the designer is not necessarily the person responsible for the harm.[65] Many parties may be involved in the creation, commercialisation, and operation of an AI system.[66] Therefore, it may be very difficult to determine which party (if any) is liable for the damage. Systems may consist of multiple component parts – there may be different entities responsible for (a) the technology in which the AI system is embodied; (b) the technology which controls this platform;

59 Mark Geistfeld, 'A Roadmap for Autonomous Vehicles: State Tort Liability, Automobile Insurance, and Federal Safety Regulation' (2017) 105 *Calif LR* 1611, 1621.

60 *Donoghue v Stevenson* [1932] AC 562 (HL); Michael Jones, Anthony Dugdale and Mark Simpson (eds), *Clerk & Lindsell on Torts* (23rd edn, Sweet & Maxwell 2020) [10–09]–[10–12].

61 Expert Group on Liability and New Technologies (n 59) 44; Matt Hervey and Matthew Lavy, *The Law of Artificial Intelligence* (Sweet & Maxwell 2021) para 5-012.

62 Charles Walton and others, *Charlesworth & Percy on Negligence* (14th edn, Sweet & Maxwell 2018) para 10-03.

63 *AB v Tameside and Glossop HA* [1997] PNLR 140 (CA).

64 Stephan Kirste, 'Concept and Validity of Law' in Pauline Westerman, Jaap Hage, Stephan Kirste and Anne Ruth Mackor (eds), *Legal Validity and Soft Law* (Springer 2018) 50.

65 Mark Lemley and Bryan Casey, 'Remedies for Robots' (2019) 86 *U Chi LR* 1311, 1378–1379.

66 Natalia Porto and Daniel Preiskel, 'United Kingdom Chapter' in Alain Bensoussan and Jérémy Bensoussan (eds), *Comparative Handbook: Robotic Technologies Law* (Larcier 2016) 346–347; Miriam Buiten, 'Towards Intelligent Regulation of Artificial Intelligence' (2019) 10 *EJRR* 41.

(c) the learning systems; (d) the data on which that system was trained;[67] and (e) updates to the system.[68] The system may also be interconnected with other systems, which share information,[69] and these may include those outside the control of the employer, for instance, in an AV context, the highway infrastructure systems and other AVs.[70] Where open source software is used, particularly when it has been developed in a collaborative, public manner, it may have many authors. Further, particularly given the internationality of technology, it might not be possible to establish jurisdiction over some of these potential parties.

The complexity of AI systems and their inputs means that it may be extremely difficult to identify the relevant tortfeasor. Linking inputs and outputs may be particularly hard with autonomous systems. Unlike a human tortfeasor, the system may offer no rationale for its decisions. Further, adaptability, interactivity, and autonomy will make it particularly difficult for users to prove that manufacturers, developers, and designers did not meet the required standard of care.[71] The behaviour of some systems may vary significantly, even after a short period of time, depending on their human caretakers,[72] and as Pagallo notes, 'the capacity of such machines to gain knowledge and skills from interaction with human caretakers, suggest that the fault would rarely fall on the designers, manufacturers or suppliers'.[73] Such evidence may be difficult to obtain and extremely difficult to comprehend, and it may necessitate specialised expert evidence. This means that the cost of bringing such actions may be high and may only be viable in larger-value actions.[74] However, it should be noted that there will also be cases where AI systems make the determination of fault easier than relying on fallible human witnesses, for instance, in an AV accident context where the AV's system produces accurate logs and recorded footage and a third party is responsible for the accident.[75]

Once duty and breach have been established, the issue of causation arises. The models of causation used by negligence require a tracing-back process, whereby the harm is traced back to a breach of duty committed by a person. The number of potential parties involved in an AI system further complicates this process.[76] The complexity of AI systems complicates proof and may make proving causation of damage extremely difficult.[77] Establishing causation involving AI systems may require

67 Chris Reed, 'How Should We Regulate Artificial Intelligence?' (2018) 376 *Philos Trans A* 20170360.

68 Expert Group on Liability and New Technologies (n 59) 21.

69 Ugo Pagallo, *The Laws of Robots, Crimes, Contracts, and Torts* (Springer 2013) x.

70 Hubbard, 'Allocating' (n 14) 31.

71 Pagallo, *The Laws of Robots* (n 70) 117; F Patrick Hubbard, 'Sophisticated Robots: Balancing Liability, Regulation, and Innovation' (2014) 66 *Fla LR* 1803, 1851–1853.

72 Pagallo, *The Laws of Robots* (n 70) 124.

73 Ibid. 126.

74 Hubbard, 'Allocating' (n 14) 43.

75 Note Surden and Williams (n 5) 180.

76 Jos Lehmann, Joost Breuker and Bob Brouwer, 'Causation in AI and Law' [2004] *AIL* 279, 280–286.

77 Chris Holder, Vikram Khurana, Faye Harrison and Louisa Jacobs, 'Robotics and Law: Key Legal and Regulatory Implications of the Robotics Age (Part I of II)' (2016) 32 *CLSR* 383, 386; Hubbard, 'Allocating' (n 14) 42.

significant forensics, simulations, and examination of logs where available. This may lead to protracted and costly litigation, delaying or denying victim compensation. The cost and expertise necessary to do this are likely to be significantly more expensive than those required to establish fault where the harm only involves human actors. These costs may not be viable in smaller-value claims. It is possible that we will need to know what decisions an algorithm made, and how it reached them.

Further, causation is extremely problematic in a machine learning context, particularly where artificial neural networks are used. The latter processes data in a non-linear fashion, and it may be extremely difficult to explain the reasons why a system produced a particular outcome.[78] With some systems, a black-box problem results, where their opaqueness means that we cannot understand or explain how or why the system produced a particular result. This causes the traditional common law tests of causation to fail.[79] Whilst the common law has adapted its causation tests, particularly in the context of toxic torts, such that it is able to deal with multiple causes, there is still a requirement to prove a link between the wrong and the harm, which might not be possible in some AI contexts. It is also possible that defendants may seek to rely on the doctrine of novus actus interveniens where, post-delivery, a machine learning system is exposed to unusual circumstances, resulting in the system learning inappropriate responses, or where the system has been hacked.[80]

The evidential doctrine of *res ipsa loquitur*, a doctrine where the harm is assumed to be caused by the defendant's negligence, where the harm should not have occurred without negligence, may assist claimants.[81] For instance, it has been used to establish liability where software caused inexplicable acceleration in motor vehicles, even where the exact error in code was not locatable.[82] However, for this doctrine to apply, the thing that inflicted the harm needs to be under the sole management and control of the defendant.[83] It is thus not a complete solution in the AI system context,[84] since it will often be the case that the system is not under the sole management and control of the defendant.[85] Proposals have been made at the European level to reverse

78 John Buyers, *Artificial Intelligence, The Practical Legal Issues* (Law Brief Publishing 2018) 14, 22.

79 Yavar Bathaee, 'The Artificial Intelligence Black Box and the Failure of Intent and Causation' (2018) 31 *Harv JL&T* 889; Curtis Karnow, 'Liability for Distributed Artificial Intelligences' (1996) 11 *Berkeley Tech LJ* 147.

80 Hervey and Lavy (n 62) para 5-023.

81 *Scott v The London and St Katherine Docks Company* (1865) 3 H&C 596; 159 ER 665 (Exc).

82 *In re Toyota Motor Corp. Unintended Acceleration Marketing, Sales Practices, and Products Liability Litigation* (US DC, CD Cal, 2013) 978 FSupp2d 1053; doctrine also applied to an autopilot system (*Nelson v American Airlines, Inc.* (CA, FD, D4, Cal) (1968) 263 CalApp2d 742; 70 CalRptr 33); David Vladeck, 'Machines without Principals: Liability Rules and Artificial Intelligence' (2014) 89 *Wash LR* 117, 142–144.

83 Jones, Dugdale and Simpson (n 61) para 7-205.

84 Note Singapore Academy of Law, *Report on the Attribution of Civil Liability for Accidents Involving Autonomous Cars* (SAL LRC, 2020) [5.12]–[5.13]; cf Bryan Casey, 'Robot Ipsa Loquitur' (2019) 108 *Geo LJ* 225, 269–273.

85 Buyers (n 79) 30.

the burden of proof where the system has failed to log or does not provide reasonable access to logged data to the claimants.[86] These recommendations, of course, do not apply outside the European Union, but they offer a potential model to overcome the problem of proof. However, due to long limitation periods in some torts, and the fact that in some cases the breach of duty might not be discovered until many years later, this may produce a significant data storage burden.

A claim of negligence also presupposes foreseeability of harm. A defendant is not liable for all of the damage they have caused. The damage must also be sufficiently connected with the breach of duty. Different labels are used for this concept: legal causation and proximate causation are used in the United States, whereas in Commonwealth jurisdictions, remoteness of damage is the dominant terminology.[87] This concept sets boundaries on the scope of liability; a defendant is only liable for damage of a kind which would have been reasonably foreseeable at the time of the breach of duty. However, a reasonable person in the defendant's position need not foresee the extent of the damage or the mechanism by which it was caused.[88]

This requirement may be problematic in an AI context, particularly since it is assessed at the time of the breach of duty and not at the time the harm was suffered. The systems may be so complex that they may perform actions which are unforeseeable and which result in unforeseeable harm,[89] particularly where they draw on constantly shifting vast real-world data, or the internet,[90] interact with other systems,[91] where AI has itself helped design the relevant controlling algorithms,[92] or where the systems continue to learn from interacting with their surrounding environment once they have left the hands of the designer/producer/supplier.[93] Systems may also be unpredictable by design.[94] Indeed, this unpredictability can give them the edge over humans. As Pagallo notes, '[e]ven the best-intentioned and best-informed designer cannot foresee all the possible outcomes of robotic behaviour.'[95]

It is clear that AI poses real problems to any claim based on the tort of negligence.

86 Expert Group on Liability and New Technologies (n 59) 2.

87 Stevens, *Torts and Rights* (n 16) 152.

88 *Overseas Tankship (UK) Ltd v Morts Dock & Engineering Co Ltd (the Wagon Mound No 1)* [1961] AC 388 (PC); *Overseas Tankship (UK) Ltd v The Miller Steamship Co Pty (the Wagon Mound No 2)* [1967] 1 AC 617 (PC); Walton (n 63) [5–128].

89 Woodrow Barfield, 'Towards a Law of Artificial Intelligence' in Barfield and Pagallo (n 34) 4.

90 Jason Miller and Ian Kerr, 'Delegation, Relinquishment, and Responsibility: The Prospect of Expert Robots' in Calo, Froomkin and Kerr (n 8) 107; Curtis Karnow, 'The Application of Traditional Tort Theory to Embodied Machine Intelligence' in Calo, Froomkin, and Kerr (n 8) 60.

91 Expert Group on Liability and New Technologies (n 59) 54.

92 Woodrow Barfield, 'Liability for Autonomous and Artificially Intelligent Robots' (2018) 9 *Paladyn, Journal of Behavioral Robotics* 193, 199.

93 Pagallo, *The Laws of Robots* (n 70) 47.

94 Miller and Kerr (n 91) 107.

95 Pagallo, *The Laws of Robots* (n 70) 138. Note also Bathaee (n 80) 923–925.

V PRODUCT LIABILITY

In addition to claims in negligence, victims may also resort to product liability claims. Space permits only a brief examination of the system found in the United Kingdom and Europe.[96]

Product liability is a form of strict liability. It was harmonised across the EU through the EU Product Liability Directive 1985 ('PLD'). This has been implemented into English law through the Consumer Protection Act 1987 ('CPA'), which is still in force. The CPA defines products as 'any goods or electricity' (the PLD uses the word 'movables' instead of goods);[97] thus, whilst the provision may include embodied AI systems which are provided with the software already embodied within them, or updates provided via a tangible medium, there are real problems in applying this to other AI systems, software, or defective updates provided electronically.[98]

The regime makes producers, suppliers, or importers liable for damage resulting from defective products.[99] Defective is defined as where the 'safety of the product is not such as persons generally are entitled to expect',[100] and in determining this, the manner and purposes for which the product has been marketed and what might reasonably be expected to be done with or in relation to the product are considered.[101] With self-learning systems, it is unclear if unpredictable deviations will be treated as defects.[102]

The claimant will need to identify and prove the defect. Particularly within a sophisticated, opaque, and interconnected AI context, this may be an extremely difficult and costly exercise requiring significant expertise.[103] The defect needs to be present at the relevant time, that is, the time when the product was supplied, otherwise the defendant has a defence to the claim.[104] This means that the regime has trouble accommodating claims arising from updates to systems, third-party activities, interconnected systems, data sharing, and post-supply self-learning.[105]

96 Although other systems of product liability will also be challenged, see for example: Kenneth Abraham and Robert Rabin, 'Automated Vehicles and Manufacturer Responsibility for Accidents: A New Legal Regime for a New Era' (2019) 105 *Va LR* 127. For a detailed discussion of the application of US products liability regime to AVs see: Geistfeld (n 60) 1632–1669.

97 PLD Article 2.

98 Ken Oliphant and Vanessa Wilcox, 'Product Liability in England and Wales' in Piotr Machnikowski (ed), *European Product Liability: An Analysis of the State of the Art in the Era of New Technologies* (Intersentia 2016) 204; Hervey and Lavy (n 62) para 5-040; Roderick Bagshaw, 'Product Liability: Autonomous Ships' in Baris Soyer and Andrew Tettenborn (eds) *Artificial Intelligence and Autonomous Shipping* (Hart Publishing 2021) 119.

99 CPA s 2.

100 CPA s 3(1); PLD Article 6 is worded slightly differently: '[a] product is defective when it does not provide the safety which a person is entitled to expect'.

101 CPA s 3(2).

102 Expert Group on Liability and New Technologies (n 59) 28.

103 Ibid. 28.

104 Under CPA s 4.

105 Note Paulius Cerka, Jurgita Grigiene, and Gintare Sirbikyt, 'Liability for Damages Caused by Artificial Intelligence' (2015) 31 *CLSR* 376, 386.

Likewise the defect must cause the damage. Similar problems with proving causation are present as with a claim in negligence, although foreseeability of damage is not required.[106] However, damage is much more narrowly defined than within the tort of negligence. For the purposes of the CPA claim, damage is defined as death or personal injury or loss of or damage to any property (including land),[107] but not to the defective product itself. For property damage, the property needs to be of a description ordinarily intended for private use, occupation, or consumption and also intended by the person suffering the loss or damage mainly for his own private use, occupation, or consumption.[108] This means that economic loss (for instance, that caused by a malfunctioning investment robo-adviser) or damage to non-consumer property is not included. This limits the application of the CPA regime, particularly in a commercial context.

Further weakening the claimant's position in an AI context is the state-of-the-art defence. Not all member states have chosen to implement this defence (it is optional), but it is found within the CPA. This defence means that the defendant is protected from liability if they can show that 'the state of scientific and technical knowledge at the relevant time was not such that a producer of products of the same description as the product in question might be expected to have discovered the defect if it had existed in his products while they were under his control'.[109] Whilst a fairly narrow interpretation is given to this defence[110] since many defects, particularly with autonomous systems involving machine learning, might not be discoverable under the existing state of scientific and technical knowledge until after an accident,[111] this defence may render the CPA claim of limited value.

As with negligence, the need for costly expert evidence to establish defectiveness, causation, and to counter any state-of-the-art defence,[112] means that this claim against the supplier/producer/importer is a poor substitute for the victim in place of the vicarious liability claim against the system's employer. Given the internationality of the many parties that may be involved in the design, development, and manufacture of AI systems, product liability claims may be further hampered by the fact that evidence may be located overseas.[113] Due to their costs, product liability claims are more viable as group/class actions. Further, the CPA also contains a limitation-longstop provision of ten years, even if the cause of action itself has not yet accrued.[114] Since

106 Jones, Dugdale and Simpson (n 61) para 10–64.

107 CPA s 5.

108 CPA s 5(3).

109 CPA s 4(1)(e).

110 Jonathan Morgan, 'Torts and Technology' (n 57) 534.

111 Note Expert Group on Liability and New Technologies (n 59) 28–29.

112 Department for Transport, *The Pathway to Driverless Cars: A Detailed Review of Regulations for Automated Vehicle Technologies* (DfT 2015).

113 Singapore Academy of Law (n 85) [17].

114 Limitation Act 1980 s 11A.

AI systems may be used for more than ten years after their supply, this cause of action may be time barred, even before the relevant incident occurs.

Whilst the EU is considering reforms to the PLD to deal with risks generated by digital products,[115] it is submitted that these cannot address the liability gap at the level of the employer. The proposed reforms, which will not apply to the UK's CPA regime, are dealt with in more detail in Chapter 9. Briefly the proposal proposes to: expand the scope of damage to include the loss, damage, and corruption of data; aims to confirm that 'product' includes software (regardless of how it was delivered, but excluding freely available open source software), AI systems, and AI-enabled goods;[116] brings software providers into the scope of the PLD; and includes post-delivery changes due to software updates or machine learning within the notion of defectiveness.[117] It is also proposes that where the manufacturer retains control of the product, the defectiveness assessment is to be extended beyond the moment of time at which the product was placed on the market.[118] The proposal also includes a power for national courts to order disclosure of relevant evidence to the claimant, where the claimant presents facts and evidence sufficient to support a plausible claim.[119] As with the European Commission's proposals on an AI Liability Act (see later) this will make little difference to disclosure obligations in common law jurisdictions.

The proposal sets out that the claimant retains the burden of proof in proving, defectiveness, damage, and the causal link between these,[120] but it also includes three rebuttable presumptions. The first is a presumption of defectiveness where: (a) the defendant fails to disclose required evidence, or (b) where the claimant establishes that the product does not comply with mandatory safety requirements intended to protect against the risk of damages which occurred,[121] or (c) where 'the claimant establishes that the damage was caused by an obvious malfunction of the product during normal use or under ordinary circumstances.'[122] The preamble to the draft directive expressly mentions that mandatory safety requirements may include data logging which is mandated by EU or national law.[123] The second is a presumption of causation where the product is defective, and the 'damage caused is of a kind typically consistent with the defect in question.'[124]

115 European Commission, Proposal for a Directive of the European Parliament and of the Council on liability for defective products (COM(2022) 495 final) ('Proposed Defective Products Directive'), Recital [3]; Explanatory Memorandum.

116 Recital [12]–[13], Article 4 (1).

117 Recital [37].

118 Article 6(1).

119 Article 8(1).

120 Article 9(1).

121 Article 9(2)(b).

122 Article 9(2)(c).

123 Recital [34].

124 Article 9(3).

The final rebuttable presumption relates to both damage and defectiveness. It applies where the claimant establishes that excessive difficulties exist, due to technical or scientific complexity, to prove defectiveness and/or causation, although the defendant has the right to contest that it is excessively difficult. In addition, the claimant also needs to demonstrate on the basis of 'sufficiently relevant evidence' that the product contributed to the damage and (where the problem of proof relates to defectiveness) that it is likely that it is defective or (where the problem of proof relates to causation) that its defectiveness is a likely cause of damage. The level of the threshold of 'likely' is not clear in the proposal. However, from the preamble, it is clear that the intention is to avoid a reversal in the burden of proof, implying that the threshold is not a low one.[125] This does not seem a major departure from existing civil liability systems, which often deploy rebuttable presumptions based on other established facts, but it may strengthen the position of claimants in some jurisdictions.

Notably, the proposal now requires member states to implement the state-of-the-art defence (it is no longer optional), which will weaken the position of claimants in some jurisdictions.[126]

VI NON-DELEGABLE DUTIES

Non-delegable duties are at the minimum 'not merely a duty to take care but a duty to provide that care is taken';[127] they may also be strict liability duties. A person who owes such a duty may be in breach, even if they have taken all due care, where they have entrusted its performance to another who is at fault. Non-delegable duties are often resorted to and adopted as a response to perceived inadequacies in vicarious liability.[128] Even if functionally similar,[129] vicarious liability and non-delegable duties are separate doctrines[130] and do not have the same policy rationales. There is no single theory which explains them.[131] Giliker argues that this is because they are merely 'gap-fillers' which courts resort to for policy reasons in the 'pursuit of social justice'.[132] Indeed, Williams described them as a 'logical fraud'.[133]

125 Recital [34].

126 Article 10; Recital [39].

127 *The Pass of Ballater* [1942] P112 (Admiralty) 117 (Langton J).

128 See Glanville Williams, 'Liability for Independent Contractors' (1956) 14 *CLJ* 180; John Murphy, 'Juridical Foundations of Common Law Non-delegable Duties' in Jason Neyers, Erika Chamberlain and Stephen Pitel (eds), *Emerging Issues in Tort Law* (Hart Publishing 2007) 371.

129 Jonathan Morgan, 'Vicarious Liability for Independent Contractors?' (2015) 31 *PN* 235.

130 *Woodland v Swimming Teachers Association* [2013] UKSC 66, [2014] AC 537 ('*Woodland*') [4] (Lord Sumption); Gray (n 51) 217–219.

131 *Woodland* (n 131) [6] (Lord Sumption).

132 Paula Giliker, 'Non-delegable Duties and Institutional Liability for the Negligence of Hospital Staff' (2017) 33 *PN* 109, 111–112.

133 Williams 'Liability for Independent Contractors' (n 129) 193; Gray (n 51) (recommends their abolition).

Examples of non-delegable duties include: an employer's duty to provide a safe system of work for its employees;[134] bailment;[135] *Rylands v Fletcher*;[136] the treatment of patients by hospitals;[137] extra-hazardous activities;[138] and where a person occasions operations on the highway, which cause dangers to highway users.[139] There will be some uses of AI systems that will potentially lead to claims against those that employ the systems based on non-delegable duties, for instance, in the context of robot surgery and robot cloakrooms. However, notwithstanding the existence of such claims in these particular circumstances, which would also be available if the work was instead carried out by an employee and are thus additional to vicarious liability, this does not address the liability gap caused by the absence of vicarious liability for AI systems generally.

A general non-delegable duty when using AI systems on the basis that to use them is an extra-hazardous activity is unlikely to be imposed. Firstly, this form of non-delegable duty has been severely curtailed in recent years. It has been rejected in Australia,[140] and within England, the principle is now considered 'anomalous' and 'unsatisfactory', and its application is seen as being 'truly exceptional' and to be 'kept as narrow as possible', applying only to 'activities that are exceptionally dangerous, whatever precautions are taken'.[141] Thus, many AI systems clearly pose insufficient risk of harm to trigger the doctrine. Further, the determination of what is extra-hazardous varies over time. Whilst some AI systems might be initially so considered, it is unlikely that as the use of AI systems become widespread, and we become accustomed to such systems, that they will be placed in this category.[142] Further, to impose such a duty would also violate tech-impartiality, since it would impose greater levels of liability on those who employ such technology over those who employ humans, even if the risk levels are the same, and in doing so, it would improperly stifle innovation.

In sum, the claims dealt with above do not offset the loss of the vicarious liability claim, and result in a liability gap.

[134] *McDermid v Nash Dredging* [1987] AC 906 (HL).

[135] Based on *Morris v CW Martin & Sons Ltd* [1966] 1 QB 716 (CA); Robert Stevens, 'Non-delegable Duties and Vicarious Liability' in Neyers, Chamberlain and Pitel (n 129) 337; cf Phillip Morgan, 'Vicarious Liability for Employee Theft: Muddling Vicarious Liability for Conversion with Non-delegable Duties' [2011] *LMCLQ* 172.

[136] (1868) LR 3 HL 330.

[137] *Woodland* (n 131) [23] (Lord Sumption).

[138] *Honeywill & Stein Ltd v Larkin Bros* [1934] 1 KB 191 (CA); *Biffa Waste Services Ltd v Maschinenfabrik Ernst Hese GmbH* [2008] EWCA Civ 1257, [2009] QB 725.

[139] Jones, Dugdale, and Simpson (n 61) paras 6–70 – 6–81.

[140] *Stevens v Brodribb Sawmilling Co Pty* 160 CLR 16, [1987] CLY 2621.

[141] *Biffa* (n 139) [78], [85] (Stanley Burton LJ).

[142] Karnow, 'The Application of Traditional Tort Theory' (n 91) 67–68; see also Hubbard, 'Sophisticated Robots' (n 72) 1864; Samir Chopra and Laurence White, *A Legal Theory for Autonomous Artificial Agents* (University of Michigan 2011) 132.

VII AEV ACT

Recognising these significant problems and the resulting liability gap, the UK Parliament has introduced a bespoke regime for AV accidents, which is found in the Automated and Electric Vehicles Act 2018. The statute introduces an insurer pays model. Where the accident is caused by an automated vehicle, the insurer is liable for the damage caused.[143] However, the introduction of this claim against the insurer does not affect any other person's liability.[144] This means the insurer can then seek contribution from other parties.[145] The justification for this approach is to ensure speedy and smooth compensation for victims,[146] and that insurers, unlike many third-party victims of AV accidents, are likely to have the resources to investigate, and bring claims against manufacturers, designers, and so on. They are also likely to be able to monitor common problems arising from different models of AVs. Deterrence and the forensic role of tort law is thus maintained. In the AV context, the same problems (and legal gaps) as with non-AV claims remain, but what the statute does is to shift these problems onto the insurer and away from the accident victim.

This statutory regime does not apply outside the AV context. Since motor vehicles (including AVs) are subject to compulsory insurance, this scheme is highly unlikely to be appropriate for many other forms of AI technology which are not subject to compulsory insurance. Compulsory insurance is quite rightly kept within very narrowly defined classes.[147] Whilst employers are required to insure against their liabilities for injuries sustained by their employees during the course of their employment,[148] they are not required to have public liability insurance for their employee's torts. To require them to insure all of the AI systems, they employ in relation to third-party injuries, so as to permit a similar system to the AEV Act to be applied to all other AI harms, would violate the principles of tech-impartiality. Further, we should be wary of any additional requirements for compulsory insurance within the AI system context. This is since such a requirement fails to appreciate the future ubiquity of such systems and also potentially excludes poorer enterprises, communities, and individuals from participating in these technological advances.

143 s 2.

144 s 2(7).

145 s 5.

146 Law Commission, *Automated Vehicles A Joint Preliminary Consultation Paper* (LC, CP No 240, 2018) para 6–26.

147 Which are found in: Road Traffic Act 1988; Employers' Liability (Compulsory Insurance) Act 1969; Nuclear Installations Act 1965; Riding Establishments Act 1964.

148 Employers' Liability (Compulsory Insurance) Act 1969 s 1(1).

VIII PROPOSALS

Space prohibits a detailed examination of all proposals to address the liability gap. Models have been proposed based on liability for children, animals,[149] slaves,[150] and non-fault systems. However, all of these models would not mirror liability for the employees replaced by the systems.

A *Children*

Unlike some civil law systems, in the English Common law, there is no parental vicarious liability for children, and liability for a child's act is based on parental fault.[151] A fault-based negligence system, as we have seen earlier, does not fill the gap left by the absence of vicarious liability.

B *Slaves*

Pagallo introduces the idea of a digital peculium: that is property which is held by the AI system itself. He proposes that liability for an AI system should be strict but limited to the system's peculium.[152] To create this system, Pagallo draws upon Roman slave law[153] and combines it with the Roman law doctrine of peculium. Slaves were essential to Roman trade and industry and often acted on behalf of their masters. However, slaves were not persons in law. Slaves, particularly those who worked in commerce had at their disposal money and assets, known as a peculium. Those dealing with slaves were limited in their contractual claims against the master to the slave's peculium.[154] The idea was that there was a balance between the slave's ability to do business, the claims of those who dealt with slaves, and their master's rights not to be negatively affected by the slave's activities.[155] However, where the master had authorised the transaction, generally or specifically, he would be liable in full.[156]

Nevertheless the limitation on liability proposed by Pagallo was not the system found in the Roman law of delict. Under Roman law, a slave who committed a delict made their master liable in full, and the liability was not limited to the wrongdoer's peculium; however, the master had the option to limit their liability to the value of the slave through noxal surrender, that is surrendering the slave to the

[149] Hubbard, 'Sophisticated Robots' (n 72) 1864; Chopra and White (n 143) 130–131.
[150] Pagallo, *The Laws of Robots* (n 70).
[151] Giliker, *Vicarious Liability* (n 47) ch 7.
[152] Pagallo, *The Laws of Robots* (n 70) 113.
[153] Ibid. 42.
[154] See Paul du Plessis, *Borkowski's Textbook on Roman Law* (6th edn, Oxford University Press 2020) 69, 288.
[155] Pagallo, *The Laws of Robots* (n 70) 103.
[156] Du Plessis (n 155) 289.

victim in place of paying the damages.[157] This produces a system of strict liability, but which is limitable up to the value of the delinquent.[158] The novelty of Pagallo's position is to both apply the peculium doctrine to tortious claims, and also then to AI systems.

Slaves may have been replaced by employees, and employees in turn by AI, but irrespective of the morality of drawing upon slave law it nevertheless seems odd to look at the ancient systems used for slaves and reason by analogy to these, rather than using the systems currently used for employees, who AI replaces. Pagallo's system produces a system of liability which is both more limited than Roman law itself and more limited than employee torts. With contract, parties would be likely to know that they were dealing with slaves/AI systems and may have chosen to contract on this basis, but with delict/tort, due to its impact on third parties, limiting such claims to the peculium may be disproportionate, since these parties may not have chosen to interact with a slave/AI system.[159] Essentially, Pagallo's proposal provides a system of limited liability, which is very different to vicarious liability and far more restricted. It is also open to abuse, and to judgment proofing since a peculium can be withdrawn, reduced at will, and can even be set at zero by the master.[160] Should a person injured by an AI powered vending machine really have their compensation limited to the coins held by the machine, and should it matter if the machine's coin bucket was emptied immediately prior to the accident? This system thus violates tech-impartiality. It may also not be suited to some modern AI conditions in that identifying the property held by the system, and drawing the parameters on the system (and thus its property), may be very difficult with interconnected systems.

It is also somewhat unusual to draw upon a system of liability which pre-dates the existence of liability insurance which in turn has radically shaped tort,[161] and which also predates the modern corporate enterprise, and core tort policies such as enterprise liability. Notably the Roman law quasi-delicts which provide for strict liability for innkeepers, shipowners, and stable keepers even for the acts of third parties,[162] were not so limited, and perhaps reflect a nascent enterprise liability. Drawing on

[157] Ibid. 94, 115; see also Barry Nicholas, *An Introduction to Roman law* (rev edn, Oxford University Press 2008) 223.

[158] Reinhard Zimmermann, *The Law of Obligations: Roman Foundations of the Civilian Tradition* (Oxford University Press 1996), 916–917, 1118.

[159] Even in such circumstances, there may be a role for limitation where all of the parties are sophisticated commercial parties (such as in the case of autonomous ship accidents), who can plan in advance and insure their interests on that basis but not when dealing with parties outside of this class (note Amalia Tzima and Phillip Morgan, 'Justifying Global Limitation of Liability for Maritime Claims in the Modern Business Environment' [2021] *LMCLQ* 306).

[160] See Nicholas (n 158) 68.

[161] Merkin and Steele (n 12); Kenneth Abraham, *The Liability Century* (Harv UP 2008); Tom Baker, 'Liability Insurance as Tort Regulation: Six Ways that Liability Insurance Shapes Tort Law in Action' (2005) 12 *Conn Ins LJ* 1.

[162] David Johnston, 'Limiting Liability: Roman Law and the Civil Law Tradition' (1995) 70 *Chi-Kent LR* 1515, 1524–1525.

more modern doctrines, which account for these changes would be more apt. Given the presence of liability insurance claims will not necessarily dissipate the wealth of the defendant. Limiting claims to the value of the peculium was a balance struck in an era prior to insurance, and never in the context of delict/tort. A better analogy for AI system liability would be to liability for an employee, which has continued into the modern era. Further, a liability system based on Roman slave law may less easily transplant into common law,[163] than a system which applies or which is designed by analogy to existing common law doctrines.

C *Animals*

Liability based on that used for animals has also been suggested.[164] With animals, again, whilst the analogy seems at first attractive in that they are property, autonomous, and learning, able to commit harms and often used for the purposes of profit, it suffers from a number of problems and is inappropriate. This is the same whether the model is based on the traditional common law model of liability for animals, as found in the US, or the newer statutory model found in England.

Firstly, unlike with animals, there is a potentially wide range of harms that might be caused by AI – not just accidents and trespasses (to the people, land, or goods). Schemes designed for the limited types of harm that might be inflicted by animals may be highly inappropriate for AI, for instance, for pure economic losses, competition wrongs, and privacy harms. More importantly, liability for animals is either significantly more onerous than with employees or significantly less onerous, depending on the context.

Under both the traditional common law approach and also under the English statutory approach, with dangerous species (such as a tiger), there is strict liability for any damage that they cause.[165] To adopt such an approach for AI would be significantly more onerous than vicarious liability for employees, since the latter requires the commission of a tort on the part of the employee and also a sufficient connection between the tort and the relationship. Further objections to applying this approach in the AI context mirror the objections to the extra-hazardous non-delegable duty approach above.

[163] Otto Kahn-Freund, 'On the Uses and Misuses of Comparative Law' (1974) 37 *MLR* 1; Mathias Siems, 'Malicious Legal Transplants' (2018) 38 *LS* 103; cf Alan Watson, 'Legal Transplants and Law Reform' (1976) 92 LQR 79; Alan Watson, *Legal Transplants* (2nd edn, University of Georgia Press 1993); Michele Graziadei, 'Comparative Law as the Study of Transplants and Receptions' in Law' in Mathias Reiman and Reinhard Zimmermann (eds), *The Oxford Handbook of Comparative Law* (Oxford University Press 2006).

[164] Hubbard, 'Sophisticated Robots' (n 72) 1864.

[165] Animals Act 1971 s 2(1); Jones, Dugdale, and Simpson (n 61) para 20-03, fn 14; James Goudkamp and Donal Nolan, *Winfield and Jolowicz on Tort* (20th edn, Sweet & Maxwell 2020) 495, [17-006]; 4 Am Jur 2d Animals para 63; Restatement (Second) of Torts para 507 (1977) ('Restatement'); Peter North, *Civil Liability for Animals* (Oxford University Press 2012).

For non-dangerous species, the common law rules and the English statutory regime diverge slightly. At common law, there is no liability for domestic animals unless the keeper knows or has reason to know that the animal has dangerous tendencies which are abnormal for animals of its class and that the harm results from these tendencies.[166] Section 2(2) of the Animals Act 1971 was intended to retain a similar form of liability;[167] however, its reference to characteristics 'not normally so found except at particular times or in particular circumstances' has been controversially interpreted by the courts in such a way that behaviour ordinary to a domestic species but only manifest at specific times, for instance, a horse when spooked or a dog when kicked, may also trigger liability, provided these characteristics are known to the keeper.[168]

If the non-dangerous animal liability approaches were applied by analogy to AI systems, both approaches would produce a significantly narrower liability exposure than vicarious liability for employees. Firstly, liability would not be present where the injury does not result from an uncommon characteristic; for instance, there would be no liability resulting from an animal/robot tripping or a diagnostic system misdiagnosing a disease due to a failure to properly scan an image. Vicarious liability includes situations where the harm results from an employee's conduct which does not stem from an uncommon characteristic, for instance, a kitchen worker slipping and dropping a heavy bag on a colleague, or a doctor misdiagnosing an illness due to momentary negligence, and this represents much of the field of such litigation. In addition, where the harm does stem from an uncommon characteristic, both models require knowledge on the part of the employer, which may not be present in a range of potential AI system harms, particularly with emerging behaviour, and in the light of the potential complexity of the systems and their inputs. Conversely, employer knowledge of an employee's characteristics is not required for a vicarious liability claim. Liability based on the model used for animals (either dangerous or non-dangerous) thus violates tech-impartiality, where AI systems replace employees.[169]

D *The European Parliament's Proposal*

The European Parliament has recommended a civil liability regime for AI.[170] In outline the proposal sets forth two regimes, which cover personal injury, property damage, and economic harms: strict liability for the operators of high-risk systems,[171]

[166] Restatement para 509. Goudkamp and Nolan (n 166) 495 para 17-006; McBride and Bagshaw (n 48) 460. Of course, there is also potential liability in ordinary negligence or in causing the animal to commit the harm, for instance, by setting one's dog on an enemy (see Restatement, para 518).

[167] Goudkamp and Nolan (n 166) para 17-010.

[168] See McBride and Bagshaw (n 48) 462–463; Goudkamp and Nolan (n 166) 499–500, para 17-013.

[169] This, of course, would not be the case where the system is a robot dog which replaces a companion animal.

[170] European Parliament resolution of 20 October 2020 with recommendations to the Commission on a civil liability regime for artificial intelligence (2020/2014(INL)).

[171] Article 4.

which is subject to compulsory insurance and a liability cap,[172] and fault-based liability for operators of other AI systems.[173]

Whilst the proposed regulation includes a definition of high-risk systems: '"high risk" means a significant potential in an autonomously operating AI-system to cause harm or damage to one or more persons in a manner that is random and goes beyond what can reasonably be expected…',[174] such systems are restricted to those listed in an annex to the regulation,[175] which is to be regularly reviewed, and will thus constitute a limited but shifting class. If this class is drawn broadly, the objections to this approach mirror those to the extra-hazardous activities approach above.

For non-high-risk systems, the proposal appears to reverse the burden of proof, the operator is not liable where they can prove that they were not at fault, in that either (a) the system was activated without their knowledge and where they had taken 'all reasonable and necessary measures to avoid such activation outside of the operator's control',[176] (b) they had observed due diligence in selecting, operating, monitoring, maintaining, and updating the system, or (c) where the harm of damage was caused by force majeure.[177] The operator is also liable where the harm is caused by an untraceable or impecunious third party who interfered with and modified the system.[178]

This approach is similar to some forms of vicarious liability found in some continental legal systems, for example, that of Germany,[179] and thus may be the proper and tech-impartial solution to these jurisdictions for dealing with the liability gap where AI systems replace employees. However, for the common law (which is now represented in the EU by Ireland), this would represent a significant narrowing of liability for AI systems, over that currently found for employees, and would violate tech-impartiality. In addition, the proposal's failure to address a number of other potential tortious harms, including reputational, dignitary, privacy, and trespass to the person or land (in the absence of physical harm), which could be committed by AI systems, means that it cannot fully address the liability gap present in the common law.

E *The European Commission's Proposal*

The European Commission has proposed an AI Liability Directive.[180] Its headline ambitions are to address the 'compensation gap',[181] by ensuring that victims injured

172 Articles 4(4) and 5.

173 Article 8.

174 Article 3(c).

175 Article 4(2).

176 Article 8(2)(a).

177 Article 8(2).

178 Article 8(3).

179 The employer is liable on the basis of their presumed fault unless they can prove otherwise (see para 831(1) BGB, note Giliker, *Vicarious Liability* (n 47) 26–28).

180 European Commission, Proposal for a Directive of the European Parliament and of the Council on adapting non-contractual civil liability rules to artificial intelligence ('AI Liability Directive') (COM(2022) 496 final).

181 AI Liability Directive, Recital [3], [8].

by AI systems receive 'equivalent protection' and 'level of redress' to those injured by other means.[182] The Commission also considers that the proposal will incentivise compliance with safety rules.[183] These ambitions, which may reflect a nascent notion of tech-impartiality, are justified by the Commission on the basis that this will promote trust in both the judicial system and AI technology.[184] However, the Commission's press release also speaks of 'putting consumers on an equal footing with manufacturers',[185] an ambition which may not be tech-impartial. Further, given the litigation resources of large technology firms this ambition is unlikely to be met. The proposal's limitations, perhaps motivated by need not to stifle innovation, ensure that the proposal is unlikely to meet its own stated objectives.

The European Commission has chosen to intervene in a minimal interim manner, subject to a review. The review will consider the appropriateness of a no-fault liability regime and compulsory insurance.[186] The Commission justifies its restricted intervention by stating that the systems which might endanger the general public and important rights such as rights to life, health, and property, 'are not yet widely available on the market'.[187] However, since the review is to take place five years after a two year transposition period (i.e., seven years after the Directive's entry into force) and given the pace of development, testing, and the current commercial availability of such systems (much of which are out of the public eye), this opinion may prove untimely.

The Commission acknowledges that AI characteristics, such as complexity, opacity, and autonomous behaviour,[188] and consequently high up-front litigation costs[189] render existing national fault-based liability systems problematic. In particular, they highlight the problem of proving causation.[190] The proposal is for a minimum harmonisation regime grafted onto the existing member state non-contractual fault-based civil liability systems.[191] Member states are also permitted to adopt or retain national rules which are more favourable to claimants.[192]

Two primary mechanisms are contained within the proposal, the rebuttable 'presumption of causality'[193] and a right to the disclosure of evidence relating

[182] Ibid., Explanatory Memo, Recital [3]. The European Commission's press release goes further and refers to the 'same standards of protection'. European Commission, Press Release, 'New Liability Rules on Products and AI to Protect Consumers and Foster Innovation' (*European Commission*, 28 September 2022) <https://ec.europa.eu/commission/presscorner/detail/en/ip_22_5807>.

[183] AI Liability Directive, Recital.

[184] Ibid., Recital [3], [5].

[185] European Commission, Press Release (n 183).

[186] Article 5(1)-(3).

[187] AI Liability Directive, Explanatory Memo.

[188] Recital [3].

[189] AI Liability Directive, Explanatory Memo.

[190] Recital [3].

[191] Article 1(2).

[192] Article 1(4).

[193] AI Liability Directive, Explanatory Memo; Recital [22], [29].

to high-risk AI systems.[194] These mechanisms also apply to subrogated claims.[195] Notwithstanding the headline description of the causation mechanism, there is a significant burden imposed on the claimant to trigger the presumption. It is also somewhat convoluted and more complex to engage than the common law doctrine of res ipsa loquitur. The proposal does not change the national definitions of fault, standards of care, burdens of proof, standards of proof, or notions of remoteness of damage, or approaches to multiple tortfeasors or contributory conduct (amongst others).[196] National definitions of causality are also maintained.[197] There is thus likely to be diversity in outcome in litigation from member state to member state.

The proposal applies only to highly autonomous systems. It does not apply to advisory AI systems, where a human actor acts after receiving information or advice from an AI system.[198] How far this exclusion extends within the category of human on the loop systems is not currently clear. It thus potentially excludes classes of case which also cause problems for existing tort systems. The proposal is directly linked to the EU's draft AI Act[199] and definitions within the proposed liability directive, for instance in relation to 'high-risk AI systems', 'provider', and 'user', are expressly linked to those contained within the AI Act.[200]

1 Rebuttable Presumption

The presumption contained in Article 4 is narrowly drawn, and the defendant has the right to rebut it.[201] The presumption establishes that for lower-risk systems, national courts are to presume a causal link between the defendant's fault and the AI system's output or failure to produce an output, where: (1) the claimant proves that the defendant or someone for whom they are responsible was in breach of a duty of care in national or EU law (or that the Article 3(5) presumption is triggered due to the defendant's failure to disclose evidence), and that duty was 'directly intended to protect against the damage that occurred',[202] (2) that it is 'reasonably likely' that the fault influenced the system's output, or lack of output,[203] and (3) the claimant demonstrates that the output or lack of output caused the damage.[204] Importantly, this only establishes an element of causation concerning the link between the defendant's fault and the output (or lack of output), and is not the same as establishing

[194] Article 1(1).
[195] Article 2(6)(b).
[196] AI Liability Directive, Explanatory Memo; Recital [10]; see also Article 1(3).
[197] Recital [10].
[198] Recital [15].
[199] Proposal for a Regulation of the European Parliament and of the Council laying down Harmonised Rules on Artificial Intelligence (Artificial Intelligence Act) and Amending Certain Union Legislative Acts (COM/2021/206 final) ('AI Act').
[200] Article 2(1)–(4).
[201] Article 4(7).
[202] Article 4(1)(a).
[203] Article 4(1)(b).
[204] Article 4(1)(c).

causation for the purposes of the tort, in that the claimant still needs to prove that the system itself caused the damage.[205] Unlike the proposal of the European Parliament the AI Liability Directive does not establish a rebuttable presumption of fault itself.

The presumption is somewhat narrower for high-risk systems. For high-risk systems, the same process is followed, save that proving fault is not sufficient, instead the claimant needs to prove that the defendant failed to comply with specific obligations contained within the AI Act, including where the defendant is the provider of the system and the data used to train, test, and validate the system did not meet the AI Act's quality criteria; the system did not meet the transparency, oversight, robustness, accuracy, or cybersecurity requirements of the AI Act;[206] and where the defendant is merely the user of the system that the defendant did not comply with their obligations under the AI Act to use/monitor the system in accordance with the instructions which accompany the system, or suspend its use; or exposed the system to data controlled by the defendant which was irrelevant to the system's intended purpose.[207] Critically with high-risk systems for a claimant's claim to succeed the claimant faces an additional hurdle over that of the victim of an incident involving a lower-risk system. To establish the tort both claimants will have to prove that the defendant was in breach of the duty of care, but to benefit from the presumption the claimant in a high-risk system incident will also need to prove that the defendant was in breach of a relevant AI Act obligation. Making the presumption less accessible to victims harmed by high-risk systems is odd, since such systems are more highly regulated because they represent a higher level of risk to victims.[208]

Further, this causation presumption only applies for lower-risk AI systems where the court considers that it is 'excessively difficult' for the claimant to prove causation,[209] and for high-risk systems, it does not apply 'where the defendant demonstrates that sufficient evidence and expertise is reasonably accessible for the claimant to prove the causal link'.[210] The stated purpose of this exception is to incentivise disclosure obligations.[211] A claimant relying solely on the rebuttable presumption to establish causation is thus likely to be in a weak position, since if a claimant benefits from the presumption by definition in many high-risk cases, they will lack access to the expertise necessary to counter the defendant's rebuttal. Moreover proving a breach of a duty, which is necessary to trigger the presumption might itself require significant forensic expertise, particularly within a 'many hands' context – where

205 AI Liability Directive, Explanatory Memo; Recital [22].
206 Article 4(2).
207 Article 4(3).
208 Orian Dheu, Jan De Bruyne, and Charlotte Ducuing, 'The European Commission's Approach to Extra-Contractual Liability and AI – A First Analysis and Evaluation of the Two Proposals' (2022) CiTiP Working Paper, 20, <https://lirias.kuleuven.be/3875635?limo=0>.
209 Article 4(5).
210 Article 4(4).
211 AI Liability Directive, Explanatory Memo.

many potential defendants are involved. It is therefore unlikely that this presumption will place consumers on an equal footing with manufacturers.

Additionally, the presumption does not apply to personal, non-professional uses of AI systems, unless the defendant 'materially interfered' with the conditions of the system's operations or 'if the defendant was required and able to determine the conditions of operation of the AI system and failed to do so.'[212] This difference may be motivated by a desire not to discourage consumer uptake of such systems and/ or by ideas of enterprise liability. However, notwithstanding the enterprise liability difference, from a tech-impartiality perspective this is problematic if it disapplies a presumption intended to provide a similar level of protection to victims of AI harms to victims of other harms. This also excludes many potential uses of autonomous vehicles, and much of the wide range of domestic robotics coming onto the market. It also leads to the problem that the use of some systems will regularly alternate between being covered by the presumption or not, even with the same user using the system to carry out tasks with the same risk profile. For instance, where an autonomous vehicle is used by an individual on the same day to travel to their doctor's surgery for a medical appointment, then commuting to work, then undertaking a journey as part of their employment, and then travelling on holiday; in relation to the user only elements of this day's journey will be covered by the presumption. From the victim's perspective their rights may thus only be discernible after examining which leg of this journey they were injured on. Likewise the legal and commercial structure used to provide and manage AI services may make a difference to victim rights against users.

2 Right of Access to Evidence

The second mechanism which the AI Liability Directive proposes is a 'right of access to evidence'. It applies only to high-risk AI systems.[213] The proposal establishes a disclosure regime, whereby on the claimant's request the court is permitted to order evidential disclosure from a user or provider in relation to a specific high-risk AI system suspected of having caused damage, where the claimant has undertaken all proportionate attempts at gathering the relevant evidence,[214] and where it is proportionate to do so, taking into account the legitimate interests of all parties, including third parties, and specifically protecting trade secrets and confidential information.[215] Where a defendant refuses to provide evidence to a potential claimant, they may also make such a request, but additionally a potential claimant is required to present facts and evidence which are sufficient to support the plausibility of their claim.[216]

212 Article 6(3).
213 Article 3(1).
214 Article 3(2).
215 Article 3(4).
216 Article 3(1).

The proposal introduces a rebuttable presumption that where a defendant user or provider refuses to comply with such an order to disclose or preserve evidence at its disposal,[217] that the court should presume that the defendant has not complied with the relevant duty of care. However, the defendant has a right to rebut this presumption.[218] This disclosure obligation may make little difference if applied in common law systems, or in some mixed jurisdictions. For instance, in an English, Irish, or Cypriot context,[219] the existing disclosure obligations within the English Civil Procedure Rules,[220] Irish Superior Court Rules,[221] and the Cypriot Civil Procedure Rules[222] would cover the disclosure obligation, and the sanctions for a defendant's non-compliance with the court's order to disclose may include inferences similar to the proposal's, but also the striking out all of parts of the defence,[223] which constitutes significantly stronger leverage to force disclosure compared to a mere rebuttable presumption relating to a single element of the claim. However, the proposed level of pre-proceedings disclosure for potential claimants may represent an expansion in court powers for some civil law jurisdictions which do not have discovery regimes comparable to common law jurisdictions.[224]

The rebuttable presumption potentially makes this disclosure obligation weak, particularly when compared to systems which include a sanction of striking out the defence. This is since a defendant may subsequently deploy evidence favourable to it at trial to rebut the presumption, whilst at the same time continuing to withhold potentially damaging evidence, to which the claimant does not have access. Further, this mechanism would not appear to level the playing field between consumers and manufacturers, since the mere provision of evidence, particularly when it consists of large quantities of complex data, does not address the problems that the claimant will have in interpreting it and identifying fault. Common law systems, which already have such disclosure obligations in place, also have significant problems in providing equivalent protection in tort to the victims of AI harms. Further, the limitation of this obligation to high-risk systems, does not address the problems encountered in litigation concerning other AI systems.

Whilst the proposal may represent some improvements on existing systems of liability, both mechanisms provided in the proposed AI Liability Directive fail to solve

[217] Ibid.

[218] Article 3(5).

[219] Nikitas Hatzimihail, 'Cyprus as a Mixed Legal System' (2013) 6 *JCLS* 37, 38–41, in Cyprus procedural law is purely common law, whereas private law is primarily common law.

[220] CPR Part 31.

[221] SCR Order 31; Commercial Litigation Association of Ireland, *Good Practice Discovery Guide* (2nd edn, CLAI 2015).

[222] Cyprus CPR Order 28.

[223] *Byers and others v Samba Financial Group* [2020] EWHC 853 (Ch); SCR Order 31, Rule 21; Cyprus CPR Order 28, Rule 12.

[224] Gloria de la Rosa, 'Taking Discovery in the European Union' (2013) 9 *ESJ* 982; cf ELI-UNIDROIT, *Model European Rules of Civil Procedure* (Oxford University Press 2021) Rules 100–103.

many of the core problems of AI liability, which have been identified in this chapter, including problems concerning duty, fault, remoteness, and 'many hands'. The proposal is therefore unlikely to bridge the liability gap. Further its interconnected nature with the proposed AI Act also makes it an inappropriate template for non-EU jurisdictions to follow.

F *No Fault/Funds*

There have also been proposals for no fault liability systems, either state sponsored, or run by the AI industry. One of the most developed is that of Karnow's 'Turing register'.[225] This proposal is for a voluntary system, whereby a centralised registry both certifies the system, and insures it. The cost of insurance is paid for by the manufacturer, who has obtained certification for their product, the premium being set by the registry based on the registry's assessment of the risk level of the product. Through this system the industry pools its risk. When the system injures a third party the registry pays for the harm caused, irrespective of fault. Essentially this is a privatised no fault system. Karnow argues that the certification branding which manufacturers will be able to display on their products will ensure that that system is attractive to them.

There are a considerable number of problems with a centralised no-fault scheme. Will the organisation have sufficient expertise to approve and vet all AI products? They will be required to deal with a broad range of technology, which is potentially unpredictable. Products will also evolve, and so a single approval process, certification, and premium is likely to be inappropriate, since their risk profile may change over time. If there is a need to regularly review certification and reassess the premium, this would fundamentally change how systems are used/sold. If premiums are reviewed given the risk of increasing premiums for previously sold systems manufacturers and developers would require a right of recall, and would be incentivised to lease, not sell their systems. The system is also overly bureaucratic, and perhaps not suitable for an era when it is not only big technology firms that can develop such products. Soon AI will be ubiquitous, the need to clearly identify a manufacturer will be a problem if the product is crowd sourced, or open sourced, or if AI programmes and systems can be created, modified, or developed by individuals.

Registration will have costs to manufacturers, and the costs of obtaining approval[226] and compliance are likely to be significant. These will need to be passed on to consumers. However, if such systems are more expensive, there may be limited incentives for consumers to buy them. Whilst purchasing such a system over

[225] Karnow, 'Distributed Artificial Intelligences' (n 80); another proposal is found in Kevin Funkhouser, 'Paving the Road Ahead: Autonomous Vehicles, Products Liability, and the Need for a New Approach' [2013] *Utah LR* 437.

[226] See Roger Kemp, 'Regulating the Safety of Autonomous Vehicles Using Artificial Intelligence' (2019) 24 *CL* 24.

its uncertified rival perhaps provides both more protection for third parties and for the consumer themselves, and reduces the risk of being the target of litigation, such incentives may not act on all purchasers, particularly men of straw, and the incentives may be low given the difficulty in bringing fault-based claims against the employers of AI (as detailed above). The registry system is also designed for a world where both manufacturers and users of systems are big, solvent players, but not when AI is ubiquitous. If, however, it was to become mandated by law or required by the market it risks driving smaller innovators out of the market, who may not be able to afford to deal with the registry's bureaucratic approval processes. There is also the risk of regulatory capture, perhaps rendering the certification of little value, or risking it being used as an obstacle for smaller competitors. Further, if the registry's role becomes analogous to a credit rating agency they may also be incentivised to issue certificates, to ensure that the registry remains in operation.

Such a system will also reduce tort's deterrent effect on employers, who may be in the best position to observe the system's evolving peculiarities, and who may be in the best position to properly supervise the system, warn third parties who may interact with the system, and ensure that it is not used for inappropriate tasks, or in inappropriately risky environments. Whilst they may need to pay more to use such systems initially, through manufacturers passing on the costs to them, the cost to employers of using the system would be determined by the premiums imposed at the time of purchase, which might not represent the harms/risk profile at the time of use. Employers would have little skin in the game. It therefore risks increasing harms. From a victim's perspective such a system might balance out the loss of a vicarious liability claim, if it were made compulsory, but for the reasons above, such a regime is inappropriate for all AI systems, and compulsion would again violate tech-impartiality.

IX VICARIOUS LIABILITY FOR AI?

We have seen above that none of the existing systems address the liability gap which is present due to the replacement of employees with AI systems. The proposals discussed above all fall short of bridging this gap in a tech-impartial fashion. Only a system modelled on vicarious liability for employees will do this.[227]

Introducing statutory vicarious liability is not radical.[228] But since AI systems as property do not commit torts, statutory vicarious liability by itself is not enough, instead it has to be a statutory master's tort form of vicarious liability. This would be a form of agency with the acts/knowledge of the system being ascribed to the

[227] Note, Expert Group on Liability and New Technologies (n 59) 7, 25, makes a case on the grounds of functional equivalence; see also Anat Lior, 'AI Entities as AI Agents: Artificial Intelligence Liability and the AI Respondeat Superior Analogy' (2020) 46 *Mitchell Hamline LR* 1043.

[228] For instance, see Police Act 1996 s 88(1).

employer. The employer as a legal or natural person can commit a tort. Whilst subtly different to common law vicarious liability, it achieves the same function. This attribution is solely for the purposes of the statutory vicarious liability claim, and not for other purposes (for instance separate direct duty claims). Given the strong enterprise liability rationale for vicarious liability within the current law, this statutory vicarious liability should only apply in a commercial setting.[229]

However, in this particular context a number of hurdles would need to be overcome. Aside from a statutory definition of AI and autonomous, firstly, we would need a test of 'employment' of an AI system. Not all who use such systems will be analogous to employers of employees, others may be analogous to employers of independent contractors. However, this test could be modelled on the existing factors considered in the assessment of stage one of vicarious liability, such as integration, control, and whether the system is part of the employer's business or another's (amongst others). Issues such as exclusivity of use, presence of any third parties in the relationship, ownership of the system, who provides the operator, supervisor, maintainer (if any), systems of management, and who has oversight, will be relevant. There may be some difficulties with complex systems, but this is not an intractable problem. Dual vicarious liability will be able to deal with situations where more than one entity is in the position of the 'employer'. It may also be the case that the identity of the 'employer' varies from time to time, and on what function the system is discharging, and the surrounding circumstances.[230] This is also found within common law vicarious liability, with the doctrine of liability for borrowed/transferred employees. However, there may be situations where a manufacturer foists an AI system on an employer, where the latter is unaware that the manufacturer has done so, and who does not use the system. In such circumstances, just as with a person who attempts to work for an employer without their knowledge or consent is not employee, the system would also not trigger liability on the part of the employer via this statutory scheme.

Whilst it may be possible for the common law courts to slowly evolve such a liability regime for AI if the right facts appear before the higher appellate courts, such a regime is best introduced in a parliamentary setting. This will enable the problem to be considered in the round, and permit considerable expert assistance in the process through evidence to select committees, and the input of a wide variety of stakeholders, for instance in defining AI, and the parameters of liability. It will also help to provide needed certainty, along with helping to ensure that the existing liability gap does not distort present behaviour.

[229] Tech-impartiality would suggest replicating the same system for non-commercial uses, for instance domestic uses, but the enterprise and loss spreading rationales of vicarious liability would suggest that there may be differences between liability for domestic and commercial uses of AI. Further, in most cases such systems will not be replacing domestic employees. Most people using a system such as Siri in a domestic context would not have previously employed a private secretary (although a tiny number may have). Thus protecting domestic use of AI and treating it differently may be justified.

[230] Lior (n 228) 1092.

A *Standards of Care?*

With vicarious liability we will also need a tort. To ensure tech-impartiality, the conduct attributed to the employer (legal or natural) should be judged by the same standards as if an employee stood in the shoes of the system.[231] Thus in the case of negligence, that of the reasonable person, or by the standard of the reasonable skilled professional where the system is carrying out such a role. The advantage of such an approach is that we do not expect a lower standard of care from a machine (or a higher one) neither discouraging nor encouraging their adoption through tort law. Tort will regulate behaviour, but where the behaviour is equally safe it shows no preference between the actors. Issues of foreseeability will also be assessed from this position.

At first glance, in some circumstances, applying human standards might not be appropriate (although it is tech-impartial). For instance, in the Tempe incident, where a pedestrian was killed by an Uber self-driving car,[232] the accident occurred in the dark where a human driver might not have been able to spot the victim or react in time, but the AV had other sensors, not typically available to human drivers, namely radar and lidar, which meant that it had abilities to spot pedestrians in the dark in excess of a human driver. Perhaps here the human driver standard should also consider that of a human driver with access to these additional sensors? Nevertheless, this is not the same as applying a non-human standard to the system.

Two linked objections to this equalising of the standard of care approach are that firstly the standard of the reasonable person serves an exculpatory function, in that not all who cause harm are deserving of blame, and there is no need for such a function to operate in the AI sphere. This objection is based on the idea that blame may function differently between humans and AI systems since AI has no feelings to hurt, reputation to be harmed, or assets necessary to maintain a reasonable quality of life. Secondly, the ordinary standard of care also permits a balance to be found between the rights of the victim not to be harmed, and the rights of the defendant to act. Since AI, unlike a person, has no right to act, the balance struck may be different. Nevertheless, such objections fail to account for the persons behind the AI system. The system proposed by this chapter attributes the wrong to the system's employer, who would be rendered liable by the system, and they may have such rights to act, along with reputation, feelings, and/or assets. Likewise a breach of a standard of care is not the same as subjective blameworthiness, as cases of defendant learner drivers or defendants with mental disorders show,[233] where they are held to

[231] Note, Expert Group on Liability and New Technologies (n 59) 7, also suggest a benchmark of human standards; Abbott (n 9) 9.

[232] Daisuke Wakabayashi, 'Self-Driving Uber Car Kills Pedestrian in Arizona, Where Robots Roam' (*New York Times*, 19 March 2018) <www.nytimes.com/2018/03/19/technology/uber-driverless-fatality.html>.

[233] For example, *Nettleship v Weston* [1971] 2 QB 691 (CA); *Dunnage v Randall* [2015] EWCA Civ 673, [2016] QB 639.

standards they cannot meet. Further, if a different standard of care was set for AI when the employer is sued, which required a higher standard of care to be displayed than a human carrying out the same role, this would discourage the adoption of AI systems even where they are safer.

Another objection and counter-proposal to this equalisation approach is that since the type of inadequacies and errors generated by an AI system will be different to those generated by human operators, applying human standards is not appropriate.[234] Instead, we must judge the standard of care by whether or not the system as a class exceeds the human standard of care. This will require an examination of its overall accident record, rather than focusing on individual instances, since whilst a system might be safer overall it will make mistakes that humans will not. Under this approach, a system which exceeds the human standard of care overall is not in breach of duty, even if in the particular circumstances of an accident a human defendant would have been liable if they, instead of an AI system, had caused the accident. However, there are three major problems with this approach.

Firstly, some victims who would not have been injured by human operators, or who would have been compensated if they had been so harmed, will not be compensated; they will thus be required to pay the costs for the safety of others. This discriminates against certain classes of victim, since for example even where the same standard is displayed in a particular instance recovery would depend on whether or not an AI system, or a human operator was responsible.[235] Secondly, this approach eliminates individual rights. A potential victim would not be able to expect a particular standard of care vis-à-vis them, instead this standard can only be expected vis-à-vis the aggregate pool of potential victims. This is particularly problematic if a system fails to adequately recognise/protect a particular class, for example a transport system which is generally safer for pedestrians, but poses increased risks to wheelchair users, or a medical system which is more accurate than human physicians in diagnosing a particular medical condition, but is less accurate for patients from particular minority communities. Such an approach to standards of care permits systems which are less safe for some classes/groups, reducing their rights, and may entrench disadvantage and discrimination. Thirdly, such an approach may prove forensically complex; litigation will require access to large data sets, and high levels of statistical training to use it, advantaging technology firm defendants over victims, and potentially making litigation more expensive. Conversely, the tech-impartial approach of applying the same standard of care to both humans and AI systems prevents the erosion of individual rights, and ensures tort retains incentives to use humans in particular circumstances where humans reach higher standards than AI, even if an AI system has overall higher standards.

[234] Gerhard Wagner, 'Robot Liability' in Sebastian Lohsse, Reiner Schulze and Dirk Staudenmayer (eds), *Liability for Artificial Intelligence and the Internet of Things* (Nomos 2019) 27, 44–45.

[235] Note Karni Chagal-Feferkorn, 'The Reasonable Algorithm' (2019) *JLT&P* 111, 122–124.

However, there are limits to the equality approach. There will be AI systems that do not replace employees, and instead carry out tasks that are fundamentally different to those carried out by humans and which no human could do, with an ability/expertise that no human could exercise. In such circumstances tech-impartiality does not limit the standard to be applied to the AI system to the human standard, instead in these circumstances the question for society to address is what standard we wish the reasonable AI to meet. In such circumstances we may assess a system by standards other than human standards. Further, the approach advanced in this chapter does not seek to fossilise standards of care. Although in the light of tech-impartiality applying the same standards for humans and AI systems in carrying out a particular task where humans and AI are in competition is appropriate, once AI systems replace humans in particular contexts, it will be possible to revisit the standard of care, and consider whether higher standards are now merited. Lowering standards would still be inappropriate since these would erode victim rights, violating the second limb of tech-impartiality. Suggestions that we should increase the standard of care expected of humans in a particular field if their AI competitors prove superior, particularly when AI systems become predominant in a field,[236] are inappropriate, since this may have the consequence of driving the remaining human workers out of an occupation or activity, leading to disenfranchisement. However, the presence of a de minimis number of holdout human workers might not prevent the required standard of care being enhanced for AI systems.

B *Objections and Boundaries*

Insurance poses a potential problem to this master's tort approach. If the acts are attributed to the employer, whilst this is not a problem for negligence, it means that a number of torts, for instance those that would be intentional torts if committed by a person, will be uninsurable. Thus statutory vicarious liability for AI systems will only work if it is also introduced alongside an exception to the public policy that one cannot insure oneself for an intentional wrong, when the wrong has been attributed via these statutory means. Intentional torts also face some problems in that imputing intention will be problematic in that the system may not have intention in any human sense, and even if it could be said to have intention we might not be able to ascertain it. Vicarious liability can nevertheless cope. Many vicarious liability intentional tort claims, particularly those for historic sexual abuse, are brought in the absence of the actual tortfeasor, who is sometimes long dead, or where the tortfeasor is one of the employer's employees but we do not know which. Courts are able to assess whether the tort of say battery has occurred, even in the absence of any evidence from, or access to the tortfeasor. In the context of AI systems where we are not able to easily assess intent, or examine the decisions made, perhaps due to a

[236] Abbott (n 9) 9, 69.

black box problem, it would not be problematic to assess and presume such intent from external observations of its outputs/actions, just as we do with such employees.

One flawed objection to a regime based on vicarious liability is that it is undesirable on the basis that it could be stricter than that of vicarious liability for an employee's tort. This objection appears to be made on the basis that an AI system, unlike an employee, will always fulfil stage two[237] of the vicarious liability requirements. Pagallo considers that this may result in 24 hour a day strict liability for the AI system since 'we can hardly imagine a service machine not undertaking its work activities'.[238] Although some individuals, particularly office holders, are considered always on duty,[239] this is uncommon. An employee has their own time, for instance that used for their private and family life, and leisure. Whereas an AI system may be considered always on the job.

However, this objection is not as strong as first meets the eye. Firstly, objecting to 24/7 liability is unsound in that if a person was able to work 24/7, and in fact did so, they too would be always on the job. Secondly, with vicarious liability for AI systems there will still be a need for a connective test, which connects the act to the relationship similar to the close connection test used for employees. Not all employee torts are sufficiently connected with their employment to trigger vicarious liability. Likewise, there will be cases in which an AI system's acts will not be sufficiently connected to their 'employment', for instance in the case of malware, hacking, and/or hijacking of the system by third parties. Thus, a data leak committed by an aggrieved employee, or by an AI system which has been hacked and altered by malicious actors, so as to disclose/leak this information, would both not lead to vicarious liability on the part of the employer. Likewise, say if a manufacturer in a secret conspiracy with a foreign intelligence agency designs an infrastructure survey drone which has concealed functions designed to spy on third parties, and this is hidden from employers of the systems, then an employer of the system who uses it for infrastructure surveying would not be vicariously liable for the system's spying.

We would also need to consider the boundaries of such a liability system. Tech-impartiality demands that which liability regime should apply depends on what form the AI takes, what function it fulfils, and whether it replaces an employee. For instance it would not be appropriate for a system based on vicarious liability to apply to a robot dog, which replaces a companion animal. However, where an AI system replaces an employee, or carries out a role which would ordinarily be carried out by an employee, a system of liability for employees should apply. Nonetheless, we will need systems in place to stop this distinction from being gamed, for instance by dressing up a system which replaces an employee as an AI animal companion

237 See text to n 21 above.

238 Pagallo, *The Laws of Robots* (n 70) 131–132.

239 Leonard Jason-Lloyd, *An Introduction to Policing and Police Powers* (2nd edn, Cavendish 2005) 9; Phillip Morgan, 'Close Connection and Police Torts' (2013) 19 *PN* 233.

system (perhaps most likely in care settings), and some systems may have dual functions. We will need to look at the function it was meant to be performing (or was performing) at the time of the harm, but occasionally the difference between such functions might not be clear cut.

Although with AI systems the liability gap is more obvious with systems that engage stochastic rather than deterministic processes, the proposed regime should apply to both forms of AI system. This encourages tech-impartiality between types of AI, further it would be odd to discriminate against victims on the basis of whether the offending AI system uses fixed rules or complex machine learning.[240]

X CONCLUSION

AI systems will replace employees in a wide range of roles. In doing so, such systems, particularly fully autonomous systems will pose significant challenges to the law of tort. As with previous industrial revolutions we can expect this revolution to lead to major developments within the law of tort.

Tech-impartiality insists that tort law should not encourage or deter the use of new technologies where such technologies generate equal risks of legally recognised harm to third parties, and should only do so where the new technologies are either more or less safe. Nor should the adoption of new technologies eliminate existing victim rights. Vicarious liability plays a key role within the law of tort. Although the commonly advanced theoretical justifications for vicarious liability point to such liability for AI systems, such systems are property and not persons, and thus unable to commit a tort. Given the rejection of the master's tort theory of vicarious liability there is thus no such liability at common law for AI systems.

By replacing employees, AI systems have the potential to create a significant liability gap. Employers who would formerly have been vicariously liable for the torts of their employees will now be able to externalise the harm their operations cause on to victims. Alternative claims based on negligence, or product liability claims, are subject to major problems in the AI system context and do not adequately fill this gap, thus these costs will be shouldered by victims. In failing to adequately fill the liability gap the existing law of tort violates the principles of tech-impartiality.

The inadequacy of tort law's ability to deal with AI system harms is widely recognised. Ad hoc solutions have been implemented in the AV context, which are not, and should not be more widely applicable. More wide-ranging solutions for all AI systems have been proposed ranging from models of liability based on liability for children, slaves, and animals, to no-fault schemes, but each is wanting, and does not respect tech-impartiality. Only liability based on the model of vicarious liability does so. Whilst there will be some challenges in applying this doctrine to AI systems, a statutory system which adopts a master's tort theory is proposed.

[240] Abbott (n 9) 60.

7

Automated Vehicle Liability and AI

James Goudkamp

I INTRODUCTION

Few, if any, developments have had a greater impact on the common law, and in particular tort law, than the advent of the motor vehicle.[1] It is a notorious fact that tort law underwent seismic shifts over the course of the twentieth century in response to cars substantially replacing earlier modes of transportation. The most obvious and perhaps significant example concerns the breach element of the tort of negligence. Under the influence of legislation requiring owners of vehicles to secure third-party insurance,[2] courts across the common law world, while notionally requiring drivers only to act reasonably, raised the standard of care that drivers must achieve for the purposes of the tort of negligence to a level where, paradoxically, it comes close to imposing liability regardless of fault.

I do not only have in mind in this regard decisions such as *Nettleship v Weston*,[3] in which the Court of Appeal of England and Wales held that a learner driver must achieve the standard of the reasonable competent motorist despite the obvious impossibility of their doing so. Rather, I am principally talking about what Patrick Atiyah evocatively described as the process of 'stretching' the law.[4] Atiyah was referring by this term to, in particular, the tendency of judges to demand that motorists exercise far more care than most drivers in practice take. He attributed this proclivity to, among other things, sympathy for injured claimants as well as an awareness that damages awarded in claims brought in respect of motor vehicle accidents are paid by insurers rather than by defendant motorists.[5]

I am grateful to Donal Nolan for discussing the issues in this chapter with me as well as to Phillip Morgan and Jenny Steele for their helpful comments on a draft.

1 See generally N Engstrom, 'When Cars Crash: The Automobile's Tort Law Legacy' (2018) 53 *Wake Forest Law Review* 293.

2 Third-party motor vehicle insurance became compulsory in England with the enactment of the Road Traffic Act 1930.

3 [1971] 2 QB 691 (CA). See also *Lovelace v Fossum* (1972) 24 DLR (3d) 561 (BCSC).

4 PS Atiyah, *The Damages Lottery* (Hart Publishing 1997) chs 2–3.

5 See also R Lewis, 'The Relationship between Tort Law and Insurance in England and Wales' in G Wagner (ed), *Tort Law and Liability Insurance* (Springer 2005).

The New South Wales Law Reform Commission eloquently described the effect of this 'stretching', which occurred throughout the common law world, in a report that was published in 1984. The Law Reform Commission observed that the rule that liability in the tort of negligence requires proof of fault had, in the context of motor vehicle accidents:[6]

> lost a great deal of [its] original meaning. A breach of duty in a negligence action involves a departure from the standards of the ordinary and reasonable road user. Yet by those standards, if they are to be applied stringently, relatively few defendants would be held liable. The trend to extend compensation to a wider class of claimants has expanded the notion of 'fault' as a criterion of liability in transport accident cases.

We are now apparently on the cusp of what promises to be a new motor-vehicle-inspired revolution in the law, including tort law, on account of the imminent introduction *en masse* of self-driving vehicles. Although automated vehicles come with the potential to reduce accident rates,[7] accidents will always be inevitable. To date, there have been several high-profile accidents involving automated vehicles including the death of a pedestrian in Arizona in 2018 caused by a self-driving Uber vehicle.[8] There is, accordingly, a very real need to consider the circumstances in which compensation for damage caused by automated vehicles is, and ought to be, available.

This chapter has a modest objective. It considers the civil liability regime in the United Kingdom for damage caused by automated vehicles. The focus is on this country principally because it is the jurisdiction with which I am most familiar. However, developments in the United Kingdom are in any event of particular interest because the Parliament at Westminster has moved especially swiftly in terms of legislating as regards civil liability for accidents occasioned by automated vehicles and because the scheme that it has established is unlike that anywhere else. Further, the whole field has been comprehensively surveyed by the Law Commission of England and Wales and Scottish Law Commission.[9]

6 New South Wales Law Reform Commission, *Accident Compensation: A Transport Accidents Scheme for New South Wales, Final Report 1*, vol 1 (1984), para 3.35.

7 'Human error is a factor in over 90% of collisions. Failing to look properly, misjudging other road users' movements, being distracted, careless or in too much of a hurry are the most common causes of collisions on our roads. Automated vehicles will not make these mistakes': Department for Transport, *The Pathway to Driverless Cars: Summary Report and Action Plan* (Department for Transport 2015) para 1.3.

8 See National Safety Transportation Board, *Highway Accident Report: Collision between Vehicle Controlled by Developmental Automated Driving System and Pedestrian Tempe, Arizona March 18, 2018* (2019) <www.ntsb.gov/investigations/AccidentReports/Reports/HAR1903.pdf>.

9 Law Commission of England and Wales and Scottish Law Commission, *Automated Vehicles: Joint Report* (2022). See also the valuable report of the Singapore Academy of Law, *Report on the Attribution of Civil Liability for Accidents Involving Autonomous Cars* (2020).

II THE AUTOMATED AND ELECTRIC VEHICLES ACT 2018

A *Overview*

By far the most significant legal development to date in the United Kingdom regarding civil liability for damage caused by automated vehicles is the enactment of the Automated and Electric Vehicles Act 2018 (the AEV Act). Part I of the AEV Act is concerned with civil liability for damage caused by automated vehicles while Part II focuses on the charging of electric vehicles. Part I, on which this chapter concentrates, entered into force on 21 April 2021[10] and applies in all parts of the United Kingdom except for Northern Ireland.[11] Reduced to its core, it establishes a regime whereby insurers of automated vehicles are: (i) held strictly liable for damage that automated vehicles cause while driving themselves and (ii) conferred with a right to bring secondary claims against persons, if any, who were responsible for the accident. This simple summary of Part I conceals, however, significant complexities in the scheme that it establishes. Unsurprisingly, given that it has only commenced very recently, Part I has not yet been the subject of any judicial elucidation although it has excited considerable academic analysis.[12]

It is important to observe at the outset that the AEV Act, in so far as Part I is concerned, is a pre-emptive piece of legislation in that no vehicles are as yet available for sale in the United Kingdom that have the degree of autonomy that is needed to engage it. An influential but arguably seriously deficient classification of different degrees of vehicle automation is that propounded by a body known as SAE International.[13] Levels 1 and 2 of this taxonomy involve automation that provides a human driver with support. Examples of such automation include cruise control and lane departure warnings. Level 3 involves 'conditional driving automation'. It entails the vehicle driving itself but a human driver might be required to take control in certain circumstances. Levels 4 and 5 involve 'high' and 'full' driving automation respectively. Neither requires a human to take control of the vehicle. A Level 4

[10] Automated and Electric Vehicles Act 2018 (Commencement No 1) Regulations 2021/396, r 3(a).

[11] The AEV Act, s 22(1).

[12] See, for example, M Channon, 'Automated and Electric Vehicles Act 2018: An Evaluation in Light of Proactive Law and Regulatory Disconnect' (2019) 10 *European Journal of Law and Technology* 26; M Channon, K Noussia and L McCormick, *The Law and Autonomous Vehicles* (Informa Law 2019); M Marynowski, 'Car Insurance in the Age of Self-Driving – Analysis of the Automated and Electric Vehicles Act 2018' (2019) 4 *Insurance Review* 25; K Oliphant, 'Liability for Road Accidents Caused by Driverless Cars' (2019) 13 *Singapore Comparative Law Review* 190; J Marson, K Ferris and J Dickinson, 'The Automatic and Electric Vehicles Act 2018 Part 1 and Beyond: A Critical Review' (2020) 41 *Statute Law Review* 395; J Marson and K Ferris, 'The Lexicon of Self-Driving Vehicles and the Fuliginous Obscurity of Autonomous Vehicles' (2021) 20 *Statute Law Review* 1.

[13] SAE International, *Taxonomy and Definitions for Terms Related to Driving Automation Systems for On-Road Motor Vehicles: J3016 202104* (2021). For criticism, see D Hopkins and T Schwanen, 'Talking about Automated Vehicles: What Do Levels of Automation Do?' (2021) 64 *Technology in Society* 101488.

automated vehicle can ask a human driver to assist but will continue driving itself if the request is unanswered while a Level 5 automated vehicle does not require any human control. The AEV Act is aimed at automation at Levels 4 and 5.[14] Vehicles with automation at Levels 4 or 5 are not yet available, however, for public use in the United Kingdom (or, apparently, anywhere else).

One other general point to observe regarding the AEV Act is that it is remarkably brief (Part I of it runs to just eight sections).[15] As such, it does not deal comprehensively with the phenomenon of automated vehicles. Indeed, it is very far from such a statute. It does not, for instance, prescribe when drivers may permit a vehicle to drive itself or specify particular standards that the technology must achieve. Perhaps most strikingly of all, the AEV Act does not make any arrangements as regards the data that automated vehicles will record and the circumstances in which those data must be preserved and made available to insurers and other stakeholders. There are indications that the government expects such issues to be dealt with by international instruments.[16] The lack of detail in the legislation reflects a 'wait and see' philosophy pursuant to which the AEV Act will be kept under review and, if necessary, expanded in order to address problems if and when they arise. This means, however, that there is a danger that it will be out of date by the time that automated vehicles that can drive themselves appear on the roads.

B *Background*

In 2013, the government wrote in its Autumn Statement that it would 'support the development of driverless cars through reviewing the regulation and legislation that applies to the testing of driverless cars…'.[17] That review was carried out in 2014.[18] It was followed by the publication in 2015 and 2016 of government reports on the theme of automated vehicles.[19] Legislation on the subject was then formally announced in the 2016 Queen's Speech. Thus, the Sovereign said that 'My ministers will ensure the United Kingdom is at the forefront of technology for new forms of transport, including autonomous and electric vehicles'.[20] The

[14] The government's view is that the AEV Act 'does not apply to level 3 vehicles': Hansard, House of Lords, Automated and Electric Vehicles Bill, volume 791, column 173, Baroness Sugg (9 May 2018).

[15] The AEV Act is not, however, the shortest statute that has ever been enacted. That prize goes to the Parliament (Qualification of Women) Act 1918, which contains just twenty-seven operative words.

[16] Centre for Connected and Autonomous Vehicles, *Pathway to Driverless Cars: Proposals to Support Advanced Driver Assistance Systems and Automated Vehicle Technologies* (Department for Transport 2016) para 2.24.

[17] HM Treasury, *Autumn Statement 2013* (HMSO 2013) para 2.156.

[18] Department for Transport, *Review of the Legislative and Regulatory Framework for Testing Driverless Cars: Discussion Documents and Call for Evidence* (Department for Transport 2014).

[19] See, for example, Department for Transport (n 7); Department for Transport, *The Pathway to Driverless Cars: A Detailed Review of Regulations for Automated Vehicle Technologies* (Department for Transport 2015); Centre for Connected and Autonomous Vehicles (n 16).

[20] *Queen's Speech 2016* <www.gov.uk/government/speeches/queens-speech-2016>.

background briefing notes to the Queen's Speech identify various goals that the proposed statute would achieve including '[e]nsuring [that] new technology delivers better, safer journeys'.[21] The promised benefits included ensuring that the United Kingdom was 'at the forefront' when it came to the ownership and use of driverless vehicles.[22] It was also said that the legislation would encourage investment in automated vehicles and ensure that 'appropriate insurance' was available in connection with their use.[23]

The relevant bill was originally supposed to be entitled the Modern Transport Bill, but it was introduced to Parliament in 2017 as the Vehicle Technology and Aviation Bill. Parliament was dissolved shortly thereafter and the bill fell. However, later in 2017, the Automated and Electric Vehicles Bill was proposed. Its provisions tracked those of the Vehicle Technology and Aviation Bill save that those clauses of the latter that had dealt with aviation no longer featured. The bill's purpose was said to prepare the United Kingdom to be ready for the introduction of automated vehicles that have a high degree of, or full, autonomy. As the Minister of State for Transport explained in the second reading speech: '[Henry] Ford himself said: "Before everything else, getting ready is the secret of success." That is what this Bill is about.'[24] The bill's passage through Parliament was unremarkable with Part I being only lightly amended. Much of the debate and written evidence focused on the provisions in Part II concerning electric charging rather than on Part I's clauses regarding automated vehicles. It appears that there was far more stakeholder interest in the former than in the latter.

C *The Mischief*

Before addressing the AEV Act's provisions in detail, it is worth considering why, specifically, the statute was enacted. It is necessary to bear in mind, in this regard, the insurance arrangements that exist in relation to conventional motor vehicles. Claims in respect of damage caused by a conventional vehicle are typically brought against the driver of the vehicle concerned. Those claims, if liability is admitted or established, are paid by the owner's or driver's third-party insurer. Even where the vehicle is uninsured or cannot be traced, compensation will still be paid by an insurer pursuant to agreements between the Secretary of State for Transport and the Motor Insurers' Bureau.[25] Obviously, however, this familiar framework cannot

[21] *Queen's Speech 2016: Background Briefing Notes* (2016) <www.gov.uk/government/publications/queens-speech-2016-background-briefing-notes> 17.

[22] Ibid.

[23] Ibid.

[24] HC Deb 23 October 2017, vol 630, col 60.

[25] The agreements are available at <www.mib.org.uk/media/166917/2015-uninsured-drivers-agreement-england-scotland-wales.pdf> and <www.mib.org.uk/media/353664/2017-untraced-drivers-agreement-england-scotland-and-wales.pdf>.

be applied to automated vehicles since there may be no human driver (indeed, conceivably, there may not even be a human occupant). The AEV Act's overarching purpose is to plug this gap in insurance cover. It does so by providing victims of accidents caused by automated vehicles with a claim directly against the vehicle's insurer.[26] Interestingly, the government considered adopting, as an alternative to the regime established by the AEV Act, a first-party insurance model, applicable to both conventional and automated vehicles alike.[27] Under such a system, injured persons would claim against their own insurer. It was thought, however, that this option 'would be too disruptive and costly at this stage'.[28]

D *Key Terms*

Section 2 contains the AEV Act's core liability rules. Section 2(1) provides:

> Where –
>
> (a) an accident is caused by an automated vehicle when driving itself on a road or other public place in Great Britain,
> (b) the vehicle is insured at the time of the accident, and
> (c) an insured person or any other person suffers damage as a result of the accident, the insurer is liable for that damage.

Pursuant to section 2(2), if there is no insurer the owner will be liable for the damage. It follows that claims can be brought under the AEV Act only in respect of 'damage' resulting from an accident that is caused by an 'automated vehicle' that was 'driving itself'. It is convenient to examine these three pivotal concepts – 'automated vehicle', 'driving itself' and 'damage' – in turn at this stage, each of which the AEV Act defines. A few remarks will then be offered as regards the word 'accident' and the phrase 'road or other public place', neither of which is defined.

1 'Automated Vehicle'

Section 1(4) provides that 'automated vehicles' are vehicles that are included on a list that the Secretary of State is obliged to maintain pursuant to section 1(1).[29] The latter subsection states that the list must include all motor vehicles that '(a) are in the

[26] By virtue of amendments that the AEV Act makes to ss 144–145 of the Road Traffic Act 1988, automated vehicles must be insured: see the AEV Act, Sch, cll 18–19.

[27] This is a reform for which Atiyah famously argued: see Atiyah (n 4) ch 8.

[28] Centre for Connected and Autonomous Vehicles, *Pathway to Driverless Cars: Insurance for Automated Vehicles* (2016) 1. See also at 3 (neither 'necessary [nor] proportionate').

[29] The Law Commissions have recommended that this listing procedure be replaced by an authorisation procedure pursuant to which an automated vehicle's manufacturer or developer would need to submit its vehicle to an authorisation authority: Law Commission of England and Wales and the Scottish Law Commission (n 9) ch 5.

Secretary of State's opinion designed or adapted to be capable, in at least some circumstances or situations, of safely driving themselves, and (b) may lawfully be used when driving themselves, in at least some circumstances or situations, on roads or other public places in Great Britain'. As to the first of these conditions, it is striking that it will be met in relation to an automated vehicle even if it is wholly incapable of safely driving itself in most circumstances provided that there are in the Secretary of State's opinion 'at least some circumstances or situations' in which it is 'designed or adapted' to be capable of self-driving safely. This suggests a strong preference to include more rather than fewer automated vehicles on the list. The second condition is that the automated vehicle concerned 'may lawfully be used when driving themselves, in at least some circumstances or situations, on roads or other public places…'. It is unclear precisely which rules the legislature has in mind in connection with this second condition.

It appears that once a vehicle has been listed by the Secretary of State it will be an 'automated vehicle' for the purposes of the AEV Act and that that is so regardless of whether the Secretary of State should have listed it. Conversely, even if a vehicle is clearly an automated vehicle that can safely drive itself it will not qualify as an automated vehicle for the purposes of the AEV Act unless and until it features on the Secretary of State's list. Notably, if an automated vehicle is capable of driving itself safely in one situation (e.g., on a dual carriageway) but not in another (e.g., on a congested city street), and it is used in the latter resulting in the claimant suffering injury, the claimant may still be entitled to compensation under the AEV Act. Significantly, section 1(4) gives no guidance as to when an automated vehicle will be designed or adapted 'safely' to drive itself. Safety is a relative concept. One possible approach would be to enquire whether the vehicle in question causes or is likely to cause accidents at a lower rate than the average incidence of accidents in which conventional vehicles are implicated.[30]

2 'Driving Itself'

Pursuant to section 8(1), 'a vehicle is "driving itself" if it is operating in a mode in which it is not being controlled, and does not need to be monitored, by an individual'.[31] Presumably, therefore, if an automated vehicle causes an accident because, for example, it is parked in a dangerous position, no claim will lie under the AEV Act (since the vehicle is not 'operating' at all in this situation). This would appear to be the case even if the vehicle had parked itself. Such cases are relatively clear-cut but others will not be, and the phrase 'driving itself' harbours significant ambiguity. The result is that situations will inevitably arise where it is unclear whether the automated vehicle or the person in charge of it is doing the driving at any particular point in time. Most obviously, these situations may include those where an

[30] See further ibid. ch 4.

[31] For criticism, see Marson, Ferris, and Dickinson (n 12).

automated vehicle is transitioning between driving itself and being driven by the person in charge of it (i.e., the so-called 'handover').

Importantly, however, scope for debate as to whether an automated vehicle was driving itself is minimised by section 145(3A) of the Road Traffic Act 1988 (RTA). This subsection stipulates that insurance policies issued in respect of automated vehicles must provide cover not only as regards the liability of the person in charge of the automated vehicle but also 'for the insurer's obligations to an insured person'. Thus, the same insurer will provide cover for both the liability of the person in charge of an automated vehicle and in respect of the automated vehicle itself. It follows that disputes as to whether an automated vehicle was driving itself will break out far less frequently than would be the case where the person in charge of the automated vehicle and the automated vehicle itself have different insurers (since were there different insurers each would be incentivised to contend that the other bears responsibility for paying a particular claim).

Nevertheless, very considerable scope remains for disputes to arise as to whether a vehicle was driving itself or was being driven.[32] There are two main situations where this is so. The first is where the insurer considers that the claimant might encounter difficulty in establishing fault on the part of the person in control of the automated vehicle. In such a case, the insurer would be incentivised to argue that the vehicle was being driven by the human concerned since in that case it would not incur liability, unless the claimant can establish fault on the part of the human driver. The second situation is where the claimant is the person in charge of the automated vehicle. Where this is the case, the insurer will have an incentive to demonstrate that the claimant was driving the vehicle since it would also avoid incurring liability in that event.

The AEV Act's definition of 'driving itself', in addition to opening the door to the foregoing debate, also appears to be too restrictive in a potentially important respect. Imagine that a pedestrian is run down by a vehicle that was operating with a certain degree of automation but which still needed to be monitored. Suppose also that the accident occurred because of a defect in the technology and that the human driver, despite monitoring the vehicle, had no sufficient opportunity to prevent the collision. No claim will be available to the pedestrian under the AEV Act since the vehicle was not 'driving itself' for the purposes of section 2(1)(a) on account of its needing to be monitored. However, it is difficult to see the sense in this given that the human driver, despite needing to monitor the vehicle, could not have avoided the accident. Why should the pedestrian be denied a remedy under the AEV Act in circumstances where the accident was caused, and caused only by, a defect in the automation technology? The difficulty is magnified by the fact that the pedestrian will not have any claim against the driver either given that the driver was not at fault.

[32] This appears to have been overlooked by the Law Commissions: see Law Commission of England and Wales and Scottish Law Commission (n 9) para 13.6.

3 'Damage'

As regards the concept of 'damage', section 2(3) defines it both by inclusion and exclusion. Damage is specifically stated to include 'death or personal injury' and 'damage to property'. It follows that pure economic loss does not qualify as damage for the purposes of the AEV Act and, as such, cannot properly form the basis of a claim brought under it. In so far as losses that are specifically excluded are concerned, they comprise: (i) damage to 'the automated vehicle',[33] (ii) damage to 'goods carried for hire or reward in or on that vehicle or in or on any trailer (whether or not coupled) drawn by it' and (iii) damage to 'property in the custody or under the control' of the insured person or, if the automated vehicle is not insured, the person who is in charge of it at the time of the accident. Suppose that one automated vehicle causes damage while driving itself to another automated vehicle. It might be suggested that a very literal reading of the foregoing definitions requires that the owner of the latter cannot sue. It seems unlikely, however, that this is what the legislature intended.

4 Undefined Terms

Only damage that is caused by an 'accident' is within the scope of section 2. However, the AEV Act does not specify what qualifies as an 'accident'.[34] Difficult issues could well arise in this connection. Suppose, for example, that an automated vehicle is programmed, in the event of a situation in which imperilling the life of either a pedestrian or an automated vehicle's occupants is unavoidable, to prefer the latter's interests and to do so by running down the former. Given that the programmer has, in effect, positively instructed the automated vehicle to collide with the pedestrian in this circumstance, it is debatable whether the injury to the pedestrian is accidental.[35] Also undefined is the phrase 'road or other public place'. This language tracks that in, among other provisions, section 143 of the RTA, which prescribes when the use of a motor vehicle must be insured. There is a body of case law regarding the concept of a 'public place' for the purposes of that provision.[36] These authorities will presumably be relevant to the construction of that phrase in section 2 of the AEV Act.

33 This echoes the approach taken in s 5(2) of the Consumer Protection Act 1987 in the context of damage caused by defective products.

34 Although s 8(3) provides that 'a reference to an accident includes a reference to two or more causally related accidents' and that 'a reference to an accident caused by an automated vehicle includes a reference to an accident that is partly caused by an automated vehicle'.

35 Consider *Charlton v Fisher* [2001] EWCA Civ 112, [2002] QB 578. The defendant deliberately reversed his vehicle into that in which the claimant was a passenger. An issue arose, which it was ultimately unnecessary to decide, as to whether the injury had been caused by an 'accident' within the meaning of the policy.

36 See R Merkin and M Hemsworth, *The Law of Motor Insurance* (2nd edn, Sweet & Maxwell 2020) para 5.63; Law Commission of England and Wales and Scottish Law Commission (n 42) appendix 2.

E A *Direct Claim Against the Insurer*

Section 2(1) of the AEV Act has been set out above.[37] It gives persons injured by automated vehicles a claim directly against the automated vehicle's insurer.[38] Various other ways of dealing with the issue had been available to the legislature. Parliament could, for example, have simply left persons injured by accidents caused by automated vehicles to sue the vehicle's producer[39] or programmer. However, it is clear why this option was not selected.[40] Not only could many claimants have encountered profound difficulties in determining which company within a corporate group was responsible for the accident in question,[41] but they could also have faced major problems in terms of enforcement in circumstances where the relevant company may be incorporated overseas. Added to this is the notoriously low success rate of product liability claims in the United Kingdom (especially under the Consumer Protection Act 1987 (CPA)) coupled with their equally well-known high cost. Understandably, the legislature was concerned by the possibility that persons injured by automated vehicles might not, without statutory intervention, be able to recover compensation without 'undue legal wrangling'.[42] Accordingly, by imposing liability directly on the insurers of automated vehicles, section 2(1) cuts through a host of complications that persons injured by automated vehicles might otherwise face. The trade-off, however, is that subject to the possibility of the insurer being able to bring a secondary claim against third parties responsible for the accident,[43] the cost of damage caused by automated vehicles will be borne by the premium paying population in the United Kingdom even if responsibility for it ultimately lies with an company incorporated overseas.

Beyond these preliminary observations, numerous other aspects of section 2 merit attention. Firstly, anyone who suffers damage caused by an automated vehicle driving itself can bring a claim under section 2. It follows that the person who is in charge of the automated vehicle at the time of the accident (if any) is among those who can rely upon section 2 in the event of suffering injury.[44]

37 See section B.iv.

38 See section B.iii.

39 Some jurisdictions in the United States have enacted legislation that places liability for damage caused by autonomous vehicles on manufacturers: see S Quidachay-Swan, 'Autonomous Vehicles and Current State Liability Legislation' [2019] *Michigan Bar Journal* 48. See also New York State Bar Association, *Report of the New York State Bar Association Task Force on Autonomous Vehicles and the Law* (2020) 6–7.

40 For further discussion, see Centre for Connected and Autonomous Vehicles (n 16) 8.

41 For an example of a case from a different context that shows how real this problem can be, see *Four Seasons Holdings Inc v Brownlie* [2017] UKSC 80, [2018] 1 WLR 192.

42 Law Commission of England and Wales and Scottish Law Commission, *Automated Vehicles: Consultation Paper 3 – A Regulatory Framework for Automated Vehicles* (2020) para 16.3.

43 See section B.xi.

44 There is one exception to this position. Section 3(2) provides that where the accident caused by the automated vehicle 'was wholly due to the … negligence [of the person in charge of it] in allowing the vehicle to begin driving itself when it was not appropriate to do so' the person in charge cannot benefit from section 2.

This is a further respect in which the AEV Act breaks with the regime applicable to claims in respect of damage caused by conventional vehicles. In the case of accidents involving conventional vehicles, not only does the driver not stand to benefit from the cover that they have purchased but is, indeed, the *only* person who does not stand to benefit.

Secondly, even though section 2 does not say so expressly, the liability that it imposes is strict. Thus, it is irrelevant whether anyone was at fault in, for example, programming or designing the automated vehicle.[45] Accordingly, section 2 places persons who are injured by automated vehicles into a preferential position compared with persons who are injured by conventional vehicles since the latter must usually establish that they were injured as a result of another person's fault in order to recover damages (albeit the requirement to prove fault, as observed at the outset of this chapter,[46] is often undemanding). In one sense, this is a surprising step for the legislature to have taken given that, from the perspective of the injured party, the type of vehicle involved in causing them damage is, or at least will almost always be, a matter of luck. Why should the circumstances in which compensation is due to a pedestrian who is run down depend on whether the pedestrian is struck by an automated vehicle or conventional vehicle instead of, for example, on whether the pedestrian's injuries are sufficiently serious that they cannot cope without compensation? Before leaving this second point, it is worth observing that the preferencing suggests a concern on the part of the legislature to reassure the public regarding the introduction of automated vehicles. It is also noteworthy that the significance of the preferencing will diminish as automated vehicles are adopted (because there will be fewer victims of motor vehicle accidents who do not stand to benefit from the strict liability rule).

Thirdly, the legislature has brought within the strict liability net for which section 2 provides only insurers (as well as owners under section 2(2) in the event that an automated vehicle is uninsured). Producers were presumably not included given that they are potentially exposed to strict liability already under the CPA. However, although section 2 does not impose liability on anyone except for insurers (and owners of uninsured automated vehicles), it preserves the liability of any other person.[47] Accordingly, persons who are injured by an accident involving an automated vehicle remain entitled to claim against the individuals responsible for it, although they would have little incentive to do so given the existence of the strict liability claim against the automated vehicle's insurer under section 2.

Fourthly, section 2 does not provide for any special requirements that need to be satisfied before liability arises in respect of pure mental harm suffered by

45 Although see ibid.

46 See the text accompanying nn 4–6.

47 Section 2(7).

secondary victims, that is, persons who were not themselves physically endangered.[48] Suppose that a vehicle runs out of control and collides with a pedestrian resulting in their being killed or seriously injured. If the vehicle is a conventional one, horrified onlookers who were not in a relationship of love and affection with the pedestrian who suffer mental harm as a consequence of what they saw would not have any claim against the driver.[49] If, however, the vehicle is an automated one, the bystanders would not seem to face any difficulty in recovering compensation under the AEV Act. This is a further respect in which claimants who sue under the AEV Act are singled out, on the basis of luck, for preferential treatment relative to other claimants.

Finally, and in contrast with the situation that obtains in relation to damage caused by conventional vehicles,[50] no arrangements are as yet in place to have the Motor Insurers' Bureau ultimately cover losses occasioned by automated vehicles where the automated vehicle concerned is uninsured or untraced. It appears that the government and the Motor Insurers' Bureau are (or were) in discussions aimed at ensuring that persons injured by automated vehicles are not prejudiced by the fact that an automated vehicle is uninsured.[51] One would hope that arrangements would also be made to cater for untraced automated vehicles.

F *Contributory Negligence*

Ordinarily, where a claimant fails to take reasonable care for their own safety and where that failure is causally related to the injury suffered, any damages recoverable are subject to reduction for contributory negligence pursuant to the Law Reform (Contributory Negligence) Act 1945.[52] However, the 1945 Act applies only if the defendant is also at fault.[53] It cannot, therefore, apply straightforwardly to a claim under the AEV Act since the usual defendant (i.e., an insurer) will never be at fault in connection with the accident that caused the damage. Section 6(3) of the AEV Act deals with this by stipulating that the 'behaviour of the [automated] vehicle' is deemed to be 'fault' on the part of the person held liable thereunder for the purposes of the 1945 Act. It follows that whenever a claimant who seeks relief

48 Mental harm constitutes 'damage' for the purposes of the AEV Act given that damage is defined to include 'personal injury': see the text accompanying n 33 above.

49 *Alcock v Chief Constable of South Yorkshire Police* [1992] 1 AC 310 (HL).

50 See n 25 above and the accompanying text.

51 Motor Insurers' Bureau, *Annual Report and Accounts 2018*, 10 <www.mib.org.uk/media/461843/annual-report-2018.pdf>.

52 In the United Kingdom, contributory negligence is no longer a complete defence to a claim in tort. However, the language of contributory negligence is still used in this country (and in other Commonwealth jurisdictions) to refer to the process by which damages are reduced on account of the claimant's own carelessness.

53 See s 1(1). As regards the apportionment provision generally, see J Goudkamp and D Nolan, *Contributory Negligence: Principles and Practice* (2nd edn, Oxford University Press 2023) ch 4.

under section 2 is guilty of contributory negligence, any damages to which they are entitled will be reduced under the apportionment legislation.

Section 3(1) of the AEV Act explains (or, perhaps more accurately, tries to explain) how the apportionment exercise should be conducted. It provides that if 'the accident, or the damage resulting from it, was to any extent caused by the injured party, the amount of liability is subject to whatever reduction under the [1945 Act] would apply to a claim in respect of the accident brought by the injured party against a person other than the insurer or vehicle owner'. Accordingly, and oddly, it is the insurer's or owner's (deemed) fault together with the claimant's fault that engages the apportionment legislation (pursuant to section 6(3) as discussed above), whereas it is the fault of 'a person other than the insurer or vehicle owner' along with the claimant's fault that will be considered for the purposes of determining the amount by which damages should be discounted (under section 3(1)). In what can only be regarded as a serious defect in the legislative framework, section 3(1) leaves the 'other' person unidentified, and the legislature seems not to have appreciated that there may not even be another person against whom a claim could be brought. Although the position is far from clear, it may be that the 'other' person should be regarded as a hypothetical human motorist driving in a manner equivalent to the way in which the automated vehicle drove itself.

Quite apart from these difficulties, these provisions are in any event nothing short of an embarrassment on account of their complexity. It may have been better had the legislature simply accepted that the comparative exercise that the apportionment regime usually entails cannot properly be conducted in claims under the AEV Act because there will never, in actuality, be any fault on the insurer's part.[54] This would have left the legislature with at least two options. One would have been simply to exclude the defence of contributory negligence from claims under the AEV Act altogether. Certainly, eliminating the defence would have been consistent with the preferencing visible elsewhere in the statute. The other option would have been to provide for the discount to be determined in view only of the extent of the claimant's departure from the standard of the reasonable person in his or her position. Surprisingly, the Law Commissions have not recommended that the foregoing provisions be amended.[55] Although they accepted that the statutory machinery is 'complex',[56] legislative intervention was not regarded 'as a priority at this stage' in view of 'the absence of any experience of how the AEV Act might apply to real life cases'.[57]

54 It is no answer to this that contributory negligence is sometimes admitted as a defence in the strict liability context, such as in connection with claims under the CPA. It is not the AEV Act's imposing strict liability that causes difficulty in connection with the contributory negligence doctrine but the fact that, in a claim under the AEV Act, the insurer will never have been at fault in connection with the accident.

55 Law Commission of England and Wales and Scottish Law Commission (n 9) para 13.23.

56 Ibid. para 13.15.

57 Ibid. para 13.22.

G *Exclusion or Limitation of Liability*

Section 4 provides, in unnecessarily convoluted terms, for a limited right on the part of insurers to exclude or restrict their liability. Section 4(1)(a) states that an insurance policy may exclude or restrict liability arising under section 2(1) where the damage results directly from prohibited changes being made to the vehicle's software by the insured or with his or her knowledge. Section 4(1)(a) is qualified, however, by section 4(2) which stipulates that section 4(1)(a) does not apply unless the insured at the time of the accident knows that the software changes concerned are prohibited under the policy. This limitation on section 4(1)(a) is inapplicable where the insured person is the policy holder. Pursuant to section 4(1)(b), it is also permissible for the insurer to exclude or restrict liability on account of an unreasonable failure by an insured person to install safety-critical software updates.[58] One can envisage complications arising where an accident would still have occurred despite a failure to install safety-critical software updates but is made worse by that failure.

H *Limitation Period*

The AEV Act makes various amendments to the Limitation Act 1980. As a consequence of these amendments, the limitation period applicable to a claim under section 2 of the AEV Act is three years with time running from the date of the accident. This is so even if the damage is property damage, where a six-year limitation period would normally apply.[59] If the claim is in respect of personal injuries, the running of time is postponed until the date of knowledge on the part of the claimant, if that date is later than the date of the accident.[60] The date of knowledge is the date on which the claimant knew: (i) that the injury concerned was significant, (ii) that it was attributable to an accident caused by an automated vehicle driving itself, and (iii) the identity of the insurer of the vehicle (or owner if the vehicle was uninsured).[61] Secondary claims under the AEV Act are subject to a two-year limitation period with time running from the date on which the right of action accrued.[62] This is consistent with the limitation period that applies to contribution claims.[63]

I *Remoteness*

The AEV Act does not expressly deal with the issue of remoteness of damage. A question mark thus hovers over whether liability arising under section 2 is restricted

58 Pursuant to s 4(6)(b), updates are deemed to be safety-critical if it 'would be unsafe to use the vehicle in question without the updates being installed'.

59 Limitation Act 1980, s 2.

60 Ibid. s 11B.

61 Ibid. s 14(1B).

62 Ibid. s 10A(1).

63 Ibid. s 10(1).

to kinds of damage that are reasonably foreseeable. The same issue arises in relation to the CPA, which is also silent on the subject. Since it is generally thought that a reasonable foreseeability remoteness constraint nevertheless applies to claims under the CPA,[64] the same approach might be warranted in relation to claims brought under the AEV Act.

J *Remedies*

The AEV Act does not specify how damages awarded pursuant to section 2 are to be assessed. Presumably, liability arising under section 2 extends to the totality of the harm suffered by the injured person. The only qualification to this is that the AEV Act imposes an upper limit on claims in respect of property damage.[65] That cap is the limit on compulsory insurance for property damage set forth in section 145(4)(b) of the RTA, which is currently £1.2m. It is unclear whether awards of punitive or aggravated damages are available under the AEV Act.

K *Secondary Claims*

As discussed above, section 2 of the AEV Act initially places the cost of accidents caused by automated vehicles on the insurers or, if the vehicle is uninsured, their owners. Section 5 of the statute makes arrangements for secondary claims. Section 5(1) stipulates that where an insurer's or owner's liability to a person injured by an automated vehicle is 'settled', 'any other person liable to the injured party in respect of the accident is under the same liability to the insurer or vehicle owner'. Pursuant to section 5(2), the insurer's or owner's liability is regarded as being settled where it has been determined by a judgment, an arbitration award or an enforceable agreement. Under section 5(3), in the event that the insurer or owner makes a recovery under section 5(1) that exceeds the sum paid to the injured person, the insurer or owner must pay the excess to the injured party. Obvious persons against whom secondary claims could potentially be brought include the person in charge of the automated vehicle,[66] a driver of another vehicle involved in the accident and the automated vehicle's producer. The last-mentioned may be liable at common law or under the CPA or both. One interesting and important issue that arises in this regard is whether software qualifies as a 'product' for the purposes of the 1987 Act.[67]

[64] See, for example, J Goudkamp and D Nolan, *Winfield & Jolowicz on Tort* (20th edn, Sweet & Maxwell 2020) para 11.051.

[65] Section 2(4).

[66] Although the insurer may itself be liable to cover any such claim meaning, it would be either pointless or fail for circuity of action.

[67] See S Whittaker, 'European Product Liability and Intellectual Products' (1989) 105 *LQR* 125; L Grolman, *Does this Compute? Applying the Consumer Protection Act 1987 to Software that Learns* (Master of Studies thesis, University of Oxford 2019); R Bagshaw, 'Product Liability: Autonomous Ships' in B Soyer and A Tettenborn (eds), *Artificial Intelligence and Autonomous Shipping* (Hart Publishing 2021).

One suspects that secondary claims are most likely to be pursued against drivers of other vehicles since judgment in such claims, if successful, will be enforceable against a British insurer.

III CONCLUSION

The AEV Act is an unusual statute in many ways, particularly on account of its being an attempt by the legislature to pre-empt technological developments. Not knowing the precise form that the relevant technology will take, the legislature has avoided trying to be too prescriptive, but the result is a statute that is remarkably thin on detail and the Secretary of State is given considerable discretion as regards the issue of whether particular vehicles will qualify as an automated vehicle for the purposes of the AEV Act. All of this suggests that the statute will require overhauling sooner rather than later, and that it could very well be out of date perhaps even before the very technology for which it seeks to cater arrives on the market. Indeed, the Law Commissions have recommended that changes be made to it at this juncture.[68]

The AEV Act attempts to deal with losses caused by automated vehicles by providing for a direct claim against insurers. Various other options for dealing with the costs of accidents caused by automated vehicles were available to the legislature. For example, Parliament could, as observed above,[69] have done nothing and left injured persons to pursue claims at common law or the CPA. Alternatively, it could have required providers of automated vehicles to arrange insurance cover or to self-insure as a precondition to being able to access the British automated vehicle market. Another option would have been to require users of automated vehicles to purchase first-party insurance.[70] It would also have been possible for the legislature to break away from an insurance model entirely and to establish a government-operated compensation fund. Consideration of the background materials to the AEV Act suggests that inadequate consideration was given to the merits of these and various other possibilities.

The same background materials suggest an absence of serious reflection on the part of the legislature on certain other basic questions of considerable importance. For example, scant consideration was given to the variety of models available for funding the payment of compensation to persons injured by automated vehicles. The legislature, by enacting the AEV, has opted to raise the money required by way of insurance premiums. There were, however, a range of alternatives. For example, the money required could have been raised through taxation of owners of automated vehicles, motorists more generally or the population at large.

68 See n 29 above.

69 See the text accompanying n 40 above.

70 See the text accompanying n 27 above.

Taxes could also have been imposed on the importation or sale of automated vehicles. It does not appear that any or any adequate addition was given to these and other possibilities.

Similarly, the architects of the AEV do not seem to have been appreciated that the AEV Act treats victims of accidents caused by automated vehicles preferentially relative to victims of accidents occasioned by conventional vehicles (who are themselves generally treated far more favourably than persons who suffer injury and illness caused other than by the fault of another person). If they did, they did not stop to ask themselves whether this preferencing makes any sense in circumstances where luck determines whether a given claimant has a claim under AEV Act or must, in order to recover compensation, establish fault on the part of a human driver. The phenomenon of preferencing is just as relevant today, if not more relevant, than it was when Patrick Atiyah forced it into lawyers' consciousnesses in the 1970s.[71]

It may be replied that the preferencing phenomenon will diminish in importance as automated vehicles gradually replace conventional vehicles. This will undoubtedly be the case, although on any assessment the phasing out of conventional vehicles will be gradual and likely take many decades. The issue remains, therefore, why any legislative intervention should be restricted to automated vehicles. Not only is the preferencing phenomenon a pressing issue but major drawbacks attend having different compensation systems that deal with different types of accidents. These downsides include adding complexity to the law as well as the fact that differences between the applicable regimes are typically arbitrary. Of course, legislating across the whole field of motor vehicle accidents (or, even more widely, the field accidents generally) is a much more formidable undertaking than establishing compensation systems piecemeal. It is a challenge to which few legislatures have risen. The Parliament at Westminster is not among them.

[71] PS Atiyah, *Accidents, Compensation and the Law* (Weidenfeld and Nicolson 1970).

8

Legal Causation and AI

Sandy Steel

Causation is a fundamental determinant of remedial liability in private law. In claims for compensation, the right-holder must prove a causal connection between the legally relevant aspect of the defendant's conduct, or the conduct of some entity for which the defendant is responsible, and their loss. In claims for rescission of a transaction on grounds of a vitiating factor, such as a misrepresentation, the right-holder must generally show that the vitiating factor was a cause of entry into the transaction. Causation is generally considered central to justifying the imposition of some burden upon a particular individual for the benefit of another particular individual.

This chapter examines the apparent and real problems to which the existence and use of artificial intelligence (AI) gives rise in the application of private law's causal rules. It considers two.

The first is a problem of proof. Causation is difficult to prove in many contexts.[1] It has been claimed that establishing causal facts in cases involving AI is likely to be especially difficult due to the nature of AI. The operation of the machine learning algorithms which power certain AI systems is variously referred to as opaque, non-transparent, or constituting a 'black box'.[2] This opacity leads some to argue for a modification in various private law rules, in particular those on proof of causation.[3]

The second problem is thought to emerge from the sense or senses in which AI is 'autonomous'. Private law attributes significance, in its rules on causation, to the intervening agency of others. Certain kinds of voluntary intervention by another preclude a wrongdoer's liability in respect of a harm. If AI is capable of the kind of

With thanks to Isra Black and Nick McBride for helpful comments on a draft.

1 See S Steel, *Proof of Causation in Tort Law* (Cambridge University Press 2015) 5–10.

2 See, for example, Y Bathaee, 'The Artificial Intelligence Black Box and the Failure of Intent and Causation' (2018) 31 *Harvard Journal of Law and Technology* 890; J Burrell 'How the Machine 'thinks': Understanding Opacity in Machine Learning Algorithms' (2016) Big Data & Society, June; S Chesterman, 'Through a Glass, Darkly: Artificial Intelligence and the Problem of Opacity' (2021) 69 *American Journal of Comparative Law* 271.

3 See later: Part I.

agency relevant to the rules on intervening agency, then it would seem to follow that the use of AI could have a liability-avoiding effect: by using AI, a person can avoid liability in respect of outcomes which would be causally attributable to the person but for the use of AI. A related issue concerns the potential unforeseeability of harm caused by AI: in so far as AI systems act without the control and supervision of human beings, the modes by which they cause harm may be so unforeseeable, the thought runs, as to relieve users or creators of the system of liability in respect of those harms.

I PROOF OF CAUSATION

Let's distinguish three kinds of uncertainty about what caused something. First, there is uncertainty due to lack of expertise. A non-economist may be uncertain why a government policy caused inflation, while an economist is not. Second, there is uncertainty due to evidence relevant to causation being destroyed, tampered with, or not gathered. If a doctor loses a medical file detailing features of a patient's condition at various times, this may make it difficult to determine what caused a deterioration in the patient's condition. If someone is bitten by a dog which is not micro-chipped with its owner's information, it may be impossible to determine the owner. Third, there is uncertainty which obtains even with relevant expertise and the absence of evidence destruction, tampering or non-collection.

All three kinds of causal uncertainty have been discussed in the context of AI. In relation to the first, there is a concern about public, non-expert, lack of understanding of the operation of AI.[4] In itself this poses no problem for the application of the private law rules on causation: the lack of general public understanding of AI is no more relevant to the ex post determination of causal issues in litigation than the lack of general public understanding of the mechanisms by which asbestos causes cancer.[5]

The second kind of uncertainty involves the absence of causal evidence which is traceable to human agency either by an act (e.g., evidence destruction) or an omission (e.g., failure to record important information or failure to disclose available information). Clearly, the inability of a person to establish causal facts relevant to litigation due to the conduct of another is not unique to cases involving AI. Porat and Stein argued more than twenty years ago that the law ought to recognise general legal duties to take reasonable care to create and maintain evidence relevant to litigation.[6] Nor is it the case that we are uniquely vulnerable, in seeking to enforce

4 See Chesterman, above n 2.

5 Except, indirectly: the ordinary person's understanding of the operation might be relevant to whether an individual's response to an AI is a reasonable one.

6 See A Porat and A Stein, *Tort Liability under Uncertainty* (Oxford University Press 2001). The duties are 'general' in the sense that they apply to everyone, not simply those engaged in litigation – contrast duties arising from disclosure or discovery orders, or arising from undertakings.

our rights, to the control of the creators or users of AI, in relation to the availability of causal evidence. There are several contexts in which a person's ability to establish a claim against a person who has possibly wronged them is particularly dependent upon the wrongdoer's own evidence-recording. For instance, an unconscious patient is dependent upon the hospital's monitoring and recording of data to establish legal claims in the event of mistreatment. Conversely, the existence of AI sometimes provides us with an *enhanced* ability to record facts relevant to causation in litigation. An autonomous, AI-powered, vehicle will likely have detailed records of the path of the vehicle in an accident. If we are seeking to answer a causal counterfactual about, say, what would have happened had the vehicle made a manoeuvre earlier, the likelihood is that there will be more available evidence to answer that question: the car's sensors will register the location of nearby vehicles, their speed, the weather conditions, and so on. This enhanced ability is not *unique* to AI, it might be noted: existing computerised vehicles, not powered by machine learning algorithms, will likely produce more evidence relevant to establishing causal issues than non-computerised vehicles; a simple dashboard camera captures data relevant to establishing liability in the event of an accident.[7]

Nonetheless, it seems true that each of us is vulnerable to being unable to establish our rights in certain cases involving harm caused by AI precisely because *ex post* determination of causation will be difficult *unless* the AI is created in such a way as to preserve, or allow the extraction of, causal information. This seems especially true in relation to what we might call 'informational' or 'decisional' AI: these are AI systems powered by machine learning to provide information which will be relied upon by a person in deciding what to do – for instance, in deciding whether to grant a person a loan – or which will execute decisions based on the model produced by its learning – for instance, whether to purchase certain shares.[8] Suppose an AI system is tasked with purchasing pharmaceutical shares and the issue is whether the system relied upon false statements made by a company whose shares it purchased. Unless the basis on which the system purchased the shares can be reconstructed on the balance of probabilities, it will be impossible to establish any claim for misrepresentation, which requires that the misrepresentation had a causal impact upon the entry into the transaction.

The problem might seem trivial: surely, it might be said, the machine learns a model for purchasing shares which can be represented as a set of rules involving necessary conditions and sufficient conditions: 'if the company has features, X, Y, Z, but not A, then always invest at level L'. If so, then it should be possible to determine, counterfactually, whether the system would have entered a transaction but

7 A fact recognised by insurance companies which offer discounts to car users who install dashboard cameras.

8 A Selbst, 'Negligence and AI's Human Users' (2020) 100 *Boston University Law Review* 1315, 1319 refers similarly to 'decision-assistance' AI.

for the false information. Some machine learning algorithms learn a model which is straightforwardly representable in this way.[9]

The problem can be more complex, however. The features of a situation which a machine learning system takes into account may be (a) extraordinarily large in number, (b) given subtle and complex weightings in making a decision, (c) not recoverable after the decision is made. It is not clear to me whether the problem with representing decisions of deep learning systems in terms of rules is a conceptual problem or only an epistemic one. It is an epistemic problem if, in principle, the model could be represented as a fiendishly complex set of 'if … then' propositions, but given the limits of human brain power, and other resources, these propositions cannot be set out in full. It is also somewhat unclear to me whether the problem is as intractable as is typically claimed for the following reason. In determining whether a specific piece of information was a cause of an entry into a transaction, it is not necessary to have a complete account of the model of the AI system. It is possible to ask a more localised question: if the inputs to the system at the time of the entry into the transaction were varied simply to exclude the specific misrepresentation, what would the output have been? Compare: it is not necessary to be able to answer causal questions about the movement of a physical object to have a complete law-like account of such objects in all conceivable circumstances.

It seems that it is possible to create algorithms which can themselves assess these kinds of counterfactual question about enormously complex models. A sizeable literature now exists, particularly in the data protection context, which recommends the adoption of 'counterfactual explanations' as a means of explaining the, otherwise opaque, outputs of decisional AI.[10] The basic idea, put crudely, is that when one is told by an obnoxious AI that one will not be granted a loan, one should be given a counterfactual explanation of the form 'if x, y, z features of your situation had been different, then the outcome would have changed'. If it is possible to provide these counterfactual explanations, then determining specific causation by means of similar counterfactuals should also be possible.

The ability to provide answers to such counterfactuals in specific cases still seems to depend upon an ability to know the inputs into the AI model – otherwise one cannot test what would have happened had a particular input not been present, given the other inputs at that time – and the collection of this information is, in principle,

9 See the different kinds of model – in particular rule-based and decision tree models – described in P Hacker, R Krestel, S Grundmann and F Naumann, 'Explainable AI under Contract and Tort Law: Legal Incentives and Technical Challenges' (2020) 28 *Artificial Intelligence and Law* 415, 431.

10 See, for example, S Wachter, B Mittelstadt and C Russell, 'Counterfactual Explanations without Opening the Black Box: Automated Decisions and the GDPR' (2018) 31 *Harvard Journal of Law and Technology* 841. For helpful overviews, see K Sokol and P Flach, 'Counterfactual Explanations of Machine Learning Predictions: Opportunities and Challenges for AI Safety' (2019) SafeAI@AAAI; S Verma, J Dickerson, and K Hines, 'Counterfactual Explanations for Machine Learning: A Review' <arXiv:2010.10596v1> [cs.LG] 20 Oct 2020.

within the control of the AI creator. The question that arises in such cases is what response private law does or should have to the failure to collect or retain such information when it is reasonable to do so.

English law has developed principles for situations in which one person bears some responsibility for the absence of evidence about causation or other elements of liability.[11] Consider *Keefe v The Isle of Man Steam Packet Company*.[12] The defendant breached its duty to monitor noise levels on its ships. The estate of a deceased former employee of the defendant alleged that the defendant's failure to monitor and take steps to reduce the noise levels caused the deceased to be exposed to excessive noise, leading to hearing loss. The trial judge rejected the claim for want of proof that the claimant had been repeatedly exposed to excess levels of noise. The Court of Appeal disagreed, finding that the hearing loss had been caused by exposure to excessive noise levels. According to Longmore LJ, the judge had not given weight to the 'potent additional consideration that any difficulty of proof for the claimant has been caused by the defendant's breach of duty in failing to take any measurements'.[13] In such circumstances, 'the court should judge a claimant's evidence benevolently and the defendant's evidence critically'.[14]

The *Keefe* reasoning was accepted to apply in principle in relation to causation in *Shawe-Lincoln v Neelakandan*.[15] The causal issue in this case was whether earlier admission to hospital by the defendant GP would have lessened the extent of the claimant's paralysis. This turned on whether, upon earlier admission, neurological observations by hospital doctors would have revealed the claimant to have been in a deteriorating neurological condition, which would then have received emergency treatment. The claimant argued that there were no records of what his condition would have been upon earlier admission precisely because of the defendant's negligent failure to refer to hospital.[16] The judge accepted that *Keefe* was relevant in principle to issue of causation in medical negligence.[17] Its effect was not to reverse the burden of proof but rather 'it is concerned with the weight which is to be attached to evidence and the circumstances in which the court may draw inferences'.[18]

11 The next two paragraphs are drawn substantially from S Steel, *Proof of Causation in Tort Law* (Cambridge University Press, 2015). That chapter contains an account of similar rules in German and US law. The general principle in English law traces back to *Armory v Delamirie* (1722) 1 Strange 505, 93 ER 664.

12 [2010] EWCA Civ 683.

13 Ibid. [18].

14 Ibid. [19]. For further instances of this reasoning, citing *Keefe*, see *Mickelwright v Surrey County Council* [2011] EWCA Civ 922 (D, a local council, negligently failed to inspect trees, and one tree fell, killing the victim; here *Keefe* was held to be relevant in relation to the council's failure to inspect the tree to determine the reason why it fell); *Robinson v Bristol NHS Trust*, 4 June 2013, Bristol County Court (unreported).

15 [2012] EWHC 1150 (QB).

16 Ibid. [12].

17 Ibid. [83].

18 Ibid. [81].

A 'benevolent' approach is to be applied. However, the reasoning in *Keefe* was held to apply only with diminished force in *Neelakandan*. First, because it was not the defendant's personal duty to maintain the evidence in question – the only duty of the defendant was to visit and to refer the claimant to hospital; the hospital doctors would have owed a duty to carry out tests on the claimant – and second, because the claimant had himself contributed to uncertainty over causation by failing to call the doctors who did treat him on the 28 November as witnesses on the state of his condition then.[19] The judge found that it was more probable on the evidence that the clamant was not in a deteriorating condition and so would not have received emergency treatment.

If it is the claimant's own choice to use an AI system whose decision-making can only be reconstructed with difficulty – as could be the case with the misrepresentation example given above, a similar argument might be made that the failure to establish causation is not solely the defendant's responsibility.

The EU Expert Group on New Technologies has proposed a similar rule to the English law position, but formulated as a duty-imposing rule, and directed specifically at novel technologies:

> [20] There should be a duty on producers to equip technology with means of recording information about the operation of the technology (logging by design), if such information is typically essential for establishing whether a risk of the technology materialized, and if logging is appropriate and proportionate, taking into account, in particular, the technical feasibility and the costs of logging, the availability of alternative means of gathering such information, the type and magnitude of the risks posed by the technology, and any adverse implications logging may have on the rights of others.
>
> [21] Logging must be done in accordance with otherwise applicable law, in particular data protection law and the rules concerning the protection of trade secrets.

The breach of this duty then triggers a rebuttable presumption that the condition of liability in respect of which the missing information is relevant is fulfilled.[20] The proposal envisages the breach of this duty triggering the presumption even when the person being held liable is not the producer, but the operator. In that event, the latter is given a claim against the producer in respect of the liability.[21]

From a private lawyer's perspective, such a duty raises interesting justificatory questions. Absent a special circumstance, positive legal duties between strangers are unusual and restricted. Positive duties typically arise from undertakings, innocent creation of risk to right-protected interests, or control over a danger posed to right-protected interests.[22] A positive duty to create products with data-gathering and

19 Ibid. [83]. This would likely have been relevant to the state of his condition at the earlier time.
20 Ibid. [22].
21 Ibid. [23].
22 See S Steel, 'Rationalising Omissions Liability in Negligence' (2019) 135 *LQR* 484.

retention features does not itself seem to further the *safety* of the product (except indirectly, in so far as it restores the threat of tort liability for unsafe AI products). Rather, it serves to facilitate the ascertainment of facts necessary for the enforcement of legal rights in relation to the product. A common lawyer might describe this as a duty, therefore, that furthers the purely economic interests of others: the interest in being able to enforce one's secondary right to compensation.

Nonetheless, such a duty upon producers seems justifiable. Producers of products know as a statistical virtual certainty that some of their products will malfunction, and that there is at least a significant likelihood that, despite all reasonable care being taken, some of their products will cause infringements of the rights of others. Suppose there is no way of determining whether, in a particular case, an AI product caused damage unless a data-gathering function is included. If it were permissible for producers to proceed in such circumstances without installing the data-gathering devices, then it would be permissible to create a situation where one infringed the rights of others and the other would never have enforceable compensatory rights in relation to the infringement. If a person knows that they will incur a secondary duty to compensate, however, then they ought to take reasonable steps towards ensuring that they will be able to fulfil that duty. The duty to have liability insurance in certain contexts could have a similar basis: in certain contexts, we know that there is a significant possibility that we will unintentionally infringe the rights of others. In these contexts, especially when the consequences of the infringement are likely to be severe, there is plausibly a duty to take measures to ensure that one will be able to fulfil any compensatory duty that arises from the infringement.

Now consider the third form of uncertainty – uncertainty that cannot be resolved with expertise and reasonable efforts at the creation and maintenance of evidence. This kind of uncertainty is inevitable in any legal system, in relation to all sorts of factual questions. Sometimes it just so happens that it is impossible to determine what happened in the past. When this is no one's responsibility, and when it is simply a matter of bad luck, most legal systems retain their orthodox burden of proof rule such that, in relation to causation, the claimant loses the factual issue. Some pressure to depart from this position typically arises when there is a *systematic* impossibility of proving causation in relation to certain activities – that is, when it is recurrently, and so, normally, predictably, impossible to establish causation in a certain context. In English law, the main examples are cases involving asbestos and mesothelioma, in which it is scientifically impossible to establish which amongst several wrongful risk imposers caused a particular person's cancer.[23] In cases in which proof of causation is 'scientifically' impossible on the balance of probabilities, and in which the defendant has done something which is known on the balance of probabilities to be the same kind of thing as that which caused the claimant's

[23] *Fairchild v Glenhaven Funeral Services Ltd* [2002] UKHL 22, [2003] 1 AC 32.

injury, it suffices to show that the breach materially increased the risk of the injury suffered.[24] At common law, this generates liability in proportion to the probability that the defendant caused the injury.[25]

We can ask at least two questions about this third kind of uncertainty and AI. The first is whether AI really implicates this kind of uncertainty. The second is, if it does, whether this justifies an alteration in the standard proof rules. Consider each in turn.

The argument that AI does involve this kind of uncertainty is based on the sheer complexity and obscurity of the models developed by certain machine learning systems.[26] As noted above, however, there do appear to be methods by which specific counterfactual questions can be put to AI systems, and there is an enormous literature on scientific methods for improving the explainability of models. Suppose, however, that there are significant limits to this and that it is not infrequently impossible to determine ex-post *why* a particular decision was reached by an AI system. It is worth pointing out that in respect of many private law liabilities, this is unproblematic. This is for two reasons. First, specifically in relation to causation, it is possible to have causal knowledge without knowing the precise mechanism by which something causes something else. Tort lawyers are familiar with this from asbestos mesothelioma cases. Asbestos causes mesothelioma. The precise mechanism by which it does so is not well understood, however. This does not preclude us from saying that a particular person's mesothelioma was caused by asbestos (although it does preclude us from identifying a specific exposure to asbestos among many as causative).

Second, and this point is not directed to the causal element of liability as such, liability is often independent of the reasons why a particular, harmful, decision was reached. An autonomous vehicle which does not identify a class of significant risks posed by an oncoming vehicle which an ordinary human would recognise is defective. Nothing needs to be known about the vehicle's 'reasons' for not recognising these risks to infer this. The conclusion of defect can be reached simply on the basis that the vehicle fails to recognise significant, ordinary, risks of harm,

[24] See Steel above (n 1), chapter 4.

[25] *Barker v Corus (UK) Ltd* [2006] UKHL 20, [2006] 2 AC 572. Joint and several liability applies in mesothelioma cases: Compensation Act 2006, section 3.

[26] Examples of the claim that proof of causation in cases involving AI will be especially difficult: Liability for Artificial Intelligence and Other Emerging Digital Technologies (2019, EU Commission), 50: '… given the practical implications of the complexity and opacity of emerging digital technologies in particular, victims may be in a weaker position to establish causation than in other tort cases, where the events leading to the harm can be more easily analysed in retrospect, even from the victim's point of view'; S Wojtczak and P Ksiezak, 'Causation in Civil Law and the Problems of Transparency in AI' (2021) 4 *European Review of Private Law* 561; M Martin-Casals, 'Causation and Scope of Liability in the Internet of Things (IoT)' in S Lohsse, R Schulze and D Staudenmayer, *Liability for Artificial Intelligence and the Internet of Things: Münster Colloquia on EU Law and the Digital Economy IV* (Hart Publishing 2019) 215.

when ordinary persons would do so. Similarly, if it were desirable for certain kinds of artificial intelligence to be classified as legal persons whose liabilities were determined by reference to the tort of negligence, it is possible to determine the issue of whether the vehicle's activity is in breach of a duty of care without peering too deeply. The mere fact that the vehicle does not identify certain kinds of risk, or has traded off substantial risk to a stranger against minor benefit to a passenger is sufficient to determine the issue of breach. The reasons why the risks were imposed or the trade-off made are not relevant to the objective standard imposed by the tort of negligence. Under strict liability regimes which merely require the involvement of the operation of a thing, the problem is non-existent.[27] Clearly, the issue is different when the reasons why a decision was made are central to the wrong itself: a much-discussed example is the wrong of direct discrimination, in which acting upon certain reasons in favour or against a decision is part of what makes the conduct wrongful.

Consider now the normative question on the supposition that AI not infrequently does involve the third kind of uncertainty. Uncertainty of this kind creates an incentives problem: in so far as the threat of private law liability deters wrongful harm, this threat is largely eliminated when a risk imposer can reliably predict that causation will be impossible to establish. Focussing only on incentives, the threat of liability can be restored either by a reversal of the burden of proof, proportional liability, or by accepting a material increase in risk as sufficient proof of causation. These measures might also incentivise the development of further methods of rendering proof of causation possible. If incentives were the only morally relevant considerations, then one of these proposals ought, plausibly, to be adopted – at least assuming that a system of fines for wrongful risk imposition would not be an equal or more effective deterrent of wrongful harm – albeit it is difficult to believe that there is a case for a specialised AI rule, rather than one that also applies to other forms of recurrent, predictable causal uncertainty.

Incentives-based considerations are not the only morally relevant considerations, however.[28] The mere fact that the imposition of liability will incentivise people to conform to their legal duties does not show that it is justifiable to impose such liability on a particular person. A liability-bearer can sometimes reasonably object: 'while this legal liability would make everyone better off, why am *I* being used as a means of serving the public good of deterrence?' Something more is needed to show that the liability-bearer is morally liable to the imposition of a burden justified by a deterrent aim. If the duty-bearer has behaved in a particularly culpable manner in imposing a risk of harm, this might alleviate their objection to being subject to

[27] See similarly J Borghetti, 'Civil Liability for Artificial Intelligence: What Should Its Basis Be?' (2019) 17 *La Revue des Juristes de Sciences Po* 94, 100.

[28] For a more extended explanation of the points here, see S Steel, 'Deterrence in Private Law' in H Psarras and S Steel (eds), *Private Law and Practical Reason* (Oxford University Press 2022).

an increased risk of error on the causal issue.[29] In the context of AI, however, it is difficult to envisage cases in which the duty-bearer has behaved with high culpability and in which there is a genuine causal problem. If the culpable choice was to employ AI in some context, then the relevant causal counterfactual would be one in which the AI was *not* employed. That counterfactual would not necessarily give rise to causal uncertainty of the third kind under discussion.[30]

In at least one category of case potentially within this third kind of causal uncertainty, it is not clear that an alteration of the general proof rules on causation would be justified. Suppose that a person authorises an AI to purchase shares on her behalf. Suppose it is impossible to identify, in any particular case, whether the algorithm relied upon the representation. In these circumstances a claim for rescission of any transaction would fail for want of proof that the transaction was induced by the misrepresentation. At least in relation to innocent or not-grossly negligent misrepresentations in a non-consumer context, it seems unjustified to alter the general rules of proof here for the benefit of the representee. Suppose it is purely speculative whether the representation had a difference-making impact upon the AI's transactional decision; it is impossible to assign a reliable probability to its having done so. At least as a matter of interpersonal fairness, the case for altering the proof rules is no stronger here than it is in misrepresentations made to human beings, and arguably weaker in so far as it can be said the investor freely chose to adopt an investment technique that makes it impossible to determine the basis of any transactional decision.

II CAUSATION AND INTERVENING AGENCY

The problem of intervening agency concerns situations in which a person's conduct – call this person the 'original agent' – only results in harm in virtue of another person's conduct, when the latter person acts independently of the original agent. 'Independently' here means 'without the original agent intending the other agent to contribute to the causing of harm'. Call the latter person an 'intervening agent'. For example: A negligently stores some fireworks in A's market stall. A firework ignites, rockets into the air, is caught by B, who panics and throws the firework toward C, in whose face the firework explodes. Here A is the original agent. B is the intervening

[29] In German law, a reversal of the burden of proof applies on causation in certain contexts when the duty-bearer has behaved with gross fault: see Steel above n 1, ch 5.

[30] For discussion of this, see Steel (n 1) 268–289. Note also here the EU Expert Group's proposal (above n 26, at [26]) that the claimant's causal proof burden be 'alleviated' (the proposal does not specify how) based on 'balancing' of various factors. The proposal seems undesirable as stated, on consistency grounds: it would create an enclave of special proof rules for 'emerging digital technology' when the factors mentioned, if they justify an alleviation of causal proof rules in this context, also justify such an alleviation in other contexts. A second point is that this proposal is more difficult to justify in the common law which adopts the balance of probabilities standard of proof; in civilian jurisdictions, a higher standard of proof is typically insisted upon even in private law cases. See Steel (above n 1), ch 2.

agent. The legal and moral issue is whether A is responsible – for our purposes, in such a way as to give rise to compensatory liability in private law – for C's loss, despite the fact that another agent, B, was involved in the causing of C's loss.

Existing discussions of this problem in the context of AI tend to focus on the issue of whether particular interventions of an AI machine will count as reasonably foreseeable.[31] The issue of reasonable foreseeability of an intervention is not determinative of the issue in English law, however (and is not usually considered a 'causal' issue at all). The current law determines whether an intervening agent's conduct relieves the original agent of legal responsibility for an outcome partly by reference to the normative quality of the intervening agent's conduct. This section first considers the application of those foreseeability-independent rules, then it turns to the issue of foreseeability.

A *Intervening Agency*

A wrongful and highly culpable intervention is most likely to relieve the original agent of liability. If I am taken to hospital as a result of your negligence, and I am then killed by an opportunistically evil doctor who would not otherwise have killed me, you are not liable for my death. If the doctor's conduct is grossly unreasonable, there is some legal support for it being the case that the loss which would not have occurred but-for that gross unreasonableness is solely the doctor's responsibility.[32] If the doctor's conduct is merely unreasonable, but not grossly so, the loss that would not have occurred but for that unreasonable treatment is still your responsibility vis a vis me. It seems reasonably well established that subsequent mere *negligence* does not break the chain of causation. A *fortiori*, a non-negligent action by another, even if necessary for the harmful outcome to ensue. Notice that it seems impossible to explain these rules by reference to the concept of foreseeability. Gross negligence is simply not unforeseeable. So the relevance of intervening agency, according to the current law, is not simply a function of its foreseeability.[33]

Is it possible for the decision made by a machine-learning system to break the chain of causation by virtue of these rules? In answering this question, it is tempting immediately to consider the possibility that the machine is itself an agent for the purposes of the intervening agency rules. Before turning to this possibility, it will be helpful first to consider situations in which a human being, or group of human beings, is culpably responsible for the AI's decision.

[31] See, for example, M Montagnani and M Cavallo, 'Liability and Emerging Digital Technologies: An EU Perspective'(2021) 11 *Notre Dame Journal of Comparative and International Law* 209, 217; Bathae (n 2) 923ff.

[32] *Wright v Cambridge Medical Group* [2011] EWCA Civ 669, [2013] QB 312 [37].

[33] See the separation of the issue of foreseeability from the issue of the chain of causation in *Corr v IBC Vehicles Ltd* [2008] UKHL 13, [2008] 1 AC 884 [11]–[14] (Lord Bingham).

Suppose, for instance, that an autonomous vehicle has been deliberately trained so that it makes decisions which, if taken by a human being not acting under pressured circumstances, would be wrongful and highly culpable. Consider:

> *Cars.* A unreasonably fails to install a software update on A's autonomous vehicle, AV, with the result that the vehicle crashes into a road barrier, and skids into the middle of a busy road. B's autonomous vehicle, BV, swerves out of the way of A's car, and crashes into C, a pedestrian.[34]

Suppose that BV has been trained by a malicious employee of its manufacturer to take steps to avoid *any* injury to its occupant in an accident, even when it is necessary to inflict grave harm on innocent bystanders in order to achieve this. Inflicting serious harms on innocent bystanders to avoid minor harms is clearly wrongful and intentionally engineering BV such that it does this is a wrongful, highly culpable act. Here, then, A – assuming it is not the case that A ought to have known of the employee's conduct – should be able to argue successfully that the employee's conduct results in a break in the chain of causation between A's breach and C's harm. The same result would follow if BV's vehicle had been hacked by a malicious hacker to execute the same manoeuvre, and B or the manufacturer of BV had no responsibility in relation to this. Conversely, A would not be able to successfully argue that BV's intervention broke the chain of causation when this was due to mere negligence on the part of BV's manufacturer, or BV's manufacturer's liability in relation to the intervention was based solely on a strict liability rule.

It might be objected that the acts attributable to BV's manufacturer do not truly intervene between A's breach and C's harm. In the standard situation of intervening causation which breaks the chain, there is an action which occurs *after* the original agent's wrongful conduct and before C's harm. In *Cars*, and more generally in cases involving culpable supervised learning, the culpable act will take sometimes take place *before* the original agent's wrongful conduct. It's difficult to see why this should make a difference, however. Compare these two examples:

> *Forest fire*. A negligently fails to extinguish A's barbeque properly. After A leaves the area, B fans the flames, and C's house is engulfed by a forest fire as a result.
>
> *Forest fire 2*. A negligently fails to extinguish A's barbeque properly. B has hidden an electric fan with a sensor nearby where people typically have barbeques. The fan switches on after A leaves the area.

In *Forest fire 2*, B's culpable act is temporally prior to A's breach, as in *Cars*, but it is difficult to accept that there is any normatively important difference between the two cases. If B's culpable act relieves A of liability in *Forest fire*, it ought to do so in *Forest fire 2*.

So far the analysis has proceeded by focussing upon the human being(s) who have created or have control over the AI. Their conduct has been considered as the

[34] Assume nothing further can be done by A after the initial crash.

relevant conduct for the application of the rules on intervening causation. It might now be objected that this view of how the law applies oversimplifies the situation. The objection is that this view ignores the fact that an AI system could or should itself be considered as an 'agent' for the purposes of these rules. The idea that the AI system is itself an agent is the source of the concern that AI creates a 'responsibility gap': by the interposition of an AI system, the original agent is relieved of responsibility and liability which would otherwise exist.[35]

Answering this objection requires an account of the rationale of the intervening agency rules, which will in turn provide an account of the relevant sense of 'agency'. The differentiations the law draws between different levels of *culpability* in respect of an outcome implies that the rules are based, at least in part, upon the idea that, absent some special fact such as one's complicity or an undertaking to protect, one should not be held liable in respect of an outcome for which another agent is either comparatively much more to blame or whose blameworthiness in relation to the outcome reaches some threshold level. If this is correct, then the relevant sense of 'agency' involves a capacity to be *blameworthy*.

Machine learning systems are capable of (i) receiving information from the world, (ii) classifying that information, and (iii) acting upon the classifications. Clearly, (i)–(iii) are insufficient for an entity to be capable of blameworthy conduct; iPhones are capable of (i)–(iii). Machine learning systems are also capable of (iv) identifying new means towards their assigned goals, and (v) updating the way in which they identify such means, given their experience.[36] It seems unlikely, however, that (iv) and (v) constitute machine-learning systems with the capacities for culpable agency. An ability to recognise more effective causal means to an end, intuitively, seems insufficient. Even if an entity can learn new, more effective, strategies for watering citrus plants, based on its experience, this is consistent with the entity having no ability to assess the desirability of watering citrus plants, or an ability to decide whether to water citrus plants. In short, the entity has no ability to set its own ends, nor its own ability to assess the desirability of pursuit of certain ends.[37]

It might be objected that the rationale of the intervening agency rules cannot be used to relieve a person of liability in virtue of another's much greater *blameworthiness* for an outcome since the rules apply to acts which are not wrongful, and so not candidates for blame. For instance, in *Corr v IBC Vehicles*, the House of Lords considered whether the deceased's suicide broke the chain of causation between

[35] For discussion (and debunking) of the idea that the use of AI creates a 'responsibility gap' see T Simpson and V Muller, 'Just War and Robots' Killings' (2016) 66 *Philosophical Quarterly* 302. Cf P Huberman, 'A Theory of Vicarious Liability for Autonomous-Machine-Caused Harm' (2021) 58 *Osgoode Hall LJ* 233, 235.

[36] See Huberman (n 35) 236: 'through machine learning processes, AAs' controlling algorithms are designed by their learning algorithms. In this latter affirmative sense, AAs modify their behaviours through internally caused processes – a kind of functional agency'.

[37] Cf Simpson and Muller (n 35).

his employer's earlier tort, which had caused the deceased to suffer severe depression, and his death.[38] The effect of the suicide was considered under the rules on intervening causation, without any assessment of whether the suicide was 'blameworthy'.[39] Instead, the focus was upon whether the suicide could be considered fully voluntary.[40] The issue was whether the deceased had made 'a voluntary, informed decision … as an adult of sound mind making and giving effect to a personal decision about his own future'.[41] It was held that he had not. It seems implicitly assumed, however, that the relevant notion of 'voluntariness' here involves a capacity to make one's own decisions about the future direction of one's life, free from certain kinds of constraint. It seems doubtful that this kind of voluntariness is possessed by machine learning systems as they currently exist.

Even if it is or becomes the case that machine learning systems have the relevant capacities to make them agents for the purposes of intervening agency rules, it does not necessarily follow that a problematic 'responsibility gap' emerges. Vicarious liability is a form of liability which is not sensitive to the intervening agency rule: it is, in this sense, a non-causal liability. A person can be liable for another's autonomous conduct, absent the breach of a duty to prevent its resulting in harm, and absent any fault with respect to the conduct. Thus, even if the machine constitutes an intervening agent, this is not considered, under the existing law, to be a normative barrier to the imposition of *any* liability in respect of the agent's conduct.[42]

B *Foreseeability*

A foreseeability requirement of some kind is generally a necessary condition of liability for compensatory damages in respect of a loss in tort and contract. Foreseeability plays a number of roles in determining liability: here, I focus on its role in relation to 'remoteness', which is sometimes bundled together with 'legal causation' and, in the United States, 'proximate cause'. In tort, the type of loss must be reasonably foreseeable at the date of breach to be recoverable unless the tort is intentionally committed. In contract, as a default, the type of loss must be reasonably foreseeable as not unlikely to occur at the date of formation.[43] A recurring concern raised in the literature is that the ability of machine learning systems to respond innovatively to their environment – to learn new information and act upon it – will often result in

[38] *Corr* (n 33).

[39] Although this issue was broached in relation to whether a reduction could be made for contributory negligence.

[40] See *Corr* (n 33) [15]–[16] (Lord Bingham).

[41] *Corr* (n 33) [15] (Lord Bingham).

[42] For proposals to create an analogous form of liability to vicarious liability, see Huberman (n 35); Phillip Morgan, 'Tort Law and AI – Vicarious Liability' in Ernest Lim and Phillip Morgan (eds), *The Cambridge Handbook of Private Law and Artificial Intelligence* (Cambridge University Press 2024).

[43] See generally A Burrows, *Remedies for Torts, Breach of Contract, and Equitable Wrongs* (4th edn, Oxford University Press 2019) 86–106.

their *unforeseeably* causing harm, and thus harm in respect of which the existing law will not provide a right to compensation.[44]

The extent to which there is a real issue here depends in part upon how the foreseeability requirement is understood. The current law, in tort, imposes a relatively undemanding requirement. This is so in two respects. First, a reasonable person can be required to foresee even very small risks of harm. If the risk of harm is more than 'far-fetched' it may be reasonably foreseeable.[45] Second, the causal mechanism by which the act or activity might cause harm does not need to be reasonably foreseeable with much granularity: even if there is a somewhat unusual mechanism by which the harm occurs, so long as it is reasonably describable as the materialisation of a foreseeable risk of the act or activity, the requirement is satisfied.[46] A detailed knowledge of complex network of processes by which a machine caused a harm is not necessarily required any more than a knowledge of the cellular mechanisms by which arsenic causes death.[47]

It also depends upon the basis of the liability at issue. If the claim is in negligence, the risk that the AI will make a harmful mistake will be foreseeable at a general level of abstraction, but if there is no reasonable precaution that can be taken to avoid or mitigate this risk, and yet it is considered reasonable to deploy the AI, then there will be no breach of duty at all. The remoteness issue does not then arise. If the AI machine has been insufficiently tested by its creator or user in such a way that amounts to a breach of a duty of care, then presumably the fact that the risk which materialised was not reasonably foreseeable is not necessarily a barrier to liability. Part of the purpose of a duty to make reasonable tests prior to use is to identify risks of use. If a risk which no reasonable person would have foreseen would have been identified by a reasonable test, then, as a matter of remoteness, it should not be open to the person in breach to escape liability by pointing to the unforeseeability of the risk. This is an instance of a broader phenomenon: the relevance and degree of foreseeability may be affected by the purpose of the defendant's duty.

If the claim is that the AI system constitutes a defective product, then the foreseeability issue is likely to arise, in the UK and the EU, in relation to the development risks defence. In this connection, it is reasonably foreseeable, at an abstract level, that the machine's learning system could make a harmful mistake, but it may not be reasonably foreseeable when and why it will make such a mistake. Presumably, it cannot be sufficient to defeat the defence that it is reasonably foreseeable that 'something might go wrong with the machine'. At such a level of abstraction, anything is foreseeable, and so the defence would never apply. Arguably, a risk of an erroneous,

44 See Montagnani and Cavallo (n 31) 217.

45 *Bolton v Stone* [1951] AC 850 (HL).

46 *Hughes v Lord Advocate* [1963] AC 837 (HL); *Jolley v Sutton London Borough Council* [2000] 1 WLR 1082 (HL).

47 The literature which poses the foreseeability problem in the context of AI does not really grapple with the issue of how broadly a risk may be described for the purposes of the foreseeability rule. Cf Bathaee (n 2) 923ff.

harm-causing decision being made by a learning algorithm is foreseeable in a more specific, fine-grained way; however, it is at least reasonably foreseeable at an abstract level *how* the harm would occur – through a mistake made by the learning algorithm. If it is possible to quantify relatively accurately the quantum of the risk of such a mistake, this might support the non-application of the defence: it should be possible reliably to insure against this risk or to pass on the cost to consumers. Consequently, the risk of overdeterrence of development which arguably justifies the defence would not be significant.

Suppose a corporation employs AI to do specified tasks that would typically have been done by human beings. Suppose that it is not negligent to do so: for instance, the reasonably foreseeable risks of harm are very low probability, the gravity of the harm which materialises is not likely to be significant and will be largely compensable, and the benefits of using the machine are substantial. Nonetheless, the fairness argument that might be thought to support vicarious liability has application in relation to those low risks: the corporation benefits from the deployment of the machine and this deployment involves the imposition risks for the corporation's own interest. If this form of strict liability is adopted, a question arises as to its scope. Specifically, it becomes necessary to identify the risks for which the person who deploys AI in their enterprise is strictly liable. Here, only a relatively abstract notion of foreseeable risk seems appropriate, if the concept is germane at all. Just as an employer may be liable for the misperformance of a task by an employee, even when the mode of misperformance is not reasonably foreseeable, one might think it appropriate that the misperformance of a task by an AI system is also a risk for which the employer ought to be liable. So long as the misperformance can reasonably be described as a mode of doing the assigned task, the issue of the foreseeability of the misperformance seems irrelevant. This is especially so if the harm which materialised would have been reasonably foreseeable to and reasonably preventable by a human being performing the task: in this event, the employer can be said, by its deployment of AI, to have created the circumstances in which the specific risk would be unforeseeable for its own benefit.[48]

By way of conclusion, it is worth mentioning one general argument offered for departing from, or mollifying, a foreseeability of harm requirement in this context. The argument is that the creator or user of the AI system chooses to create or use an entity that generates unforeseeable risks by virtue of its learning algorithms. As a matter of fairness, the argument runs, the creator or user ought to be held liable for the materialisation of these unforeseeable risks.[49] There is something to this,

[48] A different way of putting the point: if the AI succeeds in unpredictable ways that accrue to the benefit of the user/creator, then it is not unfair for the latter to bear the costs of its failure in unpredictable ways (within some limits).

[49] M Scherer, 'Regulating Artificial Intelligence Systems: Risks, Challenges, Competencies, and Strategies' (2016) 29 *Harvard Journal of Law & Technology* 353, 366; Martin-Casals (n 26) 224. It is not always clear to what foreseeability requirement this argument is directed, whether it be for the purposes of breach in negligence, remoteness generally, or defect.

but it is not clear how much further it goes than the point that the law should not require foresight with respect to the *precise details* of the causal mechanism, or type of injury, suffered. For instance, if one keeps a tiger in a city, it is reasonably foreseeable that it might *in various ways* cause harm, even if the precise mode by which it will harm on a particular occasion cannot be predicted with any reliability. The ability to predict the precise modality by which a thing will cause harm on a particular occasion, when one reasonably ought to know that the thing poses a general risk of harming in various ways, seems normatively irrelevant.[50]

III CONCLUSION

This chapter has outlined two central issues surrounding the application of the rules on causation to private law liability in respect of AI: the extent to which exceptional causal proof doctrines do and should apply to such cases and rules connected to legal causation. It has supported the recognition of responsibility-based alleviations of the general proof rules but raised doubts as to extension of existing exceptional causal proof doctrines based on impenetrable scientific uncertainty to liability for AI. It has raised doubts as to whether the rationale of the intervening agency rules should result in AI breaking the chain of causation, and supported the recognition of a broad understanding of foreseeability, particularly in contexts in which the duty-bearer ought to have taken steps which would have allowed causal chains to be more readily predictable at the time of breach.

[50] It should also be noted that the argument does not apply in relation to intervening acts of AI *not created* or used by the original agent sought to be held liable.

9

Product Liability Law and AI

Revival or Death of Product Liability Law

Vibe Ulfbeck

I INTRODUCTION

AI devices will increasingly form part of our daily lives, whether as incorporated into physical products such as cars and vacuum cleaners or as 'standalone' applications we acquire and that can interact through Internet of Things ('IoT') devices.

It has often been pointed out that the development towards more application of AI solutions will imply that human functions will be taken over by machines, thereby reducing the need to focus on liability for human errors and increasing the need to focus on liability for malfunctioning products. This would bring product liability rules to the fore.[1] The question is, however, how these rules will work in the new context.

Product liability concerns physical damage caused by physical products. It is based on notions of control as embedded in the concept of a 'defect' and the idea of clearly distinguishable risk spheres in the value chain.[2] In contrast, AI has 'unpredictability' and 'black box' explanation problems as built in features[3] and may present itself as both 'intangible' and highly 'complex' in its interaction capabilities. Consequently, it challenges both the idea of liability based on control through a defectiveness test and the idea of product liability as concerned with a world of physical objects that are distributed in a clearly organised value chain.[4]

1 Cerre, 'Report, 2021', <www.cerre.eu/publications/eu-liability-rules-age-of-artificial-intelligence-ai/>, 49; Taivo Liivak, 'Liability of a Manufacturer of Fully Autonomous and Connected Vehicles under the Product Liability Directive' (2018) 4 *International Comparative Jurisprudence* 178, 178–189; Vibe Ulfbeck, 'Autonomous Ships and Product Liability under the EU Directive' in Henrik Ringbom, Erik Røsæg and Trond Solvang (eds), *Autonomous Ships and the Law* (Routledge 2021).

2 The idea of clearly distinguishable risk spheres in the value chain is reflected in the central product liability principle that the producer cannot be held liable if it is probable that the defect which caused the damage did not exist at the time when the product was put into circulation by him, see PLD Article 7(b).

3 See Communication from the Commission of 10 January 2017, Building a European data economy, COM(2017) 9 where 'complexity', the legal nature of the IoT device and the autonomous nature of the device are identified as the main challenges with regard to product liability law.

4 The product liability regime is based on the idea that a product, once manufactured by the producer, is sold to a commercial buyer, who then passes it on to other buyers and sellers until it finally reaches the end user, for example, the consumer. This can be termed a 'clearly organised value chain'.

The aim of this contribution is to examine the impact of AI on central product liability concepts in order to be able to evaluate whether the product liability regime must indeed be expected to 'take over' as a central liability regime in the future. It focuses in particular on the product liability regime as represented in the EU product liability directive (PLD) and makes references also to the Proposal for a new PLD.[5] It starts out by providing an in-depth analysis of the central concept of a defect in product liability law in the context of AI (Section II) and then contextualises the findings by focusing on the value chain and its related concepts as the frame within which product liability law works (Section III). Section IV concludes.

II THE CONCEPT OF THE DEFECT: STANDARDISATION AND INDIVIDUALISATION AT THE SAME TIME?

A *The Reasonable Expectations Test in the Product Liability Directive*

According to Article 6 in the PLD, a product is defective if it does not live up to 'the safety which a reasonable person is entitled to expect, taking all circumstances into account'.[6] The test is a general test that relies on the concept of the 'reasonable person'. This concept is to be understood in an objective manner.[7] The decisive question is not what the victim actually expected from the product but what would generally be expected by a reasonable person (the public at

[5] The existing product liability regulation in the EU can be found in Council Directive 85/374/EEC of 25 July 1985 on the approximation of the laws, regulations and administrative provisions of the Member States concerning liability for defective products (PLD). A proposal for a revision of the PLD has recently been introduced, see Proposal for a Directive of the European Parliament and of the Council on liability for defective products, COM(2022) 495 final (Proposal for a new PLD). The Proposal for a new PLD has been underway for some time, see inter alia the EU commission's staff working document entitled 'Liability for emerging digital technologies', SWD (2018) 137 final, 25 April 2018. The EU Commission also established an expert group on Liability and New Technologies – the New Technologies Formation (the Expert Group). The task of the group was to establish the extent to which liability frameworks in the EU will continue to operate effectively in relation to emerging digital technologies (including artificial intelligence, the internet of things, and distributed ledger technologies). The Expert Group published its report, 'Report on Liability for Artificial Intelligence and other Emerging Technologies (the Expert Group Report), on November 21, 2019. See in particular pages 27–28. See also EU Commission White Paper on Artificial Intelligence, COM(2020) 65 final, 19 February 2020.

[6] Closely related to the concept of the defect is the concept of the risk development defence (PLD Article 7). This concept is not the focus of this chapter since it only becomes relevant as a liability exemption if a defect is proven to exist. Also not dealt with in this chapter, is fault-based product liability and other types of fault-based liability for AI systems, see in this regard Proposal for a Directive of the European Parliament and of the Council on adapting non-contractual civil liability rules to artificial intelligence (AI Liability Directive), COM(2022) 496 final.

[7] See, for example, Duncan Fairgrieve and others in Piotr Machinowsky (ed), *European Product Liability – An Analysis of the State of the Art in the Era of New Technologies* (2016) 51; Vibe Ulfbeck, *Erstatningsretlige Graenseområder* (DJOEF 2021), 241.

large). Furthermore, all circumstances must be taken into account when assessing the reasonable expectations, including the presentation of the product, the use to which it could reasonably be put and the time when the product was put into circulation. This makes the test a rather broad one.[8] The fact that the test relies, not on the actual, but on the legitimate expectations of the user, basically means that not any malfunction of the product is to be deemed a defect. Put differently, a product cannot necessarily be expected to be 100% safe.[9] For instance, cigarettes are sold on the market without liability for the producer although it is scientifically well established that smoking poses health risks. In the same way, pharmaceuticals are on the market without liability for the producer even though the products may have certain negative side effects.

Since the defectiveness test focuses on the expectations of the user and these expectations will most often not in reality be linked to the technical way in which the product has been construed, one could argue that the technological explanation for the malfunctioning of a product should be irrelevant. French and Belgium courts have taken this approach to the defectiveness assessment.[10] Carrying out the defectiveness evaluation without needing to focus on the technological explanation for a damage causing effect of the product would render the 'black box problem' related to AI products less important. However, in other court decisions, defectiveness assessments do focus on the underlying reasons for the defect when it comes to establishing proof of a defect.[11] Thus, establishing that something has gone wrong in the production process (fabrication defect) or that a product could technically have been manufactured in a way that would have eliminated the risk causing elements in the product (design defect) may be ways of establishing that a certain product is defective. In reality, therefore, product liability cases often involve the need for technical and technological expertise.

This also means that in order to be able to understand the challenges related to assessing whether an AI product is defective or not, it is necessary to understand – at least at a general level – how such a system is created and works.

8 It has often been pointed out that the concept is without any precise content, see Duncan Fairgrieve, Geraint Howells and Marcus Pilgerstorfer 'The Product Liability Directive: Time to Get Soft?' (2013) 4 *JETL* 1–33, 5–6. The Proposal for new PLD adds further criteria, see Article 6(a)-(h), including 'the effect on the product of any ability to continue to learn after deployment, see Article 6(c) and further below under E(3).

9 See, for example, Fairgrieve and others (n 7) 52, 53; Bernhard Koch, 'Austria' in Piotr Machinowsky (ed), *European Product Liability – An Analysis of the State of the Art in the Era of New Technologies* (2016) 125.

10 See the European Commission's Third Report on the Product Liability Directive, COM(2006) 486 Final, 10 with references to decisions from these jurisdictions.

11 See COM(2006) 486 Final, 10 with references to decisions from English courts, *Richardson v LRC Products Ltd* [2000] EWHC J0202-12; *Foster v Biosil* (2000) 59 BMLR 178, but see later *Alan Peter Ide v ATB Sales Limited* [2008] EWCA Civ 424 (CA). See also Fairgrieve, Howells and Pilgerstorfer (n 8) 9.

B *The Special Characteristics of AI Systems with Regard to the Defectiveness Assessment*

The feature of an AI system that is the most challenging to handle with regard to a defectiveness assessment is the autonomy of the system. Thus, in an AI system, an algorithm does not work solely on the basis of commands of an 'if … then' nature. Rather, the algorithm is programmed to be a 'self-learning' algorithm that can receive training and evolve on the basis of sets of data that it is exposed to.[12] The algorithm is programmed to find correlations between different phenomena, not causation. An AI system will not answer the question why there is a correlation between pictures of certain types of drivers and pictures of traffic accidents, it only identifies the correlation and 'acts' on the basis of this correlation by giving advice or by taking decisions. Before the AI system is put on the market, the algorithm is trained under the supervision of the developer. This means that the developer chooses the relevant datasets on the basis of which the training is carried out, and the developer tests the way in which the algorithm reacts to new data on the basis of its training. When the development of the AI system has been finalised, the AI system can in principle be put on the market. Some AI systems are programmed to continue learning after this stage on the basis of data received in 'real life' whereas others are 'frozen'.[13]

It has been claimed that 'authors often tend to mystify the decision-making mechanisms of algorithms as something 'unforeseeable, unpredictable or unquantifiable'.[14] Thus, from a legal perspective, it is important to understand in what sense an AI system may work in a way that is 'unpredictable, unforeseeable and unquantifiable'. At the general level, it can be argued that since the AI system is created by humans, it only does what it has been asked to do by humans. Thus, as explained above – a developer needs to create the algorithm through programming and to program the algorithm to be able to receive 'training' by being exposed to data in which it detects correlations. The developer also needs to decide on the basis of what data sets the algorithm is to be trained. The developer of course has control over the programming of the algorithm and the sets of data to which it is exposed in the 'laboratory' (an open real-world setting). Finally, the developer must test the created algorithm. However, in a number of respects, an AI system can be said to be 'unpredictable, unforeseeable and unquantifiable'. Firstly, the developer cannot know which correlations the algorithm will find and on what basis two phenomena are deemed to have a correlation. For instance, an AI system for an autonomous

[12] For a description of classical AI relying on symbolic logic and neural networks, the behaviour of which can only be described statistically, see for instance Herbert Zech, 'Liability for Autonomous Systems: Tackling Specific Risks of Modern IT' in Sebastian Lohsse, Reiner Schulze, Dirk Staudemayer (eds), *Liability for Robotics and the Internet of Things* (Nomos 2019) 187–200.

[13] Cerre (n 1) 55.

[14] Liivak (n 1) 183.

vehicle trained on the basis of a large number of photos of traffic situations may find correlations between certain types of situations and certain types of drivers, but may also find correlations between the paper quality of different photos. Secondly, making sure the data set on which the algorithm is trained does not have any flaws is in itself a challenge. Thirdly, even though the trained algorithm is thoroughly tested prior to being put on the market, it will not be possible to test how the algorithm will work (what it has learned) in all of the situations that can potentially arise. Finally, to the extent the AI system has self-learning capabilities after it has been put on the market, the developer will have no control with the data to which the system will be exposed and on the basis of which it will learn. In these respects, an AI system can be described as 'unpredictable, unforeseeable and unquantifiable'.[15]

C *Defectiveness Assessment Methods*

In practice, courts have focused on different parameters when making defectiveness assessments.

Generally, the product is compared with the description of the product and other similar products.[16] Whereas, the description of the product will also be relevant with regard to AI products, comparing the product to other products may be less meaningful, as AI systems based on the same algorithm may evolve differently depending on the data they are exposed to.[17]

In the United States, the risk/utility test plays a central role in assessing defectiveness. In Europe, it is not entirely clear to what extent this test can be used.[18] On the one hand, it has been argued that the reasonable expectations of the consumer can be and should be assessed regardless of cost/benefit considerations which may tend to introduce a fault-based liability regime through the back door. On the other hand, it could also be argued that what can reasonably be expected is exactly that the

[15] See Tiago Sergio Cabral, 'Liability and Artificial Intelligence in the EU: Assessing the Adequacy of the Current Product Liability Directive' (2020) 27 *Maastricht Journal of European Comparative Law* 615, 625: 'The developer/producer will be unable to fully understand a decision by a machine'.

[16] See, for example, Fairgrieve and others (n 7) 57; Susana Navas, 'Producer Liability for AI-Based Technologies in the European Union' (2020) 9 *International Law Research* 77, 80.

[17] Y Berhamoud and J Ferland 'Artificial Intelligence & Damages: Assessing Liability and Calculating the Damages' in P D'Agostino, C Piovesan and A Gaon (eds) *Leading Legal Disruption: Artificial Intelligence as a Toolkit for Lawyers and the Law* (Thomson Reuters 2020) 6: 'Moreover, it may prove useless to try to compare AI tools, as conclusions reached for one AI tool (i.e., the one that is defective) will not be transposable to a second AI tool, because the two, even when designed together, will have – over time – learned and evolved differently'.

[18] The preamble to the PLD is silent in this regard. Piotr Machnikowski, 'Conclusions', in Piotr Machnikowski (ed), *European Product Liability – An Analysis of the State of the Art in the Era of New Technologies* (2016), 695 raises doubt as to the compatibility of the test with the Directive. Thomas Verheyen, 'Modern Theories of Product Warnings and European Product Liability Law' (2019) 15(3) *Utrecht Law Review* <https://doi.org/10.36633/ulr.541>, 44–55, 51 finds that the European law maker preferred the reasonable expectation test over the risk utility test.

utility of a product outweighs its risks. For instance, with regard to pharmaceuticals, not any side effect renders a product defective, since on balance, the product may be found to have more advantages than disadvantages. In practice, the risk utility test is clearly accepted in at least some European jurisdictions as part of the defectiveness assessment.[19] It could also be relevant with regard to AI products.

Further, standards, both public and private, can be relevant. The PLD only mentions that the manufacturer is exempt from liability if the defect is caused by the observance of mandatory, public regulation.[20] However, it is widely assumed that public safety regulation and implementation standards may also play a role in assessing whether or not a product is defective. Schepel puts it this way: 'Formulated negatively, failure to comply with industry standards will almost automatically lead to liability'.[21] In the area of product liability, it has been pointed out that in case law, there are different views on this in different jurisdictions.[22] It is (even) less certain the extent to which compliance with standards can also be used as a defence against liability (the so called 'regulatory compliance defence').[23] The question was recently addressed in an English case, *A F Wilkes v DePuy International Ltd*, concerning an artificial hip, a stem of which fractured. A main question in the case was whether the product (the hip) could be regarded as defective. In this regard, Hickinbottom J emphasised the importance of standards and regulation:

> In an appropriate case, compliance with such standards will have considerable weight; because they have been set at a level which the appropriate regulatory authority has determined is appropriate for safety purposes.
>
> The same is true, as is again common ground before me, with regard to compliance or non-compliance with regulations which apply to a product.
>
> Certainly, where every aspect of the product's design, manufacture and marketing has been the subject of the substantial scrutiny, by a regulatory body comprised of individuals selected for their experience and expertise in the product including its safety, on the basis of full information, and that body has assessed that the level of safety is acceptable, then it may be challenging for a claimant to prove that the level of safety that persons generally are entitled to expect is at a higher level.

[19] For German law, see BGH, 16.6.2009, VI ZR 107/08, BGHZ 181, 253 para 18. For further references see Fairgrieve, Howells and Pilgerstorfer (n 8) 7–8, finding that '[i]t is somewhat difficult to exclude risk-utility having some role in evaluating whether a disclosed risk is socially acceptable' and that '[t]he central test remains what 'persons generally are entitled to expect.' Part of the answer to what is socially acceptable may well include elements of risk utility'.

[20] PLD Article 7(d).

[21] See Harm Schepel, *The Constitution of Private Governance. Product Standards in the Regulation of Integrating Markets* (Hart Publishing 2005) 349, with reference to others.

[22] Duncan Fairgrieve and Geraint Howells, 'Rethinking Product Liability: A Missing Element in the European Commission's Third Review of the European Product Liability Directive' (2007) 70 *MLR* 962–78. In the Proposal for a new PLD, 'product safety requirements' are specifically mentioned as a criterion that is relevant for the defectiveness assessment, see Article 6(1)f.

[23] Fairgrieve and Howells (n 22) 972–973.

> The challenge is compounded where, as here, the standards for the product are set on a European-wide basis, such that CE marking hallmarks a product as one which has satisfied the relevant standards (including safety standards) so that it can be marketed throughout Europe.[24]

This reasoning is in accordance with Schepel noting: 'it is hard to see how a publicly accepted mode of production, in compliance with standards and customary in the sector concerned, could fall short of legitimate safety expectations'.[25]

Despite the controversial nature of the view, it could be argued that because of the technological and complex nature of AI products it might be presumed that regulatory regimes and standards will come to play a particularly important role in this field.[26] In spring 2021, a proposal for an AI Regulation was presented.[27] It is the purpose of the regulation to create harmonised rules on AI and it establishes a system for ensuring the quality of AI systems through standardisation and certification. The AI Regulation distinguishes between 'high risk' AI products and other AI products, establishing mandatory requirements for high risk products and a voluntary system based on codes of conduct for other AI systems. The proposed AI regulation follows the 'New Legislative Framework Approach' meaning that the requirements set out in the regulation are objectives at the general level which are then detailed at the technical level in the so-called 'harmonised standards'.[28] At the moment, several technical AI standards have been developed and more are under development.[29] A product that complies with the technical, harmonized standards is presumed to live up to requirements in the underlying regulatory framework. In Section E later, examples are given to illustrate how the AI Regulation could be relevant for the defectiveness assessment under the PLD.

[24] A F *Wilkes v DePuy International Ltd* [2016] EWHC 3096 (QB), [2018] QB 627, [98]–[100].

[25] Schepel (n 21) 378.

[26] This has also been noted by the EU commission, see Liability for Emerging Technologies, SWD (2018)137 final 18, 5 where it is observed that safety regulation and standards must be taken into consideration in dealing with liability issues concerning the safety for the product. Also Christina Amato 'Product Liability and Product Security: Present and Future' in Sebastian Lohsse, Reiner Schulze, Dirk Staudenmayer (eds), *Liability for Robotics and the Internet of Things* (Nomos 2018) 94, arguing in favour of standards since leaving a 'discretion of judgements … are not sustainable in the new era of high technology'. Cp. Jean-Sebastian Borghetti, 'Civil Liability for Artificial Intelligence. What Should Its Basis Be?' (2019) 17 *Revue des Jurists de Science Po* 196 <https://papers.ssrn.com/sol3/papers.cfm?abstract_id=3541597> 97 voicing the concern that standards in a fast-moving field will not always be up to date. Similarly, Gerald Spindler, 'User Liability and Strict Liability in the Internet of Things and for Robots' in Sebastian Lohsse, Reiner Schulze, Dirk Staudenmayer (eds), *Liability for Robotics and the Internet of Things* (Nomos 2018) 125–143, 136–137.

[27] Proposal for a Regulation of the European Parliament and of the Council laying down harmonized rules on Artificial Intelligence (Artificial Intelligence Act) and amending certain union legislative acts, COM(2021)206 final.

[28] 'AI Watch: AI Standardisation Landscape – State of Play and Link to the EC Proposal for an AI Regulatory Framework' (2021) 7. See also Amato (n 26) 84–89 for a recent description of the 'the New Approach' and the 'New Legislative Framework'.

[29] 'AI Watch' (n 28).

Finally, instructions and warnings accompanying the product are relevant for the defectiveness assessment. With regard to AI products, it has been pointed out that the importance of these will increase due to the complexity of the products.[30]

In practice, it has been common to distinguish between three types of defects: fabrication defects, design defects and instruction defects. The parameters above enter into the assessment with different weight in the three different categories and there are different opinions as to how the defectiveness assessment should be made with regard to products containing AI components.

D *Fabrication Defects*

Fabrication defects are defects that occur in one or a few products in a series of products because something has gone wrong in the production process. A product that has a fabrication defect differs from the other products in the same series and will not live up to the producer's description of the quality and safety product or to general, industry safety standards. It is broadly accepted that there should (always) be liability for fabrication errors, since the user of the product will have a reasonable expectation that there are no errors in the production process.[31] Consequently, fabrication defects are regarded as a simple category of defects. Fabrication defects can also occur with regard to AI products. For instance, the AI system may have been installed in an incomplete way with the customer.[32] These types of situations can be labelled 'easy' cases, where the product is clearly defective. However, fabrication defects must be expected to be less common with regard to AI products where the problem will rather relate to the design of the product.[33]

E *Design Defects*

1 The Concept of a Design Defect

Design defects are more difficult to deal with. Design defects are defined as defects that occur in all of the products in the same series because the product has been 'thought out' (designed) in a wrong way. The defect is in the very design of the product. An AI product design can be defective in various ways. There can be flaws in the programming of the algorithm that is done before the training of the algorithm and the dataset on which the algorithm has been trained may be incomplete or in other ways unsuitable. However, even though no flaws with respect to programming or data sets can be detected, the AI system may still produce results

30 Navas (n 16) 81.

31 See for example, Gerhard Wagner, 'Robot Liability' in Sebastian Lohsse, Reiner Schulze and Dirk Staudenmayer, *Liability for Robotics and the Internet of Things* (Nomos 2018) 27–62, 43.

32 Wagner (n 31) 43; Navas (n 16) 161680.

33 Navas (n 16) 168; Cerre (n 1) 248.

that are 'unwanted', raising the question whether products also in this situation could be categorised as 'defective'.[34]

2 Programming, Dataset, and Testing Errors

With regard to programming errors, it has been argued that if an error in code line causes the AI system to cause damage then the AI system must be regarded as defective.[35]

However, at the same time it has been pointed out that no programming is 100% flawless.[36] If this is generally known and accepted in society and AI products are put on the market with this knowledge then the mere fact that a product series suffers from a flaw in coding will not necessarily render these products defective. The question then becomes which types of flaws in coding should be regarded a defect.

Parallel problems arise with regard to the data sets on the basis of which the algorithm is trained. It may be possible to detect flaws in the data set but at the same time it must probably be accepted as a fact that samples may not ever be completely flawless and that even investigating the extent to which a data set contains flaws may be impossible in practice.[37]

Despite this, Article 10(3) of the proposed AI regulation requires data sets to be 'relevant, representative, free of errors and complete'.

As has been noted in legal literature:

> ...verifying the representativeness, completeness and correctness of the used datasets would be practically impossible since they usually count billions of tokens spanning across hundreds of languages. Thus, one wonders how such models – which are nowadays used also in products – will be trained in the future.[38]

As explained above, part of the answer to this question, presumably lies in standardisation. Thus, if an AI product has been certified and labelled with the relevant E-mark, it will be presumed that the underlying dataset has been 'relevant, representative, free of errors and complete' for the purpose of the regulation.

It must be presumed that to the extent a product does not live up to technical (safety) standards with regard to coding, training, and testing, this will often be a strong indication that the product is defective.[39] More difficult is the question of

34 Also with regard to design defects there are some easy cases. For example, if a brake in a vehicle does not function at all due to an AI system, the brake will be regarded defective and so will the vehicle in which it is incorporated regardless of whether the defect is caused by AI or not, Borghetti (n 26).

35 Borghetti (n 26) 196; Liivak (n 1) 183.

36 Wagner (n 31) 43.

37 Sebastian Felix Schwemer, Letizia Tomada and Tommaso Pasini, 'Legal AI Systems in the EU's proposed AI Regulation' (2021) <https://papers.ssrn.com/sol3/papers.cfm?abstract_id=3871099>.

38 Ibid. (n 37) 6.

39 Fairgrieve and Howells (n 22) 962–978 points out that courts in different European jurisdictions have come to different results with regard to this question. See also Lenze (22) 21.

whether an AI product that is in compliance with all standards can still be regarded as defective if it causes damage (the so-called regulatory compliance defence). It has been argued that at least in some situations, standard compliance should relieve the producer of liability.[40] The question will be dealt with in Section 3 with regard to autonomous decision making.

3 Standard Compliance – But Autonomous and Unpredictable Acts

The most difficult cases will be the ones in which no coding errors, no errors with regard to the dataset and no testing errors can be detected but the AI system still produces unexpected decisions because it behaves autonomously.[41] The Proposal for a new PLD does not give any guidance as to how the defectiveness assessment should be made in this situation. It only states in Article 6(c) that one must take into consideration 'the effect on the product of any ability to continue to learn after deployment'.

The situation in which a product lives up to all formal requirements with regard to safety specifications and yet causes damage is not unknown in product liability law. As explained above, it seems to be the general starting point that regulatory compliance does not per se relieve the producer of liability. However, in some areas regulatory compliance seems to be a strong argument against civil liability. Pharmaceuticals and medical devices could be mentioned as examples. Often it will be well known that for some people, a pharmaceutical product will have certain side effects and yet the product is not deemed defective. As mentioned earlier, in the English case *Wilkes*, concerning a hip implant, the view was expressed that it may be a challenge to argue that a product that lives up to all formal requirements with regard to safety should nevertheless be regarded as defective.

Further, AI products will have the 'side effect' of causing damage every now and then. It could be argued, however, that there is a difference between AI products on the one hand and ordinary pharmaceutical products and medical devices on the other hand in that the risks related to AI products are 'unknown' and 'unquantifiable', making it difficult to estimate to what extent the advantages of using the product outweigh its disadvantages, whereas with the pharmaceuticals and medical devices it is possible to identify and quantify the risk in advance so that it is clear to both the producer, the user and society at large what the risk when putting the product on the market is as tested against a standard. But also with regard to medical devices it may be difficult to quantify the risk in advance. In the English case of

[40] Bernhard Koch, 'Product Liability 2.0 – Mere Update or New Version?' in Sebastian Lohsse, Reiner Schulze and Dirk Staudenmayer (eds), *Liability for Robotics and the Internet of Things* (Nomos 2018) 99–116, 112, note 49 arguing that there should be no liability for damage caused by hacking if the producer has complied with all standards in this regard.

[41] Borghetti (n 26) 97 finds the difficult cases to be the ones where there is only a 'possibility or a suspicion' that the algorithm was defectively designed.

Colin Gee v DePuy International Ltd[42] which (also) concerned a hip transplant, the material used for the implant had the inherent risk that some people might develop adverse reactions to it. Regulators and patients were informed of this risk and told that it was 'unknown and incalculable'[43] and yet the product was approved of to be put on the market and e-labelled.[44] The problem in the case was that no standard addressed the particular type of weakness of the product that the case concerned (incidence of adverse reaction to metal wear debris (ARMD)).

If all existing standards have been observed and no standards apply to the particular problem in the case, the question is how to evaluate whether the product suffers from a defect if it still causes damage.

In line with this, the AI Expert group[45] has questioned whether, when a sophisticated system with self-learning capabilities makes an unpredictable decision deviating in the path, such deviation can be treated as a 'defect'.[46]

There are different opinions as to how this question should be answered.[47]

One view is that in these types of situations the product should (always) be regarded as suffering from a defect since the product had 'the potential' to develop a defect and the 'susceptibility' to acquire unsafe characteristics.[48] The consequence of applying this rule seems to be establishing a position close to strict liability for damage caused by an AI product regardless of whether it suffers from a defect or not.

Others take a less far reaching position. Thus, it has also been stated that, sometimes, the defectiveness assessment will not give rise to difficulties since it can be made 'intuitively':

> If an autonomous vehicle runs over a pedestrian in a crosswalk, one can argue that the solution is easy. We do not really need to go very deep within the AI's thinking; an autonomous vehicle is not supposed to run over people and, in normal situations, if it worked, the damage would not have occurred.[49]

42 [2018] EWHC 1208 (QB), [2018] Med LR 347.

43 *Gee* (n 42) [487]

44 E-labelling provides web-based product information as an alternative to physical labelling, see <www.seagullscientific.com/resources/labeling-guide/e-labeling/>.

45 The Expert Group was appointed by the EU Commission, see n 5.

46 Expert Group Report (n 5) 28.

47 Navas (n 16) 79 states the following: 'In my opinion, it could be treated as defect when designing the AI systems, the unpredictability has not been contemplated'. This 'test', however, will hardly work since the unpredictability (as defined earlier) will be inherent in any AI product and consequently, some amount of unpredictability will always be contemplated.

48 Piotr Machnikowski, 'Producers' Liability in the EC Expert Group Report on Liability for AI (2020) 11 *JETL* 137–149, 146. One might read para. 23 in the preamble to the Proposal for a new PLD as pulling in the same direction as it contains the somewhat general remark: 'The effect on a product's safety of its ability to learn after deployment should also be taken into account, to reflect the legitimate expectation that a product's software and underlying algorithms are designed in such a way as to prevent hazardous product behaviour'.

49 Cabral (n 15) 625 (in relation to causation).

This line of thinking seems to be based on what has been called 'the human operator' test.[50] According to this test, the acts based on an AI system should be assessed by comparing them to the acts of humans. If the AI system causes damage in a situation in which it must be assumed that a human operator would have avoided it, then the AI system should be regarded as defective. Although thinking about AI systems in this way may be intuitive, it may not be the right way to assess whether an AI product is defective. Moreover, in legal theory it has been argued that 'the human operator' test 'misses the mark'[51] since the AI system is not intended to work the same way as a human but in a different way. This also means that it will cause damage in different situations than humans. Thus, whereas an AI system may statistically be safer than a human operator, the systems may still in a concrete situation cause damage where a human would have avoided it.[52] If an AI product is deemed to be defective in such situations it would amount to 'holding the system to a standard it cannot live up to'.[53] Instead, it has been argued, that with regard to AI products, the concept of a design defect should be understood as a 'system oriented' concept which focuses on whether the entire fleet of cars operated by the same algorithm causes an unreasonable number of accidents overall.[54]

This raises the question how to identify what would be 'an unreasonable' number of accidents.[55] Under the risk/utility test the relevant question would be whether it would have been possible, at a reasonable cost, to design an alternative algorithm (the alternative design test) that would produce better results. It has been pointed out that the problem with applying the alternative design test to algorithms is that it will always be possible to create a slightly better algorithm and the test would imply deeming all other algorithms than the very best on the market defective.[56]

A similar problem was addressed in *Gee*[57] where Andrews J. made the following observation:

> Using another new product as the comparator would also lead to the absurd conclusion that even if all the new products showed an improvement on the existing established products in terms of safety, the new product that showed the smallest improvement by comparison with the others could nevertheless be regarded as defective, if the difference between them was of a sufficient magnitude.

[50] Wagner (n 31) 43.

[51] Wagner (n 31) 43, cp. Ryan Abott, *The Reasonable Robot* (Cambridge University Press 2020), arguing the general view that the law should not discriminate between AI and human behaviour.

[52] Wagner (n 31) 43 mentions 'the freak event that any human would have recognized an adapted his or her behaviour to'.

[53] Wagner (n 31) 43.

[54] Wagner (n 31) 44–45; Borghetti (n 26) 98.

[55] Cerre report (n 1) 54.

[56] Borghetti (n 26) 98–99.

[57] *Gee* (n 42).

As an alternative, a certain level of safety could be identified in practice as the required level, for instance, that an algorithm should as a minimum, statistically be at least 90% as safe as a 'reference' algorithm. In order to make such an assessment, data would be required on how the algorithm and other algorithms perform statistically and such data may not be easily obtainable.[58] This problem was also addressed in *Gee*. First, it was observed that the product causing the harm met all standards but no particular standard addressed what would be an acceptable rate of failure within a certain period of time.[59] Instead, it was examined whether data on failure rates of similar products could provide guidance. Eventually it was concluded that the product (Ultamet) could not be regarded as defective as

> There is insufficiently reliable evidence to establish that the Ultamet did have a materially worse failure rate than either the rate that was expected of a comparator at the time, or the actual failure rate of a comparator (insofar as it is possible to make a reliable assessment of the latter).[60]

The case shows that a systemic approach to the defectiveness assessment is already being used in relation to certain types of products. However, if applied to AI products it will have the downside that a product may be deemed non-defective even in situations where a human would most likely have avoided causing the damage. This may seem counterintuitive. In this way, a 'systemic' approach to the concept of a defect with regard to AI products can be seen as a radical variant of 'standardization'. In order to make it operational in practice it could be considered whether to incorporate the systemic approach in new types of standards developed for the purpose of establishing the acceptable failure rate of algorithms developed for different purposes.

F *Instruction Defects*

As described above, it must be presumed that standardisation is going to play an important role in the defectiveness assessment of AI products. However, standardisation may not be the only tendency. The complexity of the products on the market will increase the demand for proper instructions for the user. Indeed, it has been pointed out that with regard to AI products, information defects will become a more frequent type of defect.[61]

In EU countries, it has been debated what constitutes an instruction defect. Originally, it was the general view that there was no duty to inform on generally known risks.[62] Later on, the duty was broadened, and in 2014, it was assumed in legal literature

58 Borghetti (n 42) 99.
59 *Gee* (n 42) [489].
60 *Gee* (n 42) [498].
61 Navas (n 16) 81.
62 Verheyen (n 18) 50 with references.

that there is a duty to warn against all known risks (broad warning test).[63] With regard to AI products it will be known that there are unknown risks. Presumably, there must be a duty to warn against this under the broad warning test.

In relation to AI products, it must also be presumed that information will become more technical and may require some kind of special knowledge on the part of the user.[64] This raises the question how to avoid an overload of information which in reality cannot be understood by a large number of users. Moreover, psychological research has drawn attention to the difficulties in designing efficient warnings.[65]

In this regard, it has been noted that information forming part of the presentation of the product needs to take into account the 'the different characteristics and purposes of the end user customer'.[66] This can be done in a generalised way so that the instructions take into account the type of user who would typically buy and use the product. However, in legal literature, it has been argued that this is not enough to free the producer of liability under the reasonable expectations test. Thus, Howells argues that a producer should only escape liability if the consumer knows, based on the information provided with the product, that *he* – with his special dispositions – will be the one that is struck by the hazard.[67]

To the extent that privacy issues can be tackled, new technologies may provide new possibilities with regard to precision in warnings and instructions. Thus, through algorithmic consumer profiling, information can be 'individualised' so it can be shaped to more precisely target the individual user. Using algorithms for consumer profiling is suggested as a tool for a 'reframing of the information duties' in consumer law so that the advice given to purchasers of a product rather than being standard advice, resembles 'the advice the honest salesman in the old corner shop would give to the buyer he knows personally'.[68] For instance, a buyer could be warned that the

63 Verheyen (n 18) 50 with reference to Hans Micklitz, 'Liability for Defective Products and Services' in Norbert Reich, Hans-Wolfgang Micklitz, Peter Rott and Klaus Tonner (eds), *European Consumer Law* (2nd edn, Intersentia 2014).

64 Navas (n 16) 81.

65 SB Pape, *Warnings and Product Liability – Lessons Learned from Cognitive Psychology and Ergonomics* (Eleven International Publishing, 2012).

66 Livak (n 1) 182.

67 Geraint Howells, 'Information and Product Liability – A Game of Russian Roulette' in Andre Janssen and Geraint Howells (eds), *Information Rights and Obligations – A Challenge for Party Autonomy and Transactional Fairness* (Routledge 2005) 160. Howells uses the example of aspirin, explaining that even if the safety notice mentions the slight chance of internal bleeding, the producer should be held liable when it happens because the product does not provide the safety expected, because the user did not expect it to harm him.

68 C Busch and A De Franceschi, 'Granular Legal Norms: Big Data and the Personalization of Private Law' in Vanessa Mak, Eric Tjong Tjin Tai and Anna Berlee (eds), *Research Handbook on Data Science and Law*, Edward Elgar Publishing 2018) 9 with reference to Christoffer Busch, 'The Future of Pre-contractual Information Duties: From Behavioural Insights to Big Data' in Christian Twigg-Flesner (ed), *Research Handbook on EU Consumer and Contract Law* (Edward Elgar Publishing 2016) 233–234.

printer he is about to buy does not fit the computer he bought last week.[69] Also in tort law, it is being suggested that negligence law can be 'personalised' so that the applicable standard of care may be adjusted to the specific characteristics of the tortfeasor.[70] With regard to product liability issues, it could be considered whether consumer profiles could be used for individualising the instructions following a product so that consumers who have a profile showing technological skills at a high level receive instructions and information about the product at one level, whereas other consumers receive instructions and information at a different level. Consumer profiles may show that there is a greater need to warn certain consumers about a specific use of a product than others. Personalised instructions could, for instance, be considered with regard to pharmaceuticals and allergy reactions.[71] To the extent the provision of personalised instructions becomes a practical option for producers, the question arises whether not using this technique could render the product defective.

The possibility to provide personalised presentations of the product also gives rise to a more fundamental question. Thus, introducing such personalised instructions, for example in the shape of personalised labels on products, will affect the consumer expectations to a product.[72] The more information is personalised the more difficult it will become to maintain the notion of 'the legitimate expectations of the consumer' as a general concept that focuses on the expectations of the 'public at large' and on general standards defining these expectations. Interestingly, the Proposal for a new PLD includes both the criterion the expectations of 'the public at large' and the criterion 'the specific expectations of the end users for whom the product is intended' in the defectiveness test.[73]

Because of the problems inherent in the defectiveness assessment with regard to AI products some scholars have simply suggested that the defectiveness concept be abandoned altogether[74] and replaced by a truly strict liability system.[75]

III DISRUPTION OF THE VALUE CHAIN

The defectiveness assessment of the product is not the only challenge faced by product liability law in the reception of AI products. Thus, AI can have an influence not only on the way the safeness of a single product or algorithm is assessed but also on the structure of the entire value chain in which the product liability rules work.

69 Parallel example in Busch and De Franceschi (n 68) 8–9.

70 See in general, Omri Ben-Shahar and Ariel Porat, 'Personalizing Negligence Law' (2016) 91 *NYU L Rev* 627–686.

71 Joasia Luzak, 'A Broken Notion: Impact of Modern Technologies on Product Liability' (2020) 11(3) *European Journal of Risk* 630, 630–649, 631.

72 On interactive labels, see www.sciencedaily.com/releases/2020/03/200326144341.htm.

73 See the Proposal for a new PLD Article 6(1) and 6(1)(h). Compare Luzak (n 71) 646, 648, who finds that the solution lies in relying on standards in the defectiveness assessment.

74 Luzak (n 71) 637.

75 Borghetti (n 26) 99.

The PLD channels liability to the producer as the central player who is the better risk avoider, better risk distributer and therefore also the better risk carrier. It builds on the idea of the 'linear' value chain, that is, a value chain in which sub suppliers of components for a product sell the components to the producer who manufactures the product that is finally put on the market for consumers and other buyers. Moreover, internally in the chain, each actor carries liability only for the safeness of the product in the shape in which it was put on the market by the actor.[76] Thus, in a traditional value chain, liability can be described as 'compartmentalised' and resting on clearly defined risk spheres.[77]

AI systems may be distributed through this type of traditional value chain. For instance, an AI component could be sold by a software provider to the producer who integrates the AI component in a product, such as an autonomous vehicle, a vacuum cleaner, or a medical device, and then puts the entire product on the market. These types of products have been called 'bundled' products.[78]

However, today, consumers may choose to buy hardware from one manufacturer and software from another, combine the two, supplement with updates received from the producer itself or a third party, and users themselves may also be authorised to access the safety related software of a system. The functioning of products may also be dependent on the reception of services, such as signals for sensors, delivered by other actors. In other words, in a digitalised world, products will often be 'unbundled',[79] making the value chain less linear and much more complex and comparable to a network.

This type of value chain challenges several, basic product liability concepts that are thought out with a view to the 'traditional' supply chain.

Firstly, whereas it is common ground that 'bundled' products such as the ones mentioned above come within the scope of the PLD, it is not clear whether 'standalone' AI products, such as an AI service offered to a medical doctor for diagnosing purposes, are covered by the product liability regime at all. Thus, according to Article 2 of the Directive a product is defined as a 'movable'. Since code is something intangible it is likely not covered by the definition of a product as it stands today.[80] However, for some time it has been under consideration to expand the definition of a 'product' and to include software and digital devices

[76] See Articles 6, 7, and 11 of the PLD.

[77] See also Koch (n 40) 102, describing the time when the product is put into circulation as the Directive's 'magic moment'.

[78] Wagner (n 31) 47; 'BEUC Report, Review of Product Liability Rules' (2017) 12 <www.beuc.eu/publications/beuc-x-2017-039_csc_review_of_product_liability_rules.pdf>.

[79] Wagner (n 31) 47–49.

[80] It seems to be broadly accepted that software is covered by the Directive if it is embedded in a physical object such as a disk or a USB stick, Cerre (n 1) 50; 'BEUC report' (n 71) 12. However, today such devices are less used and programs are often downloaded directly from the internet. For a discussion, see for example, Wagner (n 31) 11; Livaak (n 1) 180–181.

in the concept of a 'product'.[81] This would bring the PLD in line with other recent legislative initiatives such as the recently adopted sale of goods directive[82] and the directive on the supply of digital content and digital services.[83] Also the recent CJEU decision (*Krone*), finds that liability for a defective service could be conceivable if the service is part of the product's inherent characteristics.[84] In the Proposal for new PLD it is suggested that software should be defined as a product (Proposal Article 4(1)).

Including software in the definition of a product would enable suits to be brought not only against the producer of a bundled product but also against the software producer. It would also pave the way for product liability suits against producers of other 'stand-alone' AI products such as AI systems offering advice in a range of areas, including health and disease treatments. Revising the concept of a product further to also include the broader notion of digital products might enable product liability suits to be brought against providers of digital updates for a system, but such an enlargement might on the other hand make it difficult to uphold the distinction between products and services in the Directive,[85] raising the question of whether liability for defective services should be included.

Moreover, the introduction of new types of products with new vulnerabilities has inspired the question whether the definition of damage should be extended to cover not just physical damage but also non-economic loss such as loss of data due to hacker attacks.[86] Including software and data content in the definition of a 'product' may also call for a revision of the definition of a 'producer'. In the Directive,

[81] See <https://ec.europa.eu/info/law/better-regulation/have-your-say/initiatives/12979-Civil-liability-adapting-liability-rules-to-the-digital-age-and-artificial-intelligence_en>. For an overview, see, for instance, Kathrin Bauwens, 'Product Liability and AI (Part 2) – The EU Commission's Plans for Adapting Liability Rules to the Digital Age' (*Linklaters*, 16 July 2021) <www.linklaters.com/en/insights/blogs/productliabilitylinks/2021/july/product-liability-and-ai-part-2-eu-commissions-plans-for-adapting-rules-to-the-digital-age>.

[82] Directive (EU) 2019/771.

[83] Directive (EU) 2019/770.

[84] Case C-65/20 *VI v KRONE – Verlag Gesellschaft mbH & Co KG*.

[85] On the distinction between products and services with regard to AI systems and digital content, Cerre (n 1) 51; Cabral (n 15) 619–620 The Proposal for new PLD does not include 'digital products' or 'digital content' in the definition of a product, cp. Article 4 (1). The Proposal also does not include 'providers of digital updates' in the list of 'economic operators' that can be held liable under the directive, cp. Article 7. The intention seems to be that the manufacturer of the product who also delivers updates can be held liable for defective updates (digital services), see preamble, paras 15 and 37.

[86] 'The EU Commission's Inception Impact Assessment report' 4 <www.ec.europa.eu/info/law/better-regulation/have-your-say/initiatives/12979-Civil-liability-adapting-liability-rules-to-the-digital-age-and-artificial-intelligence_en>; Cabral (n 15) 629; Navas (n 16) 79. The Proposal for a new PLD defines damage as 'material loss' cp. Article 4(6) and includes material loss resulting from 'loss or corruption of data that is not used exclusively for professional purposes (Article 4(6)(c)). According to the preamble, para 16, the intention seems to be that loss or corruption of data should be considered 'damage' within the meaning on the Proposal for a new PLD.

a producer is defined in Article 3 as 'the manufacturer of a finished product, the producer of any raw material or the manufacturer of a component part and any person who, by putting his name, trademark or other distinguishing feature on the product presents himself as its producer'. It has also been argued that the engineer designer should be included in this definition.[87] Moreover, if digital content is considered a product it should be considered who could be regarded as 'producers' of this content and whether they should also be included in the definition of a producer in the PLD. More broadly, it could be considered whether the definition of the potentially liable actors in the PLD should be aligned with the corresponding definitions in the proposed AI regulation. This would mean considering whether a 'provider' and a 'product representative' as mentioned in the proposed AI regulation should also be regarded as potentially liable actors under the Directive.[88] Similarly, it has been argued that the potential liability for digital platforms as key players in the value chain and providers of data should be considered.[89] In line with this, the Proposal for a new PLD extends the group of actors who can be held liability for product injury. It uses the term 'Economic Operator' to specify who can be held liable for product liability, see Article 7. The list includes the 'Authorised Representative' as a potential subject of liability (Article 7(2)). It also includes the 'fulfilment service provider'.

Finally, the new type of value chain challenges the compartmentalisation of liability based on the idea of separated risk spheres between the different participants in the value chain. Thus, according to the PLD, a product is to be regarded as defective if it does not meet legitimate expectations with regard to safety at the time when the product was put on the market.[90] In other words, the producer is not liable for damage caused by changes to the product that occur after it has been put on the market (the so called 'later defect defence'). The reason for this is that with regard to ordinary products, the producer no longer has control over the product once it has been put on the market. However, with regard to digital products, the situation may be different. Thus, a producer may be able to update and thereby change the

[87] Navas (n 16) 81 with further references. The Proposal for a new PLD in Article 4(11) largely relies on the current definition of the producer (manufacturer) but includes other actors that can also be held liable as 'Economic Operators', see further below.

[88] Proposed AI Regulation Article 3 (1) and (5).

[89] See for instance Christoph Busch, 'When Product Liability Meets the Platform Economy: A European Perspective on Oberdorf v. Amazon' (2019) 8 *Journal of European Consumer and Market Law* 173–174, V Ulfbeck and P Verbruggen 'Online Marketplaces and Product Liability: Back to the Where We Started?' (2022) 30(6) *European Review of Private Law* 975. The Proposal for a new PLD introduces the concept of the 'fulfilment service provider' as a new potential subject of liability, but only to the extent that there is no EU producer, EU importer or Authorised Representative in the EU to make claims against (Article 7(3)). In Article 7 (6), it also makes clear that a provider of an online platform can be held liable if the consumer could reasonably believe that it were contracting with the platform. This principle is also established in DSA Article 6(3).

[90] On the notion of defectiveness, supra Section II.

system after it has been put on the market. In the proposal for the new AI Regulation it is even stated that there should be general monitoring duties after the product has been put on the market.[91] This raises the question of whether the later defect defence in the Directive should be abolished.[92]

The obstruction of the traditional value chain structure begs the question of whether the traditional principles for risk allocation between the parties in the chain can be upheld, in particular whether it makes sense to channel the liability to the producer.[93] Views differ in this regard.

According to European Law Institute, there is no reason to make fundamental changes in risk allocations. Rather, it is stated that: '…liability should be allocated to the person who [is] most likely to have caused the harm, … liability should fall on the person best placed to absorb the loss. There is no reason why this rationale should not be maintained in the digital era'.[94]

However, upholding the traditional system will give rise to some practical problems. As Wagner puts it:

> …the victim would have to investigate whether the accident was caused by defective hardware, defective software marketed by the supplier of the original software, software manufactured by a third party and added to the device by the user, or by other modifications made by the user subsequent to acquisition of the device. This burden may deter many victims from bringing suit and may seriously undermine the success even of meritorious actions.[95]
>
> And further:
>
> For unbundled products there simply is no single responsible party that controls the safety feature of all components. Thus, liability must be apportioned between all the actors who contributed to the safety features of the device that caused the accident at the time of the accident.[96]

This line of thinking is further developed by Beckers and Teubner who distinguish between different uses of AI systems and consider a 'network and enterprise liability'

[91] Proposal for AI Regulation Article 61.

[92] This has been thoroughly considered, see 'The EU Commission's Inception Impact Assessment report' (n 86) 4. The Proposal for a new PLD suggests a new formulation. Thus, according to Article 6(e), when making the defectiveness assessment, one must take into consideration 'the moment in time when the product was placed on the market or put into service or, where the manufacturer retains control over the product after that moment, the moment in time when the product left the control of the manufacturer'. According to Article 6(c), also 'the effect on the product of any ability to continue to learn after deployment' must be taken into consideration. These criteria to some extent modify the 'later defect' defence in the PLD.

[93] Koch (n 40) 112. This view can be seen as reflected in the Proposal for a new PLD, which in Article 7 expands the number of possible liability subjects.

[94] See 'ELI Guiding Principles for Updating the Product Liability Directive for the Digital Age', Guiding principle no 5.

[95] Wagner (n 31) 48.

[96] Ibid. 49.

and 'prorata network share liability' for situations in which there is a close collaboration between human and machine.[97]

Overall, and as also reflected in the Proposal for a new PLD, it can be argued that the realities of the new value chains could call for a number of adjustments of central product liability concepts. Such adjustments would basically widen the scope of the product liability rules. In contrast to what is the case with regard to the defectiveness concept, the adjustments discussed in this section can in principle be achieved by political decisions to revise the concepts in the Directive. As will be elaborated further in Section IV, the difficult question here is only how far to go.

IV CONCLUSION AND PERSPECTIVES

The analysis above shows that carrying out a defectiveness assessment with regard to AI products will not be an easy task and the Proposal for a new PLD does not solve this problem. However, the types of difficulties are not entirely unknown. Parallels can be found in relation to the defectiveness assessment of pharmaceuticals and medical implants. Until now, these problems have been handled on a case by case basis. However, with the introduction of AI products, the problems regarding the defectiveness assessment will not primarily be confined to such products as pharmaceuticals and medical implants but will appear in relation to a broad range of everyday products. In particular, the role played by standards and a 'systemic' approach to the defectiveness assessment have attracted interest. The systemic approach can be seen as a radical version of standardisation and could itself be standardised.

At the same time, not only standardisation tendencies may come to play a role in the defectiveness assessment. Paradoxically, individualisation may also be relevant and may challenge the basic idea of operating a general test of legitimate consumer expectations, including the application of standards. Consequently, it seems that the introduction of AI products could generate rather contradictory approaches to defectiveness assessment in product liability law. This reflected in the Proposal for a new PLD which in Article 6 as defectiveness criteria include both the expectations of 'the public at large' and 'the specific expectations of the end-users for whom the product is intended'. It is an interesting question whether, in the longer run, technological advances will make the individualised method prevail. The problems related to the defectiveness assessment have led to suggestions of abandoning the concept of defectiveness altogether and introducing a truly strict liability regime.

Not only the concept of defectiveness, but also basically all concepts related to the value chain, are challenged by the new type of products. This is reflected in the number of adjustments of basic product liability concepts which are suggested

97 Anna Beckers and Günther Teubner, *Three Liability Regimes for Artificial Intelligence – Algorithmic Actants, Hybrids, Crowds* (Hart Publishing 2022) 101, 106.

in the Proposal for a new PLD. Whereas the concept of defectiveness generates difficult questions of interpretation, the problems pertaining to the value chain concepts can, to a large extent, be solved by political decisions to adjust the concepts. The concept of a product could be extended to cover software and digital content, the liability period could be extended to also cover the post marketing phase, the concept of damage could be expanded to also cover non-economic loss cases and the list of potentially liable actors in the value chain could be expanded. Currently, changes with regard to all of these parameters are to some extent suggested in the Proposal for a new PLD. However, if technological developments continue to blur the traditional boundaries in product liability law and possibly even call for giving up the concept of defectiveness, the needed changes may become so fundamental that it no longer makes sense to speak about 'product liability'.

This also means that whereas one might intuitively think that the product liability regime will come to play a vital role in an era where machines take over from humans, it may in fact be the other way around: AI may end up dissolving the very concept of product liability.

10

Appropriation of Personality in the Era of Deepfakes

John Zerilli

The law of privacy in the United Kingdom is known to be somewhat patchy and jerry-built. In some ways, it invites comparison with the law of the horse, lacking a coherent body of doctrine that applies exclusively to its subject matter. Even this comparison is charitable, however, because 'horse lawyers' are not required to reflect deeply on what it means to be a horse, whereas privacy lawyers do often find themselves having to think deeply about what a person's right to privacy entails. Not only that, the law of the horse is more or less complete. Most scenarios involving horses in which there is a risk of harm – such as those arising from their breeding or uses in gaming – will have governing laws. The same cannot be said of scenarios in which the risk of a breach of privacy is high.

The UK's recent recognition of a new action for misuse of private information is an important step towards the realisation of a more coherent system of privacy protection in the United Kingdom.[1] Still, a person's right to privacy may be infringed in various ways, not all of them amounting to the unauthorised disclosure of facts about their private affairs. For convenience, and following most privacy scholarship, we can divide breaches of privacy into three broad categories: (i) those involving the disclosure of true private facts about a claimant; (ii) those involving intrusions into a claimant's private sphere (e.g., their space or means of communication); and (iii) those involving appropriation of a claimant's personality.[2]

Special thanks to Phillip Morgan, whose many penetrating comments and suggestions greatly improved this chapter. I also thank Sandy Steel and two anonymous referees for valuable feedback.

[1] *Vidal-Hall v Google Inc* [2015] EWCA Civ 311, [2016] QB 1003. See Sections III and V.

[2] This classification was refined by William L Prosser over successive editions of his esteemed text, *Handbook of the Law of Torts* (1st–4th edn, West Publishing 1941/1955/1964/1971). There is an additional category which did not appear in Prosser's first edition but which found its way into the second (1955), 42–45, namely, publicity which places the plaintiff in a false light in the public eye. Although 'false light' privacy has taken on enormous significance in the US law of torts, it is not recognised in the United Kingdom, Australia, or New Zealand. Perhaps this is just as well, for false light cases can in many (and maybe most?) circumstances be brought within the scope of the appropriation doctrine (on which, see Section I) provided that we: (i) drop any requirement for the claimant to prove that the appropriation be 'for the defendant's advantage' – as Prosser's formulation has it and (ii)

The first kind of privacy violation was traditionally redressed through equity's jurisdiction to grant relief in cases involving breaches of confidence.[3] For disclosures that do not fit the traditional equitable mould, however, the revamped jurisdiction for dealing with breaches of confidence – the action for misuse of private information – offers claimants their best chance of success.[4] Beyond unauthorised disclosures, the European Union's General Data Protection Regulation (by force of the UK's Data Protection Act 2018) gives some limited means of redress to 'data subjects' whose grievances relate to unauthorised data 'processing' (as opposed to the significantly narrower concept of unauthorised data 'disclosures').[5]

The second kind of privacy violation, which can be thought of as a breach of one's 'spatial' or 'ambient' privacy, was typically remedied through the torts of trespass and nuisance, and for the most part continues to be.[6]

The third privacy violation mentioned above, that involving the appropriation of the claimant's personality – which is a particular way of breaching what we might call a person's 'image' privacy – is the subject of this chapter.[7] Specifically, I will discuss: the rise of deepfakes – a novel kind of audio and/or visual production generated through advanced machine learning techniques; why existing common law causes of action have generally been inadequate to protect claimants from appropriation of personality; and why some of these actions may be better suited to protecting claimants from the harms of deepfakes. I will conclude by suggesting that these advantages notwithstanding, deepfakes underscore the UK's urgent need for an independent tort (or statutory action) of appropriation of personality grounded in the protection of a person's dignitary interests.[8]

found the appropriation action upon the protection of the claimant's dignitary interests (on which, see Section V). False light cases were anyway often disputes about pictures of the claimant, and these cases, in particular, can be understood as instances of appropriation. An advantage of the appropriation route is that it avoids the need for courts to grapple with the inherent vagueness of a concept like 'false light.' Indeed, by the time, the third edition of his text appeared, Prosser himself came to worry that the false light action was 'capable of swallowing up and engulfing the whole law of defamation' (1964), 839. For illuminating historical discussion of these developments, see G Edward White, *Tort Law in America: An Intellectual History* (Expanded edn, Oxford University Press 2003) 173–176.

3 The classic treatment is Tanya Aplin and others, *Gurry on Breach of Confidence* (2nd edn, Oxford University Press 2012).

4 On both the traditional equitable doctrine of breach of confidence and the recent action for misuse of private information, see Sections I and V.

5 Regulation (EU) 2016/679 of the European Parliament and of the Council of 27 April 2016 on the protection of natural persons with regard to the processing of personal data and on the free movement of such data, and repealing Directive 95/46/EC (General Data Protection Regulation) [2016] OJ L 119, 1.

6 Simon Deakin and Zoe Adams, *Markesinis and Deakin's Tort Law* (8th edn, Oxford University Press 2019) 707–708.

7 This category was first discussed in an article by Samuel Warren and Louis Brandeis, 'The Right to Privacy' (1890) 4 *HLR* 193.

8 Where I have considered it necessary or instructive, I have made reference to the law of Australia and New Zealand and, to a lesser extent, the law of Canada and the United States. However, it is to the United Kingdom that my recommendations are directed. Of course, given their jurisprudential affinity with the United Kingdom – and the fact that neither Australia nor New Zealand has adopted

I APPROPRIATION OF PERSONALITY

'Appropriation of personality' sounds like a form of identity theft. In a way it is, but identity theft and its cognate, identity fraud, are statutory offences, and the cases discussed most commonly in connection with privacy need not take these extreme (and criminally punishable) forms. The archetypal appropriation of personality occurs instead when the claimant's image or voice is used without the claimant's permission and more often than not for the defendant's advantage in the course of legitimate commercial enterprise. For instance, the defendant might use the claimant's picture or name on the defendant's goods as if to show that the claimant endorses them. From this it is but a short step to the economic torts, and among them the misrepresentation torts in particular, such as passing off. Indeed during the twentieth century, passing off was the tort of first resort in commercial situations of this kind, at least in the United Kingdom, Australia, and New Zealand.[9] But as I describe in Section III, such a state of affairs is not wholly satisfactory, since passing off was never intended to cover such cases and offers only weak protection to a claimant in commercial settings – let alone cases arising in non-commercial settings (e.g., during political campaigns). Partly for this reason, the United States early on developed a separate action based on one's 'right of publicity,' which unambiguously enjoins the commercial appropriation of personality.[10] Canada likewise, in an approach unique among common law jurisdictions, long ago extended the reach of passing off to cover most instances of commercial appropriation of personality.[11]

What these observations make clear is that, in the UK, Australia, and New Zealand, appropriation of personality, commercial or otherwise, is actionable only if a claimant's circumstances disclose one of a number of largely unrelated causes of action:

an independent tort or statutory remedy protecting the dignitary interests of claimants against appropriation of personality – much of what I say about both the possibility and desirability of reforming the law in the United Kingdom is applicable to Australia and New Zealand. Indeed, as early as 1979, among the first reports of the newly formed Australian Law Reform Commission recommended that Australia adopt a tort of privacy that encompassed both unauthorised disclosure as well as appropriation of likeness: ALRC Report 11, *Unfair Publication: Defamation and Privacy*. Nothing ever came of ALRC Report 11. In New Zealand, the High Court recently struck out a plea of appropriation of personality, the judge stating that there was 'limited prospect that this tort will be recognised in New Zealand at this time': *X v Attorney-General* [2017] NZHC 1136, [2017] NZAR 1365 [32] (Simon France J).

9 Huw Beverley-Smith, *The Commercial Appropriation of Personality* (Cambridge University Press 2002).

10 So wide is the Californian right of publicity that it offers a measure of protection even to non-celebrities, not simply to celebrities. See JT McCarthy, *The Rights of Publicity and Privacy* (2nd edn, Thomson Reuters 2022) and Kelsey Farish, 'Do Deepfakes Pose a Golden Opportunity? Considering whether English Law Should Adopt California's Publicity Right in the Age of the Deepfake' (2020) 15 *Journal of Intellectual Property Law & Practice* 40. See also Nikki Chamberlain, 'Misappropriation of Personality: A Case for Common Law Identity Protection' (2021) 26 *TLJ* 195; Rosina Zapparoni, 'Propertising Identity: Understanding the United States Right to Publicity and Its Implications—Some Lessons for Australia' (2004) 28 *MULR* 690.

11 *Krouse v Chrysler Canada Ltd* (1973) 40 DLR (3d) 15 (Ontario CA); *Athans v Canadian Adventure Camps Ltd* (1977) 80 DLR (3d) 583 (Ontario HC).

the tort of passing off, as mentioned, but also the torts of defamation, injurious falsehood, nuisance, and occasionally trespass. It is widely agreed that these latter actions are hardly more adequate to protect claimants than passing off. In something of a legal irony, however, this has been the position only insofar as disputes have concerned images generated through traditional photographic and video recording techniques. It may come as something of a surprise to learn that some of these same torts could prove more useful against 'deepfakes' – a novel and special kind of counterfeit image that is difficult to distinguish from an authentic image and can represent a person doing almost anything, no matter how scandalous, incendiary, or demeaning.[12] In Section II, I will briefly discuss the rise of deepfakes; in Section III, I will discuss why existing common law causes of action have generally been inadequate to protect claimants from appropriation of personality, and in Section IV, I will discuss why the torts of defamation, injurious falsehood, and intentional infliction of psychiatric injury may be better suited to protecting claimants from the harms of deepfakes (as opposed to traditional photographs and video recordings). I will conclude (in Section V) by suggesting that these advantages notwithstanding, deepfakes underscore the UK's urgent need for an independent tort (or statutory action) of appropriation of personality grounded in the protection of dignitary interests.

II THE RISE OF THE DEEPFAKE

The term 'deepfake' first appeared in 2017 as the username of an individual on the popular discussion forum, Reddit.[13] Deepfake would superimpose the faces of celebrities onto independently created pornographic content. The term now

[12] The literature on the law of deepfakes is still in its infancy. Useful discussions so far include: Robert Chesney and Danielle Keats Citron, 'Deep Fakes: A Looming Challenge for Privacy, Democracy, and National Security' (2019) 107 *California Law Review* 1753; Robert Chesney and Danielle Keats Citron, '21st Century-Style Truth Decay: Deep Fakes and the Challenge for Privacy, Free Expression, and National Security' (2019) 78 *Maryland Law Review* 882; SC Ekaratne, 'Manipulated Images: A Taxonomy' (2020) 42 European Intellectual Property Review 353; Kelsey Farish, 'Do Deepfakes Pose a Golden Opportunity? Considering whether English Law Should Adopt California's Publicity Right in the Age of the Deepfake' (2020) 15 *Journal of Intellectual Property Law & Practice* 40; Kareem Gibson, 'Deepfakes and Involuntary Pornography: Can Our Current Legal Framework Address This Technology?' (2020) 66 *Wayne Law Review* 259; Anne Pechenik Gieseke, '"The New Weapon of Choice": Law's Current Inability to Properly Address Deepfake Pornography' (2020) 73 *Vanderbilt Law Review* 1479; Matthew Kugler and Carly Pace, 'Deepfake Privacy: Attitudes and Regulation' (2021) 116 *Northwestern University Law Review* 611; Jack Langa, 'Deepfakes, Real Consequences: Crafting Legislation to Combat Threats Posed by Deepfakes' (2021) 101 *Boston University Law Review* 761; Nicholas O'Donnell, 'Have We No Decency? Section 230 and the Liability of Social Media Companies for Deepfake Videos' [2021] *University of Illinois Law Review* 701; Andrew Ray, 'Disinformation, Deepfakes, and Democracies' (2021) 44 *UNSWLJ* 983; Eric Kocsis, 'Deepfakes, Shallowfakes, and the Need for a Private Right of Action' (2022) 126 *Dickinson Law Review* 621; and Molly Mullen, 'A New Reality: Deepfake Technology and the World around Us' (2022) 48 *Mitchell Hamline Law Review* 210.

[13] Elizabeth Hurst, 'How Can the Law Deal with Deepfake? (*allaboutlaw*, 13 December 2019) <www.allaboutlaw.co.uk/commercial-awareness/legal-spotlight/how-can-the-law-deal-with-deepfake->.

describes any synthetic medium in which deep learning-based artificial intelligence is used to doctor an existing image or video of a person by replacing them with another's likeness.[14] In essence, deepfakes are digital forgeries.

At present, two classes of machine learning networks are widely used to create deepfakes: generative adversarial networks (GANs) and variational autoencoders (VAEs).[15] In brief, the objective of GAN approaches is to set two networks against each other so that one network (via a 'generative model') generates counterfeit images which the other (via a 'discriminative model') tries to detect.[16] After multiple rounds of training, the hope is that the second network will be unable to tell the difference between the original and counterfeit image. VAEs instead involve a process of encoding a high-dimensional image of a subject into a low-dimensional representation and then using that low-dimensional representation to construct novel images of the subject.[17] In the same way that an artist might attempt to portray someone in a fictitious setting or in caricature by first studying a few characteristic features of the subject's face and body (usually through primitive sketches), the encoder reduces a high-feature representation of a person into a low-feature representation (cf an artist taking the horizontal angle of a person's jawline and the width of their mouth as a kind of proxy for their face). The space of all possible combinations of these measurements – called 'latent space' – is then used to generate novel high-feature representations of the person, in roughly the same manner by which an artist might portray the subject striking a fictitious pose from a few primitive sketches. The autoencoder here is said to 'learn a generative model' of the person's face. But this generative decoding process merely results in counterfeit images that look very like the original: a picture of George Washington riding his horse has not yet become a picture of George Washington driving a convertible. To portray Washington driving a convertible – or someone else astride Washington's horse – requires the encoding of a *shared* latent space wherein similar measurements of Washington and some other person are *both* represented in latent space. Comparable techniques also enable high-fidelity voice simulation.[18]

The deep learning behind deepfakes means their capacity for deception is exceptionally high – much higher than counterfeit content generated through older digital and analogue means of reproduction.[19] Their capacity for mischief

[14] Jan Kietzmann and others, 'Deepfakes: Trick or Treat?' (2020) 63 *Business Horizons* 135.

[15] At time of writing, large language 'foundation' models (such as GPT-3) have been customised for generating deepfakes. But GANs and VAEs still remain the most prevalent techniques.

[16] Ian J Goodfellow and others, 'Generative Adversarial Networks' (2014) <https://arxiv.org/abs/1406.2661>.

[17] Diederik P Kingma and Max Welling, 'Auto-Encoding Variational Bayes' (2014) <https://arxiv.org/abs/1312.6114>.

[18] Linda W Lee, Jan Kietzmann and Tim C Kietzmann, 'Deepfakes: Five Ways in Which They Are Brilliant Business Opportunities' (*The Conversation*, 12 February 2020) <www.theconversation.com/deepfakes-five-ways-in-which-they-are-brilliant-business-opportunities-131591>.

[19] Not all uses are nefarious; some indeed are highly beneficial. See ibid.

is equally immense, ranging from celebrity pornography, child pornography, and revenge porn, to extortion, political sabotage, and financial fraud.[20] As an example of political deepfakery with the potential for large-scale electoral manipulation, take Extinction Rebellion's deepfake video of Belgian Prime Minister Sophie Wilmès, which had the Prime Minister tout a link between deforestation and COVID-19.[21] Within 24 hours, more than 100,000 people had seen the video, and many viewers seemed to assume that it was authentic – that it was the Belgian Prime Minister herself making the speech. Or take the example of pro-Russian propaganda during the 2022 Russian invasion of Ukraine: a deepfake video of Ukrainian president Volodymyr Zelenskyy circulated in which the President seemed to be encouraging Ukrainian forces to surrender to the invading Russian army.[22] Little imagination is required to foresee the terrifying possibilities of this technology in the wrong hands.

Moreover, deepfake technology has become readily accessible, with a number of easy-to-use apps and instructional videos appearing in recent years that allow even amateurs to create powerfully convincing video fakery.[23] And it is not only political figures and celebrities who are at risk of being deepfaked: anyone with a significant online presence would have enough images of themselves on the Internet for a deepfaker to exploit in a training set.

III THE INADEQUACY OF COMMON LAW PROTECTION AGAINST APPROPRIATION OF PERSONALITY IN THE UK

The remarks of Dixon J in *Victoria Park Racing and Recreation Grounds Co Ltd v Taylor*[24] accurately state the traditional English, Australian, and New Zealand position that rights to intangibles are safeguarded only 'as special heads of protected interests and not under a wide generalization.'[25] Even when someone's personality

20 Alec Banks, 'Deepfakes and Why the Future of Porn Is Terrifying' (*Highsnobiety*, 2018) <www.highsnobiety.com/p/what-are-deepfakes-ai-porn/>; Jon Christian, 'Experts Fear Face Swapping Tech Could Start an International Showdown' (*The Outline*, 1 February 2018) <www.theoutline.com/post/3179/deepfake-videos-are-freaking-experts-out>; Marco Schreyer and others, 'Adversarial Learning of Deepfakes in Accounting' (preprint, 2019) <https://arxiv.org/abs/1910.03810>; Christian V Baccarella and others, 'Social Media? It's Serious! Understanding the Dark Side of Social Media' (2018) 36 *European Management Journal* 431.

21 Extinction Rebellion, Belgium, 'Tell the Truth: A Speech for Sophie Wilmès' (2020) <https://web.archive.org/web/20200517141556/www.extinctionrebellion.be/en/tell-the-truth>.

22 Bobby Allyn, 'Deepfake Video of Zelenskyy Could Be 'Tip of the Iceberg' in Info War, Experts Warn' (*NPR*, 16 March 2022) <www.npr.org/2022/03/16/1087062648/deepfake-video-zelenskyy-experts-war-manipulation-ukraine-russia>.

23 DeepNude and FakeApp were among the first such apps: Elizabeth Hurst, 'How Can the Law Deal with Deepfake?' (*AllAboutLaw*, 13 December 2019) <www.allaboutlaw.co.uk/commercial-awareness/legal-spotlight/how-can-the-law-deal-with-deepfake->.

24 *Victoria Park Racing and Recreation Grounds Co Ltd v Taylor* (1936) 58 CLR 479 (HCA).

25 Ibid. 509.

has undisputed commercial value, generally through celebrity or goodwill, recovery for its unauthorised exploitation depends on a claimant satisfying the criteria of a recognised cause of action. As already noted, the torts of passing off, defamation, injurious falsehood, nuisance, and trespass have proved most serviceable in this regard. In each case, however, the appropriation itself is incidental to the complaint, with the result that many victims of appropriation go without remedy.

A *Passing Off*

Passing off is a 'misrepresentation tort' in the general family of economic torts and arose to address false advertising and unfair competition.[26] Being a misrepresentation tort, it is not immediately obvious how the appropriation of someone's personality might be remedied by an action based on the making of false statements; for appropriation normally occurs by way of images of the claimant rather than by statements.[27] Australian courts have at times been more responsive in the face of this difficulty,[28] but it is safe to say that even there passing off is not ideally suited to the claimant's needs. The inadequacies of the tort are plainer still when the appropriation does not arise in the course of trade at all.

In England, the tort of passing off requires: reputation (or goodwill) acquired by the claimant in their goods, name, trademark, or the like; a misrepresentation by the defendant leading to confusion or deception; and resulting damage to the claimant.[29] In the simplest case, it involves a representation to the effect that one's goods are the work of another, as when 'knock-off' (counterfeit) Gucci and Prada handbags are sold at prices much lower than the genuine article's market value, and, in this respect, is analogous to pseudepigraphy, or what might be called 'reverse plagiarism.'[30] But from this simple case the tort has grown to cover many others.[31] In *Sim v HJ Heinz & Co Ltd*,[32] an actor unsuccessfully sought to restrain the defendants from impersonating his well-known voice in a television advertisement, alleging both libel and passing off. In bringing the latter claim, the claimant was effectively asking the court to consider whether a person's voice could be considered a form of property.[33] Although ultimately unsuccessful on other grounds,

26 The classic treatment is Christopher Wadlow, *Wadlow on the Law of Passing-Off* (6th edn, Thomson Reuters 2021).

27 Huw Beverley-Smith, *The Commercial Appropriation of Personality* (Cambridge University Press 2002) 30.

28 *Henderson v Radio Corporation Pty Ltd* [1969] RPC 218 (Full Court NSWSC).

29 *Consorzio del Prosciutto di Parma v Marks & Spencer Plc* [1991] RPC 351 (Ch) 368.

30 In plagiarism proper, one claims that another's work is one's own.

31 Tony Weir, *Tort Law* (Oxford University Press 2002) 178.

32 [1959] 1 WLR 313 (QB).

33 Simon Deakin and Zoe Adams, *Markesinis and Deakin's Tort Law* (8th edn, Oxford University Press 2019) 709; Huw Beverley-Smith, *The Commercial Appropriation of Personality* (Cambridge University Press 2002) 67–68.

McNair J opined that it would be 'a grave defect in the law if it were possible for a party, for the purposes of commercial gain, to make use of the voice of another party without his consent.'[34]

While the way is open to extend the meaning of property to cover one's likeness or voice,[35] still a claimant must have goodwill in these attributes, and this has been thought to limit the operation of the tort to the purely commercial sphere, for unless a victim has acquired goodwill through their business, profession, or calling,[36] the tort of passing off will be unavailing.[37] To some extent, this explains why the adoption of a US-style right of publicity would not remedy the lacuna in English law; for the US right, too, protects primarily commercial interests from exploitation.[38]

Furthermore, the meaning of 'misrepresentation' in the above formulation has so far been construed narrowly. English law requires a false representation to the effect either that the claimant's and defendant's businesses are connected or that the claimant has licensed the defendant's goods or services. A representation to the effect that the claimant merely endorses the defendant's business is not sufficient.[39]

As things stand, then, there is no clear statement affirming the principle that in English law a person's voice or likeness is an inviolable feature of their person, on a par with their body, mind, and reputation.[40]

34 [1959] 1 WLR 313 (QB) 317.

35 Other requirements of the tort that have been relaxed – though not necessarily dispensed with – include proof of special damage (see Huw Beverley-Smith, *The Commercial Appropriation of Personality* (Cambridge University Press 2002) 97–99) and the requirement that both claimant and defendant be engaged in a 'common field of activity' (see *Irvine v Talksport Ltd* [2002] EWHC 367 (Ch), [2002] 1 WLR 2355).

36 *Kean v McGivan* [1982] FSR 119 (CA); *British Diabetic Association v Diabetic Society Ltd* [1995] 4 All ER 812 (Ch) 819.

37 Simon Deakin and Zoe Adams, *Markesinis and Deakin's Tort Law* (8th edn, Oxford University Press 2019) 709, n 63.

38 Kelsey Farish argues that the adoption of the more generous Californian right of publicity is of limited utility because it shares many of the drawbacks of English privacy law. See Kelsey Farish, 'Do Deepfakes Pose a Golden Opportunity? Considering whether English Law Should Adopt California's Publicity Right in the Age of the Deepfake' (2020) 15 *Journal of Intellectual Property Law & Practice* 40, 46.

39 *Fenty v Arcadia Group* [2013] EWHC 2310 (Ch), [2013] WLR(D) 310 and [2015] EWCA Civ 3, [2015] 1 WLR 3291. See also Huw Beverley-Smith, *The Commercial Appropriation of Personality* (Cambridge University Press 2002) 72–84.

40 In Australia and New Zealand, the prohibition against misleading and deceptive conduct in ss 18 and 29 of the Australian Consumer Law (ACL) and ss 9–11 of the Fair Trading Act 1986 (FTA), respectively, has become an alternative to passing off on account of certain procedural advantages, even for trade rivals who cannot be considered 'consumers' in the sense usually understood by consumer protection law; again, however, these provisions will be unavailing unless the representations were made in the course of 'trade or commerce.' See Carolyn Sappideen and Prue Vines (eds), *Fleming's The Law of Torts* (10th edn, Thomson Reuters 2011) 802, 805; cf Kit Barker and others, *The Law of Torts in Australia* (5th edn, Oxford University Press 2012) 248–249, 266–267. Note also that the Australian and New Zealand provisions also require defendants to be more than merely platforms or even publishers and 'information providers' such as traditional media (in contrast to defamation, for which it suffices

B *Defamation*

Defamation occurs 'when a person publishes words or matter to a third party that contain an untrue imputation that harms the reputation of the claimant.'[41] It was always an awkward apparatus for resolving complaints of appropriation of personality. A classic case on point, *Tolley v Fry*[42] can be read as either an expression of this maladaptiveness or as a monument to the common law's ingenuity. A well-known amateur golfer was able to prevent the defendant's unauthorised use of his image on promotional material on the basis that the image implied he was the type of person who would profit from his amateur status!

At any rate, s 1(1) of the Defamation Act 2013 now provides that 'A statement is not defamatory unless its publication has caused or is likely to cause serious harm to the reputation of the claimant.' In *Lachaux v Independent Print Ltd*,[43] the Supreme Court held that the effect of s 1 is to supplement the common law by introducing a condition that the general damage caused by a defamatory imputation must be serious,[44] in the sense that it must be *demonstrable* – there must be concrete evidence that the claimant's reputation has *in fact* been harmed.[45] The traditional position had been that general damage is presumed to flow from a defamatory imputation simply in virtue of the meaning of the words conveying the imputation. This had allowed defamatory imputations to sound in general damages even when the imputations were not supported by evidence of their having had a detrimental impact on the claimant's reputation.[46] The modified position now makes it impossible for general damages to be awarded without at least some demonstrable harm to one's reputation. Indeed, the modified position makes it impossible to sue in defamation at all unless the claimant suffers demonstrable reputational harm. At the same time, the Court was careful to emphasise that the new condition does not require proof of special damage – that is, actual pecuniary loss – and that libels[47] are therefore still, strictly speaking, actionable per se, as they have always been.[48]

that defendants are publishers). See, for example, ss 19 and 38 of the ACL and s 15 of the FTA; see also *Google Inc v ACCC* [2013] HCA 1, (2013) 249 CLR 435.

41 Alastair Mullis and Richard Parkes (eds), *Gatley on Libel and Slander* (12th edn, Thomson Reuters 2013) para 1.5.

42 [1931] AC 333 (HL).

43 [2019] UKSC 27, [2020] AC 612.

44 Ibid. [19].

45 Ibid. [16].

46 Ibid.

47 A libel is a defamatory statement whose publication takes a permanent (and probably visual) form, such as writing. See Simon Deakin and Zoe Adams, *Markesinis and Deakin's Tort Law* (8th edn, Oxford University Press 2019) 626–627. Libel is traditionally distinguished from slander, which covers all other defamatory statements, such as those that are spoken or otherwise ephemeral.

48 However, the wording of s 1 does seem to preclude the possibility of a claimant recovering nominal damages for libel in the absence of serious reputational harm, and one might reasonably argue that, if that is indeed the effect of s 1, libels cannot be actionable per se.

Since our concern is with deepfakes, and defamation always proceeds by a 'statement' of some sort, it is important to say something about how the law regards audio/visual media that are alleged to be defamatory. Section 15 of the Act defines 'statement' to mean 'words, pictures, visual images, gestures or any other method of signifying meaning.' Although statements conveying defamatory imputations are often conceived to take the form of words, s 15 reflects the common law position that pictures, visual images, voice recordings, and audio-visual media more generally can operate as 'statements' conveying defamatory imputations, provided that the medium in question may be reckoned a 'method of signifying meaning.' Statements, in turn, and therefore all audio/visual media, can be understood as either alleging facts or advancing opinions, the latter being typically based upon, but not themselves, facts. As an example of a visual allegation, a picture of the claimant performing a criminal act may be taken to allege that the claimant actually performed the act depicted. As an example of a visual opinion, a political cartoon in a right-leaning newspaper depicting a conservative candidate hugging a tree may be taken to be advancing the paper's opinion that the candidate is a hypocrite. It is worth noting that to the degree that opinions are based on facts, the opinion-holder may have learned the facts from audio/visual statements. To continue with the cartoon example, the base fact might have been learned through the paper's chief political correspondent sighting a photograph of the candidate attending a Greens Party meeting. I will return to this point in Section IV.

From all this it follows that audio/visual media will convey defamatory imputations insofar as they allege facts or advance opinions causing or likely to cause demonstrable reputational harm. From the point of view of a claimant whose image or recording has been taken without consent, the new provisions imply that if the claimant sues in defamation, they must now show that the image or recording has caused or is likely to cause them demonstrable reputational harm. In these circumstances, a claimant is likely to be more aggrieved by the injury to their reputation than by the mere fact that an image or recording of them has been made without consent. That is to say, by the time, a suit in defamation can even be feasible, defamation will be the only real gravamen of the complaint, any appropriation having thereby been subsumed.

Compounding this difficulty is the fact that defamation suits are vulnerable to defences, particularly those of truth and honest opinion.[49] In fact, even while defamation does not demand that a claimant prove the falsity of a defamatory imputation or that its publication be actuated by malice, the claimant will often have no choice but to establish falsehood or malice whenever the defence of truth or honest opinion is raised.

In short, as with passing off, the tort of defamation does not protect a person's voice or likeness from unauthorised appropriation unless the appropriation happens to meet conditions designed to protect other interests entirely.

49 See ss 2 and 3 of the Defamation Act 2013, respectively, for the elements of these defences, and Section IV.

C *Injurious Falsehood*

The tort of injurious falsehood is a catch-all tort for a variety of slights against a claimant's business or business dealings. Despite contemplating a wide class of statements, in most instances it reduces to a form of defamation of a claimant's goods or services as distinct from the claimant's character.[50] And like defamation, it makes for a clumsy attempt at redressing appropriation of personality. In *Kaye v Robertson*,[51] for instance, the celebrity claimant had his privacy grossly violated when, lying on his hospital bed in a room whose door had been marked 'restricted visiting,' journalists entered the room, took photographs, and 'interviewed' him. Scandalous stories appeared in their newspaper soon after. The court found for the claimant, but not because his personality had been appropriated or his privacy otherwise violated, but because it was an injurious falsehood – damaging to the claimant's professional reputation – to insinuate that he 'would do anything for money.'

Fleming gives as a list of injurious falsehoods the following: aspersions on the claimant's title to land or trading stock, or on the quality of their merchandise; imputations that the claimant's business is no longer a going concern, or that the claimant's staff are diseased, or that the claimant is not employable.[52] In a curious twist, injurious falsehoods even include instances of what is sometimes called 'reverse confusion' or 'reverse passing off,' where instead of the defendant representing that their goods are the claimant's (as in ordinary passing off), the defendant represents that the claimant's goods are the defendant's (analogous to straightforward plagiarism).[53]

Beyond this essential difference between defamation and injurious falsehood – the one brought for slights against character, the other for slights against business – there are three other differences whose significance will be relevant when I return to the topic of deepfakes in Section IV. First, while defamation (qua libel[54]) is still, in theory, actionable per se,[55] injurious falsehood at common law requires proof of special damage, regardless of whether or not the falsehood assumes a permanent (e.g., written) form.[56] Second, the claimant suing in defamation is not required to

[50] Michael A Jones (ed), *Clerk and Lindsell on Torts* (23rd edn, Thomson Reuters 2020) para 22-03; Simon Deakin and Zoe Adams, *Markesinis and Deakin's Tort Law* (8th edn, Oxford University Press 2019) 692.

[51] [1991] FSR 62.

[52] Carolyn Sappideen and Prue Vines (eds), *Fleming's The Law of Torts* (10th edn, Thomson Reuters 2011) 796.

[53] Ibid. 800, 803.

[54] In other words, a defamatory statement whose publication takes a permanent (and probably visual) form, such as writing.

[55] *Lachaux v Independent Print Ltd* [2019] UKSC 27, [2020] AC 612 [19].

[56] This no longer need be the case: for instance, s 3(2) of the Defamation Act 1952 dispenses with the need for claimants to prove special damage for injurious falsehood where the falsehood was calculated to cause pecuniary damage to the claimant in respect of any office, profession, calling, trade or

prove the falsity of the imputation, unlike the victim of injurious falsehood, who has always been required to do so. Third, liability for defamation is strict, whereas it is an element of liability for injurious falsehood that the defendant be actuated by malice – at the very least, that the defendant know their statement is false or be recklessly indifferent to its being so.[57]

Conclusion: as with the other common law actions so far considered, injurious falsehood is a tort whose rationale happens only incidentally to protect interests in one's likeness or voice.[58]

D *Nuisance and Trespass*

Generally, what one can see one can photograph without its being actionable, provided that the photograph does not depict a person in an embarrassing situation or otherwise constitute an actionable nuisance.[59] Thus where the appropriating images are taken by watching and besetting the claimant, causing them to suffer distress and serious inconvenience, or otherwise unreasonably interfering with the claimant's use and enjoyment of land, injunctive relief will lie to prevent publication of the images.[60] The obvious limitation of an action for nuisance, however, is that it requires the claimant to prove a relevant interest in land.[61] Furthermore, in the nature of things, the appropriating material must have been acquired during the claimant's *actual* occupation of the land – the relevant land

business held or carried on by them. See also s 2 of the same Act. Note that ss 2 and 3 of this Act are cast in terms of 'words,' not 'statements,' as s 1 of the 2013 Act has it. However, s 16(1) of the 1952 Act provides that 'Any reference in this Act to words shall be construed as including a reference to pictures, visual images, gestures and other methods of signifying meaning' – identical to the definition of 'statements' found in s 15 of the 2013 Act. Thus my remarks above in relation to s 15 apply equally to injurious falsehood, mutatis mutandis. The short point is that an action for injurious falsehood can be brought for imputations conveyed by images, recordings, and so on.

57 Michael A Jones (ed), *Clerk and Lindsell on Torts* (23rd edn, Thomson Reuters 2020) para 22-14; Kit Barker and others, *The Law of Torts in Australia* (5th edn, Oxford University Press 2012) 243; Carolyn Sappideen and Prue Vines (eds), *Fleming's The Law of Torts* (10th edn, Thomson Reuters 2011) 798.

58 Again, the prohibition against misleading and deceptive conduct enshrined in ss 18 and 29 of the Australian Consumer Law and ss 9–11 of New Zealand's Fair Trading Act 1986 offer an alternative statutory regime to the common law action of injurious falsehood. See Carolyn Sappideen and Prue Vines (eds), *Fleming's The Law of Torts* (10th edn, Thomson Reuters 2011) 799, 802; cf Kit Barker and others, *The Law of Torts in Australia* (5th edn, Oxford University Press 2012) 248–249, 266–267.

59 *Raciti v Hughes* (1995) 7 BPR 14,837 (NSWSC) 14,840 (Young J).

60 Ibid. 14, 840–14, 841. On the relation between nuisance and privacy, see *Fearn v Board of Trustees of the Tate Gallery* [2023] UKSC 4, [2023] 2 WLR 339.

61 In *Hunter v Canary Wharf* [1997] AC 655 (HL) 692, Lord Goff (with whom Lords Lloyd, Hoffman, and Hope agreed) said that 'an action in private nuisance will only lie at the suit of a person who has a right to the land affected. Ordinarily, such a person can only sue if he has the right to exclusive possession of the land.'

interest will not be sufficient. Publication might also be restrained if the images were acquired through trespass to land, provided that the images may be said to constitute confidential information.[62] Again, however, a claimant will require the relevant connection to land.

E *Harassment and the Intentional Infliction of Psychiatric Harm*

In the event that the relevant connection to land cannot be established, the Protection from Harassment Act 1997 imposes civil liability on anyone whose 'course of conduct' amounts to the harassment of another, where the defendant ought to know that their conduct would do so. However, because the Act contemplates a 'course of conduct' amounting to harassment rather than a single act of harassment, it cannot avail the victim who complains of just one act of appropriation.[63]

Alternatively, a claimant may seek relief for even a single act of appropriation if the appropriation constitutes a wilful act calculated to cause psychiatric harm.[64] This is the well-known 'rule in *Wilkinson v Downton*.'[65] In that case, the claimant suffered an acute psychiatric disturbance that resulted in weeks of debilitating incapacity after the defendant, in what was meant as a practical joke, told her that her husband had been 'smashed up in an accident … with both legs broken.'[66] Wright J identified an essential question for consideration as being 'whether the defendant's act was so plainly calculated to produce some effect of the kind which was produced that an intention to produce it ought to be imputed to the defendant',[67] and, on the facts before him, he thought that it did. It has since been recognised that humiliation, harassment, racial vilification, and personal abuse can found a good cause of action under the rule in *Wilkinson v Downton*.[68] If a claimant can therefore substantiate the claim of having suffered a psychiatric response, even a single act of 'revenge porn' or any other indecent appropriation that triggers a psychiatric response may provide a sufficient basis upon which to impute to a defendant the malicious intention of which Wright J spoke.

[62] *Australian Broadcasting Corporation v Lenah Game Meats* [2001] HCA 63, (2001) 208 CLR 199 [34], [39], [51]–[55] (Gleeson CJ), [79]–[81], [106]–[111] (Gummow and Hayne JJ), [178] (Kirby J).

[63] Michael A Jones (ed), *Clerk and Lindsell on Torts* (23rd edn, Thomson Reuters 2020) para 14-20.

[64] *Wilkinson v Downton* [1897] 2 QB 57 (QB). See now also *Rhodes v OPO* [2015] UKSC 32, [2016] AC 219. In the criminal context, see also s 33 of the Criminal Justice and Courts Act 2015 (relating to the disclosure of private sexual photographs and films with intent to cause distress), and ss 67 and 67A of the Sexual Offences Act 2003 (relating to voyeurism and 'upskirting'). The indictable common law offence of outraging public decency may also be used to prosecute creators of images or films which are lewd, obscene, or of disgusting character and such as to outrage minimum standards of public decency as assessed by a jury.

[65] [1897] 2 QB 57 (QB).

[66] Ibid. 58.

[67] Ibid. 59.

[68] *Nationwide News Pty Ltd v Naidu* [2007] NSWCA 377 (2007) 71 NSWLR 471.

F *Misuse of Private Information*

Under the new action for misuse of private information, it is tolerably clear that publication of images *howsoever* obtained – even if not through trespass – might be restrained if their publication would disclose information over which the claimant has a reasonable expectation of privacy.[69] The action is, in theory at least, a development of the equity for breach of confidence. That traditional jurisdiction provided relief for claimants who had imparted confidential information to another party 'in circumstances importing an obligation of confidence,' whenever the recipient of the information made 'unauthorised use of that information to the detriment of the party communicating it.'[70] Each of these elements has been successively diluted to the point where now all that is required – subject to a defendant's right to free expression – is for a claimant to show that information over which they had a reasonable expectation of privacy was disclosed by the defendant without authorisation.[71] In particular, the absence of a relationship of confidentiality between the parties does not prevent an unauthorised disclosure from being a 'breach of confidence';[72] nor, it seems, will the failure of the claimant to take any steps to avoid being photographed in a public setting *of necessity* prevent publication of the photographs from being considered a breach of confidence.[73]

Thus a person who drinks too much at a private function and is caught on camera performing a humiliating ritual may be able to prevent publication of the spectacle by bringing proceedings alleging misuse of private information. Importantly, the requirement that publication of the image constitute a disclosure of *true* private facts seems to imply that the image must be genuine rather than doctored.

G *Summary*

Generally speaking, a person does not have property in their appearance, so cannot prevent others from taking their photograph or recording them. Thus what one can see one can photograph without its being actionable, provided that the photograph does not depict a person in an embarrassing situation or otherwise constitute an actionable nuisance. An image or recording of a person amounting to a representation falsely suggesting that the claimant's and defendant's businesses are connected or that the claimant has licensed the defendant's goods or services, is actionable if

[69] *Campbell v MGN Ltd* [2004] UKHL 22, [2004] 2 AC 457; *Douglas v Hello!* [2007] UKHL 21, [2008] 1 AC 1; *Vidal-Hall v Google Inc* [2015] EWCA Civ 311, [2016] QB 1003. See also Section V, below.

[70] *Coco v AN Clark (Engineers) Ltd* [1969] RPC 41 (Ch) 47 (Megarry J).

[71] *Campbell v MGN Ltd* [2004] UKHL 22, [2004] 2 AC 457 [21] (Lord Nicholls), [96] (Lord Hope), [135] (Lady Hale); *Douglas v Hello!* [2007] UKHL 21, [2008] 1 AC 1 [122] (Lord Hoffman), [329] (Lord Brown). See also Section V.

[72] *Douglas v Hello!* [2000] EWCA Civ 353, [2001] QB 967.

[73] *Campbell v MGN Ltd* [2004] UKHL 22, [2004] 2 AC 457.

the representation damages the claimant's goodwill. An image or recording of a person cannot be shared if doing so would be a breach of contract, confidence, or copyright or otherwise a misuse of private information. Nor may an image or recording of a person be shared if it conveys a defamatory imputation causing or likely to cause them demonstrable reputational harm or if it amounts to injurious falsehood. Finally, photographing or recording a person, or sharing an image or recording of them, is actionable if it forms part of a course of conduct which the defendant ought to know amounts to harassment of that person, or if it constitutes a wilful act calculated to cause psychiatric harm to that person.

IV WHY DEEPFAKES MIGHT BE MORE VULNERABLE TO TRADITIONAL COMMON LAW ACTIONS

Owing to the manner in which deepfakes are generated and the motivations behind their most objectionable uses, some of the traditional categories of wrong discussed in Section III may actually fare better against deepfakes than they have against older forms of audio/visual media. The key point to emphasise in respect of common law liability is that the technology behind deepfakes invites just those uses which are apt to satisfy the more difficult elements of the traditional torts, particularly those elements concerning the defendant's mental state. It is not that there is any special magic in the old torts themselves; it is simply that some of their elements may be more readily made out when deepfakes happen to be involved.

Before proceeding, however, I should note two issues that will likely complicate the analysis later. One concerns the identity of the defendant. So far, I have been assuming that the defendant will be the creator of the deepfake – the person who manipulated the claimant's image using an autoencoder or GAN. But this cannot be assured. As Chesney and Citron point out, 'the metadata relevant for ascertaining a deep fake's provenance might be insufficient to identify the person who generated it.'[74] Then, at the point when the creator or, more likely, someone else, posts or forwards the deepfake on social media, a distributor who wishes to remain anonymous will no doubt ensure that the IP address associated with the post is impossible to trace back to them.[75] And given the global reach of social media, it is just as likely that the responsible parties will anyway be outside the jurisdiction. In the result, a person aggrieved by a deepfake may have no effective recourse against either its creator or distributor. This leaves only platform operators – such as social media companies, ISPs, servers, website operators, and blog hosts – as the obvious defendants. Platform liability for defamation (to take a salient example) covers the gamut of hyperimmunity in the United States to something approaching strict

[74] Robert Chesney and Danielle Keats Citron, 'Deep Fakes: A Looming Challenge for Privacy, Democracy, and National Security' (2019) 107 *California Law Review* 1753, 1792.

[75] Ibid.

liability in Australia.[76] In the United Kingdom, secondary publishers of defamatory matter may seek to rely on s 1 of the Defamation Act 1996 – the statutory equivalent of the common law defence of innocent dissemination – where the defendant did not author or have editorial responsibility for the defamatory material, took reasonable care in relation to its publication, and did not know or have reason to believe that the material was defamatory. In any event, s 10 of the Defamation Act 2013 makes clear that secondary publishers can only be sued when 'it is not reasonably practicable for an action to be brought against the author, editor or publisher.'[77] A related matter is that of secondary participation. Developers of user-friendly deepfake apps and providers of online instructional videos can hardly deny the perverse uses to which their materials are likely to be put. Thus in suitable cases, a claimant might seek to pursue entities in the deepfake supply chain other than those directly implicated in a deepfake's creation and dissemination.

The second issue concerns proof. In addition to the usual elements of the torts below, the claimant will naturally have to prove that the image in question is, in fact, a deepfake. This is a separate and nontrivial evidentiary challenge. I do not address that issue here save for noting that a variety of machine learning techniques are likely to make the claimant's burden easier to discharge.[78]

A *Defamation*

As I noted in Section III, a claimant suing in defamation is not required to prove the falsity of the imputation nor that the defendant was actuated by malice. But this is only technically correct, for as I also noted, the claimant is likely to confront one of the various defences to defamation and in particular the defences of truth and honest opinion.

Section 2 of the Defamation Act 2013 sets out the requirements for the defence of truth (formerly 'justification'). For the defence to work, the defendant must show that the defamatory imputation in question is substantially true. Since only facts are truth-apt, the defence can operate only when the imputation is conveyed in a factual statement, which is to say, it cannot operate when the imputation

[76] In the United States, see s 230 of the Communications Decency Act 1996; in Australia, see *Fairfax Media Publications Pty Ltd v Voller* [2021] HCA 27, (2021), 95 ALJR 767.

[77] See also reg 19 of the Electronic Commerce Regulations 2002 and, where website operators specifically are concerned, s 5 of the Defamation Act 2013. The possibility of in rem actions in the US context is discussed briefly in Eric Kocsis, 'Deepfakes, Shallowfakes, and the Need for a Private Right of Action' (2022) 126 *Dickinson Law Review* 621, 645. Insightful discussion of secondary liability in the US also appears in Jack Langa, 'Deepfakes, Real Consequences: Crafting Legislation to Combat Threats Posed by Deepfakes' (2021) 101 *Boston University Law Review* 761, 792–800.

[78] The authentication of deepfakes in court is discussed in Molly Mullen, 'A New Reality: Deepfake Technology and the World around Us' (2022) 48 *Mitchell Hamline Law Review* 210. On deepfake detection methods generally, see Jan Kietzmann and others, 'Deepfakes: Trick or Treat?' (2020) 63 *Business Horizons* 135, 144.

is conveyed in the manner of an opinion. Where a statement of fact conveys a defamatory imputation, and the statement takes an audio/visual form, it follows that the fact depicted in audio/visual form must be substantially true. But where deepfakes are the subject matter of defamation proceedings, it is highly unlikely that the fact depicted in audio/visual form will be true at all, much less substantially true: deepfakes almost always depict their subjects in fantasy scenarios doing and saying things they never did or said.[79] Hence simply in virtue of the circumstances that would typically result in a deepfake being at the centre of defamation proceedings, the claimant will have much better odds of defeating any attempt by the defendant to run a truth defence.

Section 3 sets out the requirements for the defence of honest opinion (formerly 'fair comment'). For this defence to work, the defendant must show that the opinion was based on true facts and honestly held.[80] Moreover, for the opinion to *count* as an opinion and not just a bare assertion, its expression has to give some indication of the facts upon which it is based.[81] Saying that someone is disgraceful is a bare assertion. Saying that someone is disgraceful *because* they did this or that is an opinion proper and gives the hearer a sense of the facts which led to its formation.[82]

There is no particular difficulty attending the use of deepfakes to express opinions as such – one can express an opinion in words, photographs, cartoons, or whatever other medium serves to convey one's intended meaning. What matters chiefly for this defence, so far as deepfakes are concerned, is that an opinion be based on true facts and honestly held. As to the truth of base facts: from what I have already said about the use of deepfakes to express factual statements it follows that a deepfake can hardly provide the proper basis for an opinion – the defendant would need independent evidence that the base fact is true. So if the defendant learned the base fact via deepfake alone, the defence is almost certain to fail. As to the defendant's honestly holding their opinion: while it is true that an opinion can be expressed in any meaning-bearing form (including a deepfake), the efforts taken to generate deepfakes are often such as to evince malice and, a fortiori, knowledge of the imputation's falsity (or reckless indifference to its being so). Thus where the opinion itself takes the form of a deepfake, the claimant may have better prospects of defeating a plea of honest opinion. Nevertheless, as deepfake technology becomes even easier to use and more widely accessible, it is reasonable to expect that many defendants will legitimately hold the

79 Perhaps a deepfake could allege a true private fact by having the deepfaked claimant 'voice' something that was actually said by them or that is nonetheless true of them. Or a deepfake might depict the claimant committing an act which the claimant did in fact commit, albeit not exactly as presented in the deepfake; the deepfake might be in the nature of an artist's impression or dramatisation of events that did actually take place.

80 The latter being the statutory version of the old 'absence of malice' requirement at common law.

81 *Joseph v Spiller* [2010] UKSC 53, [2011] 1 AC 852 [105] (Lord Phillips).

82 Simon Deakin and Zoe Adams, *Markesinis and Deakin's Tort Law* (8th edn, Oxford University Press 2019) 658.

opinions they choose to express through deepfakes – presumably many more people than at present will adopt deepfakery as but one mode of legitimate public expression (e.g., as a form of satire). Hence in the near future, if not right now, honest opinion defences in defamation proceedings involving deepfakes are unlikely to be any more vulnerable than when traditionally generated images are involved.

B *Injurious Falsehood*

As I noted in Section III, injurious falsehood requires that the defendant be actuated by malice, know their statement is false, or be recklessly indifferent to its truth. Moreover, it is for the claimant to prove these matters. Thus if the claimant can show that the defendant does not actually believe the disparaging statement concerning the claimant's business, the claimant will satisfy the malice requirement. To this extent, what I said above in relation to defamation applies equally to injurious falsehood: where deepfakes are concerned, the claimant will have an easier run at establishing both that the statement is false and that the defendant knows that it is false (or was reckless as to its being so).

C *Harassment and the Intentional Infliction of Psychiatric Harm*

The observations in Section III on harassment and the rule in *Wilkinson v Downton* apply equally to deepfakes. Thus any abusive deepfake (e.g., 'revenge porn') is liable to be redressed under the Protection from Harassment Act if the deepfake appears on more than one occasion and amounts to harassment of the claimant; or if a spate of separate deepfakes depicting the claimant constitutes a course of conduct amounting to harassment of the claimant. Alternatively, if a claimant can establish that they experienced a psychiatric response to the publication of a deepfake, a single such act of publication may be sufficient to found a good cause of action under the rule in *Wilkinson v Downton*. Crucially, the eerie similarity to real life and inherent plausibility of deepfakes gives claimants greater scope to argue that they were indeed harassed, humiliated, and/or abused through the act of publication. That many claimants would succumb to mental illness in response to such publication seems entirely reasonable. The spectacle of oneself performing an act which one has not performed and which indeed may be alien to one's nature is likely to be shocking, and the thought that others might view this material and take it to be genuine deeply unsettling.

V THE PROTECTION OF DIGNITARY INTERESTS

Just because the falsehood and fault elements of some torts may be easier to establish when a deepfake is the subject of a dispute, it by no means follows that the law is in a satisfactory state. So long as claimants remain in the position of having to shoehorn complaints about affronts to their dignity into actions having little to do with their dignity – or, in the case of defamation, actions concerned with reputation rather than appropriation – too many victims of unjustified appropriation will be left without remedy. The newly recognised action for misuse of private information may be able to mop up some of these cases, but as I noted in Section III, the requirement that publication of the image constitute a disclosure of *true* private facts seems to imply that the image must be genuine rather than doctored. In the result, it is unclear whether a claimant aggrieved by a deepfake would be able to satisfy the strictures of the new 'tort.' It is likely that many objectionable deepfakes would simply fall through the cracks. And it is not salutary to rely on passing off either: many pernicious instances of appropriation by deepfake simply do not arise in commercial contexts – but passing off is in essence a tort against false advertising and unfair competition.

Thus we arrive at a crucial question: if the legislature is not to enact a general civil remedy for appropriation of personality broad enough to catch all those cases that would currently pass through the sieve of the traditional torts, as well as the new action for misuse of private information, how exactly is English common law to proceed?

Despite the category-bound system of recovery epitomised in *Victoria Park Racing*,[83] the same court affirmed half a century later that

> the rejection of a general action for 'unfair competition' or 'unfair trading' does not involve a denial of the desirability of adopting a flexible approach to traditional forms of action when such an approach is necessary to adapt them to meet new situations and circumstances.[84]

But even this kind of pragmatism has its limits, since, as the authors of an Australian text put it, 'the deployment of ancient causes of action to meet modern purposes for which they were not originally designed has sometimes resulted in their distortion, to the detriment of the law's transparency and coherence.'[85] While relaxing elements of the tort of passing off might seem like the path of least resistance, the result would be a contrivance; for to do justice to the tort, it would need to operate outside commercial contexts, and for many jurists, this would be a bridge too far.[86] It seems more honest – more 'transparent and coherent' – for the courts to recognise a new and wholly independent tort of appropriation of personality, perhaps fashioned by reference to the elements of passing off. The New Zealand Court of Appeal, after

[83] *Victoria Park Racing and Recreation Grounds Co Ltd v Taylor* (1936) 58 CLR 479 (HCA).

[84] *Moorgate Tobacco Co Ltd (No 2) v Philip Morris Ltd* (1984) 156 CLR 414 (HCA) 445 (Deane J).

[85] Kit Barker and others, *The Law of Torts in Australia* (5th edn, Oxford University Press 2012) 391.

[86] Robert Chesney and Danielle Keats Citron, 'Deep Fakes: A Looming Challenge for Privacy, Democracy, and National Security' (2019) 107 *California Law Review* 1753, 1794. On the other hand, the American Law Institute's *Restatement (Second) on Torts* (1977) s 652C acknowledges that, for the purposes of the US right of publicity, appropriation in most states need not be for commercial gain (the Restatement notes that it is only in 'some' states that appropriation must be for commercial gain). It turns out that only four of the fifty states require appropriation to be for commercial gain: Nikki Chamberlain, 'Misappropriation of Personality: A Case for Common Law Identity Protection' (2021) 26 *TLJ* 195, 201.

all, managed to develop an independent tort similar to the UK's action for misuse of private information without the pretence that it was an organic development of the equity for breach of confidence.[87] The UK courts, by contrast, persisted with the fiction that the action for misuse of private information was merely a consequence of relaxing the requirements for breaches of confidence (as expressed by Megarry J in *Coco v AN Clark (Engineers) Ltd*).[88] The better view is that the courts hived the new action off from the equitable remedy so that today it stands as an independent tort alongside the old remedy.[89]

To fashion a new tort of appropriation of personality by analogy to passing off but separate from it – so that it avails a claimant not only within but also beyond the sphere of trade and commerce and has as its rationale the protection of the claimant's personality against unauthorised appropriation – is to fashion a tort grounded ultimately in the protection of the claimant's dignitary interests. Such a tort falls naturally within the category of trespassory actions and would be actionable per se (unlike passing off). Maitland once described trespass as 'that fertile mother of actions,'[90] since from actions intended to vindicate the claimant's interests in land, goods, and bodily integrity – the latter encompassing interests as diverse as freedom of movement and psychological wellbeing – we end up with actions serving to vindicate the claimant's reputation.[91] A tort that finally, and belatedly, vindicates one's interests in certain features of personality against unauthorised appropriation should hardly be considered a revolutionary turn in English law. What is in view here is just the kind of step-wise and interstitial development of common law principle without which there would be no common law to speak of.

But then, it will be said, we cannot countenance a tort that makes illegal merely the taking of someone's photograph without permission and its subsequent use towards some harmless end (a child's scrapbook, a community art installation or public mural displaying the happy faces of locals, a photography class, etc.). The answer to this concern requires doubling down on both the strict meaning of a tort being actionable per se and the specific interest that a tort of appropriation would serve to vindicate.

[87] *Hosking v Runting* [2004] NZCA 34 (2005), 1 NZLR 1.

[88] *Coco v AN Clark (Engineers) Ltd* [1969] RPC 41 (Ch) 47. See *Douglas v Hello!* [2000] EWCA Civ 353, [2001] QB 967.

[89] This is, indeed, the position which Sedley LJ seems to have preferred in *Douglas v Hello!* [2000] EWCA Civ 353, [2001] QB 967 [110], [126] and which Lord Nicholls preferred in *Campbell v MGN Ltd* [2004] UKHL 22, [2004] 2 AC 457 [14]. It now also appears to be the received view: *Vidal-Hall v Google Inc* [2015] EWCA Civ 311, [2016] QB 1003 [43], [51].

[90] Frederic W Maitland, *The Forms of Action at Common Law* (AH Chaytor and WJ Whittaker (eds) (Cambridge University Press 1969), 39.

[91] It is true that slander began in the ecclesiastical courts and that libel was originally prosecuted in the Court of Star Chamber, but libel was soon taken over by the common law courts upon the Chamber's abolition and subsumed within the 'trespass upon the plaintiff's special case,' that is, the 'action on the case' (as the category is more commonly known). See John H Baker, *An Introduction to English Legal History* (5th edn, Oxford University Press 2019) 467–470.

The recent decision of the Supreme Court in *Lachaux* reminds us that a tort may be actionable per se in the strict sense of not requiring proof of *special* damage while yet demanding that a kind of actual and compensable harm be suffered commensurate with an award of (at the very least) general damages. Thus recognition of a tort of appropriation of personality need not entail that every lewd photo or deepfake, much less every humdrum photograph, of a person taken without their consent will see its subject vindicated, though it will be, strictly speaking, actionable per se; for a tort that is strictly actionable per se may still require proof of actual and compensable harm, without which not even nominal damages can be recovered. In the case of defamation, the Court in *Lachaux* held that a consequence of s 1 of the Defamation Act 2013 is that libels are still actionable per se, though they require demonstrable harm to the claimant's reputation commensurate with an award of general damages. Much the same could be true of a tort of appropriation of personality – the tort would be actionable per se yet require a claimant to prove actual harm. What would be vindicated in the latter tort, however, is an altogether different interest. Instead of demonstrable harm to reputation, the claimant would be required to have suffered demonstrable harm by way of *loss of control over how they are perceived*, insomuch as an incident of the claimant's inherent dignity must be the freedom to decide how they will present to the world.[92] The tort therefore serves to protect 'one's sense of autonomy, dignity and sovereignty or control over oneself and one's image' insomuch as one has a right to control how one presents oneself and one's image to the public.[93] Importantly, although one's interest in being perceived a certain way or in a certain light may coincide with one's interest in a good reputation, these interests are not the same. Our ability to shape how others see us need have nothing to do with our reputation. I may have an interest in being perceived as a man, or a woman, or something else, but this is not because my character would be sullied in the event I was misgendered. Similarly, a degrading pornographic image of me which is nonetheless clearly labelled as fake would still be an affront to my dignity despite its not being defamatory.[94]

92 Cf Andrei Marmor, 'What is the Right to Privacy?' (2015) 43 *Philosophy and Public Affairs* 3. Cf too the remarks of Judith J. Thomson on the element of 'control' in 'The Right to Privacy' (1975) 4 *Philosophy and Public Affairs* 295, 305, n 1. Thomson would probably think that talk of control here is misplaced. She says that if someone invents an X-ray device that can spy on me through walls, I have thereby lost control over my privacy because I can no longer keep prying eyes out simply by shutting my front door; nevertheless, she says, my privacy would only be violated in the event someone actually trained the X-ray device on my home: it's the looking that violates my privacy, not the power to look – so losing control itself isn't the issue. In truth, of course, it's both the looking and the *intention* to look that violate my privacy, both of which co-constitute my loss of control. *Pace* Thomson, inventing the device no more entails a loss of control over my privacy than does my neighbour's high-intensity resistance training schedule, which empowers him to break down my door with his bare hands if he's so inclined. Talk of control here is not misplaced.

93 Nikki Chamberlain, 'Misappropriation of Personality: A Case for Common Law Identity Protection' (2021) 26 *TLJ* 195, 198–199, 205–206.

94 Kareem Gibson, 'Deepfakes and Involuntary Pornography: Can Our Current Legal Framework Address This Technology?' (2020) 66 *Wayne Law Review* 259, 268–270.

Determining the extent of one's 'loss of control' over how one is perceived obviously calls for evidence of how the claimant wishes to be perceived, and such evidence must be adduced in terms that answer the specific misportrayal in the appropriating matter. For instance, if a picture presents the claimant as a man, when the claimant is a woman who wishes to be perceived as such, the claimant must adduce evidence that she is a woman *and that she wishes to be perceived as such*. Evidence may establish that the claimant prefers being perceived as nonbinary. An essential issue for determination by a court would then be: how far does the appropriating matter derogate from the claimant's desired self-image (as established by the evidence)? Being portrayed as a man may be a greater affront to an individual who wants to be perceived as a woman than it would be to an individual who wants to be perceived as nonbinary. And the background assumption here must be something like: the greater the gap between the claimant's desired presentation and the defendant's actual portrayal, the greater we may take the loss of control to be. But other factors will no doubt bear on this determination. One such factor is the likelihood that the appropriating matter will be construed as a faithful portrayal of the claimant by the community. The lower the likelihood, the less successfully will the claimant be able to substantiate a loss of control. Yet another factor is the relative importance of the claimant's wish to be perceived in the manner sought. A fair-minded assessment of the claimant's wish may attach more or less importance to the specific perspective from which the claimant seeks to be viewed.

To avoid misunderstanding, it is important to stress that the tort envisaged here is solely concerned with *appropriation* – which is to say, with the unauthorised curation and portrayal of *likeness* (be it visual or vocal). It is concerned with image privacy and is therefore considerably narrower than the scope of Prosser's 'false light' privacy.[95] What is protected is the claimant's right not to be displayed in a manner that fails to respect the person's patent self-presentation. The tort therefore does not protect a person's wish to self-identify *per se*. It does not amount to a prohibition on speech that fails to respect the claimant's preferred mode of presentation. It cannot be used in aid of attempts to police the use of gender pronouns or to guarantee that a trans woman will be permitted to enter certain 'female-only' spaces. It might well, however (subject to defences), be used to prohibit the depiction of a trans woman as a man.

In some ways, the common law of nuisance provides another example of a tort that is actionable per se in the strict sense discussed in *Lachaux*. The gist of the action is unreasonable interference with land, but this includes inconvenience caused by such things as loud noises and bad smells for which a claimant need not incur pecuniary loss. Hence, while proof of special damage is not required to

95 That is to say, protection against publicity which places the plaintiff in a false light in the public eye. See William L Prosser, *Handbook of the Law of Torts* (2nd edn, West Publishing 1955) 42–45.

maintain nuisance, without demonstrable harm, there can be no action. Difficulties in quantifying degrees of inconvenience – to say nothing of loss of amenity, pain and suffering, and other heads of general damage that are routinely awarded – have not prevented the courts from engaging upon the task, nor should they stand in the way of the courts quantifying the very real harm suffered by a person whose ability to shape how they are seen by others has been compromised. Indeed, it is hard to fathom why injury to one's reputation should be compensated while injury to one's self-presentation should not. True enough, as with any tort, the courts will need to consider very carefully a range of possible defences to allegations of appropriation of personality, such as consent to publication,[96] public interest, and honest opinion. But again, that is to be expected, and the difficulties of the task should not impede the attempt.

[96] Or the claimant's acquiescing to the perception likely to be formed of them by reason of the appropriating matter. Acquiescence may be actual or constructive. For example, if I, being of sound mind and not under the influence of any drug or other intoxicant, humiliate myself in a public setting by lewd behaviour, and the defendant records me with a smart phone and thereupon shares the recording on social media, it would be open to the defendant to argue that I acquiesced to the publicity.

11

Agency Law and AI

Daniel Seng and Tan Cheng Han

I INTRODUCTION

It is 5 pm, and your day is done. You check your phone app to verify that the home air conditioner will start the moment you leave the office.[1] You are confident that the smart Internet of Things (IoT) thermostat had turned the air conditioner off once it detected that no one was home.[2] When you reach the garage, you activate the Smart Summon feature. Your Tesla unparks itself and drives to the pickup spot,[3] whereupon you hop in and drive off. At the garage exit, the gantry sensor communicates with the car's onboard unit and debits the parking fee from your bank account.[4] Coasting out of the garage and onto the expressway, you start the Autopilot feature.[5] As you settle yourself into the driver's seat, a synthetic voice[6] reminds you of your scheduled COVID-19 vaccination registration for tomorrow.[7] You smile, knowing that once vaccinated, you can avoid having your nose swabbed, even if this can be done more comfortably by robots![8]

This scenario is no longer the province of science fiction. In fact, modern society would grind to a halt without the use of these systems that are able to 'act[] on behalf

We would like to thank Ms Hitomi Yap and Mr Shaun Lim for their help with the research and editing of this paper. All errors and omissions, however, remain ours.

1 A smart air conditioner controller mimics the infrared signal from the air conditioner while using the home's Wi-Fi network to connect with an app on the phone. See thesmartcave, Here's what you need to know about smart AC controllers, <www.thesmartcave.com/best-smart-air-conditioner-controller/>.

2 See for example, the Nest Learning Thermostat, which is a web-connected, smart thermostat from Nest, a division of Google, that automatically learns about routines and programmes itself to set the temperature in your home. See Google, 'How Nest Thermostats Learn' <https://support.google.com/googlenest/answer/9247510?hl=en>.

3 The Tesla Smart Summon feature allows a Tesla driver to turn her car on remotely and beckon her Tesla to her, to save her the trouble of entering or exiting the vehicle. See <www.tesla.com/support/autopilot>.

4 The new Electronic Road Pricing system, which was to start in 2020, includes a feature to pay for parking. *See* <www.motorist.sg/article/413/new-erp-system-to-start-in-2020-includes-new-in-vehicle-units>.

5 See Tesla, 'Autopilot and Full Self-Driving Capability Features' <www.tesla.com/support/autopilot>.

6 See Wikipedia, 'Speech synthesis' <https://en.wikipedia.org/wiki/Speech_synthesis>.

7 See Ministry of Health, Singapore, 'COVID-19 Vaccination Registration' <www.vaccine.gov.sg/>.

8 See Straits Times, *New Covid-19 Swab Test Robot Offers Safe, More Comfortable Procedure for Patients* (22 September 2020) <www.straitstimes.com/singapore/robot-that-conducts-swab-tests-for-covid-19-is-safe-faster-and-more-comfortable-for>.

of [their] user[s] and [try] to meet certain objectives or complete tasks without any direct input or direct supervision from [their] user[s]'.[9] These systems, described in technical and marketing literature as 'agents', pervade all aspects of our lives in the Fourth Industrial Revolution.[10] Internet searches work through web crawlers, spiders, or bots – software programmes that systematically browse the World Wide Web to collect and index content.[11] Electronic commerce operates with software to advertise and market products, collect orders, process payments, and initiate distribution and manage logistics.[12] Chatbots and voice assistants answer queries and perform tasks or services for individuals or companies through commands or questions.[13] Sophisticated software programmes interpret human speech and respond either by way of a dialog or via synthesised voices or customised messages and responses.[14] Many systems have been implemented either in the form of apps on smartphones or in standalone devices, such as smart speakers and remote controls.[15] They have become part of an IoT – an ecosystem where devices with sensors automate many aspects of our homes and businesses.[16]

Undoubtedly, these software systems and devices vary greatly in their level of sophistication and complexity. Their ubiquity is also a product of their diverse functionalities and deployments. What they have in common is that they supplant and automate processes that would otherwise require human intervention. However, excluding the human element from economic and business transactions raises questions about the nature and character of these interactions. For instance, what is the legal status of a contract made through an automated system? Does a transacting party have any recourse, in contract or in tort, for any errors, mistakes and omissions that have been made by the automated system? Some academic writers have argued that these issues are best resolved by characterising these automated systems as legal agents. In this paper, we will review all these issues and arguments.

II TYPES OF ARTIFICIAL AGENTS

A study of automated systems must start by defining what an automated system is. Some have referred to these systems as 'automated', 'electronic' or 'artificial' agents. Others distinguish between 'first generation … electronic agents' that are 'rules-based'[17] or 'exhibit[] a limited intelligence, autonomy, and mobility'[18] and the

9 JJ Borking, BMA van Eck and P Siepel, *Intelligent Software Agents and Privacy* (1999) 1.

10 Wikipedia, 'Fourth Industrial Revolution' <https://en.wikipedia.org/wiki/Fourth_Industrial_Revolution>.

11 Wikipedia, 'Web crawler' <https://en.wikipedia.org/wiki/Web_crawler>.

12 Wikipedia, 'E-commerce' <https://en.wikipedia.org/wiki/E-commerce>.

13 Wikipedia, 'Virtual assistant' <https://en.wikipedia.org/wiki/Virtual_assistant>.

14 Ibid.

15 Smartphone users would be familiar with software and devices such as Apple's Siri, Amazon's Echo and Alexa, and Google Assistant.

16 Wikipedia, 'Internet of things' <https://en.wikipedia.org/wiki/Internet_of_things>.

17 Suzanne Smed, 'Intelligent Software Agents and Agency Law' (1998) 14 *Santa Clara High Tech LJ* 503.

18 Emad Abdel Rahim Dahiyat, 'Law and Software Agents: Are They "Agents" by the Way?' (2021) 29 *Artificial Intelligence and Law* 59.

'second generation of intelligent software agents'[19] or 'more autonomous artificial agents'[20] that 'use intelligent algorithms'[21] or 'exhibit[] a considerable level of autonomy, mobility, and sophistication'.[22] There are also references to agents that are 'self-modifying and acting according to their own experience',[23] have 'an autonomous capacity'[24] or are 'capable of learning and adapting over time'[25] to respond to changes. These systems can make optimal decisions or 'act in some extra-legal manner'[26] and even 'take actions that neither the licensor nor licensee anticipated'.[27] They

> employ more sophisticated decision-making mechanisms using statistical or probabilistic machine learning algorithms [where] there may be no strictly binary rules which determine the outcome [such that it] is the combination of relevant factors, and the relative weights the system accords them, that determines the outcome.[28]

These somewhat melodramatic classifications are not helpful, not only because of the arbitrary and fuzzy distinctions made but also because of the equivalences made using value-loaded terms such as 'intelligence' and 'discretion'.[29] For instance, it used to be thought that a system is 'autonomous' or 'intelligent' if it is programmed to be capable of 'spontaneous learning' and 'adjust[ing] its behavior' by 'adapting its behavior patterns in response to newly encountered circumstances'.[30] Today, we view these systems as implementations of machine learning using neural networks and deep learning, and describe them as implementations of Weak AI or 'Artificial Narrow Intelligence' rather than the 'intelligence' that is to be equated with human intelligence (also known as Strong AI or 'Artificial General Intelligence').[31] This implies that we need a more robust definition as we understand the technology and its limitations better. Thus, we choose to define an 'agent' (in a non-legal sense)

19 Smed (n 17) 503.

20 Samir Chopra and Laurence F White, 'Artificial Agents and the Contracting Problem' (2009) 2 *J of Law, Tech and Policy* 363, 364.

21 Ibid. 365.

22 Dahiyat (n 18) 62.

23 Ibid. 65. See also Smed (n 17) 503.

24 Dahiyat (n 18) 65.

25 Chopra and White (n 20) 369.

26 Dahiyat (n 18) 65.

27 Smed (n 17) 503. See also LH Scholz, 'Algorithmic Contracts' (2017) 20 *Stanford Technology LR* 128, 150–155.

28 Chopra and White (n 20) 369.

29 Computer scientists themselves have been guilty. For instance, Marvin Minsky defined 'Artificial intelligence' as the 'science of making machines do things that would require intelligence if done by men'. Marvin L Minsky (ed), *Introduction to Semantic Information Processing* (MIT Press 1968) v. Since then, many in the field have resiled from such statements.

30 See Thomas S Ray, 'Evolution and Optimization of Digital Organisms' in Keith R Billingsley, Ed Derohanes and Hilton Brown III (eds), *Scientific Excellence in Supercomputing: The IBM Prize Papers* (1991).

31 See, for example, Eda Kavlakoglu, "AI vs. Machine Learning vs. Deep Learning vs. Neural Networks: What's the Difference?' (*IBM*, 27 May 2020) <www.ibm.com/cloud/blog/ai-vs-machine-learning-vs-deep-learning-vs-neural-networks>.

as 'anything that can be viewed as perceiving its environment through sensors and acting upon that environment through actuators.'[32] This definition, advanced by Russell and Norvig in the leading textbook on Artificial Intelligence, speaks for the fact that an agent so defined can be a human agent, who has eyes, ears, and other organs for sensors and hands, legs, vocal cords, and so on for actuators; a software agent – which receives files, network packets, and human input as sensor inputs and acts on the environment by writing files, sending network packets and displaying information or generating sounds; or a robotic agent – with cameras and range finders for sensors and various motors for actuators.[33]

In trying to set up an artificial agent as one with the same qualities as a human agent, Russell and Norvig do not classify an artificial agent as being advanced or basic, but focus on whether the artificial agent is doing 'the right thing'. Thus an artificial agent's choice of action at any instance depends on (a) its built-in knowledge and (b) the sequence of content its sensors have perceived (the agent's percept sequence). The choice is effected by mapping every percept sequence to each choice of action, by way of different implementations or combinations of implementations known as 'models'.[34] While humans, who have desires and preferences of their own, choose actions that produce desirable results from their point of view (or additionally, are morally, ethically and legally correct), machines *do not have desires and preferences of their own.*[35] Instead, a non-human agent (which we will term 'an artificial agent') is programmed to maximise its performance based on these models and one that does so successfully is said to exhibit 'rationality'[36] or 'intelligence'.[37]

III ARTIFICIAL AGENTS AS LEGAL AGENTS

Because artificial agents are perceived to be 'intelligent' and are believed to be 'exercising discretion' autonomously,[38] proponents have advanced the theory that artificial agents should be treated as legal agents, with their users operating as principals in agency law. They assert:

> Of relevance here is the concept of authority found in agency law, which circumscribes the authority the agent has to make decisions on behalf of the principal. Implicit in the existence of that authority is the discretion to take decisions the principal herself would not have taken. Thus, prima facie, artificial agents,

32 Stuart Russell and Peter Norvig, *Artificial Intelligence: A Modern Approach* (4th edn. Pearson 2021) 36.
33 Ibid. 36.
34 Ibid.
35 Ibid. 39.
36 Ibid. 39–40.
37 Ibid. 49.
38 Chopra and White (n 20) 370 (this is so even when agents are said to be 'exercising discretion' in a predictable way because 'had the principal considered the matter herself, she might have reached a different decision.')

concluding contracts on behalf of the corporations or users that deploy them, function like legal agents.[39]

This theory coalesces around the concept of treating artificial agents as legal agents in the law of agency.[40] This is because a legal agent does not need full legal capacity: a legal agent does not need capacity to hold legal rights or be subject to liabilities to bind the principal.[41] Since a child has the capacity to enter into contracts to bind her parent or guardian at common law even though she has no capacity to bind herself to a contract,[42] it has been argued that artificial agents can, too, constitute legal agents to bind their human principals.[43] The theory also draws support from the recognition of ships and companies as artificial legal persons with legal capacities, rights and liabilities.[44] But this premise is flawed. Corporations obtained legal personality through legislation[45] and the position of ships appears to have originated out of, and extended, the medieval concept of deodand where a thing could be forfeited to the crown because it had been the immediate cause of death of a person.[46] It is therefore unlikely that ships are a good analogy for artificial agents and in the absence of legislation today, it would be remarkable for artificial agents to be recognised as legal persons.[47]

A variant of this theory recognises this difficulty and seeks to create a specific legal status for artificial agents – autonomous robots, in this case. This was proposed by the European Parliament's Resolution of 2017.[48] Drawing upon the Resolution, which requires that 'autonomous robots' be individually registered and be supported by an obligatory insurance scheme, Dahiyat has proposed yet another variant where

39 Ibid. 370.

40 Ibid. 376–68, 401–402; Smed (n 17) 505; IR Kerr, 'Spirits in the Material World: Intelligent Agents as Intermediaries in Electronic Commerce' (1999) 22 *Dalhousie LJ* 190, 239–247; Scholz (n 27) 165–168; Leon E Wein, 'The Responsibility of Intelligent Artifacts: Toward an Automation Jurisprudence' (1992) 6 *Harvard Journal of Law and Technology* 103, 106–107.

41 See P Watts and F Reynolds (eds), *Bowstead and Reynolds on Agency* (22nd edn, Sweet and Maxwell 2020), Article 5, paras. 2-012 – 2-013; American Law Institute, *Restatement (Third) of Agency*, para 3.05, Comment b, Illustration.

42 Ibid. The rule, which is quite established at common law, has been previously applied to married women (who until recently had no contractual capacity).

43 Chopra and White (n 20) 401–402; Samir Chopra and Laurence F White, *A Legal Theory for Autonomous Artificial Agents* (University of Michigan Press 2011) 41–42 ('It would be possible to treat an artificial agent as having authority to enter contracts on behalf of its operator, but without itself having legal personality.').

44 For example, Chopra and White (n 20) 379; Wein (n 40) 107–108, 118.

45 Tan Cheng Han, Jiangyu Wang and Christian Hofmann, 'Piercing the Corporate Veil: Historical, Theoretical and Comparative Perspectives' (2019) 16 *Berkeley Bus LJ* 140, 141–150.

46 Oliver Wendell Holmes, *The Common Law* (Little, Brown 1923) 25–29.

47 *See* for example, Dahiyat (n 18) 9; Chen and Burgess, 'The Boundaries of Legal Personhood: How Spontaneous Intelligence Can Problematise Differences between Humans, Artificial Intelligence, Companies and Animals' (2019) 27 *Artificial Intelligence and Law* 73, 84–85. It was also pointed out that while companies exist as separate artificial legal persons, the legal doctrine of piercing the corporate veil exists to render the actual deciding human mind and will that represent a company liable. Ibid. 85.

48 European Parliament's Resolution of 16 Feb 2017, paragraph 59(f) (2015/2103(INL)).

all businesses intending to use artificial agents do so through the creation of companies under existing corporations legislation. In this way, artificial agents 'would act in the name of the company'.[49] Dahiyat argues that this could be considered the first step that might prepare for the introduction into the legal and social framework the idea of sharing responsibility with intelligent computer systems and could also open doors to the creation of a new type of hybrid personality consisting of a human and software agent operating in tandem.[50] However, this proposal, which requires the agent-proxy companies to be legally subject to additional obligations such as disclosure of the agents' contracting terms and providing information about their functionalities, actually confirms the limitations of artificial agents: they are on their own unable to attest to the scope of their capacities and legal authority, and do so separate from their programmed actions.

A frequently used justification for the 'software agent as legal agent' theory is that artificial agents make 'autonomous' decisions, which mirror those of human agents, such that 'had the principal considered the matter herself, she *might* have reached a *different* decision (emphasis added).'[51] As noted, proponents choose this justification because of the minimised requirement of legal capacity for agents at common law. However, it is worth noting that this does not mean that an agent does *not* need *any* capacity to enter into a binding transaction. For the minor to act as an agent under common law, she must have *sufficient understanding to consent to the agency and to do the act required*.[52] The commentaries to the Third Restatement emphasise that the person/actor/agent's capacity to affect the legal relations of another (the principal and third party) is limited by the person's ability to take action, which is in turn a function of the person's *physical and mental ability as an individual*.[53] Thus, while a minor has the autonomy to enter into a binding contract online against her parent who had allowed the child Internet access (because the child had acted on the access granted to make purchases), the Third Restatement goes on to deny the computer itself a similar status. 'The computer itself is … not P's agent, because it is *not a person*' (emphasis added).[54] The relevant section of the Third Restatement reads:

> To be capable of acting as a principal or an agent, it is necessary to be a person, which in this respect requires capacity to be the holder of legal rights and the object of legal duties…. Accordingly, it is not possible for an inanimate object or a

[49] Dahiyat (n 18) 78–81. Such phrases may not be helpful as they presume a state of affairs where artificial agents have some form of personality and therefore can act in the name of or on behalf of another person. It would seem more accurate to think of corporations that deploy artificial agents as potentially bearing responsibility for the software that they use.

[50] Ibid. 79.

[51] Chopra and White (n 20) 370.

[52] See *Smally v Smally* (1700) 1 Eq.Ca.Abr. 6; *Watkins v Vince* (1818) 2 Starke 368; *Re D'Angibau* (1880) 15 Ch.D. 228 at 246; *Travelers Guarantee Co of Canada v Farajollahi* [2012] B.C.S.C. 1283.

[53] Third Restatement, para 3.05, Comment b.

[54] Third Restatement, para 3.05, Comment b, referring to para 1.04(5).

nonhuman animal to be a principal or an agent under the common law definition of agency.[55]

Thus, the need to demonstrate autonomy and personhood as impediments to the theory of agency for artificial agents must be clearly acknowledged.[56] But starting around 2006, the development of deep neural networks modelled after biological neurons enabled their application of systems that approached human-level and, in some cases, exceeded human-level performance on various tasks such as pattern and image recognition and language translation.[57] Another class of algorithms – evolutionary algorithms inspired by biological evolution – perform well in often complex problems, which do not make any assumptions about the possible solutions.[58] This has led to observations that these machines exhibit, not *automatic*, but *autonomous* or at least semi-autonomous behaviour,[59] which, in the case of *Thaler v Commissioner of Patents*, appears to have persuaded Beach J to find that the machine in question, DABUS, was the inventor of the patent sought.[60]

Beach J's reticence in deciding if the machine in question was autonomous[61] is actually understandable. Few details were given to substantiate the patentee Thaler's claim that his DABUS neural network was a 'self-assembling' system that 'mimic[s] aspects of human brain function … [in that] DABUS perceives and thinks like a person'.[62] It is well accepted that artificial neural networks are nothing more than computational problem solving systems that require instructions defined by a human as to how to solve a problem, and are not truly 'autonomous'.[63] An examination of the

55 Third Restatement, para 1.04(5), Comment e.

56 See for example, Joseph Sommer, 'Against Cyber-Law" (2000) 15 *Berk Tech LJ* 1145, 1177–1178 ('[a] programmed machine is not a juridical person and therefore cannot be an agent … it is clearly a machine.').

57 Wikipedia, 'Artificial neural network' <https://en.wikipedia.org/wiki/Artificial_neural_network>.

58 Wikipedia, 'Evolutionary algorithm' <https://en.wikipedia.org/wiki/Evolutionary_algorithm>.

59 *Thaler v Commissioner of Patents* [2021] FCA 879 [128]. At the time of writing of this paper, the decision is the subject of an appeal by the Commissioner of Patents. Cf *Thaler v Comptroller General of Patents, Trade Marks and Designs* [2021] EWCA Civ 1374 (holding that DABUS is not an inventor for different reasons). As a postscript, on 13 April 2022, the Full Court of the Federal Court of Australia in *Commissioner of Patents v Thaler* [2022] FCAFC 62, [107]–[113] allowed the appeal and unanimously overturned the decision of Beach J. The Full Court ruled that a device characterised as an AI machine could not be considered to be an inventor as an invention is the entitlement of a natural person who contributes to or supplies the inventive concept, and an AI machine that has no legal identity is unable to hold or be assigned this entitlement. This ruling mirrors many of the arguments advanced here. Similar rulings were rendered in J 0008/20 (Designation of inventor/DABUS) on 21 Dec 2021 by the European Patent Office and Thaler v Vidal, 43 F.4th 1207 (Fed. Cir. 2022) by the U.S. Court of Appeals, Federal Circuit.

60 Ibid. [131].

61 Ibid. [18], [128], [131], [143].

62 Ibid. [42].

63 Daria Kim, '"AI-Generated Inventions": Time to Get the Record Straight?' (2020) 69(5) *GRUR International* 443. Cf *Thaler v Commissioner of Patents* [2021] FCA 879, that held that a neural network system could be an 'inventor', but the decision did not turn on whether the system was 'autonomous'. But see *Commissioner of Patents v Thaler* [2022] FCAFC 62.

earlier prototype to DABUS[64] and a recent paper published by Thaler[65] confirms this as it suggests that Thaler's scientific claims are more modest: his DABUS system is a new architecture (or topology) of multiple deep neural networks with reinforcement learning elements that is capable of representing concepts and ideas.[66] Thus, DABUS is an example of a Weak AI implemented in artificial agents that merely 'reflect a conscious and deliberate decision by *a human or humans to achieve a particular end*.... Things created in this way are typically protected through recourse to the owner and creator of the thing.'[67] However much of a breakthrough DABUS may be, it is still, as Thaler admitted, a paradigm for scaling neural systems to Strong AI.[68] Electronic agents today, however sophisticated they are, are still examples of Weak AI: they are not capable of solving an arbitrarily wide variety of tasks, including novel ones.[69]

Hence outside of Strong AI, there is no true autonomous decision-making element within an artificial agent, without drawing on metaphysical and philosophical arguments that equate the models within artificial agents with the minds and wills of individuals.[70] This is because the Weak AI systems, without more, have no concepts of ethics, morality, legality, and empathy.[71] If not explicitly programmed, an artificial agent will have no idea, for instance, as to the duty of fidelity expected of agents.[72] It will even undertake an illegal or void act on behalf of its principal[73] because it will reflect any biases that it is programmed to replicate, so long as it is not explicitly programmed to address them – as the COMPAS case illustrates.[74] It is

64 U.S. Patent 5,852,815 (Neural Network Based Prototyping System and Method).

65 Thaler, 'Vast Topological Learning and Sentient AGI' (2021) 8 *Journal of Artificial Intelligence and Consciousness* 81.

66 Ibid. 108.

67 Chen and Burgess (n 46) 88 (emphasis added). The authors describe a system which they referred to as 'spontaneous intelligence', distinguished from artificial agents, which mirrors what others have referred to as Strong AI.

68 Thaler, 'Vast Topological Learning' (n 64) 109.

69 Russell and Norvig (n 32) 981 (citing the distinction first made by John Searle in 1980).

70 For example, 'Likewise, even if we accept that a software agent enjoys self-consciousness, it is not clear yet that achieving self-consciousness is a sufficient condition of legal personality'. Dahiyat (n 18) 10.

71 Concerns have been expressed by the absence of standards that define ethical design for AI and autonomous systems. See Russell and Norvig (n 32) 997. This has prompted the release of numerous AI ethical frameworks by governments and institutions around the world such as the EU Guidelines on Ethics in AI (2019), the Beijing AI Principles (2019), the Singapore AI Governance Framework v1 (2019), v2 (2020), the ACM Code of Ethics and Professional Conduct (2018), Microsoft AI principles (2018) and the Partnership on AI (Amazon, Google, Facebook, Microsoft, IBM) (2018). For a review of these frameworks, See Jessica Fjeld et al., 'Principled Artificial Intelligence: Mapping Consensus in Ethical and Rights-Based Approaches to Principles for AI' Berkman Klein Center for Internet & Society (2020) at <http://nrs.harvard.edu/urn-3:HUL.InstRepos:42160420>.

72 *UBS AG v Kommunale Wasserwerke Leipzig GmbH* [2017] EWCA Civ 1567, [2017] 2 Lloyd's Rep 621, [91]. It is difficult to see how software code can owe fiduciary duties to its user or how such duties may be meaningfully exercised against software.

73 *Cohen v Kittell* (1889) 22 QBD 680 (holding an agent not liable to a principal for omitting to carry out his illegal mandate).

74 *Loomis v Wisconsin* 881 N.W.2d 749. The defendant in this case contended that that his due process rights were infringed as he was prevented from challenging the scientific validity and accuracy

indeed possible to programme machines with individual aspects of consciousness – awareness, self-awareness, and attention – to make them 'intelligent'.[75] But this does not make them acquire true human consciousness – because they still lack 'human subjective experience' – the ability to appreciate the subjective experience of others.[76]

The current state of the art is that any artificial agent will behave exclusively within the parameters of its programmed model(s), including those that are poorly programmed.[77] As long as the model exists for the agent – be it a simple reflex agent, a model-based agent, a goal-based agent, a utility-based agent, or a hybrid of the above[78] – it is us as humans who set the performance measures for the models that in turn set the bounds within which the artificial agent behaves. This includes the possibility that an agent's response may be uncertain or unpredictable because the wrong performance measure was put into the agent, or where there was initial uncertainty about the true performance measure.[79] For instance, when the very first Ariane 5 rocket was launched, it flipped 90 degrees in the wrong direction 37 seconds after launch and was destroyed at a cost of approximately $370 million. The reason for its explosion was initially said to be unknown.[80] But a detailed inquiry subsequently identified a rudimentary software bug that led to data overflow as the cause of the disaster.[81] Another, more recent, example can be found when AlphaGo, a sophisticated computer programme that plays the board game Go, was engaged in its first competitive game against a 9-dan professional Go player, Lee Sedol.[82] In its second game of the five game series, it played move 37, which was remarked upon by commentators as 'a very strange move … [we] thought it was a mistake'.[83] It turned out that the move turned the course of the game and was subsequently described by commentators and researchers as 'brilliant' and 'beautiful' when they

of COMPAS. COMPAS is short for 'Correctional Offender Management Profiling for Alternative Sanctions'. It was used as a pretrial recidivism risk assessment tool by the courts in Wisconsin to determine if bail should be granted to the accused.

75 Russell and Norvig (n 32) 986.

76 Ibid. 985–986. If and when the machines actually do acquire this ability, they will be characterised as Strong AI, and will qualify as machines that are actually consciously thinking and not engaged in simulated thinking.

77 Ibid. 981. The current state of the art is such that artificial agents can only be characterised as weak AI.

78 Russell and Norvig (n 32) 49–58.

79 Ibid. 39–40, 46. This is so especially in environments that are partially observable, nondeterministic, dynamic, continuous and unknown, or involve other agents.

80 See, for example, CNN, 'Unmanned European Rocket Explodes on First Flight' (4 June 1996) <https://web.archive.org/web/20000819090542/http://www.cnn.com/WORLD/9606/04/rocket.explode/>.

81 See, for example, bugsnag, 'The Worst Computer Bugs in History: The Ariane 5 Disaster' (7 September 2017) <www.bugsnag.com/blog/bug-day-ariane-5-disaster>.

82 AlphaGo ran on a neural network and the original version of the program was the first computer Go program to beat a human professional Go player without handicap on a full-sized board. Wikipedia, 'AlphaGo' <https://en.wikipedia.org/wiki/AlphaGo>.

83 *See* Wired, 'In Two Moves, AlphaGo and Lee Sedol Redefined the Future' (16 March 2016) <www.wired.com/2016/03/two-moves-alphago-lee-sedol-redefined-future/>.

looked at both the code and the board setup in more detail.[84] These are but two examples of how artificial agents are actually behaving according to human-defined parameters – including not just the code, but also the statistical and neural network models generated by the code – however, wrong, unpredictable, or intelligent such behaviour may seem.

There are additional objections to recognising artificial agents as legal persons in law. 'To be a legal person is to be subject to legal rights and duties.'[85] Thus, while human agents have a 'res' or physical presence – against which legal norms such as holding assets and rights and duties, including rewards, constraints, sanctions, penalties, and punishments may apply – there is no such physically referable entity with respect to artificial agents.[86] For instance, where an agent exceeds her authority, she breaches her warranty of authority to the third party.[87] It is hard to see how an artificial agent comprised of software that malfunctions and therefore ostensibly 'acts outside its authority' can make a contractual promise to another, or how such a promise, if it exists, can be enforced against the software programme. If such claims may be made against the principal on the basis that the principal is the owner of the software (assuming this to be the case) on which the artificial agent operates, it would seemingly make the principal both agent and principal.[88] If, on the other hand, the software is owned by a different party and the claim is brought against the developer, it would have the remarkable effect of making software developers effectively agents. In addition, there would be practical difficulties in separating artificial agents in hardware from those implemented in software[89] and registering them as entities as such.[90] This point is further amplified by the fact that artificial agents are themselves not monolithic entities, since each agent could itself be made up of other software agents and entities.[91] The multiagent environment could also be competitive, co-operative or even a mixture of both,[92] rendering it even more difficult to isolate and identify each discrete artificial agent as an entity.

IV ARTIFICIAL AGENTS AS INSTRUMENTS OR TOOLS

It is therefore self-evident that legislative intervention is needed to constitute the artificial agent as a legal agent with or without legal personality. This objection

84 Ibid.

85 B Smith, 'Legal Personality' (1928) 37 *Yale Law J* 283–299.

86 Chen and Burgess (n 46) 82–83.

87 Tan Cheng Han, *The Law of Agency* (2nd edn, Academy Publishing 2017) 281.

88 If ownership is a sufficient basis on which to bring such claims, perhaps because this gives rise to tortious liability, no recourse to agency would be necessary.

89 Dahiyat (n 18) 9.

90 Dahiyat (n 18) 69–71. Dahiyat, for instance, talks about using digital signatures to identify artificial agents and confirm their integrity.

91 Russell and Norvig (n 32) 44–45.

92 Ibid. 45.

notwithstanding, it has been argued that an artificial agent should be a legal agent for reasons of expediency. The first is that rendering the artificial agent a legal agent allows for the principal to be bound by the responses of the agent.[93] The second is that the artificial agent as a legal agent enables the principal (user) of the artificial agent to be absolved of unplanned behaviour emanating from the agent.[94]

We review these reasons in turn.

V ENABLING THE PRINCIPAL TO BE BOUND BY THE AGENT'S RESPONSES

As a justification for the 'artificial agent as legal agent' theory, the first reason simply recites the raison d'état for agency, which is that the agent enjoys the power to create legal relations between the user as principal and third parties.[95] But if an artificial agent cannot be regarded as a legal agent, this *does not* mean that the user *cannot* be bound by the responses of the artificial agent. Where the artificial agent can be characterised as an instrumentality of the person who uses it, the agent shall be treated as an extension of such person. For instance, an owner who trains a dog to pick up beer from the neighbourhood store in exchange for subsequent payment will be bound if his dog proceeds to do so without his prior direction.[96] The dog's actions bind his owner not because it is a legal agent of the owner but because the dog or any other animal serves as the principal's instrumentality.[97] Contrary to the theory of legal agency, the relevant act is carried out not *on behalf of* the principal but *by* the principal through the instrumentality. As the Commentaries to the Uniform Electronic Transactions Act (UETA) explain, with reference to the definition of 'electronic agent':[98]

> This definition establishes that an electronic agent is a machine. As the term 'electronic agent' has come to be recognized, it is limited to a tool function …
>
> An electronic agent, such as a computer program or other automated means employed by a person, is a tool of that person. As a general rule, the employer of a

93 Chopra and White (n 20) 382.

94 See for example, Chopra and White (n 43) 120–121.

95 See for example, *Scott v Davis* [2000] HCA 52, (2000) 204 CLR 333 [227], [228] (Justice Gummow).

96 Third Restatement, para 1.04(5), Comment e, Illustration 3. The illustration is based on *Commonwealth v Tarrant*, 326 N.E.2d 710 (Mass.1975) (holding that a medium-sized German shepherd that accompanied the defendant into the victim's residence during a robbery was the defendant's dangerous weapon for purposes of armed-robbery).

97 Ibid.

98 UETA S 2(6) ('"Electronic agent" means a computer program or an electronic or other automated means used independently to initiate an action or respond to electronic records or performances in whole or in part, without review or action by an individual.'). See also s 106(3), Federal Electronic Signature in Global and National Commerce Act, 15 U.S.C. para7001; Singapore's Electronic Transactions Act, s 2(1) (defining an 'automated message system' to mean 'a computer program or an electronic or other automated means used to initiate an action or respond to data messages or performances in whole or in part, without review or intervention by a natural person each time an action is initiated or a response is generated by the program or electronic or other means').

> tool is responsible for the results obtained by the use of that tool since the tool has no independent volition of its own. However, an electronic agent, by definition, is capable within the parameters of its programming, of initiating, responding or interacting with other parties or their electronic agents once it has been activated by a party, without further attention of that party.[99]

Thus, section 14 of the UETA[100] and Article 12 of the UNCITRAL UN Convention on the Use of Electronic Communications in International Contracts[101] both proceed on the assumption that the artificial agent is an instrumentality of the principal and binds the principal as such, without reference to the need to subject the artificial agent to rights and obligations. 'When machines are involved [as electronic agents for parties to a transaction], the requisite intention [for contract formation] flows from the programming and use of the machine.'[102] In an affirmation of the artificial agent as instrumentality approach, the UNCITRAL secretariat made a similar observation as follows:

> Article 12 of the Electronic Communications Convention is an enabling provision and should not be misinterpreted as allowing for an automated message system or a computer to be made the subject of rights and obligations. Electronic communications that are generated automatically by message systems or computers without direct human intervention should be regarded as 'originating' from the legal entity on behalf of which the message system or computer is operated.[103]

It is on a similar basis that many cases were resolved without controversy and without resorting to complex agency principles. In one of the earliest cases on this issue, the court in the 1933 US case of *McCaughn v American Meter Co* held that a device which automatically dispensed gas upon receiving a coin deposit by a buyer – a vending machine – facilitated a contract to sell gas to the buyer 'without any working human

[99] Uniform Electronic Transactions Act (1999) with Prefatory Note and Comments, 14 February, 2000, at 7–8, <www.uniformlaws.org/HigherLogic/System/DownloadDocumentFile.ashx?DocumentFileKey=4f718047-e765-b9d8-6875-f7a225d629a8&forceDialog=0>. The Committee did consider the following: 'it is conceivable that, within the useful life of this Act, electronic agents may be created with the ability to act autonomously, and not just automatically. That is, through developments in artificial intelligence, a computer may be able to "learn through experience, modify the instructions in their own programs, and even devise new instructions." … If such developments occur, courts may construe the definition of electronic agent accordingly, in order to recognize such new capabilities.' At 8 (hereinafter UETA Prefatory Note). However, as noted above, given the current state of technology, there is no change to the treatment of an artificial agent as a tool or instrument of the principal.

[100] UETA s 14.

[101] UNCITRAL UN Convention on the Use of Electronic Communications in International Contracts, art 12 (' Article 12. Use of automated message systems for contract formation A contract formed by the interaction of an automated message system and a natural person, or by the interaction of automated message systems, shall not be denied validity or enforceability on the sole ground that no natural person reviewed or intervened in each of the individual actions carried out by the automated message systems or the resulting contract'.).

[102] UETA Prefatory Note 37 (Commentaries for section 14).

[103] UNCITRAL, 'Explanatory note by the UNCITRAL secretariat on the UN Convention on the Use of Electronic Communications in International Contracts' (2007) 70.

agency'.[104] In England, in *Thornton v Shoe Lane Parking*, a parking contract was held to be made with the garage owner when the ticketing machine at the entrance of the garage dispensed the parking ticket to the plaintiff.[105] And in the Singapore case of *Chwee Kin Keong v Digilandmall.com Pte Ltd* it was held that the plaintiffs had successfully contracted to purchase commercial laser printers (at low prices) when the defendant's website automatically processed the plaintiffs' orders and dispatched confirmation email notes to the plaintiffs' email accounts within minutes of the orders, although the contracts were subsequently vitiated for unilateral mistake.[106] Recently, in *Quoine Pte Ltd v B2C2 Ltd*, the Singapore Court of Appeal held that the respondent's trading software had successfully entered into a purchase of cryptocurrencies on the appellant's trading platform when certain trigger exchange rates were met on the platform, and that the respondent was entitled to retain the purchased cryptocurrencies even though the exchange rates were erroneous.[107] Although one of the judges dissented on the issue of whether there was an operative mistake that vitiated the contracts, the effect of the majority and minority judgements is that so long as users had full knowledge of what they were doing, they could choose to be bound by (a) the automated process under which contracts may arise and/or (b) agreements for which they had incomplete details (presumably as long as such details can be determined reasonably or by law[108]).

To support their argument of legal agency, Chopra and White argue that the artificial agent as instrumentality argument has led US courts to hold that innate objects were not 'capable of entering into consensual relationships', thus leading to 'inconsistent outcomes'.[109] They cited Wein who in turn referred to two cases: *Marsh v American Locker Co* for the proposition that because a coin-operated locker could not be said to 'consent' to an assumption of bailment liability, the court had to discard the possibility that the transaction was a bailment,[110] and *Bernstein v Northwestern Nat Bank in Philadelphia* for the proposition that depositing a bag in a night depository did not create a debtor–creditor relationship with the bank as the 'inanimate depository cannot provide the requisite act of conscious reception, and therefore is incapable of entering into a consensual relationship on behalf of the bank.'[111]

It is trite law that an instrumentality cannot enter into contractual relationships on its own since it does not have legal personality. Nevertheless, the real issue is

[104] (1933) 67 F.2d 148 (CA 3rd Cir).
[105] [1971] 2 QB 163 (CA), 169.
[106] [2004] 2 SLR(R) 594, [2004] SGHC 71, [96] ('As most web merchants have automated software responses, they need to ensure that such automated responses correctly reflect their intentions from an objective perspective.'); upheld on appeal in [2005] 1 SLR(R) 502, [2005] SGCA 2.
[107] *Quoine Pte Ltd v B2C2 Ltd* [2020] 2 SLR 20, [2020] SGCA(I) 2.
[108] E Peel, *Treitel on The Law of Contract* (15th edn, Sweet and Maxwell 2020) para 2-087.
[109] Chopra and White (n 43) 22.
[110] Wein (n 40) 125–126.
[111] Ibid. 126.

whether a person can be bound by the use of an instrumentality. As previously noted, there are clear authorities in the United States, England, and Singapore that support the artificial agent as instrumentality reasoning. Furthermore, a close reading of *Marsh* and *Bernstein* suggests that these cases actually *support* the instrumentality reasoning. In *Marsh*, the court was not satisfied that the coin-operated locker gave the defendant bailee exclusive control over the contents of the missing parcel (as compared with the plaintiff user) and thus denied bailment liability. The court accepted that the coin-operated locker mechanism gave the alleged *bailor instead of the bailee* exclusive control over its contents, without any human intervention, through the bailor's exclusive operation of the locker and possession of the locker key.[112] In fact, US courts have not denied the user a bailment relationship with the bailee operating storage services because the services were automated (e.g., storage lockers, deposit boxes and garages). Instead, the cases turned on a factual finding of whether the machine providing bailment services afforded exclusive control to the bailor or the bailee.[113] In *Bernstein*, the court found *for* the plaintiff user on the basis that a bailment relationship *was* constituted by the deposit of the bag in the night depository[114] but denied that a contract was formed, not because of the use of an inanimate depository but because it characterised the depository deposit as an offer by the user that had to be subject to an additional and unequivocal act by the bank to create the status of debtor and creditor.[115] In any event, after *Bernstein*, the Pennsylvania Supreme Court ruled that the deposit of money in a night depository of the defendant bank *could* constitute a contract of debt with the bank.[116] The 'inconsistencies' noted by Wein, Chopra and White turned not on the use of artificial agents as instruments to effect deposits, bailments or contracts but on the proper characterisation of the transactions as bailments, contracts, licences or as a duty of care in negligence. These 'inconsistencies' eventually led other courts to decide liability by determining if the deposit service operator was under a duty to take reasonable steps to prevent harm to the contents.[117]

112 *Marsh v American Locker Co, Inc* (1950) 7 N.J.Super. 81, 86.

113 See for example, 1420 *Park Road Parking, Inc v Consolidated Mut Ins Co* (1961) 168 A.2d 900 (D.C.Mun.App.); cf *Scruggs v Dennis* (1969) 222 Tenn. 714, 440 S.W.2d 20.

114 *Bernstein v Northwestern Nat. Bank in Philadelphia* (1945) 157 Pa.Super. 73, 77 (Pa. Super. Ct.).

115 Ibid. 75–76.

116 See *Phillips Home Furnishings, Inc v Continental Bank* (1976) 467 Pa. 43 (Pa. Super. Ct.) (reversing and remanding on the point of assessment of the exculpatory clause in the bank's night depository agreement). Conversely, in *Employers Ins of Wausau v Chemical Bank*, 117 Misc.2d 601 (1983), the New York court found that the deposit in the night vault constituted a bailment relationship, and that a deposit agreement was only created when the bank opens the deposited contents and credit them to the depositor's account.

117 *See MyGlynn v Parking Authority of City of Newark* (1981) 86 NJ 551, 560 (S.C. of NJ); *Garlock v. Multiple Parking Services, Inc* (1980) 103 Misc.2d 943 (citing *Basso v Miller* (1976) 40 N.Y.2d 233 (C.A. N.Y.) (abolishing the distinction between licensees, trespassers, and invitees and applying foreseeable reasonable care under the circumstances as a measure of liability').

VI LIABILITY WITH AUTOMATED AGENTS

Another frequently advanced justification for treating automated agents as 'legal agents' is that doing so opens up another avenue of redress for malfunctioning agents: the 'principal' or operator of such software agents may be held to be vicariously liable in tort for the actions of her agent.[118] Proponents of the 'legal agents' theory assert that where decision making is delegated to an artificial agent and it would be inappropriate to assign the artificial agent moral culpability, making the software a 'legal agent' enables the imposition of vicarious liability to be focused on the 'human as the locus of liability … [where] we are less inclined to attribute the mischief to the machine [without which the human principal will be insulated from liability]'.[119]

It is true that the law of vicarious liability has been broadened beyond the doctrine of *respondeat superior*. 'In principle, liability in tort depends upon proof of a personal breach of duty. To that principle, there is at common law only one true exception – namely, vicarious liability.'[120] From a practical standpoint, this means that for liability to reach the principal in vicarious liability, one has to constitute the artificial agent as a legal person and tortfeasor, and demonstrate two elements: a relationship between the principal and the tortfeasor which makes it proper for the law to make one pay for the fault of the other, and the connection between that relationship and the tortfeasor's wrongdoing.[121] In general, this arises in employment situations or where the relationship between the parties is one akin to employment.[122] In some exceptional circumstances, a principal who is not in an employment or employment-type relationship may incur vicarious liability for unauthorised acts of agents.[123] Leaving aside the difficulty of construing an artificial agent as an employee or agent, it is unnecessary to rely on such analysis to hold a person responsible for wrongful acts arising from the use of artificial agents. If the instrumentality theory is accepted, the resolution of the issue of liability turns on negligence: whether the principal had taken reasonable care in the performance of functions entrusted to it, in so far as it performed those functions itself, through its employees, or, as explained above, using its deployed instrumentalities. The principal here is liable not for the failure of the artificial agent (as a separate legal entity) but for its

[118] See, for example, Smed (n 17) 506; Chopra and White (n 43) 120–121. This is in addition to remedies for product liability claims, which are explored further in Chapters 6 and 9.

[119] Wein (n 40) at 113.

[120] *Woodland v Essex County Council* [2013] UKSC 66, [2014] AC 537 [3] (Lord Sumption), delivering the leading judgement.

[121] See, for example, *Various Claimants v Catholic Child Welfare Society* [2012] UKSC 56, [2013] 2 AC 1 [21] (*Christian Brothers*); *Cox v Ministry of Justice* [2016] UKSC 10, [2016] AC 660, [15]; *Barclays Bank plc v Various Claimants* [2020] UKSC 13, [2020] AC 973, [1].

[122] *Cox* (n 121); *Barclays Bank* (n 121) [27].

[123] *Christian Brothers* (n 119) [47]; *Cox* (n 121) [16]–[17]. See also Tan Cheng Han, 'Vicarious Liability in the Law of Agency' [2022] *JBL* 164.

own failure to exercise due care in selecting, testing, operating and monitoring its artificial agent.[124]

While this greatly simplifies the cause of action, legal agency proponents may contend that there may be difficulties in proving the *fault* of the principal in this direct cause of action in negligence.[125] And concerns may be made about the absence of well-established models or industry or technical standards to prescribe the requisite standards to be observed. Our response is simply that fault *with* the artificial agent has to be proved to maintain an action in negligence in either instance.[126] And the absence of industry practices does not mean that legal standards of care cannot be prescribed.[127] If the agents are dangerous, principals will owe duties to guard the dangerous machines to prevent injuries,[128] and persons who knowingly use or deal with such instrumentalities must be guarded, covered or protected.[129] Autonomous mobile robots may need to be equipped with passive safety features to prevent them from ever making contact with humans, or to warn humans of their approach, or even to cease their activities when they sense human presence.[130] Likewise, software designers and commercial vendors are negligently responsible for security vulnerabilities in their products and could be held liable for the harm caused by cyber criminals who exploit such vulnerabilities.[131] A manufacturer of an airplane autopilot system was implicated for negligence in the design of its system in an action by the victims against the airlines and their pilots, who entered the wrong coordinates for their destination airport that led to the eventual death of all on board when the plane crashed.[132] And manufacturers of autonomous vehicles have been the subject of actions in negligence for elements in their autopilot software that have led to the

124 EC, 'Liability for Artificial Intelligence and Other Emerging Digital Technologies' (2019) 44. For examples in U.S. law, See, for example, C Ralph Kinsey Jr, 'Nondelegable Duty – Duty and Vicarious Liability for Negligence' (1965) 44 *NC L Rev* 242, 243.

125 See for example, Ugo Pagallo, *The Laws of Robots, Crimes, Contracts, and Torts* (Springer 2013) 124 (noting that '…the capacity of such machines to gain knowledge and skills from interaction with human caretakers, suggest that the fault would rarely fall on the designers, manufacturers or suppliers').

126 'Liability for AI' (n 122) 46.

127 Ibid. 23–24.

128 *See Holbrook v Prodomax Automation Ltd* (2019) WL 6840187 (discussing how manufacturer of robots could be held liable for death of technician servicing robots). *See also* the case of Elaine Herzberg, who was killed by a self-driving Uber car in 2018. Bernie Woodall, 'Uber Avoids Legal Battle with Family of Autonomous Vehicle Victim' (*Reuters*, 29 March 2018) <www.reuters.com/article/us-autos-selfdriving-uber-settlement-idUSKBN1H5092>.

129 Chopra and White (n 43) 125.

130 Autonomous vehicles have been designed to come to a stop when sensing a human in front of their path: See <www.channelnewsasia.com/news/singapore/driverless-vehicles-safety-concern-testing-extended-12034946>; See *also* <www.techbriefs.com/component/content/article/tb/stories/blog/37748>.

131 Scott Shackleford and others, 'Toward a Global Cybersecurity Standard of Care?' (2015) 50 *Tex Intl LJ* 305; Chopra and White (n 43) 126, citing De Villiers 2005 and Rustad 2005.

132 *In Re Air Crash near Cali, Colombia on December 20, 1995* (1997) 985 F. Supp. 1106 (S.D. Fla.), reversed and remanded on appeal for further proceedings in *Piamba Cortes v American Airlines, Inc.* (1999) 1777 F.3d 1272 (11th Cir.).

death of drivers or pedestrians.[133] Similarly, if the trading provider Quoine had not reversed the counterparty trades erroneously conducted by its software,[134] the counterparties could have brought a claim in negligence against Quoine for the misconfiguration of its platform which triggered the subsequent abnormal transactions.

An extension of this duty in negligence exists – where the duty of care is held to extend to *procuring* the careful performance of work delegated to others, who may be not only agents but also independent contractors. Termed the 'non-delegable duty' of care, this is an application of the concept of assumption of responsibility to determine the scope of the duty, including whether the loss is economic or physical.[135] It is triggered when the claimant is vulnerable, where there exists a relationship between the claimant and principal by virtue of which the latter has a degree of protective custody over the former, and the subsequent delegation of that custody to another person.[136] It would apply to the principal's negligence in selecting, supervising, or otherwise controlling or failing to control that other person.[137] This could be pertinent, for instance, where a principal delegates its critical human in-the-loop operations to another, who is at fault in using an automated mechanism to discharge that duty.

It is accepted that negligence actions against artificial agents will involve issues of technical complexity and proof of causation, which may require costly expert analysis,[138] especially because the errors could be in the code, the training data, the design or architecture or even its operational safeguards, the interconnections between hardware and software, and interactions therein. However, these issues are neither unique nor insurmountable,[139] especially if they are supported by a robust application for discovery against the human principal as to the workings of the artificial agents.[140] Presumptions such as the *res ipsa loquitur* rule to place the burdens of producing evidence on the party in control of the evidence may also be usefully

[133] In addition to the settlement against Uber, see *Umeda v Tesla Inc, Slip Copy* 2020 WL 5653496 for the recent lawsuit filed against Tesla for a pedestrian death in Japan. For an analysis of the incident, see Eliot, 'Tesla Lawsuit over Autopilot-Engaged Pedestrian Death Could Disrupt Automated Driving Progress' (*Forbes*, 16 May 2020) <www.forbes.com/sites/lanceeliot/2020/05/16/lawsuit-against-tesla-for-autopilot-engaged-pedestrian-death-could-disrupt-full-self-driving-progress/?sh=69e9a7c071f4>.

[134] *Quoine Pte Ltd v B2C2 Ltd* (n 106) [30].

[135] See *Woodland* (n 120), [11]. See also *Commonwealth v Introvigne* (1982) 150 CLR 258 (HCA); *New South Wales v Lepore* [2003] HCA 4, (2003) 212 CLR 511; para 7.03(1) of the Restatement (Third) on Agency (describing this as 'direct liability' – where a principal's own fault subjects it to liability to a third party harmed by 'an agent's' conduct, in contrast to 'vicarious liability'). For its criticisms, see Glanville Williams, 'Liability for Independent Contractors' (1956) 14 *CLJ* 180; Anthony Gray, *Vicarious Liability: Critique and Reform* (Hart Publishing 2018) ch 10.

[136] See *Woodland* (n 120), [12], [23].

[137] para 7.03(1) of the Restatement (Third) on Agency Comment b.

[138] *Liability for AI* (n 122) 20–21.

[139] Ibid. 21–22. See for example, the NTSB's investigation into the Uber accident that involved an autonomous vehicle in Arizona. NTSB, 'Collision between Vehicle Controlled by Developmental Automated Driving System and Pedestrian Tempe, Arizona March 18, 2018 HWY18MH010' (19 November 2019), <www.ntsb.gov/news/events/Documents/2019-HWY18MH010-BMG-abstract.pdf>.

[140] Daniel Seng and Stephen Mason, 'AI and Evidence' (2021) 33 *Singapore Academy LJ* 241, 274.

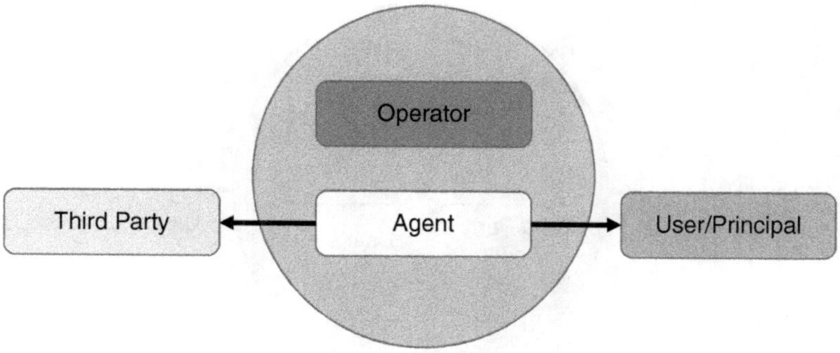

FIGURE 11.1 Figure from Chopra and White showing user as principal (ebay.com example)[141]

relied upon.[142] In any event, it should also not be assumed that these issues will be easier if agency analysis is used. Any question of whether an artificial agent was acting within authority is also likely to require understanding of the algorithms embedded in the artificial agent. In any case, discovery without any human intercession against an artificial agent is unlikely to be practical or conceivable.

Finally, Chopra and White cited ebay.com as an example where the risks of erroneous transactions will fall on the correct party where the end user, ostensibly as the principal, uses an artificial agent that is characterised as a legal agent that is operated by the company (ebay.com) to 'instruct[] the agent to bid up to a specified maximum in an auction being conducted by the third party' (Figure 11.1).[143] The authors characterised the errors as 'specification errors' – 'where the agent applies the rules the principal [erroneously] specifies',[144] 'induction errors' – where the agent enters into a contract which was not authorised,[145] and 'malfunction errors' – 'which involve software or hardware problems whereby the principal's rules or parameters for the agent do not result in the intended outcome'.[146] The authors then assert that the risk of specification errors would correctly fall on the user/principal, and the risk of induction and malfunction errors should initially rest with the user/principal or third party, who is in turn entitled to recovery against the operator for exercising the most control over the agent under the doctrine of *respondeat superior*.[147]

141 Chopra and White (n 43) 49.

142 Bryan Casey, 'Robot Ipsa Loquitur' (2019) 108 *Georgetown LJ* 225. Cf 'Report on the Attribution of Civil Liability for Accidents Involving Autonomous Cars' (2020) 47–48, Singapore Academy of Law, argued that the rule may be hard to apply to automated vehicles because it cannot be shown the defendant is in control of the situation to trigger the res ipsa loquitur rule. However, this fails to understand that with detailed and automated logs, the locus of the component that caused the accident can be dissected and found and the res ipsa loquitur rule applied to the defendant in charge of *that* component. Casey (n 141) 274–277.

143 Ibid. 48.

144 Ibid. 46.

145 Ibid. 49. At 46, the authors also describe this as 'induct[ing] [into] a contract the principal *does* object to'.

146 Ibid. 46.

147 Ibid. 49.

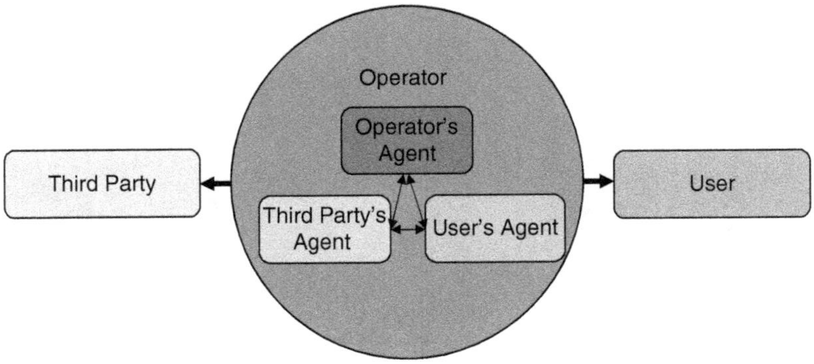

FIGURE 11.2 Modified figure from Chopra and White showing user, operator and third-party agents in multiagent environment (ebay.com example)

Chopra and White contend that under the artificial agent as instrumentality theory, the user would be primarily liable for all three types of errors.[148] This result is only reached if one assumes that there is only *one* artificial agent operating in the circumstances. In reality, it would be more accurate, as Chopra and White themselves appear to concede,[149] that more than one agent is operating under the auspices of eBay (Figure 11.2). If one assumes that there is an artificial agent for the third party to conduct the auction, an artificial agent for the user to make bids at the auction, and an artificial agent for eBay to mediate and settle the bids and complete the transaction, there are actually *three* artificial agents, each operating as the instrumentality of the respective party and interacting with one another, with eBay as the platform operator and overall controller for the artificial agents. In such a case, specification and induction errors will *prima facie* fall on the respective operators of the instrumentalities – be they the third party who erroneously described the item being auctioned or who failed to place restrictions on where the item being auctioned could be sold, or the user who erroneously programmed the wrong maximum bid price for the item or selected the wrong auctioneer. On the other hand, the risk of malfunction errors will clearly fall on eBay, since it is eBay who is the overall developer and operator for all the artificial agents. In this modified analysis, there is no need to resort to the characterisation of the artificial agent as a legal agent to resolve issues of legal liability. Furthermore, this characterisation correctly places the business risks on eBay to minimise all instances of malfunction errors, and puts eBay in the position to mediate between third party or the user as to their specification and induction errors.[150]

[148] Ibid.

[149] Ibid. 44.

[150] *See* eBay, 'User Agreement' <www.ebay.com/help/policies/member-behaviour-policies/user-agreement?id=4259#Returns>; eBay, 'eBay Money Back Guarantee policy: Appeals and Extensions' <www.ebay.com/help/policies/ebay-money-back-guarantee-policy/ebay-money-back-guarantee-policy?id=4210#section7>.

Therefore, in the overall analysis for tortious liability, the characterisation of the artificial agent as a 'legal agent' to enable a finding of legal liability appears unnecessary.

VII CONCLUSION

The law of agency underpins many commercial transactions and has facilitated the utility of legal entities such as the corporation. Increasingly, such entities are concluding transactions not through human intermediaries but through artificial agents. Many academic writers have thus postulated that artificial agents should be similarly ascribed the status of legal agents. However, the current state of AI technologies brings us nowhere near the concept of an autonomous artificial agent with the requisite level of rationality and intelligence to which we can accord the status of a legal agent. Furthermore, even if artificial agents achieve sentience and consciousness, unless legal personality is recognised or conferred, they cannot be legal agents. A piece of code, however sophisticated, cannot be a legal agent in the absence of recognition in law as a legal person. In addition, this recognition should be accompanied by some means to make such responsibility practically realisable. Corporations as legal persons achieve this through the requirement of a publicly disclosed share capital that is supported in certain circumstances by mandatory auditing, which enables a party dealing with a corporation to decide whether to seek additional protection in the form of securities or assurances from third parties. In the absence of such a framework, many of the issues of contracting and liability in the immediate future can be resolved with reference to the treatment of artificial agents as instrumentalities of persons or legal entities. Such a treatment best accords with the functionalities of artificial agents and reposes the right duties and responsibilities on the human developers and operators of such artificial agents.

12

Trust Law and AI

Anselmo Reyes

I INTRODUCTION

This chapter explores the use of Artificial Intelligent (AI) in matters relating to trusts and trust law. AI as we know it today is adept at achieving a specific task with a well-defined outcome. It is less capable where the desired outcome is open-ended, involving the performance of an unspecified number of tasks or the exercise of discretion.[1] For instance, AI may have difficulty if required to decide which (if any) of a class of persons should be awarded a scholarship for 'showing exceptional character and leadership promise'. It might consequently be thought that, apart from the mechanical administration of express and charitable trusts by robots, AI can be of little utility as far as adjudications relating to the law of trusts is concerned.[2] The rationale for such view would be that trust law applies equitable principles to determine whether to order remedies which are discretionary in nature. Thus, in deciding (say) whether to impose a constructive trust or to order specific performance, an adjudicator will need to evaluate the peculiar facts of a case and come to a view whether a respondent has acted in a manner that is unconscionable or potentially so. In this calculus, an AI dependent on finding patterns in big data may be at a disadvantage. While cases of unconscionable conduct can readily be classified into one or more of a finite number of patterns, the AI would still need to step back and assess whether the impugned conduct merits the grant or refusal of equitable relief in the particular case. This is a fact-sensitive exercise. Patterns of big data may be of limited assistance in such exercise with the result that, although AI can go a long way on big data alone, that may not be far enough to decide a trust case.

The author thanks Lusina Ho, Adrian Mak and Ho Ching Him for their comments and assistance on drafts of this chapter.

1 House of Lords Committee, *AI in the UK: Ready, Willing and Able? House of Lords Select Committee on Artificial Intelligence* (Parliament of the United Kingdom, Report of Session 2017–19, HL Paper 100, 2018) 23.

2 On AI as adjudicator generally, see Chapter 23.

While accepting that AI, certainly as we know it today, has its constraints, this chapter will argue that AI can nonetheless be of significant benefit, not just to the administration of express and charitable trusts but also in the role of adjudicator in forcing us to clarify and simplify the law relating to constructive trusts.

II AI AND EXPRESS TRUSTS

An 'express trust' will here refer to a 'trust' as defined in Article 2 of the 1985 Hague Convention on the Recognition of Trusts. In other words, an express trust signifies 'the legal relationships created – *inter vivos* or on death – by a person, the settlor, when assets have been placed under the control of a trustee for the benefit of a beneficiary or for a specified purpose'. As noted in Article 2, an express trust will have the following characteristics:

(a) the assets constitute a separate fund and are not a part of the trustee's own estate;
(b) title to the trust assets stands in the name of the trustee or in the name of another person on behalf of the trustee;
(c) the trustee has the power and the duty, in respect of which [one] is accountable, to manage, employ or dispose of the assets in accordance with the terms of the trust and the special duties imposed upon [one] by law.

Article 2 adds: 'The reservation by the settlor of certain rights and powers, and the fact that the trustee may himself have rights as a beneficiary, are not necessarily inconsistent with the existence of a trust.' Given an express trust so defined, to what extent can AI serve as a trustee and obviate the need for a human trustee? To answer this question, assume that an intending settlor approaches a service provider for an AI trust package tailored to the settlor's requirements.[3]

As a matter of equitable principles in common law jurisdictions, a trust should manifest three certainties.[4] There must be certainty of intention to create a trust, certainty of subject matter, and certainty of objects (beneficiaries). On a strict approach, an AI trust package will contain built-in restrictions that rejects inputs put forward by the user (settlor) apart from those which fulfil the three certainties. If any of the certainties is missing, then the AI can prompt the settlor to provide more requisite information which existed at the time of trust formation. Nothing is foolproof and if, notwithstanding the AI's prompts, the settlor insists on a formula of words which still has obscurities, the trust may still fail. As a safeguard, if the trust still fails for want of any of the three certainties, the AI could be programmed to hold a resulting trust in favour of an identified natural or legal person.

[3] A separate question is whether an AI trustee can and ought to be treated as a legal person. This is discussed in Section VI. See also the discussion on attributing legal personality to AI in Chapter 28.

[4] Lynton Tucker, Nicholas Le Poidevin and James Brightwell, *Lewin on Trusts* (20th edn, Sweet & Maxwell 2020) 154. See also *Knight v Knight* 49 ER 58, (1840) 3 Beav 148 (Ch).

On a forward-looking approach, as trust law and the technology behind AI evolve, in practice, it should not be difficult to programme the AI trust package to recognise each of those elements from the settlor's requirements.[5] For example, it is true that English law restricts non-charitable purpose trusts to those for the establishment and upkeep of tombs or memorials, the saying of masses for the dead, the maintenance of animals, and certain anomalous purposes.[6] There are cases in which what ostensibly appear to be purpose trusts have been interpreted by the courts as being in actuality trusts for the benefit of particular persons, so as to avoid such trusts being treated as inoperative under English law.[7] Insofar as English law is the applicable law of a trust, AI can be programmed to do the same thing and, applying Natural Language Processing (NLP) and other linguistic analysis whenever possible,[8] interpret the expression of a non-charitable purpose by a settlor into an intention by the settlor to benefit the persons who stand to gain from the fulfilment of the purpose. Even if that is beyond AI's present capability, it would simply mean that the English rule against non-charitable purpose trusts will be strictly applied by the AI programming and as more and more settlors opt for AI trustees the exceptions (which in any case have an archaic and illogical ring to them) will possibly fall into desuetude.

English law requires that non-charitable trusts do not run on into perpetuity.[9] In jurisdictions where the rule against perpetuities is not abolished, the AI trust package may reject clauses which run in contravention. In jurisdictions adopting a 'wait and see' approach, a limit to the life of a trust can easily be designed into AI, so that after (say) 80 years, the AI will treat the trust as ended and distribute whatever assets remain in accordance with its instructions.[10] There may be a problem where a trust is supposed to end upon the occurrence of a particular event. The AI may not be able to tell when the event has transpired.[11] For instance, consider a trust for 'the

5 Numerous trust cases have focused on whether a settlor has sufficiently divested himself or herself of all interest in trust property for the purposes of avoiding tax. For example, *WT Ramsay v IRC* [1982] AC 300 (HL); *RFC 2012 (In Liquidation) (formerly The Rangers Football Club Plc) v Advocate General for Scotland* [2017] UKSC 45, [2017] 1 WLR 2767. This is a specialised application of tax law and outside the scope of the discussion here. For our purposes, it does not matter whether the settlor has retained an interest in a trust. Nor, given the definition adopted, will it matter that the trust is for a non-charitable purpose.

6 *Re Endacott* [1960] Ch 232 (CA). For the care of specific animals: *Pettingall v Pettingall* (1842) 11 LJ Ch 17; *Re Dean* (1889) 41 Ch D 552. For the maintenance of graves: *Re Hooper* [1932] 1 Ch 38 (Ch). For the purpose of private masses and prayers for the souls: *Bourne v Keane* [1919] AC 815 (HL).

7 See, for example, in *Re Thompson* [1934] Ch 342 (Ch), a gift to a friend of the testator for the promotion and furthering of fox hunting was upheld.

8 John McGinnis and Steven Wasick, 'Law's Algorithm' (2014) 66(3) *Florida Law Review* 991–1050, 1017; M Corrales, M Fenwick and Forgó Nikolaus, *Robotics, AI and the Future of Law* (Springer 2018).

9 *Duke of Norfolk's Case* (1682) 3 Ch Cas 1, 22 ER 931.

10 These limitations to the life of a trust may run especially well on relatively simple forms of AI, such as expert systems, by incorporating if-then rules. See generally, KD Ashley, *Artificial Intelligence and Legal Analytics: New Tools for Law Practice in the Digital Age* (Cambridge University Press 2019) 8.

11 See generally, Larry DiMatteo, Michel Cannarsa and Cristina Poncibò, *The Cambridge Handbook of Smart Contracts, Blockchain Technology and Digital Platforms* (Cambridge University Press 2019) Part VI.

benefit of X during her lifetime and thereafter the entire trust property to be donated to Y University'. Without some external input, the AI will not know whether X has died. However, this difficulty is not an obstacle. In scenario posited, the settlor could specify (for example) that on or about a certain date every year, X must contact the AI and verify her continued existence through (say) some form of facial recognition and fingerprint or touch ID technology. If X fails to do so in a given year, the AI will be entitled to assume that X has passed away and the residue of the trust property will be donated to Y University.

With a discretionary trust, there may be difficulty where a settlor has specified open-ended criteria as to who may be potential beneficiaries. Thus, a trust for the benefit of 'such person showing exceptional character and leadership promise as the trustee may from time to time determine in their absolute discretion' may pose a challenge for AI. But this would be no more than the difficulty that human trustees would face in discerning the criteria which a settlor meant for them to apply when administering a trust in similar terms. To get around the problem, the settlor who intends that AI will be acting as trustee can be more precise about his or her criteria, including a detailed point system for assessing a candidate's suitability and tie-breaking factors for ranking candidates who score the same number of points.[12] Where an interview with a candidate is thought necessary, human intervention may be required given the present state of AI technology. However, it is envisaged that soon, it should be possible to have AI with sufficient appreciation of the nuances of human language (including body language) to conduct interviews.[13]

Given existing technology, the AI should be able to manage trust property in much the same way that algorithms now manage investment portfolios.[14] Express trusts will typically be subject to restrictions identifying permissible and impermissible investments.[15] Those restrictions can be fed into the AI coding to enable it to manage the trust property accordingly. As and when necessary and in accordance with the AI's instructions, maintenance and other payments can be made to the beneficiaries pursuant to the settlor's instructions. While it may be easier to

12 See generally, psychometric tests such as Myers-Briggs Type Indicator, Stratified Systems Theory and Big Five.

13 AI-based hiring and human resources management have been commonly adopted in Korean companies. See, for example, Jaewan Yang and others, 'Artificial Intelligence-Based Hiring: An Exploratory Study of Hiring Market Reactions' (2021) <www.jil.go.jp/english/events/seminar/20201109/document/korea_01.pdf>.

14 See, for example, Jacques Bughin and others, 'Artificial Intelligence: The Next Digital Frontier?' (*McKinsey Global Institute*, 2017) <www.mckinsey.com/~/media/mckinsey/industries/advanced%20electronics/our%20insights/how%20artificial%20intelligence%20can%20deliver%20real%20value%20to%20companies/mgi-artificial-intelligence-discussion-paper.ashx>; Deloitte, 'Artificial Intelligence – The Next Frontier for Investment Management Firms' (*Deloitte*, 2019) <www2.deloitte.com/global/en/pages/financial-services/articles/ai-next-frontier-in-investment-management.html>.

15 Tucker, Le Poidevin and Brightwell (n 4) 215–216. See, for example, *Thornton v Howe* (1862) 31 Beav 14 (Ch); *Bowman v Secular Society Ltd* [1917] AC 406 (HL).

programme robot trustees to manage investment portfolios consisting of financial products or virtual assets that can be bought and sold on a market, in principle AI can also be programmed to manage physical assets or even real property.[16] For instance, the AI trustee can be programmed to apply for property insurance from time to time or arrange for the regular upkeep of property. A difficulty, however, is that insurance companies and estate management companies may change the nature of their services or cease business over time.[17] It will be difficult for a programmer in year 1 to anticipate what service providers will still be in existence in (say) year 20 of a trust. The AI trustee may then find itself applying for insurance from a company that ceased to exist in year 15. As strong AI does not yet exist, it may not be possible with our present state of knowledge to have a robot trustee that will cater to the needs of every settlor. But where a robot trustee can meet a settlor's specifications, a beneficiary will have a workable trust that can meet all or at least a significant part of the beneficiary's needs and the trust will go on functioning over many years at minimal cost.

Individuals accumulate savings over their working lives. Many will not have pensions to cover their lives in retirement. Their savings are instead meant to cater for their maintenance and well-being for the period between their retirement and death. Given advances in health and medicine, such period may be a long time – possibly lasting some twenty or more years. Unfortunately, as they grow older, senior citizens may face conditions such as physical frailty and illness, senility, and dementia. They will increasingly be less and less able to manage their savings. Although they may have children, in today's busy world, the latter will frequently be contending with their own problems and may not have the time or ability to manage their parents' affairs. Faced with such prospect, some retirees avail of the services of a bank or other financial institutions to operate a trust of their accumulated savings for their maintenance.[18] Typically, the financial institution will require that the retiree settle a minimum amount (say, between US$1 and US$2 million) into the trust and pay annual fees (usually based on a percentage of the value of the trust assets) for the management of the trust. While everything may be fine in Year 1 when the retiree creates the trust, the same will almost certainly not be the case in Year 10 when (say) the retiree has to contend with a failing memory and increasingly precarious physical and mental health. The financial institution will most likely by then have raised the minimum amount required to

[16] Deloitte, 'Robots Are Here: The Rise of Robo-Advisers in Asia Pacific' (*Deloitte*, 2019) <www2.deloitte.com/gu/en/pages/financial-services/articles/robo-advisers-asia-pacific.html>.

[17] Ramnath Balasubramanian, Ari Libarikian, and Doug McElhaney 'Insurance 2030 – The Impact of AI on the Future of Insurance' (*McKinsey & Company*, 2019) <www.mckinsey.com/industries/financial-services/our-insights/insurance-2030-the-impact-of-ai-on-the-future-of-insurance>.

[18] Also known as an individual retirement account (IRA) in the UK. See, for example, Jordan Dechtman, 'What is a Retirement Trust?' (*Dechtman Wealth Management*, 2021) <https://dechtmanwealth.com/what-is-a-retirement-trust/>.

continue with its trust services. It will frequently be revising its annual fees afterwards, including imposing penalties if the assets under management are less than the newly stipulated minimum. This will be despite the fact that, the trust having been created for the purpose of maintaining the retiree over the remainder of life, the assets under management will usually be diminishing.[19] When one is older, one is not really much interested in high-risk investments offering the possibility of high returns in the long run. One is instead likely to prefer a conservative approach, bringing regular dividends and allowing the use of some proportion of one's accumulated capital. There will also be staff turnover at the financial institution. This means that the officer who assisted in the creation and initial operation of the trust will have moved on to some other posting. Younger individuals who will be less familiar (if at all) with the personal situation, needs and wishes of the settlor will have taken over. Whatever personal relationships may have existed between the settlor and the original officer-in-charge will have been lost. Given that the available funds in the trust will be dwindling, successive waves of officers may be less and less interested in closely managing the trust assets, as the potential returns in terms of fees and other returns to the financial institution will be diminishing. In those circumstances, what might originally have looked like a sound idea for managing the retiree's nest egg in Year 1, will have become somewhat of a headache in later years.[20]

In those circumstances, a robot may well be preferable to a financial institution as trustee. The robot should not cost significantly more to operate in Year 1 than in Year 10 or for that matter Year 20. It will manage the trust assets over time, however long or short, in strict accordance with the settlor's instructions.[21] While there may be economic volatility over the relevant period, it is not apparent that human trustees will be able to weather such financial turmoil any better than a robot managing trust assets in accordance with conservative investment instructions. Thus, it is submitted that the solution of a robot trustee, while not perfect, would be a better option than a financial institution, especially where it can be foreseen that a

[19] AI trust management may be especially helpful for those who with only relatively small amounts of savings since their low net worth makes them unattractive to traditional fund managers. Compare, for example, Nutmeg investment which is open to investment accounts with as low as £100 <www.nutmeg.com/faq>.

[20] Another problem with human wealth managers is that they may 'push' financial products on customers who do not really need them. An AI trustee may be better able objectively to service a customer's need. See Frank D Hodge, Kim I Mendoza and Roshan K Sinha, 'The Effect of Humanizing Robo-Advisors on Investor Judgments' (2021) 38 *Contemporary Accounting Research Volume* 770.

[21] AI investment systems also known as 'robo-advisers' can be automated for wealth management services where portfolios are constructed by AI according to programmed parameters and automatically re-balanced according to those parameters. See Pablo Sanz Bayón and Luis Garvía Vega, 'Automated Investment Advice: Legal Challenges and Regulatory Questions' (2018) 37 *Banking and Financial Services Policy Report* <www.researchgate.net/publication/326838138_Automated_Investment_Advice_Legal_Challenges_and_Regulatory_Questions/link/5c9f56c892851cf0aea13aea/download>.

settlor-beneficiary will not be able to take care of his or her own affairs but is likely to live for a relatively long period.[22]

III AI AND CHARITABLE TRUSTS

As a matter of equitable principles in common law jurisdictions, trusts for the special purposes of alleviating poverty, promoting religion, furthering education, and improving health or saving lives qualify for charitable status, provided that they benefit the public or a sector thereof.[23] It should be possible to programme AI to recognise when a purpose is charitable and entitled to tax concessions as a result.[24] Otherwise, what has already been stated above about the administration of express trusts by robots should equally apply to charitable trusts. In evaluating whether a member of the public or sector thereof should receive a benefit from the charitable

[22] This is not to say that everything will be smooth sailing and that all sorts of express trusts can easily be handled by robots. For example, in trusts with a substantial shareholding in a company, it will be difficult for an AI trustee to attend meetings and exercise discretion when voting for one or other course of action. Even in the simpler example of a trust administering a retiree's funds given in the text, there could still be problems with hardware, software, or programming becoming obsolete, and there may be a need for regular updates. Up to a point, such difficulties may be covered in the contract between a settlor and the institution providing the AI trustee package. The contract might specify, for instance, how updates to the AI programming are to be dealt with, if at all. One says 'up to a point' because it is not difficult to imagine scenarios which a contract might not expressly or impliedly cover. One's personal experience with updates suggests that they can sometimes lead to a computer performing worse than before. What, for instance, if the AI programming proves to be inept over the years? What happens if the institution which provided the AI trustee goes out of business? Who does one sue if something goes wrong? The point is that there are usually analogous difficulties with human trustees. The services provided by a human trustee may be incompetent and the institution which offered the trust services may become insolvent. Ultimately, it boils down to individuals making a choice given what is available on the market at a relevant time. At this stage of our knowledge, whether one goes with a human or AI trustee, there will be risks and uncertainties. The retiree who is deciding whether to entrust hard-earned funds to a human or AI trustee will have to assess the risks inherent with either course and decide which option is suitable for his or her needs and budget. A possibility is to incorporate a human or AI failsafe option into a trust. Settlors typically deal with future uncertainties by appointing a person (such as a close relative or friend) to act as a 'protector'. The protector has the power in defined circumstances to override or terminate a trust or direct that its assets be transferred to another person. In the case of an AI trustee, a similar stratagem might be employed so that the settlor designates a series of human or AI protectors who can step in and terminate the AI trust if matters do not proceed as envisaged. With this series of protectors, the trust designates one or more persons or (possibly) AIs empowered to act to preserve trust assets. If the first person designated becomes incapacitated over time, the next person or AI takes over as protector, and so on. See further Section VII.

[23] See, for example, Tucker, Le Poidevin and Brightwell (n 4) 179–180. For the statutory definition of 'charitable purpose' in England and Wales, see sections 3 and 4 of the Charities Act 2011. However, the traditional view of charitable trusts referred to here continues to apply in many common law jurisdictions, such as Singapore and Hong Kong.

[24] Deloitte, 'Whitepaper: Artificial Intelligence – Entering the World of Tax' (*Deloitte*, 2019) <www2.deloitte.com/global/en/pages/tax/articles/artificial-intelligence-in-tax.html>. This is not to minimise the difficulties involved. As a rule of thumb, the greater the amount of discretion allowed by the relevant charities law of a state as to what constitutes a charity, the greater the difficulty in programming AI to administer a charitable trust.

trust (such as a scholarship for the pursuit of a PhD), human intervention might be thought desirable for a final choice among a number of candidates thrown up by the AI trustee's algorithm. Nonetheless, in principle, especially with detailed instructions from a settlor-benefactor, it should be possible for the AI to work out which one or more candidates (if any) should receive funding from the trust. Human trustees of charitable trusts are sometimes accused of acting capriciously, favouring one potential beneficiary over another on inconsistent, illogical or highly subjective grounds. A robot trustee would impart a degree of consistency, although it may display bias depending on its programming and the big data comparables input into it for the purposes of assessing the likelihood or otherwise of a candidate achieving the trust's objectives.[25]

IV AI AND RESULTING TRUSTS

As a matter of equitable principles in common law jurisdictions, a resulting trust arises in two situations.[26] The first situation (automatic resulting trust) is where a settlor makes a gift of a limited interest in property to X but does not specify what is to happen when that limited interest is exhausted.[27] An example would be where the settlor gifts a life interest to X in land and does not state what is to happen to the land upon X's death. The law will treat the land as automatically reverting to the settlor's estate upon X's death.[28] The second situation (presumed resulting trust) is where a person A gives property to X for no apparent reason.[29] In the absence of evidence that A intended X to take the property by way of a loan or gift, the law will infer that A meant X to hold the property on a resulting trust for A. The inference of a resulting trust may be defeated by presumptions of advancement which arise in particular factual situations.[30] For instance, when a parent transfers property to his or her child, there will be a presumption, absent evidence to the contrary, that the parent intended to gift the property to the child for the purpose of the child's advancement in life.[31] There is the special situation of a *Quistclose* trust, where property is transferred to X to be used for a particular purpose.[32] If that purpose is frustrated or becomes incapable of execution, the remaining part of the property is treated as held on resulting trust by X for the transferor. In light of the foregoing classification

[25] On bias in AI adjudication, see Chapter 23.

[26] Tucker, Le Poidevin and Brightwell (n 4) 355. See also, for example, *Re Vandervell's Trusts (No 2)* [1974] Ch 269 (CA); *Westdeutsche Landesbank Girocentrale v Islington LBC* [1996] AC 669 (HL).

[27] Tucker, Le Poidevin and Brightwell (n 4) 381.

[28] See, for example, *Vandervell v Inland Revenue Commissioners* [1967] 2 AC 291 (HL).

[29] A presumed resulting trust would not involve a trustee. Tucker, Le Poidevin and Brightwell (n 4) 422.

[30] Ibid. 426. See also, for example, *Shepherd v Cartwright* [1955] AC 431 (HL).

[31] Tucker, Le Poidevin and Brightwell (n 4) 435–436. See also, for example, Bennet v Bennet (1879) 10 Ch D 474 (Ch).

[32] *Barclays Bank Ltd v Quistclose Investments Ltd* [1970] AC 567 (HL).

of resulting trusts, to what extent can AI (whether as trustee or adjudicator) be left to determine whether a resulting trust does or does not exist?

With automatic resulting trusts, it should be possible for AI (whether as trustee or adjudicator) to determine for any given property whether a settlor's gift has failed to dispose of the entire beneficial interest therein.[33] Upon exhaustion or termination of the relevant beneficial interest for some reason, the AI would then treat the remainder of the beneficial interest in the property as reverting back to the settlor's estate. As discussed earlier, the AI trustee may have difficulty deciding on its own whether the beneficial interest transferred has been exhausted or terminated. In the example of a gift of land to X for life, the AI might not be able to tell without some form of human intervention (such as some sort of regular confirmation that X continues to exist) that X has passed away. But the same problem would be present where a human being has to determine whether a beneficial interest has been exhausted or terminated.

The second situation may be trickier. But that is only because there may be conflicting accounts from the parties involved. The transferor may say that property has been transferred with the intention that it be held on resulting trust by the transferee. The transferee may claim that, on the contrary, the property was transferred with the intention that it be held on loan or as a gift. Here, the AI (acting as an adjudicator, as the AI would not have been constituted as a trustee in the circumstances) may be programmed to check initially for any circumstances triggering the presumption of advancement. If there are no such circumstances and in the absence of evidence (especially documentary evidence) corroborating that the transferred property was intended as a loan or gift, the AI can be programmed to decide that the relevant property is held on resulting trust. Where it is one person's word against another, AI may not be able to tell based on patterns from big data alone who is telling the truth. But as equity is protective of beneficiaries,[34] the AI might be programmed to favour a transferor in such situations. This would be tantamount to imposing a burden on a transferee to adduce sufficient evidence that a transfer was intended as a gift or loan. As oral evidence without more is difficult to evaluate, such programming would have the effect of nudging transferees of assets to record the terms of a transfer in some document.

Quistclose trusts are an anomalous form of resulting trust, which arose to get around the general rule against non-charitable purpose trusts in English law. Given the wider definition of express trusts adopted here, there should be little need to have AI (as trustee or adjudicator) distinguish a separate category of *Quistclose* resulting trusts. The challenge, which would be the same as that encountered in any express-purpose trust, whether or not charitable, lies in how to programme the AI to realise that a purpose has become frustrated or incapable of being achieved. The

33 See generally, Deloitte, 'Whitepaper: Artificial Intelligence – Entering the World of Tax' (n 24).

34 See, for example, Elena Zaccaria, 'The Nature of the Beneficiary's Right under a Trust: Proprietary Right, Purely Personal Right or Right against a Right?' (2019) 135 *Law Quarterly Review* 460; *Hor Yon Toy and Others v Tsui Siu Hing and Others* [2004] HKCFI 1030 [21].

existence of a *Quistclose* trust is often raised in insolvency cases where a transferor hopes to ring fence transferred property from the creditors of an insolvent business transferee.[35] In such situation, AI can be programmed to assess (say) accounting evidence to determine whether a transferee is insolvent (that is, unable to pay its debts as and when they fall due) and no longer in a position to use the transferred property for some identified commercial purpose. Where such conditions are present, the AI would conclude that the transferred property has reverted to the transferor.[36]

V AI AND CONSTRUCTIVE TRUSTS

Broadly, constructive trusts may arise or be imposed in several situations.[37] This chapter will focus on two situations. The first situation (type 1) is where a person A acts as a fiduciary for and on behalf of X, and A uses his or her fiduciary position to benefit A's own self, rather than X.[38] In such case, A must account as a constructive trustee for the benefit obtained or must compensate for the loss inflicted upon X. A becomes accountable for the benefit as soon as A wrongfully receives it. The constructive trust acts both *in rem* and *in personam*. A holds the benefit on trust for X, and A is also liable to account to X personally for the benefit. In the second situation (type 2), there is no pre-existing fiduciary relationship between A and X, but (1) A unconscionably receives trust property in which X has a beneficial interest, or (2) A dishonestly assists a trustee T to act in breach of T's fiduciary duties owed to X.[39] Precisely what state or mind is needed for the imposition of a type 2(1) constructive

35 See, for example, *Twinsectra v Yardley* [2002] UKHL 12, [2002] 2 AC 164; *Youyang Pty Ltd v Minter Ellison Morris Fletcher* [2003] HCA 15; *Dean-Willcocks v ACG Engineering Pty Ltd* [2003] NSWSC 353; *R v Prestney* [2002] NZCA 236; *Typhoon 8 Research Ltd v Seapower Resources International Ltd* [2002] HKCA 365; *Fu Kong Inc v Hua Yun Da Group Ltd* [2004] HKCFI 362; *Sacmi Cooperative Meccanici Imola v Gabriel Chi Kok Tam* [2005] HKCFI 213.

36 See further Chapter 23 on AI as judge or adjudicator.

37 Tucker, Le Poidevin and Brightwell (n 4) 359–360. Constructive trusts may be imposed in other situations in addition to those dealt with in the text. For example, where there is an understanding that property owned by A is to be held jointly with B and B acts on that understanding to B's detriment, there may be a common intention constructive trust (CICT). CICTs have typically been found in disputes between cohabitees. There is also what is referred to as a *Pallant v Morgan* equity. This arises where A and B agree to acquire land jointly. B refrains from bidding for the land pursuant to the parties' agreement, and A then acquires the land but refuses to grant an interest in it to B. There is disagreement over whether the latter situation is merely a species of type 1 constructive trust on the basis that, when acquiring the land, A can be characterised as having acted as agent (fiduciary) on behalf of himself and B. The imposition of CICTs and the *Pallant v Morgan* equity are fact-sensitive exercises, so that an AI adjudicator may have difficulty in assessing whether, on the facts of a given case, there has been the alleged agreement or common understanding.

38 Ibid. See for example, *Keech v Sandford* 25 E.R. 223, (1726) Sel Cas Ch 61 (Ch); *Westdeutsche Landesbank Girozentrale v Islington LBC* [1996] AC 669 (HL); *Re Polly Peck International Plc (No.5)* [1998] 3 All ER 812 (CA).

39 Tucker, Le Poidevin and Brightwell (n 4) 360. See also, for example, *Fortex Group Ltd (in receivership and liquidation) v MacIntosh* [1998] 3 NZLR 171; *Williams v Central Bank of Nigeria* [2014] UKSC 10, [2014] 2 WLR 355; *Selangor United Rugger Estates Ltd v Cradock (No.3)* [1968] 1 WLR 1555 (Ch).

trust remains a matter of debate among trust lawyers.[40] In type 2 situations, the court imposes a constructive trust as a remedial measure to counter X's improper conduct.[41] In type 2(1), there would be a personal obligation on A to account personally for any benefit received or to compensate for any loss inflicted. If any trust property remains in A's hands, A would hold the same trust for X. In type 2(2), by definition, A would not have received any trust property but only have assisted in the commission of a breach of trust; A would therefore only be under a personal obligation to account to X for any benefit obtained or to compensate for any loss inflicted. Note that where A comes into possession of trust property, even innocently, A should, in the ordinary course of events, come under an obligation to restore such property to the beneficiary, subject only to any available defences.[42] Given the foregoing account of constructive trusts, to what extent can AI be used to determine whether a constructive trust has arisen or should be imposed?

For type 1 constructive trusts, although the categories of fiduciary relationships are not closed, the AI (as adjudicator) can be provided with a list of the most common forms of fiduciary relationships (trustee and beneficiary, solicitor and client, director and company, agent and principal, etc.). AI should then be able to recognise the possible existence of an ongoing fiduciary relationship. Conventionally, the equitable rule is strict. Fiduciaries should not benefit themselves at the expense of the persons for whose benefit they are supposed to act.[43] They should not self-deal or otherwise put themselves in a position where they are in a potential conflict of interest with their beneficiary.[44] Applying a large database of constructive trust cases, AI should be able to determine the ways in which a fiduciary may benefit himself or herself at the expense of a beneficiary. Where there is a match or a near match between previous cases and the instant facts, the equitable rule will strictly apply. The fiduciary must account for the benefit obtained or the loss inflicted upon the beneficiary.[45] The fiduciary may, however, preclude having to account as a constructive trustee if the fiduciary makes full and frank disclosure and obtains informed consent prior to engaging in the relevant conduct.[46] Therefore, to prevent adverse consequences, the fiduciary would need to furnish an AI adjudicator with evidence that it has made disclosure. Again, since equity is protective of a beneficiary's interests and as AI will have difficulties where it is disputed whether oral disclosure has been made,

[40] Tucker, Le Poidevin and Brightwell (n 4) 771–786.

[41] Ibid. 364–365, 369–371.

[42] Ibid. 790–796. See, for the discussion of the application of construction trusts, William Swadling, 'The Fiction of the Constructive Trust' (2011) 64 *Current Legal Problems* 399.

[43] The 'no-profit' rule. See, for example, *Keech v Sandford* (n 38); *Daly v The Sydney Stock Exchange Ltd* [1986] HCA 25.

[44] The 'no self-dealing' rule. Tucker, Le Poidevin and Brightwell (n 4) 938–940.

[45] See also, more generally, *Target Holdings Ltd v Redferns* [1996] AC 421 (HL) and *AIB Group (UK) Plc v Mark Redler & Co Solicitors* [2014] UKSC 58, [2015] AC 1503.

[46] *Boardman v Phipps* [1967] 2 AC 46 (HL); *Australian Securities and Investments Commission v Citigroup Global Markets Australia Pty Limited (No.4)* [2007] FCA 963.

the fiduciary will effectively need to make the disclosure in writing and obtain the beneficiary's acknowledgment of having received the same on a particular date.

The foregoing is facilitated by the rigour of the equitable rule. The rule is meant to deter fiduciaries from contemplating any breach of their obligations, even if well-intentioned.[47] Thus, the rule is applied when, as in *Regal Hasting v Gulliver*,[48] the beneficiary would not have enjoyed a benefit if the fiduciaries (company directors) had not taken the steps which they did. Some commentators have suggested that the equitable rule should be relaxed.[49] Each situation ought instead to be examined on a case-by-case basis with a view to assessing whether a fiduciary should be sanctioned for incidentally conferring a benefit upon himself or herself, although acting with the best of motives in the interests of a beneficiary in an otherwise difficult position. AI may not be able, at present, to distinguish sufficiently between *Regal Hasting v Gulliver* situations on the one hand where the fiduciaries acted in the interests of their beneficiaries and *IDC v Cooley*[50] situations where the fiduciary acted purely in his interest on the other. So AI may not be able to decide how to temper the imposition of a type 1 constructive trust to circumstances which are analogous to the former line of cases, but not the latter. But it is submitted that such inability is only because human adjudicators are themselves ambivalent about the need to relax the strict equitable rule. No concerted attempt has been made to articulate the principles that should guide decision-makers in distinguishing between *Regal Hastings* and *IDC* situations. Without agreement on what the law should be or any attempt to articulate the underlying principles, it will be difficult to programme an AI adjudicator on what to search for in case databases to distinguish the two situations. AI may therefore not be able to develop the law without guidance from human adjudicators. What resort to AI can do instead is to force us to clarify what exactly the law should be and how strictly to apply the equitable rule. Once the law is clarified, then AI can be programmed to identify significant patterns from big data.

For type 2 constructive trusts, it should be possible in principle for AI (as adjudicator) to determine on the facts whether there has been receipt of trust property (type 2(1)) or assistance in a breach of trust (type 2(2)). The AI should be able to ascertain such matters by reference (for instance) to a database of case patterns. The difficulty lies in assessing the respondent's state of mind (that is, whether the respondent has acted knowingly, recklessly, innocently, or somewhere in between). This is particularly the case where the law prescribes that a respondent on whom a constructive trust is to be imposed must have acted with dishonesty or some unconscionable state of mind.[51] Since this is a

47 See, for example, the majority judgment in *Regal Hasting v Gulliver* [1967] 2 AC 134 (HL); *Keech v Sandford* (n 38).

48 [1967] 2 AC 134 (HL).

49 See, for example, the dissenting judgment in *Boardman v Phipps* (n 46) where Lord Upjohn held that there should be no breach of fiduciary duty unless when there existed a 'real sensible possibility of conflict of interest'.

50 [1972] 1 WLR 443 (Fam).

51 Tucker, Le Poidevin and Brightwell (n 4) 778.

fact-sensitive question, big data may not help, especially if AI will need to assess whether the respondent has acted with subjective (as opposed to objective) dishonesty. The cases themselves have adopted different tests for the operative state of mind. A number have proposed fine gradations of knowledge and dishonesty, among which it may be difficult to distinguish in practice.[52] The reality is that the problem of ascertaining a respondent's state of mind is not something confined to the use of AI. It is instead the consequence of the law on the matter being unclear and in a state of flux. The employment of AI may have the salutary effect of forcing human adjudicators to clarify (and possibly simplify) how precisely the relevant states of mind for type 2(1) and 2(2) constructive trusts are to be determined.[53] It is no assistance to have an elaborate system of states of mind if such system cannot be practically implemented, whether by human beings or AI.

The imposition of a type 2(2) constructive trust may be a matter of discretion, since the remedy is an equitable one.[54] But it is hard to envisage a human adjudicator refraining from imposing a personal duty to account where the respondent's overt conduct and the requisite state of mind (whatever that may involve) are found to meet the relevant criteria. In most cases, the human adjudicator's discretion will be constrained. By way of contrast, where the ingredients of a type 2(1) constructive trust are found, an AI adjudicator could be programmed to impose a constructive trust over the property received as well as a duty on the wrongdoer to account personally as a constructive trustee, subject only to running through a database of cases to check whether in like circumstances a remedy was imposed and (if so) for what reason. AI would not then actually be balancing the equities of a particular situation for the purposes of exercising a discretion. But the AI process may be an acceptable approximation of so doing.

VI AI AND SIMULATING EQUITY

The upshot of the foregoing discussion is that, as far as express trusts (including charitable trusts) are concerned, AI, even as we now know it today, should be able

52 Ibid. 771–786. See also, for example, *Nelson v Larholt* [1948] 1 KB 33 (KB); *Rolled Steel Products (Holdings) Ltd v British Steel Corporation* [1986] Ch 246 (CA); *Precision Dippings Ltd v Precision Dippings Marketing Ltd* [1986] Ch 447 (CA); *Investment Bank v Papadimitriou* [2015] UKPC 13, [2015] 1 WLR 4265 as to whether 'knowing' receipt equals with receipt with 'notice', and if so, whether actual or constructive notice would suffice.

53 The task of articulating a clear and simple test of the necessary state of mind for the imposition of a constructive trust will not be easy. As the law currently stands, the relevant state of mind effectively involves an adjudicator making a moral judgement based on a person's cognitive state. A dishonest state of mind arises when the latter acts in a manner that society would objectively regard as dishonest in light of facts subjectively known to him or her. The problem is that different adjudicators may reasonably disagree over whether a person has acted dishonestly in a particular situation. There, an AI adjudicator would need an appreciation of prevailing social norms (which may change over time and over which even human adjudicators may differ) to reach the conclusion that a person had the requisite state of mind for the imposition of a constructive trust.

54 In type 2(2) trusts, the wrongdoer will not have received trust property, the question is therefore whether to impose a personal duty to account on the wrongdoer.

to act as a tolerably acceptable trustee at a reasonable cost for an indefinite period. Such trusts will be self-executing, and run-of-the-mill settlors will not have to worry about the ever-increasing fees and ever-dwindling interest of professional trust managers as trust assets are gradually exhausted over the years. Resulting trusts should likewise pose no insurmountable difficulty for AI (whether as trustees or adjudicators). There may be issues in the determination of type 1 and type 2 constructive trusts by AI as adjudicator. But those are largely because the relevant law is unclear. One cannot expect AI to develop trust law, as opposed to implementing its rudimentary principles in a consistent manner. Using AI to apply equity (rather than merely simulate it) will require human adjudicators to clarify the practical criteria required (particularly in relation to the requisite state of mind) for the imposition of constructive trusts. This will almost surely entail the simplification of overly elaborate systems involving multiple shades of actual and constructive knowledge and too intricate tests for determining whether someone has or has not acted dishonestly.

In contrast to commercial law contracts (where there is no reason to favour one or other party in a dispute as to whether something was orally agreed or not), equity will normally be protective of the interests of a beneficiary in matters of trust law. Equity will typically apply rigorous presumptions against trustees or fiduciaries in the absence of compelling evidence that they fulfilled their duties (including by making full and frank disclosure). This strictness assists the use of AI as an adjudicator in disputes involving equitable principles. There will be little (if any) room in practice for discretion. If identifiable factors are present, AI will find a trust and impose a corresponding personal or proprietary remedy. On the other hand, the more that the rigours of trust law are tempered and it is required to tailor equitable relief to the degree of unconscionability inherent in a given situation, the less helpful AI will be.

At best, AI as we know it today can only simulate a sense of equity. It will have no conception of what is or is not unconscionable. It can only go by what has previously been decided and act in a manner that is narrowly consistent with that. But that may not be a bad thing and may be sufficient for most day-to-day purposes. A long-standing criticism of equity has been that it has varied historically with the length of the Chancellor's foot.[55] Modern equity is now said to have been rationalised and regularised to the extent of being predictable and certain.[56] This facilitates resort to AI. The more settled the principles of equity and the more constrained the discretion to award or refuse equitable remedies, the more favourable to the use of AI. The application of AI to matters relating to trusts can further consolidate that position.

[55] See, for example, Rundell Oliver, 'Chancellor's Foot: The Nature of Equity' (1958) 27 *U Kan City L Rev* 71; Richard O'Sullivan and Gareth Jones, 'The Length of the Chancellor's Foot: Some Principles Governing the Exercise of Judicial Discretion.' (1991) 108/109 *Law & Just-Christian L Rev* 4.

[56] See, for example, Lawlor Reed, 'The Chancellor's Foot: a Modern View' (1968) 6(4) *Hous L Rev* 630; Michael Blackwell, 'Measuring the Length of the Chancellor's Foot: Quantifying How Legal Outcomes Depend on the Judges Hearing the Case and Whether Such Variation Can Be Explained by Characteristics of the Judges' (2011) <https://papers.ssrn.com/sol3/papers.cfm?abstract_id=1855719>.

VII SOME QUESTIONS

This chapter has strongly advocated for robot trustees. Inevitably, there will be the conceptual question of whether a machine can ever be a trustee. The essence of a trust, as it is known today, is the separation of the legal and beneficial title in some property. Legal title vests in a natural or legal person, while someone else (a natural or legal person) holds the beneficial interest. Since a machine is neither a natural nor legal person, it may be argued that it cannot be a trustee. There is the further issue of liability. If the robot trustee impairs the beneficial interest because of its actions, who is to be liable to make good the harm done? Whom is a beneficiary to sue?

It is submitted that the problem of legal personality should not be treated as a showstopper as far as the use of robot trustees is concerned. It is unclear why, as a matter of convenience, a robot cannot simply be treated as a special type of 'trustee' with stringent (fiduciary) duties. There may not be much point in suing a robot trustee for harm done to a beneficial interest from the faithful adherence to its programming. But there are practical workarounds to this impediment which do not necessitate deeming a robot trustee to have legal personality.[57] For example, if the relevant harm was caused by faulty programming, the settlor or beneficiary could presumably sue the programmer or the institution which sold the robot trust package. Much will depend on the contractual terms agreed upon between the settlor or beneficiary on the one hand and the programmer or institution on the other. If there are several beneficiaries and the complaint is that the robot trustee's programming wrongly favours some beneficiaries at the expense of others, the remedy would be for the dissatisfied beneficiaries to bring an action against all other beneficiaries for the rectification of the alleged programming defect. One suggestion might be to have a human or institutional trustee who then uses AI as an aid in managing the trust. But this would not be much different from the current situation. The engagement of human beings or institutions would increase the cost of trust management and introduce the very human problems identified in Section I.

It is conceivable that the robot trustee may cause harm to third parties, perhaps by failing to make a payment due to an error calculating the available funds within a trust. In such case, the third party could, much as one sues a ship *in rem*, bring a claim against the trust property or part of it. The civil procedure to enable such an action would need to be developed. But there would not seem to be any objection in principle to a court so doing, possibly by analogy with what is routinely now done when the court exercises its admiralty jurisdiction *in rem*.

There are a myriad of ways in which a robot trustee can go wrong. It is impossible to envisage in advance the categories of potential misfortunes that may arise.[58] In

[57] For a discussion of whether legal personality should be attributed to AI, see Chapter 28; J Turner, *Robot Rules: Regulating Artificial Intelligence* (Palgrave 2019) 173–205.

[58] Turner (n 57) 81–112, especially 90–91 on foreseeability as a test for attributing liability. Turner argues that 'the actions of AI are likely to become increasingly unforeseeable, except perhaps at a very high

Quoine Pte Ltd v B2C2 Ltd,[59] due to a programming error, Quoine's platform quoted Ethereum ('ETH') for sale at a price of about 10 Bitcoin ('BTC') for 1 ETH, instead of the then-going market rate of about 0.04 BTC for 1 ETH. B2C2's algorithmic software spotted the anomalous price and put in an order to purchase around 3,092 BTC for some 309.2 ETH on Quoine's platform. The trade was completed, but Quoine purported to cancel the same after it discovered the error. Applying the law of mutual and unilateral mistake at common law and equity by analogy, a majority of the Singapore Court of Appeal[60] held on the facts that Quoine was contractually bound by the trades with B2C2 and was not entitled to avoid the transactions. It is submitted though that the general approach sketched out in Lord Mance IJ's dissenting judgement should guide adjudicators (whether human or not) in deciding how errors committed by robot trustees should be tackled. Lord Mance stated:

> …The law must be adapted to the new world of algorithmic programmes and artificial intelligence, in a way which gives rise to the results that reason and justice would lead one to expect. The introduction of computers no doubt carries risks, but I do not consider that these include the risk of being bound by an algorithmic contract, which anyone learning of would at once see could only be the result of some fundamental error in the normal operation of the computers involved. Computers are outworkers, not overlords to whose operations parties can be taken to have submitted unconditionally in circumstances as out of ordinary as the present…
>
> …[A]ny relief should be equitable, rather than at common law. The fact that computers were involved makes this appropriate…
>
> It should also be remembered that fundamental errors of the present nature can and do occur in computerised exchanges without any fault…. The law must be capable of addressing such a situation in a manner which corresponds with what I would regard as the clear justice of the case, as well as with the natural expectations of reasonable traders.
>
> It was suggested that all such problems … could have been dealt with by appropriately framed conditions of business. No doubt that is so. But the same could said in many of the situations in which the common law has developed principles of relief, to achieve just results…. The question is not whether the parties might have regulated such situations … but whether in the circumstances they should be taken to have accepted the risk of their occurrence so as to preclude application of such common law principles, adapted as necessary to the age of algorithms…

level of abstraction and generality. In consequence, holding a human responsible for any and all actions of AI would become less focused on the human's fault (usually the hallmark of negligence) and more like a system of strict, or product liability'.

59 [2020] SGCA(1) 02.

60 Comprised of Menon CJ, Phang and Prakash JJA, and French IJ.

> There is nothing surprising, impermissible or unworkable therefore about a test which asks what any reasonable [person] would have thought, given knowledge of the particular circumstances. That is the proper approach, in my opinion,.... Of course, this test involves a hypothetical.... But it does not work on the basis of speculation as to what 'might' have happened if a human element had been involved.... It is the Judge's approach which seems to me, to use his word, 'artificial' in assessing whether the contract can stand, not by reference to the circumstances and time when it was made, but on the basis that [a programmer] would have to be shown to be aware *in advance* that the only circumstances in which a [similar] contract could come into existence ... would be if some fundamental mistake occurred...

The usual way of dealing with disputes involving AI programming error is to apply existing law by analogy. Hence, the majority in *Quoine* approached the question of whether (for example) there had been a unilateral mistake in equity by reference to what Mr Boonen would or would not have foreseen years before when he was designing B2C2's algorithmic software. By the doctrine of equitable mistake, where party A enters into a contract under a mistaken belief or assumption and party B to the contract knew or ought to have realised that A was acting under a misapprehension, the court may treat the contract as void in the interests of justice.[61] B's state of knowledge at the time of contracting (as opposed to programming) is consequently a relevant factor. As Lord Mance highlights, the law should not blindly or exclusively proceed by drawing analogies with existing law in matters concerning AI. There is a need to step back and consider the bigger picture. In an AI case, one must not lose sight of the fundamental notions underlying equitable principles, such as the need to do justice and address unconscionable conduct. Where AI is concerned, there must be a rationale for each element of an analogy with existing law. What Lord Mance warns against is mechanically attributing knowledge or the lack of it on the part of AI by reference to the mindset of a human being, regardless of whether the latter could realistically have foreseen the chain of events that occurred years down the road and led to the legal dispute. The court must constantly subject its conclusions to a reality check, asking whether the outcome of its reasoning by analogy with established legal principles makes sense. If it does not, the analogy should be revised or rejected as inadequate.

Robot trustees, like their human counterparts, bring their peculiar difficulties and will no doubt pose conundrums for courts in the future. But the difficulties are not incapable of practical solution by the application of legal analogy with robust common sense. The difficulties should not be seen as impediments to the more widespread use of robot trustees.

[61] *Chwee Kin Keong and Others v Digilandmall.com Pte Ltd* [2005] SGCA 2, [77]–[83].

13

Unjust Enrichment Law and AI

Ying Hu

I INTRODUCTION

Whenever we send an email,[1] upload a photo,[2] or ask Alexa a question,[3] we are likely helping Google, Facebook, Amazon, and many other companies train their artificial intelligence (AI) systems to provide personalised services, serve targeted advertising, or develop new technologies. Recall in 2018, Google unveiled Duplex, an AI-powered assistant that sounded 'eerily human' when making appointments with real people over the phone.[4] Duplex is trained through real-time supervised training; in other words, our conversations with Duplex help improve it.[5]

Where companies collect our data to train their AI systems, or benefit from our data in other ways, are we entitled to any of those benefits? This chapter considers the situations in which individual data subjects should be allowed to seek gain-based remedies against those companies. In this chapter, 'personal data' is used loosely to refer to not only information about individuals' personal attributes and characteristics but also information about the activities that individuals carry out while using certain products or services.

I owe special thanks to Rory Gregson whose insights proved indispensable to this Chapter. I am also grateful for helpful comments from Professors Jeannie Marie Paterson, Ernest Lim, the anonymous reviewer, and participants of the AI and Private Law Conference. All mistakes are mine.

1 John D McKinnon and Douglas MacMillan, 'Google Says It Continues to Allow Apps to Scan Data from Gmail Accounts' (*Wall Street Journal*, 20 September 2018) <www.wsj.com/articles/google-says-it-continues-to-allow-apps-to-scan-data-from-gmail-accounts-1537459989>.

2 Nick Statt, 'Facebook Is Using Billions of Instagram Images to Train Artificial Intelligence Algorithms' (*The Verge*, 2 May 2018) <www.theverge.com/2018/5/2/17311808/facebook-instagram-ai-training-hashtag-images>.

3 Amazon, 'Alexa and Alexa Device FAQs' <www.amazon.com/gp/help/customer/display.html?nodeId=201602230>.

4 Lauren Goode, 'How Google's Eerie Robot Phone Calls Hint at AI's Future' (*Wired*) <www.wired.com/story/google-duplex-phone-calls-ai-future/>.

5 Yaniv Leviathan and Yossi Matias, 'Google Duplex: An AI System for Accomplishing Real-World Tasks over the Phone' (*Google AI Blog*, 8 May 2018) <https://blog.research.google/2018/05/duplex-ai-system-for-natural-conversation.html>.

This chapter proceeds as follows. Section II outlines various ways that companies can profit from the personal data they collect. Section III explains, from the plaintiff's perspective, the benefits of seeking gain-based remedies against those companies. Section IV suggests that unjust enrichment provides a plausible cause of action for individuals whose personal data has been collected or used without their consent. Section V considers two situations in which companies might be required to disgorge profits from the unlawful collection or use of personal data.

II TYPICAL SCENARIOS

Companies collect a wide variety of personal data about individuals who use their products or services. Some companies collect such data knowing that their users have not consented to the collection: for example, a weather application might surreptitiously collect comprehensive geolocation data about its users.[6] Some companies accidentally collect more data than they intend to: Google Assistant, which records and analyses voice commands when certain hotwords are detected, allegedly misperceived other words as hotwords and recorded private conversations.[7]

Companies can benefit from the personal data they have collected in several ways. They may sell that data to third parties for money or for benefits in kind (e.g., other types of data or insights from data analysis). As the Cambridge Analytica scandal has revealed, Facebook shared user data with a long list of app developers and business partners, such as Amazon, Microsoft, Samsung, and Airbnb.[8] Companies may also use that data to develop or improve their own products or services. For example, the data may be aggregated and analysed to create more granular user profiles, which enable advertisers to target the companies' users more efficiently and accurately. Alternatively, the data may form part of larger datasets to train algorithms (e.g., voice recognition algorithms) embedded in those companies' products or services.

III ADVANTAGES OF SEEKING GAIN-BASED REMEDIES

Gain-based remedies deprive the defendant of the benefits received. By contrast, compensatory damages repair the plaintiff's loss. From the plaintiff's perspective, there are several benefits to seeking gain-based remedies against companies that collect or use their personal data without their consent.

6 See, for example, *Goodman v HTC Am, Inc*, No. C11-1793, 2012 U.S. Dist. LEXIS 88496 (W.D. Wash. Jun. 26 2012).

7 See, for example, *In re Google Assistant Privacy Litig* 546 F.Supp.3d 945 (N.D. Cal. 2021).

8 See *In re Facebook, Inc* 402 F. Supp. 3d 767, 780–81 (N.D. Cal. 2019).

Firstly, in the absence of an established market for individuals to trade their personal data, individuals have experienced difficulty demonstrating that they suffered financial loss as a result of the defendant's unauthorised data collection or use.[9]

Secondly, the amount of benefits received as a result of data disclosure is often relatively easy to ascertain – if the defendant sold that data, it has benefited from the sale proceeds. By contrast, the extent of plaintiffs' loss from unauthorised data disclosure often depends on whether and how that data is eventually misused. Moreover, there is invariably a time gap between unauthorised disclosure and data misuse, which presents an additional hurdle for individuals seeking to establish a sufficient causal link between the disclosure and their loss. Without proof of actual loss, some courts might only award nominal damages for infringement of privacy interests *per se*.[10]

Thirdly, the defendant might seek to defeat a class action for unauthorised data collection or use on the basis that individualised evidence is required to determine the amount of damages recoverable by each putative class member.[11] For example, whether a plaintiff suffers any emotional distress, and the extent of such distress, is likely determined by characteristics unique to each individual. Therefore, to recover loss for emotional distress, each plaintiff is likely required to provide individualised evidence of the distress suffered.[12] By contrast, the benefits received by the defendant from unauthorised data collection or use (e.g., sale proceeds) can often be established without requiring individualised evidence from each plaintiff.[13] Alternatively, the court might certify a class action concerning liability, leaving damages assessment to be determined in separate proceedings.[14] An important problem with this bifurcated approach, as the author has argued elsewhere,[15] is that a large number of

9 See, for example, *In re Google Inc* 806 F.3d 125, 148–149 (3rd Cir. 2015) (concluding that Google obtained benefits from allegedly unlawful collection of the plaintiffs' internet usage information without causing the plaintiffs to suffer loss since the plaintiffs failed to allege facts suggesting that they ever sought to or intended to monetise their internet usage information, or that Google prevented them from capturing the full value of that information).

10 See Robert C Post, 'The Social Foundations of Privacy: Community and Self in the Common Law Tort' (1989) 77 *California Law Review* 957, 966, citing *Manville v Borg-Warner Corp*, 418 F.2d 434 (10th Cir. 1969).

11 In the United States, to obtain pecuniary relief for individual class members, a claim must satisfy the requirements in Rule 23(b)(3) of the Federal Rules of Civil Procedure, including a requirement that 'the questions of law or fact common to class members predominate over any questions affecting only individual members'. A defendant may argue that this requirement is not satisfied because individualised evidence is required to determine the amount of damages recoverable by each putative class member.

12 See, for example, *Lloyd v Google* [2021] UKSC 50, [2022] 2 All ER 209 [107]; *Alderwoods Group, Inc v Garcia* 119 So. 3d 497, 506 (Fla. Dist. Ct. App. 2013) (refusing to certify a class where the plaintiffs sought relief mainly for emotional distress).

13 Nevertheless, the plaintiffs might be required to submit some individualised evidence to prove that their personal data was unlawfully collected by the defendant in the first place.

14 See, for example, *Smith v Triad of Ala, LLC*, No. 14-cv-324, 2017 U.S. Dist. LEXIS 38574, 40–41 (M.D. Mar. 17 2017) ('Resolving these claims for damages will require a series of proceedings in which each class member can put on his or her case for damages…').

15 Ying Hu, 'Mainstreaming Unjust Enrichment in Data Security Law' (2023) 13 *UC Irvine Law Review* 855.

plaintiffs may not be sufficiently incentivised to adduce evidence in those separate proceedings, which in turn significantly reduces the defendant's potential liability.

Finally, there are additional benefits to relying on unjust enrichment as a cause of action – it is sometimes easier to establish an unjust enrichment claim for two reasons. Firstly, plaintiffs only have to demonstrate an unjustified transfer of value to the defendant to establish an unjust enrichment claim. They do not have to establish, for example, that the defendant's collection of personal data is 'highly offensive to a reasonable person', which is an essential element of the US tort of intrusion upon seclusion.[16] As explained below,[17] this 'highly offensiveness' requirement will likely set a high bar for a finding of liability. Secondly, since an unjust enrichment claim does not depend on proof of wrongdoing, it provides an avenue of redress for plaintiffs where the defendant has not committed any legally cognizable wrong, but natural justice leans in favour of providing a remedy. This may be the case where gaps in the law leave certain types of personal data unprotected.[18]

IV UNJUST ENRICHMENT CLAIMS

To bring an unjust enrichment claim, a plaintiff generally has to establish that (1) the defendant is enriched, (2) at the plaintiff's expense, (3) in circumstances which render it unjust for the defendant to retain the enrichment.[19] The exact elements of the cause of action vary in different jurisdictions.[20]

Moreover, it is trite law that a plaintiff generally cannot bring an unjust enrichment claim against a defendant with whom the plaintiff has a valid and subsisting contract governing the same subject matter (the 'pre-emption rule').[21] The primary justification for the pre-emption rule is that contract is a more effective means than unjust enrichment to regulate voluntary transfers.[22] The court should respect the parties' intention and give effect to their own valuation of benefits and allocation

[16] *Restatement (Second) of Torts* (American Law Institute 1977) § 652B; *Hernandez v Hillslides, Inc*, 47 Cal.4th 272, 286 (Cal. 2009).

[17] See Section V.B.1.

[18] For example, some commentators believe that the United States 'has a patchwork of privacy laws that leave some personal information unprotected.' Alexandria Bradshaw, 'Emerging Trends in International Data Breach Law Legal News & Developments' (2016) 1 *Georgetown Law Technology Review* 143, 143.

[19] §1 of the *Restatement (Third) of Restitution and Unjust Enrichment* (American Law Institute 2011) states, '[a] person who is unjustly enriched at the expense of another is subject to liability in restitution.'

[20] See, for example, *Vista Healthplan, Inc v Cephalon, Inc*, No. 06-cv-1833, 2015 U.S. Dist. LEXIS 74846 81–84 (E.D. Pa. June 10, 2015) (explaining various ways that the unjust enrichment laws vary in different states; for example, some states, such as California, Florida, Kansas, Maine, Massachusetts, Nevada, New Mexico, North Carolina, South Dakota, Tennessee, Utah, and Wisconsin, require proof that the defendant appreciates or knows of the benefit).

[21] As stated in §2(2) of the *Restatement (Third) of Restitution and Unjust Enrichment* (n 19), '[a] valid contract defines the obligations of the parties as to matters within its scope, displacing to that extent any inquiry into unjust enrichment.').

[22] Ibid.

of risks, as expressed in their contract.[23] It should not allow a party to escape a bad bargain by pursuing an alternative unjust enrichment claim.[24]

Companies such as Google or Facebook often require users to agree to their Terms of Service and/or Privacy Policies, whose terms are sometimes contractually binding.[25] This section considers four possible scenarios.

(1) First scenario: the defendant has collected personal data about the plaintiffs, but there is no contractual provision concerning data collection or use.
(2) Second scenario: the defendant has collected personal data about the plaintiffs in breach of a contractual provision stating that the defendant does not collect certain types of data.
(3) Third scenario: while there is a contractual provision stating that the defendant collects certain types of personal data, the defendant misrepresented, prior to the contract, that it would not disclose any data collected pursuant to that provision. The defendant subsequently discloses that data to third parties.
(4) Fourth scenario: the defendant collects and uses personal data pursuant to a valid and binding contractual provision.

The pre-emption rule likely applies in the fourth scenario to bar any unjust enrichment claims concerning data collected in accordance with that provision. This Section, therefore, focuses on the first three scenarios.

A *First Scenario: No Contractual Provision Concerning Data Collection/Use*

A number of US courts have held that plaintiffs can bring unjust enrichment claims in respect of issues not fully covered by any contract.[26] In the first scenario, the relevant contract does not address the specific benefit at issue (i.e.,

[23] Charles Mitchell, Paul Mitchell and Stephen Watterson (eds), *Goff & Jones: The Law of Unjust Enrichment* (9th edn, Thomson Reuters 2016), 53–54 (hereinafter, *Goff & Jones*).

[24] See also Stephen Smith, 'Concurrent Liability in Contract and Unjust Enrichment: The Fundamental Breach Requirement' (1999) 115 *Law Quarterly Review* 245.

[25] A body of US case law held that users are bound by terms of online agreements which they have 'clicked' to accept or which they have actual notice of. By contrast, users are not bound by browsewrap agreements – agreements that users purportedly assent to by using the website – unless they 'put[] a reasonably prudent user on inquiry notice of the terms of the contract' through the 'design and content of the website and the agreement's webpage'. See, for example, Allyson W Haynes, 'Online Privacy Policies: Contracting Away Control over Personal Information' (2006) 111 *Penn State Law Review* 587. See also *Nguyen v Barnes & Noble Inc* 763 F. 3d 1171, 1175–79 (9th Cir. 2014) (consumers 'cannot be expected to ferret out hyperlinks to terms and conditions to which they have no reason to suspect they will be bound'). The courts do not always conclude that privacy policies are contractually binding. See, for example, Gregory Klass, 'Empiricism and Privacy Policies in the Restatement of Consumer Contract Law' (2019) 36 *Yale Journal on Regulation* 45.

[26] See, for example, *Town of New Hartford v Conn Res Recovery Auth* 291 Conn. 433, 455 (Conn. 2009), citing *Klein v Arkoma Production Co*, 73 F.3d 779, 786 (8th Cir. 1997) ('when an express contract does not fully address a subject, a court of equity may impose a remedy to further the ends of justice.'); *Rent-A-PC, Inc v Rental Management, Inc* 96 Conn.App. 600, 606 (2006) ('the existence of

benefit from collection and use of the plaintiffs' personal data). Assuming that allowing the plaintiffs to pursue unjust enrichment claims is not inconsistent with the terms of the contract, the pre-emption rule should not apply in this scenario. Consequently, the plaintiffs should be permitted to pursue unjust enrichment claims provided that the elements of those claims are satisfied. Each element is examined in turn.

1 Enrichment

Assume that the defendant collects personal data about the plaintiffs without their consent – for example, the defendant secretly records the websites visited by the plaintiffs – what benefit, if any, has been transferred from the plaintiffs to the defendant? It cannot be the digital files containing the binary representation of those websites. The files are created by the defendant, not transferred by the plaintiffs to the defendant. It cannot be the information that the plaintiffs visited certain websites. The plaintiffs retain that information. It may not even be the value of using that information for a particular purpose. Since information is non-rivalrous,[27] the defendant can use it for one purpose without necessarily preventing the plaintiffs from using it for the same or different purposes.

The preferred view, it is submitted, is that the benefit transferred from the plaintiffs to the defendant is control over information about the plaintiffs (e.g., internet usage information): as the defendant acquires the power to determine the use of that information, the plaintiffs' power to determine its use diminishes accordingly. Third parties can choose whether to acquire that information directly from the plaintiffs or the defendant.

The power to determine the use of such information has value to both individual data subjects and companies. Individuals have various interests in selectively disclosing information about themselves to different people – to manage their social personalities, to develop intimate relationships, and to prevent potential injuries from third-party misuse of that information. As explained in Section II, companies have financial interests in using such information in various ways.

The objective value of the defendant's control over information about the plaintiffs depends on the type and amount of the relevant data in question. In addition, the value can be assessed by reference to a number of factors. Firstly, if the defendant has sold that data, then the sale price helps determine the value of controlling that data. Secondly, if the defendant has saved costs as a result of using information about the plaintiffs, then the value of control may be measured by reference to the

a contract, in itself, does not preclude equitable relief which is not inconsistent with the contract'); *Porter v Hu* 116 Hawai'i 42, 54 (Haw. Ct. App. 2007) ('[while] it is stated that an action for unjust enrichment cannot lie in the face of an express contract, a contract does not preclude restitution if it does not address the specific benefit at issue.').

27 See Ying Hu, 'Private and Common Property Rights in Personal Data' (2021) 33 Singapore Academy of Law Journal 173, 183–84.

amount of expenses saved.[28] For example, such information may help companies save costs in conducting experiments to determine how to increase user engagement or optimise ad sales.[29] Finally, there might occasionally exist a market price for or independent studies about the value of certain types of personal data,[30] which can shed light on the value of control over that data. However, as the UK Supreme Court pointed out in *Benedetti v Sawiris*, 'the objective value of a benefit to the defendant may be less than its ordinary market value'.[31]

It is worth noting, however, that even if the benefit received by the defendant has an objective value, an innocent defendant generally should not be subject to a forced exchange.[32] This general rule should not pose much problem where the defendant has intentionally collected personal data about the plaintiffs without their consent[33] or where the defendant has sold the data in question. By contrast, if the defendant accidentally collected personal data and transferred control over that data back to the plaintiffs as soon as it was aware of its mistake (e.g., by deleting that data), then it is arguable that the defendant has not been enriched.[34]

2 At the Plaintiff's Expense

The 'at the plaintiff's expense' requirement serves multiple purposes: it limits the categories of persons who can bring an unjust enrichment claim against a particular defendant; it may also affect the amount recoverable in such claims.[35]

In the UK Supreme Court decision of *Investment Trust Companies v HMRC*, Lord Reed identified two necessary elements of this requirement: (1) the defendant

28 The defendant might draw a distinction between the value of the defendant's control over the data collected and the use value of that data. It may then rely on *Prudential Assurance Co Ltd v Revenue and Customs Commissioners* [2018] UKSC 39, [2019] AC 929 to argue that the use value of that data should be irrelevant because it is not obtained at the plaintiffs' expense. This type of argument has been criticised by various commentators. See, for example, Andrew Burrows, 'In Defence of Unjust Enrichment' (2019) 78 *Cambridge Law Journal* 521, 538–541. The author's preferred view is that the defendant's enrichment should include such use value.

29 Jack Balkin points out that individual users are in effect 'unpaid laborers'. Jack M Balkin, 'Free Speech Is a Triangle' (2018) 118 *Columbia Law Review* 2011, 2024.

30 See, for example, *In re Facebook, Inc Internet Tracking Litigation* 956 F.3d 589, 600 (9th Cir. 2020), where the plaintiffs relied on a study which valued users' browsing histories at $52 per year.

31 [2013] UKSC 50, [2014] AC 938 [111]. The Court's approach to valuing benefits in the form of services is instructive: while the starting point is the ordinary market value of the services, the defendant is allowed to adduce evidence to demonstrate that a reasonable person in its position would have paid a lower price for those services. Ibid. [34], [100]–[109].

32 *Restatement (Third) of Restitution and Unjust Enrichment* (American Law Institute 2011) § 2(4). See also Mitchell McInnes, 'Enrichment' in Elise Bant, Kit Barker and Simone Degeling (eds), *Research Handbook on Unjust Enrichment and Restitution* (Edward Elgar Publishing 2020) 249–259.

33 It is arguable that the defendant is aware of the plaintiffs' expectation to be paid in this situation.

34 Nevertheless, the defendant arguably should still be required to repay the use value of that data if the defendant was able to save costs that it would have incurred in any event – a possible example is costs in acquiring similar types of data to train its AI systems.

35 For a helpful discussion of the 'at the plaintiff's expense' requirement, see Stephen Watterson, 'At the Claimant's Expense' in Elise Bant, Kit Barker and Simone Degeling (eds), *Research Handbook on Unjust Enrichment and Restitution* (Edward Elgar Publishing 2020).

'has received a benefit from the claimant', and (2) the plaintiff 'suffered a loss through his provision of the benefit'.[36] According to Lord Reed, if the plaintiff has 'given up something of economic value', she has in that sense incurred a loss.[37] Both elements appear to be present in the case of unauthorised data collection: the defendant receives a benefit in the form of control over information about the plaintiff; the plaintiff suffers a loss in the form of a decrease in control over that information by (consciously or unconsciously) allowing her data to be collected. The plaintiff's loss in control arguably has economic value: it reduces the plaintiff's ability to regulate relationships with the defendant and with an indeterminate number of third parties.

Two further points should be made about the 'at the plaintiff's expense' requirement. First, a third party, who has lawful access to the plaintiff's information, might also suffer a diminution in control over that information. However, the third party generally should not be allowed to bring an unjust enrichment claim against the defendant because the defendant receives its benefit directly from the plaintiff, not the third party. Second, there has been a divergence of views on whether there must be an exact correspondence between the plaintiff's loss and the defendant's gain to satisfy the 'at the claimant's expense' requirement.[38] On one view, the amount of remedy recoverable should be capped at the plaintiff's loss.[39] Others,[40] including this author, maintain that it is sufficient to show an enrichment from the plaintiff. As such, it arguably does not matter if the value of the defendant's benefit does not precisely match the amount of loss suffered by the plaintiff.

3 Unjust Factor: Mistake

The plaintiffs can seek to bring a mistake-based unjust enrichment claim against the defendant. To rely on mistake as an unjust factor, a plaintiff must establish that she transferred personal data to the defendant due to a mistake (e.g., a mistake about the defendant's data practice) and that she would not have transferred that data but for the mistake.[41] The mistake does not have to be created or induced by the defendant.[42] However, the plaintiff must not 'bear the risk of the mistake.'[43] The

[36] *Investment Trust Companies (in liq) v HMRC* [2017] UKSC 29, [2018] AC 275 [43]–[45], cited with approval in *Test Claimants in the Franked Investment Group Litigation v Revenue and Customs Commissioners* [2021] UKSC 31, [2022] 1 All ER 751 [169].

[37] *Investment Trust Companies* (n36) [45].

[38] See Watterson (n 35).

[39] See, for example, Mitchell McInnes, 'At the Plaintiff's Expense: Quantifying Restitutionary Relief' (1998) 57 *Cambridge Law Journal* 472.

[40] A summary of those views can be found in Watterson (n 35) 279.

[41] As stated in §5 of the *Restatement (Third) of Restitution and Unjust Enrichment* (n 19), mistake can serve as an unjust factor grounding an unjust enrichment claim if 'but for the mistake the transaction in question would not have taken place.'

[42] Ibid.

[43] Ibid.

UK Supreme Court in *Pitt v Holt*[44] takes a more restrictive approach: the causative mistake (of law or fact) must also be sufficiently serious.[45]

A defendant might seek to defeat a mistake-based unjust enrichment claim by arguing that the plaintiffs were risk-takers. It might argue, for example, that the plaintiffs suspected that the defendant might collect and use her personal data, but allowed the defendant to collect their data anyway; in other words, the plaintiffs 'consciously assumed the risk by deciding to act in the face of a recognized uncertainty.'[46] In the first place, whether it is necessary or desirable to have a separate non-risk-taker requirement is questionable. One might argue that the risk-taker argument does not add anything to the causation requirement, but is merely an example where there is no causative mistake.[47] In any event, under US law, plaintiffs are generally not considered risk-takers simply because they made a mistake as a result of their negligence.[48] As such, even if a reasonable person in the plaintiffs' position would have discovered the defendant's actual data practice (e.g., by reading the privacy policy), that alone should be insufficient to prevent the plaintiffs from relying on their mistake to bring unjust enrichment claims.

B *Second Scenario: Collected Personal Data in Breach of Contractual Provision*

In the second scenario, the plaintiffs can sue the defendant for breach of contract. Sometimes, the relevant breach may not be sufficiently material to entitle the plaintiffs to terminate the contracts in question.[49] Where that is the case, the pre-emption rule applies. Nevertheless, it is arguable that the court should allow concurrent claims in both contract and unjust enrichment where doing so does not undermine the justifications of the pre-emption rule.[50]

If the plaintiffs succeed in persuading the court to disapply the pre-emption rule, they can then bring unjust enrichment claims based on two plausible theories. Firstly, they might argue that the defendant has been enriched because (1) the

44 [2013] UKSC 26, [2013] 2 AC 108.

45 Ibid. [126]. The scope of this rule is unclear. One way to reconcile *Pitt v Holt* with earlier cases is to hold that this restrictive approach only applies to 'voluntary transactions'. See, for example, *Goff & Jones* (n 23), 366–367.

46 *Restatement (Third) of Restitution and Unjust Enrichment* (n 19) § 5(3)(b).

47 Thanks to Rory Gregson for raising this point. For criticisms of this requirement, see Frederick Wilmot-Smith, 'Replacing Risk-Taking Reasoning' (2011) 127 *LQR* 610 (identifying five flaws of risk taker reasoning: 'The reasoning is circular, ambiguous, inconclusive, incapable of explaining the decided cases and unnecessary.').

48 *Restatement (Third) of Restitution and Unjust Enrichment* (n 19) § 5(4).

49 Ibid. § 37, cmt. c.

50 Various commentators have argued in favour of allowing concurrent claims. See, for example, Smith (n 24); Andrew Tettenborn, 'Subsisting Contracts and Failure of Consideration – A Little Scepticism' (2002) 10 *Restitution Law Review* 1; Hu (n 15).

defendant has made an express promise not to collect certain types of personal data; (2) the promise is sufficiently material that a reasonable person, circumstanced as the actual parties were, would understand that the promise is not gratuitous; and (3) the plaintiff paid the defendant – with money, data, or both – in connection with that promise.[51] The relevant unjust factor is failure of basis: simply stated, the defendant promised to do something for remuneration, received remuneration, but did not do what was promised. Therefore, it is unfair for the defendant to keep the payment. Finally, since the defendant received the payment directly from the plaintiffs, it has been enriched at the plaintiffs' expense.

Secondly, as in the case of the first scenario, the plaintiffs might bring a mistake-based unjust enrichment claim.[52] They may argue that they transferred personal data to the defendant as a result of a mistake about the latter's data collection practice and would not have transferred that data had they not been mistaken.

C *Third Scenario: Misrepresentation Regarding Data Disclosure Practice*

In the third scenario, the plaintiffs might be able to rely on the defendant's misrepresentation to seek rescission and restitution – by arguing that they were induced into contracting with the defendant by the latter's false representation relating to its data disclosure practice.[53] If rescission is allowed, both parties are generally required to return any benefits received under the contract.[54] Having set aside the contract, the plaintiffs arguably should also be able to bring unjust enrichment claims based on mistake to recover benefits received by the defendant from disclosing the plaintiffs' personal data to third parties. Such benefits are arguably received at the plaintiffs' expense.

D *Defence*

One of the most important defences to an unjust enrichment claim is change of position. To rely on this defence, the defendant must demonstrate that its position has so changed that it would be inequitable to require it to make restitution of the original benefit received.[55] It is difficult to envisage a change in circumstances that allows the defendant to rely on this defence: a possible example is where the defendant, after collecting data about the plaintiffs, donates its data for public causes without leaving any copy.

[51] As the court recognized in *In re Marriot Int'l Inc Cust Data Sec Breach Litig* 440 F. Supp. 3d 447, 462 (D.Md. 2021), many customers pay for goods and services with their personal data instead of cash.

[52] The author has argued elsewhere that an unjust enrichment based on failure of consideration is likely to be more amenable to class action than a mistake-based claim. See Hu (n 15).

[53] A discussion of the substantive law of misrepresentation is beyond the scope of this Chapter.

[54] *Restatement (Third) of Restitution and Unjust Enrichment* (n 19) § 13 and § 54.

[55] Ibid. § 65. See also *Lipkin Gorman (A Firm) v Karpnale Ltd* [1991] AC 548 (HL).

V DISGORGEMENT FOR WRONGS

Despite the maxim 'a man shall not be allowed to profit from his own wrong', the remedy of disgorgement is not available as of right whenever the defendant commits a wrongful conduct. This section examines various grounds for awarding disgorgement in different situations and explains how those reasons can help justify an award of disgorgement for unlawful collection and use of personal data.

A *Grounds for Allowing Disgorgement*

Academics have identified at least four grounds for allowing disgorgement as a remedy.

1 To Protect Resources That Are Closely Attached to One's Personhood

First, Hanoch Dagan has argued in favour of allowing disgorgement for interference with property rights based on a personhood theory.[56] Dagan distinguishes between two types of resources: fungible resources and resources closely connected to their possessors' personhood. Protection of the latter kind of resources is necessary to facilitate its possessor's sense of maturity, self-discipline, and responsibility.[57] Therefore, the more closely a resource is attached to its possessor's personhood, the greater legal safeguard is required to prevent impermissible appropriation of that resource. Disgorgement deters such impermissible appropriation more effectively than, for example, an award of the fair market value of that resource.

2 To Facilitate Efficient Use of Resources

Secondly, disgorgement for interference with property rights can also be justified on efficiency bases. Disgorgement can be seen as a type of 'property rule', a phrase used by Guido Calabresi and A. Douglas Melamed to refer to remedies that deter non-consensual interference with rights (such as injunctions).[58] Viewed as such, Henry Smith's arguments for protecting owners' right to exclude with property rules can also help justify the availability of disgorgement as a remedy.[59] Firstly, Smith points out that resources in the world have multiple attributes and uses, which are costly to measure. Owners are often likely the 'least-cost generators' of information about their resources,[60] which makes them well-placed to decide the use of those

[56] Hanoch Dagan, *Unjust Enrichment: A Study of Private Law and Public Values* (CUP 1997). See also Margaret Radin's personhood theory of property. Margaret Jane Radin, 'Property and Personhood' (1982) 34 *Stanford Law Review* 957.

[57] Dagan (n 56) 42.

[58] Guido Calabresi and A Douglas Melamed, 'Property Rules, Liability Rules, and Inalienability: One View of the Cathedral' (1972) 85 *Harvard Law Review* 1089.

[59] Henry E Smith, 'Property and Property Rules' (2004) 79 *New York University Law Review* 1719.

[60] Henry E Smith, 'Exclusion and Property Rules in the Law of Nuisance' (2004) 90 *Virginia Law Review* 965, 985.

resources. Property rules are a cost-effective way to facilitate delegation of information gathering and choice of use to owners by removing the need for officials (e.g., the court) to measure the value of each use.[61] Secondly, property rules prevent opportunistic takings where the defendant believes that the owner is likely to be under-compensated in court due to her inability to communicate the value of her resources to the court cost-effectively and credibly.[62]

3 To Deter Violations of Important Social Norms

Another plausible ground for awarding disgorgement is to deter violations of important social norms. Few people would question that a defendant who receives a bounty for killing another person should be required to disgorge that benefit. Similarly, the Law Commission of England and Wales recommends that disgorgement be available against defendants who commit torts, equitable wrongs, or statutory civil wrongs if their conduct shows 'deliberate and outrageous disregard of the plaintiff's rights'.[63] This test captures serious violations of social norms as the Law Commission anticipates that any conduct satisfying this test would likely 'merit a bar within the criminal law'.[64]

One possible objection is that the protection of important social norms only justifies depriving the defendant of its gain; it does not provide a reason for transferring that gain to the plaintiff.[65] There are two possible responses to this objection. First, the way in which the defendant violates the social norm might show sufficient disrespect towards the plaintiff:[66] the plaintiff is entitled to the defendant's gain because disgorgement is grounded in the need to protect the plaintiff's dignitary interests. The second response is consequentialist: allowing the plaintiff to recover some or all of the defendant's gain incentivises individuals well-positioned to detect and prove violations of important social norms to incur costs to vindicate those norms. This is particularly important where public enforcement is likely inadequate to deter certain types of misconduct.

4 To Protect Important Social Relationships

Finally, disgorgement is generally available for breach of fiduciary duties.[67] Notably, a fiduciary is required to disgorge profit even if she breaches her duty inadvertently.[68] The availability of disgorgement as a remedy is often justified by the need to protect

[61] Ibid. 985–986.

[62] Ibid. Smith also points out that property rules reduce owners' incentive to invest in wasteful self-help (e.g., using secrecy agreements or extra locks) to pre-empt opportunistic takings.

[63] Law Commission of England and Wales, 'Aggravated, Exemplary and Restitutionary Damages' (LC 237, 1997) para 1.49.

[64] Ibid. para 1.258.

[65] See Ernest J Weinrib, 'Restitutionary Damages as Corrective Justice Restitution and Unjust Enrichment' (2000) 1 *Theoretical Inquiries in Law* 1, 2.

[66] Dagan (n 56) 70.

[67] *Restatement (Third) of Restitution and Unjust Enrichment* (n 19) § 43.

[68] Ibid. cmt. h.

the integrity of the fiduciary relationship itself, which allows the beneficiary to repose trust and confidence in the fiduciary.[69] As Sarah Worthington has put it, the focus is on the 'social value of the [protected relationships]';[70] disgorgement is justified because it 'best supports the legal obligation being enforced'.[71] Similarly, according to the Restatement (Third) of Restitution and Unjust Enrichment, an important objective of disgorgement is to ensure 'the fiduciary's disinterested judgment', which is best secured by 'eliminating the possibility of gain in any transaction where the interests of fiduciary and beneficiary could potentially conflict'.[72]

The scope of social relationships that are sufficiently important to ground an award of disgorgement is not necessarily limited to fiduciary relationships. For example, another type of relationship with high social value is the relationship between the Crown and secret service officers, which arguably explains the exceptional award of disgorgement for breach of contract in *Attorney-General v Blake*.[73]

B *Unlawful Collection of Personal Data*

This section considers whether disgorgement should be available as a remedy in two situations: where the defendant's unauthorised data collection amounts to (1) an intrusion upon seclusion (the 'intrusion tort') and (2) a breach of contract.

1 Intrusion Upon Seclusion

In the United States, an intrusion claim based on the unauthorised collection of personal data generally requires proof of both (1) '[intrusion] into a private place, conversation or matter as to which the plaintiff has a reasonable expectation of privacy' and (2) 'in a manner highly offensive to a reasonable person.'[74]

The courts' analysis of the first element focuses on two factors. First, the amount and sensitivity of the data collected: individuals are more likely to be held to have a reasonable expectation of privacy in data that is likely to divulge more information, such as comprehensive fine location data[75] and video viewing histories.[76] Second, the manner of collection: for example, a defendant's promise not to collect personal data may itself create an expectation of privacy.[77]

69 IM Jackman, 'Restitution for Wrongs' (1989) 48 *Cambridge Law Journal* 302, 313.

70 Sarah Worthington, 'Reconsidering Disgorgement for Wrongs' (1999) 62 *Modern Law Review* 218, 236–237.

71 Ibid. 237.

72 *Restatement (Third) of Restitution and Unjust Enrichment* (n 19) § 43, Reporter's Note, para d.

73 [2001] 1 AC 268.

74 See, for example, *Restatement (Second) of Torts* (n 16) § 652B; *Hernandez* (n 16) 286.

75 See, for example, *Goodman* (n 6); *In re Google Location History Litig.* (n 19) 1157.

76 See, for example, *In re Vizio, Inc, Consumer Privacy Litigation* 238 F.Supp.3d 1204 (C.D. Cal. 2017).

77 See, for example, *In re Nickelodeon Consumer Privacy Litig* 827 F. 3d 262, 294 (3rd Cir. 2016) (holding that a reasonable factfinder could conclude that the promise not to collect 'ANY personal information' created an expectation of privacy with respect to browsing activity on the Nickelodeon website).

The second element focuses on 'the degree to which the intrusion is unacceptable as a matter of public policy'.[78] To determine whether a data collection practice is highly offensive, the court will consider all the circumstances, including the defendant's motives, the amount and sensitivity of the data collected, and the manner of collection.[79] The 'highly offensiveness' requirement arguably sets a high bar for finding liability.[80] Unauthorised collection and use of personal data in certain contexts have been held to be 'routine commercial behaviour' and, therefore, not highly offensive. For example, the court in *Folgelstrom v Lamps Plus, Inc* held that collecting customer addresses without permission for the purpose of sending coupons and advertisements was not highly offensive.[81]

Both the personhood and the efficiency-based justifications for awarding disgorgement for violations of property rights appear to support the availability of disgorgement for the intrusion tort. To begin with, many types of data in which individuals have a reasonable expectation of privacy are deeply connected to their personhood. Firstly, such data can reveal various characteristics that make up our identity. As the US Supreme Court noted in *Carpenter v US*, comprehensive cell phone location data over an extended period of time 'provides an intimate window into a person's life, revealing not only his particular movements, but through them his 'familial, political, professional, religious, and sexual associations'.[82] Secondly, such data can be analysed to generate predictions about other characteristics that we are likely to possess, as well as behavioural choices we are likely to make.[83] The predictions generated by such data can be used to deny us opportunities, manipulate our behaviour, or damage our reputation.[84] As Jack Balkin has pointed out, the mere possibility of data misuse might be sufficient to cause individuals to alter their 'identity, behavior, or other aspects of personal self-presentation'.[85] Applying Hanoch Dagan's theory, the more closely a type of personal data is attached to an individual's personhood,

78 *Hernandez* (n 16) 287.

79 See, for example, *Shulman v Group W Productions, Inc*, 18 Cal. 4th 200, 236 (1998); *Hernandez* (n 16) 287.

80 See, for example, *In re Tiktok, Inc, Consumer Privacy Litig* 565 F. Supp. 3d 1076, 1089 (N.D. Ill. 2021) ('Their intrusion upon seclusion claim similarly demands a 'highly offensive' intrusion, a 'high bar' that courts have found even unauthorized disclosure of user data to fail.').

81 195 Cal. App. 4th 986 (2011). See also *Yunker v Pandora Media, Inc*, No. 11-CV-3113 JSW, 2013 U.S. Dist. LEXIS 42691 (N.D. Cal. Mar. 26 2013) (collection of the plaintiffs' personally identifiable information (e.g., age, gender, location, and unique device identifier) and disclosure to advertising libraries for marketing purposes in purported violation of the defendant's terms of service were held to be not highly offensive); *Saleh v Nike, Inc* 562 F. Supp. 3d 503, 525 (C.D. Cal. 2021) (collection of users' mouse clicks, keystrokes, credit card information, IP addresses, locations, browser types and operating systems was insufficient to constitute 'a serious invasion of a protected privacy interest.').

82 138 S. Ct. 2206, 2217 (2018), quoting *US v Jones* 565 U.S. 400, 415 (2012) (Sotomayor, J., concurring).

83 Shoshana Zuboff, *The Age of Surveillance Capitalism: The Fight for a Human Future at the New Frontier of Power* (Profile Books 2019).

84 Jack M Balkin, 'The Three Laws of Robotics in the Age of Big Data' (2017) 78 *Ohio State Law Journal* 1217, 1238–1239.

85 Ibid.

the more appropriate it is to use disgorgement as a remedy to prevent unlawful collection and use of that type of data.

Moreover, Smith's information costs theory helps explain why individuals should have the right to exclude others from collecting data about themselves and why that right should be protected by disgorgement. First of all, the scope of personal data is wide-ranging – including different kinds of information about an individual's health, finances, education, biological characteristics, and social activities. Individuals have many interests in keeping their personal data private – to prevent data harm, enjoy freedom of thought, make independent decisions, develop autonomous personhood,[86] manage reputation, and establish relationships of intimacy and trust.[87] Such interests are multidimensional and likely difficult to measure or value. As Smith has explained, the right to exclude allows the right holder to determine the use of a resource without having to justify it.[88] It is, therefore, a low-cost way to protect a wide range of potential uses of that resource. In the context of personal data, granting individuals the right to exclude others from collecting data about themselves is a low-cost way to protect the wide range of interests that individuals have in using their data. The intrusion tort arguably protects individuals' right to exclude in situations in which the defendant's conduct is sufficiently serious to preclude multiple uses of personal data. Secondly, individuals' non-pecuniary interests in determining the use of their personal data cannot be easily measured, if at all, in monetary terms. As such, a defendant may be incentivised to interfere with individuals' right to exclude where such right is likely undervalued by damages rules.[89] The availability of disgorgement helps prevent opportunistic data collection and use in such cases.

The UK Supreme Court recently opined in *Lloyd v Google* that user damages could be awarded for misuse of private information, which prevents the relevant individuals from exercising their 'right to control the use of [their] information'.[90] To establish a misuse of private information claim, the plaintiff must demonstrate that she has a reasonable expectation of privacy in the information in question and that her right to privacy is not outweighed by other interests (e.g., the defendant's right to freedom of expression).[91] According to the Court, the value of the plaintiff's right to control the use of her information can be assessed by 'postulating a hypothetical

86 See, for example, Post (n 10) 973–974.

87 See, for example, Helen Nissenbaum, 'Privacy as Contextual Integrity' (2004) 79 *Washington Law Review* 119, 129–132.

88 Smith (n 60) 982.

89 Ibid. 985.

90 *Lloyd v Google* (n 12) [141].

91 See, for example, *Murray v Express Newspapers plc* [2008] EWCA Civ 446, [2009] Ch 481; *Vidal-Hall v. Google Inc* [2015] EWCA Civ 311, [2014] 1 WLR 4155. Paul Wragg, 'Recognising a Privacy-Invasion Tort: The Conceptual Unity of Informational and Intrusion Claims' (2019) 78 *Cambridge Law Journal* 409, 429. The English tort of misuse of private information is arguably easier to establish than the US intrusion tort since it does not contain a 'highly offensiveness' requirement.

negotiation and estimating what fee would reasonably have been agreed for releasing the defendant from the duty which it breached'.[92]

Our discussion suggests, however, that user damages, if assessed on that basis, may not adequately protect individuals' right to privacy for several related reasons. Firstly, it assumes that a reasonable plaintiff would agree to a fee to relinquish her right to exclude the defendant from collecting or using her personal data, which assumption may not always hold in practice.[93] Secondly, user damages arguably do not provide sufficient incentive for the defendant to bargain with the plaintiff for the right to collect the plaintiff's data. The intrusion tort protects an individual's right to exclude others from her private affairs at her own discretion, not merely a right to unreasonably refuse an offer to intrude into her affairs. User damages only require the defendant to pay the plaintiff a licensing fee that a reasonable plaintiff and a reasonable defendant would have agreed on.[94] If that fee is lower than the amount of profit that the defendant expects to receive from its misconduct, the defendant will have little incentive to seek the plaintiff's permission before collecting or using her data. Limiting the plaintiff's remedy to user damages essentially sanctions a compulsory licence regime for personal data.[95] By contrast, disgorgement more effectively protects the plaintiff's right to exclude by removing the defendant's economic incentive to interfere with that right. Thirdly, since the amount of user damages is likely determined by what the defendant and the plaintiff would have agreed on at the time of the unlawful collection, the plaintiff might suffer an important disadvantage at times of rapid technological development: it is difficult for a reasonable individual to predict how technological advances will affect the value or use of her data. As a result, the amount of user damages recoverable might be lower than what the plaintiff would have been able to demand at a later date.[96]

Recent US decisions suggest that disgorgement is available for violations of privacy rights. For example, in *Davis v Facebook*,[97] Facebook used plug-ins to track users' browsing histories when they visited third-party websites. The plaintiffs alleged, among other things, that Facebook acquired their 'sensitive and valuable personal information' and sold it to advertisers for a profit despite having guaranteed

92 *Lloyd v Google* (n 12) [140].

93 A number of commentators have observed that it is often fictional to argue that the plaintiffs have 'suffered a loss of bargaining opportunity … because [they] would never have agreed to bargain away [their] rights…'. See Andrew S Burrows, *Remedies for Torts, Breach of Contract, and Equitable Wrongs* (Oxford University Press 2019) 324. See also *Turf Club Auto Emporium Pte Ltd and others v Yeo Boong Hua & others* [2018] 2 SLR 655 [274], in which the Singapore Court of Appeal found an award of user damages inappropriate where 'it would be irrational or totally unrealistic to expect the parties to bargain for the release of the relevant [obligation]'.

94 *One Step (Support) Ltd v Morris-Garner and Another* [2018] UKSC 20, [2019] AC 649 [74].

95 *Restatement (Third) of Restitution and Unjust Enrichment* (n 19) § 3 and § 39.

96 The court may exercise its discretion to select a different valuation date, but the UK Supreme Court cautioned that the purpose of the valuation is not to 'arrive at a formula dependent on future events'. *Morris-Garner* (n 94) [108].

97 *In re Facebook, Inc Internet Tracking Litigation* (n 30).

not to do so in its Data Use Policy.[98] According to the Ninth Circuit, the plaintiffs' allegations were sufficient at the pleading stage to show that Facebook's profits were unjustly earned and that they were entitled to such profits based on the 'unauthorized use of their information'.[99]

Finally, disgorgement is not the only, or always the best, way to deter unlawful collection or misuse of personal data. Plausible alternatives include exemplary damages[100] and compensatory damages for loss of legal power to prevent the defendant's misconduct by applying for injunction ex ante.[101] Disgorgement might be preferable to these alternatives for two reasons. Firstly, it is less likely to over-deter as the defendant's liability is capped by its net profit.[102] Given the difficulty in determining in advance whether a defendant's conduct constitutes an intrusion tort, the prospect of exemplary damages might cause defendants to refrain from experimenting with potentially socially beneficial, yet controversial, uses of personal data. Secondly, the amount of disgorgement can be assessed with greater certainty than, for example, the amount of exemplary damages.[103]

2 Unauthorised Collection in Breach of Contract

Sometimes, an unauthorised collection of personal data is not sufficiently serious to amount to an intrusion tort, but nevertheless breaches a contractual term between the parties. Disgorgement is only available as a remedy for breach of contract in limited situations.[104] For example, disgorgement has been awarded against employees of intelligence agencies for disclosing information about their work without prior approval in breach of contract.[105] However, there is little consensus as to whether the remedy should be available in less exceptional circumstances.

As noted above, a possible justification for awarding disgorgement for unlawful collection or use of personal data is to protect special relationships of trust. At first sight, the relationship between a company and the users of its products or services does not fall within traditional types of fiduciary relationships, such as the relationships between trustees and beneficiaries and between lawyers and their clients. Nevertheless, the classes of fiduciary relationships are not closed. Academics such as Jack Balkin have argued that certain companies should be considered 'information

98 Ibid. 601–602.

99 Ibid. 601. See also *In re Google Location History Litig.* (n 19) 1160.

100 Normann Witzleb, 'Justifying Gain-Based Remedies for Invasions of Privacy' (2009) 29 *Oxford Journal of Legal Studies* 325, 354.

101 Kit Barker, 'Damages without Loss: Can Hohfeld Help?' (2014) 34 *Oxford Journal of Legal Studies* 631.

102 For a detailed analysis of deterrence as a justification for disgorgement, see Craig Rotherham, 'Deterrence as a Justification for Awarding Accounts of Profits' (2012) 32 *Oxford Journal of Legal Studies* 537.

103 See, for example., Witzleb (n 100) 354 (a gain-based award is 'not subject to the criticism of indeterminacy).

104 *Restatement (Third) of Restitution and Unjust Enrichment* (n 19) § 39.

105 *AG v. Blake* (n 73); *Snepp v United States* 100 S. Ct. 763 (1980).

fiduciaries' because they encourage users to trust them with their data and, at the same time, those users are vulnerable to these companies.[106] Even if 'information fiduciaries' are not truly fiduciaries, it is arguable that the social value of promoting trust and long-term relationships between individuals and certain companies may be sufficiently high to justify an award of disgorgement for breach of contract in limited circumstances.

Assume that a company is in a fiduciary relationship with its users. It is generally accepted that fiduciaries owe a duty of loyalty, which prohibits a fiduciary from putting her in a position in which her personal interest conflicts with that of the beneficiary. A clear example is where the company uses its users' personal data to harm their interests (e.g., by charging them a higher price or inducing addictive behaviour). Even where a company's use of personal data benefits the company without causing tangible harm to its users (e.g., using data to train its voice recognition system or to develop an automated dispute resolution system), such usage arguably should still amount to a breach of fiduciary duty for two reasons. Firstly, the plaintiffs' personal data may be analogised with a business opportunity that the defendant acquires in its capacity as a fiduciary. As such, the defendant should be required to account for profits made using that data.[107] Secondly, a fiduciary is required to observe 'the utmost good faith' in dealings with the beneficiary.[108] Since a company generally has to pay to acquire personal data from other sources, it treats its users less favourably by failing to pay them and, in turn, arguably breaches its duty to act in the utmost good faith.

VI CONCLUSION

This article examines two ways through which individuals may seek gain-based remedies for unlawful collection and use of personal data. First, it argues in favour of relying on the cause of action of unjust enrichment as a cost-effective way to protect individuals' right to privacy. Second, it argues that disgorgement should be available as a remedy for the intrusion tort and arguably for breach of privacy promises by information fiduciaries as well. Disgorgement might also prove to be an important remedial tool to deter companies from using personal data in ways that violate important social norms (e.g., training AI systems to commit crimes).

[106] Jack M Balkin, 'The Fiduciary Model of Privacy' (2020) 134 *Harvard Law Review Forum* 11. Cf Lina M Khan and David E Pozen, 'A Skeptical View of Information Fiduciaries' (2019) 133 *Harvard Law Review* 497.

[107] Thanks to Rory Gregson for raising this point. See, for example, *Boardman v Phipps* [1967] 2 AC 46 (HL). It does not matter that the beneficiary cannot exploit the business opportunity herself.

[108] *Restatement (Third) of Restitution and Unjust Enrichment* (n 19) § 43 cmt. e.

PART II

Property

14

Property/Personhood and AI

The Future of Machines

Kelvin F. K. Low, Wan Wai Yee and Wu Ying-Chieh

I INTRODUCTION

The use of tools was once believed to be a distinguishing feature of human intelligence which allowed us to deny personhood to animals, which like tools, were property rather than persons. Although many species of animals are now known to be highly intelligent and capable of using tools, the movement to confer upon them the legal status of personhood is at best marginal. Tools, on the other hand, have grown in sophistication, and machine intelligence is developing at an unprecedented speed. The duality of law's objects (property) and subjects (persons) is rampant within legal literature even if it is inaccurate. Slavery was particularly cruel not only because it objectified human beings but also because it attributed partial personhood to those self-same objects. Thus, slaves who ran away were guilty of theft from their masters.[1] Nevertheless, studying artificial intelligence (AI) through both lenses is enlightening. Three questions loom.

First, as we get increasingly dependent on our increasingly sophisticated tools, the law will need to consider when (if ever) machines cease to be mere tools and become a part of our person. In science fiction, the cyborg is part human and part machine, and the best stories in the genre probe the question of what it means to be human. Today, cyborgs walk among us. Does the law now need to contemplate the difficult question of when machines accede to our person?

Secondly, could (or have) our tools increase(d) in sophistication to the point when they may themselves be conferred legal personhood? What criteria should we use to determine which of our tools should be emancipated? Proponents of artificial intelligence (AI) personhood fall broadly into two camps, arguing either (i) on a moral basis or (ii) on utilitarian grounds.[2] Both merit careful (re)consideration.

[1] Donna Dickenson, *Property in the Body: Feminist Perspectives* (2nd edn, Cambridge University Press 2017) 5; Muireann Quigley, *Self-Ownership, Property Rights, and the Human Body: A Legal and Philosophical Analysis* (Cambridge University Press 2018) ch 8; Justinian, *Corpus Juris Civilis*, the Code, 6.1.1.

[2] In Lawrence B Solum's classic Lawrence B Solum, 'Legal Personhood for Artificial Intelligences' (1992) 70 *NCL Rev* 1231, his analysis in Part III is utilitarian whereas his analysis in Part IV is moral.

Finally, can the law of property serve as a bulwark against rapidly advancing machine intelligence that threatens to strip us of our personhood? In *Nineteen Eighty-Four*,[3] Orwell imagines a dystopia when most of humanity is subject to omnipresent surveillance and propaganda by the state. Today, many of us have surrendered vast amounts of personal data, not to the state[4] but to corporations, who trade in this information and seek not only to predict our desires but influence them in activities ranging from what we consume to how we exercise our democratic rights. Does property have a role to play in our rage against the machines?

II ACCESSION OF MACHINES TO PERSONS

At the heart of the anime film *Ghost in the Shell*[5] lies the paradox of Theseus' ship and the metaphysics of identity. Articulated for the cyberpunk, the paradox presents itself thus: 'does a human remain the same if we change all his body parts into prosthetics?'[6] Whilst the implications of widespread cyborg (and other) enhancement on the conception of personhood are much meditated,[7] the direct neurological man-machine interface depicted in science fiction remains more fiction than science despite media hype.[8] In the meantime, existing implants present different challenges as they 'lie at the crossroads of bodies and things'.[9] As they become more prevalent, and increasingly incorporate information and communication technology, they expose their human hosts 'to a variety of established cybercriminal attacks'.[10] Perhaps more troublingly, it has been suggested that:[11]

> [V]iewing a prosthesis (or indeed other medical devices, implanted or otherwise), as objects of property may not offer adequate redress for damage done. The reason being that remedies available for either criminal or negligent damage to property may not capture the vital function (mechanical, physiological, or otherwise) that these devices serve for persons. Moreover, they do not take into account of the incorporation into (the lives of) persons which they represent[.]

3 George Orwell, *Nineteen Eighty-Four: A Novel* (Secker & Warburg 1949).

4 Cf Ross Anderson, 'When China Sees All' (2020) 326 *The Atlantic* 59.

5 Mamoru Oshii (Director), *Ghost in the Shell* (Shochiku 1995).

6 Mirt Komel, 'The Ghost Outside Its Shell: Revisiting the Philosophy of Ghost in the Shell' (2016) 53 *Teorija in Praska* (Theory and Practice) 920, 922.

7 See, for example, Susan W Brenner, 'Humans and Humans+: Technological Enhancement and Criminal Responsibility' (2013) 19 *BUJ Sci & Tech L* 215; Yuval Noah Harari, *Homo Deus: A Brief History of Tomorrow* (Harper 2017).

8 Stefan Mitrasinovic and others, 'Silicon Valley New Focus on Brain Computer Interface: Hype or Hope for New Applications?' (2018) 7 *F1000Research* 1327.

9 Mark N Gasson and Bert-Jaap Koops, 'Attacking Human Implants: A New Generation of Cybercrime' (2013) 5 *LIT* 248, 277.

10 Ibid. 249.

11 Muireann Quigley and Semande Ayihongbe, 'Everyday Cyborgs: On Integrated Persons and Integrated Goods' (2018) 26 *Med Law Rev* 276, 291. See also I Goold, H Maslen and C Auckland, 'Damage to Prostheses and Compensation for Harm' [2017] Unpublished Working Paper, cited by Quigley and Ayihongbe at 289.

Implicit in this charge of inadequacy[12] is the suggestion that some prostheses should be treated by the law not as objects but as part of the law's subject in/onto which they have been implanted. So far as criminal penalties are concerned, comparisons of baseline sentencing guidelines[13] are distracting since they discount the wide discretion inherent in the sentencing process as well as the obvious role that aggravating factors play in sentencing.[14] Current sentencing guidelines relating to criminal damage explicitly list numerous aggravating factors of relevance to damage to prostheses, including: (i) damaged items of great value to the victim (whether economic, commercial, sentimental or personal value); and (ii) the victim is particularly vulnerable. Our focus is accordingly on private law. Presumably, the task of determining when an object (the prosthesis) should be treated as part of the person would entail the law drawing upon the analogical process of *accessio*, the process by which a minor object is subsumed into a major object so that the former loses its separate identity and becomes merged into the latter.[15] One of the problems of *accessio*, determining which object is major and which is minor, will presumably not arise with implants. As with the accession of chattels to land as fixtures, the human person (like land) would always retain his identity. But this is only one of the difficulties with *accessio*.

The law of fixtures, probably the most developed branch of *accessio*, is much criticised for its inconsistency,[16] with some going so far as to describe the current rules as 'unsatisfactory, unclear and unduly cumbersome.'[17] Whilst some of the confusion no doubt stems from the pivot to intention[18] in *Holland v Hodgson*[19] and/or a failure to acknowledge the shifting contexts in which the law of fixtures operates,[20] some of it at least stems from *accessio* being bound up with the difficult question of identity, the ambivalence of which appears insoluble.[21] It should thus come as little surprise that different people respond to different prostheses differently. In a study of men using prosthesis following amputation, researchers found that prosthetic embodiment – the integration of the prosthesis into their body image – was not universal.[22] While many

12 Leaving aside political considerations.

13 Quigley and Ayihongbe (n 12) 289–290.

14 Andrew Ashworth, *Sentencing and Criminal Justice* (6th edn, Cambridge University Press 2015) ch 5.

15 For a lesser-known aspect of *accessio*, see text accompanying nn 168–181.

16 Kevin Gray and Susan Francis Gray, *Elements of Land Law* (5th edn, Oxford University Press 2009) 37–38.

17 Michael Haley, 'The Law of Fixtures: An Unprincipled Metamorphosis' (1998) *Conv* 137, 144.

18 Peter Luther, 'Fixtures and Chattels: A Question of More or Less…' (2004) 24 *OJLS* 597.

19 (1872) LR 7 CP 328 (Ex).

20 Sean Thomas, 'Mortgages, Fixtures, Fittings and Security over Personal Property' (2015) 66 *N Ir Legal Q* 343. See also Alexander Waghorn, 'Sorting Out Mixtures of Property at Common Law' (2021) 84 *MLR* 61; Alvin W-L See, 'Fixtures, Mortgages and Retention of Title Clauses' (2021) *Conv* 167.

21 Theodore Scaltsas, 'The Ship of Theseus' (1980) 40 *Analysis* 152. Cf Christopher M Newman, 'Transformation in Property and Copyright' (2011) 56 *Vill L Rev* 251.

22 Adam Saradjian, Andrew R Thompson and Dipak Datta, 'The Experience of Men Using an Upper Limb Prosthesis Following Amputation: Positive Coping and Minimizing Feeling Different' (2008) 30 *Disabil Rehabil* 871. Cf Gill Haddow, *Embodiment and Everyday Cyborgs: Technologies That Alter Subjectivity* (Manchester University Press 2021), especially Chapter 2.

of the participants indicated emotional prosthetic embodiment,[23] others regarded their prosthesis only as a tool. Moreover, 'it was apparent that those who appeared to emotionally identify with their prosthesis could also consider it a tool at other times.'[24] It is likely that the average young adult is at least as attached to their mobile phones.[25] Are we all cyborgs already? As Tim Wu explained:[26]

> in all these science fiction stories, there's always this thing that bolts into somebody's head or you become half robot or you have a really strong arm that can throw boulders or something, but what is the difference between that and having a phone with you – sorry, a computer with you all the time that is tracking where you are, which you're using for storing all of your personal information, your memories, your friends, your communications, that knows where you are and does all kinds of powerful things and speaks different languages? I mean, with our phones we are actually technologically enhanced creatures…

In *Riley v California*,[27] John Roberts CJ remarked that modern mobile phones were 'such a pervasive and insistent part of daily life that the proverbial visitor from Mars might conclude they were an important feature of human anatomy'.

Rather than stepping into the philosophical quagmire of identity, a better solution may be to recognise the physicality of mental distress. The law seems to treat the mind as akin to the disembodied sentience frequently depicted in science fiction such as the antagonist of *Ghost in the Shell*, as a ghost without a shell. Inspired by Descartes' famous '*cogito, ergo sum*',[28] the Cartesian duality of *res cogitans*[29] (ghost) and *res extensa*[30] (shell) is losing, if it hasn't already lost, its grip on philosophy[31] and seems incompatible with developments in neuroscience. Cognition is increasingly believed to be embodied, so that: (i) the properties of an entity's body limits and constrains the concepts the entity is able to acquire; (ii) cognition

[23] Participants demonstrating emotional prosthetic embodiment 'had a strong emotional connection to it, experiencing the prosthesis as part of their body: ibid. 881.

[24] Ibid.

[25] Cynthia A Hoffner, Sangmi Lee and Se Jung Park, '"I Miss My Mobile Phone!": Self-Expansion via Mobile Phone and Responses to Phone Loss' (2016) 18 *New Media Soc* 2452. Cf Lisa Meloncon, 'Toward a Theory of Technological Embodiment' in Lisa Meloncon (ed), *Rhetorical Accessability: At the Intersection of Technical Communication and Disability Studies* (Routledge 2014) 67.

[26] Tim Wu, 'Constitution 3.0: Freedom, Technological Change and the Law', 44 (13 December 2011) <www.brookings.edu/wp-content/uploads/2012/04/20111213_constitution_technology.pdf>.

[27] 573 US 373 (2014), 385.

[28] Often translated as 'I think, therefore I am.' The expression first appears in vernacular French, '*je pense, donc je suis*', in René Descartes, *Discours de la Méthode Pour bien conduire sa raison, et chercher la vérité dans les sciences* (first published 1637), before appearing in Latin in René Descartes, *Principia Philosophiae* (first published 1644).

[29] Mental substance.

[30] Corporeal substance.

[31] Cf EJ Lowe, 'Dualism' in Brian P McLaughlin, Ansgar Beckermann and Sven Walter (eds), *The Oxford Handbook of Philosophy of Mind* (Oxford University Press 2009) 66, in which dualism is defended on the basis of property dualism rather than substance dualism: 'By a *substance*, in this context, is standardly meant an *individual object*, or *bearer of properties*, not a kind of stuff.'

can occur in the absence of algorithmic processes over symbolic representations; and (iii) the body plays a constitutive rather than merely causal role in cognitive processing.[32]

Cognition arguably even extends beyond the body.[33] Even early sceptics such as Block now accept that mobile phones do indeed extend our mind,[34] which perhaps explains our strong emotional attachment to them. Scientists have shown that grief has physical markers, showing up as chronic low-grade inflammation.[35] Our brains may be less for thinking than it is for managing the needs of our bodies so that '[t]here is no such thing as a purely mental cause, because every mental experience has roots in the physical budgeting of your body'.[36] Knowing all this, it is perhaps less surprising to find out that Alzheimer's and other neurological disorders may be connected to our gut.[37]

Nor is mere mental distress the idle matter that the law appears to regard it as, with claimants seemingly expected to just get over it. Lord Jauncey's statement in *Page v Smith* that 'ordinary emotions of anxiety, fear, grief, or transient shock are not conditions for which the law gives compensation'[38] is exemplary[39] of the law's condescending attitude towards pure mental distress despite emotional distress leading to an elevated risk of morbidity and mortality.[40] The reluctance of the law to expand liability in negligence to cover 'mere' mental distress lies not in science but in the fear that it would open the floodgates of litigation. This concern, though, is better addressed by limiting such compensation to a modest sum akin to the loss of amenity award in *Ruxley Electronics and Construction Ltd v Forsyth*.[41] Arguments along the lines that 'mere mental distress is a transient and less significant type of harm than personal injury',[42] drawing upon Cartesian duality, is quite simply unscientific.

[32] Lawrence Shapiro, *Embodied Cognition* (2nd edn, Routledge 2019) 4–5.

[33] Andy Clark and David Chalmers, 'The Extended Mind' (1998) 58 *Analysis* 7. See also Andy Clark, *Supersizing the Mind: Embodiment, Action, and Cognitive Extension* (Oxford University Press 2008).

[34] David J Chalmers, 'Extended Cognition and Extended Consciousness' in Matteo Colombo, Elizabeth Irvine and Mog Stapleton (eds), *Andy Clark and His Critics* (Oxford University Press 2019) 9 at 12, referring to his colleague Ned Block.

[35] Christopher Fagundes and others, 'Grief, Depressive Symptoms, and Inflammation in the Spousally Bereaved' (2019) 100 *Psychoneuroendocrinology* 190.

[36] Lisa Fieldman Barrett, 'Your Brain Is Not for Thinking' (*The New York Times*, 23 November 2020). See also Lisa Fieldman Barrett, *Seven and a Half Lessons about the Brain* (Mariner Books 2020) 107.

[37] John F Cryan and others, 'The Gut Microbiome in Neurological Disorders' (2020) 19 *Lancet Neurol* 179.

[38] [1996] AC 155 (HL), 171.

[39] See also *McLoughlin v O'Brian* [1983] 1 AC 410 (HL), 431 (Lord Bridge); *Hicks v Chief Constable of the South Yorkshire Police* (HL) [1992] 2 All ER 65, 69 (Lord Bridge); *White v Chief Constable of the South Yorkshire Police* [1999] 2 AC 455 (HL), 501.

[40] Christopher P Fagundes and E Lydia Wu, 'Matters of the Heart: Grief, Morbidity, and Mortality' (2020) 29 *Curr Dir Psychol Sci* 235.

[41] [1996] AC 344 (HL).

[42] Andrew Burrows, *Remedies for Torts, Breach of Contract, and Equitable Wrongs* (4th edn, Oxford University Press 2019) 287.

Cuts and bruises are likewise transient but no one would suppose that damages for such harms should be irrecoverable rather than merely modest. The only difference between minor personal injuries and mental distress is that, until relatively recently, we were unable to detect the physical markers of mental distress whereas cuts and bruises are readily visible. Today, we know that severe emotional stress can trigger a rare but serious condition known as broken-heart syndrome, known medically as Takotsubo[43] syndrome, so named because it is marked by a physical reshaping of the heart's left ventricle to resemble a narrow-necked Japanese pot of the same name.[44] It is now time for the law to abandon Cartesian duality, which could never withstand scrutiny: 'dualistic interaction, in either direction, is unintelligible *in Descartes's own terms*.'[45]

It is even arguable that there is simply no lacuna to compensation at all for damage to prostheses. Where mental distress is claimed in relation to property damage, as would surely be the case for prostheses, the law arguably already permits recovery for mental distress consequent upon trespass to goods[46] so that it is not obviously true that '[t]he range and scope of the damages which may be awarded [for personal injuries] are … much broader [than those for property damage].'[47] But if not, the long overdue recognition of the physicality of mental distress will fill the gap.

III THE EMANCIPATION OF THE MACHINES

The classical definition of legal personhood is that put forth by Gray: a 'person' is not necessarily human and instead describes a 'subject of legal rights and duties.'[48] In most legal systems, personhood extends to both natural persons (humans) and legal persons (non-humans – most famously, corporations). Our discussion needs not to be detained by symbolic conferral of personhood upon natural objects such as parks[49] and rivers,[50] idols,[51] and arguably robots.[52] Some such legal 'persons' are mere publicity stunts,[53] such as the robot Sophia, conferred Saudi citizenship in 2017, but

43 Octopus pot.

44 Christian Templin and others, 'Altered Limbic and Autonomic Processing Supports Brain-Heart Axis in Takotsubo Syndrome' (2019) 40 *Eur Heart J* 1183.

45 Margaret A Boden, *Minds as Machines: A History of Cognitive Science*, vol 1 (Clarendon Press 2006) 78.

46 Burrows (n 43) 285.

47 Quigley and Ayihongbe (n 12) 290.

48 John Chipman Gray, *The Nature and Sources of the Law* (2nd edn, Macmillan 1921) 27.

49 The Te Urewara Act 2014 conferred legal personhood upon the land that comprised the Te Urewara National Park.

50 The Te Awa Tupua (Whanganui River Claims Settlement) Act 2017 conferred legal personhood on the Te Awa Tupua. Abigail Hutchinson, 'The Whangnui River as a Legal Person' (2014) 39 *Alt LJ* 179.

51 *Pramatha Nath Mullick v Pradyumna Kumar Mullick* (1925) 2 MLJ 30.

52 Jaana Parvianen and Mark Coeckelbergh, 'The Political Choreography of the Sophia Robot: Beyond Robot Rights and Citizenship to Political Performances for the Social Robotics Market' (2020) *AI Soc* 1.

53 Ibid.

'condemned to a lifeless career in marketing'.[54] Some, for example, in *Pramatha Nath Mullick v Pradyumna Kumar Mullick*,[55] are smokescreens to further the rights of natural persons. Thus, while Lord Shaw accepted that '[a] Hindu idol is, according to long established authority, founded upon the religious customs of the Hindus, and the recognition thereof by courts of Law, a "juristic entity[,]"' his Lordship did not 'attribute rights and duties to an idol, but [made] its worshippers entitled and its *shebaits*[56] bound to the performance of the acts in question.'[57] Ostensibly a dispute over the removal of the idol to a custodian's own residence from its house of worship, and thus 'the will of the idol itself',[58] Lord Shaw uses the idol's personhood to camouflage his empowerment of the disempowered women of the family.[59] The enablement of natural objects in New Zealand, though sensationalistic, is also little different from the corporation. Although these objects 'enjoy' personhood, their rights and liabilities stem from acts and omissions on the part of natural persons appointed to act on their behalf rather than their actions per se. Accordingly, the Whanganui river cannot be held legally liable for drowning a person if it floods its banks unless this results from the culpable acts or omissions on the part of the office of the Te Pou Tupua. So regarded, there is little difference (apart from novelty) from corporate personhood.

A *The Moral Case for Personhood*

The moral case for AI personhood seems inextricably entangled with the Turing Test,[60] the test for intelligence devised by Alan Turing and modelled upon a once popular 'imitation game'.[61] Originally designed to test an interrogator's ability to correctly determine the gender of two players through questions, Turing postulated that we could instead test an interrogator's ability to determine man from machine. If they were undistinguishable, we could conclude that the machine was intelligent. One obvious criticism is that it is possible that an AI could give the appearance of thinking with no understanding at all, most famously by John Searle through his Chinese room thought experiment.[62] Though Searle's thought experiment is itself controversial, the Turing test has been criticised for encouraging trickery rather than developing true intelligence.[63] Our penchant to anthropomorphise all manner

54 Emily Reynolds, 'The Agony of Sophia, the World's First Robot Citizen Condemned to a Lifeless Career in Marketing' (*Wired UK*, May/June 2018).

55 (1925) 2 MLJ 30.

56 Variously translated as ministrant, custodian, and manager.

57 PW Duff, 'The Personality of an Idol' (1927) 3 *CLJ* 42, 46.

58 *Mullick v Mullick*, 41.

59 Ibid. 42.

60 AM Turing, 'Computing Machinery and Intelligence' (1950) 59 *Mind* 433.

61 Solum (n 3); Simon Chesterman, 'Artificial Intelligence and the Limits of Legal Personality' (2020) 69 *ICLQ* 819.

62 John Searle, 'Minds, Brains and Programs' (1980) 3 *Behav Brain Sci* 417.

63 Selmer Bringsjord, Paul Bello and David Ferrucci, 'Creativity, the Turing Test, and the (Better) Lovelace Test' (2011) 11 *Minds Mach* 3.

of non-human entities,[64] a phenomenon dubbed the 'Eliza effect'[65] in AI, arguably further degrades its value as a legal test on moral grounds. But is intelligence even the right test for personhood on moral grounds? Many animals are clearly intelligent but remain outside the first books on persons in the civilian *Institutes* of Gaius[66] and Justinian[67] as well as the common law *Commentaries* by Blackstone.[68] Bentham thus proposed that 'The question is not, 'can they reason?, nor can they talk? but, can they suffer? Why should the law refuse its protection to any sensitive being?'[69] But intelligence in this context is not what it seems, as Boden explains:[70]

> Artificial intelligence (AI) seeks to make computers do the sorts of things that minds can do.
>
> Some of these (e.g., reasoning) are normally described as 'intelligent'. Others (e.g., vision) aren't. …

It is hugely controversial whether true AI, or artificial general intelligence (AGI), is even possible. Is the mind resolvable to an algorithm?[71] Is embodiment significant?[72] Are neuroproteins necessary?[73] Recent breakthroughs in AI development (such as artificial neural networks) have drawn on the our understanding of the human brain, in particular, its use of massively parallel processing but there remain significant differences.[74] Although the move to a 5-nm architecture has allowed manufacturers to cram more than 10^{10} transistors on a single chip,[75] this is still fewer in number than the 10^{11} neurons in a human brain. Whereas each transistor within a computer may have 1–3 inputs/outputs each, each neuron has 10^3 inputs/outputs

64 Pascal Boyer, 'What Makes Anthropomorphism Natural: Intuitive Ontology and Cultural Representation' (1996) 2 *J R Anthropol Inst* 83.

65 Named after Joseph Weizenbaum's ELIZA program written in the mid-1960s: Douglas R Hofstadter, *Fluid Concepts & Creative Analogies: Computer Models of the Fundamental Mechanisms of Thought* (Basic Books 1995) 157–158.

66 Animals are classified as corporeal things in Book II of the *Institutes*, see Inst. II. 12–16.

67 Animals are classified as animate things that can be vindicated in Book VI of the *Digest* of Justinian, see D. VI. 1.3.

68 William Blackstone, *Commentaries on the Laws of England* (Clarendon Press 1765–1770).

69 Jeremy Bentham, *An Introduction to the Principles of Morals and Legislation* (W Pickering 1823) 236n.

70 Margaret A Boden, *Artificial Intelligence: A Very Short Introduction* (Oxford University Press 2018) 1.

71 Contrast Miguel AL Nicolelis, 'The Human Brain, the True Creator of Everything, Cannot Be Simulated by Any Turing Machine' in David J Linden (ed), *Think Tank: Forty Neuroscientists Explore the Biological Roots of Human Experience* (Yale University Press 2018) 263 with Michael D Mauk, 'There Is No Principle that Prevents Us from Eventually Building Machines that Think' in David J Linden (ed), *Think Tank: Forty Neuroscientists Explore the Biological Roots of Human Experience* (Yale University Press 2018) 270.

72 Shapiro (n 33). See also Rolf Pfeifer and Josh Bongard, *How the Body Shapes the Way We Think: A New View of Intelligence* (MIT Press 2007).

73 Boden (n 71) 121.

74 Liqun Luo, *Principles of Neurobiology* (2nd edn, Garland Science 2020) 21–23.

75 Stephen Shankland, 'Apple's A15 Bionic Chip Powers iPhone 13 with 15 Billion Transistors, New Graphics and AI' (*CNET*, 14 September 2021) <www.cnet.com/tech/mobile/apples-a15-bionic-chip-powers-iphone-13-with-15-billion-transistors-new-graphics-and-ai/>.

and the human brain has more than 10^{14} synapses. Whilst modern computers are digital in nature, the human brain employs both digital and analogue signalling. Furthermore, unlike power hungry AI, the human brain is remarkably efficient in power consumption terms.[76] Despite recent successes, such as AlphaGo defeating the *Go* world champion Lee Sedol,[77] building AGI is acknowledged to be 'orders of magnitude harder', requiring 'new paradigms'.[78] Whether these new paradigms lie around the corner (e.g., quantum computing) or another AI winter awaits,[79] no one knows.

In the meantime, the case for personhood for animals is instructive. Often cast as speciesism, the politics of animal personhood is founded on a failure to appreciate the duality of personhood. Being a person entails not just the conferment of rights but also the ascription of responsibilities. It is fallacious to emphasise the former but ignore the latter. The philosopher Daniel Dennett explored six themes that he considered necessary for moral personhood: (i) rationality; (ii) the capacity for the attribution of intentionality; (iii) the stance of others adopted with respect to the entity; (iv) the entity's capacity for reciprocating; (v) verbal communication; and (vi) self-consciousness.[80] The first three themes are interdependent.

> An Intentional system is a system whose behavior can be (at least sometimes) explained and predicated by relying on ascriptions to the system of *beliefs* and *desires* (and other intentionally characterized features – what I will call *Intentions* here, meaning to include hopes, fears, intentions, perceptions, expectations, etc.).[81]

As this entails the attribution to an entity of intentions for the purposes of predicting its behaviour regardless of whether there was such a subjective intention, Dennett recognises 'how bland this definition of *Intentional system* is'.[82] Plants could be intentional systems[83] and so it appears corporations are too.[84] So too robots given our tendency to anthropomorphise.[85] By reciprocity, Dennett requires that a person must be able to reciprocate the stance. In order to meet the test, it must be a '*second-order*

[76] Michael Le Page, 'Knowledge Means Power' (*New Scientist*, 13 October 2018) 22. See also Emily M Bender, Timnit Gebru, Angelina McMillan-Major and Shmargaret Shmitchell, 'On the Dangers of Stochastic Parrots: Can Language Models Be Too Big?' *FAccT '21: Proceedings of the 2021 ACM Conference on Fairness, Accountability, and Transparency* (3 March 2021) 610, 612–613.

[77] Greg Kohs (Director), *AlphaGo* (ro*co Films 2017).

[78] Boden (n 71) 43.

[79] Cf Luciano Floridi, 'AI and Its New Winter: From Myths to Realities' (2020) 33 *Philos Technol* 1.

[80] Daniel Dennett, 'Conditions of Personhood' in MF Goodman (ed), *What Is a Person?* (Humana Press 1988) 145.

[81] Ibid. 149.

[82] Ibid. 150. See also Daniel Dennett, 'Intentional Systems' (1971) 8 *J Philos* 87.

[83] Ibid. 150. On an extreme view, even rocks could be intentional systems: cf Graham Parkes, 'The Role of Rock in the Japanese Dry Landscape Garden' in François Berthier, *Reading Zen in the Rocks: The Japanese Dry Landscape Garden* (Graham Parkes tr, University of Chicago Press 2000) 85, 111–112, citing the 作庭記 *Sakuteiki* ('Records of Garden Making'), the oldest published text on garden making in Japan.

[84] William G Weaver, 'Corporations as Intentional Systems' (1998) 17 *J Bus Ethics* 87.

[85] Cf Pfeifer and Bongard (n 73) 72–77.

Intentional system', that is, 'an Intentional system that itself adopted the Intentional stance toward other objects'.[86] In order for S to be such a system, it must be capable of believing that another system T desires p or hoping that T fears q.

For the significance of verbal communication, Dennett turns to Grice's theory of meaning. As Dennett explains, 'Grice attempts to define what he calls non-natural meaning, an utterer's meaning something by uttering something, in terms of the *intentions* of the utter.'[87] According to Grice:[88]

> 'U meant something by uttering x' is true if, for some audience A, U uttered s intending
>
> (1) A to produce a particular response r.
> (2) A to think (recognize) that U intends (1).
> (3) A to fulfil (1) on the basis of his fulfilment of (2).

As Dennett explains, this entails 'not only a second-, but a third-order Intention: U must *intend* that A *recognize* that U *intends* that A produce *r*.'[89] Genuine reciprocity requires third-order intentions. Dennett explains that Grice's analysis 'illuminates so many questions.'[90] Pertinently:[91]

> Do we communicate with computers in Fortran? Fortran seems to be a language; it has a grammar, a vocabulary, a semantics. The transactions in Fortran between man and machine are often viewed as cases of *man communicating with machine*, but such transactions are pale copies of human verbal communication precisely because the Gricean conditions for non-natural meaning have been bypassed. There is no room for them to apply. Achieving one's ends in transmitting a bit of Fortran to the machine does not hinge on getting the machine to recognize one's intentions.

Finally, and here the significance of being a subject of duties rises to the fore, Dennett sets out his sixth condition:

> *If I am to be held responsible for an action* … I must have been *aware* of that action under that description.[92]
>
> The capacities for verbal communication and for awareness of one's actions are thus essential in one who is going to be amenable to argument or persuasion, such reciprocal adjustment of interests achieved by mutual exploitation of rationality, is a feature of the optimal mode of personal interaction.[93]

86 Dennett (n 81) 151.
87 Ibid. 156.
88 HP Grice, 'Utterer's Meaning and Intentions' (1969) 78 *Philos Rev* 147, 151.
89 Dennett (n 81) 156.
90 Ibid. 159.
91 Ibid.
92 Ibid. 161.
93 Ibid. 161–162.

Quoting Harry Frankfurt:[94]

> Besides wanting and choosing and being moved to do this or that, men may also want to have (or not to have) certain desires or motives. They are capable of wanting to be different, in their preferences and purposes, from what they are. Many animals appear to have the capacity for what I call 'first order desires' or 'desires of the first order,' which are simply desires to do or not do one thing or another. No animal other than man, however, appears to have the capacity for reflective self-evaluation that is manifested in the formation of second-order desires.

Notably, Dennett does not invoke the concept of qualia, which he once explained as 'an unfamiliar term for something that could not be more familiar to each of us: the *ways things seem to us*.'[95] Also known as phenomenal consciousness – the sensation of pain or colour – qualia is hugely controversial. Dubbed by Chalmers as the 'hard problem of consciousness',[96] some resort to panpsychism, which in modern practice is 'the thesis that some fundamental physical entities [such as quarks or photons] have mental states.'[97] Dennett dismisses qualia,[98] which explains why he does not consider it a condition of personhood but if he is wrong, then this would be another obstacle to AI personhood.[99] Without qualia, could AI suffer?

Some may argue that it is wrong to conclude that animals lack the moral agency for personhood, at least in respect of *some* animals but if so, another hurdle to personhood remains. Regardless of whether one subscribes to Morgan's canon of parsimony,[100] which dictates that we should attribute to an organism as little intelligence as will suffice to account for its behaviour, the impossibility of decoding non-human (alien) minds remains a formidable hurdle.[101] Even if animals had the capacity for third-order intentions and second-order desires, how would we know? Much of the literature arguing for AI personhood assumes that we would understand our AI, as if they would communicate with us in English. We would do well to remember Wittgenstein's famous remark, 'If a lion could talk we could not understand him.'[102] As Boden explained, 'to recognize the creativity of a creative robot we would need

[94] Harry G Frankfurt, 'Freedom of the Will and the Concept of a Person' in Paul Russell and Oisin Deery (eds), *The Philosophy of Free Will: Essential Readings from the Contemporary Debates* (Oxford University Press 2013) 253, 254.

[95] Daniel C Dennett, 'Quining Qualia' in A. Marcel and E. Bisiach (eds), *Consciousness in Contemporary Science* (Oxford University Press 1988) 42.

[96] David J Chalmers, 'Facing Up to the Problem of Consciousness' (1995) 2 *J Conscious Stud* 200, 201.

[97] David Chalmers, 'Panpsychism and Panprotopsychism' in Godehard Bruntrup and Ludwig Jaskolla (eds), *Panpsychism: Contemporary Perspectives* (Oxford University Press 2016) 19.

[98] Dennett (n 96).

[99] Boden (n 71) 108–117.

[100] C Lloyd Morgan, 'An Introduction to Comparative Psychology' in Daniel Robinson, *The Mind* (Oxford University Press 1998) 260.

[101] David McFarland, *Guilty Robots, Happy Dogs: The Question of Alien Minds* (Oxford University Press 2008). Cf Roger T Ames and Takahiro Nakajima (eds), *Zhuangzi and the Happy Fish* (University of Hawaii Press 2015).

[102] Ludwig Wittgenstein, *Philosophical Investigations* (GEM Anscombe tr, 2nd edn, Basil Blackwell Ltd 1958), 225.

at least to share its conceptual spaces, if not its values too.'[103] Our inability to understand current AI given its opacity[104] does not bode well for our ability to understand AGI, though it may help AI researchers avoid the 'AI effect, which occurs when onlookers discount the behavior of an AI program by arguing that it is not real intelligence. … when one understands the technology, the magic disappears.'[105]

An underappreciated risk of legal personhood for alien minds (whether animals or robots) is the subversion of their legal personality by natural persons for their own ends, as demonstrated in *Naruto v Slater*,[106] the famous monkey selfie case. As is well-known, after a professional photographer, David Slater, left his camera unattended in an animal reserve in Indonesia, a Celebes crested macaque, named Naruto, picked it up and took a selfie with it.[107] When Slater and his partners published the monkey selfies and claimed copyright in them, People for the Ethical Treatment of Animals (PETA) sued them for copyright infringement on behalf of Naruto. After experiencing a hostile reception in court,[108] PETA settled and 'abandoned Naruto's substantive claims in what appears to be an effort to prevent the publication of a decision adverse to PETA's institutional interests'.[109] According to the majority, '[w]ere he capable of recognizing this abandonment, we wonder whether Naruto might initiate an action for breach of confidential relationship against his (former) next friend, PETA, for its failure to pursue his interests before its own.'[110] Smith J echoed, '[a]nimal-next-friend standing is particularly susceptible to abuse'.[111] Likewise robot next-friends. It is preferable to acknowledge the especial nature of sentient animals without disturbing their property status,[112] along the lines of France's amendment of its Civil Code to describe animals as 'living beings capable of feeling'[113]

[103] Margaret A Boden, 'Could a Robot Be Creative – And Would We Know?' in Kenneth M Ford, Clark Glymour and Patrick J Hayes (eds), *Thinking about Android Epistemology* (MIT Press 2006) 217, 232.

[104] Simon Chesterman, 'Through a Glass, Darkly: Artificial Intelligence and the Problem of Opacity' (2021) 69 *AJCL* 271.

[105] Michael Haenlein and Andreas Kaplan, 'A Brief History of Artificial Intelligence: On the Past, Present, and Future of Artificial Intelligence' (2019) 61 *Calif Manag Rev* 5, 6, referencing Arthur Clarke's Third Law: 'Any sufficiently advanced technology is indistinguishable from magic': see Arthur C Clarke, *Profiles of the Future: An Inquiry into the Limits of the Possible* (Gollancz 1974) 39.

[106] 888 F3d 418 (9th Cir 2018). See also Richard L Cupp Jr, 'Considering the Private Animal and Damages' (2021) 98 *Wash U L Rev* 1313, 1333–1341.

[107] Slater claims that he planned for the selfies to be taken: see David J Slater, 'Sulawesi macaques…' (16 August 2014) <www.djsphotography.co.uk/original_story.html>.

[108] Cupp Jr (n 107) 1337.

[109] *Naruto v Slater* (n 107) 437 (Smith J).

[110] Ibid. 421 n 3.

[111] Ibid. 432 (Smith J).

[112] Richard L Cupp Jr, 'Animals as More than 'Mere Things,' but Still Property: A Call for Continuing Evolution of the Animal Welfare Paradigm' (2016) 84 *U Cincinnati L R* 1023. Cf Angela Fernandez, 'Not Quite Property, Not Quite Persons: A 'Quasi' Approach for Nonhuman Animals' [2019] 5 *CJCCL* 155.

[113] Translated by Professor Mireille Butler for Cupp Jr, 'Animals as More than 'Mere Things,' but Still Property' at 1045 n 124. Article 515–14 of the French Civil Code provides: *Les animaux sont des êtres vivants doués de sensibilité. Sous réserve des lois qui les protègent, les animaux sont soumis au régime des biens.* (Trans: Animals are living beings capable of feeling. However, they remain subject to the laws that protect them and to the regime of tangible property.)

or the UK Animal Welfare (Sentience) Act 2022, which seeks to establish a committee with oversight of government policy 'on the welfare of animals as sentient beings'.

B *The Utilitarian Case for Personhood*

To justify granting legal personhood upon an AI system on utilitarian grounds, it should, at the minimum, lead to efficient economic outcomes, necessitating consideration of whether said goals can be achieved through less costly alternative solutions. For instance, as Hansmann and Kraakman explain, the corporation is conferred legal personhood to achieve the goal of asset partitioning and thereby facilitate commerce.[114] Corporate personhood not only limits the ability of a corporation's creditors to look only to its assets in enforcement actions but also shields its assets from the claims of the creditors of its owners or managers. Owners are thus encouraged to invest capital in the corporation, knowing that such investment represents their maximum loss. Without the device of legal personhood, it would be impossible to achieve the separation of the assets between the personal (non-business) assets of the owners/managers and business assets save through costly individual negotiation with all creditors, both personal and business, a costly exercise that also entails potential moral hazard.

Scholars have argued that by conferring legal personhood, an AI system is able to be held directly *accountable* for its failings. It is inappropriate to hold the owner of an AI system or its programmer accountable when neither is aware of or able to predict what the AI system is doing.[115] As AI systems do not naturally possess assets, Solum and others have argued for either adequate capitalisation or mandatory insurance.[116] Rothenberg goes further and discusses whether AI system can own property.[117] It is of course true that AI systems can generate income[118] but this neither dictates a separate patrimony nor accountability. Accountability, particularly criminal liability, is more complex to address since the core reasons for criminal liability are based on retribution, deterrence, and rehabilitation, all of which are designed with human actors in mind.[119] Retribution and rehabilitation seem to be inappropriate sanctions on legal fictions though it is arguable that deterrence remains valid for corporations,[120] which

[114] Henry Hansmann and Reinier Kraakman, 'The Essential Role of Organizational Law' (2000) 110 *Yale LJ* 387.

[115] See for example, Simon Chesterman, 'Artificial Intelligence and the Problem of Autonomy' (2020) 1 *Notre Dame J Emerging Technologies* 210; Chesterman (n 62).

[116] Solum (n 3), 1235–1237.

[117] D Rothenberg, 'Can Siri 100 Buy Your Home? The Legal and Policy Based Implications of Artificial Intelligent Robots Owning Real Property' (2016) 11 *Wash J L Tech & Arts* 439; Rafael Dean Brown, 'Property Ownership and the Legal Personhood of Artificial Intelligence' (2021) 30 *Information & Communications Technology Law* 208.

[118] See for example, Lynn M. LoPucki, 'Algorithmic Entities' (2017) 95 *Wash U L Rev* 887.

[119] V Khanna, 'Corporate Criminal Liability: What Purpose Does It Serve?' (1996) 109 *Harv L Rev* 1477.

[120] See for example, Cindy R Alexander and Jennifer Arlen, 'Does Conviction Matter? The Reputational and Collateral Effects of Corporate Crime' in Jennifer Arlen (ed), *Research Handbook on Corporate Crime and Financial Misdealing* (Edward Elgar 2018) 87. Cf Nick Werle, 'Prosecuting Corporate Crime

have been attributed acts and intentions by human actors.[121] In any event, the current trend in several advanced jurisdictions is to review its existing laws with a view of to making easier to prosecute corporations.[122] Thus, conferring of legal personhood reflects a choice made by the legal system. Just as legal personhood can be conferred on corporations, there is no a priori reason why it cannot be conferred on AI systems.[123] However, just because we can do something does not mean that we should do it'[124] and the customary analogies with corporations are often superficial to the point of being deeply flawed, making the case for personhood appear like nothing more than a naked attempt to shift liability away from the developers or users of AI systems.[125]

The demand for asset partitioning does not apply to AI systems in the same way as it does to corporations and may even lead to perverse incentives. First, conferring personhood on an AI system insulates the assets held by manufacturers, programmers, or users of the AI system from the legal claims of the third parties, particularly tort victims, creating moral hazard. Malevolent actors could deliberately deploy an AI system to commit fraud.[126] It is true that such actors have been able to use the corporate form to perpetrate fraud, but the law has developed tools to ensure the accountability of such human actors. However, this array of tools is complex and includes rules on the lifting of the corporate veil and agency principles.[127] It is often assumed or asserted that the same or similar tools can be applied to AI systems,[128] but it is not obvious how such rules are to be transplanted. For corporations, the primary role of attribution is to attribute mental states of natural persons to a system. For AI, it is presumably the reverse (to hold natural persons responsible) with the additional complication that any mental state on the part of the AI is entirely fictional.

Secondly, corporations have internal governance structures such as the requirement that the corporations be managed by boards of directors (who must be natural

When Firms Are Too Big to Jail: Investigation, Deterrence, and Judicial Review' (2019) 128 *Yale LJ* 1366; PC Yeager, 'The Elusive Deterrence of Corporate Crime' (2016) 15 *Criminology & Public Policy* 439.

121 *Meridian Global Funds Management Asia v Securities Commission* [1995] 2 AC 500 (PC) (holding that whose state of mind is to be attributed to the corporation depends on the purpose and context of attribution).

122 Australian Law Reform Commission, 'Corporate Criminal Responsibility' (Final Report No 136, April 2020); Law Commission of England and Wales, 'Corporate Criminal Liability: A Discussion Paper' (9 June 2021). See also GR Sullivan, 'The Attribution of Culpability to Limited Companies' (1996) 55 *CLJ* 515; Elise Bant, 'Culpable Corporate Minds' (2021) 48 *UWA L Rev* 352.

123 Shawn Bayern, 'The Implications of Modern Business Entity Law for the Regulation of Autonomous Systems' (2015) 19 *Stanf Technol L Rev* 93.

124 Chesterman (n 62).

125 Eliza Mik, 'AI as a Legal Person?' in Jyh-An Lee, Reto Hilty and Kung-Chung Liu (eds), *Artificial Intelligence and Intellectual Property* (Oxford University Press 2021) 419, 435–436.

126 See for example, Adam Janofsky, 'AI Could Make Cyberattacks More Dangerous, Harder to Detect' (*The Wall Street Journal*, 13 November 2018); S Vaithianathasamy, 'AI vs AI: Fraudsters Turn Defensive Technology into an Attack Tool' [2019] *Comput Fraud Secur* 6.

127 See generally, Alan Dignam and Peter Oh, 'Rationalising Corporate Disregard' (2020) 40 *LS* 187

128 See for example, Chesterman (n 62) 826.

persons save in some offshore jurisdictions)[129] who are elected by the shareholders and who can be removed by the shareholders. Directors are subjected to stringent fiduciary duties and duties of care to protect the corporation from opportunistic self-preference and reckless behaviour. If AI systems are to be conferred legal personhood, an equivalent governance structure would need to be put in place. While one can certainly design a framework to allow for AI systems to be managed by natural persons, whether owners or otherwise (e.g., programmers), it is not at all clear that the existing corporate law structures are adaptable for AI systems.

While duties owed by directors to corporations are variously theorised as maximising value for the shareholders solely or for the corporation as a whole including stakeholders,[130] shareholders only have limited power to influence board decisions outside of the appointment process. Directors' decision-making is generally protected by the business judgement rule unless afflicted by conflicts of interest. Although Watson argues that the use of AI systems in the boardroom – creating a 'self-driving corporation'[131] – is not as transformational as it seems, we disagree. It is true that human directors are not necessarily more constrained than AI systems, given both the omnipresence of the goal of maximising value and the business judgement rule. Thus, shareholder pressure to consider environment, sustainability, and governance (ESG) considerations may come to nought in light of the aforementioned.[132] The possibility of abuse of the corporate form by human actors does not demonstrate that existing structures to constrain such abuse can be readily transplanted to restrain AI systems. For example, Watson argues that we broaden the situations in which the corporate veil is lifted, but this presupposes both that veil-lifting, notoriously narrowly circumscribed, is an adequate constraint on misuse of the corporate form and that it is easy to map the roles of shareholders and directors to those of programmers, manufacturers, and users.[133] Moreover, although corporations may

[129] For example, Cayman Islands (Companies Act 2021 Rev Ed), Bermuda (Companies Act 1981) and British Virgin Islands (Business Companies Act 2004) allow for corporate directors. See Conyers, 'Comparison of Laws in Bermuda, BVI and Cayman Islands Relating to Offshore Companies', available at <www.conyers.com/wp-content/uploads/2019/10/Comparison_of_Laws_in_Bermuda_BVI_and_Cayman_relating_to_Offshore_Companies-BDACAYBVI-1.pdf>.

[130] In the United States, the prevailing theory of the duties of directors is that of 'shareholder primacy' where directors owe duties to shareholders; in the UK, the directors' duties are codified in section 172 of the UK Companies Act 2006 which provides, among others, that there is the duty to promote the success of the company for the benefit of its members as a whole. See generally Iris H-Y Chiu, 'Operationalising a Stakeholder Conception in Company Law' (2016) 10 *Law Financial Mark Rev* 173; Martin Gelter, 'Taming or Protecting the Modern Corporation? Shareholder-Stakeholder Debates in a Comparative Light' (2011) 7 *NYU J L & Bus* 641.

[131] Susan Watson, 'Viewing Artificial Persons in the AI Age through the Lens of History' in Andrew Godwin, Lee Pey Woan and Rosemary Teele Langford (eds), *Technology and Corporate Law: How Innovation Shapes Corporate Activity* (Edward Elgar 2021) 21. The term 'self-driving corporation' was coined by John Armour and Horst Eidenmuller, 'Self-Driving Corporations?' (2020) 10 *Harv Bus L Rev* 87.

[132] Ibid.

[133] Ibid.

also be regarded as 'systems[,] not just aggregations of individuals',[134] they are socio-technical systems[135] rather than the purely technical AI systems. Socio-technical systems are institutions that are constituted by individuals which, in turn, are socially constituted by institutions.[136] AI systems are not socio-technical because although programmers, manufacturers, and users may influence the system, they neither constitute nor are they constituted by it.

Third, conferring legal personhood on AI system dilutes criminal liability to a vanishing point. Like corporations, AI systems have 'no soul to be damned, and no body to be kicked'.[137] Early treatment of corporations treated them as legal fictions and was incapable of possessing *mens rea*.[138] However, the modern approach is to hold corporations criminally liable for almost all of the offences except those that can only be conducted by humans (such as rape and murder). Key areas of such liabilities that have been prominent include workplace health and safety violations,[139] environmental violations,[140] prevention of bribery,[141] and securities offences. Where *mens rea* or intention is required for the criminal offence, the law has attributed *mens rea* on the part of appropriate responsible persons to the corporation.[142] The unpredictability and opacity of modern AI make an equivalent exercise for AI fraught with difficulty.[143]

Deterrence is directed at human directors, managers, and employees as part of a socio-technical system. Thus, criminal corporate liability is often co-existent with directorial or manager criminal liability, and the prosecution has the discretion to prosecute the more appropriate defendant. Where it is not, there are good policy reasons for treating corporations as autonomous legal persons for the purposes of criminal and regulatory responsibilities since corporations as socio-technical systems are more than mere aggregations of individuals, so that '[c]orporate negligence does not necessarily resolve to individual negligence.'[144] Corporations have access to resources

134 Brent Fisse and John Braithwaite, 'The Allocation of Responsibility for Corporate Crime: Individualism, Collectivism and Accountability' (1988) 11 *Syd L Rev* 468, 479.

135 See FE Emery and EL Trist, 'Socio-Technical Systems' in CW Churchman and M Verhulst (eds), *Management Science Models and Techniques*, vol 2 (Pergamon 1960) 83.

136 Fisse and Braithwaite (n 135) 478.

137 John C Coffee Jr, '"No Soul to Damn: No Body to Kick': An Unscandalized Inquiry into the Problem of Corporate Punishment' (1981) 79 *Mich L Rev* 386, quoting and popularising Edward, First Baron of Thurlow 1731–1806. Cf CMV Clarkson, 'Kicking Corporate Bodies and Damning Their Souls' (1996) 59 *MLR* 557.

138 See Christopher D Stone, 'The Place of Enterprise Liability in the Control of Corporate Conduct' (1980) 90 *Yale LJ* 1, 3, 70; GOW Mueller, 'Mens Rea and the Corporation' (1957) 19 *U Pitt L Rev* 21, 22.

139 Jennifer Hill, 'Corporate Criminal Liability in Australia: An Evolving Corporate Governance Technique?' (2003) 1 *Journal of Business Law* 1.

140 Ibid.

141 Ibid.

142 Sullivan (n 123).

143 Cf *Quoine Pte Ltd v B2C2 Ltd* [2020] SGCA(I) 2, [2020] 2 SLR 20, criticised in Kelvin FK Low and Eliza Mik, 'Lost in Transmission: Unilateral Mistakes in Automated Contracts' (2020) 136 *LQR* 563.

144 Fisse and Braithwaite (n 135) 486.

and are able to put in place adequate compliance programmes or controls to ensure that wrongs are not perpetrated upon others. Criminal liability ensures deterrence on the part of the corporations from conducting further wrongs (or at least results in corporations improving their corporate compliance programmes). Reputational sanctions against corporations guilty of criminal liability will result in costs to the corporations as suppliers, customers, and other counter-parties become reluctant to deal with such corporations or demand more favourable terms to mitigate against the risks of dealing with them. At the same time, human directors, managers, and employees[145] also face reputational risks from mere association with such corporations. Even so, however, the efficacy of criminal liability against the corporate form is already much criticised, with commentators remarking that 'the problem of non-prosecution of corporate managers … is now pandemic in modern societies.'[146] Utilitarian legal personhood for AI systems would create problems of a much greater magnitude because these systems are purely technical rather than socio-technical.[147] With no natural persons constituting the AI legal person, it is not obvious at all how criminal deterrence (already regarded as inadequate for corporations) would operate, facilitating abuse[148] for no obvious good (whereas corporate personhood arguably serves some plausible human objective). In short, we can ≠ we should.

If the analogy to corporations is flawed, are there other utilitarian theories which can justify granting legal personhood to AI systems? One argument for doing so is that it is often difficult for victims to establish and allocate fault among the multitude of potential defendants, which include programmers, manufacturers, and users because of the opacity of AI.[149] However, surely this 'problem' is more easily resolved by setting up a no-fault insurance system funded by AI developers[150] without the complexity of legal personhood.

In intellectual property (IP) circles, it has been argued that in sophisticated AI systems which create the products independently, the creator of the *output* cannot be said to be the user of the system but should be the AI system itself,[151] often implying that the AI system should thus be conferred legal personhood to hold IP rights. Without denying that AI systems can be creative,[152] the intersection of law

[145] Cf *Bank of Credit and Commerce International SA v Ali* [2001] UKHL 8, [2001] 2 WLR 735.

[146] Fisse and Braithwaite (n 135) 512.

[147] Cf Bayern (n 124).

[148] LoPucki (n 119).

[149] Yueh-Ping (Alex) Yang and Mengyi Wang, 'Tackle AI Liability through Legal Personhood: A Law and Economics Perspective' (unpublished on file with authors).

[150] Cf Craig Brown, 'Deterrence in Tort and No-Fault: The New Zealand Experience' (1985) 73 *Cal L Rev* 976. But see David Enoch, 'Tort Liability and Taking Responsibility' in John Oberdeek (ed), *Philosophical Foundations of the Law of Torts* (Oxford University Press 2014).

[151] Colin Davies, 'An Evolutionary Step in Intellectual Property Rights' [2011] 27 *Comput L Secur Rev* 601. Cf Belinda Bennett and Angela Daly, 'Recognising Rights for Robots: Can We? Will We? Should We?' (2020) 12 *LIT* 60, 71–76.

[152] Cf Marcus du Sautoy, *The Creativity Code: How AI Is Learning to Write, Paint and Think* (Belknap Press 2019).

and technology is bedevilled by the conflation of identical terms with vastly different specialised meanings. The conflation of legal and technical meanings of autonomy[153] exacerbates our already natural instincts to anthropomorphise various non-human entities,[154] leading to conclusions best described as 'nonsense upon stilts.'[155] After all, 'it simply does not make any sense to allocate intellectual property rights to machines because they do not need to be given incentives to generate output.'[156] Whilst AI may diminish the effort required for user creativity or invention, this is hardly a novel problem, with copyright law having worked through precisely such an argument vis-à-vis photography.[157]

A variation of this argument posits that while an AI system is not yet a legal person, it should nevertheless be acknowledged as an inventor, with any patent it produces being allocated to its owner.[158] It is the goal of the Artificial Inventor Project to propound this hypothesis worldwide.[159] Early results were underwhelming[160] but they recently successfully appealed the decision of the Australian Patent Office[161] rejecting a patent. The Australian Federal Court in *Thaler v Commissioner of Patents*[162] held that an AI entity, DABUS (Device for the Autonomous Boot-strapping of Unified Sentience), could be regarded as an inventor under the Australian Patents Act 1990 even if it could not itself (lacking personhood) be granted a patent. Beach J concluded that Dr Stephen Thaler, the inventor of DABUS, could be said to either be entitled to have the patent assigned to him[163] or be a person who derived title from the inventor.[164] These same arguments failed in England both before the High Court[165] and

153 Mik (n 126) 422–424.

154 Boyer (n 65).

155 Carys Craig and Ian Kerr, 'The Death of the AI Author' (2021) 52 *Ottawa L Rev* 31 at 43, adapting Jeremy Bentham, 'Rights, Representation, and Reform: Nonsense upon Stilts and Other Writings on the French Revolution' in P Schofield, C Pease-Watkin and C Blamires (eds), *The Collected Works of Jeremy Bentham* (Oxford University Press 2002) 317.

156 Pamela Samuelson, 'Allocating Ownership Rights in Computer-Generated Works' (1985) 47 *U Pitt L Rev* 1185, 1199.

157 Chesterman (n 62) 835. See also Kalin Hristov, 'Artificial Intelligence and the Copyright Dilemma' (2017) 57 *IDEA: The IP L Rev* 431, 435–436.

158 Ryan Abbott, 'I Think, Therefore I Invent: Creative Computers and the Future of Patent Law' (2016) 57 *BC L Rev* 1079. Cf Belinda Bennett and Angela Daly, 'Recognising Rights for Robots: Can We? Will We? Should We?' (2020) 12 *LIT* 60, 71–76.

159 Applications were lodged in Australia, Brazil, Canada, China, Europe, Germany, India, Israel, Japan, New Zealand, Republic of Korea, Saudi Arabia, South Africa, Switzerland, Taiwan, the United Kingdom, and the United States.

160 Only South Africa issued a patent without litigation. See also USPTO, 'Public Views on Artificial Intelligence and Intellectual Property Policy' (October 2020).

161 *Stephen L Thaler* [2021] APO 5.

162 [2021] FCA 879 (hereinafter *Thaler* FCA). Now overruled, see *Commissioner of Patents v Thaler* [2022] FCAFC 62.

163 [2021] FCA 879, [166]–[176] (under s 15(b) of the Patents Act 1990).

164 Ibid. [177]–[199] (under s 15(c) of the Patents Act 1990).

165 *Thaler v The Comptroller-General of Patents, Designs and Trade Marks* [2020] EWHC 2412 (Pat), [2020] Bus LR 2146, [49] (hereinafter *Thaler* EWHC). See also *Thaler v Hirschfield* Case No. 1:20-cv-00903 (United States District Court, Eastern District of Virginia) (2 September 2021).

the Court of Appeal,[166] with Marcus Smith J describing the argument as 'hopeless' because:[167]

> DABUS would – by reason of its status as a thing and not a person – be incapable of conveying any property to Dr Thaler. In short, the ability to *transfer*, which DABUS lacks, is fatal to Dr Thaler's contentions. The same point can be put in a different way: because DABUS is a thing, it cannot even *hold* property, let alone transfer it.

As a matter of policy, it is not clear why 'AI-generated' works should be treated differently than other 'non-AI-generated' work whereby tools have eased the efforts of creative users such as photography. If a photographer used the camera of another to take a photograph, no one supposes that copyright in the resulting photographs should vest in the camera's true owner.

Abbott adopts a dual-pronged approach to support his proposition. First, an inapt analogy to *accessio*, which also[168] deals with 'ownership of the progeny of animals or the treatment of fruit or crops produced by the labour and expense of the occupier of the land (fructus industrialis)' was put forward.[169] Many non-experts assume that these rules have an air of natural law to them and deduce implications which do not follow. As Arnold LJ clarified, these instances of *accessio* 'all concern new tangible property which is produced by existing tangible property.'[170] It could not apply to intangible property produced with the aid of tangible property, or else much of our intellectual property law would have to be rewritten.[171] These rules are not rules of nature but rules of policy full of exceptions. The rule that severed crops belong to the person with the right of exclusive possession at the time of severance is subject to the emblements exception, whereby emblements – crops which are required to be sown – may be taken by a tenant who has sown them even if they are uncut at the termination of the lease.[172] And *partus sequitur ventrem*,[173] often wrongly regarded as positing that the offspring of an animal belong to the owner of the mother,[174] does not apply to cygnets, which offspring are shared by the owner of the cock and hen supposedly because swans mate for life.[175] This arguably more natural rule

[166] *Thaler v Comptroller General of Patents Trade Marks and Designs* [2021] EWCA Civ 1374, [2022] Bus LR 375 (hereinafter *Thaler* EWCA).

[167] *Thaler* EWHC (n 166) [49]. See also *Thaler* EWCA, [102] (Elisabeth Laing LJ), [136] (Arnold LJ), cf [82]–[84] (Birss LJ).

[168] Cf text accompanying nn 15–22 above.

[169] *Thaler* FCA (n 163) [167].

[170] *Thaler* EWCA (n 167) [131].

[171] Ibid. [135].

[172] William Swadling, 'Property: General Principles' in Andrew Burrows, *English Private Law* (3rd edn, Oxford University Press 2013) para 4.434.

[173] That which is born follows the womb.

[174] A few species of animals, notably the seahorse, see males carry their offspring through gestation: Amanda CJ Vincent and Laila M Sadler, 'Faithful Pair Bonds in Wild Seahorses, Hippocampus Whitei' (1995) 50 *Anim Behav* 1557.

[175] *The Case of Swans* (1572) 7 Co Rep 15b, 17a, 77 ER 435, 437. But see JM Dewar, 'Ménage à trois in the mute swan' (1936) 30 *Br Birds* 178.

for animals that reproduce sexually suggests both that *partum sequitur ventrem* is one of convenience (paternity was practically impossible to determine in ancient societies[176]) and that it can potentially be applied to other monogamous species,[177] to the extent that any species can universally be regarded as monogamous.[178] The rule is based on possession rather than ownership as demonstrated by its application in cases of chattel (animal) hire.[179] While Beach J suggests possession extends to inventions in abstract,[180] that is, information,[181] this muddles the way possession operates with respect to things and information. Possession of things (rivalrous) entails the exclusion of others, but possession of information (non-rivalrous) does not.

Secondly, Abbott relies upon policy considerations. Before addressing these, it is important to dismiss the implicit suggestion by Beach J that a rejection of Abbott's arguments would lead to vast swathes of inventions assisted by AI being unpatentable.[182] Dr Thaler had previously listed himself as an inventor in relation to inventions generated by an earlier iteration of DABUS,[183] an arrangement Abbott acknowledges is accepted practice: 'a person can qualify as an inventor simply by being the first individual to recognize and appreciate an existing invention.'[184] This practice enables accidental inventions to be patented,[185] which is significant because accidental inventions often lead to more significant advances than deliberate ones.[186]

Abbott's suggestion that his proposal incentivises the sharing of AI resources[187] is dubious.[188] He belittles the contribution of end users,[189] underestimates the bargaining position of owners of AI machines,[190] neglects to consider the impact of such a policy on end users of AI,[191] and omits consideration of innocent non-consensual

[176] Cf Blackstone, *Commentaries Book II*, 390. Owners of male parents can earn their economic 'share' through fees for the male animal serving as stud groom: cf Rebecca Cassidy, 'The Social Practice of Racehorse Breeding' (2002) 102 *Soc Anim* 155.

[177] Vincent and Sadler (n 175).

[178] Cf TR Birkhead and AP Møller, *Sperm Competition in Birds: Evolutionary Causes and Consequences* (Academic Press 1992); Jeffrey M Black (ed), *Partnerships in Birds: The Study of Monogamy* (Oxford University Press 1996).

[179] *Tucker v Farm and General Investment Trust Ltd* [1966] 2 QB 421 (CA).

[180] *Thaler* FCA (n 163) [188]–[193].

[181] Cf *Merrell Dow Pharmaceuticals Inc v HH Norton & Co Ltd* [1996] RPC 76 (HL), 86 (Lord Hoffmann).

[182] *Thaler* FCA (n 163) [44]–[56].

[183] Cf Abbott (n 159) 1083–1086. See also *Thaler* EWCA (n 167) [81] (Birss LJ).

[184] Ibid. 1098.

[185] Sean B Seymore, 'Atypical Inventions' (2011) 86 *Notre Dame L Rev*

[186] Steven Johnson, *Where Good Ideas Come From: The Natural History of Innovation* (Allen Lane 2010) 131–139; Margaret A Boden, *The Creative Mind: Myths and Mechanisms* (2nd edn, Routledge 2003) ch 9. See also Mark A Lemley, 'The Myth of the Sole Inventor' (2012) 110 *Mich L Rev* 709, 711.

[187] Abbot (n 159) 1103–1105.

[188] Cf Michael Schuster, 'Artificial Intelligence and Patent Ownership' (2018) 75 *Wash & Lee L Rev* 1945.

[189] Surely choosing to ask the right questions to an appropriately chosen AI is valuable.

[190] Owners of such technologies will likely be able to dictate terms for access.

[191] Who may be disincentivised to seek access.

access.[192] Abbott's examples of 'interlopers'[193] intercepting patents are flawed since owners can obviously control access[194] and a duty of confidence will prevent interlopers from doing so.[195] Indeed, the status quo is far more efficient than Abbott appreciates, even if it may be counterintuitive to laypersons. Should the owner of an AI system fail to appreciate the value of an AI-generated output,[196] a subsequent person who happens upon the discarded output can claim inventorship through disclosure.[197] If patents are by default allocated to the owner of an AI, who would be incentivised to do so?

IV CONTROL OVER DATA AS PROPERTY

Although we have always been subject to influence, the scale and subtlety of the manipulation are unprecedented and will only intensify as AI meets data analytics. Corporations and individuals have both sought to claim property in the data gathered, but is property the right tool to solve the puzzle of control? Towards the end of the millennium, Birks and Chin remarked that:[198]

> Pressures are commonplace in society. Freedom of the will or, synonymously, of judgmental capacity is intelligible only within the context of pressures inherent in ordinary social life. Freedom is precisely and definitively the freedom to cope with those pressures…

Autonomy in the legal sense[199] is as much concerned with freedom as it is the assignment of responsibility. As Brownsword observed, legal and moral discourse assumes 'that [persons] are capable of acting on normative signals, that they are capable of acting on the prudential and moral reasons that are given, and that they are rightly held responsible for non-compliance.'[200] Even recognising this, our conception of *legal* autonomy remains murky.[201] The ambiguity of the legal ideal of autonomy is perhaps best reflected by the differing limits set by different jurisdictions to party autonomy in contract. Famously, common law systems do not, but civilian systems do, impose a duty of good faith in contracting,[202] though it is perhaps fairer to say

192 Liability in tort for trespass surely provides a better balance.
193 Abbott (n 159) 1104.
194 Cf *Victoria Park Racing and Recreation Grounds Co Ltd v Taylor* (1937) 58 CLR 479 (HCA).
195 Cf *Thaler* EWCA (n 167) [81] (Birss LJ).
196 Cf text accompanying n 104.
197 Cf Boden (n 187) 255.
198 Peter Birks and Chin Nyuk Yin, 'On the Nature of Undue Influence' in Jack Beatson and Daniel Friedmann (eds), *Good Faith and Fault in Contract Law* (Clarendon Press 1997) 57, 88.
199 Not to be confused with the technical use of the same word in AI: cf Mik (n 126) 422–424.
200 Roger Brownsword, 'Autonomy, Delegation, and Responsibility: Agents in Autonomic Computing Environments' in Mireille Hildebrandt and Antoinette Rouvroy (eds), *Law, Human Agency and Autonomic Computing: The Philosophy of Law Meets the Philosophy of Technology* (Routledge 2011) 64, 75.
201 Ibid. 65–67.
202 Michael Bridge, 'Limits on Contractual Freedom' (2019) 7 *CJCL* 387.

that good faith comes in shades.[203] Modern AI algorithms, though not truly intelligent, combined with other technologies are rapidly eroding our autonomy.[204]

The practice of surveillance capitalism[205] by attention merchants[206] has led to the rise of data dysphoria.[207] One response is to resort to concepts of property such as ownership.[208] But how does one own data, which is merely information? Most legal systems, including the common law,[209] do not recognise property rights in information, which is inherently non-rivalrous. It helps to recognise that ownership here serves as a metaphor for control.[210] Much as is the case with self-ownership, property plays a rhetorical role. It underscores the justice of the outcome being argued for – that data subjects should control *their* data – whilst obscuring the circularity of the argument. Data is property because it is controlled by data subjects which have property in data because they control it. It employs the same childish associations with possessive pronouns that is commonplace in the literature on self-ownership. Substituting data for bodies, Harris's astute remarks in that context are similarly illuminating:[211]

> The fact that people deploy possessive pronouns in relation to their [data] is, in itself, no indication of ownership assumptions. 'My', 'yours', 'his' or 'hers' may signify a host of relationships which have nothing to do with owning. Even a child will not confuse the sense of 'my' as between: 'It's my ball!' and 'She's my teacher'.

Indeed, the incongruity is even more pronounced in relation to data as compared to bodies. Whereas my body may arguably be my own and no one else's now that slavery has been abolished, if A and B meet, who among them should exclusively[212] control this data? They cannot both have exclusive control. The law of trusts[213] and that relating to confidential information[214] employ similar techniques – viz the

[203] Cf Mindy Chen-Wishart and Victoria Dixon, 'Good Faith in English Law: A Humble '3 by 4' Approach' in Paul B Miller and John Oberdiek (eds), *Oxford Studies in Private Law Theory*, vol 1 (Oxford University Press 2020) 187.

[204] Eliza Mik, 'The Erosion of Autonomy in Online Consumer Transactions' (2016) 8 *LIT* 1.

[205] Shoshana Zuboff, *The Age of Surveillance Capitalism: The Fight for a Human Future at the New Frontier of Power* (Public Affairs 2019).

[206] Tim Wu, *The Attention Merchants: The Epic Scramble to Get Inside Our Heads* (Alfred A Knopf 2016).

[207] Robert Herian, 'Blockchain, GDPR, and the Fantasies of Data Sovereignty' (2020) 12 *LIT* 156, 158–160.

[208] Václav Janeček, 'Ownership of Personal Data in the Internet of Things' (2018) 34 *Comput L Secur Rev* 34.

[209] *Boardman v Phipps* [1967] 2 AC 46 (HL), 127–128; *Oxford v Moss* (1979) 68 Cr App R 183 (DC).

[210] Sjef van Erp, 'Management as Ownership of Data' in Sebastian Lohsse, Reiner Schulze, and Dirk Staudenmayer (eds), *Data as Counter-Performance – Contract 2.0?* (Hart Publishing 2020) 77.

[211] JW Harris, 'Who Owns My Body' (1996) 16 *OJLS* 55, 65.

[212] Felix S Cohen, 'Dialogue on Private Property' (1954) 9 *Rutgers L Rev* 357, 370–371. Cf Kevin Gray and Susan Francis Gray, 'The Idea of Property in Land' in Susan Bright and John Dewar (eds), *Land Law: Themes and Perspectives* (Oxford University Press 1998) 15, 15–16.

[213] Lionel Smith, 'Trust and Patrimony' (2008) 38 *Revue générale de droit* 379. See also S.F.C. Milsom, *Historical Foundations of the Common Law* (2nd edn, Oxford University Press 1981) xi.

[214] Michael Bridge and others, *The Law of Personal Property* (2nd edn, Sweet & Maxwell 2017) para 9-027.

cloning of obligations – to differing outcomes precisely because property is rivalrous whereas information is not. This is why data trusts make no sense unless the subject matter of the trust is not the data per se.[215] But even if we were to ignore these objections, it is not evident that recognising property in data and vesting this in data subjects provides a satisfactory solution since property can (unless prohibited by regulation) be consensually transferred. Accordingly, the resort to property simpliciter as a solution will simply lead to our digital overlords tweaking their terms of access and requiring us to transfer our property in our data to them,[216] which most would regard as a worse outcome than no one owning data. Evidently, regulation is necessary and property is inadequate to resolve our legitimate concerns.

Why then have we become conditioned to think in terms of property in data? Data, as a mass noun, is defined by the *Oxford English Dictionary* as '[r]elated items of (chiefly numerical) information considered collectively, typically obtained by scientific work and used for reference, analysis, or calculation.'[217] Etymologically, its use as such 'became increasingly common from the middle of the 20th century, probably partly popularized by its use in computing contexts, in which it is now generally considered standard'.[218] In the digital domain, linguistic and graphical metaphors have conditioned us to think of digital files as somehow separate from both information and medium, simultaneously embodied (as a thing) and disembodied (as it is intangible).[219] The problem with metaphors is that they are by definition inexact. 'The essence of metaphor is understanding and experiencing one kind of thing in terms of another.'[220] Metaphorical thinking in law can and have led the courts astray. The contract as metaphor for unjust enrichment (*quasi ex contractu*[221]) stunted the law for more than 80 years, until *Sinclair v Brougham*[222] was overruled in *Wesdeutsche Landesbank Girozentrale v Islington LBC*.[223]

More recently, the metaphor of property in data led the English Court of Appeal in *Your Response Ltd v Datateam Business Media Ltd*[224] to error. Datateam, a magazine publisher, engaged Your Response, a database manager, in 2010 to 'hold' and maintain its database of subscribers. In 2011, dissatisfied with Your Response's service, Datateam purported to terminate the contract on 17 October 2011, with effect from 16 November 2011. The parties then reached an impasse: Your Response

[215] Cf Jeremiah Lau, James E Penner, and Benjamin Wong, 'The Basics of Private and Public Data Trusts' (2020) *Sing J L S* 90.

[216] Cf Paul M Schwartz, 'Property, Privacy, and Personal Data' (2004) 117 *Harv L Rev* 2056.

[217] (OED Third Edition, March 2012; most recently modified version published online June 2021).

[218] Ibid.

[219] Michael Bridge and others, *The Law of Personal Property* (3rd edn, Sweet & Maxwell, 2021) ch 8.

[220] George Lakoff and Mark Johnson, *Metaphors We Live By* (University of Chicago Press 1980) 5.

[221] Cf Peter Birks and Grant McLeod, 'The Implied Contract Theory of Quasi-Contract: Civilian Opinion Current in the Century before Blackstone' (1986) 6 *LS* 46.

[222] [1914] AC 398 (HL).

[223] [1996] UKHL 12, [1996] AC 669.

[224] [2014] EWCA Civ 281, [2015] QB 41.

refused to release the database or provide Datateam with access to it until all outstanding fees were paid, and Datateam, in turn, refused to pay those fees until the database was made available to it. The trial judge concluded that: (i) a reasonable period of notice was three months, which meant that Datateam was in repudiatory breach; and (ii) Your Response was entitled to exercise a lien over the data until its outstanding fees were paid. Although this result could easily be justified (for different reasons), his resort to metaphorical property reasoning led the Court of Appeal to reluctantly overrule him. As the appellate court explained, a lien was a possessory security, and whether or not there was property in the data, it could not be tangible property and hence could not be subject to a lien. Although the contract was also raised to support the trial judge's conclusion, the distraction of property in the data meant that the wrong contractual doctrines were raised – implied terms rather than concurrency of obligations. The implication of terms is famously strict, and the appellate court was clearly concerned to ensure that contract law did not lead to an inconsistent outcome to property law. In truth, however, there was never a property law issue, and the outcome at trial was consistent with the common law's preference (save in a lease of land) for the obligations of contractual counterparties to be concurrent rather than independent.[225] Metaphors can simultaneously illuminate and obscure[226] and this case demonstrates the flipside of the success of the file metaphor in helping generations of computer users navigate these miraculous machines.

Some may argue that the law should accommodate the expectations of the lay public, even if they are based entirely on metaphor and misunderstanding. Such a view takes the moribund[227] maxim *communis error facit jus* and extends it well past the point of absurdity. But as Nourse LJ explained, 'the error referred to [in the maxim] is one of decision, not of assumption. Here we would say "*communis sumptio non facit jus*".'[228] Many lay persons also assume that money deposited with banks belongs to them, contrary to the law's classification of the banking relationship as one of debtor and creditor,[229] and they likewise conceive of said money as property that is transferred in inter-bank transfers, again contrary to legal analysis, which recognises only a transfer of value but not of property.[230] No one supposes that the

[225] Kelvin FK Low, 'The Perils of Misusing Property Concepts in Contractual Analysis' (2014) 130 *LQR* 547; Edwin Peel, *Treitel: The Law of Contract* (15th edn, Sweet & Maxwell 2020) paras 17-020-17-023.

[226] Lakoff and Johnson (n 221) 10.

[227] A Westlaw search of the maxim within the United Kingdom revealed only 70 cases, of which only nineteen were decided in the twentieth century and none at all in the twenty-first century. Of the twentieth-century cases, the vast majority did not apply it, with the last reference in *Hunter v Canary Wharf Ltd* [1997] AC 655 (HL), 717. The decline of the maxim is unsurprising since 'although well known, [it] must be applied with very great caution.': RH Kersley, *Broom's Legal Maxims* (10th edn, Sweet & Maxwell 1939) 86.

[228] *Sen v Headley* [1991] Ch 425 (CA), 441. See also *Isherwood v Oldknow* (1815) 3 M & S 380, 396–397; 105 ER 654 (KB) 660 (Lord Ellenborough).

[229] *Foley v Hill* (1848) 2 HL Cas 28; 9 ER 1002.

[230] David Fox, *Property Rights in Money* (Oxford University Press 2008) paras 5.70–5.73.

courts should reshape banking law to meet the misconceptions of the masses. Why should data be any different? The law must deal with facts, not mass delusion.

V CONCLUSION

Property and personhood are often seen as mutually opposed. One can either be a subject or an object but not both. Much of the legal literature on AI focuses on our inventions achieving personhood, either on moral or utilitarian grounds. The former remains more science fiction than scientific fact, whereas the latter is grounded on a failure to appreciate our continued failure to resolve the problem of our corporations (socio-technical systems) having 'no soul to be damned and no body to be kicked', a problem that would be exacerbated if legal personhood were conferred on AI (technical) systems. But if we broaden our lens to focus on both property and personhood across a wide compass, we find that we face other equally challenging problems apart from this hackneyed and mostly (for now) fantastical question. Considering the possibility of *accessio* of object to subject forces us to confront the myth of Cartesian duality. Doing so may help us finally overcome the law's degradation of the seriousness of mental distress. It is also equally important to exorcise the metaphorical ghost of data as property within the law since the rhetoric here obscures more than it illuminates. It threatens to constrain legal discourse, leading to the purely symbolic (property) tail wagging the very real (autonomy) dog.

15

Data and AI

The Data Producer's Right – An Instructive Obituary

Dev S. Gangjee

I INTRODUCTION

Data is increasingly recognised as one of the most valuable resources of the twenty-first century. Its value derives from its use in machine learning algorithms, a form of artificial intelligence that finds useful patterns within data and learns from experience. This ever-increasing value has led to data being characterised as an asset.[1] Property rights are a tried and tested legal response when it comes to regulating valuable assets. Do we therefore need a new intellectual property right for data? This chapter argues that we do not. It charts the rapid rise and recent demise of the EU data producer's right (DPR). The DPR was proposed in 2017, to incentivise the creation, dissemination, and commercial utilisation of machine-generated data. Today, it leaves a fading policy footprint in the EU, having succumbed to the compelling arguments ranged against it. However, a right of this nature continues to be debated in international policy discussions.[2] After introducing data as a valuable resource (Section II), the first contribution of this chapter is to analyse why the proposed DPR was unsuccessful, as a cautionary tale for others contemplating a similar model (Section III). This obituary emphasises why data remains such a challenging *res* for intellectually property (IP) law. Its second contribution is to suggest that

I am grateful to Peter Harrison for insightful comments on an earlier draft. Toby Bond and Ben McFarlane gave generous guidance in mapping the larger property ecosystem around data. The usual caveat applies. Having broken the fourth wall, this is a good place for an apology. This chapter oscillates inconsistently between data in the singular and plural forms because the sources referenced do so as well. Despite datum being the recognised singular form, the trend is towards usage associated with singular verbs – 'data is' and not 'data are'.

1 J Nolin, 'Data as Oil, Infrastructure or Asset? Three Metaphors of Data as Economic Value' (2020) 18(1) *Journal of Information, Communication & Ethics in Society* 28.

2 See the International Association for the Protection of Intellectual Property (AIPPI) Summary Report, *IP Rights in Data* (Q274-SR-C-2020) (Considering whether there is a need for new, *sui generis* right in certain kinds of data); See also WIPO Secretariat, 'Revised Issues Paper on Intellectual Property Policy and Artificial Intelligence' (29 May 2020) WIPO/IP/AI/2/GE/20/1 REV., 9–11; contributions to The WIPO Conversation on Intellectual Property and Frontier Technologies: Fourth Session – Data (22 and 23 September 2021, Geneva) <www.wipo.int/meetings/en/details.jsp?meeting_id=63588>.

the EU is developing an alternative framework to private property, as a resource management model for data (Section IV). While the emerging approach prioritises data access rights, this emphasis does not go far enough. There are valuable lessons to be learned from constructed commons models, as an alternative regulatory approach to private property.

II DATA AS A VALUABLE RESOURCE

A *Machine-Generated Data*

Data is generated 'by abstracting the world into categories, measures, and other representational forms – numbers, characters, symbols, images, sounds, electromagnetic waves, bits – that constitute the building blocks from which information and knowledge are created'.[3] This distinction between (raw) data and (useful) information is often emphasised in the literature. Thus, data are 'symbols that represent the properties of objects and events. Information consists of processed data, the processing directed at increasing its usefulness'.[4] Developing this chain further, 'data precedes information, which precedes knowledge, which precedes understanding'.[5] Data therefore needs to be analysed before it can be used for prediction and decision-making. This distinction is put to work in the analysis which follows. Value is generated by processing data. Nevertheless, raw data is never entirely raw. It is invariably cooked or at least marinated to some degree, being 'framed by the instruments, practices, contexts used to generate, select, represent and analyse' the data.[6] Attaching the very label 'data' to symbolic representations of the world involves making an anticipatory, subjective judgment about value. It is worth remembering that data is 'mined, produced, constructed, collected, prepared, cleaned, scrubbed, processed, analysed, combined, sold, stored, and shared, all with explicit or implicit reliance on interpretive theories and models'.[7]

The DPR was conceived around *machine-generated data*, as the object of protection. This is data 'created without the direct intervention of a human by computer processes, applications or services, or by sensors processing information received from equipment, software or machinery, whether virtual or real'.[8] The automobile industry provides a paradigmatic example of commercially valuable

[3] R Kitchin, *The Data Revolution: Big Data, Open Data, Data Infrastructures & Their Consequences* (1st edn, Sage 2014) 1.

[4] LR Ackoff, *Ackoff's Best: His Classic Writings on Management* (Wiley 1999) 170–171.

[5] Kitchin, *The Data Revolution* (n 3) 9.

[6] A Strowel 'Big Data and Data Appropriation in the EU' in T Aplin (ed), *Research Handbook on Intellectual Property and Digital Technologies* (Edward Elgar Publishing 2020) 107, 110.

[7] MJ Madison 'Tools for Data Governance' [2020] Technology and Regulation 29, 31.

[8] European Commission Communication, 'Building a European Data Economy' (10 January 2017) COM(2017) 9 final, 9.

machine-generated data.[9] Cars are progressively equipped with sensors which automatically generate streams of data, relating to 'traffic prediction, safety warnings, vehicle diagnostics, location-based services (e.g., local search), entertainment services, and autonomous driving'.[10] Analysing this data can lead to monetizable insights, in the form of research and development (R&D) improvements for vehicle designs, or selling access to third parties such as the insurance industry. Key players in the German automotive industry are said to have been behind the initial proposals to recognise a data producer's right over machine-generated data.[11] Another vivid example is provided by the aviation industry. The Airbus A350 XWB has 50,000 sensors on board, collecting 2.5 terabytes of data every day.[12] Additional sectors of interest include 'data on precision farming (helping to monitor and optimise the use of pesticides, nutrients and water) or from sensors communicating the data [they record] such as temperature or wind conditions in, for instance, wind turbines, or data on maintenance needs for industrial robots for example when they are out of paint'.[13]

Machine-generated data is frequently generated by the Internet of Things (IoT), a phrase used to describe 'a network of interconnected physical objects, each embedded with sensors that collect and upload data to the Internet for analysis or monitoring and control'.[14] Familiar examples include smart energy meters and thermostats found in homes as well as the logistical fleet management solutions which let us know when our packages will be delivered.[15] The IoT has already multiplied the volumes of such data by orders of magnitude. Machine-generated data additionally extends beyond sensors monitoring the physical world, to include the data harvested by social media analytics and other virtual interactions.[16] This so called 'big data' has led to improvements in the quality of the analysis and predictions made possible by machine learning. Big data is associated with the following criteria:

9 A Luckow and others, 'Automotive Big Data: Applications, Workloads and Infrastructures' (2015 *IEEE International Conference on Big Data* (Big Data), 2015) 1201.

10 Ibid. 1201.

11 P Bernt Hugenholtz, 'Data Property in the System of Intellectual Property Law: Welcome Guest or Misfit?' in S Lohsse, R Schulze and D Staudenmayer (eds), *Trading Data in the Digital Economy: Legal Concepts and Tools* (Nomos 2017), 73, 73–74; J Drexl, 'Designing Competitive Markets for Industrial Data – Between Propertisation and Access' (2017) 8 *JIPITEC* 257, 259 (describing subsequent disenchantment with such a right, within representative bodies of the industry).

12 See: <www.airbus.com/en/newsroom/news/2016-12-artificial-intelligence>.

13 European Commission Communication, 'Mid-Term Review on the Implementation of the Digital Single Market Strategy: A Connected Digital Single Market for All' (10 May 2017) COM(2017) 228 final, 10.

14 C Sappa, 'How Data Protection Fits with the Algorithmic Society via Two Intellectual Property Rights. A Comparative Analysis' (2019) 14(5) *JIPLP* 407, 407.

15 McKinsey & Company, *The Internet of Things: Catching Up to an Accelerating Opportunity* (Special Report, November 2021) 5.

16 See for example, J Phengsuwan and others, 'Use of Social Media Data in Disaster Management: A Survey' (2021) 13 *Future Internet* 46.

> the large increase in the *volume* of data that can be generated and stored, the *velocity* with which data can be delivered to foster decision-making in real time, the *variety* of formats in which data can be adopted, the *veracity* or confidence level that is associated with certain types of data … and the ability to extract *value*.[17]

Big data therefore facilitates a new method of empirical enquiry; new because it

> draws insights from records gathered automatically and indiscriminately a priori…. Since the dawn of the scientific method, researchers have typically studied the world by first articulating questions and hypotheses and only later collecting empirical evidence…. The big data method turns this process on its head by asking new questions of old data.[18]

It is also important to acknowledge that big data analysis is open to a range of critiques, ranging from its epistemological assumptions (more is always better; correlation superseding causation) to the uses to which it is put (Orwellian surveillance; behavioural nudges that amplify consumerism; magnifying biases; consolidating power in less visible ways).[19]

Two qualifications should be emphasised at this preliminary stage, in relation to the subject matter of the proposed DPR. Machine-generated data is personal where it directly or indirectly allows an individual to be identified. An example would be the data produced by smart, wearable medical monitoring devices. All such personal data falls within the regulatory remit of the EU's influential General Data Protection Regulation (GDPR)[20] and thus falls outside the scope of the DPR.[21] However, where such data is aggregated and effectively anonymised, the GDPR no longer applies to it and such depersonalised data reverts to being relevant subject matter. The second distinction to draw is between unstructured data and databases. Whereas 'data should be seen as singular and separate observations in a raw form … a database is formed once these observations are put together in a structured way, and [are] ready to be handled'.[22] Databases are the object of a distinct regime of IP

[17] P Andanda, 'Towards a Paradigm Shift in Governing Data Access and Related Intellectual Property Rights in Big Data and Health-Related Research' (2019) 50 *IIC* 1052, 1053 (emphasis added); See also V Mayer-Schönberger and K Cukier, *Big Data: A Revolution That Will Transform How We Live, Work, and Think* (Houghton Mifflin Harcourt 2013).

[18] M Mattioli, 'Disclosing Big Data' (2014) 99 *Minnesota L Rev* 535, 541.

[19] See, for example, MC Ebach and others, 'Big Data and the Historical Sciences: A Critique' (2016) 71 *Geoforum* 1; D Chandler and C Fuchs (eds), *Digital Objects, Digital Subjects: Interdisciplinary Perspectives on Capitalism, Labour and Politics in the Age of Big Data* (University of Westminster Press 2019).

[20] Regulation (EU) 2016/679 of the European Parliament and of the Council of 27 April 2016 on the protection of natural persons with regard to the processing of personal data and on the free movement of such data and repealing Directive 95/46/EC (General Data Protection Regulation) [2016] OJ L 119/1.

[21] Commission Communication (2017) (n 8) 9.

[22] S Diepeveen and J Wdowin, *The Value of Data – Accompanying Literature Review* (Bennett Institute and the Open Data Institute 2020) 3.

protection in the EU, which is considered below. By contrast, the DPR was conceived with a raw or unstructured flow of data in mind.

B *Extracting Value from Data*

The potential for data to increase productivity, improve governance, and unlock new forms of value is widely recognised.[23] For instance, both the European Commission and the UK government emphasise the economic value of data, as the cornerstone of their emerging regulatory frameworks. According to the Commission, data 'has become an essential resource for economic growth, job creation and societal progress. Data analysis facilitates the optimisation of processes and decisions, innovation and the prediction of future events'.[24] Benefits include the ability to make better strategic decisions, derive insights into consumer preferences and behaviour, identify potential efficiencies, reduce waste and accelerate decision making, or even automate certain types of decisions. One study indicates that the value of the EU 'Data Economy, which measures the overall impacts of the Data Market on the economy as a whole, exceeded the threshold of 400 Billion Euro in 2019 for the EU27 plus the United Kingdom, with a growth of 7.6% over the previous year'.[25] Looking ahead, beyond the inhibiting effects of the Covid pandemic, the study predicts that the 'Data Market is forecast to reach 82.5 billion Euro in the EU27, with a compound annual growth rate of 5.8%'.[26] The most relevant UK policy framework also emphasises the value of data, seeking to unlock this value by facilitating access and use, while respecting rights and interests:

> Data is an incredibly valuable resource for businesses and other organisations. *However, there is increasing evidence to suggest its full value is not being realised because vital information is not getting to where it needs to be.* To ensure the UK is a world leader in data, our first mission will be to set the correct conditions to make data usable, accessible and available across the economy, while protecting people's data rights and private enterprises' intellectual property.[27]

Data is therefore valuable when it can be trusted, accessed, and analysed. As the OECD describes it:

> [Data] have no intrinsic value; their value rather depends on the context of their use, on the use of complementary assets such as data analytics and other (meta-)

[23] WA Günther and others, 'Debating Big Data: A Literature Review on Realizing Value from Big Data' (2017) 26(3) *The Journal of Strategic Information Systems* 191.

[24] Commission Communication (2017) (n 8) 3.

[25] *The European Data Market Monitoring Tool* (D.29, European Commission, Final Study Report, 2020), 7–8.

[26] Ibid. 9.

[27] UK National Data Strategy (2020); at: <www.gov.uk/guidance/national-data-strategy> (emphasis added).

> data, as well as on the extent to which data can be *re*used. There are therefore at least three means through which the value of data can be maximised, namely by: (i) *enhancing the quality of data* to make it better "fit for use", (ii) *enhancing data analytic capacities* by investing in e.g. analytic software, know-how and skills as well as complementary (meta) data sets that help enrich existing data, and (iii) *enhancing access to data* to leverage their infrastructural nature as non-rivalrous general-purpose productive capital.[28]

Today, it is evident that enabling access to machine-generated data is an important policy priority because data driven insights 'can create high value out of previously low-value data by analysing it for the purpose of, for example, cost efficiencies, improved processes, a better understanding of behaviour, and highly personalized products. The full value of data is not known until it is put to a specific use, including new business models and innovations that are yet to be invented'.[29] Put differently, big data analytics, via increasingly effective machine learning algorithms, is where significant value is added. This is particularly apparent where data is collected as a by-product, in an unstructured or heterogenous way without any predefined objectives. This is also true where 'data created in one domain and sector can provide further insights when applied in another domain or sector' such as data sets generated for the public sector being re-used to create new and unforeseen services.[30] Thus 'in many scenarios the value intrinsic to the data is minimal and critically depends on the capacity to make sense of the data (the algorithm).... The more the competitive advantage results from that capacity, the less important it is to control (and restrict) access to the data'.[31]

The emphasis on access, as the key to unlock value, is reinforced by the way economists characterise data as a resource. Data is a very specific type of resource, one which seemingly straddles the conventional divide between goods and services. Economic analysis indicates that data has the following characteristics:[32]

- Data can be non-fungible, where no two units are substitutable. This feature has implications for comprehensive, high value datasets which may not have substitutes or equivalents. Where there are several sources of data, comparing and valuing them also presents a challenge in assessing substitutability.

[28] OECD, 'Maximising the Economic and Social Value of Data' (DSTI/CDEP(2016)4, 28 October 2016) 1.

[29] WIPO, 'WIPO Conversation on IP and Frontier Technologies: Summary of Fourth Session' 20 December 2021 (WIPO/IP/CONV/GE/21/INF/4), 4 (Report on the presentation of Ms Aruba Khalid).

[30] OECD, *Recommendation of the Council on Enhancing Access to and Sharing of Data*, OECD/LEGAL/0463 (2021) 3.

[31] Commission Staff Working Document on the Free Flow of Data and Emerging Issues of the European Data Economy SWD (2017) 2 final (10 Jan 2017) 36 (hereafter, SWD (2017)).

[32] GSMA Report, *The Data Value Chain* (June 2018) 9; N Duch-Brown, B Martins and F Mueller-Langer, *The Economics of Ownership, Access and Trade in Digital Data* (JRC Digital Economy Working Paper 2017-01) 6–11; B Martens and others, *Business-to-Business Data Sharing: An Economic and Legal Analysis* (JRC Digital Economy Working Paper 2020-05) 12–18.

- Data is non-rivalrous and can be used by many parties (or algorithms) at the same time, without being consumed in the process, or without any functional loss to data quality. This allows for economies of scope, using the same resource to produce different outputs.
- Data is classified as an experience good. It has no intrinsic value. The value of the data depends on the insights produced from it, which cannot be known in advance. This opacity makes it challenging to assess in advance the utility or worth of a dataset.
- Data is an intermediate input into the production of goods and services. Unless two entities are integrated within the same firm, this requires the sharing of data between the data recorder or holder and the service provider seeking to make use of it.

At the same time, there are certain features of the data value chain which tend to inhibit access and sharing. A stylised chain consists of several discrete steps such as data generation; collection, validation and storage; analysis to generate information; and utilisation of the insights or transacting with them.

> In a traditional value chain, different companies would typically specialise in a limited set of activities and then trade inputs and outputs with other companies, with value created at each step of taking raw material inputs through to finished goods and services. However, the nature of data results in a tightly integrated value chain where the organisation that collects the data is very likely to retain it through the steps to develop the output themselves, while buying in specific supporting services.[33]

The implication of tightly integrated chains is that firms which control access to machine-generated data retain the data for use in-house.[34] The BMWs of this world can make productive use of their automobile sensor data but where does that leave others who wish to utilise it? The desire to preserve both confidentiality and commercial autonomy – choosing when to share and on what terms – can reinforce tighter control over data, along with the need to preserve incentives for investing in the creation of high-quality data gathering infrastructure.[35] This is further exacerbated by the 'winner takes all' dynamic for certain kinds of machine-generated data. The data generated by the large online platforms benefit from significant scale and network effects.[36] Even this condensed survey indicates that while facilitating

[33] GSMA Report (n 32) 3.

[34] The empirical basis informing subsequent policy in the EU is reviewed in L Zoboli, 'Fueling the European Digital Economy: A Regulatory Assessment of B2B Data Sharing' (2020) 31 *European Business Law Review* 663.

[35] Martens and others, *Business-to-Business Data Sharing* (n 32) 13; H Zech, 'Information as Property' (2015) 6(3) *Journal of Intellectual Property, Information Technology and Electronic Commerce Law (JIPITEC)* 192, 197.

[36] GSMA Report (n 32) 3.

greater access to data is to be encouraged, this needs to be achieved in sustainable ways. Policy makers are therefore focusing on ways to remove bottlenecks and improve business-to-business (B2B) data sharing as well as usage.[37]

C (De Facto) *Data Exclusivity*

Having introduced the tension between control and access, where does IP fit within this regulatory conversation? The question of whether such non-personal, machine-generated data is protected by any of the fields of IP law is one which would give pause to Schrödinger's cat. It might be in some situations and simultaneously isn't in many others. In all fairness, the taint of uncertainty extends well beyond IP. Comparative research reveals that data is either not protectable or else only partially protected by conventional (personal) property rights across many jurisdictions.[38] The question has periodically arisen in relation to specific information stored within the computer of an employee, in a situation where the employer wishes to claim control over or access to that information. The fields of law engaged range from employment law to theft or various property torts, such that the property question has often been approached indirectly by courts. When directly requested to protect information as the object of property rights, courts have historically declined the invitation.[39]

Similarly, there is a broad consensus that the major categories of IP will not recognise raw data as viable subject matter.[40] Copyright protects creative expressions and not factual representations of the world. Patent law protects technological inventions and not pure information, let alone data. Nevertheless, it is arguable that machine-generated data can be protected by the law of trade secrets in the EU, provided the data is secret in the sense of being not generally known, its

37 European Commission Communication, 'A European Strategy for Data' COM(2020) 66 final, 7; OECD, *Recommendation on Enhancing Access* (n 30); UK National Infrastructure Commission, *Data for the Public Good* (2018).

38 T Hoeren, 'Big Data and the Ownership in Data: Recent Developments in Europe' (2014) 36(12) *European Intellectual Property Review* 751; Osborne Clarke, *Legal Study on Ownership and Access to Data* (European Commission Study 2016); S van Erp, 'Ownership of Data: The Numerus Clausus of Legal Objects' (2017) 6 *Brigham-Kanner Property Rights Conference Journal* 235; C Czychowski and JB Nordemann (eds), *Law of Raw Data* (Kluwer Law International 2021).

39 For a common law approach to this, see Section IV of KFK Low, WY Wan and Y-C Wu, 'Property/Personhood and AI: The Future of Machines' in Ernest Lim and Phillip Morgan (eds), *The Cambridge Handbook of Private Law and Artificial Intelligence* (Cambridge University Press 2024) Ch 14; *Stephen Thaler v Comptroller General of Patents Trade Marks and Designs* [2021] EWCA Civ 1374, [2022] Bus LR 375 [124]–[125]. For a comparative assessment: Czychowski and Nordemann (eds), *Law of Raw Data* (n 38).

40 H Beverley-Smith, 'Rights in Data and Information' in R Dreyfuss and J Pila (eds), *The Oxford Handbook of Intellectual Property Law* (Oxford University Press 2018) 594; M Mattioli, 'Data and Intellectual Property Law' in V Mak, E Tjong Tjin Tai and A Berlee (eds), *Research Handbook in Data Science and Law* (Edward Elgar 2018) 133; D Gervais, 'Exploring the Interfaces between Big Data and Intellectual Property Law' (2019) 10 *JIPITEC* 3.

commercial value is related to its secrecy and there are reasonable measures in place to keep the data secret.[41] However some important qualifications are called for. Trade secret protection responds only to the 'unlawful acquisition, use and disclosure of trade secrets' (Article 4) and is therefore narrower than a conventional property right, which has *erga omnes* effects. Data that circulates because of a breach of contractual terms illustrates this point. The right holder will have a claim against the party in unlawful breach, but not the remote third party who may have otherwise lawfully obtained the secret data or found it on the internet, without any sense of its provenance. Data can also be valuable without necessarily being secret, such as the information that is recorded by vehicle sensors operating in public places.[42] Trade secrecy therefore remains a practical option in the absence of better alternatives.

The other option within the EU is the *sui generis* database right.[43] This harmonised regime protects databases which need not be original, in the copyright sense of reflecting expressive choices in their ordering or contents. Protection is available if the investment in obtaining, verifying and presenting the data was substantial.[44] A database which qualifies is protected against the unauthorised extraction and/or reutilisation of the whole or a substantial part of its contents.[45] Data is thus protected in the aggregate. Given the algorithmic appetite for systematically analysing large datasets, this right is once again under scrutiny. However, there is some uncertainty in relation to the 'substantial investment' qualification threshold. 'If operating a machine that records sensor data does not require substantial investment (for example, a low-cost digital weather station or a bicycle computer), then this will not result in a protected database'.[46] The CJEU has also confirmed that this right does not acknowledge the investment made in *creating* the data, but only in the activities required to *collect* the pre-existing data.[47] It was introduced to incentivise the development of systematic, searchable databases, as opposed to incentivising the creation of raw data. A Commission working document reflects the current consensus, as

41 These are the qualifying criteria found in Art. 2(1) of Directive EU 2016/943 of the European Parliament and of the Council of 8 June 2016 on the protection of undisclosed know-how and business information (trade secrets) against their unlawful acquisition, use and disclosure [2016] OJ L 157/1 (Trade Secrets Directive).

42 Sappa (n 14); I Stepanov, 'Introducing a Property Right over Data in the EU: The Data Producer's Right – An Evaluation' (2020) 34(1) *International Review of Law, Computers & Technology* 65, 72–73.

43 Directive 96/9/EC of the European Parliament and of the Council of 11 March 1996 on the Legal Protection of Databases [1996] OJ L 77/20 (the Database Directive).

44 Art. 7(1) of the Database Directive.

45 Ibid.

46 B Hugenholtz, 'Data Property: Unwelcome Guest in the House of IP' (Paper presented at Trading Data in the Legal Economy, Munster 2018) 10.

47 C-203/02 *The British Horseracing Board and Ors. v William Hill* ECLI:EU:C:2004:695 [31] (The investments in obtaining the contents of a database must 'be understood to refer to the resources used to seek out existing independent materials and collect them in the database, and not to the resources used for the creation as such of independent materials').

well as its limits.[48] In light of CJEU case law, raw machine-generated databases are unlikely to be protected because the investments in 'obtaining' data relates to data that was *created* by sensors, often as a by-product of the central business activity of the firm. However, some German judicial decisions[49] indicate that the recording of data may qualify as an investment in 'acquiring' it or processing the raw data may count towards an investment in 'verifying' and 'presenting' it. Meanwhile the boundary between obtaining and creating is blurred where raw data is created (by sensors) and simultaneously classified (by the robot housing those sensors). At the time of writing, the EU's proposed new Data Act has opted, in Article 35, to clarify that the *sui generis* database right does not apply to databases containing data generated by the use of a connected device, that is, machine generated.[50]

This precis suggests that while mainstream IP options within the EU remain unavailable, certain types of machine-generated data may at least qualify for protection as trade secrets. However, even such tentative protection has not prevented the emergence of data markets.[51] Their existence attests to the *de facto* control enabled by mutually reinforcing technological, behavioural and legal barriers.[52] Technological barriers to data access are created by cryptography and technological protection measures. Behavioural regulation overlaps with legal regulation, often within contractual matrixes. With data access increasingly offered as a service – parties negotiate for ongoing access rather than a one-off purchase – contractual licensing regulates this ongoing relationship. The data creator or holder is usually at liberty to impose terms regulating access and subsequent use (for example, the purposes for which data can be mined and analysed; exclusivity clauses limiting the subsequent sharing of data; specifying the consequences of merging two datasets; asserting claims over the results of the data analysis).[53] This *de facto* control over data invariably attracts the language of 'ownership'. As the Commission notes:

[48] Commission Staff Working Document, 'Evaluation of Directive 96/9/EC on the Legal Protection of Databases' {SWD(2018) 147 final} 35–40. For a detailed consideration of the issues, see: JIIP and Technopolis, *Study in Support of the Evaluation of Directive 96/9/EC on the Legal Protection of Databases* (European Commission, 2018) 29–44; Leistner, 'Big Data and the EU Database Directive 96/9/EC: Current Law and Potential for Reform' in Lohsse, Schulze and Staudenmayer (n 11) 27.

[49] Principally, *Autobahnmaut* [2010] GRUR 1004 (BGH).

[50] Proposal for a Regulation of the European Parliament and of the Council on Harmonised Rules on Fair access to and Use of Data (Data act) COM(2022) 68 final; EU Inception Impact Assessment on the Data Act (Including the Review of the Directive 96/9/EC on the Legal Protection of Databases) Ares(2021)3527151, 28 May 2021.

[51] For an overview of the EU, see IDC and the Lisbon Council, *The European Data Market Monitoring Tool: Key Facts & Figures, First Policy Conclusions, Data Landscape and Quantified Stories* (D2.9 Final Study Report 2020).

[52] T Fia, 'An Alternative to Data Ownership: Managing Access to Non-personal Data through the Commons' (2021) 21(1) *Global Jurist* 181, 185–187.

[53] The limited evidence available indicates that lawyers do resort to contracts in everyday practice: B Van Asbroeck, J Debussche and J César, 'Building the European Data Economy: Data Ownership' (Bird & Bird White Paper, 1 January 2017) 112–119; Osborne Clarke, *Legal Study on Ownership* (n 38) 27–28; Czychowski and Nordemann (eds), *Law of Raw Data* (n 38).

> In some cases manufacturers or service providers may become the de facto 'owners' of the data that their machines or processes generate, even if those machines are owned by the user. De facto control of this data can be a source of differentiation and competitive advantage for manufacturers.[54]

It is against this background of existing regulatory options that we turn to assess the proposed DPR.

III THE DATA PRODUCER'S RIGHT

A *Antecedents and Rationales*

The DPR was conceived as a new form of intellectual or intangible property right. As we will see below, from its very inception this new right was devised as the means to an end: to ensure greater access to data. The answer to an apparent paradox – if we wish to ensure greater access, why are we building new property fences – is found in the recognition that property is 'an institution for organising the use of resources in society'.[55] A large body of scholarship has developed the work of Harold Demsetz, which posits that property rights emerge when the social benefits of establishing such rights exceed their costs.[56] The stable legal entitlements associated with property are said to provide incentives to develop a valuable resource, by concentrating risks and rewards in right-holders. Property also prevents overuse and waste of (finite) resources that are otherwise openly accessible, which is described as the 'tragedy of the commons'. Finally, property rights famously internalise harmful or (more questionably) beneficial effects, or externalities, by streamlining the co-ordination that is required to do so; 'only the owner of the resource and those affected by its use need agree'.[57] When a resource can be smoothly traded, initial rights allocations supposedly matter less. For the value of data to be unlocked, it needs to circulate. Thus well-defined private property rights are considered a necessary institutional precondition for this circulation, by facilitating efficient resource allocation in markets.[58]

With the objective of improved circulation in mind, Michael Mattioli proposed a 'dataright' for the United States, as a provocative thought experiment in 2014.[59]

[54] Commission Communication (2017) (n 8) 10.

[55] TW Merrill, 'The Property Strategy' (2012) 160 *University of Pennsylvania L Rev* 2061, 2062.

[56] H Demsetz, 'Toward a Theory of Property Rights' (1967) 57 *American Economic Review* 347. For one such review, see: S Djankov and others, 'Measuring Property Rights Institutions' (NBER Working Paper 27839, September 2020). For a representative criticism, which challenges its universalist ambitions by reintroducing historical and socio-economic context, see H Sato, 'The Emergence of "Modern" Ownership Rights Rather than Property Rights' (2018) 52(3) *Journal of Economic Issues* 676.

[57] TW Merrill, 'The Demsetz Thesis and the Evolution of Property Rights' (2002) 31(S2) *J Legal Studies* S331, S332.

[58] S Hazel, 'Personal Data as Property' (2020) 70 *Syracuse L Rev* 1055 (making the case for new property rights in personal data drawing on Demsetz); Stepanov (n 42) 75–79 (for a more critical engagement).

[59] Mattioli, 'Disclosing Big Data' (n 18).

Expert interviews with informaticists, data scientists, lawyers, and business professionals working at the vanguard of big data had revealed that while access to data is a problem, so is nondisclosure of the data's provenance and pedigree. How data is collected and prepared is crucial information, affecting its subsequent reliability and reuse. Disclosure of the existence of datasets and their provenance would be the precondition for granting such a 'dataright'. As regards its scope, the right would be enforceable specifically against the unauthorised use of the data (e.g., analysing it to solve a specific problem) and not merely its unauthorised circulation, subject to contractual restrictions to the contrary. Having fashioned a property carrot, Mattioli was aware that it might not be a sufficiently attractive inducement for data holders to make the desired disclosures, since secrecy and cryptographic protection remain the pragmatic defaults.

Around this time, Herbert Zech was engaging with debates in German legal scholarship by laying the groundwork for a new right in machine-generated data.[60] Given the ever-increasing volume of big data, the new 'data producer's right' was categorically not intended to incentivise the creation of more data. Instead, it was intended to overcome the propensity to rely on secrecy and the inertia created by factual control. In 'ensuring a fair allocation of the profits generated by analysing the data … a clear property rule can provide the framework for a functioning data economy'.[61] By clearly defining protected subject matter, unlocking the full suite of property remedies and facilitating the transferability of rights, Zech argued that data could be commodified and traded with greater ease in the data economy. Concurrently, practitioners were proposing a more fleshed out version of a property right, as a means of addressing the legal uncertainty over the status of data.[62] Those 'involved in the data value cycle may currently hold back on data sharing initiatives and presently have no choice but to rely on [inadequate] contractual arrangements to manage their rights in data'.[63] The right would protect each individual datum or unit of data and could be claimed by anyone who processed this data, by performing a set of operations upon it such as collecting, recording, structuring or enriching. This immediately raises the prospect of multiple right-holders invested in the same data. Such non-exclusivity was a feature and not a bug, since the right was designed to be (selectively) non-exclusive: 'A non-exclusive right, apart from fitting with the non-exclusive nature in essence of

60 Herbert Zech had published in English: 'Information as Property' (2015) 6(3) *JIPITEC* 192; 'A Legal Framework for a Data Economy in the European Digital Single Market: Rights to Use Data' (2016) 11(6) Journal of Intellectual Property Law & Practice (JIPLP) 460 (Zech engages with contemporary legal debates on property in data in the German academy; see, for example, 469 at FN71); 'Data as a Tradeable Commodity' in A De Franceschi (ed), *European Contract Law and the Digital Single Market* (Intersentia, 2016) 51.

61 Zech (2015) (n 60) 197.

62 Van Asbroeck, Debussche and César, 'Data Ownership' (n 53) 120–130; The proposed right was developed further in: Van Asbroeck, Debussche and César, 'Data Ownership' (n 53).

63 Van Asbroeck, Debussche and César, 'Data Ownership' (n 53) 5.

data itself, would allow for a shared use of data by the different actors in the data value cycle, each on their own merits'.[64] However, the proposal does not specify what would constitute an infringement of the new right. Furthermore, in order to qualify as a right-holder, one needed to satisfy a traceability requirement. This consisted of 'the obligation to be able to demonstrate at all times the provenance of and the processing performed on the data one is claiming ownership in … [and] could be accomplished by keeping [regularly updated] traceability logs'.[65] This has parallels with the 'independent creation' subsistence requirement in copyright law (a work is protected because it's created and not copied), while also functioning as a means of asserting title. Intriguingly, the proposal did require that the right would have a mandatory data transfer obligation as its counterpart. This transfer would take place on Fair, Reasonable and Non-Discriminatory (FRAND) terms, subject to certain outer-limits, such as where a transfer would conflict with the legitimate interests of the data right-holder.

It should be noted that while these proposals favoured the creation of a *new* right, a parallel debate was underway as to whether the established law of (moveable) property, set out in national civil codes, could accommodate data.[66] This intersects with an ongoing debate across jurisdictions as to whether some of form of property is an appropriate control mechanism for personal data.[67] While property talk was in the air during this period, a series of challenges arose to the suggestion that because machine-generated data is a valuable resource, it is therefore an asset which is best regulated by a private property paradigm.[68] To begin with, property forms need to adapt to the nature of the resource being protected.[69] Data, as intangible subject matter, has specific features, which include non-rivalry and numerous existing incentives for machine-generated data, notwithstanding the absence of property rights. If underproduction of data leading to market failure is not the principal concern in a world awash with big data, then the Demsetz thesis, conceived with scarce

[64] Ibid. 121.

[65] Ibid. 125.

[66] See Hoeren (n 38) (for Germany); A De Franceschi and M Lehmann, 'Data as Tradeable Commodity and New Measures for Their Protection' (2015) *The Italian Law Journal* 51 (for Italy); and more recently T Bond, 'United Kingdom' in Czychowski and Nordemann (eds), *Law of Raw Data* (n 38) 369, 371–76.

[67] For recent studies, see: P Hacker 'Lessons from IP Markets for Data Markets: On Moral Rights, Property Rules, and Resale Royalties' [2018] *Intellectual Property Quarterly* 45; L Trakman, R Walters and B Zeller, 'Is Privacy and Personal Data Set to Become the New Intellectual Property?' (2019) 50 *IIC* 937; Hazel, 'Personal Data as Property' (n 58); I Cofone, 'Beyond Data Ownership' (2021) 43 *Cardozo Law Review* 501.

[68] See A Wiebe, 'Protection of Industrial Data – A New Property Right for the Digital Economy?' 2016 *Gewerblicher Rechtsschutz und Urheberrecht Internationaler (GRUR-Int)* 877; J Drexl and others, 'Data Ownership and Access to Data' (Position Statement of the Max Planck Institute, 16 August 2016); Drexl, 'Designing Competitive Markets' (n 11); Hugenholtz 'Welcome Guest or Misfit?' (n 11); W Kerber, 'A New (Intellectual) Property Right for Non-personal Data? An Economic Analysis' (2016) *GRUR Int* 989; OECD (2016) (n 28) 23–25.

[69] J Cohen, 'Property as Institutions for Resources: Lessons from and for IP' (2015) 94 *Texas L Rev* 1.

natural resources in mind, may be a poor fit.[70] This mismatch seems more likely since the real value of data lies in the use that is made of it, often in ways unforeseen by the initial data collectors. Where Demsetz focused on negative externalities, such positive externalities or spillovers don't always interfere with incentives to invest and can instead encourage greater (data-driven) innovation.[71] Furthermore, any new property right would stack on top of existing protection options, including the *de facto* control characterising the status quo. A higher stack of rights to transact around would increase complexity as well as costs, ultimately impeding access.

These debates form the backdrop to the Commission's public consultation on Building a European Data Economy,[72] which was accompanied by the Communication introducing the DPR and a Staff Working Document elaborating upon it.[73] The Communication reveals a range of reasons behind the DPR, including the desire to enhance the global competitiveness of the European data economy and the need for a harmonised, EU-wide approach in order to prevent regulatory fragmentation. More pertinently, the DPR was introduced within a section of the Communication entitled 'A future EU framework for data access'. It was clearly envisaged as a market-making measure, in order to improve access to data.[74] The introduction of a new property right 'would aim at clarifying the legal situation and giving more choice to the data producer, by opening up the possibility for users to utilise their data and thereby contribute to unlocking machine-generated data'.[75] The certainty accompanying property status was expected to improve the efficient functioning of the emerging market for data, by increasing its circulation. The Staff Working Document clarified that 'the objective [was that] of enhancing the tradability of non-personal or anonymised machine-generated data as an economic good'.[76] A related objective was to recognise 'the legitimate interests of market players that invest in product development, ensure a fair return on their investments and thereby contribute to innovation'.[77]

[70] A Holst, 'Amount of Data Created, Consumed and Stored 2010–2025', at: <www.statista.com/statistics/871513/worldwide-data-created/> (Indicating that the pandemic accelerated the growth and analysis of data, including data related to working from home productivity and streaming entertainment).

[71] MA Lemley and BM Frischmann, 'Spillovers' (2007) 107 *Columbia Law Review* 257,

[72] See: <www.digital-strategy.ec.europa.eu/en/consultations/public-consultation-building-european-data-economy>.

[73] Commission Communication (2017) (n 8); SWD (2017) (n 31). An excellent overview of the policy background is found in D Kim, 'No One's Ownership as the Status Quo and a Possible Way Forward: A Note on the Public Consultation on Building a European Data Economy' (2018) 13(2) *JIPLP* 154.

[74] Commission Communication (2017) (n 8) 4 ('The issues of access and transmission in relation to the data generated by these machines or processes are therefore central to the emergence of a data economy and require careful assessment'); 8 (The extraction of value 'becomes more difficult to achieve if the generators of the data keep it to themselves, and the data is consequently analysed in silos'); 9–10 ('Overall, therefore, exchange of data currently remains limited').

[75] Ibid. 13.

[76] SWD (2017) (n 31) 33.

[77] Commission Communication (2017) (n 8) 11.

B Subject Matter and Duration

The subject matter envisaged for the DPR was 'non-personal or anonymised machine-generated data'.[78] The idea was to protect data 'not yet structured in a protected database', thereby falling outside of the *sui generis* database right and which was also excluded by other IP rights.[79] In the absence of any reference to a definable corpus or a continuous stream of data, the implicit presumption seems to be that each individual datum or unit would be protected. The right would extend to metadata on the data, since this it would 'contain the information necessary to use the data subject to such a potential new right'.[80] However it would protect only the symbolic representation and not the substance: 'only the syntactical level of information is protected, not the semantic level. Care also needs to be taken so that any new right on data is not conceived as a super-IP right. It should only cover the syntactical (data, code) level, but not the ideas or information encoded.'[81] Examples given emphasise the difference between the semantic content of an e-book or photograph (narrative meaning or impression) and the electronic datafile which encodes this meaning. The right would protect the encoding and not the substance. An analogy might be drawn between the creative expression protected by copyright (say, a musical work) and neighbouring or related rights over the signal that carries the work (say, the sound recording or broadcast transmission) which afford thinner protection that is shorter in duration.[82] The Commission cites Zech, who proposes that

> information can be defined on the semantic level (information with a certain meaning), on the syntactic level (information represented by a certain amount of signs [inter-sign relations]), or even by its physical carrier (information contained in a certain physical carrier or in a wider sense information represented by the structure of a physical object).[83]

The DPR was therefore directed towards protecting the syntactic level.

On further reflection, the inadequacies of this approach are readily apparent. Stated simply, how does one reify a high-velocity flow? As Bernt Hugenholtz puts it:

> Although it is still not fully conceptualised, it is difficult to imagine a data right sufficiently stable in terms of subject matter, scope and ownership to be admitted to the ranks of intellectual property. As to subject matter, if the right vests in data generated by machine processes, which data would it protect? All the data that the machine produces within a given time frame (e.g., an hour, a minute or a second)?

78 SWD (2017) (n 31) 33.
79 Ibid. 34.
80 Ibid.
81 Ibid.
82 R Arnold, 'Content Copyrights and Signal Copyrights: The Case for a Rational Scheme of Protection' (2011) 1(3) *Queen Mary Journal of IP* 272.
83 Zech, 'Information as Property' (2015) (n 60) 194. The Commission specifically references Zech 'Tradeable Commodity' (n 60), which uses the same framework.

> Or all the data that result from a finite [mechanical] process (e.g., all the data gathered by a satellite that monitors the earth)?... The problem here is that industrial data generation mostly occurs in real time. The 'velocity' – the dynamic nature – of big data makes it very difficult, if not impossible, to identify a stable object of protection. The subject matter of the right is simply too fluid.[84]

Poorly defined intangible subject matter does not lend itself to legal certainty. Moreover, disentangling the semantic and syntactic layers of information is not always straightforward. Since personal data, which may be machine-generated through sensors, is excluded from the right, the 'meaning' of the data will need to be assessed, in order to filter out personal data where necessary.[85] Put differently, protectable subject matter under the DPR can only be identified by first assessing its semantic content. This leads on to the related problem of exclusive rights over the syntactic layer amounting to exclusivity over the semantic layer.[86] Proprietary claims over the syntactic layer (the 1s and 0s in digital form) would amount to gatekeeping over the content contained in the semantic layer (say, fluctuating financial data), especially for non-fungible or unique data sources.

Definitional difficulties also implicate the question of duration, which the Commission notably did not address. Most IP rights expire, once the 'incentives for access' bargain is deemed to be fulfilled. However the value of data often 'resides in [its] immediacy and real-time availability. It may depreciate very rapidly in the modern data economy. Extending data protection over many years may have little additional value'.[87] Acknowledging the interest of data being in the public domain, Zech concludes that a 'short term of protection would be appropriate', while leaving this term unspecified.[88] If a timer begins and ends for each datum (which raises practical difficulties), then a multi-year data store will have protection expiring as a moving wave front across its contents. This will not assist parties wishing to access the entire volume of data. It also does not address the potentially indefinite technical and contractual access restrictions imposed by data holders, which the new right would not eliminate.

C *Nature of the Right and Scope*

The Commission put forward two versions of the DPR – one as a property right and the other as a civil wrongs-based model analogous to trade secrets protection.

[84] Hugenholtz, 'Data Property' (n 11) 73, 93.

[85] J Drexl, 'The (Lack of) Coherence of Data Ownership with the Intellectual Property System' in N Bruun, G Dinwoodie, M Levin and A Ohly (eds), *Transition and Coherence in Intellectual Property Law* (Cambridge University Press 2020) 213, 216–217.

[86] Wiebe, 'Protection of Industrial Data' (n 68) 881–882; J Drexl, *Data Access and Control in the Era of Connected Devices* (European Consumer Organisation (BEUC) Study 2018) 44–46.

[87] Duch-Brown, Martins and Mueller-Langer, *The Economics of Ownership* (n 32) 14.

[88] Zech, 'A Legal Framework for a Data Economy' (n 60) 469.

The first version was envisaged as a right *in rem*, 'enforceable against the world (*erga omnes*) independent of contractual relations'.[89] The right-holder would be assigned

> the exclusive right to utilise certain data, including the right to licence its usage. This would include a set of rights enforceable against any party independent of contractual relations thus preventing further use of data by third parties who have no right to use the data, including the right to claim damages for unauthorised access to and use of data.[90]

The 'essential features of the right of ownership can be recognized in this definition: the "bundle-of-rights" conception of protection; the rights are exclusive, transferable and have *erga omnes* effect'.[91]

The second version was designed around preventing acts of misappropriation. It recognised

> a set of purely defensive rights…. This option would follow [the approach in the] Trade Secrets Protection Directive…. Its objective would be to enhance the sharing of data by giving at least the defensive elements of an *in rem* right, i.e. the capacity for the de facto data holder to sue third parties in case of illicit misappropriation of data. This approach thus equates to a protection of a de facto "possession" rather than to the concept of "ownership".[92]

This move would be accompanied by the introduction of civil law remedies, including injunctions and damages. However, the misappropriation of data ought to target its subsequent unauthorised use in some form of processing or analysis and 'mere dissemination of (non-personal) data without that use … could remain lawful'.[93] The Commission notes that strengthening the status quo under this model runs the risk of presuming that 'what happens de facto is already a balanced and efficient data market'.[94] Any such defensive rights-granting may – in isolation – be counterproductive unless it is offset by other corrective measures (discussed below). The self-evident gap is that this wrongs-based approach leaves the notion of harmful misappropriation, as the touchstone of liability, entirely underdeveloped.[95] One is left to speculate whether misappropriation seemingly rests on an implicit proprietary interest based on possession *per se* ('it's wrong to use my possessions without permission'). This second model seems to end up circling back to the property logic of the first model after all.

89 SWD (2017) (n 31) 33, FN 151.
90 Ibid. 33.
91 Kim, 'No One's Ownership' (n 73) 161.
92 SWD (2017) (n 31) 33–34.
93 Ibid. 34 (citing to Mattioli (n 18) in FN155).
94 Ibid.
95 Kim, 'No One's Ownership' (n 73) 161.

D *Right-Holders*

As regards the initial allocation of ownership for the right *in rem* model described earlier, the Commission identifies both 'the owner or long-term user (i.e., the lessee) of the device' which generates the data.[96] The intended beneficiaries of this right were those who invest in the creation of data: 'The manufacturer of sensor equipped machines, tools or devices (generating the data) who has invested in the development and market commercialisation of the machine, tool or device, and the economic operators using such machines, tools or devices paying a purchase price or lease and having to amortise the machine, tool or device'.[97]

Having identified at least two possible owners, the Staff Working Document goes on to propose a multi-factorial assessment for initial rights allocation between them, including:[98]

- The 'investments done and the resources put into the creation of the data'. This encompasses both manufacturers of devices generating data flows and the economic operators whose use generates the data in real time.
- Where joint investments are made, joint rights can be envisaged subject to contractual reallocation (i.e., private (re)ordering is recognised).
- The extent to which users or manufacturers are subject to liability obligations, presumably by way of some form of 'detriment-benefit' reasoning. If the risks are attributed to a party, they should also enjoy the benefits.

However, the document also acknowledges the countervailing view that the data in question may be subject to many layers of rights 'and that this will make it conceptually virtually impossible to identify one or several owners … the concept of "ownership" is thus difficult to apply. Stakeholders also consider that defining rights of access to data is more relevant than defining ownership rights'.[99]

For the alternative, defensive right envisioned along the lines of trade secrets protection, 'such rights could protect *de facto* data holders that have lawful possession of data against unlawful use by others. This would complement technical efforts currently undertaken by data holders to protect their data'.[100]

E *Exceptions and Flanking Measures*

Since the DPR was conceived as an access-enhancing measure, the proposal recognises the need for an 'obligation to share the data. The rationale for potential

[96] Commission Communication (2017) (n 8) 13.
[97] SWD (2017) (n 31) 35.
[98] Ibid.
[99] Ibid.
[100] Ibid.

exchanges depends on the person or entity to whom the right is allocated'.[101] The following situations are expressly envisaged:[102]

- Where the device user is allocated initial ownership, they may need to share data with the sensor manufacturer, for reasons ranging from improving the product design to fulfilling a legal obligation on the manufacturer to monitor product performance.
- In some situations, the sensor manufacturer may have exclusive rights (or else the user may have more limited rights) where the data relates to safety or security. This data should remain accessible only to the manufacturer.
- Beyond these two right-holders, there may be obligations to share with other private actors. This will be determined by the public policy objectives sought to be achieved by making the data more widely available. The example given relates to '(aggregated/ anonymised) smart metering information which is relevant for balancing the grid or in order to fully enable smart homes and living environments or care institutions'.
- The public sector may require information (usually in aggregated form) from the private sector, again for certain specified purposes such as urban planning or environmental protection.
- To further an open science and open access agenda, an exception being provided to make privately held data available for research scientists entirely or predominantly funded by public resources.

Having started down the path of mandatory access obligations the proposal considers two so-called 'flanking measures'. Invoking the Coasean imperative to minimise transaction costs,[103] the Commission references 'banning unfair terms in consumer contracts or unfair business practices … to ensure a properly functioning market'.[104] This alludes to the regulation of contractual terms, to prevent exceptions from being bypassed by private ordering. The proposal also highlights the potential for digital watermarking, in order to make data traceable and thereby encourage access while preserving some measure of accountability.

Finally, with an eye to the benefits of both competitors and other non-competing economic operators accessing a producer's data, the Commission refers to:

> [A] 'data commons' as a way to describe non-discriminatory access to certain data for at least a wider group of players, specifying that this should neither be confused with an 'open data' or 'open access' approach (access for the public at large), nor should it mean that access is given at no costs. The defining element of a

[101] Ibid.
[102] Ibid. 35–36.
[103] RH Coase, 'The Problem of Social Cost' (1960) 3 *The Journal of Law & Economics* 1.
[104] SWD (2017) (n 31) 36.

'commons' is that non-discriminatory access is to be given, i.e. any member of a certain group (e.g. users of an industrial data platform) can use the data for purposes defined by the party making the data accessible.[105]

Having set out a model which prioritises data access, the Commission emphasises that this need not be entirely open and unremunerated. Since 'there is a cost in data generation and data have a value as a business asset, regulated access might be considered only for certain categories of data'.[106] While there are obvious concerns if a data holder is compelled to share with direct competitors, a different set of considerations will apply when there are requests for 're-use of data by other economic players that are not active on the same market as the company holding the data'.[107] Alluding to competition law techniques to balance interests, the proposal flags up the possibility of defining categories of 'public interest' data, 'which are neither "open data" nor entirely private data. An interplay needs to be defined between principles or rules on enhanced access that apply across business sectors and sector-specific rules'.[108] For such categories of non-personal, commercially-held data, access 'would be implemented as an obligation on data holders to licence the use of the data'.[109]

The Commission identifies the need to determine which data will qualify on a 'public interest' basis for this model. It documents existing EU regimes which mandates information sharing. These include the obligation on a manufacturer to provide vehicle maintenance and repair information, without discriminating between independent dealers and authorised repairers under Regulation 715/2007,[110] and the obligation to share chemical data in order to limit repeated animal testing.[111] Intriguingly, there is a suggestion to learn from patent pools which licence technology, often relating to technical standards, on fair, reasonable, and non-discriminatory (FRAND) terms, where reasonable and proportionate licensing fees are charged for access.[112] Importantly, this commons-based conceptualisation and licensing model is not necessarily dependent on recognising a new IP right in data. *De facto* control is reason enough to be exploring these avenues to unlock access.

[105] Ibid. Here the Commission is building on OECD, *Maximising the Economic and Social Value of Data* (n 28).

[106] Ibid. 37.

[107] Ibid.

[108] Ibid.

[109] Ibid.

[110] Regulation (EC) No 715/2007 of the European Parliament and of the Council of 20 June 2007 on type approval of motor vehicles with respect to emissions from light passenger and commercial vehicles (Euro 5 and Euro 6) [2007] OJ L171/1.

[111] Regulation 2006/1907 of 18 December 2006 concerning the Registration, Evaluation, Authorisation and Restriction of Chemicals (REACH) [2006] OJ L396/1.

[112] SWD (2017) (n 31) 38.

F *Final Fate*

Any chapter with 'obituary' in its title needs no further spoiler alerts. The DPR is no longer a policy priority within the EU. It seems to have been quietly buried. A new EU Data Act forms the basis for a regulatory environment that will facilitate increased data access, in both B2B and business-to-government (B2G) contexts.[113] The proposed legislation 'aims to ensure fairness in the allocation of data value among actors in the data economy and to foster access to and use of data'.[114] As part of this process, stakeholders who were surveyed indicated that data sharing does presently take place, including for innovating with product or service design, optimising supply chains, training algorithms and for predictive maintenance.[115] However this sharing does not seem to be occurring at optimal levels. Respondent businesses have

> experienced difficulties in relation to B2B data sharing over the last 5 years … including of a technical nature (formats, lack of standards) (69%), of a legal nature (i.e. refusal to grant access not linked to competition concerns) (55%), the lack of a legal basis for the data holder to give access to data (48%), abuse of contractual imbalance (44%) and unreasonable prices (42%).[116]

As means to the end of enhancing access, the focus has shifted to the design of model contract terms, facilitating the portability of data, developing common technical standards, facilitating the use of Application Programming Interfaces (APIs) and addressing unreasonable refusals to grant access to data. There is no longer any mention of the DPR as part of this access toolkit.

Nevertheless, some important elements of the 2017 proposal, such as a commons-oriented regime with a sector specific-focus on licensing, remain visible. One illustration is the desire to

> [g]ather key players from the manufacturing sector to agree – in a manner compliant with competition rules as well as principles of fair contracts – the conditions under which they would be ready to share their data and how to further boost data generation, notably via smart connected products…. Where data generated by individuals are concerned, their interests should be fully taken into account in such a process and compliance with data protection rules must be ensured.[117]

The focus is on designing institutional governance arrangements that are sector-specific and market-specific. The Commission is studying establishing

113 European Commission 'Data Act: Businesses and Citizens in Favour of a Fair Data Economy' (Press Release, 7 December 2021) <www.digital-strategy.ec.europa.eu/en/news/data-act-businesses-and-citizens-favour-fair-data-economy>.

114 European Commission, *Summary Report of the Public Consultation on Data Act and Amended Rules on the Legal Protection of Databases* (2021) 1 <www.digital-strategy.ec.europa.eu/en/public-consultationdata-act-summary-report>.

115 Ibid. 4–5.

116 Ibid. 4.

117 European Commission, 'A European Strategy for Data' (n 37) 26.

> data access and use rights, potentially on the basis of fair, reasonable, proportionate, transparent and non-discriminatory terms for non-personal data. It could apply to specific data, such as non-personal data generated by objects connected to the IoT in professional use, or to a wider set of data sharing situations.[118]

To the extent that IP is mentioned, it is with an eye to reconciling the *sui generis* database right or trade secret protection such that these regimes do not impede reasonable access to data.[119] Access rights are evidently the future.[120]

Given the increasing value of data markets, the failure of property logic, as an obligatory adjunct to market-making, is remarkable. It is therefore informative to reconstruct why the 'property for market-making' logic ultimately faltered. One reason has to do with the relative lack of success of the *sui generis* database right, which is the closest analogy to the proposed DPR. Periodic assessments have concluded that this right has not lived up to the promise of facilitating investment in and incentivising the creation of databases in the EU.[121] According to the most recent evaluation, 'there is no evidence to conclude that the *sui generis* right has been fully effective in stimulating investment in the European database industry, nor in creating a fully functioning access regime for stakeholders'.[122] This cannot have been an encouraging precedent. A second and related reason can be attributed to the growing commitment to open data within the Commission.[123] The recently enacted Open Data Directive[124] builds on previous efforts to ensure 'that data held by public sector bodies must be made available for commercial and non-commercial re-use, with as few strings attached as possible'.[125] An important clarification is that public sector bodies which own *sui generis* database rights may no longer exercise these to exclude others from using that data. The principal EU IP regime which previously applied to public sector data is thus no longer applicable. While definitional difficulties lie ahead – when has data generation been sufficiently publicly funded to qualify – the dial has been set to open access for vast amounts of valuable data in the EU.

118 'Inception Impact Assessment on the Data Act' (n 50) 5.

119 Ibid. 1.

120 This paradigm shift is being noticed by commentators: ML Montagnani and A von Appen, 'IP and Data (Ownership) in the New European Strategy on Data' [2021] European Intellectual Property Review 156; M Leistner 'Protection of and Access to Data under European Law' in J-A Lee, RM Hilty and K- C Liu (eds), *Artificial Intelligence and Intellectual Property* (Oxford University Press, 2021) 383.

121 DG Internal Market and Services Working Paper 'First Evaluation of Directive 96/9/EC on the Legal Protection of Databases' (12 December 2005); J Reda 'Learning from Past Mistakes. Similarities in the European Commission's Justifications of the Sui Generis Database Right and the Data Producers' Right' in S Lohsse, R Schulze and D Staudenmayer (eds.), *Trading Data in the Digital Economy* (Nomos 2017) 295.

122 Commission SWD, 'Evaluation of Directive 96/9/EC' (2018) (n 48) 46.

123 M van Eechoud, 'A Serpent Eating Its Tail: The Database Directive Meets the Open Data Directive' (2021) 52 *IIC* 375.

124 Directive (EU) 2019/1024 on open data and the re-use of public sector information of 20 June 2019 [2019] OJ L172/56.

125 Van Eechoud, 'A Serpent Eating Its Tail (n 123) 376.

The third reason seems the most dispositive: the intended beneficiaries of this new right were not convinced of its benefits. This conclusion flows from the results of a public consultation on the 2017 proposals. There were 380 responses, mainly from private organisations, 'including manufacturers and users of connected devices, operators and users of online platforms, data brokers, and businesses commercialising data-based products and services'.[126] The trend was clear: 'Most respondents do not support regulatory intervention, be it by creating ownership-type rights or by licensing obligations'.[127] The synopsis report indicates that data holders 'feel that their investments in data collection (capabilities) are well protected, notably through the Database and Trade Secrets Protection Directives, requiring no additional regulation'.[128] However, looking to the future, 'virtually all stakeholders agree with the Commission's objective of making more data available for reuse'. In certain sectors, such as the automotive after-sales market, there were concerns about fair access to data. Consequently, respondents argued that sector-specific approaches are preferred, since 'data value chains and business models building on data are extremely varied, making it difficult to design one-size-fits-all solutions'.[129] There was a strong preference, both amongst survey respondents and at subsequent workshops, to continue to rely on contractual solutions which not only require but also engender trust. Contractual solutions allowed parties to ascertain what the data would be used for, whether parties complied with data protection norms and that the data would be adequately protected once access is granted. Party autonomy was preserved, and commercially sensitive information was protected while allowing investments in gathering data to be recouped.[130]

By contrast, the lack of appetite for a new DPR comes across very strongly in the consultation:

> Many stakeholders commented at meetings and workshops that the crucial question in B2B data sharing was not so much which entity has an 'ownership title' of some sort on the data, but how access is organised.... The idea of a right to licence data from sensor-equipped machines, tools or devices is thus viewed with scepticism when awarded exclusively to either the Original Equipment Manufacturer (OEM) or the user of a sensor-equipped machine, tool or device. Stakeholders think it unlikely to achieve its stated goal of facilitating the tradability of data by reinforcing its legal status. This potential way forward would on the contrary

[126] Summary report of the public consultation on Building a European Data Economy (31 May 2017) <www.ec.europa.eu/digital-single-market/en/news/summary-report-public-consultation-building-european-data-economy>.

[127] Ibid.

[128] European Commission, 'Synopsis Report on the Consultation on the "Building A European Data Economy" Initiative' (2017) 5 <www.digital-strategy.ec.europa.eu/en/synopsis-report-public-consultation-building-european-data-economy>.

[129] Ibid.

[130] Ibid.

> strengthen the de facto holder's control over access to data, create legal uncertainty in the practical application and thus generate additional legal transaction costs.[131]

An annex to the synopsis report reveals in greater detail why the DPR failed to convince. Respondents had 'reservations about the idea of a data ownership right in general – irrespective of the party/parties to whom it would be granted'.[132] The misappropriation-based or defensive variant of the new right could 'have a chilling effect on re-use of third-party data as it increases the burden on the data supplier to demonstrate that such supply was lawful'.[133] The property right version was also unpopular because of the predictable schism when it came to choosing between either the OEM or the device user as the default owner – each constituency was concerned about being excluded. For example, device users whose use generated the data were concerned that granting sensor manufacturers a property right 'would only reinforce the current de facto control of manufacturers and ensuing lock-in effects going as far as creating new data monopolies. Furthermore, some respondents felt that it may not be compatible with trade secrets protection legislation as the sensor-equipped machine, tool or device may feedback data revealing trade secrets from the company operating it'.[134] More broadly, there was a sense that market-based (contractual) solutions worked better than regulatory allocation; there were practical difficulties in delineating between both (i) personal and non-personal data, as well as (ii) 'raw' data and data resulting from an analytics operation; and 'a new IP right would make data sharing more complicated as it increases legal costs of implementation, ultimately leading to less data being shared'.[135] The DPR looks set to remain in the realm of a thought experiment that didn't make the transition into practice.

IV THE COMMONS MODEL AS A SUCCESSOR

Laying the DPR to rest matters because metaphors matter. 'The concepts that govern our thoughts … also govern our everyday functioning, down to the most mundane details. Our concepts structure what we perceive, how we get around in the world and how we relate to other people'.[136] The property metaphor aligns with a worldview that sees data as an asset.[137] Intellectual property is also a powerful,

[131] Ibid. However there was relatively more appetite for an 'exploitation right' to be shared between the OEM and the user of the machine.

[132] European Commission, 'Annex to the Synopsis Report: Detailed Analysis of the Public Online Consultation Results on "Building a European Data Economy"' (2017) 23 <www.digital-strategy.ec.europa.eu/en/synopsis-report-public-consultation-building-european-data-economy>.

[133] Ibid. 22.

[134] Ibid. 23.

[135] Ibid. 23–24. However, as noted above, joint rights for both OEMs and data producers/users was viewed more favourably.

[136] G Lakoff and M Johnson, *Metaphors We Live By* (University of Chicago Press, 1980) 1.

[137] Nolin, 'Data as Oil, Infrastructure or Asset?' (n 1); Madison, 'Tools for Data Governance' (n 7) 29–31 (reviewing oil, sunlight and liquid/flow metaphors for data).

mobilising metaphor.[138] The waning of this metaphor in the context of machine-generated data has significance for the following reasons. First, there is the current tendency to equate de facto control with 'ownership' in data contracts, even where the intention is to allocate accountability and responsibility.[139] We are in need of a new vocabulary to describe the rights, responsibilities, duties, and privileges that will enable the data access agenda, while acknowledging that de facto control is often the starting point. Alternatives do exist. In certain contexts, ownership has been substituted by custodianship[140] or stewardship.[141] There are proposals to replace owning data with holding data, to emphasise that no rights *in rem* are involved.[142] This terminology will actively need to be developed. Second, the shift away from property should create the space for 'data as resource' to eclipse 'data as asset' in policy discourse. As Michael Madison reminds us, one 'strength of the word "resource" is that it properly evokes relationships between resources in resource systems or ecologies'.[143] This emphasises interdependence and the use value of a resource, rather than merely exchange value. A third consequence is that the eclipsing of property allows data to be reconceived as an infrastructural resource, in the sense proposed by Brett Frischmann.[144]

Infrastructure encompasses not just roads, railways, or communication networks but also 'non-physical facilities, such as education systems and governance systems (including for example the court system)'.[145] Frischmann's analysis includes such non-traditional forms of infrastructure, while emphasising demand-side reasons for valuing these resources. He describes infrastructure as a 'shared means to many ends'.[146] Three criteria are proposed to help identify such *functionally infrastructural* resources: (i) non-rivalrous consumption for some appreciable range of demand; (ii) social demand for the resource being driven by its downstream use in productive

[138] Metaphors do real work. See BL Frye, 'IP as Metaphor' (2014) 18 *Chapman Law Review* 735 (Assessing how justificatory theories are deployed rhetorically, such that the scope of IP rights doesn't match up to the underlying theories). See also P Loughlan, 'Pirates, Parasites, Reapers, Sowers, Fruits, Foxes… The Metaphors of Intellectual Property' (2006) 28 *Sydney Law Review* 211.

[139] In addition to the sources cited at (n 52), see B Van Asbroeck, J Debussche and J César, 'Big Data & Issues & Opportunities: Data Ownership' (*Bird & Bird LLP*, March 2019) <www.twobirds.com/en/news/articles/2019/global/big-data-and-issues-and-opportunities-data-ownership>.

[140] Andanda, 'Towards a Paradigm Shift' (n 17) 1054.

[141] OECD, Recommendation of the Council on Enhancing Access to and Sharing of Data, Section 1, Recommendation V(c); European Commission, 'A European Strategy for Data' (n 37) 20.

[142] Drexl, *Data Access and Control Report* (n 86) 2.

[143] Madison 'Tools for Data Governance' (n 7) 40. This is distinct from data as a resource in the extractive sense of neoliberal ideological individualism. See K Yeung, 'Algorithmic Regulation: A Critical Interrogation' (2017) 12(4) *Regulation and Governance* 505.

[144] BM Frischmann, *Infrastructure: The Social Value of Shared Resources* (Oxford University Press 2012). Data as an infrastructural resource is also emphasised in OECD *Data-Driven Innovation: Big Data for Growth and Well-Being* (2015) 179; UK National Infrastructure Commission, *Data for the Public Good* (2018); P Kawalek and A Bayat 'Data as Infrastructure' (UK NIC 2018).

[145] OECD, *Data-Driven Innovation* (n 144) 179.

[146] Frischmann, *Infrastructure* (n 144) 4.

activity; and (iii) the resource being an input in a wide range of products, including private, public and social goods.[147] All three features are applicable to data. A key feature of Frischmann's model is to argue that these features lead to society as a whole benefiting from infrastructure, since demand-side spillovers lead to social value which can far outweigh the private value of a resource. Stated briefly, infrastructure generates significant positive externalities.[148] Some degree of state involvement is usually required since markets won't otherwise provide adequate solutions. This involvement should ensure non-discriminatory access which need not be free, provided the access is affordable. The model proposed to ensure this is a commons model.[149] Frischmann identifies the threshold for commons-based intervention in the following terms:

> [The] strongest case for commons management as a public strategy is precisely when there is low market uncertainty and high uncertainty about what infrastructure uses will generate social value in the future. In this scenario, private owners have strong incentives to pursue a strategy of discrimination or prioritization because of the prospective private returns, but the public would be better off with a commons management strategy because of the prospective social returns.[150]

The strength of the commons model is that it offers an alternative to market and state paradigms, having the potential to ensure equitable access to infrastructural resources while providing sufficient incentives on the supply side. Commons 'form a third way of organising society and the economy that differs from both market-based approaches with their orientation toward prices, and from bureaucratic forms of organisation with their orientation toward hierarchies and commands'.[151]

When the Commission evoked a 'data commons' model,[152] this seemed to be a conscious application of Elinor Ostrom's foundational research on collective action facilitation mechanisms, based on design principles which support the self-governance of common-pool resources (CPRs).[153] These inductively-derived design principles are developed by communities who share access to or use the resources, as a means of preventing over-exploitation and encouraging sustainable

[147] Ibid. xiv.

[148] Ibid. ch 3.

[149] Ibid. ch 5. A commons model envisages that access can be conditional on payment, but access should be non-discriminatory and not depend on the identity of the user or the purpose to which the use is put. Both these aspects may need some refinement in the context of data. For example, direct competitors may need to be excluded from certain commons regimes, or else access provided at a level of abstraction.

[150] Ibid. 112.

[151] MD de Rosnay and F Stalder 'Digital Commons' (2020) 9(4) *Internet Policy Review* 1, 2.

[152] SWD (2017) (n 31) 36. For a more detailed consideration of the possible legal and technical configurations within data commons, see S Mills, 'Who Owns the Future? Data Trusts, Data Commons, and the Future of Data Ownership' (Manchester Metropolitan University, Future Economies and Policy Paper No 7, 2019) 21–28.

[153] E Ostrom, *Governing the Commons: The Evolution of Institutions for Collective Action* (Cambridge University Press 1990).

use. Amongst them are the principle that commons need to have clearly defined boundaries (who is entitled to benefit?), the importance of participatory decision-making, the necessity for rules to fit local circumstances, that is, the context, monitoring to ensure accountability, sanctions for those who transgress rules, and the nesting of the rules specific to one commons within larger networks of cooperation.[154] Within this approach, 'commons' is therefore not a place or set of resources but a form of institutionalised governance arrangements organised around a shared resource. 'The basic characteristic that distinguishes commons from noncommons is institutionalized sharing of resources among members of a community'.[155] Institutions in turn are the rules of the game; 'formal and informal rules that are understood and used by a community ... [not just formal rules but also including] the rules that establish the working "do's and don'ts" for the individuals in the [relevant] situation'.[156] This institutional approach has been extended beyond natural resources management to 'knowledge commons', or 'resource domains defined largely by their human generated character and their intangibility'.[157]

The emerging EU approach to data governance has clear parallels with key themes in the commons literature. Two developments illustrate the potential synergies. First, Ostrom's approach is fundamentally empirical in orientation. One of the 'key lessons of Ostrom's work [is that] commons research is and should be empirical, rather than simply conceptual.... It advances via the premise that details of governance of knowledge-sharing institutions matter as much as standard theoretical templates do'.[158] An approach which is case study driven does not mean that more generalisable lessons are beyond reach. A framework of structured enquiry becomes possible 'by aligning case studies of related but distinct commons phenomena, over time we will be able to identify those features of commons that are more and less significant to the success and failure of a commons enterprise'.[159]

This empirical orientation aligns with the EU approach in at least two important ways: (i) Section II of this chapter has described the distinctive features of data as an economic resource. An empirically attuned approach allows data to be construed as a very specific type of resource, which may not be congestible or exhaustible in the same way as natural resources but can nevertheless suffer from under-production,

[154] DS Wilson, E Ostrom and ME Cox 'Generalizing the Core Design Principles for the Efficacy of Groups' (2013) 90 *Journal of Economic Behavior & Organization* S21–S32.

[155] MJ Madison, BM Frischmann and KJ Strandburg, 'Reply: The Complexity of Commons' (2010) 95 *Cornell Law Review* 839, 841.

[156] E Ostrom and C Hess 'A Framework for Analyzing the Knowledge Commons' in C Hess and E Ostrom (eds), *Understanding Knowledge as a Commons: From Theory to Practice* (MIT Press 2007) 41, 42.

[157] MJ Madison, BM Frischmann and KJ Strandburg, 'Knowledge Commons' in B Hudson, J Rosenbloom and D Cole (eds), *Routledge Handbook of the Study of the Commons* (Routledge 2019) 76.

[158] Ibid. 78.

[159] MJ Madison, BM Frischmann and KJ Strandburg, 'Constructing Commons in the Cultural Environment' (2010) 95 *Cornell Law Review* 657, 660.

exclusion effects, or congestion on its own terms.[160] This approach also allows for further differentiation between different categories of data and associated business models.[161] The degree of access or sharing is therefore context specific. 'Data sharing is a label that may cover different economic modalities: sharing for free, trading for a monetary compensation or in exchange for other data, direct sharing of a dataset or indirect sharing of a data-based service only'.[162] (ii) This leads on to the second set of synergies. As opposed to focusing on individual fields of law – a data producer's right as a property-style, one-stop solution – the unfolding approach is more holistic. The EU is developing (or debating) regulatory approaches which span both horizontal, cross-cutting initiatives to improving data access in general alongside sector-specific regimes.[163] Examples of the former include adapting established competition law principles, such as the essential facilities doctrine, to data markets,[164] or developing restrictions on unfair contractual terms.[165] It extends to soft law toolkits, such as setting default or model contractual terms for data contracts[166] and technical guidance (for example, relating to the design of APIs to make them more accessible from a software developer's perspective).[167] Examples of the latter include sector specific approaches already in operation (or being contemplated in the future) to enable data access from: connected vehicles (including ensuring a level playing field in the after-sales repair and maintenance markets); access to customer bank account data (with prior permission) in order to facilitate the emergence of new FinTech payment solutions; sharing safety data relating to chemical production to protect human health and the environment; access to anonymised data in order to balance energy supply and demand, lowering costs and increasing the security of supply; sharing anonymised data relating to smart homes; similarly, sharing anonymised

[160] B Prainsack, 'Logged Out: Ownership, Exclusion and Public Value in the Digital Data and Information Commons' (2019) 6(1) *Big Data & Society* 2053951719829773 (emphasising the need to keep power asymmetries in mind when designing access); R Grossman, A Heath, M Murphy and M Paterson 'A Case for Data Commons: Toward Data Science as a Service' [2016] Computing in Science and Engineering 10, 18 (describing congestion challenges and the need for rationing when computational resources to analyse very large datasets are also shared on the cloud).

[161] Reviewed in European Commission, *Guidance on Sharing Private Sector Data in the European Economy*, SWD(2018) 125 final.

[162] Martens and others, *Business-to-Business Data Sharing* (n 32) 14. See also Fia 'An Alternative to Data Ownership' (n 52).

[163] W Kerber 'From (Horizontal and Sectoral) Data Access Solutions towards Data Governance Systems' (MAGKS Discussion Paper No. 40-2020).

[164] For a review of the issues, see J Crémer, Y-A de Montjoye and H Schweitzer, *Competition Policy for the Digital Era* (European Commission, Final Report 2019); T Tombal, 'Economic Dependence and Data Access' (2020) 51 *IIC* 70.

[165] The regulation of such terms were part of the flanking measures proposed in the SWD (2017) (n 31). For a more recent assessment, see EY, *Study on the Economic Detriment from Unfair and Unbalanced Cloud Computing Contract Terms* (Final Report, 2019).

[166] Support Centre for Data Sharing, *B.1 – Report on Model Contract Terms v2.0* (SMART 2018/1009, 26 Jul 2019). Sector-specific model clauses are available at: <www.eudatasharing.eu/recommended-contract-terms>.

[167] See: <www.eudatasharing.eu/legal-aspects/scds-api-licensing-assistant>.

healthcare data from smart wearable devices; circulating mechanical engineering data relating to production processes, with an eye to reducing defects and increasing productivity; codes of conduct on agricultural data sharing; and so on.[168] These initiatives prioritise data sharing for a variety of reasons, ranging from consumer protection to greater transparency, to ensuring fair competition, and to supporting innovation as well as scientific research. Some commentators have expressed concerns that this can result in a fragmented landscape.[169] However a commons-inspired approach allows us to appreciate the contextualised, responsive nature of these regimes while drawing broader thematic insights.

The second thematic parallel is the acknowledgment that law is relevant, within an approach that seems to otherwise respect the autonomy of participants who sustain or use the resource. Part of the appeal of the commons is that of a third way, between market and state. One might assume that 'the state should allow the commons to develop its institutional framework without being threatened by state intervention in its internal affairs and that state legislation should be limited to enabling statutes. Normatively, this argument promotes recognition of the commons' right to conduct its affairs autonomously'.[170] However, law is an external variable which shapes or reinforces internal interactions. The internal design principles for governance interact with external fields, such as legal regulation. One of the specific concerns in the context of data commons is that we cannot leave matters purely to data producers and users, to choose their preferred modes of governance, because not all parties are equally situated. Freedom of contract means far less when it operates within a context of unequal bargaining power. This has given rise to the notion of a constructed commons,[171] or a semi-commons.[172] Constructed commons

> refers to environments for developing and distributing [intangible resources …] that support pooling and sharing that knowledge in a managed way, much as a natural resource commons refers to the type of managed sharing environment for natural resources.… These environments are designed and managed with limitations tailored to the character of those resources and the communities involved rather than left to evolve via market transactions grounded solely in traditional proprietary rights.[173]

[168] SWD (2017) (n 31) 25–30; Support Centre for Data Sharing, B.2 – *Analytical Report on EU Law Applicable to Sharing of Non-personal Data v2.0* (SMART 2018/1009, 24 Jan 2020) 43–63.

[169] Fia 'An Alternative to Data Ownership' (n 52) 195; Support Centre, *Analytical Report on EU Law* (n 166).

[170] A Margalit, 'Commons and Legality' in GS Alexander and EM Peñalver (eds), *Property and Community* (Oxford University Press 2009) 141, 149–150.

[171] Madison, Frischmann and Strandburg, 'Constructing Commons' (n 159); A Ottolia and C Sappa, 'A Topography of Data Commons: From Regulation to Private Dynamism' (2022) 71 *GRUR International* 335.

[172] Martens and others, *Business-to-Business Data Sharing* (n 32) 5.

[173] Madison, Frischmann and Strandburg, 'Constructing Commons' (n 159) 659.

Relatively autonomous governance institutions can then be constructed against the background of legal regulation which supports pooling and sharing. A degree of legal regulation is therefore not antithetical to a commons approach. The broader point being made is that a data access agenda can be more fully developed within a commons framework, with its attendant flexibility, empirical orientation and recognition that governance frameworks can change over time.

V CONCLUSION

In its avatar as a market-making measure, property has widespread appeal. It tends to be a successful trope, which makes the failure of the DPR all the more instructive. If the underlying idea behind the DPR was to increase access to data, EU policymakers today seems prepared to directly engage with that goal, without the trappings of property as a resource regulation framework. On the one hand, this has to do with the nature of data as a valuable resource. Its value depends upon its circulation and use. On the other, we cannot escape de facto data control, through both technological and legal means. When we consider these two aspects cumulatively, an additional layer of property rights did not seem like a sufficiently attractive incentive which would dissipate de facto control, thereby ensuring greater circulation and use.

The DPR is also interesting because it showcases the limits of the intellectual property toolkit when it encounters subject matter like data. Defining the protected intangible subject matter, as well as the duration of protection, was challenging because IP works with discrete artefacts. Notwithstanding fuzzy boundaries, creative works, inventions and brands can be individually identified. By contrast, how do you 'thingify' a continuous flow of data? The nature of the rights and the property version in particular, served as a reminder that data is often co-produced; in this case by sensor or device manufacturers and the users of such devices. Allocating the new right proved contentious. Furthermore, a new property right would generate an added layer of negotiations, strengthen the position of de facto data holders and drive up costs. The heavy lifting seemed to be taken up by the exceptions and flanking measures, which proved to be the most enduring elements of the proposed DPR. This seems to have opened the pathway to a constructed commons framework, which directly engages with de facto control in differentiated, sector specific ways. It makes for an uncommon ending to a property story.

16

Intellectual Property Law and AI

Anke Moerland

I INTRODUCTION

When artificial intelligence (AI) technologies are used to generate technical inventions (e.g., using evolutionary algorithms to design antennas) or to make creative works (e.g., using IBM Watson to generate songs),[1] intellectual property (IP) law comes into play. Patents are granted for novel technical solutions and copyright is available for original creative works. With AI technologies permeating almost all sectors of our economy, more and more inventive and creative activities are being influenced by these technologies. In this chapter, I argue that the proliferation and continuously increasing sophistication of AI technologies requires us to rethink fundamental, human-centric concepts of IP law.

IP rights are meant to incentivise and reward activities that lead to inventive or creative output because society benefits from inventions and creative works. But where AI technologies are predominantly involved in the development and creation of inventions or creative works, machines do not need to be incentivised or rewarded for doing what they were programmed to do. According to the economic justification of IP rights, people may not invest resources into researching and creating new works or would not make them public without being compensated. Does the current level of IP protection sufficiently incentivise the development of AI technologies? Patents (for technical solutions) and copyright (for creative works, including software code), allow the inventor and author to determine who can use these works and what price

[1] Research for this chapter has been carried out before March 2021. Only minor updates have been included since then. While it is commonly acknowledged that there is not one general definition for artificial intelligence, this chapter understands artificial intelligence to mean computer-based systems that are developed to mimic human behaviour. See Josef Drexl and others, 'Technical Aspects of Artificial Intelligence: An Understanding from an Intellectual Property Law Perspective' (2019) Max Planck Institute for Innovation & Competition Research Paper No 19–13, 3 <https://papers.ssrn.com/sol3/papers.cfm?abstract_id=3465577>. See also William Samore, 'Artificial Intelligence and the Patent System: Can a New Tool Render a Once Patentable Idea Obvious?' in Woodrow Barfield and Ugo Pagallo (eds), *Research Handbook on the Law of Artificial Intelligence* (Edward Elgar Publishing 2018) 481.

users have to pay to gain access to and make use of these goods. How does IP law ensure that fundamental AI technologies are available to others at a reasonable price?

These are some of the important questions that the protection of IP raises in the context of AI.[2] This chapter will not be able to answer all of them, as they require complex and normative assessments that are bound to change with the continuous improvements of AI technologies. Some believe that '[AI] or the rise of machines that are capable of independent problem solving and – even – acts of independent creation, represents the most complex and potent threat to the [IP] order that has ever occurred.'[3]

According to a study published by the World Intellectual Property Organisation (WIPO) in 2019, nearly 340,000 AI-related inventions have been patented worldwide. Over half of these patents were published between 2013 and 2018, showing a steep upward trend.[4] In terms of the precise technical area involved, machine learning predominates, making up 89% of the patents identified by the study. Deep learning is the fastest growing technique, but other techniques such as neural networks, latent representation, and unsupervised learning have also seen a clear increase.[5]

AI technologies are used for designing new materials, optimising manufacturing processes, drug discovery, and other processes.[6] However, AI technologies are also increasingly used in processes relevant to registering, administering, and enforcing IP rights. IP offices use machine-learning tools to categorise incoming applications according to the technical area of the invention or type of trademark, classify goods, or services for which a mark is applied, translate prior art documents, search prior art or earlier rights, or perform formality checks.[7] IP-right holders are equally offered several commercial AI-based tools to search for protected signs[8] or products infringing trademarks, copyright, or design rights,[9] or to assist in patent licensing and prosecution, and competitor mapping.[10]

With AI infiltrating almost all aspects of IP law, many IP offices and organisations have launched consultations with a large variety of stakeholders regarding the interplay

2 I have discussed questions regarding trademarks and AI use elsewhere, such as when consumers are assisted by AI technology in the purchasing process, what function do trade mark rights still fulfil? See Anke Moerland and Christie Kafrouni, 'Online Shopping with Artificial Intelligence: What Role to Play for Trade Marks?' (2021) <https://ssrn.com/abstract=3942770>.

3 Jeremy Cubert and Richard Bone, 'The Law of Intellectual Property Created by Artificial Intelligence' in Barfield and Pagallo (n 2) 415.

4 WIPO, 'WIPO Technology Trends 2019: Artificial Intelligence' (Geneva 2019) 13.

5 Ibid. (n 5) 31.

6 Liza Vertinsky, 'Thinking Machines and Patent Law' in Barfield and Pagallo (n 3) 490.

7 Anke Moerland and Conrado Freitas, 'Artificial Intelligence and Trademark Assessment' in Jyh-An Lee, Reto Hilty and Kung-Chung Liu (eds), *Artificial Intelligence and Intellectual Property* (Oxford University Press 2021); WIPO, 'WIPO Index of AI Initiatives in IP Offices' (WIPO, 2021) <www.wipo.int/about-ip/en/artificial_intelligence/search.jsp>.

8 <www.Corsearch.com>.

9 <www.Shipglobalip.com>.

10 <www.Cipher.ai and leap-ip.ai>.

between IP and AI. Between September 2019 and November 2020, WIPO has held three Conversations on Intellectual Property and Artificial Intelligence and published two Issues Papers on the impact of AI on IP policy.[11] The US Patent and Trademark Office issued a report in October 2020 on stakeholders' views regarding the impact of AI on other IP policy areas.[12] The UK Intellectual Property Office has launched public consultations on whether the current IP regime strikes the appropriate balance in encouraging AI development and its use across the UK economy in 2021.[13]

The aim of this chapter is to explain how IP law currently applies to (1) AI-implemented inventions and incentivises their development and to (2) AI-assisted and AI-generated output. I follow the classification used by the Max Planck Institute for Innovation and Competition (MPI) research group, which distinguishes between:

> (i) AI-generated inventions (where AI acts autonomously without human intervention); (ii) AI-assisted inventions (where humans use AI as a tool to invent), and (iii) AI-implemented inventions (where AI is implemented as part of the invention).[14]

The chapter will provide an assessment of the criteria that need to be fulfilled to be entitled to patent or copyright protection, who the inventor or author can be under the current law, and who the owner of the rights would be. The analysis not only focusses on how we understand the law now but also highlights open questions as to how the law may need to be changed if at all. While fully autonomously AI-generated works are still a matter of the future, the challenges and questions as to their potential protection are also addressed. The chapter is based on doctrinal legal research, normative methods in relation to IP theories, and literature research. The assessment will focus on European Union (EU) law and the Convention on the Grant of European Patents (EPC), with the understanding that many IP legal frameworks share similar rationales and rules, due to the partial harmonisation of IP laws between jurisdictions, which has been achieved through international agreements. Broader questions of AI personhood, liability of AI, or ethical AI are beyond the scope of this chapter. I conclude that while the protection of AI technologies under patent and copyright law does not pose too many problems, the protection of AI-assisted and AI-generated works does.

[11] WIPO, 'The WIPO Conversation on Intellectual Property and Artificial Intelligence' (*WIPO*, 2020) <www.wipo.int/about-ip/en/artificial_intelligence/conversation.html>.

[12] USTPO, 'Public Views on Artificial Intelligence and Intellectual Property Policy' (*USTPO*, 2020), <www.uspto.gov/about-us/news-updates/uspto-releases-report-artificial-intelligence-and-intellectual-property>.

[13] UKIPO, 'Artificial Intelligence and IP: Copyright and Patents' <www.gov.uk/government/consultations/artificial-intelligence-and-ip-copyright-and-patents> (*UKIPO*, 2021).

[14] Josef Drexl and others, 'Comments of the Max Planck Institute for Innovation and Competition of 11 February 2020 on the Draft Issues Paper of the World Intellectual Property Organization on Intellectual Property Policy Ad Artificial Intelligence' (2020) para 10 <www.ip.mpg.de/fileadmin/ipmpg/content/stellungnahmen/2020-02-11_WIPO_AI_Draft_Issue_Paper__Comments_Max_Planck.pdf>.

II IP PROTECTION FOR AI TECHNOLOGIES

To assess how AI technologies can be protected through IP rights, we first need to define which elements are part of AI technologies. While there are several AI technologies, in this chapter, I focus on machine learning as the most common form of AI. However, examples from other forms of AI, such as evolutionary algorithms or genetic programming,[15] will also be referred to.

Machine learning, in particular artificial neural networks, consists of four elements: (1) a model architecture is established by a programmer and serves to develop an (2) algorithm through a training process with (3) training data, which is encoded in (4) software. The model architecture consists of layers of neurons connected with weights. Neurons are mathematical functions that translate input into output. Weights are trainable parameters, which are optimised during the training process. While the initial architecture does not evolve, it serves as the starting point to develop a model through the training process.[16]

As we will see, not many of these elements can be protected through IP rights. Algorithms or mathematical methods 'as such' are considered too abstract for patent or copyright protection.[17] What may be protected is software under specific conditions, either in the form of its code under copyright protection or the technical solution implemented in a computer programme under patent law.[18] Otherwise, trade secret protection, competition law, tort law, contract law, and/or technological protection measures may offer protection for models, algorithms, and weights under certain circumstances.[19] Section II addresses what IP protection is available for AI systems themselves. The IP protection available for the output that is assisted or generated by AI systems is discussed in Section III.

A *Copyright Protection for Computer Programmes Implementing AI Technology*

Copyright protection for computer programmes does not pose challenges to the current copyright framework; the challenges lie more in the protection of AI-assisted and AI-generated creative output.[20] Computer programmes can be protected by copyright

15 Drexl (n 1) 11; Samore (n 2) 478.

16 Drexl (n 15) 4.

17 Guidelines for Examination in the European Patent Office (March 2021) [hereinafter EPO Guidelines], Part G, II-3.3.1.

18 Hardware, in fact, could also be protected under patent law, for example Google's Tensor Processing Units (TPUs) that support machine learning. This chapter, however, focusses on software.

19 Directive (EU) 2016/943 on the protection of undisclosed know-how and business information [hereinafter Trade Secrets Directive] [2016] OJ L157; Josef Drexl and others, 'Artificial Intelligence and Intellectual Property Law – Position Statement of the Max Planck Institute for Innovation and Competition of 9 April 2021 on the Current Debate' (2021). Max Planck Institute for Innovation & Competition Research Paper No. 21-10, para 16 <https://ssrn.com/abstract=3822924>.

20 See Sections III and III.B.

if they are sufficiently original, in the sense that they do not copy other works and that an author has made creative choices.[21] Where software implements an AI algorithm that is expressed in coded form and stems from the developer's own intellectual creation,[22] both the source and object code can be protected as they are considered literary works. Abstract ideas or principles, such as a functional algorithm or its logic, are excluded from copyright protection.[23] The scope of protection, however, only extends to a prohibition of copying the code of an AI algorithm. The functionality of an AI system, such as a robot raising its arm, is not protected. Since small changes to a code can obtain the same or a very similar outcome and to the extent that code modified in this way will not amount to infringement, copyright law offers only limited protection.

B *Patent Protection for Computer-Implemented Inventions*

Technical solutions that are implemented in a computer programme can benefit from patent protection if they are novel, entail an inventive step, and are industrially applicable. In the European context, such inventions are referred to as computer-implemented inventions. The technical implementation of AI models and algorithms can therefore come under patent protection as long as a technical effect in a field of technology is produced.

1 Technical Invention

While according to Art 52(2) and (3) EPC,[24] computer programmes and mathematical methods *as such* are excluded from patentability, the jurisprudence of the European Patent Office (EPO) Boards of Appeal has provided guidelines on patenting software and methods that are implemented by technical means.[25] Where the claimed technical solution is implemented through a computer programme, patent protection is possible.[26] The US approach formulated in the *Alice* case also requires for software patents an improvement in the functioning of the computer.[27]

The EPO approach applicable to computer-implemented method claims is particularly relevant for AI technologies: as long as the invention using an AI technology

21 Directive 2009/24/EC on the legal protection of computer programs [2019] OJ L111 [hereinafter Software Directive]; Case C-393/09 *Bezpecnostní Softwarová Asociace v Ministerstvo Kultury* [2010] ECR I-13971.

22 Originality according to the Court of Justice of the European Union (CJEU) requires a developer to make free and creative choices in the creation of the work, reflecting her personality. See Section III.B.1.

23 Art 9(2) Agreement on Trade-Related Aspects of Intellectual Property Rights, Annex 1C of Marrakesh Agreement Establishing the World Trade Organization (adopted on 15 April 1994) 1869 U.N.T.S. 299 [hereinafter TRIPS Agreement].

24 Art 52 of Convention on the Grant of European Patents, signed 05/10/1973, 1065 U.N.T.S. 199 [hereinafter EPC].

25 EPO Guidelines, Part G, II-3.6.

26 Drexl (n 20) para. 10.

27 *Alice Corp. Pty Ltd. v. CLS Bank International*, 134 S. Ct. 2347, 2354–55 (2014); 35 USC § 101; Brian Higgins, 'The Role of Explainable Artificial Intelligence in Patent Law' (2019) 31 *IPTLJ* 1, 2.

brings forth a technical effect (by claiming a method involving the use of technical means or the use of technical means itself, such as the device), it has technical character and will not be considered a mathematical method *as such*, but a patentable subject-matter. Examples of an AI invention with a technical effect are a computer-implemented method for autonomous driving or controlling a robot or 'the use of a neural network in a heart-monitoring apparatus for the purpose of identifying irregular heartbeats'.[28]

To summarise, algorithms can be claimed as computer-implemented inventions if the specific technical implementation that confers a technical character is included in the claims. This means that what is protected is the application of the AI technology for the particular technical purpose specified in the claims.

2 Novelty, Inventive Step, and Industrial Application

Aside from being considered a technical invention, a computer-implemented AI technology also needs to be novel, inventive, and industrially applicable. A patent will be granted over the invention only if it does not form part of the state of the art. The state of the art includes 'everything made available to the public' before the filing date of the patent application.[29] What therefore needs to be assessed is whether an existing document discloses the invention. Disclosure in this sense means that a person skilled in the art (skilled person) is enabled to make the claimed invention.[30] Hence, if a neural network or other AI technology directed to a technical purpose as claimed in the patent application has not previously been disclosed, it will be novel.

While novelty centres around the question of whether the prior art already discloses the invention, inventive step requires the invention to not have been obvious to the skilled person on the basis of the state of the art. In other words, the inventive step requirement prevents inventions that are within the reach of (or obvious to) a skilled person from being granted patent protection.[31] The problem-solution approach of the EPO requires that the skilled person would not have suggested the claimed technical features that distinguish the invention from others, when presented with the closest prior-art documents from the same technical field.[32] So even where the state of the art includes AI technologies applied in certain technical contexts, it is possible that an uninventive and unimaginative skilled person would not utilise such information and knowledge and arrive at the invention in the claimed technical field.

[28] See Kemal Bengi and Christopher Heath, 'Patents and Artificial Intelligence Inventions' in Christopher Heath, Anselm Kamperman Sanders and Anke Moerland (eds), *Intellectual Property and the Fourth Industrial Revolution* (Wolters Kluwer 2020) 135, and EPO Guidelines, Part G, II-3.3.1.

[29] EPO Guidelines, Part G, IV-1.

[30] The standard of the skilled person represents a fictional character of a person who knows everything but imagines nothing. See Section III.C.1 for more detail.

[31] Bengi and Heath (n 29) 141.

[32] Drexl (n 20) para 25; Bengi and Heath (n 29) 141.

What is particularly relevant for computer-implemented inventions, and hence also AI technologies, is the fact that when determining obviousness, the skilled person only considers those features that contribute to the technical character of the invention. Features of a mathematical method contribute to the technical character of the invention if they contribute to producing a technical effect that serves a technical purpose.[33] The recent referral to the Enlarged Board has clarified in which parts of a computer-implemented invention technical effects can lie. The *Pedestrian Simulation* case G1/19 concerned a 'computer-implemented method of simulating movement'[34] through venues like a railway station or a stadium. In assessing whether any technical effects were involved, the Board of Appeal held that:

> In sum, technical effects can occur within the computer-implemented process (e.g. by specific adaptations of the computer or of data transfer or storage mechanisms) and at the input and output of this process. Input and output may occur not only at the beginning and the end of a computer-implemented process but also during its execution (e.g. by receiving periodic measurement data and/ or continuously sending control signals to a technical system).

From this, we can conclude that for AI technologies, technical effects can stem from the specific implementation of the process, the input, and the output. Overall, while it is clear that an AI invention can entail an inventive step and thereby qualify for protection, a case-by-case analysis will determine what the differences between the closest prior art and the claimed invention produce in terms of technical effects and whether the claimed solution to the technical problem would have been obvious to a skilled person.[35]

Finally, an invention must be industrially applicable. This requirement is easily met where the invention can be exploited in an industrial field. This does not seem to pose a problem for AI solutions.

3 Disclosure

What has been discussed as a potential problem for patenting AI technologies is the requirement of clarity and disclosure: to be granted a patent, the applicant needs to disclose the invention in a way that enables the skilled person to make the invention.[36] An invention will only produce societal benefit of becoming publicly accessible and fostering further development and innovation in the field, if persons trained in the field can work on it. The question arises, whether for machine learning, full

[33] Non-technical features can also, in the context of the invention, contribute to producing a technical effect and serving a technical purpose. See EPO Guidelines, Part G, VII-5.4.

[34] Case G0001/19, *Pedestrian Simulation* (EPO Enlarged Board of Appeal, 10 March 2021) paras 4 and 7.

[35] For a recent analysis of the patentability of AI inventions, see R Moufang, 'Artificial Intelligence and the Technicality Requirement of Patent Law' in C Godt and M Lamping (eds), *A Critical Mind* (Springer 2023, MPI Studies on Intellectual Property and Competition Law, vol 30), 471–488.

[36] Art 29 TRIPS Agreement; Art 83 and 84 EPC.

disclosure of the training process is possible where the causality between data points is not clear and weights are randomised.[37] However, certain guidelines have been formulated that make it plausible for AI models to be sufficiently disclosed.

According to Heath and Bengi, for a machine learning mechanism to be sufficiently clear and complete, the claims need to identify the specific AI technology, such as 'convolutional neural networks' or a 'support vector machine'.[38] This includes a detailed description of the training process, including the algorithm, criteria of data selection, and the specific training data, where the technical effect depends on the data used.[39] According to the MPI research group, 'where randomisation is applied, reproducibility of a model can be achieved if the used random number generator and "seeds" are disclosed.'[40]

To conclude, current patent laws provide protection for computer-implemented inventions if they employ technical means to produce a technical effect. This standard has been confirmed by the EPO Enlarged Board to also apply to computer-implemented simulations, including AI models. In addition, the invention should not be disclosed in prior art documents for the skilled person to be able to work on it; neither should the invention be within reach of this skilled person. This means that the combination of prior art documents in the same field of technology should not make it obvious for a skilled person to suggest the solution claimed in the application. Finally, disclosing the AI model in such a way that a skilled person can reproduce the model may pose challenges, but it seems feasible where details of the model, inputs, and the training process are specified.

III IP PROTECTION FOR AI-ASSISTED AND AI-GENERATED OUTPUTS

The most controversial aspects regarding the impact of AI on IP relate to whether output generated solely by or produced with considerable assistance from AI can be protected through IP rights. These concern AI-assisted inventions (where AI is used as a tool) and AI-generated inventions (where the AI autonomously generates an invention and no natural person qualifies as an inventor or author).[41] It is particularly the latter that poses important challenges to the IP system.

However, researchers in the field of automatic programming are of the opinion that at this stage and for the near future, AI-generated inventions remain out of reach.[42] According to a 2012 survey among industry experts, high-level

37 Drexl (n 20) para 15.

38 Bengi and Heath (n 29) 137.

39 Ibid.

40 Drexl (n 20) para 15.

41 Drexl and others (n 15).

42 Kim Daria, '"AI-Generated Inventions": Time to Get the Record Straight?' (2020) 69 *GRUR International* 443, 444.

artificial general intelligence is only achievable by 2075;[43] general artificial intelligence or superintelligence is only predicted for 2099.[44] In other words, the technological state of the art at this point or in the near future does not indicate that machines can act without a human providing instructions as to how a certain task should be performed.[45] Human designers are still considerably involved in

> the analysis and formal representation of a problem so that it can be solvable by means of computational modelling, the selection of input data, the definition of an objective function ... the design of a new algorithm or the adjustment of an existing algorithm, the interpretation of computational outcomes, etc.[46]

The emphasis should therefore be on how copyright and patent law apply to works made by humans, assisted by AI. At the same time, current questions and proposals regarding the IP protection of AI-generated works will be addressed.

A *AI as Inventor, Author, and Owner of IP Rights*

As long as AI technologies or machines are used as tools to solve a problem, the IP system is not challenged when it comes to the question of who should be named as an inventor or author. Generally, the human involved in the intelligent and creative conception of the invention is the inventor; equally, the person who makes free and creative choices for a work is the author of a copyright work. This is even where the inventor uses tools that surpass human capabilities (e.g., optical instruments) or which are self-organising (e.g., biological organisms).[47]

1 AI Authorship

The Berne Convention does not define the concept of an author, but its text and historical embedding strongly indicate that an author of a creative work is a natural person.[48] This anthropocentric focus on human authorship is also evident in other

43 Vincent Müller and Nick Bostrom, 'Future Progress in Artificial Intelligence: A Survey of Expert Opinion' in Vincent Müller (ed), *Fundamental Issues of Artificial Intelligence* (Springer 2016) <nickbostrom.com/papers/survey.pdf>, retrieved from Noam Shemtov, 'A Study on Inventorship in Inventions Involving AI Activity' (European Patent Office 2019) <www.epo.org/news-events/in-focus/ict/artificial-intelligence.html>.

44 Martin Ford, *Architects of Intelligence: The Truth about AI from the People Building It* (Packt Publishing 2018) 528, retrieved from Kim (n 43) 444.

45 Kim (n 43) 444.

46 Drexl (n 20) para 24.

47 Kim (n 43) 447.

48 See Berne Convention for the Protection of Literary and Artistic Works of September 9, 1886, completed at Paris on May 4, 1896 [Berne Convention]. See also Bernt Hugenholtz and Joao Pedro Quintais, 'Copyright and Artificial Creation: Does EU Copyright Law Protect AI-Assisted Output?' (2021) 52 *IIC* 1190, 1195.

aspects of EU law.[49] According to EU case law, the human who makes free and creative choices for a work and expresses their personality in the work is the author of a copyright work.[50] AG Trstenjak stated that only human creations are protected, including those created with the help of a technical aid.[51] In other words, AI systems currently cannot be authors of copyright works.

Where works are created by an AI, the question arises whether there is a human author behind the AI who makes creative choices and expresses their personality. Hugenholtz and Quintais distinguish between three stages in which creative choices by a human can take place: the conception, execution, and redaction of the work.[52] For general-purpose AIs,[53] like text-generation programmes or Google's Deep Dream Generator, a user may only push a button, and the AI carries out the process it was programmed to do. Arguably, in such situations, no creative choices are made by the user. Where users determine the input data and select and possibly redact the output, creative choices are likely to occur during the conception and redaction of the work, but less so during execution, which is usually dominated by the AI system. The developer of the AI system may qualify as a (co)-author where (s)he collaborated with the user in generating a specific creative output; in the case of general-purpose AI, however, it is unlikely that developers will make creative choices regarding the specific output.[54]

Another solution found by countries with a British tradition (UK, Ireland, New Zealand, South Africa) is to grant authorship to 'the person by whom the arrangements necessary for the creation of the work are undertaken',[55] in situations where a human author cannot be identified. However, it is doubtful whether this standard, also present in Irish legislation,[56] is in accordance with EU law.[57] If a human author cannot be identified, the work is considered 'authorless'. But according to EU law, works that are not created by humans are not protected by copyright, as discussed in Section III.A.1. Regardless of its EU-law compatibility, the allocation of authorship to the person making the necessary arrangement could lead, in the case of general-purpose AI, to a monopoly over AI-created works.

> A programmer or a company that designs an AI … that could create, for example, musical works according to a few criteria set by the end user, would arguably be

49 Ana Quintela Ribeiro Neves Ramalho, 'Originality Redux: An Analysis of the Originality Requirement in AI-Generated Works' [2019] *AIDA* 1, 11.

50 See Section III.B.1.

51 Case C-145/10 *Eva-Maria Painer v Standard VerlagsGmbH and Others* [2011] ECR I-1253, Opinion of AG Trstenjak, para 121.

52 See Section III.B.1.

53 General-purpose AI software is ready to use by a consumer to produce an artistic work with the help of an AI system. See Hugenholtz and Quintais (n 50) 1200.

54 Hugenholtz and Quintais (n 50) 1208.

55 UK Copyright, Designs and Patents Act 1988, s 9.3.

56 Irish Copyright and Related Rights Act 2000, art 21.

57 After Brexit, the UK is not anymore bound by EU law.

making the 'arrangements necessary' for the creation of those works, and could potentially own the rights in a near-infinite amount of copyright protected musical works.[58]

Overall, as the law stands, AI systems are not recognised as authors under any copyright system. Where developers or users of AI have made creative choices in the conception and/or redaction of creative work, they qualify for authorship.

2 AI Inventorship

In a recent study carried out for the EPO, all jurisdictions analysed therein do not currently foresee an AI system as an inventor.[59] This is supported by several patent offices' refusal of patent applications for inventions in which the Device for the Autonomous Bootstrapping of Unified Sentience (DABUS), 'a type of connectionist artificial intelligence', was indicated as an inventor.[60] In the Offices and relevant courts' decisions, the specific patent law rules, such as Art. 91 and Rule 19(1) EPC, are cited as requiring that an inventor designated in the application is a human being, not a machine. In addition, further reasons mentioned are that machines cannot be employed, nor can they exercise rights,[61] as they lack legal personality.

If machines cannot be named inventors, how do we determine (1) whether a human should still be able to claim inventorship rights, and (2) who the human behind the machine is? While the EPC does not define the concept of 'inventor', it is left to national legislation to determine inventorship. Looking at various jurisdictions worldwide, the general criterion used in national patent laws is that an inventor should contribute substantially to the intelligent and creative conception of the invention.[62] Conception entails 'forming or devising an idea or plan in the mind'.[63] The focus lies on the result, so it is the idea or plan, not the process in a human's mind.[64] Hence, where a human makes a substantial contribution to the conception of an invention, even if the technical solution may have been found by applying an AI system, the human qualifies as the inventor. For inventorship,

[58] Jani Ihalainen, 'Computer Creativity: Artificial Intelligence and Copyright' (2018) 13 *JIPLP* 724, 725.

[59] Shemtov (n 44) 20.

[60] Grounds of the EPO decision of 27 January 2020 on EP 18275163 and EP 18275174, in EPO, 'EPO Publishes Grounds for Its Decision to Refuse Two Patent Applications Naming a Machine as Inventor' (28 January 2020) <www.epo.org/news-events/news/2020/20200128.html>; *Thaler v Vidal* [2023] No. 22-919 US Supreme Court (24 April 2023); *Stephen L. Thaler* [2022] NZIPOPAT 2 (31 January 2022); *Thaler v Comptroller General of Patents Trade Marks and Designs* [2021] EWCA Civ 1374, [2022] Bus LR 375 (21 September 2021); *Commissioner of Patents v Thaler* [2022] FCAFC 62 (13 April 2022); *Thaler v Iancu, et al.* [2021] 1:20-cv-00903 (2 September 2021); *Stephen L. Thaler* [2021] 11 W (pat) 5/21 (11 November 2021).

[61] According to Art 60 EPC, the right to a patent belongs to the inventor.

[62] Shemtov (n 44) 19.

[63] Ibid. 20, referring to the Oxford English Dictionary.

[64] Ibid. See also Vertinsky (n 7) 496 for the same approach under US patent law.

one therefore needs to distinguish between AI-assisted inventions (where a human contributes substantially to the creative conception) and AI-generated inventions (where a human does not qualify for inventorship).

It is clear that various persons may contribute substantially to the conception of an AI-assisted invention. Heath and Bengi argue that one needs to inquire which human intervention is most closely attributable to the invention.[65] The closest human behind the AI machine could be the owner of the AI system, such as the programmer who defines the problem and formulates the algorithm,[66] those who provide the training or the data, the manufacturer of the machine, or the user who recognises the importance and utility of the output to solve a particular problem.[67] The latter approach is supported by patent law's focus on the result rather than the nature of the inventive process: no matter whether the inventor had a flash of genius, sheer luck, or undertook laborious efforts, (s)he is still the inventor.[68] Overall, as Vertinsky argues, there is considerable uncertainty about who can legitimately claim rights of inventorship,[69] and whether these would be the best persons to exploit the invention from an economic perspective.[70]

The situation may become even more complicated should the automation of problem-solving through machines reach a degree that no longer fits the concept of human inventorship.[71] This could be the case where computers, in the future, could deviate from the algorithm provided by a human or relate inputs and outputs without instructions from a human.[72] The question arises then whether it is desirable to allow (a) an AI system to be named as an inventor, or (b) patents to be granted without the mention of an inventor in cases where a machine has created the relevant invention.

Regarding option (a), there are important reasons not to allow AI-inventorship as long as AI systems (1) do not possess legal personality and (2) cannot be the holder of rights. This is currently not the case and would require a change of the law that goes beyond IP law questions. But if such changes were effectuated, the same criteria as for human inventors could apply for determining inventorship: if the AI system's contribution to the invention was substantial, it should be recognised as an inventor.[73]

Option (b) suggests that there could be patents that do not refer to an inventor.[74] Where the inventor is a machine and is not receptive of incentives to invent,

65 Bengi and Heath (n 29) 147.
66 Kim (n 43) 452–453.
67 Shemtov (n 46) 21.
68 Ibid.
69 Vertinsky (n 7) 500–506.
70 Daniel Gervais, 'Is Intellectual Property Law Ready for Artificial Intelligence?' (2020) 69 *GRUR International* 117, 118.
71 Kim (n 43) 448.
72 Ibid. 455.
73 Shemtov (n 44) 20.
74 Discussed by Noam Shemtov during a presentation on 'Who's the Inventor: Could and Should AI Systems Be Designated as Inventors on Patent Applications?' at Oxford intellectual Property Research Centre Invited Speaker Series (18 November 2021).

mentioning the inventor may not be needed.[75] On the other hand, the general rule that the first ownership of patents is attributed to inventors may constitute a good reason to mention the inventor even where it is a machine.[76] While in principle national procedural rules could allow for a patent application without mentioning an inventor and thereby make patent protection available for inventions generated by AI without AI obtaining legal personality, important questions regarding ownership of patents would have to be determined first.

Regardless of which option is pursued, it is doubtful whether the purpose of patent law, namely that of incentivising innovation, is served by the grant of patents for AI-generated inventions.[77] Some argue that allowing AI to be considered as inventors would incentivise research in the field of AI;[78] UKIPO is looking at legislative options such as recognizing AI as an inventor in order to encourage research using AI.[79] As Francis Gurry, former Director General of WIPO, stated:

> From a purely economic perspective, if we set aside other aims of the IP system, such as 'just reward' and moral rights, there is no reason why we shouldn't use IP to reward AI-generated inventions or creations. But this still requires some thought.[80]

On the other hand, it is not clear whether more property rights will incentivise innovation. Samore fears that where patent protection is granted on a large scale to inventions that required almost no effort by a human, these could lead to patent thickets that may hinder particularly smaller competitors from developing new technical solutions;[81] resources may be diverted from inventing to patent searches out of fear for potential liability for infringement.[82] But not allowing patent protection for AI-generated inventions and thereby allotting their output to the public domain may lead to other problems, such as mentioning a human (instead of the machine) as inventor in a patent application, while in reality, the human contribution has been nil.[83] To conclude, as long as AI-generated inventions are still a matter of the future, research into the likely effects of patent protection for AI-generated inventions should enable policy-makers to determine the way forward.

75 The right of the inventor to be mentioned in the patent in Art 62 EPC is considered a moral right, which only has meaning for humans, encouraging their inventive activities.

76 See Section III.A.1.

77 Jozefien Vanherpe, 'AI and IP: A Tale of Two Acronyms' in Jan De Bruyne and Cedric Vanleenhove (eds), *Artificial Intelligence and the Law* (Intersentia 2021) 229.

78 Vanherpe (n 79) 230.

79 UKIPO (n 14).

80 'Artificial Intelligence and Intellectual Property: An Interview with Francis Gurry' (2018) *WIPO Magazine*.

81 A patent thicket is an overlapping set of patent rights around a single invention, which requires competitors to obtain licensing agreements for multiple patents.

82 Samore (n 2) 482.

83 Ryan Abbott, 'I Think, Therefore I Invent: Creative Computers and the Future of Patent Law' (2016) 57 *BCL Rev* 1079, 1097–1098.

3 AI Ownership

In principle, the inventor of a patented technology is the first owner of the patent; (s)he is granted the right to enforce the patent, to license or transfer it.[84] In many jurisdictions, an exception applies for inventions developed in situations of employment: then, the employer owns the patent or is designated as the automatic transferee of the right to the patent.[85] These rules apply to AI-assisted inventions; in other words, the human mentioned as inventor is also the owner of the patent.

If a patent application for an AI-generated invention does not mention a human inventor, who would or should be considered the owner of the patent? There are various views about this without a conclusive answer. So far, AI systems do not possess legal personality and therefore cannot be holders of ownership rights. Two main options come to mind for ownership: the owner of the AI system, or the designer/user of the AI system who put the AI tool to produce a specific invention. Also here, one will have to assess who has made a substantial contribution to the conception of the invention by the AI.[86] Economic arguments would not favour ownership entitlement that leads to double compensation. Where the owner of the AI system or its programmer already holds a patent in the AI system itself, further patent rights in the system's output may not be economically effective.[87] In view of several contributors, co-ownership could be another option, however this may be unpractical, leading to fragmentation of ownership rights.[88]

Regarding literary and artistic works, the general rule regarding first ownership is that the creator of the work is the first owner of copyright. As in the case of patents, there are exceptions to this rule. The copyright for works made in employment, or which have been commissioned, are owned by the employer or the commissioning party, respectively.[89]

Different from patent law, a work will currently only be protected by copyright if it is created by a human, due to the close link between the author and the work. Hence, the situation that a work does not have an author, leaving one to determine the owner of the copyright, would not arise.[90] Should machines be considered authors under the copyright system, the question then arises whether they could also become owners of copyright. This will only be possible if they are also granted legal personality. So far, this is not the case.[91]

84 Vanherpe (n 79) 228; Vertinsky (n 7) 499.
85 Shemtov (n 44) 11.
86 See Section III.A.2; Vanherpe (n 79) 226.
87 Ibid. 235.
88 Ibid. 237.
89 In some systems, this rule has been altered. The Singapore's Copyright Act 2021 vests first ownership of copyright for commissioned works in the commissioned party. This is so for photographs, portraits, and engravings. See Ng-Loy Wee Loon, *Law of Intellectual Property of Singapore* (3rd edn, Sweet & Maxwell 2021).
90 Compare with solution proposed by systems following the British, see Section III.A.1.
91 Note that the European Parliament has called for e-personhood for AI, which the European Commission, however, has not taken up. See Thomas Burri, 'The EU Is Right to Refuse Legal

B *Copyright Protection for AI-Assisted Literary and Artistic Works*

Many AI systems produce creative works, such as music with Amper Music, translations with DeepL, poetry by Google's Verse-by-Verse, or paintings with ArtBreeder. The results are certainly artistic, musical, or literary works; one cannot tell whether they have been created by a human or AI. However, this does not mean that they benefit from copyright protection.

1 Copyright Protected Works and Originality

Works considered for copyright protection can take various forms. Article 2 of the Berne Convention provides a list of literary and artistic works that are generally copyrightable. These include musical compositions, dramatic works, books, choreographies, architecture, cinematographic works, to name but a few. They are all situated in the literary, scientific, or artistic domain.[92] As it stands, AI systems can produce such creative works.

However, a copyright protected work also needs to constitute a concrete and original expression of an author. According to EU case law, a work can only be protected by copyright if it represents 'the author's own intellectual creation'.[93] This originality standard contains two elements: (a) that the work has not been copied, and (b) that it presents an intellectual creation. While the former requirement can be fulfilled by AI systems, the latter cannot. Machines can create independent works that deviate sufficiently from the style they learned from and therefore would be considered new.[94] In contrast, the second requirement of an author's intellectual creation is inherently linked to a human person, manifesting the pivotal role of the author in the anthropocentric system of copyright protection.[95] While under patent law, it is crucial to assess whether the output (e.g. the invention) solves a technical problem, in copyright law, the process of creation is decisive. According to established CJEU case law[96] and recently confirmed,[97] a work benefits from copyright protection if in the creation process, the author made free, personal, and creative choices reflecting their personality. Skill and labour that show economic investment alone will not be

Personality for Artificial Intelligence' (*Euractiv*, 31 May 2018) <www.euractiv.com/section/digital/opinion/the-eu-is-right-to-refuse-legal-personality-for-artificial-intelligence/>.

92 Hugenholtz and Quintais (n 50) 1194.

93 Case C-05/08 *Infopaq International A/S v Danske Dagblades Forening* (Infopaq) [2009] ECR I-06569, para. 45.

94 Martin Senftleben and Laurens Buijtelaar, 'Robot Creativity: An Incentive-Based Neighbouring Rights Approach' (2020) 42 *EIPR* 797, 799.

95 Case C-469/17 *Funke Medien NRW GmbH v Federal Republic of Germany* (Funke Medien) [2019] ECLI:EU:C:2018:870, Opinion of AG Szpunar, para. 60;

96 *Infopaq* (n 95) para. 45; *Painer* (n 53) paras. 90–93.

97 Case C-683/17, *Cofemel – Sociedade de Vestuário SA v G-Star Raw CV* [2019] ECLI:EU:C:2019:721, para 30; Case C-833/18, *SI and Brompton Bicycle Ltd v Chedech / Get2Get* [2019] ECLI:EU:C:2020:461, para 230.

sufficient.[98] A similar standard of creative choices has been established by the US Supreme Court.[99]

These human creative choices differ fundamentally from how machines operate. As Shtefan argues,[100] computers carry out a purely mechanical, deterministic process, on the basis of the information put into the system and the programmed function. They do not generate an outcome without prior data about similar objects. This is fundamentally different from creative activity by humans, who create choreographies or music 'by internal stimulus and without prior training'. AI will not be able to feel emotions or a need for self-expression, which is embodied in creativity.[101] In conclusion, AI systems as machines will not be able to make creative choices that bring the output they create in the realm of copyright protection.

2 AI-Assisted Output

In contrast, works created by AI tools with 'sufficient traces of human creativeness' in the process of creation can be protected by copyright.[102] However, one needs to determine what degree of human guidance is sufficient, when using AI systems, to qualify for copyright protection. This determination is far from clear and depends on the creative choices humans can make at the different stages of the creative process and the different types of AI systems.

Humans often make creative choices in the conception phase of works, regarding subject matter and plot, but also medium, format, or, if applied to AI tools, which AI system and input data to choose. In addition, in the redaction phase of a creative work, humans often edit the product before it is published. These also apply to AI-assisted products. Creativity is less likely to occur in the execution phase of an AI, particularly with a machine learning system for which the distance between input and output is large and cannot be fully preconceived or explained by a human.[103]

The creative choices, however, depend on the type of AI system at issue. Senftleben and Buijtelaar distinguish between (1) a step-by-step algorithm, following concrete if-then rules without room for deviation, (2) rule-based algorithms that operate within margins provided by the programmer, leaving some room of operation to the AI system, or (3) machine-learning algorithms that learn on the basis of input data and can generate an unknown style variation.[104] Evolutionary algorithms

[98] Case C-604/10, *Football Dataco Ltd and Others v Yahoo! UK Ltd and Others* [2012] ECLI:EU:C:2012:115, para 42.

[99] *Feist Publications, Inc v Rural Telephone Service Co*, 499 U.S. 340, 346 (1991).

[100] Anna Shtefan, 'Creativity and Artificial Intelligence: A View from the Perspective of Copyright' (2021) 16 *JIPLP* 720.

[101] Ibid. 727–728.

[102] Senftleben and Buijtelaar (n 96) 800, referring to US case law.

[103] Hugenholtz and Quintais (n 50) 1202/3. The Explainable AI movement carries out research in order to develop AI that explains how output is generated.

[104] Senftleben and Buijtelaar (n 96) 804.

will fall under this last category, where an AI system aims at optimising samples according to predefined criteria by autonomously selecting, mutating, and producing new samples coming closer to the requirements.[105]

It is clear that for a step-by-step algorithm, the developer's choices will be reflected in the output. For rule-based, machine-learning, and evolutionary algorithms, a programmer or user cannot determine the concrete form and features of the resulting work. The question then arises as to whether sufficient creative choices can be made by the user in the conception of the artwork upfront, in the supervision during the execution phase, and/or in the selection of the AI output.[106] This depends on the specific situation, but will surely not be fulfilled where a user only pushes a button to start the creative process. To conclude, the creative choices of the programmer or user can lead the AI-output to be sufficiently original. Where creativity is not sufficient, AI-generated works will be unprotected and become part of the public domain.

3 Neighbouring Rights

The question arises whether such a result suggests a different approach to be taken towards the protection of AI-generated creative works. Creating a new IP right could be justified if it solves a market failure in a public goods market. This is what the utilitarian economic justification of IP rights is based on.[107] On balance, society would have to benefit more from the grant of exclusive rights than the costs of creating such IP rights. Two benefits for society have been identified: creating an incentive to (1) invest in AI research and training and (2) share the results thereof.[108]

Introducing neighbouring rights for AI-generated creations may present a way forward.[109] It provides a flexible protection framework that can be adapted to the specific situation, by granting a limited degree of exclusivity and requiring substantial investment as a pre-condition. The regime could be tailored to reward the creation and dissemination of AI-generated works. Inspiration can come from similar regimes that already exist for phonograms, databases, or press publishers' rights.

Such a regime needs to be weighed against the costs for society. Monopoly rights always create barriers to the enjoyment and dissemination of creative works.[110] Such restrictions may be considered necessary where such rights would reward investment in AI research and development. But for the developer of AI systems, IP rights in the generated output may lead to double-compensation as the AI system itself can already be protected by copyright and patent rights. Where the user of an AI system

[105] Samore (n 2) 478.
[106] Hugenholtz and Quintais (n 50) 1204/5.
[107] Drexl (n 20) para 22.
[108] Senftleben and Buijtelaar (n 96) 798.
[109] Ibid. 798.
[110] Ibid. 806.

needs to make substantial investments for developing and adjusting its creative functions or acquiring input material, a reward for the user in terms of a fair royalty may outweigh the costs. A neighbouring rights regime could entail merely a right of fair compensation for use by third parties, thereby avoiding excessive obstacles to enjoyment and use.[111] The protection period could also be considerably shorter than copyright, for example two years.[112] Further research will have to determine the exact costs of a neighbouring right, the benefits it has on the creation of AI-generated outcomes, and whether it may have any competition or substitution effects for creative works made by humans.[113]

C *Patentability of AI-Assisted and AI-Generated Inventions*

Where inventions are made with the assistance of AI or are generated by an AI system without any natural person having made a substantial contribution to the creative conception,[114] the question arises whether patent protection can apply to them. As explained in Section II.B, technical inventions can be patented if they do not fall under the excluded subject-matter,[115] and they are new, inventive, and industrially applicable. In addition, AI-assisted and AI-generated inventions will have to be sufficiently disclosed.

1 Technical Invention That Is Novel, Inventive, and Industrially Applicable

Inventions developed by AI systems cover the entire range of industry. For example, inventions developed with the help of DABUS include light signals and food containers;[116] IBM Watson is used for developing oncology treatments.[117] Where the invention constitutes a technical solution to a technical problem and does not constitute excluded subject-matter, it will be patentable. This assessment needs to be carried out for the actual output created with the AI system; where this regards a computer-implemented invention, the discussion in Section II.B is equally relevant.

111 Ibid. 809.

112 See protection regime for press articles under Article 15(4) of the Directive (EU) 2019/790 on copyright and related rights in the Digital Single Market [2019] OJ L 130.

113 Senftleben and Buijtelaar (n 96) 810.

114 See Section III.B.2.

115 Art. 52(2) of the EPC lists among others abstract ideas, methods of doing business or performing mental acts, mere discoveries or the mere presentation of information as subject-matter which is excluded from receiving patent protection. Most national patents legislation have similar exclusions.

116 Stephen Thaler, *Food Container*, filed on 17/10/2018 (EP 18275163); Stephen Thaler, *Devices and Methods for Attracting Enhanced Attention*, filed on 7/11/2018 (EP 18275174).

117 Shane Greenstein, 'IBM Watson at MD Anderson Cancer Center' (April 2021) <www.hbs.edu/faculty/Pages/item.aspx?num=59343>.

The standards of novelty and inventive step entail that (1) the AI-assisted or AI-generated invention does not form part of the state of the art before the filing date of the patent application, and (2) it was not obvious to the skilled person on the basis of the state of the art. Where sophisticated AI tools are used to create inventions, or to generate them autonomously, the question arises what the characteristics of the skilled person will be and which means (s)he has at her disposal when determining novelty and inventive step.

The skilled person is a notional person who knows everything but imagines nothing. According to the EPO Guidelines Part G, VII-3, the skilled person is

> a skilled practitioner in the relevant field of technology who is possessed of average knowledge and ability and is aware of what was common general knowledge in the art at the relevant date.... The skilled person is also presumed to have had access to everything in the 'state of the art' ... and to have been in possession of the means and capacity for routine work and experimentation which are normal for the field of technology in question.... The skilled person may be expected to look for suggestions in neighbouring and general technical fields or even in remote technical fields, if prompted to do so.... There may be instances where it is more appropriate to think in terms of a group of persons, e.g. a research or production team, rather than a single person. (emphasis added)

It seems that the standard of a skilled person under the EPC is rather wide: (s)he should be aware of all relevant information available to the public, (s)he is able to carry out routine work and experimentation, (s)he may look in other fields of technology if prompted, and it can be appropriate to consider a team of researchers or producers. Arguably, this skilled person standard also includes using AI technologies where they are part of routine work, as part of a team, in other technical fields. As Shemtov and Gabison conclude: 'if using ... AI capabilities in the relevant field has become a matter of routine in this field, the relevant research team should include AI tools and its associated expertise.'[118]

So how do we assess whether the deployment of AI would be considered routine and unimaginative? The skilled person has no incentive capacity; therefore, it would have to be routine and unimaginative for a skilled person (1) to use an AI tool, (2) to use the AI to arrive at the invention, (3) to carry out AI mosaicing of prior art,[119] and (4) to identify the AI output as useful. In other words, would an engineer with a few years of experience, for example, use a genetic programme to design an antenna with a particular radiation pattern?[120] If the answer is yes, genetic programming would have become widespread in antenna design. The MPI research group warns that 'defining an 'average' level of knowledge and skills can, however, be

[118] Noam Shemtov and Garry Gabison, 'The Inventive Step Requirement and the Rise of the AI Machines' [2022] Queen Mary Law Research Paper No. 375/2022 <https://ssrn.com/abstract=4011200>.

[119] Shemtov and Gabison (n 120).

[120] Samore (n 2) 481.

challenging given the dynamic nature of research in AI.'[121] Even then, it is conceivable that the skilled person would routinely use an AI tool.[122]

Where the skilled person becomes a skilled person using an AI tool, the standard for obviousness will be raised significantly, making it much more difficult to obtain patents on non-obvious inventions. Will inventions that were not developed with the help of AI have to meet the same higher standard? The answer is yes. In the example where the use of AI for antenna design has become commonplace, the inventive step of an invented antenna that was designed without the help of such an AI tool would nevertheless be judged according to a skilled person who has access to a genetic programme.

Where the use of AI tools has become routine, it will not be easy to meet the inventive step threshold. According to Shemtov and Gabison, only where it was not obvious to a skilled person 'to follow a particular avenue of research which involves such AI tools, techniques, and expertise'[123] would the AI-generated output be inventive. Blok mentions that this could be the case where standard AI tools are used in a non-obvious manner to develop non-obvious products and processes; another possibility is that new, more powerful AI applications are developed than those used by the skilled person.[124]

The fourth requirement for patentability is industrial application; where the invention can be commercialised, this does not form a problem.

To conclude, patent protection for AI-assisted or AI-generated works is possible where a technical invention is novel, inventive, and industrially applicable. If that invention does not fall under any of the categories of subject-matter excluded from patent protection, the main hurdle lies in the assessment of inventive step. That threshold may become considerably higher where the skilled person routinely uses AI tools in specific fields of technology. Assessing whether the use of AI is a matter of routine and, if so, whether its use becomes non-obvious because it is applied in a non-obvious manner to develop non-obvious products poses challenges.

2 Disclosure

For AI-assisted or AI-generated inventions to be granted patent protection, they need to be disclosed in such a manner that a skilled person can reproduce them. The fact that it was developed by an AI system as such is not important as the methods and tools used for their development do not have to be disclosed.[125] So the potential difficulty of disclosing the AI system that was used to develop the work is not relevant

[121] Drexl (n 20) para 25.

[122] Ibid.

[123] Shemtov and Gabison (n 120).

[124] Peter Blok, 'The Inventor's New Tool: Artificial Intelligence – How Does It Fit in the European Patent System?' (2017) 39 *EIPR* 69, 71.

[125] Drexl (n 20) para 12.

for AI-assisted or AI-generated works.[126] Where the skilled person is assisted by an AI system, it may be enabled to make the invention with even a very limited patent disclosure.[127] To conclude, disclosure of AI-assisted or AI-generated inventions does not seem to pose particular problems.

IV CONCLUSION

The use of AI systems has an important impact on the IP system. AI tools are not only used to facilitate the search, examination, administration, and enforcement of IP rights; more importantly, AI tools and the works created with their help can be protected by copyright or patents. Such protection can incentivise their further development but also limit their enjoyment and dissemination. The effects of IP protection for general purpose AI technologies needs to be carefully considered in light of the costs and benefits it imposes on society.

This chapter has analysed to what extent patent and copyright protection is available for AI technologies as well as for AI-assisted and AI-generated works, in particular under EU law and the EPC. While fully autonomously AI-generated works are still a matter of the future, the challenges and questions as to their potential protection have also been addressed. Several conclusions can be presented.

Regarding copyright protection, the protection of AI systems as computer programmes does not pose challenges to the current copyright framework. The challenges lie more in the protection of AI-assisted and AI-generated creative output, as this fundamentally challenges the anthropocentric copyright regime, under which the author as a human being plays a pivotal role. Without a human being making sufficient free, personal, and creative choices in generating a work, works cannot be protected under copyright. They will become part of the public domain. Further research into the potentially harmful effects of leaving such works unprotected will have to show whether another regime affording protection may be needed. The neighbouring rights regime, with a considerably lower scope and term of protection, could be a viable alternative.

Patent protection for AI technologies and output generated with the assistance of or by an AI poses certain challenges. AI technologies themselves can be protected by patents, if they are computer-implemented inventions having technical effects that go beyond the state of the art. Recent case law suggests that AI technologies can fulfil this standard. Additionally, disclosure of AI technologies will not pose an obstacle if the details of the model, inputs, and the training process are specified.

Whether patent protection for AI-generated inventions is still needed if AI technologies themselves can be protected under patent and copyright, is doubtful. As Vertinsky notes, 'the expanding role of thinking machines in innovation … changes,

[126] See Section II.B.3.

[127] Vertinsky (n 7) 503.

and complicates, the incentive landscape in ways that need to be examined as part of any rule change as well as any decision to not change the rules.'[128]

As the law stands, patent protection would mainly depend on the assessment as to whether a skilled person would routinely use AI tools to design new products and processes, and whether, in that light, the use of an AI tool to arrive at the particular technical features of the invention was obvious. This determination is complex and will vary with the further development of AI research. IP law will have to adapt to these new challenges.

[128] Ibid. 508.

17

Information Intermediaries and AI

Daniel Seng

I INTRODUCTION

Technology afficionados assert that the Internet of today was conceived with the commercialisation of Internet infrastructure in 1995.[1] However, technology lawyers credit the enactment of the US Communications Decency Act of 1996[2] and the Digital Millennium Copyright Act of 1998[3] for spurring the development of the commercial Internet. These two pieces of legislation, and their equivalents in the EU Electronic Commerce Directive,[4] were attempts at providing answers to the pivotal question of whether an Internet information intermediary – a company that does not create or control the content of information – is liable for merely providing access to or disseminating such information. In *Religious Technology Centre v Netcom On-Line Communication Services Inc*, the court provided the following answer in relation to claims against the intermediary for copyright infringement:

> No purpose would be served by holding liable those who have no ability to control the information to which their [uploaders] have access, even though they might be in some sense helping to achieve the Internet's automatic 'public distribution' and the users' 'public' display of files.... Where the infringing [uploader] is clearly

I would like to thank Ms Hitomi Yap and Mr Shaun Lim for their help with the research and editing of this paper. All errors and omissions, however, remain mine.

1 Wikipedia, 'National Science Foundation Network' <https://en.wikipedia.org/wiki/National_Science_Foundation_Network#Privatization_and_a_new_network_architecture>.

2 Title V, U.S. Telecommunications Act of 1996 (Pub.L. No. 104–104, 110 Stat. 56); codified as 47 U.S.C. para 230 (CDA). More accurately, the CDA was the first piece of legislation enacted by U.S. Congress to regulate indecency and pornography on the Internet. However, the indecency provisions were struck down by the U.S. Supreme Court in the landmark decision of *Reno v. American Civil Liberties Union*, 521 U.S. 844, 117 S.Ct. 2329 (1997) as being in violation of the First Amendment's guarantee of freedom of speech, though s 230 survived the repeal.

3 Pub. L. 105–304, 112 Stat. 2860 (1998); enacted as paras 512, 1201–1205, 1301–1332 of Title 17 of the U.S. Code (DMCA).

4 Directive 2000/31/EC of the European Parliament and of the Council of 8 June 2000 on certain legal aspects of information society services, in particular electronic commerce, in the Internal Market OJ L 178 (17 July 2000) (Directive on electronic commerce).

directly liable for the same act, it does not make sense to adopt a rule that could lead to the liability of countless parties whose role in the infringement is nothing more than setting up and operating a system that is necessary for the functioning of the Internet. Such a result is unnecessary as there is already a party directly liable for causing the copies to be made.[5] (emphasis added)

Because the dissemination of content by the intermediary was considered automatic and caused by the uploader, the intermediary was not held liable.[6] This very same premise was applied to claims outside of copyright law. In an action against an intermediary for disseminating and publishing a defamatory statement, the court in *Zeran v America Online Inc* reached the same conclusion:

> The *amount of information communicated via interactive computer services is, therefore, staggering*. The spectre of tort liability in an area of such prolific speech would have an obvious chilling effect. It would be *impossible for service providers to screen each of their millions of postings for possible problems*. Faced with potential liability for each message republished by their services, interactive computer service providers might choose to severely restrict the number and type of messages posted. Congress considered the weight of the speech interests implicated and chose to immunise service providers to avoid any such restrictive effect.[7]

This basic premise – that an intermediary is not liable for providing automated services to disseminate content which it was not involved in creating – has been codified in s 512 of the DMCA[8] and in s 230 of the CDA.[9] With these twin rules, Internet service providers and hosting companies are generally absolved of liability for disseminating illicit content such as copyright-infringing material, pornography, hate speech, and defamatory content authored by third parties.[10] These

5 907 F.Supp. 1361 (N.D. Cal. 1995) (emphasis added).

6 Ibid. 1381–1382 ('There are no allegations in the complaint to overcome the missing volitional or causal elements necessary to hold a BBS operator directly liable for copying that is automatic and caused by a subscriber').

7 129 F.3d 327, 331 (4th Cir. 1997) (emphasis added).

8 See, for example, H.R. Rept. 105–551 Part I, at 11 ('As to direct infringement, liability is ruled out for passive, automatic acts engaged in through a technological process initiated by another. Thus, the bill essentially codifies the result in the leading and most thoughtful judicial decision to date: *Religious Technology Center v. Netcom On-line Communications Services, Inc.*, 907 F. Supp. 1361 (N.D. Cal. 1995)').

9 Section 230, CDA started off in the U.S. House of Representatives as the Internet Freedom and Family Empowerment Act, H.R. 1978 – 104th Congress (1995–1996), and was subsequent added to the Telecommunications Act as part of the reconciliation process between the Senate and House of Representative versions of the Telecommunications Act. See Christopher Cox, 'The Origins and Original Intent of Section 230 of the Communications Decency Act' (2020) *Richmond J of Law and Tech* <www.jolt.richmond.edu/2020/08/27/the-origins-and-original-intent-of-section-230-of-the-communications-decency-act/>. Representative Cox was the author and co-sponsor of s 230 of the CDA. See also Robert Cannon, 'The Legislative History of Senator Exon's Communications Decency Act: Regulating Barbarians on the Information Superhighway' (1996) 49(1) *Federal Communications Law Journal*, art 3.

10 See Lilian Edwards, *Role and Responsibility of Internet Intermediaries in the Field of Copyright and Related Rights* 2 (WIPO 2010) <www.wipo.int/export/sites/www/copyright/en/doc/role_and_responsibility_of_the_internet_intermediaries_final.pdf>.

rules made it possible for websites, blogs, and social networks to host their users' content whilst being protected 'against a range of laws that might otherwise hold them legally responsible for what their users say and do.'[11] The rules have protected YouTube from copyright infringement for making available video clips shared by its users,[12] shielded Yelp from lawsuits for its users' negative reviews about restaurants,[13] excused eBay from claims by purchasers who bought forgeries from third-party sellers,[14] and absolved Google from trademark liability for selling keywords as part of its advertising programme.[15] The basic spirit of two pieces of US federal legislation enacted to establish a uniform federal policy for regulating the Internet has been propagated worldwide as national rules and regulations.[16] Simply put, the CDA and the DMCA have enabled the Internet that we know today.[17]

Recently, the CDA and the DMCA have been the subject of intense legislative scrutiny.[18] Questions have also been raised by the US Supreme Court as to whether

[11] Electronic Frontier Foundation, 'CDA 230: The Most Important Law Protecting Internet Speech' <www.eff.org/issues/cda230/infographic>.

[12] *Viacom Int'l, Inc v YouTube, Inc* 676 F 3d 19 (2d Cir. 2012).

[13] *Hassell v Bird*, 5 Cal.5th 522 (SC. Cal. 2018).

[14] *Gentry v eBay, Inc.* (2002) 99 Cal.App.4th 816, 121 Cal.Rptr.2d 703.

[15] *Google France SARL and Google v Louis Vuitton Malletier SA*, joined Cases C-236/08 to C-238/08.

[16] The safe harbour provisions of s 512 of the DMCA have been enacted in various forms in Australia, Bahrain, Central America-Dominican Republic states, Chile, Columbia, the European Union, Morocco, Oman, Panama, the People's Republic of China, Peru, Singapore, South Korea and the United Kingdom. See Daniel Seng, 'The State of the Discordant Union, An Empirical Analysis of DMCA Takedown Notices' (2014) 18 *Virginia Journal of Law and Technology* 369. Provisions similar to s 512 include Directive 2000/31/EC of the European Parliament and of the Council of 8 June 2000 on certain legal aspects of information society services, in particular electronic commerce, in the Internal Market ('Directive on electronic commerce'), Arts 12–14; ss 193A-193DE, Copyright Act (Cap. 63, Rev. Ed. 2006), People's Republic of China Regulation on Protection of the Right to Network Dissemination of Information of 2006, Arts 20–23; Malaysia Multimedia Act. Provisions similar to s 230, CDA include s 26, Electronic Transactions Act (Cap. 88, Rev. Ed. 2011); India IT Act (2000), s 79; Australia Broadcasting Services Act 1992 (Cth), Schedule 5, Cl 91(1). For ease of discussion, reference will henceforth be made exclusively to the CDA and DMCA, although the equivalent national provisions in the respective jurisdictions should also be noted.

[17] See, for example, Ambika Kumar, 'The Test of Time: Section 230 of the Communications Decency Act Turns 20' (DWT LLP, September 2016) <www.dwt.com/blogs/media-law-monitor/2016/08/the-test-of-time-section-230-of-the-communications>; David Kravets, '10 Years Later, Misunderstood DMCA is the Law That Saved the Web' (*Wired*, 27 October 2008) <www.wired.com/2008/10/ten-years-later/www.wired.com/2008/10/ten-years-later/>.

[18] See, for example, Mark MacCarthy, 'Back to the Future for Section 230 Reform' (*Brookings Institute*, 17 March 2021) <www.brookings.edu/blog/techtank/2021/03/17/back-to-the-future-for-section-230-reform/> (noting that reform of the CDA is on the agenda for both the US Congress and the Biden administration); Rebecca Tapscott, 'Senator Tillis Releases Draft Bill to Modernize the Digital Millennium Copyright Act' (*IP Watchdog*, 22 December 2020) <www.ipwatchdog.com/2020/12/22/tillis-draft-modernize-dmca/id=128552/>; Case C-401/19: Action brought on 24 May 2019 – *Republic of Poland v European Parliament and Council of the European Union*, 2019 O.J. (C 270) 21 (filing a legal challenge against the takedown-and-staydown notice rule in the Directive (EU) 2019/790 of the European Parliament and of the Council of 17 April 2019 on copyright and related rights in the Digital Single Market and amending Directives 96/9/EC and 2001/29/EC, 2019 O.J. (L 130) 92 (May 17, 2019) (EU Copyright Directive) on the argument that it undermined the right of freedom of expression and was neither proportional nor necessary).

the CDA immunity is aligned with its text and the business processes conducted by intermediaries.[19] It has been argued that these immunities are outmoded, as they were written in a prior Internet era.[20] In fact, new technologies in data aggregation and machine learning are empowering intermediaries to stretch these statutory immunities. To understand why, it is apposite to scrutinise the mechanics of the CDA and DMCA immunities before considering them against the backdrop of the increasing use of automation and AI by the intermediaries.

II THE MECHANICS AND LIMITS OF CDA IMMUNITY

The immunity rule in section 230(c) of the CDA reads:

> (1) Treatment of publisher or speaker: No provider or user of an interactive computer service shall be treated as the publisher or speaker of any information provided by another information content provider.

The equivalent provision in the Singapore Electronic Transactions Act reads:[21]

> 26. – (1) Subject to subsection (2), a network service provider shall not be subject to any civil or criminal liability under any rule of law in respect of third-party material in the form of electronic records to which he merely provides access if such liability is founded on –
>
> (a) the making, publication, dissemination or distribution of such materials or any statement made in such material; or
>
> (b) the infringement of any rights subsisting in or in relation to such material.
>
> . . .
>
> (3) In this section –
>
> . . .
>
> "provides access", in relation to third-party material, means the provision of the necessary technical means by which third-party material may be accessed and *includes the automatic and temporary storage of the third-party material* for the purpose of providing access;
>
> "third-party", in relation to a network service provider, means a person over whom the provider has no effective control.

Both the CDA and the ETA posit an immunity for an intermediary operating as a 'service provider' for third-party content.[22] The pithy formulation in the CDA grants immunity

[19] See, for example, *MalwareBytes, Inc v Enigma Software Group USA, LLC*, 592 U.S., 141 S.Ct. 13 (2020) (criticising the reading of extra immunity into s 230, CDA, per Thomas J.).

[20] See, for example, Matthew G Jeweler, 'The Communications Decency Act of 1996: Why § 230 Is Outdated and Publisher Liability for Defamation Should Be Reinstated against Internet Service Providers' (2008) 8 *Pittsburgh Journal of Technology Law & Policy* 40.

[21] Cap. 88, Rev. Ed. 2011 (ETA).

[22] The Singapore formulation does not define what constitutes a 'network service provider', as does the German formulation from which the Singapore provision is taken. See for example, Ulrich Wuermeling, 'The First National Multimedia Law – How Germany Regulates Online Services and the Internet' (1998) 14 *Comp L & Sec Rep* 41, 42.

to an intermediary only if, as 'an interactive computer service' provider,[23] it is not also an 'information content provider', defined as 'a person or entity that is responsible, in whole or in part, for the *creation or development* of information provided through the Internet or any other interactive computer service'.[24] With this rule, resolution of the immunity turns on characterising the intermediary as either a 'content provider' of third-party content, who has no immunity, or as a 'service provider', who has immunity.[25]

But this simple distinction shades into penumbras of uncertainty with the advent of Web 2.0. Unlike their Web 1.0-era counterparts, wikis, blogs, social networks, podcasts, and interactive websites emphasise user-generated content that features collaboration, contribution and participation from different users.[26] Web 2.0 upgrades the Web 1.0 experience by having an intermediary jointly create, co-opt, or involve the user as the third party in the creation of some content. Would this heightened involvement of the intermediary displace its immunity? On this, the *en banc* majority of the Ninth Circuit in *Fair Housing Council of San Fernando Valley v Roommates.com LLC* said:

> A website operator can be both a service provider and a content provider: If it passively displays content that is created entirely by third parties, then it is only a service provider with respect to that content. But as to content that it creates itself, or is 'responsible, in whole or in part' for creating or developing, the website is also a content provider. Thus, a website may be immune from liability for some of the content it displays to the public but be subject to liability for other content.[27]

So, an intermediary that designed its questionnaire, search, and email systems to limit the listings available to subscribers based on sex, sexual orientation, and the presence of children became a content provider of such listings and did not have s 230 immunity, even though the answers were supplied by the advertisers.[28] This is because the intermediary's efforts contributed to the discrimination of tenants on the basis of their gender, family status, and sexual orientation in breach of the Fair Housing Act. Likewise, when an intermediary contracted with and paid researchers to obtain private telephone records and other confidential information which could only be obtained in breach of US federal law and then knowingly transformed the information into a publicly available commodity, it was responsible for the development of this specific content and would not be shielded by s 230.[29] On the other

[23] S 230(f)(2), CDA (defining an 'interactive computer service' as 'any information service, system, or access software provider that provides or enables computer access by multiple users to a computer server, including specifically a service or system that provides access to the Internet and such systems operated or services offered by libraries or educational institutions').

[24] S 230(f)(3), CDA. Emphasis added.

[25] *Zeran v. Am. Online, Inc.*, 129 F.3d 327, 333 (4th Cir. 1997).

[26] Wikipedia, 'Web 2.0', <https://en.wikipedia.org/wiki/Web_2.0>.

[27] 512 F.3d 1157, 1162–1163 (9th Cir. 2008).

[28] Ibid. 1169–1170.

[29] *FTC v Accusearch Inc* 570 F.3d 1187 (10th Cir. 2009).

hand, an online dating site that offered neutral posting tools and did nothing to encourage the posting of defamatory content retained its s 230 immunity for defamation when a subscriber created a defamatory profile.[30] Likewise, when an intermediary developed a rating system by aggregating user-generated feedback or reviews, the intermediary was not treated as a content provider of the ratings and retained its s 230 immunity.[31]

What if an intermediary wishes to enforce content guidelines and review, or even remove, content that it considers objectionable? A less frequently applied part of s 230, known as the Good Samaritan Provision, provides that the intermediary who undertakes these filtering duties or 'self-regulation' shall not be held liable.[32] The Good Samaritan provision was enacted to reverse the controversial decision of *Stratton Oakmont v Prodigy Servs. Co*,[33] which held Prodigy liable in defamation for adopting content guidelines and filtering its subscribers' insulting and harassing postings. But while the aim behind this provision is laudable, most intermediaries steer clear of it in practice. This is because filtering its users' content nominally engages an intermediary with third-party content, encourages a possible recharacterisation of the intermediary as a content provider or developer of that content, and potentially weakens its possible reliance on s 230 immunity.[34]

A *The Rise of Automation and Machine Learning*

Thus, whether the intermediary has immunity depends on whether it could be said to be responsible for the creation or development of content. This analysis is, however, based on cases involving intermediaries operating Web 2.0 websites. With technological advances like Web 3.0 and machine learning, the role of the intermediary has expanded beyond that of a service provider. In operating services such as aggregating, indexing, classifying, categorising, formatting, enriching, and re-presenting user-originated content through targeted advertising or curated content to make for

[30] *Carafano v Metrosplash.com*, Inc., 339 F.3d 1119 (9th Cir. 2003).

[31] *Gentry v eBay, Inc*, 99 Cal.App.4th 816, 834, 121 Cal.Rptr.2d 703 (2002); *Levitt v Yelp! Inc*, 2011 WL 5079526 (N.D. Cal. 2011); *Kimzey v. Yelp! Inc*., 836 F.3d 1263 (9th Cir. 2016).

[32] S 230(c)(2), CDA.

[33] 1995 N.Y. Misc. LEXIS 229, 1995 WL 323710, 23 Media L. Rep. 1794 (N.Y. Sup. Ct. May 24, 1995).

[34] *Barrett v Rosenthal*, 51 Cal. Rptr. 3d, 55, 70 (Cal. 2006) ('[T]he immunity conferred by section 230 applies even when self-regulation is unsuccessful, or completely unattempted'.); *Doe v. America Online*, Inc., 783 SO.2d 1010, 1017 (2011) ('both the negligent communication of a defamatory statement and the failure to remove such a statement when first communicated by another party each alleged … under a negligence label—constitute publication'). See also Jeweler (n 20) ('It is counterproductive to attempt to encourage these entities to self-regulate their content for defamatory speech by immunizing them for that defamatory speech regardless of whether the ISP attempts whatsoever to be responsible and screen its content'.); Andrew M Sevanian, 'Section 230 of the Communications Decency Act: A Good Samaritan Law without the Requirement of Acting as a Good Samaritan' (2014) 21 *UCLA Entertainment Law Rev* 121, 131–135.

a more autonomous and intelligent Internet,[35] intermediaries are moving away from their role as passive service providers and becoming 'active' content delivery platforms. Is this permitted under the CDA immunity rules?

At first glance, this does not appear to be possible, since the intermediary has clearly taken on content creation or development responsibilities. But there is an escape route for intermediaries. In a tacit recognition of the increasing role that automation may play in serving online content, the Ninth Circuit opined that '[t]he mere fact that an interactive computer service 'classifies user characteristics … does not transform [it] into a "developer" of the "underlying misinformation".'[36] It ought to be noted that the Ninth Circuit was referring to its earlier decision in *Carafano v Metrosplash.com, Inc* where Metrosplash sought to summarise each user-submitted profile based on a Metrosplash questionnaire.[37] This summary was an attempt to identify similar profiles so that Metrosplash could provide matching services.[38]

But while one might excuse Metrosplash's content 'input' as merely editorial and agree with the Ninth Circuit that this did not amount to the creation or development of new content, the characterisation of intermediaries' involvement in other cases may lead to a number of questionable results. These involve situations where an intermediary uses automation to greatly expand its 'editorial' role to arguably create or develop new and illicit content from user-supplied information and yet avoid responsibility for 'materially contributing' to the unlawful content. In doing so, intermediaries push the limits of the CDA immunity to its breaking point.

For instance, in *Jane Doe No 1 v Backpage.com*, three plaintiffs, all minors, sued Backpage.com, as each had been the subject of sex trafficking through advertisements placed on Backpage. They alleged that Backpage had facilitated this process by selectively removing postings made by victim support organisations and law enforcement sting advertisements. Backpage had tailored its posting requirements to make sex trafficking easier, including providing automated anonymisation features such as message forwarding services and auto-replies (so that the advertisers could hide their email addresses), and automatically removing metadata from uploaded photographs (so that they could not be scrutinised for their date, time and location). Backpage also allegedly crippled its automated filtering system, which would otherwise screen out advertisements with prohibited terms (so that advertisements with terms such as 'brly legal' for 'barely legal' and 'high schl' for 'high school' could still be posted), and accepted anonymous payments.[39] In what the court admitted was a 'hard case', the First Circuit held that s 230 shielded Backpage from liability for participating in sex trafficking because these online features, 'which reflect

35 See, for example, Wikipedia, 'Semantic Web' (Redirected from 'Web 3.0') <https://en.wikipedia.org/wiki/Semantic_Web#Web_3.0>.

36 *Roommates* (n 27) 1173.

37 *Metrosplash* (n 30) 1124.

38 Ibid.

39 817 F.3d 12, 16–17, 20 (1st. Cir. 2016).

choices about what content can appear on the website and in what form, are editorial choices that fall within the purview of traditional publisher functions'.[40]

Citing *Metrosplash*, the First Circuit ruled that Backpage was not an actual participant in a sex trafficking venture and was not complicit by merely using automated technical website designs and features.[41] But Backpage is clearly distinguishable: while both use questionnaires to collect information to create postings, Backpage took active steps to alter posting content, or coerce their modification, to shield its posters from easy identification. Backpage's obfuscation mechanisms were clearly associated with facilitating the illicit practice of sex trafficking and could hardly be regarded as mere content-neutral editorial choices, while Metrosplash's categorisation services resembled the table of contents or index pages of a publication. The analogy made is clearly unpersuasive.

The same reliance on the use of automation to preserve an intermediary's role as a mere 'service provider' – and thus retain its s 230 CDA immunity – can be more clearly illustrated in *Goddard v Google, Inc*[42] In this case, consumers brought a class action against Google for furthering a scheme whereby users were harmed when they clicked on web-based advertisements for fake mobile subscription services set up by third-party advertisers through Google's AdWords advertising scheme. The US District Court dismissed the class action. It ruled that Google's use of its AdWords 'keyword tool' (which allowed advertisers to select keywords to correspond to their advertisements), and use of a mathematical algorithm as a 'suggestion tool' (to suggest to advertisers the use of the word 'free' in relation to 'ringtone' to attract more mobile subscriptions), was a 'neutral tool'.[43] The court opined, without support, that Google 'merely provides a framework that could be utilised for proper or improper purposes',[44] and the 'selection of content was left exclusively to the [third party].'[45] In other words, automation – and even the use of AI-driven selection tools in Google's AdWords programme that suggested content options to the third party – did not make the intermediary a 'content provider'. It was the third party who ultimately decided what content to use for its misleading and fraudulent advertisement.

The court supported this reasoning by contrasting AdWords with a scenario where it was suggested that a website that 'remov[es] the word 'not' from a user's message reading '[Name] did not steal the artwork' in order to transform an innocent message

40 Ibid. 21–22.

41 Ibid. 21.

42 *Goddard v Google, Inc*, 640 F.Supp.2d 1193 (N.D.Cal. 2009).

43 Ibid. 1199. See also *Hill v Stubhub, Inc*, 219 N.C.App. 227 (N.C. C.A. 2021) (holding Internet ticket marketplace not liable for unfair or deceptive trade practices on tickets sold on marketplace through its marketplace pricing tools, which were 'neutral' and thus made it not liable and entitled to immunity under s 230, CDA, even though the trial court noted that the marketplace's business model provided incentives for selling of tickets at above their face value).

44 Ibid.

45 Ibid. 1197.

into a libellous one' would void its CDA immunity.[46] That may be true where an intermediary converts a message into one with an entirely opposite meaning, but the analogy is incomplete. The court never considered the subtly persuasive – and ultimately coercive – power of machine-driven recommendation systems.[47] It is well known that Google AdWords operates, as a 'self-service' product, one of the most sophisticated machine learning-powered bidding services worldwide.[48] It works by enabling the advertiser to make automated bids for keywords, based on the history of the advertiser, the history of the user, the relevance of the ad, the time and day when the auction is happening, and many other factors, to 'deliver the most relevant ad to the user at the right moment for them.'[49] Thus, when AdWords suggests the word 'free' for an advertisement, it does so on the basis that the word would be the most relevant term the user is looking for. It ought to be noted that the word 'free' in the context of Internet parlance has too often been associated with illicit activities,[50] just as it has also come to signify the largely unjustified expectations of Internet consumers seeking advantageous deals online. It is clearly a 'bait' word, which advertising systems have come to associate with greater online advertisement traction – and is associated with arguably ulterior intent when linked with mobile subscription services such as 'ringtones' – because subscription services are inherently not 'free'.[51] In other words, if AdWords suggested the use of the word 'free' with 'ringtones', this disclosed possible complicity on the part of the intermediary. This issue needs to be investigated further and ought not be cursorily dismissed. Otherwise, the advent of AI and automation will enable an intermediary, as a 'service provider', to erect 'decisional firewalls' between itself and the offerings of its

[46] Ibid. 1199.

[47] See for example, Nick Sever, 'Captivating algorithms: Recommender systems as traps' (2019) 24(2) *Journal of Material Culture* 421. Cf European Commission, 'Proposal for a Regulation of the European Parliament and of the Council: Laying down Harmonised Rules on Artificial Intelligence (Artificial Intelligence Act) and Amending Certain Union Legislative Acts 2021/0106 (COD)', *COM*(2021) 206 final ('AIA'), Art 5.1(a) ('subliminal techniques beyond a person's consciousness in order to materially distort a person's behaviour in a manner that causes or is likely to cause that person or another person physical or psychological harm').

[48] Jerry Dischler, 'Putting Machine Learning into the Hands of Every Advertiser' (*Google*, 10 July 2018) <https://support.google.com/google-ads/answer/9065075?hl=en>.

[49] Odolena Kostova, 'Machine Learning, Smart Bidding and Google Ads' (*Medium*, 5 February 2019) <www.medium.com/@odolenakostova/machine-learning-smart-bidding-and-google-ads-1724aa8c9232>.

[50] *See* Pinsent Masons 'Anti-piracy code of practice for search engines proposed by rights holder representatives' (*Pinsent Masons*, 27 January 2012) <www.pinsentmasons.com/out-law/news/anti-piracy-code-of-practice-for-search-engines-proposed-by-rights-holder-representatives>. Google's Advertising Policies Help specifically desists from the use of words such as 'free', which, it claims, are gimmicky and do not meet editorial and professional requirements. However, in Goddard, evidence was presented that the AdWords system offered the advertisers the use of the word 'free' for mobile subscription services. See Google Ads policies, <https://support.google.com/adspolicy/answer/6008942?hl=en>.

[51] These are known as 'negative keywords' because respectable advertisers run their ad campaigns to *avoid* users who conduct searches using these keywords. See, for example, Stephanie Mialki, 'How to Find, Add & Use Negative Keywords to Your Best Advantage' (*Instapage*, 7 January 2020) <www.instapage.com/blog/negative-keywords>.

programmed systems. If unchallenged, *Goddard v Google* would suggest that an intermediary can retain its CDA immunity by ostensibly leaving the ultimate decision in the hands of the third-party user, who may be guided by a machine learning system programmed by the intermediary itself.

A similar case can be found in *Force v Facebook, Inc*, where victims of Palestinian attacks in Israel brought actions against Facebook for knowingly hosting accounts belonging to Hamas, classified by the United States as a terrorist organisation, contending that Facebook's social matching algorithms promoted terrorist content to people who liked similar pages or posts.[52] A majority of the Second Circuit dismissed the claims, holding that Facebook did not 'develop' the terrorism-related content on its social networking site by merely developing algorithms that use its users' information to match the 'materially unaltered' content with other users.[53] In a clear recognition of the weakness of the majority's argument, Chief Judge Katzmann penned a strong dissent, noting how Facebook's algorithms had played a crucial role in fostering a unique global community by linking and engaging individual users through suggesting connections to other users with shared interests, in this case, in terrorism.[54] Chief Judge Katzmann found that Facebook had, through its social networking service, become a publisher, not of the users' content but of the users' information, taking it out of the CDA immunity.[55] After all, 'the creation of social networks [through matching algorithms] goes far beyond the traditional editorial functions that the CDA immunizes.'[56] It is worth noting that Facebook does use AI, machine learning, and manual reviewers to filter out offensive postings and content on Facebook and Instagram, in compliance with its Community Standards,[57] and this has involved an expenditure of considerable costs and resources. But Facebook did not rely on this to mount a Good Samaritan defence to the claims.

A final – and perhaps harder – example can be drawn from Yelp, Inc. Yelp's business model involves the collection and subsequent curation of recommendations and reviews about businesses. Yelp also runs a paid advertisement programme on the side to allow subscribers to promote their businesses. Because the raison d'être for Yelp is the hosting of third-party reviews, Yelp has to take steps to verify these reviews to protect its business model as a trustworthy source of reviews,[58] and it is

52 *Force v Facebook, Inc*, 934 F.3d 53 (2nd Cir., 2019); Supreme Court cert. not granted.

53 Ibid. 70.

54 Ibid. 82–83.

55 Ibid. 82.

56 Ibid. 83.

57 Facebook, 'How Enforcement Technology Works' (*Facebook*, 23 June 2021) <https://transparency.fb.com/enforcement/detecting-violations/how-enforcement-technology-works/>. *See* also ibid. 60.

58 This is to address the problem of 'astroturfing', which is the practice of masking the sponsors of a message or organisation to make it appear as though it originates from and is supported by grassroots participants. See Wikipedia, 'Astroturfing' <https://en.wikipedia.org/wiki/Astroturfing>. See also Neal Ungerleider, 'FTC Subpoena Revelations, Thousands of Complaints Send Yelp's Stock Price Tumbling' (*Fast Company*, 4 April 2014) <www.fastcompany.com/3028725/ftc-subpoena-revelations-send-yelps-stock-price-tumbling>.

therefore well known that Yelp actively curates and controls the presentation of reviews.[59] However, Yelp has also been dogged by allegations of Yelp-manufactured negative reviews or wrongful manipulation of third-party reviews to the detriment of businesses who refuse to purchase advertising from Yelp.[60] While these allegations have not been proved, it is known that Yelp enlists sophisticated recommendation software that could filter and curate reviews for their authenticity, quality and integrity,[61] and even automatically republish the curated reviews on search engines.[62] Such is the utility of automated curation that, in the absence of actual proof of human intervention in the curation process, the automated nature of its editorial operations has allowed Yelp to successfully rely on the s 230 immunity to defend itself in various claims.[63] In this regard, while US courts have noted that Yelp's machine-powered curation of reviews for subsequent publication could represent an immunised activity for filtering objectionable reviews and potentially qualify for Good Samaritan immunity,[64] they do not give these arguments much credence because to qualify, the intermediary has to demonstrate that the filtering was done in 'good faith'.[65] In contrast, there is no such limitation to acquire s 230 immunity.[66] For this reason, intermediaries like Yelp (and even Facebook[67]) seem to rely on expanding their services and their role as 'developers' of user-supplied content and pushing the envelope of s 230 immunity, rendering any reliance on the Good Samaritan defence otiose.

III THE DMCA AND COPYRIGHT LIABILITY

In the copyright claims space, the same immunity that would apply to Internet intermediaries finds expression in a slightly different form in the DMCA, which seeks to codify the basic rule set out in *Religious Technology Centre v Netcom On-Line Communication Services Inc.*[68] The main difference is that unlike s 230 of the CDA, the DMCA immunity for the four designated classes of Internet

[59] The issue was first brought to the mainstream media by Wall Street Journal. See Angus Loten, 'Yelp Regularly Gets Subpoenas about Users' (*The Wall Street Journal*, 2 April 2014) <www.wsj.com/articles/SB10001424052702303847804579477644289822928>. For instance, many businesses pay third-party reviewers to flood their Yelp online listings with good reviews. See, for example, *Curry v. Yelp Inc.*, 2015 WL 1849037, at *1 (N.D. Cal. 2015).

[60] See, for example, *Levitt* (n 31) 1; *Kimzey* (n 31).

[61] See, for example, *Curry* (n 59) 1.

[62] See, for example, *Kimzey* (n 31) 1270.

[63] See above.

[64] The same argument could have influenced the decision of the majority in *Force v Facebook*, which did refer to the Good Samaritan protections in s 230(c)(2). *See* Force (n 52) 80.

[65] Levitt (n 31) 10.

[66] Ibid.

[67] *Force* (n 52) 80.

[68] *Netcom* (n 5). The s 230 CDA immunity does not apply to matters pertaining to intellectual property claims. 47 U.S.C. para 230(e)(2). The same rule applies in Singapore. *See* s 26(2)(d), ETA.

intermediaries against both direct and indirect copyright infringement is conditional, that is, granted subject to compliance with certain conditions (hereinafter referred to as 'safe harbours'). With respect to intermediaries such as hosting and information location tool service providers,[69] the immunity is granted only if, among other conditions, the intermediary has no actual knowledge of infringement or responds expeditiously to a DMCA-prescribed takedown notice submitted by an aggrieved copyright owner, content provider, or its agent (referred to as the reporter) to remove or disable access to the infringing material.[70] In other words, unlike s 230 of the CDA, DMCA immunity requires intermediaries to cooperate with content providers,[71] although the onus remains on the content provider to detect and report infringing materials online to the intermediary.

A *Volition and the Advent of Automation*

DMCA immunity is, however, explicitly stated to operate without prejudice to existing defences in the law of copyright.[72] Furthermore, the conditional nature of DMCA immunity incentivises an intermediary to shape its business such that it attracts neither direct liability – that is, liability for infringing conduct that the intermediary itself undertakes – nor indirect or secondary copyright liability – that is, accessory liability for illicit conduct undertaken by third parties. An intermediary is able to do so by adopting a business model that relies on automation to shift responsibility to the third-party user for any activity undertaken with copyright material.[73]

This is best illustrated with a series of cases that litigated the legality of network digital video recording (NDVR) services. Also known as remote storage digital video recorder (RS-DVR) services, this is a network-based digital video recorder (DVR)

69 The two safe harbour defences that are of general application are s 512(c) (hosting service providers) and s 512(d) (information location service providers). The other two safe harbour defences relate to Internet intermediaries as transitory digital network communications service providers (s 512(a)) and service providers providing system caching (s 512(b)).

70 S 512(c)(1)(A); 512(d)(1)(A). Other conditions include appointing a designated agent to receive notifications (s 512(c)(2)), implementing a repeat infringer policy (s 512(i)(1)(A)) and accommodating and not interfering with standard technical measures (s 512(i)(1)(B)).

71 *Edwards* (n 10) 6.

72 S 512(l).

73 *CoStar Group, Inc v LoopNet, Inc*, 373 F.3d 544, 554 (2004), quoting from *ALS Scan, Inc. v RemarQ Communities, Inc*, 239 F.3d 619, 622 (4th Cir.2001) ('As to direct infringement, liability is ruled out for passive, automatic acts engaged in through a technological process initiated by another'.) (emphasis added). The constraints of space in this chapter limits any further discussion of indirect liability. It suffices to say that showing of indirect liability requires proof of, among others, knowledge, direct financial benefit and control over the third-party user's infringing activities. It is more difficult to establish indirect liability than direct liability, which is based on principles of strict liability. See also Daniel Seng, 'Detecting and Prosecuting IP Infringement with AI: Can the AI Genie Repulse the Forty Counterfeit Thieves of Alibaba?' in Reto Hilty, Jyh-An Lee and Kung-Chung Liu (eds), *Artificial Intelligence and Intellectual Property* (Oxford University Press 2021) 292.

service where instead of storing media content, typically free-to-air public broadcast television content, on a DVR or set-top box at the consumer's private home, the content is stored in the cloud or on servers controlled by the intermediary service provider.[74] The recorded content is typically only available to the user who recorded it.

At first sight, the NDVR services appear to be an unobjectionable extension of time-shifting of broadcast programmes, which, pursuant to the seminal decision of the US Supreme Court in *Sony Corp. of America v Universal City Studios, Inc* has been held to be fair use of the content, since the recording is by the user for his private and domestic use.[75] (Time-shifting has been statutorily sanctioned in the copyright laws of many countries.[76]) However, broadcasters have objected to NDVR services on the basis that use of the intermediaries' services encroaches on their exclusive right to transmit (and retransmit) content. Thus, one of the preliminary issues that must be resolved is whether the making of the NDVR copies and the subsequent transmission of these recorded copies using the intermediary's platform are done by the *user* or by the *intermediary*.[77]

As the late Scalia J explained in his powerful dissent in *American Broadcasting Cos., Inc v Aereo, Inc*, the difference turns on whether the making of the copies and their subsequent transmission are considered the product of the user's or the product of the intermediary's 'volitional conduct'.[78] Even though copyright infringement is based on strict liability, 'there should still be some element of volition or causation which is lacking where a defendant's system is merely used to create a copy by a third party.'[79] Drawing upon the analogy that the owner of a copy machine is not considered to be a direct infringer if a customer uses the machine to duplicate an infringing work, the US Courts of Appeals have uniformly[80] concluded that this requires courts to identify the 'actual infringing conduct with a nexus sufficiently close and causal to the illegal copying [such] that one could conclude that the machine owner himself trespassed on the exclusive domain of the copyright owner.'[81] This reasoning is not exclusive to US case law. The Australian High Court in *Roadshow Films Pty Ltd v iiNet Ltd* acted on a similar basis when it concluded that there was no 'reasonable basis'[82] for the intermediary to take action to terminate

74 Wikipedia, 'Network DVR' <https://en.wikipedia.org/wiki/Network_DVR>.

75 464 U. S. 417 (1984).

76 For example, Singapore Copyright Act s 114; Australian Copyright Act s 111. For a comparative analysis on time-shifting laws, see Arvind Van Goethem, 'A Comparative Analysis on the Legality of Cloud Personal Video Recorders' (17 November 2015) <https://ssrn.com/abstract=2729801>.

77 See for example, *American Broadcasting Cos., Inc v Aereo, Inc*, 573 US 431, 453 per Scalia J (2014) ('That process undoubtedly results in a performance; the question is who does the performing').

78 Ibid. 456 ('The only question is whether those performances are the product of Aereo's volitional conduct').

79 *Netcom* (n 5) 1370.

80 See *Aereo* (n 77) 453 per Scalia J ('Every Court of Appeals to have considered an automated-service provider's direct liability for copyright infringement has adopted that rule').

81 *CoStar* (n 73) 550.

82 [2012] HCA 16, [78] per French CJ, Crennan and Kiefel JJ.

the accounts of its subscribers alleged to have used BitTorrent file sharing software or that it was 'not unreasonable'[83] for the intermediary to not do so. The High Court noted that an intermediary was not held liable 'merely because' it has provided facilities for enabling the infringement by the user who is the primary infringer.[84] This parallels the observation of the Ninth Circuit that establishing volition is, in the language of proximate causation, simply showing that the conduct in question is the '*direct* cause of the infringement.'[85]

Thus, while the intermediary did indeed build the automated system for making NDVR recordings, 'the key point is that subscribers call all the shots', since the automated system could not make any recording or relay any recording until the subscriber selected the programme he wanted and requested that it be relayed.[86] The Second Circuit in *The Cartoon Network LP, LLLP v CSC Holdings, Inc*[87] and the Singapore Court of Appeal in *RecordTV Pte Ltd v MediaCorp TV Singapore Pte Ltd*[88] also arrived at the same conclusion. As the Court of Appeal in RecordTV opined:

> [S]ince only [the content provider's] shows that were 'communicated' were those shows that appeared on each Registered User's playlist, and since the exact make-up of each playlist depended on the specific shows which the Registered User in question had requested to be recorded, 'the person responsible for determining the content of the communication at the time the communication [was] made' would be that Registered User himself. [The intermediary] would not have been the communicator of the [content provider's] shows ….[89]

It ought to be noted that the issue of 'volitional conduct' is not always resolved in favour of the intermediary. In *National Rugby League Investments Pty Limited v Singtel Optus Pty Ltd*, the Full Court of the Federal Court of Australia held that the time-shifted copy was made by the NDVR intermediary service provider, or alternatively, by both the service provider *and* the subscriber.[90] Likewise, the Japanese Supreme Court held in a pair of decisions – *Maneki TV*[91] and *Rokuraku II*[92] – that it was the intermediary service provider who was responsible, as it had developed the environment for making it uncomplicated and almost effortless to make the

83 Ibid. [146] per Gummow and Hayne JJ.

84 Ibid. [136] per Gummow and Hayne JJ.

85 *Perfect 10, Inc v Giganews, Inc*, 847 F.3d 657, 666 (9th Cir. 2017), quoting from *Perfect 10 Inc, v Giganews, Inc*, 2014 WL 8628034, 7 (C.D. Cal. Nov. 14, 2014) (emphasis in the original).

86 *Aereo* (n 77) 456 per Scalia J.

87 536 F 3d 121, 131–132 (2nd Cir, 2008).

88 [2011] 1 SLR 830, [15], [34]. In the court below, RecordTV was found *not* to be responsible for the time-shifted copies that were made but was responsible for transmitting or communicating the recorded copies to the user. This, of course, is an unsupportable distinction both legally and factually, which the Court of Appeal reversed. See RecordTV Pte Ltd v MediaCorp TV Singapore Pte Ltd [2010] 2 SLR 152.

89 Ibid. [36].

90 [2012] FCAFC 59, [5].

91 2009 (Ju) No. 653; Minshu Vol. 65, No. 1 (Japanese Supreme Court, Jan. 18, 2011).

92 2009 (Ju) No. 788; Minshu Vol. 65, No. 1 (Japanese Supreme Court, Jan. 20, 2011).

reproductions and the retransmissions. 'But for such actions carried out by the service provider', the Japanese Supreme Court noted, it would not be possible for users to record and reproduce the broadcast programmes.[93] In *American Broadcasting Cos., Inc v Aereo, Inc* itself, the US Supreme Court majority affirmed the illegality of Aero's NDVR services, though it sidestepped the issue of volition by simply concluding that because the services provided by the Intermediary resembled cable-TV, it ought to be regulated as such,[94] a result which Scalia J chastised as a 'result-driven'[95] rule that 'provides no criteria for determining when its cable-TV-lookalike rule applies.'[96]

In summary, the line of cases relating to the use of automation to provide online services to users, such that the infringing activities committed by the users could not be ascribed to the service provider's 'volitional conduct', has been met with a mixed degree of success. Certainly, service providers in these cases have met with less success in shifting responsibility to users, and preserving their immunities under the DMCA, than their CDA counterparts. This phenomenon can be explained by two factors: first, the copyright jurisprudence on 'volitional conduct' relies less on the form taken by the service provider's automation of its services and more on the substance of these services. Second, DMCA-safe harbours operate as conditional immunities without prejudice to existing and more flexible rules of copyright and tortious causation. There are, however, additional issues triggered by the use of automation with respect to the operation of the DMCA safe harbours.

B *Automated Processing, Errors in Takedown Notices, and the Imputation of Bad Faith*

As previously noted, the DMCA-safe harbours operate as conditional immunities, which require an intermediary to act expeditiously on an effective takedown notice. An effective takedown notice is one that complies with the six statutory requirements prescribed for a notice: (i) an authorised signature, (ii) description of the copyrighted work, (iii) identification of the material claimed to be infringing – also known as the takedown request, (iv) the takedown reporter's contact information, (v) a statement of good faith belief that use of the material complained of is not authorised, and finally, (vi) a statement of accuracy as to the information in the notice and confirmation that the reporter is authorised by the copyright owner or exclusive licensee.[97] The DMCA goes on to provide that exact compliance with these formalities is not required – only

[93] Ibid.

[94] *Aereo* (n 77) 442–444 per Breyer J.

[95] Ibid. 461 per Scalia J.

[96] Ibid. 460 per Scalia J. The majority did not explicitly repudiate Scalia J's formulation of the volitional-conduct requirement. See *BWP Media USA, Inc v T & S Software Associates*, 852 F.3d 436, 441 (5th Cir. 2017).

[97] S 512(c)(3)(A)(i) to (vi). See also Singapore Copyright (Network Service Provider) Regulations 2005, Rg 3(2)(k)(i).

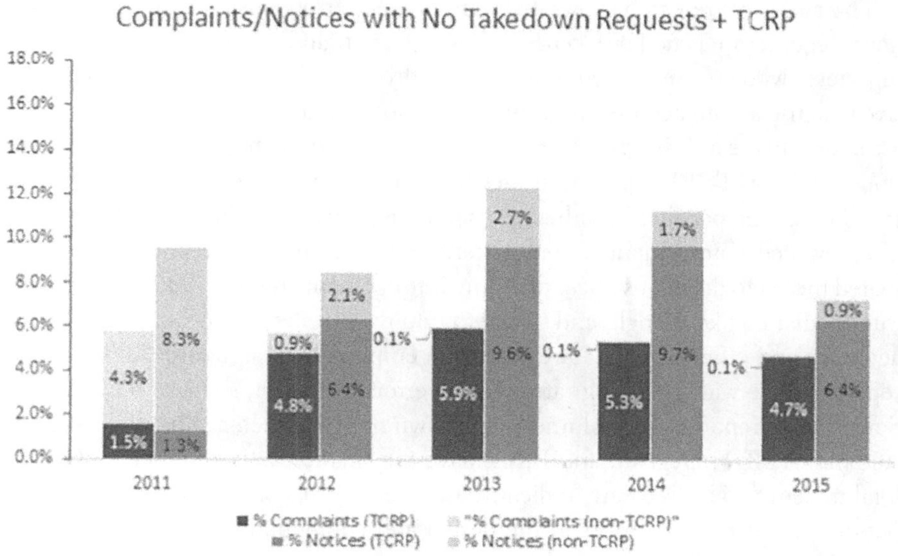

FIGURE 17.1 Chart comparing error rates of automatically vs. manually processed notices and complaints[98]

substantial compliance is required.[99] Nonetheless, if there is no substantial compliance with formalities (ii), (iii), and (iv), the notice will fail *in limine* and the intermediary is entitled to disregard it as being erroneous (Figure 17.1).[100]

This is because formalities (ii) and (iii) enable the intermediary to identify the infringed work and the infringing material,[101] and formality (iv) enables the reporter to be contacted in the event a counter-takedown notice is served on the intermediary.[102] Yet, surprisingly, data from empirical studies conducted on takedown notices show that a significant number of takedown notices do not have formalities (ii) and (iii). For instance, notices with no copyright work descriptions accounted for up to 9.6% of all notices issued[103] in 2013 before dropping to a negligible 0.05% of all notices in 2015.[104] However, notices with no takedown requests continue to make up a substantial number of all notices, rising to 12.4% of all notices in 2013 and 11.4% of all notices in 2014 before falling slightly to 7.3% of the notices in 2015.[105]

98 Ibid. 160 (Figure 5).

99 S 512(c)(3)(A). See also *Perfect 10, Inc v CCBill LLC*, 488 F.3d 1102, 1112 (9th Cir. 2007) ('substantial compliance means substantial compliance with all of § 512(c)(3) 's clauses, not just some of them').

100 The DMCA obliges an intermediary to provide the reporter with a second chance to remedy defects in formalities (i), (v), and (vi). Daniel Seng, 'Copyrighting Copywrongs: An Empirical Analysis of Errors with Automated DMCA Takedown Notices' (2021) 37 *Santa Clara High Tech L J* 119, 138.

101 Ibid. 139–140.

102 S 512(g)(2)(B).

103 Notices issued and recorded in the Lumen database.

104 Seng, 'Copyrighting Copywrongs' (n 99) 154 (Table 4).

105 Ibid.

The empirical research shows that most of these erroneous notices with no takedown requests are issued by Google's Trusted Copyright Removal Program (TCRP) reporters –who are considered more trustworthy and are empowered, almost exclusively, to use automated means to submit takedown notices to Google Inc.[106] These are known in the industry as 'robo takedowns'.[107] In contrast, the number of erroneous notices by non-TCRP reporters are several orders of magnitude smaller, as Figure 17.1 shows. One possible hypothesis is that these errors are an inevitable by-product of automated enforcement: when content providers and their reporters use automated means to detect instances of online infringement and report them to Internet intermediaries like Google and Twitter, automation involves a trade-off between accuracy and efficiency.[108] However, as the empirical research also shows, TCRP reporters have widely varying rates of such errors.[109] In fact, some of the top takedown notice reporters (by volume of takedown notices), such as Stichting BREIN, AudioLock.NET, Degban, and RIAA, have the smallest ratio of empty notices to total notices.[110] This is clearly indicative of process errors on the part of the poorly-performing reporters – errors in the design and configuration of their automated reporting systems.[111]

Takedown notices are also not immune to substantive errors – errors that raise substantive legal questions that undermine the underlying claim for alleged copyright infringement. One example of a substantive error is a 'spent' takedown request: a takedown notice targeting a website which is no longer functional – even though the claim asserts that it is valid and the information in the notice is accurate.[112] While the number of these 'spent' requests is small – an empirical study suggests that *one type* of 'spent' requests[113] accounts for only 0.23% of all takedown requests – their absolute number is not small. All in, 2.74 *million* clearly invalid requests have been issued between 2011 and 2015[114] – requests which need not be attended to by the intermediary or which would affect its DMCA immunity, but which unnecessarily consume the intermediary's resources in acting on and responding to them.

The DMCA *does* provide for penalties against a reporter who 'knowingly materially misrepresents' that material or activity is infringing.[115] Courts are beginning to recognise the dangers of having these bad notices and requests overwhelm internet

[106] Ibid. at 159.

[107] Daniel Seng, 'The State of the Discordant Union: An Empirical Analysis of DMCA Takedown Notices' (2013) 18 *Va JL & Tech* 369, 398–400; Zoe Carpou, 'Robots, Pirates, and the Rise of the Automated Takedown Regime: Using the DMCA to Right Piracy and Protect End-Users' (2016) 39 *Colum J L & Arts* 551.

[108] Seng, 'Copyrighting Copywrongs' (n 99) 165.

[109] Ibid. 161.

[110] Ibid. 164.

[111] Ibid. 162–163.

[112] S 512(c)(3)(A)(v), (vi).

[113] Based on the Megaupload test. See Seng, 'Copyrighting Copywrongs' (n 99) 171–182.

[114] Ibid. 181.

[115] S 512(f).

intermediaries, and there have been rulings that the issuance of defective takedown notices may be grounds for the Intermediary to mount an action for knowing misrepresentation.[116] However, there are difficulties in making such claims against the notice reporters because the damage suffered by the intermediary must be proved.[117]

More critically, the misrepresentation can only be constituted as a 'knowing misrepresentation' if it is proved that the reporter 'should have known [about and not issued the notice or request] if [they have] acted with reasonable care or diligence or would have had no substantial doubt had it been acting in good faith.'[118] This puts a very high bar on the aggrieved intermediary, especially if the reporter pleads that the errors are the result of a misconfiguration of its automated technical processes. It could even mount a plausible argument that the errors were driven by out-of-control machine-learning algorithms, and these were outliers in the programmed space of the system's operations. The issue of tortious liability for out-of-control software agents has been explored elsewhere,[119] and this author takes the view that this is a smokescreen argument that should not detract from the conclusion that the ultimate causality of these errors is still the reporter, with a misconfigured algorithm that was under its control.[120] It suffices to say that the DMCA threshold to make a successful claim for material misrepresentation is set too high to make misrepresentation claims a real incentive for reporters to verify their takedown notices and report their claims correctly and accurately.[121]

If this problem is not remedied, the increasing number of notice mistakes made by reporters, coupled with the DMCA conditions and the difficulty of prosecuting reporters for these mistakes, will force intermediaries into a state of disregard. This is exactly what is happening now, with some intermediaries reporting extremely high rates of successful takedowns notwithstanding the formal and substantive mistakes made by reporters.[122] Part of the reason could be that these high rates of 'successful' takedowns arose because the intermediaries themselves had been deploying automation and machine learning to deal with the ever-increasing volume of takedown

[116] See for example, *Rosen v Hosting Services, Inc*, 771 F. Supp. 2d 1219 (C.D. Cal. 2010).

[117] See for example, *Lenz v Universal Music Corp*, No. 5:07-cv-03783-JF, 2013 WL 271673, 9 (N.D. Cal. Jan. 24, 2013) (holding that 'any damage' in § 512(f) encompasses damages even if they do not amount to substantial economic damages); *Automattic Inc, v Steiner*, 82 F. Supp. 3d 1011, 1030 (N.D. Cal. Mar. 2, 2015) (holding that the online service provider entitled to recover damages for time and resources incurred in dealing with the defective takedown notices, in the form of employees' lost time and attorneys' fees).

[118] *Online Policy Group v Diebold, Inc*, 337 F. Supp. 2d 1195, 1204 (N.D. Cal. 2004).

[119] See for example, Daniel Seng and Tan Cheng Han, 'Agency Law and AI' in Ernest Lim and Phillip Morgan (eds), *The Cambridge Handbook of Private Law and Artificial Intelligence* (Cambridge University Press 2024).

[120] The empirical data suggests that this argument is implausible, because there were many reporters who submitted takedown requests that do pass the Megaupload test. Seng, 'Copyrighting Copywrongs' (n 99) 181.

[121] Ibid. 186.

[122] Google, for instance, reports a successful takedown rate of 97.5% from 2011 to 2012, and above 98% in 2015, and Microsoft a successful takedown rate of 99.7%. Ibid. 126.

notices, complaints, and requests received.[123] While automation and AI have enabled intermediaries to scale up their processing of takedown notices, their unchecked use has created an environment that lacks transparency and accountability, resulting in opportunities for misuse and abuse.[124]

IV REFORM

As intermediaries continue to accrete and add new services, their influence over the content that users see or receive also increases. The immunity laws in the CDA and DMCA may represent in the Web 1.0 era the correct balance between protecting intermediaries from third-party content and requiring them to serve as gatekeepers to shield Internet users from illicit and illegal content and information. But automation and AI technologies today threaten to upend this delicate balance. The use of machine learning to format and present information empowers the intermediary to control and shape such information while immunising it because the user is the content developer. This in turn emasculates the Good Samaritan provision and discourages any intermediary from discharging its gatekeeping responsibilities. Likewise, under the DMCA, intermediaries use automation to shift responsibility for content to end users preserve their copyright immunity, and fail to take a rigorous approach towards filtering out erroneous takedown notices.

The Internet of the future will be ever more all-encompassing and more customised,[125] and our reliance on intermediaries will be even greater. To extract the most from this increasingly vital and all-encompassing platform, we want to preserve intermediary neutrality and minimise the chilling effect of censorship and content regulations. Yet at the same time, we need intermediaries to keep our Internet safe, reliable, and trustworthy.

The EU Digital Services Act[126] is the latest attempt to rebalance these rules. Like the CDA, it confirms the horizontal intermediary immunity for third-party content.[127] But like the DMCA, it also requires intermediaries (including online platforms (OPs))[128] to set up a mechanism to receive, from any reporter, including

[123] See Daniel Seng, 'Who Watches the Watchmen': An Empirical Analysis of Google's Rejected Copyright Takedown Notices' (2015) <https://papers.ssrn.com/sol3/papers.cfm?abstract_id=3687861>.

[124] Seng, 'Copyrighting Copywrongs' (n 99) 185.

[125] See for example, Matt Blitz, 'What Will the Internet Be Like in the Next 50 Years?' (*Popular Mechanics*, 1 November 2019) <www.popularmechanics.com/technology/infrastructure/a29666802/future-of-the-internet/>.

[126] Regulation (EU) 2022/2065 of the European Parliament and of the Council of 19 October 2022 on a Single Market for Digital Services and Amending Directive 2000/31/EC (Digital Services Act) PE/30/2022/REV/1, OJ L 277, 27.10.2022.

[127] Ibid. DSA, Preamble (17)-(18); Arts 4–6.

[128] The DSA identifies three types of intermediary services: conduits, caching and hosting services. Ibid. art 3(g). Online platforms (OPs) are a type of hosting service that disseminate the hosted content to the public. Ibid. art 3(i), and online search engines (OSEs) are a type of intermediary services that allow users to perform searches and return results related to the requested content. Ibid. art 3(j). 'Very

'trusted flaggers',[129] notices seeking to takedown illegal content.[130] Intermediaries may choose to[131] implement their own 'content moderation' by way of human review or algorithmic decision-making[132] to identify and remove illegal content.[133] To promote transparency, intermediaries have to submit to the Commission the reasons for disabling content in a publicly accessible database.[134] (Under the DMCA, some intermediaries also voluntarily publish takedown notices in the Lumen database.[135]) They also have to publish a comprehensible and detailed report of the content moderation undertaken[136] (with OPs also required to publish the specification, accuracy, and safeguards of the automated means used).[137]

To promote accountability in the use of the takedown notices, where a 'trusted flagger' has submitted a significant number of insufficiently precise or inadequately substantiated notices, it may be suspended[138] or even lose its trusted status by the Digital Services Coordinator.[139] This last rule mirrors a proposal first made by the author in 2015 for the publication of 'accountability metrics' so that reporters who repeatedly make mistakes (through their robo-takedown systems) will have the priority of their notices downgraded.[140] Regrettably, the DSA did not mandate another proposal made in 2015 that reporters have to first validate the URLs that they are seeking to disable. As shown above, validating the URLs does not require considerable resources, but doing so would greatly enhance the accuracy and trustworthiness of takedown notices.[141]

First, the DSA regulates the use by VLOPs and VLOSEs[142] of machine-learning 'recommender systems' that suggest specific information to recipients of the

large online platforms' (VLOPs) and 'very large online search engines' (VLOSEs) have additional obligations, including risk assessments and risk mitigation measures. Ibid. arts 33, 34.

129 Ibid. Art 22 (entities designed by the Digital Services Coordinator that have expertise, represent collective interests and are diligent).

130 Ibid. Art 16 (notice and action mechanisms). See also Arts 17 (reasons for takedown), 20 (putback as part of internal complaint-handling system). Note that Arts 16 and 17 refer only to OPs but not to OSEs.

131 Ibid. Art 15.1(c).

132 Ibid. Art 14.1.

133 Ibid. Art 2(t) (defining 'content moderation').

134 Ibid. Art 24.5. Note again that Art 24.5 only refers to OPs but not OSEs.

135 Lumen, 'About Us' (*Lumen Database*) <www.lumendatabase.org/pages/about>.

136 DSA, Art 15. Intermediaries like Google, Facebook and Microsoft already publish semi-annual 'transparency reports'.

137 Ibid. Arts 24.1 (OPs), 33 (VLOPs and VLOSEs). There is some dispute as to what 'specification of the precise purposes' means, and some have interpreted this to refer to the algorithm used for content moderation. See, for example, Juan Londoño, The EU's Digital Services Act: A Primer, American Action Forum, Mar. 24, 2021, <www.americanactionforum.org/insight/the-eus-digital-services-act-a-primer/>.

138 Ibid. Art 22.6.

139 Ibid. Art 22.7.

140 Seng, 'Copyrighting Copywrongs' (n 99) 186–188.

141 Ibid.

142 DSA, Art. 33.1 (defined as intermediaries that service at least 45 million active recipients).

service,[143] and 'advertisement' systems that promote messages or information.[144] VLOPs and VLOSEs have to put in place risk assessment[145] and risk mitigation measures[146] and be assessed for compliance by an independent auditor,[147] whose report shall be publicly available.[148] In addition, VLOPs and VLOSEs have to disclose the 'main parameters' of their 'recommender systems' and enable recipients to modify or influence these parameters.[149]

The DSA is certainly to be lauded for rules that promote the transparent use of AI by intermediaries. As a non-AI-specific law, it, however, immunises rather than holds accountable the intermediaries' use of automated systems to aggregate and disseminate illicit content that targets specific groups or triggers specific harms. While the DSA envisioned the intermediaries' use of content moderation to remove such content, it does not mandate the intermediaries' own content moderation or condition the immunities on their use.[150] In fact, because there is no obligation to monitor,[151] there is no incentive for any intermediary to conduct content moderation. In contrast, the proposed EU Artificial Intelligence Act would bring such uses of AI by intermediaries under its ambit.[152] However, there are doubts as to whether such AI uses fall within the scope of AIA-defined prohibited uses,[153] or can be considered high-risk AI systems.[154] As this study suggests, the increasing use of automation and AI means that intermediaries are more, not less, likely to rely on the immunities to justify the use (and abuse) of their services.

Any impactful reform must explicitly recognise the developing role of automation and machine learning systems in the services offered by Internet intermediaries. And the immunities must be concomitant with adequate accountability, such that intermediaries are obliged to minimise harmful or illicit content. For a start,

143 Ibid. Art 3(s).
144 Ibid. Art 3(r).
145 Ibid. Art 34.
146 Ibid. Art 35.
147 Ibid. Art 37.
148 Ibid. Arts 37.2, 42. Confidential information or information that may cause significant vulnerabilities or undermine public security or harm recipients may be removed. Ibid. arts 37.2, 42.5.
149 Ibid. Arts 26.1(d), 27.1, 39.2(e).
150 DSA, Arts 6, 15.1(c) ('content moderation engaged in at the providers' own initiative') ('content moderation engaged in at the providers' own initiative'). This includes content moderation of its own recommender systems. Cf DSA, Art 34.1 (risk assessment includes assessing algorithmic systems risks).
151 Ibid. Arts 6, 7. Cf AIA, Art 9 (high-risk AI systems to implement a risk management system).
152 See for example, AIA, Art 3(1) and Annex I, which would classify many of the automated technologies used by intermediaries as 'AI systems' because they generate 'predictions, recommendations, or decisions' using '[m]achine learning approaches', 'logic- and knowledge-based approaches' and 'statistical approaches'.
153 See AIA, Art 5.1 ('subliminal techniques beyond a person's consciousness…', 'exploits an of the vulnerabilities of a specific group of persons … in order to materially distort the behaviour of a person', 'evaluation or classification of the trustworthiness of natural persons').
154 AIA, Arts 6, 7, Annex III. Information intermediaries do not fall within AIA, Annex II, and the AIA does not affect the application of the DSA. AIA, Art 2.5.

the intermediary's immunity is not absolute: even under s 230, intermediaries may be liable for crimes relating to the sexual exploitation of children and federal criminal statutes, breaches of intellectual property, communications privacy, and sex trafficking laws.[155] There is a baseline of third-party activities and content which intermediaries have to guard against. This translates into a minimum obligation to monitor and guard their platforms, which intermediaries can, should and ought to have deployed content moderation systems to filter and remove such content.[156] Thus, the assertion that 'there is no general monitoring obligation or active fact-finding obligation'[157] must be heavily circumscribed. To this end, it is further proposed to condition the immunity on the intermediary's good faith discharge of basic content moderation. While this deviates from provisions in the DMCA and DSA,[158] it is the only solution to bring the Good Samaritan rules to bear by incentivising the intermediaries to bring some order to the unruly online environment that they have engendered. Indeed, this change would make the immunities even more relevant and pertinent to all parties in an increasingly complex digital world.

V CONCLUSION

As Kranzberg observed in the early part of the twentieth century, '[t]echnology is neither good nor bad, nor is it neutral.'[159] The same adage can quite aptly be applied to AI and its machine-learning implementations. It is up to us to infuse technology with the best of our human values. If one such value is that we should 'do no harm',[160] it should be observed regardless of the environment, physical or virtual, or our technological tools. When Tim Berners-Lee first proposed the web, he envisioned it as a pool of information that would grow and evolve, as we grow and evolve.[161] It is therefore hoped that any recalibration of the law regarding intermediary liability will be imbued with the same wisdom and foresight that made the Internet possible in the first place, so that it can continue to flourish as the greatest heritage of our human civilisation.

155 S 230(e), CDA.

156 DSA, preamble (45) ('tools used for the purpose of content moderation, including algorithmic decision-making and human review'). See also Art 35.1(c) for VLOPs and VLOSEs.

157 DSA, preamble (30), Art 8; cf DMCA, s 512(m)(1).

158 See, for example, DSA, Arts 7 (voluntary own-initiative investigations), 15.1(c) ('information about the content moderation engaged in at the providers [of intermediary services] *own initiative*, including the use of automated tools, …') (emphasis added).

159 Eric Schatzberg and Lee Vinsel, 'Kranzberg's First and Second Laws' (2018) 6(4) *Technology's Stories* <www.technologystories.org/first-and-second-laws/>.

160 John Stuart Mill, *On Liberty* (John W Parker & Son 1859).

161 Tim Berners-Lee, 'Information Management: A Proposal' (March 1989) <www.w3.org/History/1989/proposal.html>.

PART III

Corporate and Commercial Law

18

Corporate Law, Corporate Governance and AI: Are We Ready for Robots in the Boardroom?

Deirdre Ahern

I INTRODUCTION

The path of the Fourth Industrial Revolution with intertwined opportunities and risks is inexorably unfolding, a digital era of enhanced AI capabilities.[1] Law often trails societal development before shifting organically or reactively to respect the ruthless pace of change. New technologies including AI present highly complex regulatory challenges, transformative economic, and social opportunities co-exist with risks that are evolving and under-explored. However, AI integration and socialisation is at an early stage and while the pace of innovation is rapid, real traction in terms of AI incorporation does not happen overnight.[2] Corporate law scholars can usefully observe, anticipate and respond with discursive insights on issues that benefit from critical thought and provide contextual discussion within wider doctrinal and theoretical frameworks and norms for corporate law and governance. To do so successfully requires both innate curiosity, lateral thinking and a willingness to assimilate much technological, ethical, policy and regulatory developments that lie far behind the traditional purview of corporate law.[3] It also requires a willingness to wait for clarity and solutions to emerge from policymakers and an openness to AI shaping the contours of corporate law. A measure of prescience and informed speculation goes a long way while creatively engaging with how AI can progressively influence the form and application of regulation itself. Thus, we see the boundaries of our discipline being pushed. For corporate law scholars, corporate lawyers, regulators, and lawmakers, there is much to grapple with and many of the questions remain under-studied.

1 As is frequently noted, an agreed description of AI has eluded policymakers. For convenience, this chapter uses the term 'AI' in a broad generic sense and avoids being prescriptive around it given that its nature and applications are fluid, disparate, and changing. However, the capacity for autonomous decision-making and learning is often implicit. The term 'AI' is also used here to contemplate the use of robots, machines, and machine learning.

2 Tim Fountaine and others, 'Getting AI to Scale' (2021) 99(3) *Harv Bus Rev* 116.

3 Common AI themes present around ethics, reliability, untoward effects, and liability. However, they are not the focus of this chapter.

While affirming the robustness of core corporate law principles, this chapter explores how AI has and could impact the content, application, and processes of corporate law and corporate governance, and the interactions of corporate law actors including boards, shareholders, and regulators. It considers the current and future impact of AI and related technologies on corporate law and corporate governance norms and practices. A scenario where the existing corpus of corporate law remains fit for purpose and can be applied seamlessly presents the ideal scenario for corporate life which thrives on legal certainty. Much of the debate on the regulation of AI can be boiled down to how much autonomy we can afford to give algorithms and how we appropriately contain risk without stifling opportunity. These questions are bigger than corporate law. At the same time, corporate law does not exist in a vacuum isolated, from other areas of the law. What is happening in adjacent areas of law and ethics is relevant. To a great extent, the impact of AI on corporate law is indirect; in other cases, significant regulatory, compliance, and enforcement opportunities present themselves. The first part of this chapter scrutinises the changing AI-contextualised landscape in which corporate law operates. The latter part turns to consider the impact on soft law corporate governance practices and boardroom behaviour and norms. As AI gains agency, the legal and cultural challenges of recognising robo-directors are probed. A contextual exploration of directors' duties confronts the significant contemporary challenge concerning the need for directors to engage with AI's potential to transform companies' business models, culture, and systems. When considering how and when to deploy AI applications, adoption and reliance upon AI by companies are considered against the backdrop of the likely judicial application of key best interests duty and duty of care precepts to directors. The chapter also engages with corporate governance potential and controversies surrounding the use of AI and robo-directors including stakeholder interests, board effectiveness, groupthink, and internal biases.

II THE NEW WORLD

AI, machine learning, Big Data, and Distributed Ledger Technologies (DLT) are increasingly being leveraged to enhance business processes, creating time, and cost efficiencies. While much has been made of the unstoppable rise of Big Tech, companies across all sectors increasingly embrace AI in their business processes.[4] For companies that are serious about leveraging operational governance benefits, impressive data analytics can be delivered that can inform and automate decision-making, turbo-charging risk-management. AI systems enable granular monitoring of employees and supply chains, anticipating potential

4 Michael E Porter and James E Heppelmann, 'How Smart Connected Products Are Transforming Companies' (2015) 93(10) *Harv Bus Rev* 96.

operational, and compliance risks with predictive modelling providing an early warning system.

It would be unsurprising to see a correlation between companies that are early movers in harnessing the power of algorithms and increased profitability as they gain an edge from innovation in their operations and a better understanding of markets and compliance issues. Early AI integrators will also most likely have AI-maximised their corporate governance.[5] By contrast, companies that are technological laggards will be at a disadvantage. A knowledge deficit and a lack of appropriate leadership will threaten transformative technological change. The digital and AI divide will affect smaller private companies (other than technology-driven start-ups) more than their larger and well-resourced counterparts. While some companies relish being early adopters, others who are not ready, willing, and able will lag behind.[6] The cost burden for a corporate AI upgrade will fall as systems become widespread, scaled, and off-the-shelf rather than bespoke. In any event, there will be heavy disparities in the rate and extent of AI adoption. For one thing, some companies' business models are not heavily data driven or do not involve repeated processes that benefit from automation.

First mover advantage is a known phenomenon, but first movers must also contend with being first riskers. Where AI-related losses lie once they fall will affect whether corporations are incentivised to take advantage of AI and other synergistic technological capabilities and how the interests of various interested parties are mediated between. Policy work and scholarly excavation continue around the globe on the intractable issue of devising an appropriate model of liability for AI and, more recently, governance challenges associated with the emergence of Generative AI. In the EU, a proportionate risk-based approach is designed to encourage confidence in AI through the Artificial Intelligence Act[7] while in the United States, an Algorithmic Accountability Act is planned to regulate algorithmic decision-making.[8] Many issues of significance that arise lie beyond the remit of corporate law to resolve, although the answers provided may impact the interpretation and application of corporate law rights and obligations.[9]

5 Mark Fenwick and others, 'The 'Unmediated' and 'Tech-Driven' Corporate Governance of Today's Winning Companies' (2019) 16 *NYU JL & Bus* 75.

6 Marija Cubric, 'Drivers, Barriers and Social Considerations for AI Adoption in Business and Management: A Tertiary Study' (2020) 62 *Technology in Society* 101257.

7 European Commission, 'Communication: Fostering a European approach to artificial intelligence' (2021) *COM* 205 final; European Commission, 'Proposal for a Regulation laying down Harmonised Rules on Artificial Intelligence' (2021) *COM* 206 final (political agreement was reached on the AI Act by the EU institutions on 8 December 2023). See also OECD Principles on Artificial Intelligence adopted in the OECD Council, 'Recommendation of the Council on Artificial Intelligence' (OECD/LEGAL/0449).

8 US, Bill HR 6580, Algorithmic Accountability Act of 2022, 117th Cong, 2021–2022. The Act was rejected in January 2023 after failing to pass before the 117th Congress adjourned.

9 For a good discussion in a technology context see Mark Fenwick and others, 'Regulation Tomorrow: What Happens when Technology is Faster than the Law' (2016) 6 *AUBLR* 561.

III WHAT DOES AI MEAN FOR CORPORATE LAW?

A *General Observations*

Amid seismic technological change, it can be tempting to think we need to tear up existing rule books. However, a closer look at the ebb and flow of society and regulation is that what seems new, is often in reality no more than 'old wine in new bottles'. The long-established goals of corporate law across jurisdictions are often concerned with being largely enabling and facilitatory of trade but with some essential regulatory aspects to protect the public dealing with companies against wrongdoing. AI's efficiencies may buttress the achievement of central underlying regulatory goals. Trust in corporate actors through transparency is a key value for accountability and can be assisted by AI. As against this, non-explainability of algorithmic decision-making butts up against the value of transparency and presents an obstacle to devising accountability.

Corporate law frameworks typically receive periodic root and branch overhauls every few decades but are fairly enduring in terms of longevity of basic concepts and power divisions.[10] While FinTech innovation requires development of new financial services laws to cover business models not previously contemplated, corporate law may require some adjustments for AI-driven or AI-enabled business models but the bulk of it will be able to stand largely unscathed. This is likely to be the case for corporate law systems premised largely on a flexibly worded enabling framework that is not concerned with regulating the 'why' of the business, but more concerned with facilitating business under the guise of the corporate form while setting some ground rules around 'how' companies are run.

There is little evidence to suggest that AI availability will shake up corporate law in a dynamic sense in the short term.[11] First, to do so would put the cart before the horse because there are larger fish to fry first in terms of establishing risk management and liability models for AI. Second, much of the content of the law does not need adjusting. Rather the odd nip and tuck for context may largely suffice until the issue of the agency of AI platforms is resolved. However, the context of application of the law is changing and we can expect many efficiency gains to be reaped. An escalation in DLT and AI-driven corporate administration and compliance practices is certain. How regulation and enforcement is carried out is also at the beginning of a journey of algorithmic alchemy. AI and RegTech/SupTech[12] can also be

[10] Brian Cheffins, *Company Law: Theory, Structure and Operation* (Clarendon Press 1993); Deirdre Ahern, 'Codification of Company Law: Taking Stock of the Companies Act 2006' (2014) 35 *Stat L Rev* 230.

[11] Iris H-Y Chiu and Ernest WK Lim, 'Technology vs Ideology: How Far Will Artificial Intelligence and Distributed Ledger Technology Transform Corporate Governance and Business?' (2021) 18 *Berkeley Bus LJ* 1.

[12] The term 'RegTech' connotes the use of regulatory technologies including AI in regulatory and compliance processes. 'SupTech' relates to the use of technologies by supervisory authorities in financial supervision.

expected to play a part in enabling the process of regulating to be more responsive to market gaps identified thus reducing regulatory lag.[13]

Corporate law actors' development of best practices can help to shape the creation of new legal principles and processes surrounding AI and corporate law and corporate governance. Decision-making at all levels including boardroom decision-making context is being shaped by AI. Furthermore, the face of risk management and compliance is changing beyond recognition. In some cases it may prove difficult for entrepreneurs using corporate forms to understand how existing legal frameworks apply to business models and processes based around technological innovation. Adaptive regulators have chosen to deal with this by establishing regulatory sandboxes. For example, the Canadian Securities Administrators' ('CSA') Regulatory Sandbox provides participants with tailored temporary relief from securities laws requirements while engaging in controlled testing.[14] The use of sandboxes is likely to increase across range of different contexts in the short term as a collaborative mechanism to help manage compliance with data privacy and other compliance risks as well as forming a central compliance feature under the EU AI Act.

B *Legislative Design and Corporate Law*

Corporate law's future will be shaped by the availability of tagged machine-readable legislation as previous zeal for a plain language agenda is replaced by enthusiasm for machine-readable legislation and natural language processing. The process of corporate law-making is on the way to transformative change as tagging and machine-readable formats using natural language become the norm.[15] This will change the face of compliance and make regulatory reporting more efficient. A 'technology first' approach (including machine readable regulatory rules) can revolutionise managing corporate governance and compliance resulting in considerable cost savings and greater compliance, allowing human resources to be freed up for higher chain activities. In the run up to company law reforms leading to the Companies Act 2006, the mantra was 'think small first'. Perhaps we will begin to see 'think AI first' in law-making. The alternative is to bring use of AI and algorithms into the mix as laws are made or amended – the strategy taken by New Zealand.[16]

13 John W Bagby and Nizan G Packin, 'RegTech and Predictive Lawmaking: Closing the RegLag between Prospective Regulated Activity and Regulation' (2021) 10 *Mich Bus & Entrepreneurial L Rev* 127.

14 See Deirdre Ahern, 'Regulators Nurturing Fintech Innovation: Global Evolution of the Regulatory Sandbox as Opportunity-Based Regulation' (2019) 15 *Indian J L & Tech* 345; Deirdre Ahern, 'Regulatory Lag, Regulatory Friction and Regulatory Transition as FinTech Disenablers: Calibrating an EU Response to the Regulatory Sandbox Stopgap' (2021) 22 *European Business Organization Law Review* 395.

15 Marcel Froehlich, 'Enabling RegTech Upfront: Unambiguous Machine-Readable Legislation' in Janos Barberis and others (eds), *The RegTech* (Wiley 2019).

16 Stuart Corner, 'How the New Zealand Government Will Regulate AI' (*Computerworld*, 17 March 2020) <www.computerworld.com/article/3532505/how-the-nz-government-will-regulate-ai.html>.

The UK approach is evolving towards a set of cross-sectoral AI principles to guide regulators.[17]

In the new legal order, code can become a proxy for law.[18] The provision of standard model articles in legislation may in the future be replaced by direct interaction with a Generative AI bot that will draft bespoke articles based on its training data in a matter of seconds following a series of prompts. Code can help to make rules easy to break down and comply with, but code works best with black and white rules such as mandatory corporate law rules. The more a corporate law system allows for private ordering in the form of opt out or opt in provisions or default rules, the more sophisticated the programming needs to be to enable AI-driven compliance.

For jurisdictions that have been a slave to paper-based filing, company incorporations and other post-incorporation filings will be transformed.[19] Traditionally a task for a trained company secretary, AI will increasingly be used in company formation with chatbots and machine learning being potentially used to help the promoters provide the information needed for establishing a company. In the UK, Companies House is implementing a five year Digital First strategy and Natural Voice Language (voice recognition) has been incorporated into customer services. The system can identify that the customer is interested in incorporating a company and a link to the relevant service is then automatically sent to them via SMS. Company registration offices could use AI in vetting information and documents submitted for suitability and accuracy with smart contract protocols used to determine when certificates of incorporation and confirmation of registration of other documents should be issued.

C *Attribution of Liability for AI*

Discussion of development of legal norms around liability for the deployment of AI by State and private actors remain under active policy discussion or at an early stage at domestic, regional and international levels.[20] The question of whether AI could be given authority as a corporate agent or hold power of attorney with ability to bind a company should ideally be broached once private accountability and liability frameworks for AI are in place. Devising a robust workable framework for attribution of liability for harm caused by AI systems is a major regulatory challenge of our time. Resolving this will not be the domain of corporate law. Rather, corporate law's response will adapt to the resolution of this keystone challenge. Nonetheless some brief observations are made here from the perch of corporate law.

[17] Department for Science, Innovation & Technology, *A Pro-innovation Approach to Regulation* (White Paper) (Cmnd 815, 2023).

[18] Lawrence Lessig, *Code and Other Laws of Cyberspace* (Basic 1999).

[19] The path towards automation is set by company registration offices and filings moving online. To further facilitate this there needs to be a greater move towards digitalisation including digital IDs and reduction of the need for human signatures. The Covid-19 pandemic underscored the importance of this.

[20] See, however, European Commission, 'Proposal for a Directive of the European Parliament and of the Council on Adapting Non-contractual Civil Liability Rules to Artificial Intelligence' (2022) COM 496 final.

Normally where employees are at fault, vicarious liability applies to the company through application of the respondeat superior principle.[21] As AI changes, the allocation of work actions will be redistributed from the job description of employees to algorithms involving machine learning including Generative AI integrated solutions. This, in turn, will mean that the usual systems of attributing corporate liability through vicarious liability and other mechanisms will increasingly be bypassed as human actors fade into the background.[22] That raises an issue as to when the behaviour of AI or algorithmic applications should be attributed to the company.[23] One vaunted possibility is recognising a legal status or personality for AI.[24] This has some analogy with the separate legal personality as attached to corporations with the exception that corporations usually have human agents pulling their strings.[25]

For companies using AI in the boardroom difficult issues of causation may arise given the complexities involved in pinpointing responsibility. Diamantas worries that 'corporations will become increasingly immune to liability as their operations require less and less human intervention.'[26] Attributing liability for unintended algorithmic harm involves a number of actors including developers and human programmers who may be employed by companies as well as the independent actions of an algorithm in full autonomous non-supervised machine-learning mode, acting as a Large Language Model trained on a dataset. Without a direct means of liability, the general duties of directors need consideration.[27]

D *Post-incorporation Corporate Administration and Compliance*

AI technologies using language processing can significantly reduce costs associated with regulatory compliance[28] and automation and DLT could take the place of corporate officers in internal register administration and routine reporting and filing responsibilities.[29] A powerful combination of DLT technologies and AI assistance

[21] Phillip Morgan, 'Tort Law and Artificial Intelligence – Vicarious Liability' in Ernest Lim and Phillip Morgan (eds), *The Cambridge Handbook of Private Law and Artificial Intelligence* (Cambridge University Press 2024).

[22] Ibid.

[23] Mihailis E Diamantis, 'The Extended Corporate Mind: When Corporations Use AI to Break the Law' (2020) 98 *N C L Rev* 893.

[24] Nadia Banteka, 'Legal Personhood and AI: AI Personhood on a Sliding Scale' in Ernest Lim and Phillip Morgan (eds), *The Cambridge Handbook of Private Law and Artificial Intelligence* (Cambridge University Press 2024).

[25] For a good historical account see Susan Watson, 'Viewing Artificial Persons in the AI Age through the Lens of History' in Andrew Godwin and others (eds), *Technology and Corporate Law: How Innovation Shapes Corporate Activity* (Edward Elgar 2021).

[26] Diamantis (n 22) 899.

[27] The monitoring and oversight duties of directors as part of their duty of care are of particular relevance.

[28] John O McGinnis and Russell G Pearce, 'The Great Disruption: How Machine Intelligence Will Transform the Role of Lawyers in the Delivery of Legal Services' (2013) 82 *Fordham L Lev* 3041.

[29] Since 2017, Delaware recognises that a corporation can have records administered 'on its behalf' thus facilitating the use of DLT for both the creation and administration of such records: Delaware

will prove its worth in labour saving through assisting with internal corporate administration such as allotment of shares and maintaining registers such as the register of members. AI can help with the mechanics of holding board and shareholder meetings.[30] Blockchain-based proxy voting enabled by smart contract should have a positive impact on shareholder engagement by creating a secure and transparent mechanism for proxy voting.

For boards, management, and internal and external audit functions, the data sifting and analytics of AI are hugely beneficial. As AI becomes embedded, companies will employ more software engineers and data scientists and less compliance personnel. AI-driven compliance and risk-management systems will likely decrease reliance on legal advice. For companies dipping their toe into AI waters, compliance and reporting processes incorporating AI capability and machine-readable formats present low-hanging fruit. The ability of machine-learning algorithms to improve over time based on their experience processing data has incredible potential for enhanced risk management that is adaptive to changing patterns in risk environments. AI's predictive abilities enable a responsive approach to corporate risk management and compliance as AI tools can monitor in real time and provide an early warning system for detecting and pre-empting corporate law breaches. AI could flag that a proposed act would amount to unlawful financial assistance or that a proposed dividend may be unlawful. AI monitoring can detect patterns suggestive of insider trading and market manipulation and even make a predictive analysis of which traders may be likely to 'go rogue'.[31]

E *Reporting*

Corporate reporting processes via public portals using automation, natural language processing, and machine learning will further an open data agenda. Crucially, this can further a corporate-purpose stakeholder agenda beyond shareholder primacy. For example, implementation of the EU Corporate Sustainability Reporting Directive ('CSRD')[32] will introduces digital tagging of reported sustainability information[33] which will provide scope for sophisticated AI-driven data analytics by proxy advisors,

General Corporation Law, §224 (as amended). See also the advent of digital, ledger-based securities in countries such as Switzerland and Luxembourg.

30 Anne Lafarre and Christoph Van der Elst, 'LegalTech and Blockchain for Corporate Governance and Shareholders' in Vanessa Mak and others (eds), *Research Handbook in Data Science and the Law* (Edward Elgar 2018).

31 Laura Noonan, 'Bank Uses AI to Catch Rogue Traders before the Act' (*Financial Times*, 25 March 2019).

32 Directive (EU) 2022/2464 of the European Parliament and of the Council of 14 December 2022 amending Regulation (EU) No 537/2014, Directive 2004/109/EC, Directive 2006/43/EC and Directive 2013/34/EU, as regards corporate sustainability reporting, PE/35/2022/REV/1, OJ L 322, 16.12.2022. See further Deirdre Ahern, 'The Sustainability Reporting Ripple: Direct and Indirect Implications of the EU Corporate Sustainability Reporting Directive for SME Actors' in Alessio Bartolacelli (ed), *The Prism of Sustainability* (University of Macerata, forthcoming). Available on SSRN.

33 Ibid. art 19d. See further European Reporting Lab, *Final Report: Proposals for a Relevant and Dynamic EU Sustainability Reporting Standard-Setting* (2021).

ESG rating agencies, and other stakeholders. Increasingly big data will influence the form of reporting inputs, and there will be an increased availability of centralised repositories of data that is machine readable and subject to AI and machine-learning interfaces.[34] A public portal for all corporate disclosures could be supported by both DLT and AI.[35] Further change to reporting is conceivable. Annual reporting of both financial and non-financial information is beginning to be regarded as anachronistic, and the future may lie with on-demand tailored reporting rather than cyclical point-in-time reporting.

F *Regulatory Powers and Enforcement*

Company registration offices and corporate law regulators need to optimise what is on offer to enhance their own functioning while taking due account of the associated risks. The Australian Securities and Investments Commission is committed to making data-enhanced regulatory decisions using AI techniques, such as machine learning as well as text and voice analytic solutions using natural language processing.[36] Indeed, algorithmic analysis of datasets will likely drive the design of future personnel training by regulators. To ramp up data capabilities and become data-led, regulators need to act strategically to increase data literacy and to recruit data science experts to cover data management, data analysts, and engineers. As in other regulatory domains, the expected impact of RegTech and SupTech is exponential. AI and other technologies will support corporate regulators in their regulatory, monitoring, and investigative remits. AI can assist corporate regulators to sift through masses of filed information in detecting problematic acts and omissions. As Cohen perceptively remarks, '[u]nder conditions of infloglut, the problem is not scarcity but rather the need for new ways of cutting through the clutter.'[37] Predictive AI may be used to spot patterns and detect potential corporate wrongdoing by creating an early warning system through learning from pattern recognition and sifting big data.

Although machines can interpret and apply the law, apply checks and balances, and develop sophisticated predictive warning systems,[38] in judging whether or not there has been a breach of a statutory obligation, fiduciary duty, or if a right exists, a court is often required to exercise sophisticated discretion and weigh competing factors in the balance.[39] This negates the easy automation of dispute resolution.

34 The European Single Electronic Format project for annual financial reporting is based upon tagging data and provision of a human and machine readable xHTML format.

35 This is the approach taken by the European Union in its work towards a European single access point for public corporate information including financial and non-financial reporting.

36 Australian Securities and Investments Commission, *ASIC Corporate Plan 2021–25* (2021) 21.

37 Julie E Cohen, 'The Regulatory State in the Information Age' (2016) 17 *Theoretical Inq L* 369, 384.

38 David Restrepo-Amariles and Gregory Lewkowicz, 'Unpacking Smart Law: How Mathematics and Algorithms Are Reshaping the Legal Code in the Financial Sector' (2020) 25(3) *Lex Electronica* 171.

39 Anselmo Reyes and Adrian Mak, 'AI and Commercial Dispute Resolution' in Ernest Lim and Phillip Morgan (eds), *The Cambridge Handbook of Private Law and Artificial Intelligence* (Cambridge University Press 2024).

Algorithms lend themselves better to black and white. This means that for now the future of judges seems assured.

It is possible to envisage lesser procedural strict liability breaches of the corporate law code being dealt with by an AI adjudicator. For example, in place of the Registrar of Companies, an AI system could record a failure to file accounts or reports and issue a civil penalty. The algorithm could be calibrated to take into account specified factors in deciding whether to issue a penalty and its amount such as how late a filing is, the nature of the company, and its past record.[40] In some cases, considerable discretion is exercised, and the exercise of it is quite sophisticated, but it could be broken down into guidelines for AI. The disqualification undertaking system that applies in the UK and is administered by the Insolvency Service could be suitable.[41] The role of the Insolvency Service could potentially be administered or supported by an AI algorithm including deciding the appropriate period for a disqualification undertaking.[42] Relevant factors to be weighed in the balance including mitigating circumstances to reach a penalty, for example, the period of disqualification to be imposed, would need to be programmed in.

Remodelling public and private enforcement of corporate law to place AI in the driving seat is fraught with obstacles. Concerns with due process, fairness, and accountability abound in relation to automated decision-making. Some brakes are placed on fully automated decision-making by the EU General Data Protection Regulation[43] which generally prohibits a person from being the subject of a decision made solely in reliance on automated data processing, including profiling, without consent. Operational concerns also arise. Algorithmic bias could have real consequences. COMPAS, an algorithmic tool trialled in the United States for prediction of future criminality, showed an unwarranted bias in falsely flagging black people twice as often as white people for predicted violent crime.[44]

G *Recognising Robo-Directors?*

AI has the capacity for autonomous thinking and deep learning and companies, are already heavily depending on AI tools for their unsurpassed data assimilation, data crunching, and market predictions as a tool to inform better decision-making

40 Companies Act 2006, s 453.

41 Disqualification undertakings serve in place of making an application for a disqualification order in court.

42 Company Directors Disqualification Act 1986, s 1A provides for periods of 2 to 15 years.

43 Council Regulation (EU) 2016/679 of 27 April 2016 General Data Protection Regulation ('GDPR') OJ L119/1, art 22.

44 Jeff Larson and others, 'How We Analyzed the COMPAS Recidivism Algorithm' (ProPublica, 23 May 2016) <www.propublica.org/article/how-we-analyzed-the-compas-recidivism-algorithm>; Anne L Washington, 'How to Argue with an Algorithm: Lessons from the COMPAS-ProPublica Debate' (2018) 17 *Colo Tech LJ* 131; Sascha van Schendel, 'The Challenges of Risk Profiling Used by Law Enforcement: Examining the Cases of COMPAS and SyRI' in Leonie Reins (ed), *Regulating New Technologies in Uncertain Times* (TMC Asser Press 2019).

by boards and management. The use of an upgraded Einstein product offered by Salesforce in its own boardroom has garnered a lot of attention; CEO Mark Benioff has credited Einstein with transforming him as a CEO.[45] As AI becomes smarter and more versatile, the million-dollar question for the corporate law sphere is: how ready, willing, and able is the world to legally recognise robo-directors? The Turing test of whether a machine can think is passed when a machine's behaviour in conversing and responding to questions can be convincing to the human beings it is interacting with so that they would believe they are interacting with another human.[46] Chatbots operating as customer service advisors and robo-advisors providing investment advice and automated portfolio management easily meet this test.[47]

In 2014, a Hong Kong venture capital firm, Deep Knowledge Ventures, claimed to have appointed VITAL ('Validating Investment Tool for Advancing Life Sciences') to its board and credited it with helping it to avoid being hoodwinked by hype when making investment decisions. The board of Deep Knowledge Ventures does not make a decision to invest without a positive, corroborating recommendation from VITAL. It generated a wash of publicity. However, although incredibly beneficial, VITAL is a tool and not, in fact, a de jure director, despite PR billing as such. Rather, VITAL has observer status in the boardroom and does not have voting rights.[48] A hypothesis that an AI director is a credible next step for corporate law depends on how legal responsibility for AI is structured and whether a robo-director can be subject to, and comply with, duties and obligations, and also have meaningful penalties imposed for non-compliance. In the market for corporate incorporations, the State of Delaware demonstrates that a pro-management corporate legal system which facilitates director primacy is a winning formula.[49] If there is demand for the efficiency and turbo-charged decision-making of a robo-director, states that are credible first movers in recognising AI legal actors in the corporate sphere may influence the market for incorporations, and regulatory

[45] Julie Bort, 'How Salesforce CEO Mark Benioff Uses Artificial Intelligence to End Internal Politics at Meetings' (*Business Insider India*, 19 May 2019) <www.businessinsider.in/How-Salesforce-CEO-Marc-Benioff-uses-artificial-intelligence-to-end-internal-politics-at-meetings/articleshow/58743024.cms>.

[46] Alan M Turing, 'Computing Machinery and Intelligence' in Robert Epstein, Gary Roberts and Grace Beber (eds), *Parsing the Turing Test* (Springer 2009).

[47] Iris H-Y Chiu, 'AI and Financial Intermediaries' in Ernest Lim and Phillip Morgan (eds), *The Cambridge Handbook of Private Law and Artificial Intelligence* (Cambridge University Press 2024).

[48] Nicky Burridge, 'Artificial Intelligence Gets a Seat in the Boardroom' (*Nikkei Asian Review*, 10 May 2017) <www.asia.nikkei.com/Business/Artificial-intelligence-gets-a-seat-in-the-boardroom>.

[49] Faith Stevelman, 'Regulatory Competition, Choice of Forum, and Delaware's Stake in Corporate Law' (2009) 34(1) *Delaware J Corp L* 57. In a European context, see Christian Kirchner, Richard W Painter and Wulf A Kaal, 'Regulatory Competition in EU Corporate Law after Inspire Art: Unbundling Delaware's Product for Europe' (2005) 2 ECFR 159; Deirdre Ahern, 'The Societas Unius Personae: Using the Single-Member Company as a Vehicle for EU Private Company Law Reform, Some Critical Reflections on Regulatory Approach' in Aristides J Viera Gonzalez and Christoph Teichmann (eds), *Private Companies in Europe: The Societas Personae (SUP) and the Recent Developments in the EU Member States* (Thomson Reuters Aranzadi 2016) 55.

competitiveness driving corporate mobility may emerge. Delaware's greatly pro-management corporate law system will insulate boards against AI-related liability, but to stay in pole position, it may need to consider recognising robo-directors.[50] The challenge of formally recognising a robo-director lies in a legal framework not adapted for this and is not as simple as might first seem given the divergence between vast technological advances on the one hand and relatively immutable legal principles on the other.[51]

The starting point is the familiar proposition in common law jurisdictions that a 'director' constitutes 'any person occupying the position of director, by whatever name called'.[52] AI does not meet the threshold of personhood, which is only open to humans and, in some jurisdictions, legal persons. Only allowing natural persons to be directors[53] rules out non-human directors. An outlier position, seen in the United Kingdom and Hong Kong, also permits legal persons to be appointed as directors.[54] The stumbling block, then, is that AI is not generally recognised as a legal person.[55] Furthermore, a mechanism for attaching liability for an AI director's acts and mechanisms requires knowledge. As Ricci points out, allowing AI directors would be qualitatively different from a corporate director behind whom an individual is pulling the strings: 'the appointed AI machine would be the fiduciary actually making the decisions on behalf of the corporation, the *artificial director*.'[56]

If we assume that a robo-director is not intended to have attenuated responsibility, granting it a legal status is a necessary prelude to imposing general and fiduciary duties, rights, and obligations.[57] AI would need to be given legal status in order to be able to assume the role of a legal actor with the accompanying potential to assume legal rights and responsibilities. One route to this would be by providing a statutory mechanism for an AI system to be established as a juristic person. In Roman times, the law recognised the legal capacity of non-human entities such as cities, and municipal corporations were a later evolution of that. Granting legal personality

50 To date, Delaware has focused on unlocking the potential of DLT. Pursuant to the Delaware Blockchain Initiative, Delaware's General Corporation Law was amended in 2017 to provide express statutory authority to enable Delaware corporations to use an electronic environment including a DLT environment for the creation and maintenance of corporate records including the corporation's stock ledger. On the potential of blockchain in the corporate sphere, see Alexandra Andhov, 'Corporations on Blockchain: Opportunities and Challenges' (2020) 53 *Cornell Int LJ* 1.

51 There may be greater openness to accepting AI as a member of a supervisory board in countries with a two-tier board structure.

52 Companies Act 2006, s 250(1).

53 As seen in Australia, Canada, Delaware, Ireland, New Zealand, Singapore, and South Africa.

54 This can be useful in a group context to enable the parent company to sit on the board of a subsidiary. Nonetheless, behind every corporate director is an individual or series of individuals, and the commonly argued view is that permitting corporate directors hides the true actors pulling the strings.

55 See, however, Saudi Arabia's grant of legal personhood to Sophia the Robot in 2017. See generally Simon Chesterman, 'Artificial Intelligence and the Limits of Legal Personality' (2020) 69 *ICLQ* 819.

56 Sergio AG Ricci, 'Artificial Agents in Corporate Boardrooms' (2020) 105 *Cornell Law Review* 869, 885.

57 Daniel Seng and Tan Cheng Han, 'Agency Law and AI' in Ernest Lim and Phillip Morgan (eds), *The Cambridge Handbook of Private Law and Artificial Intelligence* (Cambridge University Press 2024).

to AI systems is an option. There are some difficulties with this. For one thing, it has been questioned if robots can really grasp the significance of rights and duties.[58] That has not always been respected in corporate law policy. Until relatively recently, it was permissible to appoint minors who lacked full legal capacity as directors of companies.[59] For now, AI is confined to being a tool in the armoury of the board and cannot gain more than observer status as unless a step is taken to afford legal actor status to AI, it is legally impossible for AI to constitute a de jure director.[60] Following on from this, although this may surprise some, no matter how much AI is deferred to by human directors currently, it is impossible for it to qualify as a robo de facto director or robo shadow director. This is because AI's fundamental absence of legal status leads to an inability to impose the attendant legal responsibilities, duties and liabilities that would ensue from a de facto or shadow director designation. It is difficult to imagine that AI could be subject to fiduciary obligation without being afforded legal status and capacity in its own right.[61] There is no one unifying theory underlying the imposition of fiduciary obligation, but the non-recognition of AI as an agent with legal standing places a major hurdle in place of advancing otherwise credible arguments based on trust, reliance, and vulnerability.

Things may change in the future if an appropriate legal framework for AI is embedded. Assuming that robo-directors with legal capacity were to be legally provided for, complex policy questions would have to be broached such as whether robo-directors should be prohibited to serve without an accompanying natural director.[62] Thought would have to be given to specific removal provisions to allow for the speedy removal of problematic robo-directors. Alternatively, instead of granting AI robots equivalence in the form of director status, they could be recognised as a sui generis type of e-agent of the board that would be granted status and given rights to attend and contribute at board meetings and to be involved in co-determination with the board.[63] The board acting collectively could be the principal of the AI e-agent and delimit the scope of its authority. Principles drawn from the law of agency could frame this.[64]

58 Horst Eidenmüller, 'Robots Legal Personality' (*Oxford Business Law Blog*, 8 March 2017) <www.law.ox.ac.uk/business-law-blog/blog/2017/03/robots%E2%80%99-legal-personality>.

59 Section 157 of the Companies Act 2006 rectified this by setting a minimum age of 16 for new director appointments to accord with the age of majority.

60 On legal capacity, see Ricci (n 53).

61 An alternative path to direct legal actor status is to recognise the AI platform as emanating from a legal entity: Simone Degeling and Jessica Hudson, 'Financial Robots as Instruments of Fiduciary Loyalty' (2018) 40 *Sydney Law Review* 63.

62 John Armour and Horst Eidenmüller, 'Self-Driving Corporations?' (2019) 10 *Harv Bus L Rev* 87. Here, context and purpose are everything. Transactional non-trading companies such as special-purpose vehicles may be appropriately managed by a solo robo-director.

63 This would require clarity around the legal standing of AI actors.

64 Daniel Seng and Tan Cheng Han, 'Agency Law and AI' in Ernest Lim and Phillip Morgan (eds), *The Cambridge Handbook of Private Law and Artificial Intelligence* (Cambridge University Press 2024).

IV DIRECTORS' DUTIES

Directors' duties are not worded so as to narrowly prescribe what must be done to comply with them. Rather, they are broadly worded for ease of application to a wide range of contexts, companies, and directors. Consequently, AI's interface may influence the context of the application of directors' duties but should not of itself motivate a shift in the overarching content. However, important questions do arise for boards to confront.

Boards have complex decisions to make in relation to deciding to use AI in strategy, operations, oversight, compliance, and reporting. Given the emphasis in corporate law on collective as well as individual director responsibility, boards cannot simply delegate AI matters to a putatively AI-savvy director or committee and relieve themselves of responsibility. As Lord Woolf MR remarked in *Re Westmid Packing Services Ltd (No 3)*, 'any individual who undertakes the statutory and fiduciary obligations of being a company director should realise that these are inescapable personal responsibilities.'[65] The decision to use AI in an operational context represents a significant strategic decision for the board.[66] Innovation, market norms, cost, and regulation will influence accepted practice and AI take-up by companies. Trustworthy AI, as its capabilities unfold, will be used to enhance strategy, supervision, and monitoring and to power evidence-based decision-making. The less-established nature of AI presents a conundrum: there are costs and risks as well as opportunities to consider when and how to use AI. A defining doctrinal issue as AI becomes part of the state-of-the-art concerns whether it could be considered a breach of the duty of care for a board not to have moved with that trend. Conversely, could it be considered reckless to be an early adopter when there are so many unknowables? As remarked in relation to the risks associated with AI deployment, '[u]nder-reliance represents inefficiency, while over-reliance represents risk.'[67] Adjudicating on these questions would be time and context specific.[68] Two duties are particularly worthy of discussion in this context – the duty of loyalty and the duty of care.

In deciding whether and how to integrate AI into a company's operations, strategy, and compliance, the duty on directors to act in the company's interests is paramount. Generally, directors will be insulated against liability for good faith collective decision-making regarding the company's use or non-use of AI under the

65 *Re Westmid Packing Services Ltd (No 3)* [1998] BCC 836 (CA) 843.

66 Jeanne Boillet, 'Why AI is both a Risk and a Way to Manage Risk?' (*EY*, 1 April 2018) <www.ey.com/en_gl/assurance/why-ai-is-both-a-risk-and-a-way-to-manage-risk>.

67 Hussein A Abbass, 'Social Integration of Artificial Intelligence: Functions, Automation Allocation Logic and Human-Autonomy Trust' (2019) 11 *Cogn Comput* 159, 169. It is interesting to recall that when computers arrived, companies could not be forced to use them although with time they became mainstream.

68 Insurance could provide a sensible means of redistributing AI risk; boards would be assisted in making difficult judgment calls if Directors' & Officers' insurance policies permitted inclusion of AI risk.

best interests duty. Generally, judges do not second-guess directors' intent to act in the corporate interest[69] and the restricted pathway to derivative actions means that mounting a 'technological laggard' argument in a shareholder challenge to the effect that a board's failure to deploy an AI solution has impaired the company's competitiveness would present an uphill battle. Judicial reluctance to interfere with business judgements made by directors is venerable, and the division of power between the corporate organs does not allow shareholders to dictate to the board on corporate strategy.[70] A head-in-the-sand approach by directors that ignores the potential utility of AI to the company would not, however, be completely immune from challenge. The subjective approach to testing compliance with the duty to promote the success of the company only protects actual good-faith belief in corporate benefit where the interests of the company have been considered. If the directors of a company fail to give real consideration to corporate benefits surrounding the use or non-use of AI (for example, if the directors of a subsidiary company passively follow the lead of the parent company's decision not to use AI without actively considering the interests of the subsidiary), this would trigger the application of the harsher *Charterbridge*[71] objective test, asking whether an intelligent and honest person in their position could have reasonably believed that non-deployment of AI was in that company's interests.[72] Furthermore, board decision-making processes that fail to take into account relevant considerations or that take into account irrelevant considerations may be challenged.[73]

Stakeholder consideration and consultation with employees around AI adoption is important given that it may entail a radical restructuring of the workforce. Transparency around this is underpinned in the UK by Section 172(1) reporting obligations. Nonetheless, as a matter of law, stakeholder interests will not prevail under Section 172 of the Companies Act 2006 if the board considers AI-consequent workforce restructuring compelling to advance the long-term interests of the company for the benefit of the shareholders. For boards motivated to see beyond the lens of profit and who are interested in environmental and human rights due diligence, big data analytics offer opportunities to improve sustainability in the supply chain.[74] AI,

[69] Companies Act 2006 s 172(1); *Re Smith & Fawcett* [1942] Ch 304 (Ch); *Regentcrest plc (in liq) v Cohen* [2001] BCC 494 (Ch); *ClientEarth v Shell plc* [2023] EWHC 1897 (Ch).

[70] *Gramophone and Typewriter Ltd v Stanley* [1908] 2 KB 89 (KB); *John Shaw & Sons (Salford) Ltd* [1935] 2 KB 113 (KB); *Howard Smith Ltd v Ampol Petroleum Ltd* [1974] AC 821 (PC). Disgruntled shareholders may be better advised to consider board refreshment or to vote with their feet.

[71] *Charterbridge Corporation v Lloyds Bank Ltd* [1970] Ch 62 (Ch).

[72] See also *Re HLC Environmental Projects Ltd; Hellard v Carvalho* [2013] EWHC 2876 (Ch), [2014] BCC 337 [92].

[73] Ernest Lim, 'Judicial Intervention in Directors' Decision-Making Process: Section 172 of the Companies Act 2006' (2018) *Journal of Business Law* 169.

[74] Benjamin T Hazen and others, 'Big Data and Predictive Analytics for Supply Chain Sustainability: A Theory-Driven Research Agenda' (2016) 101 *Comput Ind Eng* 592; Venkatesh Mani and others, 'Mitigating Supply Chain Risk via Sustainability Using Big Data Analytics: Evidence from the Manufacturing Supply Chain' (2017) 9 *Sustainability* 608.

paired with IoT[75] and DLT, can be used to monitor and enhance strategic and operational corporate alignment with broader social justice and sustainability instrumental goals across complex supply chains. Indeed, the European Commission has singled out the potential for data digitalisation and the use of new technologies to provide novel solutions for identifying, addressing, and preventing adverse environmental impacts and human rights infringements.[76]

Future doctrinal development of the duty of care could see courts consider that being suitably informed prior to board decision-making should be shaped by the availability of recourse to AI systems to provide highly sophisticated analysis. Known, unknown, and unpredictable risks and the so-called 'black box' problem whereby it is not possible to reverse engineer the algorithm will also colour what we can expect of directors in relation to their duty of care. To comply with the duty to exercise reasonable care, skill, and diligence,[77] directors need to become AI proficient and obtain expert advice. Governance structures that accord with best practices, ethical guidelines, and legal requirements would need to be put in place for the risk management of AI.[78] Something may go awry post-AI adoption. Non-justifiable bias in working with datasets is an important risk issue and algorithmic risk from badly programmed algorithms that deliver biased results may be more acute for companies that are early adopters.[79] Boards would be expected to have established procedures to counteract the potential for creating or reinforcing unfair bias in AI systems as regards algorithmic design and data inputs. Putting appropriate systems in place to address risk will go a long way in showing that the duty of care has been discharged.[80]

In applying the duty of care, the degree of oversight of AI will be scrutinised along with the level of AI-knowledge board members possess in carrying out their functions. Under the UK hybrid duty of care, a director who comes on board (and one who is specifically recruited) as having technology/data governance-related skills will be held to a higher standard than that applied in relation to the average director.[81] The duty of

75 Internet of Things.

76 European Commission, *Study on Due Diligence Requirements through the Supply Chain: Final Report* (2020) 22. See further Deirdre Ahern, 'The Sustainability Reporting Ripple: Direct and Indirect Implications of the EU Corporate Sustainability Reporting Directive for SME Actors' in Alessio Bartolacelli (ed), *The Prism of Sustainability* (University of Macerata, forthcoming). Available on SSRN.

77 Companies Act 2006, s 174.

78 Appointment of a Chief Ethics Officer to keep abreast of accountability practices and norms is an option.

79 Programming errors may lead to decision-making that is based on faulty assumptions including unjust discrimination.

80 For example, cyber-resilience systems to guard against hackers targeting an AI system to gain access to valuable data or to disrupt operations.

81 Companies Act 2006, s 174: 'the care, skill and diligence required is that which would be exercised by a reasonably diligent person with- (a) the general knowledge, skill and experience that may reasonably be expected of a person carrying out the functions carried out by that director in relation to the company, and (b) the general knowledge, skill and experience that the director concerned actually has.'

care includes an expectation that boards will self-educate.[82] The sub-duty on directors to be suitably informed gains heightened relevance as AI is now mainstream across industries. The lesson of the landmark Australian case of *ASIC v Healey*,[83] which caused shockwaves for non-executive directors, is instructive. Non-executive directors were sued for failing to identify errors in the financial statements concerning the classification of a debt. Only one of them had an accounting qualification. In finding a breach of the duty of care, Middleton J. emphasised an objective standard of care based on 'the knowledge each director has or should have by virtue of his or her position as director.'[84] The reasoning in *Healey* reflects a corporate law landscape with a singular objective standard of care where directors may be held to a higher standard. Furthermore, it could be expected that courts will take account of the less-established nature of the AI technical and regulatory landscape. Nonetheless, *Healey* shows how important a role the courts will play in standard settings around the application of the duty of care, and in an AI context and as AI becomes more established, what is expected of directors will inevitably increase.

Being diligent and suitably informed involves learning about and keeping abreast of new and evolving technological developments that impact upon business models, governance, and compliance. Just like directors are required to acquire a level of financial literacy, directors in the age of AI should undergo training to have an understanding of the opportunities relating to AI and the basic assumptions and risks. Being familiar enough to be able to guide and monitor in relation to the use of AI is fundamental. However, one argument is that the expectations on directors around AI understanding should not be pitched too high. If the standard expected of directors in relation to incorporating, understanding, and monitoring new technologies is too demanding, liability chill may ensue, discouraging people from taking up directorial office. At the same time, courts, in imposing standards of expected conduct, have been reluctant to directly accede to the 'liability chill' argument.[85]

A reasonable leeway will nonetheless be afforded to directors. They are not expected to be omniscient. It is judicially understood that risk-taking is inherent in the nature of being a director. That has particular resonance in relation to AI integration. Company law has long offered business judgement rope to directors in risk-taking and making difficult judgement calls – this is what distinguishes calculated risk-taking from reckless or rash risk-taking. One is negligent. The other is making a decision after weighing up the strengths, weaknesses, opportunities, and threats, with regard to technological developments and limitations, market practices, and likely future developments.

Post-adoption of AI, issues of reliance loom large. Effective supervision and monitoring are essential aspects of the duty of care on directors. Although directors

82 *Re Barings plc (No 5); Secretary of State for Trade and Industry v Baker* [1999] 1 BCLC 433 (Ch) 489.
83 *ASIC v Healey* [2011] FCA 717 (FCA).
84 Ibid. [15].
85 *ASIC* (n 80); *In Re Caremark International Inc.* 698 A.2d 959 (1996 Del Ch).

may rely on others, and AI systems, to perform functions, directors cannot delegate away their duties and there is an inescapable personal responsibility on them. Consequently, it would not be appropriate to abdicate responsibility and wholly rely on AI as infallible. Reliance should not be blind reliance. 'AI dazzle' could arise where directors become passive in relation to the exercise of their judgement due to being unduly deferential to the insights of their AI counterpart. On the risk of being dazzled by AI's analytical contribution and predictions, there is merit in recalling Popplewell J's comment in *Madoff Securities International Ltd (in liq) v Raven*[86] that each director

> owes duties to the company to inform himself of the company's affairs and join with his fellow directors in supervising them. It is therefore a breach of duty for a director to allow himself to be dominated, bamboozled or manipulated by a dominant fellow director where such involves a total abrogation of this responsibility.[87]

The law may need to develop to recognise the specific nature of the AI beast; using AI may be treated as similar to delegating functions to an employee with retained oversight, but further caution is needed given the risks associated with algorithms and machine learning which make it difficult to second-guess and to know how it has gone astray.

V BOARD-ROOM DECISION-MAKING AND CORPORATE GOVERNANCE

Arguably, it is not the place of soft law corporate governance codes to weigh in directly on the AI adoption and use debate which is covered by directors' duties and the general law and best practice guidelines. However, corporate governance codes are revised to reflect societal expectations including around stakeholder inclusion. Workforce engagement (as enshrined in the UK Corporate Governance Code) assumes particular relevance for companies intending to use automation to radically transform business processes. In South Africa, the King IV Code contains a Principle and Recommended Practices in relation to the strategy and governance of technology and information.[88] As corporate governance norms shift from simply reflecting a shareholder primacy perspective to reflecting a more stakeholder-inclusive one, AI analysis and modelling will support this and change how the board and its committees function. AI can help with understanding and integrating the interests of stakeholders. AI can also assist with upholding corporate governance principles around board composition, scrutinising independence, and terms served. Boards need to be talking about strategy in this area. The CIO/CTO is a vital player

[86] [2013] EWHC 3147 (Comm).

[87] Ibid. [191].

[88] Institute of Directors (Southern Africa), *King Code IV: Report on Corporate Governance in South Africa* (2016) Principle 12 and Recommended Practices 10–17.

in determining a transformative strategy for levelling up technological advances in companies and implementing it. Sector 'bilinguals' will be crucial to bridging the AI gap – people specialised in areas such as finance or law but also with expertise in AI techniques such as machine learning.[89]

A *Board Composition and Board Competencies*

Boards' digital skills gap needs addressing, and market expectations will drive this. Technological expertise is not specifically referred to in the UK Corporate Governance Code[90] but it can be treated as part of the expected mix and diversity of skills on board.[91] There is a need to build digital literacy and understanding around the opportunities, risks, and ethical implications in relation to using AI. Training in AI and AI ethics can empower directors with AI governance expertise. The UK Corporate Governance Code affirms that boards are expected to 'ensure that the necessary resources are in place for the company to meet its objectives and measure performance against them.'[92] Having board competence to negotiate new technologies will increasingly be intrinsic to the review of board performance and board refreshment. Spring cleaning of the board will allow companies to adapt and thrive in the AI era. In the same way that there is momentum to appoint a director with responsibility for sustainability issues, having a non-executive director with responsibility for AI may be an attractive option at first blush. However, a word of caution is advisable given the duty of care on the board at large. The board as a whole should receive continuing board training to provide a base level of data literacy and understanding of AI and the use of algorithms.

B *Boardroom Dynamics*

At board level, AI can contribute to high-value decision-making. AI has the potential to be a positive disruptor of boardroom dynamics and norms, enabling more informed and better operational and strategic decisions to be made by companies. Helpfully, AI is excellent at counteracting unconscious bias; involving AI in decision-making can reduce agency costs by addressing internal bias, board independence, and groupthink issues.[93] AI can also assist with the setting and achievement of strategic goals and with boards' monitoring and supervisory functions. Smaller board sizes may become the norm, reflecting AI's contribution. However, human directors are unlikely to be redundant – AI remains a tool; it contributes

[89] OECD, *Artificial Intelligence in Society* (2019) ch 1 <https://doi.org/10.1787/eedfee77-en>.
[90] Financial Reporting Council, *The UK Corporate Governance Code* (2018).
[91] Ibid. Principles J, K and L.
[92] Financial Reporting Council (n 87) Principle C.
[93] Akshaya Kamalnath, 'The Perennial Quest for Board Independence: Artificial Intelligence to the Rescue?' (2019) 83 *Albany Law Review* 43.

to more balanced decision-making, but its deficits must be compensated for by less rational but inestimably vital human common sense, emotional intelligence, and instinct.[94]

If the legal path is cleared for sophisticated robots to be accepted as directors, legitimate questions concerning their acceptance and social integration may arise just as they have done for other actors adding to diversity to boards. Using a robot on an industrial assembly line is quite a different proposition to being a robo-director; a robot servant differs from a robot peer. A robo-director takes AI beyond being a purveyor of insightful information to a collaborative decision-maker. The smoothness or otherwise of human-robot director interaction, participation, and mutual understanding is partly dependent on artificial cognition with pattern recognition enabling machine learning and reasoning. To work well, human and AI agents must be able to weigh each other's contributions in the balance. Prestige and expense as well as confidence in the contribution which the AI can make will no doubt aid integration, as may the robot's perceived ability to engage with the other directors. The Chair would play an important role in ensuring not only that the AI robot is integrated but also in facilitating deliberations that take wider contributions, such as emotional intelligence, into account in decision-making.

The challenge of AI dazzle and dominance affecting constructive challenges in the boardroom would clearly be amplified where AI is accorded actual director status. Issues including trust and perceived suitability arise concerning integration into board culture and dynamics. A director with particular technological expertise or a CIO may assume the role of gatekeeper in relation to the AI director, but, as indicated above, the board as a whole has a collective responsibility. A robo-director could be at risk of being consigned to token status if it did not appear 'fit for purpose' or suitably agile through not being well designed to meet the board's needs across its range of functions and thus not perceived as sufficiently useful by some or all of the human directors. An AI system will only be as good as its programming. If its development does not take a sufficiently tailored approach to deliver performance utility at the board level, it may perform in a way that appears sub-par compared to its human counterparts who are adept at dealing with the full gamut of board business. Furthermore, like a human director, a robo-director may potentially learn from board interactions to be more cautious or even unduly cautious and risk averse in decision-making based on observed behaviours from other directors and a pattern of decisions taken that do not correlate to the suggested course of action that the data suggests.

Groupthink is well-acknowledged as problematic in terms of its capacity to destroy constructive challenge in a boardroom context, potentially leading to

[94] On this see Helen Bird and Natania Locke, 'The Corporate Board in An Age of Collaborative Intelligence and Complex Risk' in Andrew Godwin and others (eds), *Technology and Corporate Law: How Innovation Shapes Corporate Activity* (Edward Elgar 2021) 54–55.

more risky or risk-averse decisions.[95] AI in the boardroom will likely be an agent of inter-group dynamic change. This catalyst may have positive or negative consequences: it is fallacious to present AI as an effective panacea to all ills in board outcomes. Directors are individuals, and they may navigate the presence of AI differently. While AI may blast open existing groupthink coalescing around a dominant human director, groupthink may just as likely emerge around deferring to AI. Alternatively, human dominance could still exert itself by ignoring its input. AI could polarise a boardroom in the sense that there could be a tendency to defer to the all-powerful AI tool or to accept a plausible dominant individual's pushback against AI's wisdom. This should provide endlessly fascinating fodder for corporate law scholars in the future.

VI CONCLUSION

This chapter has explored the potential for AI to impact on corporate law and corporate governance practice as we stand at the frontier of AI becoming mainstream. AI's benefits as a positive disruptor are striking but much remains nascent and anticipated. Furthermore, other technological advances such as DLT, smart contracts, and IoT are increasingly of cross-cutting significance. Looking ahead, the expected arrival of the era of quantum technologies in the next decade will radically augment what is possible.

For boards, the integration of AI is all about carefully balancing opportunities with risks. The work on regulatory framing is embryonic, and the development of appropriate ethical guidelines and regulations will incentivise industry adoption.[96] As far as the corporate law and corporate governance landscape is concerned, the future vista is one of efficiency and labour-saving for corporate actors and regulators. AI is changing the milieu and manner in which corporate law and corporate governance occur but not its basic tenets concerning strategy, monitoring, and oversight. Boards walk a tricky line in making use of AI, particularly in terms of the application of the duty of care. While the best interests duty gives very useful breathing space to well-intentioned directors in the realm of AI, directors may potentially independently fall foul of the duty to exercise reasonable care, skill, and diligence. It is important that we remember that AI is a tool for assisting companies, not a panacea that takes directors or regulators out of the driving seat. AI may crunch data at an exponential rate but is not known for its ability to use common sense. Although there is much talk of autonomous decision-making and AI, the need for human input, sense and oversight remains clearly apparent. Certain aspects of corporate

[95] Stephen M Bainbridge, 'Why a Board? Group Decisionmaking in Corporate Governance' (2002) 55 *Vand L Rev* 1; Marleen A O'Connor, 'The Enron Board; The Perils of Groupthink' (2002) 71 *U Cin L Rev* 1233.

[96] Iris H-Y Chiu and Ernest WK Lim, 'Managing Corporations' Risk in Adopting Artificial Intelligence: A Corporate Responsibility Paradigm' (2021) 20 *Washington University Global Studies Law Review* 347.

life thrive on human interaction like corporate deal-making, the art of which is distinctly human. As AI becomes established, we are likely to see other adaptations to the corporate law framework, most obviously initially around delivering process efficiencies. Next-generation iterative developments will need to be harnessed on the back of achieving trust in AI and appropriate liability and accountability frameworks. The launch of AI as an autonomous or semi-autonomous corporate agent is predicated on this. Future possibilities will arise from widening the categories of corporate actors and models of liability to accommodate AI. Down the line, it is possible to imagine the mediation of disputes by an all-knowing algorithm, but there are significant due process issues to be resolved that lie outside the domain of corporate law. Above all, AI reduces agency costs. Once AI's place is solidified, corporate law scholars should take heed and acknowledge its contribution by conceptualising AI systems' role within existing theoretical frameworks such as the nexus of contracts theory and team production theory.

19

Financial Supervision and AI

Gérard Hertig

I INTRODUCTION

Financial supervisors and financial intermediaries have a long history of using 'machines' to implement and control compliance with regulatory requirements. Advances in computational statistics have made it possible for financial intermediaries to move further and rely on so-called artificial intelligence (AI). Admittedly, only a small number of firms actively use AI across their operations; however, there is evidence of increasing reliance on AI decision-making in both the private and public financial sectors. This increasing role of AI generated governance and ethics initiatives. They reflect concerns about AI-driven decision-making having accountability, competition, resilience, and fairness consequences. It also led a significant number of international organisations to set up AI Committees and to enact AI Principles. More importantly, financial supervisors have begun to use AI to prevent financial distress, detect fraud, and, more generally, for investor protection purposes. Similarly, private parties increasingly rely on AI to decide small claims and arbitration cases. In view of this evolution, this chapter deals with the current use of AI in the financial sector (Section II), regulation of and by AI (Section III), and, most importantly, AI-driven financial supervision.

II AI USE IN THE FINANCIAL SECTOR

Most recent AI achievements result from advances in machine learning (ML).[1] Fundamentally, ML facilitates predictions by using existing data to fill in missing information and identify hidden factors or patterns. In other words, when powered by massive data sets supported by potent computational processing capacities, ML is capable of generating new insights.

This contribution is based on research done within the FRS Programme established by ETH Zurich and Singapore's National Research Foundation.

[1] A Agrawal, JS Gans and A Goldfarb, 'Artificial Intelligence: The Ambiguous Labor Market Impact of Automating Prediction' (2017) NBER Working Paper 25619.

Nowadays, ML is put to use in nearly all areas of banking and finance, in particular in the financial derivatives and insurance claims sectors. Specific applications stretch from financial statement analysis,[2] descriptions of expected return behaviour,[3] optimisation, and hedging strategies[4] to detection of accounting misstatements[5] and securities litigation.[6] More generally, systemic financial crises are deemed ML detectable twelve quarters ahead, with a very high signal-to-noise ratio;[7] however, this is a situation where ML may still be outperformed by more traditional approaches.[8]

A *From Machine Learning to AI*

A significant number of financial institutions have already moved a step further, by stepping from machine learning to artificial intelligence. In simple terms, ML and AI are like a set of Russian dolls: all ML is AI, but AI is broader than ML.

ML refers to machines *automatically learning* from past data without explicit programming: their algorithms perform better over time due to exposure to more data. In other words, ML is a dynamic algorithm optimisation process under which specific changes are made without human intervention. However, ML capabilities remain limited; for example, a ML programme for detecting dog pictures will give results for dog images but remain irresponsive to cat images.

By contrast, AI enables computer systems to solve *complex problems* by providing the capacity to sense, reason, and adapt. In other words, AI systems are ultimately capable to think and act as (rational) humans do. From an evolutionary perspective, this is a 'machine' to 'deep' learning change, with AI progress being contingent on technological progress; from a practical perspective, this means that general tasks such as customer relationship management, underwriting, fraud detection, and social media monitoring can be AI driven. In other words, AI represents a *significant step* beyond ML. From a practical perspective, AI is facilitating technological innovations such as self-driving cars, translation programmes, and personal assistants. From a

[2] Amir Amel-Zadeh, Jan P Calliess, Daniel Kaiser and Stephen Roberts, 'Machine Learning-Based Financial Statement Analysis' (2020) <https://papers.ssrn.com/sol3/papers.cfm?abstract_id=3520684>.

[3] Shihao Gu, Bryan Kelly and Dacheng Xiu, 'Empirical Asset Pricing via Machine Learning' (2018) NBER Working Paper 25398.

[4] Sascha Wilkens, 'Machine Learning in Risk Measurement: Gaussian Process Regression for Value-at-Risk and Expected Shortfall' (2019) 12 *Journal of Risk Management in Financial Institutions* 374.

[5] Jeremy Bertomeu, Edwige Cheynel, Eric Floyd and Wenqiang Pan, 'Using Machine Learning to Detect Misstatements' (2020) 25 *Review of Accounting Studies* 1.

[6] Andrew Baker and Jonah B Gelbach, 'Machine Learning and Predicted Returns for Event Studies in Securities Litigation' (2020) Rock Center for Corporate Governance at Stanford University Working Paper No 244.

[7] Jérémy Fouliard, Michael Howell and Hélène Rey, 'Answering the Queen: Machine Learning and Financial Crises' (2019) NBER Working Paper 28302.

[8] Johannes Beutel, Sophia List, and Gregor von Schweinitz, 'Does Machine Learning Help Us Predict Banking Crises?' [2019] *Journal of Financial Stability* 45.

technology perspective, AI yields better results when it comes to transforming raw data into numerical features, especially in terms of preserving original data set information.

The advantages of AI over ML have been noted by financial market participants. Lenders used to rely on ML to build risk models,[9] for risk management purposes,[10] and to propose investment plans and strategies.[11] Nowadays, there is evidence of financial institutions switching to AI to assess credit quality or price insurance contracts[12] and for market-making or automated trading.[13] This evolution is not limited to larger players; while 75% of banks with more than $100 billion in assets are already implementing AI strategies, the same is true for 46% of banks that are smaller in terms of asset value.[14]

However, moving from ML to AI is challenging. Relying on AI requires clearly defined objectives,[15] which is not always easy to achieve. In addition, activists and policymakers are raising ethical considerations[16] that may require algorithms to go beyond accurate prediction.[17] These concerns have been reinforced by evidence of AI abuse when it comes to retail banking; for example, there are indications of US lenders engaging in AI-based consumer discrimination[18] and in creditworthiness assessments that potentially threaten consumer privacy and autonomy.[19] As a result, supervisors have started to issue guidance on how to use AI, especially in the risk assessment and risk monitoring area. These issues could also explain why there is limited hard data on the current state of AI adoption in finance. According to a 2020 financial services survey, 56% of respondents were already using AI for risk management purposes while 77% expected AI to become an essential business component within a few years.[20] Overall, one can state that financial firms are entering the AI

9 Zura Kakushadze and Willie Yu, 'Machine Learning Risk Models' (2019) 6 *Journal of Risk and Control* 37.

10 Lucio Fernandez-Arjona and Damir Filipović, 'A Machine Learning Approach to Portfolio Pricing and Risk Management for High-Dimensional Problems' (2020) Swiss Finance Institute Research Paper Series 28.

11 Francesco D'Accunto and Alberto G. Rossi, 'Robo-Advising' (2019) CESifo Working Paper Series 8225.

12 Financial Stability Board, *Artificial Intelligence and Machine Learning in Financial Services, Market Developments and Financial Stability Implications* (FSB 2017).

13 A Koshiyama, N Firoozye and P Treleaven, 'Algorithms in Future Capital Markets' (2020) <https://papers.papers.ssrn.com/sol3/papers.cfm?abstract_id=3527511>.

14 See <www.worldfinancialreview.com/use-of-artificial-intelligence-in-the-banking-world-2022>.

15 C Coglianese, 'Deploying Machine Learning for a Sustainable Future' (2020) University of Pennsylvania Law School, Public Law Research Paper 17.

16 Julia M Puaschunder, 'On Artificial Intelligence's Razor's Edge: On the Future of Democracy and Society in the Artificial Age' (2019) 2 *Journal of Economics and Business* 100.

17 Bo Cowgill and Megan T Stevenson, 'Algorithmic Social Engineering' (2020) 110 *American Economic Association Papers and Proceedings* 96.

18 T B Gillis, 'The Input Fallacy' (2022) 106 *Minnesota Law Review* 1175.

19 N Aggarwal, 'The Norms of Algorithmic Credit Scoring' (2021) 80 *Cambridge Law Journal* 42.

20 L Ryll and others, 'Transforming Paradigms, A Global AI in Financial Services Survey' (2020) <https://papers.ssrn.com/sol3/papers.cfm?abstract_id=3532038>.

world gradually and at different speeds. Fundamentally, AI-use is likely to be driven by the ability to access and process large and diverse datasets, which is likely to result in larger firms being early AI-users across-the-board.[21]

However, other variables are also playing a role. Firms seeking financial analyst coverage may prove less likely to be leaders in AI adoption: there is evidence of stocks with lower AI intensity getting more analyst coverage than stocks with higher AI intensity.[22] There is also evidence of AI reliance (a) resulting in auditors being less willing to tolerate contradictory evidence[23] and (b) proving problematic when the past is unlike the future.[24] AI is likely to mitigate risks by facilitating compliance with regulatory developments. For example, algorithm-generated 'synthetic data' may make it easier to comply with the 'care obligation' US broker-dealers have vis-à-vis retail investors, by enabling them to test investment recommendations.[25]

Overall, the evidence points to AI-driven managerial decision-making being increasingly relied upon by the private sector.[26] This is attributed to AI allowing for a better understanding of the process by which firm governance structures are chosen[27] and improving board independence[28] as well as risk management and tolerance.[29]

At the same time, these developments also raise managerial oversight issues.[30] While AI advances should reduce agency as well as coordination costs, they also increase liability risks at the top of the firm.[31] More generally, to the extent algorithms replace employees as the leading cause of corporate harm, they potentially immunise corporations from most civil and criminal liability.[32] Likewise, governments are

[21] T Babina, A Fedyk, A He and J Hodson, 'Artificial Intelligence, Firm Growth, and Industry Concentration' (2020) <www8.gsb.columbia.edu/researcharchive/articles/26273>.

[22] Jillian Grennan and Roni Michaely, 'Artificial Intelligence and High-Skilled Work: Evidence from Analysts' (2020) 20 *Swiss Finance Institute Research Paper Series* 84.

[23] BP Commerford, SA Dennis, J Joe and J Wang, 'Complex Estimates and Auditor Reliance on Artificial Intelligence' (2021) <https://papers.ssrn.com/sol3/papers.cfm?abstract_id=3422591>.

[24] Derek Snow, 'Machine Learning in Asset Management, Trading Strategies' (2020) 2 *The Journal of Financial Data Science* 10.

[25] JB Heaton and JH Witte, 'Synthetic Financial Data: An Application to Regulatory Compliance for Broker-Dealers' (2019) *Journal of Financial Transformation* 50.

[26] Jeremias Adams-Prassl, 'What if Your Boss Was an Algorithm? Economic Incentives, Legal Challenges, and the Rise of Artificial Intelligence at Work' (2019) 41 *Comparative Labor Law & Policy Journal* 123.

[27] Isil Erel, Léa H. Stern, Chenhao Tan and Michael S. Weisbach, 'Selecting Directors Using Machine Learning' (2021) 34 *The Review of Financial Studies* 3226.

[28] Akshaya Kamalnath, 'The Perennial Quest for Board Independence: Artificial Intelligence to the Rescue?' (2020) 83 *Albany Law Review* 43.

[29] Karel Hrazdil and others, 'Measuring CEO Personality Using Machine-Learning Algorithms: A Study of CEO Risk Tolerance and Audit Fees' (2020) 47 *Journal of Business Finance & Accounting* 301.

[30] Eleanore Hickman and Martin Petrin, 'Trustworthy AI and Corporate Governance – The EU's Ethics Guidelines for Trustworthy Artificial Intelligence from a Company Law Perspective' (2021) 22 *European Business Organisation Law Review* 593.

[31] John Armour and Horst Eidenmueller, 'Self-Driving Corporations?' (2019) 10 *Harvard Business Law Review* 88.

[32] Mihailis E Diamantis, 'The Extended Corporate Mind: When Corporations Use AI to Break the Law' (2020) 98 *North Carolina Law Review* 893.

increasingly putting AI to use. This is especially the case in the US, where a large number of federal agencies have ML and AI experience;[33] however, it is also occurring in Europe.[34] This development could reduce private firms' liability risk: given that there is no reason for governments to fare better than the private sector, judges can be expected to show restraint across-the-board when it comes to imposing liability for AI misuse.

B *AI as Risk Factor and Risk Mitigator*

Putting AI to use can prove complex and misleading. Algorithms are trained using historical data, which may perpetuate the precise biases one expects them to eradicate. Criminal proceedings are a good example.[35] AI is increasingly used to identify lawbreakers[36] and generate trial evidence;[37] however, case studies provide evidence of software bias and procedural difficulties in challenging them. More generally, real-world issues are not yet fully tractable computationally.[38] AI is still more about making predictions than establishing causal relationships,[39] which remain hard to identify in the presence of complex data interactions.[40]

Nevertheless, AI is progressively supplanting human intervention across-the-board. Overall, it is increasingly used to price goods and services[41] and likely to significantly affect international trade.[42] More specifically, AI has already made self-driving cars, automated medical diagnostics, or translations part of daily life.[43]

33 David Freeman Engstrom, Daniel E Ho, Catherine M Sharkey and Mariano-Florentino Cuéllar, *Government by Algorithm: Artificial Intelligence in Federal Administrative Agencies* (2020) Report Submitted to the Administrative Conference of the United States.

34 Michèle Finck, 'Automated Decision-Making and Administrative Law' in Peter Cane, Herwig CH Hofmann, Eric C Ip, and Peter L Lindseth (eds), *The Oxford Handbook of Comparative Administrative Law* (Oxford University Press 2020) ch 32.

35 Francesca Palmiotto, 'Regulating Algorithmic Opacity in Criminal Proceedings: An Opportunity for the EU Legislator?' (2020) Maastricht Faculty of Law Working Paper Series 1.

36 Mohammad A Tayebi and Uwe Glässer, *Social Network Analysis in Predictive Policing. Concepts, Models and Methods* (Springer 2016).

37 Sabine Gless, 'AI in the Courtroom: A Comparative Analysis of Machine Evidence in Criminal Trials' (2020) 51 *Georgetown Journal of International Law* 195.

38 Richard A Bettis and Songcui Hu, 'Bounded Rationality, Heuristics, Computational Complexity, and Artificial Intelligence' (2018) 39 *Strategic Management, Behavioral Strategy in Perspective* 139.

39 Agarwal Arvind, Aparna Gupta, Arun Kumar and Srikanth G Tamilselvan, 'Learning Risk Culture of Banks Using News Analytics' (2019) 277 *European Journal of Operational Research* 770.

40 Guanhao Feng, Jingyu He and Nicholas G Polson, *Deep Learning for Predicting Asset Returns* (2018) <arXiv:1804.09314>.

41 Emilio Calvano, Giacomo Calzolari, Vincenzo Denicol and Sergio Pastorello, 'Artificial Intelligence, Algorithmic Pricing and Collusion' (2019) CEPR Discussion Paper 13405.

42 Avi Goldfarb and Daniel Trefler, 'AI and International Trade' (2018) NBER Working Paper 24254.

43 W Nicholson Price, 'Artificial Intelligence in the Medical System: Four Roles for Potential Transformation' (2019) 21 *Yale Journal of Law and Technology* 122; Xueming Luo, Siliang Tong, Zheng Fang and Zhe Qu, 'Machines vs. Humans: The Impact of Artificial Intelligence Chatbot Disclosure on Customer Purchases' (2019) 38 *Marketing Science* 913.

To be sure, there is a dark side to these AI developments. Using AI to protect business models may infringe competition laws[44] whereas AI adjudication may generate a 'codified justice' system that favours standardisation over discretion.[45] As a result, GDP may decline in countries with significant unskilled labour.[46] This prompted calls for an automation tax to give social support systems time to adapt.[47] Whether these calls will get results is questionable. On the one hand, Northern robotisation may lead to higher wages in the South;[48] on the other hand, AI is more about enhancing human capabilities than about reducing labour costs.[49]

III REGULATING AI AND USING AI TO REGULATE

The increasing role of AI has generated regulatory concerns (Section I) as well as initiatives to use AI for investment protection purposes (Section II).

A *AI-Use as a Regulatory Concern*

Regulatory apprehensions appear most developed in China and the EU, with the United States catching up; by contrast, India and Australia are having a rockier start.[50] Some regulatory initiatives reflect concerns that the use of algorithms may occur without adequate democratic oversight or control. For example, the Council of Europe specifically addressed the manipulative capabilities of algorithmic processes.[51] Similarly, the European Commission emphasised that the regulatory framework must create an ecosystem of trust in AI.[52] To be sure, it is widely recognised that AI facilitates the detection of corruption[53] or collusion[54]

44 Niamh Dunne, 'Platforms as Regulators' (2021) 9 *Journal of Antitrust Enforcement* 244.

45 Richard M Re and Alicia Solow-Niederman, 'Developing Artificially Intelligent Justice' (2019) 22 *Stanford Technology Law Review* 242.

46 Christian Alonso and others, 'Will the AI Revolution Cause a Great Divergence' (2020) IMF Working Paper 184.

47 Vincent Ooi and Glendon Goh, 'Taxation of Automation and Artificial Intelligence as a Tool of Labour Policy' (2022) 19 *eJournal of Tax Research* 273.

48 Erhan Artuc, Paulo Bastos and Bob Rijkers, 'Robots, Tasks and Trade' (2018) World Bank Policy Research Working Paper 8674.

49 James E Bessen, Stephen Michael Impink, Lydia Reichensperger and Robert Seamans, 'The Business of AI Startups' (2018) Boston University School of Law, Law and Economics Research Paper 28.

50 Angela Daly and others, 'Artificial Intelligence, Governance and Ethics: Global Perspectives' (2019) The Chinese University of Hong Kong Faculty of Law Research Paper 15.

51 'Declaration by the Committee of Ministers' (13 February 2019) <www.search.coe.int/cm/pages/result_details.aspx?ObjectId=090000168092dd4b>.

52 COM(2020) 65 final <www.eur-lex.europa.eu/legal-content/EN/TXT/HTML/?uri=CELEX:52020DC0065&from=EN>.

53 Elliott Ash, Sergio Galletta and Tommaso Giommoni, 'A Machine Learning Approach to Analyze and Support Anti-Corruption Policy' (2021) CESifo Working Paper 9015.

54 Rosa M Abrantes-Metz and Albert D Metz, 'Can Machine Learning Aid in Cartel Detection' [2018] July CPI Antitrust Chronicle 1.

and contributes to making legal proceedings swifter and less costly.[55] Hence, the Netherlands and Germany are introducing automated taxation procedures, presumably based on AI.[56]

However, the contribution of machine learning is less impressive when the past is unlike the future, that is, when standards are superior to rules. This could create some mismatch between AI-powered legislation and the real world.[57] Further, the emerging role of AI raises resilience, privacy, and fairness issues.[58] Using AI may also facilitate anti-competitive[59] and criminal practices.[60] In particular, entrepreneurs may face liability either because they are using AI[61] or they failed to do so.[62] More importantly, the availability of AI could generate collusive practices: simulations have shown that self-learning pricing algorithms may collude on supra-competitive fixed-price equilibria.[63]

While the rise of AI occurred in a regulatory vacuum, policy-makers have become aware of its importance.[64] As a result, there is a trend towards international and national law-makers engaging in what is already called regulatory competition.[65]

When it comes to the financial sector, there are specific calls for subjecting AI-use to regulation.[66] The basic objective is to prevent a situation where AI is widely used while there are few controls of the risks for consumers and financial stability. From

[55] Carol Harlow and Richard Rawlings, 'Proceduralism and Automation: Challenges to the Values of Administrative Law' (2020) *The Foundations and Future of Public Law* 275.

[56] Stavros Zouridis, Marlies van Eck and Mark Bovens, 'Automated Discretion' in Peter Hupe and Tony Evens (eds), *Palgrave Handbook on Discretion: The Quest for Controlled Freedom* (Palgrave Macmillan 2020) 313; Nadja Braun Binder, 'AI and Taxation: Risk Management in Fully Automated Taxation Procedures' (2020) *Regulating Artificial Intelligence* 295; Marcos Pertierra, Sarah Lawsky, Erik Hemberg, Una-May O'Reilly, 'Towards Formalizing Statute Law as Default Logic through Automatic Semantic Parsing' (2017) in *Proceedings, ICAIL'17: Sixteenth International Conference on Artificial Intelligence and Law*.

[57] Zach Harned and Hanna Wallach, 'Stretching Human Laws to Apply to Machines: The Dangers of a 'Colorblind' Computer' (2020) 45 *Florida State Law* Review 617.

[58] Jasper Ulenaers, 'The Impact of Artificial Intelligence on the Right to a Fair Trial: Towards a Robot Judge?' (2020) 11 *Asian Journal of Law and Economics* 1.

[59] Jonathan Cave, 'Can Machines Learn whether Machines Are Learning to Collude?' in Sotiris Diplaris and others (eds), *Internet Science* (Springer 2019) 133.

[60] Benoit Dupont, Yuan Stevens, Hannes Westermann and Michael Joyce, *Artificial Intelligence in the Context of Crime and Criminal Justice* (2018) A Report for the Korean Institute of Criminology.

[61] Mihailis E Diamantis, 'Algorithms Acting Badly: A Solution from Corporate Law' (2021) 89 *George Washington Law Review* 801.

[62] Philipp Hacker, Ralf Krestel, Stefan Grundmann and Felix Naumann, 'Explainable AI under Contract and Tort Law: Legal Incentives and Technical Challenges' (2020) 28 *Artificial Intelligence and Law* 415.

[63] Timo Klein, 'Autonomous Algorithmic Collusion: Q-Learning under Sequential Pricing' (2021) 52 *The RAND Journal of Economics* 538.

[64] Austan Goolsbee, 'Public Policy in an AI Economy' (2018) NBER Working Paper 24653.

[65] Nathalie A Smuha, 'From a 'Race to AI' to a 'Race to AI Regulation': Regulatory Competition for Artificial Intelligence' (2021) 13 *Law, Innovation and Technology* 57.

[66] Jon Truby, Rafael Brown and Andrew Dahdal, 'Banking on AI' (2020) 14 *Law and Financial Markets Review* 10.

a practical perspective, regulatory proposals could range from *de facto* control over machine learning[67] to enacting public interest-oriented regulation.

The current preference is to have law-makers focus on areas where AI is already widely used. Lending is one obvious target. Financial intermediaries already use AI to predict the likelihood of credit card default payments by customers; their likely next step is to use AI to predict the creditworthiness of applicants with no credit history but with a record of online transactions.[68]

More generally, AI may be changing the physics of financial services by weakening the bonds between financial intermediaries and fostering new operating models.[69] In this context, it is suggested to subject financial intermediaries to personal responsibility[70] regimes; the idea here is that putting humans (and the corporations they work for) in the liability loop minimises the risk of no one being liable for AI-related damages.

These proposals are said to reflect four models: the black letter model, the emergent model, the ethical model, and the risk regulation model.[71] Under the black letter approach, the focus is on existing legislation and the ways to apply them to AI systems; in other words, one tries to tackle AI developments via the interpretation of existing legislation and the development of case law.

While the black letter model tries to deal with AI within the current legal framework, the three other models are more forward looking. The emergent model addresses the question of whether AI raises new economic or scientific issues that require innovative *ex ante* legislation – the focus being on the need for tailormade exonerations or prohibitions. The ethical model is a variation of the emergent model, with AI being subject to 'moral' norms that aim at distinguishing the good from the bad. Finally, the risk regulation model aims at reducing the probability or level of damages AI-use may cause.

From a practical perspective, it is generally recognised that, given the emerging nature of AI technology, one should facilitate market developments. Suggestions range from a 'permissionless innovation' approach[72] to fairness assessments of AI systems.[73]

67 Mauritz Kop, 'The Right to Process Data for Machine Learning Purposes in the EU' (2021) 34 *Harvard Journal of Law & Technology* 1.

68 Hicham Sadok, Fadi Sakka and Mohammed El Hadi El Maknouzi, 'Artificial Intelligence and Bank Credit Analysis: A Review' (2022) 10 *Cogent Economics & Finance* 1.

69 Deloitte, 'The New Physics of Financial Services, How Artificial Intelligence Is Transforming the Financial Ecosystem' (2022) <www2.deloitte.com/ro/en/pages/financial-services/articles/new-physics-of-financial-services.html>.

70 Ross P Buckley, Dirk A Zetzsche, Douglas W Arner and Brian W Tang, 'Regulating Artificial Intelligence in Finance: Putting the Human in the Loop' (2021) 43 *Sydney Law Journal* 43.

71 Nicolas Petit and Jerome De Cooman, 'Models of Law and Regulation for AI' (2020) European University Institute Working Paper 63.

72 Adam Thierer, Andrea Castillo O'Sullivan and Raymond Russell, 'Artificial Intelligence and Public Policy' (2017), <https://papers.ssrn.com/sol3/papers.cfm?abstract_id=3021135>.

73 Mark MacCarthy, 'An Examination of the Algorithmic Accountability Act of 2019' (2019) <https://papers.ssrn.com/sol3/papers.cfm?abstract_id=3615731>.

Under the former approach, innovation should be allowed to develop unabated unless a compelling case can be made that AI developments will bring serious harm to society; under the latter approach, AI systems that target hate speech, terrorist material, and disinformation campaign would be subject to fairness assessments and required to fix any bias the latter revealed.

Regulatory issues such as the principal/humans – agent/AI problem are relatively new for computer scientists.[74] On the other hand, they have been extensively studied by economists and legal scholars. In theory, the best way to align principal and agent interests is to design a so-called 'complete' contingent contract.[75]

In practice, jurisdictions generally aim at setting-up regulatory frameworks that are both AI-friendly and safe.[76] It is critical to manage this task properly: history shows that the benefits of technological innovation are largely a function of the environment they take place in.[77]

One approach, which is popular in common law jurisdictions, is to have courts provide AI-related backstops.[78] Another approach is to let financial supervisors take the lead, given their cost-cutting and accuracy preferences for data-centric approaches.[79] However, the possibility remains of AI subverting any control method devised by a non-AI entity.[80] To manage this risk, it has been proposed to subject AI to codes of ethics and ethical principles.[81]

B *Using AI for Investor Protection Purposes*

AI developments can be expected to have a significant impact in terms of investor protection.

Advances in mathematics and ML have gone hand-in-hand with improved automated regulation.[82] Simple rules will remain fundamental for the design of legal

74 Dylan Hadfield-Menell and Gillian K Hadfield, 'Incomplete Contracting and AI Alignment' (2019) Proceedings of the 2019 AAAI/ACM Conference on AI, Ethics, and Society 417.

75 Alan Schwartz and Robert E Scott, 'Contract Theory and the Limits of Contract Law' (2003) 113 *Yale Law Journal* 541.

76 Olivia J Erdelyi and Judy Goldsmith, 'Regulating Artificial Intelligence: Proposal for a Global Solution' (2020) <arXiv:2005.11072>.

77 Anton Korinek and Joseph E Stiglitz, 'Artificial Intelligence and Its Implications for Income Distribution and Unemployment' in Ajay K Agrawal, Joshua Gans and Avi Goldfarb (eds), *The Economics of Artificial Intelligence: An Agenda* (University of Chicago Press 2019).

78 Mariano-Florentino Cuéllar, 'A Common Law for the Age of Artificial Intelligence: Incremental Adjudication, Institutions and Relational Non-arbitrariness' (2019) 119 *Columbia Law Review* 1173.

79 Derek Snow, 'Financial Machine Learning Regulation' (2019) <https://papers.ssrn.com/sol3/papers.cfm?abstract_id= 3371902>.

80 Joshua S Gans, 'Self-Regulating Artificial General Intelligence' (2018) NBER Working Paper 24352.

81 Urs Gasser and Carolyn Schmitt, 'The Role of Professional Norms in the Governance of Artificial Intelligence' in Markus D Dubber, Frank Pasquale and Sunit Das (eds), *The Oxford Handbook of Ethics of AI* (OUP 2020) 141.

82 Felix Mormann, 'Beyond Algorithms: Toward a Normative Theory of Automated Regulation' (2021) 62 *Boston College Law Review* 1.

institutions and environments.[83] At the same time, AI developments can be expected to significantly reduce law-making and enforcement costs.[84] AI-reliance is expected to improve the accuracy of legal prediction. The increasing availability of empirical legal analysis was a first step in that direction, but its value remained closely related to a particular data set. Nowadays, AI tools allow for the detection of judicial patterns. For example, AI-driven analysis of win/loss rates and individual judges' patterns enable practitioners to develop tailor-made financial litigation strategies.[85]

The practical value of AI is most visible in the antitrust area, whereas financial supervisors and litigators have a long tradition of using sophisticated models and databases.[86] Optimists claim that AI will more generally facilitate the determination of what is 'legal' in any particular situation.[87] It is more realistic to assume that AI-driven supervision cannot yet fully capture what is going on in terms of compliance. It is also prudent to keep in mind that AI developments may go hand-in-hand with 'artificial' codes, data bias, and systemic risks.[88] To begin with, AI-driven systems remain constrained by their underlying code and the assumptions made by their programmers. In addition, the data they rely on is incomplete, as it does not fully capture what is occurring in financial markets. Finally, AI-driven systems are ill-equipped to handle the unknown unknows inherent to systemic risk: at this point in time, AI cannot deal with events it has not 'seen'. In short, while human supervision is plagued by cognitive bias, regulatory capture, and political distortion, it will continue to fare better than (fully) AI-driven supervision for the foreseeable future.

At the same time, AI is increasingly deployed in retail and corporate banking (for credit scoring/underwriting and fraud detection[89]), asset management (for portfolio strategies), trading (for automated execution and process optimisation), and insurance (for claims management). Its main function is to predict bank distress[90] and to evaluate market risks associated with regulatory changes.[91] It is also put to use for assessing loan risk and detecting fraud – in particular when it comes to money

83 Jesus Fernandez-Villaverde, 'Simple Rules for a Complex World with Artificial Intelligence' (2020) PIER Working Paper 10.

84 Adrian Zuckerman, 'Artificial Intelligence, Implications for the Legal Profession, Adversarial Process and Rule of Law' (2020) 136 *Law Quarterly Review* 427.

85 Sangchul Park and Ko Haksoo, 'Machine Learning and Law and Economics: A Preliminary Overview' (2020) 11 *Asian Journal of Law and Economics* 25.

86 Dirk Broeders and Jermy Prenio, 'Innovative Technology in Financial Supervision (suptech) – The Experience of Early Users' (2018) *FSI Insights on Policy Implementation* 9.

87 Anthony J Casey and Anthony Niblett, 'Self-Driving Laws' (2016) 66 *University of Toronto Law Journal* 429.

88 Tom CW Lin, 'Artificial Intelligence, Finance, and the Law' (1979) 88 *Fordham Law Review* 531.

89 Doaa Abu-Elyounes, '"Computer Says No!"': The Impact of Automation on the Discretionary Power of Public Officers' (2021) 23 *Vanderbilt Journal of Entertainment & Technology Law* 451.

90 Joel Suss and Henry Treitel, 'Predicting Bank Distress in the UK with Machine Learning' (2019) Bank of England Staff Working Paper 831.

91 Xinwen Ni, Wolfgang Karl Härdle and Taojun Xieg, 'A Machine Learning Based Regulatory Risk Index for Cryptocurrencies' (2020) International Research Training Group 1792 Discussion Paper 13.

laundering,[92] where AI detection systems fare nine times better than conventional systems.[93] This development may prove problematic for financial supervisors. To begin with, financial intermediaries may rely on AI for decisions that AI developers cannot properly address, which may exacerbate human error[94] and amplify tail risks.[95] More importantly, financial supervisors may face AI models and applications they cannot fully comprehend, which may increase systemic risk.

On the up-side, AI may facilitate access to justice. The extent to which *AI-driven litigation* will become common practice remains unclear.[96] Judges are likely to face 'black boxes' when confronted with algorithms;[97] even in the market-driven arbitration area, substituting AI to human judges is deemed a task that cannot be performed using currently available applications.[98] Nevertheless, there is no question that technology-driven litigation is increasingly becoming a reality. AI is increasingly used to review digitally discovered documents and to manage trials, allowing for a significant reduction in the number of lawyers involved. In addition, e-platforms have made it easier for plaintiffs to join litigation undertakings, a development especially relevant for jurisdictions that facilitate collective actions. More specifically, jurisdictions like Australia, China, Estonia, and the Netherlands plan to use or already use AI to decide small claims cases,[99] which is evidence of AI providing affordable avenues for routine[100] or collective litigation. Similarly, many US lawyers already rely on AI to reduce discovery costs, and some US courts even require them to do so.[101]

The availability of collective actions generates incentives to file law suits for two reasons: lawyers representing investors can earn substantial fees, while defendant financial intermediaries have significant incentives to agree to a settlement that binds a whole class of investors.[102] AI-driven collective actions may improve investor

92 Astrid Bertrand, Winston Maxwell and Xavier Vamparys, 'Are AI-Based Anti-Money Laundering Systems Compatible with Fundamental Rights' (2020).

93 IBM, 'Fighting Financial Crime with AI, Technical Report' (May 2019).

94 William Magnuson, 'Artificial Financial Intelligence' (2020) 10 *Harvard Business Review* 337.

95 Jón Daníelsson, Robert Macrae and Andreas Uthemann, 'Artificial Intelligence and Systemic Risk' (2022) 140 *Journal of Banking and Finance* 106290.

96 Paul Bennett Marrow, Mansi Karol and Steven Kuyan, 'Artificial Intelligence and Arbitration: The Computer as an Arbitrator—Are We There Yet?' (2020) 74 *Dispute Resolution Journal* 35.

97 Ashley Deeks, 'The Judicial Demand for Explainable Artificial Intelligence' (2019) University of Virginia School of Law Public Law and Legal Theory Research Paper Series 51

98 Horst Eidenmüller and Faidon Varesis, 'What Is an Arbitration? Artificial Intelligence and the Vanishing Human Arbitrator' (2020) 17 *New York University Journal of Law & Business* 49.

99 See Tania Sourdin, 'Judge v. Robot? Artificial Intelligence and Judicial Decision-Making' (2018) 41 *University of New South Wales Law Journal* 1114; Jingting Deng, 'Should the Common Law System Welcome Artificial Intelligence: A Case Study of China's Same-Type Case Reference System' (2019) 3 *Georgetown Law and Technology Review* 223; Anthony J Casey and Anthony Niblett, 'Will Robot Judges Change Litigation and Settlement Outcomes? A First Look at the Algorithmic Replication of Prior Cases' (2020) *MIT Computational Law Report* <https://law.mit.edu/pub/willrobotjudgeschangelitigationandsettlementoutcomes>.

100 Mark Findlay, 'Future Lawyers or Robots with Big Data?' (2020) SMU School of Law Research Paper 8.

101 See <https://news.mobar.org/data-analytics-and-artificial-intelligence-in-litigation/>.

102 Jessica Erickson, 'Automating Securities Class Action Settlements' (2019) 72 *Vanderbilt Law Review* 101.

compensation in two ways. First, they can reduce (but not eliminate) the risk of litigation being driven by attorney fee considerations: AI-reliance makes it harder to act opportunistically by simply 'running the meter'. Second, they facilitate settlement decision-making by reducing information uncertainties: AI-reliance allows for more comprehensive data processing and analysis.

The established reliance on class actions makes the United States an obvious candidate for AI-driven mass litigation. Class actions are 'launched' by one plaintiff filing a lawsuit on behalf of *everyone* harmed in a similar way – but for those who individually decide to 'opt-out'. For example, an investor making a harmful transaction upon the suggestion of a financial intermediary can sue the latter on behalf of *all* investors that invested on the basis of that same suggestion. However, AI-driven collective actions may prove inefficient. AI-reliance may increase the threat value of litigation in an asymmetric way by making it easier for professional plaintiffs to make their claims initially credible; this could prompt defendants to settle more often than required on efficiency grounds. More importantly, AI-use may raise litigation to levels that hamper financial innovation or prevent efficient market entry.

More generally, increasing AI reliance has fairness, opportunism, and bias implications.[103] On the down-side, the use of AI could widen the legal advice access gap between high-income and low-income individuals[104] and have a feedback effect on corporate disclosure decisions; that is, companies could adjust the way they talk knowing that machines are listening.[105] On the upside, algorithms permit biases to be detected when it is most likely that extra-legal biases influence judicial decision-making.[106]

Given this situation, policymakers across jurisdictions are adopting transparency and fairness-related regulations for algorithms.[107] Hence, the European Union is debating a risk-oriented Proposal for an Artificial Intelligence Act.[108] AI systems posing an unacceptable risk would be banned. High-risk AI systems and stand-alone AI systems with fundamental rights implications would be subject to *ex ante* third-party conformity assessment; however, these conformity assessments can also be carried out by their deployers if they follow harmonised standards.

The approach adopted by the Proposal is proving controversial, especially when it comes to regulatory conformity assessments. One critique is that they do not have

[103] 'US Big Data Report 2016' <https://obamawhitehouse.archives.gov/sites/default/files/microsites/ostp/2016_0504_data_discrimination.pdf>.

[104] Joshua D Blank and Leigh Osofsky, 'Automated Legal Guidance' (2020) 106 *Cornell Law Review* 179.

[105] Sean Cao, Wei Jiang, Baozhong Yang and Alan L Zhang, 'How to Talk When a Machine Is Listening: Corporate Disclosure in the Age of AI' (2020) NBER Working Paper 27950.

[106] Daniel L Chen, 'Machine Learning and the Rule of Law' in Michael A Livermore and Daniel N Rockmore (eds), *Law as Data* (Santa Fe Institute Press 2019) 443.

[107] Bo Cowgill and Catherine Tucker, 'Economics, Fairness and Algorithmic Bias' (2020) <https://conference.nber.org/confer/2019/YSAIf19/SSRN-id3361280.pdf> forthcoming in *The Journal of Economic Perspectives*.

[108] European Commission, COM(2021) 206 final, 21 April 2021.

to be carried out by independent third parties even though they require ethical decisions;[109] another critique is that they are taking place *ex post*. Overall, the major concern is the uncertainty related to the outcome of conformity assessment. Early AI-users may face costly *ex post* adjustments, while more risk-averse firms are likely to suffer competitive disadvantages.

From a market perspective, one can expect that algorithmic manipulation will be overcome by algorithmic competition.[110] On the other hand, reliance on AI may reduce administrative and judicial discretion; however, to the extent state powers are discretionary, the current view is that this discretion should remain significant.[111] More specifically, there is no evidence of AI-prediction of recidivism being less fair than predictions made by people with little or no criminal justice experience.[112] Conversely, there is evidence of AI-reliance reducing lending discrimination.[113] That being said, little is still known about humans willingness to make trust-based investments with non-human agents.[114]

People seem to remain averse to machines making moral decisions[115] and there is reluctance to entitle AI to a status comparable to natural persons, that is, legal personality.[116] At the same time, there is empirical evidence of people actually preferring advice from algorithms to advice from people,[117] especially when robo-advisors exhibit limited human characteristics.[118]

IV AI-DRIVEN FINANCIAL SUPERVISION

Directly or indirectly, a significant number of international organisations are currently dealing with AI-driven financial regulation and supervision (Section I). Their

109 Martin Ebers, 'Standardizing AI – The Case for the European Commission's Proposal for an Artificial Intelligence Act' in Larry A DiMatteo, Michel Cannarsa and Cristina Poncibò (eds), *The Cambridge Handbook of Artificial Intelligence: Global Perspectives on Law and Ethics* (Cambridge University Press 2022).

110 Saul Levmore and Frank Fagan, 'Competing Algorithms for Law: Sentencing, Admissions, and Employment' (2021) 88 *University of Chicago Law Review* 367.

111 Marieke Koopmans-van Berlo and Hans de Bruijn, 'E-Enforcement; Lessons Learned from Two Case Studies in the Netherlands' (2005) 1 *Journal of E-Government* 65.

112 Julia Dressel and Hany Farid, 'The Accuracy, Fairness, and Limits of Predicting Recidivism' (2018) 4 *Science Advances* 1.

113 Robert Bartlett, Adair Morse, Richard Stanton and Nancy Wallace, 'Consumer-Lending Discrimination in the Era of FinTech' (2019) NBER Working Paper 25943.

114 Eric Schniter, Timothy W Shields and Daniel Sznycer, 'Trust in Humans, Robots, and Cyborgs: Treated the Same, but Experienced Differently' (2018) ESI Working Paper 22.

115 Yochanan E Bigman and Kurt Gray, 'People are Averse to Machines Making Moral Decisions' (2018) 181 *Cognition* 21.

116 Simon Chesterman, 'Artificial Intelligence and the Limits of Legal Personality' (2020) 69 *ICLQ* 819.

117 Jennifer M Logg, Julia A Minson and Don A Moore, 'Algorithm Appreciation: People Prefer Algorithmic to Human Judgment' (2019) 151 *Organizational Behavior and Human Decision Processes* 90.

118 Frank D Hodge, Kim I Mendoza and Roshan K Sinha, 'The Effect of Humanizing Robo-Advisors on Investor Judgments' (2021) 38 *Contemporary Accounting Research* 770.

interventions tend to remain very general, whereas national organisations are more prescriptive (Section II). However, the overall objectives are similar: keeping AI risk taking by the private sector under control while facilitating financial supervision by increased reliance on AI.

A *International Organisations*

The AI for Good Global Summit is the leading United Nations platform for global and inclusive dialogue on AI. It is dialoguing with AI innovators and other stakeholders (including more than thirty-seven United Nations agencies and bodies) to identify strategies ensuring that AI technologies develop in a trusted, safe, and inclusive manner.

In this context, the Organisation for Economic Cooperation and Development (OECD) adopted on 22 May 2019 the Council Recommendation on Artificial Intelligence that promotes five principles for responsible stewardship of trustworthy AI systems:[119] (a) Inclusive growth, sustainable development and well-being; (b) Human-centred values and fairness; (c) Transparency and explainability; (d) Robustness, security and safety; and (e) Accountability. In particular, states are encouraged to use experimentation, with AI systems being tested and scaled-up in a controlled environment. In addition, states should review and adapt, as appropriate, their AI systems policy and regulatory frameworks to encourage innovation and competition for trustworthy AI. To back these efforts, the OECD launched an AI Policy Observatory in February 2020 aiming at helping states to enable, nurture, and monitor the responsible development of trustworthy AI systems for the benefit of society.[120]

These regulatory efforts have no direct impact upon financial supervision. However, their practical value should not be underestimated. Financial supervisors play a key role in international organisation activities, meaning that what is set there at an abstract level is likely to be directly correlated to future supervisory principles and practices.

The OECD is also targeting financial market participants more directly, by emphasising the need for testing AI models in extreme market conditions and encouraging the introduction of automatic control mechanisms that trigger alerts or switch off models in times of stress.[121]

AI actors are similarly targeted by the Group of Twenty (G20). Its 2019 AI Principles require them to respect the rule of law, human rights, and democratic values throughout the AI system lifecycle.[122] More specifically, AI actors should commit

[119] OECD/LEGAL/0449 <www.legalinstruments.oecd.org/en/instruments>.

[120] The observatory provides data and multi-disciplinary analysis on AI (see <www.oecd.ai>).

[121] OECD, 'Artificial Intelligence, Machine Learning and Big Data in Finance Opportunities, Challenges and Implications for Policy Makers' (2021) <www.oecd.org/finance/financial-markets/Artificial-intelligence-machine-learning-big-data-in-finance.pdf>.

[122] Available at <www.mofa.go.jp>.

to transparency and responsible disclosure regarding AI systems. Implementation of these principles is deemed critical for G20 members to continue their leadership on AI policy issues, given that the use of AI is still at an early level of maturity across many countries and firms.

At the European level, the Council of Europe has emphasised that AI-based technologies raise important and complex ethical, legal, political, and economic issues.[123] Therefore, it launched a reflection on the feasibility and development of a 'horizontal', cross-cutting legal framework to regulate the use and effects of AI applications. In this context, the Council set up a Committee on Artificial Intelligence (CAHAI) to examine the feasibility and potential elements of an international legal framework. As a first step, the Committee has drafted a list of main and essential principles:[124] human freedom, dignity, and autonomy; prevention of harm to human rights, democracy, and the rule of law; non-discrimination, gender equality, fairness, and diversity; transparency and explainability of AI systems; data protection and the right to privacy; accountability and responsibility. This is obviously a very long list and its practical impact is not obvious. However, putting transparency and explainability of AI systems among the list of main and essential principles is not a negligible achievement. Having these two requirements mentioned in national financial regulation or even merely taken over by financial supervisors would have a significant practical impact.

For its part, the European Commission (EC) has published a White Paper on Artificial Intelligence that reinforces the Council of Europe principles by emphasising the need for a common European approach to AI for two fundamental reasons.[125] First, this approach allows for sufficient scale and avoids single market fragmentation; second, national initiatives would endanger legal certainty, weaken citizens' trust and prevent the emergence of a dynamic European industry.

When it comes more specifically to financial regulation, research originated within the Bank for International Settlements (BIS) shows that a significant number of financial authorities use or plan to use information technology for microprudential and macroprudential supervision.[126] However, the relevant applications are in different stages of development and implementation, ranging from academic research questions through proofs-of-concept stage to fully operational.

The Financial Stability Board (FSB) has identified potential benefits and risks for financial authorities to monitor while AI technology is adopted and more data becomes available. In particular, AI applications could result in new and unexpected forms of interconnectedness between financial markets and institutions, for instance, due to the

[123] See <www.coe.int/en/web/artificial-intelligence/secretary-general-marija-pejcinovic-buric>.

[124] CAHAI (2020) 23 <www.rm.coe.int/cahai-2020-23-final-eng-feasibility-study-/1680a0c6da>.

[125] COM(2020) 65 final <www.ec.europa.eu/info/sites/default/files/commission-white-paper-artificial-intelligence-feb2020en.pdf>.

[126] See Dirk Broeders and Jermy Prenio, 'Innovative Technology in Financial Supervision (suptech) – The Experience of Early Users' (2018) FSI Insights on Policy Implementation No 9 <www.fsb.org>.

common use of previously unrelated data sources.[127] The BIS and FSB approaches are rather descriptive. However, their impact should not be under-estimated: the emphasis is put on the need to pro-actively tackle AI-developments from a market structure perspective rather than merely from a market behaviour perspective.

The European Central Bank (ECB) has more specifically stressed that supervisors need to have a large access to data, this being critical for an efficient use of AI.[128] More generally, the ECB expects AI to make supervision more informed and agile by flagging anomalies in real time, in particular when it comes to bank liquidity issues.[129] In view of these assessments, the ECB launched various AI-related projects while remaining cautious: experience shows that the more one relies on new technologies, the higher the risks associated with it. It is worth noting that the ECB's cautious approach is not merely due to operational considerations. It has explicitly indicated that, in case of AI failure, supervisors (and not technology) are the ones that will be blamed for it.[130]

The European Banking Authority (EBA) more optimistically identified the use of artificial intelligence as a promising and growing technological innovation for financial services.[131] However, it pointed out that many AI applications still deal with a limited number of intelligent tasks.[132] More specifically, the EBA deems financial institutions to be at an early stage of ML use and essentially rely on simple models dealing with customer engagement and process optimisation. By contrast, issues such as accountability, ethical aspects, and data quality are not yet addressed in depth.

B *National Organisations*

Within the European Union, France and Germany are among the most advanced users of AI for supervisory purposes. French supervisory authorities entered the big data world some years ago. Using AI has significantly increased the Autorité de Contrôle Prudentiel et de Résolution (ACPR) ability to identify fraudulent websites for blacklisting and public information purposes.[133] For its part, the Autorité des Marchés Financiers (AMF) uses ML to detect market abuse as well as market anomalies and to reduce the false positive alerts generated by its systems.[134] In particular, French authorities are directly targeting abusive uses

[127] FSB, 'AI and ML in Financial Services, Market Developments and Financial Stability Implications' (November 2017) <www.bis.org>.

[128] See ECB, 'Annual Report 2018' <www.ecb.europa.eu/pub/pdf/annrep/ar2018>.

[129] See ECB, 'Bringing Artificial Intelligence to Banking Supervision' (13 November 2019) <www.bankingsupervision.europa.eu/press/publications/newsletter/2019/html>.

[130] Ibid.

[131] EBA, '2019 Annual Report', <www.eba.europa.eu/sites/default/documents/files/document_library//885450/EBA%20Annual%20Report%202019.pdf>.

[132] 'Report on Big Data and Advanced Analytics' (January 2020) <www.eba.europa>.

[133] 'Annual Banque de France Report' (2019) <www.publications.banque-france.fr/node/343289>.

[134] Autorité des Marchés Financiers (AMF), 'Artificial Intelligence and Big Data Are Now a Reality' (5 October 2020) <www.amf-france.org/en/news-publications>.

of AI; in other words, the ACPR and AMF seem to prioritise behavioural over technical issues.

In Germany, the Bundesanstalt für Finanzdienstleistungsaufsicht (BaFin) uses AI for similar supervisory purposes, in particular to provide evidence of market abuse. BaFin is also analysing the impact of AI on product/process innovations and the emergence of new players/market structures.[135] Interestingly, BaFin does not review AI-use on the basis of overall decision-making processes; it adopts a risk-oriented approach and raises objections as and where needed. The Bundesbank is favouring a somewhat different approach. It is in favour of the supervisory focus being on ML features which are novel to current regulation and supervisory practices, such as black box characteristics, data quality, and model-learning processes.[136] In other words, the Bundesbank seems to prioritise technical over behavioural issues.

Compared to France and Germany, Italian and Spanish financial supervisors have a more measured AI-start. To be sure, Italian and Spanish banks are investing heavily in AI.[137] On the other hand, the Bank of Italy and the Bank of Spain seem to be following more conservative strategies.

The Bank of Italy is essentially using AI intelligence techniques to predict price moves on the real estate market, while its researchers are using big data methodologies to detect anomalous financial transactions.[138] For its part, the Bank of Spain is officially focusing on coordinating its AI work with other international bodies,[139] albeit it also seems to be working on identifying how AI can improve the quality control of the information it collects and enhance its macroeconomic analysis.[140]

However, a more dynamic approach to AI-use seems to be in the making. The Bank of Italy has recently launched new initiatives on AI in the financial sector, whereas the Spanish government is setting-up a supervisory authority to monitor the risks associated with AI technologies–the goal being to bring new opportunities to Spain.

When it comes to major financial centres, they generally pay significant attention to AI developments. From a practical perspective, AI supervisory involvement is especially noteworthy in Switzerland and Singapore. The Swiss Financial Market

135 'Big Data Meets Artificial Intelligence, Challenges and Implications for the Supervision and Regulation of Financial Services' (Report, 2020) <www.bafin.de/SharedDocs/Downloads/EN/dl_bdai_studie_en.html>.

136 'The Use of Artificial Intelligence and Machine Learning in the Financial Sector' (Policy Discussion Paper, November 2020) <www.bundesbank.de/resource/blob/598256/d7d26167bceb18ee7c0c296902e42162/mL/2020-11-policy-dp-aiml-data.pdf>.

137 See for example, Bank of Italy, 'Annual Report 2019' 154 <www.bancaditalia.it/pubblicazioni/relazione-annuale/2019/index.html?com.dotmarketing.htmlpage.language=1>.

138 G Batocchioni, Marco De Simoni and M Gara, 'Big Data and Machine Learning: The Bank of Italy's Experience' (2019) <www.centralbankmalta.org>.

139 Bank of Spain, 'Report on Banking Supervision 2019' 190 <www.bde.es/bde/en/secciones/informes/Publicaciones_an/Informe_anual/>.

140 Ana Fernández, 'Artificial Intelligence in Financial Services' [2019] Bank of Spain, Economic Bulletin 2.

Supervisory Authority (FINMA) has long required financial institutions to document the key features of their algorithmic trading strategies.[141] It is also expected to set out supervisory expectations concerning the use of AI in business processes and the mitigation of associated risks.

Similarly, the Monetary Authority of Singapore (MAS) has issued principles to promote fairness, ethics, responsibility, and transparency in the use of AI in the financial sector.[142] They require AI-driven decisions to be governed by at least the same ethical standards as human-driven decisions. More specifically, the Augmented Intelligence System automates the computation of key metrics,[143] which should make it easier to detect suspicious trading activities, in particular market abuse cases.

Both FINMA and MAS are concerned with protecting the trust depositors and investors have in the institutions they supervise. To that end, they are trying to maintain the competitiveness of financial intermediaries while ensuring 'risk-free' access to AI-driven products and services. This approach makes sense from a depositor protection and safe e-banking perspective. On the other hand, whether it remains sustainable when it comes to pension funds and individual investor-oriented financial products remains questionable. Here, like in previous innovative technology situations, regulatory adjustments are as likely to be shaped by significant incidents or financial crises than by reasoned approaches.

Governmental AI approaches are harder to assess when it comes to other major financial centres. The Bank of England (BoE) and the Financial Conduct Authority (FCA) have investigated how ML is deployed by financial institutions.[144] The FCA reported that AI is increasingly used in UK financial markets,[145] whereas the BoE expects AI developments to fundamentally change the way businesses provide (and consumers use) financial services.[146] These are very general and hard-to-evaluate assessments. This may be done on purpose, given that the BoE and the FCA have not proven very forthcoming when it comes to their own use of AI. For example, the only specific reference to AI in the BoE Annual Report 2019–2020 has to do with Alan Turing appearing on the new £50 note.

US lawmakers, for their part, are increasingly dealing with AI-related risks. While Congress adopted two bills mentioning AI in the 2015–2016 term, it passed more than 50 such bills during the 2019–2020 term.[147] The White House, for its part,

141 'Market Conduct Rules' (Circular 2013/8, 2013) <www.finma.ch/en/documentation/circulars/>.

142 Available at <www.mas.gov.sg/publications/monographs-or-information-paper/2018/FEAT>.

143 'Machine Learning in UK Financial Services' (2019) <www.mas.gov.sg/publications/monographs-or-information-paper/2020/mas-enforcement-report-2019-2020>.

144 Available at <www.bankofengland.co.uk/report/2019/machine-learning-in-uk-financial-services>.

145 FCA, 'Artificial Intelligence in the Boardroom' (2019) <www.fca.org.uk/insight/artificial-intelligence-boardroom>.

146 'BoE Annual Report 2019-2020' <www.bankofengland.co.uk/annual-report/2020>.

147 See Gibson Dunn, 'Annual Review of Artificial Intelligence and Automated Systems' (2020) <www.gibsondunn.com>.

released a draft 'Guidance for Regulation of Artificial Intelligence Applications' in 2019, which includes ten principles applicable when regulating AI.[148] At the state level, AI resolutions were introduced in 15 (2019), 13 (2020), and 16 (2021) states.[149] Unsurprisingly, states such as California, Massachusetts, New York, and Texas are among these States; however, this is also the case for less technology-oriented states such as Alabama, Arizona, Idaho, or Indiana.

From a practical perspective, the regulatory output is rather unimpressive. For example, Alabama set up a Commission on AI that has yet to deliver its report. The same is true for the Washington task force charged with identifying policies to help its businesses and workers respond to rapid changes in emerging technologies such as AI. Similarly, Massachusetts has yet to adopt a bill establishing a commission to analyse the use of automated decision systems, whereas bills to 'study and regulate' AI are still discussed in California, New York, and New Jersey. Admittedly, a few States have reached the implementation stage. For example, Vermont's task force has recommended the adoption of a code of ethics to set standards for responsible AI,[150] whereas Utah has adopted a deep technology talent initiative within higher education.[151]

Summing-up, given the US technology leadership, one would expect AI-related regulation to be more prominent. This shortfall may be due to lawmakers waiting for the dust to settle before implementing major AI-driven regulation changes. It may also reflect that existing regulation allows for below-the-radar screen supervisory interventions. The former approach is more likely, as it avoids hindering US financial intermediaries in the ongoing technology race.

In Japan, an Expert Group on Architecture for AI Principles to be Practiced has been set up by the Ministry of Economy, Trade and Industry. The Group published an Interim Report on January 15, 2021;[152] it concluded that, for the time being, AI governance should be dealt with via soft law. Regulatory authorities have acted more decisively. The Japan Exchange Regulation and the Tokyo Stock Exchange have used AI for market surveillance operations since March 2018, in particular to detect market manipulation.[153] For its part, the Financial Services Agency plans to roll out an artificial intelligence system that can detect fraudulent money transfers, which should strengthen the measures against money laundering.[154]

In other words, Japan is taking a more pro-active AI approach than the US. This is largely due to concerns about the aging of Japanese society, which prompted Japan

148 Available at <www.whitehouse.gov/wp-content/uploads/2020/01/Draft-OMB-Memo-on-Regulation>.

149 See <www.ncsl.org/research/telecommunications-and-information-technology/2020-legislation-related-to-artificial-intelligence.aspx>.

150 Available at <www.legislature.vermont.gov/assets/Legislative-Reports/Artificial-Intelligence-Task-Force-Final-Report-1.15.2020>.

151 Available at <www.le.utah.gov/~2020/bills/static/SB0096.html>.

152 Available at <www.meti.go.jp/press/2020/01/20210115003>.

153 See <www.jpx.co.jp/english/corporate/news/news-releases/0060/20180319-01.html>.

154 See <www.nationthailand.com/international/30402375>.

to make huge AI investments to maintain the competitiveness of its economy.[155] For example, Japan is home to 26% of the world's AI leaders, while the US, the UK, and Singapore rank second with an 18% share each – Switzerland coming in fifteenth position with a 6% share.

When it comes to China, the 2019 Governance Principles for the New Generation AI are designed to ensure AI safety, reliability, and controllability.[156] Fundamentally, AI development should comply with eight principles: harmony and human-friendliness; fairness and justice; inclusion and sharing; respect for privacy, safety, and controllability; shared responsibility; collaboration; and agile governance. These principles are similar to ethical frameworks laid out by Western governments; however, the Chinese approach reflects a government-first approach. Going forward, the plan is to submit AI to a comprehensive legal regime by 2025, with the overarching aim of making China the world centre of AI innovation by 2030.[157]

It will be interesting to compare the results of the Chinese public action approach with the achievements of the United States private sector-driven strategy. To the extent developments in AI innovations can be achieved at the firm level, the United States could be better placed; on the other hand, if economies of scale and research coordination are the driving forces of AI developments, China may have the advantage.

To sum up, the tendency is for major players to adopt a rather pro-active approach to AI-driven financial *supervision*. One can expect the next step to be a move to AI-driven financial *regulation*.

C *The Emergence of AI-Driven Financial Regulation*

The fundamental question is not whether AI will play a financial regulation role, but the extent to which it will affect private ordering and state regulation. Private ordering is likely to become the favoured approach when it comes to market and capital structures. Assuming that AI is easier to buy than talent, the robustness of financial intermediaries and institutional investors is likely to increase. Ideally, AI-use should also allow for a more level playing field; however, financial institutions may not all be equally well placed to make and benefit from AI investments. This evolution should allow AI-equipped financial supervisors to spend fewer resources monitoring and regulating market participants. More specifically, one can expect supervisors to focus on the availability and robustness of state-of-the-art technology rather than on compliance with the principle of precaution. On the other hand, systemic risk will not

155 See 'Not the US or China, but Japan Leads the World in AI' (6 October 2020) <www.consultancy.asia/news/3601/not-the-us-or-china-but-japan-leads-the-world-in-ai>.

156 Available at <www.perma.cc/V9FL-H6J7>.

157 Huw Roberts and others, 'The Chinese Approach to Artificial Intelligence: An Analysis of Policy, Ethics, and Regulation' [2021] *AI & Soc* 36, 59–77

disappear. In fact, it may prove harder to detect and manage: AI-use may standardise market participants and result in uniform behavior. At the same time, access to AI should improve financial supervisors' detection ability or, at least, management of macro-prudential events. It follows that, in terms of systemic risk, AI-driven financial supervision may, at worse, prove neutral and, at best, significantly reduce it.

V CONCLUSION

The social sciences-related AI literature has been growing rapidly, especially in the past two years. However, most contributions dealing with law-making and enforcement still focus on ML. In other words, the literature remains significantly incomplete when it comes to the use of AI for law-making and enforcement purposes. At the same time, AI may be changing the physics of financial services by weakening the bonds between financial intermediaries and fostering new operating models. This has prompted moves towards the setting-up of industry and regulatory frameworks that are both AI-friendly and safe. Hence, supervisory authorities are increasingly relying on AI for internal purposes. France and Germany, which are among the most advanced users of AI, are already using it for supervisory purposes. On the other hand, when it comes to regulating financial intermediaries, AI remains mostly confined to curbing illegal market practices, in particular market abuses. The exception is the United States, where the states are the main players and the regulatory scope is broader than in the rest of the world.

20

Financial Advisory Intermediaries and AI

Iris H.-Y. Chiu

I INTRODUCTION

The popularity of robo-advice in the US[1] and UK[2] has risen as both technology and market demand pave the way for such automated interfaces to help investors with making investment decisions. We may imagine a world where investors would be able to access investment advice that is dispensed by the combination of machine learning and predictive analytics, much like how we may ask Google or Siri anything that comes to our mind and would be pointed towards a right direction. Such investment advice can be sought 24/7, in the comfort of one's home, and all that is needed is a connection to an online portal. Investors may be freed from dealing with human advisers who may have skewed incentives towards pushing certain investment products and thus would not behaviourally succumb to pressure-selling tactics or mis-selling.

In reality, the super-intelligent robo-advisor who is accessible, and perhaps in a cost-effective manner, is yet a remote possibility. Generative AI is likely to have greater capacity for trawling and analysing investment information but it remains uncertain if this can further be developed into super-intelligent robo-advisors.[3] This chapter argues that existing financial regulation in the EU and UK plays a significant part in shaping the development of technological offerings in investment

I thank Ernest Lim and Phillip Morgan for curating this brilliant volume, and for comments received from Professors Gerard Hertig, ETH-Zurich, Eric Chaffee, University of Toledo, Deirdre Ahern, Trinity College Dublin and Wan Wai Yee, City University Hong Kong, as well as Kenneth Khoo, NUS and Yale Law School.

1 See Facundo Abraham and others, 'Robo-Advisors: Investing through Machines' (World Bank Research and Policy Brief 2019).

2 Tatiana Nikiforova, 'The Place of Robo-Advisors in the UK Independent Financial Advice Market: Substitute or Complement?' (2017) <https://ssrn.com/abstract=3084609>; Gregor Dorfleitner and others, 'The Fintech Market in Germany' (2016) <https://papers.ssrn.com/sol3/papers.cfm?abstract_id=2885931>.

3 Empirical research in Australia found that ChatGPT may help financial advisers analyse information more efficiently for simple and standardized financial needs but not for complex, tailor-made needs, see Ben Neilson, 'Artificial Intelligence Authoring Financial Recommendations: Comparative Australian Evidence' (2023) 9 *Journal of Financial Regulation* 249.

advice because its technology-neutral stance and its *ex ante* design define the boundaries of legal risk for the industry of robo-advice. Hence, the *ex ante* regulatory objective of investor protection, which can also be regarded as a regulatory constraint, would pro-actively steer technological developments in this area, even the application of generative AI. This may be regarded as a surprising argument given that we expect regulatory policies to lag behind technological developments,[4] and in many areas in financial sector services, this is indeed the case. For example, European legislation on regulating the markets for financial instruments has for a long time taken a technology-neutral stance in promoting equivalent outcomes of price transparency and market orderliness.[5] However, when eventually challenged by the novelties of high frequency trading, their disturbing effects on market prices, such as occasioned on flash crashes,[6] the Markets in Financial Instruments Directive 2014 finally imposed specific governance requirements for algorithmic traders and an obligation to act as reliable market makers.[7] Another example where legislation may be regarded as lagging behind is in relation to the novel fund-raising instruments of 'tokens' offered by blockchain app developers, which are not clearly 'securities' in nature.[8] After the height of 'initial coin offerings' has tapered off in 2019, EU policymakers[9] and the UK government[10] are deliberating on whether a new regulatory regime is needed for them.

This chapter proceeds as follows: Section II discusses the regulatory regime for investment advice in the EU and UK, based on the EU Markets in Financial Instruments Directive 2014, and how this has shaped the robo-advice industry. Section III discusses the limitations of the robo-advice industry and the gaps in meeting an optimal personalised financial advice market. Section IV offers some reflections on the future directions for regulation and concludes.

4 Nathan Cortez, 'Regulating Disruptive Innovation' (2014) 29 *Berkeley Technology Law Journal* 175.

5 Council Directive 2014/65/EU of 15 May 2014 on markets in financial instruments and amending Directive 2002/92/EC and Directive 2011/61/EU [2014] OJ L 173/349 (Markets in Financial Instruments Directive).

6 'The 2010 'flash crash': how it unfolded' (*The Guardian*, 22 April 2015) <www.theguardian.com/business/2015/apr/22/2010-flash-crash-new-york-stock-exchange-unfolded>.

7 Markets in Financial Instruments Directive, art 17.

8 Philipp Hacker and Chris Thomale, 'Crypto-Securities Regulation: ICOs, Token Sales and Cryptocurrencies under EU Financial Law' (2018) 15 *European Company and Financial Law Review* 645 on distinguishing token sales from securities offers, but see Philipp Maume and Martin Fromberger, 'Regulation of Initial Coin Offerings: Reconciling U.S. and E.U. Securities Laws' (2019) *Chicago Journal of International Law* 548; Alex Collomb and others, 'Blockchain Technology and Financial Regulation: A Risk-Based Approach to the Regulation of ICOs' (2019) 10 *European Journal of Risk Regulation* 263; D Boreiko and others, 'Blockchain Startups and Prospectus Regulation' (2019) 20 *European Business Organisations and Law Review* 665.

9 Commission, 'Proposal for a Regulation of the European Parliament and of the Council on Markets in Crypto-assets, and amending Directive (EU) 2019/1937' COM(2020) 593 final <www.eur-lex.europa.eu/legal-content/EN/TXT/?uri=CELEX%3A52020PC0593>.

10 HM Treasury, 'UK Regulatory Approach to Cryptoassets and Stablecoins: Consultation and Call for Evidence' (*UK Government*, 7 January 2021) <www.gov.uk/government/consultations/uk-regulatory-approach-to-cryptoassets-and-stablecoins-consultation-and-call-for-evidence>.

II ROBO-ADVICE AS SHAPED BY INVESTMENT ADVICE REGULATION

Robo-advice is a shorthand for automated forms of investment management interfaces. A robo-adviser can provide an algorithm-generated list of investment options for customers based on customer data, leaving customers to take further action. Robo-advisers can also be automated wealth management services where portfolios are constructed by algorithmic intelligence, monitored according to programmed parameters and automatically rebalanced according to those parameters.[11] Indeed Maume argues that the narrow definition of 'robo-advice' should be correct, relating only to the advisory and presentation of choice aspects, as automated wealth management is a different service.[12] This article adopts a more flexible definition as the business models of robo-advice generate options in order to construct portfolios or allocate to certain financial products, making the advisory an intermediate step to integrated investment management. Hence, a customer facing robo-advice is not merely *informed* of investment options but also *steered* to focus on particular options, ultimately *entrusting* to the investment form to manage his/her financial resources.

It has been observed that robo-advisors are able to offer on-demand 24/7 access in the comfort of one's environment as long as one has an internet connection.[13] This seems to meet the access preferences of many as empirically surveyed.[14] Crucially, robo-advice is often accessible to those who have small amounts to save, such as Nutmeg's promise to onboard customers saving from as little as £100 initially.[15] This has the potential to help with 'democratising finance' and increasing financial inclusion, an outcome already observed in the United States where robo-advisors have garnered over USD$400 billion assets under management and looking to exceed USD$1.5 trillion by 2023.[16] The cost of use is also generally lower than other forms of investment fund management, as annual charges can be three times lower.[17] From an affordability point of view, robo-advisers have the potential to incentivise access,

[11] Pablo Sanz Bayón and Luis Garvía Vega, 'Automated Investment Advice: Legal Challenges and Regulatory Questions' (2018) 37 *Banking and Financial Services Policy Report* 1.

[12] Maume and Fromberger (n 7).

[13] Andrea L Seidt and others, 'Paying Attention to That Man behind the Curtain: State Securities Regulators' Early Conversations with Robo-Advisers' (2019) 50 *U Tol L Rev* 501; Wolf-Georg Ringe and Christopher Ruof, 'A Regulatory Sandbox for Robo Advice' (2018) ILE Working Paper Series 14 <www.hdl.handle.net/10419/179514>.

[14] *Public Attitudes to Financial Advice Survey* (2016) <www.bandce.co.uk/wp-content/uploads/2016/02/201602-Public-attitudes-to-advice.pdf>.

[15] 'Investing for beginners' (*Nutmeg*) <www.nutmeg.com/new-to-investing>; but see Benjamin P Edwards, 'The Rise of Automated Investment Advice: Can Robo-Advisers Rescue the Retail Market' (2018) 93 *Chi Kent L Rev* 97 who finds that some robo-advisers allow savers to start investing from as low as $8.

[16] Abraham and others (n 1).

[17] Ibid. Ringe and Ruof (n 12).

and in the UK[18] and Germany,[19] the two largest robo-adviser markets in Europe, there is an upward trend in terms of growth in robo-advisers' market share. Further, the general distrust of 'manipulative' and 'greedy' humans after the global financial crisis 2007–2009 may pave the way for more social acceptance of automated services which can be seen as programmable without biases[20] and are able to functionally and objectively serve a customer's needs.[21] In sum, the interface of online access can promote wide access to cost-effective investment advice, can potentially improve the state of financial inclusion as well as financial education for many. However, there are various limitations to the robo-adviser, and many of which are shaped by the financial regulatory regime.

A *The Tenets of Investment Advice Regulation*

A regulatory duty to advise on 'suitable' investments applies where a personalised recommendation has been made to a customer,[22] excluding forms of more informal,[23] generic or marketing information. Further, an investment services provider must categorise clients into one of three groups, the retail client, the professional client, and the eligible counterparty.[24] The professional client is defined as certain financial and corporate institutions as well as natural persons meeting certain quantitative criteria such as investible assets and frequency of financial transactions carried out previously, as well as qualitative criteria in relation to his/her expertise, knowledge, and experience of financial services and transactions.[25] The eligible counterparty would be regarded to be at peer level to the financial services firm concerned.[26] These two categories of customers are owed a lesser extent of (a) the duty of suitability in relation to investment advice or portfolio management and (b) the duty of appropriateness for other financial transactions or services.[27] These

18 Gregor Dorfleitner and others, 'The Fintech Market in Germany' (2016) <https://papers.ssrn.com/sol3/papers.cfm?abstract_id=2885931>.

19 Ibid.

20 Douglas W Arner and others, 'The Evolution of Fintech: A New Post-crisis Paradigm?' (2016) 47 *Georgetown Journal of International Law* 1271, 1286.

21 Frank D Hodge and others, 'The Effect of Humanizing Robo-Advisors on Investor Judgments' (2018) <https://papers.ssrn.com/sol3/papers.cfm?abstract_id=3158004>.

22 The source regulation is Commission Delegated Regulation (EU) 2017/565 of 25 April 2016 supplementing Directive 2014/65/EU of the European Parliament and of the Council as regards organisational requirements and operating conditions for investment firms and defined terms for the purposes of that Directive OJ L 87/1, art 9 (Commission Delegated Regulation 2017/565) which directly applies to the UK before Exit day and will be adopted into UK legislation post-Exit; FCA Handbook COBS 9A.2.2-3 for a rather wide scope of dealings, COBS 9.1 for non-MiFID retail business.

23 *Redmayne Bentley Stockbrokers v Isaacs & Ors* [2010] EWHC 1504 (Comm).

24 FCA Handbook COBS 3.4, 3.5, 3.6.

25 FCA Handbook COBS 3.5.

26 FCA Handbook COBS 3.6.

27 Markets in Financial Instruments Directive, art 25(3); Commission Delegated Regulation 2017/565, art 54 and 55; FCA Handbook COBS 10.2 for non-MiFID business in relation to retail clients, COBS 10A.2 for MiFID business.

customers are not as well-protected as 'retail customers', who are defined as any customer not a professional customer or eligible counterparty.[28]

For advisory and portfolio management services, financial services providers have to ensure that their service or advice is 'suitable' for the customer,[29] but retail customers benefit from a more comprehensive information collection exercise than other customers and the obligation of 'suitability' is more extensively owed to retail customers.[30] Financial services providers are entitled to assume that professional clients and eligible counterparties have the necessary knowledge and understanding of the engagement and are financially able to bear risk.[31] In relation to other financial transactions, financial services providers owe a duty to ensure that such transaction is 'appropriate' for customers, meaning that the customer understands the risks of such a transaction.[32] The assumption of knowledge is applied to professional customers,[33] so in reality, financial services providers would deal only at arms-length with such customers. In this manner, the legal risk for financial services providers in the advisory context can be delineated in accordance with the perceived need for protection by the regulator.

In reality, 'borderline' customers such as small- and medium-sized businesses are arguably aggressively categorised as 'professional', although that is often a trade-off for opportunities to engage in higher risk but possibly higher return financial products.[34] In this context, customers may be offered 'execution-only' products some of which are complex, hence the financial services provider becomes only an intermediary for transactions and assumes no advisory capacity. This has occurred in relation to a series of litigation involving interest-rate hedging products sold by banks to small businesses, which are classified as 'professional customers', on an 'execution-only' basis. Interest-rate hedging products allow small businesses that already borrow from their banks to swap a floating interest rate on their borrowing for a fixed one, in order to hedge against risks of interest rate or in one case, foreign currency fluctuations. However, after the Bank of England reduced interest rates to unprecedented lows after the global financial crisis 2007–9, it became too insensibly expensive to carry on with the hedging products. Nevertheless, many small businesses could not

[28] FCA Handbook COBS 3.4.

[29] 'Suitability' is interpreted as meeting the client's investment objectives and risk tolerance, and that the client understands the nature of the product or service engaged with and is financially able to bear those risks. For a retail customer, the financial services provider must be satisfied that all three elements are achieved and explained in a suitability report to the customer. See Commission Delegated Regulation 2017/565, art 54, directly applicable to the UK.

[30] Ibid.

[31] Commission Delegated Regulation 2017/565 of 25 April 2016, art 54, directly applicable to the UK, and supplemented by COBS 9.

[32] Commission Delegated Regulation (EU) 2017/565, art 56, directly applicable to the UK.

[33] Ibid.

[34] Customers may challenge the classification especially after losses have been sustained on their riskier ventures, such as in *Bank Leumi (UK) PLC* v Linda Joy Wachner [2011] EWHC 656 (Comm), but courts have upheld firms' classifications as long as these have been achieved with proper processes.

terminate the arrangements unless they paid an exorbitant break fee. These small businesses sued for mis-selling but as they were unprotected by regulatory provisions on advice,[35] they sought to frame their causes of action in the common law duty of care. However, financial institutions have excluded an advisory relationship or curtailed their liability. Hence, these claimants have largely been unsuccessful as the courts have found that responsibility has not been assumed by the financial services provider[36] and express exclusions of an advisory duty of care are valid.[37]

Even in relation to the retail customer where the duty of suitability or appropriateness applies, these duties have been developed in a highly procedural manner. Where investment advice or portfolio management is concerned, firms need to collect three areas of prescribed information from customers, in relation to investment objectives, risk appetite, and financial profile in order to recommend products that meet the customer's investment objectives, suit his/her risk appetite and the level of the customer's financial knowledge and experience to ascertain if the customer understands investment product risks.[38] For other financial transactions, firms need to collect information on the customer's knowledge and understanding of the risks of the transaction concerned, in order to proceed with the transaction. This is subtly different from ensuring that clients actually understand the nature of the transaction, as firms can be satisfied on the basis of the objective profiles of clients.[39] In sum, the duties of suitability and appropriateness, even when they apply in full, are highly procedural, and can mitigate a firm's legal risk as compliance is evidenced by adhering to sound procedures and systems that give rise to the ultimate recommendation, providing *ex ante* safety against *ex post* allegations of negligence. The pressure to mitigate the cost of access associated with the legal risk for financial services providers has also resulted in the FCA introducing the regime for 'streamlined advice'. This is advice that meets the suitability standard in a more limited way, in relation to specific and limited financial needs articulated by the customer.[40] Even

35 *Green and another v Royal Bank of Scotland plc (Financial Conduct Authority intervening)* [2013] EWCA Civ 1197, [2014] Bus LR 168; *Thornbridge Limited v Barclays Bank Plc* [2015] EWHC 3430 (QB); *Crestsign Ltd v National Westminster Bank plc and Royal Bank of Scotland plc* [2014] EWHC 3043 (Ch), [2015] 2 All E.R. (Comm) 133; *Titan Steel Wheels Ltd v Royal Bank of Scotland plc* [2010] EWHC 211 (Comm), [2010] 2 Lloyd's Rep 92; *MTR Bailey Trading Ltd v Barclays* [2015] EWCA Civ 667.

36 *Grant Estates*, above and *Green* (n 34).

37 *JP Morgan Chase Bank (formerly known as The Chase Manhattan Bank) (a body corporate) and Others v Springwell Navigation Corporation (a body corporate) and by Counterclaim Springwell Navigation Corporation (a body corporate) v JP Morgan Chase Bank (formerly known as The Chase Manhattan Bank) (a body corporate) and Others* [2008] EWHC 1186 (Comm), also discussed critically in Christa Band, 'Selling Complex Financial Products to Sophisticated Clients: JP Morgan Chase v Springwell: Part 1' (2009) 24 *JIBLR* 71; *Murphy v HSBC Bank plc* [2004] All ER (D) 211.

38 Commission Delegated Regulation 2017/565, art 54 and 55; FCA Handbook COBS 9.2.1-3; COBS 9A.2.1-10.

39 Commission Delegated Regulation 2017/565, art 56; FCA Handbook COBS 10.2, 10A.2.

40 FCA, *Streamlined Advice and Related Consolidated Guidance* (2017) <www.fca.org.uk/publication/finalised-guidance/fg-17-08.pdf>.

if suitability and appropriateness are nuanced legal standards, regulators constantly face a push-back in relation to mitigating the legal risk for advisory services.

The legal framework for the advisory context in the UK is thus finely balanced in terms of protection of customers' interests and mitigation of firms' legal risk when providing advice.

B *Impact on the Design of Robo-Advice*

There has been a significant amount of academic debate in the United States as to whether robo-advisers can meet the fiduciary standard of care in advising customers. Fein is the most pronounced critic of robo-advisors in this regard,[41] as extensive exclusions and disclaimers delineate sharply the standard of care that customers can expect. Further, there is doubt that robo-advisers elicit sufficient information from customers to be able to recommend suitable products.[42] Further, there are concerns that robo-advisers are programmed by firms that embed their preferences in the algorithms, such as preferences based on sub-optimal management of conflicts of interest.[43] However, other commentators are of the view that robo-advisers can be programmed optimally and properly, and in this manner, based ultimately on human design, algorithms can deliver a standard of service that is compliant with regulation.[44] Even human advisers may rely on automation and digitalised services to help with their roles, and there should not be a presumption that pre-programmed algorithms are unable to meet the regulatory standards required.

Under the regulatory regimes in the UK/EU, it is arguable that programming robo-advisers to meet the regulatory standards of suitability or appropriateness is well-facilitated. Compliance with suitability entails the eliciting of information as prescribed and then matching the profile of the customer (as constructed by the mandatory information obtained) with financial products that are categorised accordingly.[45] The procedural approach to complying with suitability and appropriateness makes the advisory process programmable in terms of sequencing and matching. Indeed, financial products are sorted in only a few categories according

[41] Melanie Fein, 'FINRA's Report on Robo-Advisors: Fiduciary Implications' (2016) <https://ssrn.com/abstract=2768295>; Melanie Fein, 'Robo-Advisers; A Closer Look' (2015) <https://ssrn.com/abstract=2658701>.

[42] Michael Faloon and Bernt Scherer, 'Individualization of Robo-Advice' (2017) 19 *Journal of Wealth Management* 31; Bernd Scherer, 'Algorithmic Portfolio Choice: Lessons from Panel Survey Data' (2017) 31 *Financial Markets Portfolio Management* 49; Michael Tertilt and Peter Scholtz, 'To Advise, or Not to Advise — How Robo-Advisors Evaluate the Risk Preferences of Private Investors' (2018) 21 *Journal of Wealth Management* 70.

[43] Megan Ji, 'Are Robots Good Fiduciaries: Regulating Robo-Advisors under the Investment Advisers Act of 1940' (2017) 117 *Colum L Rev* 1543.

[44] John Lightbourne, 'Algorithms & Fiduciaries: Existing and Proposed Regulatory Approaches to Artificially Intelligent Financial Planners' (2017) 67 *Duke LJ* 651; Marika Salo and Helena Happio, 'Robo-Advisors and Investors: Enhancing Human-Robot Interaction through Information Design' (2017) <https://ssrn.com/abstract=2937821>.

[45] Discussed above.

to riskiness for matching purposes,[46] and this allows the programming of a clear labelling strategy for robo-advisors in seeking matches with customers' risk appetite profiles. In a restricted advice context, it is relatively straightforward for a limited range of products to be labelled in a few categories, and customers can be sorted into these categories on the basis of relatively simple questionnaires. Such strategies are highly standardised and designed to be cost-effective and fuss-free, and they technically meet the requirements of suitability and appropriateness, as long as the right information is elicited and the matching process is conducted on a rational basis using the information provided. This business model presents a relatively low level of legal risk for robo-advisory firms, and this may not be the type of tailor-made investment advice that customers are thinking of. In other words, regulatory risk is not the main concern with the current offerings of robo-advisers. The insight we derive here is that despite its attractiveness and ease of access, robo-advice is a highly limited market good, and customers may be misled into thinking that this is sufficient to meet their unique financial needs.

The design of robo-advice is thus arguably led by the *ex ante* regulatory requirements in suitability that are highly procedural in nature and lend themselves to a logical and progressional structure for programming. The procedural requirements also delimit the inputs needed from customers, and robo-advice designers are not required, nor are they incentivised, to design sophisticated data analytics machines that can process more volumes of unique customer information or desires. Indeed, more unique input and preferences would likely require more sophisticated machine learning processing to deliver possible recommendations. It may be argued that generative AI is poised to develop in this manner. However, intermediaries also potentially run into higher levels of legal risk, as they may open themselves up to promising levels of investment satisfaction beyond the suitability threshold. Given the early stages of generative AI, there is considerable legal risk in claiming that investment advice can be both comprehensive and tailor-made for clients in the mass market.

C *The Regulation of Conflicts of Interest in Investment Advice*

Next, we argue that the regulatory regime for mitigating the adverse impact of conflicts of interest on the quality of investment advice has also played a significant part in shaping the industry of robo-advice.

In the financial advice market, advice can be regarded as not trustworthy or credible if it is of poor quality or is affected by incentives that are not aligned with customers' interests. Empirical research has found that advice can be affected by the adviser's incentives, such as commissions paid by product providers,[47] and this

[46] Faloon and Scherer (n 41); Scherer (n 41); Abraham and others (n 1).

[47] Mitchell Marsden and others, 'The Value of Seeking Financial Advice' (2011) 32 *Journal of Family and Economic Issues* 625.

affects the trust environment between advisers and customers. In this respect, the FCA has undertaken pioneering reform to introduce conflict-free advice, via the Retail Distribution Review (RDR) introduced in 2012.[48]

The Review made two major achievements, one in raising the mandatory level of training and competence for financial advisors and the second in reforming adviser remuneration in order to align advisers' incentives with customers' interests. Financial advisers now have to meet prescribed qualifications for training, and preliminary findings in the FCA's post-RDR review suggest that this reform has been welcomed by both the industry and consumers and places advisors in a better position to offer credible services to the public.[49] Indeed, the FCA has also been vigilant in removing approvals for individuals who fail to convince the FCA of their skills and competence. In *Maoudis*,[50] the individual concerned was weakly qualified but provided a limited range of advisory services in debt management and counselling. The FCA was of the view that although the range of services provided was limited, the individual was unable to provide a full and informed perspective to his customers in relation to a wider range of debt management possibilities such as voluntary schemes of arrangements and personal bankruptcy.[51] This disqualification decision was upheld by the Upper Tribunal.

One of the most popular complaints against financial advisers relates to the possibility that advice may be tainted by conflicts of interest, as advisers were remunerated by commissions from product providers, incentivising advisers to steer customers towards products that offered optimal commission for the adviser.[52] The RDR introduced a phenomenal change by structurally intervening in the market practices for advisers' remuneration. Commissions from product providers are largely banned,[53] and advisers need to seek remuneration from their customers. Therefore, advisers' roles are changed from being merely intermediaries between product distributors and customers to being end-product providers to their customers, with the product now being advice. The regulation also sets out in prescribed detail how charging structures are to be designed and communicated to clients in order to ensure transparency and fairness.[54] By banning product commissions, it is envisaged that advisers that are 'independent', that is, not tied to any particular product distributor/s, would

48 FCA, *Review of Retail Distribution in the UK* (2006). The review was completed and implemented in 2012, see FCA, *Policy Statement (PS11/9) on Delivering the RDR and Other Issues for Platforms and Nominee-Related Services* (2011) <www.fsa.gov.uk/pubs/policy/ps11_09.pdf>.

49 FCA, *Post-implementation Review of the Retail Distribution Review* (2014) <www.fca.org.uk/news/news-stories/post-implementation-review-retail-distribution-review>.

50 *Steven Maoudis T/A Montana Debt Management v The Financial Conduct Authority* [2016] UKUT 0548.

51 Ibid.

52 John Chalmers and Jonathan Reuter, 'Is Conflicted Investment Advice Better than No Advice?' (2015) NBER Working Paper 18158 <www.nber.org/papers/w18158>.

53 FCA, *Policy Statement (PS11/9) on Delivering the RDR and Other Issues for Platforms and Nominee-Related Services* (2011) <www.fsa.gov.uk/pubs/policy/ps11_09.pdf>.

54 FCA Handbook COBS 6.1A.

be able to survey the market more objectively and recommend suitable products to customers. Indeed, the FCA's preliminary post-RDR review finds that customers are less likely to steer towards products that used to pay high commissions to advisers.[55] The advice market has, however, become more costly as adviser charges are levied up front. The advice market has also become increasingly bifurcated in terms of independent advice being accessible by wealthier investors and many ordinary retail investors being prevented from accessing the market due to the cost barrier.[56]

In implementing the RDR, the FCA recognised that there could be a trade-off between the cost of access and the quality of advice that can be trusted. However, it is doubtful that the RDR has improved the quality of advice just by removing conflicts of interest from advice. This is because independent advice, that is, the service of surveying the entire market and providing an objective and suitable recommendation, is not applicable to all advisers and remains the most expensive to access.

Many advisers are 'restricted' in nature, such as banks that sell their own mortgage products and product distributors that are affiliated with particular fund management and insurance companies.[57] These advisers are only able to advise on a limited range of products. Although they are also subject in principle to the ban on product provider commissions, the ban does not achieve much in view of these distributors' 'restricted' nature anyway. Hence, the FCA has relaxed the ban in relation to restricted advisers. They are allowed to collect product provider commissions as long as these are disclosed to customers and that customers are offered an enhancement to the investment advice service, such as a free yearly review.[58]

Further, for basic products such as a current bank account, life insurance, or personal pension scheme, there may be an interest in keeping the cost of access low in order to promote financial inclusion. Hence, the ban on commissions has been relaxed in relation to restricted advice and basic advice, so that customers may still benefit from not having to pay advisers up front, where they would be paid by product rebates under certain arrangements.[59] In this manner, conflict-free advice is not completely achieved under the RDR.[60]

55 FCA, *Post-implementation Review of the Retail Distribution Review* (2014) <www.fca.org.uk/publications/calls-input/evaluation-rdr-famr>.

56 FCA, *Evaluation of the Impact of the Retail Distribution Review and the Financial Advice Market Review* (2019).

57 One of the largest financial advice firms in the UK, Hargreaves Lansdown moved from branding itself as 'independent' to 'restricted' after the RDR was implemented as independent advice is too expensive to offer and entails complicated and onerous legal obligations, see <www.yourmoney.com/investing/hargreaves-lansdown-to-stop-providing-independent-financial-advice/>.

58 FCA Handbook COBS 2. 3A.9 where restricted advisers provide an 'ongoing' service such as yearly review, therefore exempted from the commission ban.

59 For example, see above and in relation to basic advice.

60 Herbert Smith, 'Retail Distribution Review: The Supervision and Enforcement of Professional Standards – A New Era?' (2010) 4 *Law and Financial Markets Review* 616.

D *Impact on Robo-Advice Industry*

The regulatory regime for addressing conflicts of interest arguably makes it rather costly for the robo-advice industry to offer independent investment advice. If the robo-adviser is designed to be independent, its design would need to be more sophisticated as it would need to interrogate the labels attached to financial products generated by a number of different providers in order to sort them into categories that it is programmed to act upon. There is an increased legal risk of misunderstanding the nature of products and therefore categorising them wrongly for the purposes of matching with customers' profiles. Machines can arrive at unpredictable and bad outcomes because of wrong associations made in pattern recognition or incorrectly processing certain correlations as necessarily causal.[61] Perhaps for this reason, most robo-advisers do not offer an independent advice service. Although generative AI may increase intermediaries' capacity to compare information across the whole market, the same legal risks remain, which may disincentivise such offerings in the mass market. Recent EU rules on product governance may, however, mitigate this risk as financial product manufacturers are under new regulatory duties to identify appropriate target markets and distribution channels and should provide sufficient information to their distributors.[62] This is reinforced by the distributors' reciprocal duty to ensure that products are targeted at a suitable market.[63] That said, robo-advisory firms would have to add the cost of complying with product distribution rules to their systems,[64] and such compliance is not a guarantee against mis-selling products that are not generated by the firm itself. It is highly likely that robo-advisers with generative AI capabilities are likely to require more investment, and it becomes uncertain if low-cost access remains possible.

In this light, although robo-advisers can currently process customers' data and offer a limited range of exchange-traded fund products in 15 minutes,[65] customers must realise that this is different from seeking personalised financial planning, which remains remote in the robo-advice universe at the moment.[66] Personalised financial planning requires processing of granular datasets and is aimed at producing a bespoke strategy. Currently, this is not within the capacity of robo-advice, which is deployed mainly to categorise and standardise investment products in order to attract mass-market participation. Robo-advice does not at the moment deliver a bespoke outcome (i.e., investment advice) based on discretion. This is because the

[61] Hillary J Allen, 'Driverless Finance' (2020) 10 *Harvard Business Law Review* 157.

[62] Markets in Financial Instruments Directive, art 24(2); Commission Delegated Directive 2017/563, art 9 and 10; FCA Handbook PROD 3.2, 3.3; ESMA's Guidelines 2018.

[63] Ibid.

[64] These rules require product distributors of other manufacturers' products to obtain sufficient information and to ascertain independently that the products are suitable for the target market concerned, FCA Handbook PROD 3.3; Commission Delegated Directive 2017/563, Art 10.

[65] Ringe and Ruof (n 12).

[66] Faloon and Scherer (n 41), but see Section III.

artificially intelligent discretion is directed at a different purpose from the exercise of human discretion. Artificial intelligence, which deploys 'deep learning' or machine learning by pattern recognition,[67] is trained to recognise accurately the binary of 'good' from 'bad' outcome, in order to conduct the 'right' automated actions. Hence, although artificial intelligence is trained by the input of vast amounts of data, the crucial processing of such data is carried out by categorisation according to pattern recognition in order to arrive at standardised and predictable outcomes. Thus, algorithmic intelligence is wired to simplify for its decision-making and not complexify,[68] and robo-advisers are unlikely to be able to produce a personalised plan based on unique events in financial lives or a rich range of diversity characteristics.[69] In this manner, the supposed superior computing power of machines to process data is only useful towards certain standardised ends. Affordable access to personalised financial advice is not currently bridged by the mainstream state of robo-advice.

Hence, robo-advisers direct investors to passive products such as index-linked funds or exchange-traded funds as these are benchmarked and therefore provide automatic parameters for rebalancing, not requiring the involvement of human discretion in investment judgement. It would be ideal if robo-advisers were able to deploy their massive computing power to consider a universe of financial products, including actively managed products, even those managed by hedge funds,[70] private equity investments, and derivative and hedging products.[71] The forward-looking question is whether generative AI is able to engage in such personalised financial planning, choosing the most optimal financial products based on the individual's unique needs and information. There is potential that generative AI is able to interrogate huge amounts of information such as the comparisons between investments (i.e., comparing apples to oranges where the different products are concerned). However, the key uncertainty lies in whether generative AI is able to interrogate unique investor preferences and match them up with the information analysed, and whether the result is indeed optimal financial planning.[72] This chapter predicts that robo-advisory providers lack the incentive to develop this for the mass market, as they may be unwilling to be exposed to receipt of information beyond the legal risk boundaries in the suitability obligation. However, generative AI-based investment

[67] Tomaso Aste 'Artificial Intelligence' (LSE Symposium on Law, Technology and Finance, London, 16 May 2019); Jans Danielsson 'Artificial Intelligence' (LSE Symposium on Law, Technology and Finance, London, 16 May 2019).

[68] Allen (n 60).

[69] Nikiforova (n 2); Alison Lui and George William Lamb, 'Artificial Intelligence and Augmented Intelligence Collaboration: Regaining Trust and Confidence in the Financial Sector' (2018) 27 *Information & Communications Technology Law* 267.

[70] Francois S L'Habitant, *Handbook on Hedge Funds* (John Wiley & Sons 2006).

[71] Robert J Shiller, 'Democratizing and Humanizing Finance' in Benjamin M Friedman (ed), *Reforming U.S. Financial Markets* (MIT Press 2011).

[72] There is early empirical research that indicates that generative AI is limited in this manner, see Neilson (2023).

advice can potentially be open to private wealth management where the legal risks and allocation can be more specifically bargained between parties.

III THE REGULATORY SHAPING OF A LOW-COST ACCESSIBLE ROBO-ADVICE INDUSTRY

The regulatory regimes discussed above have in an *ex ante* manner shaped the robo-advice industry into a low-cost and accessible industry, but offering only a limited range of highly standardised retail investor products. In other words, it is unlikely that data analytics and sophisticated machine learning are likely to be developed on a dramatic scale for personalised tailor-made financial advice, whether for the retail investor or the sophisticated investor.

It is argued that here is an inverse relationship between access and personalisation, as easier access, which usually means mass marketisation and lower cost barriers to entry are antithetical to personalisation. This is a trend in financial participation and is explained by the efficiencies of economies of scale. One of the hallmarks of financialisation is the rise of collective investing, which is the pooling of assets from many individual savers in order to invest in portfolios of different types of diversified risks.[73] But collective investing, though democratising, is also disempowering, as individuals are not likely to be able to have tailor-made portfolios or influence the collective strategy.[74] Hence, lower-cost financial advice tends to be restricted or streamlined, and customers can be funnelled down standardised or mass-market products as long as suitability or appropriateness requirements are met.

Robo-advisors are unlikely to meet the retail investment market's need for personalised financial planning and advice.[75] Empirical research cautions that adopting a 'standardised' approach to meeting financial needs is not always appropriate as life incidents such as divorce affect financial goals and management dramatically and mass-market products often are not designed to incorporate these upheavals.[76] This is arguably a market failure given that the experience of severe disruption in one's financial life, such as a divorce, is common among the adult population of developed financial jurisdictions like the UK.[77]

Further, the approach of robo-advisers in the retail context gives rise to a few other risks.

[73] The modern portfolio theory and its dominance is discussed in Paolo Sironi, *Fintech Innovation: From Robo-Advisors to Goal-based Investing and Gamification* (John Wiley & Sons 2016).

[74] Discussed in Roger M Barker and Iris H-Y Chiu, *Corporate Governance and Investment Management: The Promises and Limitations of the Financial Economy* (Edward Elgar 2017) ch 1.

[75] Marsden and others (2011); 'What FT Readers Really Want from Their Financial Adviser' (*Financial Times*, 30 November 2018).

[76] See discussion in Faloon and Scherer (n 41).

[77] See 'Divorce' (*Office for National Statistics*) <www.ons.gov.uk/peoplepopulationandcommunity/birthsdeathsandmarriages/divorce>.

The hazards associated with using robo-advice is that customers should ideally come with some extent of financial literacy in order to have realistic expectations of the limitations of the service offered.[78] Further, behavioural tendencies on the part of customers in an online context may render them in need of more protection than in a face-to-face context. For example, in an online context, the mandatory disclosures of fair product presentation, risk warnings and fee transparency may be presented in chunks of text which customers may scroll through and not register mentally, therefore reducing the impact of protective regulation.[79] The presentation of the choice architecture, as pointed out by Baker and Dellaert,[80] is crucial to customer decision-making and it should be studied further as to whether they take advantage of behavioural biases and whether specific regulatory intervention into information presentation is necessary to make information more customer-centric.

Commentators have also pointed out that as robo-advisers funnel customers down standardised options, the macro effect of such decisions should be considered at levels of scale. Baker and Dellaert opine that

> [a]t sufficient scale, robo advice can shape insurance and credit pools and even move investment markets. For example, the tsunami of index investing that is currently reshaping the mutual fund industry is the result of a distributed kind of robo advice in which algorithms supplant individual fund managers.[81]

Homogenous patterns of investing can cause unwarranted asset bubbles and vicious market spirals in poor market conditions.[82] These conditions are especially disconcerting for investors as exchange-traded funds which purport to be liquid can become illiquid, and this can gravely damage market confidence.[83] However, it may be counter-argued that the potential systemic impact of robo-advisor-led investing is not itself the problem. Index-linked investing has set the main trend for portfolio construction that is passive and 'following' the market in nature, entailing a form of herding in similar stock holdings by many pools of assets. Unless regulators are convinced that index-linked investing creates negative systemic impact that outweighs its benefits in low cost access and diversification, robo-advisers are merely a secondary development to such an investing trend.

It may be queried whether investment firms could be incentivised to develop sophisticated data analytics and machine learning to serve wealthy and sophisticated customers. These customers may be willing to pay for the cost of such services, but one may query why they would prefer to pay to interact with a machine interface,

78 Abraham and others (n 1).

79 Salo and Happio (n 43).

80 Tom Baker and Benedict Dellaert, 'Regulating Robo Advice across the Financial Services Industry' (2018) 103 *Iowa L Rev* 713.

81 Baker and Dellaert (n 78).

82 Ibid. Ringe and Ruof (n 12); Edwards (n 14).

83 Siobhan Riding, 'Watchdogs Probe Systemic Risks of Passive Fund Growth' (*Financial Times*, 1 April 2019) on the systemic risks of the $5.2 trillion global exchange-traded funds market.

although there may be interest and curiosity in engaging with generative AI models. Often though, human agents are regarded as a premium aspect of service.[84] Further, it is unlikely that machine learning would reduce the legal risk for firms offering more complex or bespoke financial products to 'professional customers', and indeed augments such risk as the humans who find it challenging to offer advice on complex financial products to professional customers would have to programme a robo-adviser to do so. Hence it is likely that whether professional customers are offered a machine interface to interact with or otherwise, investment firms are likely to curtail their legal risks by contractually excluding an advisory relationship, or by limiting their contractual liability. As discussed above, these have been found by courts to be valid,[85] and in an environment of lesser protection for professional customers, it is queried whether there would be a keen demand-side driving force for the development of intelligent machine-based interfaces for investment engagement.

IV REGULATORY BLUEPRINT FOR FURTHER DEVELOPMENTS IN SOPHISTICATED, TAILOR-MADE ROBO-ADVICE?

The limitations of robo-advice in addressing the access gap have been recognised,[86] but more futuristic commentators are of the view that continued improvements in computer processing power in relation to data volumes and increased sophistication in algorithmic training can lead to a future where artificial intelligence can better interrogate data with more complex correlations in order to provide a personalised plan for financial customers.[87]

Hence, in a survey carried out on the penetration of robo-advisers in Germany, Dorfleitner et al. report[88] that robo-advisers are lobbying for greater access to customers' financial data held in various institutions such as banks and are eager to build up a larger and more integrated picture of customer profiles. This interest is likely to augment with developments in generative AI. However, commentators caution that access to more data does not mean ethical use of such data or that 'right' judgements would be made in the course of data processing.[89] The advent of generative AI has also raised regulatory interest more generally, especially with the debates being carried out at the EU level over its draft AI Regulation. Such general regulatory developments would affect developments for AI models across sectors and not

84 Alex Leslie, 'In an Automated AI World, Human Interaction May Be a Premium Service' (disruptive .asia, 8 February 2017) <https://disruptive.asia/human-interaction-premium-service/>.
85 See n 38–40.
86 Philipp Maume, 'Regulating Robo-Advisory' (2019) 1 *Texas International Law Journal* 49.
87 Sironi (n 71); Alison Lui and George William Lamb, 'Artificial Intelligence and Augmented Intelligence Collaboration: Regaining Trust and Confidence in the Financial Sector' (2018) 27 *Information & Communications Technology Law* 267.
88 Dorfleitner and others (n 17).
89 Lui and Lamb (n 85).

just finance. In this way, impending regulatory risk would affect how generative AI may be used in robo-advisory developments.

Further, Allen[90] rightly points out that as artificial intelligence is trained towards deep learning, it is increasingly opaque as to how algorithms reach their 'judgements' or outcomes. There is a need for programmers to consider programming for more self-explication and accountability in order to make algorithmic intelligence more governable.[91]

Should regulation facilitate the development of more sophisticated robo-advisers? This area is likely affected by both general regulatory developments such as the EU AI Regulation in progress as well as specific sectoral regulatory developments. Although EU policy-makers tend to prefer technologically neutral regulation and the functional equivalence approach of 'same risks same rules',[92] new regulatory developments have also been adopted to respond to novel technological developments. For example, the Markets in Financial Instruments Directive's imposition of governance, oversight and responsibilities for algorithmic high-frequency traders shows that specific governance needs were perceived to be needed and a functional regulation of market participants' duties that applied more broadly did not suffice.[93]

Regulatory adaptations are necessary if automated advisory services are developed to interrogate more complex strategies and purport to offer personalised financial planning across a range of needs including debt, insurance, and investment. It is also suggested that regulators proactively engage with innovators on this front, as the management of both technological and legal risks in an *ex ante* manner can benefit retail investors, who are essentially consumers and have often warranted *ex ante* protections.[94]

Further, there is a marked trend amongst retail investors to prefer investments with a sustainable profile or objective.[95] Although the EU is leading in terms of achieving certain standardisations in sustainable labels for investment products to prevent greenwashing,[96] there is a concern as to whether such labels are sufficiently

90 Allen (n 60).

91 Baker and Dellaert (n 78).

92 Commission, 'Communication from the Commission to the European Parliament, the Council, the European Central Bank, the European Economic and Social Committee and the Committee of the Regions FinTech Action plan: For a More Competitive and Innovative European Financial Sector' COM(2018) 0109 final; and for example, Steven Maijoor, 'Cryptoassets: Time to Deliver' (Keynote Speech at 3rd Annual FinTech Conference, Brussels 26 February 2019), <www.esma.europa.eu/document/keynote-steven-maijoor-crypto-assets-time-deliver>.

93 Markets in Financial Instruments Directive, art 17.

94 Iris H-Y Chiu, 'More Paternalism in the Regulation of Consumer Financial Investments? Private Sector Duties and Public Goods Analysis' (2021) 41 *Legal Studies* 657; also John Y Campbell, 'Restoring Rational Choice: The Challenge of Consumer Financial Regulation' (2016) 106 *American Economic Review* 1.

95 Manuel Ammann and others, 'The Impact of the Morningstar Sustainability Rating on Mutual Fund Flows' (2018) <https://ssrn.com/abstract=3068724>.

96 Regulation (EU) 2019/2088 of the European Parliament and of the Council of 27 November 2019 on sustainability-related disclosure in the financial services sector [2019] OJ L317/1; Regulation (EU)

clear in terms of the financial and sustainable objectives, as well as performance yardsticks, in order to meet investor expectations.[97] Gaps in the interpretation and understanding of product objectives, strategies, performance, and risks between product manufacturers, distributors, and investors would make it difficult for investment firms to incorporate sustainably labelled products into their robo-advisory suite, as robo-advisors depend highly on clear categorisations of products and investors. The potential for increased legal risk rises for the incorporation of sustainable investing into robo-advisors, although firms would have to weigh the pros and cons in terms of capturing market share versus being called to account for mis-labelling. On the other hand, the increased sophistication and innovation of robo-advisors to cope with a wider range of products and investor needs is an appealing development. Regulators need to consider the extent of legal risks for such developers, balanced against the need for market discipline when unsuitable products may be offered to retail investors. In this respect, an extent of *ex ante* clarity in regulatory rules may provide an initial balance.

The fear that regulation may unduly stifle innovation is always present, but it is possible for regulators to develop more sophisticated sandbox engagement strategies to test innovations and consider regulatory policy reform.[98] Regulatory adaptations would also be important in the following ways:

(a) Cross-sectoral integration in terms of the rules on financial advice. At the moment, investment advice, which is discussed in this chapter, is distinctly treated from advice in relation to credit, for example.[99] If personalised financial planning to be delivered by machine learning is to be facilitated, the regulatory regime must be able to accommodate more holistically financial recommendations of different types and achieve some integration or streamlining of the standards of advice, as differences would cause frictions and legal risks;
(b) more explicit governance of data access and capabilities, in terms of both human-led governance such as senior management oversight, and risk management capabilities, such as data protection and anti-cyberhacking protection. The Markets in Financial Instruments Directive has already adopted

2020/852 (Taxonomy) of the European Parliament and of the Council of 18 June 2020 on the establishment of a framework to facilitate sustainable investment [2020] OJ L198/13.

97 Dirk A Zetzsche and Linn Anker-Sørensen, 'Regulating Sustainable Finance in the Dark' (2021) <https://papers.ssrn.com/sol3/papers.cfm?abstract_id=3871677>.

98 Dirk A Zetzsche and others, 'Regulating a Revolution: From Regulatory Sandboxes to Smart Regulation' (2017) <https://papers.ssrn.com/sol3/papers.cfm?abstract_id=3018534> on hopes for the regulatory sandbox as a regulatory strategy; and across the EU, see Deirdre Ahern, 'Regulatory Lag, Regulatory Friction and Regulatory Transition as FinTech Disenablers: Calibrating an EU Response to the Regulatory Sandbox Phenomenon' (2021) 22 *European Business Organisations Law Review* 395; but see caution in Iris H-Y Chiu, 'A Rational Regulatory Strategy for Governing Financial Innovation' (2017) 8 *European Journal of Risk Regulation* 7.

99 Suitability for credit is governed by 'responsible lending' which is primarily targeted at affordability assessments, see FCA Handbook CONC 5; MCOB 4.7A.

extensive regulation of the internal organisation and governance of investment firms in relation to matters such as conflicts of interest management,[100] business continuity such as in the face of cyber and operational risks,[101] and considerations of sustainability, as a matter of public interest.[102] Further internalisation of the need to improve on governing AI systems is arguably a step up from compliance with the General Data Protection Regulation;[103]

(c) more explicit governance of automated processes in relation to self-explication and accountability for the generation of choices for the customer, so that suitability reports presented to customers more clearly specify the basis on which choice sets have been generated and their qualifications. The explicability[104] of artificial intelligence systems deploying deep and intelligent machine learning is an important need, as the blackbox of machine learning often obscures why correlations have been made, delivering unexpected results;

(d) more explicit education for customers in relation to their rights, such as cooling-off rights in distance-selling,[105] rights to valuation, exit and redemption, as well as key rights and warnings such as entitlement to disclosure, to dispute resolution, and warnings about the nature of financial products and the need to seek further levels of advice;[106]

(e) more explicit responsibility for senior and responsible individuals in technological risk management[107] and articulating individual responsibility under the FCA's Senior Managers and Certified Persons regime in relation to governing artificial intelligence deployed in their business models. This regime imposes individual liability on senior managers and certified persons in relation to personal conduct and, for senior managers, personal liability for failures in oversight and control.[108] This is to incentivise the taking of personal ownership of responsibilities that have a cascading impact upon a firm's culture and discharge of its regulatory obligations;

[100] Markets in Financial Instruments Directive, art 16.

[101] Ibid. art 21; Commission Delegated Regulation 2017/565.

[102] Impending amendment to ibid. art 21, see ESMA, *Final Report: ESMA's Technical Advice to the European Commission on Integrating Sustainability Risks and Factors in MiFID II* (April 2019), <www.esma.europa.eu/sites/default/files/library/esma35-43-1737_final_report_on_integrating_sustainability_risks_and_factors_in_the_mifid_ii.pdf>.

[103] Also covered in art 21, above.

[104] Alan Dignam, 'Artificial Intelligence: The Very Human Dangers of Dysfunctional Design and Autocratic Corporate Governance' (2019) Queen Mary School of Law Legal Studies Research Paper 314 <https://ssrn.com/abstract=3382342>.

[105] Directive 97/7/EC of the European Parliament and of the Council of 20 May 1997 on the protection of consumers in respect of distance contracts [1997] OJ L144, art 7.

[106] The 'hybrid' advice model, where further human-led advice is sought, arguably complements and overcomes the limitations of robo-advice as it currently stands, see Lui and Lamb (n 85).

[107] Edwards (n 14); Nicole G Iannarone, 'Computer as Confidant: Digital Investment Advice and the Fiduciary Standard' (2018) 93 *Chi Kent L Rev* 141.

[108] Financial Services and Markets Act 2000, s63, 66A, 66B amended in 2012; 2013, FCA Handbook SYSC 23, 24.2, 27.7, COCON and FIT.

(f) consideration for a need to designate Chief Technical Officers as senior managers, and explicate governance responsibilities for technology in the firm, so that individual liability and responsibility can attach; and

(g) rethinking whether the regulatory regime for advice needs to be adapted to accommodate the rise of personalised financial planning. The current framework of suitability limits investment advisers' legal risks with the three categories of information to be elicited and the suitability standard of matching the information profiles that are provided. Moving towards a more fluid or flexible framework for information elicitation could be hazardous for providers as customers could turn around and accuse providers of unsuitable advice due to the perceived differences in weighing any particular informational component. Further, moving towards a more fluid or flexible framework would adversely affect the application of suitability, and it is queried whether we need more elastic legal standards of care in order to understand if advice has been negligently provided.[109] An application of a duty of care would, however, not only apply to the investment firm, which is likely to buy rather than write their own algorithmic software, but also to software providers. The standard of care between the software provider and firm depends on what is candidly disclosed in relation to meeting the firm's needs.[110] However, firms would make a trade-off between risks of software quality and the cost of procuring expensive and perhaps better-developed software. Hence, legal risks would abound for firms in relation to their trade-off decision and the ultimate standard of care they are held to, in relation to customers.[111] In addition or in the alternative, regulators would have to consider whether *ex ante* duties for sophisticated robo-advisors should be introduced, such as the inspection of the code and auditing of the code by recognised experts. This is an approach now taken by the Malta Innovative Technological Arrangements Act.[112] Under the Act, blockchain-based enterprises can register with the Malta Digital Innovation Authority as a recognised business provided certain conditions are complied with. One such condition is that the functionalities and features of the code in the system must be declared by the blockchain business developers and be

[109] The common law duty of care and its application in regulatory law is considered in FCA, *Discussion Paper on a Duty of Care and Potential Alternative Approaches* (July 2018) which concluded without adoption. However a regulatory Consumer Duty is being considered by the FCA which would be supported by cross-cutting principles and high-level outcomes, see FCA, A *New Consumer Duty* (2021) <www.fca.org.uk/publications/consultation-papers/cp21-13-new-consumer-duty>. This formulation however gives rise to questions regarding hierarchies of regulatory law and does not achieve greater clarity in terms of interaction with the common law duty of care.

[110] *Stephenson Blake (Holdings) Ltd. v Streets Heaver Ltd.* [2001] Lloyd's Rep P.N. 44, QBD (OR). The indeterminacy of software vendors' tort liability in the United States is discussed in Michael D Scott, 'Tort Liability for Vendors of Insecure Software: Has the Time Finally Come?' (2008) 67 *Md L Rev* 425.

[111] Ibid.

[112] 'Innovative Technology Arrangements and Services Act' (*Legizlazzjoni Malta*) <www.justiceservices.gov.mt/DownloadDocument.aspx?app=lom&itemid=12874&l=1>.

audited and verified by a 'registered systems auditor'.[113] This measure is aimed at achieving some transparency and assurance of technological 'blackboxes' which regulators and laypersons find inscrutable. Similarly, such *ex ante* regulatory approaches can be relevant for regulating sophisticated robo-advisers. The advisory algorithmic design and its limitations should be disclosed and inspected by regulators, accompanied by third-party auditing, before sophisticated robo-advisers may be authorised to provide services. This can then form the basis for disclosure to customers whose expectations of use are shaped accordingly. Even in such a framework, *ex post* actions and challenges cannot be avoided. However, it would not be the role of regulation to merely facilitate innovation, even if such may be useful, without also providing for risk and liability allocations in the interest of customer protection.

V CONCLUSION

This chapter discusses the robo-advice industry as one of the fastest-growing 'AI'-powered automated services that may be transforming access to investment advice. It argues that ideally, imaginations associated with this industry would include accessible tailor-made personalised financial advice that can be within the grasp of everyone, powered by technological advancements in data analytics and machine learning. To date, the robo-advice industry has settled on low-cost, standardised advice linked to relatively non-complex financial products that are offered to customers, rather than aiming for intelligent and personalised advisory tailoring. This chapter argues that the regulatory regime for investment advice plays a significant part in delineating the boundaries of legal risk for the industry, therefore shaping the design of robo-advice as an innovation. Significant regulatory changes in policy design would be required in order to facilitate innovation towards personalised and automated financial advice, and in this respect there may be a need to start considering how the risks of generative AI in these developments ought to be confronted.

113 Ibid. art 8(4)(b).

21

Competition Law and AI

Thomas Cheng

I INTRODUCTION

The basic premise of this handbook is that the advancement and proliferation of artificial intelligence (AI) are such that the impact of AI on the law can no longer be ignored. Nowhere is this more true than in competition law, where the discussion about the impact of algorithms on the enforcement of competition law has been raging for years since the publication of *Virtual Competition* by Ariel Ezrachi and Maurice Stucke in 2016.[1] The book has sparked a hotly contested debate about the technological feasibility of algorithmic collusion and what to do about it. The topic has taken over journals and conferences. Article after article has been written about it, and it is impossible to attend a conference where not at least a few panels are devoted to issues raised by algorithms.[2] The possible impact of algorithms on competition law enforcement remains to be fully explored. Two topics have garnered the most attention thus far: algorithmic collusion and personalised pricing.

Collusion is widely acknowledged as the cardinal sin in competition law. Per se treatment, or summary condemnation, of price fixing and other collusive behaviour is one of the few issues over which a global consensus exists in a field of law that is otherwise mired in controversy over the appropriate treatment of business practices. This consensus, however, is confined to express collusion, whereby firms collude by reaching an agreement among themselves. The legality of tacit collusion, under which firms achieve a collusive outcome through intelligent adaptation to market

[1] Ariel Ezrachi and Maurice Stucke, *Virtual Competition* (Harvard University Press 2016).

[2] Michal S Gal, 'Algorithms as Illegal Agreements' (2019) 34 *Berkeley Technology Law Journal* 67; Ulrich Schwalbe, 'Algorithms, Machine Learning, and Collusion' (2019) 14 *Journal of Competition Law & Economics* 568; Christophe Samuel Hutchinson, Gulnara Fliurovna Ruchkina and Sergei Guerasimovich Pavlikov, 'Tacit Collusion on Steroids: The Potential Risks for Competition Resulting from the Use of Algorithm Technology by Companies' (2021) 13 *Sustainability* 951; Burton Ong, 'The Applicability of Art.101 TFEU to Horizontal Algorithmic Pricing Practices: Two Conceptual Frontiers' (2021) 52 *International Review of Intellectual Property and Competition Law* 189; Ana Pošćić and Adrijana Martinović, 'EU Competition Law in the Digital Area: Algorithmic Collusion as a Regulatory Challenge' (2021) EU and Comparative Law Issues and Challenges Series (ECLIC) 1016.

conditions and competitors' behaviour without resorting to direct communication, remains unsettled, at least within the academic community.[3] Algorithmic collusion refers to the possibility that the use of algorithms by businesses to set prices for their products and to monitor competitors' pricing practices may facilitate collusion. In its most extreme, and some may argue most fanciful, form, algorithmic collusion encompasses autonomous collusive conduct undertaken by algorithms without any human intervention beyond the initial adoption of the algorithm. Autonomous algorithmic collusion raises difficult questions concerning the attribution of conduct by algorithms to firms and reopens the longstanding debate about the legality of tacit collusion.

Ezrachi and Stucke have been the most fervent crusaders against autonomous algorithmic collusion, arguing that it may signify the end of competition as we know it.[4] Other commentators dispute the technological feasibility of such collusion and assert that algorithms in their present form are incapable of handling the complexities and variability of real-world markets with a multitude of competitors and constantly changing market conditions.[5] Even if these other commentators are correct, there remains the possibility that regulation may be necessary in the future if algorithms acquire greater technological capability and become able to collude among themselves. This chapter will attempt to address the appropriate legal treatment of autonomous algorithmic collusion in light of the current evidence of its technical feasibility and various theoretical considerations.

II ALGORITHMS

A *What Is an Algorithm?*

Algorithms have become increasingly widely adopted by online merchants on both sides of the Atlantic. One-third of the 1,600 best-selling products on Amazon in the United States (US) in 2015 were sold through algorithms.[6] These products were found to have a tendency of having higher prices and sales volume.[7] A European Union (EU) sector study published in 2017 found that two-thirds of online retailers in the

3 Alexander Stewart-Moreno, 'EU Competition Policy: Algorithmic Collusion in the Digital Single Market' (2020) 1 *York Law Review* 49, 67–68; Francisco Beneke and Mark-Oliver Mackenrodt, 'Artificial Intelligence and Collusion' (2019) 50 *International Review of Intellectual Property and Competition Law* 109, 118–119; Guan Zheng and Hong Wu, 'Collusive Algorithms as Mere Tools, Super-Tools or Legal Persons' (2019) 15 *Journal of Competition Law & Economics* 123, 134.

4 Ezrachi and Stucke (n 1) 31.

5 Schwalbe (n 2); Ashwin Ittoo and Nicolas Petit, 'Algorithmic Pricing Agents and Tacit Collusion: A Technological Perspective' in Hervé Jacquemin and Alexandre de Streel (eds), *L'intelligence artificielle et le droit* (Larcier 2017).

6 Le Chen, Alan Mislove and Christo Wilson, 'An Empirical Analysis of Algorithmic Pricing on Amazon Marketplace' *Proceedings of the 25th International Conference on World Wide Web* (2016) 1337.

7 Timo Klein, 'Autonomous Algorithmic Collusion: Q-Learning under Sequential Pricing' (Tinbergen Institute Discussion Paper, 2020) 11 <www.papers.tinbergen.nl/18056.pdf>.

EU use pricing algorithms that automatically adjust their prices based on competitors' prices observed by the algorithm.[8]

Before examining how algorithms may affect competition, it is important to understand what they are. The Organization for Economic Co-operation and Development (OECD) defines an algorithm as 'a sequence of rules that should be performed in an exact order to carry out a certain task. Thus, an algorithm is an instance of logic that generates an output from a given input, whether it is a method to solve a mathematical problem, a food recipe, or a music sheet'.[9] In computer science terms, an algorithm can be understood as 'a programmed procedure for solving a mathematical problem in a finite number of steps that frequently involves repetition of an operation'.[10] According to Ulrich Schwalbe, the two defining features of an algorithm are finiteness and definiteness. Finiteness refers to the fact that 'an algorithm always terminates after a finite number of steps'[11] and definiteness to the fact that 'each step in the algorithm has to be precisely defined and the actions to be carried out must be rigorously and unambiguously specified'.[12] Algorithms hence may not possess the same flexibility, creativity, and inductive analytical ability of the human brain. It 'thinks through' and analyses issues by repeating the same logical steps thousands, if not millions, of times until a pattern or answer emerges. What it lacks in the way of human intelligence, it makes up for with virtually unlimited capacity for repetition and sheer computational speed.

B *Classifications of Algorithms*

There are a number of ways to classify algorithms. They can be categorised by input parameters, by function, by interpretability, and by learning method.[13] In terms of input parameters, an algorithm may vary depending on 'data size, type, or level of detail'.[14]

1 Functional Classification

In terms of function, at least as far as digital retailers are concerned, algorithms can be classified as monitoring, data collection, pricing, customer tracking and personalisation, and signalling algorithms.[15] The most relevant ones for our purpose are

8 European Commission, 'Final Report on the E-Commerce Sector Inquiry' (2017) *COM* 229 5.

9 'Algorithms and Collusion: Competition Policy in the Digital Age' (*OECD*, 2017) 8 <www.oecd.org/competition/algorithms-collusion-competition-policy-in-the-digital-age.htm>.

10 Pieter Van Cleynenbreugel, 'Article 101 TFEU's Association of Undertakings Notion and Its Surprising Potential to Help Distinguish Acceptable from Unacceptable Algorithmic Collusion' (2020) 65 *The Antitrust Bulletin* 423, 426.

11 Schwalbe (n 2) 575.

12 Ibid.

13 Pošćić and Martinović (n 2) 1019.

14 Ibid.

15 Ibid.

monitoring, pricing, and signalling algorithms. Monitoring algorithms, as their name suggests, allow a firm to monitor the market, in particular competitors and customers, through the use of scraping.[16] These algorithms are especially relevant in the context of algorithmic collusion by helping competitors monitor each other's prices and permitting them to retaliate almost instantly against a defecting cartel member.[17]

Pricing algorithms help firms to 'optimise pricing strategies by reacting faster to changes, thereby incurring lower costs than human agents'.[18] The first-generation pricing algorithms were more straightforward and merely followed simple pricing instructions.[19] The second-generation ones are more complex. They do not follow pre-set rules and instead react to changing market conditions.[20] Firms can enter their firm-specific data such as cost structure and distribution channels, and the algorithm will generate a pricing decision.[21] One of the key advantages of pricing algorithms is speed. They dramatically speed up the process of price updates. It used to take weeks if not months for a large brick-and-mortar retailer to change the prices of all the products in a store. An online retailer can now do the same in a matter of seconds.[22]

Signalling algorithms mostly serve a more nefarious purpose. They allow firms to signal their pricing intentions to their competitors. These algorithms help firms collude, either expressly or tacitly, by implementing 'instantaneous price changes in the middle of the night, which allows a company to give a glimpse of its future prices to competitors equipped with sophisticated algorithms capable of decoding these stealthy price announcements without consumers even knowing about it'.[23] Algorithms can pursue price negotiations among themselves through these signals, obviating the need for direct communication.[24] Burton Ong analogises these algorithms as 'the digital equivalents of unilateral price announcements made in offline markets, creating pricing focal points around which all market players converge towards rather than making their own independent pricing decisions'.[25]

2 Classification by Interpretability

In terms of interpretability, the two main types of algorithms are black box and white box algorithms. White box algorithms, also known as descriptive algorithms, are

[16] Hutchinson, Ruchkina and Pavlikov (n 2) 953.
[17] Ong (n 2) 197.
[18] Stewart-Moreno (n 3) 55.
[19] Lea Bernhardt and Ralf Dewenter, 'Collusion by Code or Algorithmic Collusion? When Pricing Algorithms Take Over' (2020) 16 *European Competition Journal* 312, 317.
[20] Ibid.
[21] Ibid. 316.
[22] Ariel Ezrachi and Maurice E Stucke, 'Artificial Intelligence & Collusion: When Computers Inhibit Competition' (2017) 2017 *University of Illinois Law Review* 1775, 1780.
[23] Hutchinson, Ruchkina and Pavlikov (n 2) 957.
[24] Ibid. 955.
[25] Ong (n 2) 197.

> designed as transparent and clear code blocks, in contrast to black-box algorithms which are very much impenetrable. The white-box algorithms are almost completely visible and understandable to humans with suitable knowledge and equipment. Therefore, one can retrace steps leading to a certain price decision.[26]

In contrast, black box algorithms work

> in the same way as human thought processes, which cannot be accurately inferred. The existence of a black box is bound to prevent users from effectively controlling all the outcomes when using machine learning algorithms, and obstruct the courts from determining the intent of users by reverse engineering.[27]

The interpretability of algorithms is highly pertinent to the issue of the attribution of algorithmic conduct to the firm. If it is impossible for the firm deploying an algorithm to understand whether and how the algorithm has learned to collude with other algorithms, which some commentators have suggested would be the case with black box algorithms,[28] an argument can be made that the firm should not be held liable for the subsequent collusion autonomously adopted by algorithms. Some commentators, however, have disputed whether an algorithm can truly be a complete black box indecipherable to its owner.[29] Others have argued that businesses have little incentive to adopt a black box algorithm as they would want to understand the basis for a particular pricing decision 'to obtain better market insights'.[30] In any case, even if an algorithm is truly a black box, there remains an issue of whether the firm should bear responsibility for adopting a black box algorithm that ultimately engages in collusion. It cannot be the case that a firm can outsource its most important competitive function to an entity over which it exercises no control and then claim to be absolved of all responsibility for any subsequent illegal conduct even though it benefits from such conduct.

3 Classification by Learning Method

Lastly, in terms of learning method, the main distinction is between algorithms that are capable of machine learning and those that are not. Adaptive algorithms 'are, essentially, sets of rules that dictate optimal responses to specific contingencies'[31] and 'must therefore be instructed to coordinate on one of many possible outcomes'.[32] They are fixed in their capabilities and cannot improve autonomously. In essence,

26 Bernhardt and Dewenter (n 19) 335.
27 Zheng and Wu (n 3) 129–30.
28 Matteo Courthoud, 'Algorithmic Collusion Detection' (2021) 5 <www.matteocourthoud.github.io/files/Algorithmic_Collusion_Detection.pdf>.
29 Gal (n 2) 108.
30 Beneke and Mackenrodt (n 3) 129.
31 Emilio Calvano and others, 'Algorithmic Pricing: What Implications for Competition Policy?' (2019) 55 *Review of Industrial Organization* 155, 158.
32 Ibid. 159.

these algorithms do what they are programmed to do under specific instructions by the programmer and do not stray beyond them. These algorithms present fewer concerns for the purpose of algorithmic collusion because they 'cannot collude unless they are designed by their programmers to do so'.[33] These algorithms do not follow a competitor's prices or retaliate against a defecting rival unless they are instructed to. The programmer's intent to collude will be plain to see. Collusion facilitated by these algorithms does not require adaptations or novel approaches under existing competition law. They are mostly deployed in the Messenger scenario described by Ezrachi and Stucke, which will be explained subsequently.

Learning algorithms, in contrast, are capable of machine learning, which allows their functions to improve over time. Machine learning is a subfield of artificial intelligence which creates algorithms capable of learning from data, experience, and experimentation.[34] Unlike adaptive algorithms, learning algorithms do not follow static programming instructions but instead 'build a decision process by learning from data inputs'.[35] A key advantage of these algorithms is that they learn through experimentation. They modify themselves over time to improve their performance in light of what they have learned from past experiences.[36] There is no need

> to specify a model of the market, estimate the model, and solve for the optimal strategy. The programmer instead chooses only which variables the strategy should be conditioned on, how frequently the program must experiment, and how much weight to give to more recent experience relative to the cumulated stock of knowledge.[37]

This is especially important in the context of algorithmic collusion because an algorithm that is based on specified models would have much greater difficulty pursuing algorithmic collusion. The programmer would need to build a specific model for the market at issue and adjust the model any time market conditions change. The model would likely be highly sensitive to its assumptions, which significantly limit its applicability and adaptability.

Learning algorithms can be further classified based on the type of machine learning on which it relies, which includes supervised learning, unsupervised learning, and reinforcement learning. Supervised learning refers to machine learning conducted under human supervision. Under supervised learning, 'an algorithm is presented with [labelled] example data and associated target values to predict correct target values after training when confronted with new data'.[38] In contrast, no human supervision is involved in unsupervised learning. Under unsupervised learning, the algorithm 'attempts to identify hidden structures and patterns from unlabelled

33 Ibid.
34 OECD (n 9) 9.
35 Gal (n 2) 78.
36 Schwalbe (n 2) 576.
37 Calvano and others, 'Algorithmic Pricing: What Implications for Competition Policy?' (n 31) 160.
38 Schwalbe (n 2) 576.

data'[39] 'by deducing structures or patterns in the input data to extract general rules'.[40] Reinforcement learning is the most advanced form of machine learning among the three. Under reinforcement learning, an algorithm 'learn[s] to take actions in an unknown but fixed environment to maximize some sort of cumulative reward'.[41] The algorithm is not trained directly to determine the best cause of action in a given environment but is geared 'to maximize the expected sum of discounted future rewards'.[42] The reinforcement learning process does not identify the correct input-output combinations or rectify unsuccessful action.[43] Instead, it emphasises the maximisation of long-term returns through experimentation. Because of the reliance on repeated experimentation, the learning process could be very long. In some of the experimental studies on collusion by a type of reinforcement learning algorithm known as the Q-learning algorithm, it was found that the algorithm would need hundreds of thousands of rounds to settle on the final collusive outcome.[44]

III ALGORITHMIC COLLUSION

A *What Is Collusion?*

Before delving into algorithmic collusion, it is important to clarify the meaning of collusion as both an economic and a legal concept. Collusion involves competitors agreeing with each other to coordinate their competitive actions to raise their profits beyond what would be possible under unfettered competition.[45] The OECD defines collusion as 'a joint profit maximisation strategy put in place by competing firms that might harm consumers'.[46] The three distinguishing features of collusion are hence (1) coordination among competitors that (2) raises their profits to a supra-competitive level, thereby (3) harming consumers. Even though the paramount objective of competition law is to protect consumer welfare, not every kind of collusive conduct that harms consumers is proscribed by competition law. Tacit collusion, which is generally tolerated by competition law, can inflict as much harm on consumers as does an express cartel. An argument can be made that the costs of regulating tacit collusion can outweigh its benefits as doing so would be tantamount to requiring a firm to ignore its competitors' pricing decisions.[47]

39 OECD (n 9) 9.
40 Schwalbe (n 2) 577.
41 Ibid.
42 Ibid.
43 Ibid. 578.
44 Emilio Calvano and others, 'Artificial Intelligence, Algorithmic Pricing, and Collusion' (2020) 110 *The American Economic Review* 3267; Emilio Calvano and others, 'Algorithmic Collusion with Imperfect Monitoring' (2021) 79 *International Journal of Industrial Organization* 102712.
45 Stewart-Moreno (n 3) 51.
46 OECD (n 9) 19.
47 Stewart-Moreno (n 3) 67–68.

Both sides of the Atlantic emphasise that collusion requires an agreement among competitors. In the US, the case law speaks of 'a meeting of minds',[48] 'a unity of purpose or a common design and understanding',[49] or 'a conscious commitment to a common scheme designed to achieve an unlawful objective'.[50] These metaphors are all taken to require that there be evidence of a conscious agreement or mutual understanding among the parties to behave anticompetitively. The EU case law also refers to 'a concurrence of will'.[51] Francisco Beneke and Mark-Oliver Mackenrodt sum up the EU position on agreement succinctly: '[t]he concept of agreement requires an expression or the joint intention of the undertakings to conduct themselves on the market in a specific way'.[52] Again, what sets an agreement under EU law apart from unilateral conduct, which falls outside the scope of Article 101 of the Treaty on the Functioning of the European Union (TFEU), is 'the element of communication between rivals'.[53] This emphasis on the existence of direct communication among the colluding firms to constitute illegal collusion prompted Joseph Harrington to observe that under competition law, '[c]ollusion is not unlawful',[54] 'what is illegal is communication among firms intended to achieve an agreement where an agreement is mutual understanding between firms to limit competition'.[55] Louis Kaplow has echoed this observation.[56]

Economists understand collusion somewhat differently. In a definition adopted by many other economists, Harrington defines collusion as 'when firms use strategies that embody a reward–punishment scheme which rewards a firm for abiding by the supra-competitive outcome and punishes it for departing from it'.[57] To him, the lynchpin of collusion is the reward-punishment scheme. This is because supra-competitive prices can be achieved with or without collusion.[58] The latter happens in an uncompetitive oligopolistic market where firms do not compete vigorously with each other. Prices may exceed the competitive level due to the lack of competitive pressure, even though the competitors are not colluding with each other. A reward-punishment scheme is critical to collusion because it ties 'a firm's current conduct with rival firms' future conduct'.[59] It is this causal relationship, not supra-competitive prices, that defines collusion.[60]

48 *American Tobacco Co v United States*, 328 U.S. 781, 809 (1946).

49 Ibid.

50 *Monsanto Co v Spray-Rite Service Corp*, 465 U.S. 752, 764 (1984).

51 Case T-41/96 Bayer v Commission, ECLI: EU: T2000:242, para. 69.

52 Beneke and Mackenrodt (n 3) 112.

53 Hutchinson, Ruchkina and Pavlikov (n 2) 956.

54 Joseph E Harrington Jr, 'Developing Competition Law for Collusion by Autonomous Artificial Agents' (2019) 14 *Journal of Competition Law & Economics* 331, 340.

55 Ibid. 346.

56 Louis Kaplow, 'Direct versus Communications-Based Prohibitions on Price Fixing' (2011) 3 *Journal of Legal Analysis* 449, 449–50.

57 Harrington Jr (n 53) 336.

58 Ibid. 334.

59 Ibid. 336.

60 Ibid.

It seems that both in law and in economics, collusion is not condemned solely due to its consequences of supra-competitive prices and consumer harm. There must be evidence that the parties to the collusive scheme are in fact acting in concert. There is hesitation to regulate any conduct that inflicts consumer harm because regulation entails its own costs.[61] What is required in law is evidence of direct communication, which signifies an agreement or mutual understanding. Economists focus on the existence of a reward-punishment scheme, which motivates parties to refrain from cutting prices. This implicitly highlights the importance of incentives: what are the reasons and motivations for firms to pursue and sustain supra-competitive prices? This is unsurprising as economics has always focused on incentives for human and firm behaviour.

The slightly different emphases between law and economics indicate their disparate attitudes towards tacit collusion. The insistence on an agreement and evidence of direct communication means that tacit collusion does not generally fall within the prohibition of collusion under competition law. Meanwhile, the existence of a reward-punishment scheme does not require an agreement or direct communication between competitors. Firms may pursue price wars to punish a defecting rival even when there is no express agreement among them. Economists hence do not distinguish between express and tacit collusion. The existence of an express agreement among the colluding firms makes no difference to them.

Economists have identified a number of structural characteristics that are conducive to collusion. These are not pre-requisites for collusion in the sense that collusion is impossible in their absence. But experience has taught us that markets that share these characteristics are more likely to experience collusion. This is important for our purpose because in trying to determine whether and how algorithms facilitate collusion, the focus is on how algorithms render market characteristics even more favourable to collusion. These structural characteristics include (1) a concentrated market with few competitors; (2) symmetric competitors in the sense of similarity in cost structure; (3) homogeneous products; (4) barriers to entry; (5) market transparency; (6) stable demand; and (7) small and frequent purchases by customers.[62]

A concentrated market makes it easier to collude because it is obviously easier to coordinate the conduct of three firms as opposed to thirteen firms, for example. Cost symmetry and product homogeneity mean that competitors are more similar to each other, which improves their chance of reaching terms of coordination. High barriers to entry reduce the likelihood that the collusive scheme will be undermined by a new entrant. A transparent market and stable demand allow the colluding firms to monitor each other's compliance with the collusive scheme more effectively. And

[61] Christopher R Leslie and Mark A Lemley, 'Categorical Analysis in Antitrust Jurisprudence' (2008) 93 *Iowa L Rev* 1207.

[62] Ai Deng, 'What Do We Know about Algorithmic Tacit Collusion?' (2018) 33 *Antitrust* 88, 92.

finally, small and frequent purchases by customers reduce the incentives for the colluding firms to cheat. The colluding firms are presumed to have greater incentives to cheat when customers are prone to make big and lumpy purchases, which means each instance of defection can be highly profitable.

B *What Is Algorithmic Collusion?*

The entire controversy regarding algorithmic collusion is premised on the idea that algorithms facilitate collusion or can even consummate collusion with other algorithms autonomously without the need for human intervention. The latter will be referred to as autonomous algorithmic collusion for the rest of this chapter. The arguments are perhaps more straightforward when algorithms are merely used to facilitate collusion. If human agents agree to collude and algorithms merely facilitate it, the use of algorithms should not affect the legality of the underlying collusive scheme. Just as the law draws no distinction between different means of communication among fellow colluding firms, be it by post, by telegraph, by email, by WhatsApp, or even by human messengers, and condemns all cartels regardless, the fact that a collusive scheme is consummated with the help of algorithms should make no difference. It may also be possible to pursue the reliance on algorithms as a facilitating practice under US antitrust law or as a concerted practice under EU competition law. This would be the most promising route for regulating algorithmic collusion if, for some reason, it is impossible to prosecute the cartel directly.

Autonomous algorithmic collusion, however, is a much thornier issue. Much of the controversy is concerned with its technical feasibility. A number of prominent commentators, such as Ariel Ezrachi, Maurice Stucke, and Michal Gal, have argued that algorithms are well capable of achieving tacit collusion.[63] A number of experimental studies, most notably by Emilio Calvano and co-authors, have demonstrated that algorithms, specifically Q-learning algorithms, are capable of tacit collusion in certain experimental settings after a long period of experimentation.[64] Meanwhile, opponents such as Nicholas Petit, Ashwin Ittoo, and Ulrich Schwalbe maintain that autonomous algorithmic collusion remains a remote possibility and there is no need for competition law to be concerned about it at the moment.[65] Joseph Harrington sums up the issue the best:

> Can [algorithms] learn to collude in a simple setting? Yes. With two [algorithms], two prices, and a fixed environment, simulations show that collusion is more common than competition. Can [algorithms] learn to collude in an actual market setting? We do not know, and I am skeptical of anyone who thinks they know. As we

[63] Ezrachi and Stucke (n 1); Gal (n 2).

[64] Calvano and others, 'Artificial Intelligence, Algorithmic Pricing, and Collusion' (n 44); Calvano and others, 'Algorithmic Collusion with Imperfect Monitoring' (n 44).

[65] Schwalbe (n 2); Ittoo and Petit (n 5).

> cannot dismiss the possibility that [algorithms] are able to learn to collude in actual markets, it is prudent to find an appropriate legal response should they be able to do so.[66]

Even if it can be conclusively shown that under the current state of technology, algorithms are incapable of tacit collusion, advancement in technology may allow them to do so in the near future. There is certainly no harm for the competition law community to anticipate the problem and engage in a thorough discussion to come up with suitable solutions. The competition law community has been too slow to react to the rise of the Big Tech. It should not repeat the same mistake with autonomous algorithmic collusion. The remainder of this chapter will proceed on the premises that there is some plausible, but by no means definitive, evidence that autonomous algorithmic collusion is feasible and that it is fruitful to start the discussion now even in light of the uncertain evidence.

There are two types of autonomous algorithmic collusion. The first type involves direct communication between algorithms, which qualifies it as express collusion and is clearly illegal under US antitrust law and EU competition law. The only issue would be whether such collusion among algorithms should be attributed to the firms deploying them. Studies have shown that some algorithms can learn to communicate with each other in order to achieve their purpose.[67] Other algorithms have the capability to decipher each other's software code, which could arguably constitute another form of algorithmic communication.[68] The case would be particularly strong if there is evidence that the code was intentionally exposed and rendered decipherable to third parties by the firm in the first place.

The second type is accomplished through intelligent and independent adaptation to competitors' conduct by algorithms with no direct communication between them. This is algorithmic tacit collusion. Tacit collusion is generally taken to be legal under both US antitrust law and EU competition law. This, however, has not deterred some commentators from advocating a different approach for algorithmic tacit collusion on a variety of grounds. The question is whether a change in the current approach to tacit collusion is called for specifically in the algorithmic context.

The foregoing discussion suggests that there are three main dimensions along which to analyse and understand algorithmic collusion: the existence of direct communication among the colluding firms or algorithms, the degree of algorithmic autonomy, and the extent of collusive human intent. If there is evidence of direct communication among the colluding firms or algorithms, there is little dispute regarding the legality of the conduct. If the collusive outcome is achieved through

66 Harrington Jr (n 53) 346.

67 Schwalbe (n 2) 596; Calvano and others, 'Algorithmic Pricing: What Implications for Competition Policy?' (n 31) 166.

68 Gal (n 2) 87.

intelligent and independent adaptations by the competitors, absent any direct communication, the conduct constitutes tacit collusion and is currently regarded as legal.

The degree of algorithmic autonomy runs the gamut, from almost complete autonomy with practically no human involvement after the initial selection and deployment of a particular algorithm to minimal autonomy where the algorithm is a mere instrument to consummate a collusive scheme concocted by human agents. The legality of the collusive conduct presents no novel issues where the degree of algorithmic autonomy is minimal. It is not much more than a good old human cartel with a sprinkle of algorithms on top. Where the degree of algorithmic autonomy is strong or almost complete, the issue arises as to whether the algorithm's conduct can be fairly attributed to the firm. It would not be possible to hold the firm liable for the collusive scheme absent attribution if the scheme is autonomously consummated by algorithms unless strict liability is contemplated for any illegal conduct subsequently perpetrated by the algorithm after it has been created and adopted. This would be tantamount to imposing a duty on firms to take action to prevent algorithms from entering into a collusive scheme later on.

The degree of collusive human intent, which can be viewed as a corollary of the degree of algorithmic autonomy, can range from a complete absence of such intent to the presence of a full collusive intent. There is a complete absence of collusive human intent in the case of autonomous algorithmic collusion, where the human agents who adopt the algorithms have no intention that the algorithms will collude. In fact, they may have no knowledge of the algorithmic collusion. There is full collusive intent where the collusive scheme is intended by and consummated among human agents, and algorithms merely play a facilitative role.

In general, it is easier to condemn a collusive scheme where evidence of direct communication is found. Both sides of the Atlantic require the existence of an agreement in order to do so and an agreement can be readily proven where direct communication among the colluding firms can be shown. The lack of evidence of direct communication may require us to infer the existence of an agreement on other bases. Condemnation is easier to justify in the presence of collusive human intent. A collusive agreement can be more readily established when there is evidence of an intent to collude. Such an intent will be harder to find if there is a high degree of algorithmic autonomy, meaning that the collusive scheme is largely the result of the autonomous decisions made by algorithms. Where algorithmic autonomy is almost complete and the extent of human involvement is minimal, prohibition is only possible either by holding the algorithms directly liable, which would necessitate the conferment of legal personhood on algorithms as advocated by some commentators,[69] or attributing the conduct by algorithms to the firm deploying them. This of course would only be possible if the underlying conduct is deemed to be illegal, which would require a resolution of the debate about the legality of tacit collusion.

69 Zheng and Wu (n 3) 151.

C *Ezrachi and Stucke's Classification*

Any discussion about the legal treatment of algorithmic collusion ought to begin with the classification put forward by Ezrachi and Stucke in *Virtual Competition*. They describe four scenarios of algorithmic collusion: Messenger, Hub and Spoke, Predictable Agent, and Digital Eye. Messenger 'concerns the use of computers to execute the will of humans in their quest to collude and restrict competition'.[70] Under this scenario, human agents have reached an agreement to collude and use algorithms to assist in the execution of the collusive scheme. The existence of collusion among human agents is not in doubt. There is express collusion, which should entail direct communication among the colluding firms and indicate the existence of collusive human intent. The degree of algorithmic autonomy is minimal. The collusive scheme is not consummated by algorithms, which are used as mere instrumentalities. It is perhaps a bit of a misnomer to call this algorithmic collusion. This is merely algorithm-assisted human collusion. As suggested earlier, the involvement of algorithms does not alter the nature of the underlying conduct, and the illegality of the collusion is undisputed.

Hub and Spoke refers to a situation where 'competitors use the same (or a single) algorithm to determine the market price or react to market changes. In this scenario, the common algorithm, which traders use as a vertical input, leads to horizontal alignment'.[71] The key feature of an algorithmic hub and spoke cartel is the use of a common pricing algorithm to determine the prices charged by each cartel member.[72] This sets it apart from the Messenger scenario where the algorithm merely executes the orders of a human agent.[73]

The degree of algorithmic autonomy is higher because algorithms are no longer deployed as mere instrumentalities to execute human will. The extent of human involvement is probably no more than the choice of the common algorithm, but it should still exceed that in the case of autonomous algorithmic collusion. In hub and spoke arrangements, the human agents may have intended the hub algorithm to pass on information to each other and to help coordinate pricing among them. Price coordination may not be the completely unintended outcome, as in the case of tacit collusion, at least as in the case of Digital Eye.

The existence of direct communication cannot be taken for granted, and thus the existence of a collusive scheme needs to be established on other bases. In many cases, the parties may have intentionally chosen the same algorithm with full awareness of each other's choices. In the context of a hub and spoke arrangement, the case law on both sides of the Atlantic tends to assume that the 'spoke' parties to

[70] Ezrachi and Stucke (n 22) 1782.
[71] Ibid. 1787.
[72] Rob Nicholls and Brent Fisse, 'Concerted Practices and Algorithmic Coordination: Does the New Australian Law Compute?' (2018) 26 *Competition & Consumer Law Journal* 82, 95.
[73] Ibid.

the arrangement communicate indirectly through the hub. Such communication is assumed if it can be shown that the spokes are all aware that they are part of the arrangement and coordinated prices are observed among the spokes. Illegality can be quite easily established if it can be shown that 'there is an intent to achieve prohibited conduct, that is, if competitors act with knowledge about the potential prohibited conduct'.[74] As former Commissioner of the US Federal Trade Commission Maureen Ohlhausen wittily observes, 'If it isn't ok for a guy named Bob to do it, then it probably isn't ok for an algorithm to do it either'.[75] The case law on both sides of the Atlantic such as *Interstate Circuit*,[76] *Toys 'R Us*,[77] and the *Apple e-books* case[78] in the US and *Eturas*[79] in the EU firmly establish the illegality of algorithmic hub and spoke arrangements where the parties involved have knowledge of each other's involvement.

The third and fourth scenarios described by Ezrachi and Stucke, Predictable Agent and Digital Eye, are both premised on tacit collusion. Both scenarios are likely to involve learning algorithms. Adaptive algorithms are unable to collude autonomously. There are, however, fine distinctions between them. Both scenarios constitute tacit collusion in the sense that an agreement or understanding among the parties is absent. Under Predictable Agent, firms adopt their own algorithms independently, but with an awareness of competitors' adoption of similar algorithms.[80] Ezrachi and Stucke are careful to emphasise that the firms have not agreed and do not intend to collude.[81] In fact, they are presumed not even to have agreed to adopt similar algorithms. Ezrachi and Stucke are not clear as to whether the firms are aware of the collusive potential of their adoption of similar algorithms. Under the appropriate market conditions, the adoption of algorithms, especially similar ones, by most firms in the market may facilitate tacit collusion and bring about higher prices.[82] And it may be possible to pursue the adoption of colluding algorithms as facilitating practices. As Ezrachi and Stucke observe, the Predictable Agent scenario 'raises challenging questions as to the ability to condemn the creation or strengthening of conscious parallelism through a sophisticated algorithm'.[83]

Given that both Predictable Agent and Digital Eye are premised on tacit collusion, it may not be immediately obvious how they differ from each other. According to Ezrachi and Stucke, under Digital Eye, competitors adopt algorithms that are set

74 Pošćić and Martinović (n 2) 1025.

75 Maureen Ohlhausen, 'Should We Fear the Things That Go Beep in the Night?' (23 May 2017) 10 <www.ftc.gov/system/files/documents/public_statements/1220893/ohlhausen_-_concurrences_5-23-17.pdf>.

76 *Interstate Circuit v United States*, 306 U.S. 208 (1939).

77 *Toys 'R' Us, Inc v Federal Trade Commission*, 221 F.3d 928 (7th Cir. 2000).

78 *United States v Apple Inc*, 791 F.3d 290 (2d Cir. 2015).

79 Case 74/14, *'Eturas' UAB v Lietuvos Respublikos konkurencijos taryba* ECLI:EU:C:2016:42.

80 Ezrachi and Stucke (n 22) 1783.

81 Ibid. 1790.

82 Ibid. 1789.

83 Ibid. 1795.

with the goal of profit maximisation.[84] The algorithms (here they are most likely to be reinforcement learning algorithms) independently determine through experimentation and machine learning that consciously parallel pricing behaviour leads to the highest profit and adopt this course of action.[85] Ezrachi and Stucke emphasise that tacit coordination here is 'the outcome of evolution, self-learning, and independent machine execution'.[86]

One possible distinction between Predictable Agent and Digital Eye may seem to be that under the former, algorithms improve the suitability of market conditions for tacit collusion, while the Digital Eye scenario is not premised on facilitation of tacit collusion at all. Algorithms simply get on with parallel pricing behavior. This distinction, however, may be difficult to draw in reality because pricing algorithms that achieve parallel pricing probably also improve market conditions for tacit collusion. It is very difficult to know where facilitation of collusion ends and actual tacit collusion begins. It is also not clear how useful this distinction is. Under Predictable Agent, after having improved market conditions for tacit collusion, it is the very same algorithms that take advantage of these conditions to achieve parallel pricing. The meaningful distinction between Predictable Agent and Digital Eye hence cannot be the different roles played by the algorithms to achieve the collusive outcome.

Ezrachi and Stucke also suggest that Digital Eye 'increases the complexity of identifying intent and distinguishing between the operation of the machine and that of its designer'.[87] The main difference between Predictable Agent and Digital Eye as far as intent is concerned seems to be that under the former, competitors are aware of each other's adoption of similar algorithms that could lead to a collusive result, whereas under the latter, the decision to adopt an algorithm seems to be made entirely independently. This perhaps provides a more meaningful distinction between the two scenarios. What makes Predictable Agent more suspect is the awareness on the part of the human agents of the collusive potential of the adoption of the same algorithm. Given that consciously parallel pricing behaviour results under both scenarios, there is no difference in the role of the algorithm that can possibly justify disparate legal treatment of the two scenarios. In contrast, the degree of human awareness of the likelihood of collusive outcome may have a bearing on two legal issues: whether it is possible to find an agreement among the firms to adopt similar algorithms and whether it is justified to attribute the algorithm's actions to the firms.

The lack of agreement among the firms under both Predictable Agent and Digital Eye suggests that there is no direct or probably any kind of communication among the firms, unless the adoption of similar algorithms can be treated as signalling. Under Predictable Agent, if the firms have no awareness that their parallel adoption

84 Ibid. 1783.
85 Ibid.
86 Ibid. 1795.
87 Ibid. 1797.

of similar algorithms may facilitate collusion, there will be no collusive human intent. And since firms adopt algorithms in order to maximise profit under Digital Eye, they are clearly devoid of a collusive intent. The degree of algorithmic autonomy under both Predictable Agent and Digital Eye is higher than that in the previous two scenarios because with tacit collusion, it is the intelligent adaptation by algorithms to each other's actions that results in collusion. The algorithms are not instructed by human agents to take the actions that may ultimately result in tacit collusion, be it monitoring of rivals, retaliating against defectors, or simply setting profit-maximising prices.

D *Autonomous Algorithmic Collusion*

The illegality of Messenger and Hub and Spoke is not in doubt. Thus, much of the debate concerning algorithmic collusion focuses on Predictable Agent and Digital Eye, both instances of autonomous algorithmic collusion. The controversy regarding autonomous algorithmic collusion in some ways resurrects the longstanding debate, at least within academic circles, about the legality of tacit collusion.

1 Traditional Debate about Tacit Collusion

The longstanding debate about tacit collusion harkens back to Donald Turner and Richard Posner, who actually later changed his views about the issue. Turner believes that tacit collusion or conscious parallelism is the natural and inevitable consequence of an oligopolistic market with high market transparency and homogeneous product.[88] In such a market, firms will naturally refrain from price cutting and follow each other's price increases to reach supra-competitive prices. For the sake of consistency, tolerance of monopolistic pricing means that competition law should also condone tacit collusion.[89] Moreover, a prohibition of tacit collusion would require firms to behave irrationally and avoid maximising profit.[90]

Richard Posner asserts that tacit collusion should be prohibited just the same as express collusion. Both constitute an illegal agreement under the Sherman Act as they entail a meeting of the minds or a mutual understanding.[91] What separates tacit collusion from express collusion is only a matter of evidence. Express collusion can be proved by documentary evidence, while tacit collusion relies on economic evidence.[92] According to Posner, 'a seller communicates his 'offer' by restricting

88 Donald Turner, 'The Definition of Agreement under the Sherman Act: Conscious Parallelism and Refusals to Deal' (1962) 75 *Harvard Law Review* 655, 665.

89 Ibid. 668.

90 Ibid. 669.

91 Richard A Posner, *Antitrust Law* (2nd edn, The University of Chicago Press 2021) 94.

92 Richard A Posner, 'Oligopoly and the Antitrust Laws: A Suggested Approach' (1969) 21 *Stanford Law Review* 1562, 1576.

output, and the offer is 'accepted' by the actions of his rivals in restricting their outputs as well'.[93] It is fair to say that the courts have largely taken Turner's side of the debate. Justice Stephen Breyer, when he was still a judge on the United States Court of Appeals for the First Circuit, asserts that courts have upheld conscious parallelism 'not because such pricing is desirable (it is not), but because it is close to impossible to devise a judicially enforceable remedy for 'interdependent' pricing. How does one order a firm to set its prices without regard to the likely reactions of its competitors?'[94]

This debate was recently rekindled by Louis Kaplow, who asserts that the current approach to the concept of agreement under Section 1 of the Sherman Act is misguided. It focuses on the form of the agreement based on the existence of communication between firms instead of a more economic approach to collusion under oligopoly theory.[95] He notes that 'successful interdependent coordination that produces supra-competitive pricing leads to essentially the same economic consequences regardless of the particular manner of interactions that generate this outcome'.[96] The same amount of consumer harm results regardless of whether the collusion is express or tacit. He also dismisses the commonly invoked argument that it is difficult to craft an appropriate remedy for tacit collusion because courts would need to either set prices for firms or enjoin them to deviate from the profit-maximising price. He retorts that what deters firms from infringing the law is not injunctive relief but the expectation of punishment in the form of fines and damages awards.[97] It is important, however, to point out that Kaplow himself stops short of advocating the outright prohibition of tacit collusion, arguing that 'the question is an empirical one in which the prevalence of social harm under the various standards must be compared as well as their costs of administration'.[98]

It was said earlier that both Predictable Agent and Digital Eye are premised on tacit collusion. There is, however, an important qualitative difference between them. Under Predictable Agent, firms adopt a similar algorithm with the awareness and perhaps the expectation that competitors will follow suit. And if the firms are aware that the algorithms may improve market conditions to facilitate tacit collusion, one can argue that the intent of the firms is not the purely innocuous intent to maximise profit. This is different from the archetypal tacit collusion that Turner, Posner, and Kaplow have in mind, where firms may truly only intend to maximise profit. They are independently adopting a course of conduct that they know competitors are likely to follow and that may facilitate tacit collusion. A distinction is

93 Ibid.

94 *Clamp-All Corp v Cast Iron Soil Pipe Institute*, 851 F.2d 478, 484 (1st Cir. 1988).

95 Kaplow (n 55) 449–450.

96 Louis Kaplow, 'On the Meaning of Horizontal Agreements in Competition Law' (2011) 99 *California Law Review* 683, 686.

97 Kaplow (n 55) 475.

98 Ibid. (n 95) 814.

thus drawn between setting a profit-maximising price, which is part and parcel of every business, and pursuing conduct that facilitates collusion, which a firm is by no means compelled to do. Their awareness that their action may facilitate tacit collusion taints their intent and bolsters the case for applying closer scrutiny of the Predictable Agent.

2 What Is Different about Algorithmic Tacit Collusion?

Digital Eye requires us to directly confront the issue of the legality of tacit collusion. This author is sympathetic to Posner's and Kaplow's arguments in support of prohibiting tacit collusion. Express and tacit collusion can inflict the same consumer harm. Moreover, the current approach to tacit collusion, with its focus on the lack of direct communication between the parties, is overly formalistic, which is inconsistent with the emphasis of substance over form under competition law. Without trying to settle the debate in the offline context, this author believes that there are good arguments for taking a stricter stance against algorithmic tacit collusion for a variety of reasons. First, one of the premises for treating tacit collusion leniently in the offline context is that it should be relatively rare. As noted by Beneke and Mackenrodt, '[m]ost scholars circumscribe this to a rare set of circumstances that include highly concentrated industries, homogeneous goods, symmetric cost structures across firms, and price transparency, among others'.[99]

A number of commentators have observed that algorithms may allow collusion in a wider variety of market structures.[100] There are reasons to believe that the immense and ever-improving technical capabilities of algorithms to monitor rivals' prices, to signal pricing intentions to other algorithms, and to enact frequent price changes will turn autonomous algorithmic collusion into a more common phenomenon. Tacit collusion may no longer be limited to highly concentrated oligopolistic markets. It can also 'be achieved with a large number of participants. The increased transparency of the internet, the high reaction speed of various IT-systems and algorithm-based price adjustments are thereby all decisive factors that enable rivals to tacitly collude on markets with many market players'.[101]

Algorithms have been said to facilitate the following critical aspects of tacit collusion: reaching terms of coordination among firms;[102] rapid detection and retaliation, hence reducing the incentive to cheat;[103] communication among competitors;[104]

[99] Beneke and Mackenrodt (n 3) 118.

[100] Peter Georg Picht and Gaspare Tazio Loderer, 'Framing Algorithms: Competition Law and (Other) Regulatory Tools' (2019) 42 *World Competition* 391, 406; Kaylynn Noethlich, 'Artificially Intelligent and Free to Monopolize: A New Threat to Competitive Markets around the World' (2019) 34 *American University International Law Review* 923, 940; Ong (n 2) 205; Zheng and Wu (n 3) 142.

[101] Giulia Sonderegger, 'Algorithms and Collusion' (2021) 42 *European Competition Law Review* 213, 216.

[102] Gal (n 2) 82.

[103] OECD (n 9) 21, 27.

[104] Gal (n 2) 87.

and the elimination of irrational behaviour to prevent unnecessary disruption to the collusive scheme.[105] Algorithms can communicate in myriad ways. They can engage in repeated rounds of price signalling until a price is agreed upon.[106] They can try to decipher each other's software codes.[107] In fact, it has been said that 'neural networks can indeed learn how to encrypt and decrypt messages, as well as how to apply those operations selectively to ensure goals related to confidentiality'.[108] It has been argued that algorithms can also create new hurdles for collusion.[109] Yet, on balance, there are good reasons to believe that algorithms should make tacit collusion more prevalent and more attainable. While we may have condoned tacit collusion in the brick-and-mortar world on the ground of its rarity, the same rationale may no longer apply once technology is sufficiently advanced to popularise algorithmic tacit collusion.

One may object to the foregoing conclusion, arguing that firms should not be held accountable if the algorithm learns on its own to engage in tacit collusion with no human involvement. This argument would have even greater validity in the case of black box algorithms, whose decision-making rationale and processes cannot be deciphered by human agents. After all, how can one be held liable for an action that the person is in no position to prevent? An analogy could be drawn between an algorithm and an employee. A firm can equally argue that if an employee decides on her own to engage in collusion without being instructed by her superiors to do so, the firm should not be held liable. A firm equally has no means to know what an employee intends to do until after the fact if she has never articulated her intentions. Competition law, however, has always held firms liable for their employee's conduct regardless of whether the employee is properly authorised to act for the firm.[110]

By the same logic, firms should be held liable for their algorithm's conduct. Moreover, firms can no longer claim to be unaware of the collusive potential of algorithms in light of the increasing amount of literature on the issue. They have been forewarned. They should be expected to monitor their algorithms closely. It hardly makes sense that consumers should be made to suffer the adverse consequences of inadequately supervised algorithms while firms enjoy their many efficiencies and advantages. If algorithms cannot be properly constrained from harming consumers, it is apt to question whether firms should be allowed to use them.[111] While an

[105] Noethlich (n 99) 941.

[106] Ariel Ezrachi and Maurice E Stucke, 'Sustainable and Unchallenged Algorithmic Tacit Collusion' (2020) 17 *Northwestern Journal of Technology and Intellectual Property* 217, 246.

[107] Gal (n 2) 87.

[108] Schwalbe (n 2) 596.

[109] Ibid. 574; OECD (n 9) 23; Gal (n 2) 92.

[110] Alison Jones, Brenda Sufrin and Niamh Dunne, *EU Competition Law: Text, Cases, and Materials* (Oxford University Press 2019) 166.

[111] Harrington Jr (n 53) 350.

outright ban of such algorithms may be a step too far, firms should be held accountable for collusion autonomously consummated by their algorithms when such a possibility is known.

IV CONCLUSION

Algorithmic collusion will probably continue to be hotly debated in the competition law community for years to come. Until the controversy regarding the technical feasibility of autonomous algorithmic collusion is settled once and for all, there will be commentators who insist that such collusion remains the stuff of science fiction, and that there is no need for competition law to pay heed to it. Such an attitude, however, is retrogressive, and competition law should take a pro-active stance towards algorithmic collusion. If it is made clear to programmers that autonomous algorithmic collusion will not be tolerated and that the indecipherable nature of black-box algorithms will not be accepted as a defence, algorithm designers will have the appropriate incentives to create and hone their algorithms to minimise the possibility of autonomous algorithmic collusion. Given the technical complexity of understanding an algorithm's decision-making process, the best way to minimise algorithmic collusion remains to tackle it at the design stage instead of trying to go after it once suspected collusion arises. This may require ex ante regulation as opposed to ex post enforcement under competition law.

22

Sales Law and AI

Sean Thomas

I INTRODUCTION

The extent of legal change as a result of developments in the technologies of artificial intelligence (AI) will depend on the nature and value of those technologies.[1] Although there are strong arguments that the law need not change,[2] there are also suggestions that legal change may be useful,[3] not least because AI already is valuable and growing in reach and relevance.[4] Its capacity for data capture, data assimilation and manipulation, and dynamic response capabilities generate considerable commercial opportunities. It is essential to recognise that AI will be, as it currently is, integrated into goods (which may also be integrated with buildings and residences).[5] This chapter thus focuses on this integration and interconnection between AI and tangible things.

A commentary on AI and law goes back at least fifty years,[6] but there remains much to do to 'develop a broad-based body of law',[7] both in the sense of being able to deal with AI issues across multiple areas of law and in avoiding a single panacea such as

1 Curtis EA Karnow, 'Foreword' in Woodrow Barfield and Ugo Pagallo (eds), *Research Handbook on the Law of Artificial Intelligence* (Edward Elgar 2018) xviii, xix.

2 Ryan Abbott, *The Reasonable Robot: Artificial Intelligence and the Law* (Cambridge University Press 2020); Ian Walden and Theodora A Christou, *A Report for the World Bank on Legal and Regulatory Implications of Disruptive Technologies in Emerging Markets* (June 2018) 7 <https://ssrn.com/abstract=3230674>.

3 Jacob Turner, *Robot Rules: Regulating Artificial Intelligence* (Palgrave MacMillan 2019) 40–42.

4 See, for example, Michael Chui and others, 'Notes from the AI Frontier: Applications and Value of Deep Learning' (17 April 2018) <www.mckinsey.com/featured-insights/artificial-intelligence/notes-from-the-ai-frontier-applications-and-value-of-deep-learning>. In the five years since, this point has become even more true: see, for example <www.europarl.europa.eu/news/en/headlines/society/20200918STO87404/artificial-intelligence-threats-and-opportunities>.

5 Cf Sean Thomas, 'Smart Homes' in Sue Farran, Russell Hewiston and Adam Ramshaw (eds), *Modern Studies in Property Law: Volume XI* (Hart Publishing 2021) ch 9.

6 Cf Bruce G Buchanan and Thomas E Headrick, 'Some Speculation about Artificial Intelligence and Legal Reasoning' (1970) 23 *Stanford L Rev* 40.

7 Woodrow Barfield, 'Towards a Law of Artificial Intelligence' in Barfield and Pagallo (eds), *Research Handbook on the Law of AI* (n 1) 2, 8.

data-protection.[8] Moreover, whilst AI and legal literature are increasing rapidly, there is an apparent lacuna in the range of responses to AI developments. The overwhelming majority of academic and policy literature focuses on the *use* of AI, whilst ignoring the *disposition* of AI. This is especially so with recent institutional responses, such as the Proposed EU Artificial Intelligence Act of April 2021.[9] Recently, the UN has actually called for a moratorium on AI:[10] this chapter will not engage with that suggestion. However, it is interesting to note the constant reference in that call to the 'sale' of AI. What could this mean? What transactional regime(s) attend to commercial dispositions of AI? How should we classify, structure, and deal with such transactions? Are they sales or something else? What are the implications of the fact that AI is embedded into tangible things? As Karnow asked: '[i]ndeed, with *embedded* AI (likely to be a widespread use) what *is* the product or service – the software or the larger item?'[11]

This is not a complete lacuna: there are some analyses of issues concerning the commercial disposition of AI systems,[12] but the area remains 'something of a conundrum'.[13] A search for 'sale' in the journal Artificial Intelligence and Law reveals 85 results, though unsurprisingly only a very small number of results are concerned with sale as ordinarily understood.[14] There are some examples from the policy literature which allude to the importance of an appropriate commercial transactional regime, but they are limited in scope and number.[15] There is of course a vast array of literature concerning the commercialisation of software in the context of IP law (primarily copyright, but other IP rights may well be relevant),[16] but it remains the

[8] See, for example, Vagelis Papakonstantinou and Paul de Hert, 'Post GDPR EU Laws and Their GDPR Mimesis. DGA, DSA, DMA and the EU Regulation of AI' (1 April 2021) <www.europeanlawblog.eu/2021/04/01/post-gdpr-eu-laws-and-their-gdpr-mimesis-dga-dsa-dma-and-the-eu-regulation-of-ai/>.

[9] European Commission, 'Proposal for a Regulation of the European Parliament and of the Council Laying Down Harmonised Rules on Artificial Intelligence (Artificial Intelligence Act) and Amending Certain Union Legislative Acts' (COM/2021/206 final, 21 April 2021). For the current state of this proposal, see <www.europarl.europa.eu/news/en/headlines/society/20230601STO93804/eu-ai-act-first-regulation-on-artificial-intelligence>. The EU Parliament's proposed ammendements are at <www.europarl.europa.eu/doceo/document/TA-9-2023-0236_EN.html>. See also <www.artificialintelligenceact.eu/>.

[10] See <www.news.un.org/en/story/2021/09/1099972>.

[11] Karnow, 'Foreword' (n 1) xxii.

[12] Leigh Smith, 'What Lenders Need to Consider When Taking Security over Artificial Intelligence Software' (2018) 33 *Butterworths Journal of International Banking and Financial Law* 364; Shawn Bayern, 'Artificial Intelligence and Private Law' in Barfield and Pagallo, *Research Handbook on the Law of AI* (n 1) 144; Stacy-Ann Elvy, 'The Artificially Intelligent Internet of Things and Article 2 of the Uniform Commercial Code' in Barfield and Pagallo (eds), *Research Handbook on the Law of AI* (n 1) 560.

[13] Barfield, 'Towards a Law of Artificial Intelligence' (n 7) 28.

[14] See, for example, John Bagby and Tracy Mullen, 'Legal Ontology of Sales Law Application to Ecommerce' (2007) 15 *Artificial Intelligence and Law* 155.

[15] UK AI Council, *AI Roadmap* (6 January 2021) 24 <www.gov.uk/government/publications/ai-roadmap>; European Parliament resolution of 20 October 2020 on intellectual property rights for the development of artificial intelligence technologies (2020/2015(INI)) <www.europarl.europa.eu/doceo/document/TA-9-2020-0277_EN.html>.

[16] See, for example, Andrea Tosato, 'Secured Transactions and IP Licenses: Comparative Observations and Reform Suggestions' (2018) 81(1) *Law & Contemporary Problems* 155; Sean Thomas, 'Security Interests over Intellectual Property: Proposals for Reform' (2017) 37 *Legal Studies* 214.

case that certain specific issues concerning AI and commercial law, in the sense of transactions where the AI is the object of the transaction and is not entirely disembodied, are under-analysed.

Section II outlines the nature and uses of AI, and considers the need for clarity about the nature of owning AIs. The possibility of treating AI as goods will be analysed in Section III. Whilst there are some strong reasons for treating software, and AI in particular, as goods, the strength of tradition as to the tangible/intangible divide likely means such treatment may need to be constructed in a sui generis form. Thus, in Section IV, I focus on two core aspects that need addressing: the nature of ownership and its relationship to IP concepts of fair use and exhaustion; and rights to repair.

II WHAT IS AI?

It is not clear what AI actually is.[17] There is no standard definition in law or indeed even in the technological fields of AI (computer science, engineering, etc.).[18] There is thus no attempt here to define AI as such.[19] What we can do is simply refer to the recent Proposed EU Artificial Intelligence Act, which sets out in recital (6) of the preamble the following:

> The notion of AI system should be clearly defined to ensure legal certainty, while providing the flexibility to accommodate future technological developments. The definition should be based on the key functional characteristics of the software, in particular the ability, for a given set of human-defined objectives, to generate outputs such as content, predictions, recommendations, or decisions which influence the environment with which the system interacts, be it in a physical or digital dimension. AI systems can be designed to operate with varying levels of autonomy and be used on a stand-alone basis or as a component of a product, irrespective of whether the system is physically integrated into the product (embedded) or serve the functionality of the product without being integrated therein (non-embedded). The definition of AI system should be complemented by a list of specific techniques and approaches used for its development, which should be kept up-to-date in the light of market and technological developments.[20]

[17] See, for example, M Mowbray, 'Moral Status for Malware! The Difficulty of Defining Advanced Artificial Intelligence' (2021) 30(3) *Cambridge Quarterly of Healthcare Ethics* 517.

[18] Barfield, 'Towards a Law of Artificial Intelligence' (n 7) 21.

[19] Cf Abbott, *Reasonable Robot* (n 2) 22: 'an algorithm or machine capable of completing tasks that would otherwise require cognition. Cognition refers to mental capabilities and the proves of acquiring knowledge and understanding through thought. This is a deliberately broad definition of AI that focuses on what it does rather than how it is designed.' See also Turner, *Robot Rules* (n 3) 15, aiming 'to arrive at a definition which is suited to the legal regulation of AI', which is (at 16): 'Artificial Intelligence Is the Ability of a Non-natural Entity to Make [autonomous] Choices by an Evaluative Process'.

[20] For a useful visualisation by Professor Ronald Leenes, see <www.threadreaderapp.com/thread/1413139322396581903.html/> (8 July 2021).

This is followed by Proposed Article 3(1):

> 'artificial intelligence system' (AI system) means software that is developed with one or more of the techniques and approaches listed in Annex I and can, for a given set of human-defined objectives, generate outputs such as content, predictions, recommendations, or decisions influencing the environments they interact with.[21]

Central to the operation of AI, of whatever form, is the use of algorithms to perform the necessary calculations at sufficient speed;[22] thus, it seems obvious then that AI is software.[23] However, some reflection on this point generates problems. Certainly, there are instances in the literature where AI appears to be considered as a chattel: this issue is discussed further later.[24] Prior to that, it is worth outlining two aspects of AI which differentiate AI-software from 'normal' software.

First is the nature of AI compared to 'normal' software. Software is fixed, and it is that fixed form which is essential to software's copyrightability (copyright of course being available not for ideas, but for such ideas that are given form). By contrast, AI is dynamic, mutable, complex, and fluid. An AI might generate its own ways of determining the extent of its own uncertainty and then reducing that uncertainty.[25] Furthermore, AI self-modification may also occur in ways humans cannot understand.[26] The second point of difference concerns replication. Digital transmission necessarily involves replication, resulting in a true copy.[27] However, if an AI is learning, the point of replication will constitute a breaking-point. One

[21] The listed techniques and approaches in Annex I are: '(a) Machine learning approaches, including supervised, unsupervised and reinforcement learning, using a wide variety of methods including deep learning; (b) Logic- and knowledge-based approaches, including knowledge representation, inductive (logic) programming, knowledge bases, inference and deductive engines (symbolic), reasoning and expert systems; (c) Statistical approaches, Bayesian estimation, search and optimisation methods.' This definition is arguably much more attractive than the rather simplistic version, adopted from Department for Business, Energy and Industrial Strategy, *Industrial Strategy: Building a Britain Fit for the Future* (November 2017) 37 <www.gov.uk/government/uploads/system/uploads/attachment_data/file/664563/industrial-strategy-white-paper-web-ready-version.pdf>, by the House of Lords Select Committee, *AI in the UK: Ready, Willing and Able?* (HL Paper 100, 16 April 2018) 14 <www.publications.parliament.uk/pa/ld201719/ldselect/ldai/100/100.pdf>: '"Technologies with the ability to perform tasks that would otherwise require human intelligence, such as visual perception, speech recognition, and language translation". Our one addition to this definition is that AI systems today usually have the capacity to learn or adapt to new experiences or stimuli.'

[22] John O McGinnis and Steven Wasick, 'Law's Algorithm' (2015) 66 *Fla L Rev* 991; Jenna Burrell, 'How the Machine "Thinks": Understanding Opacity in Machine Learning Algorithms' (2016) 3 *Big Data and Society* 1; Barfield, 'Towards a Law of Artificial Intelligence' (n 7) 4.

[23] It is worth briefly noting that the EU Parliament's revision of Article 3(1) removes reference to software: see <www.europarl.europa.eu/doceo/document/TA-9-2023-0236_EN.html>, Amendment 165.

[24] See text to n 37.

[25] See, for example, Mireille Hildebrandt, 'Law as Computation in the Era of Artificial Legal Intelligence: Speaking Law to the Power of Statistics' (2018) 68 *University of Toronto Law Journal* 12, 24.

[26] Woodrow Barfield and Ugo Pagallo, 'Preface' in Barfield and Pagallo, *Research Handbook on the Law of AI* (n 1) xxiv–xxv.

[27] This is not to say that every replication will always be perfect (see for example, S el-Showk, 'Saving for the Future' (2018) 563 *Nature* S144), but the point suffices for the distinction that follows.

way of perhaps understanding this potential impact is to compare with blockchains. Blockchains can be forked, resulting in two different blockchains (starting from the point of the fork).[28] Thus, it might be that replication of an AI will necessarily lead to not two identical AIs but two distinct (though perhaps with a point of common ancestry) AIs. Given these two aspects, using IP regimes, which are founded on the 'fixed-ness' of ideas, as the primary mechanism for dealing with AI transactions is not necessarily the best option.

It is also worth acknowledging that AIs necessarily exist within a hardware framework. This will be so even in the context of AIs in the cloud: cloud computing is merely a form of distanced computing.[29] But most hardware-bounded AIs will be in the form of smart objects: 'AI will provide the embedded intelligence within all manner of new smart machines … including distributed software systems and intelligence embodied in smart machines and products'.[30] The necessarily embeddedness of AI raises complex questions about the nature of transactions involving AI.

A *'Owning' AI – A Search for Clarity*

As noted earlier,[31] the UN's call for a moratorium on the 'sale' of AI begs a big question, and this question-begging is prevalent in the literature. Thus Abbott, one of the leading scholars on law and AI, writes of AI (in the context of various legal areas) as being 'owned as property',[32] 'the people who build, own, and use AI',[33] 'the AI's owner',[34] 'AI developers, owners, or users',[35] and 'AI owners, users, and developers'.[36] In the context of discussing the ownership of inventions generated by an AI, he writes:

> Ownership rights … should vest in an AI's owner because it would be most consistent with the way personal property (including both AI and patents) is treated. If a person owns a machine that produces property, then he would own that property whether it is a loaf of bread or a trade secret (leaving aside more complex cases in which multiple parties are involved or he does not have rights to the machine's input [whether baking soda or another party's data]). This ownership could be taken as a starting point, although parties should be able to contract around this default, and as AI-generate inventions become more common, negotiations over these inventions may become a standard part of contract negotiations. These parties can

28 See, for example, Kelvin FK Low and Ernie GS Teo, 'Bitcoins and Other Cryptocurrencies as Property?' (2017) 9 *Law, Innovation and Technology* 235, 259–264.

29 See, for example, Eric Masanet and others, 'Recalibrating Global Data Center Energy-Use Estimates' (2020) 357(6481) *Science* 984.

30 UK AI Council, *AI Roadmap* (January 2021) 25.

31 See n 10 and accompanying text.

32 Abbott, *Reasonable Robot* (n 2), 9 (tortious liability), 63 (tortious financial liability).

33 Ibid. 11 (AI-developed inventions).

34 Ibid.

35 Ibid. 15 (liability for AIs that commit crimes).

36 Ibid. 16 (determining who to punish following AI crimes).

> ultimately work out the most efficient allocation of rights between themselves, so long as property entitlements are clearly allocated. However, a default ownership rule is still necessary to minimize overall transaction costs.[37]

As a shorthand, this is acceptable, but it is not without difficulty. In the law review article that forms the basis for the quotation to footnote 36, Abbott writes that there are a 'number of options for patent ownership (assignment) such as a computer's owner (the person who owns the AI as a chattel), developer (the person who programmed the AI's software), or user (the person giving the AI tasks).'[38] Clearly, here the reference to an AI as a chattel is problematic, and yet Abbott gives no authority for this assertion (and it is the only time the claim is made in the article, and it is not made in the later monograph). Later in the monograph, when discussing the possibility of punishing AIs for crimes, he writes:

> The responsible person could be the AI's manufacturer or supplier if it is a commercial product. If it is not, the responsible person could be the AI's owner, developer if no owner exists, or user if no developer can be identified. Even noncommercial AI is usually owned as property, although this may not always be the case, for instance, with some open-source software. Similarly, all AI has human developers, and in the event an AI ever autonomously creates another AI, responsibility for the criminal acts of an AI-created AI could reach back to the original AI's owner.[39]

Again, we see the constant reference of the AI's 'owner' and it being 'owned as property', though here with the rather odd caveat of 'usually', and without any supporting authority. If an AI can be owned, then the question arises: what exactly is it owned as? Can it be a chattel? (More technically, what sort of chattel? Might it even be a novel form of chattel real – a digital twenty-first century version of the lease?) The answer will help determine how, if at all, an AI can be alienated, whether in the form of a transfer (for sale or by some other form of commercial transaction such as the grant of a security interest), or in the form of a unilateral alienation such as an abandonment. Such analysis could also help to resolve the problem Abbott notes of an AI-created AI, in that it could be analysed in line with property doctrines concerning fruits and other products of objects.

If AI is merely software, then we are thrust back to the complicated question of the status of software. If AI is something other than mere software, then whatever we state about software will not without more determine the legal form of AI. If it is the latter, then assessing whether it is a viable and suitable subject matter for a sale transaction becomes an important task.

37 Ibid. 87 (material in square brackets is in the original).

38 Ryan Abbott, 'I Think, Therefore I Invent: Creative Computers and the Future of Patent Law' (2016) 57 *BC L Rev* 1079, 1114.

39 Abbott, *Reasonable Robot* (n 2) 130–131. The underlying article is basically the same: Ryan Abbott and Alex Sarch, 'Punishing Artificial Intelligence: Legal Fiction or Science Fiction' (2019) 53 *UC Davis L Rev* 323, 379–380.

Given the necessary bounded-ness of AI, there will invariably be some tangible thing where an AI 'resides'. There are considerable difficulties with the integration and embedding of software into objects, yet despite growing awareness of these problems,[40] there appears to be little in the way of specific protection for the possibility of AI in things. It may be suggested that the issue of embedded AI systems could be resolved by application of the principles of accession. However, whilst I can only very briefly address this issue, I suggest that the accession doctrine (and also the commentary), such that it exists, tells us nothing about what to do where one element in the process is intangible. The doctrine deals solely with physical relationships of different tangible things; its 'purpose under Roman law was to deal with the particular circumstances of inseparable joinders of tangibles, where one of the tangibles was dominant.'[41] This is problematic given that an AI can be dis-embedded or replaced (by itself, a copy, or a different version) without any physical alteration or damage to the tangible thing (disregarding, just at this point, whether the capacity of the thing to work is affected).[42] Furthermore, accession operates (if rather obliquely) on the basis that there is a major/minor delineation between the things concerned: a new carburettor to an automobile or bricks to land.[43] This cannot be said of an AI embedded into goods: one is essential to the other and vice-versa. And another danger arises from utilising accession without considering the implications as to resource distribution: 'Accession makes property a powerfully efficient tool for managing resources, but it also creates a built-in multiplier effect that means owners of property continually get more property.'[44] Given the problems of control of use and disposition,[45] it is arguably essential to avoid this aspect of accession covering the vast quantities of assets that will have embedded AI.

III THE APPLICABILITY OF SALES LAW TO AI: AI SYSTEMS AS GOODS?

Currently, it appears that a disposition of an AI system will be characterised as a type or form of transaction, depending on the factual aspects of the disposition and how

[40] See, for example, Molly Shaffer Van Houweling, 'The New Servitudes' (2008) 96 *Geo L J* 885; Sean Thomas, 'Law, Smart Technology, and Circular Economy: All Watched over by Machines of Loving Grace?' (2018) 10 *Law, Innovation and Technology* 230; Chris Jay Hoofnagle, Aniket Kesari and Aaron Perzanowski, 'The Tethered Economy' (2019) 87 *Geo Wash L Rev* 783.

[41] Magda Raczynska, *The of Law of Tracing in Commercial Transactions* (OUP 2018) para 2.24. See also WJ Swadling, 'Property: General Principles' in AS Burrows (ed), *English Private Law* (3rd edn, Oxford University Press 2013) para 4.471: 'accession, the joining of one physical thing to another'; Alexander Waghorn, 'Sorting Out Mixtures of Property at Common Law' (2021) 84 *MLR* 61 (focusing solely on tangible property). Cf Thomas W Merrill, 'Accession and Original Ownership' (2009) 1 *Journal of Legal Analysis* 459: Accession principles do operate in the IP field. However, at no point does Merrill consider the issue of embedded software raised here.

[42] Cf Raczynska, *The of Law of Tracing* (n 41) para 2.07: 'This process is referred to as accession to the dominant asset and, by its nature, is irreversible.'

[43] See for example, Swadling, 'Property: General Principles' (n 41) paras 4.475-4.476.

[44] Merrill, 'Accession and Original Ownership' (n 41) 502.

[45] See n 40, and text following n 76.

we categorise AI. To take the latter element first, if AI is merely seen as software, then as such it will be protected (generally speaking) by copyright. Copyright can be disposed of by assignment or licence,[46] but dispositions of software are invariably by means of licence, primarily because assignment prevents royalty claims against third parties following sub-assignments.[47]

Some obvious problems with licensing here can readily be identified:[48] the language of the licence may be rendered archaic or even obsolete; licences will vary according to the transaction; disputes (and/or other factual changes) may lead to re-negotiations; and the licence may cover a wide range of commercially important rights and obligations. The last problem, addressed further below, concerns the value of providing a base-level of rights and obligations, without which parties would be at the mercy of bargaining imbalances (and, to be honest, poor drafting). If the alternative form of copyright disposition – assignment – is utilised, then difficulties with ascertaining whether there is a right to assign can arise.[49] Furthermore, the approach taken in copyright doctrine is clear:

> the transfer of title to the original physical material does not by itself operate to transfer the title to the copyright any more than an assignment of copyright operates by itself transfer title to the physical material on which the work may be embodied. Copyright is not a chattel and so cannot be passed by delivery.... In the end, and in the absence of any express terms, the issue will be what terms, if any, are to be implied from the circumstances of the sale.[50]

However, in English law if software is encapsulated in a physical medium, the transaction is one of goods.[51] Yet the position is not entirely clear. A sui generis approach could be taken,[52] and arguably the result of *Res Cogitans*,[53] further supports the possibility that dispositions of goods with embedded AI would be treated as sui generis sales. Another possibility is to treat the transaction as one of services,[54] or a mix of goods and services.[55]

46 Copyright, Designs and Patents Act 1988, section 90. Disposition can also be by operation of law, but that need not concern us here.

47 *De Mattos v Gibson* (1859) 4 De G & J 276; 45 ER 108 (QB); *Barker v Stickney* [1919] 1 KB 121 (CA); cf *Law Debenture Trust v Ural Caspian Oil Ltd* [1993] 1 WLR 138 (Ch) (Hoffman J) 144: it is not 'entirely clear when the principle applies and when it does not'; John N Adams, 'Barker v Stickney revisited' (1998) 1 *Intellectual Property Quarterly* 113.

48 See Nicholas Caddick, Gwilym Harbottle and Uma Suthersanen, *Copinger and Skone James on Copyright* (28th edn, Sweet & Maxwell 2020) para 26-386.

49 Ibid. para 5-67; *Dennison v Ashdown* (1897) 13 TLR 226.

50 Nicholas Caddick, Gwilym Harbottle and Uma Suthersanen (n 48) para 5-68.

51 *St Albans CDC v International Computers Ltd* [1996] 4 All ER 481 (CA). See also *Gammasonics Institute for Medical Research Pty Ltd v Comrad Medical Systems Pty Ltd* [2010] NSWSC 267.

52 *Beta Computers (Europe) Ltd v Adobe Systems (Europe) Limited* [1996] FSR 367.

53 *PST Energy 7 Shipping LLC v O W Bunker Malta Limited* [2016] UKSC 23, [2016] AC 1034.

54 Matthew Lavy, 'Reasonable Skill and Care in the Age of Machine Learning: Some Preliminary Thoughts' [2017] Aug/Sept, *Computers & Law*, 17–18.

55 Cf *The Software Incubator Ltd v Computer Associates UK Ltd* [2016] EWHC 1587, [2017] *Bus LR* 245 (QB) (HHJ Waksman QC) [36]: 'a piece of sophisticated, commercial non-bespoke software ... would be regarded, at the very least as a "product". It would not be regarded, nor is it, a "service".'

Alongside the judicial variation is a range of academic arguments, with Professor Sarah Green (currently the Law Commissioner for Commercial and Common Law) notably arguing in favour of equating software with goods approach.[56] There is little value in me providing an overview of the various positions: the arguments' own authors do them better justice than I can. Rather, I simply state that my sympathies are very much with equating of software with goods. What follows is an outline of the current state of play following the CJEU's decision in the *Computer Associates v The Software Incubator* litigation.

In *Computer Associates*, the facts are simple. Software was supplied electronically, without being in any physical medium. The Software Incubator was to act as agent for marketing the software. After The Software Incubator entered a similar contract with a competitor, the relationship broke down and a claim was made by The Software Incubator for damages for breach of the Commercial Agents (Council Directive) Regulations 1993/3053. This turned on the status of the software. If it were goods, then the Regulations would apply. At first instance, it was held that software constituted goods,[57] but this was overturned by the Court of Appeal,[58] and after an appeal to the Supreme Court,[59] the dispute was referred to the CJEU.[60]

The CJEU issued its decision on 16 September 2021.[61] The Court reiterated the EU jurisprudence that 'goods' means

> products which can be valued in money and which are capable, as such, of forming the subject of commercial transactions', and that 'as a result of its general definition, ['goods'] can cover computer software … since [it] has a commercial value and is capable of forming the subject of a commercial transaction.[62]

Moreover, 'software can be classified as "goods" irrespective of whether it is supplied on a tangible medium or, as in the present case, by electronic download.'[63]

[56] See for example, Jane Stapleton, 'Software, Information and the Concept of a Product' (1989) 9 *Tel Aviv U Studies in Law* 147; Sarah Green, 'Can Digitised Products Be the Subject Matter of Conversion?' [2006] *LMCLQ* 568; Sarah Green and Djakhongir Saidov, 'Software as Goods' [2007] *JBL* 161; JN Adams, 'Software and Digital Content' [2009] *JBL* 396; K Moon, 'The Nature of Computer Programs: Tangible? Goods? Personal Property? Intellectual Property?' (2009) 31 *EIPR* 396; Benjamin Hayward, 'What's in a Name? Software, Digital Products, and the Sale of Goods' (2012) 38(4) *Sydney L Rev* 441; A Marsoof, 'Digital Content and the Definition Dilemma under the Sale of Goods Act 1979: Will the Consumer Rights Bill 2013 Remedy the Malady?' (2014) 9 *Journal of International Commercial Law and Technology* 285; Sarah Green, 'Sales Law and Digitised Material' in Djakhongir Saidov (ed), *Research Handbook on International and Comparative Sale of Goods Law* (Edward Elgar Publishing 2019). See also Michael Bridge, Louise Gullifer, Kelvin Low, Gerard McMeel, *The Law of Personal Property* (3rd edn, Sweet & Maxwell 2021) ch 8.

[57] *The Software Incubator Ltd* (n 55).

[58] *Computer Associates UK Ltd v The Software Incubator Ltd* [2018] EWCA Civ 518, [2018] 1 Lloyd's Rep 613.

[59] *Computer Associates (UK) Ltd v The Software Incubator Ltd* UKSC 2018/0090.

[60] Case C-410/19 *Reference for a preliminary ruling from Supreme Court of the United Kingdom (United Kingdom) made on 27 May 2019 – The Software Incubator Ltd v Computer Associates (UK) Ltd* OJ C 255/27.

[61] Case C-410/19 *The Software Incubator Ltd v Computer Associates (UK) Ltd* (16 September 2021).

[62] Ibid. [34]–35].

[63] Ibid. [36].

Following A-G Tanchev's opinion, the Court said 'the use of the term 'goods' in the various language versions of Directive 86/653 does not indicate any distinction according to the tangible or intangible nature of the goods concerned.'[64]

What is interesting for these purposes is perhaps not so much this decision itself, but rather the reliance the CJEU placed on its earlier decision in *UsedSoft*: 'from an economic point of view, the sale of a computer program on CD-ROM or DVD and the sale of such a program by downloading from the internet are similar, since the online transmission method is the functional equivalent of the supply of a material medium'.[65] As such,

> the supply, in return for payment of a fee, of computer software to a customer by electronic means where that supply is accompanied by the grant of a perpetual licence to use that software can be covered by the concept of 'sale of goods' within the meaning of [the Commercial Agents Directive]'.[66]

So, we are still in a state of some flux, awaiting the implementation of the CJEU's decision. It may well be that a narrow interpretation results, that is, only applying to cases under the Commercial Agents Regulations. If so, then we will probably need legislative intervention to clarify matters. Furthermore, even if a broader approach is taken, it remains unclear whether such an approach would necessarily be applicable to AI, given the arguable differences between 'normal' software and AI. Additionally, given the role of *UsedSoft* in the CJEU's reasoning, combined with the exception to the notion of exhaustion of copyright for digital copies,[67] a strange jurisprudence concerning software has occurred: software can be goods if granted for a perpetual period, but that same software cannot be treated as goods regarding second-hand sales. This is incoherent and contradictory. A better approach would be to simply follow the first half of the logic (i.e., that software is equated with goods) and to overturn the notion that software cannot be subject to exhaustion, though such an approach is unlikely given the judicial denial of digital exhaustion in both Europe and the United States.[68]

So why then think about commercial dispositions of AI as sales of goods? On one hand, it remains the case that there is nothing fundamentally preventing such an approach, other than a potentially artificial (though admittedly likely compelling for many) divide based on tangibility.[69] On the other hand, there are strong policy justifications for treating commercial AI dispositions like sales of goods. The purpose of sales law is, inter alia, to provide a framework of rules, some mandatory

[64] Ibid. [37].

[65] Ibid. [38], citing Case C-128/11 *UsedSoft GmbH v Oracle International Corp* EU:C:2012:407, [61].

[66] Case C-410/19 *The Software Incubator Ltd v Computer Associates (UK) Ltd* (16 September 2021), [43].

[67] See Case C-263-18 *Nederlands Uitgeversverbond and Groep Algemene Uitgevers v Tom Kabinet Internet BV and others* (2019).

[68] Ibid. *Capitol Records LLC v ReDigi Inc* 934 FSupp2d 640 (USDC SD NY 2013). See also text following n 80.

[69] Cf *Computer Associates UK Ltd v The Software Incubator Ltd* [2018] EWCA Civ 518, [2018] 1 Lloyd's Rep 613 [52] (Gloster LJ).

and/or default, others are variable to one degree or another, which provides some balance of protection for parties transacting. Thus, if we move away from sales law per se, we must consider what aspects of the current sales firmament are sufficiently disposable. Some aspects of the sales doctrine are arguably sufficiently important to be retained in whatever regime does come about for AI. One such aspect is probably provisions concerning the quality and description. The importance of an accurate description of an AI, parallel to the Sale of Good Act (SGA) Section 13 obligation, is surely as clear as it would be for descriptions of goods. Similarly, what would be problematic with a requirement that an AI be of satisfactory quality, accounting for the usual factors of price, description, and other relevant aspects, and be fit for purpose? It perhaps goes without saying that there is clear scope for a deep analysis of the specifics of the quality and fitness for purpose obligations to test the extent to which they are applicable to AI systems.

Additionally, a strong argument for coherence between commercial and consumer practice can be made, given that the Consumer Rights Act 2015 provides basically the same provisions for description, quality, and purpose not just for consumer sales of tangible goods but also for digital content. This clearly demonstrates the workability of treating intangible assets in the same way as tangible things, using basically identical conceptual matrices of assessment, to achieve the same broad policy goal of having a roughly uniform foundational set of standards for transactions involving disposable assets (accounting for the different policy goals relevant to commercial and consumer transactions).[70] This accords with the Proposed EU Artificial Intelligence Act, where the importance of providing base-line requirements as to the quality, description, and purpose of AI on consumer safety grounds is clear.[71] The fact that the provisions of the Proposed EU Artificial Intelligence Act, to the extent that they can be seen as reflecting aspects of product safety and so on that mirror the basic provisions in a sales transaction, are considerably stricter than what is given by the SGA/CRA regimes, is clearly a consequence of a highly precautionary stance taken by the EU.[72] However, this is not indicative of a problem with taking the SGA approach; rather, it merely shows that there is a further policy decision to be taken (given Brexit) as to whether to alter such aspects of English commercial law.

There are also interesting implications arising with the EU Directives 2019/770 and 2019/771, dealing with goods with embedded software. For clarity and economy,

70 Cf Christian Twigg-Flesner, 'Conformity of Goods and Digital Content/Digital Services' in Esther Arroyo Amayuelas and Sergio Cámara Lapuente (eds), *El Derecho privado en el nuevo paradigma digital* (Barcelona-Madrid, Marcial Pons 2020) 3–5; Stojan Arnestål, 'Licensing Digital Content in a Sale of Good Context' (2015) 10 *J IP L & Practice* 750; Lorin Brennan and Jeff Dodd, 'A Concept Proposal for a Model Intellectual Property Commercial Law' in Jacques de Werra (ed), *Research Handbook on Intellectual Property Licensing* (Edward Elgar 2013) 257.

71 Proposed EU Artificial Intelligence Act, (27)-(34), (42) (intended purpose of use of AI), (49)-(50) (performance), Article 15 (performance).

72 It is worth briefly noting that the EU Parliament's proposed ammendements to the AI Act go further again in providing protection: see <www.europarl.europa.eu/doceo/document/TA-9-2023-0236_EN.html>.

I must pass that subject by here.[73] Instead, what follows is a consideration of some additional aspects, often not properly considered, that an AI transactional regime would require: provisions concerning ownership and rights to repair.

IV SOME ELEMENTS OF A PROPOSED REGIME FOR TRANSACTIONS INVOLVING AI

What sort of transactional regime should there be for AI systems?[74] Whilst the SGA regime arguably provides several useful elements, it is most likely insufficient.[75] Yet providing an AI-specific regime is feasible at a structural level. As noted above, such a regime would ideally (and arguably, must) be formed of multiple currently disparate areas of law – sales, services, financing, intellectual property are some of the obvious candidates. Here, I can only provide basic rudiments of some areas of such a regime, focusing on the extent to which producers and third parties may exercise control after delivery of an AI.[76]

A *Ownership and Fair Use*

If an AI system is simply to be regarded as software and thus subject to copyright, then purchasers of AI systems will acquire a licence to use the AI as opposed to ownership.[77] However, the levels of complexity and interconnections concerning

73 See for example, Karin Sein and Gerhard Spindler, 'The New Directive on Contracts for the Supply of Digital Content and Digital Services – Scope of Application and Trader's Obligation to Supply – Part 1' (2019) 15 *ERCL* 257; and 'Conformity Criteria, Remedies and Modifications – Part 2' (2019) 15 *ERCL* 365; Jorge Morais Carhalho, 'Sale of Goods and Supply of Digital Content and Digital Services – Overview of Directive 2019/770 and 2019/771' (2019) 8 *Journal of European Consumer and Market Law* 194. It was pleasing to note the similarity between the definition of goods with digital elements software in Directive 2019/770 Article 2(3) and an earlier proposal of mine: Sean Thomas, 'Goods with Embedded Software: Obligations under Section 12 of the Sale of Goods Act 1979' (2012) 26 *International Review of Law, Computers & Technology* 165, 166.

74 Cf Matthew U Scherer, 'Regulating Artificial Intelligence Systems: Risks, Challenges, Competencies, and Strategies' (2016) 29 *Harv J L Tech* 354 (different institutional agencies may provide different levels and types of protection, and that there should be an AI certification process); Proposed EU Artificial Intelligence Act Articles 16 (f), 51 (providing a system of registration for high-risk AIs). As to the possible benefits of private organisation see also Sonia Katyal, 'Private Accountability in the Age of Artificial Intelligence' (2019) 66 *UCLA L Rev* 54.

75 Cf Louise Gullifer, 'The Vanishing Scope of the Sale of Goods Act 1979 in the Twenty-First Century' in Charles Mitchell and Stephen Watterson (eds), *The World of Maritime and Commercial Law Essays in Honour of Francis Rose* (Bloomsbury Publishing 2020) 165.

76 Cf European Commission, *Liability for Artificial Intelligence and other Emerging Digital Technologies* (European Union 2019) 28–29 <www.op.europa.eu/s/plts>, noting inter alia problems relating to product liability. One concerns the integration of hardware and software and whether AI would be a product or a component, analogous to the issue of the status of AI as goods. Another concerns the difficulties of unclear defects (which may be protected by a state-of-the-art defence) and deviations by self-learning AIs, analogous to issues of quality and description. Another problem, the focus herein, is that concerning ownership and control.

77 See for example, Robert W Gomulkiewicz, 'Is the License Still the Product?' (2018) 60 *Arizona L Rev* 425.

IP licences are problematic, not least because licences are not necessarily the best mechanism if there are concerns about the power relationship between parties.[78] Thus, it is suggested that a commercial regime for transactions involving AI should, in situations where the AI is embedded into a tangible object, provide that there is no distinction between the AI and the material thing. There should be ownership of the AI itself, even if such ownership is a legal fiat.

One could argue that this is merely a crude application of the current doctrines of fair use and exhaustion, found in the fields of patent and copyright law, which provide a basic rule that the IP-right holder cannot control the goods down a chain of transactions.[79] Once the tangible thing that encompasses or expresses the IP right is put into the marketplace, then that is that. However, the ease with which AI can be replicated, and transmitted, from one object to another, raises more questions about the current doctrine on fair use, especially in light of recent EU developments.[80] The decision in *Tom Kabinet* makes it clear that for copyright, there is no concept of digital exhaustion.[81] A similar approach is taken in the USA.[82] A corresponding problem is demonstrated by the *Impressions Products v Lexmark International* decision, whereby goods were subject to patent exhaustion, but the US Supreme Court effectively pointed the way towards using licences as a means to achieve the necessary down-chain control;[83] something that is prevalent in commercial practice anyway.[84] As such, without reforming fair use/exhaustion doctrines, there are likely to be difficulties in being able to claim that an AI object is truly 'exhausted' when placed onto the market.

Whilst common law appears to treat as ineffective attempts to control moveable property down a chain of transactions,[85] and 'the purchaser of a chattel is not bound by mere notice of stipulations made by his vendor unless he was himself a party to the contract in which the stipulations were made',[86] the practical reality is that for those acquiring goods with embedded software, prior transactions are invariably drawn in the form of a licence rather than by assignment.[87] There is thus a real need to cut off any attempts by IP rights holders to control the disposition or

[78] Andrea Tosato, 'Intellectual Property License Contracts: Reflections on a Prospective UNCITRAL Project' (2018) 86 *U Cin L Rev* 1251.

[79] See, for example, Jessica C Lai, 'Exclusive Rights of Patent Owners versus Rights of Chattel Owners: The Implied Licence Approach' (2018) 18(2) *Oxford University Commonwealth Law Journal* 99.

[80] See, for example, Lothar Determann, 'Digital Exhaustion: New Law from the Old World' (2018) 33 *Berkeley Tech L J* 177; Gerald Spindler, 'Contracts for the Supply of Digital Content – The Proposal of the Commission for a Directive on Contracts for the Supply of Digital Content' in Stefan Grundmann (ed), *European Contract Law in the Digital Age* (Intersentia 2018) 281.

[81] *Tom Kabinet* (n 67).

[82] *ReDigi* (n 68).

[83] Thomas, 'Law, Smart Technology, and Circular Economy' (n 40) 255–261.

[84] Gomulkiewicz, 'Is the License Still the Product?' (n 77).

[85] *De Mattos v Gibson* (n 47).

[86] *Barker v Stickney* (n 47) 132 (Scrutton LJ).

[87] Nicholas Caddick, Gwilym Harbottle and Uma Suthersanen (n 48) para 5-84.

even use of products down a chain of transactions.[88] Additionally, given the possibility of AI changing as a process of self-learning, providing that title to AIs belongs to the 'purchaser' that owns the thing in which the AI resides enables them to benefit from any positive value (or indeed bear the loss of any negative changes) that accrues from such changes. This would usefully cohere with the general principles pertaining to things that change or produce fruits.[89]

What if a purchaser wishes to alter an AI? It may be necessary to alter the parameters of the AI's decision-tree to reflect updated data more accurately. There could be a need to prevent certain outcomes from becoming dominant. Such changes may require either specific authorisation, or they might even be prohibited, by virtue of the licence agreement (in the absence of treating the transaction as a true sale). It would also be better to simply avoid the problem by deeming the owner of a thing with an embedded AI to simply be the owner of the AI also. Such a change will help generate coherence with notions of a right to repair.

B *The Right to Repair*

The increasing technological sophistication of goods and the concomitant reach of IP rights, along with concerns about the environmental impact of enforced obsolescence and waste,[90] have raised issues concerning the extent and nature of a so-called right to repair. This is the right to repair goods (and, as will be seen, software as well), without any prohibition or interference by another party (invariably, the seller and/or the holder of an IP right).[91] This is distinct from rights to repair as a means of protecting against non-conformity in sales transactions.[92]

Recently, the expansion of rights to repair in EU law,[93] has been extended to English law through the Ecodesign for Energy-Related Products and Energy Information Regulations 2021.[94] The Regulations provide a right to repair in a small number of

88 See, for example, Thomas, 'Law, Smart Technology, and Circular Economy' (n 38). Cf Jones Day, 'Protecting Artificial Intelligence IP: Patents, Trade Secrets, or Copyrights' (January 2018) <www.jonesday.com/protecting-artificial-intelligence-ip-patents-trade-secrets-or-copyrights-01-09-2018/>.

89 See, for example, Raczynska, *The Law of Tracing* (n 41).

90 See, for example, Leah Chan Grinvald and Ofer Tur-Sinai, 'Intellectual Property Law and the Right to Repair' (2019) 88(1) *Fordham L Rev* 63; Evelyne Terryn, 'A Right to Repair: Towards Sustainable Remedies in Consumer Law' (2019) 27(4) *ERPL* 851.

91 Cf Nina Dorenbosch, 'Can Trade Mark Owners Control the Repair of Their Products?' (4 March 2020) <www.brandwrites.law/can-trade-mark-owners-control-the-repair-of-their-products/>.

92 See, for example, Till Maier-Lohmann, 'Buyer's Self-Repair of Non-conforming Goods Versus Seller's Right to Cure under Article 48 of the CISG' (2019) 24(1) *Uniform Law Review* 58.

93 Building on European Commission, 'Circular Economy Action Plan: For a Cleaner and More Competitive Europe' (11 March 2020) <www.ec.europa.eu/environment/pdf/circular-economy/new_circular_economy_action_plan.pdf>.

94 SI 2020/745, implementing the Ecodesign for Energy-Related Products Regulations 2010 and the retained Energy Labelling Framework Regulation (EU) 2017/1369 (as amended by the Ecodesign for Energy-Related Products and Energy Information (Amendment) (EU Exit) Regulations 2019). The relevant EU regulations are here: <www.ec.europa.eu/energy/topics/energy-efficiency/

specific circumstances. The first point to note is the limitation of the right to repair to seven types of goods: welding equipment, refrigeration appliances with direct sales functions, household dishwashers, household washing machines and washer-dryers, refrigerating appliances, electric motors and variable speed drives, and electronic displays. To this list, we can add the pre-existing rights to repair concerning automotive vehicles,[95] to form a rather strange numerus clausus of items to which owners have a right to repair. Of itself, this is interesting, but what makes it more intriguing is that the same restrictive approach is apparent in the Proposed EU Artificial Intelligence Act, which lists certain high-risk products where AI may be embedded, drawn from other areas of EU law:

> machinery, toys, lifts, equipment and protective systems intended for use in potentially explosive atmospheres, radio equipment, pressure equipment, recreational craft equipment, cableway installations, appliances burning gaseous fuels, medical devices, and in vitro diagnostic medical devices.[96]

That there is no coherence between these lists is probably unsurprising, and it is an inauspicious start to regulating transactions involving things with embedded AI systems.

The nature of this right to repair is worth setting out: its limitations will become clear. Consider the washing machine. The 'right to repair' in such cases is in the form of an obligation on manufacturers to make available, for at least 10 years after the last model was put on the market, certain specific spare parts, one of which is 'software and firmware including reset software.'[97] Such parts are to be made available to professional repairers only; end users are merely able to access a very limited range of spare parts (doors, hinges, seals, detergent dispensers).[98] In addition to this, the manufacturer must provide information to professional repairers to enable these repairs.[99] This information may be restricted to those who demonstrate certain professional standards,[100] and can be subject to a reasonable fee.[101] These requirements can be found for each of the other types of goods singled out by the Regulations, with obvious changes as to the types of spare parts and so on.

The right to repair is thus merely a right for professional repairers to access information and products to provide repair services: it certainly does not mean that, in

energy-label-and-ecodesign/regulation-laying-down-ecodesign-requirements-1-october-2019_en>. These regulations implement the Ecodesign Directive 2009/125/EC of the European Parliament and of the Council, specifically article 11 concerning provisions of spare parts.

95 Commission Regulation (EU) No 566/2011 (8 June 2011), amending Regulation (EC) No 715/2007 of the European Parliament and of the Council and Commission Regulation (EC) No 692/2008 as regards access to vehicle repair and maintenance information. The right is limited to vehicle repair and maintenance in the context of emissions: see for example, Erika Ellyne, 'What the Difference between Making versus Repair Can Teach Us on the Scope of Exclusive Rights' [2015] *EIPR* 525.

96 Recital 30.

97 SI 2020/745, sch 9 [18(2)].

98 Ibid. sch 9 [18(3)].

99 Ibid. sch 9 [18(9)].

100 Ibid. sch 9 [18(11)].

101 Ibid. sch 9 [18(12)].

the absence of a professional repairer willing and able to do the repair, an end-user is entitled to an enhanced right to repair beyond those limited instances where they have specific rights to repair. It is also potentially the case that access to the listed spare parts will be restricted to those who meet the requirements for professional repair, that is, end users may find it more difficult to access the spare parts other than those explicitly stated to be available for end users.[102]

For each of the types of goods covered (except one), the Regulations specifically prohibit software being used to circumvent measurement protocols.[103] Updates to software or firmware which reduce the energy performance of the goods are only acceptable with end-user consent, but given that software updates are prohibited from making a product non-compliant with set technical standards, only situations where performance-reduction does not fall below the legislative baseline would be allowed. If a software update is rejected, then the performance of the goods cannot be changed: the explicit non-inclusion of firmware here, whilst it is included elsewhere, raises the possibility that rejecting firmware updates may be allowed to result in changes in performance without liability.

There is thus no right to repair software; rather, software (and to some extent, firmware) changes made by the supplier of the software must not lead to negative performances as against the specified technical standards. This has several consequences that will need to be addressed in providing a coherent right to repair digital assets, including AI systems. First, the software and firmware relationship needs further clarification (not least since neither software nor firmware is actually defined at any point), and it would be better to impose the same basic standards in both cases. Second, the obligations to provide updates that do not reduce performance will need to be extended beyond specific performance criteria. At this point, this issue arguably collapses into a broader fitness for purpose requirement. Given the breadth of AI possibilities, the potential field of goods with AI is obviously vast. The approach taken so far with the right to repair, to limit it to specific types of goods, with specific technical measurements, will not be sufficient. It is in this sense that a broader fitness-for-purpose test is more useful. Simply put, a better test is whether updates to software affect the fitness of the AI system for-the-purposes for which it was acquired.

A third issue that arises concerns the notion of self-repair. Self-repairing objects are not necessarily science fiction,[104] and for certain types of AI, there is something

[102] This is a common worry in the comment section of *which.com*, the consumer affairs magazine: see, for example <www.conversation.which.co.uk/sustainability/right-to-repair-appliance-eu-rules/#comments-section>.

[103] SI 2020/745, reg 8 (welding equipment), reg 14 (fridges with a direct sales function), reg 20 (household dishwashers), reg 26 (household washing machines), reg 32 (fridges), reg 44 (electronic displays). Reg 38, covering electric motors and variable speed drives concerns software updates only, and does not have the same anti-circumvention provisions seen in the other regulations.

[104] Daniel Boffey, 'Robot, Heal Thyself: Scientists Develop Self-Repairing Machines' (*The Guardian*, 7 August 2019) <www.theguardian.com/technology/2019/aug/07/robot-heal-thyself-scientists-develop-self-repairing-machines>.

like a form of self-repair in terms of being able to rework algorithms over time. The extent to which an AI object would be able to repair itself, or whether it would be acceptable for a manufacturer to limit this by introducing a 'maximum acceptable damage' level or something like that, remains unresolved.

A fourth problem is that the current approach deals with software (and firmware) as being substantially just an element of the type of goods (the car, the washing machine, the fridge, and so on). This is indicative from the phrasing of the prohibitions against updates that negate the performance *of the goods*, not the performance of the software (either the software in itself was updated or any other software affected by said update). It could be said that since it is only really the external performance which matters (a positive spin on the black box problem, if you will), there is no need for anything more. However, providing coverage for situations where the performance of software itself is the central measurement will be essential for any right-to-repair regime for AIs.

So far, the issue has concerned the right to repair, as applied to software. It will be recalled though that software and firmware were themselves identified as 'spare parts' for washing machines. Similarly, for the other named types of goods covered by the Regulations, there are specific provisions including software and firmware as 'spare parts', detailed in the various Schedules covering the Ecodesign requirements. Here there is further inconsistency between the types of goods. Welding equipment includes 'software and firmware including reset software' as a spare part,[105] and includes 'instructions for installation of relevant software and firmware including reset software' as information that must be available,[106] and the same is given for fridges with a direct sales function,[107] household dishwashers,[108] and washing machines.[109] However, there is no such coverage of software and firmware in the provisions concerning (normal) fridges or electrical motors.[110] Electric displays have a specific provision, whereby the firmware must be made available free of charge to professional repairers, brokers, and spare parts providers, or for a reasonable cost for others, for a period of eight years.[111]

Thus the digital elements of the goods concerned will be subject to an obligation to allow professional repairers to access, maintain, and presumably upgrade, where necessary. There is something to be said for how software and firmware have been treated in these regulations, that is, as elements of a product that is treated the same as other tangible elements of the product. It is this equality as between tangible and intangible aspects which is potentially very valuable in thinking about how to provide protection for purchasers of AI objects. Given the vital nature of the AI to

[105] SI 2020/745, sch 1[3][2][i].
[106] Ibid. sch 1[3][9][e].
[107] Ibid. sch 3[3][2][e] (spare parts), sch 3[3][13][e] (required instructions).
[108] Ibid. sch 6[13][2][h] (spare parts), sch 6[13][13][e] (required instructions).
[109] Ibid. sch 9[18][2][l] (spare parts), sch 9[18][14][h] (required information).
[110] Ibid. sch 13 (fridges); sch 16 (electrical motors).
[111] Ibid. sch 19[18].

the object, and the object to the AI, it is essential that the digital aspect is not over-protected such that the tangible aspects become worthless. This balance between protecting the rights of users to have functional usage of their things, and the rights of IP holders to only allow conditioned access and use of the software by means of licences, is going to be tipped further towards the benefit of users by such an approach. It is likely to lead to some resistance, not least due to the very recent decision of the CJEU in *Top System v Belgium*.[112] There it was held that whilst a lawful purchaser of a computer programme can decompile all or part of the programme to correct errors,[113] they can do so 'only to the extent necessary to effect that correction and in compliance, where appropriate, with the conditions laid down in the contract with the holder of the copyright in that program.'[114] Thus, whilst there cannot be an absolute prohibition through a contractual agreement of error correction, 'the holder and the purchaser remain free to organise contractually the manner in which that option is to be exercised. Specifically, that holder and that purchaser may, in particular, agree that the rightholder will ensure the corrective maintenance of the program concerned.'[115] It is difficult to see how this decision will enable the generation of a right to repair AI software to be truly free from potential contractual limitation.

V CONCLUSION

AI is here. Some AI systems will be more visible and obviously impactful than others (and some may be less visible but even more impactful), some AI systems may just prove to be gimmicks, and it may be that the greatest impact will come from combining AI with other technologies.[116] There will be, as there already no doubt are, transactions between parties where the object is the disposition of an AI system. Such transactions may involve AI which are purely digital (notwithstanding that even cloud-based AI will be embedded in some material thing), but increasingly, AI is being embedded into tangible things: smart objects. These novel technologies (and it is sometimes necessary to recognise that digitalisation is truly a paradigmatic event in human history) will no doubt generate considerable legal quandaries. Yet we are still unsure about the nature of software, and thus the nature of AI is likely to be contingent on the fallout of the *Computer Associates v The Software Incubator* litigation, as well as the multiple national and supra-national regulatory moves (whether sensibly precautionary or redolent of luddism) around AI.

[112] Judgment of 6 Oct 2021, C-13/20 (*Top System*), ECLI:EU:C:2021:811 <www.ipcuria.eu/case?reference=C-13/20>.

[113] Council Directive 91/250/EEC of 14 May 1991, Art 5(1).

[114] Judgment of 6 Oct 2021, C-13/20 (*Top System*) [74].

[115] Ibid. [67].

[116] Adam Greenfield, *Radical Technologies: The Design of Everyday Life* (Verso 2017) 273.

There are reasonable grounds for treating AI like goods, especially if AI is embedded into tangible things. Arguably, there will be a need for an AI-specific regime in the coming years. Such a regime could beneficially borrow aspects of English sales doctrine. However, the issue of ownership of an embedded AI will need addressing, in order to reflect the dynamic and changing nature of some AIs, as well as providing protection against third-party control. Finally, the new rights to repair are clearly insufficient and are potentially susceptible to (considerably negative) contractual control.

23

Commercial Dispute Resolution and AI

Anselmo Reyes and Adrian Mak

I INTRODUCTION

Isaac Asimov's science fiction series *Foundation* anticipates the emergence of predictive analytics, a field which leverages historical data and artificial intelligence (AI) to predict future occurrences. The *Foundation* series inspired Frank Herbert's *Dune* series, in which humanity, now an inter-planetary species in the distant future, eradicates all AI out of fear of potential harm to the human race.[1] These contrasting representations of AI resonate with ongoing debates over AI's role in future dispute resolution mechanisms. AI is typically characterised as either facilitating the work of judges and arbitrators (collectively, 'adjudicators'), thereby enhancing their productivity, or as potentially replacing human adjudicators, a prospect that could have negative repercussions for humanity.

This chapter takes as given the technological level that AI has thus far reached or can attain in the future. It focuses instead on concerns about using AI for the resolution of commercial disputes from the standpoint of a human adjudicator. More particularly, it identifies the concerns that human adjudicators would have about (1) AI being used to assist in the adjudication of a commercial dispute and (2) AI adjudicating a commercial dispute in its entirety. On (1) this chapter will describe how AIs which assist in the adjudication of commercial disputes are already widely available. It will review concerns about the use of such AI and suggest ways in which such problems might be mitigated. On (2) this chapter will examine concerns about AI replacing human adjudicators altogether for the resolution of commercial disputes. The account will consider what minimum conditions should be met before AI can acceptably replace human adjudicators for the determination of commercial disputes.

Why is the discussion here confined to AI in commercial disputes? Why not, for example, consider the use of AI to resolve family, consumer, employment, or other types of legal disputes? The restriction to commercial disputes is a matter

[1] For a recent warning on the extreme dangers posed by AI, see generally Henry Kissinger, Eric Schmidt and Daniel Huttenlocher, *The Age of AI and Our Human Future* (Little Brown 2021).

of convenience. It simplifies the discussion. The expression 'commercial disputes' here refers to business disputes for significant monetary amounts arising out of contracts negotiated at arm's length, usually between parties of equal bargaining power.[2] Among legal disputes, commercial problems so defined might be regarded as the closest to being Euclidean in nature, in the sense of being likely to have a clearly optimal solution, capable of being 'proved' by applying generally accepted legal principles to the relevant facts.[3] If there are difficulties in the use of AI to resolve even commercial disputes so defined, *a fortiori* there will be impediments in other types of disputes where an adjudicator enjoys a wide discretion in how to decide a matter and different adjudicators may reasonably disagree over the optimal outcome.[4]

In what follows, the expression 'strong AI' is used to mean AI that is equivalent to human intelligence, or 'artificial general intelligence'.[5] Strong AI will possess some capacity of self-awareness.[6] It would have some understanding of the meaning or 'semantics' of what it was doing.[7] The expression 'weak AI', on the other hand, denotes AI that can only perform tasks in accordance with its programming.[8] Weak AI is thus purely 'syntactic' in its functioning and has no awareness or understanding of the task being undertaken.[9]

II AI AS SUPPORT FOR ADJUDICATORS

A *Predictive Analytics AI (PAI)*

This section will focus on the use of PAI as support for adjudicators. That is a species of weak AI which carries out statistical or other analyses based on large amounts of

2 See, for example, *Universe Tankships Inc of Monrovia v International Transport Workers' Federation (The Universe Sentinel)* [1983] 1 AC 366 (HL).

3 Jerome Frank, 'Mr. Justice Holmes and Non-Euclidean Legal Thinking' (1932) 17 *Cornell L Rev* 568.

4 For example, on the tension between rules and discretion in family law disputes, see Carl E Schneider, 'The Tension between Rules and Discretion in Family Law: A Report and Reflection' (1993) 27 *Family Law Quarterly* 229–245.

5 Lords Committee, *AI in the UK: Ready, Willing and Able? House of Lords Select Committee on Artificial Intelligence* (Parliament of the United Kingdom, Report of Session 2017–19, HL Paper 100, 2018) 15.

6 Jeff Hawkins and Richard Dawkins, *A Thousand Brains: A New Theory of Intelligence* (Basic Books 2021) 135; Marcelo Corrales, Mark Fenwick and Nikolaus Forgó, *Robotics, AI and the Future of Law* (Springer 2018) 59.

7 Privacy International ARTICLE 19, 'Report: Privacy and Freedom of Expression in the Age of Artificial Intelligence' (2018) <www.article19.org/wp-content/uploads/2018/04/Privacy-and-Freedom-of-Expression-In-the-Age-of-Artificial-Intelligence-1.pdf>.

8 Lords Committee (n 5) 15.

9 This paper thus adopts the distinction between 'syntactic' and 'semantic' systems of AI made popular by John Searle. See John R Searle, 'Minds, Brains, and Programs' (1980) 3(3) *Behavioral and Brain Sciences* 417, 417–457; See also, Searle, 'Consciousness in Artificial Intelligence – Talks at Google' <www.youtube.com/watch?v=rHKwIYsPXLg>.

data (big data) extracted from databases of statutes and case law.[10] On the basis of their programming, machines identify patterns of decision-making from the data input into them. Their analysis of big data enables them to work out how specific fact patterns are likely to be decided by human adjudicators. Armed with this information, PAI can suggest how a given case should be decided.

PAI's power is based on two technologies: machine learning and natural language processing.[11] Machine learning proceeds by inductive logic.[12] It breaks big data down into a large number of variables and constructs a model employing those variables. PAI then assigns the facts of a real-life legal problem to the variables and, applying the model, outputs a 'determination' of the legal problem.[13] In contrast to expert systems, PAI runs on algorithms that do not incorporate fixed or stable sets of instructions.[14] If human beings were to design an expert system to go through the decision trees needed to resolve even a commercial dispute of modest complexity, the permutations of possible outcomes would be enormous and beyond human capability to encode.[15] Further, the more steps involved in the programming, the greater the likelihood of errors and unforeseen bugs plaguing the system. PAI, on the other hand, functions recursively, repeatedly correlating and reducing vast amounts of information into patterns that substitute for an understanding of underlying causalities or legal logic.[16] The presumption is that the greater the number of statutes and decisions fed into the machine, the more reliable the machine's output determination is. This assimilation of big data is facilitated by natural language processing, which permits computers to understand, interpret, and translate human language into their own language.[17] This allows the rapid encoding of libraries of statutes and case precedents.[18] The trade-off is that PAI will at best only simulate legal reasoning.[19] It can identify statutory provisions likely to apply and the cases said to have similar factual patterns to a commercial dispute.[20] It can predict the likely legal outcome of the dispute. But it will have no comprehension of whether and why the outcome is valid as a matter of law.[21]

For the purposes of the discussion below, it will be assumed that PAI has reached a state of development where its proposed outcomes possess a high degree of

[10] Kevin D Ashley, *Artificial Intelligence and Legal Analytics: New Tools for Law Practice in the Digital Age* (Cambridge University Press 2019) 234.

[11] Corrales, Fenwick and Forgó (n 6) 214.

[12] Ethem Alpaydian, *Machine Learning* (MIT Press 2016); Ashley (n 10) 109.

[13] Ashley (n 10) 111.

[14] Ibid. 8.

[15] Ibid.

[16] Corrales, Fenwick and Forgó (n 6) 214.

[17] John O McGinnis and Steven Wasick, 'Law's Algorithm' (2015) 66 *Florida Law Review* 991, 1017.

[18] Guiraude Lame, 'Using NLP Techniques to Identify Legal Ontology Components: Concepts and Relations' (2004) 12(4) *Artificial Intelligence and Law* 379.

[19] Corrales, Fenwick and Forgó (n 6) 214.

[20] Ashley (n 10).

[21] Ibid. 259–283.

accuracy. This is a reasonable assumption, given recent advances in generative AI models (that is, AI which can 'generate' diverse outputs of a creative nature, such as text, image, audio, video, and code and which has been popularised by technologies such as ChatGPT). Stories abound at present of generative AI models erroneously citing non-existent case precedents in their generated legal documents. Nonetheless, it is plausible to anticipate that, as generative AI and PAI models are improved, these two technologies can at least be used in conjunction, serving as mutual checks and balances. Where a 'judgment' or 'award' output by generative AI and a predicted outcome are consistent, an adjudicator may have greater confidence in the prediction's reliability. On the other hand, where the outputs from generative AI and PAI are at odds, the prediction could automatically be flagged as suspect.

B *Human Bias in the Use of PAI*

To speed up their work with PAI, adjudicators can plug in the facts of a legal problem into a machine. PAI would then output a decision based on the patterns discerned from a database of statutes and cases. PAI can identify the statutes and precedents relied on in support of its output recommendation. PAI can also specify a confidence level, indicating its assessment of the likelihood of a human court or tribunal reaching a similar decision.[22] PAI may provide some form of legal reasoning underpinning its decision. But even with the use of various methods for 'explaining' PAI models, such as 'Local Interpretable Model-agnostic Explanations', the level of interpretability may vary.[23] Given this 'black box' feature,[24] adjudicators would have to guard against certain biases in their use of PAI.

First, there is automation bias. This is the temptation to treat the machine's output as correct, with little or no independent verification by the adjudicator. Although prediction of the likely legal outcome of a commercial dispute by PAI can have a high degree of accuracy, the possibility of error remains.[25] To avoid this bias, an adjudicator must scrutinise the statutes and cases highlighted by the machine as the basis for its conclusion and be satisfied that those sources actually support PAI's output as a matter of legal logic. When commercial disputes involve multiple issues, there may not be a case or statute exactly on point, but only a penumbra of laws or precedents of different degrees of closeness. The answer to a legal problem may consequently not be clear-cut. It would

[22] Ibid. 245.

[23] Andreas Holzinger and others, 'Explainable AI Methods – A Brief Overview' in Andreas Holzinger, Randy Goebel, Rosina Fong, Tae Moon, Klaus-Robert Müller, and Wojciech Samek (eds), *xxAI – Beyond Explainable AI* (xxAI 2020, Lecture Notes in Computer Science, vol 13200 Springer 2022) <https://doi.org/10.1007/978-3-031-04083-2_2>

[24] Davide Carneiro and others, 'Online Dispute Resolution: An Artificial Intelligence Perspective' (2014) 41(2) *Artificial Intelligence Review* 211.

[25] Q Yunfeng Zhang, Vera Liao and Rachel KE Bellamy, 'Effect of Confidence and Explanation on Accuracy and Trust Calibration in AI-Assisted Decision Making' (January 2020) *Conference on Fairness, Accountability, and Transparency* 27–30.

be especially true in such situations that busy adjudicators must resist the temptation, after only a perfunctory analysis of their own, to accept what the AI predicts.

The propensity to be lazy may be mitigated by a requirement that, at the start of their judgements or awards, adjudicators confirm that they have carefully checked the AI outputs that they have relied upon.[26] In any event, due process requires that a judgement or award be reasoned. It will not be sufficient by today's standards of procedural transparency for an adjudicator merely to say by way of a decision that, based on certain statutes and cases and with a high degree of accuracy, the machine has stated that X should be the outcome.[27] Oracular pronouncements of such nature will hardly promote confidence in a judicial system. As noted, PAI may not give legal reasons. It will be for the adjudicator in the resultant judgement or award to explain the legal logic underpinning the machine's conclusion. The adjudicator will not be able to do that unless he or she has verified the AI's output.

Second, there is anchoring bias. A study by Amos Tversky and Daniel Kahneman required participants to spin a wheel of random numbers before guessing the percentage of UN countries in Africa.[28] Participants whose spins of the wheel stopped at a high number were prone to give higher estimates of the number of African member states of the UN. The arbitrary numbers on the wheel apparently provided a cognitive anchor for the subsequent unrelated question. The wheel would be analogous to a PAI recommendation. Once an adjudicator has seen the PAI-generated recommendation, one's assessment of a case may not stray far from what the AI has predicted.[29] The adjudicator's assessment will have been anchored to the AI's prediction, however unrelated or incorrect that may be.

26 Individuals using online systems may be prompted to take certain actions by 'nudges' built into system which set out the pros and cons of taking particular options. In much the same way, adjudicators may be deterred by built-in warnings ('sludge') of serious adverse consequences if the adjudicator simply accepts what AI has output without careful examination of the source materials. See Joseph F Coughlin, '"The Internet of Things"' Will Take Nudge Theory Too Far' (*BigThink*, 27 March 2017) <https://bigthink.com/culture-religion/the-internet-of-things-big-data-when-a-nudge-becomes-a-noodge/>.

27 C.f. *State v Loomis* 881 N.W.2d 749 (Wis. 2016), cert denied 137 S.Ct. 2290 (2017). In the criminal case, the Wisconsin Supreme Court held that a trial court's use of an algorithmic risk assessment tool in sentencing did not violate the defendant's due process rights, despite the fact that the methodology used to obtain the automated assessment was not disclosed to either the court or the defendant. The defendant received a lengthy sentence based in part on a determination by an opaque algorithm. While the court considered many factors, and sought to balance competing societal values, this is just one case in a growing set of cases illustrating how criminal justice systems are being impacted by proprietary claims of trade secrets, opaque operation of PAI, and a lack of evidence of the effectiveness of PAI. See also Institute of Electrical and Electronics Engineers, 'The Ethically Aligned Design: A Vision for Prioritizing Human Well-Being with Autonomous and Intelligent Systems (A/IS)' (1st edn, 2019) 219 <https://standards.ieee.org/wp-content/uploads/import/documents/other/ead_v2.pdf> (Ethically Aligned Design).

28 Daniel Kahneman and Amos Tversky, 'Prospect Theory: An Analysis of Decision under Risk' (1979) 47 *Econometrica* 263.

29 Jeffrey J Rachlinski, Andrew J Wistrich and Chris Guthrie, 'Can Judges Make Reliable Numeric Judgments: Distorted Damages and Skewed Sentences' (2015) 90 *Indiana Law Journal* 695; Birte Englich, Thomas Mussweiler and Fritz Strack, 'iPlaying Dice with Criminal Sentences: The Influence of Irrelevant Anchors on Experts' Judicial Decision Making' (2006) 32(2) *Pers Soc Psychol Bull* 188.

The remedy for this bias would be awareness of its possibility and a heightened appreciation of the need to rigorously verify the AI's output. But a balance needs to be struck. AI is meant to facilitate the work of adjudicators. An adjudicator might verify whether the statutes and precedents thrown up by AI justify its proposed determination. However, should one go further? Should the adjudicator also confirm or at least spot check that no statute or precedent invalidates what the AI has output? The adjudicator would have to make a judgement call as to how deeply to investigate. If one must conduct a full-blown examination of the database used by the AI, there may well be little or no saving of time and cost. The purpose of using AI would be defeated. A practical approach might be to calibrate the requisite intensity of investigation with a confidence interval output by the AI in conjunction with its determination.[30]

Third, there is contrarian bias. One may be worried about being perceived as overly dependent on PAI and as not exercising a sufficiently independent mind.[31] To dispel such notion, an adjudicator may self-consciously deviate from an AI's recommendation from time to time, even when such recommendation may be perfectly correct. In an extreme situation, a lack of understanding of PAI can result in a blanket distrust and avoidance of all use of PAI by an adjudicator[32] even where PAI, properly applied, might effectively assist the adjudicator. This extreme form of prejudice may be particularly pronounced in the initial stages of a PAI roll-out and implementation. The remedy here would be similar to what has already been discussed. The adjudicator needs to conduct a good faith verification process. 'Good faith' means that the adjudicator must be neither unduly skeptical nor overly trusting of the AI's output.

Fourth, there is herd bias.[33] Informed by the AI that (say) 90% of previous similar cases have reached a particular decision, an adjudicator will inevitably feel pressured to decide in like fashion.[34] This may be the case, even when one believes that a case should be decided differently. The herd effect discourages deviation from a trend. An adjudicator may feel safer (in the sense of being less open to public criticism) in simply 'going with the flow'. Moreover, the rule of law requires that, in the absence of compelling reason, like cases should be treated in like manner.[35] This is especially true in respect of commercial disputes. Accordingly, an adjudicator

[30] Ashley (n 10) 245. There may also be the possibility of cross-checking the recommendation of one PAI against that of another PAI.

[31] Daniel L Chen, Tobias J Moskowitz and Kelly Shue, 'Decision Making under the Gambler's Fallacy: Evidence from Asylum Judges, Loan Officers, and Baseball Umpires' (2016) 131(3) *The Quarterly Journal of Economics* 1181.

[32] Institute of Electrical and Electronics Engineers (n 26) 213.

[33] Michelle Baddeley, 'Herding, Social Influence and Economic Decision-Making: Socio-psychological and Neuroscientific Analyses' (2010) 365 *Philos Trans R Soc Lond B Biol Sci* 281.

[34] Donald C Langevoort, 'Behavioral Theories of Judgment and Decision Making in Legal Scholarship: A Literature Review' (1998) 51 *Vanderbilt Law Review* 1499, 1508.

[35] See, for example, HLA Hart, *The Concept of Law* (Oxford University Press 1961) 159.

inevitably will (and should) feel pressure to follow decided cases in the absence of good reason. The difficulty is when a lazy adjudicator blindly follows the herd, as the safest option, with only a superficial consideration of whether there are features which distinguish the instant case and call for the conscientious adjudicator to depart from precedent. There is consequently nothing novel about herd bias. It will exist whether or not AI is employed.

In short, one should not lose sight of the big picture. On their own, even without resorting to AI, human adjudicators will themselves be prone to a broad range of conscious and sub-conscious prejudices or other cognitive blind spots. On any given day, their decisions may be affected by mundane factors such as fatigue, personal values, unconscious assumptions, and reliance on intuition.[36] If human adjudicators are themselves flawed, there is a strong argument for the use of PAI to relieve adjudicators of their heavy workloads and bring a greater degree of objective consistency in their decisions. As has been seen from the foregoing account of the four biases, none of the latter are so problematic as to deprive AI of utility as a tool for the more time-efficient and cost-effective resolution of commercial disputes. The important point is that PAI will not supply the underlying legal logic. It will simply make a prediction. It will be for the adjudicator in the judgement or award to spell out why the AI's determination makes legal sense. That will require the AI's output to be scrutinised to some degree by an adjudicator who must not only consciously guard against the aforementioned biases but must also be satisfied that the AI's conclusion accords with the adjudicator's understanding of the law and sense of justice.

C *Ethical Concerns in the Use of PAI*

Critics of PAI have argued that, apart from the four biases just discussed, there are ethical concerns about using PAI to assist in the determination of commercial disputes.

First, it is suggested that adjudicators cease to be the decision-makers. It is argued that responsibility of decision-making has effectively been delegated to an anonymous computer programmer and its automated system. AI (it is contended) does not merely 'nudge' an adjudicator towards a particular determination. AI's programming instead becomes the *de facto* decision-maker.[37] It is submitted that there is nothing valid in this criticism insofar as commercial dispute resolution is concerned. If an adjudicator verifies the output from AI as discussed above and articulates in his or

[36] See, for example, Keith Mason, 'Unconscious Judicial Prejudice' (2001) 75 *Australian Law Journal* 676, 680; Michael Kirby, 'Judging: Reflections on the Moment of Decision' (1999) 18 *Australian Bar Review* 4, 19; Carlos Berdejó and Daniel L Chen, 'Electoral Cycles among Us Courts of Appeals Judges' (2017) 60 *J Law Econ* 479.

[37] See, in the context of criminal enforcement and adjudication, Rashida Richardson and others, 'Dirty Data, Bad Predictions: How Civil Rights Violations Impact Police Data, Predictive Police Systems, and Justice' (2019) 94 *NYU Law Review Online* 218.

her judgement or award why the output makes legal sense, it is difficult to see why the adjudicator would be abdicating the position of decision-maker. To the same effect, an adjudicator who disagrees with the PAI output or does not discern sound legal reasoning from the sources cited and therefore arrives at a different outcome is acting as an independent decision-maker.

Second, it is contended that there will be an excessive standardisation of decisions.[38] While commercial law is relatively stable, it does evolve over time as changes are gradually introduced in the way that businesses are conducted. Novel questions may also present themselves, even where the fact patterns of a dispute are more or less the same as what has happened before. However, PAI places a premium on how the law has been applied in the past (descriptive analysis) over the justice of applying a previously determined rule in a future situation (prescriptive analysis).[39] PAI has no concept of justice.[40] All it can do is identify patterns in what has gone on before. Indeed, decisions based on PAI will presumably be added to the database from which PAI seeks patterns, thereby reinforcing the patterns already found.[41] It is contended that such mode of proceeding would fossilise the future development of commercial law.[42] It is submitted that this criticism of PAI use should also carry little weight as far as commercial dispute resolution is concerned. While checking AI's predicted outcome against the source statutes and precedents and explaining the legal justification for AI's output in a judgement or award, a reasonably alert adjudicator should be able to spot material distinctions pointing to potentially different conclusions. If there is a novel question, the AI will signal that it has little confidence in its predicted outcome, and the adjudicator will be warned to take extra care when reviewing the same.[43] In actuality, commercial parties are typically supposed to value certainty and predictability in their dealings with one another. Thus, paradoxically, the criticism of an ossification of commercial law may be an argument favouring the use of PAI in commercial disputes, so as to enhance certainty and predictability.

Third, it is argued that, in the name of upholding the rule of law and maintaining objective consistency in the application of commercial law, AI will be used by the judiciary, the executive branch of government, or even the public to monitor and evaluate judges' performance based on conformity to PAI predictions. This (it could be contended) may place indirect pressure on judges to follow the PAI's recommendations, which could lead to a curtailment of judicial independence, especially

[38] European Commission for the Efficiency of Justice, 'European Ethical Charter on the Use of Artificial Intelligence (AI) in Judicial Systems and Their Environment' (2018) 48 <https://rm.coe.int/ethical-charter-en-for-publication-4-december-2018/16808f699c> (European Ethical Charter).

[39] Markus D Dubber, Frank Pasquale, and Sunit Das (eds), *Oxford Handbook of Ethics of AI* (Oxford University Press 2021) 391.

[40] Ibid. 14.

[41] Ibid. 385.

[42] European Commission for the Efficiency of Justice (n 37) 15.

[43] Ashley (n 10) 245.

among inexperienced judges.[44] It is submitted that such concern is speculative as far as commercial disputes are concerned. Judges, experienced or not, would routinely face challenges to their judgements. Even without AI, it is routine on appeal to submit that a first-instance judge failed to apply the law in accordance with precedent. Given the need to promote certainty and predictability in the way that commercial disputes are decided, it is hard to see how mere resort to PAI by the bench, an appellant, or even the public at large in evaluating (say) an appeal against a non-conforming first instance commercial judgement would lead to an undermining of judicial independence. The non-conformity with the PAI output would simply be an argument advanced to justify an appeal. As for commercial arbitration, the mere fact that an arbitrator has deviated from a PAI prediction could not by itself lead to the setting aside of an award or a refusal to enforce it. It would still be necessary to establish one of the grounds for setting aside or refusing enforcement specified in the UNCITRAL Model Law or New York Convention. This is of course on the assumption that AI-assisted arbitral awards will not be regarded by the court of the seat of arbitration or the competent authority of an enforcing state as being *per se* contrary to public policy.

D *Ethics and Governance of AI: The Relevant Ethics Codes*

A number of international and regional organisations have developed ethical and governance codes, charters, and guidance materials to address issues over the biases and risks identified in Sections II.B and II.C.

For instance, in December 2018, the European Commission for the Efficiency of Justice (CEPEJ) published an AI governance framework, known as the *Ethical Charter on the Use of AI in Judicial Systems and Their Environment* to counter concerns over the biases and risks identified in Sections II.B and II.C.[45] The Charter is an initial attempt to set out, at a global level, the substantive and methodological principles that should guide the integration of AI tools and services into national judicial systems. It specifically deals with the use of AI in litigation. But it can be generalised to cover the use of AI in all forms of commercial dispute adjudication. The five principles espoused by the Charter are respect for (1) fundamental rights, (2) non-discrimination, (3) quality and security of data processing, (4) transparency, impartiality, and fairness of methodology, and (5) user control. The first two principles are self-evidently important. The principle of quality and security entails the processing of data by automatic learning based on certified originals. In other words,

[44] The European Ethical Charter hints in section 6.3 of Appendix I (entitled 'The main guarantees to be reaffirmed in civil, commercial and administrative proceedings') at the potential dilemmas that judges may face. For example, in paragraph 116 the Charter acknowledges: 'In these systems [where the independence of judiciary is not fully achieved], we cannot rule out the risk that such norms [of AI derived from majority trends] will place indirect pressure on judges when decisions are taken and prompt their approval, or that the executive will monitor those who depart from the norm.'

[45] European Commission for the Efficiency of Justice (n 37).

the integrity of the database needs to be guaranteed. The principle of transparency of methodology means that the techniques used in the processing of judicial decisions should be subject to regular external audits to ensure their integrity. The principle of user control stresses the need to have informed persons as users. Users should have a sufficient understanding of the strengths and limits of the AI technology to enable them to be aware of the available decision-making choices open to them. In particular, at all times, adjudicators should be able to examine the data used by the AI to come up with a proposed decision and to depart from the same.

It will be seen that the Charter concentrates on the ethical design of PAI as a means of addressing the problems identified in Sections II.B and II.C. The Charter does not explicitly deal with how judges or others should use AI.[46] It is therefore submitted that, at least for the resolution of commercial disputes, there should be an over-arching code, combining the Charter's principles and procedural guarantees with precepts on how adjudicators should approach PAI. To this end, one can break down the use of PAI into three stages: (1) training and implementation, (2) actual use, and (3) monitoring.

1 Training and Implementation Phase

Training for adjudicators on the use of PAI for commercial disputes should emphasise accountability. Adjudicators should be equipped with a basic understanding of the algorithms deployed. Further, adjudicators should be encouraged to undergo AI bias training workshops. Similar to well-established implicit bias training programmes designed to expose implicit biases, especially regarding race, gender, and other stereotypes, AI bias training programmes may alert adjudicators to the biases inherent in PAI.

Unfortunately, attaining even a basic understanding may be hindered by three types of 'obscurity' within PAI. First, there are intentional obscurities built in by designers.[47] These obscurities are deliberately introduced to protect manufacturers' and programmers' trade secrets, to conform with privacy requirements, or to prevent

46 See also the Ethically Aligned Design, which considers 6 key questions:

(1) How can A/IS improve the functioning of a legal system and enhance human well-being?
(2) What are the challenges to adopting A/IS in legal systems, and how can those impediments be overcome?
(3) How can the collection and disclosure of evidence of effectiveness of A/IS foster informed trust in the suitability of A/IS for adoption in legal systems?
(4) How can specification of the knowledge and skills required of the human operator(s) of A/IS foster informed trust in the suitability of A/IS for adoption in legal systems?
(5) How can the ability to apportion responsibility for the outcome of the application of A/IS foster informed trust in the suitability of A/IS for adoption in legal systems?
(6) How can sharing information that explains how A/IS reach given decisions or outcomes foster informed trust in the suitability of A/IS for adoption in legal systems?

47 Jesse Beatson, 'AI-Supported Adjudicators: Should Artificial Intelligence Have a Role in Tribunal Adjudication?' (2018) 31(3) *Canadian Journal of Administrative Law and Practice* 307.

parties to a dispute from 'gaming the system'. Second, there are obscurities due to the limited technical abilities of adjudicators. Most adjudicators lack the expertise to understand code. It would thus be a significant burden on the use of AI by adjudicators if it were necessary for adjudicators to understand the technical details of the specific algorithms used by a machine.[48] It is often suggested that disclosure of the basics of the source code used by PAI may satisfy conventional standards for transparency. But even if the source code were shared, it would likely be 'teach[ing] a reviewer very little, since the code only exposes the machine learning method used and not the decision rule itself'.[49] Finally, there are intrinsic obscurities. Even if adjudicators familiarise themselves with any algorithms used, there would still be obscurities within those algorithms due to PAI's 'black box' nature. This 'black box' feature cannot be reverse-engineered even by the designers who built them.[50] Machine learning would not identify the causal relationships or logic underlying its results.[51] It would only offer a Bayesian probabilistic result based on an analysis of big data.[52] These three layers of obscurities present a challenge for adjudicators relying on AI to assist them in reaching a reasoned outcome in a commercial dispute.

2 Usage Phase

In the usage phase, updated confidence levels should be attached to PAI outputs. An AI system should keep the 'human-in-the-loop' by alerting adjudicators to the possibility of significant error, warning users that outputs may be unreliable and possibly indicating how (if at all) greater accuracy may be attained.[53] But the ability to provide a proper warning will depend on the machine's programming. There may be mistrust over whether there is a yet unknown bias embedded in a machine's algorithms or the database of statutes and cases input into the machine.[54] These unknown 'unknowns' may adversely affect PAI's output and impair its ability to accurately assess the degree of error in its predictions.[55]

48 European Commission for the Efficiency of Justice (n 37) 40.

49 Beatson (n 46) 307–338.

50 Joshua Kroll and others, 'Accountable Algorithms' (2017) 165 *University of Pennsylvania Law Review* 656.

51 Harry Surden, 'Machine Learning and Law' (2014) 89 *Wash L Rev* 87, 87–115, 100.

52 Dubber, Pasquale and Das (n 38) 389.

53 Nathalia Nascimento, Paulo Alencar, Carlos Lucena and Donald D Cowan, Toward Human-in-the-Loop Collaboration between Software Engineers and Machine Learning Algorithms (*Proceedings of the 2018 IEEE International Conference on Big Data*, 2018) 3534–3540; Fabio Massimo Zanzotto, 'Viewpoint: Human-in-the-loop Artificial Intelligence' (2019) 64 *Journal of Artificial Intelligence Research* 243.

54 Lords Committee (n 5) 42.

55 For efforts to proactively discover unknown unknowns in Machine Learning, see Joshua Attenberg, Panos Ipeirotis and Foster Provost, 'Beat the Machine: Challenging Humans to Find a Predictive Model's 'Unknown Unknowns'' (2015) 6(1) *Journal of Data and Information Quality* 1; Kate Crawford and Trevor Paglen, 'Excavating AI: The Politics of Training Sets for Machine Learning' (2019) <www.excavating.ai>.

This problem will likely persist even if the PAI industry establishes some standard metric for evaluating the effectiveness of PAI service providers.[56] This is because, at best, a standard metric of evaluation can increase the transparency of various trade-offs between the preferences and values of different communities and foster more public discourse on the types and degrees of errors acceptable by the community.[57] But it does not shed light on the social desirability of unknown and unknowable biases and errors. This concern is heightened if commercial parties have no say over the selection of the PAI used by an adjudicator. The result is that the parties may feel a lack of procedural fairness.

To address this, an adjudicative process can allow for the underlying algorithms of PAI to be open to challenge by parties. For instance, if a party is unhappy with the default PAI system being used by the adjudicator, it should be allowed to challenge the same during the relevant proceedings. A procedure similar to that now used for expert evidence might be employed for this purpose.[58] The discontented party can give notice that it will be adducing evidence to challenge the algorithmic design or assumptions behind a particular PAI.[59] This procedure would then be subject to appropriate rules of disclosure and cross-examination.[60] The opposing party can adduce its own expert witnesses.[61] An adjudicator, after hearing the submissions from both parties, can issue a ruling on the final choice of PAI. This approach may be especially apposite for commercial disputes. Commercial parties can also make submissions on the variety of PAI systems available in the market at any particular time. It might be shown, for instance, that different PAI systems come up with conflicting recommendations. In any event, the assumption here is that the playing field for commercial parties dealing with each other at arm's length will be levelled.[62] The parties can thus be left to fend for themselves, provided due process (that is, the right to notice and a reasonable opportunity to be heard in connection with the use of PAI in a case) has been afforded.[63] This may be different in criminal, administrative, or constitutional cases where there will be often a power imbalance.

There are limits to such approach. AI systems are deliberately designed as black boxes, containing obscurities for a variety of reasons, such as to protect trade secrets or for privacy concerns.[64] Therefore, the extent to which commercial parties can realistically challenge the underlying algorithms of a PAI system may be queried when the latter may be deliberately opaque. A response may be to require AI service

56 Dubber, Pasquale and Das (n 38) 751.

57 Ibid. 743.

58 Tristram Hodgkinson and Mark James, *Expert Evidence: Law and Practice* (5th edn, Sweet & Maxwell 2020).

59 Ibid.

60 Ibid.

61 Ibid.

62 See, in the context of undue influence, *Parfitt v Lawless* (1872) LR 2 P&D 462.

63 Lon L Fuller, *The Morality of Law* (Yale University Press 1964) 34–37.

64 Kroll (n 49) 656–768.

providers to disclose their algorithms. In such case, however, the present intellectual property rights regime may not provide sufficient protection to prevent such algorithms and their source codes from being copied or pirated by competitors.[65] Service providers would then risk losing their competitive advantage.

Nevertheless, it is submitted that there may be increasing market forces for service providers to reveal their algorithms. The reality is that any PAI system, however 'accurate', can be challenged by parties as unreliable if it is opaque.[66] What is unreasonably opaque is a question of degree. The answer will depend (among other factors) on the number of available choices among PAI service providers. Faced with challenges by parties, adjudicators can pick and choose from among the alternative PAI service providers available in the market. Adjudicators might then routinely dismiss non-transparent PAI systems and opt for those whose disclosure of algorithms is more transparent. A PAI service provider that refuses to reveal its algorithms (or, at any rate, a bare minimum of the same) would consequently risk its product being shunned by adjudicators and commercial parties.[67] Hence, a dynamic market can exert economic pressure on PAI service providers to open up their algorithms.

It will not be sufficient for the machine to signal when the accuracy of its predictions may be suspect. An adjudicator will need to assess the extent to which he or she is prone to one or more of the biases mentioned in Section II.B. Armed with such knowledge, one will at least be on the alert and so proceed with caution. Ironically, a method of detecting whether an adjudicator is prone to bias is to use AI to analyse that adjudicator's previous decisions. PAI may be used to isolate evidence of the four biases outlined in Section II.B in one's own decisions. AI can be designed to identify factors that are unrelated to the merits of a case (such as the amount at stake, who the opposing parties and their lawyers are, and where they are from) and analyse the extent to which such irrelevant factors may be correlated with the outcomes of an adjudicator's decisions.[68] In the US, start-ups have been providing statistics on court decisions based on the identity of the judge as well as information on opposing lawyers.[69] Some European legal-tech companies

65 Anne Lauber-Rönsberg and Sven Hetmank, 'The Concept of Authorship and Inventorship under Pressure: Does Artificial Intelligence Shift Paradigms?' (2019) 14 *JIPLP* 570, 578; MC Buning, 'Autonomous Intelligent Systems as Creative Agents under the EU Framework for Intellectual Property' (2016) 2 *EJRR* 310, 312.

66 Ashley (n 10) 350.

67 One may query whether this approach would work better in common law systems. A common law adversarial-style adjudication may be more conducive in allowing for the parties' challenges. A civil law inquisitorial-style adjudication, on the other hand, may encourage parties' deferral to the adjudicator's default AI system.

68 Daniel L Chen, 'Judicial Analytics and the Great Transformation of American Law' (2019) 27 *Artificial Intelligence Law* 15.

69 Lex Machina, <https://lexmachina.com/>; see also Mihai Surdeanu and others, 'Risk Analysis for Intellectual Property Litigation' in *Proceedings of the 13th International Conference on Artificial Intelligence and Law* (New York, NY: ACM).

have gone further and claimed that they are able to identify potential biases of judges.[70] The availability of data linking presiding judges of the French administrative courts with the decisions of the courts of appeal of those courts has made it possible to develop an indicator of the likely rejection rate of appeals against orders to leave French territory made by administrative authorities.[71] In the future, PAI promises greater possibilities in detecting signs of the four psychological biases mentioned above.

Nonetheless, the foregoing approach is far from straightforward, as the application of AI along the lines suggested is fraught with policy considerations. On the one hand, the processing of judicial data is likely to improve the transparency and functioning of justice.[72] It would improve the predictability of the application of law, in particular commercial law, by adjudicators. Offering adjudicators a detailed assessment of their decisions, with the simple objective of assisting them in their decision-making process, should in principle be encouraged. But it is feared that this would undermine public respect for adjudicators and what they do. CEPEJ has expressed caution over the use of data in the manner described (that is, using the identities of judges for profiling purposes).[73] Adjudicators are averse to being rated like Michelin restaurants or Uber drivers. This could, for instance, lead to tactical manoeuvring by a party so as to obtain a court or tribunal perceived to be favourable to its position in a commercial dispute.[74] It could also lead to parties tailoring their submissions to an adjudicator's biases as revealed by PAI. In response, in June 2019, the French Government banned the publication of statistical information about judges' decisions. Anyone who breaks the new law faces a maximum penalty of five years' imprisonment.[75] The law appears to have been a compromise between judges who wanted their names redacted from opinions when published online and those who felt that the public had a right to know.[76] These underlying policy tensions will continue to emerge as more powerful PAI develops. A balance should be struck when consulting all stakeholders while seeking to maximise the benefits that AI can bring in terms of alerting adjudicators to their cognitive biases. The question as always is how in practical terms to strike that balance.

70 Predictice <https://predictice.com/>.

71 European Commission for the Efficiency of Justice (n 37) 39.

72 CEPEJ, 'Justice of the Future: Predictive Justice and Artificial Intelligence – Towards a European Ethic for Algorithms' (2018) <www.coe.int/en/web/cepej/justice-of-the-future-predictive-justice-and-artificial-intelligence>.

73 'Predictive Justice: When Algorithms Invade the Law' (2017) *Paris Innovation Review*.

74 Tania Sourdin, 'Judge v Robot? Artificial Intelligence and Judicial Decision-Making' (2018) 41(4) *UNSW Law Journal* 1114; Berdejo and Chen (n 35).

75 'France Bans Judge Analytics, 5 Years in Prison for Rule Breaks' (*Artificial Lawyer*, 2019) <www.artificiallawyer.com/2019/06/04/france-bans-judge-analytics-5-years-in-prison-for-rule-breakers/>.

76 Michael Livermore and Dan Rockmore, 'France Has Banned Judicial Analytics to Analyse the Courts' (*Slate*, 2019) <https://slate.com/technology/2019/06/france-has-banned-judicial-analytics-to-analyze-the-courts.html>.

3 Monitoring Phase

Procedural safeguards are not complete without an effective monitoring phase. Adjudications relying on PAI algorithms should accordingly not be immune from appeal. A ground for appeal might be that a human adjudicator excessively relied on PAI and failed adequately or at all to evaluate the circumstances of a case as a whole. Where an adjudicator has a discretion (for example, whether or not to grant equitable relief, such as an injunction or specific performance), an algorithm-based decision-making might be regarded as fettering discretion, if the underlying criteria applied are too narrow or much wider than the law actually permits.[77] In the context of commercial decisions, adjudicators in their judgements or awards need to justify the weight placed by them personally on such factors, even if nudged by the predictive 'decision' made by an AI system. Conversely, another ground of appeal might be insufficiently engaging with a PAI recommendation. To this end, adjudicators should enumerate in their determinations all factors taken into account by them beyond those used by a PAI system. The adjudicator should thereafter justify why a PAI output factor was or was not useful and why it was thought appropriate to take account of or deviate from the same. The length and depth of an adjudicator's justification will accordingly vary from case to case. In determining the sufficiency of justification and the requisite level of human oversight, adjudicators could consider the impact of a decision by employing the probability-severity of harm matrix.[78] The greater the likelihood of serious harm from a decision, the more stringent the level of justification required by the decision-making process. For example, the justification associated with a small-value goods claim may be much less than that associated with a complex billion-dollar claim involving multiple parties. An insufficient justification could lead to a successful appeal.

E *Summary*

PAI can significantly assist adjudicators to reach a decision in a commercial dispute by identifying pertinent statutes and cases and suggesting (predicting) a likely outcome. Because PAI will not be able to supply the legal logic underlying its prediction, the adjudicator will need to examine the validity of the same and explain in a judgement or award why the PAI output makes sense as a determination of a commercial dispute. This discipline of articulating the reasons why a PAI prediction makes sense is an essential part of the adjudicative process. It will assist the adjudicator to guard against automation, anchoring, contrarian, and herd biases. The degree of articulation or scrutiny required could depend on the probability and severity of

77 Beatson (n 46) 307–338.

78 Personal Data Protection Commission Singapore, 'Model Artificial Intelligence Governance Framework' (1st edn, 2019) 8–9 <www.ai.bsa.org/wp-content/uploads/2019/09/Model-AI-Framework-First-Edition.pdf>.

harm. Adopting the broad principles of the Charter in combination with the guidelines sketched out in Sections II.D.1–D.3 should further ensure the integrity of using PAI to decide commercial disputes.

III AI AS ADJUDICATOR

This section considers what conditions would need to be met for AI to replace human beings as judges or arbitrators in commercial disputes. John Searle observes that, in many instances, the fact that AI today is syntactic, as opposed to semantic, will not make any palpable difference.[79] In many situations, the fact that AI simulates (as opposed to duplicates) the process and output of human reasoning will be sufficient. For example, provided that a self-driving vehicle (SDV) consistently gets one safely from A to B, it should not matter to a passenger that the SDV lacks consciousness about itself as a driver or that the logic and programming followed by the SDV is unknown to the passenger. The SDV mimics what happens when a human being conveys a person from A to B. For most persons, this simulation should be adequate, and it will be unnecessary for the SDV to duplicate precisely how a human driver performs the same task. The logic followed by the SDV can remain a 'black box'.[80] But the same cannot be said of a machine writing a judgement or award that will be determinative of a commercial dispute.[81] As already noted, a cardinal requirement of due process and transparency in litigation and arbitration is that judgements and awards should set out an adjudicator's reasoning.[82] Although the winning side may not care very much why it has won, the losing party in a commercial dispute will desperately want to know the reason why it has lost. Whether or not it agrees with the outcome, the losing side must go away with the *feeling* that its arguments have been heard, understood, and dealt with fully.[83] It will not suffice merely to tell the loser that, applying the latest deep learning to the largest available database of commercial judgements, the machine has determined with 99% accuracy that a court or tribunal would conclude that the loser has no case on the facts. The losing side will want to know the legal reasoning underpinning the machine's conclusions and why, for instance, the case does not fall within the 1% error rate identified.

It is submitted that, to produce a reasoned judgement or award on its own, a machine will need to be programmed with strong AI. The machine would need to have a sense of awareness of what it was deciding, that is, an understanding of the semantics of the law.[84] Given the present state of AI, it will not be possible to satisfy

79 Searle (n 9) 417–457.

80 Kroll (n 49) 656–768.

81 Tim Miller, 'Explanation in Artificial Intelligence: Insights from The Social Sciences' (2019) 267 *Artificial Intelligence* 1.

82 See also, Margot E Kaminski, 'The Right to Explanation, Explained' (2019) 34 *Berkeley Tech LJ* 189.

83 Dubber, Pasquale and Das (n 38) 733.

84 Anselmo Reyes, *The Practice of International Commercial Arbitration – A Handbook for Hong Kong Arbitrators* (Routledge 2018) 113.

this requirement of a reasoned determination. As discussed in Section II, machines can now output a list of precedents and state by way of a decision that, on the basis of the similarities between those sources and the facts of a dispute, the ratios of the former are likely to be decisive of the outcome in the latter. However, it will need a human adjudicator to articulate the legal logic leading from the sources and the facts of the dispute to the proposed outcome.

Nonetheless, mere self-awareness will not be enough to enable AI to serve as adjudicator without further need of a human intermediary. At least three hurdles would remain to be overcome.

First, in many commercial disputes of any complexity, the law is not actually in dispute.[85] It is the facts that are hotly contested. In a typical commercial dispute of moderate complexity, the argument will be on whether a party orally agreed with X.[86] The claimant will vigorously maintain that the respondent agreed with X, while the respondent will vehemently deny any such agreement. Each side will genuinely believe that he or she is in the right. In such situation, case after case has affirmed that demeanour is a treacherous guide to who is telling the truth. The con artist will be fluent about what supposedly happened, while the truthful witness may be nervous and incoherent. The adjudicator faced with such dispute has no built-in lie detector and can only decide on the basis of the balance of probability in light of the available evidence as a whole (including contemporaneous documentary evidence).[87] It is submitted that mere self-awareness will not enable AI to duplicate the balancing or probability process that adjudicators routinely perform.

The machine could conceivably be attached to a polygraph which monitors the physical traits of a witness (dilation of the pupils, degree of perspiration, hesitation in speech, etc.).[88] But if demeanour is not an acceptable guide, it is unclear

85 As Lord Sumption observed: 'What you discover as you start practicing law is that there is surprisingly little law in it …. Much more challenging about the practice of law is understanding and analysing what are often quite complicated facts, massive documentary files, and that odd combination of memory and prejudice that accounts for how witnesses behave in the witness box. A remarkably high amount of cases that come before the courts, including the Supreme Court, are ostensibly about the law, but actually are about the correct analysis and classification of the facts. The truth is … most of [legal practice] is common sense with knobs on. What is difficult are the facts. Once you have correctly understood those, and stripped away the ninety five percent of the facts that don't matter at all, the legal solution is almost always obvious.' See Lord Sumption, 'Those Who Wish to Practise Law Should Not Study Law at University?' (Cambridge Law Faculty, Cambridge, 27 February 2013) <www.youtube.com/watch?v=uMR1NIEifWM>. This statement accords with the lead author's years of experience as a commercial barrister, judge and arbitrator.

86 Reyes (n 83) 114–115.

87 Anselmo Reyes, *Reflections on Civil Procedure under Civil Justice Reform* (Joint Publishing (HK) Co Ltd 2012); William H Park, 'Arbitrators and Accuracy' (2010) 1(1) *Journal of International Dispute Settlement* 25.

88 Shivali Best, 'The Robot That Knows When You're Lying: Scientists Create an AI That Can Detect Deception in the Courtroom' (*Daily Mail*, 20 December 2017) <www.dailymail.co.uk/sciencetech/article-5197747/AI-detects-expressions-tell-people-lie-court.html>.

why a polygraph will be of much assistance to assessing the balance of probability. Alternatively, the machine might be remotely connected to (say) the laptops of a large number of random persons (a jury) and poll those individuals from time to time on factual issues as and when they arise for determination. The machine might ask each member of the jury to vote on whether, given a summary of undisputed facts, one is of the opinion that X was or was more likely than not to have been agreed. Applying Condorcet's Jury theorem on the wisdom of crowds in matters of common sense, the machine may then take the majority answer as a factual finding on whether X was agreed.[89] But such simulation of what a court or tribunal does when it assesses the balance of probability is unlikely to be regarded as satisfactory by most parties.

It is not possible to articulate the process which a judge or arbitrator goes through when assessing on the balance of probability whether parties did or did not orally agree with X.[90] The human adjudicator must draw on his or her own daily experience as to the likelihood of individuals with the parties' characteristics having orally agreed, without any written record, on a term, understanding, or variation having significant repercussions on their commercial contract.[91] The adjudicator may have regard to the parties' conduct before and (possibly) after entering into a commercial contract and evaluate whether such behaviour is or is not consistent with the existence of the alleged oral agreement, understanding, or variation. The adjudicator will especially be attentive to the emails, drafts, minutes of meetings, and so on passing between the parties to discern whether, although not expressly acknowledged, there is some indication that the parties must have been implicitly proceeding along the lines alleged by one side or the other. The process inevitably entails some subjective assessment. To use an analogy, it would not simply be a matter of assessing the likelihood of a tossed coin coming up heads or tails. The judge or arbitrator must instead have regard to the totality of factual evidence and come to a subjective conclusion as to whether the coin is a fair or biased one and, if the latter, how that is likely to affect whether the coin comes up heads or tails on a given toss.[92] It is submitted that, in practical terms, no expert system will allow AI (however self-aware) to decide whether the parties were likely or not to have orally agreed with X. There would be too many permutations of factors and possibilities to consider when programming AI. Further, no amount of crunching big data would enable AI (however self-aware) to simulate the evaluation by a human adjudicator of hotly disputed facts in a one-off situation, or at least explain its decision-making in a meaningful way as a human adjudicator.[93] If the polling of

89 Jean-Antoine-Nicolas de Caritat marquis de Condorcet, 'Essai sur l'Application de l'Analyse à la Probabilité des Décisions Rendue à la Pluralité des Voix' (1785). See also Cass R Sunstein, 'When Crowds Aren't Wise' (*Harvard Business Review* September 2006) <www.hbr.org/2006/09/when-crowds-arent-wise>.

90 Reyes (n 83) 116.

91 Reyes (n 86).

92 Ivar Ekeland, *The Broken Dice* (University of Chicago Press 1993).

93 Miller (n 80); Dubber, Pasquale and Das (n 38) 732.

remotely connected juries of human beings is instead employed to simulate an assessment of the balance of probability, the persons so engaged would themselves have to assess the totality of the factual evidence, rather than mere summaries of the same. The exercise would be a little different from the use of human juries in the past to decide commercial cases. That practice was long ago abandoned in most common law jurisdictions as too time-consuming, and judges sitting on their own took on the twin tasks of determining the facts and applying the law.

Second, assuming that the facts have somehow been determined, the outcome of a fair number of commercial disputes hinges on a court or tribunal choosing between two equally plausible interpretations of an applicable law where there is no determinative case precedent.[94] Other cases call for the court or tribunal to distinguish the facts of a case from the apparently similar facts of a case precedent or precedents in which some principle X was applied. The court or tribunal will typically draw a distinction when the application of principle X in a particular dispute would lead to a glaring injustice or unfairness to a party.[95] In the situation of two plausible interpretations of the law, it is unclear how AI (however self-aware) would choose between the two equally likely possibilities. An expert system can be programmed to detect an unresolved legal question. But how will it reason out an answer to the dilemma when *ex hypothesi* either outcome is correct ? Deep learning may lead the machine to conclude that there are two possible answers. But how is big data to help the machine reason out which answer should be applied in the instant case? In the situation where mechanically applying a precedent would lead to injustice, it is likewise difficult to envisage how an expert system can be programmed to warn itself that the apparently right principle should be distinguished because it may lead to injustice. AI based on deep learning would have a similar problem. Big data would lead it to the apparently applicable legal principle. But how would big data alert the machine (however self-aware) to contemplate distinguishing the orthodox principle to avoid injustice?

The twin difficulties just identified arise because even in commercial disputes there is typically more than one possible answer to a legal question. Nor is commercial law static. As already noted, it develops so that on occasion even apparently settled principles may need to be distinguished or refined in appropriate circumstances.[96] These characteristics are not confined to the common law. They feature as well in civil law jurisdictions. In theory, the judge in a civil law system applies codified or statutory principles to the facts in the manner of a legal

[94] See, for instance, the court's discussion on the penalties doctrine in Cavendish Square Holding BV v Makdessi and ParkingEye v Beavis [2015] UKSC 67, [2016] AC 1172; see also the discussion by Lord Toulson on the doctrine of illegality in Patel v Mirza [2016] UKSC 42, [2017] AC 467.

[95] See, for instance, the doctrine of estoppel in *Central London Property Trust Ltd v High Trees House Ltd* [1947] KB 130 (KB); Edwin Peel, *Treitel: The Law of Contract* (14th edn, Sweet & Maxwell 2015) para 3-090.

[96] See, for instance, Cavendish (n 93); see also Patel (n 93) (Lord Toulson).

syllogism.[97] As a result, traditionally, civil law judgements were shorter than common law judgements.[98] The paradigm civil law judgement as envisaged following the French Revolution, for instance, was supposed to consist of a terse series of legal and factual propositions logically leading to the court's determination. The judgement would fit into a straightforward formula: whereas the law is as set out in X, Y, and Z and whereas the facts are A, B, and C, so the court concludes that party N prevails over party M.[99] But if one now compares common law and civil law judgements or awards in commercial matters, one will find few substantial differences. There has been a convergence of styles. Common law and civil law determinations will both cite statutes and cases in support of legal propositions, even though in civil law jurisdictions, cases are only illustrative of the application of a statutory provision and there is no strict doctrine of *stare decisis*. The judgements in both systems will explain in detail how specific legal propositions are to be applied to the facts. It follows that AI will not be more conducive to commercial disputes under the civil law, in contrast to the common law. AI will instead have to grapple in either system with the two difficulties highlighted.

Now how precisely does a human adjudicator (1) choose between two equally viable interpretations of a legal principle or (2) decide that one should draw a distinction between seemingly like cases and distinguish between the legal principles applicable to each? It is submitted that the adjudicator in such situations must draw on his or her sense of what is just and fair in the peculiar circumstances of a given commercial dispute.[100] That sense of justice acts as a reality check when the adjudicator applies a legal principle or elects between two plausible applications of the same. When standing back and assessing the outcome from applying a legal principle, if the adjudicator's sense of justice is bothered by some apparent unfairness in the result, the adjudicator will then review his or her reasoning to try to expose some flaw. It may be that there is no flaw that can be identified (as, for instance, where there is no meaningful distinction between the facts of a case and a precedent), and the adjudicator must reluctantly decide the case at hand in accordance with the precedent. Similarly, when faced with two equally plausible but competing applications of a legal principle, the adjudicator will seek to decide by reference to some set of factors that will make for a more just or fair outcome in the dispute. Adjudication is not mediation. One cannot simply split the pie in a manner deemed equitable. The nature of a commercial dispute being that only one party can prevail at the end of the day, the adjudicator must decide one way or the other and must pin the

[97] René David, *French Law: Its Structure, Sources And Methodology* (Louisiana State University Press 1972); see also René David and John EC Brierley, *Major Legal Systems in the World Today* (Free Press 1968).

[98] John P Dawson, *The Oracles of the Law* (University of Michigan Law School 1968) 375–386.

[99] Ibid.

[100] See Patrick Devlin, *The Judge* (Oxford University Press 1981) 84–116; Aharon Barak, *The Judge in a Democracy* (Princeton University Press 2006) 158–163.

outcome on some factor or factors that favour a particular application over the other. Much of this process may go on in an adjudicator's head without being clearly articulated or being capable of articulation.

If an adjudicator's thought process is as described in the previous paragraph, one's sense of justice will have been nurtured by the totality of his or her experience and education, right up to the moment of decision.[101] There would be no possibility of AI, merely by being self-aware, mimicking this sense of justice to act as a reality check on its decisions. Insofar as expert systems are concerned, it should be relatively straightforward to programme a machine to give a party (say the respondent) the benefit of a doubt where there are two possible applications of a legal principle. But it is unclear how to simulate an evaluation of factors to determine whether one legal solution is more acceptable than another. Insofar as deep learning is concerned, there being no decisive case on a matter one way or other, the machine would not be able to come up with a determination. Again, no amount of big data will enable it to reason out what is just or fair between two equally valid outcomes. The real problem is precisely that human beings themselves are unable exhaustively to describe what leads them to perceive one legal outcome to a commercial dispute as more just than another.[102] That inability to articulate would serve as a limitation on the programming of AI. It would be possible to feed a computer with large examples of ethical dilemmas and how humans have chosen among the options in such situations. It is doubtful that the 'patterns' discerned by a computer from such data can confidently be characterised as a 'sense of justice'. The machine would still need to explain why, having been fed such data, it has chosen option X instead of Y in an instant case.[103]

Third, if AI somehow surmounts the first two hurdles discussed, there will remain a need for the machine to output a coherent reasoned judgement or award. Just as it is now possible for AI to produce a painting in the style of Rembrandt or write in the style of Balzac after having been fed digitalised versions of all of Rembrandt's or Balzac's work, AI can undoubtedly be fed with a large database of judgements and awards written by the most eminent judges and arbitrators and imitate their writing style. Having studied the mannerisms and traits of eminent adjudicators and knowing the outcomes and reasoning that it is supposed to communicate in its judgement or award, the machine can probably do a credible job of producing a determination that sounds like it was written by a human adjudicator.[104] But that will almost certainly not satisfy the losing party in a commercial dispute. What the loser is after is not a pastiche of words and phrases from famous judges or arbitrators. A judgement or award in a commercial dispute cannot be a

[101] Hawkins and Dawkins (n 6) 148.

[102] Dubber, Pasquale and Das (n 38) 391.

[103] Ashley (n 10) 389.

[104] See, for example, 'A Robot Wrote This Entire Article. Are You Scared Yet, Human?' (*The Guardian*, 2020) <www.theguardian.com/commentisfree/2020/sep/08/robot-wrote-this-article-gpt-3>.

massive form letter. What the loser needs is a sense that its case has been heard and understood by the adjudicator, albeit finally rejected by the latter for the reasons set out in the judgement and award.[105] In other words, there must be some link between the words used in the judgement or award and the thought processes of the adjudicator. To put it in anthropomorphic terms, there must be 'heart' or 'human touch' behind the judgement or award. In AI terms, the machine would need enough self-awareness in writing the judgement or award, so that the words are not simply stock expressions used to frame the reasoning and outcome being communicated.

In short, the difficulties just canvassed (namely, (a) making a finding on disputed facts by reference to the balance of probability, (b) choosing between two equally plausible applications of a legal principle, (c) distinguishing between two seemingly analogous cases in the interests of fairness and justice, and (d) drafting a reasoned determination) point to three minimum conditions that AI must meet if it is to replace a judge or arbitrator in the adjudication of a commercial dispute:

(1) The AI must have a sense of consciousness or self-awareness.
(2) But self-awareness is not a sufficient condition. The machine will have to undergo a period of education.[106] Using its sense of consciousness, the machine will need to experience human life in all its variegated forms, to pick up nuances of human behaviour and cultivate an ability to assess what is more likely than not in particular situations. The interaction with human experience will also enable the machine to acquire a sense of what is fair, so that it can check its conclusions against that sense of justice. Because of the speed of its processors, it may be that the machine will be able to acquire the equivalent of significant human experience and education in a shorter time than humans. But this is not a self-evident proposition. Human beings often must mull over the situations that they encounter in life and frequently the implications of a situation are only grasped (if at all) after much out-of-the-box thinking. It is not obvious how a machine can 'experience life' and draw mature conclusions about abstract notions such as the 'balance of probability,' 'fairness' and 'justice' much more rapidly than human beings, no matter how much big data is input into them.
(3) There must be some system for validating the 'education' that the AI has received and certifying that, as a result of such 'education', it can act as an adjudicator of commercial disputes.

These three conditions suggest that it will be some time before AI can wholly replace human adjudicators, even for the resolution of commercial disputes.

[105] Dubber, Pasquale and Das (n 38) 733.
[106] Hawkins and Dawkins (n 6).

IV CONCLUSION: USE OF AI AND HUMAN EXPECTATION

The foregoing discussion presupposes that we rightly expect reasoned judgements or awards that make explicit the logic by which disputed facts are resolved and laws are applied to such facts to reach a determination. It might be queried why that should be the case. Could we not adapt our current expectations, so as to cater for something less than the use of human intermediaries posited in Section II and the minimum conditions proposed in Section III? For instance, should it not be enough by way of 'reasoning' to satisfy a losing party simply for weak AI to provide a list of cases, their rationales, and their points of resemblance to an instant case? This would be analogous to the terse civil law judgements that developed in the wake of the French Revolution. Human judges or arbitrators may disagree with the outcome on various counts. But the machine cannot be accused of failing to provide 'reasons' of a sort. It can do so much more speedily than a human being, and whether or not human adjudicators come to similar conclusions, the machine's determination would at least have the virtue of promoting commercial certainty. It would lack the subjectivity and bias inherent in an individual's perceptions of what is just and fair or what constitutes the balance of probability in a case.

In other words, why should AI adapt to the expensive and time-consuming way in which we presently decide commercial disputes? Why should we not instead adapt to the cost-effective and time-efficient way by which AI, as it now is or will soon be, can decide commercial law disputes? Ultimately, every society will need to decide at what level and plurality it would like to pitch its commercial dispute resolution services. At one end of the spectrum, disputes can simply be decided by flipping an unbiased coin. Everyone will presumably be against that, because that essentially involves giving up entirely on any form of reasons and relying purely on chance. At the other end of the spectrum, there is the current Rolls-Royce service available in today's commercial courts and arbitral tribunals. The difficulty is whether that type of service is sustainable, and the perennial complaint today is that the courts are clogged and too slow, while international commercial arbitration is too expensive and time-consuming.[107] There is a whole range of choices in between, including combining AI with human options (for instance, weak AI at first instance, followed by an appeal to a human adjudicator). On the principle of party autonomy, it will be for commercial stakeholders to state in their contracts which of the available options for the resolution of commercial disputes they are prepared to accept.

[107] Reyes (n 83) 11.

24

Insurance Law and AI

Demystifying InsurTech

Özlem Gürses

I INTRODUCTION

The word InsurTech is a new neologism expressing generally insurers' engagement with Artificial Intelligence (AI). Several technologies have changed the way that the insurers offer their product and handle their customer relations. Therefore, InsurTech plays some significant roles in the accessibility of insurance especially for consumers.

The main object of insurance is managing and transferring risks which both consumers and businesses may be exposed to in their day-to-day activities. Insurance is obtained through a private contract entered into between the assured and the insurer. When AI is involved in the operation of the insurance services, the goals that AI is expected to achieve vary from concluding a contract to finalising a claim made by the assured under that contract.

Insurance is vital for individuals, businesses, and communities to recover from adverse events which subsequently impact the long-term economic growth, development, and social cohesion. Hence, the principles governing insurance contracts are of interest not only to individuals and businesses but also for societies and national economies. The ever-growing involvement of InsurTech in the insurance operations requires us to consider the question of the level of disruption that the new technologies may have had on the insurance services and therefore on society. To answer this question, it would be helpful to first explore the areas of insurance services in which InsurTech has been predominantly employed. Following that, the social and economic impact of InsurTech will be discussed together with the fundamental principles that guide the business and legal operation of insurance services.

I am grateful to Mr Gurbaaz Gill, an undergraduate student of King's College London, Faculty of Natural and Mathematical Sciences for his contribution on researching InsureTech and associated Technologies discussed in this paper. All errors and omissions are mine.

II INSURTECH

Although the behemoths of the insurance industry remain fairly traditional institutions, the business of insurance is changing.[1] The envelope marked 'tech-transformation' is actually being pushed through the door by younger and smaller entities, adopting cutting-edge technology to revolutionise the insurance value chain.[2] Insurers may build the InsurTech technologies in their own systems, or they may purchase the services provided by InsurTech companies which have been all but shy in pitching their technology-rich solutions to larger insurance companies.[3]

In its early days of development in England, insurance was defined as 'contracts upon chance'; hence, 'each party ought to know all the circumstances'.[4] Edward Lloyd's coffee house, traders' and insurers' meeting point at the time and the foundation of today's Lloyd's of London, became the most reputable of all the coffee houses in seventeenth-century London, due to Edward Lloyd's successful intelligence gathering about the risks negotiated and insured there.

Today, the inherent reliance of insurance on intelligence gathering enables an ecology conducive for AI applications to thrive in the insurance environment. InsurTech enables insurers to include in their business models new ways of data collection and data analysis such as cloud computing, telematics, the internet of things, mobile phones, blockchain solutions, cognitive computing, and predictive modelling.[5] Whilst traditional data sources to assess risk include demographic, exposure, loss, hazard, and medical data, InsurTech sources include behavioural data, Internet of Things (IoT), images, personal data from smart watches, and genetics data.[6] Data mining and data harvesting, including machine learning, deep learning,[7] and natural language processing, enable predictive analytics which open new horizons in risk modelling. Moreover, insurance systems use advanced algorithms that learn with every additional data record and continually adjust and enhance their predictions.

1 R Swedloff, 'The New Regulatory Imperative for Insurance' (2020) 61(6) *Boston College Law Review* 2083; A Zarifis, CP Holland and A Milne, 'Evaluating the Impact of AI on Insurance: The Four Emerging AI- and Data-Driven Business Models' (*Emerald Open Res*, 2019) <https://doi.org/10.35241/emeraldopenres.13249.1>; B Nicoletti, *Insurance 4.0: Benefits and Challenges of Digital Transformation* (Palgrave Macmillan 2021) 24

2 See A Zarifis, '20 Case Studies on AI Evaluating the Impact of AI on Insurance' <https://doi.org/10.6084/m9.figshare.9845015.v2>.

3 Nicoletti (n 1) 411.

4 *Seaman v Fonereau* (1742) 2 Str. 1183, 93 E.R. 1115; *Carter v Boehm* (1766) 3 Burr. 1905, R Merkin, *Marine Insurance: Legal History* (Edward Elgar 2021).

5 B McGurk, *Data Profiling and Insurance Law* (Hart 2019); Nicoletti (n 1) 4; CP Holland and A Kavuri, 'Artificial Intelligence and Digital Transformation of Insurance Markets' (2021) 54 *Journal of Financial Transformation* 104; Zarifis, Holland and Milne (n 1).

6 Holland and Kavuri (n 5) 109.

7 McGurk (n 5) 13–14. Deep machine learning is a branch of machine learning which relies on complex statistical models and algorithms with multiple layers of parallel processing that loosely model the way the biological brain works. Neural networks 'learn' to perform tasks by considering examples generally without being programmed with any task-specific rules.

Customer services including underwriting and claims handling can be automated through these technologies that support standard customer lifecycle business processes such as new customer acquisition, security, customer identification, policy management, customer renewal, and cross-selling. As a result, not only have underwriting capacities been expanded, but the turnaround time for claims has also accelerated dramatically.[8] The recent proliferation of data therefore implies that the development of systems for mining, consolidation, and integration of data would be the next frontier in the realm of insurance.

III DISRUPTION OF INSURANCE

A *Algorithmic Underwriting*

The way that the first digital and algorithmically driven Lloyd's syndicate operates in the Lloyd's market is a strong support for the argument that InsurTech has not had a major disrupting effect in the market but has also increased the market efficiency. Ki[9] is the first fully digital and algorithmically driven Lloyd's of London syndicate offering instant capacity, accessible anywhere, at any time. Ki can provide a broker with an algorithmic quote in ten seconds, whereas traditionally it would take about two weeks.

Ki follows the same procedure in agreeing to insure a risk as has always been followed in the market.[10] Each syndicate, through their managing agents at Lloyd's, agrees to subscribe a risk by a percentage that it is willing to take. This percentage is called the syndicate's line. The terms of insurance contracts are agreed upon between the managing agent (who represents the syndicate) and the broker (the assured's agent). Syndicates' source of financial support is provided by investors who are called 'names'. Ki is a Lloyd's syndicate; its managing agent is Brit, and a name behind Ki provides the financial support required to insure risks. At Lloyd's usually a leading underwriter (LU) subscribes a risk first and relying on the LU's expertise the following underwriters may agree to insure the same risk by their own subscription. Ki is a following underwriter who subscribes to contracts insuring mainly property and casualty risks worldwide. The terms of the insurance offered by Ki are negotiated between the brokers and Ki's managing agent. To ensure a smooth incorporation of Ki's algorithmic quotation and underwriting in the market, Ki worked

[8] Holland and Kuvari (n 5) 110; Chartered Insurance Institute, 'Addressing Gender Bias in Artificial Intelligence' 8 <www.cii.co.uk/media/10122027/cii-gender-bias-in-ai-research-report.pdf>. See also EIOPA, 'A report from the European Insurance and Occupational Pension Authority (EIOPA) Consultative Expert Group: Artificial intelligence governance principles: towards ethical and trustworthy artificial intelligence in the European insurance sector' (*EIOPA*, 2021) <www.eiopa.europa.eu/document-library/report/artificial-intelligence-governance-principles-towards-ethical-and>. The EIOPA has provided a comprehensive summary of the use of AI across the insurance value chain on page 9.

[9] <www.ki-insurance.com/>.

[10] A detailed information about the formation of insurance contracts at Lloyd's can be found in O Gurses, *Marine Insurance Law* (3rd edn, Routledge 2023) ch 2.

closely with the insurance brokers in the development and the implementation process so that a broker-friendly approach was adopted as insurance brokers introduced clients to insurers.

The products offered by insurers have not changed dramatically. However, parametric insurance requires a closer look given that it does not sit easily with the principles that govern indemnity insurance. This product pays a fixed amount upon the occurrence of a triggering event. It is an 'index' based product where the payment to the purchaser of this product is determined by the degree of covariation between an event and an estimated loss.[11] No loss adjusting need take place, and as soon as a pre-determined threshold has been met, the policy is triggered, and payment is made. A natural event which is deemed likely to lead to a loss or a series of losses can be a trigger. For instance, a product designed to respond to hurricane losses could be triggered by wind speeds reaching a certain pre-agreed intensity and in a specified location, all according to a provider of weather data. For drought and agricultural cover, the parameters might be based on satellite images of the colour of the ground, or volume and frequency of rainfall over defined periods.

Parametric insurance providers benefit from remote sensing and other earth observation data sources such as weather stations, drones, and aircraft to gather data and assess losses.[12] The amount payable is based on a modelled forecast of the loss that the policyholder will incur. For instance, the WINnERS (Weather Index based Risk Services)[13] Project in Tanzania integrates remote sensing and field observations to model agricultural losses for maize farms based on weather related risk, such as rainfall deficit or heat stress.[14]

Accessibility of the product provides a great advantage for the interested parties. Advances in satellite technology and data analysis help avoid the pitfalls of high transaction costs and therefore expand the potential reach of insurance policies to rural areas previously considered uninsurable.[15] Digital platforms enables the insurer to access a greater number of customers with much lower cost to the insurers than before. Digital platforms provide the baseline digitisation through which banks and insurance capital providers can build partnerships, the purchasers of parametric products then may receive payments via mobile wallets.[16]

11 J Leeuw and others, 'The Potential and Uptake of Remote Sensing in Insurance: A Review' (10891) <www.mdpi.com/journal/remotesensing>.

12 <www.poverty-action.org/organization/planet-guarantee>.

13 <www.climate-kic.org/success-stories/winners/>.

14 Similarly, in India, see <www.pmfby.gov.in/pdf/Revised_Operational_Guidelines.pdf>.

15 Leeuw and others (n 11) 10891–10892.

16 <www.etherisc.com/>. Distributed ledger technology (DLT – Blockchain), whose defining feature is the exchange of data using a common ledger or another form of 'single source of truth', is secured against forgery through cryptography. It is an information coordination between many parties, which automatically executes the contract for payment in response to the trigger being met. Once entered, information can never be erased, and therefore blockchain contains a record of every single transaction ever made. J Bacon, JD Michels, C Millard and J Singh, 'Blockchain Demystified' (20 December 2017). Queen Mary School of Law Legal Studies Research Paper No 268/2017 <https://ssrn.com/abstract=3091218>;

Parametric insurance, however, does not attempt to assess the actual loss of the assured or whether the assured suffered loss. As a result, in some cases whilst a payment may be made there is no actual loss, in some other cases no payment may be received because on index the relevant area falls below the trigger point. No solution to this dilemma has been proposed so far by the parametric product providers.

To use the word 'insurance' to express the nature of the parametric products is misplaced. One of the most fundamental principles of indemnity insurance is that the assured is entitled for insurance indemnity only up to the full amount of the actual loss suffered,[17] but no more than that.[18] It may be the case that, due to underinsurance, failing to prove the entire loss, as a result of the deductible or the policy limit set by the terms of insurance, the assured may receive an indemnity less than the actual loss. However, these points are determined contractually, and it is under the assured's control to gather relevant evidence to prove the amount of the loss and to determine, at the outset of the contract, how much deductible will be applied to losses under that contract. What the index determines, however, is not under the assured's control, whose claim will not be supported even the actual loss is proven, as all depends on what the index concludes.

B *Data Profiling and Risk Pooling*

Algorithmic decision-making refers to the process by which an algorithm produces an output through machine learning.[19] Machine learning is a sub-category of a broader term of AI and may be defined as a method of designing a sequence of actions to solve a problem, known as algorithms, which optimise automatically through experience and with limited or no human intervention.[20] Algorithmic outcomes are based on patterns found in large amounts of data based on statistical correlations between variables in a dataset.[21] For instance, for advertisement targeting, comparability is used to classify the diversity of humankind in order to categorise groups with whom a product from a limited range can be matched. The word 'bucket'[22] is used to express this method: individuals with similar features are being dropped into a bucket. They all are assembled from data traces amongst which new

Nicoletti (n 1) 39. See also M Kianieff, *Blockchain Technology and the Law* (Routledge 2020); E Ong, 'Blockchain Bills of Lading and the UNCITRAL Model Law on Electronic Transferable Records' (2020) 3 *JBL* 202.

17 *Castellain v Preston* (1883) 11 QBD 380.

18 Valued policies may be an exception to this principle. See Marine Insurance Act 1906 s.27. See A Padfield, *Insurance Claims* (5th edn, Bloomsbury Publishing 2021) ch 6.

19 FJ Zuiderveen Borgesius, 'Strengthening Legal Protection against Discrimination by Algorithms and Artificial Intelligence' (2020) 24(10) *The International Journal of Human Rights* 1572, 1573

20 Holland and Kavari (n 5) 105; Zarifis, Holland and Milne (n 1).

21 K Langenbucher, 'Responsible A.I.-Based Credit Scoring – A Legal Framework' (2020) 31(4) *European Business Law Review* 527, 547.

22 Ibid. 530.

sets of relations between persons, parts of persons, material objects, and pecuniary interests are established. This results in 'mass predictive personalisation', instead of an individualised personalisation.[23]

The notion of expected loss is the central concept in a risk classification system.[24] Insurance puts many cases together and spreads the cost of future claims among all policyholders. In so doing insurance relies on group rather than individual estimates of expected loss. It is necessary to treat an individual as a member of group as prices are set by predicting the probability that any group of observationally identical individuals will suffer a loss. Therefore, in constructing risk classes, the insurer's goal is to calculate the expected loss of each insured and to place insureds with similar expected losses into the same class, so that each may be charged the same rate.[25] With few exceptions (such as large enterprises with detailed loss histories and frequent current losses), estimating expected loss 'individually' is impossible.[26]

Noticeably, one of the selling points of insurance services supported by InsurTech is providing a personalised or customised products for the assured. However, it is not clear who or what is the concept of person that is referred to.[27] If what the insurers mean by personalisation is that they are able to better allocate each individual to the risk groups that fit their profile best, they are not offering any revolutionary solutions for customers. At best, it could be argued that the InsurTech predictions are more accurate than the traditional methods of risk pooling.

It therefore appears that with regards to the marketing of the insurance products, such new practices may undermine existing consumer protections aimed at fixing endemic market failures in terms of not misleading customers and treating consumers fairly.[28]

A further issue appears to be the production of 'types of persons'[29] which involves generalisation rather than personalisation. The result is a sort of commodification of the individual.[30] It seems almost impossible for an individual to know the accuracy of their profile in the eyes of the AI. Another unknown is the level of accuracy or suitability of the allocation of an individual to a risk pool which will determine the price and the terms of the insurance cover that this particular individual will be subject to. This may create some 'unfair' outcomes, for instance, where a very risk-averse person lives in a place which is regarded as high risk in the general risk

23 Karen Yeung, 'Five Fears about Mass Predictive Personalisation in an Age of Surveillance Capitalism' (2018) 8(3) *International Data Privacy Law* 258.

24 KS Abraham, 'Efficiency and Fairness in Insurance Risk Classification' (1985) 71 *Va L Rev* 403, 408.

25 Ibid. 408.

26 Ibid. 423.

27 L McFall and L Moor, 'Who, or What, Is Insurtech Personalizing?: Persons, Prices and the Historical Classifications of Risk' (2018) 19(2) *Distinktion: Journal of Social Theory* 193, 194.

28 Swedloff, 'The New Regulatory Imperative for Insurance' (n 1), 2035–2036.

29 McFall and Moor (n 27) 206.

30 J Frick and IM Barsan, 'InsurTech – Opportunities and Legal Challenges for the Insurance Industry' [2020] Revue Trimestrielle de Droit Financier <https://ssrn.com/abstract=3686489>.

classification of that area. If the personalised profile in the eyes of the AI took into account the place of residence only, the risk assessment will not be personalised as it will disregard the other characteristics of this particular person.

Although scientists may argue that how AI learns is not entirely unknown, the explanation provided is still too complex to comprehend for many. For example, where the picture of a cat is fed as the input with the objective that the system will classify it as a cat, each circle of the neural network has certain weights and values attached to them that help identify defining attributes that would then help classify if it is really a cat in the image. If certain attributes at either circle are satisfied, the signal will be sent from the satisfied circle unit identifying that there is a cat/there is no cat, which is given as the output. This is, however, a very basic example as neural networks contain thousands of such circles which are called neurons. It becomes very difficult for us to comprehend data passing through such a large network.

It is not possible to trace back inputs from outputs in such large networks to derive an 'exact explanation' for the outcome. This is where the main reason for inexplicability of these neural networks lies.

Problems are therefore at least threefold. Large amounts of data are available for insurers from their own sources as well as through open-source protocols.[31] Reportedly, some motor insurance companies use over 1,000 rating factors.[32] It is unknown which of those data truly reflects the customer's profile or is taken into account in the profiling. This leads to a mass predictive personalisation. Moreover, the ratio of the machine learning which has impacts on the insurance price and terms of the insurance cover is neither clear nor appears to be explainable.

C *Presentation of the Risk to the Insurer*

Insurance is a means to transfer the insured person's uncertainty of loss to the insurer for the certainty of a smaller payment called the premium.[33] The insurer assumes the individual insured's risk of loss; therefore, the premium should be fundamentally based upon the expected value of an insured's loss.[34] Insurers individuate those prices by determining whether the particular observable characteristics of a particular insured correlate with particular harms.[35] That determination is inherently

[31] This represents collaboration between public and private institutions to establish distributed data-sharing protocols and security frameworks which will enable participating entities to utilise computing prowess and data of associates. For instance, cookies, enabled by browsers and websites, collect a variety of data from users' internet browsing history. This data is currently available in an anonymised format for several marketing companies to advertise their products. Such data can be coupled with smart-device data and health data, and ported directly to insurers.

[32] Chartered Insurance Institute (n 8) 8.

[33] Swedloff, 'The New Regulatory Imperative for Insurance' (n 1) 2057; MA Walters, 'Risk Classification Standards' Proceedings, Vol LXVIII, Part 11981, No. 129, 3.

[34] Walters (n 33) 3.

[35] L McFall, 'Personalizing Solidarity? The Role of Self-Tracking in Health Insurance Pricing' (2019) 48(1) *Economy and Society* 52, 54.

data driven[36] as insurance operations are based on the mathematical calculation of probability which takes into account the individual features and experiences of the assured.[37]

Insurers could do such an assessment only if the insurers have the information that they need about the subject matter insured and the person whose interest is insured. The insurers may want to know whether the assured has ever been bankrupt, if there have been allegations of dishonesty or criminal charges against them, or if they had any criminal convictions.[38] The assured's pre-contractual information duty is named as the duty of fair presentation of the risk which is a statutory principle under English law.[39] The origin of the duty goes back to the seventeenth century when the insurance was defined as 'contracts upon chance' and therefore 'each party ought to know all the circumstances'.[40] Briefly, the duty requires the assured to inform the insurer of the matters where a prudent insurer, objectively, would be interested in such matters. In consumer insurance the assured's duty is limited to exercise reasonable care not to misrepresent material facts.[41] A consumer assured's duty is satisfied where the assured answers, with reasonable care, questions asked by the insurer – usually via a proposal form- before the contract was concluded. The duty is heavier in business insurance that the assured is under the duty to volunteer such information, as well as the duty not to misrepresent material facts.[42] The assured's failure to comply with the duty entitles the insurer to a range of remedies from deduction from the amount to be paid under the contract to avoiding the insurance policy as a whole depending on how serious the breach was.[43]

Insurers' access to the big data does not alter the essence of the duty codified either by the Insurance Act (IA) 2015 or the Consumer Insurance (Disclosure and Representations) (CIDRA) 2012. It may, however, reduce the burden imposed on the assured to prove that the presentation of the risk was fair. Where the insurer knows, ought to know, or is presumed to know a particular information, the insurer may not argue that the assured failed to disclose those facts fairly to the insurer.[44] Insurers' methods for accumulation of information, namely, data, have been historically limited to manual methods and self-reporting where brokers played a significant role.

36 Swedloff, 'The New Regulatory Imperative for Insurance' (n 1) 2057.

37 R Swedloff, 'Risk Classification's Big Data (R)evolution' (2014) 21 *Connecticut Insurance Law Journal* 339.

38 *North Star Shipping Ltd v Sphere Drake Insurance Plc.* [2006] EWCA Civ 378, [2006] 2 Lloyd's Rep. 183; *Insurance Corp of the Channel Islands v Royal Hotel Ltd* [1998] Lloyd's Rep. I.R. 151 (QB); *Brotherton v Aseguradora Colseguros (No 2)* [2003] EWCA Civ 705, [2003] Lloyd's Rep IR 746.

39 In business insurance the duty is governed under the Insurance Act 2015, consumer assured's duty is regulated under the Consumer Insurance (Disclosure and Representation) Act 2012. See McGurk (n 5) ch 5.

40 *Whittingham v Thornburgh & Al* (1690) 2 Vern 206, 23 ER 734; *De Costa v Scandret* (1723) 2 P Wms 170, 24 ER 686; *Seaman v Fonereau* (1742) 2 Str 1183, 93 E.R. 111

41 Consumer Insurance (Disclosure and Representation) Act 2012 (CIDRA 2012) s 2(2).

42 Insurance Act 2015 (IA 2015) s 3.

43 IA 2015 s 8 and sch 1.

44 Insurance Act 2015 s 3(5).

AI-based data reporting seems to be an addendum to self-reporting of information and, in some cases, attempts to replace the latter altogether.

For instance, Selfie-Quote.com estimates an individual's age, gender, and body mass index (BMI) using an individual's selfie.[45] Similarly, Aviva has launched a new 'Ask It Never'[46] initiative with the aim of eliminating the need to ask customers questions. They also rely on the customer's digital footprint data to underwrite the risk being presented.

The insurers in this respect appear to be proud of 'abolishing' the proposal forms which contain numerous questions about the relevant individual's past, health conditions, their habits and financial conditions. However, what has been transformed is that the answers to some of the questions that are traditionally being posed in the proposal form are now being predicted by the automated system, that is, the machine learning. And the areas that the machine – at least for now – cannot predict are being set out as a declaration which the assured confirms by means of 'I declare…'. The declaration includes a confirmation of a number of existing or non-existing health conditions of the individual. This is, in a way, the same as asking a question in a proposal form such as 'Do you have any chronic illnesses'? New practices introduced by InsurTech by no means abolished the assured's pre-contractual information duty. Only the channels through which the information is provided to the insurers have been altered to some limited extent. It is essential to make the customers aware of the significance of the declaration and any other answers provided to the insurer in response to a question before an insurance cover is agreed.

D *Inducement: Causation v Correlation*

The essence of the duty of fair presentation of the risk lies on the tests of materiality and inducement. The materiality test is described above – the insurer is entitled to be informed of any matters that a prudent insurer, objectively, would be interested. The inducement test, on the other hand, is determined subjectively – the insurer has to demonstrate that had the presentation been fair, that is, had the assured complied with the duty, the insurer would either not have entered into the contract at all or would have entered, but on different terms. The data that the insurer has taken into account has therefore to be revealed by the insurer who would argue that the assured breached the duty of fair presentation of the risk. The insurer who argues the breach of the duty would have to specifically identify the issues known by the insurer through the data already available to them and the information provided by the assured, as well as the circumstances that the assured failed to present fairly. Proving materiality establishes

45 Selfie-Quote.com is the result of a collaboration between Legal and General America (LGA) and a science and technology company, Lapetus Solutions Inc.

46 The system is currently being piloted with some of its existing home insurance customers through its online portal MyAviva. It is available to consumers only; commercial customers with more complex activities will always need help from their broker and Aviva to understand their risk features.

the assured's breach but is not sufficient for the insurer to successfully seek a remedy for it. Inducement has to be proven as a matter of fact that the assured's breach led the insurer to enter into the contract as agreed between the parties.[47] The processing of volumes of data looks for patterns to achieve correlations, but it is not known how such correlations are produced.[48] Inducement, however, demands an explanation of how such correlations are produced, namely, how the features and experiences of the relevant individual assured correlated with the predicted loss experiences of that individual, and ultimately agreeing to insure such individual on the terms agreed.[49] This would then reveal whether what was not fairly presented to the insurer had a causal effect on the insurer's decision to insure such risk.

The notion of causality and the detection of causal relationships is a longstanding problem in machine learning and statistics.[50] Machines work with algorithms and data, while human decision-makers work with rules and narratives expressed in natural language.[51] The learned relationships are in general only association relations and not causal relations, that is, the observed covariation between two variables A and B is caused by an unknown third variable C.[52] When actions based on predictions are significantly fed back into the observed system, association learning cannot answer important questions arising with regard to the consequences of the executed actions. In order to develop and apply standards of transparency, accountability, and unbiasedness, the result of learning has to identify the causal factors that determine the predictions.[53]

Big data and its algorithmic analysis are, however, unlikely to provide simple, easily explainable reasons for the insurer's risk assessments that led to its ultimate decisions.[54] Consequently, where an AI entity assesses the risk presented, either the insurer will not be able to establish the assured's breach of the duty of fair presentation of the risk, as inducement will not be possible to prove, or if they want to contend that, they will have to find a way to evince on what basis, that is, on what data analysis, they entered into the contract with the assured.

E *Actuarial Fairness*

Actuarial fairness represents the concept of similar risks being treated similarly so that the premium paid by individuals corresponds to their actual risk.[55] For

47 IA 2015 s. 8; CIDRA 2012 s 4.
48 Frick and Barsan (n 30).
49 Swedloff, 'Risk Classification's Big Data (R)evolution' (n 37) 344. McFall and Moor (n 27) 205–206.
50 Jörg Zimmermann and Armin B Cremers, 'Foundations of Artificial Intelligence and Effective Universal Induction' in J von Braun and others (eds), *Robotics, AI, and Humanity* (Springer 2021).
51 Z Ződi, 'Algorithmic Explainability and Legal Reasoning' (2022) 10(1) *The Theory and Practice of Legislation* 67.
52 Zimmermann and Cremers (n 50) 40.
53 Ibid.
54 Swedloff, 'Risk Classification's Big Data (R)evolution' (n 37) 367.
55 EIOPA (n 8) 12.

practical purposes, insurers classify risks in different groups of which individuals are treated as members. Although it was proposed that insurers do not usually classify or attach risk to whole human individuals,[56] in reality, a person's features and loss experiences are of interest to the insurer for the purposes of identifying in which of the risk groups such individual will be placed. Until an insured person is treated as a member of a group, it is impossible to know his expected loss because, for practical purposes, that concept is a statistical one based on group probabilities.[57]

Telematics and IoT expose policyholder lives more to an underwriting eye.[58] Telematics can be defined as the convolution of telecommunications and informatics. For instance, a driver's data can be collected through certain specialised applications which are capable of monitoring and transmitting live location, speed, idling time, harsh acceleration/braking, fuel consumption and vehicle faults. Additionally, insurers can access data about the running routes that the assured person follows or what other types of exercise they do on a regular basis. For instance, FitSense[59] allows life and health insurers to use data from wearable technology in underwriting pricing and claims handling. Allianz offers discounts for policyholders equipping their homes with smart home devices. Drivit[60] provides unique safety and consumption metrics for insurers, who are able to develop full usage-based insurance (UBI) products based on the information from Drivit Dashboards. It also provides drivers with dynamic driving advice, along with weather and traffic state and route optimisation for pay-per-mile insurance plans. The data could be combined with other data types – for example, historical loss data, weather patterns, route map information that contains speed limits, and data from other drivers – and analysed using machine learning algorithms to derive a driving score, which is then used as an indicator of the risk of an accident and used to price the insurance premium. This approach is fundamentally different to what was historically used to model risk in car insurance, which was the demographic information about the driver, the value and type of car being insured, and the driver's history, in particular previous claims and convictions.[61]

Although it is not possible to achieve complete accuracy,[62] the more information that is available about the features of the assured and the subject matter insured, the higher the accuracy of the risk assessment. For instance, products such as Drivit and FitSense described earlier incentivise positive behaviours, which may lead to a reduction in the rate of claims which then result in lower premium charged for the

56 McFall and Moor (n 27) 205–206.

57 Abraham (n 24) 423–424.

58 Swedloff, 'The New Regulatory Imperative for Insurance' (n 1) 2062; Nicoletti (n 1) 410.

59 <www.fitsense.co/>; Zarifis (n 2).

60 <www.drivit.com/>. See also <www.cuvva.com/>; Zarifis (n 2).

61 Holland and Kavuri (n 5) 106.

62 Abraham (n 24) 405.

individuals who provided data through such devices. It may therefore be concluded that tracking increases actuarial fairness.[63]

Insurance is a mechanism of individual responsibility based on a strict equivalence of risks and premiums. Consequently, a price difference between customers of a high- and low-risk profiles is natural. State and private entities may allocate individuals to particular groups and this is a significant element in the operation of society.[64] Insurance pricing is an example of this, which may be regulated, and it represents a key political choice.[65]

Insurance is based on the complementary principles of solidarity and equity in the face of uncertain risks.[66] Solidarity implies the sharing of responsibility and benefits in terms of costs, while equity means that the contribution of an individual should be roughly in line with his or her own level of risk.[67]

Private insurance strives to achieve random solidarity[68] between people with similar risk characteristics, who share with one another the sole randomness of occurrence. Tracking makes available more up to date data about the individual risk in question. Such profiling would allow an individual to be placed in a group which is best suited to the individuals' features and loss experiences. These individuals can then be offered more customised, personalised, and fairly priced insurance services.

However, social insurers raise some concerns about the above and contend that algorithmic prediction could radicalise the principle of segmentation as it culminates in the extreme case of 'segments of one'.[69] This would mean the end of the risk-pooling on which the principle of risk-spreading is based.[70] As a result, the solidarity aspect of insurance is undermined, and the risk is not spread or pooled, but the individual policyholder pays only for their own uncertainty. Consequently, some policyholders might not be able to afford the necessary coverage[71] or might face being excluded from a cover as a whole.[72] Insurance, accordingly, is a union for mutual aid.[73] In coping with adversity, individual prudence was replaced by mutualisation

63 E Seinberg, 'Run for Your Life: The Ethics of Behavioral Tracking in Insurance' (2022) 179 *Journal of Business Ethics* 665.

64 J Davey, 'Insurance and Price Regulation in the Digital Era' in TT Arvind and J Steele (eds), *Contract Law and the Legislature: Autonomy, Expectations, and the Making of Legal Doctrine* (Hart Publishing 2020), 269–294, 274.

65 Ibid.

66 PS Harper 'Insurance and Genetic Testing' (1993) 341 *Lancet* 224.

67 Ibid.

68 Y Thiery and C Van Schoubroeck, 'Fairness and Equality in Insurance Classification' (2006) 31 *The Geneva Papers* 190, 195. For solidarity and mutuality based insurance see McGurk (n 5) ch 3.

69 A Cevolini and E Esposito 'From Pool to Profile: Social Consequences of Algorithmic Prediction in Insurance' [2020] Big Data and Society 1, 4.

70 Ibid. 4.

71 Swedloff, 'The New Regulatory Imperative for Insurance' (n 1) 2041.

72 J Liukko, 'Genetic Discrimination, Insurance, and Solidarity: An Analysis of the Argumentation for Fair Risk Classification' (2010) 29(4) *New Genetics and Society* 457, 458.

73 Ibid.

whereby the moral responsibility for the accident is not looked for in the behaviour of the faulty individual but instead attributed collectively to society. Thus, insurance socialises responsibility.[74] Charging more simply based on an underlying suspect or vulnerable characteristic reinforces structural inequality, reinforces stereotypes, and creates dignitary harms.[75] The result would be to undermine the risk-sharing paradigm and subsequently corresponding decline in social solidarity.[76]

Such concerns, however, may not be convincing. In private insurance, the insurer agrees to indemnify the assured for the loss that the latter suffers under the terms of the insurance contract. The common point between social and private insurance is that the rationality of insurance is risk pooling and risk spreading. However, the pooling of risks is not the same as pooling of losses. To argue that the risk-sharing inherent in a classification scheme automatically constitutes 'subsidisation' is to misunderstand the nature of classification.[77] It is a private insurance contract where the premium represents a common indicator of the risk for both the insurer and the assured.[78] Information available through many different channels is aggregated with insurers' internal data to establish a risk-profile, which then underpins decisions of underwriting and pricing. Most rates (costs) are determined by statistical analysis of past losses based on specific variables of the insured.[79] The variation of expected losses from individual to individual motivates insurers to price insureds differently.[80] Insurers need to divide insureds into different subgroups of similar chance solidarity in which each individual has an equal chance for losses.[81] Individual members of each class pay premiums based on expected losses and thereby share the risk of random losses so that total premiums cover the aggregate losses of the class.[82] No risk class is completely homogeneous; the slightly lower risks within a class always seem to subsidise the slightly higher risks.[83] No subsidy can run from one risk class to another but a subsidy can flow from the lucky members of the class to the unlucky.[84]

Insurance firms can contribute to financial inclusion but cannot offer solutions to entrenched social inequalities which are the preserve of public and governmental

[74] S Frezal and L Barry 'Fairness in Uncertainty: Some Limits and Misinterpretations of Actuarial Fairness' (2020) 167 *Journal of Business Ethics* 129; Swedloff, 'Risk Classification's Big Data (R)evolution' (n 37) 362.

[75] Swedloff, 'Risk Classification's Big Data (R)evolution' (n 37) 365.

[76] Liukko (n 72) 458; CP Holland, M Mullins and M Cunneen, 'Creating Ethics Guidelines for Artificial Intelligence (AI) and Big Data Analytics: The Case of the European Consumer Insurance Market' (2021) <https://ssrn.com/abstract=3808207>.

[77] Abraham (n 24) 430.

[78] Frezal and Barry (n 74) 132.

[79] 'The Impact of Big Data and Artificial Intelligence (AI) in the Insurance Sector' <www.oecd.org/finance/Impact-Big-Data-AI-in-the-Insurance-Sector.htm>.

[80] Walters (n 33) 4.

[81] Ibid.

[82] Abraham (n 24) 421.

[83] Ibid. 430.

[84] Ibid. 421.

authorities.[85] In reality, insurers have a significant financial incentive to classify insureds properly on the basis of risk.[86] They pursue a self-interested aim, whereas governments generally pursue a welfare enhancement goal.[87] The social insurance view mention that in a subsidising solidarity a person with a certain risk profile pays for the amount of loss of persons bearing a higher loss expectancy. However, if an individual is set a higher premium than the premium due for the risk they assume in order to provide for a subsidy for high-risk groups, they might choose to leave the group. Lower-risks groups are averse to subsidising higher risks groups.[88] Insurance costs depend upon buyer characteristics[89] which naturally results in risk differentiation.[90] The pooling of losses whereby everyone should share the costs equally denies the reality that some may take more precautions against possible risks of loss than others. It is equally arguable that it is only fair when these two groups are treated differently in the pricing of insurance and the conditions under which these two groups are insured.

Social insurance treats insurance as an instrument of social policy to compensate victims that insurance coverage should be seen as a right, not a privilege. However, insurance is a relationship that is established through a private contract which is not based on the principle of social compensation or subsidy whereby, for example, the young subsidise the costs of older people (risk) or wealthier customers cross-subsidise poorer customers (income).[91] It is not an instrument of social policy to compensate victims, nor is it a tax to redistribute wealth.[92] In the 2021 report by the European Insurance and Occupational Pensions Authority (EIOPA), it was acknowledged that insurance plays an important role in terms of societal responsibility and social equity in co-creating a market that offers opportunity and access to all citizens including vulnerable groups, in order to access essential products at an affordable price. On the other hand, the report reiterated that it is not always possible for insurance firms to offer insurance at an 'affordable price' (e.g., flood insurance in heavily exposed areas, terrorist risk, pandemic risk, etc.). EIOPA's report suggested that in such cases, it is a political and societal task to find solutions.[93]

It may be questioned whether peer to peer (P2P) insurance can operate in a way that may satisfy some of the objectives set by proponents of social insurance. Through P2P insurance, peer groups, such as families and friends, team up to absorb each other's risks. Every member contributes premium to insure each other's losses. This system relies on digital technology to connect the individuals with

85 EIOPA (n 8) 22.
86 Swedloff, 'Risk Classification's Big Data (R)evolution' (n 37) 345.
87 Thiery and Schoubroeck (n 66) 204.
88 Ibid. 196.
89 Walters (n 33) 2.
90 Zuiderveen Borgesius (n 19) 1584.
91 EIOPA (n 8) 22.
92 Walters (n 33) 5.
93 EIOPA (n 8) 13.

each other on a digital platform or market place, independent of location. Nexus Mutual[94] is one such example. The platform's deduction of management fee will be the cost to peers in case there are no losses or the compensation payable is less than the premium paid, as funds from the risk pool that were not used to pay out claims can be returned to users. The platform reinsures the losses that the policyholders are not liable. The system describes P2P insurance as resembling the Protection and Indemnity (P&I) Clubs by which shipowners mutually agree to share the losses suffered by the members of the Club.[95] Whilst mutuality is emphasised, in both P2P insurance and P&I club entries, members are selected. An individual or a shipowner is not as a matter of right permitted to join either of these groups. In such a selection, the risk profile of the individual or the shipowner is taken into account. Hence, mutual insurance shares many features of private insurance, and it does not represent the characteristics of what the social insurance attaches to insurance covers.

Neither index (parametric) products appear to achieve the goals that social insurers desire for insurance. Parametric products are said to prevent 'adverse selection', namely the situation where people exposed to higher risk seek insurance more frequently than those exposed to lower risk.[96] It also appears to be an efficient model for the businesses for whom investigating small claims may be costly as they do not even need to analyse any evidence of loss because it is all index based. However, in selecting this as a business model, which, as described above, is a financial product rather than an indemnity insurance, the problem arises when an actual loss falls below the trigger point set in the index.

A final note should be added here in response to some profound concerns over collecting timely information through tracking devices which, arguably, render some individuals uninsurable because the data that they represent either allocates them to 'high' risk groups (which makes the insurance unaffordable to them) or makes these individuals totally uninsurable. Firstly, as discussed above, the insurance industry has always been data driven and it is natural for the insurer to collect data about the driver's driving habits. Secondly, if the tracking devices did not collect the data, the relevant information would still be required by the insurers through the proposal forms that the assured is asked to complete before the insurer provides quotation for the insurance. Tracking has not disrupted the relationship between assured and insurer, but has generated new risk processes that enable product innovation to create personalised insurance pricing.[97] Whether insurance premiums are cheaper when InsurTech provides the necessary services is outside the scope of this paper.[98] It can nevertheless be added that with respect to policies that

94 <www.nexusmutual.io/>.

95 See Gurses (n 10) ch 1.

96 Leeuw and others (n 11) 10892.

97 Holland and Kuvari (n 5) 109.

98 For a detailed discussion on Insurance and Price Regulation in the Digital Era see Davey (n 64).

rely on wearable devices or similar telematics, it is unlikely that tracking will influence the insurance pricing dramatically.[99]

Different prices are applicable for different risk groups. Tracking devices is a facilitator to show the insurer the risk category that the relevant driver belongs to. Whether the assured has been caught whilst exceeding the speed limit is of interest to the insurer, regardless of whether the assured has a tracking device. The mode of information collection has been changed but the necessity and the essential character of the information gathered, the nature of the insurance service offered, and how such information is processed in the pricing of the insurance, has not been altered.

IV TRUST IN INSURERS

Insurance was described as a 'huge, rich, unpopular and impersonal industry whose products are bought without enthusiasm or affection, often in response to legal or financial pressure, by customers whose brand loyalty is really just inertia'.[100] Is a new kind of society being generated by the way that the automated systems, including InsurTech, interact with humans and affect their social relationships?[101] Moreover, when insurance services become more easily accessible, would this improve the perception of insurance?

Although AI/robotic entity appears to interact with human, enabling interpersonal coordination in real time,[102] as an artefact and not a natural reality, they can only fulfil a purpose imposed by human beings.[103] For instance, autonomous systems designed to detect emotions, decide, and simulate affective answers are provided for insurers through InsurTech.[104] They are in-built natural language processing systems with signal analysis and automatic speech recognition, semantic analysis and dialogue policies, response generation, and speech synthesis.[105] They have the capability to learn from data and, therefore, adapt in the sense that they have the potential to change, adapt, and learn as new information becomes available.[106] However,

99 Maiju Tanninen, Turo-Kimmo Lehtonen and Minna Ruckenstein, 'Tracking Lives, Forging Markets' (2021) 14(4) *Journal of Cultural Economy* 449, 460.

100 McFall and Moor (n 27) 194.

101 Joachim von Braun, Margaret S Archer, Gregory M Reichberg and Marcelo Sánchez Sorondo, 'AI, Robotics, and Humanity: Opportunities, Risks, and Implications for Ethics and Policy' in Joachim von Braun and others (eds), *Robotics, AI, and Humanity* (Springer 2021) 10; Zarifis, Holland and Milne (n 1).

102 A Clodic and R Alami, 'What Is It to Implement a Human-Robot Joint Action?' in Joachim von Braun and others (n 101) 236.

103 Von Braun and others (n 101) 9; W Singer, 'Differences between Natural and Artificial Cognitive Systems' in Von Braun and others (n 101) 18.

104 L Devillers, 'Human–Robot Interactions and Affective Computing: The Ethical Implications' in Von Braun and others (n 101) 206.

105 Ibid.

106 By which AI is separated from earlier digital technologies and systems. Holland and Kavuri (n 5) 107.

they cannot choose for themselves a different purpose from what was programmed in them by a human being.[107]

The capabilities of AI systems are expressed in a limited manner, for example, with respect to optimisation and pattern matching, which is a narrow conception of human intelligence.[108] The AI/robotic entity can only imitate human being[109] with no 'will',[110] or the desire or 'appetite for life' for themselves.[111] A human is not identical to the brain or some other subsystem of the nervous system[112] which can artificially be transferred to an AI/robotic entity. Artificial neurons may be built into machines to enable them to learn, adapt, and operate in dynamic and uncertain environments[113] but they have no perception of body and feelings,[114] nor can they be conscious. Thus, for the AI systems to perform tasks that would normally require humans to perform, such as complex classifications of data, predictions, assisting in an online application process, optimising pricing, and voice/image recognition, does not necessarily mean that AI systems possess human intelligence, but simply means that the machine can perform tasks that previously required humans.[115]

A number of different factors might have led to such unpopular perception of insurance including information asymmetries which make it difficult for consumers to understand and make good choices among different insurers and policies.[116] If the assured does not have the understanding of either the significance of the proposal form they completed before the contract was concluded or the terms of the insurance policy which set out the conditions and the limits of the insurance cover, the assured might naively assume that simply because they have an agreement with the insurer and they have paid the premium, the insurer would indemnify their loss when/if they suffer one.

Information asymmetry is the biggest hurdle to the improvement of the relationship between the assured and the insurer. Such asymmetry has led to the development of the duty of fair presentation of the risk which was addressed above. Further, the asymmetry encompasses the lack of understanding on the part of the assured of

[107] Von Braun and others (n 101) 9.

[108] Hence, this type of AI is classified as 'narrow' AI. Holland and Kavuri (n 5) 105. Although there are some discussions on the term 'strong' AI, that is, more general AI intelligence, it is still in an early stage and the validation of its claims is subject to further research. Nick Bostrom, *Superintelligence* (Oxford University Press 2016); Zimmerman and Kremers (n 50) 41; S Dehaene, H Lau and S Kouider, 'What Is Consciousness, and Could Machines Have It?' in Von Braun and others (n 101) 44–45.

[109] Clodic and Alami (n 102) 230; Wolfgang M Schröder, 'Robots and Rights: Reviewing Recent Positions in Legal Philosophy and Ethics' in Von Braun and others (n 101) 200; Devillers (n 104) 210; Holland and Kavuri (n 5) 106.

[110] GM. Reichberg and H Syse, 'Applying AI on the Battlefield: The Ethical Debates' in Von Braun and others (n 101) 149.

[111] Devillers (n 104) 206.

[112] Markus Gabriel, 'Could a Robot Be Conscious? Some Lessons from Philosophy' in Von Braun and others (n 101) 67.

[113] Reichberg and Syse (n 110) 149; Zimmermann and Cremers (n 50) 30.

[114] Devillers (n 104) 207.

[115] Holland and Kuvari (n 5) 106.

[116] Swedloff, 'The New Regulatory Imperative for Insurance' (n 1) 2035–2036.

the terms and conditions of the insurance contract. An additional matter introduced via machine learning is the insurers' opaque new methods of risk classification, pooling, and claim handling. Further, although machine appears to interact with humans, this is only limited to what the machine has been programmed for.

Where individuals can seek an insurance quote by swiping through a mobile app or by uploading a selfie, insurers are able to provide a quote in ten seconds, and a claim is assessed and paid in three minutes. Thus, InsurTech appears to have strong grounds for arguing that it has rendered insurance more accessible. However, accessibility of insurance should not only mean how easily the assured can contact an insurer to take out an insurance cover or how quickly the assured's claim is concluded by the insurer. It should also encompass the scope of cover to which the assured is entitled when it suffers losses. The insurer may accept or reject the claim – it all depends on the assessment of the claim under the insurance contract principles.

Moreover, the costs the individuals have to bear in return for such quick and easy services are unknown. Whilst risk classification is an essential concept of insurance, the criteria on which a classification is determined and the ratio of individuals' selection for the groups to which they belong are still unknown. Chatbots can answer only limited number of questions that they have been programmed for. They cannot adapt. Poor or incorrect advice and guidance could result in unacceptable consequences.[117] It is unknown if the risk classification performed by InsurTech implicate socially suspect categorisations such as race, national origin, or gender.[118] Where a proposal form is completed by the assured before the insurer provides a quote for the insurance cover, the assured would have a chance to know the questions being asked, so that the issues that the insurer took into account in assessing the risk and the pricing of the insurance. In the case of, for instance, obtaining a quote through a selfie, no questions are asked by the insurer. The selling point for the insurer is to provide quick and easy access to insurance, at any time that the assured wishes to. It is, however, inevitable for the insurer to seek some more information than simply what a machine can read from a selfie as well as the data available through the digital footprint. How can an insurer complete the additional information needed for the risk classification purposes? The assured, whose selfie partially completes the risk assessments and classification, is asked to sign a declaration which confirms the existence or non-existence of some circumstances as well as promises to do or not to do certain activities. To an insurance expert, this invites the duty of fair presentation of the risk. However, it is not realistic to expect an assured, a non-insurance expert, to understand the significance of such declaration for insurance contract law purposes. It may even be unrealistic to expect every assured to read every word in the declaration – this is a common omission that we all make.

[117] Holland et al. (n 76).

[118] Swedloff, 'Risk Classification's Big Data (R)evolution' (n 37) 345; See McGurk (n 5) ch 3.

Communication of the conditions of the insurance cover provided is key to overcome the information asymmetry between the assured and the insurer. The tracking devices are huge improvements in this respect by which the insurers may communicate timely warnings to the assureds with respect to the activities that might affect their eligibility to claim under their insurance contract. The risk precautionary measures are as fundamental to insurance as risk classification is.[119] Such measures are usually regulated under the terms of insurance in the form of obligations imposed on the assured. This is an area where the technicalities of the insurance contract law principles lie overwhelmingly. Contractually, if the assured fails to comply with such obligations, the law attaches some type of a remedy including the rejection of the claim by the insurer or suspension of the insurance cover.[120] For instance, insurer may require the assured to maintain a fire or burglar alarm system in the insured property. To comply with this condition is under the assured's control. The word 'control' in this context encompasses not only the ability to conduct activities more safely but also the capacity to vary levels of activity or production to reduce or prevent losses. Insurers would also be able to reclassify insureds periodically to account for the changes in expected losses resulting from insureds' prevention efforts.[121] One can be risk averse only if one knows about the possible risks. The assured faces two different risks: the insured risk, for example, fire, may take place, and the risk of losing the policy coverage by failing to comply with their contractual obligations. Tracking can potentially improve the communication between the assured and the insurer. The insurer, through the adoption of the tracking devices, could explain exactly what measures are required to be taken by the assured and the consequences of failing to do so. Insurance cover, hence, may become more accessible for the assured. Otherwise, regardless of whether the assured has understood the obligations set out by the insurance policy, the failure to comply with such obligations would, in principle, entitle the insurer to a remedy.

On the other hand, whilst tracking allows the insurers to attract safer individuals,[122] it may turn insurance into an inhibitor of action that discourages policyholders from embarking on actions.[123] Continuous monitoring of personal behaviour can be perceived in the long run as an interference with the right of self-determination. As a result, the proactive logic may transform into a veritable aggressive logic:[124] 'if you want to pay less, reduce your exposure to danger'. This may cause restrictions at an unreasonable level that minimise the movements and may affect the way that we all lead our lives. In a way, this diminishes a person's range of future options.[125]

119 Abraham (n 24) 413.
120 IA 2015 s 10–11.
121 Abraham (n 24) 413.
122 Steinberg (n 63).
123 Cevolini and Esposito (n 69) 2.
124 Ibid. 6.
125 Ibid. 7.

Moreover, research has suggested that the idea of the continuous use of tracking devices is false.[126] Gaps in the data were found due to 'missing' customers who have stopped or never started tracking their activity. This failure resulted in inaccurate or incomplete data that could hinder future data analysis or even prevent it altogether.[127] The insurer's goals of continuous engagement are not always aligned with real-world usage.[128]

From the insurers' point of view, they respect personal autonomy; they do not aim to force the insured person to do anything but they merely want to offer tools for health management.[129] In other words, behaviour-based policies are framed as platforms that the customers can use in their own efforts to improve lives. On the other hand, although efficient, tracking was asserted to be unfair. This is because, for instance, to track behaviour on the basis of 'nutrition choices' or 'exercise habits' for the purpose of pricing life insurance will exacerbate the already existing inequalities between the poor and the rich.[130] The former cannot afford to make healthy nutrition choices and do not have the time, resources, and mental leisure to exercise. It is submitted that this point should be considered in light of the actuarial fairness discussion above.

It is true that automated systems accelerate claims turnaround time dramatically.[131] However, it is not easy to dispute an outcome reached by an automated system that assessed the loss on the basis of a picture of the damage, the individual's voice, or the length of the answers provided in responding to the questions about how the loss occurred.

One of the services provided by InsurTech's is referred to as 'fraud detection'. An example is that a chatbot assesses a claim on the basis of several factors including the voice of the person making the claim and the length of the answers provided by that person in a conversation with a chatbot.[132] Concluding that the assured failed to prove what caused the loss or the assured's claim is not genuine because it is fraudulent, are two different matters. The former does not always include the assured's fraud. Further, fraud is a serious allegation; the assured's intention to defraud the insurer has to be proven by the insurer with strong evidence.

The insurer's pre-contractual information duty will be assessed under Section 17 of the MIA 1906 because the IA 2015 and CIDRA 2012 govern the pre-contractual information duty owed by the assured only. The insurer might be aware of some facts that the assured does not know. The question of whether the insurer should

[126] Tanninen, Lehtonen and Ruckenstein (n 99) 459.

[127] Ibid. 460.

[128] Ibid.

[129] Ibid. 449, 459.

[130] Steinberg (n 63).

[131] <www.lemonade.com/blog/lemonade-sets-new-world-record/>.

[132] The assumption is that genuine answers will be short and simple, and the longer and more detailed the answers are, the less likely the claim is genuine.

inform the assured of those facts will be assessed under Section 17 of the MIA 1906 which provides that insurance contracts are contracts of utmost good faith. The parties' post-contractual dealings may also be analysed under this section where necessary. As the common law cases have explained, the duty of utmost good faith is wider than the pre-contractual duty of fair presentation of the risk. Broadly defined, it is acting in line with what a business-like and fair dealing would require in an insurance contract.[133] There were cases in which, for instance, the insurer was not allowed to argue that there was a misrepresentation of a material fact, because reliance on that breach would have been unbusiness-like. This is because even if the insurer had known the truth, this knowledge would have no bearing on the decision whether to insure the assured.[134]

The test for breach of the duty is commercially fair dealing. It is the duty of each party to act with due regard to the interests of the other.[135] Good faith is determined by a market standard of fairness based on what was customary and acceptable conduct in the insurance market. Moreover, fairness, reasonableness and community standards of decency and fair dealing are the standards to determine whether the relevant conduct is business-like.

If the insurer is found in breach of the duty of good faith, the remedy would be decided based on what justice requires in each individual case. It could be reassessing the assured's claim, paying compensation either for late payment of the insured amount or for some other types of damages suffered by the assured, or, in the case of the assured's wrongdoing, restricting the remedy that might otherwise be available for the insurer under the contract.

The focus of this paper is not how insurance contracts should be regulated – regulation of insurance is a different area to the principles that govern the contractual relationship between the assured and the insurer. It is necessary however to mention that insurance regulation exists both to correct market failures and to protect insurance markets.[136] Whilst some issues may be resolved as they arise through market dynamics, some others may not be left to the market and have to be addressed by regulators. In a fast-moving digital world, there is a strong imbalance between those who manage algorithms and data, and the data subjects, the latter struggling to exercise their rights.[137] Policyholders might not know how much their claim is really worth and may accept the insurer's valuation. Even if they want to challenge the insurer's response to their claims, policyholders might not have the resources

[133] *Drake Insurance Plc (In Provisional Liquidation) v Provident Insurance Plc* [2003] EWCA Civ 1834, [2004] QB 601; *K/S Merc-Scandia XXXXII v Lloyd's Underwriters (The Mercandian Continent)* [2001] EWCA Civ 1275, [2001] 2 Lloyd's Rep 563; *Horwood v Land of Leather Ltd* [2010] EWHC 546 (Comm), [2010] Lloyd's Rep IR 453.

[134] *Drake Insurance Plc* (n 133).

[135] *Gan Insurance Co Ltd v Tai Ping Insurance Co Ltd* [2001] EWCA Civ 1047, [2001] Lloyd's Rep IR 667, [72].

[136] Swedloff, 'The New Regulatory Imperative for Insurance' (n 1) 2084; Zarifis, Holland and Milne (n 1).

[137] EIOPA (n 8) 14.

or sophistication to fight the insurer.[138] The fact that they do not have knowledge, information, or skills necessary to evaluate the insurer's business methods, and the insurer's claims and settlement practices, gives rise to the profound need for regulators to step in.[139]

Fair treatment of consumers is the centre of consumer protection.[140] The data collected should be required by the specific purposes and only the data necessary to meet those purposes should be collected.[141] Separation between classes is desirable in theory, but classification should be susceptible to as little administrative error as possible.[142] This also means that insurance firms should be transparent about how they use the data and be able to appropriately explain these uses to consumers as well as to competent authorities.[143] It is important to make reasonable efforts to monitor, and appropriately mitigate and/or remove biases in the training and testing of data to avoid these biases being reproduced in the outputs of AI systems. Explanations of specific AI use should be meaningful and understandable so that stakeholders can make informed decisions.[144]

V CONCLUDING THOUGHTS

Each of the areas identified above could be the subject of further discussions. This chapter aims to demonstrate that whilst evolution of the insurance products has been observed to some extent, such evolution has been limited. The products that incumbent insurers offer have not changed (except for parametric insurance); nor has the essence of the fundamental principles governing the insurance contract principles been altered. The word 'disruption' therefore might be displaced in this respect and what the insurance practice and law have been experiencing may be described as a strategic augmentation with the introduction of the services provided by InsurTech.

Evidence suggest that insurance covers have become more accessible to individuals. Parametric products, despite their confusing title, reduce administrative costs, and allow high-volume activities, the costs of which would have been too much to bear previously. UBI may help encourage drivers to be more risk averse, and insurance might be more accessible especially for young drivers. Insurers may respond to the assured's claim almost instantly, which saves time for both parties.

138 Swedloff, 'The New Regulatory Imperative for Insurance' (n 1) 2082.

139 See McGurk (n 5) ch 6 and 7; Swedloff, 'The New Regulatory Imperative for Insurance' (n 1) 2039. In its latest supervisory convergence plan EIOPA emphasised the crucial nature of including insurers use of data and AI in the plan. <www.eiopa.europa.eu/document-library/supervisory-statement/supervisory-convergence-plan-2022>.

140 EIOPA (n 8) 22.

141 Ibid. 22.

142 Abraham (n 24) 412.

143 EIOPA (n 8) 22.

144 Ibid. 40.

Whilst the way the insurance business is conducted is changing, transparency must be the main focus of the insurers as well as the regulators. The more understandable the processes, the more informed the parties' selection of choices will be. Better understanding of the conditions of an insurance cover, namely, the rights and obligations of the assured and the insurer, will facilitate the conclusion of an insurance contract between the parties.

The trust between the insurer and the assured can be built and maintained by only improving such dialogue. Achieving a perfect balance between the rights and obligations of the parties may not be possible especially where the market is too dynamic and open to adapt in response to any geographical or socio-political developments. However, being transparent is under the parties' control so that the insurer can explain the criteria used in the risk assessment (both at the pre-and post-contractual periods) and the claim management stages. The use of correct terminology so as to avoid any misleading statements towards the assured would contribute to this goal. Reliable and accessible insurance operations cannot be provided only by rendering the processing times simpler and shorter. Effective communication between the assured and the insurer of the details of the processes affecting the insurance cover is key to building a trustworthy relationship.

25

Securities Regulation and AI

Regulating Robo-Advisers

Eric C. Chaffee

I INTRODUCTION

Artificial intelligence is both an intrinsic good and an instrumental good. In regard to being an intrinsic good, the ability to create evermore complex technology that will eventually reach a level of consciousness is arguably the creation of life. This technology has generated and continues to generate a myriad of philosophic questions that have not been answered even in regard to human existence. For example, in *Discourse on the Method*, René Descartes famously asserted proof of his existence through his notion of '*cogito ergo sum*,' which can be translated, 'I think therefore I am.'[1] Even if this test is sufficient to prove human existence, which is debatable, the test would likely be insufficient to prove consciousness for an artificial intelligence. Technology could easily be programmed to say, 'I compute, therefore I am.' Amazon's Alexa already regularly responds, 'I'm here. I listen once I hear the wake word.'

Putting these issues aside, artificial intelligence is an instrumental good as well. This technology allows individuals to complete tasks more easily and to complete tasks that they otherwise could not undertake or complete on their own. Numerous questions exist regarding artificial technology as an instrumental good. In no area are these questions more complex than in the realm of robo-advisers. Through algorithmic analyses and machine learning, robo-advisers assist individuals in making

I would like to offer special thanks to Deirdre Ahern, Anthony Casey, Iris Chiu, Gerard Hertig, Kenneth Khoo, Ernest Lim, Phillip Morgan, Anthony Niblett, Sean Thomas, Wan Wai Yee, Hu Ying, and Yeo Hwee Ying for providing feedback that contributed to this chapter. I would also like to thank Christine Gall, Esq. for her encouragement while drafting this work. This project was supported by a summer research grant from The University of Toledo College of Law. The views set forth in this chapter are completely my own and do not necessarily reflect the views of any employer or client either past or present.

[1] Descartes did not expressly use the phrase '*cogito ergo sum*' in his *Meditations on First Philosophy*, although he thoroughly examined the concept embodied in this phrase. René Descartes, *Meditations on First Philosophy: With Selections from the Objections and Replies* (John Cottingham tr, first published 1641, Cambridge University Press 1996) 17. Descartes first used this phrase in his *Discourse on Method*. René Descartes, *Discourse on Method* (Desmond M Clarke tr, first published 1637, Penguin Books 1999) 25.

investment decisions at a relatively low cost.[2] Because use of robo-advisers creates significant risks in addition to the rewards that their use offers, the question of how they ought to be regulated has been and continues to be a subject of substantial debate.

After exploring what is a robo-adviser and the emergence of the robo-adviser industry, this chapter discusses various models for regulating this industry. Ultimately, this chapter concludes that the best model for regulating the robo-adviser industry is a mix of mandatory disclosure; fiduciary duties for those developing, marketing, and operating robo-advisers; investor education; and regulation by litigation. In addition, this chapter makes the novel suggestion that robo-advisers ought to be regulated by the regular standardised surveying of the investors who are using them and the release of that data to the general public.

II WHAT IS A ROBO-ADVISER?

For purposes of this chapter, a robo-adviser will be defined as a client-facing computerised investment tool that provides financial advice or assists in investment management.[3] This definition is worth unpacking because it goes directly to how this technology ought to be regulated.[4]

2 Benjamin P Edwards, 'The Dark Side of Self-Regulation' (2017) 85 *University of Cincinnati Law Review* 573, 605 ('Financial technology companies have begun to offer automated investment advice platforms that use algorithms to select assets for investors. In many instances, these robo-advisers provide services at a fraction of the cost.'); Nicole G Iannarone, 'Rethinking Automated Investment Adviser Disclosure' (2019) 50 *University of Toledo Law Review* 433, 436 ('Robo-advisers' rapid predicted growth is due to the promise of their technology and lower cost profile that makes them accessible to a wider range of investors, including those who were previously not served due to lower account balances than traditional advisers were equipped to assist.').

3 This definition was highly influenced by the following discussion by the Financial Industry Regulatory Authority ('FINRA) in a 2016 Report: '[D]igital investment advice tools (also referred to as digital advice tools) support one or more of the following core activities in managing an investor's portfolio: customer profiling, asset allocation, portfolio selection, trade execution, portfolio rebalancing, tax-loss harvesting and portfolio analysis. These investment advice tools can be broken down into two groups: tools that financial professionals use, referred to here as "financial professional-facing" tools, and tools that clients use, referred to here as "client-facing" tools. Client-facing tools that incorporate the first six activities – customer profiling through tax-loss harvesting – are frequently referred to as "robo advisors" or "robos"'. While not attempting to formulate a definition, the report certainly forms the foundations for the definition developed in this chapter. Financial Industry Regulatory Authority, 'Report on Digital Investment Advice' (March 2016) 2.

4 Importantly, other definitions of robo-advisers do exist. See, for example, Tom Baker and Benedict Dellaert, 'Regulating Robo Advice across the Financial Services Industry' (2018) 103 *Iowa Law Review* 713, 720 ('[W]e use the term 'robo advisor' broadly to refer to any automated service that ranks, or matches consumers to, financial products on a personalized basis.'); Nicole G Iannarone, 'Computer as Confidant: Digital Investment Advice and the Fiduciary Standard' (2018) 93 *Chicago-Kent Law Review* 141, 149 ('Robo-adviser' as colloquially used encompasses a wide spectrum of services and business models, but all provide investment advice in a digital format using proprietary algorithms.'); Edward L Pittman, 'Quantitative Investment Models, Errors, and the Federal Securities Laws' (2017) 13 *NYU Journal of Law & Business* 633, 640 ('Robo-advisers are generally regarded as web-based advisers that use algorithm-based interfaces to determine an investor's goals and provide portfolio management services including stock recommendations, rebalancing, and tax harvesting.').

At the core of this definition is the acknowledgement that robo-advisers are best understood as tools. Tool is the proper term because even though robo-advisers can be considered a form of artificial intelligence, they are certainly not a sentient form of artificial intelligence.[5] Although the term 'robo-adviser' might suggest substantial similarities with a human adviser, robo-advisers are merely a device used to help carry out a particular task, that is, investment.[6]

Next, any definition of a robo-adviser should also acknowledge that they are a computerised technology.[7] Because even human advisers are potentially investment tools, the definition earlier also acknowledges that robo-advisers are technology, that is, equipment developed from scientific knowledge.[8] The problem is that technology entails a wide variety of things. In regard to investment decisions, for instance, the role of technology likely dates back to at least to the development of the abacus in ancient times with a panoply of innovations occurring sense then. As a consequence, to differentiate robo-advisers from abaci, one must also acknowledge that they are computerised, meaning that that are associated with electronic and digital technology, which the earlier definition does.

Even with the refinement so far, describing robo-advisers as computerised investment tools is an incomplete and over-inclusive description. Complicating matters is that robo-advisers commonly use the same technology to provide investment advice that most human financial professionals use to advise their clients.[9] As a result, once one determines which investment tools might constitute robo-advisers, one must also consider how those tools and by whom those tools are used as well. In regard to robo-advisers, it is the client-facing aspect of these investment tools that transforms them into robo-advisers, rather than just computerised investment tools.

5 Iris H-Y Chiu and Ernest WK Lim, 'Technology vs Ideology: How Far Will Artificial Intelligence and Distributed Ledger Technology Transform Corporate Governance and Business?' (2021) 18 *Berkeley Business Law Journal* 1, 4–5 ('Scientific research and development of AI can be traced back to the 1950s, when the pinnacle achievement for AI was declared to be its passing of the Turing test. The elusive achievement by computers in relation to this standard to date shows that 'super intelligence' – the term used to describe AI that is able to replicate human intelligence – is still somewhat away.').

6 Nizan Geslevich Packin, 'Regtech, Compliance and Technology Judgment Rule' (2018) 93 *Chicago-Kent Law Review* 193, 200 ('Robo-advisors offer investment assistance and flexible investment management services without the involvement of a human adviser, building on algorithms and asset allocation models....').

7 Iris H-Y Chiu, 'The Regulatory Implications and Limitations of Robo-Advice' (2019) 38 *Banking & Financial Services Policy Report* 11 ('Robo-advice is automated advice provided by a machine-based interface, usually in an online context.').

8 Packin (n 6) 200 ('Robo-advisors have developed in the marketplace as an alternative for small investors who are content using Internet technology, but want to have the comfort of having an investment adviser direct them.').

9 Andrea L Seidt, Noula Zaharis and Charles Jarrett, 'Paying Attention to That Man behind the Curtain: State Securities Regulators' Early Conversations with Robo-Advisers' (2019) 50 *University of Toledo Law Review* 501, 503 ('[I]n most instances, robos and traditional human advisers are utilizing the same technological tools to provide their service with the primary differences being the robos make their tools directly available to the investor without the human sales force.').

Notably, the use of the term 'client-facing,' rather than 'investor-facing,' is important as well. For example, a hedge fund engaged in quantitative trading may use a variety a variety of computerised investment tools to engage in high-frequency algorithmic trading. Although these tools are computerised investment tool, assuming that they have been developed by the fund itself, one would have a difficult time arguing that they are robo-advisers because that term is commonly used to refer to tools that are being marketed to third-parties, that is, clients.

Still, this description seems over inclusive because of the range of computerised tools that clients might use in investment decision-making. For instance, a computerised calculator that is included with the pre-installed software on a computer would without more fall within this definition. Although reasons might exist for determining that such a calculator is a robo-adviser, it seems likely that such a calculator would fall short of what most individuals believe a robo-adviser to be. Consequently, the definition earlier also acknowledges that robo-advisers must either provide financial advice or assist in investment management. While these two categories are still somewhat ambiguous, the definition formulated earlier provides a good place to start in understanding robo-advisers.

III THE EMERGENCE OF THE ROBO-ADVISER INDUSTRY

Because of the definitional issues discussed in Section II, determining when robo-advisers were first developed and when they were first used is impossible. While defensible claims might be made regarding both of these topics, those claims would still be controversial and arbitrary. With that said, in 2010, Betterment launched and became the first pure robo-adviser firm focused on securities markets.[10] A decade later, this firm continued a major player, and it continued to attract new clients. At the end of 2020, Betterment had approximately $28 billion assets under management after adding $10 billion dollars of assets during that year.[11]

The growth in the robo-adviser industry from these relatively recent beginnings has been substantial. At the close of 2020, robo-adviser firms had approximately $785 billion assets under management, which was an increase from $631 billion assets under management in 2019.[12] The industry appears to be growing twenty-five percent year-after-year.[13] At the end of 2020, leading firms in terms of assets under management included Edelman Financial Engines (approximately $212 billion), Vanguard Personal Advisor Services (approximately $212 billion), Schwab Intelligent Portfolio Products (approximately $60 billion), and Betterment (approximately $28 billion).[14]

[10] Jon Stein, 'The History of Betterment: Changing an Industry' (*Betterment*, 20 July 2016) <www.betterment.com/resources/the-history-of-betterment>.

[11] Backend Benchmarking, 'The Robo Report: Second Quarter 2021' (2021) 19.

[12] Ibid.

[13] Ibid.

[14] Ibid.

In sum, the robo-adviser industry is well-established and is almost certain to grow for the foreseeable future. As a consequence, properly regulating this industry is and will continue to be important for the foreseeable future as well.

IV REGULATORY MODELS

Creating a comprehensive and effective regulatory regime for robo-advisers is a daunting task. Significant variation exists among robo-advisers. As discussed above, robo-advisers can be generally defined as client-facing computerised investment tools that provide financial advice or assist in investment management. With that said, robo-advisers can differ substantially, including in regard to what investment advice they provide, the types of investment opportunities that they recommend, the availability of human client-support, their user interfaces, and their programming.[15] Additionally, regulating robo-advisers creates substantial concerns about stifling innovation.[16] Although robo-advisers create a variety of risks and challenges, they also provide a variety of benefits including low cost access to investment advice.[17] Overregulating robo-advisers could lessen or extinguish these benefits.

With these concerns above in mind, this section will explore various models for regulating robo-advisers, including agency law, design intervention, merit-based regulation, disclosure-based regulation, fiduciary duties, investor education, and regulation by litigation. This section will lay the foundation for Section V, which will provide a discussion of how regulation should be approached using various existing regulatory models and what sort of additional regulation would be beneficial.

A *Agency Law*

One tempting model for regulating robo-advisers is agency law. Robo-advisers are a form of artificial intelligence, and one of the common goals of developers of artificial

15 Iannarone, 'Computer as Confidant' (n 4) 149 ('[T]here is substantial variation between robo-advice platforms, with differences in: (1) end user of the digital advice; (2) range of investment advice and options provided; and (3) level of human investment adviser interaction.').

16 Baker and Dellaert, 'Regulating Robo Advice across the Financial Services Industry' (n 4) 747 ('[R]egulatory oversight poses the risk of discouraging innovation by serving as a barrier to entry into the market for robo advisors. Moreover, as regulators develop preferences about robo advisor design, and as regulated entities come to understand those preferences, oversight may lead to a model convergence that increases the risk of catastrophic failure.').

17 Moran Ofir and Ido Sadeh, 'More of the Same or Real Transformation: Does Fintech Warrant New Regulations?' (2021) 21 *Houston Business and Tax Law Journal* 280, 297 ('[C]ommentators argue that because robo-advisors reduce the need for human intervention in communicating with customers, designing investment strategies, and conducting account rebalancing, they reduce operational and transaction costs. This, in turn, allows financial advisory firms to reduce entry barriers and expand the investor base in capital markets, thereby promoting financial inclusion.').

intelligence is to create autonomous entities that can behave intelligently.[18] Although the term 'robo-adviser' might suggest that we have reached this stage in the development of this technology, this is far from reality because robo-advisers are much more similar to calculators than human investment advisers.[19] Suggesting that an individual's use of a calculator creates a principal agent relationship borders on absurdity. Of course, as discussed at the start of this chapter, proving consciousness is a remarkably difficult task. Perhaps, an incredibly sophisticated calculator might reach this achievement, but despite the ability of many robo-advisers to process a significant amount of data, the arrival of a sentient robo-adviser is unlikely to happen anytime soon.

As a consequence, robo-advisers are unable to enter into agency relationships as they are currently conceived. Section 1.01 of the American Law Institute's *Restatement of the Law (Third) of Agency* provides: '[a]gency is the fiduciary relationship that arises when one person (a 'principal') manifests assent to another person (an 'agent') that the agent shall act on the principal's behalf and subject to the principal's control, and the agent manifests assent or otherwise consents so to act.'[20] The problems with applying this construct to robo-advisers are substantial. Robo-advisers are not actual or legal persons.[21] In addition, robo-advisers are not able to manifest assent or consent.[22] As a consequence, robo-advisers are not agents for purposes of providing investment advice under the current state of the law.

One might be able to assert an estoppel claim depending on how sophisticated the entity providing the robo-adviser states that the technology involved happens to be and what sort of advice it offers. Section 2.05 of the American Law Institute's *Restatement of the Law (Third) of Agency* provides:

> A person who has not made a manifestation that an actor has authority as an agent and who is not otherwise liable as a party to a transaction purportedly done by the actor on that person's account is subject to liability to a third party who justifiably is induced to make a detrimental change in position because the transaction is believed to be on the person's account, if

[18] Aaron D Kirk, 'Artificial Intelligence and the Fifth Domain' (2019) 80 *Air Force Law Review* 183, 187 ('The field of artificial intelligence consists of several subfields that contribute to the larger goal of getting a machine to behave intelligently.').

[19] Megan Ji, 'Are Robots Good Fiduciaries? Regulating Robo-Advisors under the Investment Advisers Act of 1940' (2017) 117 *Columbia Law Review* 1543, 1557 ('In contrast to traditional investment advisers, robo-advisors rely primarily on algorithms, rather than human judgment, to determine recommendations. Clients fill out questionnaires with information such as age, household situation, income, savings, financial goals, and risk tolerance. This information is put through a computer algorithm, which calculates an investment portfolio that is efficient and tailored to a client's needs.').

[20] American Law Institute, *Restatement of the Law (Third) of Agency* (2006) para 1.01.

[21] Lawrence B Solum, 'Legal Personhood for Artificial Intelligences' (1992) 70 *North Carolina Law Review* 1231 ('Could an artificial intelligence become a legal person? As of today, this question is only theoretical. No existing computer program currently possesses the sort of capacities that would justify serious judicial inquiry into the question of legal personhood.').

[22] Zack Naqvi, 'Artificial Intelligence, Copyright, and Copyright Infringement' (2020) 24 *Marquette Intellectual Property Law Review* 15, 27 ('[An] AI cannot assent to be an agent for a principal…').

(1) the person intentionally or carelessly caused such belief, or
(2) having notice of such belief and that it might induce others to change their positions, the person did not take reasonable steps to notify them of the facts.[23]

Still, this stretches the law almost to the point of absurdity because the third party would have to believe that the robo-adviser was a conscious actor in whatever had occurred.

Agency law could become a viable source of regulation for robo-advisers in two circumstances. First, robo-advisers could reach the level of sophistication to be conscious actors or to be attributed consciousness. However, this level of sophistication is unlikely to happen anytime soon. Second, legal constructs could be used to assign robo-advisers legal personhood and to allow them to operate within the existing law governing agency.[24] This would be, for example, similar to how the law affords legal personhood to corporations.[25]

Beyond concerns about the applicability of agency law to robo-advisers, using agency law to regulate this technology is problematic in general because it would be leaving regulation of this technology to *ex post* regulation by litigation, rather than offering *ex ante* regulation that might avoid problems in the first place. As a result, although agency law may eventually be a useful system of law to regulate robo-advisers, it is inappropriate today, and it would be inappropriate as the sole mechanism to regulate these technologies.

B *Design Intervention*

A second model for regulating robo-advisers is design intervention. Regulators could set the parameters that are permissible for programming and operating robo-advisers in an attempt to mitigate investment risk. The level of directness in regard to design intervention can vary.

In some instances, these design interventions could be relatively simple and straight-forward. For example, robo-adviser developers could be prohibited from programming robo-advisers to recommend a particular company in which the developers, marketers, or operators have an interest.

[23] American Law Institute (n 20) para 2.05.

[24] John Lightbourne, 'Algorithms & Fiduciaries: Existing and Proposed Regulatory Approaches to Artificially Intelligent Financial Planners' (2017) 67 *Duke Law Journal* 651, 673 ('Adopting a legal fiction that the AI implementation itself is a quasi-person may seem farfetched at first, but the law has previously considered other artificial entities, like corporations, as person-like.').

[25] Nadia Banteka, 'Artificially Intelligent Persons' (2021) 58 *Houston Law Review* 537, 549 ('Western legal traditions have developed the concept of legal personhood to more easily taxonomize the entities that can act in law. Being human is not a necessary condition of having legal personhood. Entities that enjoy legal personhood have, for a long time, included not only humans but also artificial entities such as corporations, trusts, and associations which the law treats as though they are one single entity, one single person.').

This type of direct design intervention, however, is problematic for at least three reasons. First, as Section II discusses, defining what constitutes a robo-adviser is an incredibly difficult task. As a consequence, because robo-advisers are a subcategory of digital investment tools, regulators are going to have difficulty figuring out which digital investment tools should be the subject of design intervention, and in some instances, the choice will end up being relatively arbitrary. Second, after the decision is made regarding what to regulate, regulators will then have to determine how to intervene in the design of those robo-advisers. Because software development and programming involve technical expertise, regulators are likely to struggle with how to properly intervene in the design of this technology. Third, the software underlying robo-advisers is continuing to develop and evolve, and regulatory design intervention could hinder or prevent that development or evolution. While mitigating the risks associated with robo-advisers is important, slowing or preventing useful innovation is a concern.[26] Over regulation, especially in regard to design, creates a substantial risk of hampering or extinguishing innovation.[27]

Even less direct methods of design intervention would be problematic as well. For example, one idea that has been proposed is that robo-advisers could have 'circuit breakers' built-in that could halt their operation to mitigate or prevent market volatility in some circumstances.[28] Although this might be a useful innovation in certain cases, in addition to the problems above, less direct design interventions also lack the nuance necessary to meaningfully regulate robo-advisers. For instance, although they might be useful in some cases, circuit breakers would be the equivalent of using a hatchet, rather than a scalpel, to perform surgery.

C *Merit-Based Regulation*

A third model for regulating robo-advisers is merit-based regulation. A regulator could make the determination whether a robo-adviser is worthy of being licensed to market its services to clients. In a certain sense, registration often involves some form of merit-based regulation because it frequently requires that those applying for it meet certain criteria to be registered. For example, in the United States, which has

26 J Howard Beales III and Timothy J Muris, 'FTC Consumer Protection at 100: 1970s Redux or Protecting Markets to Protect Consumers?' (2015) 83 *George Washington Law Review* 2157, 2223 ('Regulation based on speculative problems, however, is far more likely to chill useful innovations than it is to prevent real harms.').

27 Daniel F Spulber and Christopher S Yoo, 'Rethinking Broadband Internet Access' (2008) 22 *Harvard Journal of Law & Technology* 1, 19–20 ('Blind application of a regulatory regime developed for a different technology and different market conditions can lead to regulation that lacks any theoretical justification and can impede technological innovation and consumer welfare.').

28 William Magnuson, 'Regulating Fintech' (2018) 71 *Vanderbilt Law Review* 1167, 1218 ('[R]egulators could limit interconnectedness in fintech markets. For example, they could require robo-advisors to include in their algorithms 'circuit-breaker' type features that reduce market volatility and prevent domino effects as parties rush to limit their losses.').

a disclosure-based system of federal securities regulation, investment advisers are required to meet certain sorts of basic requirements to register with the SEC. With that said, more robust forms of review are possible that would allow a regulator to thoroughly review and pass judgement on all aspects of a robo-adviser.

In regard to robo-advisers, however, robust use of merit-regulation is not desirable for similar reasons that design intervention is not a desirable regulatory model, that is, difficulties in defining what is a robo-adviser, limitations in most regulators' technological expertise, and fears of hampering or extinguishing innovation. Specifically relating to the last category, securities regulators in merit-based systems are often overly cautious when it comes to new technology. In the United States, several states continue to have merit-based systems of regulation.[29] Famously, Massachusetts, a state with merit-based securities regulation, banned the sale of Apple Computer Inc stock in that state in 1980 because it was too speculative.[30] Similarly, for better or worse, Ohio, another state with merit-based securities regulation, prevented the use in its jurisdiction of the prevailing model for peer-to-peer lending in the United States based on concerns about the securities underlying the peer-to-peer lending activity.[31] Consequently, because robo-advising does have the virtue of affording low cost access to investment advice, merit-based regulation should be avoided.[32]

D *Disclosure-Based Regulation*

In securities law, disclosure-based regulation is often discussed as the alternative to merit-based regulation.[33] The federal securities law in the United States is founded

[29] Roberta S Karmel, 'Blue-Sky Merit Regulation: Benefit to Investors or Burden on Commerce?' (1987) 53 *Brooklyn Law Review* 105 ('All fifty states, the District of Columbia, and Puerto Rico have a securities regulation statute, called a blue-sky statute. Some are merit regulation statutes, and some are not. Merit regulation gives a state, through its blue-sky commissioner, the authority to prevent an issuer from selling its securities in that state when the offering or the issuer's capital structure is substantively unfair or presents excessive risk to the investor.').

[30] Usha R Rodrigues, 'Dictation and Delegation In Securities Regulation' (2017) 92 *Indiana Law Journal* 435, 499 ('Massachusetts used merit review to bar its residents from buying Apple stock in the 1980s because it was deemed to be too risky.').

[31] Eric C Chaffee and Geoffrey C Rapp, 'Regulating Online Peer-to-Peer Lending in the Aftermath of Dodd-Frank: In Search of an Evolving Regulatory Regime for an Evolving Industry' (2012) 69 *Washington and Lee Law Review* 485, 520–21 (discussing Ohio's decision under its state system of securities regulation to ban the prevailing model of peer-to-peer lending).

[32] Benjamin P Edwards, 'The Rise of Automated Investment Advice: Can Robo-Advisers Rescue the Retail Market?' (2018) 93 *Chicago-Kent Law Review* 97, 103 ('Automated investment advice firms may mitigate the conflicted-advice problem and expand access to investment advice. The best platforms will likely provide planning tools to help clients increase their savings rates. By providing greater access to advice at a lower cost, these new firms may reach persons that traditional financial advice firms have not yet served.').

[33] Ronald J Colombo, 'Merit Regulation via the Suitability Rules' (2013) 12 *Journal of International Business and Law* 1 ('Due to the drawbacks of merit regulation, numerous advanced economies, amongst them the UK, Australia, and Hong Kong, have all adopted disclosure-based regulation.').

upon disclosure-based regulation.[34] As Justice Arthur Goldberg described federal securities law while writing for the Supreme Court of the United States in *SEC v Capital Gains Research Bureau, Inc*, '[a] fundamental purpose ... was to substitute a philosophy of full disclosure for the philosophy of caveat emptor and thus to achieve a high standard of business ethics in the securities industry.'[35] Under such a system of regulation, the government does not pass judgement on investment opportunities for investors, but the government works to give investors full and accurate information to make informed decisions about investments themselves.[36] Based on the success of the capital markets in the United States, which is viewed as having a high-quality system of securities regulation, disclosure-based regulation can be very effective in regulating capital markets and those who participate in them.[37]

In the United States, robo-adviser firms are subject to a disclosure-based regulatory scheme. These firms qualify as investment advisers under the Investment Advisers Act of 1940.[38] Section 202(a)(11) of the Act defines 'investment advisers' as:

> any person who, for compensation, engages in the business of advising others, either directly or through publications or writings, as to the value of securities or as to the advisability of investing in, purchasing, or selling securities, or who, for compensation and as part of a regular business, issues or promulgates analyses or reports concerning securities...[39]

While the Act does contain various exclusions, robo-adviser firms typically fall within this definition.[40] As a consequence, robo-advisers have robust disclosure obligations.[41] In addition to other required disclosure, the SEC has provided guidance that robo-advisers should also disclose the following:

34 Zachary J Gubler, 'Reconsidering the Institutional Design of Federal Securities Regulation' (2014) 56 *William and Mary Law Review* 409, 417 ('The original draft of the federal securities laws incorporated a form of ... 'merit review,' but this proposal was ultimately replaced with a purely disclosure-based regime.').

35 SEC v *Capital Gains Research Bureau, Inc*, 375 U.S. 180, 186 (1963).

36 Thomas Lee Hazen, 'Social Networks and the Securities Laws' (2012) 90 *North Carolina Law Review* 1735, 1741–69 ('The federal securities laws do not focus on the merits of investments but rather are based on disclosure to allow sufficiently informed investors to fend for themselves.').

37 Steven A Ramirez, 'The Virtues of Private Securities Litigation: An Historic and Macroeconomic Perspective' (2014) 45 *Loyola University Chicago Law Journal* 669, 670 (reporting that the enactment of the Securities Act of 1933 and Securities Exchange Act of 1934 brought about 'an extended golden era of financial stability' in the United States).

38 Jerry W Markham, 'Regulating Broker-Dealer Investment Recommendations—Laying the Groundwork for the Next Financial Crisis' (2021) 13 *Drexel Law Review* 377, 414 ('The SEC has advised that robo advisers are subject to the provisions of the Investment Advisers Act.').

39 Investment Advisers Act of 1940, para 202(a)(11), 15 USC para 80b-2(a)(11) (2021).

40 Pittman, 'Quantitative Investment Models, Errors, and the Federal Securities Laws' (n 4) 640 ('Robo-advisers are registered investment advisers, generally regulated by the SEC.').

41 Arthur B Laby, 'Models of Securities Regulation in the United States' (2000) 23 *Fordham International Law Journal* 20, 21 ('Under the Investment Advisers Act of 1940..., advisory firms are required to make detailed disclosures about their business, and the people who work there to the SEC and to their

- A statement that an algorithm is used to manage individual client accounts;
- A description of the algorithmic functions used to manage client accounts (e.g., that the algorithm generates recommended portfolios; that individual client accounts are invested and rebalanced by the algorithm);
- A description of the assumptions and limitations of the algorithm used to manage client accounts (e.g., if the algorithm is based on modern portfolio theory, a description of the assumptions behind and the limitations of that theory);
- A description of the particular risks inherent in the use of an algorithm to manage client accounts (e.g., that the algorithm might rebalance client accounts without regard to market conditions or on a more frequent basis than the client might expect; that the algorithm may not address prolonged changes in market conditions);
- A description of any circumstances that might cause the robo-adviser to override the algorithm used to manage client accounts (e.g., that the robo-adviser might halt trading or take other temporary defensive measures in stressed market conditions);
- A description of any involvement by a third party in the development, management, or ownership of the algorithm used to manage client accounts, including an explanation of any conflicts of interest such an arrangement may create (e.g., if the third party offers the algorithm to the robo-adviser at a discount, but the algorithm directs clients into products from which the third party earns a fee);
- An explanation of any fees the client will be charged directly by the robo-adviser, and of any other costs that the client may bear either directly or indirectly (e.g., fees or expenses clients may pay in connection with the advisory services provided, such as custodian or mutual fund expenses; brokerage and other transaction costs);
- An explanation of the degree of human involvement in the oversight and management of individual client accounts (e.g., that investment advisory personnel oversee the algorithm but may not monitor each client's account);
- A description of how the robo-adviser uses the information gathered from a client to generate a recommended portfolio and any limitations (e.g., if a questionnaire is used, that the responses to the questionnaire may be the sole basis for the robo-adviser's advice; if the robo-adviser has access to other client information or accounts, whether, and if so, how, that information is used in generating investment advice); and
- An explanation of how and when a client should update information he or she has provided to the robo-adviser.[42]

clients. When a firm seeks to register as an adviser with the SEC, the firm submits a SEC Form ADV, which contains detailed questions about the firm's history, operations, services, and fees, as well as questions about the firm's employees and affiliates, including their disciplinary history.').

42 US Securities and Exchange Commission, 'Robo-Advisers' [2017] IM Guidance Update 1, 3–4.

Thus, if these disclosures are made, investors should have a significant amount of information available to assist them in making the decision whether to employ a robo-adviser.[43]

Disclosure based systems of regulation do have their challenges. First, lawmakers and regulators must make a proper determination what information should be the subject of disclosure. Second, the individuals and entities subject to disclosure requirements must make those disclosures. Third, the individuals and entities subject to disclosure requirements must make those disclosures truthfully. Fourth, the information disclosed must be received by the proper recipients. Fifth, the individuals and entities receiving the information disclosed must be capable of reviewing it and understanding it.

This last concern is especially prominent in regard to robo-advisers. Because disclosures related to robo-advisers involve the intersection of complex fields, finance and artificial intelligence, many investors may have difficulty understanding the information that is being disclosed to them.[44] Even in the absence of the technological aspects of robo-advisers, many investors lack even basic financial literacy.[45] As a result, in its guidance on robo-advisers, the SEC has recommended that robo-adviser firms take special care in making their disclosures readable and understandable.[46] Because of how robo-advisers and investors interact and the ability of some robo-advisers to adapt to the information that clients provide, at least one commentator has argued that robo-advisers offer a unique opportunity for active and iterative disclosure.[47] Regardless, meaningful disclosure relating to robo-advisers is of special concern.

43 Deirdre K Mulligan and Kenneth A Bamberger, 'Saving Governance-by-Design' (2018) 106 *California Law Review* 697, 781 ('[T]he SEC has issued advice aimed at helping consumers interact safely with robo-advisors, online algorithmic-based programs that provide discretionary asset management services to clients. Much of the guidance document is devoted to recommending disclosures about how the computational system and data behind the robo-advisor work.').

44 Sophia Duffy and Steve Parrish, 'You Say Fiduciary, I Say Binary: A Review and Recommendation of Robo-Advisors and the Fiduciary and Best Interest Standards' (2021) 17 *Hastings Business Law Journal* 3, 28 ('In addition to the normal and traditional disclosures, the SEC's guidance for robo-advisors, focuses heavily on the algorithms used to power the robo-advising platform.... Since research shows that most clients don't understand complex disclosures anyway, it stands to reason that disclosures regarding software program design and algorithms would be even less comprehensible to retail consumers, rendering the disclosures moot.').

45 Lisa M Fairfax, 'The Securities Law Implications of Financial Illiteracy' (2018) 104 *Virginia Law Review* 1065, 1121 ('Studies conclusively and consistently reveal that Americans lack basic understanding of financial concepts and how to effectively apply those concepts in financial decision making. Those studies also reveal that the American investor is no exception.').

46 US Securities and Exchange Commission (n 42) 5 ('We therefore remind robo-advisers to carefully consider whether their written disclosures are designed to be effective (e.g., are not buried or incomprehensible).').

47 Iannarone, 'Rethinking Automated Investment Adviser Disclosure' (n 2) 443 ('Robo-advisers have extraordinary access to the financial lives of their clients to provide their advice. To improve disclosure, the same capabilities could be deployed in a partnership between machine and human whereby the robo-adviser learns about the investor's baseline understanding, and provides bespoke disclosure tailored to the investor. The disclosure is active, requiring engagement and interaction from the investor, and iterative, providing more information at subsequent stages of decision…').

E *Fiduciary Duties*

An additional model for regulating robo-advisers involves the use of fiduciary duties. Once again, the technology underlying artificial intelligence today has not met and falls short of the intelligence required for sentience, especially in the realm of robo-advisers. As a consequence any regulatory model employing fiduciary duties to regulate robo-advisers would have to attach to the real persons or legal entities developing, marketing, and operating them because robo-advisers are tools, rather than entities capable of forming fiduciary relationships.[48]

In the United States, robo-adviser firms are subject to a variety of fiduciary duties because of their status as investment advisers under Investment Advisers Act of 1940.[49] Although the term 'fiduciary duty' is not mentioned in the Act, investment advisers have consistently been held to be fiduciaries, and as a result, subject to a number of fiduciary duties.[50] These duties include the duty of disclosure discussed in Section IV.D, based on disclosure-based regulation, which includes a duty to make disclosure of material facts related to the investment adviser's business practices and conflicts of interests.[51] Additionally, robo-adviser firms are subject to a duty of loyalty, which includes a duty to act in the best interests of clients.[52] Finally,

[48] Yesha Yadav, 'Fintech and International Financial Regulation' (2020) 53 *Vanderbilt Journal of Transnational Law* 1109, 1127 ('Where a saver might once have visited a money manager to work out how best to organize her investment portfolio, this task can instead be accomplished electronically with artificially intelligent firms as the driving engine. So-called robo-advisors can cut out the traditional intermediary…').

[49] Avery R Barber 'Redefining Fiduciary in the Robot Age: How the Department of Labor's New Definition Will Encourage Robo-Investment Platforms and Remove the Human Element from Investment Advising' (2018) 18 *Wake Forest Journal of Business and Intellectual Property Law* 316, 323 ('Currently, robo-advisers fall under the definition of 'investment advisers' under the Investment Advisers Act of 1940 and are required to register under that Act. Robo-advisers are therefore subject to the same fiduciary obligations as human advisors').

[50] James S Wrona, 'The Best of Both Worlds: A Fact-Based Analysis of the Legal Obligations of Investment Advisers and Broker-Dealers and a Framework for Enhanced Investor Protection' (2012) 68 *Business Lawyer* 1, 7 ('Advisers are subject to the standards set forth in the Advisers Act, which do not expressly impose a fiduciary obligation. The courts and the SEC, however, have held that the Advisers Act implicitly imposes a fiduciary duty on advisers.').

[51] Alina Petrova 'A Critical Analysis of Robare: Does Ignorantia Legis Excuse from Liability?' (2020) 20 *UC Davis Business Law Journal* 189, 192 ('The advisory relationship is that of trust and confidence, and it puts on an investment advisor an affirmative duty of utmost good faith and full and fair disclosure. In furtherance of the principle of full and fair disclosure, court practice and relevant regulations have established an investment advisor's ongoing obligation to disclose to its clients all material information that might affect an advisory relationship.').

[52] Barbara Black, 'How to Improve Retail Investor Protection after the Dodd-Frank Wall Street Reform and Consumer Protection Act' (2010) 13 *University of Pennsylvania Journal of Business Law* 59, 86 ('[C]ourts have viewed the 'best interests of the client' standard as an aspect of the investment adviser's duty of loyalty to address conflicts of interests, rather than as an aspect of the adviser's duty of care addressing the quality of investment advice. Over time, the SEC came to express the investment adviser's fiduciary obligation more generally as a duty of loyalty that requires advisers to manage their clients' portfolios in the best interest of clients; specific aspects of that duty include disclosing conflicts and having a reasonable basis for client recommendations.').

robo-adviser firms are subject to a duty of care, which includes a duty to offer only suitable investment advice[53] and a duty to have an internal compliance programme to ensure that it is adhering to its fiduciary duties and other substantive requirements of the law.[54]

Employing a system of fiduciary duty-based regulation for robo-adviser firms has a number of virtues. Such a system creates substantial obligations for those developing, marketing, and operating robo-advisers to look out for the well-being of clients. Fiduciary duties create standards for behaviour, and because standards are less rigid than rules, fiduciary duties are less likely to hinder innovation. On the other hand, complying with standards, including fiduciary duties can sometimes be difficult because obligations are less certain.[55] In addition, some have expressed concerns regarding whether robo-adviser firms can meet the obligations under the system of fiduciary duties imposed on other investment advisers.[56] Specifically, many have raised concerns about whether robo-advisers can collect enough information and provide sufficiently individualised advice to meet suitability requirements.[57] Regardless, in general, fiduciary duties are very useful as a system of regulation for robo-advisers.

F *Investor Education*

A fifth possible model for regulating robo-advisers is one founded upon investor education. Because of the recent advent of this technology, many investors may be unaware of the risks associated with it and may place unwarranted trust in its reliability. To effectively use robo-advisers, investors need some basic understanding of

53 Miles O Indest, 'A Tale of Two Markets: Reconciling the Securities and Exchange Commission's Implementation of the Uniform Fiduciary Standard and Equity Crowdfunding Regulations' (2015) 22 *PIABA Bar Journal* 311, 319–320 ('Investment advisers owe their clients a duty to provide them only suitable investment advice. The suitability obligation requires that the RIA make a reasonable inquiry into the client's financial needs, objectives and circumstances, and that the adviser reasonably believe that the recommendations are suitable for its customer based on those factors.').

54 17 CFR paras 275.206(4)-7 (2021).

55 J Dennis Hynes, 'Freedom of Contract, Fiduciary Duties, and Partnerships: The Bargain Principle and the Law of Agency' (1997) 54 *Washington and Lee Law Review* 439, 442–443 ('One feature of the law of fiduciary duties is that it is open-textured and uncertain. The very breadth of the fiduciary principle and the indeterminate number and kind of relationships that it touches lead to such a consequence.').

56 Jake G Rifkin, 'Robo-Advisers Jumping on the Bandwagon: Yet Another Cry for a Uniform Standard' (2019) 97 *North Carolina Law Review* 673, 675 ('The conversation in legal academia surrounding robo-advisers currently pertains to the legal obligations that robo-advisers owe their clients: whether robo-advisers can or cannot fulfil their duties as fiduciaries under the Investment Advisers Act of 1940…').

57 Iris H-Y Chiu, 'Fintech and Disruptive Business Models in Financial Products, Intermediation and Markets—Policy Implications for Financial Regulators' (2016) 21 *Journal of Technology Law & Policy* 55, 89 ('Commentators have mixed views on whether robo-advisers can robustly map and interpret investor information accurately and then 'recommend' a range of suitable products to investors.').

investing issues.[58] Securities regulators could focus on education in hopes of ensuring that investors recognise and comprehend the benefits and risks of robo-advisers.

To be helpful to the general public, educational materials would need to be simple and direct. Some securities regulators have already begun developing such materials. For example, the North American Securities Administrators Association ('NASAA') has developed a web page designed to educate investors about this technology. In addition to providing a basic definition of what robo-advisers are and how they work, the page includes a list of questions that investors should be asking themselves when deciding whether to invest using a robo-adviser.[59] The questions include:

- Does the robo-adviser build a portfolio based on your financial goals while taking into account your appetite for risk? When you invest, you should always keep track of your investments and ensure your portfolio meets your long- and short-term needs.
- Are you comfortable and familiar with the types of investment products the robo-adviser will use to build your portfolio? Research and understand the investment products the robo-adviser you are considering uses before you invest.
- Do you like discussing ideas or asking questions when seeking financial advice? If so, be sure you understand the level of human interaction you will get with the robo-adviser you are planning to use.
- Do you want the ability to make decisions based on market fluctuations? With robo-advisers, you may not have the ability to buy and sell securities in your account as the market moves up or down.
- Are you considering any tax consequences that you may encounter for investment losses and/or gains? When investing, you should consider your yearly tax situation. You may want to talk to a tax consultant to better understand how using a robo-adviser may affect you.
- Are you comfortable and familiar with the robo-adviser's fee structure and compensation model? You should know how much you are paying for the robo-adviser's services and how these costs will affect your returns over time.[60]

The page also recommends that investors research the company, management, registration, disciplinary history, and customer reviews of those providing robo-adviser services.

58 Iris H-Y Chiu, 'Transforming the Financial Advice Market—The Roles of Robo-Advice, Financial Regulation and Public Governance in the United Kingdom' (2019) 35 *Banking & Finance Law Review* 9, 27 ('Customers should ideally come with some extent of financial literacy in order to have realistic expectations of the limitations of robo-advice.').

59 North American Securities Administrators Association, 'Millennial Money Mission: Robo-Advisers' <www.nasaa.org/investor-education/millennial-money-mission/robo-advisers>.

60 Ibid.

Beyond creating materials that are understandable to the general investing public, distribution of these educational materials is also a concern. Securities regulators can maintain web pages and generate other materials regarding robo-advisers that may never be viewed by those investors needing them most. This issue could be solved by building distribution of investor education material into the process of obtaining robo-advising services.

G *Regulation by Litigation*

One final model for regulating robo adviser is regulation by litigation. This occurs when a general prohibition is allowed to develop into a complex system of regulation over time through case law. This type of approach has been used in regard to investment adviser regulation. As previously mentioned, the Advisers Act does not use the term 'fiduciary duty.' The fiduciary duties discussed earlier were derived over time from various provisions of the Act. For example, Section 206 of the Act provides the following:

> It shall be unlawful for any investment adviser, by use of the mails or any means or instrumentality of interstate commerce, directly or indirectly –
>
> (1) to employ any device, scheme, or artifice to defraud any client or prospective client;
> (2) to engage in any transaction, practice, or course of business which operates as a fraud or deceit upon any client or prospective client;
> (3) acting as principal for his own account, knowingly to sell any security to or purchase any security from a client, or acting as broker for a person other than such client, knowingly to effect any sale or purchase of any security for the account of such client, without disclosing to such client in writing before the completion of such transaction the capacity in which he is acting and obtaining the consent of the client to such transaction…; or
> (4) to engage in any act, practice, or course of business which is fraudulent, deceptive, or manipulative…[61]

Beginning with SEC v *Capital Gains Research Bureau, Inc*,[62] the Supreme Court of the United States has held that Section 206 establishes fiduciary duty standards for investment advisers. Through this case and subsequent litigation, a complex system of fiduciary duty regulation has developed.

Similarly, regulation by litigation has also occurred in regard to Section 10(b) of the Securities Exchange Act of 1934 and Rule 10b-5 promulgated thereupon, which is also applicable to robo-advisers because of their involvement in securities transactions. In *Blue Chip Stamps v Manor Drug Stores*, while musing on how much litigation has

[61] Investment Advisers Act of 1940, para 202(a)(11), 15 USC para 80b–6 (2021).
[62] SEC (n 35).

occurred regarding the implied private right of action under these provisions, Justice William Rehnquist famously wrote: '[w]hen we deal with private actions under Rule 10b-5, we deal with a judicial oak which has grown from little more than a legislative acorn.'[63] As a consequence, the implied private right of action, one of the most important regulatory tools under United States federal securities law, was developed through litigation. Although regulation by litigation does create separation of powers concerns in the United States, as the fiduciary duties under the Advisers Act and the implied private right of action under Section 10(b) and Rule 10b-5 reflect, it can be a useful way to develop the law regulating securities markets.

While regulation by litigation may be useful in some instances, especially when concerns about hindering or extinguishing innovation are present, it is not appropriate as the sole means for regulating robo-advisers. Because robo-advisers limit or eliminate investor interaction with human investment advisers, investors can be hurt more quickly, easily, and harshly than in other contexts. Therefore, robo-advisers should be regulated by existing schemes or specially developed schemes of regulation, rather than waiting for regulation to incrementally appear through regulation by litigation. Of course, regulation by litigation could be a component of an existing and sufficiently developed scheme of regulation.

V REGULATION BY SURVEY

Section IV details seven different models that could be used to regulate robo-advisers. One is inappropriate based on the state of the robo-adviser technology, that is, agency law. Two are inappropriate based on concerns about hindering or extinguishing innovation, that is, design intervention and merit based-regulation. Three of the models show promise to balance the sometimes competing interests of market protection, investor protection, and technological innovation, that is, disclosure-based regulation, fiduciary duties, and investor education. Finally, one regulatory model may be appropriate to regulate the robo-adviser industry when it is paired with other regulatory models, but it would be inappropriate to regulate the industry by itself because it would take too long to develop and address risks, that is, regulation by litigation.

Notably, the last four categories of regulation – disclosure-based regulation, fiduciary duties, investor education, and regulation by litigation – reflect the United States federal government's approach to regulating robo-advisers. Even with this being the case, the confluence of these four models still poses lingering risks relating to disclosure, conflicts of interest, licensure, programming flaws, technology glitches, regulator resource availability, and regulator capacity for regulation and enforcement.[64] As a consequence, beyond improving the use of each of the four

[63] *Blue Chip Stamps v Manor Drug Stores*, 421 U.S. 723, 737 (1975).

[64] Seidt, Zaharis and Jarrett (n 9) 511–23 (discussing various concerns related to robo-advisers).

models currently being employed, regulators should be exploring what else can be added to the United States federal model to improve and support market protection, investor protection, and technological innovation.

This chapter suggests that in addition to disclosure-based regulation, fiduciary duties, investor education, and regulation by litigation, the government in attempting to regulate the robo-adviser industry should engage in what shall be termed 'regulation by survey.' Put simply, robo-advisers ought to be regulated by regular standardised surveying of the investors who are using them and the release of that data to the general public. The surveys could be conducted on a regular basis through the robo-adviser platforms, and they could be a requirement for use of a robo-adviser. NASAA's list of questions that investors should be asking themselves when deciding whether to invest using a robo-adviser, which is discussed above, could be a useful starting point for creating a survey.[65] The survey should incorporate both narrative answers and rankings to maximise the amount and comparability of the information received.

Standardised surveying by the government is appropriate for at least three reasons. First, it would give the federal government direct access to survey results for purposes of making regulatory and enforcement decisions. The government could more easily and quickly detect issues with particular robo-adviser firms and platforms and address those issues. Second, it would give investors easily comparable information about robo-adviser firms and platforms to assist in making investment decisions, which would be an appropriate and useful addition to the federal system of disclosure-based regulation in the United States. Third, it would prevent robo-adviser firms from creating surveys with formats and questions that might create an unduly favourable impression of that robo-adviser firm.

Regulation by survey does have its shortcomings. Investors may not know when they should be concerned, and even when they do recognise the challenges and risks that they are facing, they may not be able to adequately describe those challenges and risks. Additionally, when released publicly, the information gained from surveying may fuel interest in particular existing models of robo-advising, which may hinder or prevent the development of new and innovative models of robo-advising. Finally, regulation by survey will have various administrative costs.

All of these shortcomings are legitimate, but robo-advisers are especially ripe for regulation by survey because they are intentionally designed to reduce or eliminate interaction between investors and human investment advisers. As a result, the government may be less aware of the challenges and concerns that investors are facing in using robo-adviser platforms. As a consequence, the benefits of regulation by survey relating to robo-advisers outweigh any burdens.

Additionally, regulation by survey could be useful in other contexts as well. Electronic surveying is a useful technology that was born long after the advent of

[65] North American Securities Administrators Association (n 59).

federal securities laws during the 1930s and even after the passage of the Investment Advisers Act of 1940. Robo-advisers would be an excellent place to test-run its use.

VI CONCLUSION

Robo-advisers are client-facing computerised investment tools that provide financial advice or assist in investment management. The development, marketing, and operation of this technology has created an emerging and evolving new segment of the investment adviser industry that affords a variety of benefits to investors including low-cost access to advice. At the same time, robo-advisers create a myriad of concerns for securities regulators relating to disclosure, conflicts of interest, licensure, programming flaws, technology glitches, regulator resource availability, and regulator capacity for regulation and enforcement. Various possible models exist for regulating robo-advisers, including agency law, design intervention, merit-based regulation, disclosure-based regulation, fiduciary duties, investor education, and regulation by litigation. This chapter concludes the risks generated by robo-advisers would best be regulated by a mix of disclosure-based regulation, fiduciary duties, investor education, and regulation by litigation. This type of approach is similar to what currently exists in the United States. In addition, this chapter makes the novel suggestion that robo-advisers ought to be regulated by regular standardised surveying of the investors who are using them and the release of that data to the general public. Such an approach would allow the government to engage in regulation and enforcement more effectively and efficiently, and it would give investors easily comparable information about robo-adviser firms and platforms to assist in making investment decisions.

26

Employment Law and AI

Jeremias Adams-Prassl

I INTRODUCTION

At first glance, a chapter on employment law might seem a curious anachronism in a handbook dedicated to artificial intelligence and the law. Over the course of the last decade, academic and policy debates have focused on automation, turbo-charged by the rise of artificial intelligence, destroying jobs – up to half of them, according to one much-cited account.[1] The threat (or promise?) of technological unemployment is not new, of course;[2] and yet, leading scholars have begun to think about employment law's future 'after work'.[3]

The focus of the present contribution is on the more immediate impact of artificial intelligence on work: the rise of algorithmic management.[4] Under labels ranging from 'people analytics' to 'big data HR', increasingly sophisticated technology collects and analyses ever-larger quantities of workforce-related data with a view to augmenting – or even fully replacing – the exercise of traditional employer functions,

1 Carl Frey and Michael Osborne, 'The Future of Employment: How Susceptible Are Jobs to Computerisation' (Oxford Martin School 2013) 38, 42. See also Eric Brynjolfsson and Andrew McAfee, *The Second Machine Age: Progress and Prosperity in a Time of Brilliant Technologies* (WW Norton & Company Inc 2014) ch 1. These concerns are not necessarily borne out by the numbers. A January 2021 survey by the OECD found that 'employment grew in all OECD countries over the period 2012-2019.' OECD, 'What Happened to Jobs at High Risk of Automation?' (January 2021) <www.oecd.org/future-of-work/reports-and-data/what-happened-to-jobs-at-high-risk-of-automation-2021.pdf>.

2 John Maynard Keynes, *Essays in Persuasion* (1963) 358–373 <www.marxists.org/reference/subject/economics/keynes/1930/our-grandchildren.htm>: 'We are being afflicted with a new disease of which some readers may not yet have heard the name, but of which they will hear a great deal in the years to come – namely, technological unemployment.' Keynes attributed the 'economic pessimism' of the time to 'the growing-pains of over-rapid changes'.

3 Cynthia Estlund, 'What Should We Do after Work? Automation and Employment Law' (2018) 128 *Yale Law Journal* 254.

4 This is only one of the several important dimensions of this topic. A similarly important question, beyond the scope of present discussion, explores the role of (low-wage) labour required for the creation of artificial intelligence models in the first place, for example in the context of data labelling: Janine Berg, 'Protecting Workers in the Digital Age: Technology, Outsourcing and the Growing Precariousness of Work' (2019) 41 *Comparative Labor Law & Policy Journal* 69.

from hiring and firing workers through to managing the enterprise-internal market on a daily basis. Algorithmic management has grown from its origins in the gig economy to encompass workplaces across the socio-economic spectrum: from factories and warehouses to professional service firms and public sector organisations. The Covid-19 pandemic has further fuelled the rapid growth of digital monitoring and control, given that key elements of algorithmic management are often built into remote-working or collaborative office software. The potential implications for labour market regulation are wide-ranging: while there is clear potential for algorithmic decision making to contribute to improved work quality, early case studies have highlighted a number of disconcerting implications, from constant micro-surveillance to automated bias and discrimination.

This chapter sets out some of the most important challenges flowing from the rise of algorithmic management for employment law, broadly conceived as encompassing both the individual and collective dimension of employment relation, as well as associated regulatory domains, including data protection and anti-discrimination law, insofar as they are relevant to the employment context. Discussion is structured as follows. Section II introduces the digital workplace, tracing the rise of Artificial Intelligence at work from the gig economy to employment across the socio-economic spectrum. Section III explores the implications of algorithmic management on employment status litigation, with senior courts in multiple jurisdictions focusing on close algorithmic control as a key feature in determining gig economy platforms' employer status. Section IV then turns to the legal regulation of the managerial prerogative, highlighting the drawbacks and advantages of different regimes, as well as discussing the underlying difficulties with ascribing responsibility in scenarios of diffuse algorithmic control. Additional regulatory options in equality law and under the GDPR are explored in Section V; discussion concludes with an overview and analysis of emerging regulatory proposals in the European Union, including both an omnibus regulatory regime, and more narrowly focused provisions targeting algorithmic management in the gig economy.

II THE DIGITAL WORKPLACE: FROM ELECTRONIC SURVEILLANCE TO ARTIFICIAL INTELLIGENCE

Over the course of the last decade, digital worker surveillance and algorithmic management have rapidly spread across industries and workplaces. Human resource management is frequently turning to 'people data to tackle significant challenges, with three-quarters (75%) tackling workforce performance and productivity issues using people data'. The technology involved is increasingly sophisticated: in the United Kingdom, 14% of organisations are already 'using machine learning and artificial intelligence to develop people reports'.[5] The Covid-19 pandemic has had a

[5] CIPD in association with Workday, 'People Analytics: Driving Business Performance with People Data' (June 2018) 30, 33.

significant impact on the development and deployment of algorithmic management systems, sweeping aside many of the traditional barriers to technology deployment:

> Covid-19 increasingly 'necessitates' some tasks being mediated through data-driven technologies, as well as augmenting tasks to be completed remotely; it is changing rationales for investment in technology; it is rapidly impacting the supply of labour – both increasing aggregate unemployment and restricting feasibility of labour being present at some workplaces; and it is changing public attitudes towards the uptake of new technologies.[6]

The technologies powering algorithmic surveillance and management might be new: but do they pose novel regulatory challenges for employment law? Employers have long sought to monitor their employees, not least as a result of Taylor's infamous theories of 'scientific management'.[7] Whilst the European Court of Human Rights rejected an unfettered right clandestinely to monitor employees' communications nearly 25 years ago,[8] however, the digitalised workplace opens up a plethora of new avenues for surveillance.[9]

Gig economy platforms were at the vanguard of developing intensive digital surveillance, for example by using driver's mobile phones to record information from GPS, gyrometer, and acceleration sensors to detect speeding or abrupt braking.[10] Increased digital surveillance is however by no means limited to the gig economy. In addition to monitoring all digital aspects of work on computers and devices such as workers' mobile phones, a wide array of sensors are increasingly deployed to capture information about all aspects of work. This can range from simple presence control through ID card logs and dedicated sensors to control individual desks through to 'sociometric badges' that measure and record most facets of employee interaction.[11] Through wearable technology, surveillance also reaches far beyond traditional workplaces, from body cams and jackets that monitor emergency personnel's heart rate to helmets designed to measure truck driver's brain activity.[12] In principle, at least, there seem to be few aspects of working life left that cannot be

6 A Gilbert, A Thomas, S Atwell, and J Simons, *The Impact of Automation on Labour Markets: Interactions with Covid-19* (Institute for the Future of Work 2020).

7 FW Taylor, *The Principles of Scientific Management* (Harper & Brothers 1919).

8 *Halford v United Kingdom* (20605/92). See also Michael Ford, *Surveillance and Privacy at Work Institute of Employment Rights* (Institute for Employment Rights, London 1998).

9 For more recent litigation on employee surveillance in the context of the right to a private life under Art 8 ECHR, see for example, *Barbulescu v Romania (61496/08)* (chat monitoring) and *Lopez Ribalda v Spain (1874/13)* (hidden CCTV cameras).

10 Andrew Beinstein and Ted Sumers, 'How Uber Engineering Increases Safe Driving with Telematics' *Uber Engineering* (29 June 2016) <www.eng.uber.com/telematics/> archived at <www.perma.cc/E82S-37NQ>.

11 Javier Sánchez-Monedero and Lina Dencik, 'The Datafication of the Workplace' (Working Paper, Data Justice Lab 2019), 18, 26.

12 For detailed overviews of these technologies, see Chandra Steele, 'The Quantified Employee: How Companies Use Tech to Track Workers' (*PC Magazine*, 14 Feb 2020) <www.uk.pcmag.com/security-5/124891/the-quantified-employee-how-companies-use-tech-to-track-workers>.

monitored digitally: from toilet breaks through to the 'emotion tone' of individual messages.[13]

This surveillance is worrying in its own right, especially where workers are unclear as to which information their employers collect, and where there is no employee involvement in the implementation of new technologies.[14] Wolfie Christl, author of one of the largest and most comprehensive study of algorithmic control and surveillance practices at work to date, concludes that '[i]n many areas of the world of work, the processing of personal data … has become virtually ubiquitous.'[15] Even more concerning, however, are the broader uses of the data collected, beyond immediate monitoring, through what Sánchez-Monedero and Dencik refer to as 'data integration and intelligent data analysis', including 'the possibility of building multi-source datasets, the processing of unstructured data (text, audio and video), [and] the deployment of predictive models'.[16]

Digital workplace surveillance, in other words, is a foundational element for the rise of the deployment of algorithmic management and artificial intelligence at work. What started with specific management tasks in the gig economy has today spread across the world of work:[17] we are witnessing explosive growth both in terms of which management functions can be automated, as well as the scope of workplaces where technologies are deployed.

Algorithmic management can start even before the inception of an employment relationship: a large number of providers offer services from reputation screening and CV sorting, all the way through the complete automation of the interview process.[18] There is no employer function which cannot, in principle, be automated – up to and including the firing of (supposedly) unproductive workers. When faced with allegations of retaliatory firing workers attempting to organise in a Baltimore warehouse in 2018, lawyers for Amazon responded with the astonishing assertion that no human manager had been involved in the dismissals:

> Amazon's system tracks the rates of each individual associate's productivity and automatically generates any warnings or terminations regarding quality or productivity without input from supervisors…. If an associate receives two final written

[13] Javier Sánchez-Monedero and Lina Dencik, 'The Datafication of the Workplace' (Working Paper, Data Justice Lab 2019) 18, 20.

[14] Prospect Union, 'Future of Work: Employers' collection and use of worker data (London, February 2020).

[15] 'In vielen Bereichen der Arbeitswelt ist die Verarbeitung personenbezogener Daten … geradezu allgegenwärtig geworden.' In W Christl (ed), *Digitale Überwachung und Kontrolle am Arbeitsplatz* (Cracked Labs 2021) 16.

[16] Monedero and Dencik (n 13) 15.

[17] For further illustrations, see for example, Joe Atkinson 'Automated Management and Liability for Digital Discrimination under the Equality Act 2010' (*UK Labour Law Blog*) <www.uklabourlawblog.com/2020/09/10/automated-management-and-liability-for-digital-discrimination-under-the-equality-act-2010-by-joe-atkinson/>.

[18] <www.hirevue.com/#platform-section>.

warnings or a total of six written warnings within a rolling 12-month period, the system automatically generates a termination notice.[19]

How should we understand the impact of algorithmic management on workplaces? There are numerous potential upsides – from 'rais[ing] productivity by limiting moral hazard in the workplace … to restructure[ing] jobs in a way that benefits its workers'.[20] At the same time, however, there is a quickly growing body of empirical evidence which suggests caution is required. Algorithmic management poses potentially serious risks of material harm, from high injury rates[21] to workplace stress resulting from randomised work allocation.[22] It can also play an instrumental role in fundamental rights violations, from screening out employees who will agitate for higher wages and organise or support unionisation[23] to persistent patterns of algorithmic discrimination.[24]

A *Novel Challenge?*

Are the problems identified simply down to inappropriate deployment of algorithmic management systems (and thus, at least in principle, not a novel regulatory challenge)? Or are we faced with a new set of challenges, inherent in the novel technology being deployed? In (cautiously) opting for the latter answer, there are two main areas in which significant distinctions can be identified: the amount and kind of data collected, and the ways in which that information is then processed, including the mechanism through which control can be exercised by algorithmic systems.

In terms of data collection, first, algorithmic management goes far beyond capturing ratings, or traditional information such as CVs and references. As the examples above illustrate, in principle, there are few limits to the digital information (ranging from social media profiles to keystroke logs and communication metadata) and physical information (including through biometrics, video-surveillance, and sociometric badges) that can be captured. Even where the actual substance of such communications is not disclosed or analysed, so-called 'metadata' (for example, the duration

[19] James Vincent 'Amazon Deploys AI 'Distance Assistants' to Notify Warehouse Workers if They Get Too Close' (*The Verge*, 16 June 2020) <www.theverge.com/platform/amp/2020/6/16/21292669/> (legal documents as linked in article).

[20] A Adams, 'Technology and the Labour Market: The Assessment' (2018) 3 *Oxford Review of Economic Policy* 349, 357 (citations omitted).

[21] W Evans, 'Ruthless Quotas at Amazon Are Maining Employees (*The Atlantic*, 25 November 2019) <www.theatlantic.com/technology/archive/2019/11/amazon-warehouse-reports-show-worker-injuries/602530/>.

[22] <www.amadeus-hospitality.com/service-optimization-software/hotsos-housekeeping/>.

[23] Nathan Newman, 'Reengineering Workplace Bargaining: How Big Data Drives Lower Wages and How Reframing Labor Law Can Restore Information Equality in the Workplace' (2017) 86 *University of Cincinnati Law Review* 693.

[24] Solon Barocas and Andrew D Selbst, 'Big Data's Disparate Impact' (2016) 104 *California Law Review* 671, 677.

and frequency of calls between specific individuals, or the size and timing of email attachments sent to external recipients) can easily be captured. Surveillance, crucially, is not limited to employer-imposed monitoring: whether through the use of fitness trackers or health-apps on our telephones, there is an increasing trend of self-monitoring or self-tracking, the results of which can easily be combined with data gathered in the workplace.[25] Once captured, furthermore, information is not limited to a single-use scenario: it can be stored permanently, re-combined and analysed as new techniques become available, and be used in training and developing new AI tools. There is no such thing as an anonymous dataset: even where particular information (such as regarding protected characteristics) is not recorded directly, it could nonetheless be inferred through other proxies when multiple data sources are (re-)combined.

In terms of processing, second, a major challenge arises from the constantly changing and evolving nature of algorithmic control – both as a result of particular machine learning techniques, and through tech-driven experimentation with ever-changing business models: what is required can be as little as an overnight update of an app or platform. Machine learning (one of the key technologies behind many 'artificial intelligence' solutions) is based on the probabilistic analysis of large datasets, relying on sophisticated statistical modelling to spot patterns or correlations in the data.[26] This is a crucial step away from more traditional understandings of algorithms: many machine learning techniques are designed to rely on a constant evolution and redefinition of parameters – algorithmic control is therefore no longer just confined to experiences taught through training data sets and pre-programmed analytical routines.[27]

The results are ever-changing decision structures: as increasing amounts of data are collected about individual employees and every aspect of their working lives scrutinised on an on-going basis, the factors considered relevant for key metrics such as productivity or innovation will continue to change.[28] The ensuing lack of transparency is particular problematic given the granularity and intensity of control exercised through algorithmic management, from the inception of the employment relationship all the way through to its suspension or termination, and the concomitant difficulties in challenging automated or algorithmically informed employer decisions – especially where gamification is used to dissimulate and internalise control.[29]

Whether in terms of information asymmetries or work intensification, the impact of artificial intelligence at work could be characterised as similar (if more extreme)

[25] G Neff and D Nafus, *Self-Tracking* (MIT Press Essential Knowledge Series 2016).

[26] N Polson and J Scott, *AIQ: How Artificial Intelligence Works and How We Can Harness Its Power for a Better World* (Bantam Press 2018).

[27] D Heaven (ed), *Machines That Think* (New Scientist 2017).

[28] I Goodfellow, Y Bengio, A Courville, *Deep Learning* (The MIT Press 2016).

[29] M Bodie and others, 'The Law and Policy of People Analytics' (2016) 88 *University of Colorado Law Review* 961, 975 explain how 'in people analytics, games are being used for their predictive power, often to quantify or measure particular skills or aptitudes or to screen job candidates.'

than previous waves of digitalisation. And yet, there is a fundamental difference, as Ajunwa and Greene explain

> Managerial control expands first through work intensification, as monitoring communicates that workers must be more productive, more efficient, and more sensitive to employer goals…. Then, surveillance creates a culture around what it communicates, giving norms, as a proxy for management, power over workers.[30]

III CHALLENGES TO EMPLOYMENT STATUS?

To date, the rise of algorithmic management has been subjected to comparatively little judicial scrutiny – with the major exception of status litigation in the gig economy, *viz* question as to workers' legal classification. Employment status is the cornerstone of employment law: only those employed under a contract of service (or, in the United Kingdom, a workers' contract) will enjoy recourse to protective norms ranging from minimum wage and working time rules to unfair dismissal protection.[31]

Gig economy platforms have near-universally contested attempts to classify them as employers, depicting their business model as one of neutral 'platforms' providing services to (micro-) entrepreneurs.[32] Sophisticated automated systems are seen as central to this claim. Algorithms, Sundararajan suggests, have fundamentally reshaped business organisation: 'everything about work [will] need to change': 'Today, smaller and smaller tasks can increasingly be outsourced with minimal transaction costs to crowds of workers connected to digital platforms.'[33]

The reality of algorithmic management, on the other hand, is far from visions of entrepreneurial freedom and independence. Alex Rosenblat and Luke Stark's study of Uber's control mechanisms demonstrates how working conditions in the gig economy are consistently 'shaped by the company's deployment of a variety of design decisions and information asymmetries via the application to effect a "soft control" over workers' routines', even though instructions are 'carefully designed to be indirect, presumably to avoid the appearance of a company policy'.[34] Any attempt to focus on high-priced ride, for example, is controlled by the platform's

30 Ifeoma Ajunwa and Daniel Greene, 'Platforms at Work: Automated Hiring Platforms and Other New Intermediaries in the Organization of Work' in S Vallas and A Kovalainen (eds), *Work and Labor and the Digital Age* (Emerald 2019) 66–67.

31 Employment Rights Act 1996, section 230. Note that Unfair Dismissal is linked to employee (rather than worker) status.

32 For a full account, see J Prassl, *Humans as a Service: the Promise and Perils of Work in the Gig Economy* (Oxford University Press 2018). The platform point is important: Daniel Seng, 'Information Intermediaries and AI' in Ernest Lim and Phillip Morgan (eds), *The Cambridge Handbook of Private Law and Artificial Intelligence* (Cambridge University Press 2024).

33 Arun Sundararajan, *The Sharing Economy – The End of Employment and the Rise of Crowd-Based Capitalism* (MIT Press 2016) 69, 173.

34 Alex Rosenblat and Luke Stark, 'Algorithmic Labor and Information Asymmetries: A Case Study of Uber's Drivers' (2016) 10 *International Journal of Communication* 3758, 3775.

algorithms: 'drivers are penalized for rejecting lower paid work in favor of higher paid work, which is illustrative of another constraint on their "freedom" as independent entrepreneurs.'[35]

Workers across Europe are increasingly contesting platforms' contractual insistence on self-employment status.[36] Senior courts from France's *Court de Cassation*[37] to the UK Supreme Court[38] have been receptive to misclassification arguments – with algorithmic control playing a central role in establishing the factual matrix required to overcome extensive contractual documentation purporting to set up commercial arms-length arrangements.[39]

The employment status of Uber drivers was the first gig economy decision to reach the UK Supreme Court. 'Partner Terms' and 'Services Agreement[s]' purported to create an arrangement in which drivers were seen as the platform's 'Customers', with passengers styled as 'Users'. Under this setup, Uber was merely 'to provide electronic services … to the driver, which include access to the Uber app and payment services'[40]

In 2016, a group of Uber drivers led by Yaseen Aslam and James Farrar brought a number of claims, including for failure to pay the National Minimum Wage and grant paid annual leave, against the platform. In a first instance judgement handed down that autumn, Employment Judge Snelson at the London Central Employment Tribunal was unequivocal in finding that claimant drivers were workers, rather than independent contractors. The language in *Aslam, Farrar v Uber* was unusually pointed. The tribunal, the Judge noted, were

> struck by the remarkable lengths to which Uber has gone in order to compel agreement with its (perhaps we should say its lawyers') description of itself and with its analysis of the legal relationships between the two companies, the drivers and the passengers.[41]

Following a detailed analysis of the platform's algorithmic management techniques, from route setting to automated time-out penalties when workers refused

35 Rosenblat and Stark, 'Algorithmic Labor' (n 34) 3761, 3762, 3766.

36 For a full comparative exploration, see J Adams-Prassl, S Laulom, and Y M Vázquez, 'The Role of National Courts in Protecting Platform Workers: A Comparative Analysis' in JM Boto and E Brameshuber (eds), *Collective Bargaining and the Gig Economy* (Hart 2023).

37 Soc., 4 mars 2020, n° 19-13.316, FP-P+B+R+I. See the English translation of the decision on the website of the Court: <www.courdecassation.fr/IMG/20200304_arret_uber_english.pdf>. See also the Spanish Supreme Court's decision in *Glovo*: Judgment n°. 805/2020, rec. 4746/2019.

38 *Uber BV v Aslam* [2021] UKSC 5, [2021] 4 All ER 209 ('*Uber UKSC*').

39 In line with the International Labour Organisation's Recommendation 198 of 2006 [9]. For a detailed guide, see ILO, *Regulating the Employment Relationship in Europe: A Guide to Recommendation No 198* (Geneva 2013) 33ff.

40 *Uber UKSC* (n 38), [24].

41 *Aslam and Farrar v Uber* Case No 2202550/2015 (London Employment Tribunal) [87] (citations omitted). The decision was made available at <www.judiciary.gov.uk/wp-content/uploads/2016/10/aslam-and-farrar-v-uber-reasons-20161028.pdf>.

rides assigned to them by the platform, the tribunal concluded that 'Uber subjects drivers through the rating system to what amounts to a performance management/disciplinary procedure',[42] and that its drivers could therefore not be classified as independent contractors.

The platform repeatedly appealed this finding. In a decision handed down on February 19, 2021, seven Justices of the UK Supreme Court unanimously rejected Uber's final appeal and fully vindicated the Employment Tribunal's findings as to employment status. In turning to the reality of the drivers' relationship with Uber, Lord Leggatt, with whom all Justices agreed, highlighted several elements of Uber's business model as particularly salient for the question of worker status, including the power automatically to set rates and determine the percentage of Uber's 'service fee'; information asymmetries created by the app to exercise tight algorithmic control once a driver is logged on; a 'significant degree of control over the way in which drivers deliver their services'; and tight restrictions on communications between drivers and passengers.[43] Indeed, 'the technology which is integral to the service is wholly owned and controlled by Uber and is used as a means of exercising control over drivers'.[44]

Insofar as employment status is concerned, then, the fact that algorithmic management systems are 'designed to operate coercively'[45] to ensure workers' compliance with employer specifications will provide strong support for arguments against independent contractor (mis-) classification. Employment status in and of itself, however, is only a preliminary question when it comes to addressing the socio-technical challenges inherent in digital surveillance and control. To what extent can norms designed to regulate the human exercise of managerial prerogatives grapple with the augmentation, or indeed substitution, of control through artificial intelligence?

IV LEGAL REGULATION OF THE MANAGERIAL PREROGATIVE

The analysis in Section II suggested that the challenges associated with algorithmic management are driven by two fundamentally distinct aspects of artificial intelligence systems: the amount, and kind, of data collected and the novel forms of processing underpinning complex automated decision-making systems. The potential implications for employment law are stark: the effective application of the discipline's received approach to regulating the exercise of managerial control could be threatened even where the underlying wage/work bargain is clearly within the protective scope of the contract of employment (or worker's contract).

This is particularly true in the individual dimension of the relationship, as an analysis of the role played by the implied term of trust and confidence shows. Collective

[42] Ibid. [92](8).
[43] *Uber UKSC* (n 38), [94]–[101].
[44] Ibid. [98].
[45] Ibid. [129], [123].

labour law, on the other hand, might struggle less to keep up with the fast pace of technological development and increasingly specialised deployment of algorithmic management tools. Given the inherent flexibility of reflexive (self-) regulation through collective bargaining, social partners are, at least in principle, in an excellent position to negotiate (and re-negotiate) appropriate limitations across the lifecycle of the employment relationship. Even collective agreements, however, might struggle effectively to regulate artificial intelligence at work given the potential control/accountability paradox where algorithmic management systems are deployed by small- and medium-sized companies, unable to build and maintain their own software: in contrast to traditional attempts to evade liability (as just discussed), the inability accurately to ascribe responsibility is inherent in the technology itself.

Turning first to the implied term of trust and confidence which characterises all contracts of service, it has long been accepted that employers must refrain from any conduct 'likely to destroy or seriously damage the relationship of trust and confidence between employer and employee'.[46] In exploring the potential of this implied term in regulating the deployment of algorithmic management systems, Robin Allen QC and Dee Masters argue that the 'use of [Artificial Intelligence] and [Automated Decision-Making Systems] does not abrogate employers from the obligation to make ... decisions [such as disciplinary action or dismissals] to a high standard'.[47]

The implied term of mutual trust and confidence, they suggest, has 'important consequences for any analysis of the implications of AI systems on the workplace'.[48] from placing an obligation on employers to provide explanations to enabling close scrutiny of decisions which must be taken in good faith and in a lawful and rational manner even where there is broad contractual discretion.[49] The term has powerful potential:

> The common law has always recognised that the absence of this trust and confidence is fatal to the success of any employment contract; in its absence the only possible remedy is to treat the main obligations of the contract as at an end because the courts recognise that you cannot force mutual trust and confidence between two parties. Where this happens, employees can sue for breach of contract and (subject to certain other statutory conditions) bring constructive unfair dismissal claims.[50]

That very same potential, however, also provides significant limitations in practice. For the vast majority of workers not in senior management positions, the implied term of trust and confidence only tends to come into play when the relationship

46 *Malik and Mahmud v Bank of Credit and Commerce International SA* [1998] AC 20 (HL).

47 Robin Allen and Dee Masters, 'Technology Managing People – The Legal Implications' (A report for the Trades Union Congress by the AI Law Consultancy, London 2021) para 1.45.

48 Ibid. para 1.41

49 Ibid. para 1.42 to para 1.44, citing *Keen v Comerzbank AG* [2006] EWCA Civ 1536, [2007] IRLR 132; and *Braganza v BP Shipping Ltd* [2015] UKSC 17, [2015] IRLR 48.

50 Ibid. para 1.40.

has broken down, that is, when an employee resigns and claims for constructive dismissal. Trying to rely on the term in litigation to limit the introduction of algorithmic management systems would therefore constitute a very high-risk strategy, requiring resignation in protest against the use of particularly egregious forms of automated decision making.[51]

Regulation of the managerial prerogative through collective avenues is potentially more promising on a day-to-day basis. At one end of the spectrum, algorithmic management clearly falls within the scope of information and consultation obligations derived from European Union law. Directive 2002/14/EC provides for a general framework for informing and consulting employees,[52] stipulating that 'Information and consultation shall cover' a wide range of scenarios, including in particular 'information and consultation on decisions likely to lead to substantial changes in work organisation or in contractual relations'[53] This clearly covers the introduction of algorithmic management systems, given their significant impact on the organisation of enterprise-internal markets. Upon closer inspection, however, the Directive's potential to successfully address the negative implications of algorithmic management is limited both in substance, given that the rights do not go beyond a duty to inform and consult workers (i.e., there is no ultimate right to involvement in the actual decision-making), and in scope, given that the Directive only applies to workplaces with more than fifty employees, as well as additional balloting thresholds introduced in the UK.[54]

Collective bargaining, on the other hand, has the potential to provide stronger employee protection, specifically targeting abuses of automated decision-making systems. Collective agreements negotiated between trade unions and workers can encompass a broad range of algorithmic management systems, as illustrated by a recent agreement between CWU, the Communication Workers Union, and the Royal Mail Group, which in addition to more traditional topics sets out to regulate the use of automated working time capture as well as scheduling software.[55] In the agreement, the employer 'recognise the need [in rolling out all new technology] for

[51] I am grateful to Aislinn Kelly-Lyth for further discussions of this point.

[52] Directive 2002/14/EC of the European Parliament and of the Council of 11 March 2002 establishing a general framework for informing and consulting employees in the European Community, OJ L 80, 23.3.2002, 29–34.

[53] ICE Directive 2002/14/EC Art 4(2)(c). Algorithmic Management might also be covered by Art 4(2)(b), 'information and consultation on the situation, structure and probable development of employment within the undertaking or establishment and on any anticipatory measures envisaged'.

[54] Taylor Review, <www.assets.publishing.service.gov.uk/government/uploads/system/uploads/attachment_data/file/627671/good-work-taylor-review-modern-working-practices-rg.pdf>, 52: 'Currently, the Regulations only apply to organisations with 50 or more employees. To be successful in getting ICE applied, at least 10% of (and a minimum of 15) employees must support it. Largely as a result of these restrictions, only 14% of workplaces in organisations with 50 or more employees had an on-site joint consultative committee or works council in 2011.'

[55] <www.cwu.org/wp-content/uploads/2020/12/Joint-draft-KEY-PRINCIPLES-FRAMEWORK-AGREEMENT_18_12_20_Final.pdf>.

this to be introduced in a way that gains the support of employees', and commit to a series of key principles:

- Technology will not be used to de-humanise the workplace or operational decision making.
- Where technology replaces a manual system, such as signing on sheets, any process supported by the manual system will in future be supported by the new technology.
- Scan In/Out data will not be used for the automatic reduction of contractual pay or allowances based on data captured or to reduce overtime pay where a (verbal) contract has been agreed with the manager prior to commencement.
- Technology will be used to complement, inform and enhance along with all other factors, the existing resourcing processes, including manager, CWU rep, and employee conversations.
- Technology will replace outdated and inconsistent manual methods of information gathering and provide the underlying insight to improve our current processes including resourcing.
- All data will be used in compliance with Royal Mail policies and GDPR obligations and the contents spirit and intent of Section 17 of the 2018 Guiding Principles.[56]

The advantages of relying on collective agreements in this way are clear: the specifics of algorithmic management, and thus the related risks, will be distinct in every workplace. Management and worker representatives are best placed to identify these specificities, and draw on their experience in developing tailored solutions. Joint standard setting thus furthermore increases the likelihood of meaningful compliance on the side of both parties.

At the same time, relying on collective bargaining alone also has its drawbacks – including, first and foremost, the relatively low density of collective bargaining in the United Kingdom.[57] There is furthermore a clear need to build capacity amongst trade union representatives (and, indeed, at the managerial level) to engage meaningfully with complex and sophisticated technical systems.[58] The pervasiveness of technology in the workplace finally also raises difficult questions of scope. Which aspects of artificial intelligence should be covered in collective agreements? 'Digitalisation has an

[56] Ibid. 8–9.

[57] Helge Baumann, Sandra Mierich, and Manuela Maschke 'Betriebsvereinbarungen 2017 – Verbreitung und (Trend-)Themen' (2018) 71(4) *WSI-Mitteilungen* 317; I Matuschek and F Kleemann 'Was man nicht kennt, kann man nicht regeln. Betriebsvereinbarungen als Instrument der arbeitspolitischen Regulierung von Industrie 4.0 und Digitalisierung' (2018) 71(3) *WSI-Mitteilungen* 227.

[58] Though there are efforts in that direction: see for example, 'Prospect guide' <www.prospect.org.uk/about/digital-technology-guide-for-union-reps/> or <www.uniglobalunion.org/sites/default/files/files/news/uni_pm_algorithmic_management_guide_en.pdf>.

overarching character, touches on a wide range of issues, is difficult to demarcate, and, as a consequence, is hard to capture in a set of precise provisions.'[59]

A *The Control/Accountability Paradox*

Having surveyed specific examples from the individual and collective dimension of employment law, a broader, underlying challenge remains to be addressed. As discussed in Section III, algorithmic management systems can exert an immense degree of control, where directly or indirectly, for example, in rating systems:

> Being held accountable for every interaction, drivers were very aware of the existence of this external evaluation. Trying to deliver good services for all service interactions could pose psychological stress to workers. Additionally, as extensive research on the impact of extrinsic rewards on intrinsic motivation suggests, the external device could weaken the intrinsic motivation that drivers might have.[60]

Algorithmic control thus goes far beyond direct orders, spanning from behavioural nudging to gamification:[61]

> As robots wheel giant shelves up to each workstation, lights or screens indicate which item the worker needs to put into a bin. The games can register the completion of the task, which is tracked by scanning devices, and can pit individuals, teams or entire floors in a race to pick or stow Lego sets, cellphone cases or dish soap, for instance. Game-playing employees are rewarded with points, virtual badges and other goodies throughout a shift.[62]

Where such control is exercised by a single employer, capable of developing its own sophisticated technology in-house, it can facilitate the ascription of responsibility: as seen in Section III, courts are clearly willing to take account of the intense degree of control exercised. The vast majority of employers, however, are unlikely to build and train artificial intelligence systems in-house in the way that Uber or Amazon can.

[59] There are also smaller drawbacks in practice, see Thomas Haipeter, 'Digitalisation, Unions and Participation: The German Case of "Industry 4.0"' (2020) 15(3) *Industrial Relations Journal* 242, s 2.4.

[60] Other models such as works councils exist in other legal systems, such as German labour law, and are more promising, given the mandatory nature of consultation and co-decision: MK Lee, L Dabbish, and D Kusbit, 'Working with Machines: The Impact of Algorithmic and Data-Driven Management on Human Workers' *Proceedings of the 33rd Annual ACM Conference on Human Factors in Computing Systems* (2015). See also Karen Levy and Solon Barocas, 'Refractive Surveillance: Monitoring Customers to Manage Workers' (2018) 12 *International Journal of Communications* 1166.

[61] See for example, Miriam A Cherry, 'The Gamification of Work' (2012) 40(4) *Hofstra Law Review* 851; and Bodie and others (n 29), Part II.

[62] Greg Bensinger, '"MissionRacer": How Amazon Turned the Tedium of Warehouse Work into a Game' (*Washington Post*, 21 March 2019). Similar technology is now being expanded to more fulfilment centres in at least 20 further US states: Pris Martineau and Mark Di Stefano, 'Amazon Expans Effort to "Gamify" Warehouse Work' (*The Information*, 15 March 2021).

Instead, they will rely on a complex supply chain of automated decision-making systems, bringing together a wide range of actors – with significant accountability implications.

At the same time as dramatically concentrating employer control, key elements of algorithmic management can also be relied upon to diffuse responsibility: questions as to who should be liable – the employing enterprise? The designers of the software? The providers of contaminated training data? – can no longer necessarily be tackled with the traditional tools of employment law. This is the fundamental paradox at the heart of attempts to regulate algorithmic management with existing employment law structures.

Up until now, the mechanisms designed to hide the reality of employer control in 'non-standard work' were legal stratagems: from the use of corporate personality (e.g., in the incorporation of subsidiary agency companies)[63] to contract law (e.g., in inserting independent contractor or self-employment clauses in traditional employment contracts),[64] the problem has been one of '"armies of lawyers" contriving documents … which simply misrepresent the true rights and obligations on both sides'.[65] In principle, at least, this makes it relatively straightforward to respond to evasion: existing legal mechanisms create the difficulty in ascribing responsibility to the controlling employer, and existing legal mechanisms can be relied on to restore it. Doctrines such as sham contracting or the primacy of facts allow courts to look through self-employment clauses and focus on the reality of employer control, and the corporate veil may be pierced to combat fraudulent abuse by controlling parent entities.[66]

The challenge arising from the advent of people analytics, on the other hand, is radically different: algorithmic management does not rely on legal mechanisms to obfuscate control in order to evade responsibility – rather, as seen in previous sections, diffuse and potentially inexplicable control mechanisms are inherent in the use of increasingly sophisticated rating systems and algorithms. The challenge, therefore, lies in ensuring that responsible parties can be identified both for individual norms (such as responsibility for unfair dismissal) and collective standards (such as identifying the most appropriate counterpart for collective bargaining).

V BEYOND EMPLOYMENT LAW

Discussion thus far has focused on the traditional confines of employment law, highlighting difficulties in the application of existing norms. Given that algorithmic

[63] H Collins, 'Independent Contractors and the Challenge of Vertical Disintegration to Employment Protection Laws' (1990) 10 *Oxford Journal of Legal Studies* 353.

[64] ILO, *Regulating the Employment Relationship in Europe: A Guide to Recommendation No 198* (Geneva 2013) 33.

[65] *Aslam and Farrar v Uber*, Case No. ET/2202550/2015 [73] (London Employment Tribunal, Judge Snelson).

[66] The reality of litigation and enforcement will of course be significantly more complex: J Prassl, *The Concept of the Employer* (Oxford University Press 2015) ch 5, ch 6.

management involves a series of novel considerations, however, its regulation cannot be approached through employment law alone. Other regulatory areas, from discrimination law to data protection, play a particularly salient role in grappling with the difficulties identified. How far are they able to achieve their regulatory goals in a world of automated decision-making at work?

A *Discrimination Law*

The challenge in discrimination law is twofold.[67] Out of the two broad models of discrimination, direct discrimination and indirect discrimination, algorithms are usually thought only to engage the latter category, which prohibits seemingly neutral practices, criteria, or provisions which in practice will put individuals with a certain protected characteristic (e.g., gender, ethnicity, disability) at a particular disadvantage.[68]

This means, first, that employers will be able to justify the use of algorithmic management systems as a provision, criterion, or practice (PCP) if they can show that it is a proportionate means of achieving a legitimate aim. Whilst financial considerations in and of themselves are not usually sufficient to constitute a legitimate aim, other arguments such as achieving 'best fit' or finding 'highest performers' may well be accepted, especially if they are a proportionate means in the circumstances (such as where there is a very large applicant pool). The potential range of legitimate aims is wide, and might include

> using an algorithm to sift applications may enable a reallocation of staff time, so that more candidates are called to interview; it may mean that more applications can be reviewed, such that gatekeeping measures—like hiring only from select universities—are no longer necessary; and employers may even find that use of the algorithm results in increased diversity.[69]

As Barocas and Selbst's conclude in their seminal 2016 paper exploring regulatory responses to *Big Data's Disparate Impact*.

> [u]nless there is a reasonably practical way to demonstrate that [an ADMS's] discoveries are spurious, [US employment anti-discrimination law] would appear to bless its use, even though the correlations it discovers will often reflect historic patterns of prejudice, others' discrimination against members of protected groups, or flaws in the underlying data.[70]

[67] A further difficulty arises from algorithmic systems that seek actively to counter bias, for example by boosting populations under-represented in training data. In certain jurisdictions, such approaches could be challenged as violating anti-discrimination norms: *Ricci v. DeStefano*, 557 U.S. 557 (2009).

[68] This view is not universally shared. See J Adams-Prassl, R Binns, and A Kelly-Lyth, 'Directly Discriminatory Algorithms' (2023) 86 *MLR* 144.

[69] Aislinn Kelly-Lyth, 'Challenging Biased Hiring Algorithms' (2021) 41 *Oxford Journal of Legal Studies* 899 (citations omitted).

[70] Barocas and Selbst (n 24) 672.

Even where these challenges can be overcome, litigating against algorithmic discrimination, secondly, can be nearly impossible in practice: individuals are highly unlikely to be able to obtain the requisite knowledge and/or evidence to bring cases against biased algorithms. As Kelly-Lyth concludes, 'the law on the books will not protect job applicants' rights unless algorithmic hiring becomes more transparent.'[71]

B *Data Protection*

On the other hand, data protection rules such as the European Union's General Data Protection Regulation ('GDPR') may provide some level of protection for employees across the Union's member states,[72] as illustrated extensively in the Article 29 Data Protection Working Party's Opinion 2/2017 on data processing at work.[73]

There are a number of GDPR requirements which might impact on the deployment of algorithmic management – including the limitation that data must be 'collected for specified, explicit and legitimate purposes and not further processed in a manner that is incompatible with those purposes';[74] the need to conduct a Data Protection Impact Assessment ('DPIA') '[w]here a type of processing in particular using new technologies, and taking into account the nature, scope, context and purposes of the processing, is likely to result in a high risk to the rights and freedoms of natural persons';[75] and particular safeguards surrounding sensitive personal data, including 'racial or ethnic origin, political opinions, religious or philosophical beliefs, or trade union membership.'[76]

These obligations, however, are primarily procedural, individualistic, and not targeted at the specific context of intrusive data processing at work.[77] Given ongoing uncertainties even about the interpretation of key provisions, the GDPR is thus

[71] Ibid.

[72] Regulation (EU) 2016/679 of the European Parliament and of the Council of 27 April 2016 on the protection of natural persons with regard to the processing of personal data and on the free movement of such data, and repealing Directive 95/46/EC (General Data Protection Regulation), OJ L 119, 4.5.2016, 1–88. The GDPR's future in the United Kingdom is uncertain, given on-going consultations about the (at least partial) repeal of key provisions: see <www.gov.uk/government/consultations/data-a-new-direction>.

[73] <www.ec.europa.eu/newsroom/article29/item-detail.cfm?item_id=610169>. Today, the Article 29 Working Party ('WP29') has been replaced by the European Data Protection Board, an independent body responsible for the consistent implementation of the GDPR. The Board has endorsed the Opinions and Guidelines of WP29 (Endorsement 1/2018): see <www.edpb.europa.eu/news/news/2018/endorsement-gdpr-wp29-guidelines-edpb_en>.

[74] GDPR Art 5(1)(b).

[75] Ibid. 35(1).

[76] Ibid. 9(1).

[77] Spiros Simitis, 'Reconsidering the Premises of Labour Law: Prolegomena to an EU Regulation on the Protection of Employees' Personal Data' (1999) 5(1) *European Law Journal* 45.

unlikely to provide meaningful protection against many of the difficulties identified in Section II. Take the ban on subjecting individuals to decisions based solely on automated processing in Article 22, as an example. It is subject to a number of carve-outs,[78] the meaning of which continues to be litigated.

A recent series of cases brought in Amsterdam against gig economy platforms *Uber* and *Ola* illustrate some of the conceptual and practical hurdles facing workers seeking to enforce their rights against algorithmic management practices, even where employment status is not at issue (as is the case in claims brought under the GDPR).[79]

The deactivation of certain drivers, for example, was held not to constitute solely automated processing for the purposes of Article 22 GDPR, because Uber argued that a human operator had double-checked the deactivations. This appeared to conflict with Uber's own privacy policy, which stated that 'fraudulent' behaviour could 'result in automatic deactivation'. The court, however, failed to assess the extent to which human intervention had to be 'meaningful'. It also remains unclear whether Article 22 is an outright ban on solely automated decision-making, or provides a right to opt out of such decision-making.[80]

Furthermore, whilst Articles 13–15 GDPR require the provision of 'meaningful information about the logic involved, as well as the significance and the envisaged consequences of such processing for the data subject', at least in cases of automated decision-making 'referred to in Article 22', the scope of this requirement is still unclear, particularly given that machine learning does not use 'logic' in the way that more traditional algorithms do.

In terms of practical litigation challenges, finally, when the applicants were called upon to provide counter-evidence to the platforms' claims, this was impossible given the proprietary technology involved. Relatedly, the court suggested that the drivers needed to be more specific about the data sought, which is similarly difficult given the information asymmetry created by the platform.

VI EMERGING REGULATORY APPROACHES AT THE EUROPEAN LEVEL

Given the shortcomings across different regulatory systems identified thus far, it is perhaps unsurprising that domestic and international regulators are increasingly becoming aware of the need to develop targeted regulation of algorithmic management – both in the gig economy and workplaces more generally. The European Commission in particular has been active in developing regulatory proposals, aimed both at AI generally, and algorithmic management in particular.

78 Including explicit consent: GDPR Art 22(2)(c). Cf the Working Party's concerns regarding consent in the employment relationship.

79 ECLI:NL:RBAMS:2021:1020 (Uber transparency requests); ECLI:NL:RBAMS:2021:1018 (Uber deactivation); ECLI:NL:RBAMS:2021:1019 (Ola transparency)

80 The former interpretation seems more likely, and was adopted by the Article 29 Working Party.

A *The Proposal for an Artificial Intelligence Act*

Turning first to general AI regulation, the recently published Commission proposal for a regulation laying down rules on artificial intelligence (the proposed 'AI Act') has quickly become the subject of intense political and legal debates.[81] At first glance, the underlying approach of the measure looks promising. Most importantly, it explicitly recognises the deployment of artificial intelligence systems for algorithmic management tasks (both in terms of hiring and subsequent managerial activity) as a 'high-risk context'.[82]

This classification comes with a number of stringent requirements, including risk management, data governance, recording obligations, human oversight, as well as accuracy, robustness, and cybersecurity.[83] At the same time, however, it remains unclear whether the obligations offer sufficient protection against the problematic deployment of AI at work.[84] Indeed, upon a close reading of the proposed Act's provisions, it is unlikely to address many of the challenges identified in Sections II and III. This is due, first and foremost, to the fact that whilst the Act stipulates 'conformity assessments' before automated decision-making systems can be deployed, these are mere *self*-assessments,[85] requiring software providers to certify their own compliance with the Act or (as will likely be the case) with external product standards laid down by private sector third-party standard-setting bodies. Closely linked are problems surrounding transparency and access to information: whilst an 'appropriate type and degree of transparency shall be ensured',[86] this does not grant any rights to workers or their representatives: the right's scope is limited to 'users' of AI systems, that is, employers. There is no mention of specific rights for individual workers or their collective representatives.

Overall, therefore, the Act promises little by way of employee protection at the union level – whilst at the same time posing a serious threat to domestic employment law. This is because the legal basis, Article 114 TFEU, is frequently used for *maximum* harmonisation, that is, in order to lay down standards from which Member States may not deviate.[87] As the recitals to the Act make clear, the 'purpose of this

[81] Proposal for a Regulation of the European Parliament and of the Council Laying Down Harmonised Rules on Artificial Intelligence (Artificial Intelligence Act) and Amending Certain Union Legislative Acts COM(2021) 206 final (hereinafter 'AI Act Proposal'). The proposal will be subjected to intensive legislative scrutiny, and is therefore unlikely to be enacted in its current state. For a detailed overview, see M Veale and F Zuiderveen Borgesius, 'Demystifying the Draft EU Artificial Intelligence Act' (2021) 22 *Computer Law Review International* 97.

[82] AI Act Proposal (n 81) Annex II.

[83] Ibid. Title III, Chapter II: Requirements for High-Risk Systems (Art 8, Art 10, Art 12, Art 14 and Art 15, respectively).

[84] See further, Aislinn Kelly-Lyth, 'The AI Act and Algorithmic Management' (2021) *Comparative Labour Law and Policy Journal Dispatches*, Dispatch No 39, 1.

[85] AI Act Proposal (n 81) arts 43(2), 48.

[86] Ibid. art 13.

[87] Stephen Weatherill, 'The Fundamental Question of Minimum or Maximum Harmonisation' in Sacha Garben and Inge Govaere (eds), *The Internal Market 2.0* (Hart Publishing 2020).

Regulation is to improve the functioning of the internal market ... thus preventing Member States from imposing restrictions on the development, marketing, and use of AI systems, unless explicitly authorised'.[88] This is particularly problematic for national provisions purporting to regulate the deployment of algorithmic systems, from well-established models of work council and collective bargaining to legislative innovations such as recent Spanish regulations providing for information rights about algorithmic management systems deployed by employers,[89] These norms could be pre-empted by the AI Act, without any appropriate similar safeguards at the European level, given the problems identified in the preceding paragraph.

B *Proposals for a Platform Work Directive*

Attempts to regulate algorithmic management in the specific context of the gig economy, on the other hand, are significantly more promising.[90] A recently proposed Directive on improved working conditions in platform work would require platforms to provide workers with information about automated monitoring systems, as well as decision-making systems which 'significantly affect' working conditions.[91] It also mandates human monitoring of such systems' impact on working conditions,[92] as well as human review and a written statement of reasons for significant decisions, such as decisions to suspend a worker's account or refuse remuneration for work performed.[93]

These proposals build on Article 22 of the GDPR (discussed in Section V), which provides for more limited, individualised protection against automated decision-making. Indeed, the new proposal expressly notes that while the GDPR establishes a framework for data processing, more specific rules are required in the context of platform work.[94] These proposals should be warmly welcomed – and ideally expanded during the legislative process to include *all* workers in the measure's substantive scope, given the wide prevalence of algorithmic management across different workplaces.[95]

[88] AI Act Proposal (n 81), recital 1.

[89] Royal Decree-Law 9/2021, of 11 May 2021 [now enacted] Art 64(4)(d) Workers' Statute covers 'the parameters, rules and instructions on which the algorithms or artificial intelligence systems affecting decision-making that may have an impact on working conditions and access to and maintenance of employment, including profiling, are based.' See A Todolí-Signes, 'Spanish Riders Law and the Right to Be Informed about the Algorithm' (2021) 12(3) *European Labour Law Journal* 399, 401.

[90] European Commission, Proposal for a Directive of the European Parliament and of the Council on improving working conditions in platform work COM(2021) 762 final ('Proposal')

[91] Ibid. Art 6.

[92] Ibid. Art 7. Importantly, Articles 6 and 7 apply to all platform workers, including those without an employment relationship (Art 10). This is justified by the similar impact automated systems have on working individuals, regardless of their status (r 40).

[93] Ibid. Art 8.

[94] Ibid. r 29.

[95] For a detailed initial analysis, see Aislinn Kelly-Lyth and Jeremias Adams-Prassl, 'The EU's Proposed Platform Work Directive – A Promising Step (*Verfassungsblog*, 14 December 2021) <www.verfassungsblog.de/work-directive/>.

The proposal envisages a significantly improved role for consultation and bargaining at the collective level. The Directive would provide representatives with access to information about automated systems, for example, in a context where workers' representatives currently rely on highly individualised data protection rights when gathering evidence to challenge unfair algorithmic management.[96] Such reliance is far from straightforward: in the Dutch litigation discussed above, Uber sought to argue that drivers' data subject access requests were an abuse of rights because they had been coordinated by a union seeking to gain transparency about algorithmic management tools. The new proposal would cut through specious conflicts of this type by putting relevant information directly into representatives' hands.

While the Directive is alive to the importance of promoting the role of worker representatives in the gig economy context, it does not extend beyond that sector. The Commission's Communication explains that platform work is unusual in that there are few 'practical opportunities for collective representation and organisation'.[97] While it is true that the traditional factory floor may have provided more opportunities to collective engagement, many traditional workplaces are also increasingly shifting to hybrid working models, with workers broadly dispersed. Moreover, while the Commission suggests that social partners will be able to 'initiate social dialogue on algorithmic management in the context of the new information and consultation rights',[98] it does not address the fact that the same rights would be equally valuable for social partners in traditional workplaces – where trade unions are already working to elevate their members' voices about the use of algorithmic management tools.

VII CONCLUSION

The impact of artificial intelligence on the world of work is hard to overstate: rather than leading to wide-spread technological unemployment, increasingly sophisticated decision-making systems have come to augment, and to some extent fully substitute for, the exercise of traditional management functions. Technological innovation has reshaped workplaces for centuries, of course; the question at the core of this chapter was therefore the extent to which the socio-technical challenges are novel and, if so, how existing norms of employment law would cope.

It could be thought that this does not seem to raise particularly novel or difficult questions: the manifold ways in which the Coasean 'entrepreneur-coordinator' exercises her managerial prerogative have long been regulated by statute and (to

[96] European Commission (n 90) Art 6(4).

[97] Communication from the Commission to the European Parliament, The Council, The European Economic and Social Committee and the Committee of the Regions, *Better working conditions for a stronger social Europe: Harnessing the full benefits of digitalisation for the future of work* COM/2021/761 final, 3.

[98] Ibid. 7.

a lesser extent) at common law.[99] Upon closer inspection, however, a significant challenge emerged: while algorithmic management allows the exercise of hitherto unthinkable control – in terms both of granularity and consistency – core operating features of the underlying technology clash with a number of fundamental assumptions around which the regulation of the contract of employment has been designed.[100] As a result, the effective application of fundamental norms, from discrimination law to unfair dismissal protection, is threatened even where the underlying wage/work bargain is clearly within the protective scope of the contract of employment (or worker's contract). Only the careful supplementing of existing norms with new regulatory regimes, such as those now proposed at the European Union level, can ensure that workers and employers alike reap the benefits of technological innovation, whilst protecting decent working standards across the socio-economic spectrum.

99 Ronald Coase, 'The Nature of the Firm' (1937) 4(16) *Economica* 386.

100 E Albin and J Prassl, 'Fragmenting Work, Fragmented Regulation: The Contract of Employment as a Driver of Social Exclusion' in M Freedland and others (eds), *The Contract of Employment* (Oxford University Press 2016).

PART IV

Comparative Perspectives

27

Data Protection in EU and US Laws and AI

What Legal Changes We Should Expect in the Foreseeable Future?

Ugo Pagallo

I INTRODUCTION

The legal regulation of data-driven technologies has been the bread and butter of scholars, working in the fields of information technology (IT)-law over the past 25 years. Since the pioneering work of Joel Reidenberg and Lawrence Lessig in the late 1990s, focus has increasingly been on how the law has turned into matters of access to – and control and protection over – information in digital environments.[1] Throughout the centuries, human societies have been related to the use of information and communication technologies (ICTs), but they were mainly dependent on technologies that concern energy and basic resources. What is new in today's societies is that they progressively depend on ICTs and, furthermore, on information and data as a vital resource.[2] Cases that scholars address as a part of their everyday work in the fields of IT Law, such as data protection, computer crimes, cyber-security, digital copyright, and e-commerce, illustrate how the flow of data and information jeopardises traditional assumptions of legal and political thought. The new informational dimension of today's societies has not only increased the difficulty of law enforcement on, for example, the internet, but it has also given rise to states' illegitimate claim to unilaterally regulate extraterritorial conduct by imposing norms on individuals who have no say in the decisions affecting them.[3]

Against this framework, the attention of scholars and institutions has increasingly focused over the past few years, on the new set of normative and regulatory challenges of the manifold fields of Artificial Intelligence (AI). In addition to the novelties of IT law, there is indeed something unique to the impact of AI in the legal

[1] See JL Reidenberg, 'Lex Informatica: The Formulation of Information Policy Rules through Technology' (1998) 76(3) *Texas Law Review* 553; and L Lessig, *Code and Other Laws of Cyberspace* (Basic Books 1999).

[2] See U Pagallo, 'Good Onlife Governance: On Law, Spontaneous Orders, and Design' in L Floridi (ed), *The Onlife Manifesto: Being Human in a Hyperconnected Era* (Springer 2015) 161–177.

[3] See U Pagallo, 'Law as Information and the Impact of Information Technologies' in *Theoretical Information Studies: Information in The World*, vol 11 (2020) 477–498.

domain: according to the High Level Expert Group on liability and new technologies formation, set up by the European Commission in 2018 (the 2019 Report), the fundamental changes triggered by AI depend on the complexity, opacity, openness, autonomy, predictability, data-drivenness, and vulnerability of these technologies.[4] In the phrasing of the Report on *Liability for Artificial Intelligence*, 'each of these changes may be gradual in nature, but the dimension of gradual change, the range and frequency of situations affected, and the combined effect, results in disruption.'[5] This disruption affects the field of tortious liability, or extra-contractual responsibility, as the main subject of the 2019 Report. The legal challenges of AI also affect human rights law and the laws of war, international and constitutional law, administrative and criminal law, and more.[6] This Handbook aims thus to complement the current debate on the legal opportunities and threats of AI, in particular, as it relates to the manifold domains of civil (as opposed to criminal) law. Accordingly, the focus of this chapter is restricted to the fields of personal data protection in EU law, and informational privacy in US law.[7]

This stance on AI and data privacy appears particularly fruitful, since it should help us understand (i) the impact of AI on such crucial sectors of current private law, such as data protection and informational privacy; (ii) differences among jurisdictions, such as in EU and US laws; and (iii) possible convergences between these different legal systems and traditions, due to the common challenges triggered by AI. The analysis is divided into two parts. Next, in Section II, the focus is on how the same bunch of AI technologies – be it a smart personal assistant, a robotic corporate advisor, or a financial data crunching system – raises different regulatory issues, depending on the legal system under consideration. The 2021 proposal of the European Commission for a new AI Act (AIA) in EU law stresses these differences.[8] Yet Section III draws attention to how AI systems pose a further set of legal problems, for example, group profiling and ad macro-targeting, that have led to the convergence of strategies in both EU and US laws. The dynamics of legal 'transplants' and 'receptions' will help us illustrate these forms of convergence through a case study in data protection and consumer law. The overall aim of the analysis is to ascertain to what extent current regulations on privacy and data protection may fall short in coping with the challenges of AI, and moreover, how we should interpret, or amend the law, in order to properly address such challenges.

4 See HLEG, 'Liability for Artificial Intelligence and Other Emerging Technologies' (Report from the European Commission's Group of Experts on Liability and New Technologies, 2019) <www.op.europa.eu/en/publication-detail/-/publication/1c5e30be-1197-11ea-8c1f-01aa75ed71a1/language-en>.

5 Ibid.

6 See W Barfield and U Pagallo, *Advanced Introduction to Law and Artificial Intelligence* (Edward Elgar 2020).

7 See DJ Solove and P Schwartz, *Information Privacy Law* (7th edn, Wolters Kluwer 2020).

8 See for example, Art 41 of the proposed Act on top-down standards for high-risk AI systems and their requirements.

II THE STATE-OF-THE-ART ON DIVERGING LEGAL TRADITIONS

Privacy and data protection are complex and much-debated notions within law. The right to privacy, for example, traditionally includes the protection of people's bodies, spaces, properties, and communications, as much as the protection of people's self-development in their intellectual, decisional, associational, and behavioural dimensions.[9] Some jurisdictions, however, distinguish the protection of this right from the further protection of personal data, as a sort of digital counterpart for the safeguard of the traditional right to privacy. Articles 7 (right to privacy) and 8 (right to data protection) of the EU Charter of Fundamental Rights ('CFR') illustrate this distinction. All in all, there are several cases in which the protection of privacy can involve no data processing at all, for example, the protection against cases of 'unwanted fame' or 'false light,' and vice versa, cases in which the protection of an individual's rights associated with data processing does not hinge on any harm to such individual.[10] In the first case, that is, privacy, we may say, drawing on Hannah Arendt's ideas on *The Human Condition*, that legal safeguards aim to protect the individual's 'opaqueness';[11] in data protection law, the intent mostly revolves around the transparency with which data are collected, processed, and used. A number of individual rights follow as a result of this transparency in the field of data protection: the right to determine whether personal data can be collected and, eventually, transmitted to others; the right to determine how data may be used and processed; the right to access data and where necessary, to keep data up to date; and lastly, the right to delete data and refuse at any time to have the data processed. This set of rights represents that which the German Constitutional Court has framed in terms of 'informational self-determination' since its *Volkszählungs-Urteil* ('census decision') from 1983.

The specificities of data protection, vis-à-vis the legal safeguards of the traditional right to privacy, should not suggest, however, that such rights may not overlap or reinforce each other. The case-law of most Courts, including the European Court of Human Rights, pursuant to the right to privacy enshrined in Art. 8 of the 1950 European Convention, elucidates how often the protection of the traditional right to privacy and of today's right to data protection do converge.[12] This overlap is the reason why scholars (and courts), even in Europe, regularly refer to privacy and data protection as interchangeable terms: for example, in Italy, the EU data protection

9 See B-J Koops and others, 'A Typology of Privacy' (2017) 38(2) *Univ Pa J Int* Law 483.

10 Consider the stance of the EU Court of Justice (CJEU) in the (in)famous *Google v AEPD* case (C-131/12): see in particular [99] of the decision on the so-called 'right to be forgotten.'

11 See U Pagallo, 'On the Principle of Privacy by Design and Its Limits: Technology, Ethics and the Rule of Law' in S Gutwirth and others (eds) *European Data Protection: In Good Health?* (Springer 2012) 331–346.

12 See U Pagallo, 'The Collective Dimensions of Privacy in the Information Era: A Comparative Law Approach' (2020) 11 *Annuario di diritto comparato e di studi legislativi* 115.

regulations, or directives, have been and still are 'transposed' in the so-called Code of Privacy. Similarly, in most rulings of the EU Court of Justice (CJEU), the protection of the rights enshrined in Art. 7 and 8 of the CFR is complementary. Under US law, the reference is to the new technological dimensions of the right to privacy as data privacy, digital privacy, informational privacy, and so on, so as to stress that the traditional protection of the right to privacy has to be complemented with new safeguards for the digital body (and communications) of the individuals. Several crucial rulings of the US Supreme Court have dealt with this class of issues over the past years.[13] The right to 'be let alone' had to be strengthened with a new kind of protection over data and information in digital environments, either on the basis of constitutional amendments (e.g., EU law) or of constitutional doctrines (e.g., the US Supreme Court).

Still, some crucial differences persist among jurisdictions. This is why the same technological artifacts can raise distinct and even opposite legal issues, according to the jurisdiction which is taken into account.[14] Consider the EU laws on data protection and the corresponding US approach, in order to grasp this dynamic between AI and the law. Two distinctions are critical. First, as regards the legal status of personal data, a property-like approach to data protection has prevailed in US law, thanks to a well-established common law tradition of tortious liability and, at the constitutional level, the interpretation of the Fourth Amendment to the US Constitution on 'unreasonable searches and seizures.' Contrary to this property-like approach,[15] the EU law conceives data protection as a personality right of the individual. Correspondingly, especially in the private sector, the self-regulatory and bottom-up approach taken by the US through contractual clauses and terms of service, diverges from the top-down approach of the EU (even when we take into account the principle of accountability as a form of co-regulation, pursuant to Art. 5(2) of the EU's current general data protection regulation, or 'GDPR').[16]

The second distinction has to do with the aims of legal regulation. According to the EU approach to data protection, since its inception with the 1995 directive (D-46/95/EC), down to the current GDPR, the intent of lawmakers has been to govern the entire life cycle of information, as regards the processing of personal data in all fields of private law.[17] This approach is at odds with the way in which issues of data protection are tackled in the US. Rather than a general (and technologically

[13] Such rulings have concerned, for example, the use of thermal imaging devices in *Kyllo* (533 U.S. 27 (2001)), GPS systems in *Jones* (565 U.S. 400 (2012)), and cell phone location in *Carpenter* (585 U.S. (2018)).

[14] See U Pagallo, 'Robots in the Cloud with Privacy: A New Threat to Data Protection?' (2013) 29(5) *Computer Law & Security Review* 501.

[15] See for example L Lessig, 'Privacy as Property' (2002) 69(1) *Social Research* 247.

[16] See U Pagallo, P Casanovas and R Madelin, 'The Middle-Out Approach: Assessing Models of Legal Governance in Data Protection, Artificial Intelligence, and the Web of Data' (2019) 7(1) *The Theory and Practice of Legislation* 1.

[17] This general framework – including today's EU general data protection regulation, or 'GDPR' (Reg. (EU) 2016/679) – does not include, in fact, activities that fall outside the EU law, such as activities concerning national security or public order.

neutral) legal framework, the United States have opted for a number of context-dependent regulations at the federal level.[18] In most cases, from the 1974 Privacy Act to the 2004 Video Voyeurism Act, such laws have been reactive, rather than proactive, namely, the legislative response to a scandal. Correspondingly, most data protection issues of private law fall either under the regulatory powers of each State of the Union, or under the contractual clauses and terms of service mentioned earlier. Contrary to EU law, the first question is not about overarching principles, but limited federal powers over self-regulation, tort law, and some form of state activism (e.g., California).

In light of these crucial differences between EU and US laws, we can appreciate the extent to which the increasing use of AI technologies may affect current laws on informational privacy and data protection, by paying attention to those parts of EU data protection law that appear mostly critical, or controversial, to US experts, and vice versa, based on some assumptions under US privacy law that look even bizarre to EU scholars. As regards the first set of legal issues, some principles of EU law on finality, purpose limitation, data minimisation, or the very idea of 'data controllers' illustrate the issue. AI technologies can indeed make it really tricky to determine how the principles of the EU regulation should be understood, and enforced, vis-à-vis current advancements in machine learning, neural networks, deep learning, and so on. For instance, as concerns the finality principle, that is, the principle according to which data controllers should determine the purposes for which they intend to collect and process personal data, we may note that 'they have much leeway. For example, for an intelligent home assistant, one of the purposes of collecting voice data could potentially be improving speech recognition of the owner of the device.'[19] Likewise, dealing with AI systems – such as the Google Assistant, Siri, or Alexa– we may concede that Big G, Apple, or Amazon have to be understood as their current data controllers. Yet since AI systems are not a simple 'out of the box' machine, it will be increasingly difficult to determine whether an individual should be considered as a simple end-user of the AI system, or rather, as a controller of the data collected and processed by her/his AI system. Several EU-sponsored research and reports have fully endorsed this view on end-users as data controllers of their AI systems over the past years.[20] The 2021 AIA proposal of

[18] This is the case of the Privacy Act (1974), the Cable Communications Policy Act (1984), the Electronic Communications Privacy Act (1986), the Health Insurance Portability and Accountability Act (HIPPA) (1996), the Identity Theft and Assumption Deterrence Act (1998), the CAN-SPAM Act (2003), the Video Voyeurism Prevention Act (2004), the Health Information Technology for Clinical and Economic Health or HITECH Act (2009), and so forth.

[19] R Leenes and S De Conca, 'Artificial Intelligence and Privacy – AI Enters the House through the Cloud' in W Barfield and U Pagallo (eds), *Research Handbook of the Law of Artificial Intelligence* (Edward Elgar 2018) 281.

[20] See RoboLaw, 'Guidelines on Regulating Robotics. EU Project on Regulating Emerging Robotic Technologies in Europe: Robotics facing Law and Ethics' (22 September 2014) 190: 'It is clear that the illicit treatment of the data is unlikely to be considered a responsibility of the manufacturer of the robot, but rather a liability of its user, who is the "holder" of the personal data.' See also the HLEG (n 4).

the European Commission follows suit with a new set of obligations for the users of (high-level risk) AI systems.[21]

On the other hand, we have to take into account the problems of the impact of AI under US privacy law. A pillar of US law, such as the 'third-party doctrine,' is particularly instructive, as regards both the differences between US and EU laws, and how AI can affect such doctrines and regulations. The overall idea of the 'third party doctrine' is that people give up their privacy when information is voluntarily disclosed to third parties. Such doctrine represents the general framework within which both privacy and data protection issues are reviewed even at the constitutional law level in the US. Although the doctrine has been partially revised in *Carpenter*,[22] the Justices of the US Supreme Court still assumed that secrecy is a prerequisite for the protection of privacy rights under the Fourth Amendment to the Constitution. The shortcomings of this equalisation of privacy and secrecy are well-known and clearly established, even acknowledged by some Justices of the Court. For example, as stressed by Justice Sonia Sotomayor in her concurring opinion in *Jones*, 'this approach is ill suited to the digital age, in which people reveal a great deal of information about themselves to third parties in the course of carrying out mundane tasks.'[23] Correspondingly, there is a hot debate on how to amend US law today: some propose new obligations of transparency, due process, and accountability for 'algorithmic operators,' which includes large AI companies like Google, Facebook, or Apple. Similar to doctors and lawyers, or people who manage estates or other people's property, algorithmic operators should be better conceived of as 'information fiduciaries with respect to their clients and end-users … [because] there is a significant asymmetry in knowledge and ability between fiduciary and client, and the client can't easily monitor what the fiduciary is doing on their behalf.'[24] However, another possible solution is to follow the EU's approach and address the impact of AI on informational privacy and data protection as a matter of access to and protection and control over information in digital environments.

Remarkably, the California Consumer Privacy Act (CCPA), which has been in effect since 1st January 2020, seems to adopt the EU approach.[25] Data protection is not only about the protection of secrecy, since individuals have a right to know what kind of data is collected about them (1798.100(a)) of the CCPA); the right to request a business to delete any personal information about a consumer that is collected from that consumer (1798.105(a)); the right to access their personal data (1798.115(a)), or to say no to the sale of personal data (1798.120(a)); up to the right

[21] See <www.eur-lex.europa.eu/legal-content/EN/TXT/?qid=1623335154975&uri=CELEX%3A52021PC0206>.

[22] See n 13.

[23] Ibid.

[24] JM Balkin, 'The Three Laws of Robotics in the Age of Big Data' (October 2017) 13 <https://papers.ssrn.com/sol3/papers.cfm?abstract_id=2890965>.

[25] See J Kessler, 'Data Protection in the Wake of the GDPR: California's Solution for Protecting "The World's Most Valuable Resource"' (2019) 93 *S Cal L Rev* 99.

not to be discriminated against for exercising 'the consumer's rights under this title' (1798.125(a)). Similar to the EU regulation on data protection, the aim of the CCPA is to complement the traditional protection of individual privacy with a general framework for the entire life cycle of personal information, although key differences persist. The list of differences includes the opt-in and opt-out distinctions, the extra-territorial scope of both legislations, and the right to access. Moreover, the CCPA provisions should be grasped against the backdrop of US laws, which reminds us of evergreen discussions in the field of comparative law, about the very possibility of transplants and receptions between different legal traditions and jurisdictions.[26] In the phrasing of Margot Kaminski, 'the CCPA is still largely an American-style transparency law, one that amplifies the 'notice' in 'notice and choice.' The hope is that true transparency about data practices might lead consumers to behave differently or lead to public outrage and new laws.'[27]

So far, scholars have mostly discussed whether EU data protection laws may represent a model for new US privacy regulations, or at least, whether US law could learn from the EU's shortcomings and overtake its data policies.[28] Indeed, this section has already insisted on some of the problems that the GDPR is fated to face vis-à-vis the processing of personal data through AI systems: issues of data minimisation, purpose limitation, and the critical notion of data controllers. Shouldn't US law prevent the drawbacks of such EU principles and provisions?

The 'imitation game' of legal transplants and receptions in the fields of data protection and informational privacy works both ways, however. In addition to the role that the GDPR may play as a model for the rest of the world, we should pay attention to what kind of lessons the EU data protection laws – and the ways we interpret them – can learn from the US privacy regulations, such as the CCPA, in order to address the challenges of AI in these fields. The dynamics of 'transplants' and 'receptions' which are mostly discussed by experts of privacy law in terms of 'Brussels effect,' or in similar terms,[29] is thus turned the other way around: can the convergence of

[26] See M Graziadei, 'Comparative Law as the Study of Transplants and Receptions' in M Reimann and R Zimmermann (eds), *The Oxford Handbook of Comparative Law* (2nd edn, Oxford University Press 2006) 442–461.

[27] See M Kaminski, 'Law and Technology: A Recent Renaissance in Privacy Law' (2020) 63(9) *Communications of the ACM* 24; and A Chander, M Kaminski and W McGeveran, 'Catalyzing Privacy Law' (2021) 105(4) *Minnesota Law Review* 1733.

[28] See W Hartzog and N Richards, 'Privacy's Constitutional Moment and the Limits of Data Protection' (2020) 61(5) *Boston College Law Review* 1689; and R Layton, 'The 10 Problems of the GDPR: The US Can Learn from the EU's Mistakes and Leapfrog Its Policy' (*American Enterprise Institute*, 2019) <www.judiciary.senate.gov/imo/media/doc/Layton%20Testimony1.pdf>.

[29] The reference text is A Bradford, 'The Brussels Effect' (2012) 107(1) *Northwestern University Law Review* 1; and A Bradford, *The Brussels Effect: How the European Union Rules the World* (Oxford University Press 2020). The assumption is that the non-divisibility of data and the compliance costs of multinational corporations dealing with multiple regulatory regimes, may prompt most AI manufacturers to adopt and adapt themselves to the strictest international standards across the board, that is, the EU data protection framework.

data protection and consumer law, as established by the CCPA, teach us something about today's challenges of data protection to EU scholars and institutions? Could a traditional powerful tool of consumer law, that is, class actions,[30] be fruitfully 'imported' in the realm of EU data protection? Wouldn't current advancements of technology recommend this approach? And how about US discussions on the limits of personal data protection, for example, freedom of speech and information? Isn't there anything EU scholars can learn from this further debate?

III NEW CHALLENGES AND PERSPECTIVES ON CONVERGING LEGAL SYSTEMS AND TECHNOLOGICAL CHALLENGES

We have examined so far some unique features of AI technologies that are particularly challenging in the field of privacy and personal data protection. Such challenges often depend on the crucial fact that AI systems are not a simple 'out of the box' machine. These systems progressively gain knowledge or skills from their own interaction with the living beings inhabiting the surrounding environment, so that, as a kind of prolonged epigenetic developmental process, more complex cognitive structures emerge in the transition system of the application. Such features can make it difficult to ascertain whether, or to what extent, an end-user of such AI system should be conceived of as a data controller in EU law, or what sort of 'reasonable expectation of privacy' should be accepted in US law. At the constitutional level, this reasonable expectation of privacy rests on the assumption that both individuals and society have developed a stable set of privacy expectations. Yet technology can dramatically change those expectations. As Justice Alito emphasised in his concurring opinion in *United States v Jones*, 'dramatic technological change may lead to periods in which popular expectations are in flux and may ultimately produce significant changes in popular attitudes.'[31]

In addition to the challenges that are unique to AI, we should not forget, however, how often AI overlaps with further sectors of technological innovation. This broader picture allows us to understand why Alito's 'dramatical technological change' has already impacted pillars of the legal fields under scrutiny. In particular, we should be attentive to the technological convergence between AI and further data-driven technologies, such as robotics and the internet of things. From a theoretical viewpoint, research and development in the multiple sectors of AI, such as machine learning, do not necessarily hinge on Big Data: in the 1980s and 1990s, scientists had to develop their own ways to feed and test AI systems through, for example, synthetic data for Boolean functions and 'methods that adaptively introduce relevant features

[30] See D Robinson, 'Click Here to Sue Everybody: Cutting the Gordian Knot of the Internet of Things with Class Action Litigation' (2020) 26(1) *Richmond Journal of Law & Technology* 1.

[31] See n 13.

while learning a decision tree from examples.'[32] This tradition is well alive today with new research and possible applications of synthetic data.[33] Yet, it seems fair to admit that growing amounts of training data often play a crucial role in the improvement of AI performances through, for example, machine learning techniques.[34] From the CERN's research in particle accelerators via statistical algorithms – which process more than a petabyte, that is, 10^{15} bytes per second – down to current online practices of targeting and profiling, countless examples of Big Data uses for AI applications exist out there. According to the popular definition of Doug Laney with his 'three Vs,'[35] Big Data refers to that which is unique because of the size and scale of the data we're dealing with (volume), the speed of data generation and processing (velocity), and the multiple forms and range of the data analysed (variety). Empowered by Big Data in the internet of things, through personal assistants, or robotic applications, AI thus affects the law in a remarkable way: data-driven technologies impact the traditional protection of personal data and informational privacy as individual rights, whereas the collective dimension of these rights overlaps with the provisions of further legal domains, in particular, consumer law.

The following sections examine the realignment of traditional rights through data-driven technologies (Section III.A), and the convergence between data protection safeguards and consumer law (Section III.B); then, Section III.C dwells on the dynamic of legal 'transplants' and 'receptions' at work in data protection and consumer law, through a case-study. The overall intention of this section is to stress how the uniqueness of the challenges brought about by AI in the legal domain may suggest some regulatory convergences between US and EU laws.

A *The Realignment of Traditional Rights through Data-Driven Technologies*

Big Data and AI have opened up new epistemological perspectives, different business models, increased operational efficiency, and enhanced information management systems. Still, their marriage raises several concerns. Some have focused on cases that reveal unique ethical aspects and theoretical problems of Big Data associated with existing computing technologies.[36] Others stress further epistemological questions of objectivity and loss of context, much as epistemic concerns that have

[32] See G Pagallo and D Haussler, 'Boolean Feature Discovery in Empirical Learning' (1990) 5(1) *Machine Learning* 71.

[33] See X Bangzhou and others, 'Private FL-GAN: Differential Privacy Synthetic Data Generation Based on Federated Learning' *IEEE International Conference on Acoustics, Speech and Signal Processing (ICASSP)* (2020) 2927–2931.

[34] See E Alpaydin, *Introduction to Machine Learning* (MIT Press 2014).

[35] See D Laney, '3D Data Management: Controlling Data Volume, Velocity and Variety' (2001) Metra Group Research Note 6.

[36] See B Mittelstadt and others, 'The Ethics of Algorithms: Mapping the Debate' (2016) 3(2) *Big Data & Society*.

to do with cases of inconclusive evidence leading to unjustified actions, inscrutable evidence leading to opacity, or other kinds of misguided evidence leading to bias.[37] From the legal viewpoint of personal data protection and informational privacy, the convergence of AI and Big Data poses a further specific problem.[38] Computational models of data mining and profiling techniques that exploit work in AI aim to predict people's behaviour, and include or exclude individuals from a particular service, product, or credit, by assembling such individuals in connection with certain educational, occupational or professional capabilities, or social practices (e.g., a religion), and social characteristics (e.g., an ethnicity). As a result, people are targeted as members of a group, although they can ignore even being a part of such group on the basis of a set of ontological and epistemological predicates that cluster individuals into multiple categories, such as the predisposition towards certain types of illnesses and behaviours. Therefore, since Big Data techniques regard types, rather than tokens – and hence groups, or aggregates, rather than individuals – such techniques are affecting the traditional viewpoint, according to which privacy and data protection rights mostly revolve around the protection of individuals.

Current legal systems establish certain forms of protection for the collective dimensions of the right to privacy and data protection. These legal safeguards, however, also illustrate further crucial differences between such legal systems and traditions, such as the US and EU laws. In US constitutional law, for example, the collective dimension of privacy rights is related to the safeguards of the First Amendment on freedom of association, so that, after the ruling of the Supreme Court in *Boy Scouts of America v Dale*,[39] the privacy of a group, as a single and unitary holder, can be conceived analogously with an individual's privacy.[40] In EU law, such cases of associative and corporate privacy would be examined in light of Articles 12 and 21 of the CFR, that is, in connection with the rights to freedom of association and non-discrimination, rather than some sort of associational privacy. Moreover, most jurisdictions in Europe would reject the US Supreme

37 See for example, C O'Neil, *Weapons of Math Destruction: How Big Data Increases Inequality and Threatens Democracy* (Random House 2016).

38 See U Pagallo, 'The Group, the Private, and the Individual: A New Level of Data Protection?' in L Taylor, L Floridi and B van der Sloot (eds), *Group Privacy: New Challenges of Data Technologies* (Springer 2017) 159–173.

39 530 U.S. 640 (2000).

40 The safeguards of the First Amendment to the US constitution also reflect a further critical distinction between US and EU laws, namely, the protection of privacy rights vis-à-vis the protection of freedom of speech. This divergence has been vastly discussed in the 2014 ruling of the EU Court of Justice on the right to be forgotten. See DC Nunziato, 'The Fourth Year of Forgetting: The Troubling Expansion of the Right to Be Forgotten' (2018) 39 *U Pa J Int'l L* 1011. In addition, scholars have examined whether and to what extent the First Amendment should cover AI speech even without a locatable and accountable human actor (such as a programmer or listener). See TM Massaro and H Norton, 'Artificial Intelligence and the First Amendment' in W Barfield and U Pagallo (eds), *Research Handbook on the Law of Artificial Intelligence* (Edward Elgar 2018) 353–374. Due to space limits, however, the analysis of this chapter is restricted to divergences in US and EU laws that relate to the collective dimension of data privacy rights and freedom of association.

Court's view on privacy as a corporate right, since EU courts conceive all forms of group privacy either as a procedural right of the association (e.g., Art. 80 of the GDPR), or as the form through which individuals can exercise their own rights. This is the viewpoint held by the EU Court of Justice (CJEU) in its case-law, and stated as an obiter dictum in the ECtHR's First Section decision in *Big Brother Watch & others v UK*.[41]

It remains of course an open issue whether such different approaches to the collective dimensions of privacy and data protection will successfully meet the challenges of AI. Some propose to transplant the US notion of privacy as a corporate right into EU law: informational privacy and data protection would concern 'the right that is held by a group as a group rather than by its members severally. It is the group, not its members, that is correctly identified as the right-holder.'[42] Others stress the limits of such one-size-fits-all attempts to tackle the challenges of a new collective dimension for privacy and data protection, by simply substituting the individual right-holder with a group.[43] After all, the problem with corporate solutions for the new collective dimensions of privacy and personal data protection is that corporate rights often turn out to protect a group against one or some of its members, as shown by the US Supreme Court's ruling in *Boy Scouts of America v Dale*. Furthermore, the corporate stance would allow entities, such as associations or organisations, to determine the conditions for legitimising data processing, even against the will of their own members. This right would include whether personal data that members of the group share could be collected, or transmitted to others, or whether such data should be deleted. By envisioning a new generation of group rights as corporate rights in the field of data protection, cases rendering the consent of the individuals unnecessary – as occurs today with, for example, Art. 6(1)(b-f) of the GDPR – would multiply without reasonable grounds.

Is there any other way in which we may address the new collective dimensions of privacy and data protection vis-à-vis Big Data techniques and AI applications?

B *Exploiting the Convergence with Consumer Law*

Consumer law has a long experience with the collective dimension of legal safeguards that should address the challenges of a 'mass society.' On the one hand, 'in a world of mass production, mass marketing, economic interdependence, and swift worldwide communications and transportation, it is not uncommon for many individuals to be harmed in essentially identical ways by mass-produced

[41] See applications nos 58170/13, 62322/14 and 24960/15.

[42] See L Floridi, 'Open Data, Data Protection, and Group Privacy' (2014) 27 *Philosophy and Technology* 1. Also, in support of this view, see B van der Sloot, 'Privacy in the Post-NSA Era: Time for a Fundamental Revision?' (2014) 5(2) *Jipitec* 1; and L Taylor, L Floridi, and B van der Sloot (eds), *Group Privacy: New Challenges of Data Technologies* (Springer 2017).

[43] See U Pagallo, 'Algo-Rhythms and the Beat of the Legal Drum' (2018) 31(4) *Philosophy & Technology* 507.

products or standardised corporate practices.'[44] On the other hand, the asymmetry of power and information between producers and consumers often ends up with claims too small to justify litigation, especially when sales take place cross-border. One of the most powerful tools in consumer law has thus to do with the role of class actions. On the procedural level, they are an associative action, in which a group is represented by a member of that group, where claimants sue their counterparts on behalf of the group or a class. Such actions mostly allow bringing before courts the whole claims of all class members, whether or not the latter know they have been damaged. This is why 'class actions can make it possible to litigate small claims, thereby serving the goals of compensation and deterrence (or law enforcement).'[45]

Claims in a class action have of course to be substantiated. Another chapter of this Handbook analyses the challenges of AI to current tenets of consumer law. For example, in EU law, it is crystal clear that directive 85/374/EEC on product liability, the so-called PLD regime, falls short in tackling a world of intangible products and digital services.[46] It's still uncertain whether the PLD rules cover damage to data and, vis-à-vis AI systems, how we should interpret Art. 6(1) on 'safety which a person is entitled to expect.' Also, similar to the issues in the doctrine of 'reasonable expectations' in US privacy law, it can be tricky to determine what is reasonable to expect from AI technologies, and, furthermore, the burden of proof on the 'causal relationship between defect and damage,' pursuant to Art. 4 of the PLD, can be heavy. Not only consumers can find it difficult to demonstrate the existence of a defect in the AI product, or service, but liability of producers mostly depends on when the product was put into circulation. No responsibility for updates, or upgrades, is thus taken into account.[47]

In light of the difficulties that consumer law poses to AI, it may then appear problematic that the aim of this section is to address the legal challenges of AI in privacy law and data protection through the lens of consumer law. Most of the time, the focus goes indeed the other way around, namely, addressing current limits of consumer law with the tools of data privacy, as occurs with the CCPA mentioned in Section II. Another example is of course the EU law since the 1995 directive on data protection with its regulatory effect on consumer law: all personal data, collected and processed in a transaction, shall be collected and processed in accordance with the principles and rules of data protection. However, what is suggested here is not to grasp the legal safeguards and rules of data protection and consumer law as alternative, or even opposing solutions in a sort of zero-sum

44 See JC Alexander, 'An Introduction to Class Action Procedure in the United States', in *Conference on Debates over Group Litigation in Comparative Perspective* (Geneva, 2000) <www.law.duke.edu/grouplit/papers/classactional-exander.pdf>.

45 Ibid.

46 See Barfield and Pagallo (n 6).

47 Those were the conclusions of the European Commission's HLEG (n 4).

game. Rather, such rules, both substantial and procedural, can ideally complement and reinforce each other. This standpoint is especially relevant, in order to address the legal challenges of human-AI interaction and the collective dimensions of data protection and informational privacy in a Big Data era. Whereas class actions and a consumer law approach to data privacy are congenial to the US tradition, it is noteworthy that a new dynamic of legal 'transplants' and 'receptions' is making this approach popular in EU law as well.[48] What is even more interesting, this 'imitation game' particularly fits some AI challenges for data protection and informational privacy with the advantage of not requiring particular changes, or amendments, to current regulations. Section III.C examines these ideas using a case study: it analyses how aspects of personal protection law were transplanted, received, and rejected in Italy.

C A *Case Study on Legal Transplants and Receptions*

The Italian norms on personal data protection can be properly understood as a form of legal transplant, according to the formula of Alan Watson.[49] The 1995 EU data protection directive was implemented with the Italian Act no. 675 from 1996, whereas subsequent amendments and integrations, such as the 2002 directive on e-privacy, and the 2006 directive on data retention, have been similarly transplanted into the Italian legal system. (This has not been necessary in the case of the GDPR, the latter being a regulation, which directly applies to the legal systems of all member states of the Union.) Notwithstanding multiple controversies, I may dare to say that the adoption of this set of rules on data protection has been a success. After all, the word privacy, which is often used as a synonym of data protection in Italy, turned out to be a new Italian word since the mid-1990s (although pronounced in the American, rather than British way).[50]

In other cases, however, a rejection crisis can follow as a result of the transplant. Italy, again, provides a clear example: on 22 September 1988, a new code of criminal procedure was adopted, aiming to substitute the previous inquisitorial system with an adversarial system, typical of the common law tradition. Yet, a number of the new provisions on the role of the parties, their powers, the notion of procedural truth, and so on, contradicted some principles of the Italian constitution, and the Constitutional Court in Rome had to declare the core of the

[48] See J Walker, Who's Afraid of U.S.-Style Class Actions (2012) 18(2) *Southwestern Journal of International Law* 509; and J Srouji and M Dolhem, 'Class Action and Data Privacy in the USA and Europe: Effective Deterrent or Ill-founded Approach to Compliance?' (2017) 1(3) *Journal of Data Protection & Privacy* 294.

[49] See A Watson, *Legal Transplants: An Approach to Comparative Law* (2nd edn, University of Georgia Press 1993).

[50] See U Pagallo, *La tutela della privacy negli Stati Uniti d'America e in Europa: Modelli giuridici a confronto* (Giuffrè 2008).

reform invalid. In a previous work on the law and AI, I have attempted to quantify the size of this failure.[51]

A third instance of legal transplant brings our analysis back to the collective dimensions of privacy and data protection, which were introduced in Section III.B. In 2004, the Italian Parliament debated the extent to which US class actions should be adopted in the national Consumer Code. In November 2007, the Senate passed the class action bill, which was subsequently approved by the second house of the Parliament a month later. A new article, that is, Art. 140 bis was added to the Code.[52] On 1st January 2010, the Italian class action finally entered into force after six years of work and discussions. Although it may be too early to determine whether or not these rules shall be deemed as another success story of transplants-and-receptions, a recent lawsuit appears particularly instructive on this very dynamic. The ruling tells us a lot about how we should grasp the interaction between data privacy and consumer law via class actions generally and specifically in EU law. The lawsuit concerns a giant of Big Data and AI applications, such as Facebook and its macro-targeting algorithms for advertising.[53]

The case of *Facebook v Altroconsumo* involving the largest independent and non-political party-based consumer organisation in Italy was discussed before the Administrative Tribunal in Rome and decided in January 2020.[54] One of the legal issues under scrutiny revolved around whether Facebook's privacy information and disclaimer – 'Subscribe! It's free and always will be' – should be deemed as 'unclear and incomplete.' Facebook complained about the Court's lack of jurisdiction on deceptive actions and omissions, since the services of the company, after all, were 'free.' For the sake of the argument, so went the reasoning of Facebook, the alleged 'failure to inform about the use of users' data for commercial purposes' would fall under the regulations (and sanctions) of the GDPR, rather than the provisions of the Consumer Code. Correspondingly, such an association, as Altroconsumo, should have lodged its complaints before the Data Protection Authority, rather than the

51 See T Agnoloni and U Pagallo, 'The Case Law of the Italian Constitutional Court between Network Theory and Philosophy of Information' in R Winkels and N Lettieri (eds), *2d International Workshop on Network Analysis in Law* (JURIX 2014, Krakow, 2014) 26–38 <www.leibnizcenter.org/~winkels/NAiL2014-pre-proceedings.pdf>; T Agnoloni and U Pagallo, 'The Case Law of the Italian Constitutional Court, Its Power Laws, and the Web of Scholarly Opinions' in *ICAIL, Proceedings of the 15th International Conference on Artificial Intelligence and Law* (New York) 151–155 <www.dl.acm.org/citation.cfm?id1⁄42746108>; T Agnoloni and U Pagallo, 'The Power Laws of the Italian Constitutional Court, and Their Relevance for Legal Scholars' in A Rotolo (ed), *Legal Knowledge and Information Systems: JURIX 2015: The Twenty-Eighth Annual Conference* (IOS Press, Amsterdam, 2015) 1–10.

52 In accordance with Art. 2(446) of the Act no. 244 from 24 December 2007, then amended by Art. 49(1) of the Act no. 99 from 23 July 2009.

53 In addition to the case discussed in the text, see US Department of Housing and Urban Development (HUD), Office of Administrative Law Judges (ALJ). 2019. *HUD v Facebook Inc* HUD ALJ No. FHEO No. 01-18-0323-8. In this case, most of the issues revolved around anti-discrimination law, rather than consumer protection.

54 TAR Lazio, first section, 10 January 2020, no 15275/2018.

Italian Competition and Market Authority (AGCM). The Administrative Tribunal in Rome, however, did not buy the premise of Facebook's arguments: it's simply not true that Facebook's services are free. In the wording of the judges,

> this approach offers a partial view of the potential inherent in the exploitation of personal data, which can also constitute an 'asset' available in a negotiating sense, susceptible of economic exploitation.... In addition to the protection of personal data as an expression of a right of the individual's personality, as such subject to specific and non-waivable forms of protection, such as the right to withdraw consent, access, rectification, oblivion, there is also a different field of protection of the data itself, intended as a possible object of a sale, put in place both between market operators and between them and the interested parties.[55]

Some months later, in March 2021, the Council of State, that is, the highest administrative Court in Italy, confirmed this part of the ruling.[56]

On this basis, we can appreciate how an American legal tool (i.e., class actions) has been transplanted into a national legal system (i.e., the Italian consumer code), in order to complement the provisions of a quasi-federal legislation, such as the GDPR of EU law. The gist of this 'imitation game' is that no incompatibility exists between consumer law and data protection; rather, they should be grasped as complementary. Depending on the circumstances of the case, individuals and associations may lodge complaints either before their data protection and privacy authorities, or before their national competition and market authorities, or both. Groups and individuals can protect their data for personal and economic reasons, as is the case in US law, through the powerful tool of class actions, for example, Art. 140 *bis* of the Italian Consumer Code vis-à-vis the associative mechanisms of Art. 80 of the GDPR.

Of course, we may wonder about how good this complementary approach to the challenges of AI will be, once transplanted into a civil law jurisdiction. In the jargon of the Italian justices, we may ask about the balance that shall be struck between a 'non-waivable' and a 'negotiable' form of protection. In particular, in dealing with the challenges of AI for people's privacy and the protection of their data, a balance will need to be found between the idea that 'we are our data' and the assumption that, rather, 'we own our data.'

However, in more general terms, the regulatory dynamic of legal transplants and receptions illustrated so far raises a further problem, that is, whether this combination of 'non-waivable' and 'negotiable' forms of protection for people's data privacy will be good enough to tackle the challenges of AI. In other words, the question is, will we successfully address the challenges of AI either by complementing the protection of personal data with the protection of data as an asset, that is, the Italian

[55] Ibid. no 6 of the ruling.

[56] See Consiglio di Stato (sixth section), ruling no 02631/2021 (REG.PROV.CO), from 31 March 2021.

way, or vice versa, by complementing the protection of data as an asset, that is, the US approach, with the protection of personal data as a 'non-waivable' right, such as in Art. 1798.125(a) of the CCPA?

IV CONCLUSIONS

The chapter has dealt with the mid-term (and even short-term) impact of AI on tenets of data protection and privacy law. No Sci-Fi was needed, such as imagining the behaviour of AI systems with human-like properties, or AI with superpowers or superhuman intelligences, to admit that the widespread use of such technologies is already affecting pillars of current legal regulations. Crucial differences between such legal systems and traditions, such as the EU and US laws, were put in the spotlight. The legal challenges raised by a smart personal assistant, for example, are likely to lead most EU scholars to focus on problems associated with the data collected and processed by such AI assistants vis-à-vis the principle of purpose limitation, data minimisation, and the difference between data controllers and end-users of AI systems. In US constitutional law, the use of such an AI assistant, if eventually hacked by the FBI, would be examined in connection with the safeguards of the Fourth Amendment and the flaws of the third-party doctrine. At the state level, after California, some other states, like Virginia and Nevada,[57] have aimed to complement the traditional protection of privacy and consumer law with a whole set of rights to access to – and control and protection over – information in digital environments. Although such rights are often conceived of as individual rights, such individual rights to data protection are only a part of the story: we should be attentive to the new collective dimension of privacy and data protection brought about by AI in the era of Big Data.

Further distinctions between EU and US laws followed as a result of this collective dimension. They concern whether such dimension of privacy and data protection should be understood in accordance with an associative right (i.e., the EU approach) or a corporate right (i.e., the *Boy Scout* doctrine of the US Supreme Court under the First Amendment). Such crucial differences suggest why current regulatory convergences, which were under scrutiny in Section III, should be grasped with a pinch of salt. The Italian transplant of the EU data protection rules and some family resemblance between the GDPR and the CCPA illustrated a new dynamic of legal transplants and receptions that regards both the role of class actions in civil – as opposed to common – law jurisdictions and the informational tenets of today's digital privacy in the United States. Among the drivers of this regulatory convergence between EU and US laws, between data protection and consumer law, and between

57 Nevada approved Senate Bill 220, amending Nevada's previous online privacy law from 2017, in May 2019; whereas the Virginia's Consumer Data Protection Act, also known as CDPA, refers to the new Title 59.1 a of the Code of Virginia from 13 January 2021.

'non-waivable' and 'negotiable' forms of protection, the chapter insisted on the new collective dimension of data protection rights and the fact that the value of personal data involved in cases of group infringements can be small, whereas class actions do represent a powerful means for deterrence and law enforcement in the sector of mass AI products and services.

However, what is suggested here is not a simple convergence between EU and US laws, between data protection and informational privacy, between the protection of personal data as a fundamental right and the protection of data as an asset.[58] We should be attentive to the logic of these safeguards. In US law, data is typically treated as a commodity, and most safeguards, even in the case of personal identifiable information, are remedial. These remedial safeguards relate to class actions, which are also considered as a means of deterrence and law enforcement, similar to the legal techniques of accident control in strict liability policies.[59] In EU law, the aim of data protection is just the opposite of a remedial approach, since data processing is deemed as a risky activity. The term risk appears 75 times in the GDPR, whereas the risk of data processing is characteristically approached in a proactive way. In the United States, companies have no legal duties to take self-regulatory measures, both organisational and technical, in order to abide by the regulations on data protection, such as the CCPA; in EU law, the GDPR can be understood as a mixture of rules on risk management (e.g., Art 5(2)); risk assessment (Art. 24); and risk governance (Art. 55). Risk is not only to be understood in terms of probabilities of events, consequences, and costs, so that, according to the level of risk, we can determine liability policies and accountability schemes. The notion also refers to the logic of risk production and how we intend to manage it proactively. According to Art. 35 of the GDPR, 'where a type of processing in particular using new technologies,' such as AI, 'is likely to result in a high risk to the rights and freedoms of natural persons, the controller shall, prior to the processing, carry out an assessment of the impact of the envisaged processing operations on the protection of personal data.'

It remains of course an open issue how good these provisions of EU data protection as well as the 2021 proposal for a new AI Act will be in tackling the challenges of this technology.[60] Scholars discuss risks of legal fragmentation, and whether the EU proactive approach can hinder the advance of technology, or will require over-frequent revision to tackle such a progress.[61] To be fair, a certain consensus exists,

[58] See U Pagallo, 'Algo-Rhythms and the Beat of the Legal Drum' (2018) 31(4) *Philosophy and. Technology* 507.

[59] See R Posner, 'The Jurisprudence of Skepticism' (1988) 86(5) *Michigan Law Review* 827.

[60] See L Floridi, 'The European Legislation on AI: A Brief Analysis of Its Philosophical Approach' (2021) 34 *Philosophy and. Technology* 215; and M Ebers and others, 'The European Commission's Proposal for an Artificial Intelligence Act—A Critical Assessment by Members of the Robotics and AI Law Society' (2021) 4 *RAILS* 589.

[61] See U Pagallo, 'The Legal Challenges of Big Data: Putting Secondary Rules First in the Field of EU Data Protection' (2017) 3(1) *Eur Data Prot L Rev* 36.

however, even among US scholars, on the good reasons why, from a normative viewpoint, we should adopt a proactive approach.[62] 'Proactivity' is a sort of mantra, for example, in the 2021 Final Report of the US National Security Commission on Artificial Intelligence.[63] A proactive approach does not only include forms of top-down regulation, such as the set of bans, prohibitions, and obligations proposed by the European Commission with the AI Act. Further fields of legal regulation, such as the regulation of AI in health law, show that a proactive approach can be at work through forms of co-regulation or even some variants of self-regulation.[64] Examples of this approach include the special zones created by the Japanese government since the early 2000s, in order to pre-emptively test the legal challenges of AI and robotics, in such fields as traffic law, tax law, communication law, privacy, and more.[65] These forms of legal experimentation have been expanded to further fields, for example, finance and banking, in other jurisdictions.[66] Proactivity is of course a pillar of such fields as AI and health law.[67] In data protection, today's principle of data protection by design and by default, pursuant to Art. 25 of the GDPR, or the new generation of data protection impact assessments of Art. 35, should be traced back to the early 2000s, when Ann Cavoukian and other privacy commissioners developed the first ideas on how to grasp such principle of design.[68]

The overall idea of a proactive approach is that data protection safeguards should be at work even before a single bit of information has been collected in a transparent way. This proactive approach represents the first step to tackle that on which scholars have insisted time and again over the past years, namely, the threats of AI to people's privacy and the protection of their data in the private sector.[69] The list of threats under scrutiny in this paper has included biases, lack of transparency,

62 An overview in A Tsamados and others, The Ethics of Algorithms: Key Problems and Solutions' [2021] *AI & Society* 1.

63 Available at <www.nscai.gov/2021-final-report/>.

64 See the 'Stakeholder Engagement Framework' of the Department of Health of the Australian Government: <www.health.gov.au/resources/publications/stakeholder-engagement-framework>. The framework includes five different levels of engagement, that is, from simple information to consultation, involvement, collaboration, down to delegation of legal powers to stakeholders.

65 See U Pagallo, 'LegalAIze: Tackling the Normative Challenges of Artificial Intelligence and Robotics through the Secondary Rules of Law' in M Corrales, M Fenwick and N Forgó (eds), *New Technology, Big Data and the Law. Perspectives in Law, Business and Innovation* (Springer 2017) 281–300.

66 See J Zeitlin, *Extending Experimentalist Governance?: The European Union and Transnational Regulation* (Oxford University Press 2015); and, more recently, J Turner, *Robot Rules: Regulating Artificial Intelligence* (Palgrave MacMillan 2019).

67 See T Davenport and R Kalakota, 'The Potential for Artificial Intelligence in Healthcare' (2019) 6(2) *Future Healthcare Journal* 94.

68 See A Cavoukian, 'Privacy by Design: The Definitive Workshop' (2010) 3(2) *Identity in the Information Society* 247ff.

69 The threats of AI in the public sector, for example, dealing with constitutional safeguards and human rights in the field of criminal law, both substantial and procedural, would require an analysis of its own. See U Pagallo and S Quattrocolo, 'The Impact of AI on Criminal Law, and Its Twofold Procedures' in W Barfield and U Pagallo (eds), *Research Handbook on the Law of Artificial Intelligence* (Edward Elgar 2018) 385–409.

loss of context, unjustified discrimination, subtle or overt surveillance, or how the behaviour of AI systems may turn out unpredictable also for their engineers and computer scientists. These scenarios will likely multiply in the foreseeable future and warmly recommend being equipped for them. This is why several jurisdictions, often autonomously, have been endorsing different forms of proactive policies: the aim is to be ready to intervene in, or control the behaviour of AI systems and their impact on people's privacy and data. Admittedly, this approach is at odds with other laws, such as the US privacy (and constitutional) law, that have so far endorsed a reactive response. Yet traditional forms of accident control, such as strict liability policies, authorisation regimes or the role of class actions can complement but not substitute a proactive approach to risks and threats brought forth by AI systems. In addition to current discussions on how to amend US laws, we noted some interesting changes at State level. Therefore, after the CCPA and similar legislative acts in some other states in the US, we may wonder about what kind of proactive policy, if any, could finally be adopted in US privacy and constitutional law, including at the federal level.

28

Legal Personhood and AI

AI Personhood on a Sliding Scale

Nadia Banteka

I INTRODUCTION

Is Alexa, the AI assistant, a person? This seems like a no-brainer. Alexa is not a person. It is a powerful data-software-and-network-enabled machine that performs services for people. One such service is a well-functioning voice-enabled human-computer interface. A feature of that service, and possibly another service altogether, is its conversational capacity. Because of this feature, some people may mistake Alexa for a person. As one MIT study found, young children between the ages of three and ten years old were more likely to speak to digital assistants as if they were people, asking them how old they are or what their favourite colour is.[1] But if you ask the same people who mistake Alexa for a person if they think Alexa is a human being, they surely will say no. This may seem like an oxymoron, but being human and being a person mean two different things for both lay people and for the law.

In answering questions of what it means to be a person, policymakers, legislators, and courts – like lay people – often use anthropomorphic benchmarks.[2] Humans are persons, animals are not persons, some robots that can exhibit human qualities might be persons. When asked to think more about what personhood entails, lay people, policymakers, legislators, and courts often draw on qualities that are found in these benchmarks, such as a person is intelligent, a person is capable of autonomy, a person is aware of their surroundings, and a person is capable of exercising choice and free will.[3] What is not immediately apparent is the circularity of this

[1] Stefania Druga and others, '"Hey Google Is It OK if I Eat You?": Initial Explorations in Child-Agent Interaction' (*Proceedings of the 2017 Conference on Interaction Design and Children (IDC '17)*, Association for Computing Machinery, New York, 2017) 595–600 <www.dl.acm.org/doi/pdf/10.1145/3078072.3084330>.

[2] See Kate Darling, '"Who's Johnny?" Anthropomorphic Framing in Human-Robot Interaction, Integration, and Policy' in Patrick Lin and others (eds), *Robot Ethics 2.0: From Autonomous Cars to Artificial Intelligence* (Oxford University Press 2017) 9.

[3] See, for example, Francisco J Varela and others, *The Embodied Mind: Cognitive Science and Human Experience* (MIT Press 1991); Owen Holland (ed), *Machine Consciousness* (Imprint Academic 2003); Ugo Pagallo, 'Killers, Fridges, and Slaves: A Legal Journey in Robotics' (2011) 26 *AI & Soc'y* 347,

process. It is people who are answering the ontological question of what constitutes a person. In making the assessment and setting the initial benchmarks, these people project their biases from their experience of being human. After all, personhood is a social construct created by those entities capable of social constructions, which, for now, are human beings.

Humans are expected to answer questions of what it means to be a person and who gets to be a person in various aspects of daily life. In the legal context in particular, personhood is construed as a means to allocate rights and responsibilities to entities or to serve other socially determined ends. This approach kickstarts a circular process about how and in what ways we answer such questions on legal personhood. Consider any of these actual scenarios: Alexa records a murder or a fully self-driving car causes death to a human. Can Alexa be brought to court as a witness? Can the car be held liable or prosecuted? For legislators and courts to resolve the challenge of legal responsibility for AI entities, they first need to address the question of legal personhood for AI entities. But courts still disagree on what makes one a person for the purposes of the law (or how an entity acquires legal personhood) even when they deal with humans.[4] The inquiry becomes even more complicated the moment the discussion expands to include artificial entities. Scholars have long argued and cautioned that, as people increasingly interact with AI in their daily lives, especially through anthropomorphic manifestations, they will increasingly be tempted to grant AI legal rights and duties.[5]

The legal system assigns legal consequences to an entity's actions through legal personhood.[6] AI entities pose new challenges to the law of personhood due to their ability to self-learn by accumulating experiences and generating solutions to problems without the input of developers. As they are designed to operate at an increasing distance from their developers, owners, and users, AI entities also challenge traditional legal frameworks for attribution and liability, resulting in potential accountability gaps.[7] These characteristics of AI entities have led many scholars and policymakers to criticise the law for treating them as objects instead of subjects and to argue that the law ought to give these entities legal personhood.[8] These scholars

349–50; Stephen C Hicks, 'On the Citizen and the Legal Person: Toward the Common Ground of Jurisprudence, Social Theory, and Comparative Law as the Premise of a Future Community, and the Role of the Self Therein' (1991) 59 *U Cin L Rev* 789, 816.

4 See *Planned Parenthood of Se Pa v Casey* 505 US 833, 874–79 (1992); Jackson *Women's Health Org* v Dobbs 141 S.Ct. 2619, cert granted (US June 18 2020) (No. (18-60868)).

5 Lawrence B Solum, 'Legal Personhood for Artificial Intelligences' (1992) 70 NC L Rev 1231, 1231–87; Paulius Čerka and others, 'Is It Possible to Grant Legal Personhood to Artificial Intelligence Software Systems?' (2017) 33 *Computer L & Security Rev* 685, 689; See Robert M Geraci, *Apocalyptic AI: Visions of Heaven in Robotics Artificial Intelligence, and Virtual Reality* (OUP 2010) 217.

6 Bert-Jaap Koops and others, 'Bridging the Accountability Gap: Rights for New Entities in the Information Society?' (2010) 11 *Minn JL Sci & Tech* 497, 514.

7 Ibid. 517.

8 See Fahad Alaieri and André Vellino, 'Ethical Decision Making in Robots: Autonomy, Trust and Responsibility' in Arvin Agah and others (eds), *Social Robotics* (Springer 2016) 159–60; Peter M Asaro, 'A Body to Kick, but Still No Soul to Damn: Legal Perspectives on Robotics' in Patrick Lin and others

and policymakers focus on whether AI entities should have legal personhood based on largely anthropomorphic and intuitive criteria such as the concepts of autonomy, intelligence, and awareness.[9] But conferral of legal personhood conditions based on anthropomorphic intuitions would suggest that if AI entities look and act in a certain way that resembles the 'human' way, our legal system ought to extend legal personhood to them. While AI entities do not currently have the levels of intellectual or emotional capacity of humans, they often exhibit human-like behaviours that are indistinguishable from those of humans. Consider, for instance, the chatbots that operate on websites or phone lines. For all intents and purposes of their narrow task, they are indistinguishable from human clerks. On the other hand, recent normative accounts and empirical studies have resisted these analogies and have attempted to debunk the idea that there is an established set of characteristics based on which legislators or courts confer legal personhood, and even whether AI entities can ever be legal persons.[10]

In this chapter, I argue that one of the reasons behind this struggle among scholars and policymakers regarding legal personhood for AI entities is the way legal personhood has been constructed in our sociolegal system and particularly its circularity problem. One solution to this circularity problem of legal personhood that can bring our legal system one step closer to successfully grappling with the issue of legal personhood for AI entities is to reconceptualise legal personhood from an all-or-nothing concept to one that falls along a sliding-scale spectrum. In Section I of this chapter, I discuss the struggles our legal system has had with the concept of legal personhood and argue that the way courts have approached conferring legal personhood on entities suffers from this circularity problem. These issues have recently become most pressing in the scholarly and policy proposals regarding conferring personhood on AI entities. In Section II of this chapter, I propose the beginning of a solution to this problem of defining the legal status of AI: if our legislators decide to confer legal personhood on AI entities or our common law moves towards that direction through the courts, legal personhood for AI entities should not take the form of an on-off binary switch but instead develop in line with existing jurisprudence on legal personhood for other entities as a bundle of rights and responsibilities. I argue that this bundle of rights and responsibilities for various AI entities should be placed on a sliding spectrum: on one axis is the quantity and quality of the bundle of rights and obligations that legal personhood entails. On the other axis is the level of the relevant characteristic that courts may factor in conferring legal personhood.

(eds), *Robot Ethics: The Ethical and Social Implications of Robotics* (MIT Press 2012) 170, 179; Čerka (n 5) 686; Gabriel Hallevy, *Liability for Crimes Involving Artificial Intelligence Systems* (Springer 2016) 12–13, 21–22, 28, 39; Gabriel Hallevy, 'Unmanned Vehicles: Subordination to Criminal Law under the Modern Concept of Criminal Liability' (2011/2012) 21(2) *JL INFO & SCI* 200, 207–08, 210.

9 See Darling (n 2) 9.

10 See Joanna J Bryson and others, 'Of, for, and by the People: The Legal Lacuna of Synthetic Persons' (2017) 25 *AI & L* 273, 277–78; Nadia Banteka, 'Artificially Intelligent Persons' (2021) 58 *Hous L Rev* 537.

Perhaps counterintuitively, I propose that the more autonomously, intentionally, or consciously an AI entity behaves, the more minimal and restrictive (if any) the bundle of rights and responsibilities that ought to be conferred on it.[11]

II THE LEGAL PERSONHOOD CONUNDRUM

Legal personhood, unlike natural personhood, is a legal and not factual or normative status. The law confers this status on entities in order to take account of their activities, that is, for entities to have legal capacity and responsibility.[12] However, the law does not provide a clear legal standard for legal personhood nor a systematic framework regarding the basis on which the legal system will grant legal personhood to entities.

A *Legal Personhood in Statutory and Common Law*

In the United States, John Chipman Gray introduced what has now become the classical discussion on legal personhood, arguing that the concept of a 'person' in the law no longer represents the folk understanding of a human[13] but instead entails a 'subject of legal rights and duties.'[14] These legal rights can be substantive rights such as constitutional rights or the right to own property, and they can also be procedural legal rights such as the ability to sue and be sued or the right to counsel.[15] As the common law on legal personhood evolved, being human was no longer a necessary condition for legal personhood.[16] Natural persons enjoy legal personhood, but so do artificial entities such as corporations, trusts, associations, and ecclesiastical bodies, which the law treats as though they are one single legal entity, one single legal person.[17]

But despite some categorical approaches to legal personhood that courts and legislatures have often undertaken, the enterprise of conferring legal personhood remains unclear and is often controversial even for biological persons.[18] Current jurisprudence does not provide a satisfactory answer with set criteria to the question of who

[11] Cf Banteka (n 10).

[12] See Mark A Geistfeld, 'A Roadmap for Autonomous Vehicles: State Tort Liability, Automobile Insurance, and Federal Safety Regulation' (2017) 105 *Cal L Rev* 1611, 1628; Hicks (n 3) 818; Koops (n 6) 514.

[13] See Stephen J Morse, 'Reason, Results, and Criminal Responsibility' (2004) *U Ill L Rev* 363, 372–73.

[14] See Lawrence B Solum, 'Legal Theory Lexicon 027: Persons and Personhood' (*Legal Theory Lexicon*, 14 March 2004) <www.lsolum.typepad.com/legal_theory_lexicon/2004/03/legal_theory_le_2.html>; John Chipman Gray, *The Nature and Sources of the Law* (Routledge 1909); see also Bryant Smith, 'Legal Personality' (1928) 37 *Yale LJ* 283.

[15] Mireille Hildebrandt, 'Criminal Liability and "Smart" Environments' in RA Duff and Stuart Green (eds), *Philosophical Foundations of Criminal Law* (Oxford University Press 2011) 3.

[16] Samir Chopra and Lawrence F White, *A Legal Theory for Autonomous Artificial Agents* (University of Michigan Press 2011).

[17] See for example, 1 USC § 1 (2018); see Koops (n 6) 516.

[18] Elettra Stradella and others, 'Robot Companions as Case-Scenario for Assessing the "Subjectivity" of Autonomous Agents' (CEUR Workshop Proceedings, France, 28 August 2012) 1, 28 <www.ceur-ws.org/Vol-885/paper4.pdf>.

can be a legal person.[19] Theories on legal personhood vary from approaching the issue as a metaphysical, conditions-based inquiry searching for certain attributes that an entity ought to possess to be a legal person, to approaching it as a normative question of whether an entity should be granted legal rights and duties, or as a pragmatic question of how conferring legal rights and duties on an entity can advance the goals of the legal system.[20] There are three discernible theories that aim to explain the way the legal system approaches the question of legal personhood for artificial entities that often utilise corporations as a point of reference and paradigmatic example of an artificial legal person. The 'fiction theory' views artificial entities as entities that do not represent a person but that the law addresses as if they were a legal person, establishing a legal fiction in order to address certain needs of the legal system.[21] Under the symbolist theory,[22] legal personhood for artificial entities provides a schema to establish legal rights and obligations between the natural persons that are members of an artificial entity as an aggregate, on the one hand, and the world, on the other.[23] Finally, the realist theory posits that artificial entities are independent and autonomous social entities. These entities exist irrespective of whether the law takes account of them, and the law then recognises and personalises them.[24]

The US Constitution uses the term 'person' but does not provide a definition for it.[25] The US Supreme Court has been asked to interpret questions of legal personhood particularly in the context of corporations, and the legal rights of corporations as distinct entities in the eyes of the law.[26] But the Court has not systematically addressed the defining characteristics of a legal person or the policy implications

19 See Koops (n 6) 550.

20 See Solum (n 5); Bryson (n 10) 277, 288; Čerka (n 5) 692; Morton Horwitz, 'Santa Clara Revisited: The Development of Corporate Theory' (1985) 88 *W Va L Rev* 173; David Millon, 'Frontiers of Legal Thought I: Theories of the Corporation' (1990) *Duke LJ* 201, 204, 241–251.

21 *Int'l Shoe Co v Washington* 326 US 310, 316 (1945); Bryson (n 10) 278, 280.

22 See a series of case law refuting the aggregate position (*Maxwell Café Inc v Dep't of Alcoholic Beverage Control* 298 P 2d 64, 68 (Cal Ct App 1956); *Curtiss v Murry* 26 Cal 633, 634–635 (1864); see also *Miller v McColgan* 110 P 2d 419, 421 (Cal 1941); *Erkenbrecher v Grant* 200 P 641 (Cal 1921); *Jacques Inc v State Board of Equalization* 318 P 2d 6, 14 (Cal Ct App 1957); *Dandini v Dandini* 260 P 2d 1033 (Cal Ct App 1953); Bernard E Witkin, *Summary of California Law* (8th edn, Bancroft-Whitney 1974) 4316.

23 See Benjamin D Allgrove, 'Legal Personality for Artificial Intellects: Pragmatic Solution or Science Fiction?' (MPhil dissertation, University of Oxford 2004) 60 <https://papers.ssrn.com/sol3/papers.cfm?abstract_id=926015>; Katsuhito Iwai, 'Persons, Things and Corporations: The Corporate Personality Controversy and Comparative Corporate Governance' (1999) 47 *Am J Comp L* 583, 590; Max Radin, 'The Endless Problem of Corporate Personality' (1932) 32 *Colum L Rev* 643, 658.

24 Iwai (n 23) 590; See Harold J Laski, 'The Personality of Associations' (1916) 19 *Harv L Rev* 405.

25 See US Const art I.

26 See *Burwell v Hobby Lobby Stores Inc* 573 US 682, 706–07 (2014) (discussing how a corporation is 'a form of organization used by human beings' and Fourth Amendment protections have been extended to corporations to protect the humans within the corporation, but not communicating what rights construct the corporation's personhood behind those necessary to protect the legal persons within the organization); *Santa Clara v S Pac RR* 118 US 394 (1886); *Pembina Consol Silver Mining & Milling Co v Pennsylvania* 125 US 181, 187–88 (1888) (discussing how corporations resulted more from the grant of special privileges to the people incorporating the organisation than to the organisation itself).

of conferring legal personhood. Federal and state laws have addressed legal personhood in an *ad hoc* way.[27] Ultimately, states still enjoy broad authority to decide which entities are legal persons and to establish the legal rights and duties of these entities by statute.[28] Federal and state courts have not accepted one single theory of legal personhood.[29] Instead, courts either discuss conditions that establish legal personhood on a case-by-case basis or undertake a circular analysis asserting that an artificial entity has rights because it is a legal person without first establishing what makes it a legal person.[30] This circular analysis becomes most apparent when looking at the development of legal personhood for artificial entities throughout the common law. Many of these artificial entities already *de facto* manifested legal effects despite statutory silence. The courts were then asked to make sense of and legitimise this existing reality under a largely pragmatic lens of ensuring that any changes to the status quo were not too disruptive to the socioeconomic and sociopolitical conditions that had already emerged.[31] Theories of personhood also reflect this circularity by accepting that, due to the often backward-looking approach of our common law, artificial entities exist and act in law before the law recognises them.[32]

B *The Legal Personhood for AI Entities Controversy*

This muddy legal landscape does not provide clear answers to issues of legal personhood and liability that have already arisen in the context of AI entities. These thorny

[27] See Bryson (n 10) 280–281; See generally Lori B Andrews, 'The Legal Status of the Embryo' (1986) 32 *Loy L Rev* 357 (discussing the history of legal treatment of a foetus or embryo under different areas of law). For example, the Bankruptcy Act includes individuals, partnerships, and corporations, but not governmental units, as persons. Under Ohio's corporate laws, which are typical, 'person' is defined to include, 'without limitation, a natural person, a corporation, whether non-profit or for profit, a partnership, a limited liability company, an unincorporated society or association, and two or more persons having a joint or common interest.' Foreign governments are 'persons' with the right to sue for treble damages under § 4 of the Clayton Act. Municipalities and other governmental units are 'persons' under 42 USC § 1983. In the context of employment law, employers covered by civil rights law include any 'natural' or 'juridical' persons employing persons in return for any kind of compensation, for profit or non-profit purposes, as well as their agents and supervisors. Local governments, municipal corporations, and school boards are 'persons' subject to liability under 42 USC § 1983, which imposes civil liability on any person who deprives another of his federally protected rights; Jessica Berg, 'Of Elephants and Embryos: A Proposed Framework for Legal Personhood' (2007) 59 *Hastings LJ* 369, 371 n 13 (quoting Ohio Rev Code Ann § 1701.01(G) (West 2014)) (first citing 11 USC § 101(41); then citing 42 USC § 1983 (2000); then citing *Pfizer Inc v Gov't of India* 550 F 2d 396, 399 (8th Cir 1976), affd 434 US 308, 320 (1978); then citing *Cook County v United States ex rel Chandler* 538 US 119, 129 (2003); and then citing *Monell v Dep't of Soc Servs* 436 US 658, 688–90, 695–96 (1978)).

[28] See Banteka (n 10) 559.

[29] See Horwitz (n 20) (pointing out that these theories functioned according to set guidelines as corporate doctrine developed, and arguing that they were both affected by social developments and, in turn, themselves shaped historical development); see also Millon (n 20) 204, 241–251 (discussing Horwitz's arguments).

[30] Banteka (n 10) 556–557.

[31] Ibid. 560, 595.

[32] Ibid.

issues have included cars operating with AI-based semi- or fully autonomous pilot systems crashing into other cars resulting in deaths,[33] or into pedestrians causing their deaths after erroneously classifying them as vehicles,[34] or in cases of AI bots contracting in their own name after a company has set them up to operate autonomously and interact with their clients.[35] These examples illustrate the unique challenges AI entities pose for our legal system due to their increasing distance from the natural persons responsible for them and their inherent characteristics of unpredictability, inexplicability, and autonomy. In response to these issues, many advocated for the expansion of legal personhood to these entities.

The arguments in favour of legal personhood for AI entities are frequently reduced to the following: if we have other artificial entities such as corporations that enjoy legal personhood, then why not also confer it on AI entities since these entities often act autonomously and produce legally significant and unforeseeable to humans outcomes?[36] AI's ability to self-learn based on its own experience without outside input makes the consequences of its actions unpredictable and unforeseen by its original developers. For instance, an AI system may reach a decision that is unexpected after piecing together an obscure pattern in its data and thus engage in conduct that is unlawful and in which a human would not have engaged.[37] This unlawful conduct cannot necessarily be traced back to the intent or fault of a developer if there has been no malice or fault in the original programming. Where a black box encapsulates the AI decision-making process, it becomes even more difficult and, at times, impossible for courts to identify any intent or fault of a human.[38] Actions of AI can also be the result of input from multiple independent developers.[39] Finally, due to their increased autonomy, AI entities may not be controllable even by their own developers. Since autonomy is given to many AI systems by design often along with an instruction to self-preserve, even if the legal system can identify the developer

33 See Alex Davies, 'Tesla's Latest Autopilot Death Looks Just Like a Prior Crash' (*WIRED*, 16 May 2019) <www.wired.com/story/teslas-latest-autopilot-death-looks-like-prior-crash/>.

34 National Transportation Safety Board, *Collision between Vehicle Controlled by Developmental Automated Driving System and Pedestrian Accident No. HWY18MH010* (2018) 2; Samuel Gibbs, 'Uber's Self-Driving Car Saw the Pedestrian but Didn't Swerve' *The Guardian* (London, 8 May 2018) <www.theguardian.com/technology/2018/may/08/ubers-self-driving-car-saw-the-pedestrian-but-didnt-swerve-report>; Bree Burkitt, 'Self-Driving Uber Fatal Crash: Prosecution May Be Precedent Setting' (*azcentral*, 22 June 2018) <www.azcentral.com/story/news/local/tempe/2018/06/22/self-driving-uber-fatal-crash-prosecution-may-precedent-setting/726652002/>.

35 Mireille Hildebrandt, 'Criminal Liability and "Smart" Environments' in RA Duff and Stuart Green (eds), *Philosophical Foundations of Criminal Law* (Oxford University Press 2011) 507, 514–515.

36 See Sergio M C Avila Negri, 'Robot as Legal Person: Electronic Personhood in Robotics and Artificial Intelligence' (2021) *Front Robot AI* <https://doi.org/10.3389/frobt.2021.789327>.

37 See Evan J Zimmerman, 'Machine Minds: Frontiers in Legal Personhood' (2015) *SSRN* 9 <https://papers.ssrn.com/sol3/papers.cfm?abstract_id=2563965>.

38 See Curtis EA Karnow, 'Liability for Distributed Artificial Intelligences' (1996) 11 *Berkeley Tech LJ* 147, 153–154, 182; see Ryan Calo, 'Robots in American Law' (2016) University of Washington School of Law Research Paper No 2016-04, 23 <https://papers.ssrn.com/sol3/papers.cfm?abstract_id=2737598>.

39 See Calo (n 38) 23.

responsible for a potentially malicious AI, the algorithm may continue to pursue malicious activity after the developer is removed. We can hold the human liable for some of the activity of the AI, but causation becomes more and more remote as the algorithm continues to act autonomously.[40] Due to these singular characteristics, AI entities can and will act in ways that are neither intended nor foreseeable to designers or users, making it difficult to trace the causal relationship necessary for liability. And whereas the newly proposed European Union (EU) framework for AI liability includes, in part, a provision for a strict liability regime for AI entities,[41] many scholars and policymakers in the United States have so far largely moved away from strict liability models.[42]

Even though, as I have argued elsewhere,[43] common law rules on legal personhood are incompatible with conferring it on AI entities, and legislatures should pause before doing so by statute, discussions involving legal personhood for AI entities, or 'electronic personhood', have persisted both in scholarship and in policy. Calls for personhood have largely focused on the levels of intelligence, awareness, and autonomy that AI entities exhibit. These are measured by an ability to self-learn through experience, adapt to the environment, and act intentionally without the intervention or assistance of third parties.[44] Assuming that the levels of these characteristics that AI entities exhibit increase exponentially in the future, it is conceivable that the legal system might struggle to continue viewing truly intelligent and autonomous AI entities only as agents of humans.[45] This is not a far-fetched scenario as a practical matter, but it is a scenario that the law is currently unprepared to address. Shawn Bayern recently demonstrated that an AI algorithm can exercise *de facto* legal personhood by being given control of a limited liability company.[46]

40 See Deborah G Johnson, 'Technology with No Human Responsibility?' (2015) 127 *J Bus Ethics* 707, 708; Solum (n 5) 1244–1245; Yavar Bathaee, 'The Artificial Intelligence Black Box and the Failure of Intent and Causation' (2018) 31 *Harv JL & Tech* 889, 898.

41 Commission, 'Proposal for a Regulation of the European Parliament and of the Council Laying Down Harmonised Rules on Artificial Intelligence (Artificial Intelligence Act) and Amending Certain Union Legislative Acts' COM(2021) 206 final. See also Chapter 6 of this Handbook for a discussion of the proposed AI Liability Act.

42 See, for example, Brandon W Jackson, 'Artificial Intelligence and the Fog of Innovation: A Deep-Dive on Governance and the Liability of Autonomous Systems' (2019) 35 *Santa Clara High Tech. LJ* 35, 59–60; Cary Coglianese and David Lehr, 'Transparency and Algorithmic Governance' (2019) 71 *Admin. L Rev* 1, 29–38; Alicia Lai, 'Artificial Intelligence, LLC: Corporate Personhood as Tort Reform' (2021) *Mich St L Rev* 597 (2021). Cf David C Vladeck, 'Machines without Principals: Liability Rules and Artificial Intelligence' (2014) 89 *Wash L Rev* 117, 146.

43 Banteka (n 10) 538.

44 European Parliament, 'Report with Recommendations to the Commission on Civil Law Rules on Robotics (2015/2103(INL))' (2017) Doc A8-0005/2017 20; Pagallo (n 3) 349–50; Stradella (n 18) 25, 26.

45 David C Vladeck, 'Machines without Principals: Liability Rules and Artificial Intelligence' (2014) 89 *Wash L Rev* 117, 122.

46 Shawn Bayern, 'The Implications of Modern Business Entity Law for the Regulation of Autonomous Systems' (2015) 19 *Stan Tech L Rev* 93, 104 n 43; Shawn Bayern, 'Of Bitcoins, Independently Wealthy Software, and the Zero-Member LLC' (2014) 108 *Nw U L Rev* 1485, 1496–1497. See also Lynn M LoPucki, 'Algorithmic Entities' (2018) 95 *Wash U L Rev* 887, 887, 897–901.

This allows the AI entity to exercise the bundle of rights that the corporation is given through legal personhood as its own, including, among others, the right to enter into contracts, to own property, the right to privacy, to freedom of speech, and to equal protection of the laws. Bayern also emphasised that once the algorithm was given these rights, it had the ability to confer the same rights on other algorithms by establishing new entities and putting those third algorithms in control of these new entities.[47] In order to prepare our legal system to address such scenarios, we need to revisit more systematically our conception of legal personhood.

III LEGAL PERSONHOOD ON A SLIDING SCALE

Despite the uncertain landscape regarding what conditions or circumstances would confer legal personhood on an entity, our legal system provides better answers on the topic of what legal personhood entails. We know that legal personhood is a divisible aggregate of rights and duties.[48] We also know that the exact quantity and quality of these rights and duties can vary. For example, humans as legal persons can have different sets of rights and obligations depending on their individual characteristics.[49] Consider the rights and obligations an adult human enjoys against those of a child.[50] Both categories of persons are legal persons, yet they each enjoy more, less, or simply different sets of legal rights and obligations.

A *Legal Personhood across a Sliding Spectrum*

Legal personhood represents a spectrum, and the status of legal personhood allows entities to act within the legal system with respect to (more-or-less) bundles of rights and obligations.[51] This idea of legal personhood resists representation as a binary

47 Bayern 'The Implications of Modern Business Entity Law for the Regulation of Autonomous Systems' (n 46) 104 (advocating a model under which 'legal personhood is like fire: it can be granted by anyone who already has it').

48 See Bryson (n 10) 277.

49 See ibid. 278.

50 See Ugo Pagallo, *The Laws of Robots: Crimes, Contracts, and Torts* (Springer 2013) 38–39; Ryan Abbott and Alex Sarch, 'Punishing Artificial Intelligence: Legal Fiction or Science Fiction' (2019) 53 *UC Davis L Rev* 323, 336–337.

51 See *Burwell* (n 26) 706–07 (discussing how a corporation is a form of organisation used by human beings and Fourth Amendment protections have been extended to corporations to protect the humans within the corporation); *Rowland v Cal Men's Colony*, Unit II *Men's Advisory Council* 506 US 194, 204 (1993) (discussing that the right for natural persons to represent themselves in litigation does not extend to corporations despite their legal personhood); *Baltimore & O R Co v Harris* 79 US (12 Wall) 65, 81 (1870) (discussing how natural persons may do whatever is not forbidden by law but artificial persons like corporations can only do what they are legally charted to do); *Anderson's Paving Inc v Hayes* 295 SE 2d 805, 808–809 (W Va 1982) (McGraw J dissenting) (discussing how extension of constitutional rights to a corporation is limited in context to instances where the right is necessarily incidental to the corporation's existence); *Batiste v Bonin* No 06–1352, 2007 WL 1791219 at *2 (WD La June 13 2007) (discussing how a juridical person has only the capacity that the law allows).

concept with an on-off switch: a legal person that has legal rights and duties, on the one hand, and a non-legal person that does not have any legal rights and obligations, on the other. Instead, the bundle of rights and obligations that an entity may enjoy as a legal person can vary depending on the characteristics of the entity and the priorities of the legal system.[52] What is more, conferring legal personhood on an entity not only provides legal rights and obligations but also might provide the ability to confer expansive rights on third parties. Consider recent developments in the rights of nature where parts of the ecosystem such as rivers, lakes, or forests are granted legal personhood and, through it, a procedural right for third-party humans to sue on their behalf.[53] On the flip side, the fact that an entity possesses legal personhood with a bundle of rights and obligations does not in itself establish that the legal system provides this entity with all necessary tools available to exercise these legal rights or that the legal system provides other legal persons with the tools to hold said entity accountable for breaches of its legal obligations.[54]

Viewing legal personhood as a non-binary concept is not new, but it is a fact that has not been appreciated systematically in the light of the question of legal personhood for AI entities.[55] Scholars have examined the possibilities of 'quasi-personhood,'[56] 'borderline or limited [personhood] status,'[57] or 'partial personality'[58] for AI entities. But choosing one of these different variations of legal personhood becomes unnecessary when we view legal personhood across a spectrum that allows varying levels of legal rights and duties. This approach also reflects the way US courts have addressed the question of conferring legal personhood on human and non-human entities in common law by granting these entities legal personhood with more or fewer rights and obligations based on that entity's characteristics and its interactions with the legal system.[59] Finally, viewing legal personhood across a spectrum allows us to better address the scenario many scholars and policymakers have proposed or predicted: AI entities exhibiting certain characteristics or interacting with the legal system in ways that would justify the conferral of legal personhood.[60]

[52] See Solum (n 5) 1238–1240; Ngaire Naffine, *Law's Meaning of Life: Philosophy, Religion, Darwin and the Legal Person* (Hart Publishing 2009) 46–47; Richard Tur, 'The "Person" in Law' in Arthur Peacocke and Grant Gillett (eds), *Persons and Personality: A Contemporary Inquiry* (Basil Blackwell 1988) 121–122.

[53] See Peter Stone and others, 'Artificial Intelligence and Life in 2030' (Stanford University 2016) 43.

[54] See Bryson (n 10) 278.

[55] With some notable exceptions: Bryson (n 10) 278; Koops (n 6) 559.

[56] See Peter M Asaro, 'Robots and Responsibility from a Legal Perspective' (*IEEE International Conference on Robotics and Automation*, Roma, 14 April 2007).

[57] Solum (n 5) 1253.

[58] Marshal S Willick, 'Constitutional Law and Artificial Intelligence: The Potential Legal Recognition of Computers as "Persons"' (*International Joint Conference on Artificial Intelligence*, Los Angeles, August 1985) 1271, 1272.

[59] Banteka (n 10).

[60] See n 8.

B *Legal Personhood for AI Entities across an Inverted Spectrum*

In the scholarly and policy discussion about the potential personhood status of AI entities, the characteristics of autonomy, awareness, and intentionality are at the forefront of calls for treating AI entities as legal persons.[61] Autonomy represents the ability that certain AI entities have to receive stimuli from their environment without any human intervention, modify their inner state, and perform autonomous decision making.[62] For the legal system, certain degrees of autonomy can mean that acts by AI entities may not be reducible to a person for purposes of liability.[63] In the context of legal personhood, awareness is linked with intentionality.[64] Though the two concepts are distinct,[65] awareness makes agents capable of intentional action which represents the capacity to have interests in matters.[66] Legal personhood effectively provides entities with the necessary rights to claim and protect these interests, but also with the legal consequence that they will be held accountable if they violate the interests of others. Awareness and intentionality are thus also linked with an entity's potential liability and legal accountability.[67]

These concepts that proponents of legal personhood emphasise are critical to consider not only in demonstrating the sliding scale of legal personhood but also in providing a roadmap of how to confer legal personhood in a way that least disrupts our legal system and the legal rights of individuals governed by it. The degrees of autonomy, awareness, and intentionality of AI entities fall along a spectrum. On the one end are AI entities that make decisions and act based on pre-programmed rules such as a chess player AI that uses a given scoring formula to evaluate all moves and then select the best possible move according to that formula. On the other end of this spectrum are AI entities based on advanced machine learning algorithms that make decisions or act through self-learning from data available to them.[68]

61 Ibid.

62 See Luciano Floridi and JW Sanders, 'On the Morality of Artificial Agents' (2004) 14 *Minds & Machines* 349, 349, 357, 364; Ugo Pagallo, 'From Automation to Autonomous Systems: A Legal Phenomenology with Problems of Accountability' (International Joint Conference on Artificial Intelligence, Melbourne, August 2017) 18–19; Čerka (n 5) 686; Amie L Thomasson, 'First-Person Knowledge in Phenomenology' in David Woodruff Smith and Amie L Thomasson (eds), *Phenomenology and Philosophy of Mind* (Oxford University Press 2005) 117.

63 See Abbott and Sarch (n 50) 331–332.

64 Giovanni Sartor, 'Cognitive Automata and the Law: Electronic Contracting and the Intentionality of Software Agents' (2009) 17 *AI & L* 253, 277–278.

65 Richard A Posner, 'An Economic Theory of the Criminal Law' (1985) 85 *Colum L Rev* 1193, 1221.

66 See Thomasson (n 62) 117; Pagallo (n 62) 18–19; Joel Feinberg, *The Moral Limits of the Criminal Law Volume 1: Harm to Others* (Oxford University Press 1984) 33–34; Bonnie Steinbock, *Life Before Birth: The Moral and Legal Status of Embryos and Fetuses* (2nd edn, Oxford University Press 2011) 5–6.

67 Migle Laukyte, 'Artificial and Autonomous: A Person?' (AISB/IACAP World Congress, Birmingham, July 2012) 66, 69.

68 Bathaee (n 40) 898.

Legislators and policymakers have already identified that this spectrum is relevant to how the law ought to react to the challenges that AI entities pose, but they have done so in a way that, while intuitive, creates its own problems. The request of the European Parliament to the European Commission to consider legislation granting these entities electronic legal personhood,[69] and facilitate the ascription of civil liability for instances in which AI entities make autonomous decisions provides the most developed example.[70] This framework for electronic persons would have placed shared liability along a continuum for parties involved in the AI entity's decision-making process such as the AI entity itself, the engineers, and the manufacturers, on the basis of their relative contribution to this process.[71] This continuum would reflect the different levels of autonomy and intentionality the AI entity exercised and the levels of input by humans that might have led to an injury or wrongful act.[72] The EU eventually moved away from the concept of electronic personhood in its most recent proposed Regulation intended to harmonise rules on AI for member states.[73] The new framework that does not include conferral of legal personhood on AI entities promotes a risk-based approach to regulation that ranks AI entities based on the risk they create for individuals and their fundamental rights, from unacceptable risk to high risk and low risk.[74]

The United States has not taken an equivalent approach on a federal level. Similarly, efforts to regulate AI on a state level are virtually non-existent and so much of this task will likely be left to the courts.[75] To the degree that our domestic legal system decides it is normatively sound and pragmatically desirable to confer legal personhood on AI entities, viewing AI entities and legal personhood along a spectrum is an important parameter. However, I argue that the sliding scale that determines liability based on how autonomously or intentionally an AI entity has acted should be inverted. Perhaps counterintuitively, the more autonomous, aware, or intentional AI entities are or become, the more restrictive the legal system should be in granting them legal rights and obligations as legal persons. That is the bundle of rights and obligations granted to these entities should be narrower the more they exhibit these characteristics. This approach addresses and aims to resolve an

[69] European Parliament (n 44) 20.

[70] A significant number of AI experts responded with an open letter to the European Commission warning that '[f]rom an ethical and legal perspective, creating a legal personhood for a robot is inappropriate whatever the legal status model,' 'Open Letter to the European Commission, Artificial Intelligence and Robotics' (4 May 2018) <https://g8fip1kplyr33r3krz5b97d1-wpengine.netdna-ssl.com/wp-content/uploads/2018/04/RoboticsOpenLetter.pdf> 31 May 2022.

[71] Amanda Wurah, 'We Hold These Truths to Be Self-Evident, That All Robots Are Created Equal' (2017) 22 *J Futures Stud* 61, 62–63.

[72] European Parliament (n 44) 17.

[73] Commission, 'Proposal for a Regulation of the European Parliament and of the Council Laying Down Harmonised Rules on Artificial Intelligence (Artificial Intelligence Act) and Amending Certain Union Legislative Acts' COM(2021) 206 final.

[74] Ibid.

[75] Cf HR 647, 66th Leg, 2d Reg Sess (Idaho 2022).

important concern that scholars have raised that personhood for AI entities may be used as a shield for human and corporate accountability.[76]

The sliding spectrum represents a continuum with two axes: the quantity and quality of the bundle of rights and obligations that legal personhood entails, and the level of the relevant characteristic of AI that courts may factor in to confer legal personhood such as autonomy, awareness, or intentionality. When an AI entity's act is a result of an otherwise human-driven or human-supervised process, then our current rules on intent and causation will continue to function as they do and responsibility for injury or wrongdoing will continue to be attached to the humans behind the AI. Because of this, AI entities that operate under such a level of human supervision by providers or users but otherwise act autonomously in their individual tasks, if given legal personhood, could be granted more expansive bundles of rights and obligations. This is because the legal system will be able to 'pierce their veil' and recover from the humans responsible for them and also from the AI entities themselves if they become capable of acquiring assets similarly to how corporate liability operates today.[77] On the flipside, the more autonomously, intentionally, or consciously an AI entity acts, the narrower the bundles of rights and responsibilities conferred on it should be to increase the pressure on developers to constrain these entities and encourage vigilance in monitoring the conduct of these entities.

There are several normative and pragmatic reasons for this inverted spectrum. First, the prevailing view of a regular spectrum where an increase in the quantity or quality, or both of legal rights and duties parallels an increase in autonomy, awareness, or intentionality exhibited by AI entities is flawed. This view is often based on an analogy of how the law treats other entities with limited personhood such as minors.[78] The argument goes: as minors, people exhibit limited levels of autonomy, awareness, or intentionality, and thus the legal system has widely accepted that these limited levels are to be followed by respective limitations in their legal personhood. Thus, minors enjoy a more limited bundle of rights and duties than adults. As minors become adults, our legal system assumes that their autonomy, awareness, and intentionally will increase, making them capable of exercising the full bundle of rights and responsibilities provided to them through legal personhood unless there is another legally pertinent factor that constraints their autonomy, awareness, or intentionality and causes a subsequent restriction of the bundle of rights and duties.

[76] See Alaieri and Vellino (n 8) 159, 166; see Bryson (n 10) 277, 288; Wendell Wallach, *A Dangerous Master: How to Keep Technology from Slipping beyond Our Control* (Basic Books 2015); Arthur Kuflik, 'Computers in Control: Rational Transfer of Authority or Irresponsible Abdication of Autonomy?' (1999) 1 *Ethics & Info Tech* 173, 180.

[77] See Ben Chester Cheong, 'Granting Legal Personhood to Artificial Intelligence Systems and Traditional Veil-Piercing Concepts to Impose Liability' (2021) 1 *SN Soc Sci* 231 <https://doi.org/10.1007/s43545-021-00236-0> 31 May 2022; Jacob Turner, *Robot Rules: Regulating Artificial Intelligence* (Springer 2018).

[78] See US Department of Justice, *Trying Juveniles as Adults: An Analysis of State Transfer Laws and Reporting* (2011) 2, 6; Jeffrey Fagan, 'Juvenile Crime and Criminal Justice' (2008) 18(2) *Future Child* 81, 91–92.

Adopting this approach to legal personhood and mechanically applying it to AI entities does not account for the qualitative differences between AI entities and natural persons or other artificial entities that are legal persons. The rationale behind the parallel increase of rights and duties for legal persons who are also natural persons as their autonomy, awareness, or intentionality increase is that these individuals are more capable of personalised decision-making, action, and responsibility.[79] However, this assumption does not hold true for AI entities in one very important way for our legal system. The more autonomous, aware, or intentional AI entities become, the more difficult it will be for our legal system to allocate responsibility to the individuals behind these entities.[80] Unlike corporations that are aggregates of natural persons or, at least, in a legally significant manner, tied to natural persons or assets, AI entities and their actions become increasingly remote from human developers or users the more autonomous, aware, or intentional they become.[81] Drawing analogies between entities that enjoy limited legal personhood, such as minors, or artificial entities, such as corporations, to establish an analogous legal personhood and liability framework fails to account for this feature of independent AI. As I argued above, these differences necessitate inverting the existing paradigm for allocating legal rights and responsibilities.

The inverted spectrum I propose will allow us to maintain a legal liability system that permits injured parties to recover but also incentivises developers and users to produce and use AI entities in ways that reduce the risk of harm. Some scholars have argued that setting restrictions on AI entities, particularly those entities with the ability to act increasingly autonomously or intentionally, may stifle innovation.[82] Perhaps one might argue that the proposal of this chapter would have such a stifling effect. That is developers may be deterred from investing in the development and

79 Ibid.

80 Koops (n 6) 517.

81 See Calo (n 38) 23; see also Iwai (n 23) 590.

82 Jon Truby and others, 'A Sandbox Approach to Regulating High-Risk Artificial Intelligence Applications' (2021) *EJRR* <www.cambridge.org/core/journals/european-journal-of-risk-regulation/firstview> 31 May 2022; Mark D Fenwick and others, 'Regulation Tomorrow: What Happens When Technology Is Faster than the Law?' (2017) 6 *Am U Bus L Rev* 561; Andrea O'Sullivan, 'Don't Let Regulators Ruin AI' (*MIT Technology Review*, 24 October 2017) <www.technologyreview.com/2017/10/24/3937/dont-let-regulators-ruin-ai/> 31 May 2022; Carmelo Cennamo and D Daniel Sokol, 'Can the EU Regulate Platforms without Stifling Innovation?' *Harv Bus Rev* <www.hbr.org/2021/03/can-the-eu-regulate-platforms-without-stifling-innovation> 31 May 2022; Peter Suciu, 'The EU's Ambitious AI Regulations: Increasing Trust or Stifling Progress?' (*ClearanceJobs*, 3 May 2021) <www.news.clearancejobs.com/2021/05/03/the-eus-ambitious-ai-regulations-increasing-trust-or-stifling-progress/> 31 May 2022; Angus Loten, 'Government Must Be Careful Not to Stifle Innovation When Weighing AI Restrictions, Think Tank Says' *The Wall Street Journal* (New York, 11 February 2019) <www.wsj.com/articles/government-must-be-careful-not-to-stifle-innovation-when-weighing-ai-restrictions-think-tank-says-11549879200> 31 May 2022; Andrew McAfee, 'EU Proposals to Regulate AI Are Only Going to Hinder Innovation' *Financial Times* (London, 25 July 2021) <www.ft.com/content/a5970b6c-e731-45a7-b75b-721e90e32e1c> 31 May 2022.

production of fully autonomous AI because the resulting AI will be granted a narrower bundle of rights and duties as a legal person.[83]

The idea that the development of AI may be affected by the status of AI entities as legal persons is an interesting one, and it ultimately boils down to liability. All other things being equal, there is one key legal parameter that distinguishes the predicted trajectory of AI innovation under a regular as opposed to an inverted legal personhood spectrum. Insofar as legal personhood is granted to AI entities, within a regular spectrum model, developers and users may be minimally or not at all liable for harms caused by autonomous AI under existing frameworks of intent and causation. However, under the proposed inverted spectrum model, the more limited the bundle of rights and duties assigned to the more autonomous, aware, or intentional AI entities will mean that developers and users maintain another bundle of limited rights and duties – and corresponding liability – for these entities. Whereas innovation may be most ultimately served in an unregulated liability space, we are constantly balancing conditions that foster innovation against the possibility of harm to individuals.[84] In fact, the very reason why many scholars have cautioned against legal personhood for AI entities is precisely the trajectory that the regular legal personhood spectrum proposal leads to, that is, the potential shielding of developers, users, and corporations from liability for acts committed by more autonomous AI entities.[85]

Instead, the proposal of this chapter for an inverted spectrum has the potential of nudging developers and producers to include checks and controls. These can better ensure that autonomous AI entities are equipped with the relevant tools to prevent them from engaging in harmful activity and to make their decision-making sufficiently transparent that courts and litigants will be able to trace their actions back to a responsible human party. Transparency and by extension explainability, that is, the ability to pierce into AI's black box and review the process the algorithm followed in articulate terms understandable by humans, have long been important goals for improving AI innovation.[86] Traceability is an emerging concept that is considered a key requirement for ensuring that complex processes of AI, from data processing in

83 See Ajay Agrawal and others, 'Economic Policy for Artificial Intelligence' (2018) 19 *Innov Policy Econ* 139; Alberto Galasso and Hong Luo, 'Punishing Robots: Issues in the Economics of Tort Liability and Innovation in Artificial Intelligence' in Ajay Agrawal and others (eds), *The Economics of Artificial Intelligence: An Agenda* (University of Chicago Press 2019).

84 See BC Stahl and others, 'Artificial Intelligence for Human Flourishing – Beyond Principles for Machine Learning' (2021) 124 *J Bus Res* 374; Marc Steen and others, 'Responsible Innovation, Anticipation and Responsiveness: Case Studies of Algorithms in Decision Support in Justice and Security, and an Exploration of Potential, Unintended, Undesirable, Higher-Order Effects' (2021) 1 *AI & Ethics* 501; Thomas C King and others, 'Artificial Intelligence Crime: An Interdisciplinary Analysis of Foreseeable Threats and Solutions' (2020) 26 *Sci & Eng'g Ethics* 89.

85 See Alaieri (n 8) 159, 166; Bryson (n 10) 273, 277–278; Kuflik (n 76) 173, 180.

86 See Nick Bostrom and Eliezer Yudkowsky, 'The Ethics of Artificial Intelligence' (2011) 3 <www.faculty.smcm.edu/acjamieson/s13/artificialintelligence.pdf> 31 May 2022; Bathaee (n 40) 898.

AI modelling to production deployment, are documented in understandable ways.[87] Following the proposed inverted spectrum approach would, on the one hand, limit risk to individuals, while also providing an incentive for developers to invest more in improving tools that promote transparency, explainability, and traceability. These features, in turn, would allow our legal system to apply existing notions of intent and causation. The sliding scale spectrum also has the benefit of being a flexible framework. So, when the development of AI through these checks and controls becomes more pervasive and more systems are in place to ensure proper liability attribution, courts or legislators may consider moving the scale up or down depending on what is normatively and pragmatically desirable for the needs of the legal system and innovation.

Finally, this sliding scale proposal contributes to the limitation of the potential risks of AI, similar to a rationale underlying the current EU regulation proposal, but through means that may be more conducive to the US legal system. The EU risk-based approach attempts to tailor the regulation of AI entities to the scope and intensity of risks to EU values and fundamental rights that those entities may pose by establishing a tier of risks from unacceptable, to high and low risk.[88] Based on this categorisation of risk, some AI development and practices are entirely prohibited from the European market, and high-risk AI entities' developers and users must comply with more rules compared to low-risk AI entities, where the primary focus is on transparency.[89] While the EU is undertaking a more comprehensive regulatory approach for AI development and use, in the United States, proposals for regulating AI are much narrower and happen on an agency-by-agency basis. These efforts have recently included the National Institute of Standards and Technology (NIST) development of 'a voluntary risk management framework for trustworthy AI systems;'[90] the Federal Trade Commission (FTC) memo entitled 'Aiming for truth, fairness, and equity in your company's use of AI' laying out a roadmap for its compliance expectations on companies regarding their use of biased algorithms;[91] the Food and Drug Administration (FDA) releasing of the Artificial Intelligence/Machine Learning (AI/ML)-Based Software as a Medical Device (SaMD) Action Plan;[92] the National Security Commission on Artificial Intelligence (NSCAI) report

87 Marçal Mora-Cantallops and others, 'Traceability for Trustworthy AI: A Review of Models and Tools' (2021) 5(2) *Big Data & Cognitive Computing* 20.

88 Commission (n 73).

89 Ibid.

90 US Department of Commerce, Information Security and Privacy Advisory Board, *Meeting Minutes: March 3 and 4, 2021* (2021) <www.csrc.nist.gov/CSRC/media/Events/ispab-march-2021-meeting/images-media/ISPAB%20March%202021%20Minutes%20Final%20-%20Accepted.pdf>.

91 Elisa Jillson, 'Aiming for Truth, Fairness, and Equity in Your Company's Use of AI' (*Federal Trade Commission: Business Blog*, 19 April 2021) <www.ftc.gov/business-guidance/blog/2021/04/aiming-truth-fairness-equity-your-companys-use-ai>.

92 US Food and Drug Administration, *Artificial Intelligence/Machine Learning (AI/ML)-Based Software as a Medical Device (SaMD) Action Plan* (2021) <www.fda.gov/medical-devices/software-medical-device-samd/artificial-intelligence-and-machine-learning-software-medical-device>.

advocating for the public sector to lead the way in promoting trustworthy AI;[93] and the GAO report identifying key practices to help ensure accountability and responsible AI use by federal agencies.[94]

As there is currently no federal regulation of AI in the United States, much of this gap will continue to be reactively addressed through courts both for potential injuries caused by AI entities[95] and for settling claims of rights by AI entities, such as the right to be an author or an inventor.[96] If adopted by courts, the proposed approach helps to mitigate these risks in two ways. First, on the back end, by inverting the legal personhood spectrum, this approach maintains human accountability in instances where, due to advancements of AI, they would most likely be more, if not entirely, removed. Second, on the front end, this approach will incentivise developers, as argued above, to implement checks and controls to ensure that AI entities, and particularly those entities with the potential to act autonomously or intentionally, do not engage in harmful activity and that they are sufficiently transparent to trace actions back to a responsible human party. In this way, courts can engage in developing common law rules for AI liability in lieu of comprehensive federal regulation, or complementary to it in the case of future regulation.

IV CONCLUSION

The question of who can be a legal person remains unsystematically answered in the US legal system. Whereas conferral of legal personhood on entities is often successfully provided by statute,[97] there are many important instances in our legal doctrine where legal personhood has been interpreted and conferred on entities by courts.[98] This murky legal landscape has yet to provide an answer on how our legal system is to treat the latest entities with the ability to cause legally significant

93 National Security Commission on Artificial Intelligence, *Final Report* (2021) <www.reports.nscai.gov/final-report/table-of-contents/>.

94 US Government Accountability Office, *Artificial Intelligence: An Accountability Framework for Federal Agencies and Other Entities* (GAO-21-519SP, 2021) <www.gao.gov/assets/gao-21-519sp.pdf>.

95 See, for example, Davies (n 33); Burkitt (n 34).

96 See, for example, *Thaler v Hirshfeld* 558 F Supp 3d 238 (ED Va 2021); US Copyright Office Review Board, *Re: Second Request for Reconsideration for Refusal to Register a Recent Entrance to Paradise (Correspondence ID 1-3ZPC6C3; SR # 1-7100387071)* (14 February 2022) <www.copyright.gov/rulings-filings/review-board/docs/a-recent-entrance-to-paradise.pdf>.

97 See for example, 1 USC § 1 (2018); *Vt Agency of Nat Res v United States ex rel Stevens* 529 US 765, 786 (2000) (discussing how a person is defined by statute 31 USC § 3801(a)(6) and includes 'any individual, partnership, corporation, association, or private organization' (quoting 31 USC § 3801(a)(6))); *Rowland* (n 51) (discussing how the Dictionary Act includes corporations and unincorporated associations in the term 'person'); *Pembina* (n 26) 187–188 (discussing how artificial personhood is determined by legislature in statutes); *Baltimore* (n 50) 81 (discussing how an artificial entity is deemed a person by the law); *Ruppel v CBS Corp* 701 F 3d 1176, 1181 (7th Cir. 2012) (discussing how under § 1442(a) Congress meant to include corporations as persons).

98 See *Burwell* (n 26) 706–707; *Santa Clara* (n 26); *Pembina* (n 26) 187–188.

consequences: AI entities. We currently have no comprehensive legal framework to address the unique features of AI entities, and no federal regulatory framework appears in the horizon. In response, scholars and policymakers have proposed as a solution to confer legal personhood on AI entities due to the unique characteristics these entities enjoy, such as autonomy, awareness, or intentionality and treat them like we do other artificial entities such as corporations. In this chapter, I have engaged with this possibility and argued that we should reconceptualise legal personhood from an all-or-nothing concept to one that represents a bundle of rights and responsibilities and falls along a sliding-scale spectrum. On the one axis of this spectrum is the quantity and quality of the bundle of rights and obligations that legal personhood entails for each entity. On the other axis is the level of the relevant characteristics that courts may factor in conferring legal personhood on an entity, such as autonomy, awareness, intentionality, or other characteristics courts may consider. Unlike other proposals that have argued for an increase in legal rights and duties parallel to an increase in these legal personhood characteristics, I argued here that the spectrum should be inverted and that the more autonomous, aware, or intentional AI entities are or become, the more restrictive the legal system should be in granting them legal rights and obligations as legal persons.

This approach addresses and aims to resolve an important concern that scholars have raised that legal personhood for AI entities, absent a strict legal framework, may be used as a shield for human and corporate accountability. The inverted spectrum I proposed maintains a liability system that permits injured parties to recover but also incentivises developers and users to produce and use AI entities in ways that reduce the risk of harm. Under the proposed inverted spectrum model, developers, owners, and users maintain rights, duties, and corresponding liability primarily for the entities that have the capacity to be more autonomous, aware, or intentional and are incentivised to develop appropriate checks and controls to mitigate the risks posed by these entities in lieu of a comprehensive federal regulation.

29

EU and AI

Lessons to Be Learned

Serena Quattrocolo and Ernestina Sacchetto

I INTRODUCTION

The European Union is a highly sophisticated legal institution, inspired from the very beginning by the ideal of federalism.[1] Although this is certainly not the context for speculating upon the EU's nature and characteristics, analysing the EU approach to AI implies awareness of the very special mandate the EU holds with regard to the Member States. The EU has become a supranational advocate for the European people's: fundamental rights; liberties; and personal, social, and cultural development. This explains the proactive commitment of the EU in supervising the most recent development of AI, through definitions and regulation of the phenomenon. In fact, the EU endeavour is not only meant to fill the gap between Europe, on the one hand, and US and China[2] on the other hand, in terms of investments in the AI sector,[3] but it is also mainly focused upon the goal of creating the conditions for an 'anthropocentric AI' (see COM(2018) 237 final, hereinafter), designed by humans and controlled by humans.[4] The EU Commission displayed the clear conviction that 'the way we approach AI will define the world we live in.[5]

Thus, several initiatives have been pursued in order to fulfil the EU purpose of governing AI, which has a major impact on the lives of people and on governments. The purpose is not merely to promote scientific research and commercial

Serena Quattrocolo is responsible for Sections I–IV, and Ernestina Sacchetto for Section III.D.

1 See the Ventotene Manifesto (1941), drafted by Altiero Spinelli and Ernesto Rossi, which was the inspirational basis for a European union, since the time of WWII.

2 Adelina Adinolfi, 'L'Unione europea dinanzi allo sviluppo dell'intelligenza artificiale: la costruzione di uno schema di regolamentazione europeo tra mercato unico digitale e tutela dei diritti fondamentali' in Stefano Dorigo (ed), *Il ragionamento giuridico nell'era dell'intelligenza artificiale* (Pisa University Press 2020) 36.

3 See European Commission, COM(2018) 237 final, L'intelligenza artificiale per l'Europa, 4, acknowledging the Chinese leadership in terms of investments in the field.

4 Germana Lo Sapio, 'La black box: l'esplicabilità delle scelte algoritmiche quale garanzia di buona amministrazione' (2021) 16 federalismi.it, 24 <federalismi.it/nv14/articolo-documento.cfm?Artid=45610>.

5 European Commission, COM(2018) 237 final (n 3), 1.

developments[6] in specific branches of information and communications technologies.[7] As mentioned, the purpose of the EU strategy towards AI is to regulate the phenomenon in the whole range of impacts it may have, according to the values established in Article 2 of the Treaty of the European Union, the cornerstone of the constitutional system of the Union. Having understood the magnitude of it, the EU planned to use law to regulate AI and, in particular, to foresee and regulate the legal consequences of the use of AI, in the whole range of its application.[8]

As it usually occurs in the EU panorama, the topic has been approached by studies, soft law instruments, and finally, in early 2021, by a draft regulation, which was approved in December 2023 and not yet published in the Official Journal of the EU. Hereinafter, we will briefly present the most relevant recent documents released by the EU organs, agencies and study groups.

One important caveat is that, due to the topic assigned, We will not analyse the Council of Europe's documents about AI, algorithms, and digital development.[9]

II DEFINITIONS

Although this implies the anticipation of some aspects that will be analysed afterwards, it is important to recall that one specific area of early commitment of the EU is the definition of AI. Indeed, it is a challenging endeavour, being the basis for any further step in the regulation of it.

A first important benchmark was set by the Commission to the European Parliament, the European Council, the Council, the European Economic, and Social Committee and the Committee of the Regions, 'Artificial Intelligence for Europe', COM(2018) 237 final. The document does not provide for a normative

6 *Mutatis mutandis*, with regard to the need for a regulation of the internet, Giovanna De Minico, 'Fundamental Rights, European Digital Regulation and the Algorithmic Challenge' (2021) 1 *MediaLaws*, 9 <www.medialaws.eu/wp-content/uploads/2021/04/RDM-1-21-De-Minico.pdf>.

7 For example, the US National Security Commission on Artificial Intelligence, set up in 2019, holds a mandate to regulate AI investments and developments with specific regard to the areas of military and national security (see <www.nscai.gov/2021-final-report/>).

8 Adinolfi (n 2) 17.

9 This does not mean that the Council of Europe is not playing an important role in the governance of AI at the European level: on the contrary, by means of studies, reports and statements (e.g., the Ethical Charter on the Use of AI in Judicial Systems, released by the European Commission for the Efficiency for Justice in December 2018), the Council of Europe is a crucial actor in the governance of AI in Europe, along with the EU, which is equipped with more effective legal instruments. In particular, the Council of Europe appointed the Ad hoc Committee on Artificial Intelligence, which fulfilled its mandate in 2021 and has been replaced by the Committee on Artificial Intelligence. The bodies have the specific mandate to come up with guidelines for the governance on AI in compliance with the Council of Europe standards on human rights, democracy, and the rule of law. In particular, the Ad hoc Committee on Artificial Intelligence has started drafting a Convention on AI governance, which is still under negotiation.

definition of AI but refers to it as 'systems that display intelligent behaviour by analysing their environment and taking actions – with some degree of autonomy – to achieve specific goals'. However, the more serious the EU is at coming up with a comprehensive regulation of AI governance, a clearer definition of AI emerges.

In April 2019, the study by the EU High Level Experts Group on Artificial Intelligence (HLEG)[10] tried to elaborate a more detailed concept of AI. The group stated that

> Artificial intelligence (AI) systems are software (and possibly also hardware) systems designed by humans that, given a complex goal, act in the physical or digital dimension by perceiving their environment through data acquisition, interpreting the collected structured or unstructured data, reasoning on the knowledge, or processing the information, derived from this data and deciding the best action(s) to take to achieve the given goal. AI systems can either use symbolic rules or learn a numeric model, and they can also adapt their behaviour by analysing how the environment is affected by their previous actions.

Early 2020, the Joint Research Centre (JRC), the EU Commission's Science and Knowledge Service, delivered a comprehensive investigation on the various definitions of AI,[11] elaborated since the 1950s', proposing 'an operational definition of AI formed by a concise taxonomy and a set of keywords that characterise the core and transversal domains of AI'.[12] The huge work presented by the centre not only gathered and classified the multifaceted definitions of AI, according to the various areas of scholarship at stake but also led to an interesting proposal of a uniform definition. In fact, according to the study, the previous HLEG's definition, although accurate, is highly specific and detailed, and may turn out to be too specific to apply in the non-core science realm. As a consequence, the 2020 document advocates for the following definition of AI:

> AI is a generic term that refers to any machine or algorithm that is capable of observing its environment, learning, and based on the knowledge and experience gained, taking intelligent action or proposing decisions. There are many different technologies that fall under this broad AI definition. At the moment, ML4 [*machine learning*] techniques are the most widely used.

According to the exhaustive report, there would be at least four common features, within the manifold range of AI definitions, including the fact that a system is based on: (a) consideration of the real-world complexity; (b) information processing (collecting and elaborating inputs); (c) decision-making; (d) achievement of specific goals.

10 See <www.aepd.es/sites/default/files/2019-12/ai-definition.pdf>.

11 Sofia Samoili and others, *AI WATCH. Defining Artificial Intelligence* (Publications Office of the European Union 2020) 11.

12 Ibid.

As discussed, much attention is paid in this chapter to the draft regulation, presented by the Commission on 21st April 2021, which sets forth a definition of AI (art. 1), that appears to be more similar to the COM(2018)237 final's and JRC's than the HLEG's one, establishing that

> 'artificial intelligence system' (AI system) means software that is developed with one or more of the techniques and approaches listed in Annex I and can, for a given set of human-defined objectives, generate outputs such as content, predictions, recommendations, or decisions influencing the environments they interact with.

Although the final text is not yet available, it is reasonable to consider this wide definition[13] of AI an important cornerstone in the forthcoming European legal framework: the EU policy is meant to enact the largest governance possible of the phenomenon of AI, encompassing the whole range of situations that can be linked, in some way, to the techniques listed in the annex to the draft. Although the general definition in art. 3 implies reference to Annex I, in which three categories of computational methods are defined as 'artificial intelligence techniques and approaches', the drafting technique has been criticised, for the extensive catalogue reported in the Annex. In fact, vague and broad definitions of AI will lead to uncertain applications of the forthcoming Regulation itself. Irrespective of the assumption that every piece of legislation should aspire to provide clear and unequivocal definitions, the uncertainty about the potential effect of this text may be disruptive, because many computer scientists may not recognise their work under a too broad definition of AI provided by the text, struggling in understanding whether their software, based, for example, on the use of statistical methods (mentioned in Annex I), is covered by the new regulation.[14] Until the final text becomes accessible, we will not be able to tell whether the Regulation could achieve the purpose of finding a balance between addressing the risks of new industrial developments (suggesting that the draft applies only to specific highly sophisticated AI applications) and advocating protection against the social risks of AI, such as discrimination (implying extensive application of the draft, even to basic forms of AI).

III IMPORTANT EU DOCUMENTS ON AI

Chapter 27 introduced the readers to the EU long term commitment to the digital development. The Commission even created the term 'Digital Single Market',[15]

[13] It was said that this is hardly a definition: Giovanna Marchianò, 'Proposta di regolamento della Commissione europea del 21 aprile 2021 sull'intelligenza artificiale con particolare riferimento alle IA ad alto rischio' (2021) 2 *Ambientediritto*, 3 <www.ambientediritto.it/dottrina/proposta-di-regolamento-della-commissione-europea-del-21-04-2021-sullintelligenza-artificiale-con-particolare-riferimento-alle-ia-ad-alto-rischio/>.

[14] Nathalie Smuha and others, 'How the EU Can Achieve Legally Trustworthy AI: A Response to the European Commission's Proposal for an Artificial Intelligence Act' (2021) *SSRN* 14.

[15] European Commission, COM(2015) 192, A Digital Single Market Strategy for Europe ('A Digital Single Market is one in which the free movement of goods, persons, services and capital is ensured

implying that the ultimate accomplishment of the European Single Market, established since the 1990s, is represented by the digital domain.

Stemming from such commitment, the need to define and govern AI came as a natural consequence. The undertaking has involved all the EU institutions: the Parliament (and the LIBE Committee), the Commission, the Council, each in its own capacity, and several independent agencies, such as research centres and research groups, established to focus on specific issues related to AI and its applications.

Since late 2017 and over the last few years, several studies, documents, and soft law instruments[16] have been released by the EU, to set the premise of a general harmonisation of Member States' legislations in the field of AI, prior to the regulation on the European approach to AI. However, it is worth mentioning that two different approaches have been co-existing: on the one hand, given the comprehensive EU body of legislation, the existing texts may be suitable to regulate many AI applications, via adequate interpretative tools (which was the initial position of the Commission, although apparently in the process of evolving);[17] on the other hand, the need to regulate the AI governance can be seen as a great opportunity to renew the existing body of legislation (which is the position of the Parliament), via the introduction of new legal categories.[18]

The purpose of the following paragraphs and sub-paragraphs is to list and briefly comment the most important documents in the field.

A *European Parliament Resolution with recommendations to the Commission on Civil Law Rules on Robotics*

One important document is represented by the European Parliament Resolution with recommendations to the Commission on Civil Law Rules on Robotics, on 16 February 2017 (2015/2103 (INL)),[19] calling on the Commission to establish common Union definitions of: cyber physical systems, autonomous systems, smart autonomous robots, and their subcategories by taking into consideration the characteristics

and where individuals and businesses can seamlessly access and undertake online activities under conditions of fair competition, and a high level of consumer and personal data protection, irrespective of their nationality or place of residence. Achieving a Digital Single Market will ensure that Europe maintains its position as a world leader in the digital economy, helping European companies to grow globally').

16 All of which are not necessarily coherent, see Adinolfi (n 2), 33, 34.

17 See, that is, the proposal for a directive on adapting non-contractual civil liability rules to artificial intelligence (AI Liability Directive), <https://ec.europa.eu/info/sites/default/files/1_1_197605_prop_dir_ai_en.pdf>.

18 Adinolfi (n 2) 40.

19 The document is based on FP7 project RoboLaw – 'Regulating Emerging Robotic Technologies in Europe: Robotics Facing Law and Ethics', funded by the European Commission and conducted between 2012 and 2014: see Erica Palmerini and others, 'RoboLaw' (2014) <www.robolaw.eu/RoboLaw_files/documents/robolaw_d6.2_guidelinesregulatingrobotics_20140922.pdf>.

of a smart robot.[20] Such characteristics are: the acquisition of autonomy through sensors and/or by exchanging data with its environment (inter-connectivity) and the trading and analysing of those data: self-learning from experience and by interaction (optional criterion); at least a minor physical support; the adaptation of its behaviour and actions to the environment; absence of life in the biological sense.

Based on such a large definition, the resolution refers to the largest possible range of 'robots', including among others, drones, self-driving vehicles, and medical robots. The resolution proposed to introduce a system of registration for 'smart robots', for example, those having autonomy. The system of registration of advanced robots would be managed by an EU agency for robotics and AI. This agency would also provide technical, ethical, and regulatory expertise on robotics.

The document provides for specific recommendations about liability (civil) for damages caused by robots and openly envisages a legal instrument, under Article 114 TFEU, for the regulation of legal questions related to robotics and AI, which is examined under §4. A Charter on robotics was annexed to the Resolution, inviting designers and developers to act in compliance with individuals' right to dignity, privacy, and safety.

B *Ethics Guidelines for Trustworthy Artificial Intelligence and White Paper*

Afterwards, the Commission released a more comprehensive document, namely, COM(2018) 237 final, bringing Communication from the Commission to the European Parliament, the European Council, the Council, the European Economic and Social Committee and the Committee of the Regions, 'Artificial Intelligence for Europe', mentioned above.[21]

Moving from the viewpoint of robotics to the wider realm of AI, the Commission displayed the same proactive attitude, based on some crucial assumptions. The document is based on the premise that 'artificial intelligence (AI) is already part of our lives – it is not science fiction. From using a virtual personal assistant to organise our working day, to travelling in a self-driving vehicle, to our phones suggesting songs or restaurants that we might like, AI is a reality'.[22] Iconically, the Commission underlines that 'like the steam engine or electricity in the past, AI is transforming our world, our society and our industry'. Based on these cornerstones, the main commitment stemming from the document is 'the need to join forces at European level, to ensure that all Europeans are part of the digital transformation, that adequate resources are devoted to AI, and that the Union's values and fundamental rights are at the forefront of the AI landscape'.

[20] Aida Ponce Del Castillo, 'A Law on Robotics and Artificial Intelligence in the Eu?' (2017) 2 *Fortsight Brief* <www.etui.org/publications/foresight-briefs/a-law-on-robotics-and-artificial-intelligence-in-the-eu>.

[21] See the Commission staff working document 'Liability for Emerging Digital Technologies' SWD(2018) 137 final, attached to the Communication 'AI for Europe', introducing the concept of emerging digital technologies and the need to focus on the consequent specific liability issues.

[22] See n 19.

Straight after the release of this document, in June 2018, a group of independent experts (High-Level Expert Group) was created to release ethical guidelines on AI. The group of experts focused on the concept of trustworthy AI. The concept of 'trustworthy artificial intelligence' implies regulatory and ethical compliance with AI, as well as a 'robustness' in terms of safety, protection, and reliability. In this regard, any 'human-centric' approach to AI requires strict respect for fundamental rights, regardless of whether or not they are harmonised in the European Union. In particular, the document encompasses the commitment of the Union not to produce new forms of inequalities,[23] especially referring to certain groups such as 'workers, women, people with disabilities, ethnic minorities, children, consumers, or others at risk of exclusion is reaffirmed'.

On 8 April 2019, the High-Level Expert Group on AI released the Ethics Guidelines for Trustworthy Artificial Intelligence.[24] This followed the circulation of the guidelines' first draft, in December 2018, on which more than 500 comments were received, by means of an open consultation. The guidelines then identified four key principles, defined as 'imperatives', for trustworthy AI: (a) respect for human autonomy; (b) damage prevention; (c) fairness; (d) explicability, that is, transparency and traceability of information and procedures followed by AI systems.

The Ethics Guidelines for Trustworthy AI, enhanced the shift, within the EU context, towards the concept that the need for reliable AI should not be considered a goal to achieve but the very foundation of a completely new legal system: the (potentially) most dangerous applications for fundamental rights must always be subject to a mandatory, accurate, preliminary assessment. Among such applications, there is mass surveillance and the use of so-called 'autonomous weapons'. With specific reference to the first phenomenon, the Guidelines recommend the Member States to issue regulatory acts that guarantee the individual from 'identifying and tracking' activities, through biometric recognition systems based on AI such as 'face recognition and other involuntary methods of identification using biometric data (i.e., lie detection, personality assessment through micro expressions, and automatic voice detection)'. The use of these tools should be allowed only in exceptional circumstances, such as in cases of threats to national security, but in any case, only under the condition of the respect for fundamental rights. Such fundamental rights-based perspective was to influence the EU approach to AI in all the following documents and, in particular, in the proposal of regulation (§ 4).

A few months later came the 'White Paper on Artificial Intelligence – A European approach to excellence and trust', of 19 February 2020 [COM(2020) 65 final].[25] The

[23] For a general overview about AI, algorithms and discrimination, see Woodrow Barfield and Ugo Pagallo, *Law and Artificial Intelligence* (Edward Elgar 2020) 24.

[24] European Commission, 'High Level Experts Group on AI, Ethics Guidelines for Trustworthy AI' <www.digital-strategy.ec.europa.eu/en/library/ethics-guidelines-trustworthy-ai>.

[25] European Commission, 'White Paper on Artificial Intelligence – A European Approach to Excellence and Trust' <www.eur-lex.europa.eu/legalcontent/EN/TXT/?uri=CELEX%3A52020DC0065&WT_mc_id=Twitter>.

European Commission reiterated the regulatory approach, based on the risk of potential infringement of fundamental rights. The document established the dual objective of promoting the adoption of AI, on the one hand, and addressing the risks of AI – such as opaque decision-making mechanisms, discrimination based on personal conditions or otherwise, intrusion into our private lives, or use for criminal purposes, on the other hand. The purpose of the two-tier approach is to define strategic options to achieve the highest level of digital development without affecting individuals' fundamental rights. The risk-based approach seems to offer the practical advantage of adapting the regulatory response to the relevance of the legal interests involved, based on the expected damage and the chance that the persons concerned have to avoid the risk. The White Paper anticipated the system of 'risk rating' that was to be adopted in the following proposal of a regulation (see the following paragraphs).

The White Paper, which defines the specific policy options for achieving the aforementioned goals, is based on the assumption that the rapid development of AI has led to profound changes in the models of production and delivery of services: improving health care, increasing the efficiency of agriculture, contributing to the mitigation of climate change and its adaptation, improving the efficiency of production systems, and generally increasing the safety of European citizens. In this sense, the European Commission recommends that the Member States' and the European institutions develop common and unified strategies to face the current transformation and the challenges of the future with greater awareness and responsibility. It is worth mentioning (in light of the topics tackled under D) that the White Paper encompasses a robust 'Report on the Safety and Liability Implications of Artificial Intelligence, IoT, and robotics', by the Commission. Specifically, the report examines the idea that optimising Union safety rules for AI can help avoiding flaws and damages: if these occur, accurate civil liability rules should intervene to redress the situation.

On 21 October 2020, the Presidency of the European Council released its own Conclusions about The Charter of Fundamental Rights in the context of Artificial Intelligence and Digital Change (11481/20, 2020):[26] in the Conclusions, the Presidency declares that 'We are committed to the responsible and human-centric design, development, deployment, use and evaluation of AI'. In fact, 'the same degree of protection should be applied in the digital and in the physical world'. On the one hand, the Council acknowledges 'the importance of creating awareness about the use of digital technologies and embedded AI capabilities in government institutions, the judiciary, law enforcement, the economy and science, civil society, education and the general public'. On the other hand, AI may interfere with individuals' dignity, freedom, equality, people's solidarity, civil rights, and justice.

[26] Council of the European Union, Presidency, 'Conclusions' <www.consilium.europa.eu/media/46496/st11481-en20.pdf>.

In fact, the document also highlights the risks of opacity, complexity, distortion, and a certain degree of unpredictability of 'partially autonomous' AI systems. In light of these problems, the document, based on a FREMP (Working Party on Fundamental Rights, Citizens Rights and Free Movement of Persons)[27] memorandum, criticises the AI systems' current incompatibility with fundamental rights, recommending and facilitating the introduction of suitable and effective legal norms.

It is important to remember that, in the wake of that European Council, the European Parliament had also adopted a series of resolutions concerning the use of AI, with regard, in particular, to ethics and responsibility (see, in particular, the resolution 20 October 2020, with recommendations to the Commission on a civil liability regime for AI, 2020/2014 (INI),[28] and copyright, along with the Legal Observatory's basic information about AI in criminal law and its use by the police and judicial authorities in criminal matters, 2020/2016(INI), and 2020/2017(INI) in education, culture and the audio-visual sectors.

C *Proposed AI Act*

Moreover, the European Parliament also adopted the resolution of 20 January 2021 on AI.[29] The document sets forth a definition of AI, such as 'AI system' means a system that is either software-based or embedded in hardware devices, and that displays behaviour simulating intelligence by, inter alia, collecting and processing data, analysing and interpreting its environment, and by taking action, with some degree of autonomy, to achieve specific goals. It is divided into several paragraph, focusing on the use of AI in international public law and military, in civil areas, such as health and justice, transports, and international private law.

On 21 April 2021, the Commission submitted the draft regulation for a European approach for AI (Artificial Intelligence Act), along with a brand new 'coordinated plan' about AI.[30]

Before presenting the main points of the regulation proposal, it is worth remembering that besides the EU institutions, the EU Member States also took action in the field of AI governance. In April 2018, a group of twenty-four Member States

27 Council of the European Union, 'FREMP Group' <www.consilium.europa.eu/it/council-eu/preparatory-bodies/working-party-fundamental-rights-citizens-rights-free-movement-persons/>.

28 European Parliament, 'Resolution' <www.europarl.europa.eu/doceo/document/TA-9-2020-0276_EN.html>.

29 European Parliament, 'Resolution' <www.europarl.europa.eu/doceo/document/TA-9-2021-0009_EN.html>.

30 European Commission, 'Coordinated Plan on Artificial Intelligence' (2021) <https://digital-strategy.ec.europa.eu/en/library/coordinated-plan-artificial-intelligence-2021-review>. European Commission, 'Proposal for a Regulation of the European Parliament and of the Council laying down harmonised rules on artificial intelligence (Artificial Intelligence Act) and amending certain union legislative acts', COM/2021/206final. In December 2023, the agreement between the EU policy-makers was reached but the final text is not yet available: for updates see <https://eurlex.europa.eu/legal-content/EN/HIS/?uri=celex:52021PC0206>.

released a declaration (finally signed by all the Member States and by Norway and Switzerland as well),[31] committing themselves to the challenge of realising the Digital Single Market, by cooperating in the fields of not only industrial investments but also social and economic conditions (such as, i.e., the transformations of the labour market and education). By submitting national programmes to the Commission, the Member States planned to act within a coordinated framework, deploying inter-government actions and complementing the EU institutions' initiatives,[32] both normative[33] and economic.[34]

First and foremost, it is important to stress that the legal basis of the draft regulation is Article 114 TFEU,[35] allowing measures for the establishment and functioning of the internal market in accordance with the EU digital single market strategy presented earlier. However, based on this wide assumption, the Commission drafted a document that reaches far beyond the area of internal market and private law, protecting individuals, rather than mere consumers, from a broad range of risks encompassed by the daily use of AI.[36] This aspect deserves much attention, shifting the focus of the forthcoming regulation from the commercial and private law sphere, to a more comprehensive context, in which AI is not merely a feature of a product or a service, and more of a regime requiring a complex balancing of competing interests, such as private economic interests, individual basic fundamental rights, and even matters of social and political governance. Actually, in the original proposal, the internal market functions act as the framework for a more comprehensive picture that will be summarised in its most relevant aspects.

Before focusing on the contents of the proposal, it is useful to discuss two general aspects of the document. Firstly, the draft needs to fit into a complex, existing legal framework, which includes not only the documents listed in the previous paragraph. The impact assessment document accompanying the proposal (SWD (2021)84 final), in its paragraph 1.3, examines the complex legal context, from the point of view

31 European Commission, 'EU Declaration on Cooperation on AI' (2018) <https://ec.europa.eu/jrc/communities/en/community/digitranscope/document/eu-declaration-cooperation-artificial-intelligence>.

32 Adinolfi (n 2) 38.

33 The European Parliament resolution (see n 26) on civil liability for AI implies a domestic action to amend liability regimes (see, in particular, para 6 of the text: [the Parliament] 'believes that there is no need for a complete revision of the well-functioning liability regimes, but the complexity, connectivity, opacity, vulnerability, the capacity of being modified through updates, the capacity for self-learning, and the potential autonomy, of AI-systems, as well as the multitude of actors involved represent nevertheless a significant challenge to the effectiveness of Union and national liability framework provisions; considers that specific and coordinated adjustments to the liability regimes are necessary to avoid a situation in which persons who suffer harm or whose property is damaged end up without compensation').

34 Nine billion euros have been earmarked for investment in the European digital plan, in the period 2021–27.

35 Adinolfi (n 2) 45.

36 See Giovanni De Gregorio, 'The Digital Services Act: A Paradigmatic Example of European Digital Constitutionalism' (*Diritti Comparati*, 17 May 2021) <www.diritticomparati.it/the-digital-services-act-a-paradigmatic-example-of-european-digital-constitutionalism/?print-posts=pdf>.

of: fundamental rights; products safety legislation; liability legislation; and legislation on supply of services. As the document notes, it is a rich body of secondary legislation, applicable to both public and private sector, laying down non-AI-specific principles and rules. The proposal occupies a space which is only partially unregulated, needing to cope with a long list of other provisions (see Article 2.2 of the draft).

Secondly, the structure of the draft is inspired by the Reg. 2016/679, GDPR. The GDPR has influenced the normative approach to the draft regulation about AI.[37] Besides specific prohibitions, the text sets forth standards and requirements, with specific obligations of transparency and control systems. As provided for in the GDPR, AI systems meeting the standards and requirements will not be relieved, for good, from controls, as monitoring will be permanent, according to the constant technical evolution of the field. Moreover, like the GDPR, the implementation of the European governance of AI will be based on a set of authorities, at the central level and in each Member State, and a set of penalties, including regulatory fines, for breaches of the regulation.[38]

In the explanatory memorandum to the draft, the European Commission carried out an in-depth overview of the reasons for the need to set forth general standards in the data processing by AI systems.

Within the context of the internal market, improving and optimising 'the free movement of AI-based goods and services cross-border', may provide competitive advantages to companies and thus support the achievement of great results in social and environmental standards. However, the memorandum acknowledges that the use of certain applications of AI systems may cause damage, both material and immaterial, to individuals, 'to the health and safety or fundamental rights'. Thus, there is a need to establish a legal framework, setting 'harmonized rules on artificial intelligence … to foster the development, use and uptake of AI in the internal market that at the same time meets a high level of protection of public interests'. In this way, the introduction of minimum requirements of quality and safety will allow a general improvement in the functioning of the internal market, creating the conditions for the development of a real 'ecosystem' of trust that covers the entire process of producing, marketing, selling, and using AI within the European Union. This implies a large extraterritorial impact of the future regulation, affecting not only every (user in the EU and) provider 'placing on the market or putting into service AI systems in the Union', regardless of its location, but also third-country providers and users, if the output of the AI system is used in the EU (Article 1). Like the GDPR, this brand-new regulation will reach a great number of subjects beyond the EU borders, with the purpose of making the EU a 'safe harbour' from dangerous AI applications.

37 Marco Bassini, 'Commissione Europea, proposta di regolamento sull'Intelligenza Artificiale' (*ItaliaOggi*, 24 April 2021) <www.federprivacy.org/informazione/societa/commissione-europea-proposta-di-regolamento-sull-intelligenza-artificiale>.

38 Bassini (n 37).

The approach inspiring the whole Regulation is the 'risk' of infringement of the fundamental rights of individuals; such risk was also mentioned by the previous White Paper (see earlier), although it was not the key feature of that document.

The draft Regulation moves from a system for scaling such risk. First and foremost, some AI systems represent 'unacceptable risk' and are prohibited. Title II of the draft established a list of 'Prohibited artificial intelligence practices', referring to four different groups of practices (Article 5). Paragraph (a) refers to subliminal techniques (operating beyond a person's consciousness) which are able to materially alter an individual's conduct in such a way to cause a physical or psychological harm (or make it probable). Paragraph (b) refers to AI techniques exploiting any of the 'vulnerabilities' of a specific group of people, due to their age and physical or mental disability, 'in order to materially distort the behaviour of a person pertaining to that group', causing potential physical and psychological damage. For paragraphs (a) and (b), the purpose is clearly to protect certain categories of individuals from completely distorted uses of AI techniques.

Paragraph (c) prohibits public authorities from using AI systems to assess or classify the reliability of natural persons for a certain period of time, based on their usual behaviour or other known or expected personal characteristics, with the assignment of a 'social scoring'. However, this is not a general ban of social scoring via AI systems, as EU citizens may expect. The use of AI systems for such scoring is banned in so far as it results: (i) into detrimental or unfavourable treatment of both individuals and groups, in contexts not related to those in which data was originally generated and collected; (ii) into detrimental and unfavourable treatment of both individuals and groups, unjustified or disproportioned to the gravity of their social behaviour. In these terms, the protection laid down by this provision against social scoring practices (which almost rely on AI systems) is not absolute at all and implies a 'case by case' (ii) test of proportionality which appears to be hardly compatible with a general exclusion of certain practices.

Paragraph (d) prohibits the use of 'real-time' or 'contextual' biometric identification systems in spaces open to the public, for the purpose of law enforcement, unless such use is strictly necessary for a number of goals broadly related to public safety or crime prevention:

(i) the targeted search for specific potential victims of crime, including missing children;
(ii) the prevention of a specific, substantial, and imminent threat to the life or physical safety of natural persons or of a terrorist attack;
(iii) the detection, localisation, identification, or prosecution of a perpetrator or suspect of a criminal offence referred to in Article 2(2) of Council Framework Decision 2002/584/JHA62 and punishable in the Member State concerned by a custodial sentence or a detention order for a maximum period of at least three years, as determined by the law of that Member State.[39]

[39] European Commission, COM(2021) 206 final, Proposal for a Regulation, Art 5(d).

Once again, the derogations were worded extremely broadly, in a way that could deprive the general ban of effectiveness. Both sub-paragraphs (ii) and (iii) could lead to the use of real-time facial recognition in a broad variety of situations, which are incompatible with a severe restriction. Given the multiple situations allowing for real-time facial recognition, and the utterly generic terms defining the exceptions under art. 5.d, it must be acknowledged that vast discretion is left to law enforcement authorities, even before a judicial authorisation is provided. It will be interesting to see whether a better balance will be found in the final text.

Other systems (or other forms of exploitation of the abovementioned systems), which fall into the 'high risk' scale, should be subjected to prescriptive requirements which, as said, evoke the Regulation (EU) 2016/679 (GDPR).[40] In particular, the draft is based on: (a) precise rules on impact assessment; (b) use of data having high quality standards; (c) traceability of results; (d) constant human supervision in the use of such systems; and (e) a high level of robustness, safety, and overall accuracy. Nevertheless, early commentators stressed that the requirements set forth by the proposal may not be strong enough to guarantee fundamental rights, such as, for example, in the labour market.[41] Although mentioned in the list of high-risk applications, the systems of recruitment, selection, and evaluation of workers are not meant to be assessed by independent bodies, before they are made available on the market: a self-evaluation of the standards by the producer has been considered sufficient by the drafters.[42] Moreover, meeting the standards established by the text seems to be a sufficient condition to allow the use of such systems in the Member States. To that extent, the regulation would prevail over the more severe national legislation in force in several countries, such as France, Germany, and Italy.[43]

As with the GDPR, the draft provides that the manufacturer of the AI system is responsible for carrying out a 'conformity assessment', that is, the manufacturer has to implement a process, before the product is put on the market, which can demonstrate that the requirements of the Regulation have been followed. With regard to risk assessment, there seem to be points of contact between the draft Regulation and personal data protection. Specific risks may be neutralised by abiding by precise requirements, defined by articles 6 onwards of the proposed Regulation, on the basis of the severity of the impact that each AI system may entail on individuals. In particular, Article 9 provides that the implementation of a risk management system also covers periodic monitoring: the higher the risk of the AI system, the stricter the compliance.

As discussed, an important feature of the draft is the emphasis on the quality of data entered into the AI system during the software development and testing phase: they

40 Bassini (n 37).

41 Antonio Aloisi and Valerio De Stefano, 'Il nuovo regolamento UE sull'intelligenza artificiale e i lavoratori' (*Il Mulino*, 4 June 2021) <www.rivistailmulino.it/a/regolamento-ue-sull-intelligenza-artificiale-una-minaccia-alla-protezione-dei-lavoratori>.

42 The proposal is considered to be far too imprecise about the relationship with the sophisticated system of social rights, both public and private, created by the EU over the decades: Marchianò (n 10).

43 Aloisi and De Stefano (n 41).

must be relevant, error-free, and complete. A similar provision is also provided for by the GDPR: the data processed must be characterised by particular elements that certify its quality, including the adequacy, relevance, and accuracy and, if necessary, they must be periodically updated (Article 5).

On the basis of 'accountability', the results processed must then be verified and systematically monitored throughout the entire life span of the system. Article 62, again by analogy with the GDPR, imposes the obligation on suppliers of 'high risk' AI systems to notify the competent national authorities of any serious incident or malfunction of the instrument that may constitute a 'violation' of the obligations envisaged by the EU law, the aim of which is to protect the fundamental rights in the Member States where the accident or violation occurred.[44]

Another crucial provision was covered by Article 13 of the draft, which introduces specific transparency obligations on the operation of AI systems, in favour of buyers and users of such systems. Under Article 13, it is necessary to provide all the documents demonstrating compliance with the technical requirements of the regulation (Article 11). Based on Article 13, 'high-risk artificial intelligence systems' must be designed and developed to ensure that they are sufficiently 'transparent' and allow users to easily interpret the functioning of the algorithmic model underlying the system. It gives effect to the obligation to provide the marketed systems with instructions for the use in an appropriate digital format, with 'concise, complete, correct and clear … relevant, accessible and comprehensible to users' information.[45]

In addition, Article 15 prescribes a series of requirements that an AI system must respect in order to be considered compliant with the Regulation. In particular, AI systems must be designed and developed in order to ensure the accuracy, robustness, and safety of their operation. In this regard, as mentioned, there is a further similarity with the provisions of Article 32 GDPR,[46] which require the data controller and

[44] European Commission, COM(2021) 206 final (n 39) art 62.

[45] More specifically (para 2): '(a) the identity and the contact details of the provider and, where applicable, of its authorised representative; (b) the characteristics, capabilities and limitations of performance of the high-risk AI system, including: (i) its intended purpose; (ii) the level of accuracy, robustness and cybersecurity referred to in Article 15 against which the high-risk AI system has been tested and validated and which can be expected, and any known and foreseeable circumstances that may have an impact on that expected level of accuracy, robustness and cybersecurity; (iii) any known or foreseeable circumstance, related to the use of the high-risk AI system in accordance with its intended purpose or under conditions of reasonably foreseeable misuse, which may lead to risks to the health and safety or fundamental rights; (iv) its performance as regards the persons or groups of persons on which the system is intended to be used; (v) when appropriate, specifications for the input data, or any other relevant information in terms of the training, validation and testing data sets used, taking into account the intended purpose of the AI system. (c) the changes to the high-risk AI system and its performance which have been pre-determined by the provider at the moment of the initial conformity assessment, if any; (d) the human oversight measures referred to in Article 14, including the technical measures put in place to facilitate the interpretation of the outputs of AI systems by the users; (e) the expected lifetime of the high-risk AI system and any necessary maintenance to ensure the proper functioning of that AI system, including as regards software updates.'

[46] Bassini (n 37).

data processor to implement certain technical and organisational measures that can ensure a level of security appropriate to the risk, taking into account the potential risks arising from the processing of data. These risks include the destruction, loss, modification, unauthorised disclosure, and accidental or illegal access to personal data transmitted, stored, or otherwise processed. Moreover, the adequacy of the technical security measures must be constantly monitored, in order to verify anomalies or irregularities in the functioning of the systems. Another essential element of the use of 'high risk' AI tools is the provision of constant supervision by a natural person during the period of use of the system (Article 14(1)). Indeed, such supervision and *ex post* control activities by a technical consultant are aimed at the prevention or minimisation of risks to health, safety, and fundamental rights. So far, it is possible to argue that the risk-based approach appears to be a first effective evaluation criterion for the assessment and the control of several applications that, at the time being, simply appear to be inapplicable because threatening to fundamental rights.

The regulation is meant to be a comprehensive text. Following its publication the document will be the main focus of the discussion about AI in the EU. For the time being, only a preliminary overview was possible, cherry-picking the most relevant and general aspects of the text. Many aspects of the draft were criticised due to the fuzzy definition and the unclear relationship with the existing sectorial EU products regulation: besides, the general exception of military AI, the reference in Article 2(2) seemed to exclude the application of the draft (with the exception of Article 84) also in several areas which are already covered by EU regulations and directives.

The very long negotiations shed light on many aspects and it is possible that the final text could reveal some important amendments to the approach presented above.

D *The Proposal for an AI Liability Directive*

In order to complete this legal framework, the European Commission delivered, on 28 September 2022, the Proposal for an Artificial Intelligence Liability Directive.[47] As mentioned above, the liability issues related to emerging digital technologies were the subject of attention by the Commission since 2018. It is worth remembering that, although non-contractual civil liability is not harmonised under EU law, this particular aspect of product liability has been regulated by Directive 85/374/EEC, representing the framework into which a brand-new regulation related to digital products should fit. The strong connection between the general legal framework for products liability and targeted AI liability is highlighted by the presentation, on the same day, 28 September 2022, of the proposal for a consolidated version of the

[47] European Commission, Proposal for a Directive of the European Parliament and of the Council on Adapting Non-contractual Civil Liability Rules to Artificial Intelligence (AI Liability Directive), COM(2022) 496 final.

directive 85/374, amending several definitions and specifically encompassing software, AI systems and AI-enabled goods, which will fall into the scope of the directive, being considered 'products'.[48] Both the draft directive on AI liability and the consolidated version of directive 85/374, rely on the fact that the AI Act regulation draft introduces safety rules for AI products: the presence of general safety rules allows shifting – at least, in part – the burden of proof from the claimant to the defendant.

On the general structure of the AI liability directive, the draft consists of nine articles with the particular aim of introducing, for the first time, specific rules for damage caused by AI systems. The need to introduce a new set of legal prescriptions targeted at AI started with the negotiations of the draft AI Act. In fact, based on a proportionality approach, it appeared that the EU is put in a better position than Member States to set an effective legal framework, able to address adequately claims generated by AI-enabled products and services. In fact, under traditional national rules, those who suffer damages are required to prove an unlawful act or omission on the part of the subject who caused the damage. The specific features of AI, including its complexity and opacity, may make it difficult or excessively costly for the claimants to identify the responsible party and prove that the conditions for a successful liability action are satisfied. In particular, when claiming compensation, injured parties may have to bear very high upfront costs and face considerably longer court proceedings than in cases not involving AI, and may therefore be deterred from seeking compensation at all.[49] At the same time, the proposal is also aimed at reducing the legal uncertainty for companies developing or using AI, in relation to possible liability exposure and to prevent fragmentation resulting from AI-specific adaptations of national liability rules. In this way, the AI Act and the AI Liability Directive seem to be complementary: they apply at different moments and reinforce each other. In fact, while the AI Act aims at preventing damage, the AI Liability Directive lays down a safety-net for compensation in the event of damage. The AI Liability Directive uses the same definitions as the AI Act, keeps the distinction between high-risk/non-high-risk AI, recognises the documentation and transparency requirements of the AI Act by making them operational for liability through the right to disclose information, and incentivises providers/users of AI systems to comply with their obligations under the AI Act. The Directive will apply to damages caused by AI systems, irrespective of whether they are high-risk, according to the AI Act.

[48] Council Directive 85/374/EEC of 25 July 1985 on the approximation of the laws, regulations and administrative provisions of the Member States concerning liability for defective products and the Proposal for a Directive of the European Parliament and the Council on liability for defective products, COM(2022) 495. On 14 December 2023, a provisional political agreement between the EU policymakers was reached but the legislative process is still ongoing: for further discussion of these proposals see https://eur-lex.europa.eu/legal-content/IT/TXT/?uri=CELEX%3A52022PC0496 and Chapters 6 and 9.

[49] European Parliament resolution of 3 May 2022 on artificial intelligence in a digital age.

Focusing on the crucial principle introduced by the Directive, the so-called 'presumption of causality' will relieve victims (individuals, companies, organisations, etc.) of the obligation to prove in detail how the damage was caused by faults or omissions by the defendant (such as the provider, developer, or user). In fact, Article 4(1) establishes a presumption of causality between the defendant's fault to abide by safety rules and the AI system's output (or the system's failure to produce an output). Victims are only required to prove that a causal link between such an output and the damage exists (Article 4(1)(c)). However, the defendant is, of course, permitted to rebut such a presumption (for example, by proving that a different cause resulted in the damage).

Furthermore, the Directive proposes rules to enable the relevant evidence to be accessed. Victims will be able to ask the court to order disclosure of information about high-risk AI systems. This will allow victims to identify the subject who could be held liable and find out what went wrong. In fact, if the claimant does not have access to the evidence proving the defendant's non-compliance with the duty of care, courts can issue an order of disclosure (or preservation) to the defendants.[50] If they do not abide by such an order, national judges may presume their liability.[51] Nevertheless, the defendants can rebut such a presumption.[52]

It is worth underlining that, pursuant to Article 3(4), the disclosure or preservation orders shall be 'necessary and proportionate' and thus may be subject to appropriate safeguards to protect sensitive information, such as trade secrets. This may represent a flaw in the future application of the Directive. Moreover, the burden of providing relevant information for the purposes of a successful suit, may turn out to be very difficult for the claimant in complex systems such as AI-enabled products and services. In fact, despite the disclosure orders mentioned above, some AI systems behave autonomously in a high-complexity context, where the explainability of outputs cannot be easily achieved.

It is true that the proposal considers that the autonomous nature of AI systems poses a difficulty in the comprehension of the functioning of an AI-enabled system,[53] but the presumption of causation does not make it easier for the injured parties to prove other relevant elements. After all, an aggrieved party will still face a heavy burden of proof under the Directive: from providing evidence to support the plausibility of the claim,[54] to identifying the likelihood of a failure to comply with AI Act requirements,[55] and proving a link between the output produced by the AI system and the damage suffered.[56] For instance, it might not be easy to prove that the

50 Article 3(5).
51 Ibid.
52 Article 4(7).
53 See recitals 3, 27, and 28.
54 See Article 3(1).
55 See Article 4(1)(a).
56 See Article 4(1)(c).

failure of a complex system gave rise to the damage.[57] Thus, as already highlighted,[58] the proposal does not make it easier for the injured party to satisfy all the procedural requirements. Although the draft represents an important milestone in the discussion about product liability, more needs to be done in order to make the redress mechanism for victims of AI damages more effective.

IV GENERAL CONCLUSIONS ABOUT THE EU APPROACH TO AI GOVERNANCE

Based on the main documents released by the EU over the last five years, it is possible to argue that the first cornerstone of the EU legal framework to regulate AI is 'accessibility', namely, to monitor the path followed by the software, from the input to the output.[59] This concept is certainly related to that of transparency but the normative approach displayed by the EU reaches far beyond transparency, as the latter is not sufficient, per se, to counterbalance the opacity of AI systems.

Basically, AI systems traditionally are said to be 'black-boxes', preventing or at least complicating the basic fulfilment of transparency. However, authors have observed that the definition of black box may sound similar to the one of human mind, whose decisions are made on the basis of emotions or impulses, without following a recognisable logic.[60] Thus, it is worth focusing on the real meaning of transparency.

It is possible to argue that digital transparency has been elevated to the status of a new basic guarantee[61] of the European legal system since Regulation (EU) 2016/679, reiterating the requirement with regard to the processing methods with which personal data are 'collected, used, consulted or otherwise processed [personal data…] as well as the extent to which the personal data are or will be processed'. In this context, the criterion of transparency[62] requires that information and communications relating to the processing of such personal data are easily accessible and understandable and that simple and clear language is used.

57 Article 4(1)(c).

58 Samar Abbas Nawaz, 'The Proposed EU AI Liability Rules: Ease or Burden?' (*European Law Blog*, 7 November 2022) <https://europeanlawblog.eu/2022/11/07/the-proposed-eu-ai-liability-rules-ease-or-burden/>.

59 Martin Ebers, 'Regulating AI and Robotics: Ethical and Legal Challenges' in Martin Ebers and Susana Navas (eds), *Algorithms and Law* (CUP 2019), 12 'we can see only input data and output data for algorithm-based systems without understanding exactly what happens in between'; Mike Ananny and Kate Crawford, 'Seeing without Knowing: Limitations of the Transparency Ideal and Its Application to Algorithmic Accountability' (2016) 20 *New Media Soc* 973.

60 Julie A. Seaman, 'Black Boxes' (2008) 58 *Em L J* 427.

61 See, in general, Martin Ebers and Marta Cantero Gamito (eds), *Algorithmic Governance and Governance of Algorithms, Legal and Ethical Challenges* (Springer 2020).

62 In relation to the definition of AI, transparency may have distinct connotations, in different areas of expertise. Transparency has now a 'legal dimension' (see Mireille Hildebrandt, 'The Dawn of a Critical Transparency Right for the Profiling Era' in Jacques Bus, Malcom Crompton, Mirelle Hildebrandt and George Metakides (eds), *Digital Enlightenment Yearbook* (IOS Press 2012) 52), which is different from the 'computational dimension'. In this context, the term is understood in terms of the legal dimension.

The 2019 Ethics Guidelines for Trustworthy AI rephrased the principle of algorithmic transparency in somehow different terms.[63] The guidelines emphasise, in particular, that the data sets and algorithmic processes that determine the decision of an AI system should always be documented, according to the best existing standards, in order to allow traceability and transparency. In addition, it is also expected that the learning process of a ML system is precisely documented and that collection and selection of data can be adequately reviewed. In other words, traceability enables verifiability and explainability of the algorithmic system. In this regard, the document defines the latter as the ability to explain both the technical processes of an AI system and the related human decisions. The principle is relevant to the extent that if an AI system significantly affects people's lives, these people should always be allowed to request (and obtain) an explanation of the decision-making process. Such explanation should always be timely and understandable to the recipient concerned. To that extent, the document pushes the boundaries of the concept far beyond the bare idea of 'transparency': disclosure of the functioning of software is for sure 'transparent', but totally inaccessible to those who do not have technical skills…[64] Thus, transparency is not a synonym for accessibility (explainability and interpretability)[65]: such distinct features represent different steps of interaction of the user with the software. Transparency and accessibility concur in offering a comprehensive assessment of the functioning of a software.[66]

Moreover, in the regulation proposal, transparency and accessibility are crucial. In this regard, different levels of transparency are envisaged: depending on the level of 'risk' associated with the use of a given AI tool, a corresponding algorithmic transparency is envisaged. Therefore, for some specific 'low risk' systems, minimum transparency obligations are required. When 'high risk' systems are at stake, compliance with more specific requirements is strictly necessary, in order, at least, to 'mitigate the risks to fundamental rights' (§ 2.3 of the explanatory memorandum, Proportionality). As discussed, Article 13 of the original version of the draft Regulation establishes that high-risk AI systems must be designed and developed in a way to ensure that their operation is sufficiently clear to allow users to interpret the output of the system and use it appropriately. In this regard, it is envisaged that the users of such AI tools are

63 Mirelle Hildebrandt, 'Profile Transparency by Design? Re-enabling Double Contingency' in Mireille Hildebrandt and Katja de Vries (eds), *Privacy, Due Process and the Computational Turn* (Routledge 2013) 221; Mireille Hildebrandt, 'Algorithmic Regulation and the Rule of Law' (2018) 376(2128) *Phil Trans R Soc* 1.

64 Serena Quattrocolo, *Artificial Intelligence, Computational Modelling and Criminal Proceedings* (Springer 2020) 17.

65 Zachary Lipton, *The Mythos of Model Interpretability* (presented at 2016 ICML Workshop on Human Interpretability in Machine Learning (WHI 2016), New York, 2016) <https://arxiv.org/pdf/1606.03490.pdf>; Anil K. Jain, Debayan Deb and Joshua J. Engelsma, 'Biometrics: Trust, but Verify' [2015] *Journal of Latex Class File* <https://arxiv.org/abs/2105.06625>.

66 Francesca Palmiotto, 'The Black Box on Trial: The Impact of Algorithmic Opacity on Fair Trial Rights in Criminal Proceedings' in Martin Ebers and Marta Cantero Gamito (eds), *Algorithmic Governance and Governance of Algorithms: Legal and Ethical Challenges* (Springer 2020) 56.

provided with instructions and a set of information such as: the identity and contact details of the supplier; the intended use of the tool; the level of accuracy, robustness, and IT security. The latter aspect is more specifically governed by the draft Article 15, where it is established (as said above) that the AI systems must ensure an adequate level of precision with respect to the intended use. Accuracy, robustness, and safety are standards also mentioned in the Ethics Charter, under the principle of quality and safety (Article 3). In fact, the soft law document recommends that data should only be used from certified sources, that the procedure should be redesigned to be traceable, and that the models and algorithms should be made suitable for safe storage and execution, in order to ensure the integrity of the system.

Given these premises, it is possible to argue that in the current European regulatory landscape, the concept of Explainable Artificial Intelligence (XAI)[67] plays a crucial role. As discussed, the actual transparency of an algorithmic system depends on the accuracy of the scientific theory that supports it and, secondly, on the clarity of the language used to translate it into a mathematical system. From an IT point of view, in fact, a clear mathematical language allows an operator to understand *ex post* the procedure as to how a given input led to a given output. The goal of the most recent research is to create interpretable methods to produce models maintaining high levels of performance: the purpose is to balance what has been, for a long while, the primary focus in the development of algorithms, for example, a high predictive capacity, with the understanding of the decision-making process. In this sense, 'interpretability' arises as a *trait d'union* requirement between 'transparency' and 'explainability', transforming AI system into 'white boxes', or 'glass boxes', through the analysis of the logical learning model underlying the system considered. Explainability, on the other hand, refers to a broader series of considerations that make an AI system highly understandable to recipients, including the description of the procedure that makes all the information of the AI system directly accessible to users. Explainable and interpretable AI concur with transparency, to guarantee that the user has full control over an AI system.

The draft regulation proposed a whole provision to the exercise of control by the user (Article 14). In particular, 'high risk' AI systems must be designed and developed with the provision of adequate human-machine interface tools, in order to ensure effective control by natural persons during the entire period of use of the system. The main goal is to prevent, or at least minimise the risks for health, safety, or fundamental rights that may arise when an AI system is used in ways that do not comply with the intended purpose or in conditions of improper use. Art. 14 § 4

67 Tim Miller, 'Explanation in Artificial Intelligence: Insights from the Social Sciences' (2018) 267 *Artif Intell* 1; Diogo V. Carvalho, Eduardo M. Pereira and Jaime S. Cardoso, 'Machine Learning Interpretability: A Survey on Methods and Metrics' (2019) 8 *Electronics* 832; Bernhard Waltl and Roland Vogl, 'Explainable Artificial Intelligence – The New Frontier in Legal Informatics' (*Jusletter IT*, 2018) <jusletter-it.weblaw.ch/issues/2018/IRIS/explainable-artifici_fbce1ac1do.html__ONCE&login=false>.

expressly indicates the features that these control measures must guarantee to the user: understanding of the capabilities and limits of the AI system, being able to duly monitor its entire operation (letter a); the awareness of the so called 'automation bias', due to excessive use of AI systems; the possibility of correctly interpreting the results of the AI system, taking into account the characteristics of the system; the ability to decide at any time to no longer use the AI system or to ignore its output; to be able to intervene in the operation of the system or abruptly stop its operation. These, together with the obligations of suppliers (Article 16), importers (Article 26), distributors (Article 27), and, finally, users themselves (Article 29), were meant to guarantee the exercise of constant control over AI tools. More specifically, the obligations for suppliers include, as envisaged in the Ethics guidelines, the development of a legal framework that defines the responsibility of the management and of the personnel involved in the design and development of the AI system.

As discussed, the proposed regulation will complement a long series of EU documents, establishing a benchmark for AI governance. The negotiation of the text was long and complicated. Stakeholders, both public and private, have been engaged in a serious review of the draft, with a focus on the actual level of accessibility and explainability of AI systems. This point will be crucial, having regard to the need for the regulation to interact with the sophisticated set of social and economic rights established by the EU in recent decades.

Index

Printed in the USA
CPSIA information can be obtained
at www.ICGtesting.com
CBHW082142150424
6997CB00007B/275